FINANCIAL ACCOUNTING
An Introduction to Concepts, Methods, and Uses

THE DRYDEN ACCOUNTING LIST

* Lee, Gilbart, Hipwell, and Hales — *Accounting*

* Gaber, Walgenbach, Hanson, and Hamre — *Introduction to Accounting*

Brigham and Knechel — *Financial Accounting Using Lotus 1-2-3*

* Dauderis — *Financial Accounting: An Introduction to Decision Making*

Gaber, Davidson, Stickney, and Weil — *Financial Accounting*

Hoskin and Hughs — *Financial Accounting Cases*

Ketz, Campbell, and Baxendale — *Management Accounting*

Maher, Stickney, Weil, and Davidson — *Managerial Accounting: An Introduction to Concepts, Methods, and Uses*

* Beechy — *Canadian Advanced Financial Accounting*

Stickney — *Financial Statement Analysis*

* Clowes — *EDP Auditing*

Douglas — *Governmental and Nonprofit Accounting: Theory and Practice*

Ziebell and DeCoster — *Management Control Systems in Nonprofit Organizations*

Bloom and Elgers — *Accounting Theory and Policy: A Reader*

* Most — *Accounting Theory*

Belkaoui — *Accounting Theory*

* Skinner — *Accounting Standards in Evolution*

Everett, Boley, Duncan, and Jamison — *HBJ Federal Tax Course*

Williams and Miller — *GAAP Guide, College Edition*

Bailey and Miller — *GAAS Guide, College Edition*

FIFTH CANADIAN EDITION

FINANCIAL ACCOUNTING
AN INTRODUCTION TO CONCEPTS, METHODS, AND USES

BRIAN G. GABER, PH.D., C.A.
Wilfrid Laurier University

◆

SIDNEY DAVIDSON, PH.D., C.P.A.
University of Chicago

◆

CLYDE P. STICKNEY, D.B.A., C.P.A.
Dartmouth College

◆

ROMAN L. WEIL, PH.D., C.P.A., C.M.A.
University of Chicago

DRYDEN

A Division of Holt, Rinehart and Winston of Canada, Limited

Toronto Montreal Orlando Fort Worth
San Diego Philadelphia London Sydney Tokyo

Canadian Cataloguing in Publication Data
Main entry under title:

Financial accounting : an introduction to concepts, methods, and uses

5th Canadian ed.
Includes index.
ISBN 0-03-922934-3

1. Accounting.   I. Gaber, Brian George, 1949–

HF5635.F56 1993   657'.044   C92-094825-1

Editorial Director: Scott Duncan
Acquisitions Editor: Ronald Fitzgerald
Developmental Editor: Cheryl Teelucksingh
Editorial Assistant: Lisa Whyatt
Director of Publishing Services: Jean Lancee
Editorial Manager: Marcel Chiera
Editorial Co-ordinator: Carol Tong
Production Manager: Sue-Ann Becker
Production Co-ordinator: Denise Wake
Copy Editor: Glenn Martin
Cover and Interior Design: Dave Peters
Technical Art: Debbie Fleming
Typesetting and Assembly: Compeer Typographic Services Limited
Printing and Binding: John Deyell Company Limited

⊛ This book was printed in Canada on acid-free paper.

1 2 3 4 5   97 96 95 94 93

For our students, with thanks.

Whatever be the detail with which you cram your students, the chance of their meeting in after-life exactly that detail is almost infinitesimal; and if they do meet it, they will probably have forgotten what you taught them about it. The really useful training yields a comprehension of a few general principles with a thorough grounding in the way they apply to a variety of concrete details. In subsequent practice the students will have forgotten your particular details; but they will remember by an unconscious common sense how to apply principles to immediate circumstances.

Alfred North Whitehead
The Aims of Education and Other Essays

PREFACE

The fifth Canadian edition of *Financial Accounting* builds on a theme developed over the first four editions — an integrated approach to teaching concepts, methods, and uses of accounting. We believe that an introductory course in financial accounting should have the following objectives:

1. To help students develop sufficient understanding of the theoretical structure, concepts, and judgment underlying financial statements so that they can adapt to new and different situations.

2. To train students in accounting techniques so that they are able to prepare financial statements from straightforward transactions.

3. To teach students how to interpret, analyze, and evaluate financial accounting information in order to assist in making business decisions.

Most accounting textbooks reflect similar objectives. The critical difference relates to the relative emphasis placed on the objectives. The majority of introductory financial accounting texts stress the coverage of accounting procedures and are labelled "procedural" texts. A few emphasize concepts; in Canada, none focus primarily on uses of accounting information.

The major feature of this book is its ability to support any course emphasis — procedural, conceptual, user, or, ideally, balanced. This necessitates a large book, but we believe the flexibility it provides to instructors more than justifies its length. The book is sufficiently rich in material to support a course either entirely devoted to, or devoid of, debits and credits.

The book contains not only full treatment of all the accounting procedures typically covered in an introductory course, but also more advanced material to meet the needs of those students with backgrounds in high school accounting. The book also includes considerable discussion of the uses of accounting information. The final three chapters are devoted principally to this theme.

It is, however, the conceptual content of this book that clearly sets it apart. We attempt to explain the "why" as well as the "how" of accounting procedures. There are numerous nonquantitative discussion cases on important issues facing the accounting profession. The capstone of this conceptual approach is a new chapter on accounting theory — a first for introductory accounting texts.

Today, introductory financial accounting textbooks must serve a multipurpose role. There are three distinct categories of students who take this course:

1. Accounting majors with as much as four years of high school accounting. These students are penalized if they must go through the bookkeeping cycle and rudimentary accounting procedures again.

2. Accounting majors with no previous accounting background. These students must start their accounting studies from the beginning.

3. Nonaccounting majors who are taking the course as a required business credit or for general interest. These students want minimal exposure to the procedural aspects of accounting.

We believe that a conceptual orientation benefits all three groups. Accounting educators are also beginning to believe that an accounting curriculum that begins with concepts ultimately creates better accountants. A procedural emphasis is more suited to the intermediate accounting course, which is taken only by accounting majors.

CHANGES TO THE FIFTH EDITION

The major changes in this edition are as follows:

1. A new Chapter 5 devoted to the discussion of accounting theory and a conceptual framework for accounting.

2. An appendix to Chapter 5 deals with ethical issues facing the accounting profession. Surveys of accounting instructors have indicated that this is the topic they would most like added to the accounting curriculum.

3. An appendix to Chapter 5 discusses principles of internal control. Traditionally, this topic has been covered in the fourth year auditing course, but it is now recognized that all future managers should have exposure to objectives and procedures of control.

4. An appendix to Chapter 5 discusses systems concepts. If accounting is portrayed to students as an "information system," they should have an understanding of the implications of the term.

5. The chapter on financial statement analysis has been moved to the end of the book (Chapter 15). Surveys have shown that instructors prefer to treat this as the concluding chapter to the course.

6. The two chapters on the statement of changes in financial position have been combined into a single chapter and placed near the end of the book (Chapter 13). The one-semester course does not have time to devote two weeks to the topic, and the perceived complexity of the statement of changes in financial position by the students makes it more appropriate to cover the topic at the end of the course.

7. Self-study material at the end of each chapter will help the students bridge the gap between the chapter material and the assignments.

8. The end-of-book glossary has been replaced by a running glossary in the margins. Each chapter also contains a list of the key terms defined in that chapter, and the index identifies where the principal definition can be found for each term. The running glossary approach is preferred by students.

larger page size with expanded margins. This enhances readability and allows the students to make notes in the margins.

10. A second colour has been introduced to highlight key items. The use of colour, along with a more pleasing type-style, adds significantly to the readability of the text.

11. At least two discussion cases have been added to each chapter. These deal with qualitative issues that face the profession and act as catalysts to stimulate classroom discussion.

12. Part of the Solutions Manual has been turned into an Instructor's Manual. This contains guidance on course design and curriculum matters as well as suggested approaches to taking up the case-type questions. A separate manual for instructors facilitates placing the solutions manual on library reserve for students.

13. The end-of-book appendix on accounting for the effects of changing prices has been deleted. This is consistent with the deletion of this material from the *CICA Handbook*.

14. The end-of-book appendix containing a set of annotated financial statements has also been deleted. Surveys showed that few courses had adequate time to cover this appendix, and students had difficulty benefiting from a self-study approach.

15. Most chapters now include a section discussing accounting principles in foreign jurisdictions. The multinational nature of business today calls for a more global focus in the accounting curriculum.

16. Numerous detailed reviews by accounting instructors helped identify passages that were subsequently rewritten to improve clarity.

17. The book, of course, has been updated to reflect all accounting pronouncements in effect at the time of printing.

As you can see, a great many changes have been made to the fifth edition. We believe these contribute to a book that will enhance student learning, increase student interest in accounting as a career, and meet the pedagogical needs of accounting education in the 1990s.

ORGANIZATION OF THE BOOK

The book is divided into four major sections:

PART ONE   This consists of Chapters 1 through 4. It familiarizes students with the discipline, covers the basic accounting cycle, and introduces many of the fundamental concepts that provide the foundation for accounting.

PART TWO   This is the new Chapter 5, entitled "A Conceptual Framework for Accounting." The chapter begins with a review of the concepts introduced in the first four chapters to allow instructors to omit classroom coverage of Part One for classes with high school accounting backgrounds. The chapter then introduces students to the decision usefulness paradigm, which is the central theme of accounting today. A conceptual framework for accounting is then introduced to give students a frame of reference to evaluate the accounting techniques introduced later in the book.

PART THREE   This includes Chapters 6 through 12 and covers the various elements of financial statements. These chapters present the theoretical basis for, and the impact of, accounting procedures in addition to the methods involved.

PART FOUR   The final three chapters are devoted to the users of financial statements. Chapter 13 introduces the Statement of Changes in Financial Position. Chapter 14 discusses the impact of accounting alternatives on business decisions. Chapter 15 deals with financial statement analysis.

INSTRUCTOR'S MANUAL

The Instructor's Manual contains suggested course outlines for courses emphasizing a procedural, conceptual, or user orientation. Chapter objectives and teaching hints for many topics, discussion case guidelines, and templates for making transparencies, are included.

SOLUTIONS MANUAL

The Solutions Manual contains the solutions to all procedurally oriented questions, and is suitable for placing on library reserve.

ACKNOWLEDGEMENTS

I am first and foremost indebted to the authors of the American edition for creating such a high-quality introductory text with a conceptual focus. I am equally indebted to C.L. Mitchell, who worked on the initial Canadianization of the book.

I am grateful to the following individuals who have made contributions to the book over the first four editions:

H. Babiak	University of Toronto
M. Bundy	University of Regina
P. Cunningham	Bishop's University
C. Duncan	St. Francis Xavier University
H. Elmslie	Lakehead University
M. Erickson	Society of Management Accountants of Canada
M. Fizzell	University of Saskatchewan
B. Fleisher	Simon Fraser University
G. Gilbert	University of Toronto
J. Heaphy	McGill University
C. Heywood	Wilfrid Laurier University

M. Hilton	University of Manitoba
J. Hughes	Memorial University
B. Irvine	University of Saskatchewan
D. Kennedy	University of Waterloo
D. Lockwood	University of British Columbia
B. Mallouk	University of Toronto
A. Marshall	McGill University
J. McCutcheon	Wilfrid Laurier University
E. Peter	Memorial University
R. Rennie	University of Regina
A. Richardson	McMaster University
R. Schenk	Bishop's University
P. Secord	Saint Mary's University
T. Var	Simon Fraser University
G. Walsh	Saint Mary's University
C. Wright	

I am also grateful for the comments and suggestions from the following people who reviewed the fifth edition at various stages:

A. Clarke-Okah	Carleton University
R. Davidson	Simon Fraser University
J.P. Heaphy	McGill University
D. Herauf	Carleton University
M. Klatt	Wilfrid Laurier University
K. Lamb	Queen's University
D. Lockwood	University of British Columbia
P. Marsh	University of Calgary
A.R. Marshall	McGill University
L. White	McMaster University

Many thanks to William Banks, Wilfrid Laurier University, who provided many useful ideas on how to increase the conceptual emphasis of the book, and to Dwight Edmonds, who prepared the teaching notes in the Solutions Manual. The financial support of Wilfrid Laurier University while this revision was completed is also gratefully acknowledged.

I gratefully acknowledge the permission given by the Canadian Institute of Chartered Accountants, The Society of Management Accountants of Canada, The American Institute of Certified Public Accountants, and the Financial Accounting Standards Board in allowing me to quote or adapt from their copyright material.

The people at HBJ-Holt provided immense support in the planning and production of this edition. The book reflects the talented contributions of Scott Duncan, Editorial Director; Carol Tong, Editorial Co-ordinator; Lisa Whyatt, Editorial Assistant; Marcel Chiera, Editorial Manager; Sue-Ann Becker, Production Manager; Denise Wake, Production Co-ordinator; Glenn Martin, Copy Editor; and Dave Peters, Graphic Designer. Two individuals in particular were instrumental to the success of this book. Cheryl Teelucksingh, Developmental Editor, displayed the patience of a saint in dealing with this author. Most of the enhancements made to the fifth edition arose out of discussions at the planning stage with Ron Fitzgerald, Senior Acquisitions Editor. This book represents a major departure from the stereotypic introductory accounting text, and it took vision and courage by Ron to support these changes.

As any textbook author knows, the largest contribution of all comes from the patience and understanding of one's family over the long duration of the project. To Margaret and Cory — thank you.

Brian G. Gaber
Wilfrid Laurier University
Waterloo, Canada

PUBLISHER'S NOTE TO STUDENTS AND INSTRUCTORS

This textbook is a key component of your course. If you are the instructor of this course, you undoubtedly considered a number of texts carefully before choosing this as the one that would work best for your students and you. The authors and publishers spent considerable time and money to ensure its high quality, and we appreciate your recognition of this effort and accomplishment. Please note the copyright statement.

If you are a student, we are confident that this text will help you to meet the objectives of your course. It will also become a valuable addition to your personal library.

Since we want to hear what you think about this book, please be sure to send us the stamped reply card at the end of the text. Your input will help us to continue to publish high-quality books for your courses.

BRIEF CONTENTS

CONTENTS

Chapter Seven

Inventories: The Source of Operating Profits   406

PART ONE

ACCOUNTING CONCEPTS AND METHODS

CHAPTER ONE

OVERVIEW OF FINANCIAL STATEMENTS AND THE REPORTING PROCESS

CHAPTER OUTLINE

- The Origins of Accounting
- Distinction Between Managerial and Financial Accounting
- Forms of Business Organization
- Overview of Business Activities
- Principal Financial Statements
- Other Items in Annual Reports
- Objectives of Financial Reporting
- An International Perspective

Accounting
The process of recording, classifying, reporting, and interpreting the financial data of an organization.

Accounting is a system for *measuring* the results of business activities and *communicating* those results to interested users. You are about to begin a study of (1) the concepts and procedures used by accountants to make these measurements and (2) the principal financial statements through which the measurements are communicated. Whether or not you become an accountant yourself, you will use accounting as a tool in making production, marketing, investment, or other business decisions. The goal of your study (and this book) is to help you gain sufficient understanding of accounting concepts and procedures so that you can use accounting data effectively.

THE ORIGINS OF ACCOUNTING

The need for accounting has existed for as long as humans have engaged in transactions with one another. Even a simple barter transaction between two cave dwellers — for example, a spear for a handful of flints — required a determination of the relative worth of the items exchanged. One of the basic functions of accounting is the assignment of values to goods and/or services exchanged between people. Is a spear worth two flints, four flints, or more?

Accounting is the child of commerce, and the development of both are inexorably intertwined. Although this development has been incremental and continuous, certain milestones in history have accelerated the pace of development. These milestones are:

1. The invention of money

2. The formation of kingdoms with divine rulers

3. Taxes

4. Trading cultures

5. Joint ventures

6. Double-entry bookkeeping

7. Companies and the industrial revolution

8. Professional accounting associations

9. Legal status for accounting

The invention of money greatly facilitated commerce as well as the recording of transactions. The earliest recorded references to accounting occur in records uncovered from the Mesopotamian and Egyptian civilizations. The pharoahs who accumulated vast warehouses of valuables had scribes who kept track of the contents. The imposition of taxation on the populace required additional accounting activity. Accountants were required to serve also as paymasters to pay mercenary armies hired to wage war.

There is no doubt that the origins of modern accounting began with the advent of trading societies, such as that of the Phoenicians. To finance the building of ships, fill them with cargoes, sail to distant ports, sell the cargoes, refill the ships with different cargoes for the return voyage, dispose of the goods at home, pay the crew, and pay the profits to the financiers of the venture required a fairly refined system of accounting.

Officially, the birth of modern accounting is associated with the Venetians. They were not only a great trading nation, but also accelerated the development of trading institutions such as credit and banking. A Venetian monk, Luca Pacioli, is credited with developing the concept of double-entry bookkeeping in 1494. This system is the basis for all modern accounting systems.

After the Renaissance, the focus of accounting development shifted to the colonial empires of Spain and other European countries. Billions of dollars in gold and other resources brought back from the New World required meticulous recordkeeping systems. The commercial activities of the British empire led to the passage of the Companies Act in the 1840s. This was a momentous turning point for accounting. The Act's principal characteristic — the separation of ownership and management through the selling of stock to investors — led to a new goal for accounting. This involved stewardship reporting on the fiduciary activities of the hired managerial class back to the absentee owners. This remains a primary objective for financial accounting today. At the same time, the industrial revolution was underway, and corporations were accumulating huge amounts of capital.

Canadian Institute of Chartered Accountants (CICA)
The national organization that represents chartered accountants in Canada.

The late 1800s saw also the formation of formal associations of accountants. In 1880, the first association in North America was formed in Montreal. This was followed by the Institute of Chartered Accountants in 1883 and the **Canadian Institute of Chartered Accountants (CICA)** in 1902. These associations had a profound influence on accounting. Accounting methods became more uniform, and standards of acceptable behaviour were introduced. The professional status of accounting became largely attributable to the activities of these organizations.

The development of accounting lagged behind the growth of commerce in the "roaring '20s." To some extent, the 1929 stock market crash was caused by faulty accounting practices; the net worth on the balance sheets of some companies was overstated by as much as a third when the crash occurred. The perceived inadequacies of accounting led to government intervention into accounting in the 1930s with the passage of securities legislation and the formation of regulated stock exchanges. Such legislation also gave legal sanction to the role of the accounting associations in defining acceptable accounting practices.

The modern era of accounting began in 1940 with the publication of *Corporate Accounting Standards*,[1] the first attempt to publish an inventory of generally accepted accounting principles linked to a theoretical framework. This has been the challenge of accounting ever since. Accounting practices evolved over thousands of years in response to the needs of commerce. The development of a single unified theory of accounting that justified existing practices and that could be used to promulgate new standards has been accounting's ultimate objective. We call this the search for a conceptual framework for accounting. This text describes both this search and the practices that have been identified as generally accepted in the 1990s.

DISTINCTION BETWEEN MANAGERIAL AND FINANCIAL ACCOUNTING

The field of accounting divides into two parts: managerial accounting and financial accounting.

Managerial accounting
The accounting procedures carried out by an organization's accounting staff primarily to furnish its management with accounting analyses and reports needed for decision making.

Managerial accounting is concerned with the preparation of reports for use by persons within a firm. For example, a corporate treasurer might use a statement of projected cash receipts and disbursements in deciding whether short-term borrowing is necessary. A production manager might use a report on the productivity of various employees in deciding how a special order is to be routed through a factory. A sales manager might use a report on the cost of producing and selling different product lines in recommending the prices to be charged and the products to be emphasized by the sales staff. Users of information within a firm can specify the types of information they need for their decisions; managerial accounting reports are designed to satisfy these needs.

---

[1] W.A. Paton and A.C. Littleton (Sarasota, Florida: American Accounting Association, Monograph #3, 1940).

In contrast, **financial accounting** is concerned with the preparation of reports for use by persons outside a firm. For example, a bank may want information on the cash-generating ability of a firm in deciding whether or not to grant a loan. A potential investor may desire information on a firm's profitability before deciding to purchase its common shares.

Financial accounting reports tend to be more standardized in terms of format and content than those used in managerial accounting. The large number of uses and users of financial accounting reports creates the need for some degree of uniformity in reporting among firms.

financial accounting
Those accounting activities leading primarily to publishable, general-purpose financial statements.

DISCUSSION CASE 1

One Accounting Profession — or Three?

There are three professional accounting organizations in Canada representing approximately 140,000 licenced accountants. A member of the Canadian Institute of Chartered Accountants (CICA) is a Chartered Accountant **(CA)**. Members of The Society of Management Accountants of Canada **(SMAC)** are Certified Management Accountants **(CMA)**. Members of the Certified General Accountants' Association of Canada are Certified General Accountants **(CGA)**.

CMAs work principally in industry. CAs work in industry but are also licensed by ten provincial Acts to conduct independent audits of companies. The majority of CGAs are employed in industry, but in three provinces are also licensed to conduct audits. All three types of accountants are also found in government, the largest employer in Canada.

The three professions are marked by more similarities than differences, which is natural since any profession has many similar attributes. These include:

1. Mastery of an intellectual skill
2. Altruism (a desire to serve the public interest)
3. Self-regulation (including standards for admission, day-to-day conduct, and discipline)
4. Community sanction (which recognizes the group's professional status and grants it quasi-monopoly rights)
5. A code of ethical conduct more rigorous than that of the general population
6. Intellectual curiosity and a desire to expand the frontiers of known knowledge
7. Objectivity (a commitment to search for truth without the interference of bias)

Historically, medicine, theology, and law were deemed to be professions. In the twentieth century, other groups such as accountants, engineers, dentists, and architects have laid claim to professional status. In fact, a great many occupational classes aspire
(continued)

CA (Chartered Accountant)
Professional designation given to individuals who qualify for membership in the CICA.

SMAC (Society of Management Accountants of Canada)
The national association of accountants whose provincial associations engage in industrial and governmental accounting.

CMA (Certified Management Accountants)
Professional accounting designation offered by Society of Management Accountants in Canada. CMAs are most commonly employed in industry.

CGA (Certified General Accountant)
An accountant who has satisfied the experience, education, and examination requirements of the Certified General Accountants' Association of Canada.

(continued)

to professional status and have adopted the word "professional" in their title. However, community sanction and the right of self-regulation are granted to very few of these groups.

To be a professional accountant is a desirable goal. Accountants consistently rank in the top five occupational classes in Canada for average salary. Professions enjoy high social status and public respect, and the possession of a professional designation gives the holder considerable job mobility. The study program is long and the qualifying exams rigorous but the effort is well worth it.

Professional accountants in two Canadian provinces, British Columbia and Quebec, have recently put on ice plans for a proposed merger of the accounting bodies. In British Columbia the CAs and CMAs would have merged and in Quebec CAs, CMAs, and CGAs would have tied the knot.

Debate about the proposed mergers was just as emotional and vehement as the recent free trade debates in this country. Opposition to the union came principally from the CAs.

Alberta may turn out to be the bellwether province on this issue. The provincial government recently passed legislation requiring harmonization of many aspects of accounting practice. This may turn out to be a *de facto* merger.

Despite the temporary setbacks in BC and Quebec, the three accounting bodies in Canada will probably merge eventually. History is often the best guide to the future. On several occasions in Canadian history when there have been competing accounting bodies, merger was always the result.

More importantly, merger is in the public interest. The public has the right to demand a single standard of excellence from professional accountants. Do we have competing bodies of doctors, lawyers, or engineers? No — by definition each is a single profession, and accounting should be no different.

The CICA Long Range Strategic Planning Report holds the key to implementation. It proposes that the CA be a generalist designation (much like the GP in medicine) and then that there be separate specialist designations for tax, attestation, EDP, etc. All three current bodies could be granted the generalist designation and individuals would qualify for the individual specialist designations according to their needs and abilities. One accounting profession, one uniform standard of excellence, an idea whose time has come!

References

Reprinted with permission. From "Will Canada's Accountants Ever Merge?" *Financial Executive*, July/August 1988, copyright 1986 by Financial Executives Institute, Morristown, New Jersey, and "Meeting the Challenge of Change," *Report of the CICA Long Range Strategic Planning Committee*, 1986.

Discussion Question

How is competition between the professional accounting bodies beneficial to the accounting profession and to the public?

The most common reports for external users are the financial statements included in annual reports to shareholders (owners) and potential investors. These financial statements are prepared to conform with **generally accepted accounting principles (GAAP)**. Such "principles" have evolved over time or have been made "acceptable" by decree from an official rule-making body. The **Accounting Standards Board (ASB)** of the CICA is the principal rule-making body in Canada.

This text discusses the principles that underlie the financial statements prepared by firms for external users. We begin by studying how a typical firm carries out its business activities. We then see how the results of these business activities are measured and reported in the principal financial statements. This chapter introduces material to be covered in greater depth in later chapters. The objective is to develop the "big picture" in order to provide a perspective for the concepts and procedures discussed later.

generally accepted accounting principles (GAAP)
A group of standards or guides to action in preparing financial accounting reports. Their content and usefulness have evolved over many decades.

Accounting Standards Board (ASB)
The board of the CICA charged with the responsibility of promulgating new accounting standards for the *CICA Handbook*.

FORMS OF BUSINESS ORGANIZATION

There are three predominant forms of business organization used in Canada, and the accounting treatment of them differs to some degree. The three forms are the sole proprietorship, the partnership, and the corporation. The simplest form is the sole proprietorship, in which a business is owned by a single individual, who typically also manages the business. There are several advantages to this form of organization. It is easy and inexpensive to form, often requiring nothing more than a municipal business licence. The owner has great flexibility of action, and the recordkeeping requirements are often minimal because the business's small size makes it exempt from many government regulations. Income earned by the business is not taxed until it is declared on the personal tax return of the owner.

The great disadvantage of the sole proprietorship is that the limited access to capital makes growth difficult. A partnership is a legal agreement between two or more individuals to pool their capital to overcome this obstacle. Unfortunately, the frequently divisive issues of profit-sharing, valuation of services provided, and business policies make the accounting more complex for the partnership than it is for the other business forms. Accounting for partnerships is usually studied only in advanced accounting courses.

The predominant form of business today is the corporation. Although the costs of incorporation run into the thousands of dollars, the incorporated company enjoys many advantages. Foremost is the concept of limited legal liability for owners. Unlike the other two forms, where creditors can go after the personal assets of owners, the liability of corporate investors is limited to their investment in the company. The second major advantage is the ability to sell an unlimited number of shares to raise capital. The largest corporations today control assets totalling billions of dollars. The primary focus of this book will be on the accounting practices appropriate for the corporate form of business organization.

OVERVIEW OF BUSINESS ACTIVITIES

Financial statements for external users attempt to present in a meaningful way the results of a firm's business activities. Understanding these financial statements requires an understanding of the business activities that they attempt to reflect.

Example 1   Bill Marsh and Janet Nelson, while working toward degrees in engineering, developed a computerized mechanism for monitoring automobile engine performance. They received a patent on the device and, having recently graduated, they want to set up their own firm to manufacture and sell it. The firm will be called Marnel Corporation.[2]

Some of the more important processes that Marnel Corporation must go through are described below.

ESTABLISHING CORPORATE GOALS AND STRATEGIES

The *goals* of any firm are the targets, or end results, toward which the energies of the firm are directed. The *strategies* of the firm are the means for achieving these goals.

The detail in which goals and strategies are stated varies among firms. Some firms prefer to state goals and strategies only in general terms. For example, a firm might state that its goal is "to be more profitable than our leading competitors." Its strategy might be to mechanize production so that it could manufacture quality products at a cost lower than that of its competitors.

Often firms might be more explicit. The goal might be to achieve a certain rate of profitability. The goals might also be broader than profitability alone and include concerns for employee welfare, environmental protection, and community involvement. Strategies might be spelled out in detail, including step-by-step actions to accomplish the goals.

Marnel Corporation's goal is to develop a continuing stream of quality electronic products that can be manufactured and marketed profitably, and thereby increase the value of the firm and the wealth of its owners. Its strategies include the following:

1. All electronic devices will be manufactured by Marnel Corporation in order to ensure quality and provide some protection against other firms' attempts to duplicate the devices.

2. The sales and servicing of the devices will be carried out by the firm's sales staff to provide close working relations with customers.

3. Investments will be made in research and development to ensure the ongoing creation of new products.

---

[2] Canadian companies are required by the Companies (Corporations) Acts of the provincial and federal governments to have attached to their name Limited, Ltd., Ltée, Incorporated, Inc., Corporation, or Corp., depending on the jurisdiction of incorporation.

OBTAINING FINANCING

Before Marnel Corporation can embark on its business activities, it must obtain the necessary **funds**. The principal sources of funds are owners and creditors.

Owners

Owners provide funds to a firm and in return receive some evidence of their ownership. When a firm is organized as a corporation, ownership is evidenced by shares of common stock and the owners are called **shareholders**.[3] The firm need not repay the owners at a particular future date. Instead, the owners receive **dividends** if and when the firm decides to pay them. The owners also have a claim on all increases in the value of the firm resulting from future profitable operations. Usually, shareholders are able to sell their shares to other persons at a negotiated price.

Creditors

Unlike owners, **creditors** provide funds but require that the funds be repaid, often with interest, at a specific date. The length of time that elapses until repayment varies. Long-term creditors may provide funds and not require repayment for twenty years or more. Such borrowings are usually evidenced by a **bond**. A bond is simply an agreement in which the borrowing company promises to pay the creditors interest on the amounts borrowed at specific dates in the future and then to repay the amount borrowed at the end of some stated period of years. Banks usually lend for periods between several months and several years. Bank borrowings are usually evidenced by a **note**, in which the borrowing company promises to repay the amount borrowed plus interest at some future date. Suppliers of raw materials may not view themselves as sources of funds for a firm. Yet, when they supply raw materials but do not require payment for thirty days, they implicitly provide funds. Likewise, employees who are paid weekly or monthly and governmental units that are paid monthly or quarterly provide funds.

　　All firms must choose the proportion of funds to be obtained from owners, long-term creditors, and short-term creditors. Finance courses cover such financing decisions.

MAKING INVESTMENTS

Once a firm has obtained funds, it usually invests them in various items (assets) needed to carry out its business activities, such as the following:

1. Land, buildings, and equipment — Such investments provide a firm with a capacity to manufacture and sell its products and usually take many years to provide all of the potential services for which they were acquired.

---

[3] In other legal forms of business organization, including sole proprietorships, partnerships, and co-operatives, the owners are not called shareholders. This text illustrates the corporate form of organization unless otherwise stated, and the owners are called shareholders.

funds
Generally, cash or cash and temporary investments. Sometimes refers to working capital (current assets less current liabilities).

Owners
Those who provide funds to a firm and in return receive some evidence of their ownership.

shareholders
Those who hold shares in a limited company (a corporation); in effect, they are the owners of the corporation.

dividends
A distribution to a corporation's shareholders usually in cash but sometimes in other assets.

creditors
Those who lend funds but require the funds to be repaid.

bond
A form of interest-bearing note payable, usually issued by the borrower for relatively long periods to a group of lenders.

note
A document showing the conditions, amount, and parties involved in a loan arrangement.

2. Patents, licences, and other contractual rights — Such investments provide a firm with the legal right to use certain property or processes in pursuing its business activities.

3. Common shares or bonds of other firms — A firm might invest in other firms (thereby becoming itself an owner or creditor). Such investments might be made for a few months with temporary excess cash or for more long-term purposes.

4. Inventories — The principal goal of many business firms is to sell their products to customers.[4] In order to satisfy the needs of customers as they arise, an inventory of products must be on hand. Funds are usually not invested in specific inventory items for very long, because the items will soon be sold to customers. Because a certain amount of inventory must always be on hand, however, firms must continually invest some amount of their funds in inventory items.

5. Accounts receivable from customers — When a firm sells its products to customers who are not required to pay immediately, the firm is providing financing to its customers. Carrying a certain amount of accounts receivable may be in the best interest of the firm if sales and profits
are increased accordingly. In extending credit to customers, the firm foregoes collecting its cash right away. Funds to acquire other assets must be obtained elsewhere. Carrying accounts receivable, therefore, requires an investment of funds.

6. Cash — Most firms will leave a portion of their funds in the form of cash in chequing or savings accounts so that they can pay their bills currently, and to provide a cushion to handle unforeseen expenditures.

Managerial accounting courses cover the techniques for making proper investment decisions.

CARRYING OUT OPERATIONS

A firm obtains financing and invests the funds in various resources in order to generate profit. The following constitute the operating activities of a firm:

1. Purchasing — The purchasing department of a *merchandising* firm acquires the amounts and types of products needed by its retail stores. The purchasing department of a *manufacturing* firm acquires the amounts and types of raw materials needed in production.

2. Production — The production department in a manfacturing firm combines raw materials, labour services, and other manufacturing inputs to produce the products, or outputs, of a firm.

3. Marketing — The marketing department oversees selling the product to customers.

4. Administration — The administrative activity of a firm supports purchasing, production, marketing, and other operating departments.

---

[4] Some firms, of course, sell services instead of products (e.g., an accounting firm).

Administration might include data processing, accounting, legal services, research and development, and other activities.

Managerial accounting, marketing, and production courses cover the appropriate basis for making proper investment decisions.

SUMMARY OF BUSINESS ACTIVITIES

Figure 1.1 summarizes the four principal business activities discussed in this section and distinguishes between the short term and the long term. Although the time line dividing short- from long-term activities varies somewhat among firms, one year is generally the dividing line used, since one year is the normal interval between the preparation of full financial statements. Theoretically, the demarcation should be based on one year or one operating cycle, whichever is longer. An operating cycle is the normal length of time needed to turn cash into inventory, into receivables, and back into cash. For example, a distillery that ages its products might have an operating cycle of many years.

PRINCIPAL FINANCIAL STATEMENTS

The annual report to shareholders typically includes a letter from the firm's president summarizing activities of the past year and assessing the firm's prospects for the coming year. Also frequently included are promotional

FIGURE 1.1
Summary of Business Activities

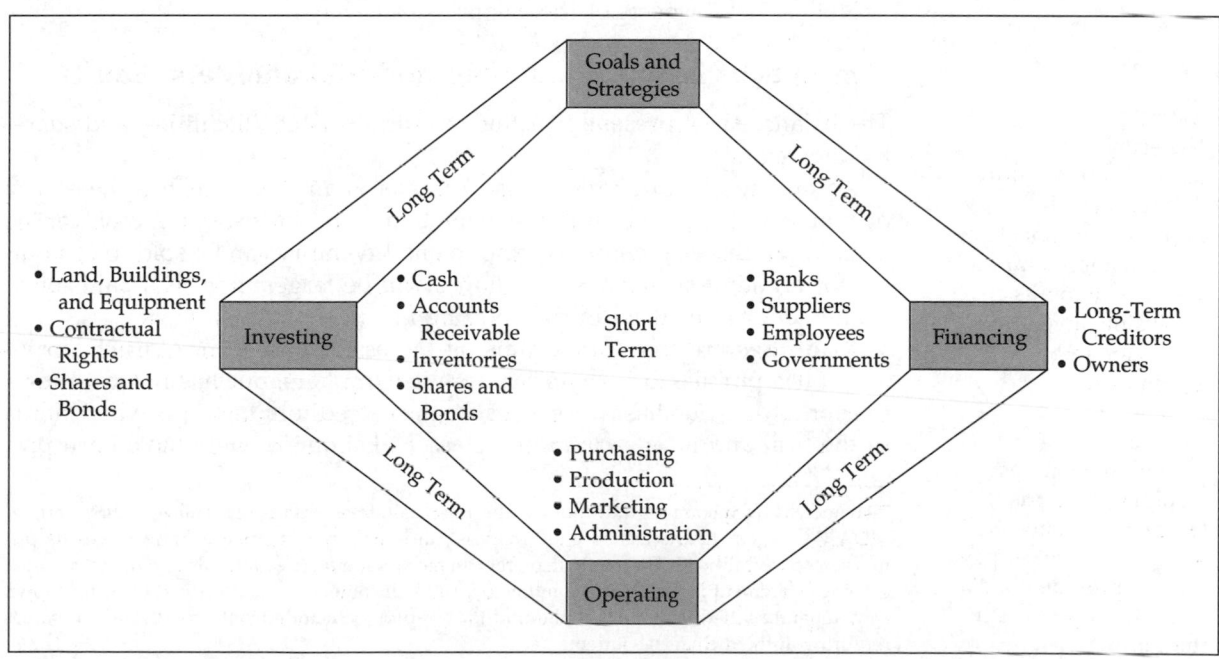

materials, such as pictures of the firm's products and employees. The section of the annual report containing the financial statements comprises the following:[5]

1. Balance sheet
2. Income statement
3. Retained earnings statement
4. Statement of changes in financial position
5. Notes to the financial statements, including various supporting schedules and explanatory comments
6. Auditor's report

BALANCE SHEET

balance sheet
A financial report showing the financial position of an entity in terms of assets, liabilities, and owners' equity at a specific date.

The **balance sheet** presents a snapshot of the financial position of the firm at an instant in time — the balance sheet date. This statement shows the accumulated wealth and the outstanding obligations of the enterprise. Each day, the balance sheet is different, reflecting further operating, financing, and investing activities. Exhibit 1.1 presents a comparative balance sheet for Marnel Corporation as of January 1, Year 1, and December 31, Year 1.

The balance sheet on January 1, Year 1, depicts Marnel Corporation on the day it was organized. Owners provided $500,000 of funds, long-term creditors provided $400,000, and suppliers provided $100,000. These funds were invested in inventories, land, building, equipment, and a patent; $70,000 was left in the firm's chequing account.

The balance sheet on December 31, Year 1, presents the financial position of Marnel Corporation at the end of the first year. The amounts for most items in the balance sheet changed between the beginning and end of the year.

Note several aspects of the balance sheet.

Concepts of Assets, Liabilities, and Shareholders' Equity

Assets
The economic resources of an entity that can usefully be expressed in monetary terms; some examples are cash, accounts receivable, inventories, and plant and equipment.

Liabilities
Current obligations resulting from past transactions that require the firm to pay money, provide goods, or perform services in the future.

The balance sheet presents a listing of a firm's assets, liabilities, and shareholders' equity.

Assets are economic resources. An asset is an item that has the ability or potential to provide future benefits to a firm. For example, cash can be used to purchase inventory or equipment. Inventory can be sold to customers for an amount that the firm hopes will be larger than was paid for it. Equipment can be used in transporting inventory to customers.

Liabilities are creditors' claims on the assets of a firm. Marnel Corporation has purchased inventories from its suppliers, but has not paid for a portion of the purchases. As a result, these creditors have provided funds to the firm and have a claim on its assets. Labour services have been pro-

---

[5] An increasingly common addition to the financial statements is the *management report*, or MDA (Management Discussion and Analysis), in which management acknowledges its primary responsibility for the content of the financial statements. Note also that the retained earnings statement is sometimes combined with the income statement instead of being shown as a separate schedule, and that the auditor's report is included only for those companies requiring audited financial statements.

EXHIBIT 1.1
MARNEL CORPORATION
Comparative Balance Sheet

	December 31, Year 1	January 1, Year 1
ASSETS		
Current Assets:		
Cash	$ 190,000	$ 70,000
Accounts Receivable	180,000	—
Inventories	270,000	100,000
Total Current Assets	$ 640,000	$ 170,000
Capital Assets		
Land	$ 30,000	$ 30,000
Buildings (net of accumulated depreciation)	380,000	400,000
Equipment (net of accumulated depreciation)	230,000	250,000
Total Property, Plant and Equipment	$ 640,000	$ 680,000
Patent (net of accumulated amortization)	120,000	150,000
Total Noncurrent Assets	$ 760,000	$ 830,000
Total Assets	$1,400,000	$1,000,000
LIABILITIES AND SHAREHOLDERS' EQUITY		
Current Liabilities		
Accounts Payable	$ 130,000	$ 100,000
Accounts Payable	30,000	—
Salaries Payable	40,000	—
Total Current Liabilities	$ 200,000	$ 100,000
Noncurrent Liabilities		
Bonds Payable (due Year 20)	450,000	400,000
Total Liabilities	$ 650,000	$ 500,000
Shareholders' Equity:		
Common Shares	$ 600,000	$ 500,000
Retained Earnings	150,000	—
Total Shareholders' Equity	$ 750,000	$ 500,000
Total Liabilities and Shareholders' Equity	$1,400,000	$1,000,000

vided by employees, but payment for these services has not been made as of December 31, Year 1. These employees likewise have provided funds to the firm and have a claim on its assets. Creditors' claims, or liabilities, result from a firm's having received benefits (cash, inventories, labour services) previously, and typically have a specified amount and date at which they must be paid.

Shareholders' equity is the owners' claim on the assets of a firm in a corporate form of business. Unlike creditors, the owners have only a residual interest. That is, owners have a claim on all assets in excess of those required to meet creditors' claims. The shareholders' equity generally comprises two parts: contributed capital and retained earnings. **Contributed capital** reflects the funds invested by shareholders for an ownership interest. The owners initally contributed $500,000 for Marnel Corporation's common shares. They invested an additional $100,000 during Year 1 for more shares.

Shareholders' equity
Proprietorship or owners' equity of a limited company. The term *stockholders' equity* is usually used by American writers.

Contributed capital
The sum of the balances in capital stock accounts plus capital contributed in excess of par (or stated) value accounts. Contrasts with donated capital.

Retained earnings
Net income over the
life of a company less
all dividends; owners'
equity less contributed
capital.

Retained earnings represent the earnings realized by a firm since its formation in excess of dividends distributed to shareholders. In other words, retained earnings are earnings reinvested by management for the benefit of shareholders. Management directs the use of a firm's assets so that, over time, more assets are received than are given up in obtaining them. This increase in assets, after any claims of creditors, belongs to the firm's owners. Most firms reinvest a large percentage of the assets generated by earnings for replacement of assets and growth rather than paying dividends.

Equality of Assets and Liabilities Plus Shareholders' Equity

As the balance sheet for Marnel Corporation shows, there is an equality between (1) assets and (2) liabilities plus shareholders' equity:

$$\text{Assets} = \text{Liabilities} + \text{Shareholders' Equity}$$

Assets reflect a firm's past investment decisions, and liabilities plus shareholders' equity reflect a firm's past financing decisions. Every dollar of funds obtained must be invested in something. Thus, we are viewing the same resources from two angles: a listing of the forms in which they are held (assets) and a listing of the parties (creditors and owners) who have provided financing and who, therefore, have a claim on those assets.

Balance Sheet Classification

The balance sheet classifies assets and liabilities as being either current or noncurrent.

Current assets
Assets that will either
be used up or con-
verted to cash within
the normal operating
cycle of the business or
one year, whichever is
longer.

Current liabilities
Obligations that,
within one year or the
operating cycle, which-
ever is longer, will
require (1) the use of
existing current assets
or (2) the creation of
other current liabilities.

Noncurrent assets
Assets that are held
and used for several
years, including land,
buildings, equipment,
patents, and long-term
investments.

Noncurrent liabilities
Liabilities that are not
due within the coming
year or operating cycle.

Current assets include cash and assets that are expected to be turned into cash, or sold, or consumed within approximately one year from the date of the balance sheet. Cash, temporary investments in securities, accounts receivable from customers, and inventories are the most common current assets. **Current liabilities** include liabilities that are expected to be paid within one year. Notes payable to banks, accounts payable to suppliers, salaries payable to employees, and taxes payable to governments are examples.

Noncurrent assets, typically held and used for several years, include land, buildings, equipment, patents, and long-term investments in securities. **Noncurrent liabilities** and shareholders' equity are a firm's longer-term sources of funds.

Valuation

The dollar amount at which each asset and liability appears on the balance sheet is based on one of two valuation bases: (1) cash, or cash equivalent, valuation, or (2) acquisition, or historical, cost valuation.

Cash is stated at the amount of cash on hand or in the bank. Accounts receivable are shown at the amount of cash expected to be collected from customers. Liabilities are generally shown at the present value of the cash required to pay the liabilities. These assets and liabilities are sometimes referred to as *monetary items* because they are valued on a cash, or cash equivalent, basis.

The remaining assets are shown either at acquisition cost or at acquisition cost net of accumulated depreciation or amortization. For example, inventories and land are stated at the amount of cash or other resources that the firm originally sacrificed to acquire those assets. Buildings, equipment, and patents are likewise stated at acquisition cost, but this amount is adjusted downward to reflect the portion of the assets' services that has been used up since acquisition.

Common stock is reported at the amount invested by owners when the firm's common shares were first issued. Retained earnings are generally the sum of all prior years' earnings in excess of dividends.

INCOME STATEMENT

The second principal financial statement is the **income statement**, which presents the results of the operating activities of a firm for a period of time. Exhibit 1.2 presents the income statement for Marnel Corporation for Year 1. This statement indicates the **net income** or **earnings** of a firm for a period of time. Net income is the difference between revenues and expenses. Note several aspects of the income statement.

Concepts of Net Income, Revenue, Expenses

The terms *net income* and *earnings* are synonyms used interchangeably in corporate annual reports and throughout this text. Generating income from operating activities is the primary goal of most business firms. The income statement provides a measure of how successful a firm was in achieving this goal for a given time span. The income statement also reports the sources and amounts of a firm's revenues and the nature and amount of a firm's expenses that net to earnings for the period.

income statement
A financial report showing the results of an entity's operations in terms of revenue, expenses, and net income for a period of time.

net income
The excess of revenue earned in a period over related expenses incurred.

earnings
Income or sometimes profit.

EXHIBIT 1.2
MARNEL CORPORATION
Income Statement for Year 1

Sales of Electronic Devices		$2,250,000
Less: Cost of Goods Sold		(1,400,000)
Gross Profit		$ 850,000
Sale of Engineering Services		140,000
		$ 990,000
Less: Selling and Administrative Expenses		
Selling Expenses	$400,000	
Administrative Expenses	200,000	600,000
Operating Profit		$ 390,000
Less: Financial Expense (net):		
Interest Expenses	$ 50,000	
Less: Interest Revenue	(10,000)	40,000
Net Income Before Income Tax		$ 350,000
Income Tax Expense		(150,000)
Net Income		$ 200,000

Revenues
The amount of cash received or claims established against customers, stemming from the provision of goods or services by the firm.

Expenses
Costs incurred for the purpose of generating revenue.

Cost of goods sold
The cost of merchandise sold to customers during the accounting period. It is calculated by adding the beginning inventory and net cost of purchases and deducting the ending inventory.

net loss
The excess of all expenses and losses for a period over all revenues and gains of the period. Negative net income.

gross profit
Net sales minus cost of goods sold.

operating profit
Calculated by deducting the operating expenses from the gross profit.

Revenues measure the inflows of assets (or reductions in liabilities) from selling goods and providing services to customers. During Year 1, Marnel Corporation sold electronic devices and provided engineering and financing services. From its customers, Marnel Corporation received either cash or promises to pay cash in the future, called Accounts Receivable from Customers. Both are assets. Thus, revenues were generated and assets increased.

Expenses measure the outflow of assets (or increases in liabilities) used up in generating revenues. **Cost of goods sold** (an expense) is a measure of the cost of inventories sold to customers. Selling expenses measure the cash payments made or the liabilities incurred to make future cash payments for marketing services received during the period. For each expense, either an asset decreases or a liability increases.

A firm strives to generate an excess of net asset inflows from revenues over net asset outflows from expenses required in generating the revenues. Net income indicates a firm's accomplishments (revenues) relative to the efforts required (expenses) in pursuing its operating activities. When expenses for a period exceed revenues, a firm incurs a **net loss**.

Classification of Revenues and Expenses

The purpose of the income statement is to provide useful information about the flows of the firm so that persons outside the company can evaluate managerial performance and construct an estimate of future performance.

Expense flows are incurred to earn revenue. Some can be identified with particular revenue transactions; for example, this is the case for the cost of goods sold, since the acquisition of the merchandise is necessary to its sale. Other expense flows, such as advertising, can be identified only with particular classes of revenue, while others, such as general management expenses, can be identified only with the general operation of the business.

To distinguish the expenses and match them to the appropriate revenue, the income statement can be segregated into steps. The first step matches the cost of goods sold with the revenue from the sale; the difference between the two represents the **gross profit**. The gross profit ratio, the ratio of gross profit to sales, will vary between industries and firms, but will alter significantly over time for one firm only if there have been dramatic changes in policy.

From the gross profit, the expenses of the operating functions, such as marketing, accounting, personnel, and general management, are deducted to derive the **operating profit** of the firm for the period. This is the second step. The operating profit is the result of the primary activities of the firm before considering the financing activities and the portion of the net income to be paid to government as income tax.

Some firms depend on the shareholders as a primary source of capital, whereas others borrow substantial sums from creditors for this purpose. The firms depending primarily on shareholders incur no interest expense, in contrast with the latter group of firms. As the third step, in order to enhance interfirm comparability and to evaluate the financial activity of a firm, the results of the financial function are deducted separately from the operating profit. The common result of the financial function is interest expense, but this expense may be offset by interest and dividends received from the investment in financial assets.

Corporations are individual legal entities and, as such, are subject to **income tax**. A full examination of corporate income tax requires a course devoted to that subject, but it will be discussed in Chapter 9. Briefly, the income tax payable by a firm is based on a fixed rate multiplied by the net income before income tax. After deducting income tax, the results of the recurring operations of the firm are presented as the *net income*. The net income represents the residual revenues attributable to the shareholders of the firm.

This **multiple-step income statement** is ordinarily used for internal reporting; the format is altered for external reporting. This multiple-step form of income statement will be used throughout this text.[6]

RETAINED EARNINGS STATEMENT

The **retained earnings statement** links the balance sheet at the beginning with that at the end of the period and the income statement. Recall that retained earnings represent the sum of prior earnings of a firm in excess of dividends paid out to the shareholders. The amount of net income helps explain the change in retained earnings between the beginning and end of the period. During Year 1, Marnel Corporation had net income of $200,000. Dividends declared and paid were $50,000. Exhibit 1.3 presents the retained earnings statement for Marnel Corporation for Year 1.

EXHIBIT 1.3
MARNEL CORPORATION
Retained Earnings Statement for Year 1

Retained Earnings, January 1, Year 1	$ 0
Add Net Income for Year 1	200,000
Subtract Dividends Declared and Paid During Year 1	(50,000)
Retained Earnings December 31, Year 1	$150,000

SUMMARY OF BALANCE SHEET AND INCOME STATEMENT

Recall that Figure 1.1 summarized the principal business activities of a firm: financing, investing, and operating. Figure 1.2 summarizes the relation between these business activities and the balance sheet and income statement.

STATEMENT OF CHANGES IN FINANCIAL POSITION

The fourth principal financial statement is the **statement of changes in financial position**. This section reports the sources (inflows) and uses (outflows) of cash during a period of time. Exhibit 1.4 presents a statement of changes in financial position for Marnel Corporation for Year 1. Operations led to an increase in cash of $50,000. (Recall that not all revenues result in an immediate increase in cash and that not all expenses result in an immediate decrease in cash.) Also, cash was received when bonds and common

income tax
An annual tax levied by the federal and provincial governments on the income of an entity. An expense, and if not yet paid, a liability.

multiple-step income statement
An income statement in which one or more intermediate subtotals (such as gross profit on sales) are derived before net income.

retained earnings statement
This statement links the balance sheet at the beginning with that at the end of the period and the income statement, and shows the changes to the Retained Earnings Account during the year.

statement of changes in financial position
A financial statement showing a firm's cash inflows and cash outflows for a specific period, classified into operating, investing, and financing categories.

---

[6] Published financial statements sometimes include single-step income statements, which are more condensed than the multiple-step version.

FIGURE 1.2
Relationship Between Business Activities and Balance Sheet and Income Statement

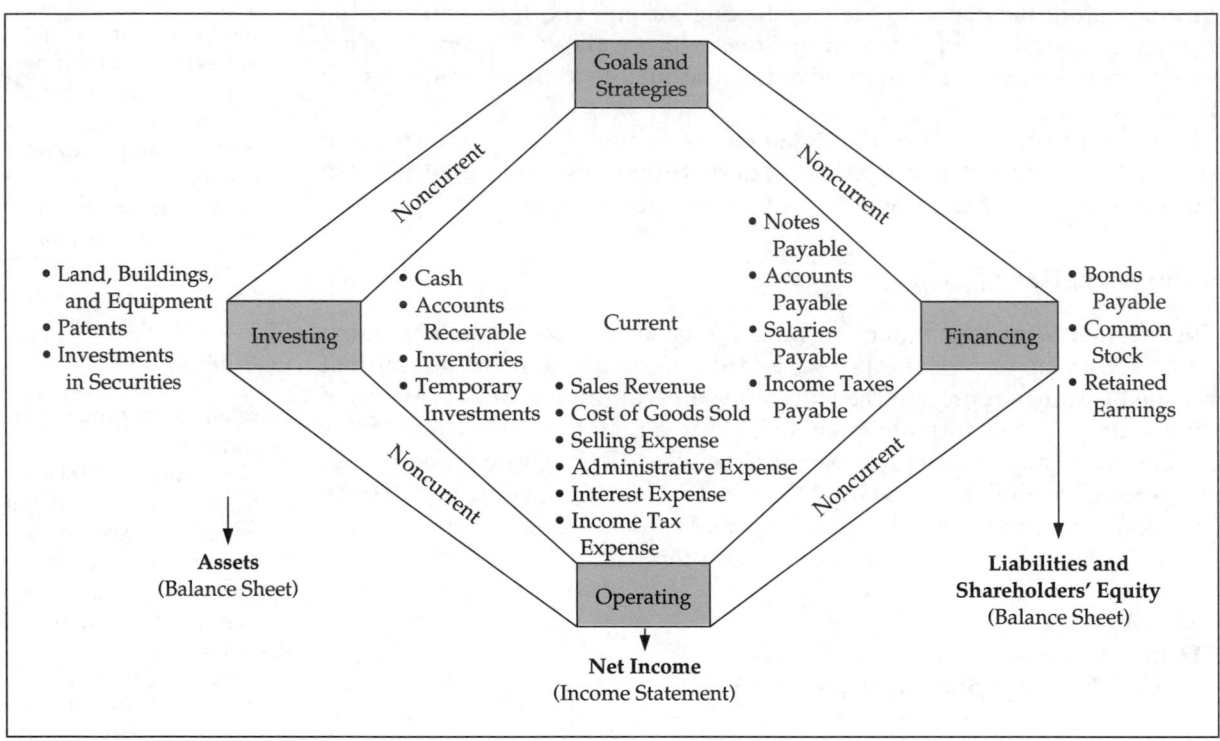

shares were issued. Cash was used to pay dividends and to acquire equipment. Of what significance is a statement explaining or analyzing the change in cash during a period of time? This might be best illustrated by an example.

EXHIBIT 1.4
MARNEL CORPORATION
Statement of Changes in Financial Position for Year 1

Cash Provided by:	
Operations	$ 50,000[a]
New Financing: Issue of Bonds	50,000
Issue of Common Shares	100,000
Sale of Noncurrent Assets	—
Total Sources	$200,000
Cash Applied to:	
Dividends	$ 50,000
Reduction in Financing	—
Acquisition of Noncurrent Assets	30,000
Total Uses	$ 80,000
Net Increase in Cash for Year 1	$120,000

[a]*Computation of this item, as well as proper formatting rules, are discussed in Chapter 13.*

Example 2 Diversified Technologies Corporation began business four years ago. In its first four years of operations, net income was $100,000, $300,000, $800,000, and $1,500,000, respectively. The company retained all of its earnings for growth. Early in the fifth year, the company learned that despite the retention of all of its earnings, it was running out of cash. A careful study of the problem revealed that the company was expanding accounts receivable, inventories, buildings, and equipment so fast that funds were not being generated quickly enough by operations to keep pace with its growth.

This example illustrates a common phenomenon for business firms. Cash may not be generated in sufficient amounts or at the proper times to finance all ongoing or growing operations. If the firm is to continue operating successfully, it must generate more funds than it spends. In some cases, the firm can borrow from creditors to replenish its cash, but future operations must generate funds to repay these loans.

Classification of Sources and Uses of Cash

Exhibit 1.4 classifies the sources and uses of cash in parallel with the three principal business activities described earlier in the chapter. Figure 1.3 graphically depicts these various sources and uses.

1. Sources: Operations — The excess of cash received from customers over the amount of cash paid to suppliers, employees, and others in carrying out a firm's operating activities is a primary source of funds for most

FIGURE 1.3
Sources and Uses of Cash

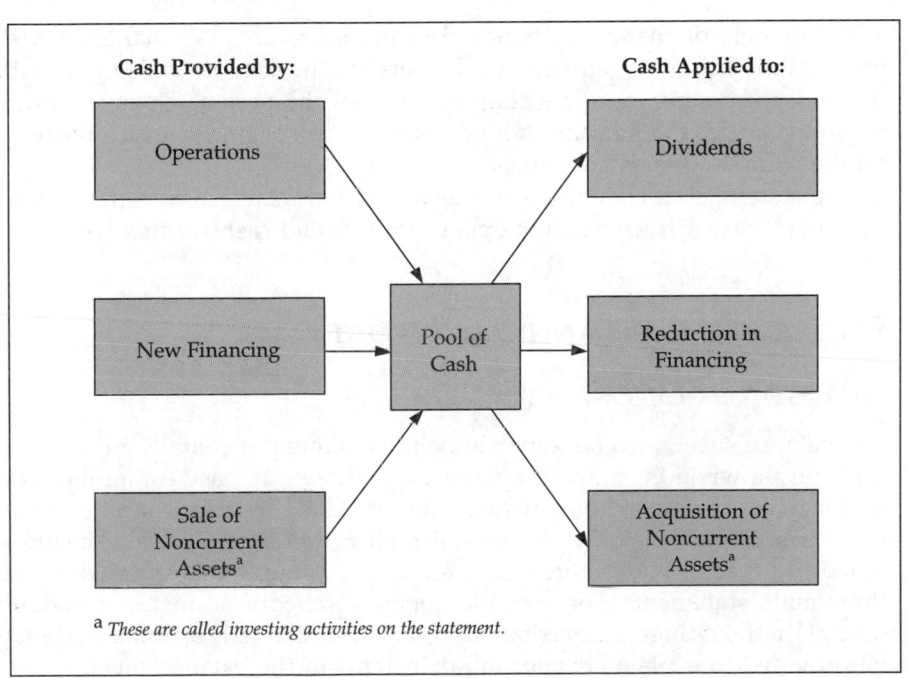

a *These are called investing activities on the statement.*

firms. Although the cash received from customers could be included among the sources and the cash paid to suppliers, employees, and others included among uses, most firms net the sources from operations against the uses from operations.

2. Sources: New Financing — Firms often obtain additional financing by issuing bonds or common shares.

3. Sources: Sale of Noncurrent Assets — The sales of land, buildings, equipment, and other noncurrent assets generate cash.

4. Uses: Dividends — Most firms whose shares are widely held by the public regularly pay dividends. The payment of dividends might be viewed as a reduction in financing, because funds potentially invested by owners (through retained earnings) are now being distributed to them.

5. Uses: Reduction in Financing — Cash is used when a firm repays noncurrent liabilities or reacquires its common shares.

6. Uses: Acquisition of Noncurrent Assets — Firms that expect either to maintain current operating levels or to grow must continually acquire buildings, equipment, and other noncurrent assets.

Some people consider the statement of changes in financial position to be the most useful of the four statements. A major purpose of annual financial statements is to present a report on the activities of management during the past year to the investors, who have entrusted their funds to management. The statement of changes best summarizes how this stewardship role was carried out and shows how these funds were deployed to produce the best possible return on investment for the owners.

Relationship to Balance Sheet and Income Statement

The statement of changes in financial position explains the change in cash between the beginning and end of the period. The statement also sets forth the major investing and financing activities of the period. Thus, the statement of changes in financial position helps explain changes in various items on the comparative balance sheet.

The statement of changes in financial position relates also to the income statement in that it shows how operations affected cash for the period.

OTHER ITEMS IN ANNUAL REPORTS

NOTES AND SUPPORTING SCHEDULES

The balance sheet, income statement, and statement of changes in financial position shown in the annual report are condensed for easy comprehension by the average reader. Some readers are interested in details omitted from these condensed versions. The annual report, therefore, typically includes schedules that provide more detail for some of the items reported in the three main statements. For example, separate schedules must be provided to explain the change in contributed capital and retained earnings, and may be provided to explain changes in other items in the balance sheet.

Every set of published financial statements also contains explanatory notes, which are an integral part of the statements. As later chapters make clear, a firm must select the accounting methods followed in preparing its financial statements from a set of generally accepted methods. The notes indicate the actual accounting methods used by the firm, and also disclose additional information that elaborates on items presented in the three principal statements. To understand fully a firm's balance sheet, income statement, and statement of changes in financial position, one must read the notes carefully. No such notes are presented for the financial statements of Marnel Corporation because they would not mean much at this stage. Do not conclude, however, that the notes are unimportant merely because they have been omitted from the statements presented in this chapter.

AUDITOR'S REPORT

The annual financial statements present a report card on the activities of management and on the performance of the firm over the course of a year. Investment and lending decisions and the operation of capital markets are largely dependent on the signals generated by these financial statements. Yet, we have the curious situation in which management prepares its own report card. Obviously, there is a natural tendency for management to want to present the financial position of the company in the most favourable light. In some cases, executive salaries are directly tied to the size of the earnings figure reported.

To add objectivity to this process, **independent auditors**, who are not employees of the corporation, are called in to make their own assessment of how fairly the financial statements portray the financial position and results of operation of the firm. Thus, the external audit adds credibility to the financial reporting process, and the **auditor's report**, contained in the annual report to the shareholders, is considered by readers to be as important as the financial statements themselves. The annual report to the shareholders contains the opinion of the independent auditor on the financial statements, supporting schedules, and notes.

The auditor's report generally follows a standard format, with some variations to meet specific circumstances. An auditor's report on the financial statements of Marnel Corporation might be as follows:

AUDITOR'S REPORT

To the Shareholders of Marnel Corporation

I have audited the balance sheet of Marnel Corporation as at December 31, 19X1, and the statements of income, retained earnings, and changes in financial position for the year then ended. These financial statements are the responsibility of the company's management. My responsibility is to express an opinion on these financial statements on the basis of my audit.

I conducted my audit in accordance with generally accepted auditing standards. Those standards require that I plan and perform an audit to obtain reasonable assurance whether the financial statements are free of material misstatement. An audit includes examining, on a test basis, evidence supporting the amounts and disclosures in the financial statements. An audit also includes assessing the accounting principles used and significant estimates

independent auditors
Professional accountants called in from outside the company to give an expert opinion on whether the financial statements are fairly presented.

auditor's report
The formal document in which an auditor expresses an opinion regarding whether financial statements of the organization present fairly its position as of a given date and the results of its operations for the period ended on that date in accordance with generally accepted accounting principles.

made by management, as well as evaluating the overall financial statement presentation.

In my opinion, these financial statements present fairly, in all material respects, the financial position of the company as at December 31, 19X1, and the results of its operations and the changes in its financial position for the year then ended in accordance with generally accepted accounting principles.

City

Date   (signed) ....*B. Hanford*..........

CHARTERED ACCOUNTANT

The report usually contains three paragraphs: an *introductory paragraph*, a *scope paragraph*, and an *opinion paragraph*. The introductory paragraph states that an audit has been performed, but it is ultimately management's responsibility to ensure the accuracy of the financial statements, even though the auditor expresses an opinion on the financial statements. The scope paragraph states that the audit was conducted in accordance with the standards of the profession, which require that the audit be planned so that it will provide *reasonable assurance* that the financial statements are free of material misstatements. This paragraph also stresses that the auditor only tests the underlying records, which precludes offering absolute assurance. The opinion paragraph expresses a professional opinion regarding whether the financial statements present *fairly*, in all *material* respects, the financial position of the company in accordance with generally accepted accounting principles (GAAP). As a general rule, if the financial statements conform to GAAP, the financial statements are fair. Hence, GAAP conformity is the basis for assessing fairness. Obviously, the auditor must have an expert understanding of what constitutes GAAP. Areas in which GAAP are ill-defined present the greatest difficulty in conducting an audit. Exceptions to the statement that the auditor's "examination was made in accordance with generally accepted auditing standards" are seldom seen in published annual reports. There are occasional references to the auditor's having relied on financial statements examined by other auditors, particularly for subsidiaries or for data from prior periods.

The opinion expressed by the auditor in the second paragraph is the heart of the auditor's report. The opinion may be *unreserved* or *reserved*. The great majority of opinions are unreserved; that is, there are no exceptions or reservations to the auditor's opinion that the statements "present fairly the financial position . . . in accordance with generally accepted accounting principles."

Reservations to the opinion result when there is a departure from GAAP, or where there is a limitation in the scope of the auditor's examination. Examples of departures from GAAP are a failure to report depreciation, an excessive provision for inventory obsolescence, or an inadequate explanation of a contingency. Examples of limitations to the scope of an auditor's examination are cases in which the auditor was appointed too late to observe the physical inventory count, the accounting records are destroyed by fire, or the auditor is not permitted to confirm the accounts receivable.

The auditor may be able to express a positive opinion on the financial statements taken as a whole, despite a reservation arising from the departure from GAAP or a limitation in the scope of this examination. In these cases, the auditor will insert a *reservation paragraph* between the scope and opinion paragraphs and qualify this opinion with an exception phrase. The reservation paragraph will explain the departure from GAAP and the impact of this departure on the financial statements, or, alternatively, provide full details of the limitation in and the reasons for the scope of the auditor's examinations.

If the departure from GAAP is so severe that it renders the statements misleading, an adverse opinion is given by the auditor. In such a case, the opinion paragraph concludes that the financial statements do not present fairly the financial position of the firm. Adverse opinions are rare in published reports.

DISCUSSION CASE 2

Good-bye to the Ink-Stained Wretch

As a profession, accounting is still a parvenu. But new recruits are being lured by power, increasing prestige, and whopping salaries. The professions in North America are lined up in a kind of informal pecking order, certified by the twin laurels of success: money and social standing. Doctors and lawyers generally occupy the uppermost ranks in the hierarchy, while teachers, architects, clerics, writers, scientists, and others fall in someplace behind. In this caste system, accountants have long been regarded as lowly unfortunates. Almost any accountant can provide a wealth of anecdotal evidence to prove the profession's reputation.

Accounting has never set the popular imagination to flights of rapturous veneration. The practitioners of other professions have all taken turns waltzing in the limelight, extolled in verse or song, held up as heroes. Yet one searches long and hard to find the accountant assigned *any* part in literature or theater, and when

he is, it's usually as a bloodless drudge — Dickens' Uriah Heep. This nineteenth-century image seems to have endured, more or less intact, into the modern era. As recently as 1960, two social scientists, conducting a government-backed survey of attitudes among 1000 students at five unnamed but "highly selective" universities, found that in the students' eyes, "The accountant is the anti-hero of the occupational world. ... The accountant is a conformist, with a minimum of social skills. ... He is rated as passive, weak, soft, shallow, and cold." Even accounting's most distinguished scholars have been apologetic about their profession. For instance, Henry Rand Hatfield's famous treatise on accounting, first delivered as a speech in 1923, is entitled "An Historical Defense of Book-keeping."

But things have been changing during the past two decades, and the profession is now in the midst

(continued)

(continued)

of a full-fledged boom in terms of size, wealth, and even status. One business magazine, not long ago, quoted the chairman of a university accounting department as saying, "Suddenly students see accounting as glamorous, sexy. Many of our best students, who would have gone to law school a couple of years ago, are now going into public accounting." The reasons are no mystery: there are plenty of job openings in accounting and the salaries are increasingly attractive.

The causes of the profession's ascent are many and varied. But generally speaking, accounting is being assigned an expanded role in society as greater answerability is demanded of all institutions both public and private.

Accounting is control, and it is being used increasingly as an instrument of social control. Thus members of the accounting profession, it is said, should be society's tribunes, ensuring that the institutions to which power and authority have been granted are properly answerable to their constituents. It may be an exaggeration to suggest, as some have, that accountants constitute a "new elite" in America. Nonetheless, it is clear that the stereotypical image of the accountant as an ink-stained wretch wearing a green eyeshade and sitting on a three-legged stool is a relic of the past.

Because of its growth and ever broadening role, accounting is a many-faceted profession these days. Some accountants work for corporations, fashioning plans, budgets, and financial statements. Others, from the accounting firms, audit those numbers, while providing tax and management consulting services on the side. Accounting firms run the gamut from sole-practitioner outfits to the Big Six concerns, employing thousands of workers and operating offices throughout the world. In addition, some accountants form a coterie of free-lance foreign-currency specialists clustered in the world's trading capitals — Hong Kong, Geneva, and other far-flung locales. Then, too, they are frequently becoming cops, as members of the state and local police, the RCMP or Revenue Canada, trying to ferret out white-collar crime. And while academia has generally been going through a period of contraction and austerity in recent years, accounting professors are in great demand.

The practice of accounting itself has become more and more complex, which tends to increase the level of specialization within the profession and adds to the demand for accountants. Fueling this trend has been the computer; it has spawned not only new techniques for gathering information, making decisions, and controlling operations, but also a vast new arena for technologically abetted crime. Tales of electronic thievery and fraud are by now well known, especially in the banking business. Crooks educated in the ways of computers have been able to tap into a bank's computer system, give the appropriate commands, and make off with millions, leaving scarcely a fingerprint in the Fortran. To cope with both the promise and the threat posed by computer technology, the large accounting firms have developed

(continued)

(continued)

cadres of computer experts in recent years. One group, for instance, may counsel a corporate client on computerized management methods, while a separate team advises it on tightening security to lessen its vulnerability to computer crooks, either outsiders or employees.

As a profession, accounting is still rapidly evolving. While it has attained considerable size and wealth, the profession is struggling uneasily to fill the larger public role that society now demands of it. How ably and actively it moves into that broader domain will be of no lit-

tle importance, particularly now that government regulation is in disrepute. The call for less regulation is a responsible tendency, it seems, only if there is some assurance that powerful private institutions can be held accountable without it. Providing that assurance is the mission of the accounting profession.

References

Adapted from Steve Lohr, "Good-Bye to the Ink-Stained Wretch," *The Atlantic*, August 1980.

Discussion Question

Why is a career in public accounting an attractive option?

OBJECTIVES OF FINANCIAL REPORTING

Financial statements, such as those discussed in this chapter, provide information to investors, creditors, and others who commit funds to a firm. The **Financial Accounting Standards Board (FASB)**, the official rule-making body in the private sector in the United States, has established a broad set of financial reporting objectives to guide the financial reporting process. Figure 1.4 summarizes these objectives, described briefly below, and their relation to the principal financial statements. Financial reporting should:

Financial Accounting Standards Board (FASB)
A U.S. nongovernmental group that promulgates authoritative rules for the general practice of financial accounting in the United States.

1. Provide information useful for making rational investment and credit decisions. This general-purpose objective states simply that financial reporting should be aimed primarily at investors and creditors and should be useful to these individuals in their decisions.

2. Provide information to help investors and creditors assess the amount, timing, and uncertainty of cash flows. This objective follows from the first by defining "useful" information more fully. It states that investors and creditors are interested primarily in the cash they will receive from investing in a firm. Those cash flows are affected by the ability of the firm to generate cash flows.

3. Provide information about the economic resources of a firm and the claims on those resources. The balance sheet satisfies this objective.

4. Provide information about a firm's operating performance during a period. The income statement accomplishes this objective.

5. Provide information about how an enterprise obtains and uses cash. The statement of changes in financial position accomplishes this objective.

6. Provide information about how management has discharged its stewardship responsibility to owners. Stewardship refers to the prudent use

FIGURE 1.4
Summary of Reporting Process and Principal Financial Statements

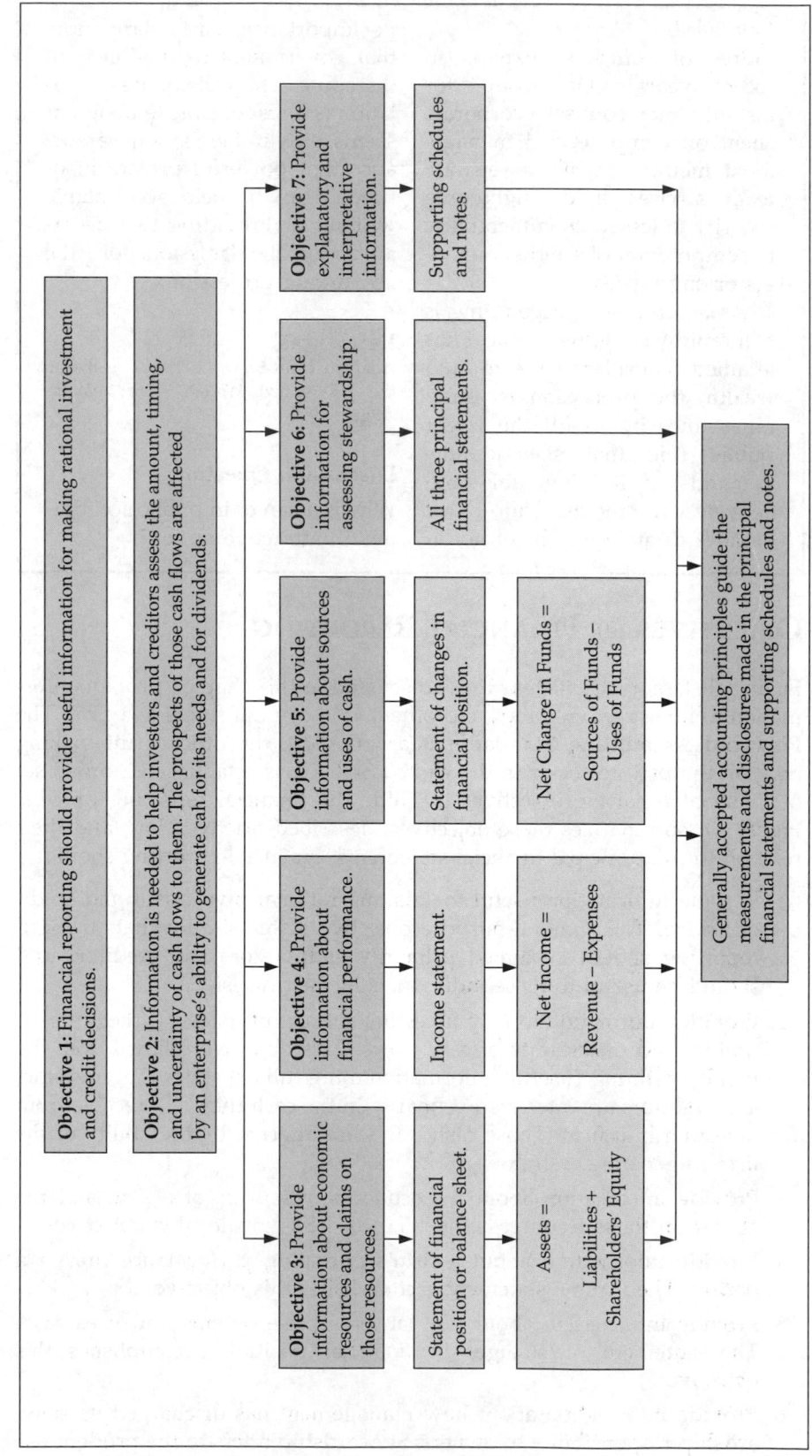

of resources entrusted to a firm. No single statement helps in assessing stewardship. Rather, owners assess stewardship using information from all three financial statements and notes.

7. Include explanations and interpretations to help users understand the financial information provided. Supporting schedules and notes to the financial statements satisfy this objective.

AN INTERNATIONAL PERSPECTIVE

The process followed for setting up accounting principles varies widely throughout the world. In some countries, the measurement rules followed for preparing the financial statements match those for computing taxable income. In other countries, a government agency that is separate from the taxing authority establishes acceptable accounting principles. In Canada and the United States, among others, the accounting profession, through its various boards and committees, plays the dominant role in setting accounting principles.

It is not surprising that the differing objectives of these standard-setting bodies (e.g., taxation, accomplishment of government's economic policy objectives, and fair reporting) result in diverse sets of accounting principles throughout the world. The International Accounting Standards Committee (IASC), a voluntary association of professional accounting organizations from many countries, has been striving to harmonize accounting principles. Although this association has no legal authority of its own, it encourages its members to exert influence on the standard-setting process within their own countries to reduce the current diversity. The Accounting Standards Board of the CICA is on official record as being committed to harmonize the *CICA Handbook* with all IASC pronouncements, except where there are special circumstances in the Canadian accounting environment that preclude such harmonization.

The balance sheet and the income statement are the principal financial statements presented by most firms around the world. Only a few countries require a statement of changes in financial position showing cash flows. Some countries, however, include a statement of sources and application of working capital.

Canada's principal trading partner is the United States. Many companies in the two countries share common ownership that requires the preparation of consolidated financial statements. With the free trade pact, the two countries will eventually act as a single common market. Fortunately, there are relatively few differences between the accounting principles of the two countries.

Other major trading blocs, such as the European Community, are emerging, and these will accelerate the move toward hamonization of accounting principles. The ideal of a single, worldwide set of accounting rules is impossible, because accounting rules are shaped to some degree by various laws and legal systems. However, we are definitely moving in the direction of an international common language of business.

SUMMARY

This chapter has provided an overview of business activities and related them to the principal financial statements included in annual reports to shareholders. Perhaps more questions have been raised than answered. It is helpful, however, to have a broad overview of the various financial statements before examining the concepts and procedures that underlie each statement.

Chapters 2 through 4 discuss and illustrate the concepts and procedures underlying the financial statements at a basic level that will allow the student to prepare the statements from a set of straightforward transactions. Chapter 5 summarizes these concepts and integrates them into a conceptual framework that proves valuable in analyzing the more complex transactions introduced in Chapters 6 through 12. The final three chapters synthesize this material, show the impact of accounting choices, and most importantly, look at financial statements from the perspective of the user.

Now we turn to the study of financial accounting. One of the most effective ways to comprehend the concepts and procedures in this book is to study carefully the numerical examples presented in each chapter and diligently work through the problems, including the self-study problem(s), at the end of each chapter.

KEY TERMS

Accounting
Canadian Institute of Chartered
    Accountants (CICA)
Managerial accounting
Financial accounting
CA (Chartered Accountant)
SMAC (Society of Management
    Accountants of Canada)
CMA (Certified Management
    Accountant)
CGA (Certified General Accountant)
Generally accepted accounting
    principles (GAAP)
Accounting Standards Board (ASB)
Funds
Owners
Shareholders
Dividends
Creditors
Bond
Note
Balance sheet
Assets
Liabilities
Shareholders' equity

Contributed capital
Retained earnings
Current assets
Current liabilities
Noncurrent assets
Noncurrent liabilities
Income statement
Net income
Earnings
Revenues
Expenses
Cost of goods sold
Net loss
Gross profit
Operating profit
Income tax
Multiple-step income statement
Retained earnings statement
Statement of changes in financial
    position
Independent auditors
Auditor's report
Financial Accounting Standards
    Board (FASB)

SELF-STUDY MATERIAL

This section contains questions, exercises, and problems to help you assess your understanding of Chapter 1. Careful review of this material will assist you in completing the homework assignments. Solutions are found at the end of the section.

QUESTIONS AND EXERCISES

True/False

For each statement, place a T or an F in the space provided to indicate whether the statement is true or false.

_T_ 1. Current liabilities include liabilities that are expected to be paid within one year.

_T_ 2. "Generally accepted accounting principles" are the accounting methods and procedures used by firms in preparing their financial statements.

_F_ 3. The income statement attempts to present an overall view of a firm's financial position at a given date.

_T_ 4. The terms net income, earnings, and profits are synonymous and are defined as the difference between revenues and expenses for a period.

_T_ 5. Financial reporting should provide useful information for making rational investment and credit decisions.

_T_ 6. One of the objectives of accounting is to help investors and creditors assess the amount, timing, and uncertainty of cash flows to them.

_T_ 7. Financial accounting is concerned with the preparation of reports that provide information to users external to the firm.

_T_ 8. If, during the audit of a firm, the auditor discovers something of a material nature that indicates the client's financial statements are erroneous or misleading, the auditor should give either a reserved or an adverse opinion.

_F_ 9. The balance sheet presents the results of earnings activity over time.

_T_ 10. Shareholders' equity is the owner's claim on the assets of the firm.

_T_ 11. The two sources of any firm's assets are the firm's creditors and owners.

_T_ 12. The statement of changes in financial position provides information about the principal financing and investing activities of a firm.

_F_ 13. The scope paragraph of the auditor's report states that the financial statements "present fairly the financial position . . . and the results of operations and the changes in financial position . . . in accordance with generally accepted accounting principles applied on a basis consistent with that of the preceding period."

_T_ 14. Retained earnings represent the sum of all prior earnings of the firm in excess of dividends.

_T_ 15. A multiple-step income statement facilitates the use of information provided in the financial statements.

_T_ 16. Noncurrent assets provide firms with long-term productive capacity.

_F_ 17. Contributed capital represents the earnings realized by a firm since its formation in excess of dividends distributed to shareholders.

_F_ 18. Acquisition of noncurrent assets is an activity that is typically a source of cash for a firm.

Matching

From the list of terms, select one term that is most closely associated with one descriptive phrase or statement that follows, and place the letter for that term in the space provided.

a. assets
b. balance sheet
c. contributed capital
d. denial of opinion or adverse opinion
e. expenses
f. financial accounting
g. income statement
h. liabilities

i. managerial accounting
j. net income
k. net loss
l. retained earnings
m. revenues
n. shareholders' equity
o. statement of changes in financial position
p. unreserved opinion

__c__ 1. Represent a measure of the assets provided by the original shareholder in exchange for an ownership interest in the firm.

__b__ 2. This financial statement presents an overall view of a company's financial position at a given date.

__a__ 3. Economic resources that have the potential or ability to provide future services or benefits to the firm.

__m__ 4. Inflows of assets (or reductions in liabilities) from selling goods and providing services to customers.

__d__ 5. Given when an auditor thinks an opinion cannot be expressed regarding the fairness of the financial statements as a whole.

__e__ 6. Outflows of assets (or increases in liabilities) used up in generating revenue.

__f__ 7. This segment of accounting is concerned with the preparation of reports that provide information to users external to the firm.

____ 8. The excess of revenues over expenses for a period.

__i__ 9. This segment of accounting is concerned with the preparation of reports that provide information to users within the firm.

__l__ 10. This item represents the earnings, or profits, realized by the firm since its formation in excess of dividends distributed to shareholders.

__o__ 11. This financial statement reports the sources and uses of cash during a period of time.

__k__ 12. Creditors' claims on the resources of the company.

__g__ 13. This financial statement presents the results of earnings activity over time.

__p__ 14. States that a firm's financial statements "present fairly the financial position and the results of operations and the changes in financial position in accordance with generally accepted accounting principles applied on a basis consistent with that of the preceding period."

__k__ 15. The excess of expenses over revenues for a period.

__n__ 16. Owners' claim on the assets of the company. The owners' claim is called a residual interest.

Multiple Choice

Choose the best answer for each question or problem and enter the identifying letter in the space provided.

__d__ 1. Which of these transactions of Corley Limited is not a use of cash?
a) purchased a tract of land
b) paid dividends to shareholders
c) reacquired some of the company's common shares
d) long-term debt was issued

2. Which of these financial statements provides information about sources and uses of cash?
   a) income statement
   b) balance sheet
   c) statement of changes in financial position
   d) all of the above

3. Which of these equations is incorrect?
   a) Shareholders' Equity = Contributed Capital + Retained Earnings
   b) Revenues − Expenses = Net Income
   c) Assets = Liabilities + Shareholders' Equity
   d) all of the above equations are correct

4. Evans Corporation's retained earnings increased by $300,000 during the year. Also during the year, dividends totalling $75,000 were declared and paid to shareholders. Evans Corporation's net income for the year was:
   a) $75,000
   b) $225,000
   c) $300,000
   d) $375,000

5. Which of the following does not describe an expense?
   a) payment of dividends to shareholders
   b) cost of merchandise sold
   c) salaries earned by employees but not yet paid
   d) depreciation for the period on the firm's building

6. Which one of these assets is not a current asset?
   a) cash
   b) land
   c) merchandise inventory
   d) accounts receivable

7. Which of these transactions of Fort Co. Ltd. is not a source of cash?
   a) additional common shares were issued
   b) additional equipment was acquired
   c) a long-term note was issued
   d) a tract of land was sold

8. Which of these persons would be least likely to receive a firm's managerial accounting reports?
   a) a creditor of the firm
   b) one of the firm's production supervisors
   c) one of the firm's vice-presidents
   d) one of the firm's salespeople

9. Revenues are a measure of the inflows of assets (or reductions in liabilities) from selling goods and providing services to customers. Which of the following is not a revenue transaction?
   a) sold merchandise for cash to a customer
   b) sold merchandise on account to a customer
   c) delivered weekly magazines to a subscriber, who had paid previously for a one-year's subscription
   d) went to the local bank and borrowed money to be used in the business

10. Which of the following would not appear on a balance sheet?
   a) retained earnings
   b) bonds payable
   c) cost of goods sold
   d) accounts receivable

 11. Coleman Inc. reports total assets and total liabilities of $225,000 and $100,000, respectively, at the conclusion of its first year of business. The company earned $75,000 during the first year and distributed $30,000 in dividends. What was the firm's contributed capital?
   a) $125,000
   b) $95,000
   c) $80,000
   d) $50,000

 12. Which of the following is not a current asset?
   a) patent
   b) inventory
   c) accounts receivable
   d) cash

 13. Which of these financial statements provides information about economic resources and claims on those resources?
   a) income statement
   b) balance sheet
   c) statement of changes in financial position
   d) all of the above

 14. Which one of these liabilities is not a current liability?
   a) mortgage payable
   b) accounts payable
   c) salaries payable
   d) taxes payable

 15. Which of the following would not appear on an income statement?
   a) rent expense
   b) salaries payable
   c) sales revenue
   d) cost of goods sold

Exercises

1. Using the information given, determine the missing amounts in each of the independent cases below:

	a	b	c
Current Assets	$150,000	$_____	$160,000
Noncurrent Assets	$225,000	$200,000	$180,000
Current Liabilities	$ 30,000	$ 50,000	$_____
Noncurrent Liabilities	$105,000	$100,000	$100,000
Contributed Capital	$_____	$110,000	$ 70,000
Retained Earnings	$ 60,000	$_____	$150,000
Shareholders' Equity	$_____	$180,000	$_____

2. Using the information given, determine the missing amounts from the income statement and retained earnings statement in each of the independent cases below:

	a	b	c
Revenues	$240,000	$270,000	$_____
Expenses	$140,000	$_____	$340,000
Net Income	$_____	$_____	$ 80,000
Retained Earnings 1/1	$ 50,000	$ 45,000	$_____
Net Income	$_____	$ 54,000	$_____
Dividends	$ 20,000	$_____	$ 64,000
Retained Earnings 12/31	$_____	$ 69,000	$ 40,000

3. Using the information given, determine the missing amounts in each of the independent cases below:

	a	b	c
Assets	$_____	$480,000	$800,000
Liabilities	$160,000	$150,000	$380,000
Contributed Capital	$100,000	$_____	$280,000
Retained Earnings 1/1	$_____	$ 0	$ 40,000
Net Income	$ 28,000	$ 75,000	$160,000
Dividends	$ 10,000	$ 36,000	$_____
Retained Earnings 12/31	$ 40,000	$_____	$_____

4. Using the information given, determine the missing amount in each of the independent cases below:

	a	b	c
Cash Provided by:			
Operations	$_____	$ 30,000	$ 90,000
New Financing	$150,000	$ 85,000	$200,000
Sale of Noncurrent Assets	$ 30,000	$ 60,000	$110,000
Cash Applied to:			
Dividends	$ 10,000	$_____	$ 70,000
Reduction in Financing	$ 90,000	$100,000	$ 80,000
Acquisition of Noncurrent Assets	$ 50,000	$ 70,000	$200,000
Increase (Decrease) in Cash	$ 75,000	$ (20,000)	$_____

5. Kirkland Corporation began operations in July 19X1. Total shareholders' equity at that time was $30,000. On December 31, 19X1, the corporation reports assets of $150,000 and liabilities of $96,000.
   a. Determine the amount of shareholders' equity as of December 31, 19X1. Has shareholders' equity increased or decreased?
   b. Give several possible explanations for the change in shareholders' equity.
   c. What items make up shareholders' equity?

PROBLEM FOR SELF-STUDY

The accounting records of Digital Electronics Corporation reveal the following:

	December 31	
	Year 2	Year 1
Balance Sheet Items:		
Accounts Payable to Suppliers	$ 295,000	$250,000
Accounts Receivable from Customers	320,000	240,000
Bonds Payable	120,000	100,000
Buildings (net of accumulated depreciation)	140,000	150,000
Cash	50,000	30,000
Common Stock	100,000	100,000
Equipment (net of accumulated depreciation)	220,000	140,000
Income Taxes Payable	70,000	40,000
Land	70,000	60,000
Merchandise Inventory	400,000	380,000
Retained Earnings	600,000	500,000
Salaries Payable	15,000	10,000
Income Statement Items for Year 2:		
Cost of Merchandise Sold	$ 620,000	
Depreciation Expense	40,000	
Income Tax Expense	100,000	
Insurance Expense	3,000	
Interest Expense	10,000	
Property Tax Expense	2,000	
Rental Revenue (rental of part of building	30,000	
Salary Expense	135,000	
Sales Revenue	1,000,000	
Dividend Information for Year 2:		
Dividends Declared and Paid	$20,000	

a. Prepare a comparative balance sheet for Digital Electronics Corporation as of December 31, Year 1 and Year 2. Classify the balance sheet items into the following categories: current assets, noncurrent assets, current liabilities, noncurrent liabilities, and shareholders' equity.

b. Prepare a multiple-step income statement for Digital Electronics Corporation for Year 2.

c. Prepare a schedule explaining the changes in retained earnings during Year 2.

ANSWERS TO SELF-STUDY QUESTIONS AND EXERCISES

True/False

1. T	6. T	11. T	16. T
2. T	7. T	12. T	17. F
3. F	8. T	13. F	18. F
4. T	9. F	14. T	
5. T	10. T	15. T	

Matching

1. c	5. d	9. i	13. g
2. b	6. e	10. l	14. p
3. a	7. f	11. o	15. k
4. m	8. j	12. h	16. n

Multiple Choice

1. d	5. a	9. d	13. b
2. c	6. b	10. c	14. a
3. d	7. b	11. c	15. b
4. d	8. a	12. a	

Exercises

1.

	a	b	c
Current Assets	$150,000	$130,000	$160,000
Noncurrent Assets	$225,000	$200,000	$180,000
Current Liabilities	$ 30,000	$ 50,000	$ 20,000
Noncurrent Liabilities	$105,000	$100,000	$100,000
Contributed Capital	$180,000	$110,000	$ 70,000
Retained Earnings	$ 60,000	$ 70,000	$150,000
Shareholders' Equity	$240,000	$180,000	$220,000

2.

	a	b	c
Revenues	$240,000	$270,000	$420,000
Expenses	$140,000	$216,000	$340,000
Net Income	$100,000	$ 54,000	$ 80,000
Retained Earnings 1/1	$ 50,000	$ 45,000	$ 24,000
Net Income	$100,000	$ 54,000	$ 80,000
Dividends	$ 20,000	$ 30,000	$ 64,000
Retained Earnings 12/31	$130,000	$ 69,000	$ 40,000

3.

	a	b	c
Assets	$300,000	$480,000	$800,000
Liabilities	$160,000	$150,000	$380,000
Contributed Capital	$100,000	$291,000	$280,000
Retained Earnings 1/1	$ 22,000	$ 0	$ 40,000
Net Income	$ 28,000	$ 75,000	$160,000
Dividends	$ 10,000	$ 36,000	$ 60,000
Retained Earnings 12/31	$ 40,000	$ 39,000	$140,000

4.

	a	b	c
Cash Provided by:			
Operations	$ 45,000	$ 30,000	$ 90,000
New Financing	$150,000	$ 85,000	$200,000
Sale of Noncurrent Assets	$ 30,000	$ 60,000	$110,000
Cash Applied to:			
Dividends	$ 10,000	$ 25,000	$ 70,000
Reduction in Financing	$ 90,000	$100,000	$ 80,000
Acquisition of Noncurrent Assets	$ 50,000	$ 70,000	$200,000
Increase (Decrease) in Cash	$ 75,000	$ (20,000)	$ 50,000

5. a. Assets at 12/31/19X1 $150,000
        Liabilities at 12/31/19X1   (96,000)
        Shareholders' equity at 12/31/19X1 $ 54,000

    Shareholders' equity has increased by $24,000 ($54,000 − $30,000) during the six-month period, July 1 to December 31.

    b. The $24,000 increase may be attributable to the company earning net income and paying no dividends or earning net income and paying dividends; or the shareholders may have made additional purchases of the company's shares; or the increase could be attributed to a combination of the above changes.

    c. Contributed capital represents the assets provided by the shareholders in exchange for an ownership interest in the firm. Retained earnings represent the earnings, or profits, realized by the firm since its formation in excess of dividends distributed to shareholders.

SUGGESTED SOLUTION TO PROBLEM FOR SELF-STUDY

Exhibit 1.5 presents a comparative balance sheet, Exhibit 1.6 presents an income statement, and Exhibit 1.7 analyzes the change in retained earnings for Digital Electronics Corporation for Year 2.

EXHIBIT 1.5
DIGITAL ELECTRONICS CORPORATION
Comparative Balance Sheet
December 31, Year 1 and Year 2

	December 31	
	Year 2	Year 1
ASSETS		
Current Assets:		
Cash	$ 50,000	$ 30,000
Accounts Receivable from Customers	320,000	240,000
Merchandise Inventory	400,000	380,000
Total Current Assets	$ 770,000	$ 650,000
Noncurrent Assets:		
Land	$ 70,000	$ 60,000
Equipment (net of accumulatd depreciation)	220,000	140,000
Buildings (net of accumulated depreciation)	140,000	150,000
Total Noncurrent Assets	$ 430,000	$ 350,000
Total Assets	$1,200,000	$1,000,000
LIABILITIES AND SHAREHOLDERS' EQUITY		
Current Liabilities:		
Accounts Payable to Suppliers	$ 295,000	$ 250,000
Salaries Payable	15,000	10,000
Income Taxes Payable	70,000	40,000
Total Current Liabilities	$ 380,000	$ 300,000
Noncurrent Liabilities:		
Bonds Payable	120,000	100,000
Total Liabilities	$ 500,000	$ 400,000
Shareholders' Equity:		
Common Shares	$ 100,000	$ 100,000
Retained Earnings	600,000	500,000
Total Shareholders' Equity	$ 700,000	$ 600,000
Total Liabilities and Shareholders' Equity	$1,200,000	$1,000,000

EXHIBIT 1.6
DIGITAL ELECTRONICS CORPORATION
Income Statement for Year 2

Sales		$1,000,000
Less: Cost of Merchandise Sold		(620,000)
Gross Profit		$ 380,000
Rental Revenue		30,000
		$ 410,000
Less: Selling and Administrative Expenses		
Salaries	$135,000	
Property Tax	2,000	
Insurance	3,000	
Depreciation	40,000	($ 180,000)
Operating Profit		$ 230,000
Less: Interest Expense		(10,000)
Net Income Before Income Tax		$ 220,000
Income Tax		(100,000)
Net Income		$ 120,000

EXHIBIT 1.7
DIGITAL ELECTRONICS CORPORATION
Retained Earnings Statement for Year 1

Retained Earnings, December 31, Year 1	$500,000
Plus Net Income	120,000
Less Dividends Declared and Paid	(20,000)
Retained Earnings, December 31, Year 2	$600,000

ASSIGNMENT MATERIAL

QUESTIONS

1. Review the meaning of the key terms listed on page 28.

2. Distinguish between financial accounting and managerial accounting. Suggest several ways in which the managers of a firm might use information presented in three principal externally directed financial statements discussed in this chapter.

3. Suggest reasons why financial accounting reports tend to be more standardized in terms of format and content than managerial accounting reports.

4. What purpose is served by having a broad set of financial reporting objectives, such as those issued by the Financial Accounting Standards Board?

5. "Asset valuation and income measurement are closely related." Explain.

6. "Operating activities can be a source of financing." Explain.

7. Does the unreserved or "clean" opinion of a chartered accountant indicate that the financial statements are free of errors and misrepresentations? Explain.

EXERCISES

8. *Preparation of personal balance sheet.* Prepare a balance sheet of your personal assets, liabilities, and owner's equity. How does the presentation of owner's equity on your balance sheet differ from that in Exhibit 1.1?

9. *Account classification.* Various items are classified on the balance sheet or income statement in one of the following ways:

   CA — Current assets
   NA — Noncurrent assets
   CL — Current liabilities
   NL — Noncurrent liabilities
   CC — Contributed capital
   RE — Retained earnings
   NI — Income statement item (revenue or expense)
   X — Item would generally not appear on balance sheet or income statement

Using the preceding letters, indicate the classification of each of the following items:
a. Factory
b. Interest revenue
c. Common shares issued by a corporation
d. Goodwill developed by a firm (see Glossary)
e. Automobiles used by sales staff
f. Cash on hand
g. Unsettled damage suit against a firm
h. Commissions earned by sales staff
i. Supplies inventory
j. Note payable, due in three months
k. Increase in market value of land held
l. Dividends
m. Employee payroll taxes payable
n. Note payable, due in six years

10. **Balance sheet relations.** Compute the missing balance sheet amounts in each of the four independent cases below:

	a	b	c	d
Noncurrent Assets	$400,000	$500,000	$340,000	?
Shareholders' Equity	?	250,000	290,000	$140,000
Total Assets	?	?	500,000	?
Current Liabilities	500,000	150,000	?*	?**
Current Assets	600,000	?	?*	?**
Noncurrent Liabilities	100,000	?	?	160,000
Total Liabilities and Shareholders' Equity	?	700,000	?	550,000

*Current assets − current liabilities = $70,000.
**Current assets − current liabilities = $80,000.

11. **Balance sheet relations.** Compute the missing balance sheet amounts in each of the four independent cases below:

	a	b	c	d
Noncurrent Assets	$700,000	$2,000,000	$340,000	?
Shareholders' Equity	?	1,550,000	380,000	$370,000
Total Assets	?	?	500,000	?
Current Liabilities	250,000	400,000	?*	?**
Current Assets	300,000	?	?*	?**
Noncurrent Liabilities	300,000	?	?	400,000
Total Liabilities and Shareholders' Equity	?	2,650,000	?	950,000

*Current assets − current liabilities = $40,000.
**Current assets − current liabilities = $70,000.

12. *Retained earnings relations.* Compute the missing amount affecting retained earnings for Year 2 in each of the independent cases below:

	a	b	c	d	e
Retained earnings, Dec. 31, Year 1	$80,000	?	$458,000	$120,000	$240,000
Net Income (Loss)	30,000	$260,000	260,000	?	(60,000)
Dividends Declared and Paid	10,000	145,000	?	35,000	?
Retained Earnings, Dec. 31, Year 2	?	766,000	598,000	110,000	180,000

13. *Retained earnings relations.* Compute the missing amount affecting retained earnings for Year 2 in each of the independent cases below:

	a	b	c	d	e
Retained Earnings, Dec. 31, Year 1	$150,000	?	$320,000	$75,000	$ 40,000
Net Income (Loss)	50,000	$125,000	180,000	?	(30,000)
Dividends Declared and Paid	20,000	75,000	?	30,000	?
Retained Earnings, Dec. 31, Year 2	?	500,000	470,000	90,000	10,000

14. *Relation of net income to balance sheet changes.* The following are the comparative balance sheets of Sweet Limited as of December 31, Year 2:

SWEET LIMITED
Comparative Balance Sheets
December 31, Year 1 and Year 2

	December 31 Year 2	Year 1
Total Assets	$800,000	$500,000
Liabilities	$160,000	$100,000
Common Stock	290,000	250,000
Retained Earnings	350,000	150,000
Total Liabilities and Shareholders' Equity	$800,000	$500,000

Dividends declared and paid during Year 2 were $60,000.
a. Compute net income for the year ending December 31, Year 2, by analyzing the change in retained earnings.
b. Demonstrate that the following relation holds true:

$$\frac{\text{Net}}{\text{Income}} = \frac{\text{Increase in}}{\text{Assets}} - \frac{\text{Increase in}}{\text{Liabilities}} - \frac{\text{Increase in}}{\text{Contributed Capital}} + \text{Dividends}$$

15. *Income statement relations.* Compute the missing amounts affecting the net income for Year 1 and each of the independent cases below:

	a	b	c	d
Sales Revenue	$500	?	$390	$260
Cost of Goods Sold	250	$60	?	190
Selling and Administrative Expenses	120	30	70	?
Income Tax Expenses	60	20	35	0
Net Income (Loss)	?	15	35	(15)

16. *Statement of changes in financial position relations.* Compute the missing amounts affecting the change in cash for Year 1 in each of the independent cases below:

	a	b	c	d
Sources of Cash:				
Operations	$500	$250	$600	$(200)*
New Financing	200	100	?	300
Sale of Noncurrent Assets	50	20	0	100

*Net use of cash for operations

	a	b	c	d
Uses of Cash:				
Dividends	100	75	200	0
Reduction in Financing	80	0	50	50
Acquisition of Noncurrent Assets	550	?	800	120
Increase (Decrease) in Cash	?	20	(50)	?

17. *Relations between financial statements.* Compute the missing information in each of the independent cases below. The letters in parentheses refer to the following:

BS — Balance Sheet
IS — Income Statement
SCFP — Statement of changes in financial position

a. Accounts Receivable, Jan. 1, Year 2 (BS) .... $ 450
   Sales on Account for Year 2 (IS) 1,700
   Collections from Customers on Account During
      Year 2 (SCFP) 1,350
   Accounts Receivable, Dec. 31, Year 2 (BS) .... ?
b. Salaries Payable, Jan. 1, Year 2 (BS) .... $ 120
   Salary Expense for Year 2 (IS) .... ?
   Payments to Salaried Employees During Year 2 (SCFP) .. 660
   Salaries Payable, Dec. 31, Year 2 (BS) 90

    c. Equipment (net of accumulated depreciation), Jan. 1,
         Year 2 (BS)   800
         Depreciation Expense for Year 2 (IS) ....   ?
         Sales of Equipment During Year 2 (SCFP)   0
         Acquisition of Equipment During Year 2 (SCFP)   250
         Equipment (net of accumulated depreciation), Dec. 31,
         Year 2 (BS)   900
    d. Retained Earnings, Jan 1, Year 2 (BS) $1,250
         Net Income for Year 2 (IS)   300
         Dividends Declared and Paid During Year 2 (BS) ....   ?
         Retained Earnings, Dec. 31, Year 2 (BS)   1,430

18. *Balance sheet relations.* Compute the missing balance sheet amounts in each of the four independent cases below:

	a	b	c	d
Total Assets	$1,000,000	?	?	$270,000
Noncurrent Liabilities	350,000	$ 25,000	?	230,000
Noncurrent Assets	?	50,000	$600,000	?
Total Liabilities and Shareholders' Equity	?	300,000	?	?
Current Liabilities	250,000	?	40,000	60,000
Shareholders' Equity	?	75,000	110,000	?
Current Assets	350,000	?	50,000	30,000

PROBLEMS AND CASES

19. *Preparation of balance sheet and income statement.* B. Stephens, L. Harris, and G. Winkle, recent graduates, set up a management consulting practice on December 31, Year 1, by issuing common shares for $750,000. The accounting records of S, H, & W Limited as of December 31, Year 2, reveal the following:

Balance Sheet Items:

Cash	$ 50,000
Accounts Receivable from Clients	165,000
Supplies Inventory	5,000
Office Equipment (net of accumulated depreciation)	85,000
Office Building (net of accumulated depreciation)	500,000
Accounts Payable to Suppliers	10,000
Payroll Taxes Payable	5,000
Income Taxes Payable	20,000
Common Stock	750,000

Income Statement Items:

Revenue from Consulting Services	$300,000
Rental Revenue (from renting part of building)	30,000
Salaries Expense	215,000
Property Taxes and Insurance Expense	30,000
Supplies Expense	10,000
Depreciation Expense	25,000
Income Tax Expense	20,000

Dividend Information:

Dividends Declared and Paid	$ 10,000

a. Prepare an income statement for S, H, & W Limited, for the year ending December 31, Year 2. Refer to Exhibit 1.2 for help in designing the format of the statement.

b. Prepare a comparative balance sheet for S, H, & W Limited on December 31, Year 1, and December 31, Year 2. Refer to Exhibit 1.1 for help in designing the format of the statement.

c. Prepare an analysis of the change in retained earnings during Year 2.

20. *Preparation of balance sheet and income statement.* The accounting records of Laser Sales Corporation reveal the following:

	December 31	
	Year 2	**Year 1**
Balance Sheet Items:		
Accounts Payable	$1,513,000	$1,247,000
Accounts Receivable	820,000	740,000
Bank Loan Payable (due April 10, Year 3)	15,000	—
Bonds Payable (due Year 16)	100,000	80,000
Building (net of accumulated depreciation)	440,000	460,000
Cash	315,000	270,000
Common Stock	1,240,000	1,190,000
Equipment (net of accumulated depreciation)	1,023,000	825,000
Income Taxes Payable	30,000	25,000
Land	50,000	40,000
Merchandise Inventory	610,000	550,000
Note Receivable (due June 15, Year 3)	20,000	—
Note Receivable (due December 31, Year 10)	100,000	100,000
Retained Earnings	470,000	430,000
Salaries Payable	32,000	28,000
Supplies Inventory	22,000	15,000

Income Statement Items for Year 2:	
Cost of Merchandise Sold	$2,611,000
Depreciation Expense	45,000
Income Tax Expense	55,000

Income Statement Items for Year 2 (continued):

Insurance Expense	8,000
Interest Expense	16,000
Interest Revenue	15,000
Payroll Tax Expense	80,000
Salary Expense	550,000
Sales Revenue	3,500,000
Supplies Expense	90,000

Dividend Information:

Dividends Declared and Paid During Year 2	$	20,000

a. Prepare a comparative balance sheet for Laser Sales Corporation as of December 31, Year 1 and Year 2. Classify the balance sheet items into the following categories: current assets, noncurrent assets, current liabilities, noncurrent liabilities, shareholders' equity.

b. Prepare a multiple-step income statement for Laser Sales Corporation for Year 2.

c. Prepare a schedule explaining, or accounting for, the change in retained earnings between the beginning and end of Year 2.

21. *Relations between principal financial statements.* The purpose of this problem is to illustrate the relations between the three principal financial statements. Exhibit 1.8 presents a comparative balance sheet for Articulation Inc. as of December 31, Year 1 and Year 2. Exhibit 1.9 presents an income statement and Exhibit 1.10 presents a statement of changes in financial position for Articulation Inc. for Year 2.

   Using amounts from these three financial statements, demonstrate that the following relations are correct:

   a. Retained earnings at the end of Year 1 plus net income for Year 2 minus dividends declared and paid for Year 2 equal retained earnings at the end of Year 2.

   b. Change in total assets equals change in total liabilities plus change in common shares plus net income minus dividends.

   c. Accounts receivable at the end of Year 1 plus sales (all on account) to customers less cash collections from customers (see statement of changes in financial position) equal accounts receivable at the end of Year 2.

   d. Buildings and equipment at the end of Year 1 plus acquisitions of buildings and equipment minus dispositions of buildings and equipment minus depreciation for Year 2 equal buildings and equipment at the end of Year 2.

   e. Bonds payable at the end of Year 1 plus new bonds issued during Year 2 minus outstanding bonds redeemed during Year 2 equal bonds payable at the end of Year 2.

   f. Common stock at the end of Year 1 plus common shares issued during Year 2 minus outstanding common shares redeemed during year 2 equal common stock at the end of Year 2.

EXHIBIT 1.8
ARTICULATION INC.
Comparative Balance Sheets
December 31, Year 1 and Year 2

	December 31	
	Year 2	Year 1
ASSETS		
Current Assets:		
Cash	$180	$ 80
Accounts Receivable from Customers	340	300
Merchandise Inventory	160	150
Total Current Assets	$680	$530
Noncurrent Assets:		
Land	$ 55	$ 40
Buildings and Equipment (net of accumulated depreciation)	165	130
Total Noncurrent Assets	$220	$170
Total Assets	$900	$700
LIABILITIES AND SHAREHOLDERS' EQUITY		
Current Liabilities:		
Accounts Payable	$350	$310
Income Taxes Payable	60	40
Total Current Liabilities	$410	$350
Noncurrent Liabilities:		
Bonds Payable	25	20
Total Liabilities	$435	$370
Shareholders' Equity:		
Common Shares	$245	$200
Retained Earnings	220	130
Total Shareholders' Equity	$465	$330
Total Liabilities and Shareholders' Equity	$900	$700

EXHIBIT 1.9
ARTICULATION INC.
Income Statement for Year 2

Sales Revenue		$1,000
Less: Cost of Goods Sold		(600)
Gross Profit		$ 400
Less: Operating Expenses		
Salaries	$100	
Depreciation	50	(150)
Operating Income		$ 250
Less: Interest Expense		(20)
Net Income Before Income Tax		$ 230
Less: Income Tax Expense		(120)
Net Income		$ 110

EXHIBIT 1.10
ARTICULATION INC.
Statement of Changes in Financial Position for Year 2

Sources of Cash:		
Operations:		
Revenues Increasing Cash	$960	
Expenses Decreasing Cash	(790)	
Total from Operations	$170	
Issue of Bonds	5	
Issue of Common Shares	45	
Total Sources		$220
Uses of Cash:		
Dividends Declared and Paid	$ 20	
Land Acquired	15	
Buildings and Equipment Acquired	85	
Total Uses		(120)
Net Change in Cash		$100

22. *Relations between financial statements.* (Adapted from materials prepared by Professor Harvey Mann.) Exhibit 1.11 presents a balance sheet as of December 31, Year 1 (columns 1 and 2), an income statement for Year 2 (column 3), a statement of changes in financial position for Year 2 (column 4), and a balance sheet as of December 31, Year 2 (columns 5 and 6) for Mann Co. Ltd.

    Compute the amounts for each of the missing items labelled **a** through **j** in the exhibit.

23. *Relation between net income and cash flows.* The ABC Co. Ltd. started the year in fine shape. The firm made widgets — just what the customer wanted. It made them for $0.75 each and sold them for $1.00. The ABC Co. Ltd. kept an inventory equal to shipments of the past 30 days, paid its bills promptly, and collected cash from customers within 30 days after the sale. The sales manager predicted a steady increase of 500 widgets each month beginning in February. It looked like a great year, and it began that way:

    January 1   Cash, $875; receivables, $1,000; inventory, $750.

    January   In January, 1,000 widgets costing $750 were sold on account for $1,000. Receivables outstanding at the beginning of the month were collected. Production totalled 1,000 units at a total cost of $750. Net income for the month was $250. The books at the end of January showed:

    February 1   Cash, $1,125; receivables, $1,000; inventory $750.

    February   This month's sales jumped, as predicted, to 1,500 units. With a corresponding stepup in production to maintain the 30-day inventory, ABC Co. Ltd. made 2,000 units at a cost of $1,500. All receivables from January sales were collected. Net income so far, $625. Now the books looked like this:

    March 1   Cash, $625; receivables, $1,500; inventory, $1,125.

EXHIBIT 1.11
MANN CO. LTD.
Financial Statements for Year 2 (Problem 22)

Account	Balance Sheet December 31, Year 1 — Assets (1)	Balance Sheet December 31, Year 1 — Liabilities + Shareholders' Equity (2)	Income Statement for Year 2	(3)	Statement of Changes in Financial Position for Year 2	(4)	Balance Sheet December 31, Year 2 — Assets (5)	Balance Sheet December 31, Year 2 — Liabilities + Shareholders' Equity (6)
Accounts Receivable	$ 200		Sales	$2,000	Collections from Customers	$1,700	a	
Inventories	300		Cost of Goods Sold	b	Purchases of Merchandise	(1,300)	$ 400	
Accounts Payable—Merchandise		$ 180			Change in Accounts Payable	40		$220
Salaries Payable		30	Salary Expense	(400)	Salaries Paid	c		40
Interest Payable		d	Interest Expense	(20)	Interest Paid	(20)		10
Income Taxes Payable		20	Income Tax Expense	(35)	Income Tax Paid	(40)		15
Other Current Liabilities		115	Other Expenses	e	Other Expenses Paid	(220)		145
					Cash from Operations	f		
Land, Building, and Equipment—Net	600		Depreciation Expense	(60)	Land, Building, and Equipment Acquired	g	740	
Bonds Payable		200			Bonds Issued	200		400
Common Shares		h			Common Shares Issued	300		600
Retained Earnings		345	Net Income	$ 35	Dividend Paid	(10)		i
Cash	100				Change in Cash	$ 60	160	
Total	$1,200	$1,200					$1,800	j

March	March sales were even better: 2,000 units. Collections: On time. Production, to adhere to the inventory policy: 2,500 units. Operating results for the month, net income of $500. Net income to date: $1,125. The books:
April 1	Cash, $250; receivables, $2,000; inventory, $1,500.
April	In April, sales jumped another 500 units to 2,500, and the manager of ABC Co. Ltd. patted the sales manager on the back. Customers were paying right on time. Production was pushed to 3,000 units, and the month's business netted $625, for a net income to date of $1,750. The manager of ABC Co. Ltd. took off for Miami before the accountant's report was issued. Suddenly a phone call came from the treasurer: "Come home! We need money!"
May 1	Cash, $0; receivables, $2,500; inventory, $1,875.

a. Prepare an analysis that explains what happened to ABC Co. Ltd. (*Hint*: Compute the amount of cash receipts and cash disbursements for each month during the period of January 1 to May 1.)

b. How can a firm show increasing net income but a decreasing amount of cash?

c. What insights are provided by the problem about the need for all three financial statements: balance sheet, income statement, and statement of changes in financial position?

24. *Preparation of balance sheet and income statement.* Keyes Manufacturing Corporation was organized on January 1, Year 1. The company issued common stock for $600,000 and long-term bonds for $400,000. The accounting records of Keyes Manufacturing Corporation as of December 31, Year 1, reveal the following:

Balance Sheet Items:

Cash	$ 50,000
Accounts Receivable from Customers	350,000
Inventories	300,000
Land	50,000
Buildings (net of depreciation)	400,000
Equipment (net of depreciation)	350,000
Accounts Payable to Suppliers	120,000
Salaries Payable to Workers	75,000
Bonds Payable	400,000
Common Stock	700,000

Income Statement Items:

Sales Revenue	$2,000,000
Cost of Goods Sold	1,200,000
Selling Expenses	200,000
Administrative Expenses	210,000
Interest Expense	40,000
Income Tax Expense	100,000

Dividend Information:

Dividends Declared and Paid	$ 45,000

a. Prepare an income statement for Keyes Manufacturing Corporation for the year ending December 31, Year 1. Refer to Exhibit 1.2 for help in designing the format of the statement.

b. Prepare a comparative balance sheet for Keyes Manufacturing Corporation on January 1, Year 1, and December 31, Year 1. Refer to Exhibit 1.1 for help in designing the format of the statement.

c. Prepare an analysis of the change in retained earnings during Year 1.

DECISION CASE 1-1

Sam Black has just completed a busy week organizing and supervising the annual April Fool's Day chicken, hot dog, and beer barbecue sponsored by the students' society of his faculty as a combination public relations, fun, and fundraising activity. The barbecue was a success. Sam had just returned from the bank, where he had deposited the proceeds of $2,810 and proudly announced that the bank balance now stood at $2,858, which represented "the most successful result of any barbecue."

The following conversation took place between Sam Black and Herbert McAlister, the president of the students' society.

"Congratulations on the successful barbecue, Sam," said McAlister. "Would you please transfer the $2,858 to the society's bank account tomorrow, so I can pay for the advance booking of the graduating class dance?"

"I can't transfer all of the money," said Black. "I still have two bills to pay — $347 for the chicken and $630 for the material needed to build the barbecue. The chicken was all sold, but the barbecue should last for another two years.

"And further," Black added, "10 of the 80 cases of beer that were delivered C.O.D. were not sold and are to be returned for a refund of $4.80 per case. And at the same time, the 65 cases of empties will be picked up, and the deposit of $0.60 a case will be returned.

"I managed to sell the 24 dozen buns left over for $0.50 a dozen to Jill Rosen for a sorority party," continued Sam. "This was half the unit cost of the 120 dozen purchased, but at least they will be used. Jill didn't have the money with her and will pay me tomorrow."

Spurred on by Herbert's interest, Black said he had also purchased barbecue sauce, condiments, and charcoal for $78 cash. Although there was a little barbecue sauce left over, it was given to the student helpers. In addition, $370 had also been spent on promoting the event.

Intent on his explanation, Sam was unaware that Bill Hahn, the society's treasurer, had sidled up and heard the story.

"From the sounds of it, last year's affair was more successful," announced Hahn. "Once you have paid your bills and repaid the $1,000 advance I gave you last week, you will have less than $900 left. This is $400 less than last year's 'Beer and Hot Dog' reported net income."

Sam was deflated by the last comment, as well as a little confused. Help Sam Black out of his confusion by preparing an income statement and a current balance sheet for the barbecue.

DECISION CASE 1-2

Your friend, Alex Demarco, has asked for your advice. He is considering purchasing a sporting goods store but knows nothing about accounting and doesn't know if this business looks like a good investment. He has obtained income statements showing net income averaging $40,000 a year. The most recent balance sheet shows assets of $180,000 and liabilities of $30,000. The current owner, Ted Dumas, is asking $200,000 for the business.

1. Alex cannot understand why he should pay more than the value of the net assets ($150,000), especially since this business is several years old and some of the assets may be worn out. What counsel can you provide him on this?

2. After examining the income statements, you notice that there is no expense shown for salary by Dumas. When questioned on this, he replied that he got enough income from his other investments that it wasn't necessary to draw a salary. What impact will this information have on the advice you offer Alex? Alex has a full-time job at the university.

CHAPTER TWO

BALANCE SHEET: PRESENTING THE INVESTMENTS AND FINANCING OF A FIRM

CHAPTER OUTLINE

- Underlying Concepts and Conventions
- Accounting Procedures for Preparing the Balance Sheet
- An Overview of the Accounting Process
- Balance Sheet Account Titles
- Analysis of Balance Sheet
- An International Perspective

Chapter 1 introduced the balance sheet, one of the three principal financial statements. Recall that the balance sheet presents a snapshot of the investments of a firm (assets) and financing of those investments (liabilities and owners' equity) as of a specific time. The balance sheet shows the following relationship:

$$\text{Assets} = \text{Liabilities} + \text{Owners' Equity}$$

Thus, a firm's resources are equated with the claims on those resources by creditors and owners. In the balance sheet, we view resources from two perspectives: a listing of the specific forms in which they are held (for example, cash, inventory, equipment), and a listing of the persons or interests that provided the financing and therefore have a claim on them (for example, suppliers, employees, governments, shareholders). Accountants often refer to liabilities plus shareholders' equity as *total equities*.

The introduction to the balance sheet in Chapter 1 left several important questions unanswered:

1. What limits are set in defining the business entity for which the balance sheet is prepared?

2. Which resources of a firm are recorded as assets?

3. What valuations are placed on these assets?

4. How are assets classified, or grouped, within the balance sheet?

5. Which claims against a firm's assets are recognized as liabilities?

6. What valuations are placed on these liabilities?

7. How are liabilities classified within the balance sheet?

8. What valuation is placed on the owners' equity in a firm, and how is the owners' equity disclosed?

In answering these questions, several accounting concepts underlying the balance sheet must be considered. This discussion not only provides a background for understanding the statement as it is currently prepared, but also permits an assessment of alternative methods of measuring financial position. After this introduction to important accounting concepts, the accounting procedures used in recording transactions and events for presentation in a balance sheet are described and illustrated.

UNDERLYING CONCEPTS AND CONVENTIONS
ACCOUNTING ENTITY

Business activities are carried on through various units, or entities. The identification of the business entity is the starting point in designing an accounting system that will provide data for financial statements. Most problems of identifying the business entity are caused by differences between the definition of the entity used in accounting, or the **accounting entity**, and the definition of the entity prescribed by law, or the *legal entity*. In accounting, we attempt to emphasize substance over form; that is, the focus is on the unit, or entity, engaged in business activity even though it may not be recognized as a separate legal entity.

accounting entity
Those people, assets, and activities devoted to a specific economic purpose and for which a separate accounting should be made.

Example 1 Joan Webster operates a hardware store in her neighbourhood as a sole proprietorship. According to the laws for sole proprietorships in most provinces, Webster's business assets and personal assets are mingled. That is, suppliers of merchandise to the hardware store can obtain payment for their claims from some or all of her personal assets if business assets are insufficient. Even so, the accounting entity is the hardware store alone, because this is the organizational unit carrying on the business activity.

Example 2 Bill White and Roger Green own and manage an apartment complex, called the Leisure Living Apartments, as a partnership. Under the partnership laws of most provinces, their personal assets as well as the business assets are subject to the claims of creditors. Even so, the accounting entity is the apartment complex alone, because this is the organizational unit carrying on the business activity.

Example 3 The Wilson Corporation operates through its subsidiaries. Each subsidiary is organized as a separate legal corporation under the laws of the government where it is located. The accounting entity is a combination (or consolidation) of Wilson Corporation and all of its subsidiary corporations, because these legally separate units operate as a single business entity. However, for purposes of internal performance evaluation by management, or to report to a given creditor, Wilson Corporation might treat each subsidiary as a separate reporting entity. Thus, the scope of the accounting entity can be related to the purpose to be served by the financial statements.

The accounting entity for which a set of financial statements has been prepared can be determined from the heading of each statement. For the three examples above, the headings might read: Webster's Hardware Store, Leisure Living Apartments, and Wilson Corporation and Consolidated Subsidiaries.

ASSET RECOGNITION

Assets are resources that have the potential for providing a firm with future economic benefits. That benefit is the ability to generate future cash inflows or to reduce future cash outflows. The resources that are recognized as assets are those (1) for which the firm has acquired rights to their future use as a result of a past transaction or exchange and (2) for which the value of the future benefits can be measured, or quantified, with a reasonable degree of precision.

Example 4   Miller Corporation sold merchandise and received a note from the customer, who agreed to pay $2,000 within four months. This note receivable is an asset of Miller Corporation, because a right has been established to receive a definite amount of cash in the future as a result of the previous sale of merchandise.

Example 5   Miller Corporation acquired manufacturing equipment costing $40,000 and agreed to pay the seller over three years. After the final payment, legal title to the equipment will be transferred to Miller Corporation. Even though Miller Corporation does not possess legal title, the equipment is Miller's asset because it has obtained the rights and responsibilities of ownership and can sustain those rights as long as the payments are made on schedule.

Example 6   Miller Corporation plans to acquire a fleet of new trucks next year to replace those wearing out. These new trucks are not yet assets, because no exchange has taken place between Miller Corporation and a supplier and, therefore, no right to the future use of the trucks has been established.

Example 7   Miller Corporation has developed a good reputation with its employees, customers, and citizens of the community. This good reputation is expected to provide benefits to the firm in its future business activities. A good reputation, however, is generally *not* recognized as an asset. Although Miller Corporation has made various expenditures in the past to develop the reputation, the future benefits are considered to be too difficult to quantify with a sufficient degree of precision to warrant recognition as an asset.

Unexecuted contracts Contracts for which performance has not yet occurred and hence for which no formal liability yet exists.

Most of the difficulties in deciding which items to recognize as assets are related to unexecuted or partially executed contracts. In Example 6, suppose that Miller Corporation entered into a contract with a local truck dealer to acquire the trucks next year at a cash price of $60,000. Miller Corporation has acquired rights to future benefits, but the contract has not been executed. **Unexecuted contracts** of this nature are generally not recognized as assets in accounting. Miller Corporation will recognize an asset for the trucks when they are received next year.

To take the illustration one step further, assume that Miller Corporation advances the truck dealer $15,000 of the purchase price upon signing the contract. Miller Corpation has acquired rights to future benefits and has exchanged cash. Current accounting practice treats the $15,000 as an advance on the purchase of equipment and reports it as an asset under a title such as Advances to Suppliers. The trucks would not be shown as assets at this time, however, because Miller Corporation is not yet deemed to have received sufficient future rights to justify their inclusion in the balance sheet. Similar asset recognition questions arise when a firm leases buildings and equipment for its own use under long-term leases or manufactures custom-design products for particular customers. Later chapters discuss these issues more fully.

Some expenditures provide future benefits to the firm but are not recognized as assets because the benefit will be used up within the forthcoming year (for instance, supplies). It is more convenient to charge these expenditures immediately as expenses against operating revenues in the income statement. Other examples of items that theoretically qualify as assets but do not get recognized as such are expenditures such as advertising where it is too difficult to measure the future benefits, or expenditures of small dollar amounts where it requires too much effort to keep track of the items on the balance sheet (for instance, hand tools).

ASSET VALUATION BASES

A monetary value must be assigned to each asset shown on the balance sheet. Several alternative **asset valuation bases** are possible.

Acquisition or Historical Cost

The **acquisition cost**, or **historical cost**, of an asset is the amount of cash payment (or cash-equivalent value of other forms of payment) made in acquiring the asset. This amount can generally be found by referring to contracts, invoices, and cancelled cheques. Because a firm is not compelled to acquire a given asset, it must expect the future benefits from that asset to be at least as large as its acquisition cost. Historical cost, then, is a lower limit on the amount that a firm considered the future benefits of the asset to be worth at the time of acquisition.

Current Replacement Cost

Each asset might be shown on the balance sheet at the current cost of replacing it. **Current replacement cost** is often referred to as an **entry value**, because it represents the amount required currently to acquire, or "enter" into, the rights to receive future benefits from the asset.

For assets purchased frequently, such as merchandise inventory, currently replacement cost can often be determined by consulting suppliers' catalogues or price lists. The replacement cost of assets purchased less frequently, such as land, buildings, and equipment, is more difficult to ascertain. A major obstacle to implementing current replacement cost is the absence of well-organized secondhand markets for many used assets. Ascertaining current replacement cost in these cases requires finding the

asset valuation bases
Principles used to determine the amounts assets should be recorded at in the accounting records.

acquisition cost
The acquisition cost of an asset is the net invoice price plus all expenditures to place and ready the asset for its intended use. The other expenditures might include legal fees, transportation charges, and installation costs.

historical cost
The money equivalent of the object given up (and/or obligations assumed) at the time of the exchange transaction.

Current replacement cost
The amount of cash or other consideration that would be needed currently to acquire the best available asset to undertake the function of the asset owned, adjusted for depreciation or amortization if appropriate.

entry value
The current cost of acquiring an asset or service at a fair market price. Replacement cost.

cost of a similar new asset and then adjusting that amount downward somehow for the services of the asset already used. There may be difficulties, however, in finding a similar asset. With technological improvements and other quality changes, equipment purchased currently will likely differ from equipment still being used but acquired ten years previously. Thus, there may be no similar equipment on the market for which replacement cost can be found. Alternatively, the current replacement cost of an asset capable of rendering equivalent services might be substituted when the replacement cost of the specific asset is not readily available. The approach, however, requires subjectivity in identifying assets with equivalent service potential.

Current Net Realizable Value

Net realizable value
An asset measure computed by subtracting the expected completion and disposable costs from the asset's estimated selling price.

Net realizable value is the amount of cash (selling price less selling costs) that the firm would receive currently if it sold each asset separately. This amount is often referred to as an **exit value**, because it reflects the amount that would be obtainable if the firm currently disposed of the asset, or "exited" ownership. In measuring net realizable value, one generally assumes that the asset is sold in an orderly fashion, rather than through a forced sale at some "distress" price.

exit value
The proceeds that would be received if assets were disposed of in an arm's-length transaction. Current selling price. Net realizable value.

Measuring net realizable value entails difficulties similar to those in measuring current replacement cost. There may be no well-organized secondhand market for used equipment, particularly when the equipment is specially designed for a single firm's needs. In this case, the current selling price of the asset (value in exchange) may be substantially less than the value of the future benefits to the firm from using the asset (value in use).

Present Value of Future Net Cash Flows

cash flows
Cash receipts minus disbursements from a given asset, or group of assets, for a given period.

Another possible valuation basis is the present value of future net **cash flows**. An asset is a resource that provides future benefits. This future benefit is the ability of an asset either to generate future net cash receipts or to reduce future cash expenditures. For example, accounts receivable from customers will lead directly to future cash receipts. Merchandise inventory can be sold for cash or promises to pay cash. Equipment can be used to manufacture products that can then be sold for cash. A building that is owned reduces future cash outflows for rental payments. Because these cash flows represent the future services, or benefits, of assets, they might be used in the valuation of assets.

present value
The estimated current worth of amounts to be received (or paid) in the future from which appropriate amounts of discount (or interest) have been deducted.

Because cash can be invested to yield interest revenue over time, today's value of a stream of future cash flows, called the **present value**, is worth less than the sum of the cash amounts to be received or saved over time. The balance sheet is to be prepared as of a current date. If future cash flows are to be used to measure an asset's value, the future net cash flows must be discounted to find their present value as of the date of the balance sheet. Chapters 9 and 10 and Appendix A discuss the discounting methodology, but the following example presents the general approach.

Example 8 Miller Corporation sold merchandise to a reliable customer, General Models Co. Ltd., who promised to pay $10,000 one year from the date of sale. General Models signed a "promissory note" to that effect and gave the note to Miller Corporation. Miller Corporation judges that the current borrowing rate of General Models is 10 percent per year. That is, a loan to General Models should yield a return to Miller Corporation of 10 percent. Miller Corporation is to receive $10,000 one year from today. The $10,000 includes both the amount initially loaned plus interest on that amount for one year. Today's value of the $10,000 to be received one year hence is not $10,000, but about $9,100. That is, $9,100 plus 10 percent interest on $9,100 equals $10,000. Hence, the *present value* of $10,000 to be received one year from today is $9,100. (Miller Corporation is indifferent about whether it receives approximately $9,100 today or $10,000 one year from today.) The asset represented by General Models' promissory note has a present value of $9,100. If the note was stated on the balance sheet at the present value of the future cash flows, it would be shown at approximately $9,100 on the date of sale.

Using discounted cash flows in the valuation of individual assets requires solving several problems. One is the difficulty caused by the uncertainty of the amounts of future cash flows. The amounts to be received can depend on whether or not competitors introduce new products, the rate of inflation, and many other factors. A second problem is allocating the cash receipts from selling a single item of merchandise inventory to all of the assets involved in its production and distribution (for example, equipment, buildings, sales staff's automobiles). A third problem is selecting the appropriate rate to be used in discounting the future cash flows back to the present. Is the interest rate at which the firm could borrow the appropriate one? Or is the rate at which the firm could invest excess cash the one that should be used? Or is the appropriate rate the firm's cost of capital (a concept introduced in managerial accounting and finance courses)? In the example above, the selected rate is General Models' borrowing rate.

Selecting the Appropriate Valuation Basis

The valuation basis selected depends on the kind of financial report being prepared.

Example 9 Miller Corporation is preparing its income tax return for the current year. The Income Tax Act and Regulations specify that acquisition or adjusted acquisition cost valuation must be used in most instances.

Example 10 A fire recently destroyed the manufacturing plant, equipment, and inventory of Miller Corporation. The firm's fire insurance policy provides coverage in an amount equal to the cost of replacing the assets that were destroyed. Current replacement cost at the time of the fire is appropriate for supporting the insurance claim.

Example 11 Miller Corporation plans to dispose of one of its manufacturing divisions because it has been operating unprofitably. In deciding on the lowest price to accept for the division, the firm considers the net realizable value of each asset.

Example 12 Brown Corporation is considering the purchase of Miller Corporation. In deciding on the highest price to be paid, Brown Corporation is interested in the present value of the future net cash flows to be realized from owning Miller Corporation.

Generally Accepted Accounting Asset Valuation Bases

The asset valuation basis appropriate for financial statements issued to shareholders and other investors is perhaps less obvious. The financial statements currently prepared by publicly held firms are based on one of two valuation bases: one for monetary assets (cash and claims to cash) and one for nonmonetary assets.

Monetary assets
Cash or cash equivalents whose monetary value remains fixed.

Monetary assets, such as cash and accounts receivable, are generally shown on the balance sheet at their present value — their current cash, or cash-equivalent, value. Cash is stated at the amount of cash on hand or in the bank. Accounts receivable from customers are stated at the amount of cash expected to be collected in the future. If the period of time until a receivable is to be collected spans more than one year, the expected future cash receipt is discounted to a present value. Most accounts receivable, however, are collected within one to three months. The amount of future cash flows is approximately equal to the present value of these flows, and the discounting process is ignored.

Nonmonetary assets
All other assets.

Nonmonetary assets, such as merchandise inventory, land, buildings, and equipment, are stated at *acquisition cost*, in some cases adjusted downward for depreciation to reflect the services of the assets that have been consumed.

The acquisition cost of an asset may include more than its invoice price. Cost includes all expenditures made or obligations incurred in order to put the asset into usable condition. Transportation cost, costs of installation, handling charges, and any other necessary and reasonable costs incurred in connection with the asset up to the time it is put into service should be considered as part of the total cost assigned to the asset. For example, the cost of an item of equipment might be calculated as follows:

Invoice Price of Equipment	$12,000
Less: 2 Percent Discount for Prompt Cash Payment	(240)
Net Invoice Price	$11,760
Transportation Cost	326
Installation Costs	735
Total Cost of Equipment	$12,821

The acquisition cost of this equipment to be recorded in the accounting records is $12,821.

Instead of disbursing cash or incurring a liability, other forms of consideration (for example, common shares, merchandise inventory, land) may be given in acquiring an asset. *In these cases, acquisition cost is measured by the market value of the consideration given or the market value of the asset received, depending on which market value is more reliably measured.*

Foundations for Acquisition Cost

Accounting's use of acquisition-cost valuations for nonmonetary assets rests on three important concepts or conventions. First, a firm is assumed to be a *going concern*. That is, it is assumed that the firm will remain in operation long enough for all of its current plans to be carried out. Any increases in the market value of assets held will be realized in the normal course of business when the firm receives higher prices for its products. Current values of the individual assets are therefore assumed to be largely unimportant. Second, acquisition-cost valuations are considered to be more objective than those obtained from using the other valuation methods. *Objectivity* in accounting refers to the ability of several independent measurers to come to the same conclusion about the valuation of an asset. Obtaining consensus on what constitutes the acquisition cost of an asset is relatively easy. Differences among measurers can arise in ascertaining an asset's current replacement cost, current net realizable value, or present value of future cash flows. Objectivity is necessary if financial statements are to be subject to audits by independent accounts. Third, acquisition cost generally provides more conservative valuations of assets (and measures of earnings) relative to the other valuation methods. Many accountants feel that the possibility of misleading financial statement users will be minimized when assets are stated at lower rather than higher amounts. Thus, *conservatism* has evolved as a convention to justify acquisition-cost valuations.

The preceding description of generally accepted valuation bases does not justify them. The valuation basis — acquisition cost, current replacement cost, current net realizable value, or present value of future cash flows — most relevant to users is an empirical question for which convincing evidence has not yet been provided. Many large, publicly held firms provide supplementary information on the current cost of their inventories, property, plant, and equipment. The required disclosure of such information is, to some extent, a response to the recognized deficiencies of historical cost valuations during periods of changing prices.

Asset Classification

The classification of assets within the balance sheet varies widely in published annual reports. The principal asset categories are described below.

Current Assets

Current assets include "those assets ordinarily realizable within one year from the date of the balance sheet or within the normal operating cycle, where that is longer than a year."[1] The operating cycle refers to the period of time that elapses for a given firm during which cash is converted into salable goods and services, goods and services are sold to customers, and customers pay for their purchases with cash. Included in current assets are cash, marketable securities held for the short term, accounts and notes receivable net of allowance for doubtful accounts, inventories of merchandise, raw materials, supplies, work in process, and finished goods and prepaid operating costs (for example, prepaid insurance and prepaid rent). Prepaid costs, or prepayments, are current assets in that if they were not paid in advance, current assets would be required within the next operating cycle to acquire those services.

---

[1] *CICA Handbook*, section 1510.

Investments

A second section of the balance sheet, labelled *Investments*, includes long-term investments in securities of other firms. For example, a firm might purchase common shares of a supplier to help assure continued availability of raw materials, or common shares of a firm in another area of business activity might be acquired to permit the acquiring firm to diversify its operations. When one corporation (the parent) owns more than 50 percent of the voting shares in another corporation (the subsidiary), a single set of "consolidated" financial statements is usually prepared.[2] That is, the specific assets, liabilities, revenues, and expenses of the subsidiary are merged, or consolidated, with those of the parent corporation. The securities shown in the Investments section of the balance sheet are therefore investments in firms whose assets and liabilities have *not* been consolidated with the parent or investor firm. Chapter 12 discusses consolidated financial statements.

The holders of a firm's long-term bonds may require that cash be set aside periodically so that sufficient funds will be available to retire the bonds at maturity. The funds are typically given to a trustee, such as a trust company, which invests the funds received. Funds set aside for this purpose are shown in a Sinking Fund account and classified under Investments on the balance sheet.

Capital Assets

plant assets
A firm's property, plant, and equipment. Also called "capital assets."

fixed assets
Plant assets.

intangible assets
A term applied by convention to a group of long-term assets that benefit operations but do not have physical existence, including patents, copyrights, franchises, trademarks, and goodwill. Part of capital assets.

Property, plant, and equipment (sometimes called **plant assets** or **fixed assets**) designates the tangible, long-lived assets *used in a firm's operations* over a period of years and generally not acquired for resale. This category includes land, buildings, machinery, automobiles, furniture, fixtures, computers, and other equipment. The amount shown on the balance sheet for each of these items (except land) is acquisition cost less accumulated depreciation since the asset was acquired. The total cost of each category is usually presented, and the accumulated depreciation is shown separately as a deduction from the acquisition cost. Land is shown at acquisition cost. Capital assets also include **intangible assets**, which include such items as patents, trademarks, franchises, and goodwill. The expenditures made by the firm in developing intangible assets are usually not recognized as assets because of the difficulty of ascertaining the existence and amount of future benefits. Only intangible assets purchased in market exchanges from other entities are recognized as assets.

LIABILITY RECOGNITION

A liability arises when a firm receives benefits or services and in exchange promises to pay the provider of those goods or services a reasonably definite amount at a reasonably definite future time. The payment is usually in cash but may be made in goods and services.

Example 13 Miller Corporation purchased merchandise inventory and agreed to pay the supplier $8,000 within 30 days. This obligation is a lia-

---

[2] The concept of *effective control* is more critical than percentage ownership of shares in determining whether consolidation is appropriate.

bility because Miller Corporation has received the goods and must pay a definite amount at a reasonably definite future time.

Example 14 Miller Corporation borrowed $4 million by issuing long-term bonds. Annual interest payments of 10 percent must be made on December 31 of each year, and the $4 million principal must be repaid in twenty years. This obligation is a liability because Miller Corporation has received the cash and must repay the debt in a definite amount at a definite future time. The interest payable on the bonds increases each day the bonds are outstanding but, at the time of the original borrowing, there is no liability. At the financial statement date, the number of days of unpaid interest will be calculated and set up as a liability on the balance sheet.

Example 15 Miller Corporation provides a three-year warranty on its products. The obligation to maintain the products under warranty plans creates a liability. The selling price for its products implicitly includes a charge for future warranty services. As customers pay the selling price, Miller Corporation receives a benefit (that is, the cash received). Past experience provides a basis for estimating the proportion of customers who will seek services under the warranty agreement and the expected cost of providing warranty services. Thus, the amount of obligation can be estimated with a reasonable degree of accuracy, and it is shown as a liability.

Example 16 Miller Corporation has signed an agreement with its employees' labour union, promising to increase wages 6 percent and to provide for medical and life insurance. This agreement does not immediately create a liability, because services have not yet been received from employees that would require any payments for wages and insurance. As labour services are received, a liability will arise.

As was the case with assets, the most troublesome questions of liability recognition relate to unexecuted contracts. The labour union agreement in Example 16 above is an unexecuted contract. Other examples include leases, pension agreements, purchase-order commitments, and employment contracts. Accounting does not currently recognize unexecuted contracts as liabilities, although the issue continues to be controversial.

LIABILITY VALUATION

Most liabilities are monetary, requiring payments of specific amounts of cash. Those due with one year or less are stated at the amount of cash expected to be paid to discharge the obligation. If the payment dates extend more than one year into the future (for example, as in the case of the bonds in Example 14 above), the liability is usually stated at the present value of the future cash outflows.

A liability that requires delivering goods or rendering services, rather than paying cash, is nonmonetary. For example, magazine publishers typically collect cash for subscriptions, promising delivery of magazines over many months. Cash is received currently, whereas the obligation under the subscription is discharged by delivering magazines in the future. Theatres and sports franchises receive cash for season tickets and promise to admit ticket holders to future performances and games. Landlords receive cash in

Advances from Customers
A preferred term for the liability account representing receipts of cash in advance of the delivery (goods) or rendering (service) that will cause revenue to be recognized. Sometimes called "deferred revenue" or "deferred income."

residual interest
The claim to remaining assets by the common shareholders of the firm after all economic obligations have been discharged.

contributed capital
The sum of the balances in capital stock accounts plus capital contributed in excess of par-value (or stated-value) accounts. Contrasts with donated capital.

share capital
Capital stock.

par-value shares
An amount specified in the corporate charter for each share and imprinted on the face of each share certificate. Par-value shares are not allowed for companies incorporated under the Canada Business Corporations Act.

contributed surplus
Capital contributions from sources other than the issuance of shares. Contributed surplus includes donated capital.

advance and promise to let tenants use the property. Such nonmonetary obligations appear among liabilities. They are stated, however, at the amount of cash received rather than at the expected cost of publishing the magazines or providing the theatrical or sporting entertainment. The title frequently used for liabilities of this type is **Advances from Customers**.

LIABILITY CLASSIFICATION

Liabilities in the balance sheet are typically classified in one of the following categories:

Current Liabilities   *Current liabilities* include "amount payable within one year from the date of the balance sheet or within the normal operating cycle, where this is longer than a year (the normal operating cycle should correspond with that used for current assets)."[3] Included in this category are liabilities to merchandise suppliers, employees, and governmental units. Notes and bonds payable are also included to the extent that they will require the use of current assets within the next year.

Long-Term Debt   Obligations having due dates or maturities more than one year after the balance sheet date are generally classified as *long-term debt*. Included are bonds, mortgages, and similar debts, as well as some obligations under long-term leases.

Other Long-Term Liabilities   Obligations not properly considered as current liabilities or long-term debt are classified as *other long-term liabilities*. Included are such items as future income taxes and some pension obligations.

OWNERS' EQUITY VALUATION AND DISCLOSURE

The owners' equity in a firm is a **residual interest**.[4] That is, the owners have a claim on all assets not required to meet the claims of creditors. The valuation of the assets and liabilities included in the balance sheet therefore determines the valuation of total owners' equity.

The remaining question concerns the manner of disclosing this total owners' equity. Accounting draws a distinction between **contributed capital** and income retained by a firm. The balance sheet for a corporation generally separates the amounts contributed directly by shareholders for an interest in the firm (that is, **share capital**) from the subsequent earnings realized by the firm in excess of dividends declared (that is, retained earnings).

In addition, where a company is authorized to issue **par-value shares**, the amount received from shareholders is further divided into the par value of the shares issued and **contributed surplus**. The par or **stated value** of a share is a somewhat arbitrary amount assigned to comply with corporation laws of each jurisdiction[5] and will rarely equal the market price of the shares at the time they are issued. As a result, the distinction between par

---

[3] *CICA Handbook*, section 1510.

[4] Although owners' equity is equal to assets minus liabilities, accounting provides an independent method for computing the amount. This method is presented in this and the next two chapters.

[5] The federal and each provincial government has the authority to incorporate companies.

or stated value and contributed surplus contains little information, but is typically shown nonetheless. The overcome this anomaly, **Companies Acts** authorize a company to issue **no-par-value shares**. When no-par-value shares are issued, the full amount received from the shareholders is included in share capital. The **Canada Business Corporations Act** requires a company to issue only no-par-value shares. (Chapter 12 discusses these finer points of accounting for owners' equity.)

Example 17 Stephens Corporation was formed on January 1, Year 1. It issued 15,000 $10 par value common shares for $10 cash per share. During Year 1, Stephens Corporation had net income of $30,000 and paid dividends of $10,000 to shareholders. The shareholders' equity section of the balance sheet of Stephens Corporation on December 31, Year 1, is as follows:

Common Shares (par value of $10 per share, 15,000 shares issued and outstanding)	$150,000
Retained Earnings	20,000
Total Shareholders' Equity	$170,000

Example 18 Instead of issuing $10 par value common shares as in Example 17, assume that Stephens Corporation issued 15,000 common shares of $1 par value for $10 cash per share. (The market price of common shares depends on the economic value of the firm and not on the par value of the shares.) The shareholders' equity section of the balance sheet of Stephens Corporation on December 31, Year 1, is as follows:

Common Shares (par value of $1 per share, 15,000 shares issued and outstanding)	$ 15,000
Contributed Surplus	135,000
Retained Earnings	20,000
Total Shareholders' Equity	$170,000

The balance sheet of firms that are organized as sole proprietorships or partnerships, rather than as corporations, do not distinguish between contributed capital and earnings retained in business.

Example 19 Instead of issuing par value shares as in Example 18, assume that Stephens Corporation issued 15,000 no-par-value shares for $10 cash per share. The shareholders' equity section of the balance sheet of Stephens Corporation on December 31, Year 1, is as follows:

Common Shares (no par value, 15,000 shares issued and outstanding)	$150,000
Retained Earnings	20,000
Total Shareholders' Equity	$170,000

Example 20 Joan Webster operates a hardware store as a sole proprietorship. She contributed $20,000 on January 1, Year 1, and used the cash to rent a building, acquire display equipment, and purchase merchandise inventory. During Year 1, she had net income of $15,000 and withdrew

stated value
A term sometimes used for the face amount of capital stock when no par value is indicated. Where there is a stated value per share, it may be set by the directors (in which case contributed surplus may come into being).

Companies Acts
The federal (CBCA) or provincial incorporating acts which govern the affairs of incorporated businesses in Canada.

no-par-value shares
Shares in which the entire sales proceeds are credited to the Common Shares account. All shares issued under the Canada Business Corporations Act are no-par-values shares.

Canada Business Corporations Act (CBCA)
The federal act that regulates the formation and conduct of corporations incorporated under it. There are also provincial corporations acts.

$10,000 cash for personal use. The owner's equity section of the balance sheet of Webster's Hardware Store on December 31, Year 1, is as follows:

Joan Webster, Capital	$25,000[a]
Total Owner's Equity	$25,000

[a]$20,000 + $15,000 − $10,000 = $25,000.

Example 21 Bill White and Roger Green own and manage an apartment complex as a partnership. Each partner contributed $50,000 cash to form the partnership on January 1, Year 1. During Year 1, net income from the apartment complex was $40,000, which the partners shared equally. Bill White withdrew $10,000 and Roger Green withdrew $5,000 from the partnership. The owners' equity section of the balance sheet on December 31, Year 1, for the apartment complex is as follows:

Bill White, Capital	$ 60,000[a]
Roger Green, Capital	65,000[b]
Total Owners' Equity	$125,000

[a]$50,000 + (0.50 × $40,000) − $10,000 = $60,000.
[b]$50,000 + (0.50 × $40,000) − $5,000 = $65,000.

DISCUSSION CASE 3

Distinctly Canadian GAAP

The differences between Canadian and U.S. GAAP are of concern to the senior financial officers who have to provide for reconciliations. According to Suresh Thadhani, the controller of Alcan, providing the two sets of figures is "a nuisance," and the reconciliation provides additional information to competitors who do not have to comply with the same standards of disclosure.

Ken Whiteside, senior vice president with TransCanada Pipe Lines, remarked that it's difficult enough to understand one bottom line. He feels that a higher corporate profit reported under Canadian GAAP, when compared with the U.S. number, raises questions about the quality of the numbers involved — which is preferable and which is right?

Why the Differences?

Why are there so many differences between Canadian and U.S. GAAP? Some standard-setters on either side of the border may be tempted to say, "Ours are better." But in most instances a definitive case for either side would be difficult to argue. Certainly, there have been some marked differences in the economic and financial development of Canada and

(continued)

(continued)

the U.S., but, again, these cannot be related directly to the differences in the two GAAPs.

Instead, it appears that standard-setting in the two countries is influenced by how each views the relative importance of the different components of the financial statements.

In any effort to set standards, there is always a trade-off between "getting it right" on the balance sheet or on the income statement. From the examples of differences cited, it becomes apparent that the Canadian leaning is towards deferral and amortization, in attempts to match revenue and expenses, to allow for cause and effect, or to recognize time and terms. The U.S. approach, on the other hand, seems to be directed more to the balance sheet, to arriving at valuations without distortions due to "matching."

One could argue that the Canadian GAAP looks at the income statement trends, while the FASB concentrates on the balance sheet snapshot. While the income statement under the U.S. GAAP, some would argue, may be subject to swings brought about by accounting standards, the U.S. GAAP balance sheet attempts to present a more meaningful report of a company's resources and obligations. The U.S. result flows from restricted definitions of assets and liabilities, combined with an income stream that has not been normalized. There is no question, however, that the effort "to get it right" on the income statements results in what some would call, with great technical precision,

"funny" items on the balance sheet. And the most misunderstood and criticized of those is, of course, deferred income taxes.

The Regulatory Climate

The regulatory surroundings of the two GAAPs are also quite different. The U.S. practice of pushdown accounting, for example, is not a result of standard-setting by the FASB; it is an instance of RAP — related accounting principles — as the practice was dictated by the Securities and Exchange Commission. In Canada, governments and regulators have retained the power to issue RAP, but have delegated the responsibility for setting both accounting and auditing standards to the CICA. In the provincial securities acts and in the federal Canada Business Corporations Act and some provincial corporations legislation, the accounting standards for Canadian profit-oriented enterprises are defined as those set out in the *CICA Handbook*.

Another contributor to the gap in GAAPs is one of the philosophy of standard-setting. Both the U.S. and Canadian models place prime importance on the use of professional judgment, but Canadian standards, in effect, place much more reliance — some would say too much reliance — on the use of the judgment.

Canadian standards are specifically designed so that they are not detailed rules. All accounting and auditing standards are contained in the *CICA Handbook*, a publication which runs to only a few hundred pages. It is not light or pleasant reading, but it is rel-

(continued)

(continued)

atively straight-forward in setting out general standards. And the CICA seldom issues supplementary technical bulletins or lengthy rationales of *Handbook* material.

Of course, it can be said that this approach is necessary for the CICA, which has 45,000 members and far fewer resources than either the FASB or the AICPA. But it is an approach in line with the early development of standard-setting in England and Scotland, where so many of Canada's early chartered accountants came from. Relative to its size, the Canadian profession does devote considerable resources not only to developing Canadian standards but also to international harmonization of accounting standards and auditing practices.

At this time [1988], however, Canada may have to make some changes in its standard-setting philosophy and practices. In Canada, as in the U.S., accountants are under a good deal of pressure from regulators and the business community. How they react and grow will help shape the financial environment in the future.

References

Reprinted with permission. From William W. Buchanan and the Canadian Institute of Chartered Accountants, "The U.S. and Canada: Two Bottom Lines (Why the Difference?)," *Financial Executive*, Sept./Oct. 1988, copyright 1988 by Financial Executives Institute, Morristown, New Jersey.

Discussion Question

Will free trade be the catalyst leading to a single GAAP for North America?

Accounting Procedures for Preparing the Balance Sheet

Now that the concepts and conventions underlying the balance sheet have been discussed, the manner in which these concepts and conventions are applied in preparing the statement can be considered. The objective is to develop a sufficient understanding of the accounting process that generates the balance sheet so that the resulting statement can be interpreted and analyzed.

Dual Effects of Transactions on the Balance Sheet Equation

The equality between total assets and total liabilities plus shareholders' equity in the balance sheet equation is maintained by reporting the effects of *each* transaction in a way that maintains the equation. Any single transaction will have one of the following four effects or some combination of these effects:

1. It increases both an asset and a liability or shareholders' equity.
2. It decreases both an asset and a liability or shareholders' equity.
3. It increases one asset and decreases another asset.
4. It increases one liability or shareholders' equity and decreases another liability or shareholders' equity.

To illustrate the dual effects of various transactions on the balance sheet equation, consider the following selected transactions for Miller Corporation during January.

1. On January 1, 10,000 no-par-value common shares are issued for $100,000 cash.
2. Equipment costing $60,000 is purchased for cash on January 5.
3. Merchandise inventory costing $15,000 is purchased from a supplier on account on January 15.
4. The supplier in (3) is paid $8,000 of the amount due on January 21.
5. The supplier in (3) accepts 700 common shares in settlement of the $7,000 amount owed.
6. A one-year fire insurance premium of $600 for coverage beginning February 1 is paid in cash on January 31.
7. Cash of $3,000 is received from a customer on January 31 for merchandise to be delivered during February.

Exhibit 2.1 illustrates the dual effects of these transactions on the balance sheet equation. Note that, after each transaction, assets equal liabilities plus shareholders' equity.

The dual effects reported for each transaction may be viewed as an outflow and an inflow. For example, common shares are issued to shareholders and cash is received from them. A cash expenditure is made and equipment is received. A promise to make a future cash payment is given to a supplier and merchandise inventory is received. Most transactions and events recorded in the accounting system result from exchanges. The accounting records reflect the inflows and outflows arising from these exchanges.

PURPOSE AND USE OF ACCOUNTS

A balance sheet could be prepared for Miller Corporation as of January 31, using information from the preceding analysis. Total assets are $110,000. To prepare a balance sheet, however, it would be necessary to retrace the effects of each transaction on total assets to ascertain what portion of the $110,000 represents cash, merchandise inventory, and equipment. Likewise, the effects of each transaction on total liabilities and shareholders' equity would have to be retraced to ascertain which liability and shareholders' equity amounts make up the $110,000 total. Even with just a few transactions during the accounting period, this approach to preparing a balance sheet would be cumbersome. Considering the thousands of transactions during the accounting period for most firms, a more practical approach to accumulating amounts for the balance sheet is necessary. To accumulate the changes that take place in each balance sheet item, the accounting system uses a device known as an **account**.

Requirement for an Account

Because a balance sheet item that changes can only increase or decrease, all an account need do is to provide for accumulating the increases and decreases that have taken place during the period for a single balance sheet

account
A record of the additions, deductions, and balances of individual assets, liabilities, owners' equity, revenue, and expenses. The basic component of a formal accounting system.

EXHIBIT 2.1
Illustration of Dual Effects of Transactions on Balance Sheet Equation

Transaction	Assets	=	Liabilities	+	Shareholders' Equity
(1) On January 1, 10,000 no-par-value common shares are issued for $100,000 cash. (Increase in both an asset and shareholders' equity.)	+$100,000		$ 0	+	$100,000
Subtotal	$100,000	=	$ 0	+	$100,000
(2) Equipment costing $60,000 is purchased for cash on January 5. (Increase in one asset and decrease in another asset.)	−60,000 +60,000				
Subtotal	$100,000	=	$ 0	+	$100,000
(3) Merchandise inventory costing $15,000 is purchased from a supplier on account on January 15. (Increase in both an asset and a liability.)	+15,000		+15,000		
Subtotal	$115,000	=	$15,000	+	$100,000
(4) The supplier in (3) is paid $8,000 of the amount due on January 21. (Decrease in both an asset and a liability.)	−8,000		−8,000		
Subtotal	$107,000	=	$ 7,000	+	$100,000
(5) The supplier in (3) accepts 700 common shares in settlement of $7,000 of the amount owed. (Increase in shareholders' equity and decrease in a liability.)			−7,000	+	7,000
Subtotal	$107,000	=	$ 0	+	$107,000
(6) A one-year fire insurance premium of $600 for coverage beginning February 1 is paid in cash on January 31. (Increase in one asset and decrease in another asset.)	+600 −600				
Subtotal	$107,000	=	$ 0	+	$107,000
(7) Cash of $3,000 is received from a customer on January 31 for merchandise to be delivered during February. (Increase in both an asset and a liability.)	+3,000		+3,000		
Total—January 31	$110,000	=	$ 3,000	+	$107,000

item. The balance carried forward from the previous statement is added to the total increases; the total decreases are deducted, and the result is the amount of the new balance for the current balance sheet. The collection of individual accounts is called a **general ledger**.

general ledger
A grouping of the accounts in which the activities of an entity are recorded.

Form of an Account

The account may take many possible forms, and several are commonly used in accounting practice.

T-account
An abbreviated form of the formal account; its use is usually limited to illustration of accounting techniques.

Perhaps the most useful form of the account for textbooks, problems, and examinations is the **T-account**. This form of the account is not used in actual practice, except perhaps for memoranda or preliminary analyses. However, it satisfies the requirement of an account and is easy to use. As the name indicates, the T-account is shaped like a T and consists of a horizontal line and a perpendicular line. The name or title of the account is written on the horizontal line. One side of the space formed by the vertical line is used to record increases in the item and the other side to record the decreases. Spaces for dates and other information can appear as well.

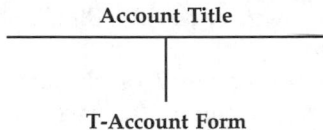

Account Title

T-Account Form

The form that the account takes in actual records depends on the type of accounting system being used. In manual systems, the account may take the form of a single "ledger" sheet with columns for recording increases and decreases. In computer systems, it may be a group of similarly coded items in a file. Whatever its form, an account contains the opening balance as well as the increases and decreases in the balance that result from the transactions of the period, and ordinarily the closing balance.

Placement of Increases and Decreases in the Account

Given the two-sided account, we must choose which side will be used to record increases and which will be used for decreases. By long-standing custom, the following rules are used:

1. Increases in assets are entered on the left side and decreases in assets on the right side.
2. Increases in liabilities are entered on the right side and decreases in liabilities on the left side.
3. Increases in owners' equity are entered on the right side and decreases in owners' equity on the left side.

This custom reflects the fact that a common format for a balance sheet shows assets on the left and liabilities and owners' equity on the right. Following this format, asset balances should appear on the left side of accounts; liability and shareholders' equity balances should appear on the right. But asset balances will appear on the left only if asset increases are recorded on the left side of the account. Similarly, right-hand liability and shareholders' equity balances can be produced only by recording liability and shareholders' equity increases on the right. When each transaction is properly analyzed with regard to its dual effects on the accounting equation and when the above three rules for recording the transaction are followed, every transaction results in equal amounts in entries on the left- and right-hand sides of various accounts.

Debit and Credit

Two terms may now be introduced: **debit (Dr.)** and **credit (Cr.)**. *Debit* means "record an entry on the left side of an account" when used as a verb and "an entry on the left side of an account" when used as a noun or adjective. *Credit* means "record an entry on the right side of an account" when used as a verb and "an entry on the right side of an account" when used as a

debit (Dr.)
(entry) An entry on the left-hand side (or in the debit column) of any account.

credit (Cr.)
(entry) An entry on the right-hand side (or in the credit column) of any account.

noun or adjective.[6] Often, however, the word *charge* is used instead of *debit*, both as a noun and as a verb. In terms of balance sheet categories, a debit or charge indicates (1) an increase in an asset, (2) a decrease in a liability, or (3) a decrease in a shareholders' equity item. A credit indicates (1) a decrease in an asset, (2) an increase in a liability, or (3) an increase in a shareholders' equity item.

In order to maintain the equality of the balance sheet equation, the amounts debited to various accounts for each transaction must equal the amounts credited to various accounts. Likewise, the sum of balances in accounts with debit balances at the end of each period must equal the sum of balances in accounts with credit balances.

Summary of Account Terminology and Procedure

The conventional use of the account form and the terms debit and credit can be summarized graphically with the use of the T-account form, as follows:

Any Asset Account			Any Liability Account	
Beginning Balance Increases + Dr.	Decreases – Cr.		Decreases – Dr.	Beginning Balances Increases + Cr.
Ending Balance				Ending Balance

Any Shareholders' Equity Account	
Decreases – Dr.	Beginning Balance Increases + Cr.
	Ending Balance

REFLECTING THE DUAL EFFECTS OF TRANSACTIONS IN THE ACCOUNTS

The manner in which the dual effects of transactions change the accounts can now be illustrated. Three separate T-accounts are created: one for assets, one for liabilities, and one for shareholders' equity. The dual effects of the transactions of Miller Corporation for January, described earlier in the chapter, are entered in the T-accounts as shown in Exhibit 2.2.

The amount entered on the left side of, or debited to, the accounts for each transaction is equal to the amount entered on the right side of, or credited to, the accounts. Recording equal amounts of debits and credits for each transaction ensures that the balance sheet equation will always be in balance. At the end of January the assets account has a debit balance of $110,000. The sum of the balances in the liabilities and shareholders' equity account is a credit balance of $110,000.

---

[6] The terms debit and credit originated in Great Britain. In early British balance sheets, amounts receivable from customers (then called *debitors*) constituted the major assets, while amounts payable to suppliers and others (then and now called *creditors*) constituted the major liabilities.

EXHIBIT 2.2
Summary T-Accounts Showing the Transactions of Miller Corporation

	Assets		= Liabilities		+ Shareholders' Equity	
	Increases (Dr.)	Decreases (Cr.)	Decreases (Dr.)	Increases (Cr.)	Decreases (Dr.)	Increases (Cr.)
(1) Issue of Common Shares for Cash	100,000					100,000
(2) Purchase of Equipment for Cash	60,000	60,000				
(3) Purchase of Merchandise on Account	15,000			15,000		
(4) Payment of Cash to Supplier in (3)		8,000	8,000			
(5) Issuance of Common Shares to Supplier in (3)			7,000			7,000
(6) Payment of Insurance Premium in Advance	600	600				
(7) Cash Received from Customer in Advance	3,000			3,000		
Balance	110,000			3,000		107,000

A balance sheet could be prepared for Miller Corporation from the information in the T-accounts. As was the case in the earlier illustration, however, it would be necessary to retrace the entries in the accounts during the period to ascertain which individual assets, liabilities, and shareholders' equity items make up the total assets of $110,000 and the total equities of $110,000.

So that the amount of each asset, liability, and shareholders' equity item can be computed directly, a separate account is used for each balance sheet item, rather than for the three broad categories alone. The recording procedure is the same, except that we must now consider which specific asset or equity account is debited and credited.

The transactions of the Miller corporation for January are recorded in Exhibit 2.3, using separate T-accounts for each balance sheet item. The number in parentheses refers to the seven transactions we have been considering for Miller Corporation.

EXHIBIT 2.3
Individual T-Accounts Showing the Transactions of Miller Corporation

Cash (Asset)				Accounts Payable (Liability)			
Increases (Dr.)		Decreases (Cr.)		Decreases (Dr.)		Increases (Cr.)	
(1)	100,000	60,000	(2)	(4)	8,000	15,000	(3)
(7)	3,000	8,000	(4)	(5)	7,000		
		600	(6)				
Balance	34,400					0	Balance

Merchandise Inventory (Asset)

Increases (Dr.)	Decreases (Cr.)
(3) 15,000	
Balance 15,000	

Advance from Customer (Liability)

Decreases (Dr.)	Increases (Cr.)
	3,000 (7)
	3,000 Balance

Prepaid Insurance (Asset)

Increases (Dr.)	Decreases (Cr.)
(6) 600	
Balance 600	

Common Shares (Shareholders' Equity)

Decreases (Dr.)	Increases (Cr.)
	100,000 (1)
	7,000 (5)
	107,000 Balance

Equipment (Asset)

Increases (Dr.)	Decreases (Cr.)
(2) 60,000	
Balance 60,000	

The balance sheet can be prepared using the amounts shown as balances in the T-accounts. The balance sheet of Miller Corporation after the seven transactions of January is shown in Exhibit 2.4.

EXHIBIT 2.4
MILLER CORPORATION
Balance Sheet, January 31

ASSETS	
Current Assets:	
Cash	$ 34,400
Merchandise Inventory	15,000
Prepaid Insurance	600
Total Current Assets	$ 50,000
Property, Plant, and Equipment	
Equipment	60,000
Total Assets	$110,000
LIABILITIES AND SHAREHOLDERS' EQUITY	
Current Liabilities:	
Advance from Customer	$ 3,000
Shareholders' Equity:	
Common Shares	107,000
Total Liabilities and Shareholders' Equity	$110,000

DISCUSSION CASE 4

A Canadian Perspective: What's the Code of Business for the '90s?

The universality of certain issues confronting business organizations today, regardless of geographic location, was demonstrated at FEI Canada's Spring Conference held in Hamilton, Ontario, May 24 to 26 [1990]. A roster of distinguished speakers discussing "Ethics and Conduct for the '90s" provided exceptional "mental edibles' relevant to all FEI members. Excerpts from the presentations follow.

Is "Business Ethics" an Oxymoron?

Calling the '90s the decade of ethics and the environment, keynote speaker Max Clarkson, professor of management at the University of Toronto, declared that business ethics is no longer an oxymoron. Further, Clarkson declared, "Ethics is not a constraint on profits."

Clarkson's experience during 30 years in business prior to becoming dean of the Faculty of Management at the University of Toronto in 1975 has provided unique insight into business management. Stating that the business of business is not just business, but "business in society," Clarkson pointed out that corporations cannot survive and prosper separate from the communities in which they operate. However, he made clear that "if you don't make a profit, you can't fulfill any social responsibilities at all."

A major research project undertaken by Clarkson has revealed that companies whose social performance was evaluated as "proactive" were more profitable in their industry over an extended period of time than those companies whose social performance was not ranked as high. "An unbalanced concentration on the bottom line was counterproductive," Clarkson reported.

This balance is not an easy concept to define, he continued. No mechanisms exist where ethical considerations and social responsibilities can be quantified in a way that will satisfy accountants, academics, or financial executives, said Clarkson.

Instead of attempting to "quantify the unquantifiable," he said, the principal elements of social responsibility and ethical performance must be defined and analyzed together with the corporate data necessary to evaluate corporate performance in an objective way. Clarkson is working on "an index of criteria" to assist companies in evaluating their performance.

The tough question, according to Clarkson, is "How do you balance your economic responsibilities and your ethical responsibilities?" Ethics are primarily a

(continued)

(continued)
matter of conduct, and behavior is the bottom line. Values generate the ground rules that guide that behavior, he continued. In a corporation, this is generally expressed as "the way we do things around here."

Concurring with the Treadway report, Clarkson stated, "Values and ethics come from the top of an organization. This is why it can be helpful to draw up codes of conduct based on statements of value and purpose.

"You must be able to tell people what you expect, and senior executives must behave in a way that is consistent with that code," he emphasized. If you have no code of conduct, it is hard to punish someone for unethical behavior, noted Clarkson. "Institutional memory" of "the way we do things" has been lost in restructurings and that has led to more codes of conduct and ethics.

References
Reprinted with permission. From "A Canadian Perspective: What's the Code of Business for the '90s?," *Technically Speaking*, Sept./Oct. 1990, copyright 1990 by Financial Executives Institute, Morristown, New Jersey.

Discussion Question
Why would anyone consider the term *business ethics* an oxymoron, and what arguments does Clarkson use against this view?

AN OVERVIEW OF THE ACCOUNTING PROCESS

The double-entry recording framework is used in processing the results of various transactions and events through the accounts so that financial statements can be prepared periodically. The accounting system designed around this recording framework generally involves the following operations:

journalizing
The process of making entries in a journal.

Posting
The process of recording entries in an account in a ledger; usually, the entries are transferred from a journal.

journal entry
An entry in the accounting records showing the accounts to be debited and credited along with the date and amounts.

1. Entering the results of each transaction in the *general journal* in the form of a *journal entry*, a process called **journalizing**.
2. **Posting** the journal entries from the general journal to the accounts in the *general ledger*.
3. Preparing a *trial balance* of the accounts in the general ledger.
4. Making *adjusting* journal entries to accounts listed in the trial balance and posting them to the appropriate general ledger accounts.
5. Preparing financial statements from a trial balance after adjusting entries.

Figure 2.1 shows these operations. Each is described further and illustrated using the transactions of Miller Corporation during January.

JOURNALIZING

Each transaction is initially recorded in the general journal in the form of a **journal entry**. The standard journal entry format is as follows:

Date Account Debited	Amount Debited	
Account Credited		Amount Credited
Explanation of transaction or event being journalized		

The **general journal** is merely a book or other device containing a listing of journal entries in chronological order. The general journal is often referred to as the "book of original entry," because transactions initially enter the accounting system through it.[7]

The journal entries for the seven transactions of Miller Corporation during January are presented below.

general journal
A grouping of the accounts in which the activities of an entity are recorded.

(1) Jan. 1	Cash		$100,000	
	Common Stock			$100,000
	10,000 no-par-value common shares are issued for cash.			
(2) Jan. 5	Equipment		$ 60,000	
	Cash			$ 60,000
	Equipment costing $60,000 is purchased for cash.			
(3) Jan. 15	Merchandise Inventory		$ 15,000	
	Accounts Payable			$ 15,000
	Merchandise inventory costing $15,000 is purchased on account.			
(4) Jan. 21	Accounts Payable		$ 8,000	
	Cash			$ 8,000
	Liabilities of $8,000 are paid for with cash.			
(5) Jan. 21	Accounts Payable		$ 7,000	
	Common Stock			$ 7,000
	700 $10 par value common shares are issued in settlement of an account payable of $7,000.			
(6) Jan. 31	Prepaid Insurance		$ 600	
	Cash			$ 600
	One-year fire insurance premium of $600 is paid in advance.			
(7) Jan. 31	Cash		$ 3,000	
	Advance from Customer			$ 3,000
	Advance of $3,000 is received from customer for merchandise to be delivered in February.			

FIGURE 2.1
Summary of the Accounting Process

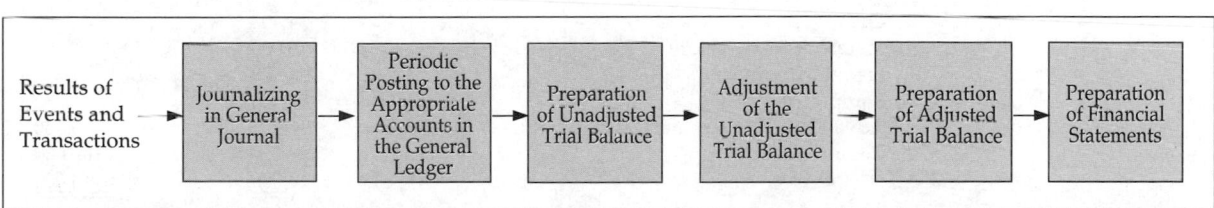

[7] In addition to the general journal, most firms also maintain *specialized journals*. These journals are used instead of the general journal where there are large numbers of similar transactions. Appendix 3.1 discusses specialized journals more fully.

Journal entries are useful for indicating the effects of various transactions on a firm's financial statements and in preparing solutions to the problems at the end of each chapter. An accounting event will not be completely understood until it is analyzed with regard to its required debits and credits and the proper journal entry is prepared. Consequently, journal entries are used as tools of analysis throughout this text.

POSTING

At periodic intervals (for example, weekly or monthly), the transactions journalized in the general journal are entered, or posted, to the individual accounts in the general ledger.[8] In manual systems, the general ledger is a book with a separate page for each account. In computerized systems, the general ledger takes the form of an access number in a computer file. The T-account described earlier serves as a useful surrogate for a general ledger account. The journal entries from the general journal of Miller Corporation would be posted to the general ledger accounts in the manner shown previously in Exhibit 2.3.

As with journal entries, T-accounts are useful tools in preparing solutions to accounting problems and are used throughout this text.

TRIAL BALANCE PREPARATION

trial balance
A list of the account titles in the general ledger, their respective debit or credit balances, and the totals of all accounts having debit balances and all accounts having credit balances.

A **trial balance** is a listing of each of the accounts in the general ledger with its balance as of a particular date. The trial balance of Miller Corporation on January 31 appears in Exhibit 2.5.

When the sum of debit account balances equals the sum of credit account balances, it is likely that the double-entry recording procedure has been carried out accurately during the period. If the trial balance is out of balance, retracing the steps followed in processing the accounting data is necessary to locate the source of the error.

EXHIBIT 2.5
MILLER CORPORATION
Unadjusted Trial Balance, January 31

Account	Amounts in Accounts with Debit Balances	Amounts in Accounts with Credit Balances
Cash	$ 34,400	
Merchandise Inventory	15,000	
Prepaid Insurance	600	
Equipment	60,000	
Advance from Customer		$ 3,000
Common Stock		107,000
Totals	$110,000	$110,000

---

[8] There are also subsidiary ledgers, discussed in Appendix 3.1.

TRIAL BALANCE ADJUSTMENT AND CORRECTION

Any errors detected in the processing of accounting data must be corrected. More frequently, adjustment is necessary to account for unrecorded events that help to measure net income for the period and financial position at the end of the period. For example, at the end of February, the Prepaid Insurance account will be adjusted downward to reflect the coverage that expired during February. This chapter and the next chapter discuss this type of adjustment more fully. Most corrections and adjustments are made by preparing an **adjusting journal entry**, entering it in the general journal, and then posting it to the general ledger accounts.

adjusting journal entry
An entry resulting from an attempt to reflect in the accounts various changes that may be appropriate, although no source document is normally available; usually, it involves accruals or deferrals.

FINANCIAL STATEMENT PREPARATION

The balance sheet and income statement can be prepared from the trial balance after adjustments and corrections. Because correcting or adjusting entries are not required for Miller Corporation, the balance sheet in Exhibit 2.4 is correct as presented. In subsequent chapters, the accounting procedures for preparing the income statement and the statement of changes in financial position are considered.

The results of various transactions and events are processed through the accounting system in a flow beginning with the journalizing operation and ending with the financial statements.

The audit of the financial statements by the independent auditor typically flows in the opposite direction. The auditor begins with the financial statements prepared by management and then traces various items back through the accounts to the source documents (for example, sales invoices, cancelled cheques) that support the entries made in the general journal. Thus, it is possible to move back and forth among source documents, journal entries, general ledger postings, and the financial statements.

BALANCE SHEET ACCOUNT TITLES

The following list shows balance sheet account titles that are commonly used. The descriptions should help you in understanding the nature of various assets, liabilities, and shareholders' equities as well as in selecting appropriate terms for solving problems. Alternative account titles can be easily devised. The list does not shown all of the account titles that are used in this book or that appear in the financial statements of publicly held firms.

ASSETS

Cash on Hand   Coins and currency, and such items as bank cheques and money orders. The latter items are merely claims against individuals or institutions, but by custom are called "cash."[9]

Cash in Bank   Strictly speaking, merely a claim against the bank for the amount deposited. Cash in bank consists of demand deposits, against which

[9] *CICA Handbook*, section 3000.

cheques can be drawn, and time deposits, usually savings accounts and certificates of deposit. In published statements, the two items Cash on Hand and Cash in Bank usually are combined under the title *Cash*.

Temporary Investments[10]   Government bonds, or shares and bonds of corporations, that the firm plans to hold for a relatively short period of time. The work **temporary** implies that they can be bought and sold readily through a security exchange such as the Toronto Stock Exchange.

Accounts Receivable[11]   Amounts due from customers of a business from the sale of goods or services. The collection of cash occurs some time after the sale. These accounts are also known as "charge accounts" or "open accounts." The general term Accounts Receivable is used in financial statements to describe the figure representing the total amount receivable from all customers but, of course, the firm keeps a separate record for each customer.

Notes Receivable[12]   Amounts due from customers or from others to whom loans have been made or credit extended, when the claim has been put into writing in the form of a promissory note.

Interest Receivable   Interest on assets such as promissory notes or bonds that has accrued, or come into existence, through the passing of time but that has not been collected as of the date of the balance sheet.

Merchandise Inventory[13]   Goods on hand that have been purchased for resale, such as canned goods on the shelves of a grocery store or suits on the racks of a clothing store.

Raw Materials Inventory   Unused materials from which manufactured products are to be made.

Work-in-Process Inventory[14]   Partially completed manufactured products.

Finished Goods Inventory[15]   Completed but unsold manufactured products.

Supplies Inventory   Lubricants, cleaning rags, abrasives, and other incidental materials used in manufacturing operations. Stationery, computer disks, pens, and other office supplies. Bags, twine, boxes, and other store supplies. Gasoline, oil, spare parts, and other delivery supplies.

Prepaid Insurance[16]   Insurance premiums paid for future coverage.

Prepaid Rent[17]   Rent paid in advance for future use of land, buildings, or equipment.

Advances to Suppliers   The general name used to indicate payments made in advance for goods to be received at a later date. If no cash is paid by a firm when it places an order, no asset is recognized.

[10] *CICA Handbook*, section 3010.
[11] *CICA Handbook*, section 3020.
[12] *CICA Handbook*, section 3020.
[13] *CICA Handbook*, section 3030.
[14] *CICA Handbook*, section 3030.
[15] *CICA Handbook*, section 3030.
[16] *CICA Handbook*, section 3040.
[17] *CICA Handbook*, section 3040.

Investment in Securities[18]   The cost of shares in other companies, where the firm's purpose is to hold the shares for relatively long periods of time.

Land[19]   Land occupied by buildings or used in operations.

Buildings[20]   Factory buildings, store buildings, garages, warehouses, and so forth.

Equipment[21]   Lathes, ovens, tools, boilers, computers, motors, bins, cranes, conveyors, automobiles, and so forth.

Furniture and Fixtures[22]   Desks, tables, chairs, counters, showcases, scales, and other such store and office equipment.

Accumulated Depreciation   This account shows the cumulative amount of the cost of long-term assets (such as buildings and equipment) that has been allocated to the costs of production or to prior periods in measuring net income. The amount in this account is subtracted from the acquisition cost of the long-term asset to which it relates in ascertaining the *net book value* of the asset to be shown in the balance sheet. This account is an example of a *contra account*.

Leasehold   The right to use property owned by someone else.

Deferred Charges[23]   Debt discount and expense, organization costs, deferred development costs, preproduction costs, and so forth. These are expenditures carried forward as assets to be expensed in future periods.

Organization Costs[24]   Amounts paid for legal and incorporation fees, for printing the share certificates, for accounting, and for any other costs incurred in organizing the business so that it can begin to function.

Deferred Development and Preproduction Costs   Expenditures made, additional to specific asset purchases, before the commencement of production or use of facilities.

Patents[25]   A right granted for up to seventeen years by the federal government to exclude others from manufacturing, using, or selling a certain process or device. Under current GAAP, research and most development costs must be treated as an expense in the year incurred, rather than being recognized as an asset with future benefits.[26] As a result, a firm that develops a patent will not normally show it as an asset. On the other hand, a firm that purchases a patent from another firm or from an individual will recognize the patent as an asset. Chapter 8 discusses this inconsistent treatment of internally developed and externally purchased patents.

Goodwill[27]   An amount paid by one firm in acquiring another business enterprise that is greater than the sum of the then-current values assignable

---

[18] *CICA Handbook,* section 3050.

[19] *CICA Handbook,* section 3060.

[20] *CICA Handbook,* section 3060.

[21] *CICA Handbook,* section 3060.

[22] *CICA Handbook,* section 3060.

[23] *CICA Handbook,* section 3070.

[24] *CICA Handbook,* section 3060.

[25] *CICA Handbook,* section 3060.

[26] *CICA Handbook,* section 3450.

[27] *CICA Handbook,* section 1580.

to individual, identifiable assets. A good reputation and other desirable attributes are generally not recognized as assets by the firm that creates or develops them. However, when one firm acquires another firm, these desirable attributes are indirectly recognized as assets, because they are a factor in the measurement of goodwill, and because they have to be paid for.

LIABILITIES

Bank Loans   Amounts borrowed from a bank, frequently payable on demand.

Accounts Payable   Amounts owed for goods or services acquired under an informal credit agreement. These accounts are usually payable within one or two months. The same items appear as Accounts Receivable on the creditors' books.

Notes Payable   The face amount of promissory notes given in connection with loans from a bank or the purchase of goods or services. The same items appear as Notes Receivable on the creditors' books.

Payroll Taxes Payable   Amounts withheld from wages and salaries of employees for payroll taxes that have not yet been remitted to tax authorities, as well as the employer's share of such taxes.

Withheld Income Taxes   Amounts withheld from wages and salaries of employees for income taxes that have not yet been remitted to the taxing authority. This is a tentative income tax on the earnings of employees, and the employer acts merely as a tax-collecting agent for the government.

Interest Payable   Interest on obligations that has accrued or accumulated with the passage of time but that has not been paid as of the date of the balance sheet. The liability for interest is customarily shown separately from the face amount of the obligation.

Income Taxes Payable[28]   The estimated liability for income taxes, accumulated and unpaid, based on the taxable income of the business from the beginning of the taxable year to the date of the balance sheet. Because sole proprietorships and partnerships do not pay income taxes directly, this term will appear only on the books of a corporation or other taxable entity.

Advances from Customers   The general name used to indicate payments received in advance for goods to be delivered or services to be furnished to customers in the future; a nonmonetary liability. If no cash is received when a customer places an order, no liability is recorded.

Rent Received in Advance   Another example of a nonmonetary liability. The business owns a building that it rents to a tenant. The tenant has prepaid the rental charge for several months in advance. The amount applicable to future months cannot be considered a component of income until the rent is earned, because service is rendered with the passage of time. Meanwhile, the advance payment results in a liability payable in services (that is, in the use of the building). On the records of the tenant, the same amount would appear as an asset, Prepaid Rent.

---

[28] *CICA Handbook*, section 3470.

Mortgage Payable   Long-term promissory notes that have been given greater protection by the pledge of specific pieces of property as security for their payment. If the loan or interest is not paid according to the agreement, the property can be sold for the benefit of the creditor.

Bonds Payable   Amounts borrowed by the business for a relatively long period of time under a formal written contract or indenture. The loan is usually obtained from a number of lenders, each of whom receives one or more bond certificates as written evidence of his or her share of the loan.

Obligation Under Capital Lease[29]   The present value of future commitments for cash payments to be made in return for the right to use property owned by someone else.

Deferred Income Taxes[30]   Certain income tax obligations are delayed beyond the current accounting period. These arise from timing differences in the deductibility of various expenses on the income statement versus the tax return, and also with respect to the period of inclusion of various revenue items.

SHAREHOLDERS' EQUITY

Common Stock[31]   Amounts received for the issue of a corporation's principal class of voting shares.

Preferred Stock[32]   Amounts received for the issue of a class of a corporation's shares that has some preference relative to the common shares. This preference is usually with respect to dividends and to assets in the event the corporation is liquidated. Sometimes, preferred shares are convertible into common shares.

Contributed Surplus[33]   Amounts received from the issuance of common or preferred shares in excess of such shares' par or stated value. This account does not appear when a company is authorized to issue only no-par-value shares, except when property is donated to the company, or credit balances result from other capital transactions such as share redemptions, sale of treasury shares, and capital reorganizations.

Retained Earnings   An account reflecting the increase in net assets since the business was organized as a result of generating earnings in excess of dividend declarations. When dividends are declared, net assets are decreased, and retained earnings are reduced by an equal amount.

Treasury Shares[34]   This account shows the cost of shares originally issued but subsequently reacquired by the corporation. Treasury shares are not

---

[29] *CICA Handbook*, section 3065.

[30] *CICA Handbook*, section 3470.

[31] Technically, this term has been discontinued in the Canadian Business Corporations Act, but it still has widespread public usage.

[32] Technically, this term has been discontinued in the Canadian Business Corporations Act, but it still has widespread public usage.

[33] *CICA Handbook*, section 3250.

[34] Treasury shares are not allowed for companies incorporated under the Canada Business Corporations Act.

entitled to dividends and are not considered to be "outstanding" shares. The cost of treasury shares is shown on the balance sheet as a deduction from the total of the other shareholders' equity accounts. Chapter 11 discusses the accounting for treasury shares.

ANALYSIS OF BALANCE SHEET

The balance sheet reflects the effects of a firm's investment and financing decisions, as well as the results of operating decisions via the changes to the retained earnings account. In general, firms attempt to balance the term structure of their financing with the term structure of their investments. For example, firms such as retail stores, with large investments in current assets (receivables and inventories), tend to use significant short-term financing. Highly capital-intensive firms, such as utilities and steel manufacturers, tend to rely heavily on long-term debt and common shares.

Short-term financing refers to obligations payable within a year of the balance sheet date. A firm will want to be sure that it will have sufficient cash available within that time period to pay the obligations. Assets classified as "current" will be the assets most likely to generate the cash needed. Likewise, long-term financing is repaid, if at all, over a longer period. Because noncurrent assets tend to generate cash over a longer period, long-term financing for these assets is appropriate.

A potential cause for concern occurs when the percentage of short-term financing begins to exceed the percentage of current assets. In this case, the firm is using short-term financing for noncurrent assets. A firm may face difficulties in obtaining sufficient cash from these noncurrent assets to meet required payments on short-term debt.

AN INTERNATIONAL PERSPECTIVE

The format of the balance sheet in come countries differs from that discussed in this chapter. In Germany and France, for example, property, plant, and equipment and other noncurrent assets appear first, followed by current assets. On the equities side, shareholders' equity appears first, followed by noncurrent and current liabilities. In the United Kingdom, the following form of the balance sheet equation characterizes the balance sheet:

$$\begin{matrix} \text{Noncurrent} \\ \text{Assets} \end{matrix} + \left(\begin{matrix} \text{Current} \\ \text{Assets} \end{matrix} - \begin{matrix} \text{Current} \\ \text{Liabilities} \end{matrix} \right) - \begin{matrix} \text{Noncurrent} \\ \text{Liabilities} \end{matrix} = \begin{matrix} \text{Shareholders'} \\ \text{Equity} \end{matrix}$$

SUMMARY

The balance sheet comprises three major classes of items — assets, liabilities, and shareholders' equity.

Resources are recognized as assets when a company has acquired rights to their future use as a result of a past transaction or exchange and when the value of the future benefits can be measured with a reasonable degree of precision. Monetary assets are, in general, stated at their current cash, or cash-equivalent, values. Nonmonetary assets are stated at acquisition cost, in most cases adjusted downward for the cost of services that have been consumed.

Liabilities represent obligations of a company to make payments of a reasonably definite amount at a reasonably definite future time for benefits already received. Shareholders' equity, the difference between total assets and total liabilities, is typically segregated for companies into contributed capital and retained earnings.

The equity of total assets and total liabilities plus shareholders' equity is maintained by recording the effect of each transaction in a dual manner in the accounts. The double-entry recording framework is summarized as follows:

Asset Accounts		=	Liability Accounts		+	Shareholders' Equity Accounts	
Increases (Debits)	Decreases (Credits)		Decreases (Debits)	Increases (Credits)		Decreases (Debits)	Increases (Credits)

The dual effects of each transaction are initially recorded in journal entry form in the general journal. These journal entries are then posted to the appropriate asset, liability, and shareholders' equity accounts in the general ledger. A trial balance of the ending balances in the general ledger accounts is prepared periodically as a check on the mathematical accuracy of the double-entry recording procedure. Any necessary adjustments of the account balances in the trial balance are then made in the general journal and posted to the accounts in the general ledger. The financial statements are prepared from the adjusted trial balance. Chapters 3 and 4 discuss the procedures for preparing the income statement. Chapter 13 discusses the statement of changes in financial position.

KEY TERMS

Accounting entity
Unexecuted contracts
Asset valuation bases
Acquisition cost
Historical cost
Current replacement cost
Entry value
Net realizable value
Exit value
Cash flows
Present value
Monetary assets

Nonmonetary assets
Plant assets
Fixed assets
Intangible assets
Advances from Customers
Residual interest
Contributed capital
Share capital
Par-value shares
Contributed surplus
Stated value
Companies Acts

No-par-value shares
Canada Business Corporations Act
  (CBCA)
Account
General ledger
T-account
Debit

Credit
Journalizing
Posting
Journal entry
General journal
Trial balance
Adjusting journal entry

SELF-STUDY MATERIAL

This section contains questions, exercises, and problems to help you assess your understanding of Chapter 2. Careful review of this material will assist you in completing the homework assignments. Solutions are found at the end of this section.

QUESTIONS AND EXERCISES

True/False

For each statement, place a T or an F in the space provided to indicate whether the statement is true of false.

_F_ 1. The balance sheet derives its name from the fact that it shows the following balance, or equality:

$$\text{Assets} + \text{Liabilities} = \text{Owners' Equity.}$$

_T_ 2. Assets can be defined as resources used by the firm for which legal title is held.

_F_ 3. Whenever a firm's good reputation has developed over many years of operation, it is acceptable to assign a value to this resource and classify it as goodwill on the balance sheet.

____ 4. The accounting entity and legal entity are often different for an organization.

____ 5. All assets found on a balance sheet are recorded at their historical cost.

____ 6. The present value of $20,000 to be received in one year at 10 percent is $22,000.

____ 7. The present value of future cash flows should be less than the total of the future cash flows.

____ 8. Cash and accounts receivable are examples of monetary assets.

____ 9. In designing an accounting system, an important starting point is the recognition of the firm as a separate economic entity, emphasizing the substance over the form of the organization.

____ 10. Some resources of a firm provide future economic benefits but are not capable of being reasonably measured or quantified and, therefore, are not classified as assets on the balance sheet.

____ 11. The historical cost of an asset always represents its future economic value to the firm.

____ 12. In measuring net realizable value, we generally assume that the asset is not being sold at a distress price.

____ 13. The valuation basis selected by a firm depends on the purpose of the financial report being prepared.

____ 14. Land is a good example of a nonmonetary asset.

____ 15. A company is considered to be a going concern when it is expected to last forever.

____ 16. The operating cycle for most companies is one year or less.

____ 17. It is acceptable for certain depreciable assets, such as buildings and machinery, to be carried on the balance sheet at either historical cost *or* historical cost adjusted downward for the benefits received by the firm since acquisition.

____ 18. Replacement cost and net realizable value are opposite approaches to determining the current value of an asset; replacement cost refers to an asset's exit value, and net realizable value refers to an asset's entry value.

_____ 19. Net realizable value is defined as the net amount of cash that could be realized from the sale of an asset.

_____ 20. The only accounts found in the investments section of the balance sheet are for the investments in the securities of other firms.

_____ 21. Intangibles are long-term assets that lack physical substance.

_____ 22. Only when intangible assets are acquired from other entities can they be recognized as assets.

_____ 23. An example of an account included in the "other long-term liability" section is future income taxes.

_____ 24. The more specialized a firm's assets, the more difficulty there is in determining either their replacement cost or their net realizable value, because a well-organized second-hand market for these items may not exist.

_____ 25. The present value of future cash flows approach to assigning values to balance sheet items is likely to be employed with current liabilities, such as accounts payable and taxes payable.

_____ 26. A piece of land acquired for use should be classified as property, plant, and equipment.

_____ 27. For an obligation to be treated as a liability, it is necessary that it can be estimated with a reasonable degree of accuracy.

_____ 28. Current liabilities are usually paid from assets classified as current.

_____ 29. The par value of a share is the same as its market value.

_____ 30. The term _charge_ can be used interchangeably with _debit_.

_____ 31. As long as a partnership has always been profitable, there will be a credit balance in the Retained Earnings account.

_____ 32. The process of posting is the transferring of amounts from T-accounts to the journal affected by the transaction.

_____ 33. If the debits and credits in a trial balance are not equal, a possible explanation is that a current asset was improperly classified as an investment.

_____ 34. Conservatism in accounting refers to the ability of several independent appraisers to come to the same conclusion about the value of an asset.

_____ 35. The general ledger is also known as the "book of original entry."

_____ 36. Treasury shares are usually shown on the balance sheet as a deduction from the total of the other shareholders' equity accounts.

_____ 37. If a firm accounts for the assets in a conservative manner, its net income is less likely to be overstated.

_____ 38. All transactions have a dual effect on the balance sheet equation, because both an asset and an equity account are affected in equal amounts in every transaction.

_____ 39. A lease transaction is an example of an unexecuted contract, which often is not recognized as a liability at the time of the agreement between the lessor and lessee.

_____ 40. Some liabilities due within one year are not classified as current liabilities.

_____ 41. A liability represents any obligation taken on by a firm.

_____ 42. Liabilities that will be discharged by the rendering of goods or services are considered nonmonetary liabilities and are stated at the amount of cash received.

_____ 43. Because owners' equity is a residual interest in the firm's assets, its valuation is dependent on the value assigned to the assets and liabilities within the balance sheet.

_____ 44. Accumulated depreciation does not represent a fund set aside to replace fixed assets after they have been fully depreciated.

___ 45. Retained earnings represent the cumulative amount of cash available for dividends.

___ 46. Liability accounts are increased by debits, are decreased by credits, and normally have a debit balance.

___ 47. A basic rule underlying the balance sheet equation is that total debits must always equal total credits.

___ 48. Because the accounts in the general ledger and the journal entries within the general journal both report the same transactions, it is not necessary to maintain both a general ledger and a general journal.

___ 49. Even if no errors have been detected in the processing of accounting data, correcting or adjusting entries may be needed at the end of a period.

___ 50. The T-account, which serves the purpose of accumulating increases and decreases for each balance sheet item, uses the following simple rule: all increases are recorded on the left, and all decreases are recorded on the right.

___ 51. The term *debit* refers to the left-hand side of a T-account for both assets and liabilities.

___ 52. Interest receivable on ten-year bonds held as portfolio investments would represent the total interest to be received over the ten-year period.

Matching

I. From the list of terms, select one term that is most closely associated with one descriptive phrase or statement that follows and place the letter for that term in the space provided.

a. accounts payable	n. temporary investments
b. accounts receivable	o. merchandise inventory
c. accumulated depreciation	p. mortgage payable
d. bonds payable	q. notes receivable
e. cash	r. organization costs
f. common shares	s. patents
g. contributed surplus	t. preferred shares
h. future income taxes	u. prepaid insurance
i. finished goods inventory	v. raw materials inventory
j. goodwill	w. retained earnings
k. income taxes payable	x. rent received in advance
l. interest payable	y. treasury shares
m. interest receivable	z. withheld income taxes

___ 1. The shares originally issued and outstanding that have been reacquired from the owners.

___ 2. The financial obligation, which accrues with the passage of time, of the company to pay for the use of borrowed money.

___ 3. A residual claim of owners having certain preferences relative to other owners' claims.

___ 4. A type of liquid asset, an example of which is a demand deposit.

___ 5. A right granted to exclude others from manufacturing, using, or selling a certain process or device.

___ 6. The balance in this account is the amount owed to the company by its customers.

___ 7. Usually debited when interest revenue is credited.

___ 8. Goods on hand that have been purchased for resale.

___ 9. Amounts owed for goods or services acquired under an informal credit agreement.

___ 10. Shares and bonds that can readily be converted into cash.

___ 11. A type of inventory for a manufacturer.

___ 12. Recorded only when another business enterprise is acquired.

___ 13. An example of long-term debt.

_____ 14. Insurance premiums paid for future coverage.

_____ 15. The amount subtracted from the cost of a fixed asset to get net book value.

_____ 16. The amount of income taxes postponed for payment to future years.

_____ 17. The amount of proceeds from the sale of shares in excess of the par value.

_____ 18. Amounts due from customers, for which the claim is in the form of a written promise to pay.

_____ 19. The estimated and unpaid liability for current income taxes.

_____ 20. Amounts paid for various fees incurred in organizing a corporation.

_____ 21. Cumulative amount of net income earned by a business since its inception in excess of dividends paid.

II. For the list of accounts below, select the balance sheet category in which that account should be classified.

a. Current Assets
b. Investments
c. Property, Plant, and Equipment
d. Intangible Assets
e. Current Liabilities

f. Long-Term Debt
g. Other Long-Term Liabilities
h. Share Capital
i. Contributed Surplus
j. Retained Earnings

_____ 1. Furniture and Fixtures

_____ 2. Liability for Pensions

_____ 3. Accumulated Depreciation

_____ 4. Future Income Taxes

_____ 5. Capitalized Lease Obligation

_____ 6. Land

_____ 7. Notes Payable (due in five years)

_____ 8. Common Stock

_____ 9. Withholding Taxes Payable

_____ 10. Cash

_____ 11. Convertible Bonds Payable (convertible into common or preferred shares)

_____ 12. Advance to Suppliers

_____ 13. Sinking Fund for Retirement of Bonds

_____ 14. Supplies

_____ 15. Prepaid Rent

_____ 16. Income Taxes Payable

_____ 17. Investment in Bonds (for a long-term purpose)

_____ 18. Interest Receivable

_____ 19. Accounts Receivable

_____ 20. Excess of Proceeds over Par Value on Issue of Preferred Shares

_____ 21. Rent Received in Advance

_____ 22. Treasury Shares

_____ 23. Temporary Investments

_____ 24. Accounts Payable

_____ 25. Organization Costs

_____ 26. Building

_____ 27. Patent

_____ 28. Mortgage Payable (due in one year)

_____ 29. Work-in-Process Inventory

_____ 30. Prepaid Insurance

_____ 31. Advances from Customers

_____ 32. Bonds Payable

Multiple Choice

Choose the best answer for each question or problem and enter the identifying letter in the space provided.

_____ 1. Which equation does not represent an acceptable presentation of the balance sheet equation?
   a) Assets − Liabilities = Owners' Equity
   b) Assets = Liabilities + Capital stock + Contributed Surplus + Retained Earnings
   c) Assets = Equities
   d) all of the above represent acceptable presentations of the balance sheet equation.

_____ 2. Which of these liabilities would be accounted for at the present value of future cash payments?
   a) accounts payable
   b) bonds payable
   c) income taxes payable
   d) withholding taxes payable

_____ 3. The Bonanza Co. Ltd. is interested in disposing of one of its subsidiaries and needs to decide on the minimum price it might be able to charge. Which valuation method would likely be used?
   a) acquisition cost
   b) net realizable value
   c) present value
   d) replacement cost

_____ 4. The balance in all assets accounts combined is $100,000 on December 1. During December, the following transactions took place:

   Purchase of $10,000 of inventory for cash.
   Purchase of $15,000 of machinery on account.
   Retirement of $20,000 in bonds with cash.

   What is the combined December 31 balance in the asset accounts?
   a) $95,000
   b) $115,000
   c) $105,000
   d) $80,000

_____ 5. The balance sheet reflects the application of various valuation methods. Which of the methods listed may be used on a balance sheet that follows generally accepted accounting principles?
   a) acquisition cost
   b) current cash equivalent value
   c) present value of future cash flows
   d) all of the above

____ 6. From the following list of accounts, determine the amount that would be properly classified as property, plant, and equipment.

Land Used in Business	$100,000
Machinery Leased from Others (no liability has been recorded)	60,000
Accumulated Depreciation	(80,000)
Inventories	124,000
Land Held for Future Plant Site	40,000
Building	200,000
Investment in Shares of Construction Co. Inc.	50,000

a) $220,000
b) $360,000
c) $260,000
d) $280,000

____ 7. Which of the following would cause an imbalance in the accounting equation?
a) recording a purchase on account at the wrong amount
b) recording a 19X1 purchase in 19X2 instead
c) posting the credit for a cash purchase at the wrong amount
d) all of the above

____ 8. All of the following assets are nonmonetary, except one. Which one?
a) accounts receivable
b) land
c) inventory
d) patent

____ 9. The concept of present value:
a) can be simply defined as value today of a stream of future cash flows
b) implies that the value of receiving cash today will be less than the value of receiving it in the future
c) is employed extensively in the valuation of assets under current generally accepted accounting principles
d) determines the minimum amount that a buyer would be willing to pay for an asset

____ 10. Different balance sheet items employ different valuation methods. Which valuation application is not generally accepted?
a) a major line of inventory has increased in value substantially above its cost and has been restated to its current replacement cost
b) machinery is stated at its historical cost less the estimated amount of benefits consumed to date
c) cash is received for goods to be delivered next month; the liability is stated at the amount of cash received and not the cost of foods to be delivered
d) common share capital is stated at the amount at which it was originally sold

____ 11. Redondo Corp. has assets and liabilities of $30,000 and $24,000, respectively. If Redondo issues an additional $3,000 worth of shares for cash, what will be the balance in shareholders' equity following this transaction?
a) $30,000
b) $27,000
c) $9,000
d) $33,000

_____ 12. Which of these statements concerning the rules of debit and credit is incorrect?
   a) debits are always recorded on the left
   b) debits reduce shareholders' equity
   c) assets have debit balances
   d) credits always mean decreases

_____ 13. From this list of selected account balances, determine the total for the shareholders' equity section of the balance sheet for Cabbage Company Ltd.

Investment in Shares of Rutabaga Limited	$ 2,500
Retained Earnings	5,000
Cash (in special bank account for a payment of dividends)	3,000
Note Payable to Suppliers	2,000
Common Stock	10,000
8% Preferred Stock	7,500

   a) $20,500
   b) $22,500
   c) $24,500
   d) $25,500

_____ 14. What account would not be found on the balance sheet of a corporation?
   a) Contributed Surplus
   b) Retained Earnings
   c) Investment in Smith Ltd. Shares
   d) Keith, Capital

_____ 15. Which of these journal entries is incorrectly recorded?

   a) Jan. 1: Cash $33,000
                    Investment in X Co Ltd. Shares $33,000
              Sales of an investment for cash.

   b) Jan. 2: Prepaid Insurance $ 750
                    Cash $ 750
              Paid in advance for a one-year insurance policy.

   c) Jan 3: Accounts Receivable $1,200
                    Merchandise Inventory $1,200
              Returned defective merchandise for credit. The
              merchandise has not yet been paid for.

   d) Jan 4: Machinery $30,500
                    Notes Payable $30,500
              Gave a one-year note to acquire machinery.

_____ 16. The following entry was made on June 15 for Cindy Inc.

   Jun. 15 Machinery $17,000
                  Accounts Payable $17,000

   This entry was made for which of these transactions?
   a) payment for purchase of machinery
   b) sale of machinery
   c) depreciation of machinery
   d) purchase of machinery

_____ 17. The Paypac Corporation failed to record the purchase of inventory on account at the end of 19X1. In which of the following ways is the balance sheet misstated?
   a) assets and liabilities are both understated
   b) assets are understated and liabilities are overstated
   c) assets and shareholders' equity are both understated
   d) assets, liabilities, and shareholders' equity are all correctly stated

Exercises

1. Indicate the effect of each of the stated transactions on the balance sheet equation in the example. After each transaction is properly recorded, compute new subtotals for the Assets, Liabilities, and Owners' Equity, being sure to maintain the equity of the equation. Use the following format:

Transaction Letter	Assets	=	Liabilities	+	Owners' Equity
(Example)	$ + 300,000				$ + 300,000
Subtotal	300,000	=			300,000

(Example) Issued 1,500 common shares of $100 par value for $300,000 cash.
   a. Purchased for $250,000 cash a building to be used for office space.
   b. Received $1,000 for a magazine subscription to be delivered to customers over the next year.
   c. Paid $2,100 in advance for one year of rent.
   d. Paid $750 to an advertising agency for a promotional campaign that will start in one month.
   e. Bought $30,000 of merchandise inventory on account.
   f. Paid $12,000 to the supplier for inventory purchases in (e) and gave a note for the remaining $18,000.
   g. Loaned $3,500 to an officer and accepted his 90-day note.
   h. Bought $5,500 of merchandise for cash.
   i. Borrowed $5,000 from the bank.

2. These balance sheet account titles may be needed in recording the ten transactions that follow. For each transaction, select those accounts that would be used in journalizing and place the letters accompanying the account title in the appropriate columns for debit and credit.

   a. Cash   h. Accounts Payable

   b. Notes Receivable   i. Notes Payable

   c. Merchandise Inventory   j. Rent Received in Advance

   d. Supplies Inventory   k. Capital Stock

   e. Prepaid Insurance   l. Contributed Surplus

   f. Machinery and Equipment   m. Retained Earnings

   g. Organization Costs

Transaction	Account Debited	Account Credited
(Example) Bought Inventory for cash.	c	a

   1. Paid the lawyers in company shares for the legal work performed in organizing the company.

Transaction	Account Debited	Account Credited
2. Advanced money to an officer, and received a 90-day note as recognition of the debt.		
3. A 120-day note was given to the bank for a loan.		
4. Acquired supplies for cash.		
5. Purchased merchandise on open account.		
6. Purchased for cash a one-year insurance policy for $300.		
7. Received a one-year advance from tenants for rental property.		
8. Owners invested $20,000 cash in the company in exchange for 2,000 shares having a par value of $5.		
9. Machinery and equipment were bought on open account.		
10. Paid off the creditors for inventory purchases.		

3. In T-account form, set up the balances for the following account for Watson Limited at January 1, 19X1. For each transaction (a–g), make the appropriate journal entry and post each entry to the proper T-accounts. Following these two steps, prepare an unadjusted trial balance at month-end.

Cash	$120,000
Notes Receivable	40,000
Merchandise Inventory	200,000
Land	60,000
Building	280,000
Accounts Payable	80,000
Notes Payable	64,000
Interest Payable	3,200
Bonds Payable	80,000
Common Shares, No Par Value	400,000
Retained Earnings	72,800

a. The note receivable of $40,000 was collected.
b. The note for $64,000 and the related accrued interest of $3,200 were paid on January 2.
c. The January 1 balance in Accounts Payable was paid during the month of January.
d. Bonds in the amount of $32,000 were issued at face value and the proceeds were used to pay for an addition to the building.
e. Merchandise inventory costing $120,000 was acquired with payment of $64,000 in cash and the remainder due in 30 days on open account.
f. The plot of land costing $60,000 was sold for $60,000.
g. An additional 800 common shares were sold for $125 per share.

4. Indicate whether or not each of the following items should be recognized as an asset. Indicate the correct answer by placing "Yes" or "No" in the space provided.
_____ 1. A union agreement that promises a higher quality of performance in the upcoming year.
_____ 2. A piece of machinery worth $1,000, originally purchased for use, but subsequently retired from use and awaiting sale.
_____ 3. The company's own shares purchased back from the original shareholders.
_____ 4. Cash held in a fund by a firm's trustee, to be used to retire bonds in five years.
_____ 5. Cash received from subscribers for publications to be shipped next year.
_____ 6. Costs incurred to develop a new patent.
_____ 7. Interest to be received for the previous six months, on a long-term note receivable.

_____ 8. The value to be derived by the firm from having a key location for selling its product.

_____ 9. The benefit to the firm of its employees receiving advanced college degrees.

_____ 10. The goodwill paid for when acquiring another business enterprise.

5. Indicate whether or not each of the following items should be recognized as a liability for the organization. Indicate the correct answer by placing a "Yes" or "No" in the space provided.

_____ 1. The obligation to pay interest next year on bonds that were issued on the balance sheet date.

_____ 2. The obligation to pay workers for services already rendered.

_____ 3. An agreement to purchase inventory in the following year.

_____ 4. An agreement to publish and ship magazines next year for cash already received.

_____ 5. The obligation to pay dividends from income earned next year.

_____ 6. Unpaid income taxes from the current year.

_____ 7. The burden of having a senile president.

_____ 8. The obligation of the president to pay for his son's traffic fines.

_____ 9. The expectation of replacing worn-out equipment.

_____ 10. The obligation to repay a loan made in the current year and due in five years.

6. From this list of account balances, prepare in proper form a balance sheet for Tommy's Memorial Park Inc.

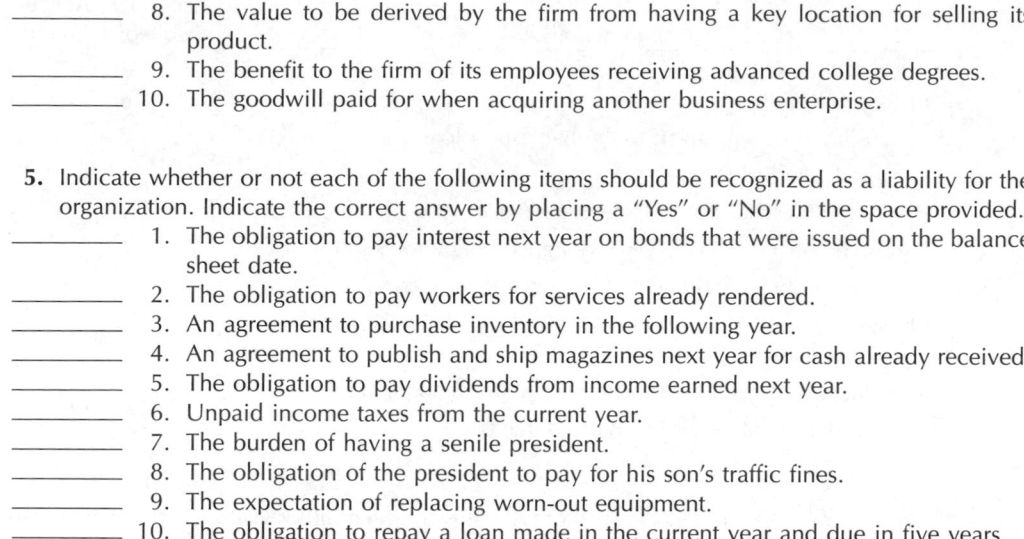

Trial Balance
December 31, 19X1

	Dr.	Cr.
Cash	$ 5,000	
Temporary Investments	15,000	
Accounts Receivable	40,000	
Building	50,000	
Notes Payable (due in 1 year)		$22,000
Patent	8,000	
Building — Accumulated Depreciation		10,000
Property Taxes Payable		6,000
Accounts Payable		31,000
Retained Earnings		77,800
Common Shares		50,000
Bonds Payable		80,000
Inventory	30,000	
Land	100,000	
Investment in Trizec Corp. Shares	28,000	
Investment in Canadian Utilities Ltd. Bonds	12,000	
Prepaid Insurance	1,000	
Withheld Income Tax		2,200
Contributed Surplus		25,000
Goodwill	15,000	
	$304,000	$304,000

PROBLEM FOR SELF-STUDY

The Electronics Appliance Corporation was organized on September 1. The following transactions occurred during the month of September.

(1) The firm issues 4,000 no-par-value common shares for $12 cash per share on September 1.

(2) The firm's lawyer is given 600 no-par-value common shares on September 2 in payment for legal services rendered in the organization of the corporation. The bill for the services is $7,200.

(3) A factory building is leased for the three years beginning October 1. Monthly rental payments are $5,000. Two months' rent is paid in advance on September 5.

(4) Raw materials are purchased on account for $6,100 on September 12.

(5) A cheque for $900 is received on September 15 from a customer as a deposit on a special order for equipment that Electronics plans to manufacture. The contract price is $4,800.

(6) Office equipment with a list price of $950 is acquired on September 20. After deducting a discount of $25 for prompt payment, a cheque is issued in full payment.

(7) The company hires three employees to begin work on October 1. A cash advance of $200 is given to one of the employees on September 28.

(8) Factory equipment costing $27,500 is purchased on September 30. A cheque for $5,000 is issued, and a long-term mortgage liability is assumed for the balance.

(9) The labour costs of installing the new equipment in (8) are $450 and are paid in cash on September 30.

  a. Prepare journal entries for each of the nine transactions.
  b. Set up T-accounts and post each of the nine journal entries.
  c. Prepare a balance sheet for Electronics Appliance Corporation as of September 30.

ANSWERS TO SELF-STUDY QUESTIONS AND EXERCISES

True/False

1. F	14. T	27. T	40. T
2. F	15. F	28. T	41. F
3. F	16. T	29. F	42. T
4. T	17. F	30. T	43. T
5. F	18. F	31. F	44. T
6. F	19. T	32. F	45. F
7. T	20. F	33. F	46. F
8. T	21. T	34. F	47. T
9. T	22. T	35. F	48. F
10. T	23. T	36. T	49. T
11. F	24. T	37. T	50. F
12. T	25. F	38. F	51. T
13. T	26. T	39. T	52. F

Matching

I.

1. y	7. m *or* e	13. d *or* p	19. k
2. l	8. o	14. u	20. r
3. t	9. a	15. c	21. w
4. e	10. n	16. h	
5. s	11. i *or* v	17. g	
6. b	12. j	18. q	

II.

1. c	9. e	17. b	25. d
2. g	10. a	18. a	26. c
3. Reduction of c	11. f	19. a	27. d
4. g	12. a	20. i	28. e
5. f	13. b	21. e	29. a
6. c	14. a	22. Reduction of (i+ h + j)	30. a
7. f	15. a	23. a	31. e
8. h	16. e	24. e	32. f

Multiple Choice

1. d	6. a	11. c	16. d
2. b	7. c	12. d	17. a
3. c	8. a	13. b	
4. a	9. a	14. d	
5. d	10. a	15. c	

Exercises

1.

Transaction Letter	Assets	=	Liabilities	+	Owners' Equity
Example	$300,000				$300,000
Subtotal	$300,000	=			$300,000
a.	+250,000				
	−250,000				
Subtotal	$300,000	=			$300,000
b.	+ 1,000		+1,000		
Subtotal	$301,000	=	$ 1,000	+	$300,000
c.	+2,100				
	−2,100				
Subtotal	$301,000	=	$ 1,000	+	$300,000
d.	+750				
	−750				
Subtotal	$301,000	=	$1,000	+	$300,000
e.	+30,000		+30,000		
Subtotal	$331,000	=	$31,000	+	$300,000
f.	−12,000		−12,000		
			−18,000		
			+18,000		
Subtotal	$319,000	=	$19,000	+	$300,000
g.	+3,500				
	−3,500				
Subtotal	$319,000	=	$19,000	+	$300,000
h.	+5,500				
	−5,500				
Subtotal	$319,000	=	$19,000	+	$300,000
i.	+5,000		+5,000		
Total	$324,000	=	$24,000	+	$300,000

2.

	Account Debited	Account Credited
1.	g	k (possibly l as well)
2	b	a
3.	a	i

	Account Debited	Account Credited
4.	d	a
5.	c	h
6.	e	a
7.	a	j
8.	a	k, l
9.	f	h
10.	h	a

3.

Cash

Bal.	120,000	67,200	(b)
(a)	40,000	80,000	(c)
(d)	320,000	320,000	(d)
(f)	60,000	64,000	(e)
(g)	100,000		
Bal.	108,800		

Notes Receivable

| Bal. | 40,000 | 40,000 | (a) |
| Bal. | 0 | | |

Merchandise Inventory

Bal.	200,000	
(e)	120,000	
Bal.	320,000	

Land

| Bal. | 60,000 | 60,000 | (f) |
| Bal. | 0 | | |

Building

Bal.	280,000	
(d)	320,000	
Bal.	600,000	

Accounts Payable

(c)	80,000	80,000	Bal.
		56,000	(e)
		56,000	Bal.

Notes Payable

| (b) | 64,000 | 64,000 | Bal. |
| | | 0 | Bal. |

Interest Payable

| (b) | 3,200 | 3,200 | Bal. |
| | | 0 | Bal. |

Bonds Payable

	80,000	Bal.
	320,000	(d)
	400,000	Bal.

Common Shares

	400,000	Bal.
	100,000	(g)
	500,000	Bal.

Retained Earnings

| | 72,800 | Bal. |
| | 72,800 | Bal. |

Journal Entries	Dr.	Cr.
a. Cash	$40,000	
Notes Receivable		$40,000
b. Notes Payable	$64,000	
Interest payable	3,200	
Cash		$67,200
c. Accounts Payable	$80,000	
Cash		$80,000

Journal Entries	Dr.	Cr.
d. Cash	$320,000	
Bonds Payable		$320,000
Building	$320,000	
Cash		$320,000
e. Merchandise Inventory	$120,000	
Cash		$64,000
Accounts Payable		56,000
f. Cash	$60,000	
Land		$60,000
g. Cash	$100,000	
Common Shares		$100,000

Watson Limited
Trial Balance
January 31, 19X1

	Debits	Credits
Cash	$ 108,800	
Merchandise Inventory	320,000	
Building	600,000	
Accounts Payable		$ 56,000
Bonds Payable		400,000
Common Shares		500,000
Retained Earnings		72,800
	$1,028,800	$1,028,800

4.
1. No	4. Yes	7. Yes	10. Yes
2. Yes	5. Yes	8. No	
3. No	6. No	9. No	

5.
1. No	4. Yes	7. No	10. Yes
2. Yes	5. No	8. No	
3. No	6. Yes	9. No	

6. Balance Sheet
Tommy's Memorial Park Inc.
December 31, 19X1

Assets

Current Assets			
Cash		$ 5,000	
Temporary Investments		15,000	
Accounts Receivable		40,000	
Inventory		30,000	
Prepaid Insurance		1,000	$ 91,000
Portfolio Investments			
Investment in Shares		$ 28,000	
Investment in Bonds		12,000	40,000
Property, Plant, & Equipment			
Land		$100,000	
Building	$50,000		
Accumulated Depreciation	(10,000)	40,000	140,000
Intangibles			
Patent		$ 8,000	
Goodwill		15,000	23,000
Total Assets			$294,000

Liabilities

Current Liabilities

Accounts Payable	$ 31,000	
Notes Payable	22,000	
Property Taxes Payable	6,000	
Withheld Income Tax	2,200	$ 61,200

Long-Term Debt

Bonds Payable		80,000
Total Liabilities		$141,200

Shareholders' Equity

Common Shares	$ 50,000	
Contributed Surplus	25,000	
Retained Earnings	77,800	
Total Shareholders' Equity		$152,800
Total Liabilities and Shareholders' Equity		$294,000

SUGGESTED SOLUTION TO PROBLEM FOR SELF-STUDY

The journal entries for the nine transactions are as follows:

(1) Sept. 1	Cash	$48,000	
	Common Stock		$48,000
	Issuance of 4,000 no-par-value common shares for $12 cash per share.		
(2) Sept. 2	Organization Costs	$ 7,200	
	Common Stock		$ 7,200
	Issuance of 600 no-par-value common shares in settlement of $7,200 lawyer's bill connected with organization of the corporation.		
(3) Sept. 5	Prepaid Rent	$10,000	
	Cash		$10,000
	Prepayment of rent for October and November on factory building.		
(4) Sept. 12	Raw Material Inventory	$ 6,100	
	Accounts Payable		$ 6,100
	Raw materials costing $6,100 are purchased on account.		
(5) Sept. 15	Cash	$ 900	
	Advances from Customers		$ 900
	An advance of $900 is received from a customer as a deposit on equipment to be manufactured in the future.		
(6) Sept. 20	Equipment	$ 925	
	Cash		$ 925
	Equipment with a list price of $950 is acquired, after a discount, for $925.		
(7) Sept. 28	Advance to Employee	$ 200	
	Cash		$ 200
	A cash advance of $200 is given to an employee beginning work on October 1.		

(8) Sept. 30	Equipment	$27,500	
	Cash		$ 5,000
	Mortgage Payable		22,500
	Acquisition of equipment for $5,000 cash and assumption of a $22,500 mortgage for the balance of the purchase price.		
(9) Sept. 30	Equipment	$ 450	
	Cash		$ 450
	Installation cost on equipment acquired in (8) of $450 is paid in cash.		

Exhibit 2.6 presents T-accounts for Electronics Appliance Corporation and shows the posting of the nine entries to the accounts. The letters A, L, and SE are added after the account titles to indicate the balance sheet category of the accounts. Exhibit 2.7 presents a balance sheet as of September 30.

EXHIBIT 2.6
T-Accounts and Transactions During September for Electronics Appliance Corporation

Cash (A)					Advances to Employees (A)			Raw Materials Inventory (A)			Prepaid Rent (A)	
(1)	48,000	10,000	(3)		(7)	200		(4)	6,100		(3)	10,000
(5)	900	925	(6)									
		200	(7)									
		5,000	(8)									
		450	(9)									
	32,325					200			6,100			10,000

Equipment (A)			Organization Costs (A)			Accounts Payable (L)			Advances from Customers (L)		
(6)	925		(2)	7,200				6,100	(4)		900	(5)
(8)	27,500										
(9)	450										
	28,875			7,200				6,100			900

Mortgage Payable (L)			Common Stock (SE)		
		22,500	(8)	48,000	(1)
				7,200	(2)
		22,500		55,200	

EXHIBIT 2.7
ELECTRONICS APPLIANCE CORPORATION
Balance Sheet, September 30

ASSETS		
Current Assets:		
Cash	$32,325	
Advances to Employees	200	
Raw Materials Inventory	6,100	
Prepaid Rent	10,000	
Total Current Assets		$48,625
Property, Plant, and Equipment:		
Equipment		28,875
Intangibles:		
Organization Costs		7,200
Total Assets		$84,700
LIABILITIES AND SHAREHOLDERS' EQUITY		
Current Liabilities:		
Accounts Payable	$6,100	
Advances from Customers	900	
Total Current Liabilities		$ 7,000
Long-Term Debt:		
Mortgage Payable		22,500
Total Liabilities		29,500
Shareholders' Equity:		
Common Shares, 4,600 no-par-value shares issued and outstanding	$55,200	
Total Shareholders' Equity		55,200
Total Liabilities and Shareholders' Equity		$84,700

ASSIGNMENT MATERIAL

QUESTIONS

1. Review the meaning of the key terms listed on pages 83–84.

2. How can you ascertain from a balance sheet whether the enterprise is a corporation, partnership, or sole proprietorship?

3. Conservatism is generally regarded as a convention in accounting. Indicate who might be hurt by conservatively stated accounting reports.

4. One of the criteria for the recognition of an asset or a liability is that there be a transaction, or exchange. What justification can you see for this requirement?

5. Accounting typically does not recognize either assets or liabilities for mutually unexecuted contracts. What justification can you see for this treatment?

6. Cash discounts taken on the purchase of merchandise or equipment are treated as a reduction in the amount recorded for the assets acquired. What justification can you see for this treatment?

7. A group of investors owns an office building, which is rented unfurnished to tenants. The building was purchased five years ago from a construction company and, at that time, was expected to have a useful life of 40 years. Indicate the procedures that might be followed in ascertaining the amount at which the building would be stated under each of the following valuation methods.
   a. Acquisition cost
   b. Current replacement cost
   c. Current net realizable value
   d. Present value of future cash flows

8. Some of the assets of one firm correspond to the liabilities of another firm. For example, an account receivable on the seller's balance sheet would be an account payable on the buyer's balance sheet. For each of the following items, indicate whether it is an asset or a liability and give the corresponding account title on the balance sheet of the other party to the transaction.
   a. Advances by Customers
   b. Bonds Payable
   c. Interest Receivable
   d. Prepaid Insurance
   e. Rental Fees Received in Advance

EXERCISES

9. *Asset recognition.*   Indicate whether or not each of the following items would be recognized as an asset by a firm according to generally accepted accounting principles.
   a. A patent on a new invention purchased from its creator.
   b. A firm's chief scientist, who has twice won the Nobel prize.
   c. The right to use a building during the coming year. The rent for the period has already been paid.
   d. An automobile acquired with the issue of a note payable. Because the note has not been paid, legal title to the automobile has not yet passed to the firm.
   e. A degree in engineering from a reputable university, awarded to the firm's chief executive.
   f. A contract signed by a customer to purchase $1,000 worth of goods next year.
   g. A favourable reputation.

10. *Asset recognition and valuation.*   Indicate whether or not each of the following immediately gives rise to an asset under generally accepted accounting principles. If an asset is recognized, state the account title and amount.
    a. A cheque for $300 has been sent to an insurance company for property insurance. The period of coverage begins next month. (Consider from the standpoint of the firm making the cash expenditure.)
    b. A cheque for $3,000 is issued as a deposit on specially designed equipment. The equipment is to have a total purchase price of $20,000 and will be completed and delivered next year. (Consider from the standpoint of the firm making the cash expenditure.)
    c. Common shares of Bell Canada Enterprises Inc. are acquired with temporary excess cash for $12,000.
    d. Merchandise inventory with a list price of $800 is acquired, with payment made in time to secure a 3 percent discount for prompt payment. Cash discounts are treated as a reduction in the acquisition cost of the inventory.
    e. A well-known scientist has been hired to manage the firm's research and development activity. Employment begins next month. One-twelfth of the annual salary of $90,000 is payable at the end of each month worked.
    f. Bonds with a face value of $200,000 are purchased for $206,000. The bonds mature in 20 years. Interest is payable by the issuer at the rate of 10 percent annually.
    g. An order for $700 worth of merchandise is received from a customer.
    h. Notice has been received from a manufacturer that raw materials billed at $2,000, with payment due in 30 days, have been shipped by freight. The buyer obtains title to the goods as soon as they are shipped by the seller.

11. *Asset recognition and valuation.* Indicate whether or not each of the following events immediately gives rise to the recognition of an asset under generally accepted accounting principles. If an asset is recognized, state the account title and amount.
    a. Raw materials with an invoice price of $4,800 are purchased on account from Greer Wholesalers.
    b. Defective raw material purchased in part **a** for $400 is returned to Greer Wholesalers and full credit is received.
    c. The bill of Greer Wholesalers (see parts **a** and **b**) is paid promptly. A discount of 2 percent offered by the seller for prompt payment is taken. Cash discounts are treated as a reduction in the acquisition cost of the raw materials.
    d. A machine is purchased for $25,000 cash.
    e. The cost of transporting the new machine in part **d** to the plant site is paid in cash, $450.
    f. Material and labour costs incurred in installing the machine in part **d** total $300 and are paid in cash.

12. *Asset recognition and valuation.* Indicate whether or not each of the following events immediately gives rise to an asset under generally accepted accounting principles. If an asset is recognized, state the account title and amount.
    a. An investment of $8,000 is made in a government bond. The bond will have a maturity value of $10,000 in three years. The firm intends to hold the bond to maturity.
    b. A cheque for $900 is sent to a landlord for two months' rent in advance. (Consider from the standpoint of the firm issuing the cheque.)
    c. A cheque for $1,000 is written to obtain an option to purchase a tract of land. The price of the land is $32,500. (Consider from the standpoint of the firm issuing the cheque.)
    d. A firm signs a four-year employment agreement with its president for $500,000 per year. The contract period begins next month. (Consider from the standpoint of the firm.)
    e. A patent has been purchased from its creator for $40,000.
    f. A patent has been received on a new invention developed by a firm. Expenditures of $40,000 have been made to develop the patented invention.
    g. Notice has been received from a supplier that materials billed at $4,000, with payment due in 30 days, have been shipped by freight. The seller retains title to the materials until received by the buyer.

13. *Asset recognition and valuation.* In each of the following transactions, give the title(s) and amount(s) of the asset(s) that would appear on the balance sheet.
    a. A firm purchases an automobile with a list price of $8,000. The dealer allows a discount of $850 from the list price for payment in cash. Dealer preparation charges on the automobile amount to an extra $200. The dealer collects a 4 percent sales tax on the price paid for the automobile and preparation charges. In addition, the dealer collects a $75 fee to be remitted to the province for this year's

licence plates and $300 for a one-year insurance policy provided by the dealer's insurance agency. The firm pays a body shop $75 for painting the firm's name on the automobile.

b. A firm acquires land that has been valued at $2 million by a real estate appraiser. The firm pays for the land by giving up shares in Imperial Oil Limited at a time when equivalent shares traded on the Toronto Stock Exchange have a market value of $2,100,000.

c. A firm acquires land that has been appraised at $2 million by a real estate appraiser. The firm pays for the land by giving up shares in Small Timers, Inc., whose shares are traded only on the Vancouver Stock Exchange. The last transaction in shares of Small Timers, Inc., occurred four days before this asset swap. Using the prices of the most recent trades, the shares of Small Timers, Inc. given in exchange for the building have a market value of $2,100.000.

14. *Liability recognition.* Indicate whether or not each of the following items is recognized as a liability according to generally accepted accounting principles.

a. An obligation to provide magazines next year to subscribers who have paid one year's subscription fees in advance. (Consider from the standpoint of the magazine publisher.)

b. The reputation for poor quality control on products manufactured.

c. An obligation to provide warranty services for three years after customers purchase the firm's products.

d. The outstanding common shares of a corporation.

e. Unpaid property taxes for the preceding year.

f. The amount payable by a firm for a television advertisement that has appeared but for which payment is not due for 30 days.

g. A tenant's obligation to maintain a rented warehouse in good repair.

h. The firm's president has an incompetent son who is employed in the business.

15. *Liability recognition and valuation.* Indicate whether or not each of the following events immediately gives rise to the recognition of a liability under generally accepted accounting principles. If a liability is recognized, state the account title and amount.

a. A company hires its president under a five-year contract beginning next month. The contract calls for $300,000 compensation per year.

b. An insurance company receives $2,000 for six months' insurance coverage in advance. (Consider from the standpoint of the insurance company.)

c. A manufacturer agrees to produce a specially designed piece of equipment for $3 million. A down payment of $300,000 is received upon signing the contract, and the remainder is due when the equipment is completed. (Consider from the standpoint of the manufacturer.)

d. Additional common shares with a par value of $75,000 are issued for $80,000.

e. Employees earned wages totalling $6,000 during the last pay period, for which they have not been paid. The employer is also liable for payroll taxes of 8 percent of the wages earned.

f. A firm signs a contract under which it agrees to sell $6,000 of merchandise to a particular customer.

16. *Liability recognition and valuation.*   Indicate whether or not each of the following events immediately gives rise to the recognition of a liability under generally accepted accounting principles. If a liability is recognized, indicate the account title and amount.

   a. A $600 cheque is received from a tenant for three months' rent in advance. (Consider from the standpoint of the lessor, or owner, of the building.)
   b. Utility services received during the past month of $240 have not been paid. (Consider from the standpoint of the firm using the utility services.)
   c. A $10,000 loan has been received from the bank, with the firm signing a note agreeing to repay the loan with interest at 8 percent in six months.
   d. A firm has signed an agreement with its employees' labour union in which it has agreed to increase the firm's contribution to the union pension fund by $20,000 per month, beginning next month. (Consider from the standpoint of the firm.)
   e. Income taxes totalling $15,000 on last year's earnings have not been paid.
   f. A firm has signed an employment contract with its controller for a three-year period beginning next month at a contract price of $200,000 per year. (Consider from the standpoint of the firm.)

17. *Liability recognition and valuation.*   Indicate whether or not each of the following events immediately gives rise to a liability under generally accepted accounting principles. If a liability is recognized, state the account title and amount.

   a. A landscaper agrees to improve land owned by a firm. The agreed price of the work is $2,500. (Consider from the standpoint of the firm owning the land.)
   b. A cheque for $36 is received for a two-year future subscription to a magazine. (Consider from the standpoint of the magazine publisher.)
   c. A construction company agrees to build a bridge for $2 million. A down payment of $200,000 is received upon signing the contract, and the remainder is due when the bridge is completed.
   d. Additional common shares with a par value of $60,000 are issued for $80,000.
   e. A firm received a 60-day, 10 percent loan of $10,000 from a local bank.
   f. A firm signs a contract to purchase at least $6,000 worth of merchandise during the next year.
   g. Refer to part **f**. An order for $1,500 of merchandise is placed with the supplier.

18. *Disclosure of owners' equity.*   The assets of a business total $700,000, and liabilities total $550,000. Present the owners' equity section of the balance sheet under the following assumptions:
   a. The business is a sole proprietorship owned by William Gleason.

 b. The business is a partnership. William Gleason has a 35 percent interest. John Morgan has a 40 percent interest, and David Johnson has a 25 percent interest.

 c. The business is a corporation. Outstanding common shares were originally issued for $80,000, of which $50,000 represented par value. The remainder of the owners' equity represents accumulated, undistributed earnings.

19. *Balance sheet classification.* Information may be classified with respect to a balance sheet in one of the following ways:

 (1) Asset.
 (2) Liability.
 (3) Shareholders' equity.
 (4) Item would not appear on the balance sheet as conventionally prepared.

Using these numbers, indicate the appropriate classification of each of the following items:

 a. Salaries payable
 b. Retained earnings
 c. Notes receivable
 d. Unfilled customers' orders (no deposits received)
 e. Land
 f. Interest payable
 g. Work-in-process inventory
 h. Mortgage payable
 i. Organization costs
 j. Advances by customers
 k. Advances to employees
 j. Patents
 m. Good credit standing
 n. Common stock

20. *Balance sheet classification.* Information may be classified with respect to a balance sheet in one of the following ways:

 (1) Asset.
 (2) Liability.
 (3) Shareholders' equity.
 (4) Item would not appear on the balance sheet as conventionally prepared.

Using these numbers, indicate the appropriate classification of each of the following items:

 a. Preferred shares
 b. Furniture and fixtures
 c. Potential liability under lawsuit (case has not yet gone to trial)
 d. Prepaid rent
 e. Contributed surplus
 f. Cash on hand
 g. Goodwill
 h. Estimated liability under warranty contract
 i. Raw materials inventory

    j. Rental fees received in advance

    k. Bonds payable

    l. Unexpired insurance

21. **Working backwards from journal entries.**   Presented below are journal entries for a series of transactions. Describe the transaction that most likely gave rise to each journal entry.

a. Equipment	$ 10,000	
Cash		$ 2,000
Note Payable		8,000
b. Cash	$ 6,000	
Accounts Receivable		$ 4,000
Advances from Customers		2,000
c. Accounts Payable	$ 2,500	
Merchandise Inventory		$ 2,500
d. Bonds Payable	$100,000	
Common Stock		$40,000
Contributed Surplus		60,000
e. Cash	$ 800	
Subscription Fees Received in Advance		$ 800
f. Prepaid Rent	$ 2,000	
Cash		$ 2,000

PROBLEMS AND CASES

22. **Journal entries for various transactions.**   Present journal entries for each of the following transactions of Mailor Corporation during April, its first month of operations.

    (1) April 2: A total of 250,000 $5 par-value common shares are issued for $8 cash per share.

    (2) April 3: A building costing $800,000 is acquired. A down payment of $200,000 is made in cash and a 10 percent note maturing in three years is signed for the balance.

    (3) April 8: A machine costing $15,000 is acquired for cash.

    (4) April 15: Merchandise inventory costing $120,000 is acquired on account from various suppliers.

    (5) April 18: A cheque for $400 is issued for insurance coverage for the period beginning May 1.

    (6) April 20: A cheque for $800 is received from a customer for merchandise to be delivered on May 5.

    (7) April 26: Invoices totalling $80,000 from the purchases on April 15 are paid, after deducting a 2 percent discount for prompt payment. Cash discounts are treated as a reduction in the acquisition cost of inventory.

    (8) April 30: The remaining invoices from the purchases on April 15 are paid after the discount period has lapsed.

23. *Journal entries for various transactions.* Present journal entries for each of the following transactions of Area Corporation. You may omit dates and explanations for the journal entries.
   (1) A total of 20,000 $10 par-value common shares are issued at par value for cash.
   (2) Land and building costing $90,000 are acquired with the payment of $25,000 cash and the assumption of a twenty-year, 8 percent mortgage for the balance. The land is to be stated at $30,000 and the building at $60,000.
   (3) A used lathe is purchased for $4,620 cash.
   (4) Raw materials costing $3,600 are acquired on account.
   (5) Defective raw materials purchased in (4) and costing $650 are returned to the supplier. The account has not yet been paid.
   (6) The supplier in (4) is paid the amount due, less a 2 percent discount for prompt payment. Cash discounts are treated as a reduction in the acquisition cost of raw materials.
   (7) A fire insurance policy providing $100,000 coverage beginning next month is obtained. The one-year premium of $625 is paid in cash.
   (8) A cheque for $2,000 is issued to Roger White to reimburse him for costs incurred in organizing and promoting the corporation.
   (9) A cheque for $600 is issued for three months' rent in advance for office space.
   (10) A patent on a machine process is purchased for $35,000 cash.
   (11) Office equipment is purchased for $950. A down payment of $250 is made, with the balance payable in 30 days.
   (12) Express Transfer Company is paid $275 for delivering the equipment purchased in (3).

24. *Journal entries for various transactions of a sole proprietorship.* Express the following transactions of Winkle Grocery Store, a sole proprietorship, in journal entry form. You may omit explanations for the journal entries.
   (1) John Winkle contributes $50,000 cash to help set up the grocery store.
   (2) A 60-day, 8 percent note is signed in return for a $10,000 loan from the bank.
   (3) A building is rented, with the annual rental of $6,000 paid in advance.
   (4) Display equipment costing $16,000 is acquired. A cheque is issued.
   (5) Merchandise inventory costing $35,000 is acquired. A cheque for $8,000 is issued, with the remainder payable in 30 days.
   (6) A contract is signed with a nearby restaurant under which the restaurant agrees to purchase $6,000 of groceries each week. A cheque is received for the first two weeks' orders in advance.

25. *Journal entries for various transactions.* Express the following independent transactions in journal entry form. If an entry is not required, indicate the reason. You may omit explanations for the journal entries.
   (1) Bonds of the Sommers Co. Ltd. with a face value of $60,000 and annual interest at the rate of 8 percent are purchased for $58,500 cash.

(2) A cheque for $2,600 is received by a fire insurance company for premiums on policy coverage over the next two years.

(3) A corporation issues 20,000 no-par-value common shares in exchange for land, building, and equipment. The land is to be stated at $30,000, the building at $180,000, and the equipment at $75,000.

(4) A contract is signed by a manufacturing firm agreeing to purchase 100 dozen machine tool parts over the next two years at a price of $60 per dozen.

(5) A total of 5,000 no-par-value preferred shares are issued to a lawyer for legal services rendered in the organization of the corporation. The bill for the services is $9,500.

(6) A coupon book, redeemable in future movie viewings, is issued for $60 cash by a movie theatre.

(7) A firm has been notified that it is being sued for $30,000 damages by a customer who incurred losses as a result of purchasing defective merchandise.

(8) Merchandise inventory costing $2,000, purchased on account, is found to be defective and returned to the supplier for full credit.

26. *Effect of transactions on balance sheet equation.* Indicate the effects of the transactions below on the balance sheet equation using the following format:

Transaction Number	Assets	=	Liabilities	+	Shareholders' Equity
(1)	+$50,000		0		+$50,000
Subtotal	$50,000 =		0	+	$50,000

(1) A total of 5,000 no-par-value common shares are issued for $50,000 cash.

(2) Equipment costing $12,000 is acquired. A down payment of $4,000 is made, with the remainder payable in six months with interest at 9 percent.

(3) Raw materials costing $6,000 are acquired on account.

(4) Installation cost of $800 on the equipment in (2) is paid in cash.

(5) The property insurance premium of $420 for the year, beginning on the first day of next month, is paid.

(6) Raw materials acquired in (3) for $700 are found to be defective and returned to the supplier for full credit. The account had not yet been paid.

(7) Invoices from the purchase in (3) totalling $4,000 are paid after deducting a 1 percent discount for prompt payment. Cash discounts are treated as a reduction in the acquisition cost of raw materials.

(8) A total of 100 no-par-value common shares are issued to the firm's attorney for services in organizing the corporation. The attorney's bill was $1,000.

(9) Customers advanced the firm $250 for merchandise to be delivered next month.

27. *Effect of transactions on balance sheet equation.* Indicate the effects of the transactions below on the balance sheet equation using the format at the top of p. 111.

Transaction Number	Assets	= Liabilities +	Shareholders' Equity
(1)	+$30,000	0	+$30,000
Subtotal	$30,000 =	0 +	$30,000

(1) A total of 3,000 no-par-value common shares are issued for $30,000 cash.

(2) Merchandise costing $24,300 is purchased on account.

(3) Store equipment costing $4,800 is acquired. A cheque for $1,000 is issued and the balance is payable over three years under an installment contract.

(4) A cheque is issued for $900 covering two months' rent in advance.

(5) Refer to transaction (3). Common shares with a market value of $3,800 are issued in full settlement of the installment contract.

(6) The merchandise supplier in transaction (2) is paid the amount due.

28. **T-account entries for various transactions.** Set up T-accounts for the following accounts. Indicate whether each account is an asset, liability, or shareholders' equity item, and enter the transactions described below:

Cash	Accounts Payable
Merchandise Inventory	Note Payable
Prepaid Insurance	Mortgage Payable
Building	Common Stock — Par Value
Equipment	Contributed Surplus

(1) A total of 30,000 $5 par-value share are issued for $8 cash per share.

(2) A building costing $300,000 is acquired. A cash payment of $60,000 is made, and a long-term mortgage is assumed for the balance of the purchase price.

(3) Equipment costing $5,000 and merchandise inventory costing $7,000 are acquired on account.

(4) A three-year fire insurance policy is taken out, and the $900 premium is paid in advance.

(5) A 90-day, 6 percent note is issued to the bank for a $10,000 loan.

(6) Payments of $8,000 are made to the supplier in (3).

29. **T-account entries and balance sheet preparation.** The Patterson Manufacturing Corporation is organized on January 1. During January, the following transactions occur:

(1) The corporation issues 15,000 no-par-value common shares for $210,000 in cash.

(2) The corporation issues 28,000 no-par-value common shares in exchange for land, building, and equipment. The land is to be stated at $80,000, the building at $220,000, and the equipment at $92,000.

(3) The corporation issues 2,000 no-par-value common shares to a lawyer in payment of legal services rendered in obtaining the corporate charter.

(4) Raw materials costing $75,000 are acquired on account from various suppliers.

(5) Manufacturing equipment with a list price of $6,000 is acquired. After deducting a $600 discount, the net amount is paid in cash.

Cash discounts are treated as a reduction in the acquisition cost of equipment.

(6) Freight charges of $350 for delivery of the equipment in (5) are paid in cash.

(7) Raw materials costing $800 are found to be defective and returned to the supplier for full credit. The raw materials had been purchased on account [see (4)], and no payment had been made as of the time that the goods were returned.

(8) A contract is signed for the rental of a fleet of automobiles beginning February 1. The rental for February of $1,400 is paid in advance.

(9) Invoices for $60,000 of raw materials purchased in (4) are paid, after deducting a discount of 3 percent for prompt payment. Cash discounts are treated as a reduction in the acquisition cost of raw materials.

(10) Fire and liability insurance coverage is obtained from Northwest Insurance Company. The two-year policy, beginning February 1, carries a $400 premium, which has not yet been paid.

(11) A contract is signed with a customer for $20,000 of merchandise that Patterson plans to manufacture. The customer advanced $4,500 toward the contract price.

(12) A warehouse costing $60,000 is acquired. A down payment of $7,000 is made, and a long-term mortgage is assumed for the balance. No principal payments are to be made on the mortgage for two years.

(13) Raw materials inventory with an original list price of $1,500 is found to be defective and returned to the supplier. This inventory has already been paid for in (9). The returned raw materials are the only items purchased from this particular supplier during January. A cash refund has not yet been received from the supplier.

(14) The firm purchased 6,000 $10 par value common shares of the General Cereal Corporation for $95,000. This investment is made as a short-term investment of excess cash. The shares of General Cereal Corporation are traded on the Toronto Stock Exchange.

The following assumptions will help you resolve certain accounting uncertainties: (i) Transactions (2) and (3) occurred on the same day as transaction (1). (ii) The invoices paid in (9) are the only purchases for which discounts were made available to the purchaser. (iii) No depreciation is recorded for January.

  a. Enter these transactions in the T-accounts. Indicate whether each account is an asset, liability, or shareholders' equity item. Cross-reference each entry to the appropriate transaction number.

  b. Prepare a balance sheet as of January 31.

30. *T-account entries and balance sheet preparation.* The Scott Products Co. Ltd. is organized in October 1. During October, the following transactions occur:

  (1) The corporation issues 20,000 $5 par value preferred shares for $7 per share in cash.

  (2) The corporation issues 200 $100 par value shares at par value for cash.

(3) The corporation gives $40,000 in cash and 5,000 common shares in exchange for land and building. The land is to be stated at $5,000 and the building at $70,000.

(4) Equipment costing $26,000 is acquired. Cash of $3,000 is paid and an 8 percent note, due in one year, is given for the balance.

(5) Transportation costs on the equipment in (4) of $800 are paid in cash.

(6) Installation costs on the equipment in (4) of $1,100 are paid in cash.

(7) Merchandise inventory costing $45,000 is acquired on account.

(8) Licence fees for the year beginning November 1 of $800 are paid in advance.

(9) Merchandise costing $1,300 from the acquisition in (7) are found to be defective and returned to the supplier for full credit. The account had not been paid.

(10) A patent is purchased from its creator for $15,000.

(11) The corporation signed an agreement to manufacture a specially designed machine for a customer for $60,000, to be delivered in January of next year. At the time of signing, the customer advanced $6,000 of the contract price.

(12) Invoices totalling $30,000 from the purchases in (7) are paid, after deducting a 2 percent discount for prompt payment. Cash discounts are treated as a reduction in the acquisition cost of inventory.

a. Enter the transactions in T-accounts. Indicate whether each account is an asset, liability, or shareholders' equity item. Cross-reference each entry to the appropriate transaction number.

b. Prepare a balance sheet for Scott Products Co. Ltd. as of October 31.

31. *T-account entries and balance sheet preparation.* The Sarwark Corporation is organized on January 1. During January, the following transactions occur:

(1) A total of 10,000 no-par-value common shares are issued for $150,000.

(2) Bonds with a face and maturity value of $100,000 are issued at face value for cash.

(3) Land and building costing $200,000 are acquired. A cheque for $80,000 is issued, with the remainder payable over twenty years. The land is assigned $20,000 and the building is assigned $180,000 of the acquisition cost.

(4) Equipment costing $40,000 is acquired. After deducting a discount of 2 percent for immediate cash payment, the net amount due is paid.

(5) Merchandise costing $25,000 is acquired on account.

(6) Merchandise costing $2,000 is found to be defective and returned to the supplier. No cash payments have yet been made to this supplier.

(7) An insurance policy for a one-year period beginning February 1 is obtained. The premium for the one-year period of $1,200 is paid.

(8) A customer placed an order for $1,500 of merchandise to be delivered in February. The customer sent a cheque of $300 with the order.

(9) Merchandise suppliers in (5) are paid $18,000 of the amounts due. The remaining suppliers will be paid in February.

   a. Enter these transactions in T-accounts. Indicate whether each account is an asset, liability, or shareholders' equity item. Cross-reference each entry to the appropriate transaction number.

   b. Prepare a balance sheet as of December 31.

32. *T-account entries and balance sheet preparation for a sole proprietorship.* The following transactions occur during March for Dryden's Book Store, a sole proprietorship, in preparation for its opening for business on April 1.

(1) H.R. Dryden contributes $6,000 in cash, 100 common shares of Western Corporation, and an inventory of books to be sold. The shares of Western Corporation are quoted on the Vancouver Stock Exchange at $15 per share on the day they are contributed, and will be sold when additional cash is needed. The books are to be stated at $2,750.

(2) Two months' rent on a store building is paid in advance in cash. The book store will occupy the building on April 1. The monthly rental is $400.

(3) Store fixtures are purchased for $4,000, of which $800 is paid in cash. A note, to be paid in ten equal monthly installments beginning May 1, is signed for the balance.

(4) Books with an invoice price of $2,600 are purchased on account.

(5) A one-year insurance policy on the store's contents beginning April 1 is purchased. The premium of $160 is paid by cheque.

(6) A cheque for $320 is issued to the Darwin Equipment Co. Ltd. for a cash register and other operating equipment.

(7) Books costing $1,800 are ordered from a publisher. Delivery is scheduled for April 15.

(8) The books purchased in (4) are paid for by cheque. Payment is made in time to obtain a 2 percent discount for prompt payment. These are the only purchases for which discounts are available. Cash discounts are treated as a reduction in the acquisition cost of the books.

(9) An operating license for the year beginning April 1 is obtained. A fee of $250 is paid by cheque.

   a. Enter these transactions in T-accounts. Indicate whether each account is an asset, liability, or owners' equity item. Cross-reference each entry to the appropriate transaction number.

   b. Prepare a balance sheet for this sole proprietorship as of March 31.

33. *T-account entries and balance sheet preparation for a partnership.* Priscilla Mullins and Miles Standish form a partnership to operate a laundry and cleaning business to be known as Pilgrim's One Day Laundry and Cleaners. The following transactions occur in late June, before the grand opening on July 1.

(1) Standish contributes $400 cash and cleaning equipment that is to be stated at $5,600.

(2) Mullins contributes $3,000 cash and a delivery truck to be stated at $2,500.

(3) The July rent for the business premises of $400 is paid in advance.

(4) Cleaning supplies are purchased on account from Wonder Chemical Ltd. for $2,500.

(5) Insurance coverage on the equipment and truck for a one-year period beginning July 1 is purchased for $425 cash.

(6) The firm borrows $2,000 from the First Canadian Bank. A 90-day, 8 percent note is signed, with principal and interest payable at maturity.

(7) The Wonder Chemical Ltd. account is paid in full after deducting a 2 percent discount for prompt payment. Cash discounts are treated as a reduction in the acquisition cost of supplies.

(8) A cash register is purchased for $700. A down payment of $100 is made, and a note is signed for the remainder, payable in ten equal installments beginning August 1.

a. Enter these transactions in T-accounts. Indicate whether each account is an asset, liability, or owners' equity item. Cross-reference each entry to the appropriate transaction number.

b. Prepare a balance sheet for the partnership as of June 30.

EXHIBIT 2.8
WESTERN SALES INC.
Balance Sheet for the Year Ended December 31, Year 5

ASSETS
Current Assets:

Cash and Certificates of Deposit	$ 86,500	
Accounts Receivable—Net	193,600	
Merchandise Inventory	322,900	$ 603,000
Investments (substantially at cost):		
Investment in Treasury Bills	$ 60,000	
Investment in Eastern Sales Corp.	196,500	256,500
Fixed Assets (at cost):		
Land	$225,000	
Buildings and Equipment—Net	842,600	1,067,600
Intangibles and Deferred Charges:		
Prepaid Insurance	$ 1,200	
Prepaid Rent	1,500	
Goodwill	2	2,702
Total Assets		$1,929,802

LIABILITIES AND SHAREHOLDERS' EQUITY
Current Liabilities:

Accounts Payable	$225,300	
Accrued Expenses	10,900	
Income Taxes Payable	89,200	$ 325,400
Long-Term Liabilities:		
Bonds Payable	$500,000	
Pensions Payable	40,600	
Contingent Liability	100,000	640,600
Shareholders' Equity:		
Common Stock—$10 par value, 50,000 shares issued and outstanding	$625,000	
Earned Surplus	338,802	963,802
Total Liabilities and Shareholders' Equity		$1,929,802

34. *Criticism of balance sheet format and disclosure.* Comment on any unusual features of the balance sheet of the Western Sales Inc. shown in Exhibit 2.8.

35. *Effect of recording errors on balance sheet equation.* Using the notation O/S (overstated), U/S (understated), or No (no effect), indicate the effects on assets, liabilities, and shareholders' equity of failing to record each of the following independent transactions or events. For example, a failure to record the issuance of common shares for $10,000 cash would be:

> Assets — U/S $10,000
> Liabilities — No
> Shareholders' equity — U/S $10,000

(1) Merchandise costing $6,000 is purchased on account.
(2) A machine costing $10,000 is acquired. A 25 percent down payment is made, with the remainder payable over five years.
(3) An order for $3,500 of merchandise is placed with a supplier.
(4) A cheque for $300 is received from a customer for merchandise to be delivered next month.
(5) A cheque for $800 is issued to cover rental of a warehouse for the next two months.
(6) Common shares with a market value of $1,500 are issued to lawyers for services rendered in setting up the firm.
(7) A note payable for $2,000, which had previously been correctly recorded on the books, is now paid in the amount of $2,000.
(8) A cheque for $1,000 is issued for the option to purchase a tract of land. The price of the land is $30,000. The option can be exercised within 90 days.

36. *Constructing a balance sheet from incomplete records.* Most of the financial records of the Rowland Novelty Company were removed by an employee who, apparently, took all of the cash on hand from the store on October 31. From supplementary records, the following information is obtained:
(1) According to the bank, cash in bank was $5,730.
(2) Amount payable to creditors was $4,720.
(3) Rowland's initial contribution to the business was $15,000, and the total interest in the business at the time of the theft was $17,500.
(4) Cost of merchandise on hand was $11,380.
(5) A one-year fire insurance policy was purchased on September 1 for $900.
(6) Furniture and fixtures were rented from the Anderson Office Supply Company for $200 per month. The rental for October has not been paid.
(7) A note for $1,200 was given by a customer. Interest due at October 31 was $45.
(8) Payments due for other customers amounted to $1,915.
(9) Rowland purchased a license from the city for $300 on July 1. The license allows retail operations for one year.
  a. Determine the probable cash shortage.

b. Prepare a well-organized balance sheet presenting the financial position immediately before the theft.

37. *Constructing statements from T-account analysis.* In early 19X3, the president of Quebec City Candle Store contacted you for assistance. On January 4, 19X3, the accountant of Quebec City Candle Store was hospitalized as a result of a traffic accident. You were hired as a consultant to prepare the financial statements for 19X2. From the company records, you found the following account balances:

	January 1, 19X1		December 31, 19X1	
	Dr.	Cr.	Dr.	Cr.
Cash	$ 6,500		$ 3,000	
Accounts receivable	35,400		32,200	
Merchandise	10,500		45,800	
Supplies	1,500		1,200	
Prepaid insurance	1,800		1,400	
Land	22,500		22,500	
Buildings	45,000		45,000	
Accumulated depreciation — buildings		$ 6,000		$ 7,200
Equipment	12,000		15,000	
Accumulated depreciation — equipment		2,000		3,000
Accounts payable		14,200		37,500
Salaries payable		1,000		1,500
Capital stock		100,000		100,000
Retained earnings		12,000		16,900
Total	$135,200	$135,200	$166,100	$166,100

Upon further investigation, you have found the following working papers prepared by the accountant:

19X2 Purchases on account:	
Merchandise	$270,000
Supplies	2,000
19X2 Cash receipts:	
Sales of merchandise	75,000
Collections of customers' accounts	300,000
19X2 Cash disbursements:	
Supplies	1,200
Delivery charges on outgoing merchandise	2,200
Insurance premium	800
Payments on account	285,000
Sales staff salaries	18,900
Utility services	2,100
Purchase of equipment	3,000

You took inventory and found that merchandise on hand on December 31, 19X2 was $65,000, and the inventory of supplies on December 31, 19X2 was $900.

Further discussion with the sales manager revealed that 19X2 sales on account were $310,000, and that unpaid salaries of the sales staff amounted to $1,000.

Other information:

Depreciation for year on building		$ 1,200
Depreciation for year on equipment		1,500
Insurance expired during year		1,200
Earnings before extraordinary items	$110,200	$110,000
Less: Dividends — 6% cumulative	(30,000)	
Subtotal	$ 80,000	$110,000
Extraordinary items	(2,900)	—
Earnings available to common shareholders, after extraordinary items	$ 77,300	$110,000
Weighted average	58,000	55,000
Earnings per share before extraordinary items	$1.38	$2.00
Earning per share after extraordinary items	$1.33	$2.00

Adapted with permission from the Society of Management Accountants of Canada.

EXHIBIT 2.9
RANKS HOVIS McDOUGALL PLC
Unadjusted Trial Balance, January 31

	August 31	
	Year 7	Year 8
Fixed Assets:		
Brand Names	—	£ 678.0
Tangible Assets	£ 422.3	463.7
Investments	3.4	.7
Total Fixed Assets	£ 425.7	£1,142.4
Current Assets:		
Stocks	215.6	234.3
Debtors	215.6	234.3
Cash	46.2	65.2
Creditors Due within One Year:		
Borrowings	(53.0)	(45.1)
Other	(266.7)	(347.3)
Net Current Assets	£ 90.7	£ 91.7
Total Assets Less Current Liabilities	£ 516.4	£1,234.1
Creditors Due after More than One Year:		
Borrowings	(133.7)	(139.8)
Other	(78.6)	(96.6)
Provisions for Liabilities	(38.9)	(19.0)
	£ 265.2	£ 978.7
Capital and Reserves:		
Called up Share Capital	£ 91.4	£ 93.2
Share Premium Account	28.0	27.5
Revaluation Reserve	24.9	522.5
Other Reserves	107.3	184.9
Minority Interests	13.6	50.5
	£ 265.2	£ 978.7

38. *Balance sheet interpretation.*   Exhibit 2.9 presents a comparative balance sheet for Ranks Hovis McDougall PLC, a major consumer products company in Great Britain.

a. Complete the following schedule summarizing the balance sheet of Ranks Hovis McDougall PLC in a format similar to that used in Canada. You need not prepare a complete balance sheet that includes individual accounts.

	August 31	
	Year 7	Year 8
Current Assets		
Noncurrent Assets	_____	_____
Total Assets	======	======
Current Liabilities		
Noncurrent Liabilities		
Shareholders' Equity	_____	_____
Total Liabilities and Shareholders' Equity	======	======

What relation do you observe in the term structure (that is, current versus noncurrent) of its assets and its liabilities plus shareholders' equity? Can you observe this relation more easily using the published balance sheet format or the format commonly used in Canada?

b. Firms in Great Britain use different account titles for certain balance sheet items. Indicate the account title commonly used in Canada for each of the following accounts appearing in the balance sheet of Ranks Hovis McDougall PLC.
   (1) Tangible Assets
   (2) Stocks
   (3) Debtors
   (4) Borrowings (due within one year)
   (5) Other Creditors (due within one year)
   (6) Borrowings (due after more than one year)
   (7) Called Up Share Capital
   (8) Share Premium Account
   (9) Other Reserves

c. Ranks Hovis McDougall PLC recognized the value of its internally-developed brand names in the amount of £678.0 million during Year 8. Give the journal entry that was likely made to recognize this intangible asset. How might the firm have valued brand names?

DECISION CASE 2-1

Saul Levi, the owner-operator of a local hardware store, is planning to add a line of mechanized gardening equipment to his present stock. The cost of purchasing this new merchandise, the higher replacement costs of inventory, and the pressing demands for payment by his creditors have made him realize that he needs more cash. He approaches the manager of the local bank to arrange for a demand bank loan of $30,000, taking with him the following balance sheet he prepared for inclusion in his income tax return.

SAUL LEVI'S HARDWARE STORE
Balance Sheet
December 31, Year 7

Assets			Liabilities and Owner's Equity	
Cash on hand and in bank		$ 780	Accounts payable	$22,970
Accounts receivable		1,210	Notes payable	6,000
Inventory		12,000	Owner's equity	11,000
Land		10,000		
Building	$50,000			
Less Accumulated				
Depreciation	43,920	6,080		
Goodwill		10,000		
		$40,070		$40,070

Saul Levi has owned the building for twenty years and lives above the store. He did not originally operate the store, but decided to do so when the business of the tenant, Sam Brown, seriously declined because of Brown's failing health. Brown had fallen behind in his rent and had incurred substantial debts to his suppliers. In December Year 7, Levi agreed to take over the business assets and liabilities in consideration for $10,000, represented by the rental arrears of $4,000 and a noninterest-bearing note payable of $6,000, which falls due in December Year 8.

The local bank manager, recognizing Levi's limited accounting background, asked a number of questions about the balance sheet, and discovered the following information:

1. Included in the cash on hand was an I.O.U. from Saul's wife for $200, which Saul's assistant had put in the till when Mrs. Levi asked for $200 for household and personal expenses.

2. In order to minimize his income tax, Levi had written off, as uncollectable, certain accounts receivable that were overdue. He estimated that he would collect 80 percent of the $2,500 overdue accounts.

3. In addition, Saul had estimated conservatively the value of his inventory. He considered that, at today's prices, he would have to pay at least $18,000 to replace the inventory that would be sold at a regular price of $27,000 (150 percent above cost). In addition, he planned to sell the obsolete merchandise at a "clear out" rate for $6,000. He had ignored this inventory when preparing his balance sheet for the income tax department.

4. Levi had made no additions to the counters, display cases, lighting fixtures, and so on, since he began operating the business. No value had been placed on these items in the balance sheet when he took over

the business because they were old but still usable, and the proceeds of the sale would have been offset by the cost of repairing the store if they were removed. However, if replaced today, these items would cost $17,000. Saul estimated that the replacement fixtures would last twice as long as the present fixtures.

5. The land and building were recorded at Saul's cost when purchased twenty years ago, although the segregation between the two was made on an arbitrary basis. He had recorded the depreciation on the building at the maximum permitted for income tax purposes. This resulted in accumulated depreciation considerably in excess of what he thought was necessary, since the building should last another twenty years without major repairs. Further, the city had assessed the land and building recently for real estate tax purposes at the current market value of $60,000, allocating $40,000 to the land and $20,000 to the building. Saul thought that the city assessment was fair, but that, if he sold the land and building at the assessed value, he would be required to pay a real estate commission of 5 percent.

6. Levi had carried $10,000 of goodwill from the balance sheet of the previous owner, Brown.

The bank manager advised Saul Levi that, if a loan was granted, it would carry interest of 20 percent but that, before he could make a final decision, he would need more realistic estimates of Saul's equity in the business.

1. Prepare a revised balance sheet for Saul Levi's Hardware Store at December 31, Year 7, to assist the bank manager in deciding on Levi's loan request.

2. Would the above balance sheet be different from that prepared in accordance with generally accepted accounting principles?

3. Do you think the bank manager would make a loan?

CHAPTER THREE

INCOME STATEMENT: REPORTING THE RESULTS OF OPERATING ACTIVITIES

CHAPTER OUTLINE

- The Accounting Period Convention
- Accounting Methods for Measuring Performance
- Measurement Principles of Accrual Accounting
- Overview of Accounting Procedures
- Illustration of the Accounting Process for a Merchandising Firm
- Appendix 3.1: Accounting Journals and Ledgers
- Appendix 3.2: Preparation of a Work Sheet

Net income
The excess of revenue earned over related expenses incurred for the period.

Revenues
The amount of cash received or claims established against customers stemming from the provision of goods or services by the firm.

Expenses
Costs incurred by a firm in the process of earning revenue.

The second principal financial statement is the income statement. This statement provides a measure of the operating performance of a firm for some particular period of time. **Net income**, or *earnings*, is equal to revenues minus expenses.

Revenues measure the net assets (assets less liabilities) that flow into a firm when goods are sold or services are rendered. **Expenses** measure the net assets used up in the process of generating revenues. As measures of operating performance, revenues reflect the services rendered by the firm, and expenses indicate the efforts required.

This chapter considers the measurement principles and accounting procedures that underlie the income statement. We begin by considering the concept of an accounting period, the span of time over which operating performance is measured. Next, two common approaches to measuring operating performance, the cash basis and the accrual basis, are described and illustrated. Finally, the accounting procedures used in applying the accrual basis of accounting are illustrated for a merchandising firm. Chapter 4 explores more fully the application of the accrual basis of accounting for manufacturing, construction, and other types of business.

THE ACCOUNTING PERIOD CONVENTION

The income statement reports operating performance over a specified period of time. Years ago, the length of this period varied substantially among firms. Income statements were prepared at the completion of some activity, such as after the round-trip voyage of a ship between England and its colonies, or at the completion of a construction project.

The operating activities of most modern firms do not divide so easily into distinguishable projects. Instead, the income-generating activity is carried on continuously. For example, a plant is acquired and used in manufacturing products for a period of forty years or more. Delivery equipment is purchased and used in transporting merchandise to customers for four, five, or more years. If the preparation of the income statement were postponed until all operating activities were completed, the report might be prepared only when the firm ceased to exist and, in any case, would be too late to help a reader appraise operating performance. An **accounting period** of uniform length facilitates timely comparisons and analyses among firms.

An accounting period of *one year* underlies the principal financial statements distributed to shareholders and potential investors. Most firms prepare their annual reports using the calendar year as the accounting period. A growing number of firms, however, use a **natural business year**. The use of a natural business year is an attempt to measure performance at a time when the cycle of earnings activities has been substantially concluded. The ending date of a natural business year varies from one firm to another. For example, the Hudson's Bay Company uses a natural business year ending January 31, which comes after completion of the Christmas shopping season; Standard Broadcasting Corporation Limited uses a year ending August 31, just before the beginning of the new radio and television season; and Union Gas Limited uses a year ending March 31, coinciding with the end of winter, the major period of natural gas sales.

Reports of performance for periods shorter than a year are frequently prepared as indicators of progress during the year. These are known as "interim reports" or "reports for interim periods." Preparing interim reports does not remove the need to prepare an annual report.

accounting period
The time period, typically one year, to which accounting reports are related.

natural business year
A fiscal year that ends during a company's period of lowest production and sales activity; more time is therefore available to prepare the financial statements.

ACCOUNTING METHODS FOR MEASURING PERFORMANCE

Some operating activities both start and finish within a given accounting period. For example, merchandise might be purchased from a supplier, the merchandise sold to a customer on account, and the account collected in cash, all within a particular accounting period. Few difficulties are encountered in measuring performance in these cases. The difference between the cash received from customers and the cash disbursed to acquire, sell, and deliver the merchandise represents earnings for this series of transactions.

Many operating activities, however, start in one accounting period and finish in another. Buildings and equipment are acquired in one period but used over a period of several years. Merchandise is sometimes purchased in one accounting period and sold during the next, with cash collected from customers during a third period. A significant problem in measuring performance for a specific accounting period is measuring the amount of revenues and expenses from operating activities that are in process at the beginning of the period or are incomplete at the end of the period. Two approaches to measuring operating performance are (1) the cash basis of accounting and (2) the accrual basis of accounting.

CASH BASIS OF ACCOUNTING

cash basis of accounting
The accounting basis in which revenue is recognized only when money is received and in which expenses are recognized only when money is paid.

Under the **cash basis of accounting**, revenues from selling goods and providing services are recognized in the period in which cash is received from customers. Expenses are reported in the period in which payments are made for merchandise, salaries, insurance, taxes, and similar items. To illustrate the measurement of performance under the cash basis of accounting, consider the following example.

Donald and Joanne Allens open a hardware store on January 1, Year 1. They contribute $20,000 in cash and borrow $12,000 from a local bank. The loan is repayable on June 30, Year 1, with interest charged at the rate of 12 percent per year. A store building is rented on January 1, and two months' rent of $40,000 is paid in advance. The premium of $2,400 for property and liability insurance coverage for the year ending December 31, Year 1 is paid on January 1. During January, merchandise costing $40,000 is acquired; $26,000 worth of merchandise is purchased for cash, and $14,000 is purchased on account. Sales to customers during January total $50,000, of which $34,000 is sold for cash and $16,000 is sold on account. The acquisition cost of merchandise sold during January is $32,000, the various employees are paid $5,000 in salaries.

Exhibit 3.1 presents a performance report for Allens' Hardware Store for the month of January, Year 1 using the cash basis. Cash receipts from sales of merchandise of $34,000 represent the portion of the total sales of $50,000 made during January that was collected in cash. Although merchandise costing $40,000 was acquired during January, only $26,000 cash was disbursed to suppliers, and only this amount is subtracted in measuring performance under the cash basis. Cash payments during January for salaries, rent, and insurance are also subtracted in measuring performance, without

EXHIBIT 3.1
ALLENS' HARDWARE STORE
Performance Measurement on a Cash Basis for the Month of January, Year 1

Cash Receipts from Sales of Merchandise		$34,000
Less: Cash payments for Merchandise and Services		
Merchandise	$26,000	
Salaries	5,000	
Rental	4,000	
Insurance	2,400	
Total Cash Payments		(37,400)
Excess of Cash Payments over Cash Receipts		($ 3,400)

regard to whether or not the services acquired were fully consumed by the end of the month. Cash payments made for merchandise and services exceeded cash receipts from customers during January by $3,400.[1]

As a basis for measuring performance for a particular accounting period (for example, January Year 1 for Allens' Hardware Store), the cash basis of accounting has two weaknesses. First, the cost of the efforts required in generating revenues is not adequately matched with those revenues. Performance of one period therefore gets mingled with the performance of preceding and succeeding periods. The store rental payment of $4,000 provides rental services for both January and February, but under the cash basis, the full amount is subtracted in measuring performance during January. Similarly, the annual insurance premium provides coverage for the full year, but under the cash basis of accounting none of this insurance cost will be subtracted in measuring performance during the months of February through December.

The longer the period over which future benefits are received, the more serious is this weakness of the cash basis of accounting. Consider, for example, the investments of a capital-intensive firm in buildings and equipment that might be used for ten, twenty, or more years. The length of time between the purchase of these assets and the collection of cash for goods produced and sold can span many years.

A second criticism of the cash basis of accounting is that it postpones unnecessarily the time when revenue is recognized. In most cases, the sale (delivery) of goods or rendering of services is the critical event in generating revenue. Collecting cash is relatively routine, or at least highly predictable. In these cases, recognizing revenue at the time of cash collection may result in reporting the effects of operating activities one or more periods after the critical revenue-generating activity has occurred. For example, sales to customers during January by Allens' Hardware Store totalled $50,000. Under the cash basis of accounting, $16,000 of this amount will not be recognized until the cash is collected during February or even later. If the creditworthiness of customers has been checked before making sales on account, the cash will probably be collected, and there is little reason to postpone recognition of the revenue.

The cash basis of accounting is used principally by lawyers, accountants, and other professional people. These professionals have relatively small investments in multiperiod assets, such as buildings and equipment, and usually collect cash from their clients soon after services are rendered. Most such firms actually use a **modified cash basis of accounting**, under which the costs of buildings, equipment, and similar items are treated as assets when purchased. A portion of the acquisition cost is then recognized as an expense when services of these assets are consumed. Except for the treatment of these long-lived assets, revenues are recognized at the time cash is received, and expenses are reported when cash disbursements are made. When calculating taxable income, professional people using the modified cash basis must further modify their reporting system by extending the accrual concept to billings for services, to expenses, and possibly to work in process that has not been billed.

modified cash basis of accounting
The cash basis of accounting with long-term assets accounted for with the accrual basis of accounting. In most cases, "cash basis of accounting" actually means "modified cash basis."

---

[1] Note that, under the cash method, financing transactions (cash received from owners and through borrowing) are not included in the performance report.

Most individuals use the cash basis of accounting for the purpose of computing personal income and personal income taxes. A business is *not* permitted to use the cash basis of accounting when calculating income subject to tax under the Income Tax Act, except for unincorporated farms and fishing operations whose owners elect to use the cash basis.

ACCRUAL BASIS OF ACCOUNTING

accrual basis of accounting
The accounting basis whereby revenue is recognized in the period earned, whether it is actually received or not, and expenses are recognized and matched with the related revenue of the period, whether they are actually paid or not.

The **accrual basis of accounting** typically recognizes revenue when goods are sold or services are rendered. It reports costs incurred as expenses in the period when the revenues that they helped produce are recognized. Thus, accrual accounting attempts to *match* expenses with associated revenues. Costs incurred that cannot be closely identified with specific revenue streams are treated as expenses of the period in which services of an asset are consumed and the future benefits of an asset disappear.

EXHIBIT 3.2
ALLENS' HARDWARE STORE
Income Statement for the Month of January
(Accrual Basis of Accounting)

Sales Revenue		$50,000
Less: Cost of Goods Sold		(32,000)
Gross Profit		$18,000
Less: Operating Expenses		
Salaries	$5,000	
Rent	2,000	
Insurance	200	(7,200)
Operating Profit		$10,800
Less: Interest Expense		(120)
Net Income		$10,680

Exhibit 3.2 presents an income statement for Allens' Hardware Store for January of Year 1 using the accrual basis of accounting. The entire $50,000 of sales during January is recognized as revenue, even though cash in that amount has not yet been received. Because the outstanding accounts receivable will probably be collected, the sale of the goods, rather than the collection of cash from customers, triggers the recognition of revenue. The merchandise sold during January cost $32,000. Recognizing this amount as an expense (cost of goods sold) matches the cost of the merchandise sold with revenue from sales. Of the advance rental payment of $4,000, only $2,000 applies to the cost of services consumed during January. The remaining rental of $2,000 applies to the month of February. Likewise, only $200 of the $2,400 insurance premium represents coverage used up during January. The remaining $2,200 of the insurance premium provides coverage for February through December and will be recognized as an expense during those months. The interest expense of $120 represents one month's interest on the $12,000 bank loan at an annual rate of 12 percent ($= \$12,000 \times 0.12 \times 1/12$). Although the interest will not be paid until the loan becomes due on June 30, Year 1, the firm benefited from having the funds

available for its use during January; an appropriate portion of the total interest cost on the loan should therefore be recognized as an expense of January. The salaries, rental, insurance, and interest expenses, unlike the cost of merchandise sold, cannot be associated directly with revenues recognized during the period. These costs are therefore reported as expenses of January to the extent that services were consumed during the month.

Note that income tax expense is missing from Allens' Hardware Store's income statement. Because the accounting entity, Allens' Hardware Store, is not a limited company, it is not considered a taxable entity under the Income Tax Act and pays no income tax. For income tax purposes, the income from Allens' Hardware Store is assumed to flow directly and completely to Donald and Joanne Allens at the end of the fiscal year. The portion of the store's income allocated to Donald will be included as part of Donald's personal income subject to income tax, and the remainder will be included as part of Joanne's personal income subject to income tax.

The accrual basis of accounting provides a better measure of operating performance for Allens' Hardware Store for the month of January than does the cash basis for two reasons:

1. Revenues more accurately reflect the results of sales activity during January.
2. Expenses are associated more closely with reported revenues.

Likewise, the accrual basis will provide a superior measure of performance for future periods, because activities of those periods will be charged with their share of the costs of rental, insurance, and other services to be consumed. Thus, the accrual basis focuses on *inflows of net assets* from operations (revenues) and the *use of net assets* in operations (expenses), regardless whether those inflows and outflows currently produce or use cash.

Most business firms, particularly those involved in merchandising and manufacturing activities, use the accrual basis of accounting. The next section examines the measurement principles of accrual accounting.

MEASUREMENT PRINCIPLES OF ACCRUAL ACCOUNTING

Reporting revenues and expenses under the accrual basis of accounting requires considering when revenues and expenses are recognized (timing questions) and how much is recognized or reported (measurement questions).

TIMING OF REVENUE RECOGNITION

The operating process for the acquisition and sale of merchandise might be depicted as shown in Figure 3.1. Revenue could conceivably be recognized at the time of purchase, sale, or cash collection; at some point(s) between these events; or even continuously. Answering the timing question requires a set of criteria for revenue recognition.

FIGURE 3.1
Earnings Process for the Acquisition and Sale of Merchandise

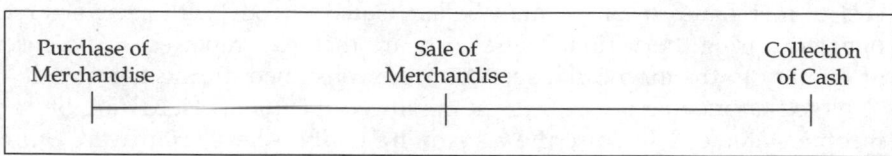

Criteria for Revenue Recognition

The criteria currently required to be met before revenue is recognized under the accrual basis of accounting are as follows:

1. All, or a substantial portion, of the services to be provided have been performed.
2. Cash, a receivable, or some other asset conducive to reasonably precise measurement has been received.

For the vast majority of firms involved in selling goods and services, revenue is recognized at the time of sale (delivery). The goods have been transferred to a buyer or the services have been performed. Future services, such as for warranties, either are insignificant or, if significant, can be estimated with reasonable precision. An exhange between an independent buyer and seller provides an objective measure of the amount of revenue. If the sale is made on account, past experience and an assessment of credit standings of customers provide a basis for predicting the amount of cash that will be collected. Thus, the criteria for revenue recognition are usually met at the time of sale.

MEASUREMENT OF REVENUE

The amount of revenue recognized is measured by the cash or cash equivalent value of other assets received from customers. As a starting point, this amount is the agreed-upon price between buyer and seller at the time of sale. Some adjustments to this amount may be necessary, however, if revenue is recognized in a period before the collection of cash.

ADJUSTMENTS TO REVENUE

Cash Discounts

cash discounts
A reduction in the amount owed to encourage early payment.

Often, the seller of merchandise offers a reduction from its invoice price for prompt payment. Such reductions are called **cash discounts**. There is nothing incongruous in the proposition that goods may have two prices: a cash price or a higher price if goods are sold on credit. The seller offers a cash discount as an incentive for prompt payment so that additional bookkeeping and collection costs can be avoided.

The goods are sold for a certain price if prompt payment is made, and a penalty is added in the form of a higher price if the payment is delayed.

The bills rendered by some public utilities illustrate this approach. The amount of cash discount made available to customers, therefore, should be considered as one of the adjustments in the measurement of net sales revenue.

The need to prepare operating statements for relatively short periods leads to alternative possibilities for recording cash discounts reported for a period. The issue is whether the amount of cash discount should be deducted from sales revenue in the period when the sales revenue is recognized or in the period of cash collection. In computing the amount of cash discounts recognized for a period, the major alternatives are the following:

1. To recognize discounts when taken by the customer, without regard to the period of sale (called the **gross price method**).

2. To estimate the total amount of discounts that will be taken on the sales made during the period (called the **allowance method**).

3. To record sales amounts reduced by all discounts made available to customers and to recognize additional revenue when a discount lapses (called the **net price method**).

Intermediate accounting texts discuss these methods.

Trade Discounts

A common business practice is to allow customers who buy in large quantity a lower unit purchase cost. For instance, Alpha Company quotes a list price of $500 for their machine, but if 100 are purchased, 20 percent reduction in list price is granted, and if more are purchased, a further 5 percent reduction is allowed. If Beta Company orders 140 machines, the invoice price will be:

On the first 100 units	
List ($500 × 100)	$50,000
Less 20%	(10,000)
	$40,000
On the next 40 units	
List ($500 × 40)	$20,000
Less 25%	(5,000)
	$15,000
Invoice gross cost	$55,000
Unit cost	$ 393

Both the sale and the purchase will be recorded at $55,000 so the **trade discount** is not reflected in the accounts. Any cash discount allowed will be calculated on the $55,000.

The advantage of trade discounts, besides stimulating volume sales, is that a sales catalogue can be published once, showing list prices. The firm can use the same catalogue for all customers and allow trade discounts as it sees fit.

gross price method
Setting up purchases/sales initially at their full amount without deducting any allowable cash discounts.

allowance method
Setting up purchases/sales initially at full amount, but setting up anticipated cash discounts as a valuation allowance.

net price method
Setting up purchases/sales initially at the full price less allowable cash discounts.

trade discount
A reduction in selling price from the full list price granted to customers who buy in large quantities usually.

Sales Returns

When a customer returns merchandise, the sale has been cancelled, and an entry that reverses the sale is appropriate. In analyzing sales activities, however, management may be interested in the amount of goods returned. If so, a sales contra account is used to accumulate the amount of returns for a particular period.

A cash refund, such as might be made in a retail store when a customer returns merchandise that had been purchased for cash, would be entered as:

Sales Returns	$23	
Cash on Hand		$23

Return of goods by a customer who buys "on account" usually involves the preparation of a credit memorandum, which is the reverse of a sales invoice. The credit memorandum lists the goods that have been returned and indicates the dollar amount that is to be allowed the customer. The entry to record the issuance of the credit is normally a debit to the **sales returns** account and a credit to the Accounts Receivable account.

Misleading sales and income amounts can result if goods are returned in a period after the period of sale. If there is no adjustment in the period of sale for estimated returns, the sales and income amounts for the period of sale are overstated, because they reflect transactions that are later cancelled. Further, sales and revenue amounts are correspondingly understated in the period when the goods are returned. An allowance method for estimated returns similar to that for estimated uncollectable accounts could be used. Because the amounts of sales returns for most businesses are usually relatively small, however, an allowance method is not often used.

Sales Allowances

A **sales allowance** is a reduction in price granted to a customer, usually after the goods have been delivered and found to be unsatisfactory or damaged. Again, as for sales returns, the effect is a reduction in the sales revenue, but it may be desirable to accumulate the amount of such adjustments as a separate item. An account, Sales Allowances, may be used for this purpose, or a combined account title, Sales Returns and Allowances, may be used. The recordkeeping problems are similar to those caused by sales returns.

sales returns & allowances
Reductions granted to customers from the amount owing because the goods were returned or were in some way sub-standard.

Presentation of Sales Adjustments in the Income Statement

In discussing the complications that accompany accounts receivable, several adjustments to sales that are accumulated in revenue contra accounts have been introduced. All of these adjustments — for cash discounts, for returns, and for allowances — are illustrated in the Alexis Co. Ltd.'s income statement in Exhibit 3.3.

EXHIBIT 3.3
Income Statement Illustration of Sales and
Sales Adjustments, Alexis Co. Ltd.
Partial Income Statement for the Year Ended June 30, Year 6

Revenues:			
Sales—Gross		$515,200	
Less: Sales Adjustments			
Cash Discounts Taken[a]	$33,900		
Allowances	11,000		
Returns	8,600		
Total Sales Adjustments		(53,500)	
Net Sales			$461,700

[a]*The gross price method is used. If the net price method were used, discounts taken would not be shown and there would be an addition to revenue for the amount of sales discounts that lapsed.*

Adjustment for Sales Allowances

The vendor may occasionally grant allowances to the purchaser to compensate for unsatisfactory merchandise. In these cases, the amount of cash the vendor eventually receives will be less than the stated selling price. The allowances are netted against the gross revenues to determine the net revenue.

DISCUSSION CASE 5

Impact of Sales Terms on Pricing

The concept of pricing is frequently confined to the identification of the price per unit charged to the customer on the sales invoice or as listed on the company's price sheet or in its catalogue. The terms and conditions of sale, often shown in fine print on the back of the invoice, are not always seen as having any direct bearing on price. In reality, they have a substantial impact on the actual price recovered, and in many instances serve to negate completely the effect of the pricing decision. Some of the sales terms are readily measurable as to the effect on price; others are not, being either hidden from view or misleading as to interpretation. In total they constitute an integral part of the pricing process, and the effects of each must be measured on a step-by-step basis to obtain the desired economic results.

One of the more obvious examples of pricing impact is the measurement of cash discounts allowed for early payment. Typical is the discount of "2% 10 days net 30." First, the discount is a direct reduction of 2% in the selling price, a reduction that will usually be taken by the customer,

(continued)

(continued)

even beyond the 10-day period allowed. Second, the offer of a 2% reduction for payment 20 days early — in 10 days rather than 30 — amounts to an annual interest rate of 36% per year, a payment for the use of money far in excess of the bank rate for funds even in times of double-digit inflation.

Taken together, these two points add up to the fact that cash discounts seldom work as intended, that in practice they routinely become nothing more than a price concession. Management is not deliberately offering 36% per annum for the use of money, but an alert customer will make the calculation properly and be quick to take advantage of it. Furthermore, the fact that many accounts take the discount well after the time allowed is evidence that customers regard it more as a price concession than a reward for early payment. Some companies attempt to charge back the unearned discount, a procedure that creates undesirable friction with their own customers, which the sales force would prefer to avoid.

Variations of the cash discount terms, such as "2% 10th prox," further complicate the picture by encouraging customers to bunch their orders around the first of the month to get the greatest leverage on the terms offered. This, obviously, can have the undesirable effect of creating peak work loads in order entry, shipping, and billing, with consequent dry periods toward month-end.

In short, cash discounts make little economic sense as payment for the use of funds and in practice become nothing more than a reduction of price. In recent years, the great majority of companies have found it to be an awkward vehicle for price adjustment and have abandoned it in favour of net terms.

References

Curtis W. Symonds, *Pricing for Profits* (New York: AMACOM Book Division, American Management Association, 1982), pp. 70–72. Reprinted with permission of Curtis W. Symonds.

Discussion Question

As company president, what would you do if your best customers started remitting after the expiry of the discount period but still deducted the cash discount from their remittances?

Adjustment for Delayed Payments

When the period between the sale of the goods or services and the time of cash collection extends over a year or more and there is no provision for explicit interest payments, the selling price probably includes an interest charge for the right to delay payment. Under the accrual basis of accounting, this interest element is recognized as interest revenue during the periods between sale and collection when the loan is outstanding. To recognize all potential revenue entirely in the period of sale would be to recognize too soon the return for services rendered over time in lending money. Thus, when cash collection is to be delayed beyond one year, the measure of revenue for the current period should be the selling price reduced to account for interest during future periods. Only the *present value* at the time of sale of the amount to be received should be recognized as revenue during the period of sale. For most accounts receivable, the period between sale and collection spans only two to three months. The interest element is likely to be relatively insignificant in these cases. As a result, in accounting practice, no reduction for interest on delayed payments is made for receivables to be collected within one year or less. This procedure is a practical expedient rather than a strict following of the underlying accounting theory.

TIMING OF EXPENSE RECOGNITION

Assets provide future benefits to the firm and thus represent **unexpired costs**. As the benefits are consumed in revenue generating process, this is noted by transferring the costs to the income statement where they are called **expired costs**, or more commonly, expenses. One of the major tasks facing accountants is to decide when to make this transfer. There are two principal expense recognition policies used:

1. Asset expirations directly associated with particular types of revenue are expenses in the period in which the revenues are recognized. This treatment is called the **matching principle**, because cost expirations are matched with revenues.

2. Asset expirations not associated with revenues are expenses of the period in which services are consumed in operations.

Product Costs

The cost of goods or merchandise sold is perhaps the easiest expense to associate with revenue. At the time of sale, the asset physically changes hands. Revenue is recognized, and the cost of the merchandise transferred is treated as an expense.

A *merchandising firm* purchases inventory and later sells it without changing its physical form. The inventory appears as an asset stated at acquisition cost on the balance sheet. Later, when the inventory is sold, the same amount of acquisition cost appears as an expense (cost of goods sold) on the income statement.

A *manufacturing firm*, on the other hand, incurs various costs in changing the physical form of the goods it produces. There are three types of cost: (1) direct material, (2) direct labour, and (3) manufacturing overhead (sometimes called indirect manufacturing costs). Direct material and direct labour costs are associated directly with particular products manufactured. Manufacturing overhead includes a mixture of costs that provide a firm with a capacity to produce. Examples of manufacturing overhead costs are expenditures for utilities, property taxes, and insurance on the factory, as well as depreciation on manufacturing plant and equipment. The services of each of these items are used up during the period while the firm is creating new assets — the inventory of goods being worked upon or held for sale. Benefits from direct material, direct labour, and manufacturing overhead are

unexpired costs
Assets.

expired costs
Expenses or losses.

matching principle
A primary objective of the accounting process, which is to show revenues and costs associated with generating those revenues in the same income statement.

product costs
The costs properly associated with the product being produced (as opposed to the period in which the costs are incurred). Product costs are period costs (expenses) when the related products are sold.

transferred to, or become part of, the asset represented by units of inventory. Because the inventory items are assets until sales are made to customers, the various direct material, direct labour, and manufacturing overhead costs incurred in producing the goods are included in the manufacturing inventory under the titles Work-in-Process Inventory and Finished Goods Inventory. Such costs, which are assets transformed from one form to another, are called **product costs**. Product costs are assets; they become expenses only when the goods in which they are embodied are sold. Chapter 4 discusses more fully the accounting for manufacturing costs.

Revenue-Related Expenses

Revenue-related expenses are those expenses that occur after a sale has been made. Some of these expenses, such as sales commissions, are known with certainty at the time of sale. Others, such as *bad debts* or *cash discounts*, can only be estimated at the time of sale because the amount of the expense depends on the future action of the customer in paying the account by the discount date, or in failing to pay. These expenses should attach to the period when the revenue is recognized and not to a later period when the specific customer's account is found to be uncollectable, or when the customer has taken advantage of the discount for prompt payment. If the recognition of these items is postponed, reported income of the subsequent periods will be reduced by an earlier decision to extend credit and discount terms to the customer. Thus, the performance of the firm for both the period of sale and the subsequent period will be measured inaccurately.

A question arises whether bad debts and cash discounts should be considered as a reduction of revenue or as a business expense. Although it may be argued theoretically that these items are reductions in revenue, since revenue should be measured on a cash-equivalent basis, the general practice is to treat them as business expenses. The general practice will be followed in the illustrations in this chapter.

Selling Costs

In most cases, the cost incurred in selling, or marketing, a firm's products relate to the units sold during the period. For example, salaries and commissions of the sales staff, sales literature used, and most advertising costs are incurred in generating revenue currently. Because these selling costs are associated with the revenues of the period, they are reported as expenses in the period when their services are used. It can be argued that some selling costs, such as advertising and other sales promotion, provide future-period benefits for a firm and should continue to be treated as assets. However, distinguishing the portion of the cost relating to the current period (to be recognized as an expense) from the portion relating to future periods (to be treated as an asset) can be extremely difficult. Accountants, therefore, treat selling and other marketing activity costs as expenses of the period when the services are used. These selling costs are treated as **period expenses** rather than as assets, even though they may enhance the future marketability of a firm's products.

period expenses
Period costs. Associated with the period in which they are incurred (rather than with the product being produced).

Administrative Costs

The costs incurred in administering the activities of the firm cannot be closely associated with units produced and sold and, like selling costs, are treated as period expenses. Examples include the president's salary, accounting and data-processing costs, and the costs of conducting various supportive activities, such as legal services and corporate planning.

Financial Costs

Some firms limit the amount of funds provided by creditors and finance the majority of asset acquisition from funds received from the issue of shares, or from the retention of income that is not paid to the shareholders as cash dividends. Other firms minimize the shareholders' contribution to asset acquisition and borrow substantial amounts with repayment obligation. The form of financing should not influence operating decisions, and financing activities are ordinarily separated from operating activities. To reflect this separation, the results of operating and financial activities may be separated in the income statement. The costs and revenues resulting from the financing activities arise from the passage of time and are treated as period expenses. Examples include interest paid on bank loans, notes payable, bonds payable, mortgages payable, and financial income from interest-bearing bank deposits, notes receivable, investment in bonds and shares of other companies, and investment in government bonds.

MEASUREMENT OF EXPENSES

Expenses represent assets consumed during the period. The amount of an expense is therefore the cost of the expired asset. Thus, the basis for expense measurement is the same as for asset valuation. Because assets are primarily stated at acquisition cost on the balance sheet, expenses are measured by the acquisition cost of the assets that were either sold or used during the period.

SUMMARY

The *amount* of income from operating activities is equal to the difference between the cash received from customers and the amount of cash paid to suppliers, employees, and other providers of goods and services. However, cash receipts from customers do not always occur in the same accounting period as the related cash expenditures to the providers of goods and services. To obtain a measure of operating performance in which outflows are matched more effectively with inflows, the accrual basis of accounting is used.

The accrual basis determines the *timing* of income recognition. Revenue is typically recognized at the time of sale under the accrual basis. Costs that can be associated directly with particular revenues become expenses in the period when revenues are recognized. The cost of acquiring or manufacturing inventory items is treated in this manner. Costs that cannot be closely associated with particular revenue streams become expenses of the period when goods or services are consumed in operations. Most selling and administrative costs are treated in this manner.

The accounting procedures for preparing the income statement are considered next.

OVERVIEW OF ACCOUNTING PROCEDURES

RELATIONSHIP BETWEEN BALANCE SHEET AND INCOME STATEMENT

balance sheet equation The algebraic expression that governs the relationship among the three principal components of the balance sheet, expressed as: assets = liabilities + owners' equity.

Net income, or earnings, for a period measures the excess of revenues (net asset inflows) over expenses (net asset outflows) from selling goods and providing services. Dividends measure the net assets distributed to shareholders. The Retained Earnings account on the balance sheet measures the cumulative excess of earnings over dividends since the firm began operations. The following disaggregation of the **balance sheet equation** helps to show the relation of revenues, expenses, and dividends to the components of the balance sheet.

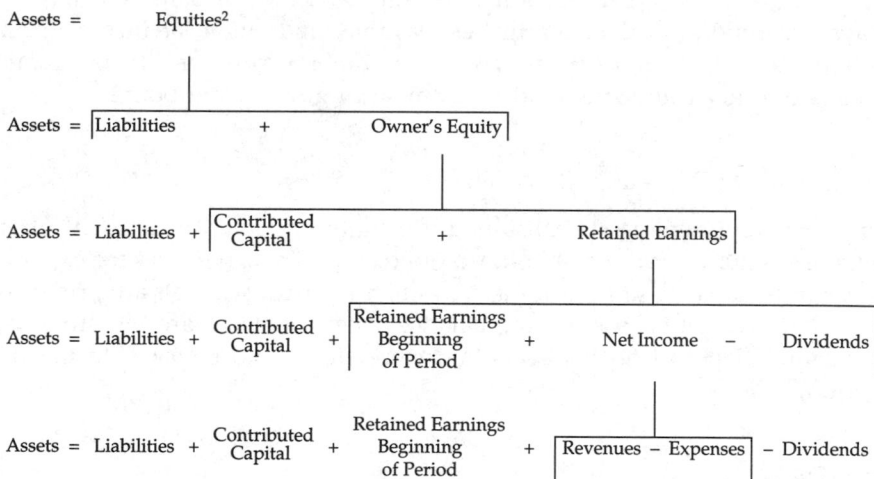

PURPOSE AND USE OF INDIVIDUAL REVENUE AND EXPENSE ACCOUNTS

Revenue and expense amounts could be recorded directly in the Retained Earnings account. For example, the sale of merchandise on account results in an increase in assets (accounts receivable) and retained earnings (sales revenue) and a decrease in assets (merchandise inventory) and retained

[2] Equities are sometimes defined as "claims to assets." Liabilities are claims by the creditors, and owner's equity relates to residual claims by the owners. The word *residual* signifies that creditors have first claim to the assets if the firm is dissolved.

earnings (cost of merchandise sold). Measuring the *amount* of net income would be relatively simple if revenues and expenses were recorded directly in the Retained Earnings account. Net income would be computed from the following equation:

$$\text{Net Income} = \frac{\text{Retained Earnings}}{\text{End of Period}} - \frac{\text{Retained Earnings}}{\text{Beginning of Period}} + \text{Dividends}$$

The income statement is not designed merely to report net income. As the equation above indicates, the amount of net income can be deduced from the change in the Retained Earnings account. Rather, the income statement is designed to report the sources and amounts of a firm's revenues, and the nature and amounts of a firm's expenses that sum to income for the period. Knowledge of the components of a firm's net income is helpful both in appraising past performance and in forecasting future performance.

To help in preparing the income statement, individual revenue and expense accounts are maintained during the accounting period. These accounts begin the accounting period with a zero balance. During the period, revenues and expenses are recorded in the accounts as they arise. At the end of the period, the balance in each revenue and expense account represents the cumulative revenues and expenses *for the period*. These amounts are reported in the income statement, which shows the net income of the period.

Because revenues and expenses are basically components of retained earnings, the balance in each revenue and expense account is transferred at the end of the period to the retained earnings account. Each revenue and expense account will then have a zero balance after the transfer. Retained earnings will be increased by the amount of net income (or decreased by the net loss) for the period.

The end result of maintaining separate revenue and expense accounts during the period and transferring their balances to the Retained Earnings account at the end of the period is the same as if revenues and expenses were initially recorded directly in the Retained Earnings account. Using separate revenue and expense accounts facilitates preparation of the income statement, which shows specific types of revenues and expenses. Once this purpose has been served, the need for separate revenue and expense accounts *for a given accounting period* has ended. Having been reduced to a zero balance at the end of the accounting period, these accounts begin the following accounting period with a zero balance and are therefore ready for entry of the revenue and expense amounts of the following period.

The process of transferring the balances in revenue and expense accounts to retained earnings is referred to as the **closing process**, because each revenue and expense account is closed, or reduced to a zero balance. Revenue and expense accounts accumulate amounts for only a single accounting period, and are therefore **temporary accounts**. On the other hand, the balance sheet accounts reflect the cumulative changes in each account from the time the firm was first organized, and are not closed each period. The balances in these accounts at the end of one period are carried over as the beginning balances of the following period. Balance sheet accounts are **permanent accounts**.

closing process
The process of determining the net income for the period. Mechanically, closing refers to the ruling off of temporary accounts in the general ledger and transferring their balances to an income summary account using closing journal entries.

temporary accounts
Accounts that do not appear on the balance sheet. Revenue and expense accounts, their adjuncts and contras, production cost accounts, income distribution accounts, and purchase-related accounts (which are closed to the various inventories). Sometimes called "nominal accounts."

permanent accounts
Accounts that appear on the balance sheet and are not closed at the end of each accounting period; contrast with temporary accounts.

DEBIT AND CREDIT PROCEDURES FOR REVENUES, EXPENSES, AND DIVIDENDS

Because revenues, expenses, and dividends are components of retained earnings, the recording procedures for these items are the same as for any other transaction affecting owner's equity accounts.

Shareholders' Equity

Decreases (Debit)	Increases (Credit)
Expenses	Issues of Share Capital
Dividends	Revenues

A transaction giving rise to revenue results in an increase in net assets (increase in assets or decrease in liabilities) and an increase in shareholders' equity. The usual journal entry to record a revenue transaction is therefore:

Asset (A) Increase or Liability (L) Decrease	Amount	
Revenue (SE)		Amount
Typical entry to recognize revenue.		

A transaction giving rise to expense results in a decrease in net assets (decrease in assets or increase in liabilities) and a decrease in shareholders' equity. The usual journal entry to record an expense is therefore:

Expense (SE)	Amount	
Asset (A) Decrease or Liability (L) Increase		Amount
Typical entry to record expense.		

Dividends result in a decrease in net assets and a decrease in shareholders' equity. As we discuss in Chapter 11, dividends may be paid either in cash or in other assets. Although the accounting procedures for dividends are similar regardless of the form of the distribution, we assume that cash is used unless information is provided to the contrary. The usual entry to record the declaration of a dividend by the board of directors of a corporation is:

Retained Earnings (SE)	Amount	
Dividends Payable (L)		Amount
Typical entry to record dividend declaration.		

The journal entry to record the actual payment of the dividend is:

Dividends Payable (L)	Amount	
Cash (A)		Amount
Typical entry to record dividend payment.		

A conceptual error sometimes made is that of treating dividends as an expense on the income statement. *Dividends are not expenses*. They are not costs incurred in *generating* revenues. Rather, they represent *distributions* of assets arising from current and prior years' operations to the owners of the firm.[3]

Before illustrating the recording procedures for revenues and expenses, it may be helpful to review briefly the steps in the accounting process.

REVIEW OF THE ACCOUNTING PROCESS

The steps in the accounting process, discussed in Chapter 2, are summarized as follows:

Journalizing   Each transaction or series of transactions during the period is recorded in journal entry form in the general journal (or in a special journal that supplements the general journal).

Posting   At periodic intervals, the entries in the general journal are posted to the accounts in the general ledger.

Trial Balance   At the end of the accounting period, the balance in each general ledger account is calculated and a trial balance is prepared. A trial balance is a listing of all accounts in the general ledger that have balances. If the recording process has been carried out properly, the total amount in accounts having debit balances must equal the total amount in accounts having credit balances.

Adjusting Entries   During the period, some accounting events may be only partially recorded, not recorded at all, or recorded incorrectly. Before the financial statements can be prepared at the end of the period, the omissions must be accounted for and the errors corrected. The entries to do this are known as **adjusting entries**. These entries are made so that revenues and expenses are reported in appropriate accounts with correct amounts, and so that balance sheet accounts show correct amounts of assets and equities at the end of the period.

Statement Preparation   The balance sheet, income statement, statement of changes in financial position, and any desired supporting schedules (for example, an analysis of changes in the Cash, Buildings and Equipment, or Retained Earnings accounts) are then prepared.

adjusting entries
Those entries resulting from an attempt to reflect in the accounts various changes that may be appropriate, although no source document is normally available; usually, they involve accruals or deferrals.

ILLUSTRATION OF THE ACCOUNTING PROCESS FOR A MERCHANDISING FIRM

Stephen's Shoe Store, Inc. has been in business since Year 1. A trial balance taken from its general ledger accounts on January 1, Year 4, the first day

---

[3] An alternative method for recording dividends is to debit an account, Dividends Declared. At the end of the accounting period, the balance in the Dividends Declared account is closed to the Retained Earnings account, thereby reducing the balance of Retained Earnings. The end result is a debit to Retained Earnings and a credit to Dividends Payable for the amount of dividends declared during the period. Because the account, Dividends Declared, is closed in a manner similar to that for an expense account at the end of the accounting period, this method of recording the dividend sometimes leads to the erroneous treatment of dividends as expenses. In this book, declarations of dividends are debited directly to Retained Earnings.

of an accounting period, is shown in Exhibit 3.4. To facilitate understanding, in this illustration the asset accounts are designated (A), the liability accounts (L), and the shareholders' equity (including revenue and expense) accounts (SE). Trial balances do not usually contain such designations.

EXHIBIT 3.4
STEPHEN'S SHOE STORE, INC.
Trial Balance
January 1, Year 4

	Accounts with Debit Balances	Accounts with Credit Balances
Cash (A)	$ 30,000	
Accounts Receivable (A)	63,000	
Merchandise Inventory (A)	175,000	
Land (A)	100,000	
Building and Equipment (A)	525,000	
Accumulated Depreciation (XA)		$ 85,000
Accounts Payable (L)		115,000
Income Tax Payable (L)		20,000
Bonds Payable (L)		100,000
Common Stock (SE)		250,000
Contributed Surplus (SE)		200,000
Retained Earnings (SE)		123,000
Total	$893,000	$893,000

Note that the revenue and expense accounts do not appear in this trial balance; they have zero balances at the beginning of an accounting period. One of the accounts in the trial balance, Accumulated Depreciation, has not previously been considered. This account is presented on the balance sheet as a deduction from Building and Equipment. (See Exhibit 3.10 for balance sheet presentation of this account.) Because of this manner of disclosure, this account is referred to as a **contra account**. A contra account accumulates amounts that are subtracted from the amount in another account. The nature and use of these contra accounts are discussed later in this illustration. The asset contra account in the trial balance (Exhibit 3.6) is designated (XA).

JOURNALIZING

The transactions of Stephen's Shoe Store during Year 4 and the appropriate journal entries at the time of the transactions follow.

1. The firm purchases merchandise on account costing $355,000.

Merchandise Inventory (A)	$355,000	
Accounts Payable (L)		$355,000

2. Sales during the year are $625,000, of which $255,000 are for cash and the remainder are on account.

Cash (A)	$225,000	
Accounts Receivable (A)	400,000	
Sales Revenue (SE)		$625,000

3. The cost of merchandise sold during Year 4 is $390,000

Cost of Goods (SE)	$390,000	
Merchandise Inventory (A)		$390,000

4. The firm pays salaries in cash of $110,000 during the year.

Salaries Expense (SE)	$110,000	
Cash (A)		$110,000

5. The firm collects cash of $325,000 from customers who had purchased on account.

Cash (A)	$325,000	
Accounts Receivable (A)		$325,000

6. The firm pays $250,000 to merchandise suppliers for purchases that have been made on account.

Accounts Payable (L)	$250,000	
Cash (A)		$250,000

7. The firm makes a payment of $20,000 to the government for Year 3 income taxes.

Income Tax Payable (L)	$20,000	
Cash (A)		$20,000

8. The firm pays a premium of $1,500 on January 1, Year 4, for a three-year property and liability insurance policy.

Prepaid Insurance (A)	$1,500	
Cash (A)		$1,500

The debit in this entry, made on January 1, Year 4, is to an asset account, because the insurance provides three years of coverage beginning on that date. The entry to reduce the Prepaid Insurance account and to record the insurance expense for Year 4 is one of the adjusting entries made at the end of the accounting period, and is illustrated later.

9. Warehouse space not needed in the company's operations is rented out for one year beginning December 1, Year 4. The annual rental of $600 is received at that time.

Cash (A)	$600	
Advances from Tenants (L)		$600

10. On December 31, Year 4, the firm pays annual interest at 8 percent on the long-term bonds outstanding: $0.08 \times \$100,000 = \$8,000$.

Interest Expense (SE)	$8,000	
Cash (A)		$8,000

11. A customer who had purchased merchandise on account for $10,000 has experienced financial difficulty and has been unable to pay for the goods on time. The customer now promises to pay $10,000 in 90 days with interest at 9 percent per year. As evidence of that promise, the customer gives a promissory note. On November 1, Year 4, Stephen's Shoe Store accepts the 90-day note for $10,000 bearing interest at 9 percent in settlement of the open account receivable.

Notes Receivable (A)	$10,000	
Accounts Receivable (A)		$10,000

12. The board of directors declared a cash dividend of $15,000 on December 28, Year 4. The dividend is to be paid on January 20, Year 5.

Retained Earnings (SE)	$15,000	
Dividends Payable (L)		$15,000

POSTING

The entries in the general journal are posted to the appropriate general ledger accounts. In this illustration, the posting operation takes place on December 31, Year 4. The T-accounts in Exhibit 3.5 show the opening balances from the trial balance in Exhibit 3.4 and the effects of transactions (1) through (12).

EXHIBIT 3.5
Stephen's Shoe Store, Inc.
T-Accounts Showing Beginning Balances, Transactions During Year 4, and Ending Balance Before Adjusting Entries

Cash (A)			
Bal. 1/1	30,000		
(2)	225,000	110,000	(4)
(5)	325,000	250,000	(6)
		20,000	(7)
		1,500	(8)
(9)	600	8,000	(10)
Bal. 12/31	191,100		

Accounts Receivable (A)			
Bal. 1/1	63,000		
(2)	400,000	325,000	(5)
		10,000	(11)
Bal. 12/31	128,000		

Notes Receivable (A)		
Bal. 1/1	0	
(11)	10,000	
Bal. 12/31	10,000	

Merchandise Inventory (A)			
Bal. 1/1	175,000		
(1)	355,000	390,000	(3)
Bal. 12/31	140,000		

Prepaid Insurance (A)		
Bal. 1/1	0	
(8)	1,500	
Bal. 12/31	1,500	

Land (A)		
Bal. 1/1	100,000	
Bal. 12/31	100,000	

Building and Equipment (A)		
Bal. 1/1	525,000	
Bal. 12/31	525,000	

Accumulated Depreciation (XA)		
	85,000	Bal. 1/1
	85,000	Bal. 12/31

Accounts Payable (L)			
		115,000	Bal. 1/1
(6)	250,000	355,000	(1)
		220,000	Bal. 12/31

Income Tax Payable (L)			
		20,000	Bal. 1/1
(7)	20,000		
		0	Bal. 12/31

Dividends Payable (L)			
		0	Bal. 1/1
		15,000	(12)
		15,000	Bal. 12/31

Advances from Tenants (L)		
	0	Bal. 1/1
	600	(9)
	600	Bal. 12/31

Bonds Payable (L)		
	100,000	Bal. 1/1
	100,000	Bal. 12/31

Common Stock (SE)		
	250,000	Bal. 1/1
	250,000	Bal. 12/31

Contributed Surplus (SE)		
	200,000	Bal. 1/1
	200,000	Bal. 12/31

Retained Earnings (SE)			
(12)	15,000	123,000	Bal. 4/1
		108,000	Bal. 12/31

Sales Revenue (SE)		
	0	Bal. 1/1
	625,000	(2)
	625,000	Bal. 12/31

Cost of Goods Sold (SE)		
Bal. 1/1	0	
(3)	390,000	
Bal. 12/31	390,000	

Salaries Expense (SE)		
Bal. 1/1	0	
(4)	110,000	
Bal. 12/31	110,000	

Interest Expense (SE)		
Bal. 1/1	0	
(10)	8,000	
Bal. 12/31	8,000	

Trial Balance Preparation

The trial balance prepared at the end of the accounting period before adjusting and closing entries is called an **unadjusted trial balance**. The unadjusted trial balance of Stephen's Shoe Store as of December 31, Year 4, appears in Exhibit 3.6. The amounts in the unadjusted trial balance are taken directly from the ending balances in the T-accounts in Exhibit 3.5.

unadjusted trial balance
A trial balance of the general ledger accounts taken before the adjusting step of the accounting cycle.

EXHIBIT 3.6
STEPHEN'S SHOE STORE, INC.
Unadjusted Trial Balance, December 31, Year 4

	Accounts with Debit Balances	Accounts with Credit Balances
Cash (A)	$ 191,000	
Accounts Receivable (A)	128,000	
Notes Receivable (A)	10,000	
Merchandise Inventory (A)	140,000	
Prepaid Insurance (A)	1,500	
Land (A)	100,000	
Building and Equipment (A)	525,000	
Accumulated Depreciation (XA)		$ 85,000
Accounts Payable (L)		220,000
Dividends Payable (L)		15,000
Advances from Tenants		600
Bonds Payable (L)		100,000
Common Stock (SE)		250,000
Contributed Surplus (SE)		200,000
Retained Earnings (SE)		108,000
Sales Revenue (SE)		625,000
Cost of Goods Sold (SE)	390,000	
Salaries Expense (SE)	110,000	
Interest Expense (SE)	8,000	
Totals	$1,603,600	$1,603,600

ADJUSTING ENTRIES

The entries in the general journal made during the year result from transactions between the firm and outsiders (for example, suppliers, employees, customers, and governmental units). Other events that continuously occur, however, involve no specific transaction to signal the requirement for a journal entry, but must be considered in measuring net income for the period and financial position at the end of the period. For example, building and equipment are used continuously in the process of generating revenue. Because the services of these assets are consumed during the period, a portion of their acquisition cost must be recorded as an expense. Similarly, insurance coverage expires continuously throughout the year. Because the services of the asset are gradually consumed, a portion of the asset, Prepaid Insurance, must be recorded as an expense.

Other kinds of events occur that affect the revenues and expenses of the period but do not involve a cash transaction with an outsider until a subsequent period. For example, salaries and wages are earned by administrative employees during the last several days of the current accounting period, but they will not be paid until the following accounting period. Such salaries and wages, although payable in the next period, are expenses of the current period when the labour services are consumed. Similarly, interest accrues on a firm's notes receivable or payable. Interest will be collected or paid in a subsequent period, but a portion of the interest should be recognized as revenue or expenses in the current period.

Adjusting entries are prepared at the end of the accounting period. These entries alter the balances in the general ledger accounts in order to recognize all revenues and expenses for the proper reporting of net income and financial position. The following sections illustrate several examples of adjusting entries for Stephen's Shoe Store.

Recognition of Accrued Revenues and Receivables

Revenue is earned as servcies are rendered. For example, rent is earned as a tenant uses the property. Interest, a "rent" for the use of money, is earned from a loan as time passes. Recording these amounts as they accrue day by day is usually not convenient, however. At the end of the accounting period, there may be some situations in which revenue has been earned but for which no entry has been made, either because cash has not been received or because the time has not arrived for a formal invoice to be sent to the customer. A claim has come into existence that, although it may not be due immediately, should appear on the balance sheet as an asset and must be reflected in the revenues of the period. The purpose of the adjusting entry for interest eventually receivable by the lender is to recognize on the balance sheet the right to receive cash in an amount equal to the interest already earned and to recognize the same amount as revenue on the income statement for the period.

Stephen's Shoe Store received a 90-day note from a customer on November 1, Year 4. At year-end, the note already appears on the trial balance. Interest earned during November and December, however, does not appear in the unadjusted trial balance. The note earns interest at the rate of 9 percent per year. By convention in business practice, interest rates stated on loans are almost always stated as annual interest rates. Also by convention, a year equal to 12 months of 30 days each, or 360 days, is usually assumed to simplify the calculation of interest earned. Interest of $150 is earned by Stephen's Shoe Store, Inc. during November and December. This amount is equal to the $10,000 principal times the 9 percent annual interest rate times the elapsed 60 days divided by 360 days ($150 = $10,000 × 0.09 × 60/360). The adjusting entry to recognize the asset, Interest Receivable, and the interest earned is:

(13) Interest Receivable (A)	$150	
Interest Revenue (SE)		$150

Recognition of Accrued Expenses and Payables

As various services are received, their cost should be reflected in the financial statements, whether or not payment has been made or an invoice received. Here, also, recording these amounts day by day is frequently not convenient. Some adjustment of expenses and liabilities will probably be necessary at the end of the accounting period.

Salaries and wages earned during the last several days of the accounting period, which will not be paid until the following accounting period, illustrate this type of adjustment. According to payroll records, employees of

Stephen's Shoe Store earned salaries of $14,000 during the last several days of Year 4 that were not recorded at year-end. The adjusting entry is:

(14) Salaries Expense (SE)	$14,000	
Salaries Payable (L)		$14,000

Other examples of this type of adjusting entry include costs incurred for utilities, taxes, and interest.

Allocation of Prepaid Operating Costs

Another type of adjustment arises because assets are required for use in the operations of the firm but are not completely used during the accounting period in which they are acquired. For example, Stephen's Shoe Store paid $1,500 on January 1, Year 4, for a three-year insurance policy. During Year 4, one-third of the coverage expired, so $500 of the premium should be removed from the asset account and reflected as insurance expense. The balance sheet on December 31, Year 4, should show $1,000 of prepaid insurance as an asset, because this portion of the premium is a future benefit — the asset of insurance coverage to be received over the next two years.

The nature of the adjusting entry to record an asset expiration as an expense depends on the recording of the original payment. If the payment resulted in a debit to an asset account, the adjusting entry must reduce the asset and increase the expense for the services used up during the accounting period. Stephen's Shoe Store had recorded in entry (8), as discussed on page 141, the payment of the insurance premium on January 1, Year 4, as follows:

(8) Prepaid Insurance (A)	$1,500	
Cash (A)		$1,500

The adjusting entry is therefore:

(15) Insurance Expenses (SE)	$500	
Prepaid Insurance (A)		$500

Insurance expense for Year 4 is $500, and prepaid insurance in the amount of $1,000 appears as an asset on the balance sheet on December 31, Year 4.

Alternative Procedure   Instead of debiting an asset account at the time the premium is paid, some firms debit an expense account. For example, Stephen's Shoe Store might have recorded the original premium payment as follows:

(8a) Insurance Expense (SE)	$1,500	
Cash (A)		$1,500

Because many operating costs become expenses in the period in which the expenditure is made (for example, monthly rent), this second procedure for recording expenditures during the year sometimes reduces the number of adjusting entries that must be made at year-end. In the situation with the insurance policy, however, not all of the $1,500 premium paid is an expense of Year 4. If the original journal entry had been (8a), the adjusting entry would have been:

(15a) Prepaid Insurance (A)	$1,000	
Insurance Expense (SE)		$1,000

After the original entry in (8a) and the adjusting entry in (15a), insurance expense for Year 4 would be reflected in the accounts at $500, and prepaid insurance at $1,000. The *result* of these two approaches to recording the original payment of the premium is the same. The *adjusting entries*, however, are quite different. (See Problem 3 for Self-Study at the end of the chapter.)

Recognition of Depreciation

When assets such as buildings, machinery, furniture, and trucks are purchased, their acquistion cost is debited to appropriate asset accounts. Although these assets may provide services for a number of years, their future benefits expire as time passes. The asset's cost is spread systematically over its estimated useful life. The charge made to the current operations for the portion of the cost of such assets consumed during the current period is called **depreciation**. Depreciation involves nothing new in principle; it is identical with the procedure for prepaid operating costs presented previously. For example, the cost of a building is a prepayment for a series of future services, and depreciation allocates the cost of the services to the periods in which services are received and used.

Various accounting methods are used in allocating the acquisition cost of long-term assets to the periods of benefit. One widely used method is the **straight-line method**. Under this procedure, an equal portion of the acquisition cost less estimated salvage value is allocated to each period of the asset's estimated useful life. The depreciation charge for each period is computed as follows:

$$\frac{\text{Acquisition Cost} - \text{Estimated Salvage Value}}{\text{Estimated Useful Life in Periods}} = \frac{\text{Depreciation Charge for}}{\text{Each Period}}$$

Internal records indicate that the Building and Equipment account of Stephen's Shoe Store comprises a store building with an acquisition cost of $400,000 and a group of items of equipment with an acquisition cost of $125,000. At the time the building was acquired, it had an estimated 40-year useful life and a zero salvage value. Depreciation expense for each year of the building's life is calculated to be:

$$\frac{\$400,000 - \$0}{40\,\text{years}} = \$10,000 \text{ per year}$$

At the time the equipment was acquired, it had an estimated useful life of six years and an estimated salvage value of $5,000. Annual depreciation is therefore:

depreciation
The decline in economic potential of limited-life assets because of wear, deterioration, and obsolescence.

straight-line method
A method of amortizing bond discount by transferring equal amounts to interest expense for equal periods of time. The concept is also applicable to depreciation.

$$\frac{\$125{,}000 - \$5{,}000}{6 \text{ years}} = \$20{,}000 \text{ per year}$$

The adjusting entry to record depreciation of $30,000 (= $10,000 + $20,000) for Year 4 is:

(16) Depreciation Expense (SE)	$30,000	
Accumulated Depreciation (XA)		$30,000

The credit in entry (16) could have been made directly to the Building and Equipment account, because the credit records the portion of the asset's cost that has expired, or become an expense, during Year 4. The same end result is achieved by crediting the Accumulated Depreciation account, a contra-asset account, then deducting the balance in this account from the acquisition cost of the assets in the Building and Equipment account on the balance sheet. Using the contra account enables the financial statements to show both the acquisition cost of the assets in use and the portion of that amount that has previously been recognized as an expense. Showing both acquisition cost and accumulated depreciation amounts separately provides a rough indication of the relative age of the firm's long-lived assets. (See Exercise 29 at the end of the chapter.)

Note that the Depreciation Expense account includes depreciation only for the current account period, while the Accumulated Depreciation account includes the cumulative depreciation charges on the present assets since acquisition.

Valuation of Liabilities

When a firm receives cash from customers before it sells merchandise or renders services, it incurs liabilities. For example, Stephen's Shoe Store received $600 on December 1, Year 4, as one year's rent on warehouse space. When the cash was received, the liability account, Advances from Tenants, was credited. One month's rent has been earned as of December 31, Year 4. The adjusting entry is:

(17) Advances from Tenants (L)	$50	
Rent Revenue (SE)		$50
To reduce liability from $600 to $550.		

The remaining $550 of the cash collected for rent is yet to be earned and appears on the December 31, Year 4 balance sheet as a liability.

Income Tax Expense

After the adjusting entries are recorded, a final entry for income tax expense is required for Stephen's Shoe Store, Inc. Corporate income tax payable for a period is based on the accounting net income before income tax of the period, adjusted for differences between accounting income and income for tax purposes. A rate specified by the Income Tax Act is applied to income for tax purposes.

For Year 4, there was no difference between accounting income before income tax and income for tax purposes. The rate of income tax was 40 percent and the income tax payable was $29,080 (= 0.40 × $72,700, from Exhibit 3.9).

(18) Income Tax Expense (SE)	$29,080	
Income Tax Payable (L)		$29,080

Correction of Errors

The process of checking, reviewing, and auditing at the end of the accounting period may uncover various errors and omissions. For example, the firm might have recorded the month's sales as $38,700 instead of $37,800. This is a very common error called a transposition error. A second common error is a slide, such as recording $37,800 as $378,000. Regardless of the nature of the error, if it is noticed before the books are closed, a simple adjusting entry will correct the records. Once the books have been closed, an adjustment to retained earnings is necessary. The latter procedure is discussed in Chapter 11. There were no errors of any type in the accounts of Stephen's Shoe Store.

Trial Balance After Adjusting Entries

The adjusting entries are posted or entered in the general ledger in the same manner as entries made during the year. A trial balance of the general ledger accounts after adjusting entries are made is called an **adjusted trial balance** and helps when preparing the financial statements. Exhibit 3.7 presents the trial balance data before and after adjusting entries for Stephen's Shoe Store. The exhibit indicates the effect of the adjustment process on the various accounts. The number in parentheses identifies the debit and credit components of each adjusting entry.

adjusted trial balance
A trial balance of the general ledger accounts taken after adjustments have been made.

Preparing Income Statement

The adjusted trial balance shows all revenue and expense accounts with their correct amounts for the period. The income statement can be prepared by listing all of the revenue accounts, listing all of the expense accounts, and showing the difference between the sum of the revenues and the sum of the expenses as net income. Revenue and expense accounts are temporary labels for portions of retained earnings. Once the adjusted trial balance has been prepared, the revenue and expense accounts have served their purpose for the current period and are closed.

CLOSING OF TEMPORARY ACCOUNTS

The closing process transfers the balances in the temporary revenue and expense accounts to Retained Earnings. A temporary account with a debit balance is closed by crediting it with the amount equal to its balance at the end of the period and debiting Retained Earnings. A temporary account with a credit balance is closed by debiting the temporary account and crediting Retained Earnings. After closing entries, the balances in all temporary

EXHIBIT 3.7
STEPHEN'S SHOE STORE, INC.
Trial Balance Before and After Adjusting Entries[a] December 31, Year 4

Accounts	Unadjusted Trial Balance		Adjusting Entries		Adjusted Trial Balance	
	Debit	Credit	Debit	Credit	Debit	Credit
Cash (A)	$ 191,100				$ 191,100	
Accounts Receivable (A)	128,000				128,000	
Notes Receivable (A)	10,000				10,000	
Interest Receivable (A)			150 (13)		150	
Merchandise Inventory (A)	140,000				140,000	
Prepaid Insurance (A)	1,500			$ 500 (15)	1,000	
Land (A)	100,000				100,000	
Building and Equipment (A)	525,000				525,000	
Accumulated Depreciation (XA)		$ 85,000		30,000 (16)		$ 115,000
Accounts Payable (L)		220,000				220,000
Salaries Payable (L)				14,000 (14)		14,000
Dividends Payable (L)		15,000				15,000
Income Tax Payable (L)				29,080 (18)		29,080
Advances from Tenants		600	50 (17)			550
Bonds Payable (L)		100,000				100,000
Common Stock (SE)		250,000				250,000
Contributed Surplus (SE)		200,000				200,000
Retained Earnings (SE)		108,000				108,000
Sales Revenue (SE)		625,000				625,000
Interest Revenue (SE)				150 (13)		150
Rent Revenue (SE)				50 (17)		50
Cost of Goods Sold (SE)	390,000				390,000	
Salaries Expense (SE)	110,000		14,000 (14)		124,000	
Interest Expense (SE)	8,000				8,000	
Insurance Expense (SE)			500 (15)		500	
Depreciation Expense (SE)			30,000 (16)		30,000	
Income Tax Expense (SE)			29,080 (18)		29,080	
Totals	$1,603,600	$1,603,600	$73,780	$73,780	$1,676,830	$1,676,830

[a]This convenient tabular form is often called a work sheet. Most work sheets are more elaborate than this one, but their purpose is the same — to display data in a form for easy computations and financial statement preparation. The typical work would not show just two final columns called Adjusted Trial Balance, but would show four columns: Income Statement Debit and Credit, and Balance Sheet Debit and Credit. The horizontal sum of the amounts in an income account is shown in the appropriate debit or credit income statement column of the work sheet. The horizontal sum of the amounts in a balance sheet account is shown in the appropriate debit or credit balance sheet column of the work sheet. See Appendix 3.2 for further explanation.

accounts are zero. The former debit (credit) balances in temporary accounts become debits (credits) in the Retained Earnings account.

Each temporary revenue and expense account could be closed by a separate entry. Some recording time is saved, however, by closing all revenue and expense accounts in a single entry as follows:

(19) Sales Revenue (SE)	$625,000	
Interest Revenue (SE)	150	
Rent Revenue (SE)	50	
Cost of Goods Sold (SE)		$390,000
Salaries Expense (SE)		124,000
Interest Expense (SE)		8,000
Insurance Expense (SE)		500
Depreciation Expense (SE)		30,000
Income Tax Expense (SE)		29,080
Retained Earnings (SE)		43,620

The amount credited to Retained Earnings is the difference between the amounts debited to revenue accounts and the amounts credited to expense accounts. This amount is the net income for the period.[4]

Alternative Closing Procedure

An alternative closing procedure uses a temporary *"Income Summary"* account. Individual revenue and expense accounts are first closed to the Income Summary account. The income statement is prepared using information on the individual revenues and expenses in the Income Summary account. The balance in the Income Summary account, representing net income for the period, is then closed to Retained Earnings.

For example, the entry to close the Sales Revenue account under this alternative procedure is:

(19a) Sales Revenue (SE)	$625,000	
Income Summary (SE)		$625,000

The entry to close the Cost of Goods Sold account is:

(19b) Income Summary (SE)	$390,000	
Cost of Goods Sold (SE)		$390,000

Similar closing entries are made for the other revenue and expense accounts. The Income Summary account will have a credit balance of

[4] The amount credited to Retained Earnings in the closing entry is called a *plug* and is equal to the net income transferred. When making some journal entries in accounting, often all debits are known, as are all but one of the credits (or vice versa). Because double-entry recording procedure requires equal debits and credits, the unknown quantity can be found by subtracting the sum of the known credits from the sum of all debits (or vice versa). This process is known as *plugging*.

EXHIBIT 3.8
Illustration of Income Summary
Account for Stephen's Shoe Store, Inc.

Income Summary Account (SE)

Cost of Goods Sold	$390,000	$625,000	Sales Revenue
Salaries Expense	124,000	150	Interest Revenue
Interest Expense	8,000	50	Rent Revenue
Insurance Expense	500	$625,200	
Depreciation Expense	30,000		
Income Tax Expense	29,080		
To Close Income	43,620		
Summary Account	$625,200		

Retained Earnings (SE)

		$123,000	Beginning Balance
Dividends	$15,000	43,620	Net Income
		$151,620	Ending Balance

$43,620 after all revenue and expense accounts have been closed. The balance in the Income Summary account is then transferred to Retained Earnings:

(19c) Income Summary (SE)	$43,620	
Retained Earnings (SE)		$43,620

The end result of both closing procedures is the same. Revenue and expense accounts, as well as the Income Summary account if one is used, have zero balances after closing entries, and the Retained Earnings account is increased by the net income for the period of $43,620. Exhibit 3.8 shows the Income Summary account for Stephen's Shoe Store after all revenue and expense accounts have been closed at the end of the period.

FINANCIAL STATEMENT PREPARATION

The income statement, balance sheet, and any desired supporting schedules can be prepared from information in the adjusted trial balance. Exhibit 3.9 presents the income statement of Stephen's Shoe Store for Year 4. Exhibit 3.10 presents the comparative balance sheets for December 31, Year 3 and Year 4. Exhibit 3.11 presents an analysis of changes in retained earnings. Companies are required to prepare comparative income statements and statements of retained earnings as well as comparative balance sheets. To simplify the illustration, single-year income and retained earnings statements are presented below.

EXHIBIT 3.9
STEPHEN'S SHOE STORE, INC.
Income Statement for the Year Ending
December 31, Year 4

Sales Revenue		$625,000
Less: Cost of Goods Sold		(390,000)
Gross Profit		$235,000
Less: Operating Expenses		
Salaries	$124,000	
Insurance	500	
Depreciation	30,000	(154,500)
Operating Profit		$ 80,500
Less: Financial Expenses		
Interest Expense	$ 8,000	
Less: Interest Earned	(150)	
Net Interest Expense	$ 7,850	
Less: Rent Earned	(50)	(7,800)
Net Income Before Income Tax		$ 72,700
Less: Income Tax Expense		(29,080)
Net Income		$ 43,620

EXHIBIT 3.10
STEPHEN'S SHOE STORE, INC.
Comparative Balance Sheet
December 31, Year 3 and Year 4

		December 31, Year 4		December 31, Year 3
ASSETS				
Current Assets:				
Cash		$191,100		$ 30,000
Accounts Receivable		128,000		63,000
Notes Receivable		10,000		—
Interest Receivable		150		—
Merchandise Inventory		140,000		175,000
Prepaid Insurance		1,000		—
Total Current Assets		$470,250		$268,000
Property, Plant, and Equipment:				
Land		$100,000		$100,000
Building and Equipment	$525,000		$525,000	
Less: Accumulated Depreciation	(115,000)		(85,000)	
Building and Equipment — net		410,000		440,000
Total Property, Plant, and Equipment		$510,000		$540,000
Total Assets		$980,250		$808,000
LIABILITIES AND SHAREHOLDERS' EQUITY				
Current Liabilities:				
Accounts Payable		$220,000		$115,000
Salaries Payable		14,000		—
Dividends Payable		15,000		—
Income Tax Payable		29,080		20,000
Advances from Tenants		550		—
Total Current Liabilities		$278,630		$135,000
Long-Term Debt:				
Bonds Payable		100,000		100,000
Total Liabilities		$378,630		$235,000
Shareholders' Equity:				
Common Stock — at par value		$250,000		$250,000
Contributed Surplus		200,000		200,000
Retained Earnings		151,620		123,000
Total Shareholders' Equity		$601,620		$573,000
Total Liabilities and Shareholders' Equity		$980,250		$808,000

EXHIBIT 3.11
STEPHEN'S SHOE STORE, INC.
Statement of Retained Earnings for the Year Ending
December 31, Year 4

Retained Earnings, December 31, Year 3		$123,000
Net Income	$43,620	
Less: Dividends	(15,000)	
Increase in Retained Earnings		28,620
Retained Earnings, December 31, Year 4		$151,620

DISCUSSION CASE 6

Computer Software for Accountants

Accounting involves the collection, recording, and summarizing of financial data about an organization — data processing. Today [1991], most organizations employ the technological assistance of computers in carrying out these activities, hence the term — *electronic data processing (EDP)*.

A computer performs the same functions as an individual in an accounting system. However, it can potentially perform them quicker, cheaper, and with less potential for error than an individual. In small companies computers are optional; in large companies they are a necessity.

The major difference between a DP and an EDP system is in storage media for the accounting data. In an EDP system, the journals and ledgers described in this chapter are stored on electromagnetic media (tape or disk). This has raised important new issues for the accountant to deal with, such as data integrity and data security.

A firm has the option of internally developing its own specialized programs for its accounting applications or purchasing "canned software" from commercial software houses. There are so many good packages available on the market today that most firms choose the latter option if they are using microcomputers.

These accounting software packages have the following general capabilities:

1. Transaction processing, journal and ledger maintenance, and financial statement preparation
2. Electronic spreadsheets
3. Database management systems

Programs that have the first capability are often referred to as general ledger packages. These packages include programs to handle the specialized journal functions we have discussed in this chapter, including receivables, payroll, payables, fixed assets, and inventory. The software will support the functions of journalizing and the updating of subsidiary ledgers, and control accounts. It can also include such functions as invoicing, preparing customer statements, and generating periodic reports. Most of the general ledger packages are quite user-friendly and relatively foolproof, so that accounting departments with little computer expertise can use them.

These systems can reduce clerical effort and errors, and some even have features that enhance internal control. A complete general ledger system can be acquired for under $500.

Some of the systems available in Canada include ACCPAC, Accounting Plus, BPI, MBSI, NewViews, Peachtree, Radio Shack, and Bedford. Every computer software store will carry one or more packages, and the sales staff can usually instruct purchasers on use.

(continued)

(continued)

Electronic spreadsheet software is used primarily for planning purposes in accounting. Such software is highly useful in "what if?" decisions. With one of these packages, the accountant can examine the effects of different sales prices, sales volumes, product costs, and so on. The computer algorithms will recast the income statement employing the new assumptions, so that the bottom-line impact of any accounting decision on income is immediately discernible.

Database management systems differ greatly in relative complexity and features. In general such a system can be used as the information management facility for the entire firm. Accounting, production, marketing, and human resources are all handled by the database system. The advantages of having one centralized information database increase with the size of the firm. Commercial packages include AB Master, RBase, dBase III Plus, Profile Plus, Watbase, and Info Star.

In Canada, there are literally dozens of small accounting software companies. Most produce products that are solid, viable alternatives to the growing number of American packages that have been "Canadianized." But the greatest problem is that most are known only regionally and are certainly not backed with the same marketing muscle of their American competition. Yet, the products represent reliable, hard-working and feature-packed products that deserve serious consideration. Here's a non-

representative sample of some of these products.

Eight years ago [1983], Edmonton's Comsoft Inc. started selling an accounting program out of an aircraft hangar, so it's no surprise that sales of its Abacus accounting system soon took off. It's now available in two versions. The high-end Abacus II package can keep financial history on sales to customers for as long as you like.

A currency-literate accounting system comes from Toronto's Informatic Systems. The company's industrial strength BCS Software can handle transactions in up to 15 different foreign currencies. You can report sales analyses and receivables listings in either the original currency or in Canadian dollars.

Business Vision is an integrated product with substantial features. The accounting is logical for neophytes, and comprehensive support is based in Toronto. Business Vision is highly recommended for first time users.

Classic Software, based in central Ontario, offers a strong, middle-priced modular software product featuring on-line local (in province) support. Our opinion is that this is a solid product and worthy of consideration as an alternative to better known names.

According to my Webster's dictionary, "mathesis" means "learning particularly mathematics." Toronto's Mathesis Inc. has developed a mathematically sound accounting program, Fiscal Knowledge, running under Microsoft's Excel spreadsheet.

(continued)

(continued)

It gives you a flexible, modifiable accounting program with all the calculation power of a spreadsheet.

For manufacturing and bill-of-material processing, Toronto's FLEX Software offers just that — flexibility. With this package, you have the capability of tailoring screens and options to your specific needs. Seldom has any package offered so much flexibility in being fitted to the user's environment.

Many small businesses have been successfully computerized using Fortune software. It is a modular package with accounting know-how. Accounting is presented in a logical, simple manner to end users. The pre-set general ledger account range generates glance sheets and income statements, and receivable, payable and inventory modules are also available. Fortune is a good introduction to computerization for timid and/or smaller businesses.

For the graphically inclined, there is NewViews from Q.W. Page Associates Inc., which offers a different approach to accounting. With the correct set-up, the client can run virtually any business, from sales of serialized items to electrical contracting — complete with inventory and invoicing. This package is a joy to the creative accounting types who like to design a set of books. But caveat emptor: correct set-up is mandatory.

Out of Peterborough, Ontario comes Shopkeeper, retailing for approximately $1,000. A small point-of-sale package with a cash drawer, it sports invoicing, accounts payable, accounts receivable and a general ledger. As with many vertical packages, the general ledger is basic in comparison with the POS system, but it's a useable, complete package.

Summation from Sumware Corporation is a fast and easy-to-use real-time accounting system. Its developers are Toronto's Murk brothers, and they've come up with one of the best-kept secrets for retail and wholesale accounting. Sumhow get your hands on it and take a look.

Another retailer's solution is TMAN, from Vancouver's Bold Point Software Ltd. Simple and inexpensive, it should ring bells for single-store establishments. It can be run as a stand-alone program or can be integrated with ACCPAC Bedford.

Vigilant Business Software comes in many flavours for just about every vertical taste. The Toronto-based software developer has complete accounting systems for wholesale distributors, professional firms, process manufacturers and many more. Billings and accounts receivables can be tracked in either Canadian or U.S. currency.

In general, an accountant no longer needs to know much about computers to enjoy the many advantages that computerized data processing can provide.

References

Includes material taken from Edward Hall, "A Land of Hewers of Wood and Creators of Software," *The Bottom Line*, May 1991, p. 20.

Discussion Question

What benefits can accounting software provide to accountants?

SUMMARY

Measurements of net income *for the period* and of financial position *at the end of the period* are interrelated. Revenues result from selling goods or rendering services to customers and lead to increases in assets or decreases in liabilities. Expenses indicate that services have been used in generating revenue and result in decreases in assets or increases in liabilities. Because revenues represent increases in owners' equity, revenue transactions are recorded by crediting (increasing) an owners' equity account for the specific type of revenue and by debiting either an asset or liability account. Expenses represent decreases in owners' equity and are recorded by debiting (decreasing) an owners' equity account for the specific type of expense and crediting either an asset or a liability account. The revenue and expense accounts accumulate the revenues earned and expenses recognized during the period.

Some events will not be recorded as part of the regular day-to-day recording process during the period because no explicit transaction between the firm and some external party (such as a customer, creditor, or governmental unit) has taken place to signal the requirement for a journal entry. Such events require an adjusting entry at the end of the period so that periodic income and financial position can be properly reported on an accrual basis. After an adjusted trial balance has been prepared, the balances in these temporary accounts are transferred, or closed, to the Retained Earnings account.

KEY TERMS

Net income
Revenues
Expenses
Accounting period
Natural business year
Cash basis of accounting
Modified cash basis of accounting
Accrual basis of accounting
Cash discounts
Gross price method
Allowance method
Net price method
Trade discount
Sales returns
Sales allowance
Unexpired costs
Expired costs
Matching principle
Product costs

Period expenses
Balance sheet equation
Closing process
Temporary accounts
Permanent accounts
Adjusting entries
Unadjusted trial balance
Depreciation
Straight-line method
Adjusted trial balance
Journal
Book of original entry
Cash receipts journal
Cash disbursements journal
Ledger
Subsidiary ledger
Controlling accounts
Work sheet

APPENDIX 3.1

ACCOUNTING JOURNALS AND LEDGERS

This appendix describes and illustrates some of the more common types of journals and ledgers used in accounting systems.

JOURNALS

The **journal** presents a chronological record of accounting events. *Journalizing* consists of analyzing the accounting events into the proper debits and credits and recording the results of the analysis in a journal. The journal contains accounting information classified by accounting event. Further, each accounting event is analyzed and recorded completely before the next one is entered. The journal is the first place in which a complete formal record of the accounting event is made. It is therefore sometimes called the **book of original entry**. By recording all information relating to each accounting event in one place, the journal provides a chronological history, or running record, of the various events and transactions of the firm. The number of transactions, even in a small business, is so large that errors are bound to occur. It would be almost impossible to locate errors if a record such as the journal were not kept. Each journal entry can be checked independently for equal debits and credits, and postings in the ledger accounts can be traced back to the journal to determine the origin, authorization, and analysis of each transaction.

The journal may take one of three possible forms: (1) two-column journal, (2) multicolumn journal, or (3) specialized journal.

journal
A tabular record in which business transactions are analyzed in terms of debits and credits and recorded in chronological order before being posted to the general ledger accounts. Also called "book of original entry."

book of original entry
Journal.

The Two-Column Journal Form

The most common journal form is the two-column form presented in Exhibit 3.12. Essentials of the two-column form are a pair of columns to record the debits and credits and a place to indicate the names of the accounts affected by the transaction. As posting is done, there will be entered in the reference (Ref.) column the number, or page, of the account to which the amount has been posted, or perhaps a check mark to indicate that the posting has been done. A transaction involving the receipt of $150 from R. Wood as payment on an account receivable is shown in Exhibit 3.12 in the two-column journal.

The two-column journal form is the one commonly used for the general journal of a firm.

Exhibit 3.12
Two-Column Journal Form

Date		Accounts and Explanation	Ref.	Debit	Credit
9	1	Cash	√	1 5 0 00	
		Accounts Receivable	√		1 5 0 00
		Collection from R. Wood on Account			

Multicolumn Journal

The process of posting, or transferring, figures from the journal to the general ledger accounts is laborious and monotonous. When the two-column journal form is used, each journal debit and credit must be copied into the general ledger individually. In practice, this simple two-column form is usually replaced by a more elaborate journal or journals. One labour-saving device is to expand the journal into a multicolumn record. The *multicolumn* journal provides several debit and several credit columns to replace the two-column form. This subdivision permits separate columns to be reserved for the entering of debits or credits in accounts, such as Cash and Sales for a merchandising firm, that are used often. A simple multicolumn journal form is shown in Exhibit 3.13. The transaction involving the receipt of cash from R. Wood on account is entered in the multicolumn journal.

Exhibit 3.13
Multicolumn Journal

Date		Explanation	Cash		Merchandise Sales		Other Accounts			
			Debit	Credit	Debit	Credit	Debit	Credit	Ref.	Account Title
9	1	Collection from R. Wood on Account	150.00					150.00		Accounts Receivable

Designing a multicolumn journal requires selecting the accounts to be allocated special columns. Columns should be provided for the debits or credits, or both, of those accounts that are used most frequently. In practice, it may not be easy to discover which will be used most often. If the business has been in operation for some time, the past transactions can be studied and a tabulation made of the number of entries to each side of each account. If there is no experience to use as a guide, an attempt is made to anticipate the types of transactions that will occur most frequently, and a tentative set of column headings is selected. In any case, the column headings may have to be changed from time to time so that the multicolumn format may be used efficiently. When only one multicolumn journal is used, two columns must always be reserved to record the debits and credits to the accounts for which specialized columns are not provided. The multicolumn journal is composed of two segments: (1) specialized columns for frequent items and (2) an attached two-column journal form to provide for all other items.

The principal advantage of using specialized columns is the saving in posting time. The posting of a column total to the general ledger takes the place of the posting of each of the individual items that appear in the column. Specialized columns also facilitate the process of journalizing, because most bookkeepers find it easier to analyze transactions when the commonly used accounts are spread across a columnar sheet. Each entry also takes less vertical space, and more entries can therefore be made on a journal page.

Specialized Journals

The advantages of specialization can be extended further by replacing the multicolumn journal by a group of specialized journals. There is no standard set of journals suitable for all firms. However, in most concerns, four specialized journals are likely to be used in addition to the general journal: cash receipts, cash disbursements, revenue recognition (particularly sales), and acquisition of goods and services (particularly purchases of merchandise and raw materials). The size of the firm and the nature of its operations will, of course, affect the number and types of specialized journals employed. Below, a cash receipts journal and a cash disbursements journal are described briefly.

Cash Receipts Journal A **cash receipts journal** provides a chronological listing of all transactions involving the receipt of cash. Exhibit 3.14 shows an example of a cash receipts journal. Each cash receipt is entered in the Cash Dr. column, and the credit entry appears in either the Accounts Receivable Cr., Sales Cr., or Other Cr. column. At periodic intervals, such as weekly or monthly, the total amount in each column is posted to the appropriate general ledger accounts. For example, at the end of September, $995 would be debited to the Cash account in the general ledger. Likewise, $225 would be credited to the Accounts Receivable account in the general ledger.

cash receipts journal
Specialized journal used to record all transactions involving cash receipts.

EXHIBIT 3.14
Cash Receipts Journal

CASH RECEIPTS JOURNAL						Page 46
Date		Explanation	Cash Dr.	Accounts Receivable Cr.	Sales Cr.	Other Cr.	Account Title
9	1	Collection from R. Wood on account	150.00	150.00			
9	5	Sale of Merchandise to Customers	250.00		250.00		
9	12	Collection from J. Smith on Account	75.00	75.00			
9	19	Receipt of Dividend from Ford Motor Company	120.00			120.00	Dividend Revenue
9	25	Sales of Merchandise to Customers	400.00		400.00		
			995.00	225.00	650.00	120.00	

Cash Disbursements Journal A **cash disbursements journal** contains a sequential listing of all cash disbursements made. If all disbursements are made by cheque (a desirable procedure for control purposes), the cash disbursements journal will list each cheque written (credits to the account) and the appropriate account debited. Exhibit 3.15 presents a typical cash disbursements journal. Each disbursement is entered in the Cash Cr. column. An entry is also made in either the Accounts Payable Dr., Selling and

cash disbursements journal
Specialized journal used to record all disbursements by a firm.

Administrative Expense Dr., or Other Dr. column. At periodic intervals, the total amount in the Cash Cr. column ($506) is posted to the credit side of the general ledger account for Cash. Similar entries are made on the debit sides of the other general ledger accounts.

EXHIBIT 3.15
Cash Disbursements Journal

| | | | | | | Selling and Adminis-trative | | |
Date	Cheque Number	Payee	Cash Cr.	Accounts Payable Dr.	Expense Dr.	Other Dr.	Account Title
9 4	246	G. Winkle	80.00		80.00		
9 7	247	Stephens Wholesale	163.00	163.00			
9 16	248	Harris Insurance	96.00			96.00	Prepaid Insurance
9 22	249	City of Norwich	62.00	62.00			
9 28	250	Burkett Supply	105.00		105.00		
			506.00	225.00	185.00	96.00	

CASH DISBURSEMENTS JOURNAL — Page 64

LEDGERS

ledger
A book of accounts. See general ledger and subsidiary ledger; contrast with journal.

A group of accounts arranged in orderly fashion is known as a **ledger**. The account is the unit of classification within the ledger for accumulating information. There are few essential requirements for the form of a ledger account. Space should be provided for the following data: account title; date of transaction; debit, credit and balance amounts; and a reference to trace the posting to its source in a journal. Space for other explanatory data may sometimes be useful. The standard ledger form presented in Exhibit 3.16 provides space for an explanation of each entry. An alternative T-account ledger form presents all debit entries on the left half of the page and credit entries on the right half. The T-account form is frequently used for class presentation but seldom found in practice.

Note that the debit to the Cash account in the ledger is equal to the total cash receipts for September taken from the Cash Receipts Journal in Exhibit 3.14. Likewise, the credit to the Cash account is equal to the total cash

EXHIBIT 3.16
Ledger Form

CASH

Date	Explanation	Ref.	Dr.	Cr.	Bal.
9 1	Balance		634.00		634.00
9 30	Cash Receipts Journal	46	995.00		1,629.00
9 30	Cash Disbursements Journal	64		506.00	1,123.00

disbursements for September listed in the Cash Disbursements Journal. The reference (Ref.) is to the appropriate page in these two specialized journals.

All firms maintain a general ledger. There is usually one ledger sheet for each balance sheet and income statement account. Some firms also maintain subsidiary ledgers. A **subsidiary ledger** contains a listing of individual items that make up the total in a general ledger account. A subsidiary accounts receivable ledger would contain a listing of the individual customers' accounts and amounts due. The sum of the amounts in the subsidiary ledger should equal the total in the general ledger account. The amounts shown in the two ledgers are reconciled periodically, and any differences are investigated and corrected. When such a system of internal checks between the general ledger and subsidiary ledgers is used, the general ledger accounts are referred to as "**controlling accounts**." Exhibit 3.17 lists some common controlling accounts. Note that the subsidiary record is not always a group of ledger accounts in the standard ledger form. It may be a group of specially designed forms.

subsidiary ledger
A group of accounts, not part of the general ledger, that explain or reflect the detail (such as individual customer balances) underlying the balance in a related control account (such as Accounts Receivable) in the general ledger.

controlling accounts
General ledger accounts, the balance of which reflects the aggregate balance of many related subsidiary accounts. Most firms maintain such records for accounts receivable and accounts payable.

EXHIBIT 3.17
Examples of Controlling Accounts

General Ledger Controlling Account	Type of Subsidiary Record
Accounts Receivable	Individual customers' ledger accounts, or a file of uncollected sales invoices.
Accounts Payable	Individual ledger accounts, or a file of unpaid purchase invoices.
Common Stock	A record of the share certificates and number of shares held by each shareholder.
Notes Receivable	A file of uncollected notes receivable, or a "register" or book in which the notes are listed.
Raw Material Inventory	Separate record card for each item in inventory used in manufacturing.
Equipment	Separate record card for each item of equipment. This is often known as a plant ledger.
Land	Separate record cards showing description and cost of each parcel of land owned.

DISCUSSION CASE 7

Micros in Accounting

The computing and processing capabilities of a microcomputer approach those of the largest mainframe of only 20 years ago [1963]. Ever smaller, faster, cheaper, and easier to use, the microcomputer has enjoyed spectacular sales growth. Microcomputer sales in North America are *(continued)*

(continued)

now [1983] running over two million units per year. And the business market — as opposed to the home or hobbyist market — is now accounting for the lion's share of sales.

The small business is an obviously large market. Long closed out from the advantages of computer processing by prohibitive cost and the need for specially trained personnel, an increasing number of small businesses now find it feasible to use microcomputers to process their basic accounting transactions, to provide ready access to necessary operating data, and to handle correspondence.

But this use — essential as it is — is only the tip of the iceberg. Microcomputers expand the options available to businesses of all sizes. Using microcomputers, management can arrange data-processing facilities with much less concern for hardware costs. A micro might be used to automate activities that for reasons of cost or confidentiality are not suitable for processing on the company's mainframe. Typical business applications include the following:

1. Forecasting, modelling, and financial statement consolidation are simplified by a microcomputer program known as an electronic spreadsheet. Once a model of relationships among a specific set of data has been established, an electronic spreadsheet program will automatically update all of the items affected by a change in one or more components. Some simple examples include the effect on the bottom line if sales double, if a division is sold, or if a union contract is settled at various possible levels.

2. Databases may be created for the use of individual executives or departments. Once a database file has been created in a common format, the information can be retrieved, summarized, sorted, rearranged, or used to prepare special purpose reports. The publications department might use a microcomputer to keep its mailing list current. Personnel data, meeting calendars, information on contracts with potential customers, tickler files, almost any type of data an individual or department needs to file and find for later use could become the subject of a microcomputer application. Applications that may not be cost-effective on the company's mainframe computer might well be practicable on a micro.

3. Graphics software available for microcomputers can reduce the time and cost associated with preparing illustrative charts for many types of presentations. The graphics capabilities of microcomputers are easily seen in the games run on home computers.

4. Security portfolio analysis, trend analysis, and plotting are possible with specialized programs. Arrangements can be made to use the microcomputer as a terminal to access data bases of specialized information maintained by outsid-
(continued)

(continued)

ers. Teleglobe and Infomart are two of the major Canadian data bases. The Source and CompuServe are available in the United States. Prestel can be accessed in the United Kingdom, and so on.

Not so long ago corporate electronic data processing was highly centralized. The high cost of the computer carried with it the need to allocate service facilities principally to priority tasks. Relatively inexpensive machines with enough processing power were simply not available. That has changed — less expensive computers have put computer power into the hands of many individuals. The power of the computer is being dispersed throughout the business organization.

Microcomputers — ever smaller and less expensive machines — are accelerating this already widespread trend. Microcomputers will not replace the mainframe computer for large-scale applications, but microcomputers are becoming so inexpensive that it is quite reasonable to automate additional activities. Distributed data processing — the use of several different computers (and now including microcomputers) in different locations all connected by transmission facilities — is becoming more and more common.

References

From *Microcomputers: Their Use and Misuse in Your Business*, Price Waterhouse, 1983, pp. 1–2.

Microcomputers have gone through several evolutionary stages, as shown in Table 3.1:

TABLE 3.1
Micro Evolution

Size	Storage Capacity	Features
Desktop	256K	no hard drive
Desktop	20MB	hard drive
Desktop	100MB	hard drive, VGA
Laptop	40MB	hard drive, battery
Notebook	20MB	hard drive, fits in briefcase

The next advance on the horizon is the use of compact disks (CDs) for storage. One CD can currently hold about 900MB, but the cost of this technology is still prohibitively expensive.

Discussion Question

Will the computer make accountants obsolete? Why or why not?

APPENDIX 3.2

PREPARATION OF A WORK SHEET

work sheet
An informal accounting document used to facilitate the preparation of financial statements.

To facilitate the preparation of the income statement and balance sheet at the end of an accounting period, a **work sheet** is often used. Exhibit 3.18 presents an example of a work sheet. This work sheet contains pairs of debit and credit columns for:

1. Unadjusted trial balance
2. Adjusting entries
3. Adjusted trial balance
4. Income statement
5. Balance sheet

All of the required procedures at the end of an accounting period can be conveniently summarized in the work sheet, facilitating the preparation of the financial statements. A work sheet does not eliminate any of the usual end-of-period procedures. Adjusting and closing entries must still be made, entered in the general journal, and posted to the appropriate general ledger accounts. The work sheet is simply a mechanism for aggregating all of the data from these end-of-period procedures and organizing it in a useful form for preparing the financial statements.

ILLUSTRATION OF WORK SHEET PREPARATION

The data presented in the chapter for Stephen's Shoe Store, Inc. are used to illustrate the preparation of a work sheet.

Unadjusted Trial Balance   The first two columns contain the account balances taken from the general ledger at the end of the period before adjusting entries have been made. The debit and credit columns are summed to ensure that the trial balance is in balance.

Adjusting Entries   The adjusting entries made at the end of the accounting period are entered in the next two columns. Note that the debits and credits for each entry are cross-referenced in the adjusting entries columns. The numbers used for cross-referencing in this case refer to the numbered journal entries in the chapter. Letters are often used as cross-references instead of numbers to avoid the possibility of confusing the amount of the adjusting entry with its cross-reference.

Adjusted Trial Balance   The amounts in the adjusted trial balance columns are the sum or net amounts for each account in the first four columns. Adjusted trial balance columns are not essential in a work sheet, but they do facilitate the completion of the income statement and balance sheet columns.

Income Statement   The amount in each income statement account in the adjusted trial balance is extended to the appropriate debit or credit column in the income statement section of the work sheet. A subtotal of the total debits (expenses) and the total credits (revenues) is then calculated. The

EXHIBIT 3.18
STEPHEN'S SHOE STORE, INC.
Work Sheet
Year Ended December 31, Year 4

Accounts	Unadjusted Trial Balance Debit	Credit	Adjusting Entries Debit	Credit	Adjusted Trial Balance Debit	Credit	Income Statement Debit	Credit	Balance Sheet Debit	Credit
Cash (A)	$ 191,100				$ 191,100				$ 191,100	
Accounts Receivable (A)	128,000				128,000				128,000	
Notes Receivable (A)	10,000				10,000				10,000	
Interest Receivable (A)			150 (13)		150				150	
Merchandise Inventory (A)	140,000				140,000				140,000	
Prepaid Insurance (A)	1,500			$ 500 (15)	1,000				1,000	
Land (A)	100,000				100,000				100,000	
Building and Equipment (A)	525,000				525,000				525,000	
Accumulated Depreciation (XA)		$ 85,000		30,000 (16)		$ 115,000				$ 115,000
Accounts Payable (L)		220,000				220,000				220,000
Salaries Payable (L)				14,000 (14)		14,000				14,000
Dividends Payable (L)		15,000				15,000				15,000
Income Tax Payable (L)				29,080 (18)		29,080				29,080
Advances from Tenants (L)		600	50 (17)			550				550
Bonds Payable (L)		100,000				100,000				100,000
Common Stock (SE)		250,000				250,000				250,000
Contributed Surplus (SE)		200,000				200,000				200,000
Retained Earnings (SE)		108,000				108,000				108,000
Sales Revenue (SE)		625,000				625,000		$625,000		
Interest Revenue (SE)				150 (13)		150		150		
Rent Revenue (SE)				50 (17)		50		50		
Cost of Goods Sold (SE)	390,000				390,000		$390,000			
Salaries Expense (SE)	110,000		14,000 (14)		124,000		124,000			
Interest Expense (SE)	8,000				8,000		8,000			
Insurance Expense (SE)			500 (15)		500		500			
Depreciation Expense (SE)			30,000 (16)		30,000		30,000			
Income Tax Expense (SE)			29,080 (18)		29,080		29,080			
Subtotals							581,580	625,200		
Net Income for the Year							43,620			43,620
Totals	$1,603,600	$1,603,630	$73,780	$73,780	$1,676,830	$1,676,830	$625,200	$625,200	$1,095,250	$1,095,250

difference between these two subtotals is net income or net loss for the period. For Stephen's Shoe Store, revenues exceed expenses by $43,620. This amount is entered in the debit column in the income statement section to equate the two income statement columns. The amount is also entered in the credit column in the balance sheet section. The placement of the net income amount in these two columns is analogous to the entry to close revenue and expense accounts to retained earnings. The credit in the balance sheet column is to "net income for the year" instead of retained earnings. Retained earnings at the end of the year must be calculated from the work sheet ($151,620 = $108,000 + $43,620).

Balance Sheet   The final step is to extend the amounts for each balance sheet account from the adjusted trial balance to the appropriate debit and credit columns in the balance sheet section of the work sheet. An equality between the debit and credit columns serves as a check on the work sheet preparation procedures.

ALTERNATIVE WORK SHEET FORMATS

The particular columns used in a work sheet depend on a firm's accounting system and the financial statements and schedules to be prepared. Two alternative work sheet formats are discussed briefly below.

Combined Income and Retained Earnings Columns

Some firms prepare a combined statement of income and retained earnings. The seventh and eighth columns in the work sheet in Exhibit 3.18 can be altered to include information for both of these statements. Exhibit 3.19 contains a partial work sheet to illustrate the procedure. Dividends declared and paid during Year 4 were $15,000. For purposes of this illustration, it is assumed that a Dividends Declared account was debited instead of Retained Earnings, when the dividend was declared. Thus, the balance in the Retained Earnings account on the trial balance at the end of Year 4 is its balance as of January 1, Year 4.

The revenues and expenses are extended from the adjusted trial balance columns to the income and retained earnings statement columns in Exhibit 3.19 in precisely the same manner as in Exhibit 3.18. The difference between the subtotals of the two columns of $43,620 is net income for the year. This amount is again entered in the debit column to equate the two columns. Instead of being entered as a credit in the balance sheet columns, as in Exhibit 3.18, the amount is entered as a credit in the income and retained earnings columns. The retained earnings amount on the adjusted trial balance, assuming dividend declarations are debited to a Dividends Declared account, is the balance on January 1, Year 4 of $123,000. This amount is entered in the credit column. The dividends declared are entered in the debit column. A second subtotal is now taken. The difference between the column totals of $151,620 is the balance in the retained earnings at the end of the year. This amount is entered in the debit column of the income and retained earnings statement section to equate the two columns. It is also entered in the credit column in the balance sheet section. The principal

EXHIBIT 3.19
STEPHEN'S SHOE STORE, INC.
Partial Work Sheet
Year Ended December 31, Year 4

Account	Income and Retained Earnings		Balance Sheet	
	Debit	Credit	Debit	Credit
Sales Revenue (OE)		$625,000		
Interest Revenue (OE)		150		
Rent Revenue (OE)		50		
Cost of Goods Sold (OE)	$390,000			
Salaries Expense (OE)	124,000			
Interest Expense (OE)	8,000			
Insurance Expense (OE)	500			
Depreciation Expense (OE)	30,000			
Income Tax Expense (OE)	29,080			
Subtotal	$581,580	$625,200		
Net Income for the Year	43,620			
Total	$625,200	$625,200		
Retained Earnings (beginning of year)		123,000		
Net Income for the Year		43,620		
Dividends Declared	15,000			
Subtotal	$640,200	$791,820		
Retained Earnings (end of year)	151,620			$151,620
Total	$791,820	$791,820		

difference between the work sheets in Exhibits 3.18 and 3.19 is that the ending balance in Retained Earnings is calculated explicitly in Exhibit 3.19, but must be calculated separately in Exhibit 3.18.

Merchandise Accounts in the Work Sheet

The illustration in the text implicitly assumed that Stephen's Shoe Store used a perpetual inventory system. Purchases of inventory items were debited to the Merchandise Inventory account. At the time of sale, the cost of the merchandise sold was credited to the Merchandise Inventory account and debited to Cost of Goods Sold. The balance in the Merchandise Inventory account consequently is constantly updated and should show the inventory on hand at all times. Chapter 7 points out that many firms use a periodic inventory system. In a periodic system, purchases of merchandise inventory are usually debited to a Purchases account. Freight-in, returns, discounts, and allowances on items purchased are debited or credited as appropriate to separate accounts. Under a periodic system, the balance in the Merchandise Inventory account at any time *during* an accounting period is its balance as of the beginning of the period. No entry is made in the Merchandise Inventory account as items are either purchased or sold. At periodic intervals, usually quarterly or annually, inventory is counted to determine the amount of inventory still on hand. Any difference between the beginning inventory plus net purchases and the amount still on hand (ending inventory) is assumed to have been sold.

To illustrate the preparation of a work sheet when a periodic inventory system is in use, assume that the following data are obtained for Stephen's Shoe Store for Year 4:

Beginning Inventory, January 1, Year 4		$175,000
Plus: Purchases	$375,000	
Freight-in	10,000	
Less: Returns	(5,000)	
Discounts	(20,000)	
Allowances	(5,000)	
Net Purchases		$355,000
Less: Ending Inventory, December 31, Year 4		(140,000)
Cost of Goods Sold		$390,000

Exhibit 3.20 presents a partial work sheet for Stephen's Shoe Store and assumes a periodic inventory system is used. The amount in the Merchandise Inventory account in the adjusted trial balance at the beginning of the year is entered in the debit column in the income statement section of the work sheet. The amounts in the Purchases, Freight-in, Returns, Discounts, and Allowances accounts are likewise entered in their appropriate debit or credit columns. The amount in the ending inventory of $140,000, as determined by physical count, is entered in the credit column in the income statement section and the debit column in the balance sheet section. The total of the amounts in the debit column in the income statement section of $560,000 (= $175,000 + $375,000 + $10,000) exceeds the total of the amounts in the credit column of $170,000 (= $140,000 + $5,000 + $20,000 + $5,000) by $390,000. This is the Cost of Goods Sold for the period. The work sheet will not show a separate line for Cost of Goods Sold. Its amount is calculated implicitly when the income statement columns are summed.

EXHIBIT 3.20
STEPHEN'S SHOE STORE, INC.
Partial Work Sheet
Year Ended December 31, Year 4

Account	Adjusted Trial Balance		Income Statement		Balance Sheet	
	Debit	Credit	Debit	Credit	Debit	Credit
Merchandise Inventory	$175,000		$175,000	$140,000	$140,000	
Purchases	375,000		375,000			
Freight-in	10,000		10,000			
Returns		$ 5,000		5,000		
Discounts		20,000		20,000		
Allowances		5,000		5,000		

DISCUSSION CASE 8

Benefits of Computers in Organizations

Significant benefits from computers can be realized by organizations if they carefully consider what they can accomplish. However, not all benefits of computers can easily be reduced to reliable dollar values. First there is the problem that future benefits can only be estimated and are therefore subject to inaccuracies in estimates. Another more important problem is that many of the benefits are intangible and virtually impossible to reduce to dollar values. For example, employees may react favourably to working with on-line VDTs in their jobs with a resultant positive impact on morale. The value of this improved morale cannot be evaluated in simple dollar terms.

Another important point about computer benefits is that they are probabilistic, i.e., dependent on many factors turning out favorably. Many things can go wrong in computer installations, even in the best-planned situations. Acts of god, government action, employee dishonesty, and/or overlooked implementation considerations all can cause serious problems in computer installations.

Computer benefits are available in all areas of operations of most organizations. The following sections discuss the more common areas. Some organizations realize more than sufficient benefits to justify computer acquisition in only one or two of these areas.

Comprehensive Information Benefits

Manual and mechanical data processing systems impose many restrictions on the amount of data which can be processed and stored economically, but a computerized system removes many of these restrictions. For example, many organizations marketing small unit-value items cannot afford to maintain detailed inventory records with manual or mechanical systems. However, modern computer systems with point-of-sale input terminals change the economics of recording sales of many small unit value inventory items completely. A retail organization can keep track of virtually every individual product sale. This information allows managers to make better inventory management decisions.

Many smaller manufacturing firms depend almost totally on personal supervision to keep production operations flowing smoothly. Several factors such as unavailable raw materials, broken machines, or employee absenteeism throw production operations into shambles. Managers must often scramble to adjust work orders to keep the available resources occupied.

Comprehensive manufacturing planning and control systems for smaller computers offer the opportunity to significantly improve scheduling, monitoring,

(continued)

(continued)

and adjusting production operations. Labour and equipment productivity improvements of 20 to 30 percent are not uncommon in smaller manufacturing firms with these systems. Investments in raw material inventories often decrease significantly with no negative impact on meeting production requirements. Figure A illustrates several types of benefits resulting from more comprehensive information being made available to managers. Each of these alone may be sufficiently important to a particular company to warrant the computer investment.

FIGURE A
Comprehensive Information Benefits

Comprehensive Information	Benefits
Customer Status Reports	Better credit management, improved cash flows, better direction for sales efforts.
Inventory Status Reports	Reduced investment in inventories, fewer stock-outs, less product obsolescence losses.
Fixed Asset Utilization Reports	Better capital investment analysis, improved scheduling of utilization, better preventive maintenance planning.
Labour Productivity Reports	Better labour force requirements planning, better incentive planning, improved counselling of problem workers.
Cash Flow Analysis Reports	Better cash requirements planning, lower borrowings, more rapid loan repayments, less interest expense.

Timely Information Benefits

Obtaining current information about finances and operations is very difficult in manual or mechanical environments simply because of delays in handling and processing data. Computers offer the opportunity to record data concerning transactions as they occur and process this data very soon after each step in processing transactions. This allows management reporting to take place on a much more timely basis and provides a means to improve decisions critically dependent on timely information, e.g., cash management. Figure B illustrates other types of benefits from more timely information.

Information in manual or mechanical data processing environments is often inconveniently located in filing cabinets or central filing departments. Computers offer the opportunity for much more information to be as readily available as the nearest VDT. Also, in manual or mechanical environments, it is often necessary to spend a great deal of time assembling information from a variety of sources. How-
(continued)

(continued)

FIGURE B
Timely Information Benefits

Timely Information	Benefits
On-line data entry	Instant availability of data on transactions in process, current status of resources, and historical references.
Daily summary reporting	Provides management with current overview of all important functional activities (e.g., sales, production, finance).
Ad hoc retrieval requests	Provides management with current information on specific matters of concern (e.g., customer status, outstanding transactions).
Daily updating of master files	Provides the basis for reporting current status of master files (e.g., customers, products, suppliers, employees).

ever, in a computer environment, even complex requests for information can be accommodated readily through data base accessing techniques.

Information Accuracy Benefits

Inaccuracies are frequent in manual or mechanical data processing systems because of carelessness, incompetence, lack of training, and many other human-related factors. However, in computer environments, computer programs may contain many editing checks to promote a very high level of accuracy and reliability of accounting data (see Figure C). Also, most computers are highly reliable in terms of functioning properly or readily detecting errors in processing caused by hardware problems.

FIGURE C
Benefits of More Accurate Information

More Accurate Information	Benefits
Computer program edits	Detects most types of clerical errors during data entry.
Control total reconciliations	Provides assurance that all financial data is being properly processed.
Data scanning techniques	Provides a means to scan computer files for unusual data that may result from input errors.
User/management output reviews	Users and managers can be more confident about the reliability of outputs.

(continued)

(continued)

Clerical Productivity Benefits

In manual or mechanical environments, each step in data processing requires large amounts of human effort. However, in a computer environment, manual effort is only substantial in the initial entry of input data to a computer system. Subsequent steps in data processing can be performed automatically by the computer (see Figure D). Depending on the nature of data processing activities in an organization, clerical productivity improvements can be very significant.

FIGURE D
Clerical Productivity Benefits

Clerical Productivity	Benefits
Typing	Word processing technology improves typing productivity substantially.
Collating	Merging is performed automatically by many different types of computer printers.
Filing	Much filing is eliminated by deleting printed outputs and using microfilm or microfiche instead.
Bookkeeping	Many clerical steps in the bookkeeping process, such as transcribing and summarizing data, are eliminated.
Document preparation	Many documents are produced automatically by computer systems.
Document checking	Clerical checking requirements are eliminated because computers perform repetitive processing functions very reliably.
Retrieving data	Looking up data in filing cabinets is eliminated and replaced by on-line retrieval of data with VDTs.

Figure E summarizes the clerical process required in many manual and computer systems. The manual system requires significant clerical effort at every step, but the computer system only requires clerical effort in the first step. The time savings beyond the initial entry of data into a computer system are evident.

FIGURE E
Impact of Automation of Clerical Procedures

Manual System	Computer System
Clerks write or type data on business documents (e.g., purchase orders, sales invoices, checks, etc.).	Clerks key data into the computer through keyboards on VDTs (a printer can produce printed outputs if so desired).

(continued)

(continued)

Manual System	Computer System
Clerks transcribe data from documents to accounting journals and ledgers (e.g., bills, cash receipts, cash payments, accounts receivable, payable, payroll, etc.).	Computer performs all transcribing functions "automatically" and prints all accounting journals and ledgers through simple request by clerks using VDTs.
Clerks summarize journals and ledgers for financial report preparation (e.g., monthly financial statements, customer statements and aged lists, stock status reports, cost accounting reports).	Computer performs all report preparation operations through simple requests by clerks using VDTs.
Clerks must hunt through filing cabinets to find necessary information to answer many kinds of questions.	Computer performs all information retrieval operations through simple requests by clerks using VDTs.

Operational Improvement Benefits

These benefits can lead to improvement of organizational efficiency and effectiveness in many ways. One organization increased its sales and profits by over 500 percent in three years largely because its new computer system provided much better information on stock availability and allowed customer orders to be shipped much more rapidly than any of its local competitors. Another company installed a manufacturing planning and control system and, two years later, found that unit production costs had decreased by almost 20 percent because of much improved production scheduling, labour utilization, and reduced overhead costs (see Figure F).

All of these specific areas can often translate into an improved

FIGURE F
Organizational Benefits

Organizational Benefits	Comments
Customer service	Availability of stock, rapid delivery of orders, status of orders.
Resource management	Equipment load balancing, cash flow analysis, credit management.
Marketing	Inventory turnover, customer activity analysis, profitability analysis.
Manufacturing	Scheduling, raw materials management, production cycle time.
Distribution	Delivery service, truck utilization, warehousing costs.
Human relations	Job status, job upgrading, employee morale.
Decision support	Simulation, data analysis, external data sources.

(continued)

(continued)

bottom-line profitability for a private organization or an improved level of efficiency and effectiveness of a public sector or not-for-profit organization. However, it is often extremely difficult or even totally impossible to anticipate the extent of benefits or quantify their potential dollar value. The decision to invest in a computer often must be made on a consensus by management that the benefit potential is worthwhile.

References

From Kenneth W. Clowes, *EDP Auditing* (Toronto: Holt, Rinehart and Winston of Canada Ltd., 1988), pp. 92–97.

Discussion Question

Do these perceived benefits accrue to all firms, can they be quantified, and are there any disadvantages to computer acquisition?

SELF-STUDY MATERIAL

This section contains questions, exercises, and problems to help you assess your understanding of Chapter 3. Careful review of this material will assist you in completing the homework assignments. Solutions are found at the end of the section.

QUESTIONS AND EXERCISES

True/False

For each statement, place a T or an F in the space provided to indicate whether the statement is true or false.

____ 1. The income statement provides a measure of the operating performance of a firm for a particular period of time.

____ 2. Expenses measure the net assets (assets less liabilities) that flow into a firm when goods are sold or services are rendered.

____ 3. Net income is produced when revenues exceed expenses.

____ 4. Expenses measure the net assets used up in the process of generating revenue.

____ 5. A natural business year for a company is always the one that coincides with the calendar year.

____ 6. For accounting purposes, the cash-basis income statement provides the most meaningful measure of operating performance during a particular period because cash flow is the most objective measure of a company's performance.

____ 7. The major difference between the cash basis and the accrual basis is in expense recognition because revenues are the same for both methods.

____ 8. Depreciation acounting attempts to adjust the ledger account balances for long-lived assets to equate to their current market value.

____ 9. The balance in the Accumulated Depreciation account represents the cumulative depreciation on the asset since acquisition.

____ 10. The adjusted trial balance is prepared from information in the income statement and balance sheet.

____ 11. Product costs are recorded as expenses of the period in which the services are consumed, because these costs rarely create assets with future benefits.

____ 12. Revenues − Expenses − Dividends = Net Income.

____ 13. Revenues reflect an increase in owners' equity and are recorded as credits.

____ 14. The Dillingham Co. Inc. recorded the purchase of a one-year insurance policy on July 1, 19X1 by debiting Prepaid Insurance. On December 31, 19X1, the company should prepare an adjusting entry that debits Insurance Expense and credits Prepaid Insurance for the amount of the expired insurance.

____ 15. Assets may be referred to as unexpired costs, while expenses may be referred to as expired costs.

____ 16. Product costs represent only the costs of raw material for a manufacturing firm.

____ 17. Assets = Liabilities + Contributed Capital + Revenues − Expenses − Dividends.

____ 18. Assets = Liabilities + Contributed Capital + Retained Earnings.

_____ 19. The balance in a revenue account is closed to Retained Earnings by a debit to the revenue account and a credit to Retained Earnings.

_____ 20. Permanent accounts, which reflect the cumulative changes in each account from the time the firm was first organized, appear on the income statement.

_____ 21. Expenses cause a decrease in owners' equity and are recorded as credits.

_____ 22. Under the accrual basis of accounting, revenue is recognized in the period when the cash is received, as opposed to when the sale is made.

_____ 23. Dividends represent distributions of earnings and decrease owners' equity.

_____ 24. The Depreciation Expense account reflects the cumulative depreciation on the asset since acquisition.

Matching

From the list of terms, select one term that is most closely associated with one descriptive phrase or statement that follows and place the letter for that term in the space provided.

a.	accrual basis	k.	matching convention
b.	accumulated depreciation	l.	natural business year
c.	adjusted trial balance	m.	owners' equity
d.	cash basis	n.	period expenses
e.	closing process	o.	permanent accounts
f.	contra accounts	p.	posting
g.	depreciation	q.	product costs
h.	dividends	r.	revenues
i.	expenses	s.	temporary accounts
j.	journalizing	t.	unadjusted trial balance

_____ 1. These accounts accumulate amounts for only a single accounting period.

_____ 2. These accounts reflect the cumulative changes in each account from the time the firm was first organized.

_____ 3. A measure of the inflow of net assets from selling goods and providing services.

_____ 4. A measure of the outflow of net assets that are used up, or consumed, in the process of generating revenues.

_____ 5. The year ends when most of the earnings activities of a firm have been substantially completed.

_____ 6. A manufacturing firm's costs of producing its product.

_____ 7. The process of transferring entries in the general journal to the accounts in the general ledger.

_____ 8. A trial balance prepared at the end of the accounting period after adjusting entries are made.

_____ 9. Recognizes revenues and expenses as cash flows (inflow and outflow) take place.

_____ 10. A trial balance prepared at the end of the accounting period before adjusting and closing entries.

_____ 11. Expenses not directly associated with particular revenues but used or consumed in an accounting period.

_____ 12. The charge made to the current operations for the portion of cost of long-lived assets consumed during the current period.

_____ 13. The balance in this account reflects the cumulative depreciation of an asset since acquisition.

_____ 14. This account represents distributions of earnings to shareholders of the firm.

_____ 15. Deduction or valuation accounts that accumulate amounts that are subtracted from another account.

_____ 16. The basis that recognizes revenues on the completion of a critical event in the earnings process.

_____ 17. Treatment of recognizing asset expirations as expenses in the same period as directly associated revenues are recognized.

_____ 18. Contributed Capital plus Retained Earnings.

_____ 19. The process of transferring the balances in revenue and expense accounts to Retained Earnings.

_____ 20. The process of recording transactions in the general journal or in a special journal.

Multiple Choice

Choose the best answer for each question or problem and enter the identifying letter in the space provided.

_____ 1. Which of these accounts is *not* closed during the closing process?
a) Wage Expense
b) Interest Revenue
c) Utility Expense
d) Accumulated Depreciation

_____ 2. Temporary revenue and expense accounts may be closed:
a) individually by separate entries to Retained Earnings
b) in a single entry to Retained Earnings
c) to a temporary Income Summary account
d) by any of the above three methods

_____ 3. Which of these transactions did not result in revenue being reported?
a) sold merchandise for cash
b) sold merchandise on account
c) collected an account receivable
d) all of the above transactions would result in revenue being reported

_____ 4. Benjamin Corp. purchased a one-year insurance policy on April 2, 19X1 for $1,000. The amount of prepaid insurance reported on the balance sheet and the amount of insurance expense reported on the income statement at December 31, 19X1 are, respectively:
a) $250; $750
b) $750; $250
c) $333; $667
d) $667; $333

_____ 5. Which of these accounts is *not* an expense?
a) Depreciation
b) Sales Salaries
c) Dividends Declared
d) Delivery Expense

_____ 6. All of the following are examples of period expenses, except:
a) administrative costs
b) inventory costs
c) accounting costs
d) selling costs

_____ 7. Which of these statements is correct?
a) Accumulated Depreciation is a permanent (balance sheet) account
b) Advances from Customers is a permanent (balance sheet) account
c) both a and b are permanent accounts
d) neither a nor b is a permanent account

_____ 8. All of the following are temporary accounts and should be closed during the closing process, except:
a) Prepaid Insurance
b) Cost of Goods Sold
c) Sales Revenue
d) Depreciation

_____ 9. The normal balances in Depreciation Expense and its related Accumulated Depreciation accounts are:
a) debit and credit, respectively
b) credit and debit, respectively
c) both have debit balances
d) both have credit balances

_____ 10. On December 26, 19X1, Caylor Limited hired three salesclerks to begin work immediately on an after-Christmas sale. The clerks were paid on January 9, 19X2. Disregarding amounts, what entry should have been made on December 31, 19X1?
a) debit Salary Expense and credit Salary Payable
b) debit Salary Expense and credit Cash
c) debit Salary Payable and credit Cash
d) debit Salary Payable and credit Salary Expense

_____ 11. The account Accumulated Depreciation reflects:
a) depreciation for the current accounting period only
b) cumulative depreciation on the asset since acquisition
c) the amount of depreciation that can be taken in future periods
d) none of the above

_____ 12. Richardson Co. Inc. completed its first year of operations in 19X1. The company distributed dividends of $25,000. If the ending balance of Retained Earnings on December 31, 19X1 is $35,000 and the company had revenues of $200,000 from 19X1 sales, the company's 19X1 expenses totalled:
a) $175,000
b) $165,000
c) $140,000
d) none of the above

_____ 13. Firms may prepare reports of performance:
a) using the calendar year as the accounting period
b) using a natural business year as the accounting period
c) for interim periods
d) answers a, b, and c are each correct under appropriate circumstances

_____ 14. In preparing its 19X1 adjusting entries, the Jesson Co. Ltd. neglected to adjust Prepaid Insurance for the amount of insurance expired during 19X1. As a result of this error:
a) 19X1 net income is understated, the balance in Retained Earnings is understated, and assets are understated
b) 19X1 net income is overstated, the balance in Retained Earnings is overstated, and assets are correctly stated

c) 19X1 net income is overstated, the balance in Retained Earnings is overstated, and assets are overstated

d) none of the above

_____ 15. In preparing its 19X1 adjusting entries, the Clark Corporation neglected to adjust rental fees received in advance for the amount of rental fees earned during 19X1. As a result of this error:

a) 19X1 net income is understated, the balance in Retained Earnings is understated, and liabilities are overstated

b) 19X1 net income is overstated, the balance in Retained Earnings is overstated, and liabilities are correctly stated

c) 19X1 net income is understated, the balance in Retained Earnings is understated, and liabilities are understated

d) none of the above

Exercises

1. Assume that the accrual basis of accounting is used and that revenue is recognized at the time goods are sold or services are rendered. Indicate the amount of expense recognized during the month of September in each of the following situations:

_____ a. During September, a wholesale company purchased $600,000 of merchandise for resale. A portion, $100,000, was the cost of goods ordered by its customers in August to be delivered in September. Customers placed orders and received goods with a cost to the wholesale company of $300,000 in September. Customers in September ordered goods with a cost of $150,000 to be delivered in October. The remaining portion of September's purchases was maintained for future express orders.

_____ b. A manufacturing firm has two insurance policies covering its property against casualties. Each policy covers a six-month period. On August 15, the premium for the first policy, $1,200, is paid to cover the period August 15 through February 15. On September 1, the second policy's premium, $900, is paid to cover the period September 1 through February 28.

_____ c. In September, a professional football team incurred a cost of $40,000 for the design and printing of its home-game tickets. The team has eight home games: two in September, three in October, two in November, and one in December.

_____ d. A swimming pool company purchased concrete supplies totalling $30,000 in August. At the end of August, there were still unused supplies totalling $25,000 and, at the end of September, there were unused supplies totalling $5,000. The remaining $5,000 worth was used in October.

_____ e. An accounting firm leases its office space. Every six months, on September 1 and March 1, it is required to pay $180,000 under the lease contract.

_____ f. Sales commissions for a cosmetics company are based on a percentage of each sales dollar generated by the sales staff. The commissions are paid at the end of each three-month period. In September, $50,000 was paid for July, August, and September sales. Sales related to commissions for the three-month period were: July, $250,000; August, $350,000; September, $400,000.

2. Assume that the accrual basis of accounting is used and revenue is recognized at the time goods are sold or services rendered. Indicate in the space provided the dollar amount of revenue recognized in the month of January. (Each case is independent.)

_____ a. In January, a company sold its product for a sales price totalling $400,000, of which $270,000 was collected in January, $100,000 in February, and the remainder in March.

_____ b. A theatrical company sells $120,000 worth of season tickets to its plays, which will be performed the second Saturday in each month for ten months beginning in January. Also, the company sells $8,000 worth of tickets for January's play.

_____ c. The Burnaby Brahmans, a professional football team, receives $300,000 for its portion of the gate receipts for the playoffs held in the previous December.

_____ d. Office Space Limited, an owner of the office buildings, collected $800,000 in January for office rental fees. Each of its customers pays four months' rental three times a year.

_____ e. On January 1, the company lends $100,000 to a customer. The customer agrees to repay the $100,000 plus 12 percent interest (total of $112,000) on December 31 of that same year.

_____ f. A computer leasing firm makes collections in the month of January of $800,000. The contract with its customers indicates that 60 percent paid for their leased computers in the month before their usage. Other customers, representing 30 percent, paid in the month of usage, and the other 10 percent of the collection represented payments in the month following the usage.

3. Indicate whether the following accounts are temporary or permanent by placing in the space provided either a T for temporary or a P for permanent.

_____ a. Retained Earnings

_____ b. Cost of Goods Sold

_____ c. Accumulated Depreciation

_____ d. Advances from Tenants

_____ e. Sales

_____ f. Depreciation Expense

_____ g. Prepaid Insurance

_____ h. Bonds Payable

_____ i. Work in Process

_____ j. Raw Materials

_____ k. Accounts Receivable

_____ l. Salaries Payable

_____ m. Sales Staff Commissions

_____ n. Finished Goods

_____ o. Interest Revenue

_____ p. Contributed Surplus

_____ q. Insurance Expense

_____ r. Delivery Expense

_____ s. Dividends Payable

_____ t. Common Stock

4. The following is a partial listing of the Brockway Limited's unadjusted and adjusted trial balances. From the information given, reconstruct the adjusting entries.

	Unadjusted Trial Balance		Adjusted Trial Balance	
	Dr.	Cr.	Dr.	Cr.
Prepaid Insurance	$ 1,500		$ 690	
Supplies on Hand	630		270	
Interest Receivable			105	
Building	78,000		78,000	
Accumulated Depreciation		$12,000		$14,000
Advances from Tenants		1,200		800
Rent Payable				2,000
Salaries Payable				900
Insurance Expense			810	
Supplies Expense			360	
Depreciation Expense			2,000	
Salaries Expense			900	
Rent Expense			2,000	
Interest Revenue				105
Rent Revenue				400

5. This adjusted trial balance is for Alton Corporation on December 31, 19X1 (accounts listed alphabetically):

Alton Corporation
Adjusted Trial Balance
December 31, 19X1

	Dr.	Cr.
Accounts Payable		$ 75,000
Accounts Receivable	$ 250,000	
Advertising Expense	15,000	
Cash	140,000	
Common Stock		250,000
Cost of Goods Sold	1,250,000	
Interest Revenue		25,000
Inventory	375,000	
Rent Expense	60,000	
Retained Earnings		562,500
Salaries Expense	450,000	
Salaries Payable		2,500
Sales		1,625,000
	$2,540,000	$2,540,000

_____ a. Prepare the necessary closing entries.

_____ b. What is the amount of the company's reported net income (or loss) for the year?

PROBLEM 1 FOR SELF-STUDY

Harris Equipment Corporation was organized on January 2, Year 2 with the issuance of 10,000 shares of $10 par-value common stock for $15 cash per share. The company maintains a perpetual inventory system. The following transactions occurred during Year 2:

(1) January 2, Year 2: The firm acquired a building costing $80,000 and equipment costing $40,000. It paid cash in the amount of $60,000 and assumed a 10 percent mortgage for the balance of the purchase price. Interest is payable on January 2 of each year, beginning one year after the purchase.

(2) January 2, Year 2: The firm bought a two-year fire insurance policy on the building and equipment. It paid the insurance premium of $1,200 for the two-year period in advance (debit an asset account).

(3) During Year 2: Merchandise acquired on account totalled $320,000. Payments to these suppliers during Year 2 totalled $270,000.

(4) During Year 2: Sales of merchandise totalled $510,000, of which $80,000 was for cash and $430,000 was on account. The cost of merchandise sold was $180,000. Collections from credit customers during Year 2 totalled $360,000.

(5) During Year 2: Salaries paid to employees totalled $80,000.

(6) During Year 2: Utility bills totalling $1,300 were paid.

(7) November 1, Year 2: A customer advanced $600 toward the purchase price of merchandise to be delivered during January, Year 3.

(8) November 1, Year 2: A customer gave a $1,000, 9 percent, 90-day note to settle an open account receivable.

(9) December 1, Year 2: The firm rented out a portion of the building for a three-month period. It received the rent for the period of $900 in advance (credit a revenue account).

Give the journal entries to record these nine transactions *during Year 2*. (Adjusting entries at the end of Year 2 are analyzed in the next self-study problem.) Omit explanations for the journal entries.

PROBLEM 2 FOR SELF-STUDY

Refer to the data for Harris Equipment Corporation in the preceding self-study problem. Give the adjusting entries on December 31, Year 2 to reflect the following items. You may omit explanations to the journal entries.

(10) The building acquired on January 2, Year 2 has a twenty-year estimated life and zero salvage value. The equipment has a seven-year estimated life and $5,000 salvage value. The straight-line depreciation method is used.

(11) Interest expense on the mortgage liability for Year 2 is recognized.

(12) Salaries earned by employees during the last three days of December total $800 and will be paid on January 4, Year 3.

(13) Interest revenue is recognized on the note receivable [see transaction **(8)** in the preceding self-study problem].

(14) An adjusting entry is made to record the proper amount of rent revenue for Year 2 [see transaction **(9)** in the preceding self-study problem].

(15) Dividends of $25,000 are declared. The dividend will be paid on January 15, Year 3 (debit Retained Earnings).

(16) Income tax expense is recorded as 40 percent of accounting income before income tax.

PROBLEM 3 FOR SELF-STUDY

To achieve efficient recording of day-to-day cash receipts and disbursements relating to operations, a firm may credit *all* cash receipts to revenue accounts and debit *all* cash disbursements to expense accounts. The efficiency stems from treating all receipts in the same way and from treating all disbursements in the same way. As a result, lower-paid clerks can be employed to make the routine and repetitive entries for receipts and disbursements. In the day-to-day recording of transactions, the clerk need not be concerned with whether a specific cash transaction reflects settlement of a past accrual, a revenue or expense correctly assigned to the current period, or a prepayment relating to a future period. Higher-paid accountants need be employed only at the end of the period to analyze the existing account balances and to construct the adjusting entries required to correct them. This process results in temporarily incorrect balances in some balance sheet and income statement accounts *during* the accounting period.

Construct the adjusting entry required for each of the following scenarios.

a. On September 1, Year 2, a tenant paid $24,000 rent for the one-year period starting at that time. The tenant debited the entire amount to Rent Expense and credited Cash. The tenant made no adjusting entries for rent between September 1 and December 31. Construct the adjusting entry to be made on December 31, Year 2 to recognize the proper balances in the Prepaid Rent and Rent Expense accounts.

b. The tenant's books for December 31, Year 2, after adjusting entries, show a balance in the Prepaid Rent account of $16,000. This amount represents rent for the period January 1 through August 31, Year 3. On September 1, Year 3, the tenant paid $30,000 for rent for the one-year period starting September 1, Year 3. The tenant debited this amount to Rent Expense and credited Cash, but made no adjusting entries for rent during Year 3. Construct the adjusting entry required on December 31, Year 3.

c. The tenant's books for December 31, Year 3, after adjusting entries, show a balance in the Prepaid Rent account of $20,000. This amount represents rent for the period January 1 through August 31, Year 4. On September 1, Year 4, the tenant paid $18,000 for rent for the *six-month* period starting September 1, Year 4. The tenant debited this amount to Rent Expense and credited Cash, but made no adjusting entries during Year 4. Construct the adjusting entry required on December 31, Year 4.

d. Whenever the firm makes payments for wages, it debits Wage Expense. At the start of April, the Wages Payable account had a balance of $5,000, representing wages earned but not paid during the last few days of March. During April, the firm paid $30,000 in wages, debiting the entire amount to Wage Expense. At the end of April, analysis of amounts earned since the last payday indicates that wages of $4,000 have been earned but not yet paid. Construct the required adjusting entry.

e. A firm purchased an insurance policy providing one year's coverage from May 1, Year 1 and debited the entire amount to Insurance Expense. After the firm made adjusting entries, the balance sheet for December 31, Year 1 correctly showed Prepaid Insurance of $3,000. Construct the adjusting entry that must be made on January 31, Year 2 if the books are closed monthly and a balance sheet is to be prepared for January 31, Year 2.

f. The recordkeeping system for an apartment building instructs the bookkeeper always to credit rent revenue when a payment is received from tenants. At the beginning of Year 3, the liability account, Advances from Tenants, had a credit balance of $25,000, representing collections from tenants for rental services to be received during Year 3. During Year 3, collections from tenants of $250,000 were all debited to Cash and credited to Rent Revenue. No adjusting entries were made during Year 3. At the end of Year 3, analysis of the individual accounts indicates that of the amounts already collected, $30,000 represents collections for rental services to be provided to tenants during Year 4. Present the required adjusting entry.

g. When the firm acquired new equipment costing $10,000 on January 1, Year 1, the bookkeeper debited Depreciation Expense and credited Cash for $10,000, but made no further entries for this equipment during Year 1. The equipment has an expected service life of five years and an estimated salvage value of zero. Construct the adjusting entry required before a balance sheet for December 31, Year 1 can be prepared.

ANSWERS TO SELF-STUDY QUESTIONS AND EXERCISES

True/False

1. T.	7. F	13. T	19. T
2. F	8. F	14. T	20. F
3. T	9. T	15. T	21. F
4. T	10. F	16. F	22. F
5. F	11. F	17. F	23. T
6. F	12. F	18. T	24. F

Matching

1. s	6. q	11. n	16. a
2. o	7. p	12. g	17. k
3. r	8. c	13. b	18. m
4. i	9. d	14. h	19. e
5. l	10. t	15. f	20. j

Multiple Choice

1. d	5. c	9. a	13. d
2. d	6. b	10. a	14. c
3. c	7. c	11. b	15. a
4. a	8. a	12. c	

Exercises

1.
a. $400,000
b. $350
c. $10,000
d. $20,000
e. $30,000
f. $20,000

2.
a. $400,000
b. $20,000
c. –0–
d. $200,000
e. $1,000
f. $240,000

3.

a. P	f. T	k. P	p. P
b. T	g. P	l. P	q. T
c. P	h. P	m. T	r. T
d. P	i. P	n. P	s. P
e. T	j. P	o. T	t. P

4.

	Dr.	Cr.
a. Insurance Expense	$810	
Prepaid Insurance		$810
To record expired insurance.		
b. Supplies Expense	$360	
Supplies on Hand		$360
To record supplies used.		
c. Interest Receivable	$105	
Interest Revenue		$105
To record interest earned and receivable.		
d. Depreciation Expense	$2,000	
Accumulated Depreciation		$2,000
To record depreciation expense.		

e. Advances from Tenants $400
       Rent Revenue $400
    To record rent revenue earned.

f. Rent Expense $2,000
       Rent Payable $2,000
    To record rent expense.

g. Salaries Expense $900
       Salaries Payable $900
    To record salaries expense.

5.   **Dr.**   **Cr.**

a. Sales $1,625,000
    Interest Revenue   25,000
       Retained Earnings $1,650,000
    To close revenue accounts.

    Retained Earnings $1,775,000
       Advertising Expense   15,000
       Cost of Goods Sold   1,250,000
       Rent Expense   60,000
       Salaries Expense   450,000
    To close expense accounts.

    Alternatively: The revenue and expense accounts may be closed to the Income Summary
    account, then the Income Summary account is closed to Retained Earnings.

b. The reported net loss is $125,000 ($1,625,000 + $25,000 − $15,000 − $1,250,000 −
    $60,000 − $450,000).

SUGGESTED SOLUTION TO PROBLEM 1 FOR SELF-STUDY

		Dr.	Cr.
(1) Jan. 2, Year 2	Building	$ 80,000	
	Equipment	40,000	
	Cash		$ 60,000
	Mortgage Payable		60,000
(2) Jan. 2, Year 2	Prepaid Insurance	1,200	
	Cash		1,200
(3) During Year 2	Merchandise Inventory	320,000	
	Accounts Payable		320,000
During Year 2	Accounts Payable	270,000	
	Cash		270,000
(4) During Year 2	Cash	80,000	
	Accounts Receivable	430,000	
	Sales Revenue		510,000
	Cost of Sales	180,000	
	Merchandise Inventory		180,000
During Year 2	Cash	360,000	
	Accounts Receivable		360,000
(5) During Year 2	Salary Expense	80,000	
	Cash		80,000
(6) During Year 2	Utilities Expense	1,300	
	Cash		1,300
(7) Nov. 1, Year 2	Cash	600	
	Advances from Customers		600
(8) Nov. 1, Year 2	Note Receivable	1,000	
	Accounts Receivable		1,000
(9) Dec. 1, Year 2	Cash	900	
	Rent Revenue		900

SUGGESTED SOLUTION TO PROBLEM 2 FOR SELF-STUDY

(10)	Depreciation Expense	4,000	
	Accumulated Depreciation		4,000
	($80,000 − $0)/20 = $4,000.		
	Depreciation Expense — Equipment	5,000	
	Accumulated Depreciation — Equipment		5,000
	($40,000 − $5,000)/7 = $5,000.		
(11)	Interest Expense	6,000	
	Interest Payable		6,000
	$60,000 × 0.10 = $6,000.		
(12)	Salary Expense	800	
	Salaries Payable		800
(13)	Interest Receivable	15	
	Interest Revenue		15
	$1,000 × 0.09 × 60/360 = $15.		
(14)	Rent Revenue	600	
	Advances from Tenants	600	
(15)	Retained Earnings	25,000	
	Dividends Payable		25,000
(16)	Income Tax Expense	93,286	
	Income Tax Payable		93,286
	0.4 × [($510,000 + $900 − $600 + $15) − ($80,000 + $800 + $1,300 + $9,000 + $180,000 + $6,000)] = $93,286.		

SUGGESTED SOLUTION TO PROBLEM 3 FOR SELF-STUDY

a. The Prepaid Rent account on the year-end balance sheet should represent eight months of prepayments. The rent per month is $2,000 (= $24,000/12), so the balance required in the Prepaid Rent account is $16,000 (= 8 × $2,000).

Prepaid Rent	$16,000	
Rent Expense		$16,000
To increase the balance in the Prepaid Rent account, reducing the amount in the Rent Expense account.		

b. The Prepaid Rent account on the balance sheet for the end of Year 3 should represent eight months of prepayments. The rent per month is $2,500 (= $30,000/12), so the required balance in the Prepaid Rent account is $20,000 (= 8 × $2,500). The balance in that account is already $16,000, so the adjusting entry must increase it by $4,000 (= $20,000 − $16,000).

Prepaid Rent	$4,000	
Rent Expense		$4,000
To increase the balance in the Prepaid Rent account, reducing the amount in the Rent Expense account.		

The Rent Expense account will have a balance at the end of Year 3 before closing entries of $26,000 (= $30,000 − $4,000). This amount comprises $16,000 (= $2,000 × 8) for rent from January through August and $10,000 (= $2,500 × 4) for rent from September through December.

c. The Prepaid Rent account on the balance sheet at the end of Year 4 should represent two months of prepayments. The rent per month is $3,000 (= $18,000/6), so the required balance in the Prepaid Rent account is $6,000 (= 2 × $3,000). The balance in that account is $20,000, so the adjusting entry must reduce it by $14,000 (= $20,000 − $6,000).

Rent Expense	$14,000	
Prepaid Rent		$14,000
To reduce the balance in the Prepaid Rent account, increasing the amount in the Rent Expense account.		

The Rent Expense account will have a balance at the end of Year 3 before closing entries of $32,000 (= $18,000 + $14,000). This amount comprises $20,000 (= $2,500 × 8) for rent from January through August and $12,000 (= $3,000 × 4) for rent from September through December.

d. The Wages Payable account should have a credit balance of $4,000 at the end of April, but it has a balance of $5,000 carried over from the end of March. The adjusting entry must reduce the balance by $1,000, which requires a debit to the Wages Payable account.

Wages Payable	$1,000	
Wage Expense		$1,000
To reduce the balance in the Wages Payable account, reducing the amount in the Wage Expense account.		

e. The Prepaid Insurance account balance of $3,000 represents four months of coverage. Thus, the cost of insurance is $750 (= $3,000/4) per month. The adjusting entry for a single month is:

Insurance Expense	$750	
Prepaid Insurance		$750

f. The Advances from Tenants account has a balance of $25,000 carried over from the start of the year. At the end of Year 3, it should have a balance of $30,000. Thus, the adjusting entry must increase the balance by $5,000, which requires a credit to the liability account.

Rent Revenue	$5,000	
Advances from Tenants		$5,000
To increase the balance in the Advances from Tenants account, reducing the amount in the Rent Revenue account.		

g. The Depreciation Expense for the year should be $2,000 (= $10,000/5). The balance in the Accumulated Depreciation account should also be $2,000 and, thus, the Depreciation Expense account must be reduced (credited) by $8,000 (= $10,000 − $2,000). The adjusting entry not only reduces recorded Depreciation Expense, but sets up the asset account and its accumulated depreciation contra account.

Equipment	$10,000	
Accumulated Depreciation		$2,000
Depreciation Expense		8,000
To reduce Depreciation Expense, setting up the asset and its contra account.		

ASSIGNMENT MATERIAL

QUESTIONS

1. Review the meaning of the key terms listed on page 158.

2. What factors would a firm likely consider in its decision to use the calendar year versus a fiscal (natural business) year as its accounting period?

3. Which of the following types of businesses are likely to have a natural business year different from the calendar year?
   a. A ski resort in British Columbia
   b. A professional basketball team
   c. A grocery store

4. Distinguish between a revenue and a cash receipt. Under what conditions will they be the same?

5. Distinguish between an expense and a cash expenditure. Under what conditions will they be the same?

6. "Cash flows determine the *amount* of revenue and expense but not the *timing* of their recognition". Explain.

7. "Accrual accounting focuses on the use, rather than the financing, of assets." Explain.

8. "Depreciation on equipment may be a product cost or a period expense, depending on the type of equipment." Explain.

9. "Revenue and expense accounts are useful accounting devices, but they could be dispensed with." What is an alternative to using them?

10. Why are revenue and expense accounts closed at the end of each accounting period?

11. Before the books have been closed for an accounting period, what types of accounts will have nonzero balances? After the books have been closed, what types of accounts will have nonzero balances?

12. If each transaction occurring during an accounting period has been recorded properly, why is there a need for adjusting entries at the end of the period?

13. What is the purpose of using contra accounts? What is the alternative to using them?

EXERCISES

14. *Relation between cash flows and revenues and expenses.* Under the accrual basis of accounting, cash receipts and disbursements may precede, coincide with, or follow the period in which revenues and expenses are recognized. Give an example of each of the following:
    a. A cash receipt that precedes the period in which revenue is recognized.
    b. A cash receipt that coincides with the period in which revenue is recognized.
    c. A cash receipt that follows the period in which revenue is recognized.
    d. A cash disbursement that precedes the period in which expense is recognized.
    e. A cash disbursement that coincides with the period in which expense is recognized.
    f. A cash disbursement that follows the period in which expense is recognized.

15. *Revenue recognition.* Assume that the accrual basis of accounting is used and that revenue is recognized at the time the goods are sold or services are rendered. How much revenue is recognized during the month of May in each of the following transactions?
    a. Collection of cash from customers during May for merchandise sold and delivered in April, $8,200.
    b. Sales of merchandise during May for cash, $9,600.
    c. Sales of merchandise during May to customers to be collected in June, $2,400.
    d. A store building is rented to a toy shop for $800 a month, effective May 1. A cheque for $1,600 for two months' rent is received on May 1.
    e. Data in part (d), except that collection is received from the tenant in June.

16. *Revenue recognition.* Assume that the accrual basis of accounting is used and that revenue is recognized at the time goods are sold or services are rendered. Indicate the amount of revenue recognized in each of the months of April, May, and June relating to the following cash receipts during May.
    a. $4,600 collected from customers for merchandise sold and delivered in April.
    b. $8,900 collected from customers for merchandise sold and delivered in May.
    c. $1,800 collected from customers for merchandise to be delivered in June.
    d. $3,600 collected from subscibers for subscription fees to magazines for the one-year period beginning April 1.
    e. Same as part (d), except that the subscription period begins May 1.
    f. Same as part (d), except that the subscription period begins June 1.

17. *Revenue recognition.* Indicate the amount of revenue, if any, recognized from each of the following related events, assuming that the accrual basis of accounting is used.
    a. A firm receives purchase orders from regular customers for $8,400 of merchandise. A 2 percent discount is allowed, and generally taken, for prompt payment.
    b. The customers' orders are filled and shipped by way of the company's trucking division.
    c. The firm sends invoices totalling $8,400 to the customers.
    d. The merchandise is received by customers in the correct quantities and according to specifications.
    e. The firm receives cheques in the amount of $8,232 (= 0.98 × $8,400) from customers in payment of the merchandise.
    f. Upon reinspection, several days later, merchandise with a gross invoice price of $600 is found to be defective by customers and returned for appropriate credit.

18. *Revenue recognition.* Indicate which of the following transactions or events immediately gives rise to the recognition of revenue under the accrual basis of accounting.
    a. The receipt of an order from a customer for merchandise.
    b. The shipment of goods that have been paid for in advance.
    c. The issue of additional common shares.
    d. The completion of a batch of men's suits by a clothing factory.
    e. The sale of tickets by a major league baseball team for a game in two weeks.
    f. Same as part **(e)**, except that sale was made by Ticket World, a ticket agent.
    g. The interest earned on a savings account between interest dates.
    h. A collection of cash from accounts receivable debtors.
    i. The rendering of accounting services to a customer on account.

19. *Expense recognition.* Give the amount of expense recognized, if any, from each of the following related events, assuming that the accrual basis of accounting is used.
    a. The purchasing department notifies the stockroom that the supply of 1 cm plywood has reached the minimum point and should be reordered.
    b. The firm sends a purchase order to Central Lumber Co. Ltd. for $10,000 of the material.
    c. The firm receives an acknowledgement of the order. It indicates that delivery will be made in fifteen days, but that the price has been raised to $10,200.
    d. The shipment of plywood arrives and is checked by the receiving department. The correct quantity has been delivered.
    e. The purchase invoice arrives. The amount of $10,200 is subject to a 2 percent discount if paid within ten days. Cash discounts are treated as a reduction in the acquisition cost of inventory.
    f. Upon reinspection, the firm finds plywood with a gross invoice price of $200 to be defective and returns it to the supplier.

g. The balance of the amount due the Central Lumber Co. Ltd. is paid in time to obtain the discount.

h. The firm sells the plywood to customers for $12,000.

20. *Expense recognition.* Assume that the accrual basis of accounting is used and that revenue is recognized at the time goods are sold or services are rendered. Indicate the amount of expense recognized during March, if any, from each of the following transactions or events.

a. An insurance premium of $1,800 is paid on March 1 for one year's coverage beginning on that date.

b. On April 3, a utilities bill totalling $460 for services during March is received.

c. Supplies totalling $700 were purchased on account during March. Of these purchases $500 was paid in March and the remainder was paid in April. On March 1, supplies were on hand that cost $300. At March 31, supplies that cost $350 were still on hand.

d. Data of (c), except that $200 of supplies were on hand at March 1.

e. Property taxes of $4,800 on an office building for the year were paid in January.

f. An advance of $250 on the April salary is paid to an employee on March 29.

21. *Expense recognition.* Assume that the accrual basis of accounting is used and that revenue is recognized at the time goods are sold or services are rendered. Indicate the amount of expense recognized in each of the months of April, May, and June relating to the following cash expenditures during May.

a. $1,900 for advertising that appeared on television programs during April.

b. $3,200 for sales commissions on sales made during May.

c. $500 for rent on delivery equipment for the month of June.

d. $600 for an insurance premium for coverage from May 1 until October 30.

e. $800 as a deposit on equipment to be delivered during June.

f. $1,200 for property taxes on an office building for the current calendar year.

22. *Income recognition.* Feltham Limited acquired used machine tools costing $75,000 from various sources. These machine tools were then sold to Mock Corporation. Delivery costs paid by Feltham Limited totalled $4,500. Mock Corporation had agreed to pay $100,000 cash for these tools. Finding itself short of cash, however, Mock Corporation offered some of its bonds to Feltham Limited. The bonds have a face value of $110,000 and mature in five years. The bonds promise 8 percent interest per year. At the time the offer was made, the bonds could have been sold in public bond markets for $98,000.

Feltham Limited accepted the offer and held the bonds for three years. During the three years, it received interest payments of $8,800 per year, or $26,400 total. At the end of the third year, Feltham Limited sold the bonds for $95,000.

a. What profit or loss did Feltham Limited recognize at the time of sale of machine tools to Mock Corporation?

b. What profit or loss would Feltham Limited have recognized at the time of the sale of machine tools if it had sold the bonds for $98,000 immediately upon receiving them?

c. What profit or loss would Feltham Limited have recognized at the time of the sale of machine tools if it had held the bonds to maturity, receiving $8,800 each year for another five years and $110,000 at the time the bonds matured?

23. *Identifying missing half of journal entries.* In the business world, many transactions are routine and repetitive. Because accounting records business transactions, many accounting entries are also routine and repetitive. Knowing one-half of an entry in the double-entry recording system often permits a reasoned guess about the other half. The items below give the account name for one-half of an entry. Indicate your best guess as to the nature of the transaction being recorded and the name of the account of the *routine* other half of the entry. Also indicate whether the other account is increased or decreased by the transaction.

   a. Debit: Cost of Goods Sold.
   b. Debit: Accounts Receivable.
   c. Credit: Accounts Receivable.
   d. Debit: Accounts Payable.
   e. Credit: Accounts Payable.
   f. Credit: Accumulated Depreciation.
   g. Debit: Retained Earnings.
   h. Credit: Prepaid Insurance.
   i. Debit: Property Taxes Payable.
   j. Debit: Merchandise Inventory.

24. *Asset versus expense recognition.* Give the journal entry that should be made upon the receipt of each of the following invoices by the South Appliance Company, assuming that no previous entry has been made.

   (1) From Western Electric Supply Company, $385, for repair parts purchased.
   (2) From Touch & Rose, chartered accountants, $800, for services in filing income tax returns.
   (3) From the Standard Electric Company, $12,365, for refrigerators purchased.
   (4) From the White Stationery Company, $250 for office supplies purchased.
   (5) From the Showy Sign Company, $540, for a neon sign acquired.
   (6) From Schutheis and Schutheis, attorneys, $1,000, for legal services in changing from the corporate to the partnership form of organization.
   (7) From the Swell Telephone Company, $65, for telephone service for next month.
   (8) From the Madison Avenue Garage, $43, for gasoline and oil used by the delivery truck.
   (9) From the Municipal Electric Department, $105, for electricity used for lighting last month.

25. *Journal entries for notes receivable and notes payable.* The General Supply Co. Inc. received a $10,000, three-month, 9 percent promissory note, dated December 1, Year 6, from Widen Stores to apply on its open accounts receivable. The fiscal year-end of both companies is December 31.

    a. Present journal entries for the General Supply Co. Inc. from December 1, Year 6 through collection at maturity. The books are closed quarterly. Include the closing entry for interest.

    b. Present journal entries for Widen Stores from December 1, Year 6 through payment at maturity. Include the closing entry for interest.

26. *Journal entries for notes payable.* Selected transactions of Burlson Limited are described below. Present dated journal entries for these transactions and adjusting entries at the end of each month from January 15, Year 2 through July 1, Year 2. Assume that only the notes indicated were outstanding during this period. The accounting period is one month.

    (1) The company issued a $6,000, two-month, 10 percent promissory note on January 15, Year 2 in lieu of payment on an account due that date to the Grey Wholesale Company.

    (2) The note in (1) and interest were paid at maturity.

    (3) The company issued a $2,000, three-month, 9 percent promissory note to the Grey Wholesale Company on the date of purchase of merchandise, April 1, Year 2.

    (4) The note in (3) and interest were paid at maturity.

27. *Journal entries for office supply inventories.* On January 1, Year 4, the Office Supplies Inventory account of the Harris Company had a balance of $4,200. During the ensuing quarter, supplies were acquired on account in the amount of $9,000. On March 31, Year 4, the inventory was taken and calculated to amount to $2,500.

    Present journal entries to record the above acquisition and adjustments at the end of March in accordance with each of the following sets of instructions, which might be established in an accounting systems manual:

    a. An expense account is to be debited at the time supplies are acquired.

    b. An asset account is to be debited at the time supplies are acquired.

28. *Journal entries for rental receipts and payments.* The Regina Realty Co. Ltd. rents office space to Maddox Consultants at the rate of $600 per month. Collections have been made for rental through April 30, Year 3. The following transactions occurred on the dates indicated:

    (1) May 1, Year 3: Collection, $600.

    (2) June 1, Year 3: Collection, $1,200.

    (3) August 1, Year 3: Collection, $1,800.

Present journal entries for the above transactions and for adjusting entries from May 1 to August 31, inclusive, as they relate to both companies, assuming that each company adjusts its books monthly.

29. **Using accumulated depreciation to estimate asset age.**
    a. Machine A costs $10,000, has accumulated depreciation of $4,000 as of year-end, and is being depreciated on a straight-line basis over ten years with an estimated salvage value of zero. How long ago was machine A acquired?
    b. Machine B has accumulated depreciation (straight-line basis) of $6,000 at year-end. The depreciation charge for the year is $2,000. The estimated salvage value of the machine at the end of its useful life is $1,000. How long ago was machine B acquired?

30. **Effect of recording errors on financial statements.** In recording transactions of Rogow Corporation during Year 7, the following errors were made:
    (1) An expenditure of $2,000 to acquire a tract of land was debited to Administrative Expenses.
    (2) Cash collections during Year 7 of $1,500 relating to sales made during Year 6 were credited to Sales Revenue of Year 7.
    (3) An expenditure of $1,200 for insurance coverage from October 1, Year 7 to September 30, Year 8 was debited to Administrative Expenses on October 1, Year 7.
    (4) Cash collections during Year 7 of $1,000 for goods to be delivered during Year 8 were credited to Sales Revenue of Year 7.
    Indicate the cumulative effect exclusive of income tax implications) of these errors on the following items in the financial statements prepared on December 31, Year 7.
    a. Current assets
    b. Property, plant, and equipment
    c. Current liabilities
    d. Sales revenue
    e. Administrative expenses
    f. Net income
    g. Retained earnings

31. **Effect of recording errors on financial statements.** In recording the adjusting entries of the Hammond Sales Company, Inc. at the end of Year 7, the following adjustments were omitted:
    (1) Depreciation on the delivery truck of $3,000.
    (2) Insurance expired on the delivery truck of $600.
    (3) Interest accrued on notes payable of $150.
    (4) Interest accrued on notes receivable of $330.
    Indicate the cumulative effect (exclusive of income tax implications) of these omissions on the following items in the financial statements prepared on December 31, Year 7.
    a. Current assets
    b. Property, plant, and equipment
    c. Current liabilities
    d. Selling and administrative expenses
    e. Net income
    f. Retained earnings

32. **Effect of recording errors on financial statements.** Using the notation O/S (overstated), U/S (understated), and NO (no effect), indicate the effects on assets, liabilities, and shareholders' equity as of December

31, Year 5 of the following independent errors or omissions. Ignore income tax implications.

   a. An expenditure of $1,200 for insurance coverage for the one-year period beginning September 1, Year 5 was debited to Administrative Expenses.

   b. Sales commissions earned and paid during December Year 5 were debited to Interest Expense.

   c. Depreciation on delivery equipment for Year 5 of $1,500 was not recorded.

   d. A cheque for $900 was received from a customer during December Year 5 for merchandise to be delivered during January Year 6. Sales Revenue was credited when the cash was received.

   e. Interest accrued on Notes Payable of $400 as of December 31, Year 5 was not recorded.

   f. Interest accrued on Notes Receivable of $560 as of December 31, Year 5 was recorded as $650.

33. **Effect of recording errors on financial statements.** Using the notation O/S (overstated), U/S (understated), and NO (no effect), indicate the effects on assets, liabilities, and shareholders' equity as of December 31, Year 3, of the following independent errors or omissions. Ignore income tax implications.

   a. An expenditure of $600 made on December 1, Year 3 for six months' rent on an automobile was debited to Prepaid Rent. No adjusting entry was made on December 31, Year 3.

   b. A microcomputer acquired on July 1, Year 3, for $6,000 was debited to Administrative Expenses. The microcomputer has an expected useful life of three years and zero estimated salvage value.

   c. The company rented out excess office space for the six-month period beginning January 1, Year 3. A rental cheque for this period of $600 was received on December 26, *Year 2* and correctly credited to Rental Fees Received in Advance. No further journal entries were made relating to this rental during Year 3.

   d. Interest accrued on Notes Receivable of $500 as of December 31, Year 3 was not recorded.

   e. A cheque for $250 was reeived from a customer on December 31, Year 3 in settlement of an account receivable. No journal entries have been made to record this cheque.

   f. An expenditure of $740 for travel on December 31, Year 3 was recorded as $470.

34. **Allocation of cost.** How should the cost of the following assets be allocated over their useful lives?

   a. A building with an estimated useful life of 30 years.

   b. A road leading to a timber tract. The road would normally last for 14 years before extensive reconstruction would be necessary, but it is expected that the timber will all be cut in 5 years.

   c. Rent prepaid for 2 years on a warehouse in Regina.

   d. A truck with an estimated service life of 144,000 kilometres.

   e. Rent prepaid for a year on a shop used for boat repairs at a summer resort. The shop is open only from June 1 to September 1.

   f. An ore deposit owned by a mining company.

35. *Reconstructing accounting records.* Most of the financial records of the Rowland Novelty Company were removed by an employee who apparently took all of the cash on hand from the store on October 31. From supplementary records, the following information is obtained:

   (1) According to the bank, cash in bank was $5,730.

   (2) Amounts payable to creditors were $4,720.

   (3) Rowland's initial contribution to the business was $15,000, and the total shareholders' equity at the time of the theft was $17,500.

   (4) Cost of merchandise on hand was $11,380.

   (5) A one-year fire insurance policy was purchased on September 1 for $900.

   (6) Furniture and fixtures are rented from the Anderson Office Supply Company for $200 per month. The rental for October has not been paid.

   (7) A note for $1,200 was given by a customer. Interest due at October 31 was $45.

   (8) Payments due from other customers amounted to $1,915.

   (9) Rowland purchased a licence from the city for $300 on July 1. The licence allows retail operations for one year.

   a. Determine the probable cash shortage.

   b. Prepare a well-organized balance sheet presenting the financial position immediately preceding the theft.

36. *Miscellaneous transactions of adjusting entries.* Prepare journal entries for each of the following sets of data.

   a. The company rents out excess office space at a rate of $3,000 per month, payable in advance at the beginning of each calendar quarter of the year. The rental payment for the first quarter was received two months late on March 1. Assume that the books are closed monthly. Present the collection entry on March 1 and the adjusting entry made at the end of each month.

   b. On March 16, a $20,000, two-month, 9 percent note was received by the company in full payment of an open account receivable. Assume that the books are closed monthly. Give all journal entries relating to the note, from March 16 until payment at maturity on May 15.

   c. The balance in the Prepaid Insurance account on January 1, Year 4, was $600. On March 1, Year 4, the company renewed its only insurance policy for another three years, beginning on that date, by payment of $14,400. Assume that the books are closed quarterly. Present journal entries for the renewal and adjusting entries for Year 4.

   d. The Repair Parts Inventory account showed a balance of $3,000 on January 1. During January, parts costing $8,000 were purchased and charged to Repair Expense. An inventory of repair parts at the end of January revealed that parts costing $3,800 were on hand. Present the adjusting entry required at the end of January.

   e. An office machine was acquired on July 1, Year 6, at a cost of $100,000. It was estimated to have a ten-year life and a $20,000 residual value. Assume that the books are closed annually. Present the adjusting entries on December 31, Year 6 and December 31, Year 7.

f. Property taxes for the calendar year are assessed on January 1 but are paid on April 1. The company's property taxes for Year 8 of $24,000 were paid as required. Assume that the books are closed quarterly. Give the journal entries relating to property taxes for Year 8.

PROBLEMS AND CASES

37. *Cash versus accrual basis of accounting.* J. Thompson opened a hardware store on January 1, Year 5. Thompson invested $10,000 and borrowed $8,000 from a local bank. The loan plus interest is repayable on June 30, Year 5, with interest at the rate of 9 percent per year.

    Thompson rented a building on January 1 and paid two months' rent in advance in the amount of $2,000. Property and liability insurance coverage for the year ending December 31, Year 5 was paid on January 1 in the amount of $1,200.

    Thompson purchased $28,000 of merchandise inventory on account on January 2 and paid $10,000 of this amount on January 25. The cost of merchandise on hand on January 31 was $15,000.

    During January, cash sales to customers totalled $20,000 and sales on account totalled $9,000. Of the sales on account, $2,000 had been collected as of January 31.

    Other costs incurred and paid in cash during January were as follows: utilities, $400; salaries, $650; taxes, $350.
    a. Prepare an income statement for January, assuming that Thompson uses the accrual basis of accounting with revenue recognized at the time goods are sold (delivered).
    b. Prepare an income statement for January, assuming that Thompson uses the cash basis of accounting.
    c. Which basis of accounting do you feel provides a better indication of the operating performance of the hardware store during January? Why?

38. *Cash versus accrual basis of accounting.* Management Consultants, Inc. opened a consulting business on July 1, Year 2. Roy Bean and Sarah Bower each contributed $7,000 cash for the firm's common shares. The corporation borrowed $8,000 from a local bank on August 1, Year 2. The loan plus interest is repayable on July 31, Year 3 with interest at the rate of 9 percent per year.

    Office space was rented on August 1, with two months' rent paid in advance. The remaining monthly rental fees of $900 per month were made on the first of each month, beginning October 1. Office equipment with a four-year life was purchased for cash on August 1 for $4,800.

    Consulting services rendered for clients between August 1 and December 31, Year 2 were billed at $15,000. Of this amount, $9,000 was collected by year-end.

    Other costs incurred and paid in cash by the end of the year were as follows: utilities, $450; salary of secretary, $7,500; supplies, $450. Unpaid bills at year-end are as follows: utilities, $80; salary of secretary, $900; supplies, $70. All supplies acquired were used. Income tax is payable at the rate of 40 percent of accounting income before income tax calculated on an accrual basis.

   a. Prepare an income statement for the five months ended December 31, Year 2, assuming that the corporation uses the accrual basis of accounting, with revenue recognized at the time services are rendered.

   b. Prepare an income statement for the five months ended December 31, Year 2, assuming that the corporation uses the cash basis of accounting.

   c. Which basis of accounting do you feel provides a better indication of operating performance of the consulting firm for the period? Why?

39. *Cash versus accrual basis of accounting.* J. Hennessey opened a retail store on January 1, Year 8. Hennessey invested $20,000 and borrowed $10,000 from a local bank. The loan plus interest is repayable on December 31, Year 9, with interest at the rate of 12 percent per year. Hennessey rented a building on January 1 and paid a year's rent in advance in the amount of $8,000. Property and liability insurance coverage for the two-year period of $2,000 was paid on January 1, Year 8.

   Hennessey purchased $84,000 of merchandise on account during Year 8 and paid $76,000 of the amount by the end of Year 8. The cost of merchandise on hand on December 31, Year 8 was $12,000.

   During Year 8, cash sales to customers were $30,000 and sales on account totalled $70,000. Of the sales account, $62,000 was collected by December 31, Year 8.

   Other costs incurred and paid in cash were salaries, $20,000; utilities, $1,500. Unpaid bills at year-end are as follows: salaries, $1,200; utilities, $120.

   a. Prepare an income statement for Year 8 assuming that the company uses the accrual basis of accounting, with revenue recognized at the time of sale.

   b. Prepare an income statement for Year 8 assuming that the company uses the cash basis of accounting.

   c. Which basis of accounting do you feel provides a better indication of operating performance for the retail store during Year 8? Why?

40. *Miscellaneous transactions and adjusting entries.* Present journal entries for each of the following separate sets of data:

   a. On January 15, Year 2, a $6,000, two-month, 12 percent note was received by the company. Present adjusting entries at the end of each month and the entry for collection at maturity.

   b. The company uses one Merchandise Inventory account to record the beginning inventory and purchases during the period. The balance in this account on December 31, Year 2, was $580,000. The inventory of merchandise on hand at that time was $60,000. Present the adjusting entry.

   c. The company rents out part of its building for office space at the rate of $900 a month, payable quarterly in advance on January 1, April 1, July 1, and October 1. The quarterly rental for the first quarter was received one month late on February 1, Year 2. Present collection and adjusting entries for the quarter. Assume that the books are adjusted monthly.

d. The company leases branch office space at $3,000 a month. Payment is made by the company on the first of each six-month period. Payment of $18,000 was made on July 1, Year 2. Present payment and adjusting entries through August 31, Year 2. Assume that the books are adjusted monthly.

e. The balance of the Prepaid Insurance account on October 1, Year 2, was $400. On December 1, Year 2, the company renewed its only insurance policy for another two years, beginning on that date, by payment of $3,000. Present journal entries for renewal and adjusting entries through December 31, Year 2. Assume that the books are adjusted quarterly at the end of March, June, September, and December.

f. The Office Supplies on Hand account had a balance of $400 on December 31, Year 2. Purchases of supplies in the amount of $580 were recorded in the Office Supplies Expense account during the month. The physical inventory of office supplies on December 31, Year 2 was $340. Present any necessary adjusting entry at December 31, Year 2.

g. An office building was constructed at a cost of $560,000. It was estimated that it would have a useful life of 50 years from the date of occupancy, October 31, Year 2, and a residual value of $80,000. Present the adjusting entry for the depreciation of the building in Year 2. Assume that the books are closed annually at December 31.

41. *Miscellaneous transactions and adjusting entries.* Give the journal entry to record each of the transactions below as well as any necessary adjusting entries on December 31, Year 6, assuming that the accounting period is the calendar year and the books are closed on December 31.

a. Harrison's Supply Company Ltd. received a 90-day note from a customer on December 1, Year 6. The note in the face amount of $3,000 replaced an open account receivable of the same amount. The note is due with interest at 9 percent per year on March 1, Year 7.

b. Thompson's Wholesale Limited purchased a two-year insurance policy on September 1, Year 6, paying the two-year premium of $9,600 in advance.

c. William's Products Inc. acquired a machine on July 1, Year 6 for $20,000 cash. The machine is expected to have a $4,000 salvage value and a four-year life.

d. Greer Electronics Ltd. acquired an automobile on September 1, Year 5 for $5,000 cash. The automobile is expected to have $1,400 salvage value and a four-year life.

e. Devine Co. Ltd. rented out excess office space for the three-month period beginning December 15, Year 6. The first month's rent of $6,400 was received on this date.

f. Prentice Products Corporation began business on November 1, Year 6. It acquired office supplies costing $5,000 on account. Of this amount, $4,000 was paid by year-end. A physical inventory indicates that office supplies costing $2,400 were on hand on December 31, Year 6.

42. *Preparation of T-account entries and adjusted trial balance.* A corporation known as the Kirby Collection Agency Ltd. is organized by Betty Kirby and Charles Stevens on January 1, Year 3. The business of the firm is to collect overdue accounts receivable of various clients on a commission basis. The following transactions occurred during January:

(1) Kirby contributes office supplies worth $3,000 and cash of $12,000. She is issued share certificates for 500 shares with a par value of $30 a share.

(2) Stevens contributes $3,000 in cash and office equipment valued at $9,000. He is issued share certificates for 400 shares.

(3) The Kirby agency collects $400 on an account that was turned over to it by the Jiggly Market. The commission earned is 50 percent of the amount collected.

(4) The stenographer's salary during the month, $600, is paid.

(5) A bill is received from Lyband and Linn, chartered accountants, for $400 to cover the cost of installing a computer system.

(6) The amount due the Jiggly Market [see **(3)**] is paid.

(7) An office is leased for the year beginning February 1, Year 3, and the rent for two months is paid in advance. A cheque is drawn for $900.

(8) An automobile is purchased on January 30 for $4,500; of this, $2,500 is paid by cheque and an installment contract, payable to the Scotch Automobile Sales Company, is signed for the balance.

a. Open T-accounts and record the transactions during January.

b. Prepare an adjusted, preclosing trial balance as of January 31, Year 3. Indicate, by "R" or "E," accounts that are revenue or expense accounts.

43. *Preparation of T-account entries and adjusted trial balance.* Bill Wilson operates a restaurant that he has rented fully equipped from its owner. The trial balance of the restaurant on November 1, Year 6, the first day of an accounting period, is as follows:

Cash	$ 6,975	
Food on Hand	5,400	
Accounts Payable, Barry Meat Company		$ 2,050
Accounts Payable, Conell Wholesale Grocery		2,378
Bill Wilson, Capital		7,947
	$12,375	$12,375

A summary of the transactions for the month of November is as follows:

(1) Cash received for meals served, $26,550.

(2) November rent paid by cheque, $4,050.

(3) Food purchased on account from the Conell Wholesale Grocery, $7,650.

(4) Maintenance to equipment paid in cash, $450.

(5) Food purchased on account from the Barry Meat Company, $4,725.

(6) Payment to Barry Meat Company, $5,650.

(7) Payment to Conell Wholesale Grocery, $8,228.

(8) Salaries for the month totalling $6,273 are paid.

(9) Cost of food used, $11,925.

a. Open T-accounts for the accounts in the trial balance and enter the beginning balance. Record the transactions for the month of November in the T-accounts, opening additional T-accounts for individual revenues and expenses as needed.

b. Prepare an adjusted, preclosing trial balance to check the accuracy of your entries.

44. *Preparation of T-account entries, adjusted trial balance, income statement, and balance sheet.* The trial balance of Safety Cleaners and Dyers at February 28, Year 6 is shown below. The books have not been closed nor have adjusting entries been made since December 31, Year 5.

Cash	$ 3,400	
Accounts Receivable	15,200	
Supplies on Hand	4,800	
Prepaid Insurance	1,200	
Equipment	65,000	
Accumulated Depreciation		$ 9,680
Accounts Payable		7,900
P.O. Grey, Capital		60,000
Sales Revenue		46,060
Salaries and Wages Expense	26,600	
Cost of Outside Work	2,040	
Advertising Expense	400	
Repairs Expense	500	
Rent Expense	1,200	
Power, Gas, and Water Expense	880	
Supplies Used	—	
Depreciation Expense	—	
Miscellaneous Expense	2,420	
	$123,640	$123,640

A summary of the transactions for the month of March, Year 6 is as follows:

(1) Sales: for cash, $14,000; on account, $5,800.

(2) Collections on account, $10,000.

(3) Purchases of outside work (cleaning done by wholesale cleaners), $800, on account.

(4) Purchases of supplies, on account, $2,800.

(5) Payments on account, $4,000.

(6) March rent paid, $600.

(7) Supplies used (for the quarter), $5,340.

(8) Depreciation (for the quarter), $2,420.

(9) March salaries and wages of $11,120 are paid.

(10) Bills received but not recorded or paid by the end of the month: advertising, $200; maintenance on equipment, $60; power, gas, and water, $380.

(11) Insurance expired (for the quarter), $400.

a. Open T-accounts and enter the trial balance amounts.

b. Record the transactions for the month of March in the T-accounts, opening additional T-accounts as needed. Cross-number the entries.

c. Prepare an adjusted, preclosing trial balance at March 31, Year 6, an income statement for the three months ending March 31, Year 6, and a balance sheet as of March 31, Year 6.

d. Enter closing entries in the T-accounts using an Income Summary account.

45. *Preparation of T-account entries, adjusted trial balance, income statement, and balance sheet.* The balance sheet accounts of Hanover Camera Repair Shop at June 30, Year 8, are as follows:

Cash	$1,920	
Repair Parts Inventory	600	
Office Supplies Inventory	80	
Equipment	2,200	
Accumulated Depreciation		$ 300
Accounts Payable		2,500
B. Greer, Capital		2,000
	$4,800	$4,800

A summary of the transactions during July is as follows:

(1) Performed repair services, for which $900 in cash was received immediately.

(2) Performed additional repair work, $200, and sent bills to customers for this amount.

(3) Paid creditors, $400.

(4) Took our insurance on equipment on July 1, and issued a cheque to cover one year's premium of $96.

(5) Paid $60 for a series of advertisements that appeared in the local newspaper during July.

(6) Issued a cheque for $130 for rent of shop space for July.

(7) Paid telephone bill for the month, $35.

(8) Collected $100 of the amount charged to customers in item (**2**).

Adjusting entries required at the end of July relate to the following:

(9) The insurance expired during July is calculated at $8.

(10) Cost of repair parts used during the month, $180.

(11) Cost of office supplies used during July, $40.

(12) Depreciation of equipment for the month is $30.

a. Open T-accounts and insert the July 1 balances. Record the transactions for the month in the T-accounts, opening additional T-accounts for individual revenue and expense accounts as needed.

b. Prepare an adjusted, preclosing trial balance at July 31, Year 8.

c. Prepare an income statement for the month of July and a balance sheet as of July 31, Year 8.

d. Enter closing entries in the T-accounts using an Income Summary account.

46. **Preparation of T-account entries, adjusted trial balance, income statement, and balance sheet.** The trial balance of Jones Shoe Repair Shop at February 28, Year 2 is shown below. The books have not been closed since December 31, Year 1.

Cash	$ 6,060	
Accounts Receivable	15,200	
Supplies Inventory	4,800	
Prepaid Insurance	900	
Equipment	65,000	
Accumulated Depreciation		$ 11,460
Accounts Payable		6,120
W.R. Jones, Capital		62,360
Sales Revenue		46,060
Salaries and Wages Expense	26,600	
Cost of Outside Work	2,040	
Advertising Expense	900	
Rent Expense	1,200	
Power, Gas, and Water Expense	880	
Supplies Used	—	
Depreciation Expense	—	
Miscellaneous Expense	2,420	
	$126,000	$126,000

A summary of the transactions during the month of March, Year 2 is as follows:

(1) Sales: for cash, $26,000; on account, $17,600.

(2) Collections on account, $22,000.

(3) Purchases of outside work (repair work done by another shoe repair shop for Jones), $1,600, on account.

(4) Purchases of supplies, on account, $2,800.

(5) Payments on account, $6,000.

(6) March rent paid, $1,200.

(7) March salaries and wages of $13,290 are paid.

Adjusting entries required at the end of March relate to the following:

(8) Supplies used (for the quarter), $4,960.

(9) Depreciation (for the quarter), $3,820.

(10) Bills received but not yet recorded or paid by the end of the month: advertising, $300; power, gas, and water, $620.

(11) Insurance expired (for the quarter), $300.

a. Open T-accounts and enter the trial balance amounts.

b. Record the transactions for the month of March in the T-accounts, opening additional T-accounts as needed. Cross-number the entries.

c. Prepare an adjusted, preclosing trial balance at March 31, Year 2, an income statement for the three months ending March 31, Year 2, and a balance sheet as of March 31, Year 2.

d. Enter closing entries in the T-accounts using an Income Summary account.

47. *Preparation of journal entries, T-accounts, adjusted trial balance, income statement, and a balance sheet.* The postclosing trial balance of Cunningham's Hardware Store Ltd. on September 30, Year 4 is as follows:

Cash	$ 88,400	
Accounts Receivable	54,500	
Merchandise Inventory	136,300	
Prepaid Insurance	800	
Equipment	420,000	
Accumulated Depreciation		$168,000
Accounts Payable		66,200
Note Payable		10,000
Salaries Payable		2,500
Capital Stock		300,000
Retained Earnings		153,300
Total	$700,000	$700,000

Transactions during October and additional information are as follows:
(1) Merchandise inventory purchased on account from various suppliers is $92,600.
(2) Sales, all on account, total $170,000; cost of merchandise sold, $73,000.
(3) Rent for the month of October of $23,500 is paid.
(4) Salaries paid to employees during October are $41,200.
(5) Accounts receivable of $68,300 are collected.
(6) Accounts payable of $77,900 are paid.
(7) Miscellaneous expenses of $6,400 are paid in cash.
(8) The premium on a one-year insurance policy was paid on June 1, Year 4.

Adjusting entries required at the end of October relate to the following:
(9) Equipment is depreciated over a ten-year life. Estimated salvage value of the equipment is considered to be negligible.
(10) Employee salaries earned during the last two days of October but not paid are $3,200. These are the only unpaid salaries at the end of October.
(11) The note payable is a 90-day, 12 percent note issued on September 30, Year 4.
(12) Merchandise inventory on hand on October 31, Year 4 totals $155,900.
(13) The company records income tax at the rate of 40 percent of accounting income before income tax.
a. Prepare general journal entries to record the transactions during October.

b. Set up T-accounts and enter the opening balances in the accounts on September 30, Year 4. Post the entries from part (a) in the T-accounts, creating additional accounts as required.

c. Prepare an unadjusted trial balance as of October 31, Year 4.

d. Prepare adjusting entries required at the end of October.

e. Enter the trial balance from part **(c)** and the adjusting entries from part **(d)** in a work sheet and complete the work sheet.

f. Prepare an income statement for the month of October.

g. Prepare a balance sheet as of October 31, Year 4.

48. *Preparation of adjusting entries and work sheet.* The following unadjusted trial balance is taken from the books of the Kathleen Clothing Company Ltd. at July 31, Year 3.

Accounts Payable		$ 12,952
Accounts Receivable	$ 18,257	
Accumulated Depreciation		8,214
Advances by Customers		540
Capital Stock		40,000
Cash	9,000	
Equipment	2,640	
Depreciation Expense	—	—
Dividends Payable	—	—
Furniture and Fixtures	12,000	
Income Tax Expense	—	—
Income Tax Payable		3,500
Insurance Expense	—	—
Leasehold	10,800	
Merchandise Cost of Goods Sold	—	—
Merchandise Inventory	49,500	
Miscellaneous Expense	188	
Prepaid Insurance	450	
Rent Expense	—	—
Retained Earnings		14,294
Salaries and Commissions Expense	2,020	
Salaries and Commissions Payable		500
Sales		25,000
Supplies Inventory	145	
	$105,000	$105,000

Additional data:

(1) Depreciation on equipment is to be calculated at 10 percent of cost per year (assume zero salvage value).

(2) Depreciation on furniture and fixtures is to be calculated at 20 percent of cost per year (assume zero salvage value).

(3) The leasehold represents long-term rent paid in advance by Kathleen. The monthly rental charge is $600.

(4) One invoice of $420 for the purchase of merchandise from the Peoria Company on account was recorded during the month as $240. The account has not yet been paid.

(5) Commissions unpaid at July 31, Year 3 are $340. All salaries have been paid. The balance in the Salaries and Commissions Payable account represents the amount of commissions unpaid at July 1.

(6) Merchandise with a sales price of $350 was recently delivered to a customer, and charged to Accounts Receivable, although the customer had paid $350 in advance.

(7) The balance in the Prepaid Insurance account relates to a three-year policy that went into effect on January 1, Year 3.

(8) A dividend of $3,000 was declared on July 31, Year 3.

(9) The inventory of merchandise on July 31, Year 3 was $33,600.

(10) The company records income tax at the rate of 40 percent of accounting income before income tax.

Prepare a work sheet incorporating adjusting journal entries at July 31, Year 3. Use only the accounts listed in the trial balance.

49. *Preparation of closing entries.* The adjusted trial balance of Life Photographers, Inc. at June 30, Year 2 is presented in Exhibit 3.21.

a. Present the journal entries to close the revenue and expense accounts directly to Retained Earnings as of June 30, Year 2.

b. Set up in T-account form the revenue, expense, and retained earnings accounts. Insert the trial balance amounts and record the closing entries from part **a**.

EXHIBIT 3.21
LIFE PHOTOGRAPHERS, INC.
Adjusted Trial Balance
June 30, Year 2

Accounts Payable		$ 3,641
Accounts Receivable	$ 3,900	
Accumulated Depreciation		1,995
Advertising Expense	1,500	
Cameras and Equipment	15,500	
Cash	2,994	
Common Stock		10,000
Depreciation Expense — Cameras and Equipment	180	
Depreciation Expense — Furniture and Fixtures	105	
Electricity Expense	300	
Equipment Repairs Expense	180	
Furniture and Fixtures	9,600	
Insurance Expense	330	
Photographic Supplies Expense	1,950	
Photographic Supplies on Hand	3,390	
Prepaid Insurance	270	
Rent Expense	1,425	
Retained Earnings		14,138
Revenue — Commercial Photography		18,090
Revenue — Printing Service		4,680
Salaries Expense	10,800	
Telephone Expense	120	
	$52,544	$52,544

50. *Working backwards to balance sheet at beginning of period.* (Problems 50 through 52 are adapted from problems by George H. Sorter.) The following data relate to the Prima Company Ltd.:

(1) Postclosing trial balance at December 31, Year 2:

Debits	
Cash	$ 10,000
Temporary Investments	20,000
Accounts Receivable	25,000
Merchandise Inventory	30,000
Prepayments for Miscellaneous Services	3,000
Land, Buildings, and Equipment	40,000
Total Debits	$128,000
Credits	
Accounts Payable (for merchandise)	$ 25,000
Interest Payable	300
Taxes Payable	4,000
Notes Payable (6 percent, long-term)	20,000
Accumulated Depreciation	16,000
Capital Stock	50,000
Retained Earnings	12,700
Total Credits	$128,000

(2) Income and retained earnings data for Year 2:

Sales		$200,000
Less: Cost of Goods Sold		(130,000)
Gross Profit		$ 70,000
Less: Operating Expenses:		
Depreciation Expense	$ 3,000	
Other	48,700	(51,700)
Operating Profit		$ 18,300
Less: Interest Expense		(1,200)
Net Income Before Income Tax		$ 17,100
Income Tax		(8,000)
Net Income		$ 9,100
Less: Dividends		(5,000)
Increase in Retained Earnings		$ 4,100

(3) Summary of cash receipts and disbursements in Year 2:

Cash Receipts		
Cash Sales	$ 47,000	
Collection from Credit Customers	150,000	
Total Receipts		$197,000

Cash Disbursements

Payment to Suppliers of Merchandise	$128,000	
Payment to Suppliers of Miscellaneous Services	49,000	
Payment of Taxes	7,500	
Payment of Interest	1,200	
Payment of Dividends	5,000	
Purchase of Temporary Investments	8,000	
Total Disbursements		198,700
Excess of Disbursements over Receipts		$ 1,700

(4) Purchases of merchandise during the period, all on account, were $127,000. All "Other Operating Expenses" were credited to Prepayments.

Prepare a balance sheet for January 1, Year 2. (*Hint:* Set up T-accounts for each of the accounts in the trial balance and enter the *ending* balances in the T-accounts. Starting with information from the income statement and statement of cash receipts and disbursements, reconstruct the transactions that took place during the year and enter the amounts in the appropriate T-accounts.)

51. *Working backwards to cash receipts and disbursements.* The Secunda Company Limited's trial balance at the beginning of Year 2 and the adjusted, preclosing trial balance at the end of Year 2 are presented below.

	12/31/Year 2	1/1/Year 2
Debits		
Cash	$ 9,000	$ 20,000
Accounts Receivable	51,000	36,000
Merchandise Inventory	60,000	45,000
Prepayments	1,000	2,000
Land, Buildings, and Equipment	40,000	40,000
Cost of Goods Sold	50,000	—
Interest Expense	3,000	—
Other Operating Expenses	29,000	—
Total Debits	$243,000	$143,000
Credits		
Accumulated Depreciation	$ 18,000	$ 16,000
Interest Payable	2,000	1,000
Accounts Payable	40,000	30,000
Mortgage Payable	17,000	20,000
Capital Stock	50,000	50,000
Retained Earnings	16,000	26,000
Sales	100,000	—
Total Credits	$243,000	$143,000

All goods and services acquired during the year were purchased on account. The Other Operating Expenses account includes depreciation charges and expirations of prepayments. Dividends declared during the year were debited to Retained Earnings.

Prepare a schedule showing all cash transactions for Year 2. (*Hint:* Set up T-accounts for each of the accounts listed in the trial balance and enter the amounts shown as of January 1, Year 2 and December 31, Year 2. Starting with the entries in revenue and expense accounts, reconstruct the transactions that took place during the year and enter the amounts in the appropriate T-accounts. The effect of earnings activities is not yet reflected in the Retained Earnings account because the trial balance is preclosing.)

52. *Working backwards to income statement.* Tertia Company Inc. presents the following incomplete postclosing trial balances, as well as a statement of cash receipts and disbursements:

	12/31/Year 2	1/1/Year 2
Debits		
Cash	$?	$?
Accounts and Notes Receivable	41,000	36,000
Merchandise Inventory	49,500	55,000
Interest Receivable	700	1,000
Prepaid Miscellaneous Services	5,200	4,000
Building, Machinery, and Equipment	47,000	47,000
Total Debits	$?	$?
Credits		
Accounts Payable (miscellaneous services)	$ 2,500	$ 2,000
Accounts Payable (merchandise)	41,000	34,000
Property Taxes Payable	1,500	1,000
Accumulated Depreciation	12,000	10,000
Mortgage Payable	30,000	35,000
Capital Stock	25,000	25,000
Retained Earnings	?	76,000
Total Credits	$211,200	$183,000

	Year 2
Cash Receipts	
1. Collection from Credit Customers	$144,000
2. Cash Sales	63,000
3. Collection of Interest	1,000
	$208,000
Less: Cash Disbursements	
4. Payment to Suppliers of Merchandise	$114,000
5. Repayment on Mortgage	5,000
6. Payment of Interest	500
7. Prepayment to Suppliers of Miscellaneous Services	57,500
8. Payment of Property Taxes	1,200
9. Payment of Dividends	2,000
	$180,200
Increase in Cash Balance for Year	$ 27,800

Prepare a combined statement of income and retained earnings for Year 2 (*Hint:* Set up T-accounts for each of the balance sheet accounts listed in the trial balance and enter the amounts shown as of January 1, Year 2 and December 31, Year 2. Starting with the cash receipts and disbursements for the year, reconstruct the transactions that took place during the year and enter them in the appropriate T-accounts. The effect of earnings activities for the year is already reflected in the Retained Earnings account, because the trial balance shown is postclosing.)

53. *Specialized journals and subsidiary ledgers.*
    a. What advantage is there to using multicolumn journals instead of two-column journals?
    b. What advantage is there to using specialized journals instead of multicolumn journals?
    c. What advantage is there to using subsidiary ledgers in conjunction with a general ledger?

54. *Specialized journals and subsidiary ledgers.* Indicate whether each of the following statements is true or false.
    a. Posting is the process of recording entries in a journal.
    b. A general journal is not needed when specialized journals are used.
    c. The balances in individual subsidiary ledger accounts are not included in the general ledger trial balance.
    d. Specialized journals are created to facilitate the recording of various types of frequent transactions.
    e. A controlling account represents a group of subsidiary ledger accounts that are kept in detail outside of the general ledger.
    f. A specialized journal must have an equal number of debit and credit columns.
    g. A journal must have at least one column for debits and at least another column for credits.
    h. The use of subsidiary ledgers facilitates the taking of a trial balance.
    i. When a controlling account is credited, one of the subsidiary ledger accounts is debited.
    j. There is usually more detail about an individual transaction in the general journal than in the general ledger.

55. *Accounting cycle with specialized journals.* The trial balance of the general ledger of the Renuit Shop, Inc., on July 1, Year 5 is as follows:

Cash	$ 700	
Supplies Inventory	425	
Tools	2,000	
Accumulated Depreciation		$ 800
Accounts Payable		625[a]
Common Shares		500

[a]Amount is payable to Handicraft Supply Company.

Retained Earnings		1,200
Repair Service Revenue		—
Cost of Repair Supplies Used	—	
Salary Expense	—	
Utilities Expense	—	
Depreciation Expense	—	
Total	$3,125	$3,125

The transactions during July are as follows:

(1) Cash is received on July 3 for repair work done, $360.

(2) Supplies are purchased on account from Handicraft Supply Company on July 10, $185.

(3) Cash payments are made on July 31 as follows: salaries, $125; utilities, $13; Handicraft Supply Company on account, $725.

(4) Cash is received for repair work done on July 31, $310.

(5) Depreciation on tools for the month is $55.

(6) The cost of supplies used during the month is $255.

   a. Open T-accounts for the accounts listed in the trial balance on July 1, Year 5, and enter the opening balances.

   b. Construct a six-column journal with the following column headings: Cash, Debit and Credit; Revenue for Repair Services, Credit; Supplies, Debit; Other Accounts, Debit and Credit. Also include columns for Date, Explanation, and Other Account Titles.

   c. Enter transactions (1) through (4) in the six-column journal.

   d. Post amounts from the six-column journal to the appropriate T-accounts.

   e. Prepare an unadjusted trial balance.

   f. Prepare a two-column general journal. Enter the adjusting entries for items (5) and (6) on July 31, Year 5.

   g. Post the adjusting entries to the T-accounts.

   h. Prepare an adjusted trial balance.

   i. Enter the closing entries on July 31, Year 5 in the general journal, then post them to the general ledger accounts.

   j. Prepare a postclosing trial balance.

56. *Specialized journals.* The most common transactions of the Beal Antique Shop, Inc. are as follows:

Sales for cash and on account.
Payments for purchases of merchandise by cash and by cheque.
Collections of cash from customers.
Payments of operating expenses by cash and by cheque.
Deposits in the bank.

Subsidiary ledgers are used for customers' accounts and operating expense accounts. The following are the transactions for July 1–31:

July 1 Cash sales, $200.
      4 Sale, on account, L.C. Jones, $80; cash sales, $60.
      6 Common shares worth $500 are issued for cash.
   11 Cash sales, $250.

15 Collection from a customer, A.C. Hines, $75.

17 Sale, on account, A.O. Brown, $85.

20 Store fixtures are purchased for $800 from the Office Supply Company. A cheque (No. 550) is issued, $200; the balance is covered by an installment contract.

23 Merchandise is purchased for $650 from the East Antique Company. Cheque (No. 551) is issued in full payment.

25 Cash sales, $200.

25 Collection from a customer, M.A. Cross, $90.

27 A note payable is issued to the bank, $1,000. The proceeds are added by the bank to the firm's account.

28 Sale, on account, W.I. Snow, $95; cash sales, $60.

29 A telephone bill is received. Cheque (No. 552) is issued, $12.

30 Merchandise is acquired from the Specialty Furniture Company, $550. Cheque (No. 553) is issued in payment of the accompanying invoice.

31 The clerk is paid for the second half of the month. Cheque (No. 554) is issued for earnings of $300, less deductions of 6 percent for payroll taxes and $45 for income tax.

a. Prepare an eleven-column journal with the following column headings: Cash (Dr. and Cr.); Accounts Receivable (Dr. and Cr.); Merchandise Inventory (Dr.); Selling and Administrative Expenses (Dr.); Sales (Cr.); Other Accounts (Dr. and Cr.). Also include columns for Date, Explanation, and Other Accounts Titles.

b. Enter each of the transactions during July in the eleven-column journal.

c. Total columns.

57. *Specialized journals, posting, trial balance (if combined with Problem 58, a mini-practice set).* E.S. Brady and R.E. Brady own and operate Brady Business Services, Inc., providing mimeographing and public stenographic services. At September 30, Year 3, the trial balance of the general ledger and the schedules of the subsidiary ledgers are as follows:

General Ledger		
Cash	$ 5,500	
Accounts Receivable	9,500	
Supplies on Hand	3,300	
Prepaid Insurance	960	
Office Equipment	19,500	
Accumulated Depreciation		$ 7,200
Accounts Payable		4,900
Equipment Contract Payable		3,000
Share Capital		10,000
Retained Earnings		13,660
Total	$38,760	$38,760

Accounts Receivable

Baum & Co.	$ 1,220
Clark's Market	300
David Bros.	—
Forest Stores	1,800
H.B. Gross	590
Moll & Co.	750
Ohio Realty	—
Porter and Sons	290
A.B. Reck	1,450
Standard Service	3,100
Total	$ 9,500

Accounts Payable

Burton, Inc.	$ 250
City Supply Co.	2,360
Mears & Co.	450
P.A. Page, Ltd.	1,080
Snell Bros.	760
Total	$ 4,900

The following transactions took place during the month of October:

October 1 Received $450 in cash for secretarial work completed and delivered today.

1 Completed and delivered mimeograph work for Moll & Company and invoiced them for $510.

2 Issued cheque (No. 100) for $600 to K.M. Bear for rent for the month of October. (Cheques are issued in serial number order.)

3 Received cheque for $1,800 from Forest Stores in payment of their account balance.

6 Issued cheques (Nos. 101–104) in payment of September 30 balances to Burton, Inc., City Supply Company, P.A. Page, Ltd., and Snell Brothers.

6 Acquired on account paper and other mimeograph supplies from City Supply Company, $1,050.

7 Cash receipts for the day were $330 for stenographic service and $1,250 for mimeograph work.

8 Received the following invoices: Mears & Company, $100, for repairs to office equipment; Burton, Inc., $480, for office supplies: P.A. Page, Ltd. $250 for mimeograph supplies.

10 Received cheques from the following customers for the September 30 balances: Baum & Company, Clark's Market, Moll & Company, Porter and Sons, and Standard Service.

10 Issued cheque (No. 105) for $150 for advertising invoice received from the *Daily Register*.

13 Issued Cheque (No. 106) for $1,500 to Hall Office Equipment, Ltd. for monthly payment on the equipment purchase contract.

13 Completed and delivered the following mimeograph jobs and invoiced the customers: Ohio Realty, $460; Davis Brothers, $200; Standard Service, $930.

14 Receipts for the day for stenographic work, $620.

15 Issued Cheque (No. 107) for $90 to Blott Typewriter Services for repairs on machines.

16 Received a cheque for $550 from S.V. Smith for mimeograph work completed and delivered today.

17 Receipts for the day: stenographic services, $100; mimeograph work, $850.

17 Issued cheques (Nos. 108, 109) to Mears & Company and P.A. Page, Ltd. for invoices of October 8.

20 Issued cheque (No. 110) to City Supply Company for invoice of October 6.

20 Purchased the following operating supplies on account: City Supply Company, $1,500; Snell Brothers, $950.

20 Issued cheque (No. 111) to a customer, S.V. Smith, as an adjustment reducing the amount he had paid for mimeograph work, $50 (adjustment because of error in calculating the charge on October 16).

21 Received a cheque from H.B. Gross for $590 in payment of September 30 balance.

21 Other cash receipts for the day: stenographic services, $440; mimeograph work, $460.

23 Issued cheque (No. 112) for $450 to Mears & Company.

24 Billed the following customers for mimeograph work completed and delivered: Clark's Market, $210; Forest Stores, $445; Moll & Company, $1,070.

24 Issued a cheque (No. 113) for $500 to N. Stewart as a dividend.

28 Cash receipts for the day: stenographic services, $270; mimeograph work, $1,500.

29 Issued a credit memo to Moll & Company for $100 as an adjustment on invoice of October 24 (incorrect rate used).

30 Issued cheque (No. 114) to Southwestern Telephone Company for telephone bill for the month, $120.

31 Paid $50 out of cash on hand for machinery repair.

31 Cash receipts for the day: mimeograph work, $435.

31 Issued cheques (Nos. 115, 116) for October salaries: E.S. Brady, $2,750; R.E. Brady, $2,500.

a. Open T-accounts for each of the general ledger accounts and insert the September 30 balances.

b. Record the October transactions in a twelve-column journal. The amount-column headings in the journal are as follows: Cash, Dr. and Cr.; Accounts Receivable, Dr. and Cr.; Accounts Payable, Dr. and Cr.; Supplies on Hand, Dr.; Sales Revenue, Cr.; Other Accounts, Dr. and Cr. There should also be columns for Date, Explanation, and Other Account Titles.

c. Post the transactions during October from the journal to the general ledger T-accounts.

d. Prepare an unadjusted trial balance of the general ledger accounts as of October 31.

58. *Adjusting and closing journal entries and trial balance.* This problem is a continuation of Problem 57. Additional information as of October 31, Year 3:

(1) Ending inventory of supplies amounts to $4,750.

(2) The insurance policy acquired on October 1, Year 2 runs for three years.

(3) Office equipment was acquired on September 30, Year 1 at a cost of $19,500. It was estimated that the salvage value of the equipment at the estimated retirement date, September 30, Year 6 would be $1,500.

(4) Income tax expense is estimated to be $600.

a. Construct a two-column general journal. Prepare any adjusting entries required on October 31, Year 3 and enter them in the general journal.

b. Post the adjusting entries to the general ledger T-accounts.

c. Prepare an adjusted preclosing trial balance.

d. Prepare the closing entries for the revenue and expense accounts, enter them in the general journal, and post them to the general ledger T-accounts.

e. Prepare a postclosing trial balance.

59. *Specialized journals.* Referring to Problem 57, prepare the following specialized journals:

(1) Cash receipts and disbursements journal with the following columns: Date; Cash on Hand, Dr. and Cr.; Accounts Receivable, Cr. (amount, name of customer); Sales Revenue, Cr.; Other Accounts, Dr. (amount, account title, explanation).

(2) Cheque register with the following columns: Date, Payee; Cheque Number; Cash in Bank, Cr.; Accounts Payable, Dr.; Other Accounts, Dr. (amount, account title, explanation).

(3) Revenue journal for use where credit is extended, with the following columns: date; name of customer; a single column for Accounts Receivable, Dr. and Sales Revenue, Cr.

(4) Invoice register with the following columns: date: name of creditor; Accounts Payable, Cr.; Supplies on Hand, Dr.; other accounts, Dr. (amount, account title, explanation).

Record the transactions during October in the appropriate journal.

60. *Subsidiary ledgers.* Refer to Problem 57. Prepare the subsidiary ledgers for Accounts Receivable and Accounts Payable as of October 31, Year 3 using the format shown in Problem 57.

61. *Financial statement impact of cash versus accrual assumption.* In Year 1, the Glitter Corporation was a newly formed jewellery company. During its first year of operations, the company did not have a qualified accountant. The first year-end closing, to say the least, was a bit chaotic.

The bookkeeper for the Glitter Corporation elected to use the cash method. The following were noted at year-end:

(1) Depreciation for the office building was not entered.

(2) Interest on an outstanding note payable was not accrued.

(3) A down payment for some jewellery to be delivered next year was recorded as sales.

(4) Although the contract was signed, the purchase of a shipment of gem stones was not recognized because the delivery date was one month after year-end.

(5) Some credit sales were not booked as revenue for the year.

(6) The company bought a large quantity of rubies and sapphires and paid in advance. The gems being shipped are not expected to arrive until three months after the year-end. By the end of the current year, because of a newly invented synthetic process for rubies, the ruby price had dropped by 20 percent. However, the sapphire price had increased by 10 percent because of a shortage in the world markets. The purchase of these gems had not been recorded.

a. Explain the difference between the cash and accrual bases of recording accounting transactions.

b. What are the effects of items 1 to 6 (listed above) on assets, liabilities, and owners' equity if accounting is done on an accrual basis? Show the direction of change and support your answer with corresponding journal entries. Use the following format:

		Impact on Accounts (Increase, Decrease or No Change)		
Item	Assets	Liabilities	Owners' Equity	Journal Entry

Adapted with permission from the Society of Management Accountants of Canada.

62. *Working backwards from trial balance to journal entries.* Majestic Bodies Fitness Club Ltd. offers free trial memberships to the general public to attract business. The customer must pay a deposit of $500 but, if not satisfied after a month, he or she can withdraw and get a full refund. The following were taken from the trial balances of Majestic Bodies Fitness Club Ltd. during the month of December Year 1.

	Unadjusted Trial Balance	Adjusted Trial Balance
Club membership sales	$122,800 cr.	$141,300 cr.
Accumulated depreciation for fitness equipment	2,700 cr.	4,000 cr.
Interest revenue	1,280 cr.	1,540 cr.
Supplies expense	2,360 dr.	1,460 dr.
Unexpired liability insurance	0	2,800 dr.
Tanning booth revenue	3,200 cr.	4,900 cr.
Office salaries	6,500 dr.	7,980 dr.
Commissions payable	400 cr.	1,430 cr.

During the Christmas season, the club was selling gift certificates to promote its business. A gift certificate for ten visits to the club's tanning facilities was selling for $50. A total of twenty certificates were sold.

During December Year 1, eighteen people used the gift certificates for a total of 40 visits.

a. Reconstruct the journal entries that probably were prepared to adjust each of the trial balance accounts above.

b. Journalize the sale of the gift certificates and the resulting revenue in December Year 1.

Adapted with permission from the Society of Management Accountants of Canada.

DECISION CASE 3-1

Your friend's mother, Mary Brooks, has opened Mary's Boutique Ltd. in a nearby shopping mall. She began her business on February 1, Year 1; she invested $20,000 in share capital and her husband, Tom, contributed another $20,000 as a loan to the firm, bearing interest at 10 percent, of which none has been paid to date.

Mary Brooks has found the boutique exciting and appears to have been successful as a business person — but how successful? She answers this question when preparing her income tax return; this in turn helps determine whether or not she should continue the business.

Brooks maintains a summary of selected transactions. This summary for the year ended January 31, Year 2 follows:

Cost of merchandise purchase on account	$34,600
Wages paid to assistant	9,200
Salary paid to M. Brooks	12,000
Rent Paid	4,800
Business taxes and licences (eleven months, Year 1)	330
Supplies purchased for cash	2,950
Miscellaneous expenses paid	6,340

During the year, Mary's Boutique Ltd. sold merchandise for $57,600 — $8,900 for cash — and collected all credit sales except $5,300. However, Mary expected to collect only $4,100 from the accounts outstanding. Mary had recorded and summarized the cost of each item of merchandise sold and, for the year, the total was $24,800. The cost of the merchandise remaining was $8,700, leaving $1,100 of purchases unaccounted for. Brooks attributed this difference to theft or failure to record the cost of the item sold. At January 31, Year 2, Mary estimated the boutique had supplies on hand that cost about $250.

The bank had deducted interest and bank charges, totalling $1,400, from the boutique's account. The major portion of this deduction was for interest on the demand loan which, at January 31, Year 2, was $10,000. This demand loan was fully secured by a government bond Mary had purchased for the firm for $10,000 when she originally organized it and had excess cash on hand. The current market value of this bond was $10,200. The firm had received $600 interest on the bond during the year and $400 additional interest had been earned to January 31, Year 2. The bank balance at January 31, Year 2 was $7,480.

When Mary's Boutique Ltd. was formed, a friendly insurance agent sold Mary Brooks a comprehensive policy for the business with a two-year premium of $480, which was paid and included in the miscellaneous expenses.

The firm had paid the previous store occupant $20,000 for the existing furniture and fixtures, which are estimated to last for ten years.

Brooks has very good relations with her suppliers, to whom she owed $6,200 at January 31, Year 2.

Income tax payable by Mary's Boutique Ltd. is calculated at 20 percent of net income before income tax.

Prepare a set of financial statements for Mary's Boutique Ltd. to show the results of the first year of business. Do you think that Mary Brooks will have a successful career as a boutique operator?

CHAPTER FOUR

INCOME STATEMENT: EXTENSIONS OF THE ACCRUAL CONCEPT

CHAPTER OUTLINE

- Accrual Basis for Manufacturers
- Accrual Basis for Long-Term Contractors
- Accrual Basis When Cash Collectability Is Extremely Uncertain
- Recognition of Revenue Between Purchase and Sale
- Summary Illustration of Income Recognition Methods
- Format and Classification Within the Income Statement
- An International Perspective

Chapter 3 points out that most business firms use an accrual, rather than a cash, basis of accounting. The two distinguishing features of the accrual basis are the following:

1. Revenue is recognized when all, or a substantial portion, of the services to be provided have been performed and cash, a receivable, or some other asset whose cash equivalent can be measured objectively has been received.

2. Expenses are recognized in the period when related revenues are recognized or, if they are not associated with a particular revenue stream, when goods or services are consumed in operations.

merchandising firms
Firms that purchase (rather than manufacture) finished goods for resale.

For most **merchandising firms,** revenue is recognized in the period when goods are sold. Expenses are then matched either directly with the revenue or with the period when goods or services are consumed. This chapter explores the application of the accrual concept to other types of businesses: firms involved in manufacturing, firms involved in long-term contract activities, and firms selling goods on an installment basis.

ACCRUAL BASIS FOR MANUFACTURERS

A **manufacturing firm** incurs various costs in changing the physical form of the goods it produces. Figure 4.1 depicts the operating cycle for a typical manufacturing firm. A firm acquires productive facilities (plant and equipment) to provide capacity to manufacture goods. Raw materials for use in production are also acquired. Converting raw materials into a salable product requires labour and other manufacturing services (for example, utilities, insurance, taxes, and depreciation on production facilities) during the period of production. The finished product is held in inventory until sold. When the good is sold, either cash is collected or a receivable from the customer arises.

Most manufacturing firms recognize revenue at the time goods are sold. At this time, the production activity has been completed, a customer has been identified, a selling price has been agreed upon, and an assessment of the customer's credit standing provides a reasonable basis for estimating the amount of cash that will be collected.

ACCOUNTING FOR MANUFACTURING COSTS

As Chapter 3 points out, a merchandising firm acquires inventory items in finished form ready for sale. The acquisition cost of these items remains in the asset account, Merchandise Inventory, until the units are sold. At the time of sale, the cost of the items sold is transferred from the asset account, Merchandise Inventory, to the expense account, Cost of Goods Sold.

A manufacturing firm, on the other hand, incurs various costs in transforming raw materials into finished products. These manufacturing costs are generally classified into **direct material** (or raw material), **direct labour**, and **manufacturing overhead**. Manufacturing overhead includes a variety of indirect costs that provide a firm with productive capacity (depreciation, insurance, and taxes on manufacturing facilities, supervisory labour, supplies for factory equipment). Until the units are sold and revenue is recognized, manufacturing costs are treated as **product costs** — assets — and accumulated in various inventory accounts.

A manufacturing firm, like a merchandising firm, incurs various selling costs (commissions for the sales staff, depreciation, insurance and taxes on

manufacturing firm
A firm that combines materials and labour to make a product as opposed to just reselling products acquired from other firms.

direct material
Materials physically making up a product.

direct labour
All labour of workers applying their skills directly to the manufacture of products. The labour of workers indirectly supporting the manufacturing process is accounted for as indirect labour, part of factory overhead.

manufacturing overhead
Costs that contribute to the manufacturing process and are allocated to work-in-process inventory.

product costs
The costs properly associated with the product being produced (as opposed to the period in which the costs are incurred). Product costs become period costs (expenses) when the related products are sold.

FIGURE 4.1
Operating Cycle for Manufacturing Firm

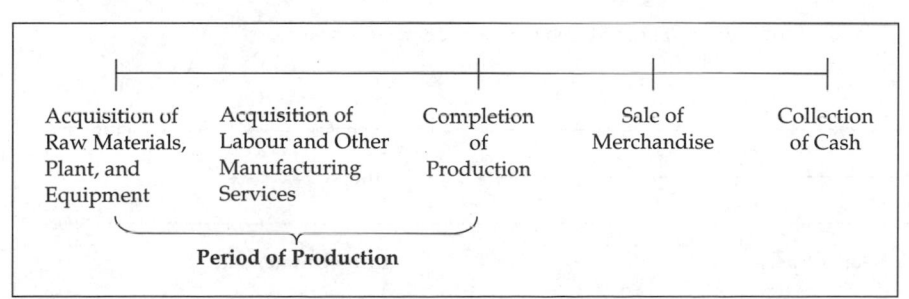

period expenses
Costs associated with the period in which they are incurred (rather than with the product being produced).

Raw Materials Inventory
Goods purchased for use in manufacturing a product.

Work-in-Process Inventory
Partly finished goods, services, or contracts that are in the process of manufacture or completion; an asset that is classified as inventory.

Finished Goods Inventory
Manufactured products ready for sale; a current asset (inventory) account.

the sales staff's automobiles) and administrative costs (salary of president, depreciation on computer facilities). Selling and administrative costs are treated as **period expenses** by both merchandising and manufacturing firms. Figure 4.2 summarizes the nature and flow of various costs for a manufacturing firm.

Separate inventory accounts are maintained by a manufacturing firm for product costs incurred at various stages of completion. The **Raw Materials Inventory** account includes the cost of raw materials purchased but not yet transferred to production. The balance in the Raw Materials Inventory account indicates the cost of raw materials on hand in the raw materials storeroom or warehouse. When raw materials are issued to producing departments, the cost of the materials is transferred from the Raw Materials Inventory account to the **Work-in-Process Inventory** account. The Work-in-Process Inventory account accumulates the costs incurred in producing units during the period. The Work-in-Process Inventory account is debited for the cost of raw materials transferred from the raw materials storeroom, the cost of direct labour services used, and the manufacturing overhead cost incurred. The Work-in-Process Inventory account is credited for the total manufacturing cost of units completed in the factory and transferred to the finished goods storeroom. The **Finished Goods Inventory** account includes the total manufacturing cost of units completed but not yet sold. The cost of units sold during the period is transferred from the Finished Goods Inventory account to the Cost-of-Goods-Sold account. Figure 4.3 shows the flow of manufacturing cost through the various inventory and other accounts.

FIGURE 4.2
Diagram of Cost Flows

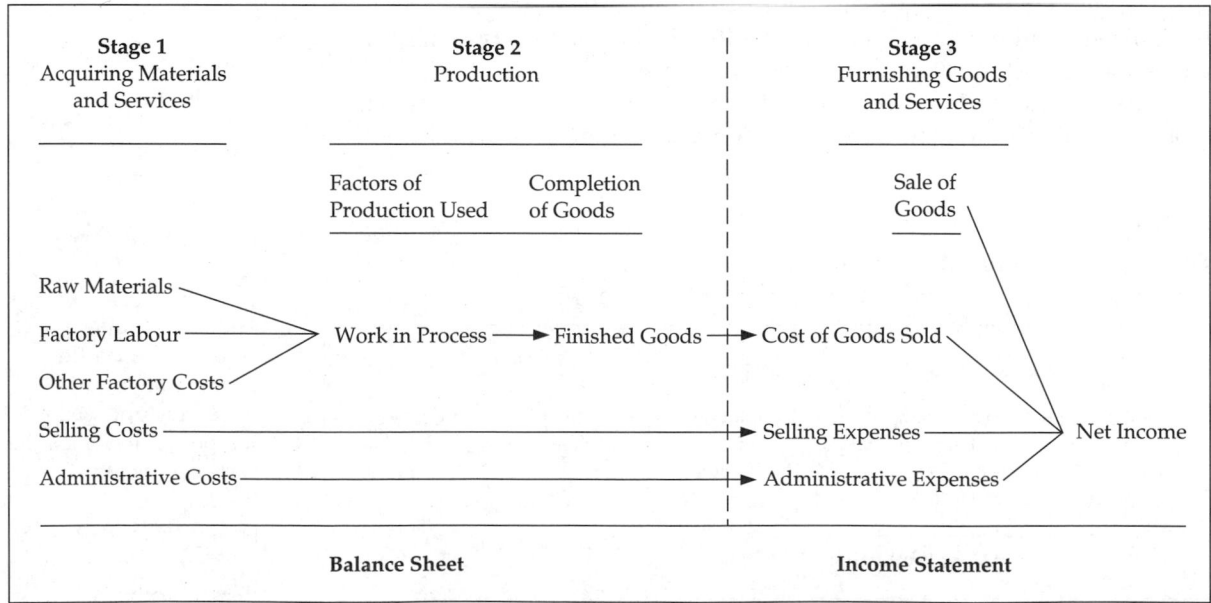

FIGURE 4.3
Flow of Manufacturing Costs Through the Accounts

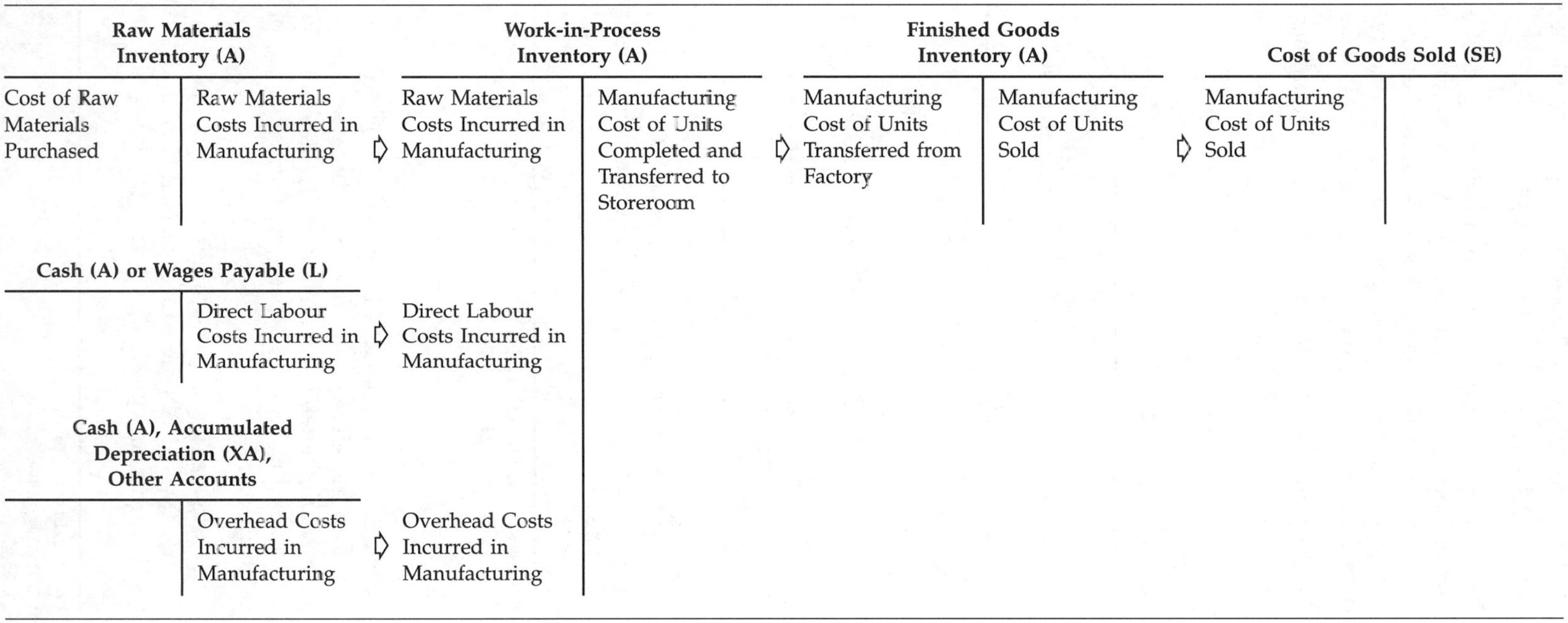

Raw Materials Inventory (A)

| Cost of Raw Materials Purchased | Raw Materials Costs Incurred in Manufacturing |

Cash (A) or Wages Payable (L)

| | Direct Labour Costs Incurred in Manufacturing |

Cash (A), Accumulated Depreciation (XA), Other Accounts

| | Overhead Costs Incurred in Manufacturing |

Work-in-Process Inventory (A)

Raw Materials Costs Incurred in Manufacturing ⇧

Direct Labour Costs Incurred in Manufacturing ⇧

Overhead Costs Incurred in Manufacturing ⇧

| Manufacturing Cost of Units Completed and Transferred to Storeroom |

Finished Goods Inventory (A)

Manufacturing Cost of Units Transferred from Factory ⇧

| Manufacturing Cost of Units Sold |

Cost of Goods Sold (SE)

Manufacturing Cost of Units Sold ⇧

ILLUSTRATION OF THE ACCOUNTING PROCESS FOR A MANUFACTURING FIRM

The accounting process for a manufacturing firm is illustrated with information about the operations of the Moon Manufacturing Co. Ltd. The company was formed on December 31 with the issuance of 10,000 no-par-value common shares for $30 per share. Transactions during January are described below, and the appropriate journal entires are provided:

1. A building costing $200,000 and equipment costing $50,000 are acquired for cash.

Building (A)	$200,000	
Equipment (A)	50,000	
Cash (A)		$250,000

2. Raw materials costing $25,000 are purchased on account.

Raw Materials Inventory (A)	$25,000	
Accounts Payable (L)		$25,000

3. Raw materials costing $20,000 are issued to producing departments.

Work-in-Process Inventory (A)	$20,000	
Raw Materials Inventory (A)		$20,000

4. The total payroll for January is $60,000. Of this amount, $40,000 is paid to factory workers, and $20,000 is paid to selling and administrative personnel.

Work-in-Process Inventory (A)	$40,000	
Salaries Expense (SE)	20,000	
Cash (A)		$60,000

Recall that nonmanufacturing costs are recorded as expenses of the period in which the services are consumed, because these costs rarely create assets with future benefits. Journal entry (4), as well as entries (5) and (6) below, illustrates the difference between the recording of a product cost and a period expense.

5. The expenditures for utilities during January are $1,200. Of this amount, $1,000 is attributable to manufacturing, and $200 to selling and administrative activities.

Work-in-Process Inventory (A)	$1,000	
Utilities Expense (SE)	200	
Cash (A)		$1,200

6. Depreciation on building and equipment during January is as follows: factory, $8,000; selling and administrative, $2,000.

Work-in-Process Inventory (A)	$8,000	
Depreciation Expense (SE)	2,000	
Accumulated Depreciation (XA)		$10,000

7. The manufacturing cost of units completed during January and transferred to the finished goods storeroom is $48,500.

Finished Goods Inventory (A)	$48,500	
Work-in-Process Inventory (A)		$48,500

8. Sales during January total $75,000, of which $25,000 is on account.

Cash (A)	$50,000	
Accounts Receivable (A)	25,000	
Sales Revenue (SE)		$75,000

9. The cost of the goods sold during January is $42,600.

Cost of Goods Sold (SE)	$42,600	
Finished Goods Inventory (A)		$42,600

10. The income tax for January is $2,000.

Income Tax Expense (SE)	$2,000	
Income Tax Payable (L)		$2,000

Exhibit 4.1 shows how the various manufacturing and other costs incurred flow through the accounts. Exhibit 4.2 presents an income statement for Moon Manufacturing Co. Ltd. for January.

EXHIBIT 4.1
MOON MANUFACTURING CO. LTD.
T-Accounts Showing Transactions During January

Raw Materials Inventory (A)					Work-in-Process Inventory (A)			
(2)	25,000	20,000	(3)		(3)	20,000	48,500	(7)
					(4)	40,000		
					(5)	1,000		
					(6)	8,000		
Bal. 1/31	5,000				Bal. 1/31	20,500		

EXHIBIT 4.1 (continued)

Finished Goods Inventory (A)			
(7)	48,500	42,600	(9)
Bal. 1/31	5,900		

Cost of Goods Sold (SE)		
(9)	42,600	
Bal. 1/31	42,600	

Cash (A)			
Bal. 1/1	300,000	250,000	(1)
(8)	50,000	60,000	(4)
		1,200	(5)
Bal. 1/31	38,800		

Accounts Receivable (A)		
(8)	25,000	
Bal. 1/31	25,000	

Building (A)		
(1)	200,000	
Bal. 1/31	200,000	

Equipment (A)		
(1)	50,000	
Bal. 1/31	50,000	

Accumulated Depreciation (XA)		
	10,000	(6)
	10,000	Bal. 1/31

Salaries Expense (SE)		
(4)	20,000	
Bal. 1/31	20,000	

Sales Revenue (SE)		
	75,000	(8)
	75,000	Bal. 1/31

Accounts Payable (L)		
	25,000	(2)
	25,000	Bal. 1/31

Utilities Expense (SE)		
(5)	200	
Bal. 1/31	200	

Depreciation Expense (SE)		
(6)	2,000	
Bal. 1/31	2,000	

Income Tax Expense (SE)		
(10)	2,000	
Bal. 1/31	2,000	

Income Tax Payable (L)		
	2,000	(10)
	2,000	Bal. 1/31

EXHIBIT 4.2
MOON MANUFACTURING CO. LTD.
Income Statement for the Month of January

Sales Revenue		$75,000
Less: Cost of Goods Sold		(42,600)
Gross Profit		$32,400
Less: Operating Expenses		
Salaries	$20,000	
Utilities	200	
Depreciation	2,000	(22,200)
Net Income Before Income Tax		$10,200
Income Tax Expense		(2,000)
Net Income		$ 8,200

SUMMARY OF THE ACCOUNTING FOR MANUFACTURING OPERATIONS

The accounting procedures for the selling and administrative costs of manufacturing firms resemble those for merchandising firms. These costs are treated as expenses of the period in which services are consumed. The accounting procedures for a manufacturing firm differ from those of a merchandising firm primarily in the treatment of inventories. A manufacturing firm incurs various costs in transforming raw materials into finished products. Until the units produced are sold, manufacturing costs are accumulated in inventory accounts — the Work-in-Process Inventory account or the Finished Goods Inventory account — depending on the stage of completion of each unit being produced. Product costs are therefore debited to inventory (asset) accounts until the time of sale.

DISCUSSION CASE 9

Job Order Costing in Service Industries

Many firms in service industries use variations of job order costing systems for accumulating costs and developing billings to customers. Manufacturing firms typically accumulate costs by job or product while service firms accumulate costs by client (accounting and law firms) or by project (engineering and architectural firms).

For example, in a public accounting firm, revenues are based on services provided by professional staff. Each staff member keeps track of all time during the workweek according to classification codes such as the following:

001-900 Charge code for each client to be billed.
    901 Unassigned (unchargeable) time.
    902 Training.
    903 Client development and promotion.
    904 Community service.
    905 Service to the institute.

In addition, a suffix system might be used; for example:

A Audit work.
B Accounting services.
C Tax services.
D Management advisory services.
E Other.

Some firms keep track of staff time to the nearest quarter hour.

In addition to the billable hours charged by professional staff, accounting firms have large administrative and support structures whose costs must also be recovered by fees billed to clients. These costs include secretarial support, library research staff, office space, computers, and even the managing partner's salary. Thus, an overhead charge is built into per diem billing rates of the professional staff. For instance, a staff assistant may be charged out

(continued)

(continued)

at $30 an hour, although his or her hourly salary may be less than half that amount.

Accounting firms do not usually detail these overhead charges when invoicing clients, although breakdowns should be available to clients who request them. This is one area in which small accounting firms and sole practitioners have a distinct advantage over national and international accounting firms. Small firms have a much lower overhead structure and can pass on these savings through lower billing rates.

Control of costs is as important in an accounting firm as in any manufacturing firm. And because labour is a service firm's product, control of costs equals control of time. It is important, therefore, for accountants and other professionals to be "clock watchers."

Discussion Question

Although having professional staff keep track of time so meticulously helps in job costing, can you think of any negative ramifications?

ACCRUAL BASIS FOR LONG-TERM CONTRACTORS

The operating cycle for a long-term contractor (for example, building construction, shipbuilding) differs from that of a manufacturing firm (depicted in Figure 4.1) in three important respects:

1. The period of construction (production) may span several accounting periods.
2. A customer is identified and a contract price agreed upon in advance (or at least in the early stages of construction).
3. Periodic payments of the contract price are often made by the buyer as work progresses.

The criteria for the recognition of revenue from long-term contracts are often satisfied during the period of construction. The existence of a contract indicates that a buyer has been identified and a price agreed upon. Either cash is collected in advance or an assessment of the customer's credit standing leads to a reasonable expectation that the contract price will be received in cash after construction is completed. Although future services required on these long-term construction contracts can be substantial at any given time, the costs to be incurred in providing these services can often be estimated with reasonable precision. In agreeing to a contract price, the firm must have some confidence in its estimates of the total costs to be incurred on the contract.

PERCENTAGE-OF-COMPLETION METHOD

When the criteria for revenue recognition are met as construction progresses, revenue is usually recognized during the period of construction using the **percentage-of-completion method**. Under the percentage-of-completion method, a portion of the total contract price, based on the degree of completion of the work during the period, is recognized as revenue each period. This proportion is based either on engineers' or architects' estimates of the degree of completion or on the ratio of costs incurred to date to the total expected costs for the contract. The actual schedule of cash collections is *not* significant for the revenue recognition process when the percentage-of-completion method is used. Even if all of the contract price is collected at completion of construction, the percentage-of-completion method may still be used as long as reasonable estimates of the amount of cash to be collected and of the costs remaining to be incurred can be made as construction progresses.

As portions of the contract price are recognized as revenues, corresponding proportions of the total estimated costs of the contract are recognized as expenses. Thus, the percentage-of-completion method follows the accrual basis of accounting, because expenses are matched with related revenues.

To illustrate the percentage-of-completion method, assume that a firm agrees to construct a bridge for $5,000,000. Estimated costs are as follows: Year 1, $1,500,000; Year 2, $2,000,000; Year 3, $500,000. Thus, the expected profit from the contract is $1,000,000 (= $5,000,000 − $1,500,000 − $2,000,000 − $500,000).

Assuming that the degree of completion is based on the percentage of total costs incurred and that actual costs are incurred as anticipated, revenue and expense from the contract are as follows:

Year	Degree of Completion	Revenue	Expense	Profit
1	$1,500,000/$4,000,000 = 37.5%	$1,875,000	$1,500,000	$ 375,000
2	$2,000,000/$4,000,000 = 50.0%	2,500,000	2,000,000	500,000
3	$500,000/$4,000,000 = 12.5%	625,000	500,000	125,000
		$5,000,000	$4,000,000	$1,000,000

COMPLETED CONTRACT METHOD

Some firms involved with construction contracts postpone the recognition of revenue until the construction project and the sale are completed. This method is the same as the completed sale basis, but is often referred to as the **completed contract method** of recognizing revenue. If the completed contract method were used in the example above, no revenue or expense from the contract would be recognized during Year 1 or Year 2. In Year 3, contract revenue of $5,000,000 and contract expenses of $4,000,000 would be recognized in measuring net income.

In some cases, the completed contract method is used because the contracts are of such short duration (such as a few months) that earnings reported with the percentage of completion method and the completed contract method are not significantly different. In these cases, the completed contract method is used because it is generally easier to implement. Firms use the completed contract method in situations in which a specific buyer has not been obtained during the periods while construction is progressing, as is sometimes the case in constructing residential housing. In these cases, future selling efforts are required and substantial uncertainty may exist

percentage-of-completion method
An accounting method used for large construction projects lasting more than one accounting period where a portion of the total revenues are recognized each period in proportion to the percentage of total contract costs incurred.

completed contract method
A revenue recognition policy used for construction-type contracts whereby no revenue is recognized until the contract has been completed.

regarding the contract price to be ultimately established and the amount of cash to be received.

The primary reason for a contractor's not using the percentrage-of-completion method when a contract exists is the uncertainty of total costs to be incurred in carrying out the project. If total costs cannot be reasonably estimated, the percentage of total costs incurred by a given date also cannot be estimated, and the percentage of services already rendered (revenue) cannot be determined.

ACCRUAL BASIS WHEN CASH COLLECTABILITY IS EXTREMELY UNCERTAIN

Occasionally, estimating the amount of cash or cash equivalent value of other assets that will be received from customers is difficult. This may occur because the future financial condition of the buyer is highly uncertain, or because the payments are spread over a very long period of time. Therefore, an objective measure of the present value of the cash to be received cannot be made at the time of the sale. Under these circumstances, revenue is recognized at the time of cash collection using either the installment method or the cost-recovery-first method described below. Unlike the cash method of accounting, however, there is an attempt to match expenses with revenues.

INSTALLMENT METHOD

installment method
Method of recording a sale transaction whereby each installment (payment on account) is recognized as part recovery of cost and part profit.

Under the **installment method**, revenue is recognized as parts of the selling price are collected in cash. At the same time, corresponding parts of the cost of the good or service sold are recognized as expenses. For example, assume that merchandise costing $60 is sold for $100. The buyer agrees to pay (ignoring interest) $20 per month for five months. Under the installment method, revenue of $20 is recognized each month as cash is received. Likewise, cost of goods sold is $12 (= $20/$100 × $60) each month. By the end of five months, total income of $40 [= 5 × ($20 − $12)] would be recognized.

The installment method is sometimes used by land development companies. These companies typically sell undeveloped land and promise to develop it over several years. The buyer makes a nominal down payment and agrees to pay the remainder of the purchase price in installments over ten, twenty, or more years. In these cases, future development of the land is a significant aspect of the earnings process. Also, substantial uncertainty often exists regarding the ultimate collectability of the installment notes, particularly those not due until several years in the future. The customer can always elect to stop making payments and merely lose the right to own the land.

COST-RECOVERY-FIRST METHOD

cost-recovery-first method
A method of revenue recognition that credits inventory as collections are received until all costs are recovered, at which time profit recognition begins.

Under circumstances in which there is great uncertainty about cash collection, the **cost-recovery-first method** of income recognition can also be used.

Under this method, costs of generating revenues are matched dollar for dollar with cash receipts until all such costs are recovered. Revenues and total expenses are equal in each period until all costs are recovered. Only when cumulative cash receipts exceed total costs will profit (that is, revenue without any matching expenses) be shown in the income statement.

To illustrate the cost-recovery-first method, refer to the example above relating to the sale of merchandise for $100. During the first three months, revenue of $20 and expenses of $20 would be recognized. By the end of the third month, cumulative cash receipts of $60 would exactly equal the cost of the merchandise sold. During the fourth and fifth months, revenue of $20 per month would be recognized, but without an offsetting expense. For the five months as a whole, total income of $40 would again be recognized, but in a different pattern than under the installment method.

USE OF INSTALLMENT AND COST-RECOVERY-FIRST METHODS

Generally accepted accounting principles permit the installment method and the cost-recovery-first method only when great uncertainty exists about cash collection. For most sales of goods and services, past experience and an assessment of customers' credit standings provide a sufficient basis for estimating the amount of cash to be received.

The installment method is allowable for income tax reporting under certain circumstances, even when cash collections are assured. Retailers and other firms selling on extended payment plans often use the installment method for income tax reporting (while recognizing revenue at the time of sale for financial reporting). The cost-recovery-first method is not permitted for income tax reporting.

RECOGNITION OF REVENUE BETWEEN PURCHASE AND SALE

The period between the aquisition or production of inventory items and the sale of the items is referred to as a *holding period* . The current market prices of these assets could change during this holding period while the items are held in inventory. Such changes are described as **holding gains** (unrealized) and **holding losses** (realized), because a transaction or exchange has not taken place.

Unrealized holding gains could be recognized as they occur. Accountants typically wait, however, until the asset is sold or exchanged in an arm's-length transaction before recognizing any gain. At that time, an inflow of net assets subject to objective measurement takes place. Because the accountant assumes that the firm is a going concern, the unrealized gain will eventually be recognized as revenue in the ordinary course of business in a future period. The recognition of revenue and the valuation of assets are therefore closely associated. Nonmonetary assets are typically stated at acquisition cost until sold. At the time of sale, an inflow of net assets occurs (for example, cash, accounts receivable), and revenue reflecting the previously unreported unrealized gain is recognized. This treatment of unrealized holding gains has the effect of shifting income from periods when the asset is held and the market price increases to the later period of sale. The

holding gains and losses
The relationship between the historical cost and the replacement cost of inventory.

longer the holding period (consider, for example, land held for several decades), the more likely it is that reported income will be shifted to later
periods.

Current accounting practices do not treat all unrealized holding losses
in the same way as unrealized holding gains. If the current market prices
of inventory items or temporary investments decrease below acquisition
cost during the holding period, the asset is usually written down with a
credit to the asset account. The matching debit recognizes the unrealized
loss in the period of price decline. This treatment of losses rests on the
convention that earnings should be reported conservatively. Considering
the estimates and predictions required in measuring revenues and
expenses, some accountants prefer to provide a conservative measure of
earnings so that statement users will not be misled into thinking the firm
is doing better than it really is.

The inconsistent treatment of unrealized gains and unrealized losses
does not seem warranted. The arguments used against recognizing unrealized gains apply equally well to unrealized losses. If gains cannot be measured objectively before sale, how can losses be measured before? If losses
can be measured objectively before sale, why cannot gains? The accounting
treatment of unrealized holding gains and losses is considered further in
Chapters 6, 7, and 12.

SUMMARY ILLUSTRATION OF INCOME RECOGNITION METHODS

**revenue recognition
policies**
The policies chosen by
the organization that
define how and when
revenue is to be recog-
nized in the financial
statements. The most
common and general
policy used is recogni-
tion when performance
has occurred.

Exhibit 4.3 illustrates the application of various **revenue recognition policies** discussed in Chapters 3 and 4. The illustration relates to a contract for
the construction of a bridge for $12 million. The expected and actual pattern
of cash receipts and disbursements under the contract is as follows:

Period	Expected and Actual Cash Receipts	Expected and Actual Cash Expenditures
1	$ 1,000,000	$1,600,000
2	1,000,000	4,000,000
3	2,000,000	4,000,000
4	4,000,000	—
5	4,000,000	—
Total	$12,000,000	$9,600,000

The contractor completed the bridge in Period 3. Exhibit 4.3 indicates the
contractor's periodic revenues, expenses, and income recognized during
each period under the contract using:

1. The cash basis of accounting

2. The percentage-of-completion method

3. The completed contract (completed sale) method
4. The installment method
5. The cost-recovery-first method

No single firm could simultaneously justify all of the five methods of income recognition for financial reporting purposes; we present them for illustrative purposes. Note that the total revenues, expenses, and income recognized for the five years are the same for all methods. In historical cost accounting over sufficiently long time periods, income is equal to cash inflows less cash outflows. The patterns of annual income differ significantly, however, depending on the accounting method.

EXHIBIT 4.3
Comprehensive Illustration of Revenue and Expense Recognition (all dollar amounts in thousands)

Period				Cash Basis of Accounting[a]		
				Revenue	Expense	Income
1				$ 1,000	$1,600	$ (600)
2				1,000	4,000	(3,000)
3				2,000	4,000	(2,000)
4				4,000	—	4,000
5				4,000	—	4,000
Total				$12,000	$9,600	$2,400

	Percentage of Completion Method			Completed Contract Method		
Period	Revenue	Expense	Income	Revenue	Expense	Income
1	$ 2,000[d]	$1,600	$ 400	—	—	—
2	5,000[e]	4,000	1,000	—	—	—
3	5,000[e]	4,000	1,000	$12,000	$9,600	$2,400
4	—	—	—	—	—	—
5	—	—	—	—	—	—
Total	$12,000	$9,600	$2,400	$12,000	$9,600	$2,400

	Installment Method[b]			Cost-Recovery-First Method[c]		
Period	Revenue	Expense	Income	Revenue	Expense	Income
1	$ 1,000	$ 800[f]	$ 200	$ 1,000	$1,000	—
2	1,000	800[f]	200	1,000	1,000	—
3	2,000	1,600[g]	400	2,000	2,000	—
4	4,000	3,200[h]	800	4,000	4,000	—
5	4,000	3,200[h]	800	4,000	1,600	$2,400
Total	$12,000	$9,000	$2,400	$12,000	$9,600	$2,400

[a]The cash basis is not allowed for tax reporting, except for farming and fishing businesses.
[b]The installment method should be used for financial reporting only if extreme uncertainty exists regarding the amount of cash to be collected from customers.
[c]The cost-recovery-first method is allowed for financial reporting only if extreme uncertainty exists regarding the amount of cash to be collected from customers. It is not permitted for tax purposes.
[d]$1,600/$9,600 × $12,000.   [f]$1,000/$12,000 × $9,600.   [h]$4,000/$12,000 × $9,600.
[e]$4,000/$9,600 × $12,000.   [g]$2,000/$12,000 × $9,600.

DISCUSSION CASE 10

Profits are OK, Says Society

In "Can Ethics and Profits Live Under the Same Roof?" (March/April [1988]), author Ralph Sorenson makes a valiant effort but is in trouble right from the title line.

"Ethics" and "profits" are not mutually exclusive words or concepts. It's a shame when we in the business community concede that fundamental argument right off the bat.

Corporations exist in our society to fulfill needs. Consider that the other alternative is to have some form of government organization fulfill those needs. Most would agree that there's no point in arguing which is more ethical.

Let's go on. Whether or not an individual corporation consciously realizes it, it has a raison d'être, a reason for being. And every company's raison d'être is different from that of the next company, but they all fit the same template: "Do something for somebody." (As an aside, the degree of success of corporations is closely aligned with how well the organization perceives and adheres to its raison d'être.)

That's all very nice, but what about profits? While raisons d'être come in all sizes and shapes, the corollary to them all is the same — the corporation must make a profit. Otherwise, how will you be able to fulfill your raison d'être tomorrow?

Conceptually, profits are society's way of saying that they like and appreciate what you are doing for them and probably would like you to continue providing similar value tomorrow. Nothing unethical about that, is there?

References

Reprinted with permission. From John G.B. Howland, "Profits are OK, says Society?" *Financial Executive*, July/August 1988, copyright 1988 by Financial Executives Institute, Morristown, New Jersey.

Discussion Question

How have recent changes in the former communist bloc countries lent credence to the author's message that profits are beneficial? When does society say that profits are not okay?

FORMAT AND CLASSIFICATION WITHIN THE INCOME STATEMENT

One of the major objectives in income statement presentation is to show the results of normal business operations as distinct from gains and losses resulting from highly infrequent or unusual transactions. Segregating these items makes it easier for financial statement users to predict future earnings performance of the company.

The income statement might contain some or all of the following additional sections or categories beyond those described previously, depending on the nature of the firm's income for the period:

1. Income before extraordinary items and discontinued operations[1]
2. Discontinued operations
3. Extraordinary gains and losses
4. Net income for the period
5. Earnings per share

The majority of income statements include only the Net Income and Earnings per Share sections. The other sections are added if necessary.

INCOME BEFORE EXTRAORDINARY ITEMS AND DISCONTINUED OPERATIONS

Revenues, gains, expenses, and losses from continuing areas of business activity of a firm are presented in the first section of the income statement. A heading such as "Net Income (or Net Earnings) for the Year" is used if there are no other sections in the income statement. This segment of the income statement should show the following amounts separately, if material:[2]

1. Sales
2. Income from investments by major class
3. Income from operating and sales-type leases
4. Government assistance credited directly to income
5. Depreciation, depletion, and amortization of leasehold improvements
6. Amortization of deferred charges and intangible assets
7. Research and development costs
8. Interest expense by class of investment
9. Gains, losses, and provisions for losses resulting from normal business activities that are both abnormal in size and caused by rare or unusual circumstances
10. Income taxes

In addition, the income statement should include the amount of income from contingent and sublease rentals, the cost of goods sold, other major operating expenses, and rentals for the year under lease obligations.

The information presented above is frequently included in the footnotes to the financial statements rather than in the body of the statement.

---

[1] If there are discontinued operations, this line is properly entitled "Income from continuing operations."

[2] *CICA Handbook*, section 1520.

DISCONTINUED OPERATIONS

continuing operations
A heading used in the income statement to distinguish income attributable to the part of the business that is ongoing from the part that has been sold or discontinued.

discontinued operations
Portions or segments of a business that have been discontinued. Separate disclosure of the results of discontinued operations should be made on the income statement.

In order to help financial statement users predict future earnings, the income statement should clearly distinguish between earnings from sources and activities that are expected to continue in future periods (**continuing operations**) and earnings from sources and activities that are not expected to do so (**discontinued operations**).[3]

Most large companies have clearly distinguishable lines of business or classes of customers. These are referred to as segments. Normally, the income statement shows the revenues and expenses from the business as a whole, although the operating results of individual segments over a certain size must be separately disclosed in the footnotes. However, when a company discontinues a segment, a separate section of the income statement should show the impact on earnings of two events:

1. *Gain or loss from operating the segment between when management decides to discontinue it and when it is actually discontinued.*

2. *Gain or loss from the actual disposal of the segment's assets.*

Both of these amounts are afforded net-of-tax treatment similar to that for extraordinary items. The reporting format would be as follows:

Income from Continuing Operations		$$
Discontinued Operation (Note X):		
Gain/Loss from Operations		
(net of income taxes):	$$	
Gain/Loss on Disposal		
(net of income taxes)	$$	
		$$
Net Income		$$

EXTRAORDINARY ITEMS

Extraordinary items
Transactions or events that are unusual in nature, occur infrequently, and are not the result of decisions of management. Gains and losses on such items are show separately, net of tax effect, in the income statement.

Unusual items
Events and transactions that are not considered to be part of normal business operations but cannot be classified as extraordinary items.

Extraordinary items are transactions and events that meet three criteria:[4]

1. *They are unusual in nature.*

2. *They occur infrequently.*

3. *They are not the result of decisions made by managers or owners.*

All three conditions must by met in order for an item to qualify as an extraordinary item. **Unusual items** are highly abnormal and significantly different from the firm's ordinary and typical activities. To determine a firm's ordinary and typical activities, we must consider such things as the type of operations, lines of business, operating policies, and the environment in which the firm operates. The operating environment includes the characteristics of the industry, the geographical location of the firm's facilities, and the types of governmental regulations imposed. A transaction or

---

[3] *CICA Handbook*, section 3475.

[4] *CICA Handbook*, section 3480.

event is considered to occur *infrequently* if the firm does not expect it to recur in the foreseeable future.

The three criteria considerably restrict the events and transactions that qualify as extraordinary items. For instance, a firm's flood loss would not be extraordinary if the facility was located on a flood plain where such an event happened every few years. On the other hand, if the flood was the result of a dam bursting, it would almost certainly be classified as an extraordinary loss. Catastrophes and "acts of God" such as floods, fires, earthquakes, and tornadoes are the most common causes of extraordinary losses. Other events that may generate extraordinary losses or gains are expropriations of property and prohibitions under newly enacted laws (such as a government ban on a product that is currently marketed).

The third condition was added by the CICA to prevent management from distorting their financial reports. Management would naturally prefer to report all gains as recurring and all losses as extraordinary. With this third condition, there are far fewer extraordinary items reported in income statements today.

Income taxes payable resulting from an extraordinary gain must be deducted from the gain and the "aftertax" total must be added to "net income before extraordinary items" to arrive at the "net income for the period." The income tax recoverable from an extraordinary loss will be treated in a similar fashion.

This method is referred to as the **net-of-tax treatment**. Suppose Fisher Ltd. had pretax income from operations of $125,000 and, in addition, suffered an extraordinary loss of $30,000 from a flood. Assuming a 40 percent income tax rate, the bottom section of the income statement would appear as follows:

net-of-tax treatment Financial statement disclosure of an item (such as extraordinary items) with the related tax payable or benefit shown adjacent to the item, rather than as part of the overall tax provision.

Income Before Taxes and Extraordinary Item		$125,000
Less: Income Taxes		(50,000)
Income Before Extraordinary Item		$ 75,000
Extraordinary Item:		
Flood Loss (Note X)	$30,000	
Less: Tax Reduction from Flood Loss	(12,000)	(18,000)
Net Income		$ 57,000

The total income taxes payable of $38,000 [($125,000 − $30,000) × 40%] is split on the statement as $50,000 on operating revenue, less a $12,000 reduction caused by claiming a flood loss. In this way, readers can readily see the tax impacts of extraordinary gains and losses.

Unusual or Nonrecurring Items   These items do not meet the strict criteria for extraordinary items mentioned above but nevertheless are considered worthy of separate disclosure in the income statement bacause of their abnormal size or the circumstances creating them. Examples of such items include gains and losses from (a) the writeoff or writedown of receivables and inventories; (b) the exchange or translation of foreign currencies into Canadian dollars; (c) the sale or abandonment of property, plant, or equipment used in the business; (d) the effects of a strike; and (e) the adjustment of long-term contract accruals. The usefulness of the income statement is enhanced by reporting items such as these as separate items in the statement.

EARNINGS PER SHARE

The two most widely used numbers in financial statements are probably net income and **earnings per share (EPS)**. These two statistics are important pieces of information in making investment decisions about a company. As the name suggests, EPS indicates the maximum current earnings that theoretically could be distributed to each shareholder after the prior claims of debt holders and preferred shareholders have been satisfied. Earnings per share data must be shown either on the face of the income statement or in a note to the financial statements cross-referenced to the income statement. With only a few exceptions, companies present this information on the face of the income statement.

Both basic and fully diluted earnings per share are to be presented in the income statement for income before extraordinary items (if relevant) and net income for the period.

The basic earnings per common share are conventionally calculated by dividing net income minus preferred share dividends by the weighted average number of outstanding common shares during the accounting period. For example, assume that a firm had a net income of $500,000 during the year 19XI. Dividends declared and paid on outstanding preferred shares were $100,000. The average number of common shares outstanding during 19XI was 1,000,000 shares. Earnings per common share would be $0.40 [= ($500,000 − $100,000) ÷ 1,000,000].

Assume now that this firm had 1,000,000 shares outstanding on January 1 but issued an additional 400,000 shares on September 1. The weighted average number of shares outstanding for the year ended December 31 would be calculated as follows:

Shares	Months Outstanding	Share Months
1,000,000	8	8,000,000
1,400,000	4	5,600,000
		13,600,000
		÷ 12
		= 1,133,333 shares

Where extraordinary items are presented in the income statement, earnings per share before extraordinary items will be shown in addition to the above. The difference between this figure and the basic earnings per common share will be the amount of extraordinary items divided by the average number of common shares outstanding.

If a firm has securities outstanding that can be converted into or exchanged for common shares, it may be required to present two sets of earnings per share amounts: **basic earnings per share** and **fully diluted earnings per share**. For example, some firms issue convertible bonds or convertible preferred shares, which can be exchanged directly for common

---

earnings per share (EPS)
Net income less any preferred dividend requirements divided by the weighted average number of common shares outstanding.

basic earnings per share
The amount of current earnings attributable to each common share outstanding during the period. This calculation does not take into account the potential effects of dilutive securities.

fully diluted earnings per share
The earnings per share of a corporation with a complex capital structure calculated on the assumption that all shareholders with dilutive securities converted them into common shares.

shares. Also, many firms have employee stock option plans under which the company's common shares may be acquired by employees under special arrangements. If these convertible securities were to be converted or stock options were to be exercised and additional common shares were issued, the amount conventionally shown as earnings per share would probably decrease, or become *diluted*. When a firm has outstanding securities that, if exchanged for common shares, would decrease earnings per share, a dual presentation of basic and fully diluted earnings per share is required.

INCOME STATEMENT FORMAT

Firms use different reporting formats in their income statements. Some firms use a **multiple-step income statement**, which presents several subtotals before reporting the amount of net income for the period. One common multiple-step format separates income from operating activities and revenues and expenses relating to investment and financing activities. The upper portion of Exhibit 4.4 presents an income statement for May Department Stores in this multiple-step format. Note that this format nets revenues from sales of merchandise and expenses related to generating these revenues to obtain operating income. It then adds interest revenues from investments and subtracts interest expenses on debt to derive income before income taxes. This reporting format attempts to capture in the income statement the distinction made in Chapter 1 (see Figure 1.1) between operating, investing, and financing activities. Other multiple-step formats are also found in annual reports.

The lower portion of Exhibit 4.4 presents a **single-step income statement** for May Department stores. This format presents and totals all revenue items, followed by all expense items. The computation of net income results from a single arithmetic step — a subtraction of total expenses from total revenues. The single-step method usually results in a more condensed presentation of the income statement.

multiple-step income statement
An income statement in which one or more intermediate accounts (such as gross profit on sales) are derived before the ordinary, continuing income is reported.

single-step income statement
A condensed form of the income statement in which the ordinary, continuing income of the business is derived in one step by subtracting total expenses.

EXHIBIT 4.4
Income Statement for May Department Stores (amounts in millions)

	Year 6	Year 7	Year 8
Multiple-Step Format:			
Sales	$10,376	$10,581	$11,742
Cost of Goods Sold	(7,533)	(7,706)	(8,453)
Gross Profit	$ 2,843	$ 2,875	$ 3,289
Selling and Administrative Expenses	(2,048)	(2,019)	(2,279)
Operating Income	$ 795	$ 856	$ 1,010
Interest Revenue	26	22	18
Interest Expense	(153)	(135)	(247)
Income Before Income Taxes	$ 668	$ 743	$ 781
Income Tax Expense	(287)	(299)	(278)
Net Income	$ 381	$ 444	$ 503

	Year 6	Year 7	Year 8
Single-Step Format:			
Sales	$10,376	$10,581	$11,742
Interest Revenue	26	22	18
Total Revenues	$10,402	$10,603	$11,760
Cost of Goods Sold	$ 7,533	$ 7,706	$ 8,453
Selling and Administrative Expenses	2,048	2,019	2,279
Interest Expense	153	135	247
Income Tax Expense	287	299	278
Total Expenses	$10,021	$10,159	$11,257
Net Income	$ 381	$ 444	$ 503

AN INTERNATIONAL PERSPECTIVE

Firms in all industrialized countries and in most developing countries around the world prepare financial statements based on the accrual basis rather than the cash basis of accounting. The particular measurement rules used in applying the accrual basis, however, differ between countries. Chapters 6 to 12 briefly discuss some of these differences.

The format and classification of income items within the income statement vary among countries. The general measurement and disclosure principles discussed in Chapters 3 and 4, however, should permit the reader to interpret and understand widely varying formats.

The income statement format and underlying principles are very similar in Canada and the United States. The major differences pertain to the frequency of extraordinary items reported and the computations of the earnings per share statistics.

Exhibit 4.5 shows the income statement for Wellcome PLC, a British pharmaceutical firm. Note the different terminology used:

Exhibit 4.5	This Book
Group Profit and Loss Account	Income Statement
Turnover	Sales Revenue
Trading Profit	Operating Income
Profit on Ordinary Activities	Income from Continuing Operations

Wellcome's Statement classifies operating costs according to their nature (for example, raw materials, labour, depreciation) instead of by functional activity (for example, cost of goods sold, selling expenses, administrative expenses). Classification by nature of expense is common in European countries. One item seldom seen in Canadian annual reports is "Change in Stocks of Finished Goods and Work in Process." Wellcome reports among its operating costs on the income statement actual raw materials, labour, and overhead costs incurred during the year. It assigns a portion of these costs to units in the Work-in-Process

Inventory and Finished Goods Inventory accounts at the end of the period. For example, at the end of Year 8, £18.7 million of costs included in various operating cost items in the income statement actually apply to units in process or in finished goods at the end of Year 8 and not to units sold. Netting this £18.7 million against the actual cost incurred results in the proper amount of costs being matched against revenues.

EXHIBIT 4.5
Wellcome PLC Group Profit and Loss Account

	Year 7	Year 8
Turnover	£1,132.4	£1,250.5
Operating Costs:		
Raw Materials and Consumables	(246.9)	(245.4)
Other External Charges	(401.5)	(424.4)
Staff Costs	(309.1)	(337.4)
Depreciation	(38.8)	(44.1)
Change in Stocks of Finished Goods and Work		
in Process	36.5	18.7
Other Operating Changes	(10.3)	(6.7)
Other Operating Income	15.0	21.7
Trading Profit	£ 177.3	£ 232.9
Net Interest Payable	(8.2)	(11.7)
Profit on Ordinary Activities Before Taxation	£ 169.1	£ 221.2
Tax on Profit from Ordinary Activities	(71.4)	(89.4)
Profit on Ordinary Activities Attributable to		
Shareholders	£ 97.7	£ 131.8

KEY TERMS

Merchandising firms	Cost-recovery-first method
Manufacturing firm	Holding gains and losses
Direct material	Revenue recognition policy
Direct labour	Continuing operations
Manufacturing overhead	Discontinued operations
Product costs	Extraordinary items
Period expenses	Unusual items
Raw Materials Inventory	Net-of-tax treatment
Work-in-Process Inventory	Earnings per share (EPS)
Finished Goods Inventory	Basic earnings per share
Percentage-of-completion method	Fully diluted earnings per share
Completed contract method	Multiple-step income statement
Installment method	Single-step income statement

SELF-STUDY MATERIAL

This section contains questions, exercises, and problems to help you assess your understanding of Chapter 4. Careful review of this material will assist you in completing the homework assignments. Solutions are found at the end of the section.

QUESTIONS AND EXERCISES

True/False

For each statement, place a T or an F in the space provided to indicate whether the statement is true or false.

_T_ 1. The cost-recovery-first method of income recognition matches costs of generating revenues dollar for dollar with cash receipts until all such costs are recovered.

_T_ 2. The balance in the Finished Goods account represents the total manufacturing cost of units completed but not sold.

_T_ 3. When materials are issued to producing departments, the Work-in-Process Inventory account is debited.

_T_ 4. The Work-in-Process Inventory account is debited for the cost of direct labour services used.

_F_ 5. The Finished Goods account accumulates the costs incurred in producing units during the period.

_T_ 6. For an item to qualify as extraordinary, it must be both a typical of the company's normal business activities and infrequent in occurrence.

_F_ 7. Gains or losses on sale of a business should not be disclosed in a separate classification on the income statement.

_T_ 8. The Raw Materials account includes the cost of raw materials purchased but not yet transferred to production.

_F_ 9. The installment method of recognizing revenue is used for both tax and financial statement purposes in every long-term payment contract sale.

_F_ 10. Earnings per share data should be considered as supplementary and therefore disclosed only at the discretion of management.

_F_ 11. The Cost-of-Goods-Sold account is debited for the total manufacturing cost of units completed and transferred to the storeroom.

___ 12. The Finished Goods account is debited for the cost of units sold during the period.

_T_ 13. The completed contract method of recognizing revenue is the same as the completed-sale basis.

_F_ 14. Product costs represent only the cost of raw materials for a manufacturing firm.

_F_ 15. The balance in the Raw Materials account represents manufacturing cost incurred on uncompleted units.

___ 16. Unrealized holding gains and losses are never recognized until a sale is made.

_F_ 17. The Raw Materials account is credited for the total manufacturing cost of units completed and transferred to the storeroom.

_T_ 18. The percentage-of-completion method of revenue recognition allows firms with long-term construction contracts to recognize a portion of the total contract price, based on the degree of completion of the work, during each accounting period of the life of the contract.

F   19. The installment method of revenue recognition allows a firm to recognize revenue from a cash sale equally over a three- to five-year period in the future.

Matching

I. Indicate by letter whether each expenditure should be classified as (a) direct material, (b) direct labour, (c) manufacturing overhead, (d) selling expense, (e) administrative expense, or (f) none of the above.

C   1. Insurance costs on factory building C ✓
b   2. Wages paid to assembly-line workers b ✓
a   3. Salary of the sales vice-president C ✗
a   4. Cost of paint for the glossy finish on the product a ✓
b   5. Salary of the painter of the product b ✓
e   6. Cost of service contract for the maintenance of the computer C ✗
e   7. Salary of the company president e ✓
d   8. Cost of oil and gasoline for sales staff cars d ✓
a   9. Raw materials for the product a ✓
C   10. Depreciation of the factory equipment C ✓
d   11. Cost of pamphlets distributed to advertise the product a ✗
f   12. Salary of the factory supervisor (person in charge of the assembly-line workers) b ✗
d   13. Sales commissions paid on each sale of the product d
C   14. Cost of cleaning supplies used to remove grease in the factory C
C   15. Cost of normal maintenance for machinery in the factory C
e   16. Salary of the company controller e
e   17. Costs of legal fees e   e
C   18. Salary of vice-president for production b
e   19. Depreciation on the company's computer e
e   20. Electricity cost for the office building e

II. Indicate by letter for each transaction or event whether it shoud be classified within the income statement as (a) income before extraordinary items or (b) extraordinary items.

a   1. Loss from sale of investment in preferred shares
b   2. Gain on sale of the company's only division for manufacturing sports equipment
b   3. Realization of taxable loss carryforward
a   4. President's salary during the year
a   5. Loss on decline in the market value of several inventory items
a   6. Gain on the sale of the vice-president's company automobile
b   7. Loss on factory and equipment in an African country when they are confiscated by that country's government
a   8. Interest received on short-term investments
b   9. Loss on damages from a flood that affected the company's factory in Winnipeg
a   10. The cost of goods sold during the year

Multiple Choice

Choose the best answer for each question or problem and enter the identifying letter in the space provided.

 1. Faulkner Co. Ltd. purchased inventory on July 1, 19X1 for $3,000. On December 31, 19X1, the inventory had a current market price of $2,250. During 19X2, the inventory was sold for $2,000. Which of these statements is true?
a) the inventory was reported on the December 31, 19X1 balance sheet at its cost of $3,000
b) when the inventory was sold during 19X2, the company reported a $1,000 loss
c) for the year ending December 31, 19X1, Faulkner recognized a $750 unrealized loss in its income statement
d) the inventory was reported on the December 31, 19X1 balance sheet at $2,000

 2. King Co. Ltd. purchased land on December 31, 19X1 for $20,000. The land had a fair market value of $24,000 one year later. On July 1, 19X3, the land was sold for $30,000. Which of these statements is true?
a) the land was carried on the books at $20,000 on December 31, 19X2
b) a $10,000 gain was recorded on July 1, 19X3 when the land was sold
c) there was an unrealized holding gain of $4,000 as of December 31, 19X2
d) all of the above statements are true

 3. If a reasonable estimate of the amount of cash to be received can be made, when should revenue be recognized?
a) at the time of sale
b) at the time of cash collection
c) at the time of cash collection, using the cost-recovery-first method
d) none of the above

 4. Which of the following is not a product cost?
a) depreciation on plant machinery
b) salary of the production vice-president
c) insurance associated with the delivery equipment
d) property taxes associated with the factory building

 5. The earnings process for a manufacturing firm includes which of the following?
a) completion of production
b) collection of cash
c) acquisition of raw materials, plant, and equipment
d) all of the above

 6. Which of the following is not a period expense?
a) salary of the sales vice-president
b) salaries of factory custodial employees
c) salaries of administrative clerical personnel
d) salaries of employees who deliver the finished product to customers

Exercises

1. The Parker Shipbuilding Co. Ltd. received a contract late in 19X1 to construct a ship for a contract price totalling $4,000,000. The contract was to be completed in 19X5. Following is a schedule of the receipts and disbursements over the life of the contract.

Year	Expected and Actual Cash Receipts	Expected and Actual Cash Expenditures
19X2	$ 500,000	$ 750,000
19X3	1,000,000	1,500,000
19X4	2,000,000	500,000
19X5	500,000	250,000
Total	$4,000,000	$3,000,000

Determine the amount of revenue, expense, and net income for each year under each of these methods of revenue recognition:

a. production (percentage-of-completion) method
b. sales (completed contract) method
c. cash-collection (installment) method
d. cash-collection (cost-recovery-first) method
e. cash basis

2. The Jones Company Inc. has completed its first year in business. Given the incomplete information in the four T-accounts, answer the questions that follow:

Raw Materials Inventory

Balance 12/31 15,000	

Work-in-Process Inventory

Labour 75,000	
Overhead 36,000	135
Balance 12/31 21,000	6

Finished Goods Inventory

135	120,000
Balance 12/31 15,000	

Cost of Goods Sold

120,000	

a. Determine the amount of goods finished during the period and transferred to Finished Goods Inventory: $ 135,000
b. Determine the amount of raw materials transferred to Work-in-Process Inventory during the period: $ 45,000
c. Determine the amount of raw materials purchased during period: $ 60,000
d. Record all journal entries for the company's manufacturing activities during the period. Assume that the $36,000 overhead cost relates to depreciation on the factory building.

PROBLEM 1 FOR SELF-STUDY

The following data relate to the manufacturing activities of the Haskell Co. Ltd. during March:

	March 31	March 1
Raw Materials Inventory	$ 46,900	$42,400
Work-in-Process Inventory	63,200	75,800
Finished Goods Inventory	46,300	44,200

	March 31	March 1
Factory Costs Incurred During the Month:		
Raw Materials Purchased	$ 60,700	
Labour Services Received	137,900	
Heat, Light, and Power	1,260	
Rent	4,100	
Expirations of Previous Factory Acquisitions and Prepayments:		
Depreciation of Factory Equipment	$ 1,800	
Prepaid Insurance Expired	1,440	
Other Data Relating to the Month:		
Sales	$400,000	
Selling and Administrative Expenses	125,000	
Estimated Income Tax Expense	25,000	

a. Calculate the cost of raw materials used during March.

b. Calculate the cost of units completed during March and transferred to the finished goods storeroom.

c. Calculate the cost of goods sold during March.

d. Calculate new income for March.

PROBLEM 2 FOR SELF-STUDY

The Brennan Construction Co. Ltd. contracted on May 15, Year 2 to build a bridge for the city for $4,500,000. Brennan estimated the cost of constructing the bridge would be $3,600,000. Brennan incurred $1,200,000 in construction costs during Year 2, $2,000,000 during Year 3, and $400,000 during Year 4 in completing the bridge. The city paid $1,000,000 during Year 2, $1,500,000 during Year 3, and the remaining $2,000,000 of the contract price at the time the bridge was completed and approved in Year 4.

a. Calculate the net income (revenue less expenses before income tax) of Brennan on the contract during Year 2, Year 3, and Year 4, assuming that the perentage-of-completion method is used.

b. Repeat (a), assuming that the completed contract method is used.

c. Repeat (a), assuming that the installment method is used.

d. Repeat (a), assuming that the cost-recovery-first method is used.

PROBLEM 3 FOR SELF-STUDY

The following information is available regarding the NEWCO Company:
    January 1, 19X1 — 50,000 common shares issued
    December 1, 19X1 — 1 for 10 stock dividend
    October 1, 19X2 — 12,000 common shares issued for cash

	Years Ended December 31	
	19X2	19X1
Earnings before extraordinary item	$110,200	$110,000

In 19X2, a major fire destroyed one of NEWCO's buildings, which is estimated to have a net loss of $2,900 (all figures are shown net of taxes). This is not included in the above earnings.

a. What earnings per share figures would be required on the December 31, 19X2 comparative income statement?

b. Assume that on January 1, 19X2, the following shares, in addition to the common shares, were outstanding: 5,000 6%, $100 par cumulative preferred shares, and 5,000 10%, $50 par non-cumulative preferred shares.

   What earnings per share figures would be required on the December 31, 19X2 comparative income statement if:

   (1) dividends were declared in 19X2?
   (2) dividends were not declared in 19X2?

ANSWERS TO SELF-STUDY QUESTIONS AND EXERCISES

True/False

1. T	6. T	11. F	16. F
2. T	7. F	12. F	17. F
3. T	8. T	13. T	18. T
4. T	9. F	14. F	19. F
5. F	10. F	15. F	

Matching

I.

1. c	6. e	11. d	16. e
2. b	7. e	12. c	17. e
3. d	8. d	13. d	18. c
4. a	9. a	14. c	19. e
5. b	10. c	15. c	20. e

II.

1. a	4. a	7. b	10. a
2. b	5. a	8. a	
3. b	6. a	9. b	

Multiple Choice

1. c	3. a	5. d	6. b
2. b	4. c		

Exercises

1. a.

Percentage-of-Completion Method

Year	Revenue	Expense	Net Income
1986	$1,000,000[a]	$ 750,000	$ 250,000
1987	2,000,000[b]	1,500,000	500,000
1988	666,667[c]	500,000	166,667
1989	333,333[d]	250,000	83,333
Total	$4,000,000	$3,000,000	$1,000,000

[a] $750,000/$3,000,000 × $4,000,000.
[b] $1,500,000/$3,000,000 × $4,000,000.
[c] $500,000/$3,000,000 × $4,000,000.
[d] $250,000/$3,000,000 × $4,000,000.

b. **Completed Contract Method**

Year	Revenue	Expense	Net Income
1986	0	0	0
1987	0	0	0
1988	0	0	0
1989	$4,000,000	$3,000,000	$1,000,000
Total	$4,000,000	$3,000,000	$1,000,000

c. **Cash Collection (Installment Method)**

Year	Revenue	Expense	Net Income
1986	$ 500,000	$ 375,000[e]	$ 125,000
1987	1,000,000	750,000[f]	250,000
1988	2,000,000	1,500,000[g]	500,000
1989	500,000	375,000[e]	125,000
Total	$4,000,000	$3,000,000	$1,000,000

[e] $500,000/$4,000,000 × $3,000,000.
[f] $1,000,000/$4,000,000 × $3,000,000.
[g] $2,000,000/$4,000,000 × $3,000,000.

d. **Cash Collection (Cost-Recovery-First Method)**

Year	Revenue	Expense	Net Income
1986	$ 500,000	$ 500,000	0
1987	1,000,000	1,000,000	0
1988	2,000,000	1,500,000	$ 500,000
1989	500,000	0	500,000
Total	$4,000,000	$3,000,000	$1,000,000

e. **Cash Basis**

Year	Revenue	Expense	Net Income (loss)
1986	$ 500,000	$ 750,000	$ (250,000)
1987	1,000,000	1,500,000	(500,000)
1988	2,000,000	500,000	1,500,000
1989	500,000	250,000	250,000
Total	$4,000,000	$3,000,000	$1,000,000

2.

Raw Materials Inventory		
Purchased 60,000		
		45,000
Balance 12/31 15,000		

Work-in-Process Inventory		
Materials 45,000		
Labour 75,000		
Overhead 36,000		135,000
Balance 12/31 21,000		

Finished Goods Inventory		
135,000	120,000	
Balance 12/31 15,000		

Cost of Goods Sold		
120,000		

a. $135,000

b. $45,000

c. $60,000

d. Journal entries:

	Dr.	Cr.
(1) Raw Materials Inventory	$ 60,000	
Cash or Accounts Payable		$ 60,000
To record purchase of raw materials.		
(2) Work-in-Process Inventory	45,000	
Raw Materials Inventory		45,000
To record cost of raw materials transferred to Work-in-Process Inventory.		
(3) Work-in-Process Inventory	75,000	
Cash or Salaries Payable		75,000
To record salaries of factory workers.		
(4) Work-in-Process Inventory	36,000	
Accumulated Depreciation		36,000
To record depreciation on factory building.		
(5) Finished Goods Inventory	135,000	
Work-in-Process Inventory		135,000
To record cost of completed units transferred to finished goods storeroom.		
(6) Cost of Goods Sold	120,000	
Finished Goods Inventory		120,000
To record cost of goods sold.		

SUGGESTED SOLUTION TO PROBLEM 1 FOR SELF-STUDY

The transactions and events relating to manufacturing activities are shown in the appropriate T-accounts in Exhibit 4.6.

EXHIBIT 4.6
T-Accounts and Transactions for Haskell Co. Ltd.[a]

Raw Materials Inventory			
Bal.	42,400		
(1)	60,700	56,200	(2)[b]
Bal.	46,900		

Work-in-Process Inventory			
Bal.	75,800		
(2)	56,200	215,300	(8)[e]
(3)	137,900		
(4)	1,260		
(5)	4,100		
(6)	1,800		
(7)	1,440		
Bal.	63,200		

Finished Goods Inventory			
Bal.	44,200		
(8)[c]	215,300	213,200	(9)[d]
Bal.	46,300		

Cost of Goods Sold		
(9)	213,200	

Prepaid Insurance		
	1,440	(7)

Cash or Various Liabilities		
	60,700	(1)
	137,900	(3)
	1,260	(4)
	4,100	(5)

Accumulated Depreciation		
	1,800	(6)

[a]Amount calculated by plugging.
[b]The cost of raw materials used is $56,200 (= $42,400 + $60,700 − $46,900).
[c]The cost of units completed during March is $215,300.
[d]The cost of units sold during March is $213,200 (= $44,200 + $215,300 − $46,300).
[e]Net income is $36,800 (= $400,000 − $213,200 − $125,000 − $125,000).

SUGGESTED SOLUTION TO PROBLEM 2 FOR SELF-STUDY

a. Percentage-of-Completion Method:

Year	Incremental Percentage Complete	Revenue Recognized	Expenses Recognized	Net Income
2	12/36 (0.333)	$1,500,000	$1,200,000	$300,000
3	20/36 (0.556)	2,500,000	2,000,000	500,000
4	4/36 (0.111)	500,000	400,000	100,000
Total	36/36 (1.000)	$4,500,000	$3,600,000	$900,000

b. Completed-Contract Method:

Year	Revenue Recognized	Expenses Recognized	Net Income
2	0	0	0
3	0	0	0
4	$4,500,000	$3,600,000	$900,000
Total	$4,500,000	$3,600,000	$900,000

c. Installment Method:

Year	Cash Collected (= Revenue)	Fraction of Cash Collected	Expenses (= Fraction × Total Cost)	Net Income
2	$1,000,000	2/9	$ 800,000	$200,000
3	1,500,000	3/9	1,200,000	300,000
4	2,000,000	4/9	1,600,000	400,000
Total	$4,500,000	1.0	$3,600,000	$900,000

d. Cost-Recovery-First Method:

Year	Cash Collected (= Revenue)	Expenses Recognized	Net Income
2	$1,000,000	$1,000,000	$ 0
3	1,500,000	1,500,000	0
4	2,000,000	1,100,000	900,000
Total	$4,500,000	$3,600,000	$900,000

SUGGESTED SOLUTION TO PROBLEM 3 FOR SELF-STUDY

		19X2 $	19X2 $
a.	Earnings before extraordinary items	$110,200	$110,000
	Extraordinary items	(2,900)	—
	Earnings after extraordinary items	$107,300	$110,000
	Outstanding common shares Weighted average		
	50,000 + 5,000		55,000
	55,000 + (12,000 × 3/12)	58,000	
	Earnings per share		
	Before extraordinary items	$1.90	$2.00
	Net earnings per share	$1.85	$2.00

		19X2 $	19X2 $
b.	Earnings before extraordinary items	$110,200	$110,000
	Less: Dividends — 6% cumulative	(30,000)	
	— 10% noncumulative	(25,000)	
	Subtotal	$ 55,200	$110,000
	Extraordinary items	(2,900)	—
	Earnings available to common shareholders, after extraordinary items	$ 52,300	$110,000
	Weighted average of common shares	58,000	55,000
	Earnings per share before extraordinary items	$0.95	$2.00
	Earnings per share after extraordinary items	$0.90	$2.00

Adapted with permission from the Society of Management Accountants of Canada.

ASSIGNMENT MATERIAL

QUESTIONS

1. Review the meaning of the key terms listed on page 243.

2. "Depreciation on equipment may be a product cost or a period expense, depending on the type of equipment." Explain.

3. Compare and contrast the Merchandise Inventory account of a merchandising firm and the Finished Goods Inventory account of a manufacturing firm.

4. The percentage-of-completion method is often used by construction companies. Why is this method of income recognition not used by a typical manufacturing firm?

5. Under both the installment method and the cost-recovery-first method, revenue is recognized when cash is received. Why, then, is the pattern of income (that is, revenues minus expenses) over time different under these two methods?

6. Compare and contrast the installment method and the cash basis of accounting.

7. "When the *total* amount of cash to be collected from a customer is highly uncertain, the cost-recovery-first method seems more appropriate than the installment method." Explain.

8. Economists typically define income as an increase in value, or wealth, while assets are held. Accountants typically recognize income when the criteria for revenue recognition are satisfied. Why does the accountants' approach to income recognition differ from that of the economists?

9. Why do income statements separate income relating to continuing operations from income relating to discontinued operations?

EXERCISES

10. *Identifying product costs and period expenses.* Indicate whether each of the following types of wages and salaries is a (1) product cost or (2) period expense:
    a. Cutting-machine operators
    b. Delivery labour
    c. Factory janitors
    d. Factory payroll clerks
    e. Factory superintendent
    f. General office secretaries
    g. Guards at factory gate

   h. Inspectors in factory
   i. Maintenance workers who service factory machinery
   j. Nightwatch force at the factory
   k. General office clerks
   l. Operator of a lift truck in the shipping room
   m. President of the firm
   n. Sales manager
   o. Shipping room workers
   p. Sweepers who clean retail store
   q. Travelling salespersons

11. *Identifying product costs and period expenses.* Indicate whether each of the following types of materials and supplies is a (1) product cost or (2) period expense:
   a. Cleaning lubricants for factory machines
   b. Paper for central office computer
   c. Glue used in assembling products
   d. Supplies used by factory janitor
   e. Gasoline used by salespersons
   f. Sales promotion pamphlets distributed
   g. Materials used in training production workers

12. *Identifying product costs, period expenses, and assets.* Indicate whether each of the following costs is a (1) period expense, (2) product cost, or (3) some balance sheet account other than those for product costs.
   a. Office supplies used
   b. Salary of factory supervisor
   c. Purchase of a fire insurance policy on the store building for the three-year period beginning next month
   d. Expiration of one month's protection of the insurance in (c)
   e. Property taxes for the current year on the factory building
   f. Wages of truck drivers who deliver finished goods to customers
   g. Wages of factory workers who install a new machine
   h. Wages of mechanics who repair and service factory machines
   i. Salary of the president of the company
   j. Depreciation of office equipment
   k. Factory supplies used

13. *Raw materials inventory transactions.* Compute the missing item in each of the independent cases below:

	a	b	c	d
Raw Materials Inventory, Jan. 1	$ 15,000	$ 76,900	$ 28,700	?
Purchases of Raw Materials	$297,000	$696,000	?	$76,700
Raw Materials Used	$290,000	?	$467,300	$71,700
Raw Materials Inventory, Dec. 31	?	$ 72,100	$ 37,900	$12,300

14. *Work-in-process inventory transactions.* Compute the missing item in each of the following independent cases.

	a	b	c	d
Work-in-Process Inventory, Jan. 1	$ 26,000	$ 55,600	$ 39,400	?
Raw Materials Used	$290,000	$700,800	$ 467,300	$ 71,700
Direct Labour Cost	$260,000	$675,800	?	$ 87,300
Manufacturing Overhead Costs	$180,000	$267,900	$ 136,900	$ 42,900
Cost of Units Completed	$724,000	?	$1,206,600	$193,400
Work-in-Process Inventory, Dec. 31	?	$ 72,300	$ 35,900	$ 41,700

15. **Finished goods inventory transactions.** Compute the missing item in each of the independent cases below.

	a	b	c	d
Finished Goods Inventory, Jan. 1	$ 71,000	$ 189,300	$ 110,300	?
Cost of Units Completed	$724,000	$1,627,800	?	$193,400
Costs of Units Sold	$701,000	?	$1,197,900	$187,200
Finished Goods Inventory, Dec. 31	?	$ 179,600	$ 119,000	$ 22,100

16. **Income computation for a manufacturing firm.** The following data relate to a manufacturing firm for a period:

Sales	$250,000
Cost of Units Completed	240,000
Costs of Units Sold	210,000
Selling and Administrative Expenses	30,000

Compute net income before income tax for the period.

17. **Income computation for a manufacturing firm.** The following data relate to the United Manufacturing Corporation for the month of April.

	April 30	April 1
Raw Materials Inventory	$10,000	0
Work-in-Process Inventory	25,000	0
Finished Goods Inventory	22,000	0

Manufacturing cost (direct material used, direct labour, manufacturing overhead) incurred during April totalled $65,000. Sales revenue for April was $25,000, and selling and administrative expenses were $2,000.
    Compute net income before income tax for April.

18. **Percentage-of-completion and completed contract methods of income recognition.** A construction company agreed to build a warehouse for $2,500,000. Expected and actual costs to construct the warehouse were as follows: Year 1, $600,000; Year 2, $1,000,000; Year 3, $400,000. The warehouse was completed in Year 3.

Compute revenue, expense, and net income before income tax for Year 1, Year 2, and Year 3 using the percentage-of-completion method and the completed contract method.

19. *Installment and cost-recovery-first methods of recognition.* A real estate firm sold a tract of land costing $80,000 to a manufacturing firm for $100,000. The manufacturing firm agreed to pay $25,000 per year for four years (plus interest).

Compute revenue, expense, and net income for each of the four years using the installment method and the cost-recovery-first method. Ignore interest and income tax.

PROBLEMS AND CASES

20. *Preparation of journal entries and income statement for a manufacturing firm.* Westside Products Inc. showed the following amounts in its inventory accounts on January 1.

Raw Materials Inventory	$15,000
Work-in-Process Inventory	65,000
Finished Goods Inventory	32,000

The following transactions occurred during January:
(1) Raw materials costing $28,500 were acquired on account.
(2) Raw materials costing $31,600 were issued to producing departments.
(3) Salaries and wages paid during January for services received during the month were as follows:

Factory Workers	$46,900
Sales Personnel	14,300
Administrative Officers	20,900

(4) Depreciation on buildings and equipment during January was as follows:

Manufacturing Facilities	$12,900
Selling Facilities	2,300
Administrative Facilities	1,800

(5) Other operating costs incurred and paid in cash were as follows:

Manufacturing	$15,600
Selling	4,900
Administrative	3,700

(6) The cost of goods manufactured and transferred to the finished goods storeroom totalled $85,100.
(7) Sales on account during January totalled $150,000.
(8) A physical inventory taken on January 31 revealed a finished goods inventory of $35,200.

a. Present journal entries to record the transactions and events during January.
b. Prepare an income statement for Westside Products Inc. for January (ignore income tax).

21. *Preparation of journal entries and an income statement for a manufacturing firm.* Southside Products Ltd. showed the following amounts in its inventory accounts on January 1.

Raw Materials Inventory	$40,000
Work-in-Process Inventory	96,000
Finished Goods Inventory	73,000

The following transactions occurred during January.
(1) Raw materials costing $122,700 were acquired on account.
(2) Raw materials costing $119,200 were issued to production.
(3) Salaries and wages paid during January for services received during the month were as follows:

Factory Workers	$87,600
Sales Personnel	18,900
Administrative Personnel	27,400

(4) Depreciation on buildings and equipment during January was as follows:

Manufacturing Facilities	$14,700
Selling Facilities	2,400
Administrative Facilities	2,900

(5) Other operating costs incurred and paid in cash were as follows:

Manufacturing	$18,200
Selling	7,300
Administrative	4,400

(6) The cost of goods completed and transferred to the finished goods storeroom totalled $234,000.
(7) Sales on account during January totalled $325,000.

(8) A physical inventory taken on January 31 revealed a finished goods inventory of $68,000.

    a. Present journal entries to record the transactions and events during January.

    b. Prepare an income statement for Southside Products Ltd. for January. (Ignore income tax.)

22. *Flow of manufacturing costs through the accounts.* The following data relate to the manufacturing activities of Cornell Ltd. during June.

	June 30	June 1
Raw Materials Inventory	$ 43,600	$ 46,900
Factory Supplies Inventory	7,700	7,600
Work-in-Process Inventory	115,200	110,900
Finished Goods Inventory	71,400	76,700

Factory costs incurred during the month:

Raw Materials Purchased	$429,000
Supplies Purchased	22,300
Labour Services Received	362,100
Heat, Light, and Power	10,300
Insurance	4,200

Expirations of previous factory acquisitions and prepayments:

Depreciation on Factory Equipment	$36,900
Prepaid Rent Expired	3,600

    a. Calculate the cost of raw materials and factory supplies used during June.

    b. Calculate the cost of units completed during June and transferred to the finished goods storeroom.

    c. Calculate the cost of goods sold during June.

23. *Flow of manufacturing costs through the accounts.* The following data relate to the activities of Myers Corporation during April.

	April 30	April 1
Raw Materials Inventory	$16,400	$18,700
Work-in-Process Inventory	72,400	66,800
Finished Goods Inventory	29,800	32,900

Factory costs incurred during the month:

Raw Materials Purchased	$87,300
Labour Services Received	66,100
Heat, Light, and Power	2,700
Depreciation	15,600

Other data relating to the month:

Sales	$250,000
Selling and Administrative Expenses	38,100

a. Calculate the cost of raw materials used during April.
b. Calculate the cost of units completed during April and transferred to the finished goods storeroom.
c. Calculate net income before income tax for April.

24. ***Preparing T-account entries, adjusted trial balance, income statement, and balance sheet for a manufacturing firm.*** On July 1, the accounts of the Tampa Manufacturing Co. Ltd. contained the following balances:

Debit Balances		**Credit Balances**	
Cash	$ 110,000	Accumulated Depreciation	$ 30,000
Accounts Receivable	220,000	Accounts Payable	56,000
Raw Materials Inventory	80,000	Wages Payable	24,000
Work-in-Process Inventory	230,000	Capital Stock	1,000,000
Finished Goods Inventory	170,000	Retained Earnings	200,000
Factory Supplies Inventory	20,000		
Manufacturing Equipment	480,000		
Total	$1,310,000	Total	$1,310,000

Transactions for the month of July are listed below in summary form:
(1) Sales, all on account, were $310,000.
(2) Labour services furnished by employees during the period (but as yet unpaid) amounted to $80,000. All labour is employed in the factory.
(3) Factory supplies were purchased for $8,500; payment was made by cheque.
(4) Raw materials purchased on account, $100,000.
(5) Collections from customers, $335,000.
(6) Payment of $108,000 was made to raw materials suppliers.
(7) Payments to employees total $78,500.
(8) Rent of the factory building for the month, $8,000, was paid.
(9) Depreciation of manufacturing equipment for the month, $12,000.
(10) Other manufacturing costs incurred and paid, $40,000.
(11) All selling and administrative services are furnished by Clark and Company for $10,000 per month. Their bill was paid by cheque.

(12) Raw materials used during month, $115,000.

(13) Factory supplies used during month, $8,000.

(14) Cost of goods completed during month, $258,000.

(15) Goods costing $261,500 were shipped to customers during the month.

(16) Estimated income tax expense for July is $15,400.

    a. Open T-accounts and record the July 1 amounts. Record transactions **(1)** through **(15)** in the T-accounts, opening additional accounts as needed.

    b. Prepare an adjusted, preclosing trial balance as of July 31.

    c. Prepare a combined statement of income and retained earnings for July.

    d. Enter closing entries in the T-accounts using an Income Summary account.

    e. Prepare a balance sheet as of July 31.

25. *Preparing T-account entries and adjusted trial balance for a manufacturing firm.* Melton Plastics Limited was incorporated on September 16. By September 30, having rented a building for its manufacturing operations, the firm was ready to begin operations. The trial balance at that date was as follows:

Cash	$387,200	
Raw Materials Inventory	19,200	
Factory Equipment	136,000	
Accounts Payable		$ 22,400
Capital Stock		520,000
	$542,400	$542,400

The following data relate only to the manufacturing operations of the firm during October:

(1) Materials purchased on account, $161,600.

(2) Wages and salaries earned during the month, $148,000.

(3) Raw materials requisitioned and put into process during the month, $168,800.

(4) Equipment was acquired during the month at a cost of $112,000. A cheque for $40,000 was issued, and an equipment contract payable in eight equal monthly installments was signed for the remainder (ignore interest).

(5) Additional payments by cheque:

Raw Materials Suppliers	$140,000
Payroll	112,420
Building Rent	6,000
Utilities	2,920
Insurance Premiums (for one year from October 1)	9,600
Miscellaneous Factory Costs	26,400
	$297,340

(6) Invoices received but unpaid at October 31:

City Water Department	$ 120
Hoster Machine Supply Co. Ltd. for additional equipment	2,400

(7) Depreciation on equipment for the month, $1,200.

(8) One month's insurance expiration is recorded.

(9) The cost of parts finished during October was $281,750.

   a. Open T-accounts and enter the amounts from the opening trial balance.

   b. Record the transactions during the month in the T-accounts, opening additional accounts as needed.

   c. Prepare an adjusted trial balance at October 31.

26. **Preparing T-account entries and financial statements for a manufacturing firm.** This problem is a continuation of Problem 25, Melton Plastics Limited. In addition to the manufacturing activities described in that problem, the following transactions relating to selling and administrtive activities occurred during October.

(10) Sales, on account, $340,600.

(11) Collections from customers, $330,000.

(12) Salaries earned during the month: sales, $30,800; office, $31,200.

(13) Payments by cheque:

Sales Salaries	$27,630
Office Salaries	27,550
Advertising during October	7,200
Rent of Office and Office Equipment for October	2,200
Office Supplies	1,600
Miscellaneous Office Costs	1,400
Miscellaneous Selling Costs	2,800
Total	$70,380

(14) The inventory of office supplies on October 31 is $800.

(15) The inventory of finished goods on October 31 is $59,000.

   a. Employing the T-accounts of Problem 25 and additional accounts as needed, record the selling and administrative activities for the month in the T-accounts.

   b. Prepare a combined statement of income and retained earnings for the month (ignore income tax).

   c. Prepare a balance sheet as of October 31.

   d. Enter closing entries in the T-accounts, using an Income Summary account.

27. **Income recognition for shipbuilder.** Maine Shipbuilding Inc. agreed on June 15, Year 2 to construct an oil tanker for Global Petroleum Co. Ltd. The contract price of $80 million is to be paid as follows: at the time of signing, $8 million; December 31, Year 3, $32 million; at completion

on June 30, Year 4, $40 million. Maine Shipbuilding Inc. incurred the following costs in constructing the tanker: Year 2: $21.6 million; Year 3: $36 million; Year 4: $14.4 million. These amounts conformed to original expectations.

Calculate the amount of revenue, expense, and net income before income tax for Year 2, Year 3, and Year 4 under each of the following revenue recognition methods:

a. Percentage-of-completion method
b. Completed contract method
c. Installment method
d. Cost-recovery-first method
e. Cash basis

Which method do you feel provides the best measure of Maine Shipbuilding Inc.'s performance under the contract? Why?

28. *Income recognition for contractor.* The Humbolt Electric Co. Ltd. received a contract late in Year 1 to build a small electricity-generating unit. The contract price was $700,000, and it was estimated that total costs would be $600,000. Estimated and actual construction time was fifteen months, and it was agreed that payments would be made by the purchaser as follows:

March 31, Year 2	$ 70,000
June 30, Year 2	105,000
September 30, Year 2	203,000
December 31, Year 2	161,000
March 31, Year 3	161,000
	$700,000

Estimated and actual costs of construction incurred by the Humbolt Electric Co. Ltd. were as follows:

January 1 — March 31, Year 2	$120,000
April 1 — June 30, Year 2	120,000
July 1 — September 30, Year 2	180,000
October 1 — December 31, Year 2	120,000
January 1 — March 31, Year 3	60,000
	$600,000

The Humbolt Electric Co. Ltd. prepares financial statements quarterly at March 31, June 30, and so forth.

Calculate the amount of revenue, expense, and net income before income tax for each quarter under each of the following methods of revenue recognition:

a. Percentage-of-completion method
b. Completed contract method

c. Installment method

d. Cost-recovery-first method

Which method do you feel provides the best measure of Humbolt's performance under this contract? Why?

Under what circumstances would the methods not selected in part **(e)** provide a better measure of performance?

29. ***Point-of-sale versus installment method of income recognition.*** The Freda Company begins business on January 1, Year 8. Activities of the company for the first two years are summarized below.

	Year 9	Year 8
Sales, All on Account	$150,000	$100,000
Collections from Customers		
On Year 8 Sales	55,000	45,000
On Year 9 Sales	60,000	
Purchases of Merchandise	120,000	90,000
Inventory of Merchandise at 12/31	57,000	30,000
All Expenses Other than Merchandise, Paid in Cash	22,000	16,000

a. Prepare income statements for Year 8 and Year 9, assuming that the company uses the acrual basis of accounting and that revenue is recognized at the time of sale (ignore income tax).

b. Prepare income statements for Year 8 and Year 9, assuming that the company uses the installment method of accounting (ignore income tax).

30. ***Income recognition over two-year period.*** The Webster Corporation produces a single product at a cost of $5 each, all of which is paid in cash when the unit is produced. The selling cost consists of a sales commission of $3 a unit and is paid in cash at the time of shipment. The selling price is $10 a unit; all sales are made on account. No uncollectable accounts are expected, and no costs are incurred at the time of collection.

During Year 2, the firm produced 200,000 units, shipped 150,000 units, and collected $1 million from customers. During Year 3, the firm produced 125,000 units, shipped 160,000 units, and collected $2 million from customers.

a. Calculate the amount of net income before tax for Year 2 and Year 3 if revenue and expense are recognized at the time of production.

b. Calculate the amount of net income before tax for Year 2 and Year 3 if revenue and expense are recognized at the time of shipment.

c. Calculate the amount of net income before tax for Year 2 and Year 3 if revenue and expense are recognized at the time of cash collection.

d. Calculate the amount of net income before tax for Year 2 and Year 3 if revenue and expense are recognized on a cash basis.

e. A firm experiencing growth in its sales volume will often produce more units during a particular period than it sells. In this way, inventories can be built up in anticipation of an even larger sales volume during the next period. Under these circumstances, will recognition of revenue and expense at the time of production, shipment, or cash collection generally result in the largest reported net income for the period? Explain.

    f. A firm experiencing decreases in its sales volume will often produce fewer units during a period than it sells in an effort to reduce the amount of inventory on hand for next period. Under these circumstances, will recognition of revenue and expense at the time of production, shipment, or cash collection generally result in the largest reported net income for a period? Explain.

31. *Classifying items in income statement.* The results of various transactions and events are usually classified within the income statement in one of the following two sections: (1) income before extraordinary items and (2) extraordinary items. Using the appropriate number, identify the classification of each of the transactions or events below. State any assumptions you think are necessary.

    a. Depreciation expense for the year on a company's automobile used by its president.

    b. Uninsured loss of a factory complex in Manitoba as a result of a flood.

    c. Gain from the sale of temporary investments.

    d. Loss from the sale of a delivery truck.

    e. Loss from the sale of a division that conducted all of the firm's research activities.

    f. Earnings during the year up to the time of sale of the division in **(e)**.

    g. Loss in excess of insurance proceeds on an automobile destroyed during an accident.

    h. Loss of plant, equipment, and inventory held in a foreign country when confiscated by the government of that country.

32. *Classifying items in income statement.* Prepare a multiple-step income statement for Nordic Enterprises, Inc. from the information shown in Exhibit 4.7 and comment on any unusual features of this statement.

33. *Revenue recognition for various types of businesses.* Discuss when revenue is likely to be recognized by firms in each of the following types of businesses:

    a. A shoe store

    b. A shipbuilding firm constructing an ice breaker under a government contract

    c. A real estate developer selling lots on long-term contracts with small down payments

    d. A barber shop

    e. An apple-growing farm

    f. A producer of television movies, where the rights to the movies for the first three years are sold to a television network and all rights thereafter revert to the producer

    g. A residential real estate developer who constructs only "speculative" houses and later sells the houses to buyers

EXHIBIT 4.7
NORDIC ENTERPRISES, INC.
Operating Results
December 31, Year 5

Revenues and Gains:

Sales Revenue	$1,964,800
Rental Revenue	366,900
Interest Revenue	4,600
Gain on Sale of Equipment	2,500
Gain on Sale of Sole Subsidiary (Less tax of $428,800)	643,200
Gain from Operations of Subsidiry (Less tax of $160,000)	240,000

Expenses and Losses:

Cost of Goods Sold	$1,432,900
Depreciation Expense	226,800
Salaries Expense	296,900
Interest Expense	6,600
Loss of Plant Due to Fire (Net of tax at 40%)	3,000
Income Tax Expense	200,000
Dividends	100,000

h. A producer of fine whiskey that ages from six to twelve years before sale

i. A credit union lending money for home mortgages

j. A travel agency

k. A printer who prints only custom-order stationery

l. A seller of trading stamps to food stores redeemable by food store customers for various household products

m. A wholesale food distributor

n. A livestock rancher

o. A shipping company that loads cargo in one accounting period, carries cargo across the ocean in a second accounting period, and unloads the cargo in a third period. The shipping is all done under contract, and cash collection of shipping charges is relatively certain.

34. *Revenue recognition for franchise.* Pickin Chicken, Incorporated and Country Delight, Incorporated both sell franchises for their chicken restaurants. Each franchisee receives the right to use the franchisor's products and to benefit from national training and advertising programs. The franchisee agrees to pay $50,000 for exclusive franchise rights in a particular city. Of this amount, $20,000 is paid upon signing the franchise agreement, and the remainder is payable in five equal annual installments of $6,000.

   Pickin Chicken, Incorporated recognizes franchise revenue as franchise agreements are signed, whereas Country Delight, Incorporated recognizes franchise revenue on an installment basis. In Year 2, both companies sold eight franchises. In Year 3, they both sold five franchises. In Year 4, neither company sold a franchise.

   a. Calculate the amount of revenue recognized by each company during Year 2, Year 3, Year 4, Year 5, Year 6, Year 7, and Year 8.

b. When do you feel that franchise revenue should be recognized? Why?

35. *Flow of manufacturing costs through the accounts.* The following data relate to the manufacturing activities of Quilt Manufacturing Company during July.

	July 1	July 31
Raw Materials Inventory	$ 56,300	$ 62,900
Factory Supplies Inventory	15,900	13,700
Work-in-Process Inventory	297,200	257,200
Finished Goods Inventory	83,700	86,200

Factory costs incurred during the month were as follows:

Raw Materials Purchased	$ 42,700
Supplies Purchased	9,200
Labour Services Received	187,600
Heat, Light, and Power	12,100
Insurance	6,000

Expirations of previous factory acquisitions and prepayments were as follows:

Depreciation on Factory Equipment	$15,000
Prepaid Rent Expired	2,000

a. Calculate the cost of raw materials and factory supplies used during July.
b. Calculate the cost of units completed during July and transferred to the finished goods storeroom.
c. Calculate the cost of goods sold during July.

36. *Income recognition for contractor.* On March 15, Year 1, Fuller Construction Company contracted to build a shopping centre at a contract price of $10 million. The schedule of expected and actual cash collections and contract costs is as follows:

Year	Cash Collections from Customers	Estimated and Actual Cost Incurred
1	$ 2,000,000	$1,200,000
2	3,000,000	3,200,000
3	4,000,000	1,600,000
4	1,000,000	2,000,000
	$10,000,000	$8,000,000

a. Calculate the amount of revenue, expense, and net income for each of the four years under the following revenue recognition methods:
    1. Percentage-of-completion method
    2. Completed contract method
    3. Installment method
    4. Cost-recovery-first method
b. Which method do you believe provides the best measure of Fuller Construction Company's performance under the contract? Why?

37. *Revenue recognition policies.*   The Omega Drilling Company of Black Squirrel, Alberta, specializes in oil-well servicing and drilling for various oil companies. Orders are usually received one to three weeks before drilling begins. The drilling time for a well ranges from three days to one month, at the end of which time all services are performed and the invoice is sent to the customer. Collection records show that 80 percent of the customers pay within 45 days, while another 20 percent usually pay within 90 days. Lately, because of the economic downturn in the oil industry, Omega has experienced many collection defaults.

The problem of when to recognize revenue has been raised at a committee meeting at Omega Drilling Company. The following are the views of several key personnel of the company:

(1) Credit and collection manager: "Currently, with the decline in oil prices, we cannot be certain of revenue collection. Therefore, we shouldn't recognize any revenue until the entire transaction has been completed, i.e., after we have been paid."

(2) Officer manager: "I think we should recognize the revenue as soon as we send the invoice to the customer. The invoice is proof that the customer owes us money."

(3) President: "I disagree. Revenue should be recognized as soon as the order is taken. We need to show the best financial picture at all times."

(4) Drilling manager: "You are all wrong. Revenue is earned throughout the entire drilling/service-billing-collection process. It should be recognized, therefore, as these stages progress. I would recommend that we recognize one third of it at the end of each of these three major and critical events."

Being the only accountant within 300 km, you are called in to resolve the company's problem.
a. For each of the above positions, indicate whether you agree or disagree and why.
b. What recommendation would you make with regard to revenue recognition for Omega Drilling Company? Give reasons.

38. *Income statement format.*   Exhibit 4.8 presents an income statement for Bayerische Motoren Works (BMW) for two recent years.
    a. Prepare an income statement for BMW for Year 6 and Year 7 in which operating revenues and expenses are separated from non-operating revenues and expenses. (See Exhibit 4.7 for a possible format.)

b. Refer to **(a)** above. Express each item in the income statement as a percentage of sales. For example, net income as a percentage of sales for Year 6 is 2.2 percent (= DM337/DM14,994).

c. How has the profitability of BMW changed from Year 6 to Year 7?

EXHIBIT 4.8
Income Statement for BMW

	Year 6	Year 7
Sales	DM14,994	DM17,657
Increase in Product Inventories	75	91
Other Operating Income	499	345
Interest Income (net of interest expense)	270	286
Total Revenues	DM15,838	DM18,379
Expenditures for Materials	DM 8,607	DM10,260
Expenditures for Personnel	3,174	3,586
Depreciation	949	1,146
Other Operating Expenditures	2,064	2,461
Total Expenses	DM14,794	DM17,453
Income from Normal Business	DM 1,044	DM 926
Income Taxes	(707)	(551)
Net Income	DM 337	DM 375

DECISION CASE 4-1

Your uncle, Bob Orsky, recently "made a killing" on the stock market and can realize his long-standing dream of becoming a gentleman farmer. He has been negotiating the purchase of Jesse Jones's farm and small dairy herd near Collingwood (Jesse is planning to retire). Until his retirement in ten years' time, however, Bob must hire a farm family to operate the farm for him; he has been advised that he should have no trouble finding a trustworthy farm family to operate the farm for him on payment of $18,000 per year.

Year 2 was a normal year for farms in the Collingwood area, and Bob believes that the following statement of cash receipts and disbursements prepared by Jesse is more or less typical of the results his farm manager could be expected to achieve.

Jesse Jones's Farm
Statement of Cash Receipts and Disbursements
For the Year Ended December 31, Year 2

Receipts:

Milk Deliveries	$60,000
Apple Deliveries	14,000
Sales of Calves (in excess of requirements)	2,500
Sale of Old, Tired Milking Cows	600 *excluded*
Proceeds of Expropriation of Land for Road Allowance	3,000
Total Cash Receipts	$80,100

Cash Disbursements:

Seed Grain	$ 900	
Cattle Food and Supplements	8,000	
Veterinary Fees	600	
Property Taxes	1,700	
Insurance on Building (three years from January 1, Year 2)	4,500	
Gas and Oil	4,000	
Spray and Chemicals	900	
Mortgage Interest ($1,000) and Principal ($10,000)	11,000	
Purchase of Tractor	~~18,000~~ 5,000 *depre*	
Cost of Replacing Two Milk Cows Hit by Lightning		
While in Pasture	~~2,000~~	51,600
Excess of Receipts over Disbursements		$28,500

Jesse's asking price for the farm is $350,000 (mortgage free), which corresponds closely to the money Bob has to invest. Bob considers that he would probably be able to earn an average of at least 15 percent per annum, before income taxes, over the next ten years in an investment with a similar risk.

The farm equipment is in good condition and today would cost $50,000 to replace new with an average life of ten years. The farm buildings are old but appear to have an unlimited life, as long as they are maintained as they have been under Jesse's ownership.

Because of a fire in one of the local apple-packing plants, Jesse has been forced to defer the delivery of 60 percent of his apple crop until January or February Year 3, an unusual event. However, he anticipates no trouble selling these apples to the packing house for the same price as those delivered to date.

Would you advise Bob to buy Jesse's farm or to wait until another farm comes on the market that would be a more profitable investment?

PART TWO

A CONCEPTUAL FRAMEWORK FOR ACCOUNTING

CHAPTER FIVE

A CONCEPTUAL FRAMEWORK FOR ACCOUNTING

CHAPTER OUTLINE

- The Objectives of Accounting
- A Conceptual Framework for Accounting
- Accounting Concepts
- The Objectives of Financial Statements
- Desirable Attributes of Financial Statements
- The Nature and Development of Generally Accepted Accounting Principles
- Professionalism and Accounting
- Appendix 5.1: Tentative Conclusions on Objectives of Financial Statements of Business Enterprises
- Appendix 5.2: Ethical Conduct
- Appendix 5.3: Accounting as a System
- Appendix 5.4: Internal Control Concepts

The first four chapters have provided an introduction to accounting. We have covered the objectives of financial accounting, basic terminology, the accounting cycle, accounting records, financial statements, and some of the theoretical concepts embodied in generally accepted accounting principles.

In this chapter, we will develop a conceptual framework for accounting. This will prove beneficial as we move through the subsequent chapters in appreciating the "why" of accounting practices in addition to the "how."

THE OBJECTIVES OF ACCOUNTING

The first sentence of this book states that "Accounting is a system for *measuring* the results of business activities and *communicating* those results to interested users." This definition contains two broad implications. First, accounting is a system. We will discuss the ramifications of that later in this chapter. Second, accounting consists of two principal activities — measuring economic performance and reporting the results of those measurements. In carrying out these two activities, there are five basic **accounting objectives** in its mandate. These are shown in Figure 5.1.

The first objective of accounting is to maximize **decision usefulness** to help people make optimal decisions involving the deployment of available resources. There are two basic categories of people using accounting information — those within the firm and those who are external to the firm. The special branch of accounting that services the information needs of insiders is called **management accounting**. The information needs of outsiders are serviced by the branch we call **financial accounting**. The principal distinctions between the two branches are timeliness and flexibility. Management receives feedback on the economic consequences of decisions on a real-time basis, almost instantaneously. In the worst-case scenario, individuals external to the firm receive feedback only at annual intervals. Management, being a single group with highly focused information needs, can tailor the format of accounting reports specifically to its needs. On the other hand, external accounting reports (the financial statements) must address the information needs of several user groups with diverse interests. The reports must also be compared with those of other firms. This creates a situation in which the need for standardization becomes the dominant force shaping this reporting process. Also, these external groups require assurances regarding the reliability of these financial reports because they do not have access to the underlying records. Objectivity becomes the other major force shaping financial reporting. This leads to a situation in which a complex series of prescribed rules evolve to ensure standardization and objectivity. We call these rules **accounting standards**. Conversely, there are no standards in management accounting. Whatever leads to better decisions is used, and what does not is discarded.

The second major objective of accounting is **stewardship**. The dominant organizational structure today is the corporation. This results in a separation of ownership of resources and day-to-day management of these resources. The latter role is entrusted to a professional managerial class.

accounting objectives
Objectives that make accounting a purposeful activity and hence strongly influence the nature of accounting activity. At its most broadly stated level, the objective of accounting is to assist people to make economic decisions. This leads to a hierarchy of increasingly detailed objectives that influence accounting procedures.

decision usefulness
The quality of financial statements that maximizes their usefulness to economic decision making.

management accounting
The accounting procedures carried out by an organization's accounting staff, primarily to furnish its management with accounting analyses and reports needed for decision making.

financial accounting
The accounting activity leading primarily to publishable, general-purpose financial statements such as the income statement, balance sheet, and statement of changes in financial position.

accounting standards
Sometimes used to refer to accounting principles or to pronouncements contained in the CICA Handbook.

FIGURE 5.1
Objectives of Accounting

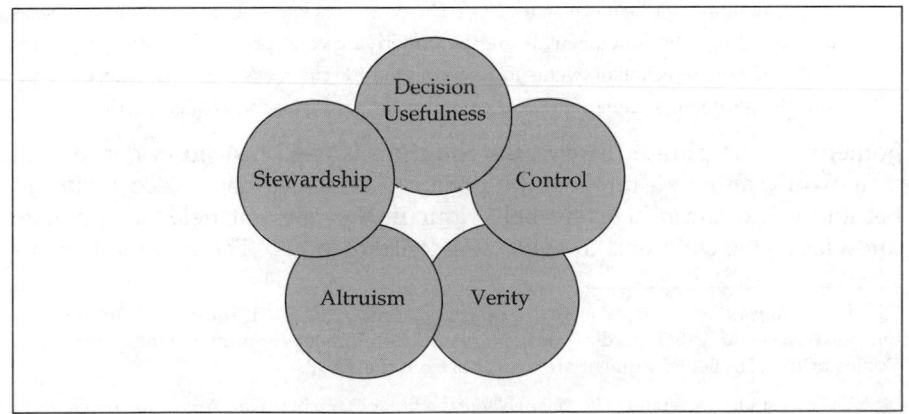

stewardship
The requirement for managers of the firm to be accountable to owners for their actions in deploying the economic resources entrusted to them.

control
Most generally, a system that prescribes desired behaviour. Also one of the primary functions associated with the management process.

verity
A state of truthfulness or faithful representation.

altruism
A fundamental trait of a true profession that implies that public interest is placed ahead of personal interest.

conceptual framework
A coherent system of interrelated objectives and concepts introduced by the FASB to help lead to consistent standards for financial accounting and reporting.

theory of accounting
A set of objectives, principles, assumptions, and so on that attempt to explain accounting as a coherent, consistent, logical activity.

This position of fiduciary trust is referred to as stewardship. A major function of accounting is to report back to resource owners on the relative success of this management group in managing these resources. This second objective of accounting, sometimes called the scorekeeping function, is not as dependent on timely information as the decision-support objective of accounting, and has perhaps hindered the evolution of a more frequent reporting cycle for financial accounting. The need for objectivity, however, is just as strong in stewardship reporting.

The third major objective of accounting as a service function in the organization is to help management manage. One of the five basic functions of a management is **control**, and the accounting system is ideally suited to assist in this process. The internal control system, to a large degree, is embedded within the accounting system. Appendix 5.4 will discuss basic principles of internal accounting control.

The fourth objective of accounting is **verity**, which means a dedication to the search for truth and accurate depiction of economic events. The nature of our capital market system creates incentive to overstate economic performance because resources flow to those firms that publish the most promising financial results. The professional nature of the accountant insists on unbiased accurate financial reporting under all circumstances.

The financial major objective of accounting is **altruism**, which is also a manifestation of accounting's professional nature. A true profession is motivated by the concept of public service. For example, when we hear of medical doctors risking their own lives to treat patients, that is altruism. Accountants typically are not profit-maximizers, because this would require a degradation of the other accounting objectives that collectively serve the best interests of society.

A CONCEPTUAL FRAMEWORK FOR ACCOUNTING

The term **conceptual framework** was popularized by the U.S. Financial Accounting Standards Board (FASB) in the 1970s. The FASB devoted over ten years and many millions of dollars attempting to create a conceptual framework. The framework was defined as follows:

> A constitution, a coherent system of interrelated objectives and fundamentals that can lead to consistent standards and that prescribes the nature, function, and limits of financial accounting and financial statements. The objectives identify the goals and purposes of accounting. The fundamentals are the underlying concepts of accounting, concepts that guide the selection of events to be accounted for, the measurement of those events, and the means of summarizing and communicating them to interested parties.[1]

Sometimes, the phrase **theory of accounting** is used instead of conceptual framework, although this may be presumptuous because a theory should be able to explain all current behaviour in the relevant field, to organize knowledge logically, and to avoid self-contradictions.[2] The pragmatic roots

---

[1] *Scope and Implications of the Conceptual Framework Project* (FASB, 1976), p. 2. Copyright by Financial Accounting Standards Board, Norwalk, Connecticut. Reprinted with permission. Copies of the complete document are available from the FASB.

[2] R.K. Mautz and H.A.Sharaf, *The Philosophy of Auditing* (Sarasota, Fla.: American Accounting Association, 1961), p. 8.

and political nature of accounting have created some accounting procedures that are contradictory and for which it is difficult to provide any theoretical justification. For instance, most accountants agree that the accounting objective of decision usefulness and the historical cost convention are contradictory. The purpose of creating a conceptual framework is, of course, to do something about these problems.

Figure 5.2 depicts our view of a conceptual framework for accounting. In the broadest sense, this framework can be viewed as a three-stage process.

GOALS → METHODS → OUTCOMES

In systems theory terminology (see Appendix 5.3), this can be described as:

INPUT → TRANSFORMATION PROCESS → OUTPUT

FIGURE 5.2
A Conceptual Framework for Accounting

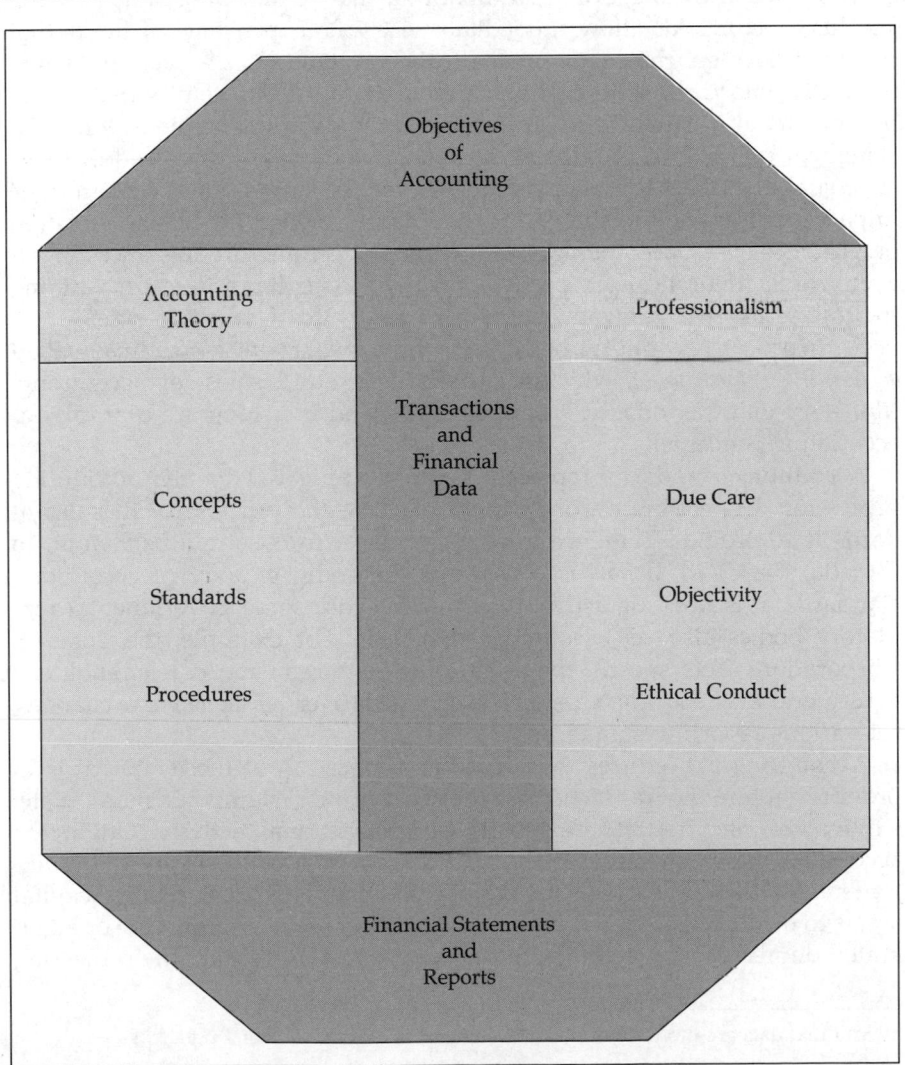

The input for accounting consists of (a) transactions and financial data and (b) accounting objectives.

The output for accounting is information.[3] Accounting information may be in the form of a single statistic, or in the form of schedules, reports, or financial statements. Regardless of the form in which it is displayed, all accounting information should satisfy at least one (but as many as possible) of the five accounting objectives. This relationship between input and output characterizes the goal-driven nature of accounting.

The transformation process that turns financial data into accounting information consists of two *filters* (again, using systems terminology). The first is accounting theory and the second is **professionalism**. A theory of accounting can be described as an interrelated framework of concepts, standards, and procedures that represents a normative expression of how unorganized financial data should be turned into organized accounting information. This section discusses accounting theory; we discuss professionalism later in this chapter.

professionalism
The state of acting professional based on the attributes associated with professional conduct.

Generally accepted accounting principles (GAAP) are closely related to a theory of accounting, but are a mix of normative and pragmatic policies. For instance, GAAP allow immediate write-off (expensing) of items that theoretically meet the requirements to be capitalized as assets and systematically amortized on the grounds of materiality. An item is deemed to be immaterial if it will have no impact on the decisions made by financial statement users. Typically, the auditor sets a materiality threshold of tolerance such that GAAP violations are ignored as long as the "bottom line" impact is below the threshold. The materiality concept allows the violation or virtually every accounting standard under certain circumstances; however, from a theoretical perspective, it is hard to justify different accounting treatments for two very similar transactions that differ only in size.

A theory of accounting starts with broad concepts (sometimes called *accounting conventions*), which set the basic ground rules for accounting. Monetary unit, periodicity, economic entity, and matching are examples of accounting concepts.

Accounting standards represent laws promulgated by the accounting profession. Depending on one's point of view, the purpose of these standards is to provide guidance to accountants or to constrain behaviour. In Canada, the *CICA Handbook* constitutes the codified body of accounting standards; it is not exhaustive, however, because some governmental regulatory bodies also set accounting standards. For example, the Business Corporations Acts specify the accounting requirements for shareholders' equity, and the Securities Commissions, which oversee the stock exchanges, set various reporting standards.

Accounting procedures
The methods required to implement accounting principles.

Accounting procedures represent the application of these standards in order to capture the transactions in the accounting system, then manipulate, summarize, and report the results of transactional activity. Often, the accountant has a choice of more than one procedure to satisfy the requirements of the standard. For example, the standard may require capital assets to be depreciated, but the accountant may select straight-line or accelerated depreciation. One of the major issues currently facing the profession

---

[3] Recall that data are input. Information is sometimes defined as useful data.

is the number of accounting methods that should be available as substitutes. Historically, the profession's attitude was that a multiplicity of accounting alternatives was needed to reflect the varying circumstances of different firms. Today, the prevailing view is that the circumstances of different firms and industries are not so different, and that uniformity of accounting methods is desirable in order to maximize the comparability of financial statements.

It is noteworthy that our accounting standards are less specific and more philosophical in nature than those of the United States and other countries. The *CICA Handbook* specifies remarkably few specific procedures, and this is by design. The profession in Canada places a high premium on the role of professional judgment and allows accountants considerable flexibility in selecting accounting procedures. The United States has unfortunately become such a litigious country that accounting procedures are spelled out in the most intricate detail. A classic illustration of this is the earnings per share computation, where the U.S. pronouncement is more than ten times the length of the Canadian pronouncement.

ACCOUNTING CONCEPTS

REVIEW OF CONCEPTS IN CHAPTERS 1 TO 4

Exhibit 5.1 identifies the major **accounting concepts** introduced in the first four chapters. We will not repeat the discussion of these concepts, but they are crucial to your understanding of accounting. You should review them carefully and, if necessary, reread the appropriate chapters and/or approach your instructor for clarification.

accounting concepts The basic assumptions derived from the economic and social environment — including the uses to which accounting information are put — that underlie the development of accounting principles.

THE OBJECTIVES OF FINANCIAL STATEMENTS

The objectives of financial statements are a subset of the objectives of accounting and therefore must be fully congruent with that broader set of objectives. The principal objectives of financial statements are to provide information to the two primary user groups — investors and creditors — so that they can make rational investing and lending decisions.[4] There are, however, numerous other groups in society who rely on financial statements. We refer to the financial statements as general purpose statements because they must try to satisfy diverse and potentially conflicting needs of these user groups. We refer to the financial statements also as external statements in recognition that they are not designed specifically to service the information needs of management; its needs are met by a separate information system — the management information system, or MIS.

The FASB decided that the specific information need of greatest concern to investors and creditors is that of the prospects for future positive net cash flows into the particular firm. The second most critical information

---

[4] *Tentative Conclusions on Objectives of Financial Statements of Business Enterprises* (Stamford, Conn.: Financial Accounting Standards Board, 1976), p. 4.

EXHIBIT 5.1
Concepts: Chapters 1 to 4

Chapter	Concept
1	Accounting as a measurement system Objectives of financial accounting Needs of financial statement users Need for standardized reporting Balance sheet showing financial position at an instant in time Assets, liabilities, and equities defined The balance sheet equation A reporting convention (current versus noncurrent) The two primary valuation bases for financial statements (cash and historical cost) Monetary versus nonmonetary items The income statement as a summary of a period's activities Matching and the relationship between revenues and expenses Sources of funds (operations, financing activities, and investment activities) The articulated nature of financial statements The seven objectives of financial reporting
2	The accounting entity concept Asset recognition criteria Asset valuation bases Asset classification bases Liability recognition criteria Liability valuation bases Liability classification bases Owners' equity valuation and disclosure bases The account The debit-credit mechanism The accounting cycle
3	The business cycle versus the reporting cycle Cash versus accrual accounting Revenue recognition criteria Expense recognition criteria
4	Accounting concepts germane to a manufacturing environment Accounting concepts germane to a contract environment Formatting conventions for financial statements

need is assessment of the effectiveness of management in carrying out its fiduciary stewardship role with regard to the resources entrusted to it. There are other objectives for financial statements (for example, support for income tax return filing), but cash flow prediction and stewardship accountability are the key objectives.

From your knowledge of accounting and financial statements at this point, do you think that the statements do a good job of satisfying these two information needs? Most people would say no. Structuring financial accounting specifically around meeting these needs is part of a major accounting objective — decision usefulness. Under the *decision usefulness paradigm*, user information requirements drive the content of financial statements. We are working in that direction, but still have a considerable distance to go. An example of a change in accounting intended to enhance decision usefulness is the change to the cash definition of funds in the statement of changes in financial position. The requirement for an **MD&A (management discussion and analysis)** section in annual reports filed with the Ontario Securities Commission is perhaps the latest example of restructuring accounting reports to better service user needs. In the MD&A, management is required to explain the economic results communicated by the financial statements.

Keeping sight of the decision usefulness paradigm and the principal objectives of financial statements is important in evaluating the appropriateness of accounting principles, policies, and practices. Many of accounting's problems in the past can be blamed on a lack of objectives-driven behaviour. If the financial statements try to be all things to all people, they end up serving the information needs of none of the user groups.

Appendix 5.1 contains an excerpt from the FASB conceptual framework document, *Tentative Conclusions on Objectives of Financial Statements of Business Enterprises,* and gives the background rationale regarding the identification of the objectives of financial reporting.

DESIRABLE ATTRIBUTES OF FINANCIAL STATEMENTS

The FASB conceptual framework project identified the qualitative attributes of financial information that are associated with sound financial statements. Seven major attributes were identified:[5]

1. Relevance
2. Understandability
3. Reliability
4. Completeness
5. Objectivity
6. Timeliness
7. Comparability

Relevance means that the financial statements should contain information that satisfies the information needs of users. The problem here, of course, is that there are numerous user groups with diverse information needs. The accounting profession has agreed to focus on investors and creditors in deciding what is relevant. One extreme view, called the events approach, would make the financial statements much more extensive in detail and let the users sort out for themselves what is and is not relevant.

Understandability means that the financial statements should not be so complex and technical that a professional accounting designation is necessary to comprehend them. This issue has been debated not only by the accounting profession, but also by the courts in litigation against public accountants. This case law has given rise to the "reasonable person" concept, which holds that the financial statements must be understandable to

MD&A (management discussion and analysis)
A section of the annual report in which management explains to shareholders the reasons for the economic performance of the firm for the period shown.

Relevance
A qualitative characteristic of accounting information; relevant information contributes to the predictive and evaluative decisions made by financial statement users.

Understandability
A basic objective of accounting that attempts to minimize the complexity of the financial statements for readers.

---

[5] *Tentative Conclusions* (FASB, 1976), p. 22.

an individual who is neither an accounting illiterate nor a trained accountant. Research by academics has shown that financial statements rate quite
low on an understandability scale and that the reading difficulty level parallels the skills necessary to earn a college degree.

Reliability
A qualitative character-
istic of accounting
information; reliable
information contains
no bias or error, and
faithfully portrays
what it intends to
represent.

Reliability refers to the confidence that statement users may have that
the statements are free of material error and/or fraud. The independent
audit is the mechanism that provides this reliability to users. Very few
investors and creditors will rely on unaudited financial statements.

Completeness
The inclusion in
reported information of
everything material
that is necessary for
faithful representation
of the relevant
phenomena.

Completeness means that users should be presented with a summary of
all economic activities for the fiscal period. Therefore, all transactions of the
period must be properly captured, summarized, and reported, and a proper
cutoff must be achieved between periods. Most controversies about completeness do not involve the numbers, but rather the accompanying footnotes. Companies have traditionally made footnote disclosures as brief as
possible, claiming that too much disclosure might give an advantage to
competitors. Evidence suggests that this competitive disadvantage seldom
arises due to footnote disclosure. On the other hand, there have been a
great many lawsuits against accountants on the basis of *insufficient* disclosure. Further, the annual reports that win awards for best presentation tend
to have extensive disclosures. What should be disclosed is a frequent source
of conflict between firms and their independent auditors. The auditor wants
voluminous disclosure, because no one ever gets sued for saying too much,
but many get sued for saying too little. You should be aware that legal
liability consequences have a real impact on the form and content of published financial statements.

Objectivity
An accounting princi-
ple requiring that,
whenever possible,
accounting entries be
based on objective
(verifiable) evidence.

Objectivity is closely related to reliability. The information presented in
the financial statements should be neutral (free of bias). Financial statements
are prepared by management, yet these statements represent a report card
on the success of management activities. This creates a natural bias on the
part of management to make the financial position of the company look as
good as possible. This bias is accentuated by the fact that management
compensation packages are often tied to profits reported in the financial
statements. Again, it is the independent audit that provides credibility and
user confidence in the financial statements. Some accounting policies actually introduce bias into the financial statements. For instance, conservatism
distorts the true economic status of a firm.

timeliness
The availability of
information to a deci-
sion maker before the
information loses its
capacity to influence
decisions.

In general, the usefulness of information is a function of its **timeliness**.
Lack of timeliness is perhaps the biggest single impediment to the usefulness of financial statements. Annual published statements are little more
than historical documents; they are useful primarily to assess management
stewardship. A study by Ball & Brown found that by the time the annual
report reaches investors, only about 15 percent of its content is news to
them. Contrast this with other findings that have shown that the stock
market reacts to new information within minutes. Investors increasingly
have turned to other, more timely sources of information, such as financial
analysts and press releases. Quarterly reports are a response to this need
for timeliness, but the objectivity requirement (external audit verification)
puts a constraint on the utility of interim financial reports.

Comparability
The quality of informa-
tion that enables users
to identify similarities
in and differences
between two sets of
economic information.

Comparability is a key requirement for financial statements. The decision model of investors and creditors is based on two principal activities

— tracking the economic performance of the firm over time, and comparing the economic performance of the firm with other firms who are potential investment/credit candidates. These users must be able to (a) distinguish between real changes in economic performance and artifactual changes attributable solely to changes in accounting policy, and (b) adjust for differences in performance between firms that are attributable to the employment of different accounting policies. Thus, a general rule of accounting is that companies should change their accounting policies as infrequently as possible and that, when they do, the change and its impact should be fully disclosed in the financial statements.

By definition, these seven attributes collectively should lead to statements that meet the test of decision usefulness.

THE NATURE AND DEVELOPMENT OF GENERALLY ACCEPTED ACCOUNTING PRINCIPLES

Generally accepted accounting principles (GAAP) are the accounting methods and procedures used by firms in preparing their financial statements. The primary source of statements of GAAP is the *CICA Handbook* prepared following due process by the Accounting Standards Board (ASB) of the Canadian Institute of Chartered Accountants (CICA). Where the Handbook makes no reference to an item, additional sources may be the Companies Acts, Securities Commission statements, prevailing Canadian practice, textbooks such as this one, and standards of other countries. This section considers the nature of these principles and the process through which they are developed.

NATURE OF ACCOUNTING PRINCIPLES

To understand the nature of **accounting principles**, contrast them with principles in fields such as physics and mathematics. In physics and other natural sciences, a principle (or theory) is evaluated by asking how well the predictions of the principle correspond with physically observed phenomena. Mathematicians evaluate a principle (or theorem) by comparing its internal consistency with the structure of definitions and underlying axioms. In accounting, principles stand or fall on their general acceptability to preparers and users of accounting reports. Unlike principles in the physical sciences, principles in accounting do not exist naturally, merely awaiting discovery. And unlike mathematics, accounting has no structure of definitions and concepts that can be used unambiguously to develop accounting principles. For example, one GAAP requires land to be stated at its acquisition cost as long as it is held by a firm. Changes in the market value of the land are not reflected in the financial statements until the land is sold. This accounting principle cannot be "proven" to be correct. It has simply been judged to be the generally acceptable method of accounting for land. Accounting principles might more aptly be called "accounting conventions."

accounting principles The rules that give guidance in the measurement, classification, and interpretation of economic information as well as communication of the results through the medium of financial statements.

DEVELOPMENT OF ACCOUNTING PRINCIPLES

Accounting principles result from an essentially political process. Various persons or groups have power, or authority, in the decision process that defines GAAP. The next few paragraphs describe the most important participants in this process.

THE COMPANIES ACTS

The fundamental and superior authorities for establishing and monitoring companies are the legislatures of the provincial and the federal governments. This authority is given expression through the Companies Acts (or Corporations Acts) that have been passed in each of the provinces and by the federal government. Attempts continue to be made to achieve uniformity in this legislation, with limited success. Because no uniform Companies Act exists, and because all laws are subject to change, references to law will be limited to the Canada Business Corporations Act enacted by the federal government. Under this Act, the authority for establishing GAAP has been delegated to the CICA, with a few minor exceptions.

THE SECURITIES COMMISSIONS

A second group concerned with GAAP is the provincial securities commissions. They have authority specified by legislation to regulate accounting practices for companies under their jurisdiction, generally limited to those companies whose securities are traded in the relevant province. There is considerable uniformity in the major practices of the provincial securities commissions. Again, the primary responsibility for establishing GAAP has been delegated by these securities commissions to the CICA.

THE CICA

The CICA is the accounting body responsible for establishing GAAP in Canada. The CICA has delegated the authority to the ASB, whose origin dates from 1946. The operation of the ASB is financed by the CICA but operates independently. The majority of the Board members are chartered accountants, but members from related associations are included to represent providers and users of financial statements.

The complex due process procedure used by the Board for setting accounting standards is summarized below:

1. An issue is identified and placed on the ASB's agenda.

2. The research staff collects and summarizes material related to the problem, including statements issued by standard-setting bodies in other countries.

3. Where major initiatives are undertaken, a Research Study by a consultant may be commissioned.

4. On completion of the Research Study, the project is allocated, where necessary, to a regional section of the ASB.

5. A regional section of the ASB, with staff support, prepares a proposal for consideration of the ASB.

6. The ASB may return the proposal to the regional section for modification or modify the proposal and prepare an Exposure Draft.

7. The Exposure Draft is circulated widely with a request for comment by a specified date.

8. The comments are analyzed by the ASB staff and considered by the ASB.

9. The ASB may modify the Exposure Draft.

10. Where the modifications are significant, a Re-Exposure Draft may be issued and the Exposure Draft Review Process repeated.

11. Where the modifications are not significant, the ASB will vote on the amended Exposure Draft and, on approval of at least two-thirds of the members, will authorize additions or revisions to the *CICA Handbook*.

12. The Handbook revisions and additions are prepared by the staff and issued to the members of the CICA in Handbook Revisions Releases that state the effective date of the revisions.

ACCOUNTING PRACTICES OF OTHER NATIONS

Canada traditionally has been influenced by the customs, laws, and culture of the United Kingdom and the United States. This influence is particularly significant in economic affairs in that, traditionally, capital and skills have been drawn from these two countries. Today, many Canadian companies are owned by American and British companies, and the shares of several Canadian companies are listed for trading on American stock exchanges. Consequently, Canadian accounting practice has drawn extensively from the British and American experiences. This has occurred not only for the traditional reasons, but also because those companies whose shares are owned by foreign companies, or are traded in American stock exchanges, are subject to the laws of those jurisdictions, including the GAAP. Significant lack of congruence between Canadian and American GAAP creates uncertainties in Canada and costly conversion processes when conforming to American practices. Consequently, when determining GAAP in Canada, members of the CICA committees must be aware of the comparable GAAP in other countries, particularly those of the United States.

Canadian accounting institutes have been active members in the International Accounting Standards Committee (IASC), whose objective is to formulate and publish accounting and auditing standards, and to promote their worldwide acceptance and observance. Although the standards issued by the committee have no legal force in Canada, the ASB supports the objective of international harmonization of accounting standards. When the IASC issues a standard, it is compared with present Canadian practice and, where a significant difference exists, serious consideration is given to incorporating the new standard in the *CICA Handbook*.

FUTURE DEVELOPMENT OF ACCOUNTING PRINCIPLES

Unless governments unexpectedly decide to exert their legal authority, we see little reason for the future development of accounting principles to differ materially from that in the past. The process will continue to be a political one, with opposing viewpoints attempting to exert influence on the decision process. Positions taken or opinions rendered by participants in this process must be not only carefully developed, but also effectively marketed if the positions are to become generally acceptable to the persons who prepare and use financial statements. To provide guidance to the stand-setting process, the ASB should strive to relate its pronouncements on particular topics to general-purpose financial reporting objectives.

The biggest future trend in accounting standard-setting will be the harmonization of international standards. This is a logical outgrowth of the internationalization of the marketplace. Global trade demands a global language of commerce.

THE EMERGING ISSUES COMMITTEE

We have mentioned that one of the potential shortcomings of financial accounting is lack of timeliness. This applies to standard-setting as well as to financial reporting practices. It is not uncommon for three or more years to elapse between the time the profession recognizes the need for a standard and its promulgation. In the meantime, financial statement users are being disserved.

To deal with this, the CICA created the **Emerging Issues Committee (EIC)**. It is empowered to deal with controversies and ambiguities in accounting by issuing guidance bulletins in a timeframe of less than a year. These pronouncements do not have the same authoritative weight as Handbook pronouncements, but they still fall under the broad umbrella we call GAAP. At the time of writing, the EIC had issued bulletins on approximately three dozen accounting controversies. In most cases, the thrust of the bulletin has been the severe restriction of the range of acceptable accounting treatments by business firms publishing financial statements.

Emerging Issues Committee (EIC) A committee of the CICA that publishes authoritative guidance on accounting issues in a more timely fashion than the Accounting Standards Board.

PROFESSIONALISM AND ACCOUNTING

One of the most overused words in the English language is "profession." Almost all occupational groups refer to themselves as professionals these days. We have the engineering profession, the landscaping profession, professional sports, and so on. The concept of a profession goes back to antiquity, however, and the requirements for membership are stringent indeed. Historically, medicine, law, and theology were the three professions. The attributes of a true profession are:

1. Altruism, which places the needs of society above the needs of the individual.

2. A systematic body of theory.

3. Professional authority over the subject matter such that lay people are unable to evaluate the quality of service rendered.

4. Community sanction, which not only recognizes the profession, but grants it monopoly status.

5. The power to self-regulate, implying full control over standards of admission, practice, and discipline.

6. A code of ethical conduct that is stricter than that of society in general.

7. Objectivity, meaning that judgments will be rendered in unbiased fashion and that the pursuit of truth is paramount.

8. Recognition as an intellectual calling that requires expert judgment on matters for which there are no simple answers as well as choices between plausible alternatives.

Accounting meets all of these requirements and is recognized by society as a profession.

We have indicated that the professional attributes of accounting, which we identified in Figure 5.2 as due care, objectivity, and ethical conduct, represent a pillar of the conceptual framework for accounting. These three attributes are the heart of the *Rules of Professional Conduct for Chartered Accountants*. The other professional accounting bodies have similar ethical codes.

Due care means devoting necessary effort to the task at hand. Although member of the public are unable to evaluate the quality of work performed by accountants, they are assured that the combination of high skill and due care will result in work of the highest quality.

Objectivity implies that the accountant will be unbiased. This is a challenging requirement for the accountant who must give a stewardship report on the activities of management to the public while being paid by management. An even higher level of objectivity is required to be a financial statement auditor. The continuous search for truth (that is, fair presentation) is part of this objectivity.

Ethical conduct is the third general attribute of professional behaviour. This implies that the accountant follows an impeccable moral code. Business ethics is a much-discussed topic today, and the consensus is that ethics are poor in business environments. The professional code of ethics of accounting sets it very much apart from the general business community.

We view professionalism as being so important to the conceptual framework because so much of financial reporting involves matters of judgment and choice. The opportunities are certainly there for using the financial statements to misrepresent true economic performance. The professional code of accountants precludes this possibility. It is often said that the greatest asset of the accounting profession is the trust it has earned from society. This is, of course, directly related to professionalism. It is very important that accountants safeguard this asset by taking all possible measures to maintain their ethical approach to dealing with the public.

SUMMARY

The main themes of this chapter have been as follows:

1. Accounting is an artifact. There are no immutable laws such as those found in the natural sciences. All laws, principles, and concepts are established by society.

2. Accounting is a service function. Accounting exists to serve the needs of people making economic decisions and should be oriented toward helping them to make the best possible decisions. This decision usefulness paradigm is the fundamental goal of accounting.

3. Accounting is the language of business. Any language needs rules, conventions, and a high degree of standardization to allow effective communication. Globalization of the marketplace will exacerbate this need for standardization.

4. Accounting is an important part of the management process. A basic function of management is exercising control, and this would not be possible without the assistance of the accounting system.

Having a conceptual framework for accounting has major benefits. First, it increases the legitimacy of accounting's status as a profession, because a theoretical structure is a necessary condition of a profession. Second, it creates a mindset that results in objectives-driven behaviour, which ultimately helps accounting fulfil its proper role in society.

We have attempted to present a conceptual framework for accounting in this chapter. The essence of this framework is the role of accounting theory and accounting's professional nature in transforming economic data into information that best serves society's needs. This is reflected in the objectives of accounting, which all revolve around the concept of public service.

We believe the test of whether a unified, coherent theory of accounting exists is whether all of our current accounting procedures can be justified in light of underlying concepts and standards, and can be shown to be congruent with the objectives of accounting. As we have indicated, there are conflicting views regarding whether there exists a defensible theory of accounting. As you proceed through the remainder of this book, you should attempt to relate the accounting procedures you encounter to this test and eventually form your own opinion.

No debate exists, however, about whether accounting is a true profession. This is a source of both pride and immense responsibility for accountants, and makes accounting a truly rewarding career choice.

We believe that the appendices to this chapter are important reading for both future preparers and future users of financial information. Appendices 5.1 and 5.2 are reprinted from two of the most influential works in accounting literature. Seminal pieces such as these should be read by students in their original form. Several references to systems and systems theory are made in this chapter, and Appendix 5.3 provides the necessary background. The inclusion of Appendix 5.4 on control may seem controversial in an accounting text, but control is an important topic to accountants today, and should be introduced before fourth-year auditing courses.

Ethics is considered a vital topic in the business and accounting curriculum today. The three discussion cases at the end of the chapter form a basis for classroom discussion on ethics.

APPENDIX 5.1

TENTATIVE CONCLUSIONS ON OBJECTIVES OF FINANCIAL STATEMENTS OF BUSINESS ENTERPRISES[6]

Financial accounting is primarily concerned with providing financial information useful to stockholders, creditors, potential stockholders and creditors, and others outside an enterprise. General purpose financial statements are the means by which the information accumulated and processed in financial accounting is periodically communicated formally to those who use the information.

Information in financial statements[7] is a particular kind of information and is necessarily subject to the limitations of financial accounting. Financial statements provide financial information — information that is primarily quantified and expressed in terms of money. The elements of financial statements are financial representations of economic things and events, measured primarily by exchange prices in past or expected exchanges or by amounts derived from exchange prices. Since business enterprises are producers and distributors of scarce (economic) resources rather than ultimate consumers, financial accounting bears on the allocation of resources to producing and distributing activities and focuses on the creation of, use of, and rights to wealth. Financial accounting does not attempt to measure the degree to which the consumption of wealth satisfies consumers' wants or to measure related concepts such as welfare or psychic income. The information in financial statements is limited by the need to measure in terms of money and also is often limited by constraints inherent in procedures, such as verification, that are commonly used to enhance the reliability or objectivity of financial statement information.

Financial accounting and financial statements are not ends in themselves but are intended to provide information that is useful to those who receive it. The objectives of financial statements stem largely from the needs of those who use the statements or information derived from them. In the following section, the italicized paragraphs are the Board's tentative conclusions on the objectives of financial statements of business enterprises. The remaining paragraphs include explanations, amplifications, or observations to support or supplement the tentative conclusions.

Financial statements of business enterprises should provide information within the limits of financial accounting, that is useful to present and potential investors and creditors in making rational investments and credit decisions. Financial statements should be comprehensible to investors and creditors who have a reasonable understanding of business and economic activities and financial accounting and who are willing to spend time and effort needed to study financial statements.

---

[6] *Tentative Conclusions on Objectives of Financial Statements of Business Enterprises* (FASB, 1976), pp. 2–6. Copyright by Financial Accounting Standards Board, Norwalk, Connecticut. Reprinted with permission. Copies of the complete document are available from the FASB.

[7] "Financial statements" in common terminology usually means "general purpose financial statements" and is used here with that meaning.

Members of numerous groups make economic decisions based on their relationships to and knowledge about business enterprises and thus have a potential interest in information provided by financial statements. Among the potential users of financial statement information are owners, lenders, suppliers, potential investors and creditors, employees, management (including directors), financial analysts and advisors, brokers, underwriters, stock exchanges, lawyers, taxing authorities, regulatory authorities, financial press and reporting agencies, labor unions, trade associations, and customers. Many of those groups are interested in essentially the same kinds of financial information. General purpose financial statements are based on the presumption that many users of financial statements have common information needs. Although investors and creditors may need essentially the same kinds of financial information as several other groups of potential users, there are reasons to focus the objectives of financial statements on the financial information needs of investors and creditors.

First, investors and creditors and their advisors are among those who use general purpose financial statements as a principal source of financial information about individual business enterprises. Some of those who use financial information in various kinds of economic decisions need specialized or detailed information and can usually obtain it. For example, management needs many kinds of specialized and detailed information to decide day-to-day matters and establish policies. But management also controls the accounting of the enterprise, and much of the accounting effort may be managerial accounting designed to help management plan and control operations. Similarly, the information needed to measure taxable income to determine tax payments according to tax law and regulations and the information needed to set rates for public utilities are both specialized information needs not usually satisfied by general purpose financial statements. But both taxing authorities and rate-making bodies have statutory authority to require the specific information they need to fulfill their functions. Many governmental regulatory bodies not concerned with taxation or rate-making also have a statutory authority to require specific information. Although not all investors and creditors need to rely on general purpose financial statements for financial information — for example, a bank or insurance company negotiating with an enterprise for a large loan or private placement of securities can often obtain desired information about the enterprise by making the information a condition for completing the transaction — most do not have access to financial information except through financial statements. To identify investors' and creditors' needs as the focal point of financial statement information greatly narrows the range of economic decisions and varied needs for specialized information that general purpose financial statements must try to satisfy, thereby increasing the possibility that the statements can reasonably satisfy the narrower range of needs.

Second, investors' and creditors' needs for financial information and the ways that they and their advisors use it are better understood than those of other groups who may rely on general purpose financial statements or information obtained from them. Little or no information is available on how customers, employees, and similar groups use information from financial statements or other sources. Despite numerous gaps that exist in the knowledge of investors' and creditors' information needs and the fact that no study has been able to identify precisely how financial statement information affects investors' and creditors' decisions and securities' prices, the essential characteristics of investment and credit decisions have been described in detail, are reasonably well understood, and have been incorporated in various investment decision models. Further, many investment and credit decisions result in transactions in markets for which detailed data are available, permitting study and analysis of the investment decision process and testing of hypotheses about it.

Financial statements are but one source of information about business enterprises. Financial statement information is a particular kind of information that is necessarily limited by the nature of financial accounting and by certain constraints on the financial accounting process. Investors, creditors, and others are therefore expected to use financial statement information in conjunction with other information about a business enterprise, the industries in which it operates, the securities markets, and the economy as a whole.

Individual investors and creditors have varying degrees of understanding of the business and economic environment, business activities, securities markets, and related matters. Their understanding of financial statements and the extent to which they use and rely on financial statement information may also vary greatly. However, an attempt to provide different financial statements for different perceived levels of investor and creditor competence would require assessments concerning those differences that could not be supported except arbitrarily. Relevant information should not be excluded from financial statements merely because it may be difficult for someone to understand or because some investors or creditors choose not to use it.

Financial statements of business enterprises should provide information that helps investors and creditors assess the prospects of receiving cash from dividends or interest and from the proceeds from the sale redemption or maturity or securities or loans. Those prospects are affected (1) by an enterprise's ability to obtain enough cash through its earning and financial activities to meet its obligations when due and its other cash operating needs, to reinvest in earning resources and activities to pay cash dividends and interest and (2) by perceptions of investors and creditors generally about that ability, which affect market prices of the enterprise's securities relative to those of other enterprises. Thus, financial accounting and financial statements should provide information that helps investors and creditors assess the enterprise's prospects of obtaining net cash inflows through its earning and financial activities.

Investment and credit decisions normally involve choices between present cash (price of a security that can be bought or sold or amount of a loan) and rights to expected future cash receipts from dividends or interest and proceeds. Investors and creditors need information to help them form rational expectations about those future cash receipts and assess the risk that the amounts or timing of the receipts may differ from expectations. Business enterprises, like investors and creditors, invest cash to earn more cash, and they receive cash as a result of the transactions and other events that affect their economic resources and obligations to transfer resources to other entities. Since an enterprise's ability to bring in cash affects both its ability to pay dividends and interest and the market prices of its securities, expected cash flows to investors and creditors are related to expected cash flows to the enterprise in which they have invested or to which they have loaned funds. Expected cash flows to investors and creditors from sale of securities are also affected by other factors that affect market prices.

Financial statements of a business enterprise should provide information about the economic resources of an enterprise, which are sources of prospective cash inflows to the enterprise; its obligations to transfer economic resources to others, which are causes of prospective cash outflows from the enterprise; and its earnings, which are the financial results of its operations and other events and conditions that affect the enterprise. Since that information is useful to investors and creditors in assessing an enterprise's ability to pay cash dividends and interest and to settle obligations when they mature, it should be the focus of financial accounting and financial statements.

Investors and creditors often use information about the past to help in assessing the prospects of an enterprise. Although investment and credit decisions reflect investors' and creditors' expectations about future enterprise performance, those expectations are commonly based at least partly on evaluations of past enterprise performance, including evaluation of how management has discharged its responsibility to stockholders for its use of enterprise resources entrusted to it, and evaluation of the enterprise's present economic resources and obligations.[8]

Financial accounting cannot directly measure the value of a business enterprise — the present value of its expected net cash receipts — because of the uncertainty of expected cash receipts and payments, particularly those expected far in the future. Nor can accounting statements that show only cash receipts and payments during a short period, such as a year, adequately indicate whether or not an enterprise's performance is successful. Enterprise earnings (net income or net profit) measured by accrual accounting, which recognizes the financial effects of transactions and other events when they occur rather than only when cash is received or paid, are usually considered a better indicator of an enterprise's present and continuing ability to bring in the cash it needs to acquire resources, produce salable output, pay for goods and services it uses, meet its other obligations, and pay cash dividends to stockholders than is information about current cash receipts and payments. Financial statements reflecting accrual accounting are composed of individual elements that represent the enterprise's economic resources, its obligations to transfer resources to other entities, inputs to and outputs from its earning activities, and the financial results of other events and circumstances. In recognizing likely cash effects of transactions and events as well as actual cash receipts and payments, accrual accounting emphasizes the incidence of the transactions or events having cash consequences rather than the cash receipts or payments themselves. That emphasis recognizes that the earning activities of an enterprise

---

[8] Investors and creditors ordinarily invest in or lend to enterprises that they expect to continue in operation. Information about the past is usually less useful in assessing prospects for the enterprise's future if it is in liquidation or is expected to enter liquidation. Then, emphasis shifts from operating or earning activities to liquidation values of the enterprise's resources and the obligations that must be met. The objectives of financial statements do not change if an enterprise shifts from expected operation to expected liquidation, but the kind of information, including measures of elements of financial statements, that is relevant may change.

during a period, as well as other events that affect periodic earnings, often do not coordinate with the cash receipts and payments of the period.

Although periodic financial measures of enterprise performance provided by accrual accounting may tend to fluctuate less than measures of net cash receipts for the same accounting periods, the purpose of accrual accounting is to measure and report changes in resources and obligations and to relate sacrifices and benefits — efforts and results — to accounting periods rather than to reduce fluctuations in reported results by averaging the results of several periods. To apply the concepts and techniques of financial analysis and to base their expectations about an enterprise's future performance on a "more representative" result, investors or creditors may average or normalize the performance of several periods or otherwise adjust the measures of enterprise performance reported in financial statements.

Financial statements of business enterprises should provide explanatory information about particular aspects of an enterprise's operations and other events and circumstances affecting it if that information is necessary to an understanding of the past financial results and financial position of the enterprise. The usefulness of financial statement information as an aid to investors and creditors in forming expectations about a business enterprise is usually enhanced by management's explanations of the information. Management has knowledge of enterprise affairs to an extent that investors, creditors, and other "outsiders" can never attain and can often increase the usefulness of financial statement information by explaining certain transactions, other events, and circumstances that affect the enterprise and their financial impact on it. In addition, financial statement information often depends on, or is affected by, management's estimates and judgment. Investors and creditors are aided in evaluating information affected by estimates and judgment by explanations of underlying assumptions or methods used, including disclosure of significant uncertainty about assumptions or estimates.

APPENDIX 5.2

ETHICAL CONDUCT[9]

[An independent auditor's various responsibilities include one type] of responsibility which flows directly from his professional status. As a professional man, he has obligations that do not rest upon the non-professional. These obligations may be stated as a series of specific rules of conduct or, in more general terms, may be described as an attitude or set of ideals. It is the purpose of this chapter to explore the ideas of ethics and ethical conduct and their applicability to auditing with a view toward expressing as succinctly as possible the essence of a concept of ethical conduct.

The theory of ethics has been a subject of interest to philosophers since the beginning of recorded thought. Because philosophers are concerned

---

[9] Excerpts from R.K. Mautz and H.A. Sharaf, *The Philosophy of Auditing* (Sarasota, Fla.: American Accounting Association, 1961), pp. 232–39.

with the good of all mankind, their discussions have been concerned with what we may call general ethics rather than with the ethics of small groups such as the members of a given profession. We cannot look, therefore, to their philosophical theories for direct solutions to our special problems. Nevertheless, their work with general ethics is of primary importance to the development of an appropriate concept in any special field. Ethical behavior in auditing or in any other activity is no more than a special application of the general notion of ethical conduct devised by philosophers for men generally. Ethical conduct in auditing draws its justification and basic nature from the general theory of ethics. Thus we are well advised to give some attention to the ideas and reasoning of some of the great philosophers on this subject.

Basis for General Theories of Ethics. At various times and by various philosophers a number of different bases for a theory of ethics have been advanced. A review of the writings of some of the great philosophers will provide guidance in understanding the rationale behind ethics and ethical conduct. Obviously, we can do little more than gain a brief glimpse of the entire field, but even this will be helpful.

Socrates was among the first to try to construct a rational basis for right conduct. He based his theory of ethics on "knowledge," and emphasized the role it plays in providing a practical guide to the ethical conduct of man. The following excerpt from *A History of Philosophy* gives insight into Socrates' thinking on ethics:

> Socrates' faith in knowledge, in clear and reasoned thinking, is strong — so strong that he sees in it the cure of all our ills. He applies his method to all human problems, particularly to the problems of morality, and seeks to find a rational basis for conduct. . . . The central thesis of the Socratic ethics is contained in the formula: "Knowledge is virtue." Right thinking is essential for right action. . . . Knowing what virtue is, he (man) will be virtuous. Knowledge is both the necessary and sufficient condition of virtue: Without knowledge virtue is impossible, and its possession insures virtuous action. "No man is voluntarily bad or involuntarily good." No man voluntarily pursues evil or that which he thinks to be evil. . . . Since virtue is knowledge it follows also that virtue is one: Knowledge is a unity, an organized system of truth and hence the several virtues are merely so many different forms of virtue as such.[10]

Hume took quite another approach. He was an empiricist and relied upon this approach in all his philosophical work. First, he aimed at explaining ethics in terms of empirically verifiable observations and relationships, what is done rather than what should be done.

> Thus Hume introduced into his ethical theory the empiricism we have found in his metaphysics and theory of knowledge. He did not ask, "What ought men do?" or "Why ought they do it?" He asked, "What do they mean when they use such terms as 'ought,' 'virtue,' 'moral?' " . . . If we can show that all the activities which are approved fall into certain classes, we shall have explained moral approbation, in exactly the same way as we explain heat by ascertaining the phenomena with which it is constantly conjoined. . . .[11]

---

[10] Frank Thilly and Ledger Wood, *A History of Philosophy*, Third Edition (New York: Henry Holt & Co., 1957), pp. 69–70.

[11] W.T. Jones, *A History of Western Philosophy* (New York: Harcourt, Brace, and Co., 1952), p. 794.

It is likely that there are those in public accounting practice today who interpret ethical conduct in much the same terms. They are interested primarily in what is being done; and they feel that if their own conduct meets the current standards of actual practice little more can be asked of them. The obvious weakness in this approach, however, is first, that "general acceptance" may not, at times, provide a reliable guide to ethical conduct or sound practice, and second, if this is stipulated as a basic guide, there will be no way to raise the level of actual conduct or practice should it once slip.

Second, Hume attacked the idea that ethical conduct could be accounted for on a basis of reason. He contended that good stems from some human sentiment, an internal taste or feeling, which makes virtue an end, desirable on its own account for the immediate satisfaction that it conveys.

> . . . the ultimate ends of human action can never, in any case, be accounted for by *reason*, but recommend themselves entirely on the sentiments and affections of mankind without any dependence on the intellectual faculties. Ask a man *why he uses exercise*; he will answer, *because he desires to keep his health*. If you then inquire *why he desires health*, he will readily reply, *because sickness is painful*. If you push your inquires further and desire a reason *why he hates pain*, it is impossible he can ever give any. This is an ultimate end and is never referred to any other object.
>
> ....
>
> Something must be desirable of its own account, and because of its immediate accord or agreement with human sentiment and affection.[12]

Besides, Hume maintained that the "personal merit" of an individual consists in the possession of qualities of character and personality useful or agreeable to the person himself or to others. He felt this was such an obvious principle as to warrant little discussion, yet he does elaborate on it somewhat and classifies "personal merit" into:[13]

1. Qualities useful to others,
2. Qualities useful to the person himself,
3. Qualities immediately agreeable to others,
4. Qualities immediately agreeable to the person himself.

In view of the fact that an auditor must deal with many other people, his professional colleagues, the staff of his firm, employees of his clients, and the general public, the importance of "personal merit" seems obvious.

John Locke developed a different theory. He reasoned that truth, ethical conduct, and moral principles are not innate. They can only be acquired through perception and conception. And although Locke recognized the role that conscience, the still small voice, plays, he argued that it was not the sole source of moral knowledge:

> Conscience is no proof of any innate moral rule. To which I answer, that I doubt not but, without being written on their hearts, many men may, by the same way that they come to the knowledge of other things, come to assent to several moral rules, and be

---

[12] *An Inquiry Concerning the Principles of Morals*, David Hume, Edited by Charles W. Hendel (Liberal Arts Press, New York, 1957), Appendix I, p. 111.

[13] *An Inquiry*, Hume, Section LX, pp. 90–91.

convinced of their obligation. Others also may come to the same mind, from their education, company, and customs to their country; which persuasion, however got, will serve to set conscience on work, which is nothing else but our opinion or judgment of the moral rectitude or pravity of our own actions. And if conscience be a proof of innate principles, contraries may be innate principles; since some men, with the same bent of conscience prosecute what others avoid.[14]

His attack on the theory that there are innate moral truths, which need no proof, is based on this logical analysis.

Moral rules need a proof; ergo, not innate — Another reason that makes me doubt of any innate principles, is that I think there cannot any one moral rule be proposed whereof a man may not justly demand a reason; which would be perfectly ridiculous and absurd, if they were innate, or so much as self-evident; . . . Should that most un- shaken rule of morality, and foundation of all social virtue, "That one should do as he would be done unto," be proposed to one who never heard it before, but yet is of capacity to understand its meaning; might be not without any absurdity ask a reason why? and were not he that proposed it bound to make out the truth and reasonableness of it to him? . . . So that the truth of all these moral rules plainly depends upon some other antecedent to them, and from which they must be deduced, which could not be if either they were innate, or so much as self-evident.[15]

Locke then propounds the basis on which he felt that ethical conduct could be judged. In his view, "law" is the criterion of judging whether any action is morally good or bad. In his words, "Moral good or evil is only the conformity of or disagreement of our voluntary actions to some law." In this respect, Locke recognizes three types of laws: the divine law, the civil law, and the law of opinion and reputation:

Good and evil . . . are nothing but pleasure or pain, or that which occasions or procures pleasure or pain to us. Moral good and evil, then, is only the conformity or disagree- ment of our voluntary actions to some law, whereby good and evil is drawn on us from the will and power of the law-maker; which good and evil, pleasure or pain, attending our observance or breach of the law, by the decree of the law-maker is what we call "rewards" and "punishment."

Moral rules — Of these moral rules or laws, to which men generally refer, and by which they judge of the rectitude or privity of their actions, there seems to be three sorts, with their different enforcement, or rewards, and punishments. . . .
(1) The divine law.
(2) The civil law.
(3) The law of opinion or reputation, if I may so call it.

By the relation they bear to the first of these, men judge whether their actions are sins or duties; by the second, whether they be criminal or innocent; and by the third, whether they be virtues or vices.[16]

---

[14] *An Essay Concerning Human Understanding*, by John Locke (edited and published by "George Routledge and Sons Ltd." New York: E.P. Dutton & Co., No date), Book I, Chapter 3, Section 8, p. 30.

[15] *An Essay*, Locke (E.P. Dutton), p. 28.

[16] *An Essay*, Locke (E.P. Dutton), pp. 279–80.

Careful analysis of the Rules of Professional Conduct would indicate that these three types of laws interjoin to provide a well-integrated foundation of such rules.[17]

Kant looks at ethical conduct from a somewhat different point of view. To him, self-imposed action conforming with one's sense of duty is the supreme source of morality. He believes that moral acts should be done, not to make the individual merely successful or happy, but because it is the individual's duty so to act. It is duty for duty's sake that ranks above all other types of motive. Duty, he conceives of as acting from respect of law. However, this is not the type of respect that arises from fear of retribution or punishment. Nor is it the type of law that is impressed from the outside. Kant uses the expression "law" as a universal guide to action which the individual accepts as binding upon himself as well as on others:

> Duty is the necessity of acting from respect for law, i.e., from a principle accepted as binding on oneself and on all other, on all occasions in which it is relevant.[18]

Thus, to Kant, once one imposes the law on himself, he needs no pressure from outside. His own will becomes an autonomous, supreme source of good. Of course the will needs some discipline and control. For this, Kant provides two rules:

(1) Act only on maxims which you can at the same time wish that they would become universal laws, and (2) So act, as to treat humanity, whether in your own person or that of another, in every case as an end, never as a means only.

These rules require the individual to treat others as he would wish to be treated and thus to put aside selfish motives.

It is difficult to synthesize out of these diverse theories any single theory or ethical conduct and it may be that this is not necessary. Perhaps it is enough that for the moment we recognize some of the basic connotations of ethical conduct with which philosophers have been concerned.

The Nature of a Profession. Writing in 1915, Abraham Flexner offered six criteria which he proposed as the identifying marks of a profession. These are: (1) intellectual operations coupled with large individual responsibilities, (2) raw materials drawn from science and learning, (3) practical application, (4) an educationally communicable technique, (5) tendency toward self-organization, and (6) increasingly altruistic motivation.[19] Independent auditing, as we have conceived of it in this monograph, certainly meets these requirements. The ethical responsibilities of the professional man are found in the first, fifth, and sixth requirement in Flexner's list. Some brief attention to these responsibilities may be in order.

We customarily discuss the responsibilities of a professional man under three headings: (1) responsibility to his client, (2) responsibility to society, (3) responsibility to other members of his profession. To these should be

---

[17] We refer with approval to H.T. Scovill, "The Accountant and His Conscience," *The Illinois Certified Public Accountant*, March, 1952, pp. 28–32.

[18] Sir David Ross, *Kant's Ethical Theory* (Oxford: Oxford University Press, Amen House, London, E.C. 4, 1954), p. 93.

[19] Abraham Flexner, "Is Social Work a Profession?" *School and Society*, Vol. I, No. 26, June 26, 1915, pp. 901–11, at 904.

added (4) responsibility to himself. If he neglects any one of these or permits any one to get out of balance with the others he is failing in the appropriate discharge of his professional responsibilities. We feel these four separately stated responsibilities can be expressed as one fundamental requirement: *to facilitate the continuation of the profession and the service it renders.*

Professional ethics are both a special application of general ethics. General ethics emphasize that there are certain guides by means of which an individual can govern his conduct. Knowledge of the ultimate outcome of his actions on himself and others, awareness of the requirements of the society in which he lives, respect for divine law, acceptance of duty, obligation to act toward others as one would want all men to act at all times, and recognition of the norms of ethical conduct in the society in which one operates all aid the individual to attain a high degree of ethical conduct. These apply to the group or the profession as well. Putting these together we obtain a concept which, in the field of ethical conduct, is similar to the concept of due audit care in the performance of an engagement.

The individual practitioner, because he claims the status of a professional man, has responsibilities beyond those of the ordinary craftsman. He has an obligation to understand the ideals and functions of his profession (we would like to think this monograph is a fair presentation of the ideals and functions of independent auditing); he has an obligation to consider the possible outcome of any proposed action; he has an obligation to refrain from those activities which detract from the healthy survival of the profession. In this it is assumed that he has the intelligence, knowledge, and experience to understand the impact which his activities may have on the profession. The practitioner who pleads ignorance of these, except in unusual cases, has largely disqualified himself from a professional status. The practioner who ignores them in deciding on a given course of action may commit negligence sufficiently gross to make fraudulent his claim of a professional status.

At this point it is instructive to turn to a fellow profession for its experience. Frequently we learn a great deal and may even spare ourselves real difficulties if we will take the time and have the courage to learn from the experience of others. Some of the experience of the legal profession is particularly useful to us in this respect.

The canons of legal ethics, in their present form, date back to the last quarter of the nineteenth century. The necessity for their development at that time was an unfortunate trend in legal practice which some described as the "movement toward the commercialization of law." The following passage by Mr. Richard Hofstadter describes the situation:

> Around the turn of the century, the professional talents of courtroom advocacy and brief-making were referred to again and again as "lost arts," as the occupation of the successful lawyer centered more and more upon counseling clients and offering business advice. General and versatile talent, less needed than in the old days, was replaced by specialized practice and the division of labor within law firms. The firms themselves grew larger; the process of concentration and combination in business, which limited profitable counseling to fewer and larger firms, engendered a like concentration in the law. Metropolitan law firms, as they grew larger and more profitable, moved into closer relationships with and became "house counsel" of large investment houses, banks, or

industrial firms, that provided them with most of their business. But the relation that was the source of profit brought with it a loss of independence to the great practitioners. The smaller independent practitioner was affected in another, still more serious way: much of his work was taken from him by real-estate, trust, and insurance companies, collection agencies, and banks, which took upon themselves larger and larger amounts of what had once been entirely legal business. . . . [20]

This trend led some of the leaders of the legal profession to take firm measures to control the drift away from appropriate professional activities:

> About 1875 the leaders of the Bar, realizing the deplorable condition into which their profession was falling, as well as the imperative necessity of taking a firm stand against the rising tide of commercialism and the growing influence of those who would turn the profession from a "branch of the administration of justice" into a "mere money-getting trade" began the movement for the re-establishment at the Bar of standards of character, education, and training, and also for the organization of bar associations all over the country.[21]

This statement emphasizes the importance of a high standard of ethical conduct for the profession and a concept that looks to protection of the service potential of the profession above all else.

We have no intention of implying that independent auditing has approached anything like the unsatisfactory state which the law had apparently reached at the time described in these quotations. The Rules of Professional Conduct of the American Institute of Certified Public Accountants, together with the strengthening force of rulings by the Securities and Exchange Commission and the stock exchanges, have done much to protect the practice of auditing. Nor do we wish to suggest that such rules be abandoned in favor of more general statements such as those we have advanced here. Such specific statements provide useful guides in day-by-day activities. It is our suggestion that a general statement such as the one mentioned here should be adopted by those who draft specific rules of conduct. It could serve as the basic guide by which such rules are tested and as the best possible guide to all practitioners in their daily pursuits when specific rules have not yet been promulgated on a given issue.

If we feel that auditing performs a useful service and that this service should be continued, we have an obligation to protect the professional institutions that make this service available to the public. We may modify or alter the nature and variety of such service if we will, but with this privilege goes an important responsibility to do so only if it is unquestionably in the best long range interest of society. A profession exists, not to compensate its members more or less handsomely, but to serve society. Dean Roscoe Pound has defined a profession as:

> A group of men pursuing a learned art as a common calling in the spirit of public service — no less a public service because it may incidentally be a means of livelihood.[22]

[20] Richard Hofstadter, *The Age of Reform* (New York: Vintage Books, Inc., 1960), pp. 158–59.

[21] Henry S. Drinker, "Legal Ethics," *The Annals of the American Academy of Political Sciences*, Vol. 297, January, 1955, pp. 37–45, at 38.

[22] Roscoe Pound, *The Lawyer From Antiquity to Modern Times* (St. Paul, Minnesota: West Publishing Company, 1953), p. 5.

As Mr. Carey points out, it is the emphasis on public service that largely distinguishes a profession from business:

> This is the concept which largely distinguishes a profession from business — that professional men assume an obligation to place public service ahead of reward.[23]

Here we have the clue to the solutions of some of the value problems facing the profession. Such problems must always be solved with the best interests of all at heart if we are to preserve the profession of independent auditing for the future good of society. And if we customarily solve such problems on any other basis we have at once renounced our right to hold professional status and sealed the ultimate doom of the profession as such.

APPENDIX 5.3

ACCOUNTING AS A SYSTEM

SYSTEMS

When people talk about accounting in an organizational context, they usually refer to the accounting **system**. An understanding of what is implied by such a phrase is useful to students of accounting. We will begin with a brief discussion of systems theory, then discuss the characteristics of accounting systems in particular.

A system can be defined as a combination of people, machines, and methods to achieve specified desirable outcomes. *Webster's Dictionary* (9th edition) defines a *system* as "an assemblage of substances that is in, or tends to, equilibrium." *Funk & Wagnall's Standard Desk Dictionary* (1983) defines it as "an orderly combination or arrangement of parts, elements, etc., into a whole; especially such combination according to some rational principle." As is evident from these definitions, a system can be almost any collection of things, as long as there is some common attribute or purpose. In business, we typically speak of the accounting system, production system, quality control system, EDP system, and so on. In fact, an entire firm can be viewed as a metasystem made up of a series of subsystems.

The top portion of Figure 5.3 depicts a simple system, illustrating the concepts of a transformation process of inputs to outputs and of system boundaries. The middle portion shows a more complex system with **feedback** capability, and the bottom portion shows the most advanced type of system with **feedforward** capability.

Feedback indicates whether the transformation process has successfully turned inputs into the desired outputs. Feedforward uses this information to adjust the transformation process accordingly. For example, if a trial balance is taken at the end of the fiscal period, this provides feedback regarding whether the debit-credit equality has been maintained in the accounting records. If each transaction is checked for debit-credit equality and adjusted

system
A collection of interrelated parts to achieve some defined purpose.

feedback
The process of informing employees about how their actual performance compares with the expected or desired level of performance in the hope that the information will reinforce desired behaviour and reduce unproductive behaviour. More generally, reporting the results of the transformation process in a system.

feedforward
The most advanced form of system, in which the feedback is used automatically to make adjustments to the transformation process.

---

[23]John L. Carey, *Professional Ethics of Certified Public Accountants* (New York: The American Institute of Accountants), p. 50.

FIGURE 5.3
Systems

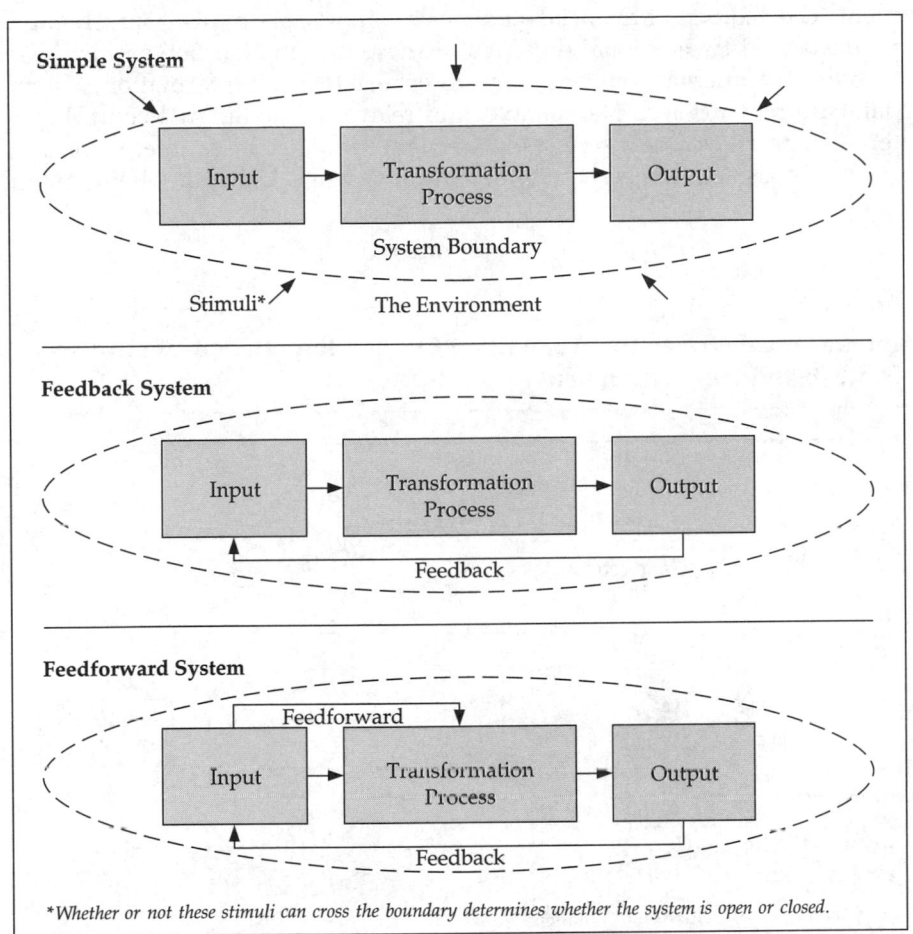

Simple System

Input → Transformation Process → Output

System Boundary

Stimuli* The Environment

Feedback System

Input → Transformation Process → Output

Feedback

Feedforward System

Feedforward

Input → Transformation Process → Output

Feedback

Whether or not these stimuli can cross the boundary determines whether the system is open or closed.

(if necessary) before submission into the accounting stream, the system is a feedforward system. For a clear illustration of these three types of systems, consider a home heating system. A fireplace is a system, a fireplace with a thermometer in the room is a feedback system, and a furnace with a thermostat is a feedforward system.

All systems are subsets of larger systems. Thus, it is necessary to define carefully the boundaries of the system being discussed. In Chapter 2, we introduced the concept of the **business entity**, which allowed us to determine which transactions and economic events should be captured by our accounting system. The business entity also defines the boundaries of our control system.

A system is an **open system** if it interacts with its environment, and a **closed system** if it does not. The accounting system is an open system.

business entity
Entity or accounting entity.

open system
One that interacts with its environment.

closed system
A relatively rare type of system that does not interact with its surrounding environment.

Figure 5.4 shows the principal interactions between the accounting system and the environment external to the firm.

Notice the interactions between the accounting system and the environment. They consist of financial statements, reports, tax returns, information requests, and transactional data. All of these information flows must pass through the internal control system to ensure that the information system database remains accurate, reliable, and relevant. The internal control system can be viewed as a screen or filter that regulates these interactions.

We are also concerned here with control systems. Using the definition of

FIGURE 5.4
Interactions Between the Accounting System, the Internal Control System, and the Environment

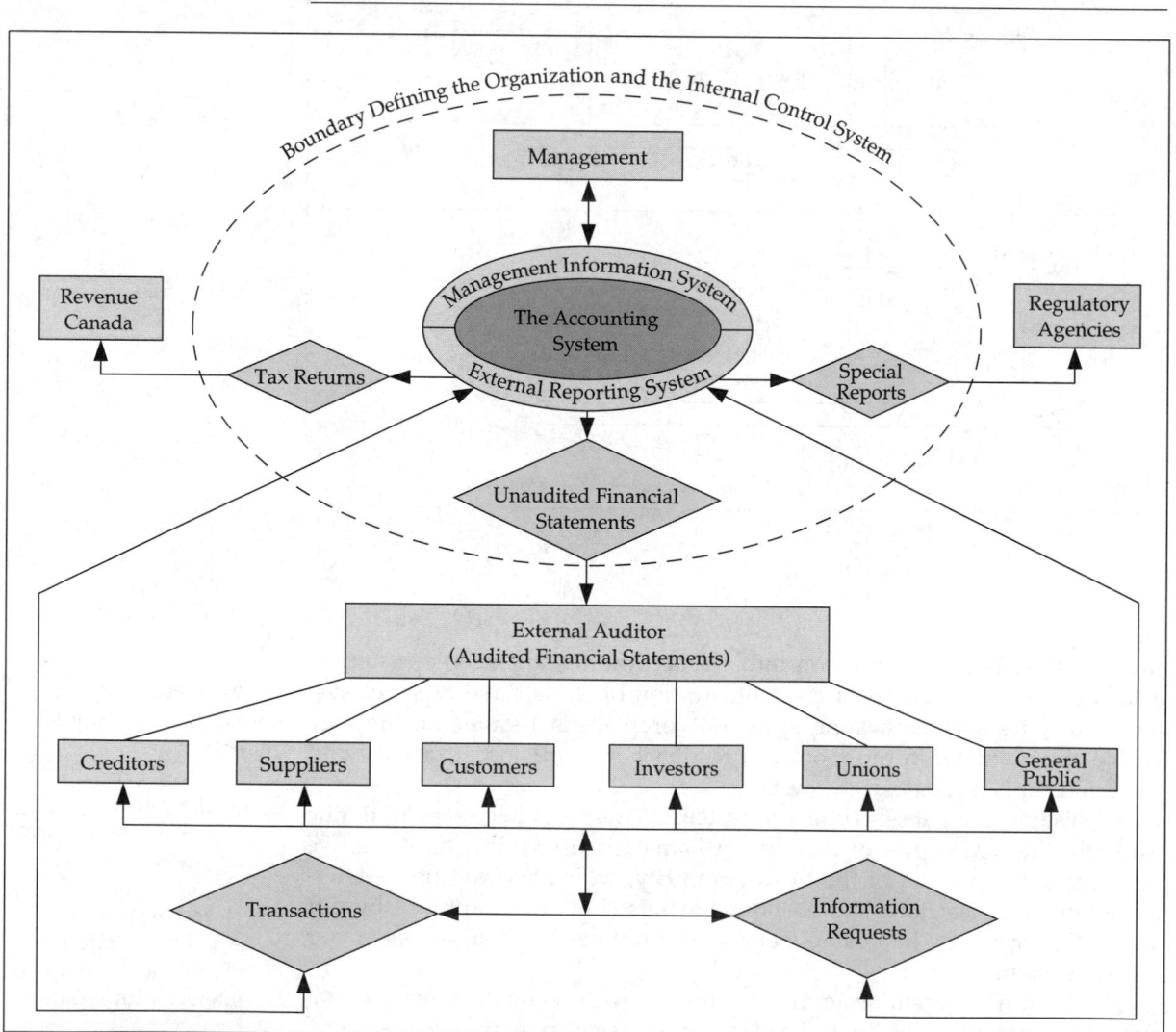

a system as a group of objects unified by a common purpose, a control system can help achieve the following:

1. Keep activity within the system attuned to its defined purpose.
2. Set criteria and standards for membership in the system.
3. Oversee evolution of the system in an orderly fashion.
4. Regulate interaction with other systems.
5. Provide feedback on the activities of the system.

An "internal" control system also has these aims. Internal controls are prescribed courses of action in reaction to different events and conditions. These courses of action must be carried out either by machines (computers) or by individuals. Ultimately, the achievement of a successful control environment is a function of the commitment of the individuals in the organization to control.

ACCOUNTING AS A SYSTEM

The accounting system is made up of the accounting policies, the accounting records, and the computers and individuals who transform raw economic activity into summarized financial reports. An accounting system (1) captures and records transactions; (2) sorts, analyzes, and summarizes transactions; and (3) updates accounting records and produces standard reports. The difference between an accounting system and an accounting information system lies in the ability to respond to nonroutine information requests from users. **Accounting information systems** are synonymous with computer database systems in that the ability to respond to casual inquiries is a key feature of database systems. The most advanced accounting information systems can analyze the results of information processing to automatically trigger other transactions and special reports to management. For instance, the system might monitor inventory levels using economic order quantity (EOQ) analysis to automatically generate purchase orders to suppliers. The future of accounting systems lies in **expert systems.** These computer-based systems mimic human intelligence and even display the capacity to learn, thus removing the human component from the system.

One common source of confusion is the difference between an accounting information system and a **management information system**. The former is a subset of the latter, which includes both financial and nonfinancial data in its database. The accounting information system can be further subdivided into the financial accounting system and the management accounting system. The primary distinction is that the financial accounting system is constrained to follow the rules of GAAP, while the management accounting system can record and manipulate data in any way that is useful to management decision making. For the sake of brevity, we will use the following acronyms throughout this book: FAS: financial accounting system; MAS: management accounting system; AIS: accounting information system; CBAIS: computer-based accounting information system; and MIS: management information system.

Accounting information systems
The collection of people, procedures, and records that produce accounting information for defined entities.

expert systems
Computer software that allows the automated processing of information and the making of routine decisions according to programmed decision rules.

management information system
A system designed to provide all levels of management with timely and reliable information required for planning, control, and evaluation of performance.

APPENDIX 5.4

INTERNAL CONTROL CONCEPTS

INTRODUCTION

Every employee of an organization has a responsibility to help the organization achieve its strategic goals. These may be numerous, but in private-sector organizations, they typically include profitability, growth, and survival. Organizations are similar to living organisms in that survival is the most fundamental and critical of all goals. It has been demonstrated countless times that no organization can survive indefinitely without a system of **internal control**.

Effective control is directly related to the basic functions of management described in Exhibit 5.2.

internal control
A plan of organization and all of the co-ordinated methods and measures adopted within a business to safeguard its assets, check the accuracy and reliability of its accounting data, promote operating efficiency, and encourage adherence to prescribed managerial policies.

EXHIBIT 5.2
The Basic Functions of Management

Planning	Selecting goals and strategies for achieving them.
Organizing	Deciding how the organization should be divided into subunits, and the positions and responsibilities associated with each subunit.
Staffing	The hiring, training, and allocation of people to fill these positions.
Directing	Giving directives and guidance to employees to assist the organization in fulfilling its tactical objectives.
Controlling	Assessment of the performance of the organization in achieving its tactical objectives and strategic goals.

Internal control can be defined as all of the plans, policies, procedures, and systems in place within the organization to:

1. Safeguard the assets of the organization.
2. Ensure reliable and accurate outputs from the organization's information system.
3. Promote efficiency in the use of resources within the organization.
4. Require adherence by employees to prescribed management directives.

The first two components of this definition are sometimes said to constitute internal accounting control and the latter two components, internal administrative control. In the past, accountants tended to be preoccupied with accounting control and managers with administrative control. Such a limited focus has proved unfortunate and has sometimes led to a lack of goal congruence between the two groups. Current thinking is that all employees of the organization should be equally focused on all four components of control. Accountants must be aware of the need to be efficient and effective in the organization, and managers must be sensitive to the importance of asset safeguarding and reliable information systems to the survival and prosperity of the organization.

WHY INCLUDE INTERNAL CONTROL IN AN ACCOUNTING COURSE?

Internal control has historically been taught in auditing courses in university business schools, which means that only students who are designated accounting majors study the topic in any depth. We firmly believe, however, that every employee in an organization should have a working knowledge of both the objectives and techniques of internal control. Without such knowledge, it becomes more difficult for the actions of the individual to be goal-congruent with the goals of the organization. As well, internal controls are designed to apply to every individual in the organization. An understanding of the philosophy of internal control is necessary to make the individual a willing participant in the process. Once the fundamental principle is internalized that control is a key prerequisite to any successful organization, employees become willing participants in the process. Typically, the introductory financial accounting course is required for all business students and the auditing courses are only electives; therefore, we believe that a full discussion of internal control is among the most important topics in this book — all business students should be exposed to it.

AN AGENCY THEORETIC MODEL OF JUSTIFICATION FOR INTERNAL CONTROL

The growth in importance and complexity of internal control has paralleled the growth in size and complexity of organizations in the twentieth century.

In the simplest form of organization, the owner is all things, including manager and employee. In such an entity, there is relatively little need for control because one person:

1. Performs all functions.

2. Has access to all information.

3. Has no significant accountability relationships to other individuals.[24]

All decision making and the consequences of such decisions are vested in this one individual. Some control is still mandatory. Every organization requires feedback on performance to survive, and feedback is an example of control. One of the reasons that the failure rate for new businesses is more than 60 percent is that these entrepreneurs with ideas for better mousetraps ignore the concept of feedback control, and costs get out of line in relation to revenues.

As soon as the individual hires an employee, control takes on an added dimension. It is unrealistic to assume that the owner-manager could supervise the employee 100 percent of the time. Therefore, a control mechanism is required to ensure the employee (a) understands the policies and procedures the employer wants followed and (b) actually follows these policies and procedures. This role of internal control as the "invisible boss" is supported by the agency theory in finance. Under this theory of human behav-

---

[24] Actually, this is an oversimplification, because even the sole proprietor is a citizen and a taxpayer, and hence has accountability to the government.

iour, organizations are viewed as consisting of two parties — the principal (our owner-manager) and the agent (our employee). The ideal organization is one in which there is total goal congruence by the principal and the agent to maximize the wealth of the firm. However, in reality, humans act to maximize self-interest; therefore, the agent can be expected not to act in the best interests of the principal. This suboptimal behaviour can include "shirking" or even fraud. The fact that the principal cannot be always physically present to observe the actions of the agent is referred to as an **information asymmetry problem**. The divergence of interests of the principal and agent results in an **incentive problem**.

There are several possibilities open to the principal to reduce this **agency problem**. One approach is to reduce the degree of information asymmetry. This can be achieved by improving the reporting structure to provide more complete and timely information on the activities of the agent. The second approach is to add an external audit to review the activities of the agent. The third approach is to design a control system under which the activities of the agent are constrained to follow prescribed policy.[25] The fourth approach is to reduce the incentive problem. This can be done by increasing the incentives for the agent to act in the best interests of the principal. Typically, this is achieved by adjusting compensation packages to tie salary to earnings levels.

This agency model is referred to as the single-person agency model. It should not be too difficult to visualize how the agency problems can be exacerbated in an organization with hundreds of thousands of employees. Internal control is a panacea to such organizations.

THE HISTORICAL DEVELOPMENT OF INTERNAL CONTROL

As indicated earlier, the development of internal control has paralleled the development of large organizations. The seminal event was the passage of the Companies Act in England in the nineteenth century. This led to the development of the **limited company** or **corporation**. A limited company is a legal entity that has the rights of a person. It can contract, sue, and be sued, and it has an indefinite life. Most important from the standpoint of control is the concept of investors contributing capital to the organization and entrusting this capital to a paid managerial class to deploy it on their behalf. This separation of ownership and management begged for the development of a control environment over this managerial class. Initially, the primary objective of control was to prevent and/or detect fraud by managers.

The other significant attribute associated with this form of legal entity is the potential to accumulate huge amounts of capital from many investors in a single firm. The late nineteenth century saw the advent of the megacorporation, created by magnates such as Carnegie, Morgan, and Rockefeller. Policies that could be informal in smaller organizations had to be formalized in these megacorporations. These large firms processed millions of transactions through the accounting records, again creating an environment ripe for the development of control systems. In the 1920s, the empha-

information asymmetry problem
A situation in which not all interested parties are dealing with an equal information set.

incentive problem
A problem identified in agency theory in motivating managers to give maximum performance and not "shirk" on the job.

agency problem
The fact that human nature is to maximize personal welfare foremost, which leads to a situation in which hired managers might not necessarily act in a way that maximizes the welfare of owners.

limited company
An incorporated firm characterized by limited legal liability and ownership by share capital.

corporation
A legal entity created by the granting of a charter from an appropriate governmental authority and owned by shareholders, who have limited liability for corporate debt.

---

[25] This option is rarely discussed in the finance literature, which suggests to the authors that a discussion of internal control is badly needed in an introductory accounting course.

sis began to switch from fraud detection to reliability of the accounting records.

The stock market crash of 1929 was the next significant milestone in the historical development of control. Millions of investors were badly hurt by this crash, and the world plunged into a great depression. Subsequent analyses showed that a major cause of the crash was overvaluation of financial position because of shoddy accounting practices, symptomatic of a lack of managerial accountability to investors. This led to government intervention in the affairs of business for the first time. The passage in 1933 of the Securities Act created severe penalties in the United States for unacceptable corporate behaviour. This again fuelled the need to expand managerial control and accountability.

Other milestones that have contributed to the need for strong systems of internal control include:

1. Watergate, the American scandal that led to the discovery of widespread unethical business practices and prompted the U.S. government to pass the Foreign Corrupt Practices Act. A feature of this Act was the requirement for corporations to have adequate systems of internal control.

2. The rapid increase of third-party liability suits against corporations. Increasingly, corporations are being sued for large amounts for following unacceptable business practices. A strong internal control environment is the best defence against such actions.

3. The development of global conglomerates with thousands of employees, which created new demands for better organizational control. More recently, the apparent advantages of the Japanese model of management has led to a thorough evaluation of the North American model. This creates new opportunities for managerial control policies.[26]

In summary, internal control has evolved with the needs of organizations. Although internal control may be optional for the single-person firm, it is an absolute necessity in the multiemployee organization. In the modern organization, internal control permeates all aspects of organizational behaviour.

A CONCEPTUAL FRAMEWORK FOR INTERNAL CONTROL

Figure 5.5 shows a conceptual framework for internal control that is analogous to the framework for accounting shown in Figure 5.1. This framework is also an example of a deductive or top-down approach to theory-building, starting from definitional concepts and using these to explain and/or justify real-world phenomena. Notice that part of the definition of internal control relates to ensuring accurate and reliable financial reports. Thus, the linkage between the accounting system and the internal control system is explicit and crucial.

---

[26] L.D. Etherington and I.M. Gordon, in *Internal Control in Canadian Corporations: A Management Perspective* (Toronto: SMAC/CICA, 1985), surveyed control practices and attitudes in 600 of Canada's largest companies. The study found that managers today view internal control as being vital to the success of their organization.

FIGURE 5.5
A Conceptual Framework for Internal Control

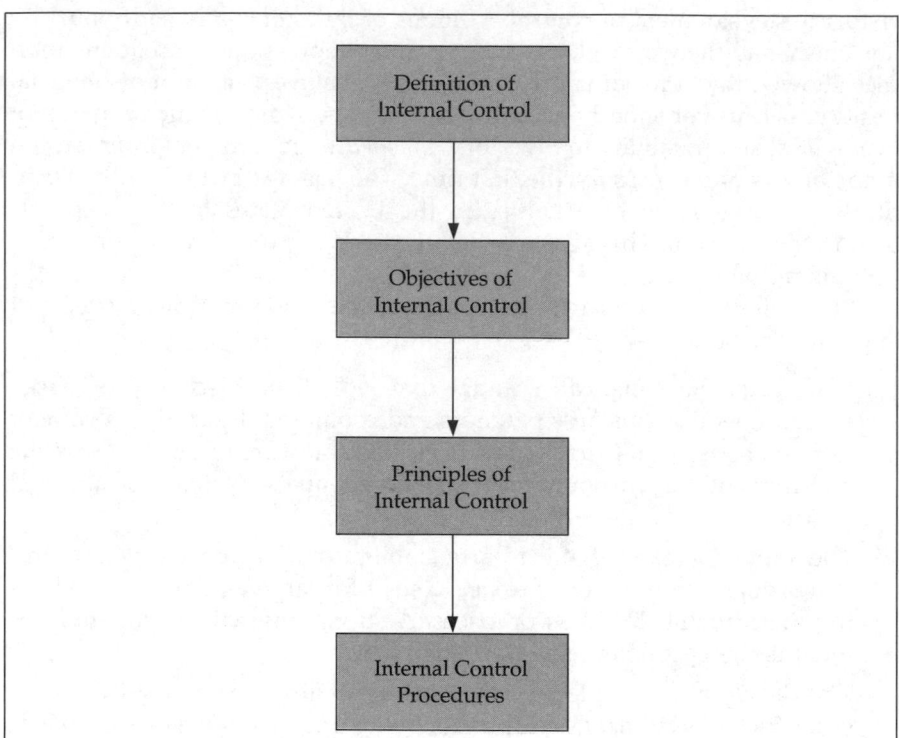

PREREQUISITES TO EFFECTIVE INTERNAL CONTROL

Many factors contribute to the success of an internal control system. Undoubtedly, the most important is the human factor. Internal control systems exist on two dimensions — on paper and in reality. It is people carrying out the prescribed policies that create the second dimension. In addition to the human factor, there are three other prerequisites to effective internal control:

Adequacy   The control procedures prescribed for the organization must be adequate for their purposes. For instance, a budget is a control mechanism. There are good and bad techniques of budgeting. Care must be taken to ensure that the superior approaches are used.

Understanding   The normative system must be documented in a clear and unambiguous fashion, and the policies must be fully communicated to those individuals in the organization who bear the primary responsibility for carrying out these policies. For example, a general control principle is managerial review and supervision, but some managers may have difficulty understanding how to implement such a policy. Precisely what activities of subordinates should be reviewed? How rigorous should the supervision be? The more detail associated with these specifications, the greater success there will be in carrying them out.

The highest degree of ambiguity results from inadequate documentation standards for organizational policies. The firm's policy manual is the most important means of documenting control policies.

Attitude Even if internal control policies are well designed and are clearly communicated to employees, commitment by the employees is still required to carry them out appropriately. This commitment represents a willingness to work toward the attainment of organizational goals and a control-conscious mindset. Commitment of this sort comes from two sources. First, people of integrity and high moral standards should be hired. Second, senior managers should lead by example and display strong control-consciousness themselves.

RESPONSIBILITY AND ACCOUNTABILITY FOR CONTROL

Primary responsibility for a well-designed, properly functioning system of internal control lies with senior management and the board of directors. This responsibility can be discharged by hands-on involvement by these groups, or by delegation to lower levels of management. The priority accorded to internal control by senior management sends a signal throughout the organization. It is often said that control is, first and foremost, a state of mind. Senior management is responsible for creating that state of mind in the organization.

Perhaps the clearest evidence of management's acceptance of its responsibility for control is shown by the increasing popularity of audit committees. These are standing committees of directors charged with the responsibility to ensure, among other things, that adequate control and reporting systems are in place.

The requirement for management to exercise its right to not only manage, but to also report periodically on the results of this activity, is referred to as **accountability**. Management is accountable to various groups, including owners, creditors, employees, customers, suppliers, and a multitude of government agencies. In addition to accountability for assets managed, management is accountable for profitability, return on investment, market position, productivity, product leadership, human resource management, legal and ethical compliance, social and environmental responsibility, tactical and strategic planning, and the attainment of all organizational goals.

accountability
The requirement that people be held responsible for their actions. Closely related to the concept of stewardship.

The importance of the primacy of senior management responsibility for the design and maintenance of adequate systems of internal control is stated in the authoritative literature: the *CICA Handbook* (section 5205.02), the Canada Business Corporations Act (sections 20 and 22), the AICPA Statement on Auditing Standards No. 1 (sections 110.02 and 320.31), and the U.S. Foreign Corrupt Practices Act (section 102).

INTERNAL CONTROL IN A COST/BENEFIT FRAMEWORK

All controls require the expenditure of money and/or effort. In addition, many controls place real or perceived constraints on employee behaviour. Control may also have an irritant or nuisance value and breed active resentment among employees (for example, an inspection of lunch buckets as employees leave the factory). Therefore, it is important to evaluate each control to ensure that the incremental benefit exceeds these costs.

In practice, the quantification of both costs and benefits into dollars is exceedingly difficult. One way to achieve this is the exposures approach, which is based on the theory of expected loss probability. First, the vulnerabilities of the firm in the event of control failures are identified. These may include lost business, loss of assets, loss of information, and even shutdown of the firm. Second, the dollar amount associated with each potential negative outcome is estimated. Third, the probability of the event actually occurring is estimated. The expected loss is the loss multiplied by the probability of the loss. This expected value is compared with the cost of one or more controls specifically aimed at preventing the negative outcome from occurring.

The subjectivity associated with the exposures approach should be obvious. To protect themselves, most firms build in a degree of control redundancy. This refers to the practice of having two or more controls that attempt to achieve the same control objective. For instance, a bank may have a safe, electronic security systems, and armed guards to protect cash. Even if one control proves inadequate — suppose the guard's gun jams — the other controls should still foil the robbers. The costs associated with control redundancy and with the cost of the internal control system overall can be viewed as a form of business insurance.

MANAGEMENT CONTROL

If one of the five basic functions of management is control, what is embodied in this concept? Controlling is measuring performance in the organization against goals and objectives, and developing procedures to facilitate the achievement of these goals. Management control occurs at two different levels — the tactical level and the strategic level. The strategic level is closely linked to goal-setting and the means of pursuing goals. The operational level of control ensures that day-to-day procedures and decisions are consistent with strategic goals.

DESIGNING A SYSTEM OF INTERNAL CONTROL

Recall that an internal control is a specific procedure or policy oriented toward satisfying one or more of the four goals of internal control. These goals are to safeguard assets, ensure a reliable and accurate information system, promote operational efficiency, and ensure that management policies and directives are followed. The number of procedures that qualify as internal controls can number in the thousands. No firm would need or could afford to institute a system incorporating all known controls. Even if cost were not a factor, there are the adverse effects of excessive control on employee morale. Ideally, every organization should develop the most frugal set of controls possible, balancing cost against effectiveness and employee freedom against constrained behaviour, to achieve the four goals of control.

In order to design such a system, an ad hoc, haphazard selection process is not appropriate. There are two techniques to ensure that the best possible system is chosen. The first technique involves the evaluation of potential controls in light of underlying control objectives. The second technique is to group controls into broad categories or classification schemes. This helps us to better understand the purpose of each control.

Objectives of Internal Control

Objectives are similar to goals, but they are more specific, and usually more linkable to specific actions and decisions. For example, profitability is a goal for any firm, but increasing annual sales by 20 percent is an objective. Some people feel that the distinction between goals and objectives is artificial. It is common to refer to all underlying motivations for controls as objectives, and we will follow that convention.

Transaction Objectives Almost all activity within an organization involves one of two things: information flows or transactions. Transactions are economic events between two or more parties resulting in the exchange of resources or future commitment to exchange resources. Buying and selling represent the two most frequent transactions engaged in by most businesses. Accordingly, most controls are oriented toward regulating either information flows or transaction flows. At one time, almost all of the attention was directed at the latter because of the direct implications for safeguarding of assets. However, now that most organizations view their information database as their most important asset, control over both activities is given equal weight.

There are four objectives underlying the control of transactions:

1. Transactions should be executed in accordance with management's specific or general authorization.
2. Access to assets should be allowed only in accordance with management's specific or general authorization.
3. Transactions should be recorded in the information system to permit generation of financial statements and to maintain accountability trails.
4. The recorded accountability for the custody and deployment of assets should be compared with the underlying assets at regular intervals.

These objectives are reflective of the process of management itself. The owners delegate power and responsibility to the board of directors, who in turn delegate to the chief executive officer (the president). This individual assembles senior, middle, and lower management teams and an employee base to assist in carrying out day-to-day activities to achieve the long-term goals of the firm. Power represents the ability to contractually commit the firm to acquire, disburse, or transform resources. The results of these resource decisions usually culminate in transactions. To the extent that any of this power is delegated by the board to managers and employees, a chain of accountability must be established so that blame or reward can always be attributed to specific individuals. A fundamental management principle is "no responsibility without authority." The other side of this adage is "no authority without responsibility." Successful organizations have explicit, unambiguous chains of accountability. The internal control system is the mechanism by which this chain is made to work.

A visible manifestation of the chain of accountability is the organization chart for the organization. This, along with the firm's policy manual, constitutes a written description of the accountability relationships in the firm. Organizations in which these two documents are not accurate and up-to-date often have poor management practices.

Transaction Cycle Objectives Transactional activity can be grouped into broad categories called cycles. The primary purpose of doing this is processing efficiency, although it may also help to reduce recording errors. Exhibit 5.3 shows the major cycles and the related ledger accounts. Let us consider one cycle, the revenue cycle, as an example. This cycle concerns all of the activities associated with exchanging goods and services with customers for consideration. It involves soliciting customer orders, shipping the goods, providing followup service for the product, setting up accounts receivable for the transactions, and eventually collecting the cash.

transaction cycles
A synonym for accounting cycles — the repetitive processes whereby economic transactions are recorded in the accounting records.

A benefit of dealing with **transaction cycles**[27] is that the broad objectives of internal control can be translated into more specific and therefore more usable objectives for each cycle. The control objectives for the revenue cycle[28] are listed in Exhibit 5.4. Careful review of these 21 control objectives should reveal that they are entirely consistent with the four broad objectives of internal control and with the control objectives for transactional activity. There is not much emphasis in these revenue cycle objectives on the safeguarding of assets, because that function has been transferred primarily to the treasury cycle. A similar set of objectives exists for each of the cycles identified in Exhibit 5.3.

EXHIBIT 5.3
Transaction Cycles

Cycle	Ledger Accounts
Treasury	Cash, Investments
Revenue	Cash, Accounts Receivable, Sales
Disbursements	Cash, various expense accounts
Payroll	Cash, Wage and Salary Expense
Inventory	Inventory, Accounts Payable
Capital Assets	Cash, Long-Term Debt, Capital Assets
General Ledger	All accounts (concerned with financial statement preparation)

The final step in the creation of the internal control system is to specify individual procedures and policies to ensure that each of these cycle objectives is achieved. We call each of these procedures *internal controls*. Exhibit 5.5 shows the individual internal control procedures supporting the first revenue cycle objective. Each of the procedures in Exhibit 5.5 can be stated as a series of even more explicit control procedures. For instance, controls supporting (8) might include specific authority placed in employee job descriptions; access passwords; keys to open rooms, cabinets, or computer terminals; and so on.

Principles of Internal Control

There are potentially several thousand procedures that could be called internal controls, and not all procedures are equally applicable to the cir-

---

[27] Be sure not to confuse these transaction cycles with the broader concept of the accounting cycle, introduced in Chapter 3.

[28] Excerpt from *A Guide for Studying and Evaluating Internal Accounting Controls* (Chicago: Arthur Andersen & Co., 1978).

EXHIBIT 5.4
--Control Objectives for the Revenue Cycle

1. Customers should be authorized in accordance with management's criteria.
2. The prices and terms of goods and services to be provided should be authorized in accordance with management's criteria.
3. Adjustments to revenues, cost of sales, selling expenses, customer accounts, and account distributions should be authorized in accordance with management's criteria.
4. Revenue cycle processing objectives should be established and maintained in accordance with management's criteria.
5. Only those customer requests for goods and services that meet management's criteria should be approved.
6. An approved request should be required before goods or services are provided.
7. Each authorized order should be accurately shipped on a timely basis.
8. All, and only, shipments made and services provided should result in a billing.
9. Each billing should be prepared accurately and promptly.
10. Accountability for cash received should be established immediately.
11. Billings should be accurately and promptly classified, summarized, and reported.
12. Costs of goods and services sold and sales-related expenses should be accurately and promptly classified, summarized, and reported.
13. Cash received should be accurately and promptly classified, summarized, and reported.
14. Adjustments to revenues, cost distributions, customer accounts, and account distributions should be accurately and promptly classified, summarized, and reported.
15. Billings, collections on account, and related adjustments should be accurately applied to the proper customers' accounts.
16. Journal entries should be prepared each accounting period for billings, costs of goods and services sold, sales-related expenses, cash received, and related adjustments.
17. Revenue journal entries should summarize and classify economic activities in accordance with management's plan.
18. Tax information derived from revenue activities should be accurately and promptly reported.
19. Recorded balances of accounts receivable, as well as related transaction activity, should be periodically substantiated and evaluated.
20. Access to cash should be permitted only in accordance with management's criteria until control is turned over to the treasury cycle.
21. Access to shipping, billing, cash collection, accounts receivable records, critical forms, processing areas, and processing procedures should be permitted only in accordance with management's criteria.

Source: *A Guide for Studying and Evaluating Internal Accounting Controls* (Chicago: Arthur Andersen & Co., 1978).

EXHIBIT 5.5
Internal Control Procedures Supporting First Cycle Control Objective

1. Clear statements of criteria should be communicated by management to employees.
2. Appropriate databases, such as approved customer lists, customer master files, and price lists, should be created and approved by management.
3. All changes to customer accounts must be approved by supervisory personnel.
4. Prenumbered standard forms with precoded key fields should be used, and physical control over these forms should be maintained.
5. The databases should be reviewed and approved by management periodically.
6. The subsidiary ledger should be reconciled to the control account on a regular basis.
7. Periodic internal audit checks, such as sending out confirmation requests to customers, should be made.
8. Access control to the databases should be established.

cumstances of all firms. Certain control procedures are sufficiently general and so universal in their applicability that we refer to them as principles of internal control. Exhibit 5.6 presents a list of such principles.

EXHIBIT 5.6
Principles and Internal Control

Principle	Explanation
1. Segregation of duties.	If no single individual is responsible for the complete recording of a transaction from start to end, the self-checking ability of the debit-credit mechanism makes it necessary to have collusion between employees to have fraud or error go undetected.
2. Separate the custody of asset function from the recording function.	Those having custody of assets have no incentive to steal if they have no access to the accounting records to make false entries covering their tracks. Similarly, employees in the recordkeeping function have no incentive to falsify the books if they have no access to the underlying assets. Once again, collusion would be necessary to circumvent the control.
3. Assets should be safeguarded.	Self-explanatory and part of the definition of internal control. Many firms wrongly interpret this as safeguarding only against outsiders. Loss of assets because of employee dishonesty is an equally serious threat.
4. Competent and reliable personnel should be hired.	Because people carry out most internal controls, the quality of the internal control environment is directly proportional to the quality of the employee group.
5. Formal system of authorization.	The power to command resources in the organization is delegated by the owners to the board and throughout the levels of management. The limits of this power and the associated accountability for actions should be clearly and unambiguously specified for each employee.
6. Managerial review.	The success of a great many internal controls depends on superiors' reviewing of the actions of subordinates or the outcome of the control procedures. Control is as much an attitude as a collection of procedures.
7. Timely recording.	The longer it takes for transactions to be captured within the accounting records, the higher the probability of data loss or error.
8. Adequate documentation.	Transactions must be recorded on appropriate paper or magnetic media to establish a proper audit trail. Controls and employee responsibilities must also be fully documented.
9. Audit.	A more formal step than managerial review. The accounting system should be subject to periodic internal or external audit so that management will be able to conclude that the four objectives of internal control have been met.
10. Budgeting.	Budgeting is a process of setting up expectations of future performance for the organization. The subsequent comparison of budgeted and actual results constitutes an extremely powerful control.

EXHIBIT 5.6 (continued)

Principle	Explanation
11. Rotation of duties and vacations.	The duties of each job should periodically be performed by others. This constitutes an effective check of each other's work.
12. Sound organizational structure.	An effective chain of command must exist with clearly defined delegation of authority and responsibility.
13. Avoid temptation.	This could also be described as "out of sight, out of mind." The basic premise is that almost all employees start out being honest, but if opportunities to be dishonest are continually placed in front of them, the temptation might become overwhelming.
14. A formal system of internal control.	The internal control system should be carefully designed to meet the needs of the organization, fully documented and communicated to employees, and regularly reviewed with regard to its effectiveness.

Impact of the Computer on Accounting

The computer has had a larger impact on the accounting function than on any other functional area of the business organization. Computers can process data much faster and much more reliably than humans, and can store large amounts of data in much less space than traditional paper-based media. These characteristics, in combination with the rapidly dropping cost of computers and their ease of use for nonsophisticated users, has led to the almost total elimination of traditional, manual accounting systems in favour of computer-based accounting information systems (CBAIS). A $500 personal computer and a $200 accounting software package is all that it takes to create and operate a CBAIS.

You may wonder, then, why we make so few references to computers in this book. It is because the computer assumes only the clerical and book-keeping functions in the accounting system. It handles transaction capture, recording, analysis, summarization, storage, and reporting. What it does not do, however, is select the basic accounting policies most appropriate for the organization, choose between alternative accounting policies, make accounting estimates, or analyze transactions in circumstances in which no codified GAAP is available for guidance. In other words, the computer has rendered the bookkeeper obsolete, but it has not reduced the role and importance of the accountant — and this is a course about accounting.

An important question is whether the addition of a computer to the accounting system enhances or degrades the internal control environment. The answer is that it can do either. There are nine attributes of computer-based processing that affect the quality of the internal control environment.[29]

---

[29] Excerpts from J.E. Boritz, *Computer Guide*, 6th ed. (Waterloo, Ont.: University of Waterloo Press, 1987).

Speed The computer allows high-speed processing, which in supercomputers can be millions of operations per second. This means that if faulty programming exists, errors can be produced at a frightening speed. On the other hand, if internal controls are built into the software instructions, they will be executed with comparable speed, greatly increasing the effectiveness of the control environment.

Consistency Computers do not make unsystematic, random errors that are associated with human activity. A computer performs its programmed instruction time after time with zero variance. On the other hand, computers are more prone than humans to systematic error. A program instruction with faulty logic will be executed over and over again with no questions asked.

Flexibility Computers lack flexibility. It is costly in terms of time and effort to develop the programs that drive the computers. If controls are embedded in these programs at the time of their original development, it is a relatively inexpensive exercise. However, if controls have to be added later, the reverse is true.

Automation As computers get more sophisticated and automate the accounting activity to a greater degree, people begin to forget that humans are still the most important element of any control system, and develop an erroneous attitude that the computer will take care of everything.

Audit Trail One of the fundamental requirements of a sound control environment is to have adequate audit trails. This means that transactions can be traced through the accounting system from source documents to books of original entry, to the ledger, and to their ultimate disposition in the financial statements. Similarly, any amount in the financial statements should be traceable back to the original transactions. In advanced computer systems, this audit trail is often absent.

Ease of Remote Access Advanced computer systems facilitate access to the database from remote, offsite terminals. This creates major headaches in maintaining security for the data.

Ease of Producing Official Documents A control system is much more effective when tight control is exercised over source documents. In addition, these documents are often elaborately preprinted, making them difficult to forge. However, the computer has the ability to create highly official-looking documents, making this traditional control less effective.

Concentration of Function As computer systems become increasingly automated and fewer people are involved, the most basic of all control principles, segregation of duties, becomes impossible. Some people believe that without segregation of duties, adequate internal control is impossible.

Microcomputer Revolution More and more accounting systems are employing microcomputers, which have major control deficiencies relative to mainframe systems. On the other hand, micros have spawned the development of micro-based computer audit software, which has significantly enhanced the control environment.

In summary, the computer has the capacity to either enhance or degrade the control environment in an accounting system. Two adages always seem to hold: (a) people are always the most important element, even in a computer-based accounting information system, and (b) controls are most effective and least expensive when added at the original design phase of computer-based systems. If used intelligently, the computer can become one of the most important elements of the system of internal control.

Internal Control Procedures

Chapter 6 will discuss the internal controls that should be in place to protect liquid assets such as cash. Refer back to the preceding objectives and principles of control when you study those procedures.

KEY TERMS

Accounting objectives
Decision usefulness
Management accounting
Financial accounting
Accounting standards
Stewardship
Control
Verity
Altruism
Conceptual framework
Theory of accounting
Professionalism
Accounting procedures
Accounting concepts
MD&A (management discussion and analysis)
Relevance
Understandability
Reliability
Completeness
Objectivity

Timeliness
Comparability
Accounting principles
Emerging Issues Committee (EIC)
System
Feedback
Feedforward
Business entity
Open system
Closed system
Accounting information systems
Expert systems
Management information system
Internal control
Information asymmetry problem
Incentive problem
Agency problem
Limited company
Corporation
Accountability
Transaction cycles

Assignment Material

Questions

1. Explain each of the key terms on page 317.

2. Explain each of the concepts identified in Exhibit 5.1.

3. What are the objectives of accounting?

4. What impact has the decision usefulness paradigm had on accounting?

5. What are the distinctions between management accounting and financial accounting?

6. What would be the impact if financial statements failed to embody the seven desirable attributes of financial information identified in this chapter?

7. How does accounting benefit by having a conceptual framework?

8. Who are the users of financial statements? Which user groups have primacy and what are their information needs?

9. What is an MD&A? What information would you like to see included in the MD&A?

10. How are accounting standards set in Canada? What is the difference between an accounting standard and an accounting principle?

11. What impact does the globalization of business have on accounting?

12. Why was there a need for the CICA to establish the Emerging Issues Committee? What impact will it have on financial reporting?

13. Can you think of any ways of improving the timeliness of financial reporting? Are your suggestions implementable?

14. What would be the implications of an organization's not having an internal control system?

15. How does the accounting system help management exercise control in the organization?

16. What specific impact does an internal control system have on the financial statements?

17. How does agency theory explain the need for internal control? Do you accept the model of human behaviour advanced by this theory?

18. Does the primary responsibility for a sound system of internal control rest with accountants?

19. How are cost/benefit considerations relevant to the design of an internal control system?

20. Economic activity in the organization consists of three things: resource flows, information flows, and transaction flows. Comment on this statement.

21. What are management's objectives with respect to the control of transactions?

22. How do the internal control system and the accounting system help achieve accountability in an organization?

23. Has the computer enhanced or degraded the quality of internal control for organizations?

24. Is accounting an art or a science?

25. How does an understanding of accounting concepts make an individual a better accountant?

26. What is meant by the claim that accounting is politicized? How does this affect financial reporting?

27. What role does government play in regulating accounting? Is this a desirable or undesirable state of affairs? Should there be more government regulation?

28. An important theory taught in business schools is the efficient market hypothesis (EMH), which suggests that the aggregate market consisting of millions of investors is sophisticated enough to see the economic substance of firm performance irrespective of what the financial statements say. The most extreme version of this hypothesis suggests that the stock market impounds all new information about a firm into its stock price within minutes. What implications does the EMH have for accounting?

29. Should financial statements users be given a greater say in standard-setting and in the content and form of financial statements?

30. Is accounting information free? If not, who pays?

31. Is financial reporting neutral (free of bias)? How can the neutrality be increased?

32. What are the characteristics of a profession? Does accounting meet those requirements?

33. Do accountants owe their first loyalty to themselves, their firm, their profession, or society? Can you envisage a scenario in which conflicting loyalties would create a moral dilemma for the accountant?

34. This chapter identified some inconsistencies in accounting that suggest theoretical problems. What were they? Can you conceive of any way to resolve them?

35. What are the advantages and disadvantages to accounting of the following underlying concepts?
    a. Accrual concept.
    b. Matching.
    c. Conservatism.
    d. Historical cost-valuation principle.

  e. Full disclosure.
  f. Materiality.
  g. Objectivity.

36. The American Accounting Association, in *A Statement of Basic Accounting Theory*, asserted that there are five standards governing the appropriateness of financial accounting information:
  a. Appropriateness to expected use.
  b. Disclosure of significant relationships.
  c. Inclusion of environmental information.
  d. Consistency of practices through time.
  e. Uniformity of practice within and among entities.
  Indicate what you think is implied by each of these criteria and assess how well these criteria mesh with the conceptual framework we have outlined in this chapter.

37. It is often said that future-oriented financial information has more relevance to economic decision-making than do historical cost-based financial statements. If decision usefulness is our goal, why do we not include future-oriented information such as budgets and forecasts in the financial statements?

38. Rank the four basic financial statements in terms of decision usefulness and support your ranking.

39. Comment on the "events" approach to financial reporting advocated by George Sorter of Columbia University, whereby financial statement users would be provided with access to essentially the entire set of accounting records and would be free to make their own summaries and draw their own inferences.

40. Some individuals claim that financial statement users would be much better off (and many accountants would be unemployed) if the range of acceptable accounting alternatives was greatly decreased. For example, why do we need three different types of depreciation methods if theorists all agree that depreciation is an arbitrary process? Comment on this hypothesis.

41. Does accounting deal with certainty or uncertainty? What is the role of professional judgment in accounting?

42. Will it ever be possible to "automate" accounting, that is, design an expert system that eliminates the need for human involvement?

43. How do accountants measure income? How precise is this measurement?

44. How do accountants value assets? How precise is this measurement?

45. How do accountants decide what qualifies as an asset?

46. What is meant by the term "time value of money"? Do financial statements give due recognition to this concept?

47. How does inflation erode the usefulness of financial statements?

48. What problems exist in trying to compare the financial statements of a Canadian company with, say, a Japanese firm?

49. What is meant by the phase "current value accounting" and what are the pro and cons of this basis of accounting in relation to historical cost-based accounting? (Hint: see discussion of asset valuation bases in Chapter 2.)

50. Ernie Entrepreneur decides to leave business school and start his own business — Ernie's Hot Dog Stand. Design an accounting system that will meet Ernie's information needs and an internal control system that will meet as many as possible of the internal control principles and objectives identified in this chapter. What changes to this system would be necessitated if Ernie had considerable success and opened a chain of fifty hot dog stands?

DISCUSSION CASE 11

Ignorance of Unwritten Laws Seen as Key Ethics Pitfall for Accountants

Although ethical risks from outside the accounting profession are increasing, how accountants deal with time is largely conditioned by matters within the profession's control, says Leonard J. Brooks, FCA, professor of business ethics and accounting at the University of Toronto.

"To handle ethical dilemmas arising from without or within the profession, an accountant must be able to identify or be aware of the ethical issues involved, then must understand the issues in sufficient depth to fully appreciate them and, finally, must be able to analyze the problems using sound processes of ethical reasoning sufficient to ensure an ethical outcome," Brooks told his audience at an ethics symposium in May.

"Unfortunately," he continued, "many matters within the profession's control are preventing student as well as graduate accountants from acquiring the knowledge and skill necessary to discharge these three aspects of ethical decision making."

Approximately 80 educators, accounting and business professionals and students gathered at the symposium to consider ways to improve the areas of ethics ambiguity and criticism in accounting and business. According to Ross A. Denham, FCA, a professor of accounting at the University of Alberta and organizer of the event, "it was a great success."

In addition to identifying the three aspects of ethical decision making, Brooks, founding editor of the *Corporate Ethics Monitor* and a member of the editorial board of the *Journal of Business Ethics*, discussed the conditions preventing accountants from successfully making ethical decisions.

"At the present time," he told his audience, "there are many *(continued)*

(continued)

university programs which do not, in a formal way, introduce students to the ethical issues facing our society and particularly the business community. Even fewer formally introduce students to those ethical dilemmas facing the accounting profession specifically."

Unless more courses providing a formal exposure to ethical issues in accounting are offered, "ethical awareness will be left to drift on a laissez-faire basis. Can the accounting profession afford the overall risk involved?" Brooks asked.

Student and graduate accountants also have difficulty in understanding ethical issues beyond recognizing that proper working papers must be retained and fees must not be charged on a contingency basis. There are, however, many more significant ethical issues an accountant ought to understand.

For example, "when confronted with an ethical dilemma, to whom is the duty of a professional accountant owed: the employer/partner, the firm, the profession, the owner/shareholder, or the public? Which code of conduct takes precedence: the employer's or the professional's? ... These are ethical dilemmas which cannot be dispensed with in short order," Brooks argued. "But how many of our accounting programs offer a significant discussion of such dilemmas?"

Brooks also asked some thought-provoking questions about the ability of accountants to apply ethical reasoning in decision making: "How many of our programs are developing in students the ability to apply practical frameworks of ethical analysis? Are practical frameworks available? Is ethical analysis being applied to practical problems which an accountant could realistically face?

"Efforts must be made to address the ethical awareness, understanding and analytical skills of both students and graduates without delay," Brooks urged, citing a recent study in the May 1991 issue of *CA Magazine* that reported that many of the accountants charged with misconduct by the disciplinary process of the Institute of Chartered Accountants of Ontario were convicted because they were unable to recognize an ethical dilemma, understand the significance of it or understand how they should analyze the problem.

James C. Gaa, an associate professor of accounting at McMaster University, also examined some of the barriers that stand in the way of developing a better understanding of ethics in accounting and improving the education of accountants.

What is needed, Gaa said, is a broader sense and a more adequate conception of ethics. "Acting in accordance with codes of conduct is not [always] sufficient," he said, nor is acting in accordance with legal rules, because no set of rules is complete and unambiguous.

According to Tim Leech, CA, managing director of NCM Control & Security Services Limited and a regular contributor to *The Bottom Line's Internal Auditing Letter*, a specialized newsletter for IA professionals, the Canadian Insti-
(continued)

(continued)
tute of Chartered Accountants should take a leading role in addressing ethics in accounting.

Fraudulent Practices

"As a practising forensic accountant, I have had the misfortune of seeing ethical failures that involved chartered accountants," Leech said. He went on to describe cases where accountants were aware of infractions of the rules of professional conduct by other accountants — such as tax evasion and time charging misrepresentations — but did not report them and cases of fraudulent and unethical practices relating to time recording and invoicing, including premium billing on assignments that were to be billed on the basis of time actually incurred and charging time to clients' accounts that was not actually worked.

Leech suggested that the provincial institutes, perhaps in cooperation with the CICA Ethics Advisory Committee, design three one-day ethical awareness and decision-making programs and that attendance at one such program be mandatory for all members.

He proposed other recommendations for discussion as well, including confidential ethics concerns hot lines, scholarships and/ or prizes for research work and/ or articles by business students on ethics related issues affecting the profession and ethics case studies accompanied by commentary and analysis in each provincial institute newsletter.

Registrants at the symposium also heard the views of individuals from outside the accounting profession. William W. May, an associate professor of religion and director of the program in business ethics at the University of Southern California, proposed a decision model providing a reasoned process for resolving ethical dilemmas, and Roger Shiner, a professor of philosophy at the University of Alberta, offered a philosopher's point of view on ethics in accounting.

"There will inevitably be conflicts between the rights of the professional person qua person and the value to society of the professional activity." But, he noted, the values of impartiality and trustworthiness "will outweigh both the interests of clients and the interests of professionals themselves."

Dr. S. Keith Ward, a founding facility member of The King's College and a consultant to the committee for the improvement of teaching and learning on ethics at the University of Alberta, explored the larger issue of ethical pluralism in a postmodern age.

"Efforts by professional associations to arrive at more or less arbitrary ethical standards, standards that are imposed upon members of the associations who may not share the beliefs that appear to underlie them, are rearguard actions that will require elaborate and onerous policing procedures. If members of a profession are not inspired by an ethical code because it is not consonant with their own beliefs, they will adhere to it reluctantly and only when someone is watching," he warned. "A post-
(continued)

(continued)

modern society which no longer believes in God or in the triumph of the human spirit through progress is not likely to warm to ethical norms based on these or any other overarching principles."

References

Linda Bellio, "Ignorance of Unwritten Laws Seen as Key Ethics Pitfall for Accountants," *The Bottom Line*, July 1991, p. 20.

Discussion Question

What are the unwritten laws and the pitfalls to which the author refers?

DISCUSSION CASE 12

It's the Detail That Counts

As the last decade of the century overtakes us, public interest in ethics is at an all-time high. Whether or not we view conscience as a luxury, we can't deny that there is a tremendous surge of public and media interest about the ethics of our institutions and of those managing them.

Voters and taxpayers read about government leaks, patronage and electoral financial improprieties, and become cynical about the ethics of their leaders. Churchgoers suffer through shocking revelations about wrongdoing by TV evangelists and priests charged with the care of children. Readers of the business pages learn of insider trading, illegal toxic waste disposal, unsafe products knowingly produced and sold, and kickbacks and bribery in corporate purchasing. Moreover, they hear that sharp practice and misrepresentation played a part in the Principal Group affair.

Is the world going to hell in a handcart? Are ethical standards plummeting to a new low? Despite some recent horror stories, probably not. There is little evidence to suggest that people in business today — or in politics, for that matter — are significantly more ethical or unethical than their forebears. Does the new interest in ethics indicate a radical change in public expectations and standards of behaviour? I doubt it, but I do think those standards are gradually becoming more stringent as the public acquires more awareness and knowledge.

The major difference today is in the availability of information — in communication. Moreover, more attention is given to that information. We work in an increasingly transparent fishbowl, and institutional activities are under a more powerful microscope than ever before. The global village is shrinking, and investigative reporting and critical jour-

(continued)

(continued)

nalistic inquiry into business activity is increasing in quantity and depth (though not always in quality). Moreover, the electronic media now give us a closer, more graphic look at the *human* results of business and political decisions. As a result of these and other factors, public concern about ethical behaviour in all of our institutions — particularly our business institutions — has increased dramatically.

Maintaining Public Trust

As citizens and as professionals, we should be concerned about what all of this is doing to the public's trust in our institutions and in those who manage them. Trust is the "glue" that holds a society together and the essential ingredient that lets our companies operate.

Moreover, a crucial connection exists between a society's competitiveness and its ethics. IBM Chairman John Akers put it well recently when he said: "Ethics and competitiveness are inseparable. We compete as a society. No society anywhere will compete very long or successfully with people stabbing each other in the back; with people trying to steal from each other; with everything requiring notarized confirmation because you can't trust the other fellow; with every little squabble ending in litigation, and with government writing reams of regulatory legislation, tying business hand and foot to keep it honest.

"That is a recipe not only for headaches in running a company, it is a recipe for a nation to become wasteful, inefficient and noncompetitive. There is no escaping this fact: The greater the measure of mutual trust and confidence in the ethics of a society, the greater its economic strength."

So we have good reason to be concerned about events and conditions that result from or contribute to reduced public trust in our corporate organizations, large and small. Public trust that our corporate intentions are honorable and ethical has eroded. There is evidence that the public no longer believes that our institutional "bottom line" goes beyond profit maximization to embrace the fulfillment of a contributive role in society. In short, consumers have begun to wonder whether business institutions exist to serve them or to exploit them.

At the same time, early indications suggest a shift in the public's priorities away from the "grab all you can get" and "shop till you drop" mentality of the '80s toward more community- and family-oriented values. Also, the public is starting to show willingness to change its actual behaviour because of environmental concerns.

George Bush might say we are evolving toward a gentler, kinder society; nevertheless, if and when these trends strengthen, corporations can expect to be subjected to even tougher standards and more exacting expectations of good ethics, public-spiritedness and service-orientation. Above all, corporations will have to demonstrate, not just declare, that their purposes and strategies are not directed solely, or even primarily, at making as much money

(continued)

(continued)

as possible, but at serving — playing a contributive, ethically positive role in society. As Polish president Lech Walesa said recently, "There is a declining world market in words. The only thing people believe now is behaviour."

The Role of Upper Management

To meet this growing challenge, corporations, through their most senior officers, must re-examine their values, fundamental purposes and strategies. In the view of Harvard's Kenneth Andrews, the principal obstacle to achieving higher standards of business ethics is management's total loyalty to the maximization of profit. The define the purpose of the corporation as exclusively economic is "a deadly oversimplification," he says, adding that it encourages overemphasis on self-interest at the expense of others.

Competition, while it can be a powerfully productive and constructive force, fosters and requires the will to win — over others. Careerism focuses attention on advantage — over others. Working and living within that worldview and value system, immature people of all ages take much too seriously what football coach Vince Lombardi once said: "Winning is not the most important thing; it's the only thing!"

Now, that's a good line for firing up a team, but as a business philosophy, it's nonsense. Another Lombardi quote puts things in perspective. He said he expected his players to have three kinds of loyalty: "to God, to their families, and to the Green Bay Packers — *in that order*." While it is healthy for us to be focused on our work and on our company's success, we should also remember there are things in life more important than any corporation. So in considering and communicating the purpose of the corporation and the role of the bottom line, top management must put profit in its proper light.

Professor Robert Solomon of the University of Texas once said: "To be sure, a business does aim to make a profit, but it does so by supplying quality goods and services, by providing jobs, and by 'fitting' in the community. To single out profits rather than productivity or public service as the central aim of business activity is just asking for trouble. Moreover, profits are not as such the ultimate goal of business activity. Profits get distributed and reinvested. Profits are a means to building the business and rewarding employees, executives and investors."

While profit is necessary, it is insufficient as a guiding principle for business conduct. It is also, of course, one of the handiest ways of keeping score, and this partially explains why it is so often thought of as synonymous with purpose. In focusing so strongly on the score, the media cover business in much the same way they cover sports — as if it were only about winning and losing. As a result, the public — and sometimes business people themselves — come to think of business as a game, and a zero-sum, win-lose game at that.

But business is more important than any game. Business involves
(continued)

(continued)

real people's lives, and it deeply affects the welfare of communities and nations. The media do us all a disservice when they cover business as sport, and business people, perhaps seduced by the media-promoted myth, make a similar mistake when they approach their work as gamesmanship. We should heed what Kenneth Blanchard and Norman Vincent Peale wrote recently on business ethics: "Managing only for profit is like playing tennis with your eye on the scoreboard and not on the ball."

Think also about the effect of this mentality on employees. Says Andrews: "When they first come to work, individuals whose moral judgment may ultimately determine their company's ethical character enter a community whose values will influence their own. The economic function of the corporation is necessarily one of those values. But if it is the only value, ethical inquiry cannot flourish. If management believes that the invisible hand of the market adequately moderates the injury done by the pursuit of self-interest, ethical policy can be dismissed as irrelevant. And if what these people see (while they are hearing about maximizing shareholder wealth) are managers dedicated to their own survival and compensation, they will naturally be more concerned about rewards than about fairness. . . .

"Under pressures to get ahead, the individual (of whose native integrity we are hopeful) is tempted to pursue advancement at the expense of others, to cut corners, to seek to win at all costs, to make things seem better than they are — to take advantage, in

sum, of the myopic evaluation of performance. . . .

"By contrast, when the corporation is defined as a socio-economic institution with responsibilities to other constituencies (employees, customers and communities, for example), policy can be established to regulate the single-minded pursuit of maximum immediate profit. The leaders of such a company speak of social responsibility, promulgate ethical policy, and make their personal values available for emulation by their juniors."

Sometimes, CEOs express concern about ethics and espouse high standards, while their somewhat disenchanted and threatened middle managers grumble that they "can't afford" to be ethical in a competitive world of actual or threatened takeovers, downsizing, "lean and mean" structures, and tough quantitative targets. However, the CEOs' statements aren't necessarily mere lip service. It's just that making general statements, however sincere, is much easier than actually making things happen. In other words, although we all tend to think in generalities, we are condemned to live in detail. And it's the detail that counts.

In business ethics, as in so many other business areas, the keys to success are persistence, consistency, communication and commitment. A corporate value system that is not continually reexamined and backed up by sound implementation strategies and systems *will* become mere lip service. Securing the commitment of staff takes persistent effort to ensure consistent application of values in the development of

(continued)

(continued)

strategy and systems. And staff commitment, as many have pointed out, is a key corporate success factor. It is also, I believe, strongly connected to building and maintaining an ethical climate in the organization.

The Role of the CFO

This brings us to the chief financial officer. If the CEO is, as he or she must be, the company's chief ethics officer, what are the roles of the CFO and of the other financial executives?

It makes sense to approach this from three separate perspectives, which admittedly overlap considerably. First, the CFO fills a general management role as a member of his or her company's top strategic management team. Second, the financial executive has specific functions in serving his or her company, functions that involve a multitude of ethical questions, issues and dilemmas. Third, all financial executives, acting as members of their profession, can have an influence on broader institutional arrangements and professional standards. The responsible financial executive must direct his or her attention to an extremely broad variety of questions — all bristling with ethical issues.

In the first of these roles — as a member of the top management team — the CFO shares the responsibility of defining and conveying the firm's vision, purpose and values. He or she must consider carefully not only shareholder value, but stakeholder values and the entire range of the firm's stakeholder responsibilities.

Often expert on present value calculations and intimate with the magic of compound interest, thoughtful financial executives can have strong influence, for good or ill, on the time horizon most emphasized in the company. Improving ethical standards is often largely a matter of raising people's sights, getting them to look at what they and the company should do in the long term. If the future consequences of present actions are properly weighed in current decisions, the results are more likely to be responsible and ethical. Long-term thinking tends to preclude many tempting "quick-fix" propositions. This is not to say, of course, that current profitability and cash-flow considerations are unimportant. It is a question of balance.

In the second role — financial executive as functional specialist — CFOs and their staff design many of the key systems whose characteristics profoundly influence almost every aspect of the company. This brings us to the crucial matter of communication. Much of what CFOs and their financial officers do actually involves communication. Their subordinates are communications officers to the same degree as any public relations director. Think about the way internal accounting systems are set up in a corporation and, more particularly, how they interconnect with compensation and reward systems. The accounting system is, after all, the primary system that tells managers at all levels about their costs and revenues. Clearly, the ways in which fixed costs and overheads are allocated — and

(continued)

(continued)

most CFOs will admit there is almost always an element of arbitrariness in this — can deeply affect the news this system delivers and, in turn, heavily influence the decisions managers make. Similarly, accounting assumptions of all sorts (basic system decisions about depreciation periods, capital investment hurdle rates and many other "accounting" matters) are crucial, though sometimes hidden, determinants of management behaviour.

Knowing this, CFOs should ask themselves, first, who is the "audience" for the news any particular accounting system will deliver and, second, will the system give accurate and truthful signals in terms of the particular audience's needs? Is the audience the shareholders? Revenue Canada? Strategic management? Unit management? Is the system design basically driven by statutory reporting requirements? By tax considerations? Or by top management's need for an accurate management information system for decision support?

If the system is designed for one set of purposes but is also used for others, it may be useful to consider whether the information delivered by the system tends to generate productive responses from middle- and lower-level managers. For example, does it tend to push them toward short-term, profit-maximizing decisions to the detriment of longer-term, broader corporate goals? Does it "export" costs to future periods? Or does it actually encourage a realistic, longer-term perspective? Are the accounting units set up and sized so that the numbers motivate managers to work cooperatively for the good of the whole? Or do they tend to incite them into revenue-grabbing, cost-shedding games *vis-à-vis* other units in the company?

In short, do the messages sent by the accounting systems designed, installed and operated by CFOs and their staff promote or discourage the behaviour they and the rest of top management consider consistent with company values and strategy? Do they promote or discourage teamwork, information sharing, good customer service and striving for quality? Do they tend to support ethically productive behaviour, or do they make it more difficult? Clearly, this particular ethical buck stops with the financial executives.

Also, CFOs are responsible for the accuracy, completeness, charity and timeliness of company financial disclosure to the investing public. And in the role of building their company's capital base, they must make some delicately balanced choices about the company's obligations to various classes of shareholders, from common shareholders (majority or minority, voting or nonvoting) through the various shades of the equity/debt spectrum to straight lenders. CFOs need not be reminded of how tricky some of these ethical choices have become.

Finally, financial executives as a group have an obligation to exert a positive ethical influence on the practices, and the standards of practice, followed in our capital markets. In these turbulent times, characterized by glob-
(continued)

(continued)

alization, tough international competition and steadily increasing complexity, the integrity, fairness and efficiency of our capital markets are crucial to us all.

And there are worrisome trends. As Robert Reich observed recently in the *New York Times*: "The changing pattern of stock ownership has encouraged mergers and acquisitions, contributing to the emphasis on immediate gains. Not long ago, the majority of stocks were owned by individuals and many of them held on to their shares for years. It was not unusual for such an investor to take a mildly proprietary interest in how his or her company was doing and what it was planning to do. Today, 70% of the volume of stock trading is done by institutions — mainly mutual funds, pension funds and insurance companies — which are under pressure to produce the short-term earnings that clients demand."

Reich went on to point out that "asset-rearranging" (as opposed to wealth-producing) activities harm productivity by expending the energy of some of our most talented citizens. "Paper entrepreneurs" are responsible for the nation's most innovative economic strategies, and the result is a "brain drain" from product to paper. Moreover, Reich says, an economy based on asset-rearranging has one particular disadvantage — it invites zero-sum games in which one group's gain is another's loss.

These are complex issues that we have been wrestling with for some time. John Maynard Keynes wrote in 1936: "When the capital development of a country becomes a byproduct of the activities of a casino, the job is likely to be ill-done." I suppose he didn't consider the record of Wall Street to be one of the triumphs of laissez-faire capitalism.

Let's hope CFOs continue to consider the changes in the capital markets and begin exerting healthy influences on the system.

Not surprisingly, many of the thoughts I have expressed here are also reflected in the Royal Bank of Canada's code of conduct, which I am proud to have helped prepare more than a decade ago. In the early pages, after an outline of the bank's commitment to such stakeholders as customers, employees, shareholders and the community, and before the substantive rules, the code lists some "basic principles" that I believe are worth repeating:

- To give good value — contributing rather than exploiting.
- To deal with people and institutions fairly and honestly.
- To recognize and respect each person's rights, individuality and human dignity.
- To be a responsible citizen.
- To be a leader, unceasingly striving for excellence in everything we do.

The rest is detail.

References

David Grier, "It's the Detail That Counts," *CA Magazine*, August 1991, pp. 45–48. Reprinted with the permission of *CA Magazine*, published by the Canadian Institute of Chartered Accountants, Toronto.

Discussion Question

What steps can CFOs take to promote high ethical standards in organizations?

DISCUSSION CASE 13

Sustainable Ethics

The environment is one of the biggest ethical challenges of our time, so it's particularly opportune that my first article as editor of the Ethics department should appear in a special environmental issue. Debate on the environment covers a wide range of subjects, including the "costs" of doing the right thing; inconvenience versus environmentally preferential choices; individual, corporate and institutional rights and obligations; damage to human health; intergenerational perspectives; whistle blowing; and a host of others.

These subjects are, to say the least, topical and are likely to remain so for the foreseeable future. Business ethics have also assumed a high profile in recent years. To confirm this, take a trip to your local bookstore and note the shelf space occupied by books on these two topics. The ethics surrounding environmental and business considerations are linked by the notion of sustainable development, which has become a buzzword for governments and for many corporations. It's a concept that involves making ethical choices and measuring costs and benefits in an environmental context — a concept, therefore, that should involve the skills of our profession.

A number of businesses are already facing these complex evaluations. If your client or employer is a large publicly traded company, or a company operating in an environmentally sensitive field, it likely already has a code of conduct and a statement of environmental policy. In some cases, it may also have a senior officer with responsibility for environmental issues.

On the other hand, if you are a CA in a public accounting firm, you probably have yet to deal with environmental issues in a significant way. The accounting profession hasn't been in the forefront in identifying and attempting to resolve ethical and environmental issues. Activity over the past several years has been confined to a few academics, a few CAs employed in industry who are involved in the "What's it going to cost to clean up the problem?" decision, and, in recent years, a very few in public practice with clients who have had to consider accounting for or disclosing environmental liabilities.

But times are changing. "We must now pay the full costs of environmentally clean production," said the Honorable James Bradley, then Minister of the Environment for Ontario at a conference sponsored by the Canadian Centre for Ethics & Corporate Policy. "To survive, we must change our environmental operating deficits to surpluses and start reducing our accumulated environmental debt." After

(continued)

(continued)

an initial question about the appropriateness of being lectured to by a politician about deficits, the reaction of an accounting professional should be, "How can I help? How can my professional skills be applied to improve ethical decision-making on the environment?"

This is the challenge now facing our professional bodies, our public accounting firms and ourselves. The CICA and at least one provincial institute are considering the issue; in other countries, the accounting profession is stirring. But much more needs to be done, and quickly. I believe the profession and its members have an important, perhaps even crucial, role to play in the 1990s in the great environmental and ethics debates.

Why CAs?

What on earth do accountants know about the environment? What gives accountants any special expertise concerning ethics? These are both good questions. Unless he or she has particular interest in those areas, a CA will likely not have much (if any) knowledge of technical or legal environmental issues. Nor does a CA necessarily know better than anyone else what is right or wrong. A CA is neither more nor less qualified to make the "right" or "best" decisions in the trade-offs that our clients and employers have to make between, say, safety and profit, or between short-term profit and the amount spent on more environmentally friendly production methods. This doesn't mean, however, that an accountant has nothing special

to bring to bear on these decisions.

While CAs aren't trained as ethicists (whatever *that* means), they do go through a training process that includes public practice, where professional values are constantly instilled. In particular, the need to consider the wider public interest along with that of a client or employer is a constant feature of a public accountant's daily life. It's also important for an employed CA, although much more difficult to apply. (The most a public accountant stands to lose from taking a stand is the client and the associated fee revenue; employed CAs put their livelihood at risk.) This objectivity and concern for wider interest is obviously important in the difficult ethical choices companies make, including environmental ones.

Despite some recent setbacks and the so-called "expectation gap," the public accounting profession is trusted and well respected. Knowledgeable users of our reports respect us not just for our expertise in accounting but for our objectivity and credibility. And I don't think this is confined to Canada. The International Federation of Accountants (IFAC) recently issued "Guidelines on Ethics for Professional Accountants," which says in the introduction: "A distinguishing mark of a profession is acceptance of its responsibility to the public. The accountancy profession's public consists of clients, credit grantors, governments, employers, employees, investors, the business and financial community, and others who rely on the objectivity and integrity of

(continued)

(continued)

professional accountants to maintain the orderly functioning of commerce. This reliance imposes a public-interest responsibility on the accountancy profession. The public interest is defined as the collective well-being of the community of people and institutions the professional accountant serves.

"A professional accountant's responsibility is not exclusively to satisfy the needs of an individual client or employer. The standards of the accountancy profession are heavily determined by the public interest. . . ."

No other profession has this combination of skills. Lawyers have many of them, but they operate, and are seen to operate, in more of an advocacy role which, in an attest engagement, a public accountant strives to avoid.

In addition, CAs are skilled at measuring things. We are knowledgeable about systems and have excellent reporting skills. We are analytical by temperament, skeptical and quick to recognize overblown rhetoric. A CA may have no particular ethical corner on a trade-off between, say, the cost of fixing a toxic-waste outflow into a lake and the benefits obtained. But consider the skills CAs can bring to such considerations: managing a team that might include experts in other fields, assigning costs to the various steps that could be taken, establishing mechanisms for managing and monitoring the process and the problem, and issuing a report that summarizes the issue in as factual and quantifiable terms as possible with respect to the costs and the expected benefits. With help from the profession in establishing standards and reporting parameters for this kind of engagement, and with a reasonable effort to become familiar with environmental issues and concepts, the CA's ability to lend credence to the information used by decision makers could significantly improve the decisions themselves. Better — or, if not better, at least more informed — decisions would result.

However, having said all this, we are dealing with issues of far greater significance than most CAs are used to. This is the challenge. As a profession, we have not yet been able to come to grips with the intuitively simple problem of current-value accounting and reporting. Issues such as how to compare an immediate cost to a benefit that won't occur until the next generation (or later) present enormous and perhaps insuperable challenges. Nonetheless, someone has to start making such decisions because concerned parties will demand it. Activists express the challenge differently — what is the cost to our children and grandchildren if we don't take measures today? We can't answer that, but we should be able to opine on the costs today and, in certain cases, we may be able to quantify some aspects of a future benefit, provided we're given criteria to report against. (For example, based on information from experts, the percentage decrease of harmful emissions could be calculated.)

We must also remember that the ultimate choices are ethical ones with which, as individuals, we may disagree. But this is the nature of ethical problems. I have

(continued)

(continued)

always been an admirer of the theory of utilitarianism. As expounded by John Stuart Mill, an action is right or wrong depending on its consequences in providing "the greatest benefit for the greatest number." The theory is in great disfavour with today's moral philosophers because it gives no clear-cut answer except when one of the actions contemplated will provide both more benefit and for more people. Unfortunately, most environmental improvements usually result in a small increase in benefits for a large number of people (including people yet to be born), and significant harm (such as high costs) to a small number of people.

There is no easy answer. This is what Mill's utilitarian principle tells us, but it also helps us recognize the dilemma. If a particular pollutant causes extreme harm to a few people (for example, Minamata disease in Japan, which resulted from mercury poisoning), the balance is tipped and society demands that action, such as shutting down the polluter, be taken. In other words, the factory's closing results from a large net swing to the "greatest benefit" side with little consideration for the "greatest number." One doesn't have to be a genius to see how the skill we have as CAs can contribute to better solutions in this type of framework.

What We Can Do

How shall we meet this challenge? If we are to play our part in dealing with environmental questions in an ethical and practical way, it's critical that our professional bodies become involved or, in the vernacular, "get serious." The CICA is starting to deal with some of these concerns. The Ontario institute sponsored a conference on the environment in January, and the issue of *CA Magazine* you have in your hands is devoted primarily to this theme. A good start, as long as the momentum is maintained or increased. These efforts must lead to a shift of environmental issues, and perhaps other ethical problems, from the fringes of our professional life into the mainstream.

This will not be an easy task, and resources, especially human ones, will be scarce. Our first priority is for the CICA and the provincial institutes to act in unison (no wheel reinventing allowed) and in an organized fashion. One suggestion is for the CICA to establish an environmental standards committee with a status equivalent to the present accounting, auditing and public sector committees. Also, the CICA should seek a role in the Prime Minister's "National Task Force on the Environment and the Economy" while the provincial institutes do the same in the various roundtables established by the provinces. There are many other influential groups, all concerned with how to implement sustainable development. Let's get involved!

Work is already under way in several areas that will help establish criteria for environmental auditing. (I hesitate to employ this term because of its frequent

(continued)

(continued)

misuse, but I use it in the sense of providing assurance that adds credibility to statements by entities, including governments, about environmental performance.) In 1986, the AICPA published its "Attestation Standards," which set the framework for auditors reporting on matters other than financial statements. The CICA has an equivalent project under way, scheduled to reach exposure draft stage in 1991. This would be an excellent framework for the aforementioned environmental standards committee to use as a basis for more detailed guidance.

Nothing, to my knowledge, yet exists concerning accounting for environmental costs and benefits other than costs incurred directly by the entity involved. Nothing on "externalities," which an economics professor in the early '60s taught me about long before I knew the difference between a debit and a credit. Since his political leanings put him somewhere between Lenin and Stalin, he placed great emphasis on pollution as a cost of production that never appeared in companies' books or financial statements — an externality.

In spite of occasional forays by academics into the area of "social accounting," an article by Daniel Blake Rubenstein in the November 1989 issue of *CA Magazine* ("Black oil, red ink," p. 28) and a very recent paper by the Chartered Association of Certified Accountants in the United Kingdom entitled, "The Greening of Accountancy — The Profession After Pearce," no real progress

has been made. A Stalinistic solution has not been forthcoming (just as well, when one considers the environmental disaster in Eastern Europe); likewise, no accounting or measurement solution has happened either. So we must still find a way to account for externalities — for the credits and debits of, say, a large company in a "company town" with no other independent source of employment. However bad the pollution caused by such a company, the social costs of closing it down are horrendous. Finding a practical way out of such ethical dilemmas cries out for social accounting techniques. The CICA should, in my view, resurrect this issue and commission a research study with a short reporting deadline to deal with it.

As for more traditional areas of concern, the Accounting Standards Committee of the CICA should make sure it has adequately dealt with the accounting for and disclosure of environmental costs and liabilities within the existing model of historical cost accounting. Even this area is fraught with difficulties. We already have accounting standards that would, in some circumstances, require providing for future environmental costs or disclosing a contingent liability. Even compliance with laws and regulations presents problems. For example, one would normally expect a breach of the law to result in a prosection, conviction (if guilty) and penalty. But it's not that simple any more. Some governments, it appears to me, have chosen to put tough environmen-

(continued)

(continued)

tal laws in place with the intention of charging only the most egregious offenders. For others, the threat of large penalties is used to pressure companies to make improvements. Perhaps a valid approach (perhaps not, and in itself an ethical issue), but one that certainly makes an accountant's life difficult in determining when liabilities should be set up or contingent liabilities disclosed. I am happy to report, however, that the CICA has established a task force to "identify how environmental issues should be accounted for and/or disclosed. . . ."

Another important area is training. A careful look should be taken at the profession's training needs in business ethics and ethical analysis generally. Perhaps credits for limited studies in environmental science and social planning should be recognized in our admissions policy.

One thing is clear. Our professional bodies should move forcefully and as fast as possible. We're late starting so we'll need real momentum on all fronts.

Public accounting firms can make important contributions. The major firms will have to provide much of the human resources to the professional bodies if the latter are to succeed. This presents a real challenge in these recessionary times. It's particularly difficult because those with some expertise in the area are in very short supply and in great demand on chargeable assignments.

Firms should encourage their partners and staff to identify ways to assist their clients with environmental issues — either as an adjunct to the attest function or on consulting assignments. They should be aware of environmental legislation and regulation that affects their clients, at least in general terms. Clients should be thinking about their public accountant when faced with major ethical decisions in the environmental area.

Public accounting firms should also ensure their own houses are in order. I have recently been involved with a task force charged with assessing and, where possible, improving environmental practices in my firm's Toronto office. "No environmental issues in an office," you might say. But think about it for a minute. I can assure you there are enough to keep us going for some time — for more than I would have thought possible. Auditors frequently ask clients whether they have a "code of ethics" and, in relevant cases, "an environmental code." Outside organizations such as EthicScan question companies about such matters and publish the results (see, for example, their bimonthly publication *The Corporate Ethics Monitor*). But how many public accounting firms have codes of conduct and/or environmental codes themselves?

It may even be appropriate to train some CAs in ethical analysis — a skill with wide application in business, but a particular relevance in major environmental decisions.

And finally, but unfortunately, it's necessary in this increasingly

(continued)

(continued)

litigious society to recognize that, by jumping into this important area, public accounting firms will be increasing their risk, even if they do solid work. This risk will have to be managed and may hold back useful developments, pending the establishment of standards and rules. We should do everything we can to try to encourage a legal environment that won't unduly hamper forward-thinking developments. At the same time, the existence of some risk can be a positive factor if it prevents us from giving assurances on matters so nebulous that our profession's reputation suffers as a result.

Whether we are CAs in public practice, industry, academe or government, the best thing we can do is heighten our own awareness by reading the original document that brought the term "sustainable development" into everyday language. *Our Common Future* was published in May 1987 by the United Nations "Brundtland" Commission, named after its chairperson, the Prime Minister of Norway. The first half is the best, but read all of it if you can, most of it if you can't. It's an astonishing document, and history may show that it was the most influential single publication of the 1980s. If it doesn't whet your appetite, forget environmental accounting and auditing — leave it to someone else.

In addition to becoming generally informed, CAs in public practice need to bring environmental and ethical thoughts to bear on their employers and clients. CAs in industry, many of whom will already have been involved with the costs of compliance with environmental laws, should take steps to ensure that all the issues that need to be addressed are being addressed and that costs and benefits are considered on a reasonable basis. (And don't forget to put out your blue box!)

Sustainable development is an immediate and long-term ethical and business issue for the profession and all its members. I believe we're uniquely positioned to offer a major contribution to the debate, and reasonable and ethical solutions to environmental problems. It's a formidable challenge, one that will lead us to change our way of thinking in a number of important respects. And there will be risks. But if we don't take up the challenge, I don't think the solutions will be as good.

I urge readers to express their views. Future articles in the Ethics department will continue to deal with some of the issues discussed here. Please don't hesitate to contribute.

References

David Selley, "Sustainable Ethics," *CA Magazine*, March 1991, pp. 71–74. Reprinted with the permission of *CA Magazine*, published by the Canadian Institute of Chartered Accountants, Toronto.

Discussion Question

What is meant by sustainable development and sustainable ethics, and how are the two concepts related?

ACCOUNTING CONCEPTS PROBLEM 1

Exhibit 5.7 presents *CICA Handbook* Section 1000, entitled "Financial Statement Concepts." Answer the following questions:

a. What contribution does Section 1000 make to accounting?

b. What are the primary objectives of financial statements?

c. Why does it help to understand the qualitative attributes of financial information?

d. Why does it help to define elements of financial statements?

e. To what does the term "recognition criteria" refer?

f. What is the measurement basis underlying financial statements in Canada?

g. What is GAAP and where does one find authoritative support to decide whether a proposed accounting treatment is within the framework of GAAP?

h. Does Section 1000 constitute a conceptual framework for accounting?

i. Is Section 1000 totally consistent with the conceptual framework presented in Chapter 5?

EXHIBIT 5.7
A. Handbook Section 1000

Financial Statement Concepts

PURPOSE AND SCOPE

.01   The purpose of this Section is to set out the concepts that underlie the development and use [of] accounting principles in the general purpose financial statements of profit oriented enterprises. The conceptual material will provide a consistent source of reference to guide the future development [of] accounting standards by the Committee.

.02   The material can also be used by preparers of financial statements and accounting practitioners in making judgments in applying generally accepted accounting principles and in establishing accounting policies in areas where there are no generally accepted accounting principles.

.03   The material does not define standards for any particular measurement or disclosure issue. Nothing in this Section overrides any specific Recommendation in other Sections of the Handbook. To the extent there may be inconsistencies between this Section and other Sections, it is intended that these will be resolved when those other Sections are reviewed by the Committee.

Financial statements

.04   Financial statements normally include a balance sheet, income statement, statement of retained earnings and statement of changes in financial position. Notes to financial statements and supporting schedules to which the financial statements are cross-referenced are an integral part of such statements.

.05   Financial statements are usually limited to information about economic transactions and events that are financial in nature and can be expressed in financial terms. Financial statements deal with measurements that may, by their nature, be imprecise and are generally based on representation of past rather than future transactions and events.

EXHIBIT 5.7 (continued)

.06 In addition to the process of providing financial statements, financial reporting includes other types of reporting, such as information outside the financial statements in annual reports, prospectuses and other material distributed with financial statements. Financial reporting is accordingly broader in scope than the process of providing financial statements. While it is recognized that many financial statement concepts also apply to other types of financial reporting, this Section does not specifically set out concepts for other types of financial reporting.

OBJECTIVE OF FINANCIAL STATEMENTS

.07 In the Canadian economic environment, the production of goods and the provision of services are, to a significant extent, carried out by investor-owned business enterprises in the private sector and to a lesser extent by government-owned business enterprises. Debt and equity markets act as an exchange mechanism for investment resources.

.08 Enterprise ownership is often segregated from management creating a need for external communication of economic information about the enterprise to investors. For the purposes of this Section, investors include present and potential debt and equity investors and their advisors. Creditors and others who do not have internal access to enterprise information also need external reports to obtain the information they require.

.09 It is not practicable to expect financial statements to satisfy the many and varied information needs of all external users of information about an enterprise. Consequently, the objective of financial statements focuses primarily on the information needs of investors and creditors. The Committee believes that financial statements prepared to satisfy these needs are often used by others who need external reporting of information about an enterprise.

.10 Investors and creditors are interested, for the purpose of making resource allocation decisions, in predicting the ability of the enterprise to generate cash flows in the future, to meet its obligations and to generate a return on investment.

.11 Investors also require information about how the management of an enterprise has discharged its stewardship responsibility to those that have provided resources to the enterprise.

Objective

.12 The objective of financial statements is to communicate information that is useful to investors and creditors in making resource allocation decisions and assessing management stewardship. Information provided in financial statements should fairly present: (1) an enterprise's economic resources, obligations and equity, (2) changes in the enterprise's economic resources, obligations and equity, and (3) the economic performance of the enterprise.

BENEFIT VERSUS COST CONSTRAINT

.13 The benefits expected to arise from providing information in financial statements should exceed the cost of doing so. This constraint applies to the development of accounting standards by the Committee and is a consideration in the preparation of financial statements in accordance with those standards. The Committee recognizes that the benefits and costs may fall to different parties and that the evaluation of benefits and costs is substantially a judgmental process.

MATERIALITY

.14 Investors and creditors are generally interested only in information that may affect their decision making. Materiality is the term used to describe the significance of information to decision makers. While materiality is a matter of judgment in the particular circumstances, as a general rule it should be judged in relation to the significance of an item in the making of decisions by an investor or creditor. If it is probable the item would change or influence a decision, it would be deemed to be material.

EXHIBIT 5.7 (continued)

QUALITATIVE CHARACTERISTICS

.15 Qualitative characteristics define and describe the attributes of information provided in financial statements that make that information useful to investors and creditors. The four qualitative characteristics are understandability, relevance, reliability and comparability.

.16 a) Understandability

Given that the objective of financial statements is to communicate information that is useful to investors and creditors, an essential characteristic of the information provided in financial statements is that it is readily understandable by investors and creditors. For this purpose, investors and creditors are assumed to have a reasonable knowledge of business and economic activities and a willingness to study the information with reasonable diligence.

.17 b) Relevance

For the information provided in financial statements to be useful, it must be relevant to the decisions made by investors and creditors. Relevance is achieved through predictive and feedback value and timeliness.

i) Predictive and feedback value

Information that helps investors and creditors to predict future cash flows has predictive value. Although the information provided in financial statements will not normally be a prediction in itself, this does not preclude the information from being useful in making predictions. The predictive value of the income statement, for example, is enhanced if unusual, abnormal or infrequent items are separately disclosed. Information that confirms or corrects the earlier predictions of investors and creditors has feedback value. Information often has both predictive and feedback value.

ii) Timeliness

For information to be useful for decision making, it must be received by the decision maker before it loses its capacity to influence decisions. The usefulness of information for decision making declines as time elapses.

.18 c) Reliability

For the information provided in financial statements to be useful, it must be reliable. Reliability is achieved through representational faithfulness, verifiability and neutrality.

i) Representational faithfulness

Representational faithfulness is achieved when transactions and events affecting the enterprise are presented in financial statements in a manner that recognizes their economic substance.

ii) Verifiability

The financial statement representation of a transaction or event is verifiable if knowledgeable and independent observers would agree, with a reasonable degree of precision, that it corresponds to and adequately reflects the actual transaction or event.

iii) Neutrality

Information is neutral when it is free from bias that would lead investors and creditors towards making predetermined decisions. Bias in measurement occurs when a measure tends to overstate or understate the item being measured. In the selection of acounting principles, bias occurs when the selection is made with the interests of particular users or with particular economic or political objectives in mind.

Financial statements that do not include everything necessary for faithful representation of transactions and events affecting the enterprise would be incomplete and, therefore, potentially biased.

The neutrality of financial statements is affected in an acceptable manner by the use of conservatism in making judgments when conditions of uncertainty exist. When uncertainty exists, estimates of a conservative nature attempt to ensure net assets or net income are not overstated. However, conservatism does not encompass the deliberate understatement of net assets or net income.

EXHIBIT 5.7 (continued)

.19   d) Comparability (including consistency)

Comparability is a characteristic of the relationship between two pieces of information rather than of a particular piece of information by itself. It enables investors and creditors to identify similarities in and differences between two sets of financial statements. Comparability is important when comparing the financial statements of two different enterprises and when comparing the financial statements of the same enterprise over two periods or at two different points in time.

.20   Comparability in financial statements of an enterprise is enhanced when the same accounting policies are used consistently from period to period. Consistency helps prevent misconceptions that might result from the application of different accounting policies in different periods. When a change in accounting policy is deemed to be appropriate, disclosure of the effects of the change is necessary to maintain comparability.

Qualitative characteristics trade-off

.21   The Committee recognizes that there is often a trade-off required in the degree to which qualitative characteristics can be achieved, particularly between relevance and reliability. For example, there is often a trade-off between the timeliness of producing financial statements and the reliability of the information reported in the statements. Generally, the objective is to achieve an appropriate balance among the characteristics. The relative importance of the characteristics in different cases is a matter of judgment.

FUNDAMENTAL CONCEPTS

The following fundamental concepts normally underlie the preparation of financial statements:

a) Accrual

Revenues and expenses are recognized in the period in which they are considered to have been earned or incurred, respectively, whether or not they have been settled by the receipt or payment of cash or its equivalent. The accrual concept encompasses deferrals that occur when the recognition of a cash receipt or payment occurs prior to the criteria for recognition of revenue or expense being satisfied (see paragraph 1000.24).

b) Matching

Revenues and expenses that are linked to each other in a cause and effect relationship are included in income in the same accounting period.

c) Going concern

Financial statements are prepared on the assumption that the enterprise will continue in operation for the foreseeable future. Assets, therefore, are normally accounted for on the basis of continued use as opposed to liquidation. The going concern concept is not applied when the enterprise is not expected to continue in operation for the foreseeable future.

d) Substance over form

Transactions and events are accounted for and presented in a manner that conveys their economic substance rather than their legal or other form.

e) Historical cost

Transactions and events are initially recognized and subsequently included in the financial statements at the value ascribed to them when they took place.

f) Nominal dollar financial capital

Capital is measured in financial terms and no adjustment is made for the effect of a change in the general purchasing power of the currency during the period. The concept of capital used in financial statements is important because income exists only after the capital of an enterprise has been maintained. Thus, income is the increase in the amount of capital at the end of the period over the beginning of the period, after excluding the effects of capital contributions and withdrawals.

EXHIBIT 5.7 (continued)

ELEMENTS OF FINANCIAL STATEMENTS

.22   Elements of financial statements are the basic categories of items portrayed in financial statements. There are two types of elements: those that describe the economic resources, obligations and equity of an enterprise at a point in time (balance sheet elements), and those that describe changes in economic resources, obligations and equity (income statement elements). A statement of changes in financial position consists primarily of changes in balance sheet elements. Notes to financial statements, while an integral part of financial statements, are not considered to be an element.

.23   The elements defined herein are the most common categories of items portrayed in financial statements. The existence of other items is not precluded. In practice, a balance sheet may include, as a category of assets or liabilities, deferred charges or credits that arise from a delay in income statement recognition. Criteria for the recognition of items in financial statements are discussed in paragraph 1000.24.

.24   Net income is the residual amount after expenses and losses are deducted from revenues and gains. Net income is important because it is frequently used as a measure of economic performance.

a) Assets

.25   Assets are resources controlled by an enterprise as a result of past transactions or events from which future economic benefits may be obtained.

.26   Assets have two essential characteristics:
   i) they embody a future benefit that involves a capacity, singly or in combination with other assets, to contribute directly or indirectly to future net cash flows; and
   ii) the transaction or event giving rise to the enterprise's right to, or control of, the benefit has already occurred.

.27   It is not essential for the future benefit to be legally enforceable for the resource to be an asset provided that the enterprise can control the use of the future benefit through other means.

b) Liabilities

.28   Liabilities are obligations of an enterprise arising from past transactions or events, the settlement of which may result in the transfer of assets, provision of services or other yielding of economic benefits in the future.

.29   Liabilities have two essential characteristics:
   i) they embody a duty or responsibility to others that entails settlement by future transfer or use of assets at a specified or determinable date, on occurrence of a specified event, or on demand; and
   ii) the transaction or event obligating the enterprise has already occurred.

.30   Liabilities do not have to be legally enforceable provided that they otherwise meet the definition of liabilities; they can be based on equitable or constructive obligations. An equitable obligation is a duty based on ethical or moral considerations. A constructive obligation is one that can be inferred from the facts in a particular situation as opposed to a contractually based obligation.

.31   c) Equity

Equity is the ownership interest in the assets of an enterprise after deducting its liabilities. It may include, for example, various types of share capital, contributed surplus and retained earnings. Capital contributions and withdrawals are equity transactions that do not give rise to revenues, expenses, gains or losses.

.32   d) Revenues

Revenues are increases in economic resources, either by way of inflows of assets or reductions of liabilities, arising in the course of the ordinary activities of an enterprise, normally from the sale of goods, the rendering of services and the use by others of enterprise resources yielding interest, royalties and dividends.

.33   e) Expenses

Expenses are decreases in economic resources, either by way of outflows of assets or incurrences of liabilities, arising in the course of the ordinary activities of an enterprise.

EXHIBIT 5.7 (continued)

.34 f) Gains

Gains are increases in equity from peripheral or incidental transactions and events affecting an enterprise and from all other transactions, events and circumstances affecting the enterprise except those that result from revenues or capital contributions.

.35 g) Losses

Losses are decreases in equity from peripheral or incidental transactions and events affecting an enterprise and from all other transactions, events and circumstances affecting the enterprise except those that result from expenses or withdrawals of capital.

RECOGNITION CRITERIA

.36 Recognition is the process of including an item in the financial statements of an enterprise. Recognition consists of a narrative description of the item in a statement (e.g., "inventory" or "sales") and the addition of the amount involved into statement totals. Similar items may be grouped together in the financial statements for the purpose of disclosure.

.37 Recognition means inclusion of an item within one or more individual statements and does not mean disclosure in the notes to the financial statements. Notes either provide further details about items recognized in the financial statements, or provide information about items that do not meet the criteria for recognition and thus are not recognized in the financial statements.

.38 The recognition criteria below provide general guidance on when an item is recognized in the financial statements. Whether any particular item is recognized or not will require the application of judgment in considering whether the specific circumstances meet the recognition criteria.

.39 The recognition criteria are as follows:

a) the item has an appropriate basis of measurement and a reasonable estimate can be made of the amount involved; and

b) for items involving obtaining or giving up future economic benefits, it is probable that such benefits will be obtained or given up.

.40 It is possible that an item will meet the definition of an element but still not be recognized in the financial statements because it is not probable that future economic benefits will be obtained or given up or because a reasonable estimate cannot be made of the amount involved.

. . .

Measurement

.44 Measurement is the process of determining the amount at which an item is recognized in the financial statements. There are a number of bases on which the amount can be measured. One of the fundamental concepts of financial statements is that they are prepared using the historical cost basis of measurement (see paragraph 1000.17).

.45 Other bases of measurement are also used but only in certain limited circumstances. The main ones are:

a) Replacement cost — the amount that would be needed currently to acquire an equivalent asset. This may be used, for example, when inventories are valued at the lower of historical cost and replacement cost.

b) Realizable value — the amount that would be received by selling the asset in the ordinary course of business. This may be used, for example, to value temporary and portfolio investments. Realizable value encompasses market value, which is a way of estimating realizable value when a market for the asset exists.

c) Present value — the discounted amount of future cash flows expected to be received from an asset or required to settle a liability. This is used, for example, to estimate the cost of pension benefits.

. . .

EXHIBIT 5.7 (continued)

GENERALLY ACCEPTED ACCOUNTING PRINCIPLES

.48 Generally accepted accounting principles is the term used to describe the basis on which financial statements are normally prepared. There are special circumstances where a different basis of accounting may be appropriate, for example, in financial statements prepared in accordance with regulatory legislation or contractual requirements.

Generally accepted accounting principles encompass the Recommendations of this Handbook and those other accounting principles that have gained general acceptance. An accounting principle not covered by the Recommendations of the Handbook is considered to have gained general acceptance when it is actually being used in similar circumstances by a significant number of enterprises in Canada.

.49 Where there is no generally accepted accounting principle for a transaction or event, accounting principles will be developed, using judgment, through the application of the concepts contained in this Section and by referring to other sources including the following:

- the Handbook;
- practice in analogous situations;
- Accounting guidelines published by the CICA Accounting Standards Steering Committee;
- International Accounting Standards published by the International Accounting Standards Committee;
- standards published by bodies authorized to establish financial accounting standards in other jurisdictions;
- CICA research studies; and
- other sources of accounting literature such as text books and journals.

Review of this material may also help determine whether an accounting principle is generally accepted.

.50 In those rare circumstances where following a Handbook Recommendation would result in misleading financial statements, generally accepted accounting principles encompass appropriate alternative principles.

Reprinted with permission. From Section 1000, "Financial Statement Concepts," from the *CICA Handbook*, the Canadian Institute of Chartered Accountants, Toronto, Canada.

PART THREE

MEASUREMENT AND REPORTING ISSUES OF FINANCIAL STATEMENT COMPONENTS

CASH, TEMPORARY INVESTMENTS, AND RECEIVABLES: THE LIQUID ASSETS

CHAPTER OUTLINE

- Liquidity
- Cash
- Internal Control Considerations for Cash
- The Bank Statement
- Summary of Accounting for Cash
- Temporary Investments
- Accounts Receivable
- Notes Receivable
- Illustration of Balance Sheet Presentation

LIQUIDITY

Liquidity
The ease with which assets can be converted into cash.

insolvent company
A company that is unable to pay debts as they come due.

Liquidity is essential for business operations. An **insolvent company**, one that cannot pay its bills and meet its commitments as they mature, will not survive no matter how large its shareholders' equity. Most bankrupt companies show positive shareholders' equity on their balance sheets at the time of bankruptcy. Bankruptcy is usually caused by an inability to meet debts as they come due. One of the most famous bankruptcies in Canada occurred when the Atlantic Acceptance Corporation Limited was placed in bankruptcy. It had almost $133 million of assets, financed by $117 million of debts and $16 million of shareholders' equity. Nevertheless, the company became insolvent because it could not meet a $5 million cheque. More recently, we have witnessed the near-bankruptcy of one of the world's largest companies, Canadian-based Olympia & York. This company, which is reputed to control about $15 billion in real estate, was unable to meet a $20 million interest payment. This precipitated a worldwide banking crisis that resulted in one hundred international bankers meeting in Toronto to discuss ways of rescheduling the company's debt. O & Y survived only because the banking community decided that it was just too large to fail. Other companies were not so fortunate. The global recession that began in 1989 caused an unprecedented number of bankruptcies in Canada. The message is clear — liquidity must take precedence over profitability to guarantee corporate survival.

"Money-like assets" are an important determinant of a firm's liquidity. Cash, temporary investments, accounts receivable, and notes receivable are the principal liquid assets of a business. These assets are generally stated at their current cash, or cash-equivalent, values on the balance sheet. This chapter explores various inclusion and valuation questions related to each of these liquid assets. The objective of the chapter is to present the methods of accounting and reporting for money-like assets so that assessments can be made of a firm's liquidity at a moment in time and changes in that liquidity over time.

CASH

Cash is the most liquid asset. It is also the most vulnerable because of its susceptibility to theft or embezzlement. Accordingly, this chapter discusses not only the accounting requirements for cash, but also the key internal control procedures that should be in place to protect this asset.

CASH INCLUSIONS AND VALUATION

To be counted as cash on the balance sheet, an item should be freely available for use as a medium of exchange. *Coins, currency, travellers' cheques,* and *undeposited cheques* qualify. Most cash is cash in the bank in the form of *demand deposits* and *savings accounts*. Although banks can restrict the immediate withdrawal of funds from savings accounts and term deposits, these items are usually sufficiently available for use as a medium of exchange to be included in cash. Cash includes *foreign currency* unless a firm's ability to use the currency is severely restricted. For example, foreign currency held by a division located in a country that forbids the outflow of funds would not be included. Also, funds set aside or restricted for a particular purpose would not be included. For example, firms are often required to establish **sinking funds** to retire outstanding debt. The cash in a sinking fund appears as Investments, rather than in Cash, on the balance sheet.

sinking funds
Cash and other assets accumulated and segregated for some specific purpose such as retiring debt.

The Cash account should exclude compensating balances. When a company borrows money from the bank, it may be asked to maintain a minimum specified balance in its bank account at all times. This compensating balance, in effect, reduces the amount of money available to the firm. Restricted balances such as these should be separately shown in Current or Noncurrent Assets, depending on the maturity date of the borrowings they support.

Once an item meets the criteria to be included in cash, there are few valuation problems. Cash is normally stated at its face amount. Foreign currency must be translated to its Canadian dollar-equivalent amount using the exchange rate in effect on the date of the balance sheet.

CASH MANAGEMENT

The management of cash involves two distinct goals. First, a firm establishes a system of internal controls to ensure that cash is safeguarded from theft or embezzlement. Typical internal control procedures include the separation of duties of individuals handling cash receipt and disbursement, depositing cash receipts immediately, disbursing cash only by authorized cheques, and preparing bank account reconciliations regularly.

Second, management wants to regulate cash balances so that neither too much nor too little cash is available at any time. Cash on hand or in chequing accounts generally does not earn interest. In fact, during inflationary periods, idle cash loses purchasing power and thus decreases in real value. A firm does not want to maintain excessive cash balances. On the other hand, a firm does not want to be short of cash and unable to meet its obligations as they become due or unable to take advantage of cash discounts.

A weekly or monthly budget of cash receipts and disbursements aids cash management. Such a budget indicates both the amounts and times when excess cash will be available for investment or when additional borrowing will become necessary.

INTERNAL CONTROL CONSIDERATIONS FOR CASH

CONTROLLING CASH RECEIPTS AND DISBURSEMENTS

The system for controlling cash receipts should be designed to ensure that all money collected for the firm benefits the firm. In most businesses, collections are received primarily through the mail in the form of bank cheques or in currency for cash sales. The need to control the collections of currency and coins is obvious. All collections for cash sales should be recorded promptly, either in a cash register or some other device that both records the receipts and locks in the amount of the collection. Other kinds of collections are more susceptible to mishandling because they occur less often. These include receipts from the sale of assets not normally intended to be sold, receipts from dividends and interest on investments, collections on notes receivable, proceeds of bank loans, and proceeds of share or bond issues.

DISCUSSION CASE 14

In-House Thieves

Few people, from corporate executives on down, realize how big employee theft is. The fact is, it's a crime that amounts to 1% of the Gross National Product, and just (continued)

(continued)

about every employee this side of sainthood will commit it some time during his or her working life. Moreover, employee theft accounts for 80% of all crime against corporations.

Security experts divide internal crime into three categories — the theft of things such as raw materials, finished products, cash, and tools; the theft of information; and fraud.

The theft of raw materials occurs primarily in the manufacturing and construction businesses. For a manufacturing firm, it most often occurs in the shipping and receiving or warehouse end of the operation, where controls are notoriously lax. With hundreds of shipments going in and out of a docking area each day, keeping an eye on materials is taxing, and the opportunity for theft astounding.

At construction sites, there are often hundreds of workers performing a wide variety of tasks and trucks coming and going with materials. It is relatively easy for an employee to slip off the job to nab some lumber, plasterboard, or insulating material and stash it in a pick-up truck, or to arrange for a commercial truck to pick up material and haul it away.

The illegal siphoning off of crude and refined oil plagues the oil industry. The measurement of how much oil goes into a tank is relatively imprecise, so employees are able, undetected, either to siphon oil from a storage tank or to pump only part of the oil in a tanker truck into a tank.

When it comes to the outright theft of money, banks are where the big action is. In one such instance, an employee in a bank's operations department fiddled with customer accounts entered in the bank computers and embezzled about $21 million in a two-year period before he was caught.

Theft of information, though less prevalent than the theft of objects or services, can be disastrous. The energy industry is a frequent target of such thefts. Seismic surveys and exploration data, which cost millions of dollars to collect, have been pilfered from major oil companies and sold to small independent drillers or to foreign concerns.

Fraudulent schemes are the most costly form of employee theft. "The creation of dummy or shell companies is on the upswing, and it is not especially difficult to arrange," says Errol M. Cook, a security expert. He tells of one executive who formed an "offshore" insurance company. This executive had the authority to place insurance, so he bought a policy from the dummy company and pocketed the premiums. Cook notes that "where phony insurance companies are used, the type of insurance placed is usually where claims would not be occurring — officers' and directors' liability and bonding insurance, for example."

Employees in a payroll department can easily rip off a company. At one hospital, a worker added the names of two friends to the payroll and managed to funnel $40,000 their way before she was caught.

(continued)

(continued)

The most distressing thing about employee theft, security experts say, is that companies make it so easy. They leave valuable items unlocked or do not check to see that supplies actually exist. "It is just astounding the number of ... corporations ... that have woefully inadequate security systems. I should know, because many of them are my clients," says August Bequai, a lawyer, author, and consultant in the area of corporate security.

References

Reprinted with permission. From *Business Month* Magazine (October 1982), copyright 1982 by Goldhirsh Group Inc., 38 Commercial Wharf, Boston, MA 02110.

Discussion Question

To what extent should relationships with employees be based on trust? What are the alternatives to trusting your employees completely?

One way to provide effective control of cash receipts would be to maintain duplicate sets of records, each under separate supervision. But doing so would be expensive. The business need not undertake this expensive control device, however, if it (1) designs its cash-handling techniques so that the monthly statement received from its bank effectively serves as a duplicate record and (2) separates the functions of cash handling and record-keeping. To use the bank statement as an effective cash-controlling device requires that all receipts be deposited promptly and all disbursements be made by cheque.

Undeposited Cash

If a firm follows the desirable practice of depositing all receipts intact each day, disbursements will usually be made only from chequing accounts. A daily record of cash on hand is desirable. Cash registers facilitate the accumulation of such cash data. There are many types, but the usual cash register is a combination of a cash drawer and a multiple-register adding machine. The transactions are normally entered by hand. Then, they are recorded and accumulated by the register so that at the end of the day, the totals are available for each of several divisions of the day's activities — the total cash sales (sometimes classified according to products or departments), total collections on account, and total sales of each salesperson.

Cash registers are being increasingly replaced by combination cash register/computer terminals, which are called point-of-sale (POS) systems. When such systems are used with bar-code scanners, the sales, cash, and inventory records are updated automatically at the time of each transaction.

Cash in Bank — Deposits

A deposit slip provides the information for preparing the journal entry to record the deposit of cash funds in the chequing account. The deposit slip should be prepared in duplicate; the bank keeps the original and the firm keeps the duplicate. The duplicate is often initialled by the bank teller and used as a receipt for the deposit of the funds. The total on the deposit slip is entered in a journal as a debit to Cash in Bank and a credit to Cash on Hand.

Cash in Bank — Issuance of Cheques

The information for the entry to record cheques drawn in payment of bills comes from the document authorizing the payment. The customary entry will be a debit to Accounts Payable and a credit to Cash in Bank.

Control of Disbursements by Cheque

All cash payments except for those of very small amounts should be made by cheque. The firm can thereby restrict the authority for payments to a few employees. Firms often provide further control by requiring that all cheques be signed by two employees. Another control device is the use of a Cash Disbursements Journal or Cheque Register in which all cheques issued are recorded. Using such a journal provides control because a single person, who is not allowed to authorize payments or to sign cheques, is responsible for recording all payments.

In any case, control over disbursements should ensure that:

1. Payments are made only by authorized persons.
2. Adequate records support each payment. Such records attest that disbursement was for goods and services procured by proper authority and actually received by the business. The records attest that payment is made in accordance with the purchase contract.
3. The transaction is entered properly in the formal account records.
4. Authorization of payment is separate from making payment, and recordkeeping is separate from both.

Petty Cash

It is inefficient for small payments to be made by cheque. Small payments may be made by cash and yet come within the cheque control system by the use of an **imprest petty cash fund**, operated as follows:

1. *Establishment of the fund*: A cheque is prepared for an amount that will provide for small cash payments for a reasonable time, and is cashed by the petty cash cashier responsible for the cash payments. The establishment of the fund is recorded by debiting Petty Cash and crediting Cash.
2. *Payments from fund*: When payments are made by the petty cash cashier, receipts or other memos are saved to show that the money was spent.
3. *Replenishment of fund*: When the cash in the fund is almost exhausted by payments, the receipts and memos are batched and totalled and reimbursement requested. A cheque will be made payable to the petty cash cashier for the total of the batched receipts and memos accompanying the request for replenishment. The cheque will be reported as a normal expenditure, with a debit to the appropriate expenses and a credit to Cash. When the cheque is cashed by the petty cash cashier, the cash in the fund will equal the amount on hand when the fund was established. If not, the petty cash fund will be replenished by the

imprest petty cash fund
A cash fund with a fixed balance that is replenished when depleted (e.g., payroll and petty cash).

amount required to restore it to its original balance, and the difference will be charged to a Cash Short and Over account.

Note that:

1. The only entry made in the petty cash account is to establish the fund or to change the total amount.
2. The petty cash cashier should have cash, receipts, and memos on hand equal to the amount of the fund.
3. The payments made by the petty cash cashier will not be recorded in the accounting records until the replenishment cheque is prepared.

For example, suppose Tworo Corp. established a petty cash fund of $100 on January 1. During January, $85 was spent on various items, such as postage and transportation. At month-end, the fund was replenished. The associated journal entries would be:

Petty Cash	$100	
Cash		$100
Miscellaneous Expenses	$ 85	
Cash		$ 85

If, at the end of February, there was $70 in expense receipts and $26 in cash, the replenishment entry would be:

Miscellaneous Expenses	$70	
Cash Short and Over	4	
Cash		$74

THE BANK STATEMENT

At the end of each month (or other regular intervals), the bank sends a statement together with the cancelled cheques that have been paid and deducted from the depositor's account, and memorandums of any other additions or deductions that have been made by the bank. When the bank statement is received, it should be compared promptly with the record of deposits, cheques drawn, and other bank items on the records of the firm.

The balance shown on the bank statement will rarely correspond to the balance of the Cash in Bank account. The two basic causes of the difference are *time lag* and *errors*. In the normal course of business activities, some items will have been recorded by either the bank or the firm without having reached the recording point on the other set of records; hence, there is a *time lag* difference. Causes of such differences include cheques outstanding (that is, cheques recorded by the drawing firm but not yet received by the bank on which they were drawn), deposits made just before the bank statement date that do not appear on the bank statement, and transactions (such as service charges and collections of notes or drafts) that have not been recorded on the firm's books. The other basic difference is caused by errors in recordkeeping by either the firm or the bank. The process of comparing the bank statement with the books is known as *reconciling* the bank account, and the schedule that is prepared to demonstrate the results of the comparing is called a **bank reconciliation**. Exhibit 6.1 shows a typical reconciliation.

EXHIBIT 6.1
LIPSCOMB CORPORATION
Bank Reconciliation
National Bank
April 1

Balance shown on bank statement, April 1		$3,941.43[a]
Deposits of March 30 and 31, not yet recorded by bank		753.25
Cheque of F. Lipscomb deducted by bank in error		102.00
		$4,796.68
Outstanding cheques:		
#2443	$ 79.67	
#2459	242.53	
#2471	131.26	
#2472	32.44	
#2473	243.55	
Less: Total outstanding cheques		(729.45)
Adjusted bank balance[a]		$4,067.23
Balance shown on books, April 1		$3,588.23
Items unrecorded on books:		
Collection of note of J.B. Ball:		
Face amount of note	$500.00	
Less collection charge	(15.00)	485.00
Less: Bank service charge for March		(24.00)
Adjusted book balance before correction of errors		$4,049.23
Cheque #2467 for $268.81 was entered in the cheque register		
as $286.81. It was issued in March to pay a bill for office		
equipment		18.00
Adjusted book balance[b]		$4,067.23

[a]Although most calculations in this book are rounded off to the nearest dollar, the bank reconciliation is one area in which cents are important. Lack of perfect balance is often symptomatic of counterbalancing errors.
[b]This is the amount that would be shown in the Cash in Bank account if a balance sheet were prepared as of April 1.

bank reconciliation
A procedure or analysis explaining the various items — such as deposits in transit, cheques outstanding, bank charges, and errors — that lead to differences between the balance shown on a bank statement and the related Cash account in the general ledger.

PREPARING THE BANK RECONCILIATION

The bank reconciliation explains the difference between the book balance of Cash in Bank and the bank's statement of the firm's cash on deposit. It indicates the required adjustments of the firm's accounts. If the bank statement is used as a control device, the bank reconciliation is the final step in the monthly procedure for controlling cash receipts and disbursements. The bank reconciliation provides a convenient summary of the adjusting entries that must be made by the firm to account for previous errors in recording cash-related transactions or for cash transactions that have not yet been recorded.

Preparing the bank reconciliation typically involves the following steps:

1. Enter at the top of the reconciliation the balance as shown on the bank statement.

2. Enter next any deposits that have not been recorded on the bank statement. Such items usually occur because the bank has prepared the statement before the deposits for the last day or two have been recorded. If there are any time or date breaks in the list of deposits for the period, the bank should be notified promptly.

3. Enter any other adjustments to the bank's balance, such as errors by the bank in recording cancelled cheques or deposits, or the return of cheques belonging to some other customer of the bank. Errors on bank statements are infrequent.

4. Obtain a subtotal.

5. List the outstanding cheques. A list should be prepared, beginning with the cheques still outstanding from the previous period and continuing with the cheques outstanding that were drawn during the current period.

6. Deduct the sum of the outstanding cheques from the subtotal obtained in step (4). The balance is the adjusted bank balance — the balance that would be shown on the bank statement if all deposits had been entered, all cheques written had been returned, and no errors had been made; it is the final figure for this first section of the statement.

7. Enter the Cash in Bank account balance as shown on the books on the bank statement date.

8. Add or deduct any errors or omissions that have been disclosed in the process of reviewing the items returned by the bank. These will include such items as company errors in recording deposits or cheques, cheques that have not been entered in the cheque register, and service charges and collection fees deducted by the bank.

9. The net result is the adjusted book balance, and it must correspond to the adjusted bank balance derived in the first section. If it does not, the search must be continued for other items that have been overlooked.

ADJUSTING ENTRIES FROM THE BANK RECONCILIATION

The bank reconciliation shows two distinct kinds of differences:

1. Differences between the balance shown on the bank statement and the adjusted bank balance.

2. Differences between the account balance on the firm's books and the adjusted book balance.

Only the second type of difference requires entries on the firm's books. Any deposits not credited by the bank will presumably have been recorded by the time the reconciliation is prepared and, in any event, represent funds that the depositor may assume are in the bank and available for use.

DISCUSSION CASE 15

The Paperless Society

Billions of paper cheques are written each year by businesses and individuals. The costs of processing this large volume of cheques have motivated financial institutions to develop systems for transferring funds among parties electronically, without the need for paper cheques. The exchange of cash through such a system is called *electronic funds transfer (EFT)*.

A typical example of EFT is the payment of a payroll. An employer firm obtains authorizations from its employees to deposit their payroll cheques directly to their chequing accounts. The firm then sends to the bank a magnetic tape coded with the appropriate payroll data. The bank's computer processes the magnetic tape, deducts the total payroll amount from the firm's chequing account, and adds each employee's payroll amount to his or her chequing account.

Banks are attempting to introduce EFT into retailing in situations in which customers typically pay for goods with a cheque at the time of purchase. At the checkout counter, the customer uses a plastic card to activate a computer terminal connected with the bank. These cards are referred to as *debit cards*. Funds to pay for the groceries are immediately transferred from the customer's chequing account to the store's account at the bank. This procedure not only eliminates the cost of processing the paper cheques for the bank, but also eliminates the risk of bad cheques for the grocery store. So far, Canadian consumers have been more resistant than American consumers to the use of debit cards.

The use of EFT will increase with the development of expanded computer networks capable of handling electronic funds transfers. The specific controls over cash transactions handled through EFT, of course, may vary from the internal control procedures under a paper cheque system. However, adequate controls are no less important in an electronic funds transfer system.

Some people foresee these debit cards entirely replacing cheques in the future. This is part of the movement to what has been called the "paperless society." An advanced version of this card is now being tested by the banks. It incorporates a keyboard on the card and an internal memory. With each use, the individual can see the current balance, a history of past transactions, and so on.

The major factor standing in the way of the paperless society is consumer fear of outside control over their cash balances. For example, there is currently a controversy over the limit of bank responsibility if an automated teller banking machine short-changes a user. The banks claim this is impossible, but there have been newspaper reports of Canadians complaining to the banks

(continued)

Entries must be made for all of the differences between the cash balance on the books and the adjusted book balance, because they represent errors or omissions. The reconciliation illustrated in Exhibit 6.1 requires adjustments for bank service charges, for the collection of a note, and for the cheque whose amount was incorrectly recorded. (The bank must, of course, correct any error on its books when the mistake is called to its attention.) The entries would be:

Bank Service Charge Expense	$ 24	
Cash in Bank		$ 24
Service charges for month of March.		
Cash in Bank	$485	
Collection Expense	15	
Notes Receivable, J.B. Ball		$500
Note collected by bank.		
Cash in Bank	$ 18	
Accounts Payable		$ 18
To correct entry of cheque #2467.		

SUMMARY OF ACCOUNTING FOR CASH

Cash is an enterprise's most vulnerable resource. An internal control system is essential to the proper management of cash, and the monthly bank statement serves as a major control. Using the bank statement as an effective control device requires depositing receipts daily and making all disbursements by cheque or through petty cash funds. By this means, the bank reconciliation serves as a control device, because the bank record will reflect the cash inflows and outflows of the enterprise.

TEMPORARY INVESTMENTS

A business may find itself with more cash than it needs for current and near-term business purposes. Rather than allow cash to remain unproductive, the business may invest some of its current excess cash in income-yielding securities, such as Canadian government bonds and treasury bills, or shares or bonds of other companies. The interest or dividends generated by these securities provide more income than the company would gain by leaving the money in the bank. Such liquid assets appear under the caption of **Temporary Investments** in the Current Asset section of the balance sheet.

A business may also acquire securities with the intention of holding them for a longer period. Such securities are treated as *long-term investments*. Thus, the classification of a security as a current or noncurrent asset is a function of management's intentions. This section considers the classification and valuation of securities held temporarily. Securities intended to be held for a longer period are considered in Chapter 12.

Temporary Investments Investments of idle cash that are readily convertible into cash on short notice should the need arise. Also called marketable securities.

CLASSIFICATION OF TEMPORARY INVESTMENTS

Securities are classified as Temporary Investments among current assets as long as they can be readily converted into cash *and* management intends to do so when it needs cash. Securities that do not meet both of these criteria are included under Long-Term Investments on the balance sheet.

Example 1 Morrissey Manufacturing Corporation invested $150,000 of temporary excess funds in Canada Treasury Bills. The bills mature in three months. This investment appears among temporary investments, because the bills can be sold at any time and, even if not sold, the cash will be collected within three months.

Example 2 Suppose that Morrissey Manufacturing Corporation had acquired twenty-year bonds of Greer Electronics Limited instead of the Canada Treasury Bills. Its intent in acquiring the bonds was the same as before: the investment of temporary excess cash. These bonds would similarly be classified as temporary investments, if they could readily be traded in an established marketplace.

Example 3 West Corporation acquired 10 percent of the outstanding shares of Haskell Corporation on the open market for $10 million. West Corporation plans to hold these shares as a long-term investment. Even if the shares of Haskell Corporation were readily marketable, they would not be classified as temporary investments, because West Corporation does not intend to turn the securities into cash within a reasonably short period. These securities appear as Long-Term Investments on the balance sheet.

In published financial statements, all securities properly classified as Temporary Investments appear together on a single line on the balance sheet. However, when temporary investments include holdings of securities issued by affiliated companies, these should be set out separately.

VALUATION OF TEMPORARY INVESTMENTS

Temporary investments are initially recorded at acquisition cost. Acquisition cost includes the purchase price plus any commissions, taxes, and other costs incurred. For example, if temporary investments were acquired for $10,000 plus $300 for commissions and taxes, the entry would be:

Temporary Investments	$10,000	
Cash		$10,300

Dividends on temporary investments become revenue when declared. Interest revenue is recognized when it is earned.[1] Assuming that a dividend of $250 was declared and $300 of interest was earned on temporary investments and these amounts were immediately received in cash, the entry is:

Cash	$550	
Dividend Revenue		$250
Interest Revenue		300

There is nothing unusual about the valuation of temporary investments at the date of acquisition or the recording of dividends and interest. The valuation of temporary investments after acquisition, however, departs from strict historical cost accounting.

LOWER OF COST AND MARKET

The *CICA Handbook* requires that "when the market value of temporary investments has declined below the carrying value, they should be carried at market value." This statement is a specific way of saying that marketable securities should be valued at the **lower of cost and market**. Under the lower of cost and market method, decreases in the market value of securities are recognized as holding losses each period as the decreases occur, even though a market transaction has not taken place.

The lower of cost and market may be interpreted as either the lower of individual cost and market, or the lower of aggregate cost and market.

Lower of Individual Cost and Market

The lower of cost and market rule is based on the concept of conservatism that requires a company to "provide for all losses but anticipate no profits." Once a loss has been provided for by reducing the carrying value of a security to market value, when lower than cost, the reduced carrying value will never be increased. When the security is sold, the gain on the sale will be calculated by comparing the proceeds to this carrying value.

Example 4   Wolfson Limited acquired temporary investments during Year 3 as shown in Exhibit 6.2.[2] The entry to record the acquisition of shares of A Ltd., B Ltd., and C Ltd. during Year 3 is:

Temporary Investments (A Ltd.)	$50,000	
Temporary Investments (B Ltd.)	30,000	
Temporary Investments (C Ltd.)	20,000	
Cash		$100,000

lower of cost and market
An accounting procedure providing for inventories or temporary investments to be carried at the balance sheet date at their acquisition price or not-realizable value, whichever is lower.

---

[1] This reflects application of the accrual concept. For convenience, many firms wait until receipt of the interest or dividend cheque. As long as the impact on revenues is not materially different, such treatment is acceptable.

[2] In reality, a firm holding these securities for four years would likely classify them as portfolio investments, a noncurrent asset. For purposes of illustration, we have shown the accounting for a portfolio of temporary investments over several years.

EXHIBIT 6.2
Data for Illustration of Accounting for Temporary Investments of Wolfson Limited

Security	Date Acquired	Acquisition Cost	Market Value			
			Dec. 31, Year 6	Dec. 31, Year 5	Dec. 31, Year 4	Dec. 31, Year 3
A Ltd.	4/1/Year 3	$ 50,000	$43,000	$52,000	$54,000	$53,000
B Ltd.	6/1/Year 3	30,000	—	—ᵃ	22,000	27,000
C Ltd.	8/1/Year 3	20,000	—ᵇ	24,000	23,000	16,000
Total		$100,000	$43,000	$76,000	$99,000	$96,000

ᵃHoldings of B Ltd. sold during Year 5 for $32,000.
ᵇHoldings of C Ltd. sold during Year 6 for $17,000.

Holding Loss

At the end of Year 3, the market value of the shares of A Ltd. increased from the date of purchase, but the market value of the shares of B Ltd. and C Ltd. declined. Applying the lower of cost and market rule, a writedown of $7,000 is required to recognize the **holding loss** on the investment in shares of B Ltd. and C Ltd. The entry to record the writedown is:

Holding Loss on Temporary Investmentsᵃ	$7,000	
Temporary Investment (B Ltd.)		$3,000
Temporary Investment (C Ltd.)		4,000
To record the reduction in carrying value of investments to market value.		

ᵃAn alternative way of recording this is to create a **valuation allowance**, instead of writing down the asset directly. Valuation allowances are used commonly with receivables. The benefit of the allowance method is that it preserves more information (the original carrying value of the asset).

holding loss
The decline in market (replacement) cost of inventory below its acquisition cost. Under GAAP, such losses are realized when a lower of cost and market comparison is performed.

valuation allowance
An allowance netted against an asset to reflect a potential loss in its value.

The holding loss appears in the income statement for Year 3 as a reduction of financial income.[3] The Temporary Investments are presented in the December 31, Year 3 balance sheet, valued at the lower of cost and market of $93,000 (= $50,000 + $27,000 + $16,000). The market value of $96,000 will be noted.

During Year 4, the market value of B Ltd. shares declined and the market value of A Ltd. and C Ltd. shares increased. To recognize the unrealized holding loss of $5,000 (= $27,000 − $22,000) on the shares of B Ltd., a writedown of $5,000 is required. The entry is:

Holding Loss on Temporary Investments	$5,000	
Temporary Investment (B Ltd.)		$5,000

[3] For income tax purposes, losses (or gains) are reported only when realized, generally by sale.

The increase in the market value of the shares of A Ltd. and C Ltd. will not be recorded. At the end of Year 4, the temporary investments have an original cost of $100,000 (= $50,000 + $30,000 + $20,000) and a carrying value (lower of individual cost and market) of $88,000 (= $50,000 + $22,000 + $16,000). The cost has been decreased by a reduction of financial income of $7,000 in Year 3 and $5,000 in Year 4. The Temporary Investments would be shown on the December 31, Year 4 balance sheet at the carrying value of $88,000 with the market value of $99,000 noted.

Realized Gain Through Sale

During Year 5, the shares of B Ltd. are sold for $32,000, the market value of A Ltd. shares declined but remain above cost, and the market value of C Ltd. shares increased. When an individual temporary investment is sold, the realized gain or loss is the difference between the selling price and the carrying value. All gains or losses are considered holding gains and losses. The entry to record the sale is:

Cash	$32,000	
Temporary Investments (B Ltd.)		$22,000
Holding Gain on Temporary Investments		10,000

The gain on sale is a combination of the unrealized holding losses provided for in Year 3 and Year 4 of $8,000 (= $3,000 + $5,000) and the realized holding gain above cost of $2,000 (= $32,000 − $30,000). The gain on the sale of temporary investments would be included in financial income for Year 5.

At December 31, Year 5, the carrying value of the temporary investments is $66,000, consisting of the cost of A Ltd. shares of $50,000 and the lowest market value of C Ltd. shares of $16,000 at December 31, Year 3. Note that the market value of A Ltd. shares has consistently exceeded cost. *The carrying value of each investment is the lower of cost and market, where market is defined as the lowest year-end price since the shares were purchased.*

During Year 6, the market values of the shares of A Ltd. declined by $9,000 (= $52,000 − $43,000) and the shares of C Ltd. were sold for $17,000. The shares in C Ltd. had a carrying value of $16,000, which represents the cost of $20,000 less the unrealized holding loss during Year 3 of $4,000. The entry to record the sale of C Ltd. shares is:

Cash	$17,000	
Temporary Investments (C Ltd.)		$16,000
Holding Gain on Temporary Investments		1,000

The decline in market value of the shares of A Ltd. during Year 6 exceeds the net unrealized holding gains because acquisition at December 31, Year 5 of $2,000 (= $52,000 − $50,000) and the market value is below cost. To recognize the net unrealized holding loss of $7,000 (= $50,000 − $43,000) on the shares of A Ltd., a writedown is required. The entry is:

Holding Loss on Temporary Investments	$7,000	
Temporary Investments (A Ltd.)		$7,000

The Temporary Investments are shown on the December 31, Year 6 balance sheet at $43,000, the market value of the shares in A Ltd. Income from temporary investments is reduced by $6,000 (= $7,000 − $1,000) as a result of the unrealized loss from holding A Ltd. and the realized gain from the sale of shares of C Ltd.

Lower of Aggregate Cost and Market

The lower of aggregate cost and market is also based on the concept of conservatism. The lower of cost and market rule is applied to the total portfolio of temporary investments rather than to each security within the portfolio. The lower of aggregate cost and market is implemented either by adjusting the carrying value of each individual security to market value when aggregate market value is less than cost, or by establishing a contra account to the total portfolio of temporary investments, usually called Allowance for Decline in Temporary Investments. Using a separate contra account enables the simultaneous identification of both the acquisition cost and the amount of decline, if any, in the market value of the portfolio of temporary investments. Separate identification of the cost of individual investments is still required because, when a security is sold, the difference between the sale price and cost must be determined to record the gain or loss realized on sale. Realized gains and losses are computed from original cost. Realized losses are charged to the contra account. Realized gains are recorded in the income statement as financial income and are offset by any unrealized holding loss added to the contra account. If the realized loss exceeds the contra account balance, a loss will be recorded. The entries to record the lower aggregate cost and market value using a contra account, based on the data provided in Exhibit 6.2, are presented below.

Example 5 Wolfson Limited acquired temporary investments during Year 3 as shown in Exhibit 6.2. The entry to record the acquisition of the shares of A Ltd., B Ltd., and C Ltd. during Year 3 is:

Temporary Investments	$100,000	
Cash		$100,000

Unrealized Holding Loss

At the end of Year 3, the aggregate cost of the portfolio of temporary investments of $100,000 is $4,000 above the aggregate market value of $96,000. Applying the lower of cost and market rule, a provision of $4,000 is required. The entry is:

Holding Loss on Temporary Investments	$4,000	
Allowance for Decline in Temporary Investments		$4,000
To record the creation of an allowance account to reduce the carrying value of temporary investments to the lower of the aggregate cost or market.		

The loss account appears in the Year 3 income statement as a reduction of financial income, and the Temporary Investments are included in current assets at $96,000 (= $100,000 − $4,000).

Unrealized Holding Gain

During Year 4, the market value of the temporary investments increased, so that at December 31 the aggregate market value exceeds the carrying value by $3,000 [= $99,000 − ($100,000 − $4,000)]. Regardless of the absence of the need for the $4,000 balance in the contra account, the balance in the contra account remains unchanged because the Allowances for Decline cannot be reduced except through sale. No entry is recorded in Year 4, and the Temporary Investments are included in current assets as $96,000, unchanged from December 31, Year 3.

Realized Holding Gain Through Sale

During Year 5, a gain was realized on the sale of B Ltd. shares. The entry to record the sale of B Ltd. shares for $32,000 is:

Cash	$32,000	
Temporary Investments		$30,000
Holding Gain on Temporary Investments		2,000

The cost of temporary investments at December 31, Year 5 is $70,000 (= $50,000 + $20,000). The market value is $76,000 and the Allowance for Decline in Temporary Investments is $4,000. Because the market value exceeds cost, the Allowance for Decline in Temporary Investments is unnecessary. However, the balance in this account is reduced only for realized losses or on the ultimate disposal of all temporary investments. Consequently, no entry is made.

The gain appears in the Year 5 income statement as an addition to financial income. The Temporary Investments are included in current assets at their carrying value of $66,000 (= $50,000 + $20,000 − $4,000), with the market value of $76,000 noted.

Realized Holding Loss Through Sale

During Year 6, the market value of the shares of A Ltd. declined to $43,000 and the company sold the C Ltd. shares for $17,000.

The balance in the Allowance for Decline in Temporary Investments absorbs the loss on sale of C Ltd. shares. The entry to record the sale is:

Cash	$17,000	
Allowance for Decline in Temporary Investments	3,000	
Temporary Investments		$20,000

The balance in the Allowance account is now $1,000 (= $4,000 − $3,000), which is insufficient to reduce the investment in shares of A Ltd. (the remaining temporary investment) to its market value. To provide for this deficiency, the allowance account is increased to $7,000 (= $50,000 − $43,000). The entry to record this increase is:

Holding Loss on Temporary Investments	$6,000	
Allowance for Decline in Temporary Investments		$6,000

The loss account appears in the Year 6 income statement as a reduction in financial income and the Temporary Investments are included in current assets at $43,000 (= $50,000 − $7,000).

Evaluation of Alternatives

Exhibit 6.3 summarizes the financial statement effect of the two alternative methods of determining and recognizing the holding gains and losses on

EXHIBIT 6.3
Items in Income Statement and Balance Sheet of Wolfson Limited Illustrating Transactions in Marketable Securities as Temporary Investments — Current Assets Under Two Alternatives

	Year 6	Year 5	Year 4	Year 3	Total
Alternative 1: Individual Cost or Market					
Excerpts from Income Statement for Year					
Dividends Earned (Assumed)	$ 6,000	$ 8,000	$10,000	$10,000	$34,000
Holding Gain (Loss) on Temporary Investments	(6,000)	10,000	(5,000)	(7,000)	(8,000)
Financial Income from Temporary Investments	$ —	$18,000	$ 5,000	$ 3,000	$26,000
Balance Sheet Item at Year-End					
Temporary Investments at Lower of Cost and Market	$43,000	$66,000	$88,000	$93,000	
(Market Value)	$43,000	$76,000	$99,000	$96,000	
Alternative 2: Aggregate Cost or Market					
Excerpts from Income Statement for Year					
Dividends Earned (Assumed)	$ 6,000	$ 8,000	$10,000	$10,000	$34,000
Holding Gain (Loss) on Temporary Investments	(6,000)	2,000	—	(4,000)	(8,000)
Financial Income from Temporary Investments	$ —	$10,000	$10,000	$ 6,000	$26,000
Balance Sheet Item at Year-End					
Temporary Investments at Lower of Cost and Market	$43,000	$66,000	$96,000	$96,000	
(Market Value)	$43,000	$76,000	$99,000	$96,000	

temporary investments and consequent balance sheet valuations. The lower of *individual* cost and market method represents the *more conservative* alternative because unrealized gains on some securities cannot offset unrealized losses on others.

A review of Exhibit 6.3 illustrates this statement. For each of Year 3 and Year 4, the lower of individual cost and market method reports the largest holding loss and the lowest balance sheet values, because the unrealized gain of A Ltd. shares cannot offset the unrealized losses in the other investments. In Year 5, both lower of cost and market alternatives report the same balance sheet values and the cumulative reductions in financial income over the three years. In Year 6, the balance sheet values reported under each alternative are the same, as the market value of the remaining security is below cost for the first time since it was purchased.

To provide full disclosure to financial statement users, the market value of temporary investments should be disclosed in addition to the carrying value.

ACCOUNTS RECEIVABLE

The third liquid asset this chapter considers is accounts receivable. Trade accounts receivable typically arise when goods or services are sold on account. The entry is:

Accounts Receivable	$250	
Sales Revenue		$250

Receivables sometimes also arise from transactions other than sales. For example, advances might be made to officers or employees; deposits might be made to guarantee performance or cover potential damages; or claims may be made against insurance companies, governmental bodies, common carriers, or others. These receivables are classified as either current assets or investments, depending on the expected collection date. This section focuses on trade accounts receivable, considering both their valuation and their management.

TRADE ACCOUNTS RECEIVABLE VALUATION

control account
A general ledger account, the balance of which reflects the aggregate balance of many related subsidiary accounts. Most firms maintain such records for accounts receivable and accounts payable.

Individual accounts receivable are initially recorded at the amount owed by each customer. The recording is made in a subsidiary ledger either as a manual accounting system (discussed in Chapter 3), or in a separately coded section of a computer memory bank. The sum of the amounts in individual customers' accounts appears in the master account, or **control account**, for Accounts Receivable. The Accounts Receivable account records the total of the amounts in individual customers' accounts.

The amount in the control account for Accounts Receivable is reduced for estimated uncollectable (doubtful) accounts, sales discounts, and sales returns and allowances. The reporting objective is to state accounts receivable at the amount expected to be collected in cash. The difference between the amounts owed by customers and the amounts expected to be collected in cash must be charged against revenue. According to the matching principle, the charge against revenue for expected uncollectable amounts, sales discounts, and sales returns and allowances is preferably made in the period when the sales occur. In this way, revenue and net income for a period will reflect the amounts expected to be collected for services rendered during the period.

RECEIVABLES MANAGEMENT

When a firm extends credit to customers, the possibility arises that one or more of them will not pay the money they owe. Usually, this occurs because the customer has liquidity problems — an inability to pay. In some cases, the customer is just unwilling to pay — because of a disagreement over the quality of goods and services received or because of dishonesty. Regardless of the reason, the firm must try to estimate at each balance sheet date the percentage of its receivables that will eventually turn out to be uncollectable. This is another example of the principle of conservatism — anticipate all losses, which result in current assets being carried at net realizable value.

Firms have some control over the amount of bad debt losses they will experience by:

1. The credit policy established.
2. The collection policy established.

The **credit policy** is a formal decision rule regarding which customers the firm will grant credit. A very liberal credit policy will boost sales but may also boost bad debts. A very stringent credit policy will have the reverse impact. Many firms will have a credit officer to judge whether potential customers should be granted credit. The objective for every firm is to find the ideal credit policy — that which maximizes net cash flow from sales.

credit policy
The policy that governs the conditions under which existing and potential customers shall be granted credit.

An aggressive collection policy can also reduce bad debts. Customers should be contacted as soon as the account is overdue. For balances long overdue, the use of a collection agency may be advisable.

These policies fall under the heading of receivables management. In general, firms that actively manage their receivables suffer fewer losses than firms that do not.

Firms use two methods of accounting for doubtful accounts: (1) the direct writeoff method and (2) the allowance method.

DIRECT WRITEOFF METHOD

The **direct writeoff method** recognizes losses from doubtful accounts in the period in which a specific customer's account is determined to be uncollectable. For example, if it is decided that the account receivable of John Mahoney for $200 has become uncollectable, the following entry will be made:

direct writeoff method
An accounting procedure in which uncollectable accounts are charged to expenses in the period they are determined to be uncollectable.

Bad Debts Expense	$200	
Accounts Receivable		$200
To record loss from an uncollectable customer's account.		

The direct writeoff method has three important shortcomings. First, the loss from doubtful accounts is usually not recognized in the period in which the sale occurs and revenue is recognized. Too much income is recognized in the period of sale and too little in the period of writeoff. Second, the amount of losses from doubtful accounts recognized in any period is susceptible to intentional misrepresentation, because it is difficult to decide when a particular account becomes uncollectable. Third, the amount of accounts receivable on the balance sheet does not reflect the amount of cash expected to be collected. The direct writeoff method is not appropriate when such losses are significant in amount, occur frequently, and are reasonably predictable. However, a firm that has not had any bad debts for several years would be able to justify using this method.

ALLOWANCE METHOD

allowance method
An accounting procedure whereby the related amount of uncollectable accounts expense is estimated and recorded in the contra asset account Allowance for Uncollectable Accounts in the period in which credit sales occur.

When amounts of uncollectables can be estimated with reasonable precision, GAAP require an alternative procedure, the **allowance method**. The allowance method involves:

1. Estimating the amount of uncollectable accounts that will occur over time in connection with the sales of each period.

2. Making an adjusting entry in the same period as the sales for the estimated uncollectable amount

3. Making a corresponding adjustment to the amount of accounts receivable so that the balance sheet figure reports the amount expected to be collected.

The entry involves a debit to Bad Debts Expense and a credit to Allowance for Doubtful Accounts, which is an account contra to the total of Accounts Receivable. The credit must be made to a contra account rather than to Accounts Receivable because no specific, individual account is being written off at the time of entry.[4] Because the Allowance for Doubtful Accounts is a contra to Accounts Receivable, its balance at the end of the period will be deducted from Accounts Receivable. Because it is assumed that an adequate allowance for doubtful accounts has been made in the absence of a contrary statement, it is not considered necessary to refer to such allowance. The Bad Debts Expense is normally shown as a Selling, or Administration, Expense.[5]

---

[4] Recall that Accounts Receivable is a "control" account showing the total of all amounts receivable from specific customers. There is a separate account for each customer in a subsidiary ledger; the Accounts Receivable account merely records their total.

[5] Views differ as to the type of account — expense or revenue contra — debited when providing for doubtful accounts. Many firms debit Bad Debts Expense and include its amount among total expenses on the income statement. Their rationale is that a certain amount of bad debts is a necessary "cost" of generating revenues. Advocates of using a revenue contra account point out that its use permits net sales to be shown at the amount of cash expected to be collected. When the provision is debited to an expense account and included among total expenses on the income statement, net sales will overstate the amount of cash expected to be received. More significantly, however, advocates of using a revenue contra account point out that uncollectable accounts cannot be an expense. Accounts that, at the time of recording, were not expected to be collected were never assets to begin with. Although the arguments for using a revenue contra account may be persuasive, Bad Debts Expense is the account debited in this book because that account is more widely used in practice. In either case, income remains the same.

To illustrate the allowance method, assume that 2 percent of the credit sales made during the current period are estimated never to be collected. If sales on account are $90,000, the entry to increase the expense and reduce the amount of Accounts Receivable to the amount expected to be collected would be:

Bad Debts Expense	$1,800	
Allowance for Doubtful Accounts		$1,800
To record the estimate of uncollectable accounts arising from		
current period's sales (0.02 × $90,000).		

When a particular customer's account is judged uncollectable, it is written off against the Allowance for Doubtful Accounts. If, for example, it is decided that a balance of $200 due from John Mahoney will not be collected, the entry to write off the account will be:

Allowance for Doubtful Accounts	$200	
Accounts Receivable		$200
To write off John Mahoney's account.		

The entry to write off specific accounts may be made during the period, as information about specific customers' accounts is obtained, or at the end of the period as an adjusting entry.

Assume that, subsequently, Mahoney wanted to reestablish his credit rating by paying the amount owed. The company would first reinstate the receivable balance by the entry:

Accounts Receivable	$200	
Allowance for Doubtful Accounts		$200
To reinstate J. Mahoney's account previously written off.		

Then, the company would record the cash receipt:

Cash	$200	
Accounts Receivable		$200
Payment on account by J. Mahoney.		

A notation would be made in the credit manager's files regarding Mahoney's payment of the account, and this would be considered in future decisions to grant Mahoney credit.

Under the allowance method, the expense for the period of sale is increased by the amount of uncollectables that is estimated to arise from that period's sales. Some time later, when the attempts at collection are finally abandoned, the specific account is written off. Net assets are not affected by writing off the specific account. The reduction in net assets took place earlier, when the Allowance for Doubtful Accounts was credited in the entry recognizing the estimated amount of eventual uncollectables.

ESTIMATING UNCOLLECTABLES

When the Allowance Method is used, accountants use two basic methods for calculating the amount of the adjustment for doubtful accounts: the percentage of sales method and the aging of accounts receivable method.

Percentage of Sales Method

percentage of sales method
A method of calculating the bad debt expense provision for the period on receivables by multiplying a historical loss rate times sales. An alternative is the aging method.

The easiest method in most cases is to multiply the total credit sales on account during the period by an appropriate percentage, because it seems reasonable to assume that doubtful account amounts will vary directly with the volume of credit business. The example on page 367 used the **percentage of sales method**. The percentage to be used is estimated by studying the experience of the business or by inquiring into the experience of similar enterprises. The rates found in use will generally be within the range of 0.25 percent to 2 percent of credit sales.

To illustrate, assume that total sales are $1,600,000, of which $1,500,000 are credit sales, and experience indicates that the appropriate percentage of doubtful accounts is 2 percent of credit sales. The entry is:

Bad Debts Expense	$30,000	
Allowance for Doubtful Accounts		$30,000
To provide for estimate of uncollectables computed		
as a percentage of sales.		

If cash sales occur in a relatively constant proportion of credit sales, the estimated uncollectables percentage, proportionately reduced, can be applied to the total sales for the period. The total amount of all sales may be more readily available than that for sales on account.

Aging of Accounts Receivable Method

aging the accounts
Classifying the accounts receivable by age for the purpose of identifying overdue accounts and/or establishing an allowance for uncollectable accounts.

A more time-consuming but more accurate method of calculating the amount of the adjustment, often called **aging the accounts**, involves classifying each customer's account as to the length of time for which the account has been uncollected. Common intervals used for classifying individual accounts receivable are:

1. Not yet due
2. Past due 30 days or less
3. Past due 31 to 60 days
4. Past due 61 to 180 days
5. Past due more than 180 days

The accountant then estimates the percentage of receivables for each interval that will eventually prove uncollectable. Presumably, the balance in the Allowance for Doubtful Accounts should be large enough to cover substantially all accounts receivable past due for more than 180 days and smaller portions of the more recent accounts. The actual portions are estimated from past experience.

As an example of the adjustment to be made, assume that the present balance in the Accounts Receivable account is $850,000 and the balance in the Allowance for Doubtful Accounts before the adjusting entry for the period is $36,000. An aging of the accounts receivable balance ($850,000), shown in Exhibit 6.4, results in an estimate that $68,000 of the accounts will probably become uncollectable. The adjustment requires that the Allowance for Doubtful Accounts balance be $68,000, an increase of $32,000. The adjusting entry at the end of the period is:

Bad Debts Expense	$32,000	
Allowance for Doubtful Accounts		$32,000
To increase Allowance account to $68,000 computed by		
an aging analysis: $68,000 − $36,000 = $32,000		

EXHIBIT 6.4
Illustration of Aging Accounts Receivable

Classification of Accounts	Amount	Estimated Uncollectable Percentage	Estimated Uncollectable Amounts
Not yet due	$680,000	0.5%	$ 3,400
1–30 days past due	60,000	6.0	3,600
31–60 days past due	30,000	25.0	7,500
61–180 days past due	50,000	50.0	25,000
Over 180 days past due	30,000	95.0	28,500
	$850,000		$68,000

Even when the percentage of sales method is used, aging the accounts should be done periodically as an occasional check on the accuracy of the percentage being used. If the aging analysis shows that the balance in the Allowance for Doubtful Accounts is apparently too large or too small, the percentage of sales to be charged to Bad Debts Expense can be lowered or raised so that the apparent error will work itself out through future adjustments.

When the percentage of sales method is used, the periodic provision for doubtful accounts (for example, $30,000) is merely added to the amounts provided in previous periods in the account, Allowance for Doubtful Accounts. When the aging method is used, the balance in the account, Allowance for Doubtful Accounts, is adjusted (for example, by $32,000) to reflect the desired ending balance. If the percentage used under the percentage of sales method reasonably reflects collection experience, the *balance* in the allowance account should be approximately the same at the end of each period under these two methods of estimating doubtful accounts. The two methods reflect different emphases for the financial statement. The percentage of sales method reflects an income statement focus, while the aging method is principally concerned with the proper balance sheet valuation.

Exhibit 6.5 illustrates the operation of the allowance method for uncollectables over two periods. In the first period, the percentage method is used. In the second period, the aging method is used. Normally, a firm would use the same method in all periods.

EXHIBIT 6.5
Review of the Allowance Method of Accounting for Doubtful Accounts

Transactions in the First Period:
(1) Credit sales are $1,000,000.
(2) Cash of $937,000 is collected from customers in payment of their accounts.
(3) At the end of the first period, it is estimated that uncollectables will be 2 percent of sales; 0.02 × $1,000,000 = $20,000.
(4) Specific accounts totalling $7,000 are written off as uncollectable.
(5) The bad debts expense and other temporary accounts are closed.

Transactions in the Second Period:
(6) Credit sales are $1,200,000.
(7) Specific accounts totalling $22,000 are written off during the period as information on their uncollectability becomes known. The debit balance of $9,000 will remain in the Allowance account until the adjusting entry is made at the end of the period; see (9).
(8) Cash of $1,100,000 is collected from customers in payment of their accounts.
(9) An aging of the accounts receivable shows that the amount in the Allowance account should be $16,000. The amount of the adjustment is $25,000. It is computed as the difference between the desired $16,000 credit balance and the current $9,000 debit balance in the Allowance account.
(10) The bad debts expense and other temporary accounts are closed.

Cash		Accounts Receivable			Allowance for Doubtful Accounts		
		(1) 1,000,000				20,000	(3)
(2) 937,000			937,000	(2)			
			7,000	(4)	(4) 7,000		
Bal. ?		Bal. 56,000				13,000	Bal.
		(6) 1,200,000					
			22,000	(7)	(7) 22,000		
(8) 1,100,000			1,100,000	(8)			
						25,000	(9)
Bal. ?		Bal. 134,000				16,000	Bal.

Bad Debts Expense			Sales Revenue		
(3) 20,000				1,000,000	(1)
	Closed	(5)	(5) Closed		
(9) 25,000				1,200,000	(6)
	Closed	(10)	(10) Closed		

TURNING RECEIVABLES INTO CASH

A firm may find itself temporarily short of cash and unable to borrow from its usual sources. In such instances, accounts receivable can be used to obtain funds. A firm may assign its accounts receivable to a bank or finance company to obtain a loan. The borrowing company physically maintains control of the accounts receivable, collects amounts remitted by customers, then forwards the proceeds to the lending institution. Alternatively, the firm may pledge its accounts receivable to the lending agency. If the borrowing firm is unable to make loan repayments when due, the lending agency has the power to sell the accounts receivable in order to obtain payment. Finally, the accounts receivable may be factored to a bank or finance company to obtain cash. In this case, the accounts receivable are, in effect, sold to the lending institution, which physically controls the receivables and collects payments from customers. If accounts receivable have been assigned or pledged, a footnote to the financial statements should indicate this fact. The collection of such accounts receivable will not increase the liquid resources available to the firm to pay general trade creditors. **Assigned receivables** and **pledged receivables** are still assets that show on the balance sheet, but **factored receivables** are considered to be sold unless there are **recourse provisions** that prevent sale recognition. Sale without recourse implies all future risks and rewards of ownership rest with the purchaser and title is deemed to have passed. Sale with recourse implies there are contingent obligations by the seller in case of default that might prevent sale recognition. For instance, if Omega Company factors a $1,000,000 receivable with recourse to Gamma Corporation which proves uncollectable, Omega must make restitution to Gamma.

NOTES RECEIVABLE

The last liquid asset considered in this chapter is notes receivable. Many business transactions involve written promises to pay sums of money at a future date. These written promises are called **promissory notes**. The holder of a promissory note has a liquid asset, notes receivable. A promissory note is a written contract in which one person, known as the **maker**, promises to pay to another person, known as the **payee**, a definite sum of money. The money may be payable either on demand or at a definite future date. A note may or may not provide for the payment of interest in addition to the principal amount.

Promissory notes are used most commonly in connection with obtaining loans at banks or other institutions, purchasing various kinds of property, and as a temporary settlement of an open or charge account balance when payment cannot be made within the usual credit period. A note may be secured by a mortgage on real estate (land and buildings) or personal property (machinery and merchandise), or by the deposit of specific collateral (*share certificates*, *bonds*, and so forth). If the **secured note** is not collected at maturity, the lender can take possession of the real estate, personal property, or other collateral, sell it, and apply the proceeds to the repayment of the note. Any proceeds in excess of the amount due under the note are then paid to the borrower. Alternatively, the note may be *unsecured*, in which case it has about the same legal status as an account receivable.

CALCULATION OF INTEREST REVENUE

Interest is the price paid for the use of borrowed funds. From the lender's point of view, it is revenue. The interest rate is usually expressed as a percentage of the principal, with the rate being stated on an annual basis. Because interest is a payment for the use of borrowed funds for a period

Assigned receivables
Receivables pledged as security for loans.

pledged receivables
Receivables earmarked as collateral for loans.

factored receivables
Receivables sold to a third party to raise immediate cash.

recourse provisions
The right to seek restitution from the original holder of a financial instrument if default occurs.

promissory notes
A written promise to pay a certain sum of money on demand or at a determinable future time.

maker
One who signs a note to borrow, or one who signs a cheque; in the latter context, synonymous with drawer.

payee
The person or entity to whom a cash payment is made or who will receive the stated amount of money on a cheque.

secured note
A financial instrument whose payment is backed by specified assets.

of time, it accrues with the passage of time. Although interest accrues every day (indeed, every time the clock ticks), firms usually record interest only at the time of payment or at the end of an accounting period.

Most short-term notes receivable from customers are based on **simple interest** calculations.[6] The general formula for the calculation of simple interest is:

$$\text{Interest} = \text{Principal} \times \text{Interest Rate} \times \text{Elapsed Time}$$

For example, the interest at the rate of 12 percent a year on $20,000 is $200 for one month, $400 for two months, $1,200 for six months, and so on. The calculation for shorter periods is complicated by the odd number of days in a year and the variations in the number of days in a month. Simple interest at the rate of 12 percent a year on $20,000 for 90 days would be $20,000 × 0.12 × 90/365, or $592, if an exact computation were made. For many purposes, especially the calculation of accrued interest, a satisfactory approximation of the correct interest can be obtained by assuming that the year has 360 days and that each month is one-twelfth of a year. Thus, 30 days is the equivalent of one month, and 60 days is the equivalent of two months, or one-sixth of a year. Under this method, the interest at 12 percent on $20,000 for 90 days would be the same as the interest for three months, or one-quarter of a year, or $600. Keep in mind that nearly all quotations of simple interest rates state the rate per year, unless some other period is specifically mentioned. In the formula for simple interest, Principal × Rate × Elapsed Time, "time" should be expressed in terms of years, or portions of a year, because the rate is the rate per year.

For the sake of uniformity and simplicity, we shall use the following rules in connection with the calculation of interest throughout the text and problems:

1. When the maturity terms are given in months, consider one month to be one-twelfth of a year, three months to be one-fourth of a year, six months to be half a year, and so on, regardless of the actual number of days in the period. This is equivalent to regarding any one-month period as being 30 days in a 360-day year.

2. When the maturity terms are given in days, use the 360-day year. Consider 30 days to be one-twelfth of a year, 60 days to be one-sixth of a year, 17 days to be 17/360 of a year, and so on. Calculate maturity dates and elapsed time by using the actual number of days.

ACCOUNTING FOR INTEREST-BEARING NOTES RECEIVABLE

Interest-bearing notes are those that indicate a face, or principal, amount together with explicit interest at a stated fair market rate for the time period stated in the note.[7] For example, the basic elements of such a note might read as follows: "Two months after date (June 30), the Suren Co. Ltd. promises to pay to the order of the Mullen Co. Inc. $3,000 with inter-

simple interest
Interest calculated on principal where interest earned during periods before maturity of the loan is neither added to the principal nor paid to the lender. Interest = Principal × Interest Rate × Time.

compound interest
Interest calculated on principal plus previously undistributed interest.

[6] Most long-term notes involve **compound interest**, which is discussed in Appendix A.

[7] Both noninterest-bearing notes, where the face amount is the same as the maturity value, and notes where the stated rate differs from the fair market rate involve compound interest calculations; Chapters 9 and 10 discuss them.

est from date at the rate of 12 percent per annum." At the maturity date, August 31, the maturity value would be the face amount of $3,000 plus interest of $60 calculated in accordance with the preceding discussion ($60 = $3,000 × 0.12 × 2/12), or a total of $3,060.

Among the transactions related to a note receivable discussed in this section are the following: receipt of note, interest recognition at an interim date, transfer before maturity, and collection at maturity date.

Receipt of Notes and Collection at Maturity

Promissory notes are usually received from customers in connection with sales or with the settlement of an open account receivable. The customer is usually the maker, but the customer may transfer a note that has been received from another. It is common practice to allow the customer full credit for the face value and accrued interest, if any, although a different value might be agreed upon in some instances.

If, on June 30, the Mullen Co. Inc. were to receive a 60-day, 12 percent note for $3,000, dated June 30, from the Suren Co. Ltd., to apply on its account, the entry would be:

June 30 Notes Receivable	$3,000	
Accounts Receivable		$3,000

Assuming that the accounting period of the Mullen Co. Inc. is the calendar year, the entry upon collection at maturity would be:

Aug. 31 Cash	$3,060	
Notes Receivable		$3,000
Interest Revenue		60

Assuming instead that the accounting period of the Mullen Co. Inc. is one month, the interest adjustment at the interim date, July 31, would be:

July 31 Interest Receivable	$30	
Interest Revenue		$30
($3,000 × 0.12 × 30/360 = $30)		

The entry upon collection at maturity would then be:

Aug. 31 Cash	$3,060	
Notes Receivable		$3,000
Interest Receivable		30
Interest Revenue		30

At the maturity date, the note may be collected (as illustrated above), renewed, partially collected with renewal of the balance, or dishonoured by the maker. These other possibilities involve more advanced accounting procedures and are not discussed in this book.

Transfer of Notes Receivable

To obtain cash, a note may be transferred to another party without recourse provisions. This procedure is equivalent to a sale of the note, because the transferor has no further liability even if the maker fails to pay at maturity.

If Mullen Co. Inc. transferred without recourse the two-month, 12 percent, $3,000 note to Lane Trust Company for $3,030 one month after the date of the note, the entry would be:

July 31 Cash	$3,030	
Notes Receivable		$3,000
Interest Revenue		30
To record transfer of note without recourse.		

Most businesses that "purchase" notes are, however, unwilling to acquire them without recourse. Such firms do not want to be responsible for investigating the credit-worthiness of the maker or for any collection efforts required for dishonoured notes. Consequently, most notes that are transferred are done so *with recourse*.

A transfer with recourse places a potential or "contingent" obligation on the transferor if the maker fails to pay at maturity. Such a transfer is not a completed transaction because of the possibility that the endorser will have to pay the note in case the maker defaults at maturity.

Chapter 9 discusses contingent obligations, such as those for notes transferred with recourse or for the potential loss arising from an unsettled damage suit. Contingent obligations do not appear in the accounts, but are merely disclosed in notes to the balance sheet.

If Mullen Co. Inc. transferred with recourse the 60-day, 12 percent $3,000 note to Lane Trust Company one month after the date of the note, the entry would be the same as if the note were transferred without recourse. If Mullen Co. Inc. prepared financial statements before Lane Trust Company collected from the maker, however, the notes to Mullen's balance sheet would contain a statement such as the following:

Contingencies. The firm is contingently liable for a note transferred and accrued interest thereon to the Lane Trust Company. The face value of the transferred note is $3,000.

ILLUSTRATION OF BALANCE SHEET PRESENTATION

The balance sheet accounts discussed in this chapter include Cash, Temporary Investments, Notes Receivable, and Accounts Receivable. Exhibit 6.6 illustrates the presentation of these items in the balance sheet, which includes all of the current assets for the Alexis Co. Ltd. as of June 30, Year 6.

EXHIBIT 6.6
Detailed Illustration of Current Assets on the Balance Sheet
Alexis Co. Ltd. Balance Sheet (Excerpts)
June 30, Year 6 and Year 5

	June 30, Year 6	June 30, Year 5
Current Assets:		
Petty Cash Funds	$ 1,000	$ 800
Cash in Bank	14,500	12,500
Term Deposits	8,000	7,500
Temporary Investments at Acquisition Cost	$30,000	$25,000
Less: Allowance for Excess of Cost of Temporary Investments over Market Value (on June 30, Year 5, market value of $31,000 exceeds cost)	(3,000)	—
Temporary Investments at Lower of Cost and Market	27,000	25,000
Notes Receivable (See Note A)	12,000	10,000
Interest and Dividends Receivable	500	400
Accounts Receivable	54,500	53,700
Merchandise Inventory*	72,000	67,000
Prepayments	4,800	4,300
Total Current Assets	$194,300	$181,200

Note A. The amount shown for Notes Receivable does not include notes with a face amount of $2,000 that have been discounted with recourse at the First National Bank. The company is contingently liable for these notes, should the makers not honour them at maturity. The estimated amount of our liability is zero.

Additional required disclosures for this item omitted here. See Chapter 7.

SUMMARY

This chapter has examined the accounting for cash and other liquid, or cash-like, assets. Among the questions addressed were the following:

1. What items are included in each of the liquid asset accounts?
2. At what amount are they stated?

KEY TERMS

Liquidity
Insolvent company
Sinking funds
Imprest petty cash fund
Bank reconciliation
Temporary Investments
Lower of cost and market
Holding loss
Valuation allowance
Control account
Credit policy
Direct writeoff method
Allowance method

Percentage of sales method
Aging the accounts
Assigned receivables
Pledged receivables
Factored receivables
Recourse provisions
Promissory notes
Maker
Payee
Secured note
Simple interest
Compound interest

SELF-STUDY MATERIAL

This section contains questions, exercises, and problems to help you assess your understanding of Chapter 6. Careful review of this material will assist you in completing the homework assignments. Solutions are located at the end of the section.

QUESTIONS AND EXERCISES

True/False

For each statement, place a T or an F in the space provided to indicate whether the statement is true or false.

_____ 1. Generally accepted accounting principles are the accounting methods and procedures used by firms in preparing their financial statements.

_____ 2. In accounting, there is a structure of definitions and concepts that can be used unambiguously to develop accounting principles.

_____ 3. The Parliament of Canada has taken the lead in developing accounting principles during the last ten years.

_____ 4. The major agency within the accounting profession for developing accounting principles is currently the Accounting Standards Board of the CICA.

_____ 5. Liquid assets are generally stated at their cash, or cash-equivalent, value on the balance sheet.

_____ 6. Bank savings accounts that have restrictions on their immediate withdrawal are treated as cash on the balance sheet.

_____ 7. Cash in a bond sinking fund is treated as a long-term investment.

_____ 8. To control cash disbursements properly, all payments should be made by cheque, except for various immaterial items that may be handled through a petty cash or change fund.

_____ 9. The appearance of the Allowance for Doubtful Accounts on the balance sheet indicates the use of the direct writeoff method.

_____ 10. Simple interest on a note is calculated by multiplying the principal amount of the note by the stated interest rate and multiplying this amount by the period of time for which the note is to be outstanding.

_____ 11. All investments in income-yielding securities are classified as current assets.

_____ 12. All temporary investments must be valued at the lower of cost and market.

_____ 13. The valuation of a portfolio of temporary investments at the lower of aggregate cost and market will usually be lower than the valuation at the lower of individual cost and market.

_____ 14. When the market value of a temporary investment exceeds its cost, the company must record a holding gain.

_____ 15. The account Allowance for Excess of Cost of Temporary Investments over Market Value must always have either a zero or credit balance.

_____ 16. The method of accounting for doubtful accounts that recognizes a loss when a customer's account has clearly been demonstrated to be uncollectable is the direct writeoff method.

_____ 17. One method of obtaining cash from accounts receivable is to pledge the accounts, a method that is equivalent to a sale.

_____ 18. Temporary investments are considered to be a firm's most liquid assets.

_____ 19. A realized loss can only occur when a security is sold, or when it is transferred from a current to a long-term classification (or vice versa).

_____ 20. A firm may report realized losses but not realized gains when accounting for temporary investments.

_____ 21. For all firms, the optimal amount of bad debts is zero.

_____ 22. When accounts are formally written off the books under the allowance method, the current assets are reduced.

_____ 23. Cash Discounts are treated as a contra to Sales Revenue.

_____ 24. If a company has deposits in transit at the end of the period, no adjusting entry should be made by the company to correct its records.

_____ 25. The control of cash receipts should be designed to ensure that all collections are deposited in the bank intact and daily.

_____ 26. A cash discount that is offered as an incentive for prompt payment is actually a form of interest expense to the buyer.

_____ 27. Cash balances should be managed in such a way that having too little cash is to be avoided but having too much cash is of no significant concern.

_____ 28. Realized losses related to temporary investments go on the income statement, but unrealized holding losses never go on the income statement.

_____ 29. A firm has a contingent liability whenever it transfers a note receivable to another party with recourse.

_____ 30. All items found on a bank reconciliation are errors.

_____ 31. An outstanding cheque is treated as a reduction from the book balance on a bank reconciliation.

_____ 32. The balance on a bank statement always represents the correct amount in a company's account and is the amount to which the company's cash account should be reconciled.

_____ 33. A bank service charge is the fee charged by the bank for a company's outstanding cheques.

_____ 34. Excess cash invested in income-yielding securities such as bonds or shares are classified as temporary investments as long as they can be readily converted into cash and management intends to do so if the need arises.

_____ 35. The computation of bad debt expense using the percentage of sales method involves multiplying the bad debt percentage times the credit sales for the period.

_____ 36. The realized gain or loss on the sale of temporary investments is the difference between the sales price and the original cost of the security.

_____ 37. The definition of cash excludes such items as demand deposits and savings accounts because these items are not physically in the firm's possession.

_____ 38. Showing temporary investments at cost is criticized for failing to recognize easily measurable changes in a firm's economic position and for giving management an opportunity to manipulate its profits for a period.

Matching

From the list of terms, select one term that is most closely associated with one of the descriptive phrases or statements that follows and place the letter for that term in the space provided.

a. accounts receivable
b. Accounting Standards Board

c. allowance for doubtful accounts
d. allowance method

e. bad debts expense
f. bank reconciliation
g. bank service charge
h. cash
i. Companies Acts
j. demand deposit
k. deposits in transit
l. direct writeoff method
m. Generally Accepted Accounting Principles (GAAP)
n. holding gain or loss
o. lower of cost and market

p. market value
q. notes receivable
r. outstanding cheque
s. pledging of accounts receivable
t. sales returns and allowances
u. simple interest formula
v. subsidiary ledger
w. temporary investments
x. time deposit
y. transfer without recourse
z. transfer with recourse

_____ 1. the current rule-making body of the accounting profession

_____ 2. the preferable method of accounting for uncollectable accounts

_____ 3. the most liquid asset

_____ 4. chequing account

_____ 5. a promise in writing for the receipt of a definite sum of money at some future point in time

_____ 6. a method by which doubtful accounts are charged to expense when they are clearly demonstrated to be uncollectable

_____ 7. investments in shares or bonds that are readily convertible into cash

_____ 8. an example of an addition to bank statement balance in a bank reconciliation

_____ 9. the required method of valuation for temporary investments

_____ 10. a negative consequence of extending credit

_____ 11. treated as a contra to sales revenue

_____ 12. usually classified as cash even though not always immediately available for withdrawal from a bank

_____ 13. a trade receivable

_____ 14. a contra to Accounts Receivable

_____ 15. an example of a reduction of the book balance in a bank reconciliation

_____ 16. the ledger that contains the detailed accounts, the total for which is shown in the controlling account in the general ledger

_____ 17. if the borrower does not repay a note when due, the lending institution can sell the accounts receivable maintained as collateral for the loan

_____ 18. Principal × Rate × Time

_____ 19. an example of a deduction from the bank statement balance in a bank reconciliation

_____ 20. transfer of a note that places a contingent liability on the transferor

Multiple Choice

Choose the best answer for each question or problem and enter the identifying letter in the space provided.

_____ 1. Which of the following is not classified as cash and shown among current assets?
a) cash on hand
b) petty cash
c) demand deposit
d) bond sinking fund

_____ 2. Which of the following is the primary formal record of generally accepted accounting principles (GAAP)?
   a) the Companies Acts
   b) the Security Commission Regulations
   c) the *CICA Handbook*
   d) common commercial accounting practice

_____ 3. Which of these methods is not normally considered a generally accepted accounting method?
   a) the direct charge-off method
   b) the aging of accounts method
   c) the percentage of sales method
   d) the lower of cost and market method (for temporary investments)

_____ 4. Beth Co. acquired temporary investments in 19X1 at a cost of $15,000. At the end of the year, their market value was $14,000. The securities were sold for $17,000 in early 19X2. If Beth employed the lower of cost and market method at the end of 19X1, what gain or loss would be recognized on the sale in 19X2?
   a) $2,000 loss
   b) $3,000 gain
   c) $1,000 loss
   d) $2,000 gain

_____ 5. The unrealized loss related to temporary investments is properly placed in which section of the balance sheet?
   a) as a contra to Temporary Investments
   b) as a Current Asset
   c) as an Other Item
   d) as a contra to Owners' Equity

_____ 6. When the market value of a temporary investment is different from its historical cost, what is the prescribed treatment, according to the *CICA Handbook*?
   a) use the market method
   b) use the cost method
   c) use the lower of cost and market method
   d) none of the above are prescribed

_____ 7. A four-month, 6 percent, $10,000 note is received by Kinko Inc. during 19X1. How much interest will Kinko Inc. earn if it holds the note to maturity?
   a) $200
   b) $150
   c) none
   d) $600

_____ 8. Which item, found on a bank reconciliation, would not involve an adjustment to the bank statement?
   a) outstanding cheques
   b) deposits in transit
   c) bank service charge
   d) a deposit credited to the company's account in error

___ 9. Realized gains and losses related to temporary investments go in which section of the income statement?
a) Sales
b) Operating Income and Expenses
c) Financial Income and Expense
d) Extraordinary Items

___ 10. Control over cash disbursements should ensure that:
a) disbursements are made only by authorized persons
b) adequate records support each disbursement
c) the disbursement is recorded in the accounting records
d) all of the statements above describe proper controls for cash disbursements

___ 11. The control of cash receipts should include which of these precautions?
a) collections for sales should be recorded promptly
b) duplicate sets of records should be maintained
c) a bank reconciliation should be prepared monthly
d) all of the above are appropriate controls for cash receipts

___ 12. Which of these events reduces total assets?
a) the return of merchandise for credit
b) the writeoff of doubtful accounts under the allowance method
c) the collection of an account receivable
d) the sale of a temporary investment for book value that is less than the original cost

___ 13. The Truth Co. purchased a temporary investment for $50,000 during 19X1. At year-end, the market value was $46,000. On December 31, 19X2, the market value had risen to $51,000. Which amount would appear on the 19X2 income statement?
a) neither a gain nor a loss
b) $4,000 loss
c) $1,000 gain
d) $5,000 gain

___ 14. The proper handling in the financial statements of the account Allowance for Doubtful Accounts is:
a) a revenue contra account
b) a selling expense
c) a contra to Accounts Receivable
d) a current liability

___ 15. Which of these accounts would not be treated as a reduction in sales revenue on the income statement?
a) Sales Allowances
b) Sales Returns
c) Bad Debts Expense
d) all of the above

___ 16. Which item, taken from a bank reconciliation, would not require a correcting entry on the company's books?
a) a cheque for $54 shown incorrectly on the bank statement as $45
b) bank service charge
c) collection of a note for the company by the bank
d) a cheque received from a customer that was deposited during the month and returned with the bank statement along with a memorandum indicating insufficient funds in the customer's account

_____ 17. Of the numerous ways of turning receivables into cash, which one is the same as an outright sale of the receivables?
   a) assignment of receivables
   b) factoring of receivables
   c) pledging of receivables
   d) collection of receivables

_____ 18. During 19X1, Christian Ltd. had $600,000 of sales, $300,000 of which were on account. The balances in its Accounts Receivable and its Allowance for Doubtful Accounts on December 31, 19X1 were $50,000 and $10,000, respectively. Past experience indicates that 5 percent of all credit sales will not be collected. What is the correct amount for Christian to debit to Bad Debts Expense?
   a) $30,000
   b) $15,000
   c) $5,000
   d) $20,000

_____ 19. Refer to Question 18, but assume that an aging of accounts indicated that $15,000 of the receivable balance would not be collected. What is the correct amount for Christian to debit to Bad Debts Expense?
   a) $20,000
   b) $10,000
   c) $15,000
   d) $5,000

_____ 20. The Green Tambourine Co. Inc. accepted a 10 percent, $50,000 note from a customer on August 1, 19X1, due on February 1, 19X2. If the accounting year ends on December 31, how much interest revenue is recorded when the note is collected?
   a) $5,000
   b) $2,500
   c) $417
   d) $835

_____ 21. At the end of 19X2, temporary investments acquired during 19X1 for $52,000 had a market value of $46,000. The market value at the end of 19X1 was $45,000. What should be recognized for 19X2 if the lower of cost and market method is being employed?
   a) a realized loss of $2,000
   b) an unrealized loss of $2,000
   c) a realized loss of $6,000
   d) neither a gain nor a loss

_____ 22. Jacobs Co. received an 8 percent, $6,000 note on September 1, 19X1, due in six months. If the year ends on December 31, 19X1, what amount of interest should be recorded at year-end?
   a) $480
   b) $240
   c) $160
   d) $80

Exercises

1. The Underhill Co. Ltd. reported sales of $1,000,000 in 19X1, of which $400,000 were for cash. It had the following balances at year end before adjustments:

Accounts Receivable $250,000
Allowance for Doubtful Accounts   (50,000)

The accounts written off as uncollectable during 19X1 totalled $45,000. Calculate the Bad Debts Expense for each method below.

   a. the direct writeoff method
   b. the percentage of sales method, where experience indicates a 5 percent rate is appropriate
   c. the aging method, where an evaluation of accounts indicates that $100,000 will not be collected
   d. same as (c), except assume that the Allowance for Doubtful Accounts has a *debit* balance of $50,000 instead of a *credit* balance

2. Prepare a bank reconciliation and all necessary adjusting entries on December 31, 19X1 for Annaheim Ltd.

   Balance per bank statement 12/31 19X1 $258,000
   Balance shown per books 12/31 19X1 $229,840

   An analysis of the cancelled cheques revealed the following: (a) $10,000 of the $16,000 of outstanding cheques for November were still outstanding on December 31, (b) $33,600 of cheques written during December had not cleared the bank by the end of the month, and (c) a $1,600 cheque for Fitzgerald Ltd. had been charged against the Annaheim Ltd. account.

   Annaheim Ltd. had placed $20,400 in the night deposit box of the bank on December 31 and had not received credit on the December statement. An analysis of the cash receipts journal revealed a $360 error in the deposit of December 20: Annaheim Ltd. recorded it as $6,720, and the correct amount shown on the bank statement was $7,080. The error related to the cheque from L. Selmon on payment of his account. The bank also included three memorandum items. The first was a credit memorandum for the note of Bob Bailey collected by the bank for Annaheim on December 28 for $7,200 plus $72 in interest. The second item was a $32 debit memorandum for the December bank service charge. The third item was also a debit memorandum. A cheque from Gus Hernandez for $1,040, received and deposited by Annaheim Ltd. during December, was returned with the statement marked insufficient funds.

3. The balances in selected accounts for Abnorma Walker Ltd. on May 1, 19X1 are as follows:

   Accounts Receivable $150,000
   Allowance for Doubtful Accounts   (80,000)

   a. A 20-day, 10 percent note from Heidi Inc. was received in early May for its $9,500 overdue account. Payment of the note plus interest was received during the month when due.
   b. Gross sales on account for the month of May were $1,400,000. Cash sales were $300,000.
   c. Customers received credit for $5,000 of merchandise purchased on account and returned during May.
   d. Customers' accounts carried in the subsidiary ledger at $850,000 were collected.
   e. Accounts receivable of $90,000 were written off as uncollectable during the month.
   f. At month-end, an aging of the accounts indicated that $30,000 would be uncollectable.
   Record the May transactions in two-column journal form.

4. Shula Inc. purchased 50,000 shares of Deco Ltd. on January 17, 19X1, at $12 per share. In addition, on August 15, 19X1, 2,200 shares of Reptilias Corp. were purchased at $100 per share. At year-end, December 31, 19X1, the market values for the Deco Ltd. and Reptilias Corp. shares were, respectively, $11 per share and $101 per share.

   On February 17, 19X2, a $0.10 per share dividend was received on the Deco Ltd. shares. On July 11, 19X2, all the shares of Deco Ltd. were sold for $13 per share. At the end of 19X2, the market value for a Reptilias Corp. share was $98.

   Record in proper journal form for Shula Inc. all original entries and year-end adjusting entries that would be needed for 19X1 and 19X2. Assume that Shula employs the lower of aggregate cost and market method and that the securities are temporary investments.

5. Assume all the same facts as in Exercise 4. Record in proper journal form for Shula Inc. all original entries and the year-end adjusting entries for 19X1 and 19X2. Assume that Shula employs the lower of individual cost or market method.

PROBLEM 1 FOR SELF-STUDY

Refer to the data in Exhibit 6.2 showing transactions in temporary investments for Wolfson Limited over four years. Assume that in addition to those transactions, Wolfson Limited purchased 1,000 shares of D Ltd. on October 1, Year 1, for $40 per share, $40,000 in total. Shares of D Ltd. had a market value of $45 per share at the end of Year 1, $36 per share at the end of Year 2, $30 per share at the end of Year 3, and $50 per share at the end of Year 4.

a. For each of the four years, determine the amount reported as Temporary Investments in the December 31 balance sheet, and the amount reported as Holding Gain or Loss on Temporary Investments in the income statement, where Wolfson Limited uses each of the following bases to value Temporary Investments: lower of individual cost and market; or lower of aggregate cost and market.

b. Assume that, during Year 5, Wolfson Limited sold the D Ltd. shares for $32,000 in place of selling the B Ltd. shares. At December 31, Year 5, the market value of the B Ltd. shares was $30,000. Compare the holding gain (loss) as originally reported and the amount reported under this alternative, under each of the bases of valuing temporary investments listed in (a) above.

PROBLEM 2 FOR SELF-STUDY

Refer to the data in Exhibit 6.5 showing sales and collection activities for two periods. At the end of the third period, the *unadjusted* trial balance included the following accounts and amounts: Accounts Receivable — $75,000 debit; Allowance for Doubtful Accounts — $8,000 debit; Bad Debts Expense — zero (adjusting entries have not yet been made); Sales Revenue — $1,300,000. No further specific accounts receivable need be written off for the period.

a. Reconstruct the transactions of the third period, assuming all sales were made on account.

b. What were the total cash collections for the third period from customers who paid their accounts?

c. Reconstruct the transactions of the third period, assuming that only $1 million of the $1.3 million total sales were made on account.

d. What were the total cash collections for the third period, including collections both from customers who paid cash and from customers who paid their accounts?

e. Does one need to know the actual split of sales between cash sales and sales on account to know the total amount of cash collected from customers (that is, the sum of cash sales and collections on account)? Why or why not?

f. Assume that 2 percent of all sales for the third period is estimated to be uncollectable. What is the adjusting entry to be made at the end of the third period for estimated uncollectables? What net balance of Accounts Receivable will appear on the balance sheet at the end of the third period?

g. Independent of the answer to (f), assume that an aging of accounts receivable indicates that the amount in the Allowance for Doubtful Accounts appropriate for the status of outstanding accounts at the end of the third period is $20,000. What is the adjusting entry to be made at the end of the third period for estimated uncollectables?

ANSWERS TO SELF-STUDY QUESTIONS AND EXERCISES

True/False

1. T	11. F	21. F	31. F
2. F	12. T	22. F	32. F
3. F	13. F	23. F	33. F
4. T	14. F	24. T	34. T
5. T	15. T	25. T	35. T
6. T	16. T	26. T	36. T
7. T	17. F	27. F	37. F
8. T	18. F	28. F	38. T
9. F	19. T	29. T	
10. T	20. F	30. F	

Matching

1. b	6. l	11. t	16. v
2. d	7. w	12. x	17. s
3. h	8. k	13. a	18. u
4. j	9. o	14. c	19. r
5. q	10. e	15. g	20. z

Multiple Choice

1. d	7. a	13. a	19. d
2. c	8. c	14. c	20. c
3. a	9. c	15. c	21. d
4. b	10. d	16. a	22. c
5. a	11. d	17. b	
6. c	12. a	18. b	

Exercises

1. a. $\underline{\$45,000}$

   b. $0.05 \times \$600,000 = \underline{\$30,000}$

   c.
Total doubtful accounts	$100,000
Credit in Allowance Account	(50,000)
	$ 50,000

   d.
Total doubtful accounts	$100,000
Debit in Allowance Account	50,000
	$150,000

2. Annaheim Ltd.
Bank Reconciliation
December 31, 19X1

Balance shown on bank statement 12/31 19X1		$258,000
Additions:		
Deposits in transit, December 31	$20,400	
Cheque of Fitzgerald incorrectly charged against the account of Annaheim Ltd.	1,600	22,000
		$280,000

Deductions:			
Outstanding cheques from November		$10,000	
Outstanding cheques from December		33,600	(43,600)
Adjusted bank balance, December 31, 19X1			$236,400
Balance shown on books 12/31 19X1			$229,840
Additions:			
Error in December 20 deposit		$ 360	
Collection of note:			
Face amount of note	$7,200		
Interest on note	72	7,272	7,632
			$237,472
Deductions:			
Bank service charge		$ 32	
Insufficient funds cheque from G. Hernandez		1,040	(1,072)
Adjusted book balance, December 31, 19X1			$236,400

	Dr.	Cr.
Adjusting Entries:		
Cash in Bank	$ 360	
Accounts Receivable		$ 360
Error in recording L. Selmon cheque on payment of account.		
Cash in Bank	$7,272	
Notes Receivable, Bob Bailey		$7,200
Interest Revenue		72
Collection by bank of Bob Bailey note plus interest.		
Bank Service Charge	$ 32	
Cash in Bank		$ 32
Bank service charge for December.		
Accounts Receivable	$1,040	
Cash in Bank		$1,040
Insufficient funds cheque of G. Hernandez.		

		Dr.	Cr.
3.	a.		
	Notes Receivable, Heidi Inc.	$ 9,500	
	Accounts Reeivable		$ 9,500
	Receipt of 10 percent, 20-day note in exchange for overdue account.		
	Cash	$ 9,553	
	Notes Receivable, Heidi Inc.		$ 9,500
	Interest Revenue		53
	Collection of Heidi Inc. note plus 20 days of interest.		
	b. Accounts Receivable	$1,100,000	
	Cash	300,000	
	Sales Revenue		$1,400,000
	Sales for May.		
	c. Sales Returns and Allowances	$ 5,000	
	Accounts Receivable		$ 5,000
	Sales returns for May.		

d. Cash $ 850,000
        Accounts Receivable $ 850,000
    Collections on account during May.

e. Allowance for Doubtful Accounts $ 90,000
        Accounts Receivable $ 90,000
    To write off doubtful accounts.

f. Bad Debts Expense $ 40,000
        Allowance for Doubtful Accounts $ 40,000
    To increase allowance to $30,000 as
    determined by aging process.

Allowance, May 2, 19X1 $80,000
Writeoff during July   90,000
Balance before adjustment   ($10,000)
Required balance, per aging of accounts   30,000
Increase in Allowance $40,000

	Dr.	Cr.

4.

01/17   Temporary Investments $600,000
19X1   Cash $600,000
        Purchase of 50,000 shares of Deco Ltd. for $12
        per share.

08/15   Temporary Investments $220,000
19X1   Cash $220,000
        Purchase of 2,200 shares of Reptilias Corp. for $100
        per share.

12/31   Unrealized Holding Loss on Valuation of
19X1   Temporary Investments $ 47,800
            Allowance for Excess of Cost of Temporary Investments
            over Market Value $ 47,800
        Recognition of unrealized holding loss on temporary
        investments from use of lower of aggregate cost and
        market method.

	Acquisition Cost	Market Value	Difference
Deco Ltd.	$600,000	$550,000	($50,000)
Reptilias Corp.	220,000	222,200	2,200
	$820,000	$772,200	($47,800)

	Dr.	Cr.

02/17   Cash $ 5,000
19X2   Dividend Income $ 5,000
        Receipt of $0.10 per share dividends on Deco Ltd.
        Shares.

07/11   Cash $650,000
19X2   Realized Holding Gain on Sale of Temporary
            Investments $ 50,000
        Temporary Investments   600,000
        Sold 50,000 shares of Deco Ltd. for $13 per
        share, resulting in a $1 per share ($13 − $12)
        gain.

12/31   No Entry
19X2

Recognition of recovery of unrealized holding loss
recognized in previous year.

Acquisition Cost Reptilias Corp.	$220,000
Market Value	215,600
Difference	$ 4,400
Credit Balance in Allowance Account	47,800
Credit Balance Required	(4,400)
Excess: No Adjustment	$ 43,400

5.

		Dr.	Cr.
01/17 19X1	Temporary Investments: Deco Ltd. Cash	$600,000	$600,000
	Purchase of 50,000 shares of Deco Ltd. for $12 per share.		
08/15 19X1	Temporary Investments: Reptilias Corp. Cash	$220,000	$220,000
	Purchase of 2,200 shares of Reptilias Corp. for $100 per share.		
12/31 19X1	Unrealized Holding Loss on Valuation of Temporary Investments Temporary Investments: Deco Ltd.	$ 50,000	$ 50,000
	Recognition of unrealized holding loss on Deco Ltd. Investment ($600,000 − $550,000)		
02/17 19X2	Cash Dividends Income	$ 5,000	$ 5,000
	Receipt of a $0.10 per share dividend on Deco Ltd. shares.		
07/11 19X2	Cash Realized Holding Gain on Sale of Temporary Investments Temporary Investments: Deco Ltd.	$650,000	$100,000 550,000
	Sold 50,000 shares of Deco Ltd. for $13 per share, resulting in a $2 per share ($13 − $11) gain over book value.		
12/31 19X2	Unrealized Holding Loss on Valuation of Temporary Investments Temporary Investments: Reptilias Corp.	$ 4,400	$ 4,400
	Recognition of unrealized holding loss on Reptilias Corp. investment ($220,000 − $215,600).		

SUGGESTED SOLUTION TO PROBLEM 1
FOR SELF-STUDY

a. See Exhibit 6.7.

EXHIBIT 6.7
Problem 1 for Self-Study
(Suggested Solution to Part a)

	Year 6	Year 5	Year 4	Year 3
Lower of Individual Cost and Market				
Balance Sheet Value at Dec. 31				
A Ltd.	$43,000^m	$ 50,000^c	$ 50,000^c	$ 50,000^c
B Ltd.	—	—	22,000^m	27,000^m
C Ltd.	—	16,000^{cv}	16,000^{cv}	16,000^m
D Ltd.	30,000^{cv}	30,000^m	36,000^m	40,000^c
Total	$73,000	$ 96,000	$124,000	$133,000
Holding Gain (Loss) During Year				
A Ltd.	$ (7,000)	$ —	$ —	$ —
B Ltd.	—	10,000	(5,000)	(3,000)
C Ltd.	1,000	—	—	(4,000)
D Ltd.	—	(6,000)	(4,000)	—
Total	$ (6,000)	$ 4,000	$ (9,000)	$ (7,000)
Lower of Aggregate Cost and Market				
Balance Sheet Value at Dec. 31				
Cost—A Ltd.	$50,000	$ 50,000	$ 50,000	$ 50,000
B Ltd.	—	—	30,000	30,000
C Ltd.	—	20,000	20,000	20,000
D Ltd.	40,000	40,000	40,000	40,000
Total	$90,000	$110,000	$140,000	$140,000
Less: Allowance for Decline	(2,000)	(5,000)	(5,000)	—
Carrying Value	$88,000^{cv}	$105,000^{cv}	$135,000^m	$140,000^c
Holding Gain (Loss) during Year				
On Sales	$ (3,000)	$ 2,000	$ —	$ —
Other	3,000	—	(5,000)	—
Total	$ —	$ 2,000	$ (5,000)	$ —

^{c} = cost; ^{m} = market value; ^{cv} = carrying value.

b. See Exhibit 6.8.

EXHIBIT 6.8
Problem 1 for Self-Study
(Suggested Solution to Part b)

Holding Gain (Loss) Reported
Year Ended December 1, Year 5

	Gain (Loss)	
	Original	Revised
Lower of Individual Cost or Market		
Investment A Ltd.	—	—
Investment B Ltd.	$10,000	—
Investment C Ltd.	—	—
Investment D Ltd.	(6,000)	$ (4,000)
Total	$ 4,000	$ (4,000)

Lower of Aggregate Cost or Market

	B Ltd.	D Ltd.
Gain (Loss on Sale of Shares):		
Sale Price	$32,000	$32,000
Less: Original Cost	(30,000)	(40,000)
Gain (Loss)	$ 2,000	$ (8,000)
Charged to Allowance for Decline	—	5,000
Holding Gain (Loss) Reported	$ 2,000	$ (3,000)

SUGGESTED SOLUTION TO PROBLEM 2 FOR SELF-STUDY

a. Sales were $1,300,000, debited to Accounts Receivable. Specific accounts receivable of $24,000 (= $16,000 credit at start of period plus $8,000 debit by the end of period) were written off with debits to the Allowance for Doubtful Accounts and credits to Accounts Receivable. Thus, the balance in accounts receivable before cash collections was $1,410,000 (= $134,000 + $1,300,000 − $24,000). Because the ending balance is actually $75,000, the cash collections from customers who bought on account are $1,335,000 (= $1,410,000 — $75,000).

b. $1,335,000, as derived above.

c. Sales were $1,300,000, debited $300,000 to Cash and $1,000,000 to Accounts Receivable. Specific accounts receivable of $24,000 were written off with debits to the Allowance for Doubtful Accounts and credits to Accounts Receivable. The amount is derived as in (a). The writeoff of specific accounts left a balance of $1,110,000 (= $134,000 + $1,000,000 − $24,000), but the actual ending balance was $75,000, so $1,035,000 (= $1,110,000 − $75,000) of accounts must have been collected in cash.

d. $1,335,000 equals $300,000 cash sales plus $1,035,000 from collections on account.

e. No. Once cash from a sale on account has been collected, the overall effect of the sale on the financial statements is identical to a cash sale. Thus, cash sales and collected credit sales have the same effects on the financial statements.

f. Bad Debts Expense	$26,000	
Allowance for Doubtful Accounts		$26,000

Amount is equal to 0.02 × $1,300,000. Ending balance in the allowance account is $18,000 (= $26,000 credit less $8,000 debit).

The net Accounts Receivable balance at the end of the third period is $57,000 (= $75,000 − $18,000).

g. Bad Debts Expense	$28,000	
Allowance for Doubtful Accounts		$28,000

A $28,000 credit is required to establish a $20,000 credit balance in an account with a tentative $8,000 debit balance.

Assignment Material

Questions

1. Review the meaning of each of the key terms listed on page 375.

2. What is the distinction between being insolvent and being bankrupt? What are the causes of insolvency?

3. Why would having excessively high cash balances be considered a poor management practice?

4. What are the preferred business practices to minimize credit losses? What is the balance that has to be struck?

5. Who has primary responsibility in the firm for ensuring that internal control over cash and marketable securities is adequate?

6. What evidence of cash control have you observed in a cafeteria? A department store? A theatre? A gas station?

7. The Tastee Delight ice cream stores prominently advertise on signs in the stores that the customer's purchase is free if the clerk does not present a receipt. Oakland's Original hot dog stand says that the customer's purchase is free if the cash register receipt contains a red star. What control purposes do such policies serve?

8. Current assets are defined as those assets that are expected to be turned into cash, or sold, or consumed within the next operating cycle. Cash is not always classified as a current asset, however. Explain.

9. Does application of the lower of cost and market valuation method to the portfolio of temporary investments or to each temporary investment individually result in the most conservative asset values and net income amounts?

10. Which of the two methods for treating uncollectable accounts (direct writeoff or allowance) implies recognizing income reductions earlier rather than later? Why?

11. a. An old adage in tennis holds that if your first serves are always good, you are not hitting them hard enough. An analogous statement in business might be that if you have no uncollectable accounts, you probably are not selling enough on credit. Comment on the validity of this statement.
    b. When are more uncollectable accounts better than fewer uncollectable accounts?
    c. When is a higher percentage of uncollectable accounts better than a lower one?

12. The customary method of accounting for sales results in adequate reporting for the returned sales when the goods are returned in the same period in which they are sold. If the goods are returned in a period subsequent to that of the sale, distortion of the reported income results. Explain how sales returns may produce each of the described effects.

13. Under what circumstances will the Allowance for Doubtful Accounts have a debit balance during the accounting period? The balance sheet figure for the Allowance for Doubtful Accounts at the end of the period should never show a debit balance. Why?

14. What is the effect on the financial statements of discounting, or transferring, a note with recourse versus without recourse?

EXERCISES

15. *Inclusions in Cash account.* Indicate if each of the following items should be included in "cash" on the balance sheet. If not, indicate how the item should be reported.
    a. Cash that has been collected from customers and is awaiting deposit in the firm's chequing account.
    b. Cash left in cash registers each day, which serves as a change fund.
    c. Cash set aside in a special savings account to accumulate funds to replace equipment as it wears out. The firm is not legally obligated to use the funds for this purpose.
    d. Cash set aside in a special savings account to accumulate funds to retire debt as it becomes due. The firm is legally obligated to use the funds for this purpose.
    e. A postdated cheque received from a customer. The cheque is dated 60 days after the date of the balance sheet.
    f. A money order received from a customer.
    g. Postage stamps.
    h. Cash held for small miscellaneous expenditures, such as freight charges and executive lunches.

16. *Inclusions in Cash account.* You are asked to compute the amount that should be shown as Cash on the balance sheet as of December 31 for Zeff Transportation Limited from the following information.
    a. Coins, currency, and cheques received from customers on December 31, but not yet deposited, $6,500.
    b. Cash held for making small miscellaneous cash expenditures. The fund normally has a balance of $100, but expenditures of $22 were made on December 31.
    c. The firm's postage meter was filled on December 31 and contains $500 of postage.
    d. The books indicate that the balance in the firm's chequing account on December 31 is $45,800. When the bank statement is received on the next January 10, it is learned that one customer's cheque for $800, which was deposited on December 28, was returned for insufficient funds. In addition, during December, the bank collected $2,200 for a note receivable from one of Zeff's customers and added

the amount to Zeff's bank account. The note had a face value of $2,000 and interest of $200.

e. Term deposit for a face value of $10,000. The deposit was acquired on July 1 of this year and matures on June 30 of next year. Simple interest of 12 percent per year accumulates on the note and is payable at maturity with the principal.

f. British sterling currency, £10,000. The exchange rate on December 31 is $1.60 per pound sterling.

17. *Bank reconciliation.*

a. Arrange the following data related to Antle Inc. in bank reconciliation form.

Adjusted Bank Balance	$6,713
Adjusted Book Balance	6,713
Balance per Bank Statement, October 31	7,873
Balance per Books, October 31	6,028
Error in Deposit of October 28; $457 Deposit Entered on Books as $547	90
Outstanding Cheques	1,305
Payroll Account Cheque Deducted from this Account in Error	145
Proceeds on Note of W.Y. Smith, Taken by the Bank for Collection,	
Less Collection Fee of $25	775

b. Present journal entries on the books of Antle Inc. to record the adjustments indicated in the bank reconciliation schedule.

18. *Bank reconciliation.*

a. Prepare a bank reconciliation schedule at July 31 for the Home Appliance Co. Ltd. from the following information:

Balance per Bank Statement, July 29	$1,240
Balance per Ledger, July 31	714
Deposit of July 30 Not Recorded by Bank	280
Debit Memo — Service Charges	8
Credit Memo — Collection of Note by Bank	300

An analysis of cancelled cheques returned with the bank statement reveals the following: Cheque #901 for purchase of supplies on account was correctly drawn for $58 but was recorded as $85. The manager wrote a cheque for traveling expenses of $95 while out of town. The cheque was not recorded. The following cheques are outstanding:

Cheque #650	$120
Cheque #721	162
Cheque #728	300
	$582

b. Journalize the adjusting entries required by the information revealed in the bank reconciliation.

19. *Bank reconciliation.* On May 31, the books of the Griffin Co. Ltd. show a debit balance in the Cash in Bank account of $4,720. The bank statement at that date shows a balance of $6,000. The deposit of May 31 of $250 is not included in the bank statement. Notice of collections made by the bank on mortgages of the company in the amount of $350, including interest of $250, and of bank service charges of $20 have not previously been received. Outstanding cheques at May 31 total $1,200.

   a. Prepare a bank reconciliation for the Griffin Co. Ltd. at May 31.
   b. Journalize the entries required upon preparation of the bank reconciliation.

20. *Classify temporary investments.* Indicate the classification of each of the securities below in the balance sheet of Bower Corporation on December 31.

   a. Treasury Bills, acquired on October 15. The bills mature next April 15.
   b. Shares of Brazil Coffee Corporation, a major supplier of raw materials for Bower Corporation's products.
   c. Shares of Overland Transportation Limited. The shares were originally acquired as a temporary investment of excess cash. Overland Transportation Limited has been so profitable that Bower Corporation plans to increase its ownership percentage and eventually obtain 51 percent of the outstanding shares.
   d. Ontario Hydro bonds that mature in three years. The bonds were acquired with a cash advance from a customer on a contract for the manufacture of machinery and will be sold, as needed, to pay costs of manufacturing. The manufacturing process will take three years.

21. *Journal entries for holdings of temporary investments.* The following list gives all events for Germont Inc's. actions with respect to its current asset portfolio of temporary investments during the period August, Year 1 through January, Year 2.

   8/21   Germont Inc. purchases 1,000 shares of Grenvil Co. Ltd. for $15 per share. In addition, it pays $150 in brokerage commissions to its stockbroker.
   9/1   The stockbroker calls Germont Inc. to report that Grenvil Co. Ltd. shares closed on the preceding day at $18 per share.
   9/30   Grenvil Co. Ltd. declares a dividend of $0.25 per share.
   10/25 Germont Inc. receives a dividend cheque for $250.
   12/31 The stockbroker calls Germont Inc. to report that Grenvil Co. Ltd. shares closed the year at $11 per share. The books are closed for the year.
   1/31   Germont Inc. sells 600 shares of Grenvil Co. Ltd. for $13 per share, the closing price for the day. Brokerage commissions, deducted from the proceeds, are $100.
   1/31   Germont Inc. prepares an up-to-date balance sheet as part of an application for a loan.

Prepare dated journal entries as required by the events described above.

22. *Journal entries for portfolio of temporary investments.* The aggregate cost and aggregate market value of the portfolio of temporary investments, current assets, of Elson Corporation at various dates appear below:

Date	Aggregate Cost	Aggregate Market Value
December 31, Year 1	$150,000	$140,000
December 31, Year 2	160,000	144,000
December 31, Year 3	170,000	185,000
December 31, Year 4	180,000	160,000

No temporary investments were sold during these years. Give the journal entry required at the end of each year, assuming that the accounting period is the calendar year.

23. *Journal entries for the allowance method.* The trial balance of the Walker Co. Ltd. at the end of its first year of operations included $20,000 of outstanding customers' accounts. An analysis reveals that 80 percent of the total credit sales of the year had been collected and that no accounts had been written off as uncollectable.

   The credit manager estimated that 2 percent of the total credit sales would be uncollectable. On the next January 31, the account of H.J. Williams, who had owed a balance of $300 for six months, was judged uncollectable and was written off.

   On July 1, the amount owed by H.J. Williams, previously written off, was collected in full.

   Present dated journal entries to record the following:
   a. Adjustment for estimated uncollectable accounts on December 31.
   b. Writeoff of the H.J. Williams account on January 31.
   c. Collection of the H.J. Williams account on July 1. Assume that it is felt that there is evidence that the account should never have been written off as uncollectable, and that total uncollectables are likely not to be different from the original estimates.

24. *Reconstructing events when allowance method is used.* The balance sheets of Wilton Corporation on December 31, Year 1 and Year 2, showed gross accounts receivable of $8,300,000 and $9,700,000 respectively. You are advised that the balances in the Allowance for Doubtful Accounts account at the beginning and end of Year 2, after closing entries, were credits of $750,000 and $930,000, respectively. The income statement for Year 2 shows that the bad debts expense was $300,000, which was 1 percent of sales. All sales are made on account. There were no recoveries during Year 2 of accounts written off in previous years.

   Give all the journal entries made during Year 2 that have an effect on Accounts Receivable and Allowance for Doubtful Accounts.

25. *Aging accounts receivable.* Love Limited's accounts receivable show the following balances by ages:

Age of Accounts	Balance Receivable
0–30 Days	$300,000
31–60 Days	75,000
61–120 Days	30,000
More than 120 Days	15,000

The credit balance in the Allowance for Doubtful Accounts is now $6,000.

Love Limited's credit maanger suggests that the following percentages be used to compute the estimates of amounts that will eventually prove uncollectable: 0–30 days, 0.5 percent; 31–60 days, 1 percent; 61–120 days, 10 percent; more than 120 days, 60 percent.

Prepare a journal entry that will carry out the credit manager's suggestion.

26. *Aging accounts receivable.* Rozay Corporation's accounts receivable show the following balances:

Age of Accounts	Balance Receivable
0–30 Days	$500,000
31–60 Days	175,000
61–120 Days	80,000
More than 120 Days	40,000

An adjusting entry based on the percentage of sales method has already been made for the period. The credit balance in the Allowance for Uncollectable Accounts is now $30,000. The Bad Debt Expense account has a balance of $35,000.

Analysis of recent collection experience suggests that the following percentages be used to compute the estimates of amounts that will eventually prove uncollectable: 0–30 days, 0.5 percent; 31–60 days, 1 percent, 61–120 days, 10 percent; more than 120 days, 40 percent.

Prepare the indicated adjusting entry.

27. *Simple interest computations.* Calculate simple interest on a base of $6,000 for the following intervals and rates, using a 360-day year.
   a. 60 days at 12 percent
   b. 90 days at 9 percent
   c. 60 days at 16 percent
   d. 15 days at 16 percent
   e. 5 months, 15 days at 12 percent

28. *Journal entries for notes.* On May 10, the Dukes Co. Ltd. receives a note from one of its customers, Salk Builders, Inc., to apply on its account. The six-month, 12 percent note for $6,000, issued on May 10, is valued at its face amount, $6,000.

On July 25, the Dukes Co. Ltd. endorses the note and transfers it with recourse to Beaver Ltd. to settle an account payable. The note is valued at its face amount plus accrued interest.

On November 12, the Dukes Co. Ltd. is notified that the note was paid at maturity.
  a. Present dated entries on the books of the Dukes Co. Ltd., assuming that it closes its books quarterly on March 31, June 30, and so on.
  b. Present dated entries on the books of Beaver Ltd., assuming that it closes its books quarterly on March 31, June 30, and so on.

29. *Effect of compensating balances on effective interest rate.* Davidoff Corporation borrowed $1 million from the local bank on July 1. The bank charged Davidoff Corporation interest at its prime lending rate of 13.5 percent. The principal and interest on the loan are repayable on the following June 30. Davidoff Corporation must maintain a $100,000 compensating balance on an interest-free chequing account at the bank during the term of the loan.
  a. What is the effective annual interest rate that Davidoff Corporation is paying on this loan?
  b. What message to Davidoff Corporation is implicit in the bank's requirement that a compensating balance be maintained?

30. *Journal entries for the allowance method.* The trial balance of the Biddle Company at the end of its first year of operations included $25,000 of outstanding customers' accounts. An analysis revealed that 90 percent of the total credit sales of the year had been collected and that no accounts had been charged off as uncollectable.

The auditor estimated that 1 percent of the total credits sales would be uncollectable. On the next January 31, the account of Robert Jesse, who had owed a balance of $500 for six months, was judged uncollectable and was written off.

On August 1, the amount owed by Robert Jesse, previously written off, was collected in full.

Present dated journal entries to record the following:
  a. Adjustment for estimated uncollectable accounts for December 31.
  b. Writeoff of the Robert Jesse account on January 31.
  c. Collection of the Robert Jesse account on August 1. Assume that it is believed there is evidence that the account should never have been written off as uncollectable and that total uncollectables are likely not to be different from the original estimates.

PROBLEMS AND CASES

31. *Bank reconciliation and journal entries.* The bank reconciliation of the Clovis Company at March 31 was as follows:

Balance per Bank Statement, March 31	$3,965
Unrecorded Deposit	475
Outstanding Cheques	820
Adjusted Bank and Book Balance, March 31	3,620

The bank statement, returned cheques, and other documents received from the bank at the end of April provide the following information:

Balance, April 29	$ 3,800
Deposit of March 31	475
Deposits of April 1–29 Including a Credit Memo for a Collection of a Note, $860	16,160
Cancelled Cheques Issued Before April 1	600
Cancelled Cheques Issued During April	16,200

The Cash in Bank account of the Clovis Company for the month of April shows deposits of $16,140 and cheques drawn of $17,015. The credit memo has not as yet been recorded on the books of the company; it represents the collection of a note with $800 face value on which $40 of the $60 total interest had already been accrued as of March 31.

a. Prepare a bank reconciliation for the Clovis Company as of April 30.

b. Present in journal entry form any adjustment of the company's books resulting from the information generated by the bank reconciliation.

32. *Journal entries and financial statement presentation of temporary investments.* The information below summarizes data about the temporary investments of Albion Corporation.

					Market Value	
Security	Date Acquired	Acquisition Cost	Date Sold	Selling Price	Dec. 31, Year 1	Dec. 31, Year 2
A	1/5/Year 1	$40,000	11/5/Year 2	$50,000	$30,000	—
B	6/12/Year 1	85,000	—	—	90,000	$82,000
C	2/22/Year 2	48,000	—	—	—	46,000
D	3/25/Year 2	25,000	12/5/Year 2	18,000	—	—
E	4/25/Year 2	36,000	—	—	—	50,000

a. Give all journal entries relating to these temporary investments during Year 1 and Year 2, assuming that the calendar year is the accounting period, when the company values temporary investments at the lower of individual cost and market; or the lower of aggregate cost and market.

b. Indicate the manner in which temporary investments would be presented in the balance sheet and related notes on December 31, Year 1 under each alternative listed in (a).

c. Indicate the manner in which temporary investments would be presented in the balance sheet and related notes on December 31, Year 2 under each alternative listed in (a).

33. *Financial statement presentation of temporary investments.* Exhibit 6.9 gives data on holdings of temporary investments of Sprouse Limited for Year 1 and Year 2. There were no sales of securities during Year 1. During Year 2, Sprouse Limited purchased new shares in Security F. During Year 2 the following sales of securities took place:

	Net Proceeds of Sale	Cost	Realized Gain (Loss)
Security A	$125,000	$100,000	$ 25,000
Security B	65,000	100,000	(35,000)
	$190,000	$200,000	$(10,000)

EXHIBIT 6.9
Data on Temporary Investments for Sprouse Limited

	Year 2		Year 1	
	Cost	Market	Cost	Market
In Current Assets:				
Security A	$100,000	$100,000	$200,000	$250,000
B	200,000	150,000	300,000	250,000
C	200,000	175,000	200,000	150,000
D	150,000	100,000	150,000	200,000
E	50,000	100,000	50,000	75,000
F	200,000	225,000	—	—
Total of Portfolio	$900,000	$850,000	$900,000	$925,000

The company wishes to determine the impact on the financial statements of valuing temporary investments at the lower of individual cost and market; or the lower of aggregate cost and market. Ignore income taxes.

a. Prepare in parallel columns for year-ends 2 and 1 the data that appear in the December 31, Year 2 balance sheet for each alternative valuation.

b. Determine the holding gains and losses that would be included in calculating net income for Year 1 and Year 2 for each alternative valuation.

34. *Effects of applying lower of cost and market to entire portfolios, rather than security by security.* Information relating to the temporary investments of TSS Limited is shown below:

Security	Date Acquired	Acquisition Cost	Date Sold	Selling Price	Market Value Dec. 31, Year 2	Market Value Dec. 31, Year 1
H	4/26/1	$18,000	2/9/2	$15,000	—	$16,000
I	5/25/1	25,000	8/10/2	26,000	—	24,000
J	11/24/1	12,000	—	—	$15,000	14,000
K	2/26/2	34,000	—	—	33,400	—
L	12/17/2	8,000	—	—	8,800	—

a. Compute the net holding gain or loss reported in the Year 1 and Year 2 income statements where the company values temporary investments at the lower of individual cost and market; the lower of aggregate cost and market; and market value.

b. Which alternative results in the most conservative asset values and measure of income?

35. *Allowance method; working "backwards."* The sales, all on account, of the Needles Inc. in Year 1, its first year of operations, were $600,000. Collections totalled $500,000. On December 31, Year 1, it was estimated that 1.5 percent of all sales would probably be uncollectable. On that date, specific accounts in the amount of $3,000 were written off.

The company's *unadjusted* trial balance (but after all nonadjusting entries were made) on December 31, Year 2 included the following accounts and balances:

Accounts Receivable (Dr.)	$60,000
Allowance for Doubtful Accounts (Dr.)	4,000
Bad Debt Expense	—
Sales (Cr.)	$700,000

In Year 2, Needles Inc. switched to the aging method for estimating uncollectables. It estimated that the Year 2 ending balance of accounts receivable contained $12,000 of probable uncollectables. You may assume, although it is not necessary to do so (why?), that all sales in Year 2 were made on account.

Present journal entries for the following:

a. Transactions and adjustments of Year 1 related to sales and customers' accounts.

b. Transactions of Year 2 resulting in the above trial balance amounts.

c. Adjustment for estimated uncollectables for Year 2.

36. *Reconstructing events when allowance method is used.* The amounts in certain accounts on January 1, and before adjusting entries on December 31, appear below:

	December 31	January 1
Accounts Receivable	$ 500,000 Dr.	$400,000 Dr.
Allowance for Doubtful Accounts	20,000 Dr.	30,000 Cr.
Bad Debt Expense	0	0
Sales	2,000,000 Cr.	0

During the year, 90 percent of sales were on account and 3 percent of credit sales are judged to be uncollectable. During the year, one account for $1,500 was collected, although it had been written off as uncollectable during the preceding year. When the written-off account was reinstated, the credit was to the Allowance account.

a. Give the journal entries made during the year that explain the changes in the four accounts as listed above.

b. Give any adjusting entries required on December 31.

37. **Estimating percentage of uncollectables.** The data in the following schedule pertain to the first eight years of Glidden Limited's credit sales and experiences with uncollectable accounts.

Year	Credit Sales	Related Uncollectable Accounts	Year	Credit Sales	Related Uncollectable Accounts
1	$200,000	$5,100	5	$500,000	$6,000
2	300,000	6,450	6	550,000	5,400
3	400,000	7,450	7	560,000	5,750
4	450,000	8,000	8	580,000	5,950

Glidden Limited has not previously used an Allowance for Doubtful Accounts but has merely charged accounts written off directly to Bad Debts Expense.

What percentage of credit sales for a year would you recommend that Glidden Limited charge to Bad Debts Expense if the allowance method were to be adopted at the end of Year 8?

38. **Decision to extend credit to a new class of customers.** The Feldman Company has a gross margin on credit sales of 30 percent. That is, cost of goods sold on account is 70 percent of sales on account. Uncollectable accounts amount to 2 percent of credit sales. If credit is extended to a new class of customers, credit sales will increase by $10,000, 8 percent of the new credit sales will be uncollectable, and all other costs, including interest to finance extra inventories, will increase by $1,000.
   a. Would Feldman Company be better or worse off if it extended credit to the new class of customer and by how much?
   b. How would your answer to part **(a)** differ if $3,000 of the $10,000 increase in credit sales had been made anyway as sales for cash? (Assume that the uncollectable amount on new credit sales is $800.)

39. **Decision to extend credit; working backwards to uncollectable rate.** The Hanrahan Company has credit sales of $100,000, a gross margin on those sales of 25 percent, with 3 percent of the credit sales uncollectable. If credit is extended to a new class of customers, sales will increase by $40,000, other expenses will increase by $2,500, and uncollectables will be 5 percent of *all* credit sales. Verify that Hanrahan Company will be $3,500 better off if it extends credit to the new customers. What percentage of the new credit sales are uncollectable?

40. **Journal entries for notes.** On November 1, Year 1, Atlas Corp. receives a note from one of its customers to apply on its open account receivable. The nine-month, 18 percent note for $8,000, issued November 1, Year 1, is valued at its face amount.

On January 31, Year 2, Atlas Corp. endorses the note and transfers it with recourse to First Canadian Bank in return for a cash payment of $8,100. The company's chequing account at this bank is increased for the proceeds, $8,100.

On August 1, Year 2, Atlas Corp. is notified by the bank that the note was collected from the customer at maturity.

Atlas Corp. closes its books annually on December 31.

Present dated journal entries on the books of Atlas Corp. relating to this note.

41. *Reconstructing events from journal entries.* Give the likely transaction or event that would result in making each of the independent journal entries below:

a.	Notes Receivable	$ 300	
	Accounts Receivable		$ 300
b.	Temporary Investments	$10,000	
	Cash		$10,000
c.	Bad Debts Expense	$ 2,300	
	Allowance for Doubtful Accounts		$ 2,300
d.	Holding Loss on Valuation of Temporary Investments	$ 4,000	
	Allowance for Excess of Cost of Temporary Investments over Market Value		$ 4,000
e.	Cash	$ 295	
	Notes Receivable		$ 285
	Interest Revenue		10
f.	Cash	$ 1,200	
	Loss on Sale of Temporary Investments	200	
	Temporary Investments		$ 1,400
g.	Allowance for Doubtful Accounts	$ 450	
	Accounts Receivable		$ 450
h.	Bad Debts Expense	$ 495	
	Accounts Receivable		$ 495
i.	Accounts Receivable	$ 285	
	Allowance for Doubtful Accounts		$ 285

42. *Management of investment portfolios to affect income and financial statement ratios.* The chief financial officer (CFO) of Easton Limited is nervous about the state of the company's financial affairs, as reflected in its tentative postclosing trial balance at the end of the current year, which appears in Exhibit 6.10. The CFO worries that the current ratio is too low.

Several years ago, the company borrowed $6 million in the form of a long-term bond issue, maturing fifteen years from now, carrying an interest rate of 7.5 percent per year. Interest rates have increased substantially since then, and comparable borrowings would now cost the firm more than 10 percent per year. The CFO worries about terms of the bond agreement that require the firm to maintain a ratio of current assets to current liabilities of at least 1.20 to 1.00. If the current ratio falls below that amount, the bond issue becomes due immediately, rather than maturing at its original maturity date, which is still fifteen years in the future. The CFO knows it will be costly to borrow new funds to replace the old.

Over the past several years, Easton Limited has acquired various holdings of temporary investments, some as current assets and some

EXHIBIT 6.10
EASTON LIMITED
Tentative Postclosing Trial Balance at Current Year-End
(dollar amounts in thousands)
(Problem 42)

	Dr.	Cr.
Allowance for Excess of Cost of Temporary Investments over Market Value (current asset contra)		$ 2,500
Current Liabilities		5,500
Portfolio Investments (noncurrent assets)	$ 3,000	
Temporary Investments (current assets), at Cost	3,500	
Noncurrent Liabilities		6,000
Other Current Assets	5,000	
Other Noncurrent Assets, Net	12,000	
Owner's Equity Accounts		9,500
Totals	$23,500	$23,500

Holdings of Equity Securities	Cost	Year-End Market Value
Current Assets:		
A Ltd.	$ 2,000	$ 600
B Inc.	1,500	400
Total	$ 3,500	$ 1,000
Noncurrent Assets:		
C Corp.	$ 1,000	$ 5,000
D Co. Ltd.	2,000	1,600
Total	$ 3,000	$ 6,600

as noncurrent assets. Data on these holdings appear in Exhibit 6.10. The decline in value of C Corp. and D. Co. Ltd. occurred during the current year and is considered temporary. The holdings of any one company were acquired in a single transaction. The CFO wonders what, if anything, can be done with the holdings of temporary investments to keep the call provision of the bond issue from being triggered.

The chief executive officer (CEO) of Easton Limited has discussed these problems with the CFO and raised another issue. The CEO's compensation package contains a bonus clause. As things now stand, the CEO will not receive a bonus because income for the year is $1.5 million short of the minimum for a bonus to be earned. Neither the CFO nor the CEO wants the firm to incur any extra income tax payments, as will become payable at a rate of 40 percent on any gains realized on sale of securities. Both the CEO and the CFO seek your advice.

a. Is the bond issue in danger of being declared due for current payment? Why or why not?

b. What actions, if any, can management of Easton Limited undertake to protect the outstanding bond issue from coming due at the end of the current year without having to pay additional income taxes? Provide journal entries that record the actions you suggest. What is the effect on income? On shareholder's equity?

c. What actions, if any, can management undertake to boost reported income sufficiently so that the CEO will receive a bonus? Provide journal entries that record the actions you suggest. How will these actions affect the current ratio?

43. *Preparing an income statement.* Selected balance sheet acounts for Richman Enterprises as at December 31 are as follows:

	19X2	19X1
Accounts receivable	$ 13,400	$ 11,500
Inventory	27,000	15,000
Accounts payable for merchandise	(14,000)	(9,000)
Accrued liabilities for operating expenses	(12,000)	(16,000)
Owner's equity (E. Richman)	(122,000)	(110,000)

An analysis of the cash account as of December 31, 19X2 revealed the following:
(1) A total of $160,000 had been paid to merchandise suppliers during the year.
(2) A total of $42,000 had been paid for operating expenses.
(3) A total of $24,000 had been withdrawn from the business by E. Richman in the form of dividends.
(4) A total of $237,000 had been collected from customers.

Depreciation on buildings and equipment is $10,000 per year. A reasonable estimate of bad debts is 4 percent of sales and is recorded in the Allowance for Doubtful Accounts Receivable account. Writeoffs of uncollectable accounts during 19X2 were $7,975. Assume that all sales, purchases, and operating expenses are made on account.
  a. Prepare in good form an income statement for 19X2 from the information given above. Ignore taxes and show all calculations.

Adapted with permission from the Society of Management Accountants of Canada.

44. *Temporary investments.* The following schedule shows the Sackman Corporation's portfolio of temporary investments as of December 31 of each year:

	19X2		19X1	
	Cost	Market	Cost	Market
Security A	$150,000	$100,000	$150,000	$135,000
B	100,000	75,000	200,000	180,000
C	50,000	80,000	50,000	60,000
D	70,000	60,000	70,000	75,000
	$370,000	$315,000	$470,000	$450,000

The initial portfolio was acquired during 19X1. During 19X2, one-half of the investment in Security B was sold for $130,000.
  The management of Sackman would like to determine the impact on income of valuing temporary investments at the lower of individual cost and market, or the lower of portfolio (i.e., aggregate) cost and market.

a. Determine the effect on income of the temporary investments for 19X1 and 19X2 using:
(i) the lower of individual cost and market.
(ii) the lower of portfolio (aggregate) cost and market.
Show all supporting calculations.
b. Determine the unrealized holding gains included in income under each valuation alternative in 19X1.
c. Prepare a journal entry to record the sale of Security B, assuming the portfolio (i.e., aggregate) method was used in 19X1.
d. One investor was heard to say, "The only section of the balance sheet that I feel confident in is the current asset section. Cash, temporary investments and accounts receivable are each specified in dollar amounts, so the reporting can't vary in any way." Comment on the validity of the investor's confidence with specific reference to each of these accounts.

Adapted with permission from the Society of Management Accountants of Canada.

DECISION CASE 6-1

Mark Wong is a recent graduate of a well-known west coast business school. After graduation, he set up a marketing consulting firm, "Mark Wong Western." On July 1, Year 1, he began the business with $12,000 in cash received from a legacy. He leased an automobile, furniture, and office equipment in order to preserve his capital. To provide for the eventual purchase of his own office building, he had limited his withdrawals from the business to $800 per month during the first year.

Having completed 12 months of frenetic activity and becoming cramped for space, Wong is considering moving to larger quarters, possibly purchased. To assist him in the purchase of office facilities, he considers it necessary to produce financial statements for a potential lender showing the first year results of his business in a favourable light. He has also been advised that he will have to prepare financial statements for income tax purposes and, in order to maximize his cash, he wants to minimize his income tax payments.

Wong has heard of the "triple-entry bookkeeping system" — one entry for the tax department, one entry for the creditors, and one for the owner. He would like to know the results of this system as applied to the first year of his business. He comes to you.

You find that Wong's financial data had been thrown out inadvertently with his market survey records. However, he advises you that the business has no debts and has the following assets:

1. Cash on hand in change fund, $200.

2. Undeposited cheque in an amount of $700 for a small market survey completed but not yet billed.

3. Balance per bank statement, $5,340. Wong believes that he issued two cheques at the end of June, totalling $873, which have not been deducted from the bank statement.

4. During the year, as his bank balance increased, he invested the excess in bonds and shares, the certificates for which he has stored in an envelope in a filing cabinet. On opening the envelope, you find a $10,000, 12 percent bond of Manning Oil Ltd. with an interest coupon attached for $600 representing six months' interest to March 31, Year 2. Attached is a note stating that the bonds had been purchased on September 30, Year 1 at par value. You call Wong's broker and she advises you that the bond could be sold at June 30, Year 2 for $9,600 plus accrued interest.

Also in the envelope is a certificate for 200 shares of Nalgoma Mines Ltd. and a broker's note attached indicating that the shares were purchased for $25 each plus brokerage of $200. The market value of the shares at June 30 amounted to $6,700.

Out of the bottom of the envelope flutters a note receivable by the company for $1,000 signed by Bill Wood dated December 31, Year 1. The note bore interest at 8 percent per annum payable at the due date, December 31, Year 2. You find that the note was received in return for a loan to Mark Wong's brother-in-law, who had planned to borrow from the finance company at 20 percent interest.

Wong maintains a copy of each invoice billed in a separate file, notes the money (if any) received, and extracts the invoice when paid in full. The file currently includes invoices totalling $5,720, of which $150 has been received in payment. Mark examines the bills and advises you that he expects to collect 90 percent of the amounts outstanding, although he could make a case that $2,500 will not be collected because it is two months overdue.

Mark Wong had no other assets except his B. Comm., good looks, and confidence.

1. Prepare statements of the business's net worth at June 30, Year 2 that could be prepared for a banker (an optimistic view), for the tax department (a pessimistic view), and for Mark Wong's private information (a realistic view). Finally, prepare a net worth statement in conformity with generally accepted accounting principles.

2. Calculate the income earned by the business according to each of the above statements.

CHAPTER SEVEN

INVENTORIES: THE SOURCE OF OPERATING PROFITS

CHAPTER OUTLINE

- Inventory Terminology
- Significance of Accounting for Inventories
- Problem 1: Costs Included in Inventory at Acquisition
- Problem 2: Bases of Inventory Valuation
- Problem 3: Timing of Computations
- Problem 4: Cost Flow Assumptions
- Identifying Operating Profit and Holding Gains
- Current Cost Basis Removes the Need for a Cost Flow Assumption
- Estimating Inventory Values When the Periodic Method Is Used
- An International Perspective

inventory
A stock of goods owned by a firm. These goods represent merchandise held for sale, raw materials, work in process, or finished goods.

merchandise inventory
Purchased goods held for resale by non-manufacturing firms.

finished goods inventory
Goods held for sale by a manufacturing firm.

raw materials inventory
Materials being stored that will become part of goods to be produced.

This chapter introduces the choices that a firm must make in accounting for inventories and shows the impact of these decisions on reported expenses and net income for the period. The choices made in accounting for inventories can make two companies that are basically alike appear to be quite different.

INVENTORY TERMINOLOGY

The term **inventory** means a stock of goods or other items owned by a firm and held for sale, or for processing before being sold, as part of a firm's ordinary business operations. Tools, for example, are inventory in the hands of a tool manufacturer or hardware store, but not in the hands of a carpenter. Marketable securities are inventory in the hands of a securities broker or dealer, but not in the hands of a manufacturer who is holding them as a temporary investment.

Goods held for sale by a retail or wholesale business are called **merchandise inventory**; goods held for sale by a manufacturing concern are called **finished goods inventory**. The inventories of manufacturing firms also include **raw materials inventory** (materials being stored that will become part of goods to be produced) and **work-in-process inventory** (partially completed products in the factory). The balance sheet may also include inventories of supplies to be consumed in administrative, selling, and manufacturing operations.

To "inventory" a stock of goods means to prepare a list of the items on hand at some specified date, to assign a unit cost to each item, and to calculate the total cost of the goods.

SIGNIFICANCE OF ACCOUNTING FOR INVENTORIES

Financial accounting attempts to measure periodic income. Accounting for inventories affects income measurement by assigning costs to various accounting periods as expenses. The total cost of goods available for sale during a period must be allocated between the current period's usage (cost of goods sold, an expense) and the amounts carried forward to future periods (end-of-period inventory, an asset during the current period, but later an expense).

INVENTORY EQUATION

The **inventory equation** aids understanding of the accounting for inventory. In the following equation, all quantities are measured in physical units.

$$\underbrace{\text{Beginning Inventory} + \text{Additions}}_{\substack{\text{Goods Available for} \\ \text{Use or Sale}}} - \text{Withdrawals} = \text{Ending Inventory}$$

inventory equation
Beginning inventory + net purchases − cost of goods sold = ending inventory. Ordinarily, additions are net purchases and withdrawals are cost of goods sold.

If we begin a period with 2,000 kilograms of sugar (beginning inventory) and we purchase (add) 4,500 kilograms during the period, there will be 6,500 (= 2,000 + 4,500) kilograms available for use. If we use (withdraw) 5,300 kilograms during the period, there should be 1,200 kilograms of sugar left at the end of the period (ending inventory). The inventory equation can also be written as:

$$\underbrace{\text{Beginning Inventory} + \text{Additions}}_{\substack{\text{Goods Available for} \\ \text{Use or Sale}}} - \text{Ending Inventory} = \text{Withdrawals}$$

If we begin the period with 2,000 kilograms of sugar, if we purchase 4,500 kilograms of sugar, and if we observe 1,200 kilograms on hand at the end of the period, we know that 5,300 (= 2,000 + 4,500 − 1,200) kilograms of sugar were used, or otherwise withdrawn from inventory, during the period. The sum of Beginning Inventory plus Additions is usually called **Goods Available for Use or Sale**. In this example, there are 6,500 kilograms of sugar available for use or sale.

If accounting were concerned merely with tracing physical quantities, there would be few conceptual problems in accounting for inventories. But, of course, accounting reports are stated in dollar amounts, not physical quantities. When prices remain constant, inventory accounting problems

Goods Available for Use or Sale
The sum of beginning inventory plus all acquisitions, or purchases, of merchandise or finished goods during an accounting period.

are minor, because all items carry the same per-unit cost. Any variation in values of inventories results only from changes in quantities. The major problems in inventory accounting arise because the unit acquisition costs of inventory items fluctuate over time.

To illustrate, suppose that an appliance store had a beginning inventory of one television set, "TV set 1," which cost $250. Suppose further that two TV sets are purchased during the period — TV set 2 for $290 and TV set 3 for $300 — and that one TV set is sold for $550. The three TV sets are exactly alike in all physical respects; only their costs differ. Assume that there is no way to know which TV set was sold.

The inventory equation can be written as follows, with all quantities measured in dollars of cost:

$$\underbrace{\begin{array}{ccc} \text{Beginning} \\ \text{Inventory} \\ \$250 \end{array} + \begin{array}{c} \text{Net} \\ \text{Purchases} \\ \$590 \end{array}}_{\begin{array}{c} \text{Cost of Goods} \\ \text{Available for Sale} \\ \$840 \end{array}} - \begin{array}{c} \text{Ending} \\ \text{Inventory} \\ ? \end{array} = \begin{array}{c} \text{Cost of} \\ \text{Goods Sold} \\ ? \end{array}$$

Because financial statements are prepared with amounts measured in dollar terms, some assumption must be made about which TV set was sold. There are at least four assumptions that can be made in applying the inventory equation to determine the Cost of Goods Sold expense for the income statement and the ending inventory for the balance sheet. Exhibit 7.1 shows these assumptions. As the inventory equation and the TV set example both show, the higher the Cost of Goods Sold, the lower must be the Ending Inventory. The particular pair of numbers that appears — one in the income statement and one in the balance sheet — reflects the *cost flow assumption*, a major accounting issue discussed below.

EXHIBIT 7.1
Assumptions for Inventory Illustrations

Assumed Item Sold	Cost of Goods Available for Sale (beginning inventory plus purchases)[a]	=	Cost of Goods Sold (income statement)	+	Ending Inventory (balance sheet)
TV Set 1	$840		$250		$590
TV Set 2	840		290		550
TV Set 3	840		300		540
"Average" TV Set	840		280[b]		560[b]

[a]*Cost of goods available for sale = cost of (TV Set 1 + TV Set 2 + TV Set 3) = ($250 + $290 + $300) = $840.*
[b] *Average cost of a TV set = $840/3 = $280.*

PROBLEMS OF INVENTORY ACCOUNTING

The remainder of this chapter discusses four problems of inventory accounting:

1. The costs to be included in acquisition cost.
2. The valuation basis to be used for items in inventory.
3. The frequency of carrying out inventory computations, periodically or perpetually.
4. The cost flow assumption used to trace the movement of costs into and out of inventory, which may not parallel the physical movement of goods.

PROBLEM 1: COSTS INCLUDED IN INVENTORY AT ACQUISITION

COMPONENTS OF INVENTORY COST

The amount on a balance sheet for inventory includes all costs incurred to acquire goods and prepare them for sale. This is sometimes called the *laid-down cost*. For a merchandising firm, such costs should include purchasing, transportation, receiving, unpacking, customs duties, inspecting, and shelving costs, as well as any bookkeeping and office costs for recording purchases.[1] Example 8 on page 56 (in Chapter 2), showing the computation of the cost of some equipment, applies to inventory as well.

For a manufacturing firm, inventory costs include direct materials, direct labour, and manufacturing overhead. In a manufacturing firm, *all* production costs are debited to Work-in-Process Inventory. The process of recording *all* manufacturing costs in Work-In-Process Inventory is straightforward. The later allocation of costs in Work-in-Process Inventory to individual items transferred to the Finished Goods Inventory is not conceptually difficult, but requires special techniques of cost accounting that are beyond the scope of this book. The procedure followed is called *absorption costing* or **full costing**.[2]

full costing
An inventory costing method used by manufacturers that includes both fixed and variable costs in the unit cost.

direct costing
The method of allocating costs that assigns only variable manufacturing costs to product and treats fixed manufacturing costs as period expenses.

---

[1] Because the amounts involved are often relatively small, and because it is difficult to assign a definite dollar amount for many of these costs to specific purchases, practice tends to restrict the actual additions to a few significant items that can easily be identified with particular goods, such as transportation costs. The costs of operating a purchasing department, the salaries and expenses of buyers, the costs of the receiving and warehousing departments, and the costs of handling and shelving are usually treated as expenses of the period in which they are incurred, even though they must be incurred to make merchandise ready for sale.

[2] An alternative procedure, known as *variable costing* or **direct costing**, may be superior for internal management purposes.

In the direct costing procedure, product costs are classified into variable manufacturing costs (those that tend to vary with output) and fixed manufacturing costs (those that tend to be relatively unaffected in the short run by the number of units produced). Nonvariable (fixed) manufacturing costs are treated in the same way as selling and administrative costs; that is, they are treated as expenses assigned to the period of incurrence rather than as costs assignable to the product produced. Nonvariable manufacturing costs are charged in their entirety against revenues in calculating net income for the period.

When absorption costing is used, unit costs of product manufactured tend to vary inversely with the total number of units produced because a given amount of fixed costs is allocated to all the units produced. The larger the number of units produced, the smaller the per-unit cost.

Managerial accounting courses discuss the criticism of absorption costing and suggested benefits of direct costing for internal management uses. Direct costing is seldom used in external reporting.

THE PURCHASE TRANSACTION

Purchases account
The account in which is recorded the acquisition price of merchandise held for resale by companies using the periodic inventory method.

The purchase transaction includes receiving goods, inspecting them, and recording the purchase. Legally, purchases should be recorded in the **Purchases account** of the formal accounting records when title to the goods passes. The timing of title passage is often a technical question whose answer depends on many circumstances of the transaction. For convenience, the accountant usually recognizes purchases only after the invoice and the goods are received and inspected. Adjustments may be made at the end of the accounting period to reflect the legal formalities for goods in transit that belong to the purchaser or for goods on hand that still belong to the seller.

MERCHANDISE PURCHASES ADJUSTMENTS

The invoice price of goods purchased seldom measures the total acquisition cost. Additional costs are incurred in transporting and handling the goods; deductions may be required for cash discounts, goods returned, and other adjustments of the invoice price. All of these adjustments could be debited or credited to the Merchandise Inventory account. Frequently, however, a number of contra and adjunct accounts are used for these adjustments so that a more complete analysis of the cost of purchases is available. Purchase Discounts, Freight-in, Purchase Returns, and Purchase Allowances accounts are used to provide the needed detail. The accounting for purchase adjustments closely parallels the accounting for sales adjustments discussed in Chapter 3.

purchase discounts
Reductions in purchase invoice price granted for prompt payment.

The largest adjustment to the invoice price of merchandise is likely to be that for **purchase discounts**. Sellers often offer a discount from the invoice price for prompt payment. For example, the terms of sale "2/10, net/30" mean that a 2 percent discount from invoice price is offered if payment is made within 10 days and, otherwise, the full invoice price is due within 30 days.[3] Purchase discounts become a reduction in the purchase price. Two alternative methods for recording purchases are the *gross price method* and the *net price method*. Problem 26 at the end of the chapter describes and illustrates these methods of recordkeeping.

PROBLEM 2: BASES OF INVENTORY VALUATION

The basis for valuing inventory — the rule for assigning a cost to a physical unit — affects both periodic net income and the amounts at which inventories appear on the balance sheet. At least five valuation bases are used for one purpose or another: acquisition cost, current cost measured by replacement cost, current cost measured by net realizable value, lower of (acquisition) cost and market, and standard cost. Some of the following discussion reviews fundamentals considered in Chapter 2. Generally accepted accounting principles require the use of the lower of cost and market basis for most purposes.

---

[3] Problem 29 at the end of Appendix A demonstrates that the interest rate implied in these terms of sales is about 45 percent per year. That is, a purchaser who does not take such a discount is borrowing money at an interest rate of about 45 percent per year. Most purchasers find it advantageous to take such discounts and to borrow elsewhere at lower rates.

DISCUSSION CASE 16

Effective Purchasing: A Direct Route to New Profits

As a financial executive, you are not responsible to increase sales. But your eye is definitely on profitability. And you have in your company a resource that can fatten the bottom line just as surely as a big sales boost — and much more quickly and directly.

The resource is your purchasing department. Consider: Typically, for every $20 million of sales, about $1 million ends up as a profit. If you can save $1 million internally, the effect on profit is as good as a $20-million sales increase. And purchasing, more than any other function, has the potential for savings that can reach into the millions — if it is used right.

That is a big "if." For while the best-managed, most successful companies have long recognized purchasing's direct impact on profit, too many others overlook the goldmine at their feet. This oversight has always been wasteful and costly. In today's competitive world economy, it can threaten a company's survival.

Also, many successful companies who are doing a good job on purchasing for the bill-of-materials frequently overlook the secondary goldmine of MRO (maintenance, repair, and operating costs) and advertising and marketing materials, where, though less dollars are spent than for bill-of-materials, frequently millions of dollars are spent. It is not unusual on this classification of materials to save as much as 25 percent. Also, MRO and advertising savings are easier to accomplish because they do not affect the product.

Why, then, do many companies fail to tap the profit potential of effective purchasing? There are many reasons, but perhaps the biggest is simply the burden of purchasing's traditional role. The purchasing department has long been considered a support or service function, existing to serve the objectives of manufacturing. Its main imperative was to assure supplies to keep production lines running. A second objective, imposed in some companies, would be to assure supplies, while at the same time reduce inventory investment. Purchasing was a tactical way to achieve the objectives of other functions. There was no recognition that purchasing could be used in a genuinely strategic way.

Inevitably, this idea of purchasing affected the way the function was conducted. It was treated largely as a clerical, rather than professional, function. It did not attract the highest-caliber people. But if it did, they soon were promoted to "faster-track" jobs in manufacturing or marketing. It was not equipped by management with the most advanced computers. Typically, for lack of both decision support and a clearly defined mission, purchasing spent 80 percent of its time

(continued)

(continued)

on activities that affected only 20 percent of the dollars it spent — and vice versa.

In a few instances, exceptional individuals in purchasing were promoted to the level of division president. This is a double-edged sword, because in order to attract exceptional people in purchasing, there must be a clear career path to top management. However, if exceptional people are "pirated" without the career path, there will not be talented layers of management in this critical function. At Travenol Laboratories, a career path was established several years ago and, to date, two directors of purchasing are now operating unit presidents. The result of this career path is an exceptional purchasing department that helps to support a high-quality, low-cost product line.

The traditional positioning of the purchasing function as a drain on profitability continues to exist. Today, this is completely out of touch with industrial reality. A new Industrial Revolution has transformed dominant industries from manufacturing to assembly. This has made effective purchasing — not production — the key to competitiveness and profitability. Companies that fail to recognize the transformation are clinging to outdated thinking, and often with disastrous financial results.

What are the trends driving this transformation? First, complexity. Most industrial products contain so many different kinds of parts, and require so many different technologies, that almost no company can any longer make most of its components cost-effectively. By choosing to buy components rather than make them, a company positions itself to benefit from the specialized capabilities and the economies of scale that outside supplies can provide.

A second trend transforming industry from manufacturing to assembly is the emergence of a truly worldwide industrial economy, including third world countries that manufacture technological products. The steady rise of new industrial nations means that American buyers have a continually expanding choice of outside suppliers — many characterized by extremely low wage costs.

The final transforming influence is competition. In the past, many companies could rely on marketing strategies emphasizing *either* quality *or* price. These days an either/or strategy is inadequate. The Japanese example has taught us that it is possible — and crucial — to compete in quality and price together. American companies are under demand from their customers to do so. To survive, they have no choice but to make the same demand of their suppliers.

IBM is a perfect example. The company manufactures very little. They design, subcontract, assemble, and support their products. The net result is a very high-quality, reasonably priced product. And IBM has shown that this strategy can work. They are virtually competing with the entire nation of Japan — and winning.

(continued)

(continued)

An Ongoing Analysis

The most effective purchasing departments have long made use of make-or-buy analyses. Whether the analysis favored making a component in-house or buying it outside depended on the individual company, its markets, its suppliers, and a great many other highly special factors. These days, for American companies, such analyses more and more tend to favor buying. We often find that as much as 50 percent of components made in-house could be purchased from outside suppliers with greater cost-effectiveness.

An effective purchasing department must be engaged in continuing make-or-buy analyses. It should treat the company's internal manufacturing operation as if it were a vendor — gathering comprehensive cost data by each stage of the production process, and comparing costs against those of outside suppliers, in the U.S. and elsewhere, to uncover opportunities for cost-effective purchases.

In the past, an ongoing make-or-buy analysis was too burdensome for most purchasing departments. Today, thanks to personal computers and a new generation of software, such analysis is only one of many easily accessible tools for effective purchasing.

Computers enable purchasing to handle vastly greater amounts of information than ever before. With the right software, targeted specifically for purchasing's objectives, a company has the power to make continuing make-or-buy analyses, as well as other strategic and tactical purchasing decisions. Here are some of these applications.

Parts Coding

Many companies don't know, in effect, what they purchase. That is, they don't have easily accessible information on the great variety of parts and components they buy for different divisions or different end uses. The result, even in the best cases, is costly duplication of purchases. Still worse, different purchases of the same or similar items may be made at a whole range of prices at different locations within the same organization, rather than at the best available price. And the company misses out on the savings possible through ganged or cluster production for longer runs.

A newly available computer-based parts coding system can solve these problems. The system gives the user a 10-character field for coding parts by family, group, and subgroup — plus a 15-character field for easy sequential part numbering. And this coding system can be expanded if larger fields are required.

With such a system, each purchased part can be given its own exclusive identification. Once the ID's are in the data base, it becomes a powerful management tool. One can review the demand and purchase history for individual parts. Families of items can be scanned to determine their budget impact, and cost-saving buying strategies can be devel-

(continued)

(continued)

oped based on volume discounts and long-term contracts.

ABC Analysis

As mentioned earlier, purchasing has sometimes been prone to devoting too much time and effort to activities that account for only small proportions of dollars spent. ABC Analysis is the best cure for this problem. This process divides all purchased items into three classes. In a typical case, if you multiply the quantity of an item purchased each year by the unit cost, and arrange the totals in descending order, you find that:

- 10 percent of the items account for 75–80 percent of the dollars spent. This is the A group.
- Another 15 percent of items account for another 15 percent of dollars spent. This is the B group.
- The other 75 percent of items purchased account for only 10–15 percent of dollars spent. This is the C group.

ABC Analysis is a detailed application of Pareto's Law, which says that in any situation a small proportion of causes produces a large share of results. Because the three classes of purchased items have such a widely different impact on spending, they deserve different management priorities. Group A should be geared to rapid inventory turnover and regular individual attention in light of current conditions of demand, supply, and technology, which can have cost-reducing potential. Group B can be con-

trolled more loosely with preset reorder points and reorder quantities. Group C should be managed to prevent stockouts with adequate buffer stocks (achievable with a low level of inventory investment), and to minimize management and clerical effort.

By tailoring purchasing and inventory policy to the cost impact of specific groups of purchased items, most companies can immediately allocate management time for cost reductions while reducing inventory investment. In addition, ABC Analysis can serve as a guide to setting management priorities and can identify opportunities for savings available through value analysis.

Value Analysis

The relationship of function, design, and cost is the focus of value analysis. It aims to reduce costs through changes in design, in materials, in manufacturing processes, or in suppliers. Value analysis requires detailed knowledge of how a purchased item is produced, and how much each stage of the production process adds to the cost. With the right computer software, this information can be at a buyer's fingertips. The user can ask "What if . . . ?" about potential changes in materials or production processes, or elimination of certain frills. Conversely, the user can model the additional cost — if any — of adding a desirable feature to the product. The right software can provide buyers with a decision support system that organizes the

(continued)

(continued)

References

Reprinted with permission from James Schacher, "Effective Purchasing: A Direct Route to New Profits," *Financial Executive*, February 1986, copyright 1986 by Financial Executives Institute, Morristown, New Jersey.

detailed knowledge required by value analysis to locate savings opportunities. The buyer can then reap the savings in any number of ways: by having the production process changed, substituting a standard part for a special part, or switching from a brand name specification to a generic of equivalent performance.

Discussion Question

"Many firms buy their way into bankruptcy." What is implied by this statement?

ACQUISITION COST BASIS

The **acquisition cost basis** values units in inventory at their historical cost until sold. In accounting, the terms *acquisition cost* and *historical cost* mean the same thing.

acquisition cost basis Inventory valued at a historical cost until sold.

Using acquisition costs implies using the *realization convention*: gains (or losses) caused by increases (or decreases) in the market value of assets do not appear in income until the particular assets are sold. When the acquisition cost basis is used, only sales transactions affect income. Any changes in the value of inventory items occurring between the time of acquisition and the time of sale are not recognized. The figure shown on the balance sheet for inventory becomes out of date to the extent that prices have changed since the items were acquired. The longer the time since acquisition, the more likely the current value of the inventory will differ from its acquisition cost.

The determination of acquisition cost depends on the components included in acquiring the unit of inventory and the cost flow assumption adopted. The former is discussed on page 409, and the latter in the section beginning on page 421.

CURRENT COST BASIS

A current cost basis values units in inventory at a current market price. Two current cost bases discussed below are (1) current entry value, often called *replacement cost*, and (2) current exit value, often called *net realizable value*. When inventories are stated at current cost, gains and losses from changes in prices are recognized during the holding period that elapses between acquisition (or production) and the time of sale.

Whereas acquisition cost for inventory shows objective, verifiable information that may be out of date, current cost shows up-to-date information, which can be more useful, but the amount shown may be more difficult to measure and to audit.

Replacement Cost (Entry Value)

replacement cost
For an asset, the current fair market price to purchase another, similar asset (with the same future benefit or service potential). Current cost.

The **replacement cost** of an item at a given time is the amount a firm would have to pay to acquire the item at that time. In computing replacement cost, one assumes a fair market (or arm's-length) transaction between a willing buyer and a willing seller. One also assumes that the inventory is bought in the customary fashion in the customary quantities. Replacement cost does not imply the forced purchase of inventory by a frantic buyer from a hoarding seller (which probably implies a premium price), purchases of abnormally large quantities (which often can be bought at a lower than normal price), or purchases of abnormally small quantities (which usually cost more per unit to acquire).

Net Realizable Value (Exit Value)

net realizable value
An asset measure computed by subtracting the expected completion and disposal costs from the asset's estimated selling price (i.e., the net proceeds on disposal).

The amount that a firm could realize as a willing seller (not a "distressed seller") in an arm's-length transaction with a willing buyer in the ordinary course of business is **net realizable value**. The measurement of net realizable value can present problems for items of inventory not yet ready for sale (for example, partially complete inventory in a manufacturing firm). Additional manufacturing costs will have to be incurred before the item can be sold. Also, a sales commission and other selling costs, such as packaging and freight costs, will probably be incurred. In these cases, net realizable value is the estimated final selling price of the inventory less the estimated costs necessary to make the item ready for sale and to sell it. Consider, as examples, agricultural products and precious metals on hand at the close of an accounting period. These are often stated at net realizable value. It may be easier to estimate a market price less selling costs than to measure the historical cost of a bushel of apples harvested from an orchard.

LOWER OF COST AND MARKET BASIS

lower of cost and market valuation basis
An accounting basis providing for inventories or temporary investments to be carried at the balance sheet date at their acquisition price or net realizable value, whichever is lower.

The **lower of cost and market valuation basis** involves the lesser of the two amounts: acquisition cost or "market value." The latter is generally measured as net realizable value. The *CICA Handbook* discourages the use of "market value" in describing inventory value because of its lack of precision. To replace "market value," the Handbook recommends that a more descriptive term be used, such as "replacement cost," "net realizable value," or "net realizable value less normal profit margin."[4]

A decline of $5,000 in the market value of inventory is recognized with the following entry:

Loss from Decline in Value of Inventory	$5,000	
Inventory		$5,000

The entry directly credits the Inventory account, not a contra account as may be done for temporary investments (explained in Chapter 6), because subsequent recoveries in market value are not recorded as gains. Under

---

[4] *CICA Handbook*, section 3030.

some approaches to inventory accounting, the above entry is not recorded explicitly; instead, the loss appears as a higher cost of goods sold. Consider, for example, the calculation in Exhibit 7.2 of cost of goods sold when beginning inventory is $19,000, purchases are $100,000, and ending inventory has a cost of $25,000 but has a replacement cost of $20,000.

EXHIBIT 7.2
Calculating Cost of Goods Sold Illustrating
Different Bases of Inventory Valuation

	Cost Basis	Lower of Cost and Market Basis
Beginning Inventory	$ 19,000	$ 19,000
Purchases	100,000	100,000
Goods Available for Sale	$119,000	$119,000
Less: Ending Inventory	(25,000)	(20,000)
Cost of Goods Sold	$ 94,000	$ 99,000

Note that cost of goods sold is $5,000 more under the lower of cost and market basis than under the acquisition cost basis. The loss of $5,000 is not reported separately, but income will be $5,000 less than when the acquisition cost basis is used. If the amount of the writedown to market is so large that the reader of the statements will be misled without separate disclosure of the decline net realizable value, the writedown can be shown as an adjustment to cost of goods sold or as a loss, separately reported as part of operating activities.

The lower of cost and market basis for inventory valuation is called a "conservative" policy because (1) losses from decreases in market value are recognized before goods are sold, but gains from increases in market value are not recorded before a sale takes place; and (2) inventory figures on the balance sheet are never greater, but may be less, than acquisition cost. That is, **holding losses** are reported currently, whereas **holding gains** are not reported until the goods are sold.

Over long enough time spans, however, income equals cash-in less cash-out. For any one unit, there is only one total gain or loss figure — the difference between its selling price and its acquisition cost; the valuation rule merely determines how this gain or loss is spread over the accounting periods between acquisition and final disposition. When the lower of cost and market basis is used, the net income of the current period may be "conservatively" lower than if the acquisition cost basis were used, but the net income of a later period, when the unit is sold, will be higher.

STANDARD COSTS

Standard cost is a predetermined estimate of what items of *manufactured* inventory *should* cost. Studies of past and estimated future cost data provide the basis for standard costs. Manufacturing firms frequently use standard cost systems for internal performance measurement and control. Manage-

holding losses/ holding gains
Difference between end-of-period price and beginning-of-period price of an asset held during the period. Realized holding gains and losses are not ordinarily separately reported in financial statements. Unrealized gains are not usually reflected in income at all. Some unrealized losses, such as on inventory or temporary investments, are reflected in income as the losses occur.

Standard cost
Those costs, usually expressed on a per-unit basis, that under ideal operating conditions should be incurred for direct material, for direct labour, and for factory overhead.

rial and cost accounting texts discuss these uses. Standard cost is also used occasionally as the valuation basis for preparing financial statements. Units in inventory may be valued at standard cost, especially in the preparation of monthly or quarterly statements.

GENERALLY ACCEPTED ACCOUNTING BASIS FOR INVENTORY VALUATION

Accounting uses a historical cost basis for most assets. Because the "market value" of some inventory items can be significantly less than acquisition cost, either because of price changes for this kind of inventory generally or because of physical deterioration of the particular items in an inventory, generally accepted accounting practice favours the use of lower of cost or market for inventory.[5] This is the same as saying that "market values" must be used in some cases. Computing market value requires either replacement cost or net realizable value amounts. Thus, generally accepted accounting principles for inventory valuation and measurement of cost of goods sold may require a combination of three valuation bases: acquisition cost, replacement cost, and net realizable value. In a period of rising prices, replacement cost and net realizable value are likely to be higher than acquisition cost, so valuation at cost and the lower of cost and market usually give the same valuation.

Current cost information is a good example of how supplementary footnote disclosures can enhance the usefulness of financial statements. Users are interested in knowing the current cost of beginning inventory, ending inventory, and cost of goods sold in notes to the financial statements even if the financial statements are based on lower of cost and market values.

PROBLEM 3: TIMING OF COMPUTATIONS

Two principal approaches to calculating the physical quantity and dollar amount of an inventory are the *periodic* inventory system and the *perpetual* inventory system. The periodic inventory system is less expensive to use than the perpetual inventory system because it involves fewer accounting computations, but the perpetual inventory system provides useful information not provided by the periodic inventory system.

PERIODIC INVENTORY SYSTEM

periodic inventory system
An accounting method for inventories in which no record is made in the Inventory account for purchases or sales of merchandise at the time of such transactions. Rather, the Inventory account is updated when a physical stocktaking is performed and closing entries are made.

In a **periodic inventory system**, the ending inventory figure for each item on hand results from making a physical count of units on hand at the end of an accounting period and multiplying the quantity on hand by the cost per unit. The cost of the total ending inventory is calculated by summing the ending inventory figure for each item. Then, the inventory equation calculates the withdrawals that represent the cost-of-goods-sold expense.

---

[5] The *CICA Handbook* makes no recommendation on inventory valuations.

The following form of the inventory equation computes the cost of goods sold under a periodic system:

$$\underbrace{\begin{array}{c}\text{Beginning} \\ \text{Inventory} \\ \text{(known)}\end{array} + \begin{array}{c}\text{Purchased} \\ \text{(known)}\end{array}}_{\begin{array}{c}\text{Goods Available} \\ \text{for Use or Sale}\end{array}} - \begin{array}{c}\text{Ending} \\ \text{Inventory} \\ \text{(counted} \\ \text{and costed)}\end{array} = \begin{array}{c}\text{Cost of} \\ \text{Goods Sold} \\ \text{(solved for)}\end{array}$$

When a periodic system is used, no entry is made for withdrawals (cost of goods sold) until the inventory on hand at the end of the accounting period is counted and costed.

To illustrate the periodic system, assume that sales during the year amounted to $165,000. The entries made to record sales during the year would have the combined effect of the following entry:

Cash and Accounts Receivable	$165,000	
Sales		$165,000
To record cash and credit sales for the year.		

At the end of the year, a physical count is taken, inventory costs are assigned, and the cost of the withdrawals is computed from the inventory equation. Exhibit 7.2 derives cost of goods sold for the lower of cost and market basis embedded in a periodic inventory system. We assume that all purchases have been debited to the Merchandise Inventory account. The cost-of-goods-sold expense is recognized in a single entry:

Cost of Goods Sold	$99,000	
Merchandise Inventory		$99,000
Cost of goods sold recognized under a periodic inventory system.		

A periodic inventory system generates no separate information to aid in controlling the amount of inventory shrinkage (the general name for losses from such causes as breakage, theft, evaporation, and waste). All goods not in the physical ending inventory count are assumed to have been either sold or used. Any losses from shrinkage appear in the cost-of-goods-sold amount. Furthermore, physically counting the inventory at the end of the accounting period can seriously interfere with normal business operations for several days. Some firms using the periodic inventory system even close down and engage a large staff in physically counting the items on hand. Preparing income statements more frequently than once a year is expensive when the inventory figures result only from physically counting inventories.[6]

---

[6] The gross profit method and retail inventory methods provide for approximating ending inventory costs when counts cannot easily be taken. These methods are outlined on pages 430 and 431.

PERPETUAL INVENTORY SYSTEM

perpetual inventory
Records on quantities and amounts of inventory that are changed or made current with each physical addition to or withdrawal from the stock of goods; an inventory so recorded.

In a **perpetual inventory** system, the cost of goods sold is calculated and recorded whenever an item is taken from inventory. A perpetual inventory system requires a constant tracing of costs as items move into and out of inventory. Such entries as the following may be made from day to day:

Accounts Receivable (or Cash)	$800	
Sales		$800
Cost of Goods Sold	$475	
Finished Goods Inventory		$475
To record the cost of goods withdrawn from inventory and sold for $800.		

After postings for a period have been completed, the balance in the Merchandise Inventory account is the cost of the goods that should be on hand. Statements can be prepared without carrying out a physical count of inventory. In a perpetual inventory system, the following form of the inventory equation computes goods expected to remain in the ending inventory after each acquisition or withdrawal:

$$\underbrace{\begin{matrix} \text{Beginning} \\ \text{Inventory} \\ \text{(known)} \end{matrix} + \begin{matrix} \text{Purchases} \\ \text{(known)} \end{matrix}}_{\begin{matrix}\text{Goods Available}\\\text{for Use or Sale}\end{matrix}} - \begin{matrix} \text{Withdrawals} \\ \text{(recorded)} \end{matrix} = \begin{matrix} \text{Ending} \\ \text{Inventory} \\ \text{(solved for)} \end{matrix}$$

Using a perpetual inventory system does not eliminate the need to take a physical inventory in which the items of inventory on hand are counted and costed. A physical count and assigning of costs to remaining items provides a check on the perpetual inventory and enables the measurement of any loss from shrinkage. The loss is the difference between the amounts in the Merchandise Inventory account and the cost of the goods actually on hand. To illustrate, assume a book balance for inventory of $10,000 and an amount based on a physical count of $9,200. The entry to record the shrinkage is:

Loss from Inventory Shrinkage	$800	
Merchandise Inventory		$800
To write down inventory from book amount of $10,000 to actual amount of $9,200.		

The credit reduces the book amount of inventory from its recorded amount, $10,000, to the correct amount, $9,200. The debit is to a Loss account or, if immaterial, to Cost of Goods Sold. In either case, it reduces net income for the current period.

Some businesses using a perpetual approach make a complete physical check at the end of the accounting period, in the same way as when a periodic approach is used. A more effective procedure is available. Rather than taking the inventory of all items at one time, the count may be staggered throughout the period. For example, a college bookstore may check actual physical amounts of textbooks and inventory account amounts at the end of the school year, whereas the comparison for beach wear might be done in November. All items should be counted at least once during every year, but not all items need to be counted at the same time. The count of a particular item should be scheduled for a time when the stock on hand is near its low point for the year.

CHOOSING BETWEEN PERIODIC AND PERPETUAL INVENTORY SYSTEMS

A perpetual inventory system helps maintain up-to-date information on quantities actually on hand. It is justified when being "out of stock" may lead to costly consequences, such as customer dissatisfaction or the need to shut down production lines. In such cases, a perpetual inventory system might keep track of the physical quantities of inventory but not the dollar amounts. Controlling losses is easier under a perpetual system because inventory records always indicate the goods that should remain. A periodic inventory system usually costs less than a perpetual inventory system, but it provides no data on shrinkages.

As is often the case in business, costs should be compared with benefits. A periodic inventory system is likely to be cost-effective when being out of stock would not be extremely costly, when there is a large volume of items with a small value per unit, or when items are hard to steal. Perpetual inventory systems are cost-effective when there is a small volume of high-value items, or when running out of stock would be costly.

As the cost of recordkeeping with computers declines, the cost of perpetual inventories declines. Their use, therefore, continues to increase.

PROBLEM 4: COST FLOW ASSUMPTIONS

SPECIFIC IDENTIFICATION AND THE NEED FOR A COST FLOW ASSUMPTION

Individual units sold can sometimes be physically matched with a specific purchase. If so, no special problems will arise in ascertaining the acquisition cost of the units withdrawn from inventory and the cost of the units still on hand. For example, cost can be marked on the unit or on its container, or the unit can be traced back to its purchase invoice or cost record. The inventory and cost of goods sold of an automobile dealer or of a dealer in diamonds or fur coats might be computed using specific identification of costs.

In most cases, however, new items are mixed with old units on shelves, in bins, or in other ways, and physical identification is impractical. Accounting traces cost flows, not the physical flow of goods. Moreover, to assume that cost flows differ from physical flows of goods may be desirable (for reasons to be discussed in this section).

Historical Costs
The money equivalent of the object given up (and/or obligations assumed) in an exchange transaction.

FLOW OF HISTORICAL COSTS

The inventory costing problem arises because of two unknowns in the inventory equation:

$$\underbrace{\begin{array}{c}\text{Beginning} \\ \text{Inventory} \\ \text{(known)}\end{array} + \begin{array}{c}\text{Net} \\ \text{Purchases} \\ \text{(known)}\end{array}}_{\begin{array}{c}\text{Goods Available} \\ \text{for Use or Sale}\end{array}} = \begin{array}{c}\text{Cost of} \\ \text{Goods Sold} \\ \text{(unknown)}\end{array} + \begin{array}{c}\text{Ending} \\ \text{Inventory} \\ \text{(unknown)}\end{array}$$

We know the costs of the beginning inventory and net purchases, but not the amounts for cost of goods sold and for ending inventory. The question is whether to compute amounts for the units in ending inventory using the most recent costs, the oldest costs, the average cost, or some other cost. Of course, the question could have been put in terms of computing amounts for the cost of goods sold, for once we place an amount on one unknown quantity, the inventory equation automatically determines the amount of the other. The sum of the two unknowns, Cost of Goods Sold and Ending Inventory, must equal the Cost of Goods Available for Sale (= Beginning Inventory plus Net Purchases). The higher the cost assigned to one unknown, the lower must be the cost assigned to the other.

When prices are changing, no historical cost-based accounting method for costing ending inventory and cost of goods sold allows the accountant to show recent costs on both the income statement and the balance sheet. For example, in a period of rising prices, if recent, higher acquisition prices are used in measuring cost of goods sold for the income statement, older, lower acquisition prices must be used in costing the ending inventory for the balance sheet. As long as cost of goods sold and ending inventory are based on acquisition costs, financial statements can present current amounts in the income statement or the balance sheet, but not in both. Of course, combinations of current and out-of-date information can appear in both statements.

If more than one purchase is made of the same item at different prices and specific identification is not feasible, some assumption must be made about the flow of costs. Using a cost flow assumption, the accountant computes the acquisition cost applicable to the units remaining in the inventory. One of three cost flow assumptions is typically used for this purpose. These cost flow assumptions are:

1. First-in, first-out (FIFO).
2. Last-in, first-out (LIFO).
3. Weighted average.

The following demonstrations of each of these methods use the TV set example introduced earlier and repeated at the top of Exhibit 7.3. The example of the three TV sets illustrates most of the important points about the cost flow assumption required in accounting for inventories and cost of goods sold. The first problem for self-study at the end of this chapter illustrates the techniques more realistically, but contains no new concepts.

EXHIBIT 7.3
Comparison of Cost Flow Assumptions Historical Cost Basis

Assumed Data

Beginning Inventory: TV Set 1 Cost	$250
Purchases: TV Set 2 Cost	290
TV Set 3 Cost	300
Cost of Goods Available for Sale	$840
Sales: One TV set—Sales Price	$550

	Cost Flow Assumption		
Financial Statements	**FIFO** (1)	**LIFO** (2)	**Weighted Average** (3)
Sales	$550	$550	$550
Cost of Goods Sold	(250)[a]	(300)[c]	(280)[b]
Gross Profit on Sales	$300	$250	$270
Ending Inventory	$590[d]	$540[f]	$560[e]

[a] *TV Set 1 costs $250.*
[b] *Average TV set costs $280 (= $840/3).*
[c] *TV Set 3 costs $300.*
[d] *TV Sets 2 and 3 cost $290 + $300 = $590.*
[e] *Two average TV sets cost 2 × $280 = $560.*
[f] *Sets 1 and 2 cost $250 + $290 = $540.*

FIRST-IN, FIRST-OUT

The first-in, first-out cost flow assumption (FIFO) assigns the cost of the earliest units acquired to the withdrawals and the cost of the most recent acquisitions to the ending inventory. This cost flow assumes that the oldest materials and goods are used first. This cost flow assumption conforms to good business practice in managing physical flows, especially in the case of items that deteriorate or become obsolete. Column (1) of Exhibit 7.3 illustrates FIFO. TV set 1 is assumed to be sold, whereas TV sets 2 and 3 are assumed to remain in inventory. The designation FIFO refers to the cost flow of units sold, not to the actual physical flow of goods.

FIFO
First-In, First-Out; an inventory-flow assumption by which ending inventory cost is determined from most recent purchases.

LAST-IN, FIRST-OUT

The last-in, first-out cost flow assumption (**LIFO**) assigns the cost of the latest units acquired to the withdrawals and the cost of the oldest units to the ending inventory. Some theorists argue that LIFO matches current costs to current revenues and therefore that LIFO better measures income. Column (2) of Exhibit 7.3 illustrates LIFO. The $300 cost of TV set 3 is assumed to leave, whereas the costs of TV sets 1 and 2 are assumed to remain in inventory. The designation of LIFO refers to the cost flow for units sold, not the actual physical flow of goods.

In a period of consistently rising prices, LIFO results in a higher cost of goods sold and a lower reported periodic income than either FIFO or

LIFO
Last-In, First-Out. An inventory valuation method that assumes that the most recently purchased goods are sold first.

weighted-average cost flow assumptions. LIFO usually does not reflect physical flows, but it used because it produces a Cost-of-Goods-Sold figure based on more up-to-date prices. In a period of rising prices, LIFO's higher (than FIFO's) Cost-of-Goods-Sold figure reduces reported income.

Revenue Canada consistently has refused to permit companies to use the LIFO method of inventory valuation when determining taxable income. Primarily because of the tax department's position, this method is used rarely in Canada. Canadian practice varies dramatically from that used in the United States, where the LIFO method of inventory valuation is accepted for income tax purposes and has become the most popular inventory valuation method.

WEIGHTED AVERAGE

weighted-average cost flow assumption
A method of inventory valuation that spreads the total dollar cost of all goods available for sale equally among all units.

Under the **weighted-average cost flow assumption**, the average of the costs of all goods available for sale (or use) during the accounting period, including the cost applicable to the beginning inventory, must be calculated.[7] The weighted-average cost is applied to the units sold and those on hand at the end of the month. Column (3) in Exhibit 7.3 illustrates the weighted-average cost flow assumption. The weighted-average cost of TV sets available for sale during the period is $280 [$= \frac{1}{3} \times$ ($250 + $290 + $300)]. Cost of Goods Sold is therefore $280, and ending inventory is $560 (= 2 × $280).

COMPARISON OF COST FLOW ASSUMPTIONS

FIFO results in balance sheet figures that are closest to current cost, because the latest purchases dominate the ending inventory amounts. The Cost-of-Goods-Sold expense tends to be out of date, however, because FIFO assumes that the earlier prices of the beginning inventory and the earliest purchases are charged to expense. FIFO usually leads to the highest reported net income of the three methods when prices are rising, and to the smallest net income when prices are falling.

Because LIFO ending inventory can contain cost of items acquired many years previously, LIFO produces balance sheet figures usually much lower than current costs. LIFO's Cost-of-Goods-Sold figure closely approximates current costs. Exhibit 7.4 summarizes the differences between FIFO and LIFO. Of the cost flow assumptions, LIFO usually implies the smallest net income when prices are rising (highest Cost of Goods Sold), and the largest when prices are falling (lowest Cost of Goods Sold). Also, LIFO results in the least fluctuation in reported income in businesses where selling prices tend to change as current prices of inventory items change.

The weighted-average cost flow assumption falls between the other two in its effect on both the balance sheet and the income statement. It is, however, much more like FIFO than like LIFO in its effects on the balance sheet. When inventory turns over rapidly, the weighted-average inventory costs reflect current prices almost as much as FIFO.

---

[7] This description is technically correct only when a periodic inventory system is used. The first problem for self-study at the end of this chapter explores the procedures for applying the weighted-average method in a perpetual inventory system.

EXHIBIT 7.4
Age of Information About Inventory Items

Cost Flow Assumption	Income Statement	Balance Sheet
FIFO	Old Prices	Current Prices
LIFO	Current Prices	Very Old Prices[a]

[a] *The oldest prices on the FIFO income statement are just over one year old in nearly all cases, and the average price on the FIFO income statement (for a year) is slightly more than $1/2$ year old. The larger the rate of inventory turnover, the closer the average age on the income statement is to $1/2$ year. LIFO balance sheet items are generally much older than the FIFO income statement items.*

IDENTIFYING OPERATING PROFIT AND HOLDING GAINS

The reported net income under FIFO is generally larger than that under LIFO during periods of rising prices. This higher reported net income is caused by including a larger realized holding gain in reported net income under FIFO than under LIFO. This section illustrates the significance of holding gains in the calculation of net income under FIFO and LIFO.

The **gross profit** (Sales minus Cost of Goods Sold) shown on the income statement is the aggregate of an operating profit and a realized holding gain (or loss).

The difference between the selling price of an item and its replacement cost at the time of sale is called **operating profit**. This operating profit gives some indication of the relative advantage that a particular firm has in the market for its goods, such as a reputation for quality or service. The difference between the current replacement cost of an item and its acquisition cost is called a *holding gain* (or *loss*). The holding gain (or loss) reflects the change in cost of an item during the period while the inventory item is held. Holding gains indicate increasing prices and the skill (or luck) of the purchasing department in timing acquisitions.

To demonstrate the calculation of the operating profit and holding gain, consider the TV set example introduced in Exhibits 7.1 and 7.3. The acquisition cost of the three items available for sale during the period is $840. Assume that one TV set is sold for $550. The replacement cost of the TV set at the time it was sold is $320. The current replacement cost at the end of the period for each item in ending inventory is $350. The top portion of Exhibit 7.5 illustrates the separation of the conventionally reported gross profit into the operating profit and the realized holding gain.

The operating profit is the difference between the $550 selling price and the $320 replacement cost at the time of sale. The operating profit of $230 is the same under both the FIFO and LIFO cost flow assumptions. The **realized holding gain** is the difference between cost of goods sold based on replacement cost and cost of goods sold based on acquisition cost. We use the adjective "realized" on the basis of the requirements of the revenue-realization principle. Gains associated with items actually sold can flow through to the income statement, but gains associated with inventory still

gross profit
Net sales minus cost of goods sold.

operating profit
The difference between the selling price of an item and its replacement cost at the time of sale.

realized holding gain
A gain that has been confirmed by an exchange transaction (i.e., a sale) and can be recognized in the income statement.

on hand cannot be formally recognized — they are unrealized. The realized holding gain under FIFO is larger than that under LIFO, because the earlier purchases at lower costs are charged to cost of goods sold under FIFO. The larger realized holding gain under FIFO explains why net income under FIFO is typically larger than that under LIFO during periods of rising prices. In conventional financial statements, the realized holding gain does *not* appear separately, as in Exhibit 7.5.

EXHIBIT 7.5
Reporting of Operating Profits and Holding Gains for TV Sets Using the Periodic Inventory Method

	Cost Flow Assumption			
	FIFO		**LIFO**	
Sales Revenue	$550		$550	
Less: Replacement Cost of Goods Sold	(320)		(320)	
Operating Profit on Sales		$230		$230
Realized Holding Gain on TV Sets:				
Replacement Cost (at time of sale) of Goods Sold	$320		$320	
Less: Acquisition Cost of Goods Sold				
(FIFO—TV Set 1; LIFO—TV Set 3)	(250)		(300)	
Realized Holding Gain on TV Sets				
(inventory profit)		70		20
Conventionally Reported Gross Profit[a]		**$300**		**$250**
Unrealized Holding Gain:				
Replacement Cost of Ending Inventory (2 × $350)	$700		$700	
Less: Acquisition Cost of Ending Inventory				
(FIFO—TV Sets 2 and 3; LIFO—TV Sets 1 and 2)	(590)		(540)	
Unrealized Holding Gain on TV Sets		110		160
Economic Profit on Sales and Holding Inventory				
of TV Sets (not reported in financial statements)		**$410**		**$410**

[a] Note that Exhibit 7.3 stops here.

unrealized holding gain
The difference between the current replacement cost of ending inventory and its acquisition cost.

The calculation of an unrealized holding gain on units in ending inventory also appears in Exhibit 7.5. The **unrealized holding gain** is the difference between the current replacement cost of the ending inventory and its acquisition cost.[8] This unrealized holding gain on ending inventory is not reported in the income statement as currently prepared under generally accepted accounting principles. The unrealized holding gain under LIFO is larger than that under FIFO, because earlier purchases with lower costs remain in ending inventory under LIFO. The sum of the operating profit plus all holding gains (both realized and unrealized), called "Economic Profit" in Exhibit 7.5, is the same under FIFO and LIFO. Most of the holding gain under FIFO (that is, the realized portion) is recognized in computing net income for each period, whereas most of the holding gain under LIFO

[8] The unrealized holding gain for a *given year* on items on hand both at the beginning and at the end of the year is the difference between year-end current cost and beginning-of-year current cost. The examples in this chapter do not illustrate this complication of unrealized holding gains in opening inventory; all items on hand at the end of the year are purchased during the year.

(that is, the unrealized portion) is not currently recognized in the income statement. Instead, under LIFO, the unrealized holding gain remains unreported, so long as the older acquisition costs are shown on the balance sheet as ending inventory.

The total increase in wealth for a period includes both realized and unrealized holding gains. That total increase ($410 in the example) is independent of the cost flow assumption, but does not appear in financial statements under currently accepted accounting principles.

CURRENT COST BASIS REMOVES THE NEED FOR A COST FLOW ASSUMPTION

The preceding sections illustrate the difficulty in constructing useful financial statements in historical cost accounting for inventory in times of changing prices. If a FIFO cost flow assumption is used, the income statement reports out-of-date cost of goods sold. If a LIFO cost flow assumption is used, the balance sheet reports out-of-date ending inventory. (See Exhibit 7.4.)

A current cost basis for inventory allows up-to-date information to be shown on both statements, eliminating the need for a cost flow assumption. But using a current cost basis eliminates the realization convention from accounting, incurs additional costs, and requires the accountant to make estimates of current costs. Some accountants find that the resulting loss of objectivity and verifiability and the additional costs of collecting the information outweigh the potential benefits from using current cost data. Other accountants think that the benefits of current data outweigh the costs of having less auditable numbers.

Exhibit 7.6 illustrates the TV set example when both cost of goods sold and ending inventory are valued at replacement cost.

The first income figure, $230, is labelled *Operating Profit*. This figure shows selling price less replacement cost of goods sold at the time of sale. This number may have significance for companies operating in unregulated environments. The significance can perhaps be best understood by considering the following assertion. If the retailer of the TV sets pays out more than $230 in other expenses, taxes, and dividends, there will be insufficient funds retained in the firm for it to replace inventory and to allow it to continue in business carrying out the same physical operations next period as it did this period. On the date of sale, a new TV set costs $320; the historical cost of the TV set sold, whether $250 or $230 or some amount in between, will not help the retailer to understand the costs required to maintain its productive assets intact, given the *current* economic conditions.

The second income item shown in Exhibit 7.6 is called *Holding Gains for Year*. Holding gains of $180 occurred during the period on the TV sets held in inventory. At the time of sale, the replacement cost of TV sets had increased to $320. Thus, the holding gain on three TV sets, on the date of sale of one of them, was $120 [= 3 × $320 − ($250 + $290 + $300)]. By the end of the accounting period, there was another $60 [= 2 × ($350 − $320)] holding gain on the two TV sets still held in inventory, because the replacement cost increased to $350 from $320.

EXHIBIT 7.6
Using Replacement Cost Data to Analyze Components of Income

Assumed Data

Beginning Inventory: TV Set 1 Cost		$250
Purchases:	TV Set 2 Cost	290
	TV Set 3 Cost	300
Historical Cost of Goods Available for Sale		$840
Sales: One TV Set for		$550
Replacement Cost of TV Sets on:		
Date of Sale		$320
At End of Period		$350

Income Statement

Sales	$550
Replacement Cost of Goods Sold	(320)
Operating Profit	$230
Holding Gains for Year[a] (see calculation below)	180
Economic Income	$410

Calculation of Holding Gains for Year

Replacement Cost at Time of Sale[a]	$ 320
Replacement Cost of Ending Inventory (2 × $350)	700
Total Replacement Cost	$1,020
Historical Cost of Goods Available for Sale	(840)
Total Holding Gains for Year	$ 180
Ending Inventory (two TV sets, $350 current cost each)	$ 700

[a] *To give some recognition to the realization convention, the total holding gain might be divided into realized and unrealized portions. To do so requires knowing the acquisition cost of the TV set sold, and that requires a cost flow assumption. As Exhibit 7.5 indicates, if a LIFO assumption is made, the realized holding gain is $20, and the realized income of $250 could be between the operating profit of $230 and the economic income of $410.*

The $410 income figure shown after the inclusions of holding gains may also be significant. It represents the increase in wealth of the firm without regard to the realization convention. Some economists define income as the change in wealth during the period. They judge realization through arm's-length transactions to be unimportant. **Economic income**, including all holding gains, is $410 in the example.

Economic income
The change in wealth during a period.

ESTIMATING INVENTORY VALUES WHEN THE PERIODIC METHOD IS USED

To count every item in inventory is generally expensive. Firms try to do it as seldom as possible, consistent with requirements of generally accepted accounting principles and proper inventory control. When the periodic inventory method is used and financial statements are to be prepared, say at the end of a month or quarter, reasonably good estimates of Ending Inventory and Cost of Goods Sold amounts can often be obtained with the various *gross profit methods* and *retail methods*. The details of these methods are covered in intermediate accounting books, but we can introduce the general idea.

DISCUSSION CASE 17

You Can Trust Your Accountant

Today, business is generally seen as a cutthroat environment with little room for ethics and integrity. Even the professions, always considered a bastion of trustworthiness, are coming under attack.

Lord Benson* attributes this to some problems of the professions' own making, but also to media sensationalism of these problems and a middle class dislike for the bourgeoisie elitist concept with which professions historically were associated.

However, accountants have been able to maintain a better than average image in the eyes of the public.

A Harris poll conducted in the United States found "that even though people tend to have little faith in the integrity and honesty of most business dealings, accountants are still seen as the moral and ethical pillars of the business community."

Professional accountants were ranked first in terms of ethics and morality, followed by university professors, bankers, and doctors. Newspaper and magazine editors and newscasters were also viewed in positive terms. Politicians and even members of the clergy were rated negatively.

Three out of four people polled believed that the accounting profession is performing better now than ever. They also credited accountants with high marks for honesty, competence, reliability, and objectivity. Take a bow, accountants!

References

*"The Professions and the Community," *Journal of Accountancy*, April 1983. "You Can Trust Your Accountant," *The Bottom Line*, January 1987, p. 36.

Discussion Question

How have accountants earned such high marks for trustworthiness?

The foundation of these estimating methods is the fact that most businesses mark up the cost of similar kinds of merchandise by a relatively constant percentage in obtaining selling prices. For example, nearly every college bookstore sets the selling price of a textbook 25 percent above its cost to the bookstore. Put another way, the manager of the bookstore would say that the gross profit (retail selling price less cost) is 20 percent of selling price.[9] To take another example, men's clothing in a department store is

---

[9] This is one of the most confusing areas in business terminology. If you bought a share of stock for $8 and sold it for $10, both you and your stockbroker would call that a 25 percent (= $2/$8) *gain*. You would compute the gain percentage with the denominator being original cost. A retailer, however, speaks of the *markup* on an item selling for $10 that cost $8 as being 20 percent (= $2/$10). The retailer uses selling price, not cost, as the denominator. It is common practice, and the effective participant in the business world will have to understand these differences in terms.

gross profit method
A procedure for estimating the cost of ending inventories by multiplying the representative cost-of-goods-sold percentage times sales and deducting that amount from goods available for sale.

likely to carry a selling price that is twice the cost to the store. The selling prices of most types of retail items are higher than the cost of the items by a relatively constant percentage. This fact is used in estimating Ending Inventory and Cost of Goods Sold.

We find it easier to illustrate the procedure than to define it. The method is illustrated in Exhibit 7.7 and is often called the **gross profit method**. The gross profit percentage is defined by:

$$\text{Gross Profit Percentage} = \frac{\text{Selling Price} - \text{Acquisition Cost}}{\text{Selling Price}}$$

Assume that the data shown at the top of Exhibit 7.7 are available from the records for a month. (The kinds of information assumed to be available would typically be available in nearly all businesses.) In this business firm, all goods carry a gross profit percentage of 25 percent. That is, if the selling price of an item is $100, it cost $75 ($25/$100 = 25 gross profit percentage).

The cost of goods sold and inventory at the end of January are computed as shown at the bottom of Exhibit 7.7. This method results in the correct figures for the Cost of Goods Sold and Ending Inventory if each item has a gross profit percentage of exactly 25 percent. The method results in approximations if the individual items have different gross profit percentages the average of which is 25 percent.

EXHIBIT 7.7
Illustration of Gross Profit Method
(Gross Profit Percentage is 25 Percent of Selling Price)

Assumed Data

Cost of Inventory, January 1	$150,000
Invoice Cost of Purchases During January	220,000
Transportation-in on Purchases During January	2,000
Invoice Cost of Purchases Made During January but Returned to Seller During January (purchase returns)	7,000
Sales Made During January	310,000
Selling Price of Goods Sold During January but Returned by Customers (sales returns)	10,000

Application of Gross Profit Method to Assumed Data

Cost of Inventory, January 1		$150,000
Net Purchases:		
Purchases	$220,000	
Plus Transportation-in	2,000	
Less: Purchase Returns	(7,000)	215,000
Total Cost of Goods Available for Sale		$365,000
Estimated Cost of Goods Sold:		
Sales	$310,000	
Less: Sales Returns by Customers	(10,000)	
Net Sales	$300,000	
Less: Estimated Gross Profit (= 0.25 × 300,000)	(75,000)	
Estimated Cost of Goods Sold		(225,000)
Estimated Cost of Ending Inventory, January 31		$140,000

A variant of the gross profit method is the **retail method**, which is widely used by retail businesses because it simplifies the recordkeeping for inventory. Such firms typically mark each item of merchandise with the retail price and record purchases at both cost and retail price. A firm can estimate its ending inventory at retail price merely by subtracting sales from the retail price of goods available for sale. To determine the inventory cost, the firm applies a cost-to-retail percentage, which is the ratio of cost to retail price of merchandise available for sale. Consider the following illustration.

retail method
A method used principally by retailers that uses a percentage of cost/selling price of merchandise available for sale, to cost ending inventory.

	Cost	Retail
Beginning inventory	$14,000	$22,000
Net cost of purchases	70,000	98,000
Cost of goods available for sale	$84,000	$120,000

$$\text{Cost-to-retail percentage} \frac{\$84,000}{\$120,000} = 70\%$$

Less: Sales during period	90,000
Estimated ending inventory at retail prices	$30,000
Applicable cost percentage	×0.70
Estimated ending inventory at cost	$21,000

The cost-to-retail percentage can also be used to compute the cost of a physical inventory taken at retail prices. Thus, the firm saves the considerable effort and cost of determining unit costs for each inventory item. For a supermarket or department store with thousands of different products on the shelves, this saving is non-trivial. Suppose that the store clerks use an adding machine to accumulate the sales value of merchandise on hand, which totals $940,000. Applying a hypothetical percentage of 60%, the cost would be estimated to be $564,000.

The accuracy of this method is dependent on the assumption that the ending inventory contains the same mix of products as did the original merchandise available for sale. It should also be pointed out that bar coding of merchandise and electronic sales registers makes estimation methods such as this unnecessary since computerized records by item are available.

AN INTERNATIONAL PERSPECTIVE

All major industrialized countries require the use of lower of cost and market as a basis for valuation of inventory. Only the United States and, to a lesser degree, Japan use the LIFO cost flow assumption in valuing inventory. The greatest variation between countries appears to relate to what costs are inventoriable for manufactured products. The tax laws of most countries are fairly explicit about how to value inventory for income tax purposes, and these tax regulations have been important in shaping accounting practices.

SUMMARY

Inventory measurements affect both the Cost-of Goods-Sold expense on the income statement for the period and the amount shown for the asset Inventory on the balance sheet at the end of the period. The sum of the two must be equal to the beginning inventory plus the cost of purchases, at least in accounting based on acquisition costs and market transactions. The allocation between expense and asset depends primarily on the valuation basis and the cost flow assumption used.

Additional inventory problems include dealing with the inclusions (absorption and variable costing) and timing inventory computations (periodic and perpetual approaches).

Common business terminology often inhibits clear thinking about the four problems because the term "inventory method" is so often used. For example, the terms "absorption costing method," "acquisition cost method," "perpetual method," and "LIFO method" are often used, but these are not alternatives to one another. An inventory method results from a combination of choices, one from each of the following:

1. *Inclusion:* absorption or variable costing.
2. *Basis:* historical cost, lower of cost and market, current cost, or standard cost, among others.
3. *Frequency of computations:* periodic or perpetual.
4. *Cost flow assumption:* FIFO, LIFO, or weighted average.

Be prepared for the ambiguous use of the term "inventory method," realizing that one of several distinctions may be at issue.

KEY TERMS

Inventory
Merchandise inventory
Finished goods inventory
Raw materials inventory
Work-in-process inventory
Inventory equation
Goods Available for Use or Sale
Full costing
Direct costing
Purchases account
Purchase discounts
Acquisition cost basis
Replacement cost
Net realizable value
Lower of cost and market
  valuation basis

Holding losses/holding gains
Standard cost
Periodic inventory system
Perpetual inventory
Historical costs
FIFO
LIFO
Weighted-average cost flow
  assumption
Gross profit
Operating profit
Realized holding gain
Unrealized holding gain
Economic income
Gross profit method
Retail method

SELF-STUDY MATERIAL

This section contains questions, exercises, and problems to help you assess your understanding of Chapter 7. Careful review of this material will assist you in completing the homework assignments. Solutions are found at the end of the section.

QUESTIONS AND EXERCISES

True/False

For each statement, place a T or an F in the space provided to indicate whether the statement is true or false.

_____ 1. To inventory a stock of goods means to prepare a list of the items on hand at some specified date, to assign a unit price to each item, and to calculate the total cost of the inventory.

_____ 2. The term inventory, as used in accounting, means a list of assets in both the current and the noncurrent categories.

_____ 3. In most cases, the total acquisition costs of inventory purchases may be measured accurately by the invoice price of merchandise.

_____ 4. As part of the statement of changes in financial position, inventory transactions either provide or use cash from operations.

_____ 5. During periods of rising prices, the unrealized holding gain recognized on the income statement using FIFO is greater than the amount recognized under LIFO.

_____ 6. A conventionally reported gross profit on sales consists of (a) a realized holding gain and (b) an unrealized holding gain.

_____ 7. FIFO has the advantage of reporting up-to-date costs for Cost of Goods Sold on the income statement and Inventory on the balance sheet.

_____ 8. The term "cost" (for merchandise) may include invoice price plus cost of transportation, as well as costs of purchasing, receiving, handling, and storage.

_____ 9. The lower of cost and market basis usually refers to valuations using a comparison of acquisition cost and net realizable value.

_____ 10. Standard-cost systems employ catalogue list prices to value inventory because control of acquisition cost is impossible.

_____ 11. Agricultural products in inventory are often valued at net realizable value, which is defined as selling price less cost of disposal.

_____ 12. The FIFO cost flow assumption assigns the cost of the most recent acquisitions to the inventory and the costs of the earliest units acquired to the withdrawals.

_____ 13. The LIFO cost flow method assumes that the business carries a certain amount of reserve stock units on hand and that current operations and sales are carried on with the use of units purchased most recently.

_____ 14. Net income under FIFO is usually smaller than that under LIFO when prices are rising.

_____ 15. FIFO, LIFO, and weighted-average cost flow assumptions relate to costs associated with withdrawals from inventory. As a result, income reports vary, but balance sheet valuations reflect little difference.

_____ 16. Under absorption costing, fixed cost per unit remains the same regardless of changes in production volume.

_____ 17. Variable costs in total change with production volume.

_____ 18. Under direct costing, all variable production costs are expensed when incurred; under absorption costing, both variable and fixed costs are expensed.

_____ 19. Direct costing and absorption costing are both used for published reports, but direct costing is used more for short-run decision making.

_____ 20. Under absorption costing, net income may increase as a result of production increases while sales remain the same.

_____ 21. A merchandise purchase (cash) discount, although more appropriately treated as a reduction of the purchase price, may also be viewed as a revenue item.

_____ 22. If one company uses the gross price method for recording purchase (cash) discounts and another company uses the net price method for an identical purchase and payment transaction, the balances in the Purchase Discounts and Purchase Discounts Lost accounts will be the same.

_____ 23. One major difference between the perpetual and periodic inventory systems is that withdrawals are recorded when assets are withdrawn under the perpetual system, whereas they are recorded only at the end of the period under the periodic system.

_____ 24. A physical inventory count is not needed under a perpetual inventory system because a continuous record is kept of items in stock.

Matching

From the list of terms, select one term that is most closely associated with one descriptive phrase or statement that follows and place the letter for that term in the space provided.

a. absorption (full) costing
b. acquisition cost basis
c. cost of goods sold
d. FIFO
e. finished goods
f. inventory
g. LIFO
h. lower of cost and market basis
i. net realizable value
j. operating profit
k. periodic inventory system
l. perpetual inventory system

m. purchases
n. purchase (cash) discounts
o. purchase (cash) discounts lost
p. raw materials
q. realized holding gain
r. replacement cost
s. shrinkage
t. standard cost
u. unrealized holding gain
v. variable (direct) costing
w. weighted-average method
x. work in process

_____ 1. A stock of goods owned by a firm and held for sale to customers.

_____ 2. The amount a firm would have to pay to acquire a replacement for an inventory item at that particular time.

_____ 3. The difference between the current replacement cost of the ending inventory and its acquisition cost.

_____ 4. The difference between the selling price of an item and its replacement cost at the time of sale.

_____ 5. The difference between cost of goods sold based on replacement cost and cost of goods sold based on acquisition cost.

_____ 6. Account title used to record discounts for early payments for merchandise, usually associated with the gross price method.

_____ 7. Materials being stored that will become a part of the goods to be produced.

_____ 8. Procedure by which a manufacturing firm includes all production costs in work in process.

_____ 9. This cost flow assumption assumes that a business carries a certain amount of reserve stock on hand and that current operations and sales are carried on with the use of units purchased most recently.

_____ 10. The portion of merchandise available for sale or use that is allocated to the current period's usage.

_____ 11. Partially completed products in the factory.

_____ 12. Selling price less costs of marketing.

_____ 13. Account title and term designating acquisition of merchandise during the accounting period.

_____ 14. Cost flow assumption that assigns the cost of the earliest units acquired to the withdrawals and the costs of the most recent acquisitions to the ending inventory.

_____ 15. Account title used to record discounts foregone, usually associated with the net price method.

_____ 16. Under this system, no entry is made for withdrawals from inventory until the end of the period.

_____ 17. A predetermined estimate of what each item of manufactured inventory should cost on the basis of past cost and planned production methods.

_____ 18. Its use entails carrying units in inventory at their acquisition costs until sold.

_____ 19. This inventory system is designed so that the cost of withdrawals is recorded at the time assets are withdrawn from inventory.

_____ 20. Goods held for sale by a manufacturing concern.

_____ 21. Inventory cost flow assumption that is physically appropriate for liquid or other types of products where distinguishing different lots is difficult.

_____ 22. Valuation basis that departs from cost when the utility of the goods is no longer as great as their cost.

_____ 23. "Losses" from inventory owing to theft, evaporation, or waste.

_____ 24. Procedure whereby a manufacturing firm charges fixed production cost to the period rather than as a cost of the product.

Multiple Choice

Choose the best answer for each question or statement fragment and enter the identifying letter in the space provided.

_____ 1. Under this cost flow assumption, the income statement reports out-of-date cost of goods sold:
   a) FIFO method
   b) LIFO method
   c) weighted-average method
   d) replacement cost method

_____ 2. The inventories of a manufacturing company include:
   a) finished goods
   b) raw materials
   c) work in process
   d) all of the above

_____ 3. The correct equation that applies to the determination of cost of goods sold is:
a) Beginning Inventory − Purchases + Ending Inventory = Cost of Goods Sold
b) Beginning Inventory + Purchases − Ending Inventory = Cost of Goods Sold
c) Beginning Inventory + Purchases + Ending Inventory = Cost of Goods sold
d) none of the above

_____ 4. Under a perpetual inventory system:
a) no entry is made as withdrawals take place
b) the cost to administer is usually less than that under the periodic method
c) a physical count of items on hand should be made from time to time
d) items in inventory are usually hard to steal

_____ 5. Which of the following is not acceptable for determination of inventory cost?
a) FIFO method
b) LIFO method
c) specific identification method
d) all of the above are acceptable

_____ 6. Characteristics of the use of current value bases to determine inventory values and cost of goods sold include all of the following, except:
a) current value basis shows current information that can be more useful
b) the information is generally easier to obtain
c) the information may be more difficult to audit
d) none of the above

_____ 7. The estimated selling price of the inventory less any estimated costs to make the item ready for sale and to sell it is the:
a) replacement cost
b) net realizable value
c) standard cost
d) market selling value

_____ 8. The amount that a firm would have to pay to acquire a replacement for an inventory item at a particular time is the:
a) replacement cost
b) net realizable value
c) standard cost
d) market selling value

_____ 9. When applying the lower of cost and market valuation method, each of the following is a factor, except:
a) replacement cost
b) net realizable value
c) standard cost
d) acquisition cost

_____ 10. A predetermined estimate of what each item of manufactured inventory should cost, on the basis of past experience and planned production methods, is the:
a) replacement cost
b) net realizable value
c) standard cost
d) acquisition cost

_____ 11. In variable costing (direct costing) for inventories for manufacturing firms, all of these are valid characteristics, except:
    a) classification of production costs into variable manufacturing costs and fixed manufacturing costs
    b) the unit cost of manufactured goods varies with the number of units produced
    c) product costs contain only variable costs
    d) unusual patterns of income do not result because the number of units produced differs from the number of units sold

_____ 12. Under this cost flow assumption, the costs assigned to the ending inventory are the costs of the earliest units acquired:
    a) FIFO method
    b) LIFO method
    c) weighted-average method
    d) replacement cost method

_____ 13. This cost flow assumption conforms to most actual physical inventory flows:
    a) FIFO method
    b) LIFO method
    c) weighted-average method
    d) replacement cost method

_____ 14. No cost flow assumption is required when this valuation method is adopted:
    a) FIFO method
    b) weighted-average method
    c) current cost method
    d) LIFO method

_____ 15. Characteristics of the use of the gross profit method of estimating inventory and cost of goods sold include all of the following, except:
    a) assuming last period's gross profit rate is continued this period
    b) applying last period's gross profit rate to the current period's sales revenue
    c) determining the cost of sales by deducting the closing inventory value from the sum of the opening inventory and purchases
    d) determining the closing inventory by deducting the estimated cost of sales from the sum of the opening inventory, net purchases, and transportation costs of purchases

_____ 16. The difference between the selling price of an item and its replacement cost at the time of sale is the:
    a) operating profit
    b) realized holding gain
    c) unrealized holding gain
    d) gross profit

_____ 17. The difference between the current replacement cost of the ending inventory and its acquisition cost is the:
    a) operating profit
    b) realized holding gain
    c) unrealized holding gain
    d) gross profit

_____ 18. Conventionally, accountants refer to the difference between sales and cost of goods sold as the:
   a) operating profit
   b) realized holding gain
   c) unrealized holding gain
   d) gross profit

_____ 19. The difference between cost of goods sold based on replacement cost and cost of goods sold based on acquisition cost is the:
   a) operating profit
   b) realized holding gain
   c) unrealized holding gain
   d) gross profit

_____ 20. During periods of rising prices, this cost flow assumption produces the highest reported net income:
   a) FIFO method
   b) LIFO method
   c) weighted-average method
   d) all produce the same net income

_____ 21. When a firm records the payment within the discount period and is using the net method of recording purchases, the result will be:
   a) a debit to Discounts Lost account
   b) a credit to Discounts Lost account
   c) a credit to Purchases Discount account
   d) no entry to Discounts Lost or Purchases Discount accounts

Exercises

1. Indicate the normal balances (either debit or credit) for each of the following:

Account	Normal Balance
a. Purchases	_____
b. Accounts Payable	_____
c. Freight-In	_____
d. Sales	_____
e. Purchases (Cash) Discount	_____
f. Purchases Allowance	_____
g. Purchases Returns	_____
h. Purchases Discounts Lost	_____
i. Finished Goods Inventory (Perpetual)	_____
j. Cost of Goods Sold	_____
k. Accounts Receivable	_____

2. Place the correct number in the space provided for each of the following:

Beginning Inventory	$ 10,000	$ (c)	$ (e)	$ 45,000	$ (i)
Net Purchases	(a)	40,000	85,000	(g)	275,000
Total Goods Available	$110,000	$45,000	$85,000	$245,000	$350,000
Ending Inventory	9,000	(d)	0	(h)	90,000
Cost of Goods Sold	$ (b)	$38,000	$ (f)	$215,000	$ (j)

a. _____	f. _____
b. _____	g. _____
c. _____	h. _____
d. _____	i. _____
e. _____	j. _____

3. The LWM Corporation purchases its merchandise from a wholesaler that allows terms of 2/10, n/30. The following transactions took place that are related to purchases in January and February, LWM's first two months of operation. The company uses a periodic inventory system.

Jan. 15	Purchased Merchandise — Gross Invoice Price	$5,000
Jan. 23	Purchased Merchandise — Gross Invoice Price	$3,000
Jan. 24	Paid January 15 Invoice	$4,900
Feb. 15	Paid January 23 Invoice	$3,000

   a. Record the foregoing transactions in general journal form, assuming that LWM Corporation uses the gross price method of recording purchases.
   b. Record the foregoing transactions in general journal form, assuming that LWM Corporation uses the net price method of recording purchases.

4. Brother Prince Limited uses LIFO inventory costing. Here are certain items of information relating to the current inventory operations:

Replacement cost of goods sold	$ 960
Acquisition cost of goods sold	900
Replacement cost of ending inventory	2,100
Acquisition cost of ending inventory	1,620
Sales revenue	1,650

   Determine: a. operating profit on sales
   b. realized holding gain
   c. conventionally reported gross profit
   d. unrealized holding gain

5. The following data were obtained from the inventory records of Austin Inc. for the month of July:

Jul. 1	Beginning Inventory	2,000 units @ $3 each
Jul. 5	Issued	500 units
Jul. 8	Purchased	1,000 units @ $4 each
Jul. 12	Purchased	300 units @ $3 each
Jul. 15	Issued	400 units
Jul. 20	Issued	800 units
Jul. 25	Issued	500 units
Jul. 30	Purchased	500 units @ $5 each

   a. Calculate the cost of July ending inventory, assuming a periodic inventory system using:
      i. FIFO cost flow assumption
      ii. LIFO cost flow assumption
      iii. weighted-average flow assumption
   b. Calculate the cost of goods sold for July, assuming a periodic inventory system using:
      i. FIFO cost flow assumption
      ii. LIFO cost flow assumption
   c. Calculate the ending inventory and cost of goods sold, assuming a perpetual inventory system using:
      i. LIFO cost flow assumption
      ii. weighted-average flow assumption

PROBLEM 1 FOR SELF-STUDY

Exhibit 7.8 presents data on beginning amounts of, additions to, and withdrawals from the inventory of Item X during June. Beginning inventory is assumed to be 100 units, costing $10 each, in all cases.[10]

  a. Compute cost of goods sold and ending inventory using a FIFO cost flow assumption. Note that periodic and perpetual approaches give the same results.

  b. Compute cost of goods sold and ending inventory using a LIFO cost flow assumption with a periodic inventory.

  c. Compute cost of goods sold and ending inventory using a LIFO cost flow assumption with a perpetual inventory.

  d. Compute cost of goods sold and ending inventory using a weighted-average cost flow assumption in a periodic inventory.

  e. Compute cost of goods sold and ending inventory using a weighted-average cost flow assumption in a perpetual inventory.

EXHIBIT 7.8
Data for Illustration of Inventory Calculations

Item X	Units	Unit Cost	Total Cost
Beginning Inventory, June 1	100	$10.00	$1,000
Purchases, June 7	400	11.00	4,400
Purchases, June 12	100	12.50	1,250
Total Goods Available for Sale at Cost	600		$6,650
Withdrawals, June 5	25		?
Withdrawals, June 10	10		?
Withdrawals, June 15	200		?
Withdrawals, June 25	260		?
Total Withdrawals During June	495		?
Ending Inventory, June 30	105		?
Replacement Cost per Unit, June 30		$13.60	

PROBLEM 2 FOR SELF-STUDY

Refer to the data for Item X in Exhibits 7.9 and 7.10 on pages 444 and 445, showing cost of goods sold and ending inventory in a periodic inventory using FIFO and LIFO cost flow assumptions, respectively. Assume that the 495 units withdrawn from inventory were sold for $15 each, $7,425 in total. Construct a schedule that both separates operating profit from holding gains and separates *realized* holding gains from *unrealized* holding gains. Show the results for FIFO and LIFO in parallel columns. The total of operating profit and realized holding gain should be equal to the gross profit reported in historical cost income statements. The total of operating profit and all holding gains should be the same for LIFO as for FIFO. Assume that the replacement cost of item X remained unchanged until a purchase was made.

---

[10] To simplify the problem, beginning inventory is shown as having the same opening valuation of $1,000 under all cost flow assumptions. If costs had varied in the past, the opening unit costs would differ across cost flow assumptions.

PROBLEM 3 FOR SELF-STUDY

Canadian Steel Ltd. uses a LIFO cost flow assumption for inventories. Its year-end financial statements show the following amounts:

Balance Sheet Inventories:	
Beginning of Year	$1,500,000
End of Year	$1,700,000
Income Statement Amounts:	
Cost of Goods Sold	$8,000,000
Income Before Taxes	800,000
The Excess of FIFO Cost over Reported LIFO Cost of Inventory:	
Beginning of Year	$1,650,000
End of Year	$1,850,000

a. Compute the inventory turnover ratio from the published financial statements based on LIFO cost flow.

b. Compute the difference in income before taxes between LIFO and FIFO.

c. Compute the inventory turnover ratio computed from the financial statements as they would appear using FIFO cost flow.

ANSWERS TO SELF-STUDY QUESTIONS AND EXERCISES

True/False

1. T	7. F	13. T	19. F
2. F	8. T	14. F	20. T
3. F	9. T	15. F	21. T
4. T	10. F	16. F	22. F
5. F	11. T	17. T	23. T
6. F	12. T	18. F	24. F

Matching

1. f	7. p	13. m	19. l
2. r	8. a	14. d	20. e
3. u	9. g	15. o	21. w
4. j	10. c	16. k	22. h
5. q	11. x	17. t	23. s
6. n	12. i	18. b	24. v

Multiple Choice

1. a	7. b	13. a	19. b
2. d	8. a	14. c	20. a
3. b	9. c	15. c	21. d
4. c	10. c	16. a	
5. d	11. b	17. c	
6. b	12. b	18. d	

Exercises

1. a. Debit	**2.** a. $100,000	
b. Credit	b. $101,000	
c. Debit	c. $ 5,000	
d. Credit	d. $ 7,000	
e. Credit	e. 0	
f. Credit	f. $ 85,000	
g. Credit	g. $200,000	
h. Debit	h. $ 30,000	
i. Debit	i. $ 75,000	
j. Debit	j. $260,000	
k. Debit		

3.

			Dr.	Cr.
a.	1/15	Merchandise Purchases	$5,000	
		Accounts Payable		$5,000
		To record purchases on account.		
	1/23	Merchandise Purchases	$3,000	
		Accounts Payable		$3,000
		To record purchases on account.		
	1/24	Accounts Payable	$5,000	
		Purchase (Cash) Discounts		$ 100
		Cash		4,900
		To pay Jan. 15 invoice within discount period.		
	2/15	Accounts Payable	$3,000	
		Cash		$3,000
		To pay Jan. 23. invoice after discount period lapsed.		
b.	1/15	Merchandise Purchases	$4,900	
		Accounts Payable		$4,900
		To record purchases on account.		
	1/23	Merchandise Purchases	$2,940	
		Accounts Payable		$2,940
		To record purchases on account.		
	1/24	Accounts Payable	$4,900	
		Cash		$4,900
		To pay Jan. 15 invoice within discount period.		
	2/15	Accounts Payable	$2,940	
		Purchase (Cash) Discounts Lost	60	
		Cash		$3,000
		To pay Jan. 23 invoice after discount period lapsed.		

4. a.
Sales Revenue	$1,650
Less: Replacement Cost of Goods Sold	(960)
Operating Profit on Sales	$ 690

b.
Replacement Cost of Goods Sold	$ 960
Less: Acquisition Cost of Goods Sold	(900)
Realized Holding Gain	$ 60

c. Sales Revenue $1,650
    Less: Acquisition Cost of Goods Sold   (900)
    Conventionally Reported Gross Profit $ 750
    (sum of a + b)

d. Replacement Cost of Ending Inventory $2,100
    Less: Acquisition Cost of Ending Inventory   (1,620)
    Unrealized Holding Gain $ 480

5. a. i.

	Available	Issued
Jul. 1 Beginning	2,000	
Jul. 5		500
Jul. 8	1,000	
Jul. 12	300	
Jul. 15		400
Jul. 20		800
Jul. 25		500
Jul. 30	500	
Total Available Units	3,800	2,200
Issued Units	(2,200)	
Units in Ending Inventory	1,600	

i.

	Units	Unit Cost	Total
	500	$5	$2,500
	300	3	900
	800	4	3,200
FIFO Ending Inventory	1,600		$6,600

ii.

	Units	Unit Cost	Total
LIFO Ending Inventory	1,600	$3	$4,800

iii.

	Units	Unit Cost	Total
	2,000	$3	$6,000
	1,000	4	4,000
	300	3	900
	500	5	2,500
	3,800		$13,400

Weighted-Average $13,400/3,800 = $3.53/unit
Ending Inventory   1,600 @ $3.53 = $5,643

b. i.

	Units	Unit Cost	Total
	2,000	$3	$6,000
	200	4	800
FIFO Cost of Goods Sold	2,200		$6,800

ii.

	Units	Unit Cost	Total
	500	$5	$2,500
	300	3	900
	1,000	4	4,000
	400	3	1,200
LIFO Cost of Goods Sold	2,200		$8,600

c. i.

Date	Purchased Units	Purchased Cost	Purchased Amount	Issued Units	Issued Cost	Issued Amount	Balance Units	Balance Cost	Balance Amount
7/1							2,000	$3	$6,000
7/5				500	$3	$1,500	1,500	3	4,500
7/8	1,000	$4	$4,000				1,500	3	4,500
							1,000	4	4,000
7/12	300	3	900				1,500	3	4,500
							1,000	4	4,000
7/15							300	3	900
				300	3	900	1,500	3	4,500
				100	4	400	900	4	3,600

c. i.

	Purchased			Issued			Balance		
Date	Units	Cost	Amount	Units	Cost	Amount	Units	Cost	Amount
7/20				800	4	3,200	1,500	3	4,500
							100	4	400
7/25				100	4	400			
				400	3	1,200	1,100	3	3,300
7/30	500	5	2,500				1,100	3	3,300
							500	5	2,500
				2,200		$7,600	1,600		$5,800

Perpetual LIFO Ending Inventory   1,600 units $5,800 cost

Perpetual LIFO Cost of Goods Sold   2,200 units $7,600 cost

c. ii.

	Purchased			Issued			Balance		
Date	Units	Cost	Amount	Units	Cost	Amount	Units	Cost	Amount
7/1							2,000	$3	$6,000
7/5				500	$3	$1,500	1,500	3	4,500
7/8	1,000	$4	$4,000				2,500	3.40	8,500
7/12	300	3	900				2,800	3.36*	9,400
7/15				400	3.36	1,344	2,400	3.36	8,056
7/20				800	3.36	2,688	1,600	3.36	5,368
7/25				500	3.36	1,680	1,100	3.36	3,688
7/30	500	5	2,500				1,600	3.87*	6,188
				2,200		$7,212	1,600		$6,188

Rounded to the nearest cent.

Perpetual Weighted-Average Ending Inventory   1,600 units $6,188 cost

Perpetual Weighted-Average Cost of Goods Sold   2,200 units $7,212 cost

SUGGESTED SOLUTION TO PROBLEM 1 FOR SELF-STUDY

a. See Exhibit 7.9.

b. See Exhibit 7.10.

c. See Exhibit 7.11.

d. See Exhibit 7.12.

e. See Exhibit 7.13.

EXHIBIT 7.9
Ending Inventory and Cost of Goods Sold Computation Using a Periodic Inventory and a FIFO Cost Flow Assumption

Item X

Ending Inventory Computation

100 Units @ $12.50 (from June 12 purchase)	$1,250
5 units @ $11.00 (from June 7 purchase)	55
Ending Inventory, June 30	$1,305

Cost of Goods Sold Computation

Cost of Goods Available for Sale	$6,650
Less: Ending Inventory	(1,305)
Cost of Goods Sold	$5,345

EXHIBIT 7.10
Ending Inventory and Cost of Goods Sold Computation
Using a Periodic Inventory and a LIFO Cost Flow Assumption

Item X

Ending Inventory Computation

100 Units @ $10.00 (from beginning inventory)	$1,000
5 units @ $11.00 (from first purchase, June 7)	55
Ending Inventory at Cost	$1,055

Cost of Goods Sold Computation

Cost of Goods Available for Sale	$6,650
Less: Ending Inventory	(1,055)
Cost of Goods Sold	$5,595

EXHIBIT 7.11
Ending Inventory and
Cost of Goods Sold Computation
Using a Perpetual Inventory
and a LIFO Cost Flow Assumption

Item X
Cost of Goods Sold Computation

Date	Received			Issued			Balance		
	Units	Cost	Amount	Units	Cost	Amount	Units	Cost	Amount
6/1							100	$10.00	$1,000
6/5				25	$10.00	$ 250	75	10.00	750
6/7	400	$11.00	$4,400				75	10.00	750
							400	11.00	4,400
6/10				10	11.00	110	75	10.00	750
							390	11.00	4,290
6/12	100	12.50	1,250				75	10.00	750
							390	11.00	4,290
							100	12.50	1,250
6/15				100	12.50	1,250	75	10.00	750
				100	11.00	1,100	290	11.00	3,190
6/25				260	11.00	2,860	75	10.00	750
Cost of Goods Sold						$5,570	30	11.00	330

Ending Inventory Computation

75 units @ $10.00	$ 750
30 units @ $11.00	330
Ending Inventory	$1,080

Alternative Cost of Goods Sold Computation

Cost of Goods Available for Sale	$6,650
Less: Ending Inventory	(1,080)
Cost of Goods Sold	$5,570

EXHIBIT 7.12

**Ending Inventory and Cost of Goods Sold Computation
Using Periodic Inventory and a
Weighted-Average Cost Flow Assumption**

Ending Inventory Computation		
6/1	100 units @ $10.00	$1,000
6/7	400 units @ $11.00	4,400
6/12	100 units @ $12.50	1,250
	600 units @ $11.08 (= $6,650/600)	$6,650
Ending inventory (105 units @ $11.08)		$1,163
Cost of Goods Sold Computation		
Cost of Goods Available for Sale		$6,650
Less: Ending Inventory		1,163
Cost of Goods Sold		$5,487[a]

[a] Because of rounding error, this number is not 495 (= 600 − 105) units × $11.08 = $5,485. In general, the weighted-average unit price should be applied either to ending inventory or to cost of goods sold. After being applied to one, the other is found from the inventory equation.

EXHIBIT 7.13

**Ending Inventory and Cost of Goods Sold Computation
Using a Perpetual Inventory and a
Moving-Average Cost Flow Assumption**

Item X
Ending Inventory and Cost of Goods Sold Computation

	Received			Issued			Balance		
Date	Units	Cost	Amount	Units	Cost	Amount	Units	Total Cost	Unit Cost[a]
6/1							100	$1,000	$10.00
6/5				25	$10.00	$ 250	75	750	10.00
6/7	400	$11.00	$4,400				475	5,150	10.84
6/10				10	10.84	108	465	5,042	10.84
6/12	100	12.50	1,250				565	6,292	11.14
6/15				200	11.14	2,228	365	4,064	11.13[b]
6/25				260	11.13	2,894	105	1,170	11.14
Cost of Goods Sold						$5,480			

Alternative Cost of Goods Sold Computation

Cost of Goods Available for Sale	$6,650
Less: Ending Inventory	(1,170)
Cost of Goods Sold	$5,480

[a] Unit cost = total cost/units.
[b] Note how the rounding effects change the unit cost even though no new units were acquired.

SUGGESTED SOLUTION TO PROBLEM 2 FOR SELF-STUDY

See Exhibit 7.14.

EXHIBIT 7.14
Reporting of Operating Profits
and Holding Gains for Item X

	Cost Flow Assumption			
	FIFO		**LIFO**	
Periodic Inventory Method				
Sales Revenue from Item X (495 × $15.00)	$7,425		$7,425	
Less: Replacement Cost of Goods Sold				
[(25 × $10.00) + (10 × $11.00)				
+ (460 × $12.50)]	(6,110)		(6,110)	
Operating Profit on Sales of Item X		$1,315		$1,315
Realized Holding Gain on Item X:				
Replacement Cost of Goods Sold	$6,110		$6,110	
Less: Acquisition Cost of Goods Sold				
(FIFO — Exhibit 7.9; LIFO — Exhibit 7.10)	5,345		5,595	
Realized Holding Gain on Item X		765		515
Conventionally Reported Gross Profit		**$2,080**		**$1,830**
Unrealized Holding Gain on Item X:				
Replacement Cost of Ending Inventory				
(105 × $13.60; see Exhibit 7.8)	$1,428		$1,428	
Less: Acquisition Cost of Ending Inventory				
(FIFO — Exhibit 7.9; LIFO — Exhibit 7.10)	(1,305)		(1,055)	
Unrealized Holding Gain on Item X		123		373
Economic Income on Sales and Holding Inventory				
of Item X		**$2,203**		**$2,203**

SUGGESTED SOLUTION TO PROBLEM 3
FOR SELF-STUDY

a. Inventory Turnover = $\dfrac{\text{Cost of Goods Sold}}{\text{Average Inventory During Year}}$

$= \dfrac{\$8,000,000}{0.5(\$1,500,000 + \$1,700,000)}$

= 5 times per year

b. Pretax income would be larger by the amount that cost of goods sold would be smaller. Cost of goods sold would be smaller by $200,000 = $1,850,000 − $1,650,000.

c. $\dfrac{\text{Inventory}}{\text{Turnover}} = \dfrac{\text{Cost of Goods Sold}}{\text{Average Inventory During Year}}$

$= \dfrac{\$8,000,000 - \$200,000}{0.5[\$1,500,000 + \$1,650,000) + (\$1,700,000 + \$1,850,000)]}$

$= \dfrac{\$7,800,000}{\$3,350,000}$

= 2.33 times per year

ASSIGNMENT MATERIAL

QUESTIONS

1. Review the meaning of each of the key terms listed on page 432.

2. Under what circumstances would the perpetual and periodic inventory systems both yield the same inventory amount if the weighted-average flow assumption were used?

3. During a period of rising prices, will the FIFO or LIFO cost flow assumption result in the higher ending inventory amount? The lower inventory amount? Assume no changes in physical quantities during the period.

4. Refer to the preceding question. Which cost flow assumption will result in the higher ending inventory amount during a period of declining prices? The lower inventory amount? Ignore the lower of cost and market method.

5. a. During a period of rising prices, will a FIFO or LIFO cost flow assumption result in the higher cost of goods sold? The lower cost of goods sold? Assume no changes in physical quantities during the period.
   b. Which cost flow assumption, LIFO or FIFO, will result in the higher cost of goods sold during a period of declining prices? The lower cost of goods sold? Ignore the lower of cost and market method.

6. "Cost flow assumptions for inventory are required only because specific identification of items sold is costly. Specific identification is theoretically superior to any cost flow assumption and eliminates the possibility for income manipulation available with some cost flow assumptions." Comment.

7. Assume that a steel manufacturer and a retailing firm have identical sales and income and that the costs of their purchased inputs of goods and services increase at the same rate. The steel company has inventory turnover of about four times per year, whereas the retailer has inventory turnover of about ten times per year.

   Which of the two firms is more likely to increase income through switching from FIFO to LIFO? Explain.

8. "LIFO provides a more meaningful income statement than FIFO, even though it provides a less meaningful balance sheet." Does it ever? Does it always?

9. Assume that the cost basis for inventory is changed from historical cost to current cost, that current costs exceed historical costs at the end of the year of change, and that all year-end inventory is sold during the following year. Ignore income tax effects.

What will be the impact of the change on net income for the year of change? On income for the following year? On total income over the two years?

10. Would you expect to find a periodic or perpetual inventory system used in each of the following situations?
    a. The greeting card department of a retail store.
    b. The fur coat department of a retail store.
    c. Supplies storeroom for an automated production line.
    d. Automobile dealership.
    e. Wholesale dealer in bulk salad oil.
    f. Grocery store.
    g. College bookstore.
    h. Diamond ring department of a jewellery store.
    i. Ballpoint pen department of a jewellery store.

11. A noted accountant once claimed that firms using a LIFO cost flow assumption will find that historical cost of goods sold is *greater than* replacement cost of goods sold computed as of the time of sale. Under what circumstances is this assertion likely to be true? (*Hint*: Compare the effects of periodic and perpetual approaches on LIFO cost of goods sold.) Do you agree that the assertion is likely to be true?

EXERCISES

12. *Journal entries for periodic and perpetual inventories.* Goods that cost $1,500 are sold for $2,000 cash. Present the normal journal entries at the time of the sale:
    a. When a periodic inventory is used.
    b. When a perpetual inventory is used.

13. *Computations involving different cost flow assumptions.* The inventory at September 1 and the purchases during September of Hanna Ltd.'s raw material were as follows:

9/1	Inventory	1,000 kg	$ 4,500
9/5	Purchased	3,000 kg	13,500
9/14	Purchased	3,500 kg	17,500
9/27	Purchased	3,000 kg	16,500
9/29	Purchased	1,000 kg	8,000

The inventory at September 30, is 1,800 kilograms.

Assume a periodic inventory system. Compute the cost of the inventory on September 30 under each of the following cost flow assumptions:
    a. FIFO
    b. Weighted Average
    c. LIFO

14. *Compute acquisition cost of inventory and record sales transaction using perpetual inventory.*   Ducru Ltd. ordered from an overseas supplier 10,000 shirts that had a list price of $12 each, requesting the normal trade discount. The invoice arrived showing a discount of 40 percent from list price. Ducru Ltd. paid its customs broker $750 for taxes and paid a trucking company $250 to deliver the goods. Later, it sold 1,000 shirts for $12 each on account. Ducru Ltd. uses a perpetual inventory system.

    Prepare journal entries to record the sales transaction.

15. *Over long enough time spans, income is cash-in less cash-out; cost flow assumptions.*   Gazin Inc. was in business for four years. Exhibit 7.15 shows its purchases and sales during that four-year period. Ignore income taxes.

EXHIBIT 7.15
GAZIN INC.
Purchases and Sales
(Exercise 15)

	Purchases		Sales	
	Units	Unit Cost	Units	Unit Cost
Year 1	12,000	$10	9,000	$15
Year 2	11,000	11	10,000	17
Year 3	10,000	12	11,000	19
Year 4	9,000	13	12,000	21
Totals	42,000		42,000	

a. Compute income for each of the four years assuming FIFO cost flow.
b. Compute income for each of the four years assuming LIFO cost flow.
c. Compare total income over the four-year period. Does the cost flow assumption matter?

16. *Over long enough time spans, income is cash-in less cash-out; cost basis for inventory.*   The Sales Co. Ltd. began business on January 1, Year 1. Information concerning merchandise inventories, purchases, and sales for the first three years of operation follows:

	Year 3	Year 2	Year 1
Sales	$450,000	$330,000	$300,000
Purchases	350,000	260,000	280,000
Inventories, Dec. 31:			
At cost	95,000	95,000	80,000
At market	100,000	80,000	75,000

a. Compute the gross profit on sales (sales minus cost of goods sold) for each year, using the lower of cost and market basis in valuing inventories.

b. Compute the gross profit on sales (sales minus cost of goods sold) for each year, using the acquisition cost basis in valuing inventories.

c. Indicate your conclusion about whether the lower of cost and market basis of valuing inventories is "conservative."

17. *When goods available for sale exceed sales, income can be manipulated, even when specific identification is used.* Langoa Limited has 300 identical TV sets available for sale during December, when it expects to sell 200 sets for $500 each. These TV sets were acquired as follows: 100 in June for $200 each, 100 in August for $300 each, and 100 in November for $250 each. Assume that sales for December are 200 units at $500 each.

a. Compute gross profit for December assuming FIFO.

b. Compute gross profit for December assuming specific identification of sales and sets sold to minimize reported income for tax purposes.

c. Compute gross profit for December assuming specific identification of sales and sets sold to maximize reported income, so as to increase the store manager's profit-sharing bonus for the year.

18. *Computations involving cost flow assumptions and periodic or perpetual approaches.* The following information concerning Arpesfeld Limited's inventory of merchandise is available:

Nov.	2	Inventory	4,000 kg @ $5
	9	Sold	3,000 kg
	16	Purchased	7,000 kg @ $6
	23	Sold	3,000 kg
	30	Sold	3,000 kg

Compute the cost of goods sold and the cost of ending inventory on November 30 for each of the following combinations of inventory systems and cost flow assumptions.

a. Periodic FIFO
b. Perpetual FIFO
c. Periodic weighted average
d. Perpetual weighted average
e. Periodic LIFO
f. Perpetual LIFO

19. *Computing cost of goods sold under various treatments of cost flows with periodic and perpetual systems.* The Central Supply Co. Ltd. has in its inventory on May 1 three units of item K, all purchased on the same date at a price of $60 per unit. Information relative to item K is as follows:

Date	Explanation	Units	Unit Cost	Tag Number
May 1	Inventory	3	$60	K-515, 516, 517
3	Purchase	2	65	K-518, 519
12	Sale	3		K-515, 518, 519
19	Purchase	2	76	K-520, 521
25	Sale	1		K-516

Compute the cost of units sold in accordance with the following:
a. Specific identification of units sold.
b. FIFO cost flow assumption and periodic inventory system.
c. FIFO cost flow assumption and perpetual inventory system.
d. LIFO cost flow assumption and periodic inventory system.
e. LIFO cost flow assumption and perpetual inventory system.
f. Weighted-average cost flow assumption and perpetual inventory system.
g. Weighted-average cost flow assumption and periodic inventory system.

20. *LIFO provides opportunity for income manipulation.* Lagrange Ltd. began the year with 20,000 units of product on hand that cost $10 each. During the year, it produced another 30,000 units at a cost of $18 each. Sales for the year were expected to total 50,000 units. During November, the company had to make a decision about production for the remainder of the year. No additional units need be produced this year beyond the 30,000 units already produced. Up to 60,000 additional units could be produced; the cost would be $22 per unit regardless of the quantity produced. The company uses a periodic LIFO inventory. Assume that sales are 50,000 units for the year at an average price of $25 per unit.
a. What production for the remainder of the year gives the largest cost of goods sold for the year? What is that cost of goods sold?
b. What production for the remainder of the year gives the smallest cost of goods sold for the year? What is that cost of goods sold?
c. Compare the gross margins implied by the two production plans devised in **(a)** and **(b)**.

21. *Calculations combining cost basis and cost flow assumptions.* The Sanlex Co. Ltd. started the year with no inventory on hand. It manufactured two batches of inventory (100 units each), which were identical except that the variable costs of producing the first batch were $120 and the variable costs of producing the second batch were $200 because of rising prices. By the end of the year, Sanlex Co. Ltd. had sold 75 units from the first batch for $300 and none of the second batch. The ending inventory had a market value of $305. Total fixed manufacturing costs for the year were $160. Under the absorption (full) costing procedure, $100 of fixed manufacturing costs allocated to units produced remained in inventory at the close of the year. Selling and administrative expenses for the year were $40.
Prepare a statement of pretax income for the Sanlex Co. Ltd. for the year under each of the following sets of assumptions:
a. FIFO, acquisition cost basis
b. LIFO, acquisition cost basis
c. FIFO, lower of cost and market basis

22. *Separating operating profit from holding gains.* On January 1, the merchandise inventory of Revsine Appliance Store consisted of 1,000 units acquired for $450 each. During the year, 2,500 additional units were acquired at an average price of $600 each while 2,300 units were

sold for $900 each. The replacement cost of these units at the time they were sold averaged $600 during the year. The replacement cost of units on December 31 was $750 per unit.

a. Calculate cost of goods sold under both FIFO and LIFO cost flow assumptions.

b. Prepare partial statements of income showing gross profit on sales as revenues less cost of goods sold with both FIFO and LIFO cost flow assumptions.

c. Prepare partial income statements separating the gross profit on sales into operating profits and realized holding gains under both FIFO and LIFO.

d. Append to the bottom of the statements prepared in part **(c)** a statement showing the amount of unrealized holding gains and the total of realized income plus unrealized holding gains.

e. If you did the above steps correctly, the totals in part **(d)** are the same for both FIFO and LIFO. Is this equality a coincidence? Why or why not?

23. **Effect of inventory errors** (*adapted from a problem by S. Zeff*). Pollack Company reported net income of $106,000 in Year 1 and $88,000 in Year 2. Early in Year 3, Pollack Company discovered that it had *overstated* its Year 1 ending inventory by $6,000 and had *understated* its Year 2 inventory by $10,000.

What should have been the company's reported net incomes for Year 1 and Year 2? Ignore income taxes.

PROBLEMS AND CASES

24. **Effect of inventory errors.** On December 30, Year 1, merchandise amounting to $1,000 was received by the Warren Co. Ltd. and was counted in its December 31 listing of all inventory items on hand. The invoice was not received until January 4, Year 2, at which time the acquisition was recorded as a Year 2 acquisition. The acquisition should have been recorded for Year 1. Assume that the error was not ever discovered by the firm. Warren Co. Ltd. uses a periodic inventory system. Indicate the effect (overstatement, understatement, none) on each of the following amounts. Ignore income taxes.

a. Inventory, 12/31/Year 1

b. Inventory, 12/31/Year 2

c. Cost of goods sold, Year 1

d. Cost of goods sold, Year 2

e. Net income, Year 1

f. Net income, Year 2

g. Accounts payable, 12/31/Year 1

h. Accounts payable, 12/31/Year 2

i. Retained earnings, 12/31/Year 2

25. *Analysis of adjunct and contra accounts used for purchases and sales.* The accounts listed below might appear in the records of a retail store. Their use is never required, but accounts such as these often provide details about purchase activity useful to management. From the name of the account and your understanding of the accounting for purchase and sales, indicate:

   a. Whether the account is a permanent account (to appear as such on the balance sheet) or a temporary account (to be closed at the end of the accounting period).
   b. The normal balance, debit or credit, in the account. If the account is a temporary one, give the normal balance before closing.
   c. If the account is a temporary one, the kind of account it is closed to — balance sheet asset, balance sheet liability, balance sheet owners' equity through a revenue account, or balance sheet owners' equity through an expense (or revenue contra) account.

   (1) Merchandise Purchases
   (2) Merchandise Purchase Allowances
   (3) Merchandise Purchase Returns
   (4) Purchase Returns
   (5) Sales Tax on Purchases
   (6) Freight-In on Purchases
   (7) Sales Allowances
   (8) Allowance for Sales Discounts
   (9) Provincial Sales Taxes Payable on Sales

   (The next three items should not be attempted until Problem 26 has been read.)

   (10) Purchase Discounts
   (11) Purchase Discounts Taken
   (12) Purchase Discounts Lost

26. *Gross and net price methods for treating purchase discounts.* The chapter mentions two alternatives for treating discounts on merchandise purchases often used in practice: (1) the gross price method, which recognizes the amount of discounts taken on payments made during the period without regard to the period of purchase, and (2) the net price method, which deducts all discounts made available from the gross purchase invoice prices at the time of purchases. This problem explains the two methods.

   Alternative 1: Gross Price Method The gross price method of accounting for purchases records invoices at the gross price and accumulates the amount of discounts taken on payments made. Suppose that goods with a gross invoice price of $1,000 are purchased, 2/10, net/30. (That is, a 2 percent discount from invoice price is offered if payment is made within ten days and the full invoice price is due, in any case, within 30 days.) The entries to record the purchase and the payment (1) under the assumption that the payment is made in time to take the discount, and (2) under the assumption that the payment is too late to take advantage of the discount, are as follows:

Gross Price Method	(1) Discount Taken		(2) Discount Not Taken	
Purchases (or Inventory)	$1,000		$1,000	
Accounts Payable		$1,000		$1,000
To record purchase.				
Accounts Payable	$1,000		$1,000	
Cash		$ 980		$1,000
Purchase Discounts (or Inventory)		20		—
To record payment.				

The balance in the Purchase Discounts account is deducted from the balance in the Purchases account in calculating net purchases for a period. Such a deduction approximates the results achieved by treating purchase discounts as a reduction in purchase price at the time of purchase. It is only an approximation because the total adjustment includes discounts taken on payments made this period, without regard to the period of purchase.

An accurate adjustment would require eliminating the discounts taken related to purchases of previous periods while including the amount of discounts available at the end of the accounting period that are expected to be taken during the following period. This refinement in the treatment of purchase discounts is seldom employed in practice.

Alternative 2: Net Price Method In recording purchases, the purchase discount is deducted from the gross purchase price immediately upon receipt of the invoice, and the net invoice price is used in the entries. The example used previously of a $1,000 invoice price for goods subject to a 2 percent cash discount would be recorded as follows under the net price method:

Net Price Method	(1) Discount Taken		(2) Discount Not Taken	
Purchases (or Inventory)	$980		$980	
Accounts Payable		$980		$ 980
To record purchase.				
Accounts Payable	$980		$980	
Purchase Discounts Lost	—		20	
Cash		$980		$1,000
To record payment.				

The balance in the Purchase Discounts Lost account could be added to the cost of the merchandise purchased and, therefore, viewed as an additional component of goods available for sale. Most accountants believe, however, that discounts lost should be shown as a general operating expense rather than as an addition to the cost of purchases, because lost discounts may indicate an inefficient office force or inadequate financing. In this book, we treat purchase discounts lost as an expense unless an explicit contrary statement is made.

a. Attempt to decide which of these two alternatives is preferable and why. You might find working part **(b)**, below, helpful in making your decision.

b. Prepare a journal form with two pairs of columns, one headed Net Price Method and the other headed Gross Price Method. Using this journal form, show summary entries for the following events in the history of Evans and Foster Ltd., furniture manufacturers.

(1) During the first year of operations, materials with a gross invoice price of $60,000 are purchased. All invoices are subject to a 2 percent cash discount if paid within ten days.

(2) Payments to creditors during the year amount to $53,000, settling $54,000 of accounts payable at gross prices.

(3) Of the $6,000, gross, in unpaid accounts at the end of the year, the discount time has expired on one invoice amounting to $400. It is expected that all other discounts will be taken. This expectation is reflected in the year-end adjustment.

(4) During the first few days of the next period, all invoices are paid in accordance with expectations.

27. *Gross and net price methods for recording purchase discounts.* (This problem should not be attempted until Problem 26 has been read.) The following are selected transactions of the Skousen Appliance Store:

(1) A shipment of refrigerators is received from the Standard Electric Corp., $15,000. Terms 2/30, n/60.

(2) Part of the shipment of **(1)** is returned. The gross invoice price of the returned goods is $1,200, and a credit memorandum for this amount is received from the Standard Electric Corp.

(3) The invoice of the Standard Electric Corp. is paid in time to take the discount.

a. Give entries on the books of the Skousen Appliance Store, assuming that the net price method is used.

b. Give entries on the books of the Skousen Appliance Store, assuming that the gross price method is used.

28. *Fundamentals of the gross margin method for approximating inventory amounts.* The merchandise inventory of Parks Store was destroyed by fire on July 4. The accounting records were saved and provided the following information:

Cost of Merchandise Inventory on Hand, January 1	$ 45,000
Purchases of Merchandise, January 1 to July 4	125,000
Sales, January 1 to July 4	180,000

The average retail markup over the cost of the goods sold during the year before the fire was 50 percent of the acquisition cost. That is, selling price equals 150 percent of cost.

a. Estimate the cost of the goods on hand at the time of the fire.

b. Give the journal entry to record the loss, assuming that it was uninsured.

c. Give the journal entry to record the loss, assuming that all goods were fully insured for their acquisition cost.

29. *Fundamentals of the retail inventory method for approximating inventory amounts.* Refer to the data in the preceding problem. Assume that the store owner does not know the average retail markup over cost for the destroyed goods. The accounting records show that the total sales revenue during the four years preceding the fire amounted to $1,000,000 and the total cost of goods sold over the same period was $650,000.

a. Assume that the ratio of sales prices to cost of goods sold for the last four years reflects this year's operations as well. Estimate the cost of the goods destroyed in the fire.

b. Assume the same facts as above, except that the $1,000,000 represents the original selling price of the goods sold during the last four years. Certain goods were marked down before sale so that the actual sales revenue was only $975,000. Assuming that the same percentage of goods was marked down by the same price percentage during the first six months of this year as in the previous four years, estimate the cost of the goods destroyed by the fire.

30. *Detailed comparison of various choices for inventory accounting.* The Harrison Corporation was organized and began retailing operations on January 1, Year 1. Purchases of merchandise inventory during Year 1 and Year 2 were as follows:

	Quantity Purchased	Unit Price	Acquisition Cost
1/10/Year 1	1,000	$10	$10,000
6/30/Year 1	400	15	6,000
10/20/Year 1	200	16	3,200
Total Year 1	1,600		$19,200

	Quantity Purchased	Unit Price	Acquisition Cost
2/18/Year 2	300	$18	$ 5,400
7/15/Year 2	100	20	2,000
12/15/Year 2	500	22	11,000
Total Year 2	900		$18,400

The number of units sold during Year 1 and Year 2 was 900 units and 1,100 units, respectively. Harrison Corporation uses a periodic inventory system.

a. Calculate the cost of goods sold during Year 1 under the FIFO cost flow assumption.

b. Calculate the cost of goods sold during Year 1 under the LIFO cost flow assumption.
c. Calculate the cost of goods sold during Year 1 under the weighted-average cost flow assumption.
d. Calculate the cost of goods sold during Year 2 under the FIFO cost flow assumption.
e. Calculate the cost of goods sold during Year 2 under the LIFO cost flow assumption.
f. Calculate the cost of goods sold during Year 2 under the weighted-average cost flow assumption.
g. For the two years taken as a whole, will FIFO or weighted-average result in reporting the larger net income? What is the difference in net income for the two-year period under FIFO as compared to weighted-average? Assume an income tax rate of 40 percent for both years.
h. Which method, weighted-average or FIFO, should Harrison Corporation probably prefer and why?

31. *Continuation of preceding problem introducing current cost concepts.* (This problem should not be attempted until Problem 30 has been done.) Assume the same data for the Harrison Corporation as given in the previous problem. In addition, assume the following:

Selling Price per Unit:	
Year 1	$25
Year 2	30
Average Current Replacement Cost:	
Year 1	$15
Year 2	20
Current Replacement Cost:	
December 31, Year 1	$17
December 31, Year 2	22

a. Prepare an analysis for Year 1 that identifies operating margins, realized holding gains and losses, and unrealized holding gains and losses for the FIFO, LIFO, and weighted-average cost flow assumptions.
b. Repeat part (a) for Year 2.
c. Demonstrate that over the two-year period, the income plus holding gains before taxes of Harrison Corporation are independent of the cost flow assumption.

32. *Impact on financial statements of the choice between a FIFO and a LIFO flow assumption.* Take 12 pieces of paper and mark each one with a number from 1 to 12 inclusive. Sort the pieces of paper into a pile with the numbers in consecutive order facing up, so that number 1 is on top and number 12 is on bottom. These 12 pieces of paper are to represent 12 identical units of merchandise purchased over three

periods at prices increasing from $1 to $12. Assume that four of the units are purchased each period for three periods, that three units are sold each period, and that a periodic inventory system is used.

   a. Compute the cost of goods sold and ending inventory amounts for each of the three periods under a FIFO flow assumption.

   b. Compute the cost of goods sold and ending inventory amounts for each of the three periods under a LIFO flow assumption.

   c. Re-sort the 12 pieces of paper into decreasing order to represent declining prices for successive purchases. Compute the cost of goods sold and ending inventory amounts for each of the three periods under a FIFO flow assumption.

   d. Repeat part (c) using a LIFO flow assumption.

   e. Convince yourself that the following are all true statements.

      (1) In periods of rising prices and increasing physical inventories, FIFO implies higher reported income than does LIFO.

      (2) In periods of declining prices and increasing physical inventories, LIFO implies higher reported income than does FIFO.

      (3) Under FIFO, current prices are reported on the balance sheet and old prices are reported on the income statement.

      (4) Under LIFO, current prices are reported on the income statement and very old prices are reported on the balance sheet.

      (5) In periods of rising prices and increasing physical inventories, the difference between FIFO and LIFO balance sheet amounts for inventory at the end of each period after the first one is larger than the differences between FIFO and LIFO reported net income for each period after the first one.

   f. Assume that in period 4, only one unit (number 13) is purchased for $13, but three are sold. What additional "truth" can you deduce from comparing LIFO and FIFO cost of goods sold when physical quantities are declining and prices are rising?

   g. The LIFO portion of Figure 7.1 represents a periodic inventory. In this part of the question, assume that in each period, the first item is acquired before any sales occur. Then one item is sold, then the two items are purchased; then one more item is sold; then the last purchase is made and the last sale occurs. (If P represents purchase and S represents sale, the sequence of events of each period is PSPPSPS.) Draw a figure similar to those in Figure 7.1 to represent a LIFO cost flow assumption coupled with a perpetual inventory system. Convince yourself that in times of rising prices, the LIFO cost of goods sold figure with a periodic inventory exceeds LIFO cost of goods sold computed with a perpetual inventory.

33. *Exploring the relation between replacement cost of goods sold and historical LIFO cost of goods sold.* The points to grasp in this problem are as follows:

   (1) LIFO cost of goods sold is generally larger in a periodic inventory than in a perpetual inventory.

   (2) LIFO cost of goods sold for most companies is insignificantly different from replacement cost of goods sold using replacement costs as of the time of sale.

FIGURE 7.1
To Aid in Understanding Problem 32

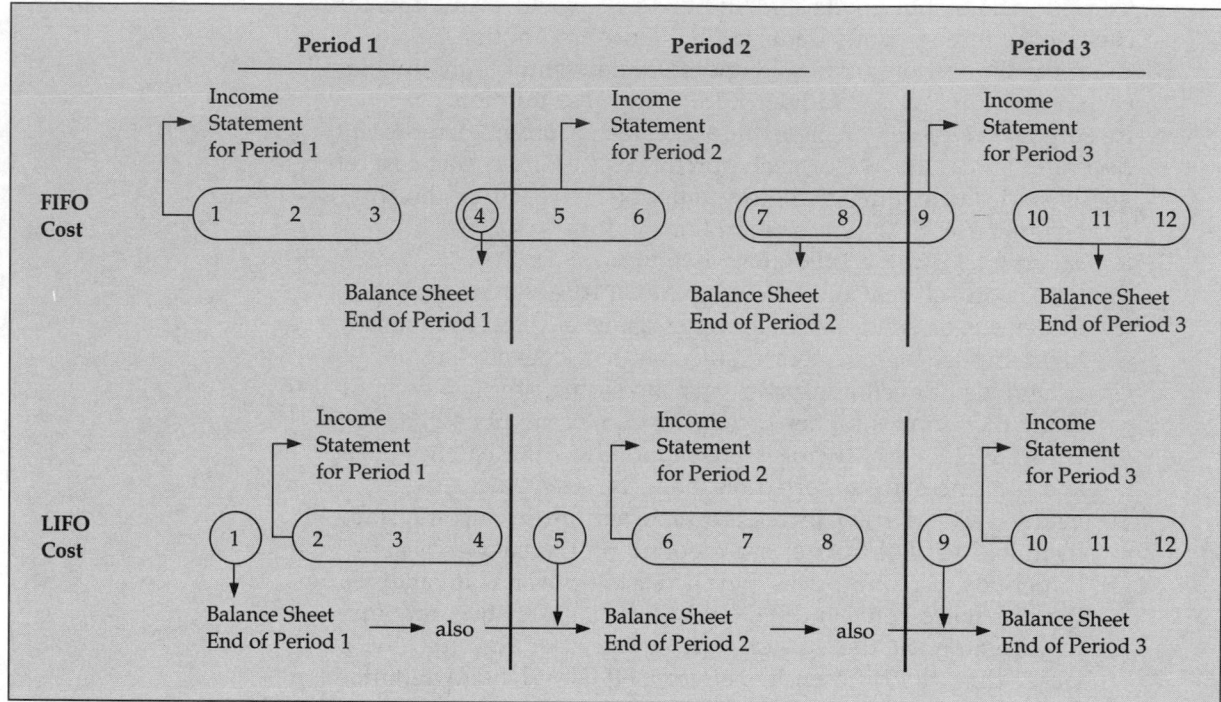

(3) Historical LIFO cost of goods sold in a periodic inventory is likely to be larger (although not significantly) than the replacement cost of goods sold using replacement cost at the time of sale.

The data in Exhibit 7.16 are hypothetical. They are constructed from ratios of an actual retailing firm selling grocery products. Sales revenue for the year is $2,820,000. All expenses (including income taxes) other than cost of goods sold are $144,000 for the year. Exhibit 7.16 shows cost of goods available for sale. The cost of the grocery items for this company increase during the year at a steady rate of about 1 percent per month. The company starts the year with an inventory equal to 1½ months' sales. These items were acquired at the end of December of Year 1 for $300,000. At the end of each month during Year 2, the firm is assumed to acquire inventory in physical quantities equal to the next month's sales requirements. We assume that all sales occur at mid-month during each month and that all purchases occur at the end of a month to be sold during the next month. (These artificial assumptions capture the reality of a firm that acquires inventory, on average, ½ month before it is sold and has an inventory turnover rate of about eight times per year.) Identical physical quantities are purchased and sold each month.

Exhibit 7.16 shows the actual cost of the items purchased at the end of each month and the replacement cost of those items if they had been acquired at mid-month.

EXHIBIT 7.16
Data for Problem 33

	Replacement Cost of Goods Measured at	
	Sales Dates (mid-month)	Purchases Dates (end of month)
December Year 1	—	$ 300,000
January Year 2	$ 201,000	202,000
February Year 2	203,000	204,000
March Year 2	205,000	206,000
April Year 2	207,000	208,000
May Year 2	209,000	210,000
June Year 2	211,000	212,000
July Year 2	213,000	214,000
August Year 2	215,000	216,000
September Year 2	217,000	218,000
October Year 2	219,000	220,000
November Year 2	221,000	222,000
December Year 2	223,000	224,000
Replacement Cost of Goods Sold at Times of Sale	$2,544,000	
Cost of Goods Available for Sale		$2,856,000

At the end of the year, ending physical inventory is equal in amount to $1\frac{1}{2}$ months' sales, which is the same as the physical quantity on hand at the start of the year.

   a. Compute LIFO historical cost of goods sold and net income for Year 2 using a periodic inventory system.
   b. Compute LIFO historical cost of goods sold and net income for Year 2 using a perpetual inventory system.
   c. Compute net income for Year 2 using replacement cost of goods sold at the time of sale.
   d. What is the percentage difference between the largest and smallest cost of goods sold figures computed in (a), (b), and (c)?
   e. What is the percentage error in using LIFO costs of goods sold to approximate replacement cost of goods sold? (Compute percentage errors for both LIFO periodic and LIFO perpetual calculations.)

34. *Comparing LIFO and FIFO with declines in inventory quantities.* The LIFO Company and the FIFO Company both manufacture paper and cardboard products. Prices of timber, paper pulp, and finished paper products have generally increased by about 5 percent per year through the start of this year. Inventory data for the beginning and end of the year are shown below:

	Inventory Amounts	
	December 31	January 1
LIFO Company Inventory (last-in, first-out; historical cost)	$15,870,000	$19,695,000
FIFO Company Inventory (first-in, first-out; lower of cost and market)	38,250,000	46,284,000

Income statements for the two companies for the year ending December 31 are as follows:

	LIFO Company	FIFO Company
Sales	$57,000,000	$129,000,000
Less: Cost of Goods Sold	(44,580,000)	(108,000,000)
Gross Profit	$12,420,000	$ 21,000,000
Less: Operating Expenses		
Depreciation	$ 5,400,000	$ 12,000,000
Other	2,220,000	5,400,000
Total	$ 7,620,000	$ 17,400,000
Net Income Before Income Tax	4,800,000	3,600,000
Income Tax (40 percent)[a]	(1,920,000)	(1,440,000)
Net Income	$ 2,880,000	$ 2,160,000

[a] Assume that the companies calculate income tax expense as a percentage of net income before income tax.

a. Assuming that the prices for timber, paper pulp, and finished paper had remained unchanged during the year, how would the two companies' respective inventory choices affect the interpretation of their financial statements for the year?

b. How would the answer to part (a) differ if prices at the end of the year had been higher than at the beginning of the year?

35. *Reconstructing underlying events from ending inventory amounts* (*adapted from CPA examination*). The Burch Corporation began a merchandising business on January 1, Year 1. It acquired merchandise costing $100,000 in Year 1, $125,000 in Year 2, and $135,000 in Year 3. Exhibit 7.17 shows information about Burch Corporation's inventory as it would appear on the balance sheet under different inventory methods. In answering each of the following questions, indicate how the answer is deduced. You may assume that in any one year, prices moved only up or down, but not both.

a. Did prices go up or down in Year 1?

b. Did prices go up or down in Year 3?

EXHIBIT 7.17
BURCH CORPORATION
Inventory Valuations for Balance Sheet
Under Various Assumptions

December 31	LIFO Cost	FIFO Cost	Lower of LIFO Cost and Market	Lower of FIFO Cost and Market
Year 1	$40,200	$40,000	$37,000	$37,000
Year 2	36,400	36,000	34,000	34,000
Year 3	41,800	44,000	41,800	44,000

    c. Which inventory method would show the highest income for Year 1?

    d. Which inventory method would show the highest income for Year 2?

    e. Which inventory method would show the highest income for Year 3?

    f. Which inventory method would show the lowest income for all three years combined?

    g. For Year 3, how much higher or lower would income be on the FIFO cost basis than it would be on the lower-of-FIFO-cost-and-market basis?

36. *Reconstructing accounting policies from financial statement data.* Data for Company A and Company B in Exhibit 7.18 are taken from the annual reports of two actual companies for a recent year. One of these companies uses a LIFO cost flow assumption for 100 percent of its inventories, and the other uses LIFO for about 45 percent of its inventories. Answer the following questions, making explicit the reasoning used in each case.

    a. From the cost of goods sold data alone, which of the companies appears to be the 100 percent LIFO company? The 45 percent LIFO company?

    b. From the ending inventory data alone, which of the companies appears to be the 100 percent LIFO company? The 45 percent LIFO company?

    c. From your answers to parts (a) and (b), draw a conclusion about which of the companies appears to be which.

    d. Note that Company A earned net income equal to 2.1 percent of sales whereas Company B earned net income equal to 7.6 percent of sales. Can you conclude that Company A is less profitable than Company B? Why or why not?

EXHIBIT 7.18
Data for Analysis of LIFO and FIFO
Effects on Financial Statements

	Dollar Amounts in Millions	
	Company A	Company B
Sales Revenue	$5,151	$5,042
Cost of Goods Sold:[a]		
Historical Cost Basis	3,638	3,720
Replacement Cost Basis	3,675	3,720
Net Income	108	383
Ending Inventory:		
Historical Cost Basis	1,026	1,245
Replacement Cost Basis	1,056	2,169
Ratio of Net Income to Revenue	2.1%	7.6%

[a] *Excludes depreciation charges.*

e. Which of the two companies is more likely to be involved in retailing, and which is more likely to be involved in manufacturing? Explain.

37. *Decision making and cost basis for inventories.* Imagine that you take frequent business trips. You have discovered a major airline's Bonus Travel Tickets, which enable the holder to fly round trip anywhere that the airline flies. These tickets are bought and sold by special ticket brokers, and their price fluctuates almost daily in the marketplace. The schedule shown here presents data on tickets purchased and used.

Ticket Number	When Bought	Price Paid	When Used
1	May	$400	May
2	May	400	?
3	May	425	June
4	June	450	July
5	June	475	August
6	June	500	September
7	July	440	?
8	August	550	?

In October, you decide to take a good friend with you on a weekend vacation to New York and to use two of the tickets you have for the trip. At the time you take the October vacation, you have three tickets in your desk drawer: numbers 2, 7, and 8. During the week of the trip, you have the option to purchase new tickets for $600 each, and your broker offers to buy tickets from you or anyone else for $480 each.

Your friend wants to reimburse you for the cost of the travel but has not made clear what is meant by "cost." Your friend does not intend to audit the cost you quote. What is the "cost" of your friend's travel under each of the following sets of facts?

a. For the trip, you use ticket numbers 2 and 8, putting the friend's name on ticket 2 and yours on ticket 8.

b. For the trip, you use ticket numbers 2 and 8, putting the friend's name on ticket 8 and yours on ticket 2.

c. Just before you depart, your broker, in tribute to your being such a good customer, offers you one ticket for the bargain price of $480 and offers to sell you other tickets for $600. You purchase the ticket, but not until after the vacation weekend. For the trip, you use ticket numbers 2 and 8, putting the friend's name on ticket 2 and yours on ticket 8.

d. Same facts as (c), except that you do purchase the bargain-priced ticket and use it during the vacation, putting your friend's mame on it.

e. Indicate how your answers to parts (a) through (d) change (if they do) when you assume that your travelling companion is a business associate, not your friend, and the trip is a business trip, not a vacation.

f. Should the cost you impose on your friend or your business associate depend on which particular ticket happens to be used in travel?

38. **Detailed comparison of various choices for inventory accounting.** The Freeman Corporation was organized and began retailing operations on January 1, Year 1. Purchases of merchandise inventory during Year 1 and Year 2 were as follows:

	Quantity Purchased	Unit Price	Acquisition Cost
1/10/Year 1	600	$10	$ 6,000
6/30/Year 1	200	12	2,400
10/20/Year 1	400	15	6,000
Total Year 1	1,200		$14,400

	Quantity Purchased	Unit Price	Acquisition Cost
2/18/Year 2	500	$18	$ 9,000
7/15/Year 2	500	20	10,000
12/15/Year 2	800	24	19,200
Total Year 2	1,800		$38,200

The number of units sold during Year 1 and Year 2 was 1,000 units and 1,500 units, respectively. Freeman Corporation uses a periodic inventory system.

a. Calculate the cost of goods sold during Year 1 under the FIFO cost flow assumption.

b. Calculate the cost of goods sold during Year 1 under the LIFO cost flow assumption.

c. Calculate the cost of goods sold during Year 1 under the weighted-average cost flow assumption.

d. Calculate the cost of goods sold during Year 2 under the FIFO cost flow assumption.

e. Calculate the cost of goods sold during Year 2 under the LIFO cost flow assumption.

f. Calculate the cost of goods sold during year 2 under the weighted-average cost flow assumption.

39. **Computation of markup ratios and holding gains/losses.** The following data pertain to the first two years of operations of the Macheral Company:

	19X2	19X1
Sales	$462,500	$331,250
Purchases	300,000	230,000
Ending Inventory:		
At Cost	75,000	22,500
At market	82,500	28,125

a. Compute Macheral Company's gross profit for 19X1 and 19X2, assuming inventory is valued at cost.
b. Express gross profit for 19X2 as a percentage of sales. What is the average markup on cost?
c. Distinguish between the terms gross profit and operating profit.
d. In 19X1, a supplier representative indicated to Macheral's management that there would be a significant price increase in its product line. Acting on this tip, Macheral made all of its 19X1 purchases within a one-week period, before any sales had occurred. Subsequently, the market value of these goods increased over the initial cost by the same percentage as reflected in Macheral's 19X1 ending inventory (i.e., market vs. cost). Compute any holding gains or losses included in the 19X1 income.

Adapted with the permission of the Society of Management Accountants of Canada.

DECISION CASE 7-1

Barbara Distributors Ltd. imports and distributes a variety of products produced in the Pacific Rim countries. Currently, the company imports about thirty lines of merchandise with about twenty varieties in each line.

The sales staff is motivated to sell the products, but must have some flexibility in setting prices to meet the competition. To provide a guide and control in setting prices and to ensure that each line makes an adequate contribution, the buyers are required to set a retail price on each item of merchandise they purchase. The salespeople are required to advise the sales manager when these prices are changed. The accounting staff makes a notation of the original retail price on all purchase invoices showing the percent markup expected. A copy of each purchase invoice with this information is given to the main buyer and to the sales manager. At the same time, a memo record of the initial retail price is made for each invoice and summarized monthly.

Unfortunately, on November 17, one of the shipments from Taiwan was piled too close to the heat register and caught fire. The fire spread quickly and by the time it was put out, the company's entire merchandise inventory was either destroyed or damaged by smoke and water.

The insurance company sent an adjustor to determine the insurance claim that should be paid under the company's insurance policy. The policy provides that the insurance company will reimburse the insured by an amount equal to the "cost" of the inventory "less salvage value." With considerable difficulty, the adjustor has taken a physical inventory of the merchandise, referred to the current invoice prices, and arrived at a cost of $293,000, which he is willing to recommend that the insurance company pay for the inventory, which would then be sold by the insurance company.

As a check on the adequacy of the adjustor's recommendation, the accountant judged that accounting information might be useful. He had the books entered up to the date of the fire and extracted the following information from them for the period from January 1, the start of the current fiscal year, to November 17.

Cost of Material Purchased (Sales Price $1,234,100)	$668,400
Freight on Merchandise Purchased	$ 68,200
Custom Duty and Brokerage	$ 80,400

The operating costs of the various functions for the year to date were as follows:

Buying Office	$ 52,300
Warehousing	$ 48,000
Marketing	$119,600
Accounting	$ 41,900
General Administration	$ 63,600

The accountant estimated that 30 percent of the warehouse cost was incurred to receive, unpack, and store incoming shipments and the remainder incurred on outgoing shipments. The benefits from the accounting and administrative functions were received by the buying, warehousing, and marketing functions in proportion to the direct operating costs incurred by these three functions.

The sales for the year to date were $1,073,400, and the sales returns, $52,800.

The balance sheet at December 31 last showed that the inventory, valued at the lower of cost and market, was $244,900. At that date, the retail value of the inventory was $428,700.

Should the company accept the insurance claim proposed by the insurance adjustor? If the claim is not accepted, what alternative claim would you propose? What uncertainties exist about the adjustor's estimate and that of the alternative you propose?

CHAPTER EIGHT

CAPITAL ASSETS: THE SOURCE OF OPERATING CAPACITY

CHAPTER OUTLINE

- Acquisition of Plant Assets
- Depreciation — Fundamental Concepts
- Depreciation Accounting Problems
- Depreciation Methods
- Repairs and Betterments
- Retirement of Assets
- The Investment Tax Credit
- Wasting Assets and Depletion
- Intangible Assets and Amortization
- An International Perspective

Capital assets
Long-term assets, comprising plant assets, natural resources, and intangible assets.

Plant assets
A firm's property, plant, and equipment. Also called "capital assets."

Wasting assets
Natural resources that have limited useful life and, hence, are subject to amortization called "depletion." Examples are timberland, oil and gas wells, and ore deposits.

Intangible assets
Capital assets lacking physical existence, including patents, copyrights, franchises, trademarks, and goodwill.

Capital assets[1] are long-lived assets used by a company to help produce product and otherwise contribute to the revenue-generating process. These assets fall into three major classes — plant assets, wasting assets, and intangible assets. **Plant assets**[2] include such items as buildings, equipment, tools, furniture, fixtures, and vehicles. **Wasting assets** are natural resource deposits such as oil wells, coal mines, uranium mines, and timber tracts. **Intangible assets** are legal rights that confer economic benefits on the firm and include items such as patents, copyrights, franchises, trademarks, and goodwill. Collectively, these three types of capital assets, along with land, constitute what is called the productive or operating capacity of the firm.

Assets are future benefits, short-lived or long-lived. A business acquires a short-lived asset, such as insurance coverage, in one period and uses up

---

[1] The CICA has recently adopted this term in the *CICA Handbook* (section 3060), although it has a long history in accounting. The *capital* of a firm normally refers to the funds contributed by owners to create it, and the shareholders' equity section of the balance sheet shows this investment. This capital is used primarily to pay for the types of assets discussed in this chapter — hence the term *capital assets*.

[2] A popular synonym for plant assets is *fixed assets*.

its benefits within a year. A long-lived asset is different; to reap its benefits, the owner uses it for several years. In these cases, the accountant allocates the cost of the asset as a charge against operations over the several accounting periods of benefit. This general process is called **amortization**. Amortization of plant assets is called **depreciation**. Amortization of the cost of wasting assets is called **depletion**, but the term *amortization* is still used in conjunction with intangible assets.

Most of this chapter deals with depreciation because plant assets are the most common long-lived assets and depreciation problems are typical of almost all other amortization problems.

The problems of plant asset valuation and depreciation measurement can be conveniently separated into the consideration of four separate kinds of events:

1. Recording the acquisition of the asset.

2. Recording the asset's use over time.

3. Recording adjustments for changes in capacity or efficiency and for repairs or improvements.

4. Recording the asset's retirement or other disposal.

amortization
The periodic, systematic charging to expense of intangible assets reflecting the decline in economic potential of the assets.

depreciation
The periodic, systematic charging to expense of plant assets reflecting the decline in economic potential of the assets.

depletion
The allocation of the cost of extracting natural resources to the units extracted.

ACQUISITION OF PLANT ASSETS

The cost of a plant asset includes all charges necessary to prepare it for rendering services, and it is often recorded in a series of transactions. Thus, the cost of a piece of equipment will be the sum of the entries to recognize the invoice price (less any discounts), transportation costs, installation charges, and any other costs incurred before the equipment is ready for use. See the example on page 58, and then consider the following, more complex, example.

Example 1 A firm incurs the following costs in searching for and acquiring a new plant site:

1. Purchase price of land and building $1,000,000

2. Fees paid to lawyer in handling purchase contracts 10,000

3. Transfer taxes paid to local real estate taxing authorities 2,000

4. Fees paid to consulting engineer for structural report on soundness of the building, its current value, and estimated cost of making needed repairs 15,000

5. Salaries earned by management personnel during the search for the site and the negotiation of its purchase 8,000

6. Profits lost on sales the company failed to make because management was distracted from serving a potential new customer during the search 20,000

7. Operating expenditures for company automobiles used during the search 75

8. Depreciation charges for company automobiles used during the search   65

9. Uninsured costs to repair automobiles damaged in a multivehicle accident during the search   3,000

The firm might accumulate and classify these costs as described below.

The firm would temporarily accumulate in a combined land and buildings account the cost for items 1, 2, 3, 5, 7, and 8. Then, the firm would split those costs into separate accounts for land and for building. This might be done using the appraisal it received in item 4. For example, if the engineer estimated the current value of the existing building to be $250,000, the firm might allocate 25 percent (= $250,000/$1,000,000) of the combined costs to the building and the rest to the land. (Accounting requires such allocation because the firm will depreciate the building, but not the land.)

Costs attributable to the building alone include item 4, the engineer's report on the building. Items 7 and 8, operating costs for the automobiles, are so small that many firms would not include them in the costs to be capitalized (set up as an asset); they would treat these costs as period expenses, following their usual procedures.

Many firms would not include item 5, salaries of company employees, in the acquisition cost of the site, but accounting theory suggests they should.

Accountants would not agree on the treatment for item 9, repair costs for the accident. Some would think it part of the cost of the site, like items 2, 7, and 8, to be allocated to the land and the building. Others would report it as expense of the period. Probably all practising accountants would classify it as expense for financial reporting so that the firm would bolster its argument for calling it a current tax deduction in computing taxable income.

Item 6, foregone profits, does not result from an expenditure. It is not incurred in an arm's-length transaction with outsiders. Historical cost accounting would not record this cost, sometimes called an **opportunity cost**, in any account.

Computing the acquisition cost of an asset acquired in a trade-in transaction presents special problems. A trade-in transaction involves both the retirement of an old asset and the acquisition of a new one. Although its problems might be discussed with acquisitions, this chapter discusses trade-in transactions in the section on retirements. Computing the acquisition cost of a **self-constructed asset** presents other problems, discussed below.

opportunity cost
The current value of the income (or costs) that could be earned (or saved) by using an asset for its best alternative use relative to the use being considered.

self-constructed asset
An asset created when a firm constructs its own building or equipment.

SELF-CONSTRUCTED ASSETS

When a firm constructs its own buildings or equipment, many entries to record the labour, material, and overhead costs will normally be required before the total cost is recorded. One of these costs may be interest paid during construction. The amount may be significant during periods of double-digit interest rates and for projects with long construction periods. The *CICA Handbook* makes no recommendation on capitalization of interest during construction and, as a consequence, there is no standard Canadian practice. Most public utilities (such as electric and gas, pipeline, telephone, and cable television) and land development companies capitalize interest during construction. A few companies in other industries also follow this practice. The amount of interest that is capitalized is usually based on the entity's actual borrowings and interest payments. It is intended to be the interest cost incurred during the assets' acquisition periods that in principle could have been avoided if the assets had not been acquired.

If there is a specific new borrowing in connection with the asset being constructed, the interest rate on that borrowing should be used. If the expenditures on plant exceed such specific new borrowings, the interest rate to be applied to such excess is the weighted average of rates applicable to other borrowings of the enterprise. If there are no specific new borrowings, the average interest rate on old borrowings is used to compute the total amount to be capitalized. The total amount of interest included cannot exceed total interest costs for the period. The **capitalization of interest** into plant during construction reduces otherwise reportable interest expense and increases income during periods of construction. In later periods, the plant will have higher depreciation charges, which reduce income.

Example 2   Assume the following long-term debt structure:

Construction Loan at 15 Percent on Building Under Construction	$1,000,000
Other Borrowings at 12 Percent Average Rate	3,600,000
Total Long-Term Debt	$4,600,000

capitalization of interest
Adding the financing costs of borrowed funds used in self-constructing capital assets to the asset cost base.

The account Building Under Construction has an average balance during the year of $3,000,000. The amount of interest to be capitalized is based on all of the new construction-related borrowings, $1,000,000, and enough of the older borrowings, $2,000,000, to bring the total to $3,000,000. The interest capitalized is computed as:

$1,000,000 × 0.15	$150,000
2,000,000 × 0.12	240,000
$3,000,000	$390,000

The entries to record interest and then to capitalize the required amounts might be:

Interest Expense	$582,000	
Interest Payable		$582,000

To record all interest as expense: $582,000 =
(0.15 × $1,000,000) + (0.12 × $3,600,000) =
$150,000 + $432,000.

Building Under Construction	$390,000	
Interest Expense		$390,000

To record interest capitalized as part of the cost of the building, reducing interest expense.

The preceding two entries might be combined as one:

Interest Expense	$192,000	
Building Under Construction	390,000	
Interest Payable		$582,000
To record interest payable, part charged to expense and part charged to the cost of the building.		

Both total interest for the year, $582,000, and the amount capitalized, $390,000, should be disclosed in notes. The income statement will report interest expense, $192,000, in the example. The amount shown in future years for depreciation of the plant will be larger than otherwise because of interest capitalization in earlier years. Over the life of the asset, from construction through retirement, total income is unaffected by capitalizing interest, because the increased income in the construction period is later exactly offset by larger depreciation charges. Over long enough time spans, total expense must equal total cash expenditure.

DEPRECIATION — FUNDAMENTAL CONCEPTS

PURPOSE OF DEPRECIATION

Most plant assets can be kept intact and in usable operating condition for more than a year but, except for land, they must eventually be retired from service. Depreciation systematically allocates the cost of these assets to the periods of their use.

Allocation of Cost

The cost of a depreciating asset is the price paid for a series of future services. The asset account is like a prepayment, similar to prepaid rent or insurance — a payment in advance for services to be received. As the asset is used in each accounting period, a portion of the investment in assets is treated as the cost of the service received and is recognized as an expense of the period or as part of the cost of goods produced during the period.

Depreciation is a process of cost allocation. This chapter discusses the problems of *allocating* the cost of assets to the periods of benefit. A depreciation problem will exist whenever (1) funds are invested in services to be rendered by a plant asset and (2) the asset, at some date in the future, must be retired from service with a residual value less than its original cost.

No uniquely correct amount for the periodic charge for depreciation can be computed. The cost of the plant asset is a *joint cost* of the several benefited periods. That is, each of the periods of the asset's use benefits from its services. There is usually no single correct way to allocate a joint cost. The depreciation process assigns periodic charges that reflect systematic calculations.

Return of Capital

A business attempts to earn both a return *of* capital and a return *on* capital. Before there can be a return *on* capital (as measured by accounting profits), all costs must be recovered. The purpose of amortization is to charge against revenues the cost of noncurrent assets. To understand the role of amortization in this process, reconsider the installment method and the cost-recovery-first method of recognizing revenue, introduced in Chapter 4. In the cost-recovery method, there is no accounting income until all costs are recovered. The accounting under cost-recovery-first charges to expense an amount equal to cash collections so that there is no accounting income until all anticipated costs have been debited to expense. In contrast, under the installment method, costs are allocated over the time of cash collections so that each dollar collected represents identical proportions of cost recovery and profits. In accounting for noncurrent assets, one might, in principle, debit expense and credit plant assets so that there is no profit until the costs of plant assets have been written off. The early periods of a noncurrent asset's life could have no income but the later periods would show no expense for plant and, consequently, larger net income. Instead, accounting estimates the life of the noncurrent asset and writes off its cost over its life, in principle allowing each period to show both cost recovery and income. The amortization process provides for the gradual return of the investment in a noncurrent asset. In historical cost accounting, the process is designed to provide a return of the cost of the asset, no more and no less.[3] But the return of costs is designed to occur over the asset's life, not entirely in the early periods of its life.

DEPRECIATION VERSUS DECLINE IN VALUE

In ordinary conversation, "depreciation" frequently means a decline in value. Over the entire service life of a plant asset, there is decline in value of the asset from acquisition until it is retired from service. The charge made to the operations of each accounting period does not result from declines in value during that period but, rather, from the process of ensuring systematic amortization of the cost. If, in a given period, an asset increases in value, there will still be depreciation during that period. There have been two partially offsetting processes: (1) a holding gain on the asset, which usually is not recognized in historical cost-based accounting, and (2) depreciation of the asset's historical cost to achieve a return of investment.

THE CASE FOR DEPRECIATION

The justification for depreciation is the decline in an asset's service potential. Because the services provided by land do not diminish over time, land

---

[3] In periods of inflation, basing depreciation charges on acquisition costs will not, in most cases, charge amounts to expense that are sufficient to maintain the productive capacity of the business. Basing depreciation on acquisition costs will enable a business to recover its initial cash investment, but not necessarily enough to replace the physical productive capacity purchased with the cash.

is not depreciated; all costs are recovered when the land is sold. Many factors lead to the retirement of assets from service, but the causes of decline in service potential can be classified as either *physical* or *functional*. The physical factors include such things as ordinary wear and tear from use, chemical action such as rust or electrolysis, and the effects of wind and rain. The most important functional (nonphysical) cause is *obsolescence*. Inventions, for example, may result in new processes that reduce the unit cost of production to the point where continued operation of old equipment is not economical, even though it may be relatively unimpaired physically. Retail stores often replace display cases and storefronts long before they are worn out in order to make the appearance of the store more attractive. Changed economic conditions may also become functional causes of depreciation, such as when an old airport becomes inadequate and must be abandoned, and a new, larger one is built to meet the requirements of heavier traffic; or when an increase in the cost of gasoline causes a reduction in demand for automobile products, which results in reduced scale of operations in automobile manufacturing.

Identifying the specific causes of depreciation is not essential for measuring it. Almost any physical asset will eventually have to be retired from service and, in some cases, the retirement will become necessary at a time when physical deterioration is negligible. Understanding the specific causes can nevertheless help in estimating an asset's useful life.

DEPRECIATION ACCOUNTING PROBLEMS

The three principle accounting problems in allocating the cost of an asset over time are:

1. Measuring the depreciable basis of the asset.
2. Estimating its useful service life.
3. Deciding on the pattern of expiration of asset cost over the useful service life.

DEPRECIABLE BASIS OF PLANT ASSETS

physical life
The period of time in which a fixed asset continues to have revenue-generating potential. Also called service life.

economic life
The time span over which the benefits of an asset are expected to be received. This may be shorter than the physical life (fixed assets) or legal life (intangible assets).

scrap value
Disposal value, assuming item is to be scrapped.

Depreciation is a process of systematically allocating the cost of an asset to the income statement through annual depreciation charges. The cost to be allocated is not the acquisition (gross) cost of the asset, but rather its net cost. Many assets generate cash proceeds when ultimately disposed of. If the asset has future revenue-generating potential in its current form, other firms may be willing to purchase it. Even if the revenue-generating potential is used up (that is, the asset is at the end of its **physical life** or **economic life**), the **scrap value** of the metal or other raw materials in the asset may generate cash flow. With the current trend toward recycling in our economy, the scrap potential of many assets has increased. Therefore, the depreciable basis of a plant asset is its gross cost reduced by any proceeds received on disposal.

Salvage value has been the term historically used to describe these disposal proceeds, but the CICA now requires a finer distinction to be made.[4] If the asset has future service potential to another firm, the proceeds are called **residual value**. If the asset has no future service potential and can only be sold for scrap, the proceeds are called **disposal value**. The rationale for this distinction will be evident when we look at the depreciation methods in the next section.

Estimating Disposal Value

Conceptually, it makes sense to depreciate an asset on the basis of its net cost (acquisition cost less disposal value). In practice, estimating the residual or disposal value of an asset ten or twenty years in the future can be difficult. When subjective estimates such as these are used as a basis for generating accounting entries, it is expected that, as better information becomes available, the calculations will be revised and the accounting records amended prospectively. We call such estimates **accounting estimates**. Many firms avoid the problem by simply assuming a zero disposal value.

One class of assets for which disposal values are normally available is automobiles. A formal market exists for used vehicles, and published guides to resale values are available.

In general, if a firm intends to dispose of an asset before the expiry of its useful life, there is more onus of the firm to estimate its residual value than would be the case if the asset were to be kept until it wore out. The salvage value is often immaterial, but the residual value may be material. For example, if a new building is purchased for $1,000,000 with an expected life of twenty years and the firm expects to dispose of it in five years, the residual value will be substantial.

In some cases, the disposal value can be negative. This scenario is becoming more common because of tougher environmental protection laws. Consider, for example, the costs associated with dismantling a nuclear power plant and disposing of radioactive materials. Negative disposal value increases the depreciable basis of the asset.

Unit of Account

Whenever feasible, depreciation should be computed for individual items such as a single building, machine, or automobile. Where similar items are in use and each one has a relatively small cost, individual calculations may be impractical and the depreciation charge is usually calculated for the group as a whole. Furniture and fixtures, tools, and telephone poles are examples of assets that are usually depreciated in groups. Group depreciation techniques are treated in more advanced financial accounting courses. The basic principles of depreciating individual items discussed here apply, however, to group depreciation situations.

Salvage value
The expected net recovery (sales proceeds minus disposal costs) of an asset at the end of its useful life.

residual value
At any time, the estimated or actual net realizable value (that is, proceeds less removal costs) of an asset, usually a depreciable plant asset. In the context of depreciation accounting, this term is equivalent to disposal value and is preferable to scrap value, because the asset need not be scrapped.

disposal value
The estimated proceeds from selling a capital asset that is unneeded or at the end of its useful service life.

accounting estimates
Subjective estimates used as a basis for generating accounting entries.

---

[4] *CICA Handbook*, section 3060.31.

ESTIMATING SERVICE LIFE

The depreciation calculation requires an estimate of the economic service life of the asset. In making the estimate, both the physical and the functional causes of depreciation must be considered. Experience with similar assets, corrected for differences in the planned intensity of use or alterations in maintenance policy, is usually the best guide for this estimate.

Despite abundant data from experience, estimating service lives for financial reporting is the most difficult task in the entire depreciation calculation. Allowing for obsolescence is particularly difficult because most obsolescence results from forces outside the firm. Estimates will probably prove to be incorrect. For this reason, estimates of useful service life of assets are reconsidered every few years.

PATTERN OF EXPIRATION OF COSTS

Once the cost is measured and both disposal value and service life are estimated, the total of depreciation charges for the whole life of the asset has been determined. If disposal value is assumed to be zero, the entire cost will be depreciated. The problem remains of selecting the pattern for allocating those charges to the specific years of the life. Depreciation based on the passage of time follows one of five basic patterns. They are labelled E, A, S, D, and N in Figures 8.1 and 8.2.

A represents *accelerated* depreciation; S, *straight-line* depreciation; and D, *decelerated* depreciation. (Understanding the terms *accelerated* and *decelerated* is easier if you compare the depreciation charges in the early years to straight-line depreciation. See Figure 8.2.) Pattern D is seldom used in financial reporting, but is useful for certain managerial accounting problems. Pattern E represents immediate expensing of the item. All costs are charged to the period in which the cost is incurred. The section on intangibles dis-

FIGURE 8.1
Patterns of Writing Off Costs: Book Value over Economic Life of Asset

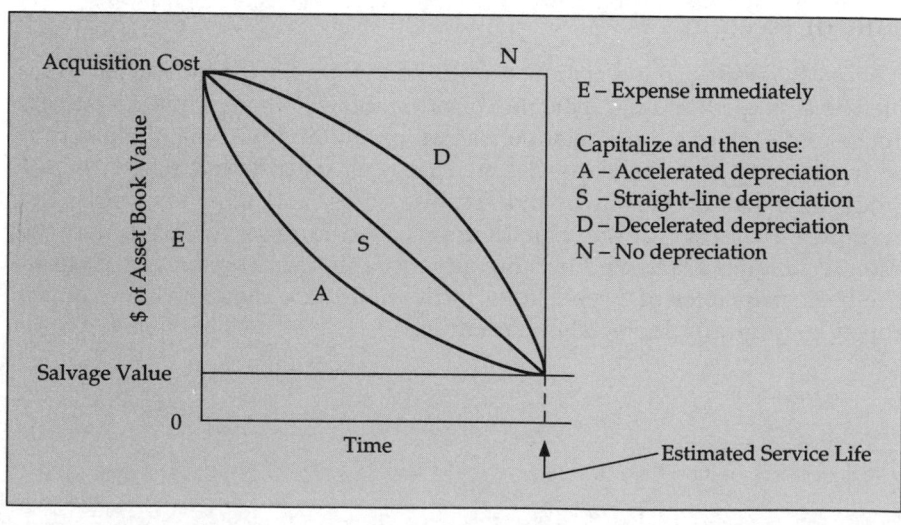

FIGURE 8.2
Patterns of Annual Depreciation Charge over Economic Life of Asset

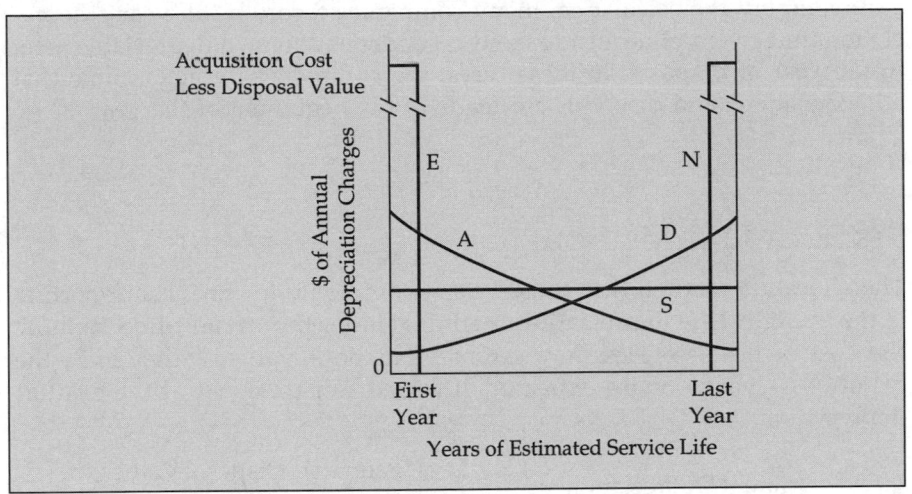

cusses this pattern. Pattern N represents the situation, such as for land, where there are no periodic amortization charges. The asset is shown on the books at acquisition cost until it is sold or otherwise retired.

DEPRECIATION METHODS

All depreciation methods systematically allocate the cost of the asset minus its estimated disposal value to the periods in which it is used. The methods discussed here are as follows:

1. Straight-line method (pattern S)
2. Activity or use method
3. Declining-balance method (pattern A)
4. Compound interest methods (pattern D)

The *CICA Handbook* actually requires two separate calculations. The amount of depreciation expense that should be charged to income is the *greater* of:

1. Cost less disposal value over the total life of the asset.
2. Cost less residual value over the useful life of the asset to the reporting entity.

The Handbook provides no rationale for this requirement, but the effect is certainly one of conservatism. For the sake of simplicity, we will assume throughout this book that whenever only one of the two values (disposal or residual) is provided, it is the one leading to the larger charge against income. Whenever alluding to the net cost of an asset, we shall use the phrase "cost less disposal value."

When a depreciable asset is acquired or retired during an accounting period, depreciation should be calculated only for that portion of the period during which the asset is used.

To simplify the calculation, many companies record a full year's depreciation in the year of acquisition and no depreciation on a depreciable asset in the year of disposal. In these cases, the companies in fact assume that all acquisitions and disposals are made at the beginning of the year.

STRAIGHT-LINE METHOD

straight-line depreciation
If the depreciable life is n periods, the periodic depreciation charge is $1/n$ of the depreciation cost, which results in equal periodic charges to income.

The allocation method that is used most commonly for financial reporting is the **straight-line depreciation** method. Under the straight-line method, the cost of the asset, less any estimated disposal value, is divided by the number of years of its expected life in order to arrive at the annual depreciation:

$$\text{Annual Depreciation} = \frac{\text{Cost Less Estimated Disposal Value}}{\text{Estimated Life in Years}}$$

For example, if a machine costs $12,000, has an estimated disposal value of $1,000, and has an expected useful life of five years, the annual depreciation will be $2,200 [= ($12,000 − $1,000)/5]. Occasionally, instead of positive disposal value, the cost of removal exceeds the gross proceeds on disposition. This excess of removal costs over gross proceeds should be added to the cost of the asset in making the calculation. Thus, if a building is constructed for $37,000,000, and it is estimated that it will cost $5,000,000 to remove it at the end of 25 years, the annual depreciation will be $1,680,000 [= ($37,000,000 + $5,000,000)/25].

Most companies take depreciation to the nearest month. For example, if an asset was acquired on March 17, the first depreciation entry would be for April.

UNITS OF ACTIVITY METHOD

Many assets are not used uniformly over time. Manufacturing plants often have seasonal variations in operation so that certain machines may be used 24 hours a day at one time and 8 hours or less a day at another time of year. Trucks are not likely to receive the same amount of use in each year of their lives. The straight-line method of depreciation may result in depreciation patterns unrelated to patterns of use.

When the rate of use varies over periods and when the total use of an asset over its life can be estimated, a depreciation charge based on actual use during the period may be used. It is commonly assumed that an equal benefit is received from each unit of use resulting in the adoption of the straight-line use method where the same cost is allocated to each unit of use. For example, depreciation of a truck for a period could be based on the ratio of kilometres driven during the period to total kilometres expected to be driven over the truck's life. The depreciation cost per unit (kilometre) of use is:

$$\text{Depreciation Cost per Activity Unit} = \frac{\text{Cost Less Estimated Disposal Value}}{\text{Estimated Number of Units}}$$

$$\begin{pmatrix} \text{Annual Depreciation} \\ \text{Expense Charged} \end{pmatrix} = \begin{pmatrix} \text{Depreciation} \\ \text{Cost per Unit} \end{pmatrix} \times \begin{pmatrix} \text{Activity Units} \\ \text{Incurred for Year} \end{pmatrix}$$

Assume that a truck costs $24,000, has an estimated disposal value of $1,200, and is expected to be driven 100,000 kilometres before it is retired from service. The depreciation per kilometre is $0.228 [=($24,000 − $1,200)/100,000]. If the truck is operated 2,000 kilometres in a given month, the depreciation charge for the month is 2,000 × $0.228 = $456.

ACCELERATED DEPRECIATION (DECLINING-BALANCE METHOD)

The earning power of some plant assets declines as the assets grow older. Cutting tools lose some of their precision; printing presses are shut down more frequently for repairs; rentals in an old office building are lower than those from a new one. Some assets provide more and better services in the early years of their lives while requiring increasing amounts of maintenance as they grow older. Where this is the case, methods that recognize larger depreciation charges in early years and progressively smaller depreciation charges later may be justified. Such methods are referred to as **accelerated depreciation** methods because the depreciation charges in the early years of the asset's life are larger than in later years. Accelerated depreciation leads to a pattern such as A in Figures 8.1 and 8.2.

For convenience, the depreciation charges for a year, however they are determined, are allocated on a straight-line basis to periods *within* the year.

The **declining-balance depreciation** method is one accelerated depreciation method. In this method, the depreciation charge is calculated by multiplying the **net book value** of the asset (cost less accumulated depreciation) at the start of each period by a fixed rate. The estimated disposal value is not subtracted from the cost in making the depreciation calculation, but the asset should not be written down below its estimated disposal value. Because the net book value declines from period to period, the result is a declining periodic charge for depreciation throughout the life of the asset.[5]

units-of-production method
The method of depreciation whereby the annual charge is related to some measure of production activity instead of the passage of time.

accelerated depreciation
Any method of calculating depreciation charges where the charges become progressively smaller in each period. An example is the declining-balance method.

declining-balance depreciation
The method of calculating the periodic depreciation charge by multiplying the book value at the start of the period by a constant percentage.

net book value
The cost less accumulated depreciation of a capital asset.

---

[5] Under the declining-balance method, as strictly applied, the fixed depreciation rate used is one that will charge the cost less disposal value of the asset over its service life. The formula for computing the rate is:

$$\text{Depreciation Rate} = 1 - \sqrt[n]{\frac{s}{c}} = 1 - \left(\frac{s}{c}\right)^{1/n}$$

In this formula, n = estimated periods of service life, s = estimated disposal value, and c = cost.

Estimates of disposal value have a profound effect on the rate. Unless a positive disposal value is assumed, the rate is 100 percent — that is, all depreciation is charged in the first period. For an asset costing $10,000 with an estimated life of five years, the depreciation is 40 percent per period if disposal value is $778, but it is 60 percent if disposal value is $102.

The effect of small changes in disposal value on the rate and the seeming mathematical complexity of the formula have resulted in widespread use of approximations or rules of thumb instead of the formula.

The rate most commonly used is the maximum one permitted for income tax purposes. If a machine costing $5,000 is purchased on January 1, Year 1 and depreciated on a declining-balance basis with a rate of 40 percent, the depreciation charges will be calculated as shown in Exhibit 8.1.

EXHIBIT 8.1
Declining-Balance Depreciation Asset with Five-Year Life

Year	Acquisition Cost (1)	Accumulated Depreciation as of Jan. 1 (2)	Net Book Value as of Jan. 1 = (1) − (2) (3)	Depreciation Rate (4)	Depreciation Charge for the Year = (3) × (4) (5)
1	$5,000	$ 0	$5,000	0.40	$2,000
2	5,000	2,000	3,000	0.40	1,200
3	5,000	3,200	1,800	0.40	720
4	5,000	3,920	1,080	0.40	432
5	5,000	4,352	648	0.40	259
6	5,000	4,611	389	—	—

The undepreciated cost as of December 31, Year 5, as shown in Exhibit 8.1, is $389 (= $648 − $259). This amount is unlikely to equal the disposal value at that time. The problem may be anticipated and solved by adjusting the depreciation charge in one or more of the later years.

With a few exceptions, the declining-balance method applied on a group basis is used when determining the maximum depreciation, called **capital cost allowance (CCA)** that may be claimed as an expense when deriving taxable income. Further details of CCA are provided below.

DECELERATED DEPRECIATION (COMPOUND INTEREST METHODS)

Compound interest depreciation methods are seldom used in financial accounting except for real estate development operations, but they are theoretically sound for many management decisions. For plant assets producing equal annual net inflows of cash, compound interest depreciation leads to a pattern like D in Figures 8.1 and 8.2. This book does not illustrate compound interest methods, but see Problem 38 at the end of this chapter.

CAPITAL COST ALLOWANCE

Under the Income Tax Act, a company is not permitted to deduct depreciation when deriving taxable income. In place of depreciation, a company may claim CCA as specified in the Act and Regulations.

When framing the CCA provisions, the government hoped to achieve three objectives. The first objective was to permit a company to deduct from taxable income, over the life of the company, the cost of using depreciable assets. The cost to be allowed was defined as the initial acquisition cost less the proceeds of the ultimate disposal. A corollary of this objective was that

capital cost allowance (CCA)
The method allowed by Revenue Canada for calculating depreciation in computing taxable income.

Compound interest depreciation
A method of depreciation designed to hold the rate of return on an asset constant.

the differences between the disposal price and the net book value of depreciable assets on the disposal date were considered to be corrections of the CCA claimed over the life of the assets rather than capital gains or losses, except to the extent that the disposal price exceeded the original cost to the company.

The second objective was to permit the company to select the pattern of allocating the cost of the asset to each year, subject only to a liberal maximum annual allowance. This annual allowance was, in most cases, double the normal straight-line rate of depreciation.

Third, the method adopted was intended to be simple for the company to compute and for the income tax department to administer, in order to reduce the cost to the company and the government of administering the regulations.

These objectives were attained by framing legislation that has the following features:

1. No allowance for depreciation is permitted as a deduction from revenue to compute taxable income, except as permitted by the CCA regulations.

2. All depreciable assets are grouped into about 35 classes, roughly on the basis of term of life of the asset from the date it was originally constructed until it was scrapped. For each class, a maximum rate of depreciation (called capital cost allowance) is permitted, varying from 1 percent to 100 percent and applied to the class as a whole.

3. The treatment of individual assets is ignored, except when an asset is sold for more than its cost to the company. In such as case, the excess of the proceeds of the disposal of the asset over the cost is considered as a capital gain, and only three-quarters of the excess is considered taxable income.

4. In computing the maximum CCA permitted to be deducted when computing taxable income, the undepreciated capital cost of a class is used as the base to which the stated rates apply. The undepreciated capital cost of a class consists of the acquisition cost of the assets in the class less the sum of the accumulated CCA claimed and the proceeds of the sales of assets of the class, reduced by any portion of the proceeds considered to be a capital gain.

5. It is assumed that all depreciable assets are purchased in the middle of the fiscal period. Consequently, only 50 percent of the CCA may be claimed in the year of acquisition. When a fiscal period is less than 12 months, a proportion of the annual amount may be claimed. With these exceptions, the balances in each class at the end of each fiscal year are used as the base for computing the maximum CCA for that year, with the full rates adopted.

The maximum CCA permitted to be claimed in any one year is computed as follows:

1. Determine the undepreciated cost at the beginning of the year for each class of asset owned by the company. This balance is available from the income tax return submitted in the previous year.

2. Add to the opening balance of the undepreciated cost of each class of assets the cost of assets purchased in that class during the year.

3. Deduct from this total for each class the proceeds of the sales of assets in the class during the year, except to the extent that a portion of the proceeds (the excess of the sale proceeds over the cost) is considered to be a capital gain. The balance of the undepreciated cost on completion of steps 1, 2, and 3 becomes the class base for CCA for that year.

4. Multiply the base for each class of asset by the rate stated in the regulations. The resultant product is the maximum CCA permitted under the Act. Examples of the rates applicable to particular classes follow:

Brick, stone, concrete buildings	Class 3	5%
Frame, stucco on frame, galvanized buildings	Class 6	10%
Furniture and machinery not otherwise specified	Class 8	20%
Automobiles and trucks	Class 10	30%

5. Deduct one-half of the CCA claimed on the cost of the assets acquired during the year less the proceeds of disposals.

6. A special situation arises when all of the assets in a class are disposed of, or when the proceeds of the sale of assets in a class exceed the undepreciated cost of the class at the beginning of the fiscal year plus the cost of additions made during the year.

   When all of the assets in a class are disposed of and the proceeds of the disposal (reduced by any capital gain) are less than the undepreciated cost of the class at the end of the year, the undepreciated cost, reduced by the proceeds of the disposal, may be deducted from taxable income in that year. On the other hand, when the proceeds of disposal (reduced by any capital gains), whether or not all of the assets of the class are disposed of, exceed the undepreciated cost of the class at the end of the year, the excess must by included in the taxable income of the year of disposal, subject to certain exceptions. For example, where an asset disposal is involuntary (resulting from, say, a fire, theft, or expropriation), special provisions apply.

A company is not required to claim any CCA in a year, but if not claimed, the benefit remains available as part of the undepreciated cost.

An illustration of the CCA claimed by CCA Limited, incorporated on January 1, Year 1, is presented in Exhibit 8.2.

The maximum CCA permitted to be deducted in deriving taxable income for assets falling in some classes is computed using the straight-line method. These asset classes were established for assets whose useful lives to the taxpayer were determined by legal contract or depletion of a nonrenewable resource, and assets for which accelerated rates of CCA were granted to encourage companies to acquire and use the specific type of asset. Examples of these classes and basis for computing their CCA follow:

Class 13 Leasehold improvements — over the life of the lease plus one renewal period (minimum five years, maximum forty years).

Class 14 Patents, franchises, licences, etc. — over the life of the asset.

Class 15 Woods assets — depreciated on the basis of a rate applied to the cords or board feet of timber cut during the year.

Class 24 Water pollution control equipment — 50 percent

EXHIBIT 8.2
CCA LIMITED
Analysis of Capital Cost Allowance
Fiscal Year-End December 31

	Class 6 10%	Class 8 20%	Class 10 30%
Jan. 1, Year 1 Purchased frame building	$100,000		
Jan. 15, Year 1 Purchased manufacturing equipment		$300,000	
Feb. 13, Year 1 Purchased: 1 fork life truck			$ 4,000
3 delivery trucks @ $5,000			15,000
1 automobile			3,000
Undepreciated capital cost, Dec. 31, Year 1	$100,000	$300,000	$22,000
Capital cost claimed for the year[a]	—	—	3,000
Undepreciated capital cost, Jan. 1, Year 2 and Dec. 31, Year 2 (there were no transactions during Year 2)	$100,000	$300,000	$22,000
Capital cost claimed for Year 2[b]	10,000	60,000	6,600
Undepreciated capital cost, Jan. 1, Year 3	$ 90,000	$240,000	$15,400
Oct. 20, Year 3 Sold building for $110,000[c]	(100,000)		
Oct. 20, Year 3 Sold machinery for $320,000[c]		(300,000)	
Dec. 20, Year 3 Sold fork lift truck for $5,000[c]			(4,000)
Dec. 20, Year 3 Sold automobile for $1,000			(1,000)
Dec. 20, Year 3 Sold 1 truck for $4,000			(4,000)
Dec. 31, Year 3 Purchased a new factory building (frame)	150,000		
Undepreciated capital cost, Dec. 31, Year 3	$140,000	$ (60,000)	$ 6,400
Capital cost claimed for Year 3[d]	5,000		
The $60,000 must be taken into current income		60,000	
Undepreciated capital cost, Jan. 1, Year 4	$135,000	—	$ 6,400
Jan. 5, Year 4 Purchased machinery		$400,000	
June 30, Year 4 Sold 2 trucks for $3,000 each	$200,000		6,000
Undepreciated capital cost, Dec. 31, Year 4	$135,000	$400,000	$ 400
Maximum capital cost allowance claimed for Year 4	13,500	40,000[f]	400[e]
Undepreciated capital cost, Jan. 1, Year 5	$121,500	$360,000	—

[a] *Because the company suffered a loss during the first year, no CCA was claimed.*
[b] *Maximum CCA claimed.*
[c] *Sale proceeds in excess of the original cost of the asset are considered to be capital gains and are exempt from taxation.*
[d] *The company achieved a small taxable income before CCA, so only enough CCA to produce a taxable income of zero was claimed.*
[e] *The entire balance may be claimed because there are no assets remaining in class 10.*
[f] *Only 50 percent of the normal CCA may be claimed in the year in which the machinery was purchased.*

Class 29 Certain machinery and equipment acquired after May 8, 1972 for use in Canada primarily in the manufacture or processing of goods — 50 percent (maximum in first year only).

Over the years, various accelerated rates have been introduced to spur the economy or to give recognition to unusual conditions (for example, double depreciation for manufacturers of defence materials in wartime). At other times, the deduction of CCA has been deferred or restricted.

FACTORS TO CONSIDER IN CHOOSING THE DEPRECIATION METHOD

Depreciation affects both income reported in the financial statements and taxable income on tax returns. The firm need not choose the same depreciation method for both financial and tax reporting purposes. If it chooses different methods for the two purposes, the difference between depreciation in the financial statements and CCA on the tax return will lead to a problem in accounting for income taxes, as discussed in Chapter 10.

Financial Reporting

Financial reporting for long-lived assets seeks an income statement that realistically measures the expiration of their benefits and provides a "reasonable" pattern of cost recovery. No one knows, however, just what portion of the service potential of a long-lived asset expires in any one period. The plant asset benefits several periods of use, and no uniquely correct way of allocating these benefits exists. All that can be said is that financial statements should report depreciation charges on the basis of reasonable estimates of asset expirations. Chapter 14 discusses more fully alternative accounting principles, including the choice of depreciation methods.

Tax Reporting

It seems clear that in selecting the amount of CCA claimed for tax reporting, the goal of the firm should be to maximize the current value of the reductions in tax payments from claiming CCA. Earlier deductions are worth more than later ones, because a dollar saved today is worth more than a dollar saved tomorrow. A firm will generally choose an amount that meets the general goal of paying the least amount of tax, as late as possible, within the law. This goal is sometimes called the *least and latest rule*.

DEPRECIATION IN MANUFACTURING ENVIRONMENTS

Accumulated Depreciation
A contra account to the related asset account, reflecting the cumulative amounts recorded as depreciation for a specific asset or group of assets.

The debit made in the entry to record periodic depreciation is usually either to an expense account or to a product cost account. In a manufacturing concern, the depreciation of factory buildings and equipment is a product cost, a part of the cost of work-in-process and finished product. Depreciation on sales equipment is a selling expense. Depreciation on office equipment is a general or administrative expense. The matching credit for periodic depreciation could, in principle, be made directly to the asset account affected, such as buildings or equipment. Although such an entry is sometimes made, usually the credit is to a contra asset account. This leaves the acquisition cost of the asset undisturbed and permits easy computation of the total amount written off through depreciation. The effect, however, is precisely the same as that of a direct credit to the asset account. **Accumulated Depreciation** is the title of the contra asset account credited.

The entry to record periodic depreciation of office facilities, a period expense, is:

Depreciation Expense	$1,500	
Accumulated Depreciation		$1,500

The entry to record periodic depreciation of manufacturing facilities, a product cost, is:

Work-in-Process Inventory[6]	$4,500	
Accumulated Depreciation		$4,500

The Depreciation Expense account is closed at the end of the accounting period as a part of the regular closing-entry procedure. The Work-in-Process Inventory account is an asset. Product costs, such as depreciation on manufacturing facilities, accumulate in the Work-in-Process account until the goods being produced are completed and transferred to Finished Goods Inventory. The Accumulated Depreciation account remains open at the end of the period and appears on the balance sheet as a deduction from the asset account to which it refers. The balance in the Accumulated Depreciation account represents the total charges before the balance sheet date for the depreciation on assets currently in use. The difference between the balance of the asset account and the balance of its accumulated depreciation account is called *net book value* of the asset.

For consistency, we will follow the practice of debiting Depreciation Expense throughout this book instead of Work-in-Process Inventory.

CHANGES IN PERIODIC DEPRECIATION

The original depreciation schedule for a particular asset may require changing. Estimates of useful life (and of disposal value as well) may be judged incorrect in the light of new information, which may become apparent at any time during the asset's life. The accuracy of the estimates improves as retirement approaches. If the change in estimate has a material impact, corrective action must be taken. The generally accepted procedure is to make no adjustment for the past estimate error, but to spread the remaining undepreciated balance less the revised estimate of disposal value over the new estimate of remaining service life of the asset.

To illustrate the accounting for changes in periodic depreciation, assume the following facts. An office machine was purchased on January 1, Year 1, for $9,200. It was estimated that the machine would be operated for fifteen years with a disposal value of $200. The depreciation charge recorded for each of the years from Year 1 through Year 5 under the straight-line method would have been $600 [= ($9,200 − $200)/15]. On December 31, Year 6, before the books are closed for the year, it is decided that a total useful life of ten years is more likely, but the disposal estimate of $200 is still reasonable.

---

[6] In actuality, the depreciation is first charged to a Factory Overhead account, which is eventually closed to Work-in-Process.

The accepted procedure for recognizing this substantial decrease in service life is to revise the future depreciation so that the correct total will be accumulated in the Accumulated Depreciation account at the end of the revised service life. No adjustments of amounts previously recorded may be made. In our example, the total amount of acquisition cost yet to be depreciated before the Year 6 adjustments is $6,000 [= $9,200 − $200) (5 × $600)]. The new estimate of the *remaining* life is five years (the year just ended plus the next four), so the new annual depreciation charge is $1,200 (= $6,000/5). The only change in the accounting procedure is to substitute the new amount of $1,200 for the former annual depreciation of $600. The depreciation entry on December 31, Year 6 and each year thereafter will be:

Depreciation Expense	$1,200	
Accumulated Depreciation		$1,200
To record depreciation for Year 6 on the basis of revised estimates.		

Figure 8.3 illustrates the revised depreciation path.

FIGURE 8.3
Illustration of Revised Depreciation Schedule.*

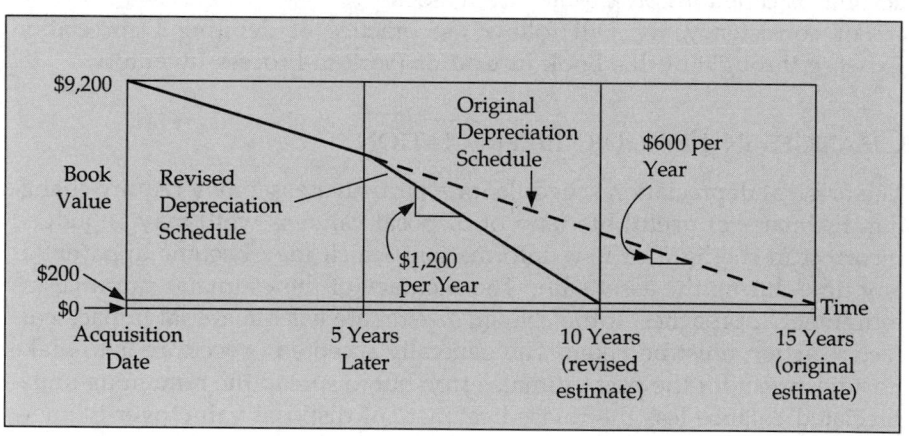

Asset's useful life estimate is decreased from 15 to 10 years at the start of Year 6. The straight-line method is used. Asset cost is $9,200 and has estimated disposal value of $200.

REPAIRS AND BETTERMENTS[7]

Depreciation is not the only cost of using a plant asset. Repair and maintenance costs during the life of the asset will be incurred. The repair policy adopted by the business will often affect the depreciation rate. If, for example, machinery, trucks, and other plant assets are checked and repaired frequently, such assets will have a longer useful life, and therefore a lower

---

[7] *CICA Handbook*, section 3060.29.

depreciation rate than otherwise. The more commonly used estimates of service life and depreciation rates assume that normal repairs will be made during the life of an asset.

Repairs must be distinguished from betterments. **Repairs** do not extend estimated service life materially or otherwise increase productive capacity. They restore future benefits to originally estimated levels. **Betterments** involve making an asset substantially better, improving its productive capacity. Repairs maintain or restore service potential; betterments extend service beyond that originally anticipated.

Whether a particular expenditure is a repair (treated as a period expense) or a betterment (treated as an asset) can be difficult to decide. The line between maintaining service and improving or extending it is not distinct. Some expenditures may both restore and extend service potential. In such cases, the portion that is deemed to be a betterment must be capitalized. Consider, for example, an aircraft engine repair during which improved alloy materials are installed where inferior alloy parts had been used before. There is frequent disagreement between Revenue Canada and taxpayers, as well as among accountants, over this question in specific situations.

UNIT OF ACCOUNT SOMETIMES DISTINGUISHES REPAIR FROM BETTERMENT

Some assets are actually composites of assets. Consider, for example, a truck, which might simplistically be thought of as a chassis, an engine, and a set of tires.

Although some major parts of a composite asset may have shorter lives than the asset as a whole, accounting for them with separate asset accounts is frequently impractical. Thus, the cost of a replacement set of tires is usually charged to repairs expense, although the tires could be treated as a separate asset. In some cases, composite assets are disaggregated for the purposes of depreciation. Exhibit 8.3 illustrates the effects on the timing and amounts of depreciation and repair expense of treating a truck either as a single asset or as a group of assets. At the time the truck was acquired, replacing the tires every second year and the engine after three years was anticipated. The repair to the windows in Year 5 was not. The truck has a six-year life and no estimated disposal value. When the truck is depreciated as a single asset, replacement of tires or the engine is a repair. When separate accounts are used, replacing the tires is a betterment, the acquisition of a new asset.

RETIREMENT OF ASSETS

When an asset is retired from service, the cost of the asset and the related amount of accumulated depreciation must be removed from the books. As part of this entry, the amount received from the sale or trade-in and any difference between that amount and book value must be recorded. The difference between the proceeds received on retirement and book value is a gain (if positive) or a loss (if negative). Before making the entry to write off the asset and its accumulated depreciation, an entry should be made to

Repairs
Expenditures to restore an asset's service potential after damage or prolonged use. If the latter, the difference between repairs and maintenance is one of degree and not of kind. Treated as an expense of the period in which it is incurred.

Betterments
Expenditures that improve the value of an asset and are hence capitalized.

Retirement of Assets
Removing the cost and depreciation costs of the asset from the books when an asset is retired from service.

bring the depreciation up to date; that is, the depreciation that has occurred between the start of the current accounting period and the date of disposition is recorded. Because of the inherent uncertainties and the insignificant amount, this entry is frequently ignored in practice.

EXHIBIT 8.3
Unit of Account Influences Depreciation and Maintenance Charges

Assumed Data
Truck: Cost $48,000; six-year life.
Engine: Cost $9,000; three-year life.
Tires: Cost $1,200; two-year life.
Windows: Repair cost $800 in Year 5.
(straight-line depreciation)

| | Depreciation of | | | | |
	Chassis	Engine	Tires	Maintenance	Total Expense
Separate Asset Accounts					
Year 1	$ 6,300[a]	$ 3,000[b]	$ 600[c]	—	$ 9,900
Year 2	6,300	3,000	600	—	9,900
Year 3	6,300	3,000	600[c]	—	9,900
Year 4	6,300	3,000[b]	600	—	9,900
Year 5	6,300	3,000	600[c]	$ 800[d]	10,700
Year 6	6,300	3,000	600	—	9,900
	$37,800	$18,000	$3,600	$ 800	$60,200
Single Asset Account	**Truck**				
Year 1	$ 8,000[e]	—	—	—	$ 8,000
Year 2	8,000	—	—	$ 1,200[f]	9,200
Year 3	8,000	—	—	9,000[g]	17,000
Year 4	8,000	—	—	1,200[f]	9,200
Year 5	8,000	—	—	800[d]	8,800
Year 6	8,000	—	—	—	8,000
	$48,000			$12,200	$60,000

[a] *Chassis ($48,000 − $9,000 − $1,200)/6.*
[b] *Engine: $9,000/3.*
[c] *Tires: $1,200/2.*
[d] *Window Repair.*
[e] *$48,000/6.*
[f] *Tires.*
[g] *Engine.*

To illustrate the retirement of an asset, assume that sales equipment that cost $5,000, was expected to last four years, and had an estimated disposal value of $200, is depreciated on a straight-line basis at $1,200 [= ($5,000 − $200)/4] per year. Depreciation has been recorded for two years, and the equipment is sold at mid-year in the third year. The depreciation from the start of the accounting period to the date of sale of $600 [= ½ × ($5,000 − $200)/4] is recorded:

Depreciation Expense	$600	
Accumulated Depreciation		$600
To record depreciation charges up to the date of sale.		

The book value of the asset is now its cost less 2.5 years of straight-line depreciation of $1,200 per year or $2,000 (= $5,000 − $3,000). The entry to record the retirement of the assets depends on the amount of the selling price.

1. Suppose that the equipment was sold for $2,000 cash. The entry to record the sale would be:

Cash	$2,000	
Accumulated Depreciation	3,000	
Equipment		$5,000

2. Suppose that the equipment was sold for $2,300. The entry to record the sale would be:

Cash	$2,300	
Accumulated Depreciation	3,000	
Equipment		$5,000
Gain on Retirement of Equipment		300

3. Suppose that the equipment was sold for $1,500. The entry to record the sale would be:

Cash	$1,500	
Accumulated Depreciation	3,000	
Loss on Retirement of Equipment	500	
Equipment		$5,000

TRADE-IN TRANSACTIONS

Instead of being sold when it is retired from service, the asset may be traded in on a new unit, a common practice for automobiles. The **trade-in transaction** can best be viewed as a sale of the old asset followed by a purchase of the new asset. The accounting for trade-in transactions determines simultaneously the gain or loss on disposal of the old asset and the acquisition cost recorded for the new asset. The procedures depend on the data available about the market value of the asset traded in and the cash equivalent cost of the new asset.

The trade-in of assets falls under the class of accounting transactions called *exchange of nonmonetary assets*. The general rule that governs the accounting is that the new asset should be set up at the fair value of the asset surrendered or of the asset acquired, whichever is more objectively determinable. The cost and accumulated depreciation of the old asset is removed, the cash changing hands is recorded, and the "plug" in the entry becomes the gain or loss recognized. If the assets exchanged are deemed similar (for example, a truck for a truck), this procedure is modified to avoid recognizing any gain. The rationale for this is that the earnings process is deemed to still be incomplete and the gain is unrealized.

trade-in transaction
The acquisition of a new asset in exchange for a used one and, perhaps, additional cash.

Using Market Value of Old Asset

fair market value
Value (price) determined at arm's length between a willing buyer and a willing seller, each acting rationally in his or her own self-interest. May be estimated in the absence of a monetary transaction.

If the **fair market value** of the old asset traded in can be found, that amount plus the cash given up generally determines the valuation of the new asset. Assume that used equipment originally costing $5,000 with $3,000 of accumulated depreciation has a fair market value of $1,300 and is traded in on a new piece of equipment, along with an additional $5,500 of cash. The new equipment had a list price of $7,300. The entries would be:

Equipment (new)	$6,800*	
Accumulated Depreciation	3,000	
Loss on Disposition of Equipment	700	
Equipment (old)		$5,000
Cash		5,500
To record trade-in of equipment.		

*$1,300 + $5,500

list price
The published or nominally quoted price for goods.

Note that the **list price** of the new equipment does not affect the entries shown above. Valuation of the used asset in established secondhand markets almost always offers more reliable information than quoted list prices.

Using Market Value of New Asset

If, however, a reliable valuation of the used asset is not available, the lowest available cash price for the new asset (which is sometimes the list price) will determine the valuation of the new asset as well as the gain or loss on disposition of the old asset. If the list price of the new equipment in the preceding example was $7,000 and there was no other reliable information available, the entries would be:

Equipment (new)	$7,000	
Accumulated Depreciation	3,000	
Loss on Disposition of Equipment	500	
Equipment (old)		$5,000
Cash		5,500
To record trade-in of equipment.		

Exchange of Similar Assets (Implied Gain)

trade-in allowance
A deduction allowed from the normal purchase price of an asset created by trading in another asset.

Assume that a drill press costing $1,000, with accumulated depreciation of $540, is traded for a new drill press. A **trade-in allowance** of $600 is granted and a cash payment of $800 is requested. The cash purchase price of the new asset is $1,400. Instead of recording the new asset at its fair value ($1,400), we would use the book value of the old asset plus the cash paid ($460 + $800). The unrealized gain of $140 would be gradually realized through lower depreciation charges ($1,260 instead of $1,400). The entry would be:

Equipment (new)	$1,260	
Accumulated Depreciation	540	
Equipment (old)		$1,000
Cash		800
To record trade-in of drill press for new model.		

The capital cost allowance regulations under the Income Tax Act ignore the accounting gain on sale on disposal of an individual asset. They require a company to deduct the lesser of the disposal proceeds and the capital cost from the undepreciated capital cost of the assets in the class, thereby reducing the undepreciated capital cost of the class. This reduction in the undepreciated capital cost subsequently diminishes the capital cost allowance that may be claimed as a deduction from income in the current and future years. Any gain or loss recorded by a company on disposal of plant assets is eliminated in computing taxable income.

THE INVESTMENT TAX CREDIT

In order to stimulate investment in machinery and equipment, the federal government has passed tax laws that permit the purchaser of machinery and equipment to claim a credit against income taxes otherwise payable. The credit reduces the purchaser's income tax liability, and the capital cost of the asset is reduced by the amount of the **investment tax credit** claimed in a year. The rate of the credit and the property eligible for the credit have varied through the years as the federal government has amended the tax laws. The examples in this section assume a 10 percent tax credit on all equipment purchases.

investment tax credit A reduction in income tax liability granted by the federal government to firms that buy new equipment.

If a firm buys $900,000 of equipment this year with an estimated service life of eight years, it will receive a $90,000 (= 0.10 × $900,000) investment tax credit. If its income tax liability shown on the tax return before the investment tax credit is $600,000, the following entry will be made:

Income Tax Expense	$600,000	
Income Tax Payable		$600,000
To record income taxes before the investment tax credit.		

The investment credit will reduce income taxes payable by $90,000 in the year in which the credit is earned, independent of the financial accounting treatment of the credit. There are two generally accepted methods of recording the investment tax credit for financial reporting — the flow-through method and the deferral method.[8] Two major options, the deferred-credit method and the cost-reduction method, are included in the deferral method.

---

[8] Problem 29 at the end of this chapter explores the theoretical possibilities one might consider in choosing the methods in practice.

flow-through method
A method of accounting for the investment tax credit whereby the credit generated by this year's asset purchases is recorded as a reduction of income tax expense for the current year.

Under the **flow-through method**, the entire investment credit realized during the year by all asset acquisitions is recorded as a reduction in income tax expense of the year. (It all "flows through" to income this year.) The entry would be:

Income Tax Payable	$90,000	
Income Tax Expense		$90,000
To record the investment tax credit (= 0.10 × $900,000) for the year.		

deferral method
The process of apportioning income taxes among periods.

The **deferral method** spreads the benefit from the investment tax credit over the years of the service life of the equipment acquired. The entire investment tax credit reduces the amount of income taxes payable in the year of acquisition, even though the reported reductions in income tax expense are spread over the years of service life. In the example, the entry in the year of acquisition, using the deferred-credit method, would be:

Income Tax Payable	$90,000	
Income Tax Expense		$11,250
Deferred Investment Tax Credit		78,750
Part (⅛ × $90,000) of investment tax credit reduces the income tax expense in first year. The remaining portion will reduce expense in later years. The entire effect on taxes payable occurs in the first year.		

The Deferred Investment Tax Credit account appears on the balance sheet either as an asset contra account or among the noncurrent liabilities. At the end of each of the seven following years, the following entry would be made:

cost-reduction method
A method of accounting for the investment tax credit whereby the credit reduces the carrying cost of the acquired asset.

Deferred Investment Tax Credit	$11,250	
Income Tax Expense		$11,250
To amortize the deferred investment tax credit. Recorded income tax expense is reduced by $11,250 in each of Years 2 through 8. Income tax payable is reduced by $90,000 in Year 1.		

deferred-credit method
A method of accounting for the investment tax credit that initially charges the entire credit to a balance sheet account. The subsequent amortization systematically reduces income tax expense over the life of the acquired asset.

The **cost-reduction method** considers the reduction in income taxes payable to be a reduction in the cost of the equipment purchased. As in the **deferred-credit method**, the cost-reduction method spreads the benefits from reduced income taxes payable over the years of service of the new equipment, but records this benefit by reducing the amount of the depreciation expense. In the example, the entry in the year of acquisition, using the cost-reduction method, would be:

Income Tax Payable	$90,000	
Machinery and Equipment		$90,000
To record the investment tax credit (= 0.10 × $900,000)		

The depreciation on the new machinery and equipment will be based on the reduced cost of $810,000 (= $900,000 − $90,000). At the end of each of the eight years of the asset's service life the following entry would be made:

Depreciation	$10,125	
Accumulated Depreciation		$10,125
To record depreciation on new machinery and equipment		
equal to ⅛ of the net cost of $810,000.		

EFFECTS OVER TIME

Income tax expense is reduced by the full amount of the investment tax credit under both methods, but over different time periods.

If the deferral approach is used, income tax expense is reduced not only by a part of this year's investment tax credit, but also by portions of the investment tax credit relating to earlier years that are still being amortized. For a firm in equilibrium (and assuming no recent change in the tax laws with regard to the investment tax credit), income tax expense and net income will be the same under the flow-through and deferral approaches. For a growing firm, the flow-through method produces higher reported net income in all years during the growth period.

If the deferral method is used, income tax expense for a growing firm will be greater than taxes paid or taxes currently payable. This excess represents an expense that does not use funds.[9]

WASTING ASSETS AND DEPLETION

The costs of finding natural resources and preparing to extract them from the earth should be capitalized and amortized. Whether all costs of exploration or the costs of only the successful explorations are capitalized into the asset accounts remains an open accounting question. Generally accepted accounting principles allow two treatments. Under the **full-costing method**, the costs of all explorations (both successful and unsuccessful) are capitalized so long as the expected benefits from the successful explorations will more than cover the cost of all explorations. Under the **successful-efforts method**, only the cost of the successful efforts is capitalized; the cost of unsuccessful exploration efforts become expenses of the period when it becomes apparent that the efforts will not result in productive sites.

full-costing method
An accounting method used in the oil and gas industry whereby the exploration costs associated with all drilling sites are capitalized whether they lead to income-producing wells or not.

successful-efforts method
An accounting method used in the oil and gas industry whereby only costs associated with successful exploration are capitalized.

---

[9] *CICA Handbook*, section 3805. Until 1984, the *CICA Handbook* made no reference to the accounting treatment of the investment tax credit. During the preceding decade, the flow-through method had become the alternative favoured by Canadian companies. In 1984, the *CICA Handbook* recognized the investment tax issue and, contrary to existing practice, recommended that the cost-reduction approach be used for fiscal years beginning on or after January 1, 1985.

Amortization of wasting assets, or natural resources, is called *depletion*. The depletion method most often used is the *units-of-production method*. For example, if $4.5 million in costs were incurred to discover an oil well that contained an estimated 1.5 million barrels of oil, the costs of $4.5 million would be amortized (depleted) at the rate of $3 (= $4,500,000/1,500,000) for each barrel of oil removed from the well. The major accounting problem for extractive industries stems from uncertainty about the eventual total of units that will result from exploratory efforts.

Intangible Assets and Amortization

Assets can provide future benefits without having physical form. Such assets are called *intangibles*. Examples are research costs, advertising costs, patents, trade secrets, know-how, trademarks, and copyrights. The first problem with intangibles is to decide:

1. Whether expenditures made to acquire or develop intangibles have future benefits and can be quantified with a sufficient degree of precision so that they should be "capitalized" (set up as assets) and amortized over time; or

2. Whether they have no future benefits and thus are expenses of the period in which the costs are incurred.

If the latter, the immediate expensing of the asset's cost appears as pattern E in Figures 8.1 and 8.2.

The second problem to solve is how to amortize the costs if they have been capitalized. Deciding on the period of amortization (the estimated service life) is difficult. Amortization of capitalized intangibles is usually recorded using the straight-line method, but other methods can be used if they seem appropriate. This section discusses some common intangibles and the issues involved in deciding whether to expense or to capitalize their costs. Amortization practices have varied widely in the past. Some industries have expensed these costs almost immediately. High technology industries such as telecommunications have treated their intangibles as having an indefinite life and as not requiring amortization. In 1990, the *CICA Handbook* began requiring amortization of all intangibles and placed a 40-year cap on amortization periods.[10]

---

[10] The origin of the 40-year limit is one of the more interesting stories in accounting history. Apparently, the Accounting Principles Board in the early 1960s was wrestling with the question of the period over which goodwill should be amortized, if at all. One of the members was reputed to have said that because goodwill is really attributable to the entrepreneurial skills of one or more key executives and the average working career of an individual is 40 years, this is the proper amortization period.

Now we see the 40-year rule applied to intangibles of all types. This illustrates an important cornerstone of accounting theory — why we do something in accounting matters less than the fact that everybody does it uniformly.

DISCUSSION CASE 18

Name That Brand

These days a good name is hard to find. The R.J. Reynolds Tobacco division of R.J. Reynolds Industries thought the perfect brand name for a new cigarette aimed at fashion-conscious, young women smokers would be Ritz, as in puttin' on the . . . Not so fast, said the Ritz Hotel in Paris, haunt of several generations of American romantics. The hotel, which, as it happens, markets a brand of cigarettes called Ritz Paris, brought a trademark infringement suit against Reynolds.

Was RJR intentionally infringing the Paris hotel's trademark? That's for the courts to decide; the suit is pending in a New York federal court. But name overlap can happen innocently these days. In the last four years alone more than 150,000 trademarks were registered with the U.S. Patent & Trademark Office. That's double the number of names registered in the preceding four years. It makes picking a name a big problem.

But be of good cheer. Some smart businesses are willing to relieve you of the problem. For a price. "The days when clients asked their advertising agencies to crank out a few names or held a company contest are over," declaims Frank Delano, chairman of the New York firm of Delano Goldman & Young, Inc. Its business is making up names. "We can clear a name in North America in about four hours and

foreign countries in about five days."

What's a name? Plenty, says Larry Goldman, Delano's partner. Apple Computer's name was a good choice, he explains, because it separated the company from thousands of others using the word computer as part of their trademark. Goldman claims he told Apple that Lisa was a poor name choice for its later product. "Too feminine," says Goldman.

Where do companies get their names? Some let their computers spew out thousands of letter combinations. Other sources include foreign words, trees, flowers, even words that don't mean anything but do imply desirable qualities — such as Ford's Merkur, which sounds, as it is intended to, German and vaguely high tech. The challenge in these cases is to match the name with the image of the product.

For big jobs, like naming cars or motorcycles, Delano Goldman & Young might charge $100,000 or more. A smaller job might cost $20,000. Clearly, the name business is profitable. Delano says that last year his company generated $1.2 million in revenues, with pretax earnings of 22%, and he expects to do $2 million in 1985.

Delano Goldman is not without competition. NameLab, Inc., in San Francisco, works from morphemes — the core semantic

(continued)

(continued)

unit within a word. For example, "tra" in transport, used by NameLab in the name Softra for a California software distributor. There are approximately 6,200 morphemes in the English language, the root of most of the 150,000-word stock of the language. Ira Bachrach, NameLab's president, says he has programmed each morpheme into his computer through the use of a notational system. The end result: coinages like Compaq (morpheme: pak, meaning small object).

"Most of the morphemes are Indo-European, the root of most of the major Western languages. By choosing the right morphemes," says Bachrach, "you can create names that have an impact worldwide." One example: Acura, the name of Honda's new luxury car. Bachrach thinks the word conveys precision — as in accurate — which was Honda's intention. Acura also meets the technical demands of a coined word, Bachrach explains. Because it ends with the suffix *a*, it is read as a noun and, therefore, a name. The word also starts and ends with the same letter, making it more memorable, and contains three clearly voiced syllables in only five letters.

Suzanne Leff, vice president of Interbrand, Inc., a New York company in the name business, points to Lozol, a drug for treating high blood pressure, manufactured by USV Laboratories, a unit of Revlon. "The name is a palindrome — it is spelled the same backwards and forwards — which is an advantage because such words tend to have pleasant sounds and are well balanced," says Leff.

Needless to say, the name was created by Leff's company.

References

Jeffrey A. Trachtenberg, "Name That Brand," *Forbes*, April 8, 1985, pages 128 and 130. Reprinted with permission of *Forbes* magazine, copyright Forbes Inc., 1985.

Discussion Question

Do you think it is rational economic behaviour to pay a company $100,000 to name your product? How would you account for this expenditure? If brand names are so important, why are supermarkets so successful in selling "no-name" products?

RESEARCH AND DEVELOPMENT

research and development (R&D)
Expenditures made for the purpose of creating or improving products. These must be expensed or capitalized, depending on the circumstance.

One common intangible is the benefit provided by expenditures on **research and development (R&D)**. Such costs are incurred for various reasons. Perhaps the firm seeks to develop a technological or marketing advance in order to have an edge on competition. Or it might wish to explore possible applications of existing technology to design a new product or improve an old one. Other research may be undertaken in response to a government contract, in preparing for bids on potential contracts, or in pursuit of "discoveries," with no specific product in mind. Whatever the reason, practically all research costs will yield their benefits, if any, in future periods. Herein lies the accounting issue: should R&D costs be charged to expense immediately as they are incurred, or should they be capitalized and amortized over future periods?

Generally accepted accounting principles[11] distinguish between the accounting treatment of research costs and development costs. Research costs result from a planned investigation undertaken with the hope of gaining new scientific or technical knowledge and understanding. Such investigation may or may not be directed toward a specific practical aim or application. Development costs result from a translation of research findings or other knowledge into a plan or design for new or substantially improved materials, devices, products, processes, systems, or services before the commencement of commercial production or use. In both cases, costs include all direct costs of a research or development project and, in addition, a fair share of overhead costs.

Generally accepted accounting principles require immediate expensing of research costs. This requirement is based on arguments that the future benefits from most research efforts are too uncertain to warrant capitalization and that writing them off as soon as possible is more conservative. Nevertheless, others consider that there must be future benefits in many cases or else efforts would not be pursued. Theoretically, research costs should be matched with the benefits produced by the research expenditures through the capitalization procedure with amortization over the benefited periods.

Development expenditures are incurred after the research phase has been completed, with a consequent reduction in the uncertainty of future benefits. In recognition of this fact, generally accepted accounting principles recommend that development costs be capitalized where they meet stringent criteria to assure reasonable future expense recovery. Under these circumstances, the development costs are amortized over future years commencing with the commercial production or use of the product or process and charged as an expense in a systematic and rational basis. The deferred development cost of each project is reviewed at the end of each accounting period to ensure that the cost will still be recovered at that time. Any cost that is not expected to be recovered should be written off as an expense of the period. Where development costs fail to meet the criteria, they will be expensed as incurred.

Where a company defers development costs, it must additionally disclose in the financial statements the unamortized balance of the development costs, the amount of development costs deferred during the year, and the amortization of development costs charged to expense during the year. It is also encouraged to present a general description of the general nature of the projects whose costs have been deferred.

ADVERTISING

Advertising expenditures are designed to increase sales currently and in the future, but there is a lag between in incurrence of these costs and their impact. The impact of advertising usually extends into subsequent periods.

Advertising
Expenditures promoting products intended to increase sales.

---

[11] *CICA Handbook*, section 3450.

brand names
Product names that are legally registered by a company and that may qualify as capital (intangible) assets by virtue of their ability to generate superior sales.

accounting rate of return
Income for a period divided by average assets during the period.

patent
An exclusive right given to the inventor of a product or process which legally prevents others from making, using, or selling the invention. Granted by the federal government for seventeen years.

Goodwill
The value that derives from a firm's ability to earn more than a normal rate of return in its industry.

Common practice immediately expenses all advertising and sales promotion costs, regardless of the timing of their impact (see pattern E in Figures 8.1 and 8.2). Those supporting this practice argue that (1) it is more conservative to do so; (2) it is almost impossible to quantify the future effects and timing of benefits derived from these costs; and (3) when these costs remain stable from year to year, income is not affected by the capitalization policy after the first few years. Nevertheless, some accountants support the capitalization treatment because doing so will better report assets and match costs with resulting benefits.

Many companies that market brand-name products to consumers own major economic assets that do not appear on their balance sheets. Consider, for example, the Procter & Gamble Corporation (P&G), which owns such well-known **brand names** as Tide and Crest. In recent years, P&G's net income has been about $1 billion and its total balance sheet assets have been about $15 billion. Thus, its **accounting rate of return** (net income divided by total assets) has been approximately 7 percent. In recent years, P&G has spent about $5 billion per year on advertising. If P&G had capitalized its advertising costs and amortized them over three years, its assets would be about $7.5 billion greater and its accounting rate of return would be only 4 percent. Therefore, one should be cautious in comparing the economic performance of firms without considering the underlying accounting policies. P&G shows that the rate of return on assets employed for companies with substantial uncapitalized intangible benefits can be misleadingly large.

Patents

A **patent** is a right obtained from the federal government to exclude others from the benefits from an invention. The legal life of patent protection may be as long as seventeen years, although the economic life of the patent may be considerably less. The accounting for patent costs depends on whether the patent was purchased from another party or developed internally. If the former, the purchase price is capitalized. If the latter, the total cost of product development and patent application is treated as an R&D cost and may be expensed or capitalized. Patent costs are usually amortized over the shorter of (1) its remaining legal life or (2) its estimated economic life. If for some reason the patent becomes worthless, the remaining capitalized cost is recognized immediately as an expense of the period. Often, the most significant component in the capitalized value of a patent is the legal expense associated with prosecuting a patent infringement suit. Some cynics claim that patents have no value until their exclusivity is tested in a court of law. If, however, the infringement suit is unsuccessful, all previously capitalized costs associated with the patent should be immediately written off.

Goodwill

Goodwill is an intangible asset that will be mentioned here only briefly. More details follow in Chapter 12. Goodwill arises from the purchase of one company or operating unit by another company and is measured as the difference between the amount paid for the acquired company as a whole and the sum of the current value of its individual assets less its liabilities. Thus, goodwill will appear in the financial statements of the company making the acquisition. Under current practice, goodwill acquired after March 1974 must be amortized over a time period not longer than 40 years.[12] Most companies use a considerably shorter amortization period. Goodwill is generally not recognized by a company that develops it, even though large expenditures for advertising and other publicity may be made annually. All such expenditures are charged to expense as incurred.

COPYRIGHTS

A **copyright** protects the owner against the unauthorized reproduction of a specific artistic or literary work. Included in the latter are the rights to computer software. A copyright lasts for the life of the author plus 50 years. The purchase price of copyrights can be substantial. For example, entertainer Michael Jackson purchased the copyrights to songs of the Beatles for $125 million. Theoretically, a firm could amortize copyrights over their legal life, which could exceed the 40-year limit, but the CICA strongly suggests that all intangibles should be amortized over 40 years or less.

copyright
Exclusive right given to the author, artist, or composer of a work of art for the lifetime of the author plus fifty years.

FRANCHISES

Franchises involve exclusive rights to market a product in a given geographic area. The rights and responsibilities are determined by the contractual agreement between the franchisor and the franchisee. Examples of franchises are Kentucky Fried Chicken, Harvey's, and Midas Mufflers. It may be argued that the franchise is the dominant form of retail business in the 1990s.

There are many controversial accounting issues associated with franchising, especially with regard to revenue recognition by the franchisor. For the franchisee, the major issue is whether any additional outlays beyond the initial franchise fee should be capitalized. These outlays could include, for example, a monthly fee for management support and technical advice. The franchise asset can be substantial in size; a McDonald's franchise probably costs in excess of $1 million. The amortization requirements are the same as for the other intangibles.

Franchises
Rights to market specific brands of products in given geographical areas.

ORGANIZATION COSTS

Expenditures incurred in launching a new business (usually a corporation) are called **organization costs**. These include legal fees, fees paid to the government, and costs associated with attracting debt or equity financing. Although the 40-year amortization limit applies, because of the relatively small amounts involved, most companies write off these costs almost immediately.

organization costs
Expenditures incurred in launching a business (usually a corporation) or in issuing shares; may include lawyers' fees, various registration fees paid to government, and other startup costs.

---

[12] *CICA Handbook*, section 1580.

DISCUSSION CASE 19

Should Human Resources Be Reflected on the Balance Sheet?

The annual report for a large firm begins with the statement: "People are our most important asset." But an analysis of the firm's financial statements reveals no human assets. The reason is simple: Everyone agrees that people are important to an organization, but no one knows how to place a monetary value on their importance.

An executive's job is to allocate and administer scarce resources to achieve a goal — that is, maximize owner wealth. But if investments in assets are distorted, decisions of managers, investors, and appraisers may not be the optimum ones. Recognition of this has stimulated interest in the valuation of intangible assets, especially human assets.

Humans fall into a large and complex category of assets known as intangibles. Included among such assets are patents, copyrights, trademarks, and a variety of intangible assets commonly listed under the term "goodwill," such as a favourable business name or location, or a group of knowledgeable or skilled employees. While important to the success and value of a firm, many of these intangible assets do not appear on a firm's balance sheet because there is usually no objective cost basis at which to value them. In addition, tax laws discourage the allocation of costs to goodwill because

goodwill, unlike equipment and other tangible assets, cannot be depreciated. Consequently, buyers tend to minimize the amount of the purchase costs allocated to goodwill in financial statements.

For many years, accountants have attempted to build human value into financial statements. Although their efforts have not been completely successful, they have generated many ideas that may be helpful to financial executives.

It wasn't until the 1960s that a theory of human resource accounting was developed. Since then, many have applied their knowledge and skills to the valuation of human resources.

Accountants generally desire to provide information to improve the decision-making ability of managers. Thus, early accounting literature defined *human resource valuation* as the process of identifying, measuring, and communicating information about human resources to assist management decision-making within an organization. Within a few years, the definition was modified to read "identifying and measuring data about human resources and communicating this information to interested parties." Interested parties are divided into two basic groups: investors and managers.

(continued)

(continued)

Research demonstrates that investors change their decisions concerning investments when human resource information about a firm is disclosed. Such a reaction would not be unusual if humans were normally considered an asset of the firm. Their inclusion as assets, however, has raised several questions. The most prominent is, obviously, what is an asset?

From the accountants' point of view, things of value should be recognized, valued, and placed on a firm's balance sheet as an asset. Valuing humans, however, creates a tremendous problem because they do not conform to the traditional definition of an asset. The classical definition of something owned by a firm cannot be applied to humans. This is true even in professional sports. A firm may own a player's contract and not the player.

When defined in terms of characteristics, assets should have utility, scarcity, and exchangeability. Arthur Andersen & Co. applied this definition to human resources and conclude that humans lack exchangeability and thus are not assets. The firm advised, however, that if obtaining and training human assets required large expenditures, these should be reported in special statements rather than in the traditional financial statements.

When analyzed from a broader, more philosophical point of view, humans can be classified as assets. The word "asset" can have many different meanings. When applied in a particular chain of reasoning, it has a known and constant meaning that is not bound by tradition, but based upon use. If assets are considered tangibles or intangibles that possess certain properties, and if accounting statements are to provide a realistic reflection of the usefulness or value of these properties, humans can be assets. If one property is that an asset should be subject to control by the firm, that control need not be absolute. For instance, goodwill is currently considered an asset, but it is subject to many forces outside the firm.

Thus, assets are something that possess utility or value. They are acquired not for their own sake, but for what they can contribute to a firm's cash flow. This definition avoids controversies over ownership, control, and exchangeability. Once it is accepted, the real challenge is measuring the value of all assets.

Human resource accounting advocates argue that a firm's value is understated when finance statements fail to recognize the value of human assets. Some accountants still reject the concept of considering humans an asset, but the more basic objection is that human valuation is too subjective or difficult to measure. Attempts to measure human value have generally been split between two theories: historical cost theory and replacement cost theory. Among accountants, the historical cost theory seems to be favored because it is similar to conventional accounting practices. Because historical costs are not as useful in making decisions about the present or future, many

(continued)

(continued)

have reason to prefer replacement cost theory.

Historical cost valuation records objective and verifiable input values. When cost theory is applied to human resource valuation, two questions arise: Which costs are relevant, and which of these costs are to be expensed or capitalized? One approach has been to classify human resource costs as either training or educational. Training costs relate to a current job, whereas educational costs relate to the preparation for advancement. Training costs are expensed, and educational costs are capitalized.

A second approach includes all recruiting, testing, training, and development costs. Whether to expense or capitalize a particular cost is determined by how long the firm is expected to benefit from the cost. A formula has been developed to calculate whether it is reasonable to assume that the benefit would exceed 12 months. If so, the cost is capitalized. This method was actually implemented by the R.G. Barry Corporation. (See Bertha Proffitt, "Human Resource Accounting in Practice at R.G. Barry Corporation," *The Woman CPA*, October 1974. Historical cost models have also been used by the Atlanta Braves, Flying Tigers Corporation, Upjohn Company, and Touche Ross & Co.)

The benefit of using the historical cost method is that it incorporates the value of human resources in financial statements. Consequently, attention is focused on both the costs and the

benefits associated with recruiting, training, and educating human resources.

The replacement cost method of human resource valuation is based upon established economic theory. People, like any other resource, have value because they are capable of providing future utility or service. Consequently, the current value of an individual to an organization can be defined as the present value of the future services he or she is expected to provide the firm.

An individual's value to a firm can be calculated by determining a "conditional value" and the probability that the individual will remain with the firm. The conditional value is the present worth of the services an individual could perform if he remains with the firm throughout his productive working life.

With the exception of cash or claims on cash, the values assigned to balance sheet assets recorded at historical costs do not represent realistic measures. The classic example is fixed investments. Their initial value is based upon cost, but all future financial statement values are determined by a variety of depreciation techniques, life expectancies, salvage values, etc. Accountants record an input cost and then allocate cost to a series of future income flows. While these allocations are frequently less than perfect, they are of some value to management, investors, appraisers, etc.

Why should human resources be treated any differently? Input costs are indeed associated with

(continued)

(continued)

the acquisition of human assets. Thus, these costs should be recognized. At issue is not whether the costs are measured perfectly or allocated exactly but whether human resources receive the value they deserve. This objective can only be accomplished if human resources are recorded and integrated with information about other assets.

Human resource valuation is of concern to people in many professions: the plant manager with high employee turnover, the financial analyst making investment recommendations, the investor deciding between alternative investment opportunities, and the business appraiser. There are no simple or exact solutions on how to appropriately report and use human resource valuations.

While recognizing that human resource valuation data are useful to managers, analysts, investors, and appraisers, accountants have spent much of their efforts debating whether humans are assets, and if they are, what about them can be measured. The accuracy of such measurements has been overly debated to the detriment of financial statement users who need human resource information to make informed investment and business decisions. If accuracy were the main issue, a strong case could be made for deleting from financial statements depreciation and inventory valuations, which are based on arbitrary historical cost assumptions.

The true value of a business is generated by an integrated valuation system that cannot be derived by merely summarizing and adding the individual valuation elements of the system. While each valuation element, including the human resource element, is important and deserves consideration, the value of a business may be greater than or less than the sum total of the individual valuation elements. Consequently, accountants should continue their efforts to place human resource valuations in financial statements. To accomplish this goal, they may need to place less emphasis upon historical cost data and more emphasis on the present value of future benefits.

References

Reprinted with permission from Charles P. Edmonds, "Should Human Resources Be Reflected on the Balance Sheet?" *Financial Executive*, January 1986, copyright 1986 by Financial Executives Institute, Morristown, New Jersey.

Discussion Question

Assume that you are the controller for a public accounting firm. Realizing that people are really the only assets the firm has, you decide to capitalize its human resources. How would you establish a value to place on the balance sheet? Do you think the users of financial statements want this type of information?

AN INTERNATIONAL PERSPECTIVE

The accounting for capital assets in most developed countries closely parallels that in Canada. Acquisition, or historical, cost is the most common valuation method. France permits periodic revaluation of capital assets to current market value. Few firms perform these revaluations, however, because they result in immediate taxation of the unrealized gains. Firms in Great Britain are also allowed to revalue their capital assets periodically, but without the adverse tax implications. Refer to Exhibit 2.9 on page 118, a balance sheet for Ranks Hovis McDougal PLC. This firm revalued its tangible assets during Year 8 (it also purchased additional tangible assets). The offsetting credit for the revaluation is to the Revaluation Reserve account, shown among Capital and Reserves on the balance sheet.

Depreciation accounting in developed countries also closely parallels that in Canada. Firms use both straight-line and accelerated-depreciation methods. When firms in Great Britain recognize depreciation on revalued plant assets, they charge the depreciation on the revalued amount above historical cost to the Revaluation Reserve account. Thus, neither the initial unrealized holding gain nor depreciation of this gain flows through the income statement. The income statement includes depreciation only on historical cost amounts.

Firms in developed foreign countries also account for intangible assets by methods similar to those used in Canada. It is the norm, for example, to expense research expenditures immediately. France and Japan, however, allow capitalization of such costs.

One recent change in the accounting for intangibles occurred in Great Britain. Firms can now place a valuation on their brand names and include this item among assets on the balance sheet. These firms must generally hire independent appraisers to obtain the needed valuations. Appraisers might base their valuations on premium prices charged customers for a brand-name product over a nonbrand-name product, on the promotion and other costs associated with launching a new brand-name product, or on the price paid in recent mergers and acquisitions of brand-name product firms.

Refer again to the balance sheet of Ranks Hovis McDougal PLC in Exhibit 2.9 on page 118. Note that fixed assets for Year 8 include £678.0 million for brand names. The offsetting credit is to the Revaluation Reserve account. As with depreciation of revalued plant assets, firms charge the amortization of brand names against the revaluation reserve account instead of to income.

The accounting practices of our largest international trading partner, the United States, are virtually identical to those in Canada for capital assets, with two notable exceptions. Many U.S. firms use tax depreciation also for book purposes. The most common method is called *sum of the years' digits*, which is an accelerated-depreciation method. Second, capitalization and amortization policies for wasting assets in the United States often reflect political incentives.

SUMMARY

Three major classes of long-lived operating assets are plant assets, wasting assets (nonrenewable natural resources), and intangibles. The major accounting problems for each class are the same: (1) calculating the cost of the asset to be capitalized as an asset, (2) estimating the total period of benefit or the amount of expected benefits, and (3) assigning the cost to the benefited periods or units produced in a systematic and reasonable fashion.

This chapter emphasizes depreciable plant assets and their depreciation. The cost figure to be charged off is reduced by any disposal value. The period (or number of units) of benefit is determined by judgment based on experience. The pattern of depreciation charges over the asset's life is usually based on some conventional method — the most common methods in practice are straight-line, declining-balance, and unit-of-production. The Income Tax Act does not permit a company to deduct depreciation when computing taxable income, but replaces it with a maximum capital cost allowance that may be claimed, using the declining-balance basis for most asset classes.

If the asset is retired before the end of the estimated service life for an amount different from its book value, a gain or loss will be recognized. Under the capital cost allowance regulations, the gain or loss will not be recognized in the year of disposal but will be deferred to the future.

Intangibles such as trademarks, copyrights, patents, and computer programs are among the most valuable resources owned by some firms. The accounting treatment of *purchased* intangibles is the same as for tangible assets. For most intangibles developed by a firm, accounting requires the immediate expensing of the development costs. This accounting drastically alters the look of some financial statements. The firms most likely to be affected are service, rather than manufacturing, companies.

KEY TERMS

Capital Assets
Plant assets
Wasting assets
Intangible assets
Amortization
Depreciation
Depletion
Opportunity cost
Self-constructed asset
Capitalization of interest
Physical life
Economic life
Scrap value
Salvage value
Residual value
Disposal value
Accounting estimates

Straight-line depreciation
Units-of-production method
Accelerated depreciation
Declining-balance depreciation
Net book value
Capital cost allowance (CCA)
Compound interest depreciation
Accumulated Depreciation
Repairs
Betterments
Retirement of assets
Trade-in transaction
Fair market value
List price
Trade-in allowance
Investment tax credit
Flow-through method

Deferral method
Cost-reduction method
Deferred-credit method
Full-costing method
Successful-efforts method
Research and development (R&D)
Advertising

Brand names
Accounting rate of return
Patent
Goodwill
Copyright
Franchises
Organization costs

SELF-STUDY MATERIAL

This section contains questions, exercises, and problems to help you assess your understanding of Chapter 8. Careful review of this material will assist you in completing the homework assignments. Solutions are found at the end of the section.

QUESTIONS AND EXERCISES

True/False

For each statement, place a T or an F in the space provided to indicate whether the statement is true or false.

_____ 1. The useful life of a tangible asset for computing depreciation should be the total number of years for which the asset is physically capable of performing.

_____ 2. The depreciation method most commonly used for financial statement purposes is the straight-line method.

_____ 3. When the rate of usage of an asset varies from period to period, a depreciation charge based on actual usage during the period may be justified.

_____ 4. Expenditures made to repair an asset should be capitalized.

_____ 5. The amount of expenses in any one year is the same whether or not interest during construction is capitalized.

_____ 6. Identifying the specific cause of depreciation is not essential for measuring it.

_____ 7. When disposal value is negative, the depreciable basis is the acquisition cost of the asset.

_____ 8. Interest costs incurred during construction of a plant asset may be capitalized.

_____ 9. If, over a year, the current value of a depreciating asset rises rather than falls, the income statement will report an appreciation gain rather than a depreciation expense.

_____ 10. Because the cost of a plant asset is a joint cost of many benefited periods, there is no single correct way to determine the amount of periodic depreciation charge.

_____ 11. The gain or loss on disposal of a depreciable asset is normally included in taxable income in the year of disposal.

_____ 12. Most firms claim the maximum capital cost allowance (CCA).

_____ 13. The term "accelerated-depreciation method" implies that the amount of depreciation per year decreases as the asset becomes older.

_____ 14. A firm is not required to use the same method of depreciation for financial accounting as for income tax purposes.

_____ 15. The goal of a firm when choosing a depreciation method for tax purposes should be to maximize the current value of the tax savings attributable to the depreciation charge.

_____ 16. The investment tax credit is an allowable deduction in the computation of taxable income.

_____ 17. Intangible assets lack physical substance.

_____ 18. When calculating CCA for tax reporting, disposal value can be ignored.

_____ 19. A major difficulty in calculating CCA is determining the useful life of an asset.

_____ 20. The production method is a type of straight-line method.

_____ 21. When a company trades in an old asset for a similar new one, generally accepted accounting principles disallow recognition of any losses.

_____ 22. The recognition of goodwill when one company acquires another should be made on the books of the company that developed the goodwill.

_____ 23. Patent costs must be amortized over the legal life of the patent, which is seventeen years.

_____ 24. When a depreciable asset is disposed of, an entry should be made to bring depreciation up to date before making the entry to remove the asset from the books.

_____ 25. When the estimated useful life of an asset is revised, the accountant must correct the books for misstated depreciation in previous years.

_____ 26. When the proceeds from the sale of an asset exceed the net book value, there is a gain on the sale.

_____ 27. The cost of testing a newly acquired piece of equipment before initial use should be expensed.

_____ 28. When the efficiency and earning power of assets decline as the assets grow older, it may be appropriate to employ an accelerated-depreciation method.

_____ 29. All research and development costs are required to be expensed when incurred for financial accounting purposes.

_____ 30. The usual entry to record depreciation on a building is to debit Depreciation Expense and to credit Building.

_____ 31. The most common depletion method for financial accounting purposes is the units-of-production method.

_____ 32. Declines in the service potential of an asset result from both physical and functional factors.

_____ 33. Compound interest methods of depreciation are examples of decelerated methods of depreciation.

_____ 34. A gain on retirement of plant assets is treated as a subtraction in determining funds from operations on the statement of changes in financial position.

_____ 35. Advertising expenditures are normally expensed when incurred.

_____ 36. Amortization of intangible assets is called "depletion."

_____ 37. Expenditures made on an asset to maintain the service level anticipated should be expensed when incurred, but costs to improve an asset should be capitalized.

_____ 38. Accounting gains and losses on disposal of assets are not recognized for tax purposes.

_____ 39. For tax purposes, the investment tax credit should, whenever possible, be taken completely in the year of purchase of qualifying property.

_____ 40. In amortizing intangible assets, only the straight-line method is acceptable for financial accounting purposes.

_____ 41. The main purpose underlying depreciation accounting is to record the decline in market values of assets over the useful life of each.

_____ 42. Because the investment in a depreciating asset is the price paid for a series of future benefits, the asset is similar in many respects to prepayments for rent and insurance.

_____ 43. Theoretically, research and development costs should probably be capitalized and amortized over future periods.

_____ 44. Under the flow-through method of accounting for the investment tax credit, the entire credit is treated as a reduction of income tax expense in the year of purchase of qualified properties.

_____ 45. The declining-balance depreciation method applies a constant rate per year times the declining book value of the asset.

Matching

From the list of terms, select one term that is most closely associated with one descriptive phrase or statement that follows and place the letter for that term in the space provided.

a. accumulated depreciation
b. advertising
c. book value
d. building under construction
e. compound interest depreciation method
f. cost allocation
g. cost-reduction approach
h. declining-balance depreciation method
i. depletion
j. depreciation
k. expense
l. flow-through method

m. goal of depreciation accounting for financial statement purposes
n. goodwill
o. income tax method
p. investment tax credit
q. obsolescence
r. patent
s. repairs
t. disposal value
u. self-constructed assets
v. trade-in allowance
w. work-in-process inventory

_____ 1. Interest may be capitalized for these items.

_____ 2. Depreciation is not a decline in value; it is a process of _____.

_____ 3. Investment tax credit treated as a reduction of income tax expense over the service life of qualifying property.

_____ 4. Amortization of natural resources.

_____ 5. Small adjustments and replacements to plant assets with little or no effect on useful life.

_____ 6. Proceeds on disposition of an asset at the end of its useful life.

_____ 7. Matching of costs with the benefits derived from the use of an asset.

_____ 8. A reduction of taxes for purchasing qualifying plant assets.

_____ 9. An intangible that appears on the balance sheet only when one company is acquired by another.

_____ 10. Account debited if depreciation is a production cost.

_____ 11. Cost less accumulated depreciation.

_____ 12. Proper accounting for all research and some development costs when incurred.

_____ 13. Depreciation method with increasing depreciation per year of useful life.

_____ 14. Recognize no accounting gains or losses on disposal of assets.

_____ 15. A functional factor in determining depreciation.

_____ 16. The account credited for depreciation.

_____ 17. Legal right to future benefits of an invention.

Multiple Choice

Choose the best answer for each question or problem and enter the identifying letter in the space provided.

_____ 1. Which of these costs would not be included in the cost of machinery?
a) invoice price
b) installation costs
c) testing of machinery before its intended use
d) all of the above would be included

____ 2. Nashua Ltd. owns a machine that has a book value of $20,000 and a fair market value of $18,000, which it trades for a new machine that has a list price of $25,000. In addition to giving up the old machine, Nashua pays $6,000 in cash. At what amount should the new machine be recorded?
a) $35,000
b) $24,000
c) $26,000
d) $18 ,000

____ 3. Assume the same facts as in question 2. What would be the amount of gain (loss) recognized for income tax purposes?
a) 0
b) $2,000 loss
c) $1,000 gain
d) $7,000 gain

____ 4. The text describes the five basic patterns for allocations of plant assets:
E — Expense immediately
S — Straight-line method
D — Declining-balance method
C — Compound interest method
N — No writeoff
Which basic pattern would be appropriate for land?
a) E
b) S
c) C
d) N

____ 5. Referring to question 4, which pattern would be appropriate for most intangibles?
a) E
b) S
c) D
d) N

____ 6. Which term is used to refer to the writeoff of intangible assets?
a) amortization
b) depreciation
c) depletion
d) writeoff

____ 7. During 19X6, Kyle Corp. traded 5,000 shares in White Corp. that had a current market value of $45,000 for a piece of land. The shares had cost Kyle Corp. $22,000 in late 19X1 and had increased to a market high of $52,000 in late 19X5. Which journal entry properly reflects this transaction?

a) Land	$45,000	
Gain on Sale		$23,000
Shares in White Corp.		22,000
b) Land	$22,000	
Shares in White Corp.		$22,000
c) Land	$45,000	
Loss on Sale	7,000	
Shares in White Corp.		$22,000
Holding Gain		30,000

d) Land	$52,000	
Shares in White Corp.		$22,000
Gain on Sale		30,000

_____ 8. Which of these factors is an example of a functional cause of depreciation?
a) wear and tear
b) inadequate size to meet current needs of the company
c) rust or decay
d) deterioration from wind or rain

_____ 9. The Lewis Co. Ltd. owns machinery that has a cost of $100,000 and accumulated depreciation of $60,000 on January 1, 19X1. On July 1, 19X1, the machinery is sold for $43,000. The straight-line depreciation method has been used during the previous six years of its service life. How much gain or loss will be recorded on the sale?
a) $3,000 gain
b) $13,000 gain
c) $22,000 loss
d) $8,000 gain

_____ 10. In selecting the best depreciation method for tax purposes, which statement is not correct?
a) the goal should be to maximize the present value of the tax savings from the depreciation deductions
b) the asset should be written off as soon as possible
c) earlier depreciation deductions are more valuable than later ones
d) a compound interest depreciation method should be employed

_____ 11. Caldwell Co. Inc. acquired a machine for $20,000 in 19X1 and has depreciated it on the straight-line basis (no disposal value) for two years based on a ten-year estimated life. In 19X3, it was determined that the remaining life was only four years instead of eight. What amount of depreciation should be recorded for 19X3, on the basis of generally accepted accounting principles?
a) $5,000
b) $4,000
c) $3,333
d) $2,000

_____ 12. Which cost may be capitalized for a self-constructed asset?
a) interest before construction
b) interest during construction
c) interest after construction
d) all of the above

_____ 13. For which of these methods may disposal value be ignored in calculating depreciation?
a) straight-line
b) compound interest
c) declining-balance
d) none of the above

_____ 14. For which depreciation method is the estimate of useful life not required?
a) straight-line
b) compound interest
c) declining-balance
d) capital cost allowance

_____ 15. Berger Ltd. buys a building on April 1, 19X1 for $100,000. The building has a physical life of 50 years, but Berger anticipates using the building for 30 years. At the end of 50 years, the building will have no disposal value, but it will have a disposal value of $5,000 in 30 years. How much depreciation would be recorded on December 31, 19X1 if the straight-line method were used?

    a) $3,167
    b) $2,000
    c) $1,500
    d) $2,375

_____ 16. On January 1, 19X1, the Ditoo Company Ltd. has machinery on the books that originally cost $200,000. During 19X1, the following expenditures were made:

Minor Repairs	$ 5,000
Improvements	10,000
Additions	37,000

How much should be recorded in the machinery account on December 31, 19X1?

    a) $252,000
    b) $247,000
    c) $237,000
    d) $215,000

_____ 17. Rigamortis Inc. purchases a piece of equipment on January 1, 19X1 at a cost of $100,000. The equipment has a five-year useful life and can be sold for $10,000 at the end of five years. How much depreciation would be recorded in the second year if Rigamortis Inc. were to use the declining-balance depreciation method at double the straight-line rate?

    a) $24,000
    b) $20,000
    c) $21,600
    d) $36,000

_____ 18. Lisel Ltd. has spent $250,000 on research during 19X1 to generate new product lines. Of the five projects worked on, one resulted in a patented item while the other four were considered unsuccessful. According to generally accepted accounting principles, how much of the $250,000 should be recognized as an expense in 19X1?

    a) $250,000
    b) 0
    c) $200,000
    d) $50,000

_____ 19. How is the gain on disposal of an asset treated on the funds statement?

    a) it is a source of funds
    b) it is a use of funds
    c) it is a subtraction in computing cash from operations
    d) it is an addition in computing cash from operations

_____ 20. In 19X1, Poor Me Corp. acquired $200,000 of new equipment having a ten-year useful life. The net income before tax and taxable income was $500,000, and the effective tax rate was 40 percent. If the investment tax credit claimed was 10 percent, what would be the amount of income tax expense for 19X1 under the cost-reduction approach?

    a) $192,000
    b) $180,000
    c) $198,000
    d) $200,000

_____ 21. Refer to question 20, but assume instead that the flow-through method is employed.
   a) $192,000
   b) $180,000
   c) $198,000
   d) $200,000

_____ 22. When the rate of usage for an asset varies greatly from period to period, the depreciation method that best matches the cost with expected benefits is:
   a) straight-line method
   b) production method
   c) declining-balance method
   d) compound interest method

_____ 23. Hostility Corp. reports its net assets at a book value of $150,000. Recent investigation revealed that the net assets had a market value of $175,000. In addition, Hostility had been offered $220,000 for the company by Conglomerate Corp. What is the amount of goodwill that should be recorded on the books of Hostility?
   a) 0
   b) $25,000
   c) $45,000
   d) $70,000

Exercises

1. The Wiley Co. Ltd. has the following relevant debt and equity structure:

Long-Term Debt (at 13%)	$5,000,000
Share Capital	6,000,000
Retained Earnings	2,500,000

Wiley is constructing a building for its own production use, which is being financed with long-term debt. During the year, the average balance in the construction accounts was $6,000,000. A construction loan for $4,000,000 was taken out at the beginning of the year, requiring the payment of interest at 14 percent.

   Determine the maximum amount of interest that should be capitalized for the year.

2. The Winters Corp. purchased some equipment on April 1, 19X1 for $78,000. The freight costs were $1,500. On receipt, the following expenditures were incurred:

Major repair before use	$ 2,300
Rearrangement of other machinery to accommodate new machine	2,000
Rewiring for new machine	500
Installation	650
Testing before productive use	
Labour	500
Materials	200
Operating costs after start of productive operations	29,000
Minor repair during operational period	820
Depreciation in first year of use	1,500

Determine the costs that should be assigned to the equipment account. Indicate how any items excluded from this account would be properly handled.

3. A truck is purchased for $8,000 and is expected to have a five-year useful life and a $1,000 disposal value at the end of that time. Further, the truck is expected to be operable for a total of 1,400 hours during the five years. Calculate the depreciation expense in each of the five years for the following depreciation methods.

   a. the straight-line method
   b. the declining-balance method with a 150 percent straight-line rate
   c. the units-of-production method, if the production units (hours) in Years 1 to 5 were 240, 280, 360, 320, and 200, respectively

4. On July 1, 19X1, the Trembly Company Ltd. purchased a machine for $20,000 that has an estimated life of eight years and a disposal value of $2,000. In early 19X2, a major improvement was made to the machine, costing $2,500. As a result, the annual capacity was expanded, but its estimated life remained unchanged. During 19X3, Trembly revised its estimated useful life to be only three remaining years and its disposal value to $1,000.
   Calculate the depreciation for 19X1, 19X2, and 19X3 using the straight-line method.

5. During 19X1, Towne Co. acquired machinery, which qualified for the 10 percent investment tax credit, at a cost of $300,000. The machinery is expected to have a ten-year useful life. The income before tax and taxable income for both 19X1 and 19X2 was determined to be $350,000 and the tax rate was 40 percent in each year.
   Prepare the necessary entries for income tax expense for both 19X1 and 19X2, assuming use of the following methods of accounting for the investment tax credit: (a) flow-through method and (b) deferred-credit method.

PROBLEM 1 FOR SELF-STUDY

Purdy Inc. acquires two used trucks from Foster Inc. Although the trucks are not identical, they both cost $15,000. Purdy Inc. knew when it negotiated the purchase price that the first truck required extensive engine repair, expected to cost about $4,000. The repair was made the week after acquisition and actually cost $4,200. Purdy Inc. thought the second truck was in normal operating condition when it negotiated the pruchase price, but discovered on using the truck that certain bearings needed replacing. The cost of this repair, made the week after acquisition, was $4,200.

   a. What costs should be recorded in the accounts for the two trucks?
   b. If the amounts recorded above are different, distinguish between the two "repairs."

PROBLEM 2 FOR SELF-STUDY

Jensen Limited purchased land with a building standing on it as the site for a new plant it planned to construct. The company received bids from several independent contractors for demolition of the old building and construction of the new one. It rejected all bids and undertook demolition and construction using company labour, facilities, and equipment.

   All transactions relating to these properties were debited or credited to a single account, Real Estate. Various items in the Real Estate account are described below. The Real Estate account is to be closed. All amounts in it should be taken out and reclassified into one of the following accounts:

   (1) Land account
   (2) Buildings account
   (3) Revenue, gain, or expense contra account

(4) Expense, loss, or revenue contra account

(5) Some other account

You may reclassify amounts of the following transactions into two or more of the above. If you use **(5)**, some other account, indicate the nature of the account.

a. Cost of land, including old building.

b. Legal fees paid to bring about purchase of land and to transfer its title.

c. Invoice cost of materials and supplies used in construction.

d. Direct labour and materials cost incurred in demolition of old building.

e. Direct costs of excavating raw land to prepare it for the foundation of the new building.

f. Discounts earned for prompty payment of item **(c)**.

g. Interest for year on notes issued to finance construction.

h. Amounts equivalent to interest on Jensen Limited's own funds used in construction that would have been invested in temporary investments if an independent contractor had been used. The amount was debited to Real Estate and credited to Interest Revenue so that the cost of the real estate would be comparable to its cost if it had been built by an independent contractor.

i. Depreciation for period of construction on trucks that were used both in construction and regular company operations.

j. Proceeds of sale of materials salvaged from old buildings were debited to Cash and credited to Real Estate.

k. Cost of building permits.

l. Salaries of certain corporate engineering executives can be allocated between Salary Expense and Real Estate. The portion debited to Real Estate represents an estimate of the portion of the time spent during the year on planning and construction activities for the new building.

m. Payments for property taxes on plant site owned by its former owner but assumed by Jensen Limited.

n. Payments for property taxes on plant site for construction period.

o. Insurance premiums to cover workers engaged in demolition and construction activities. The insurance policy contains various deductible clauses, requiring the company to pay the first $5,000 of damages from any accident.

p. Cost of injury claims for $2,000 paid by the company because the amount was less than the deductible amount in the policy.

q. Costs of new machinery to be installed in building.

r. Installation costs for the machinery above.

s. Profit on construction of new building (computed as the difference between lowest independent contractor's bid and the actual construction cost) was debited to Real Estate and credited to Construction Revenue.

PROBLEM 3 FOR SELF-STUDY

Central Electric Co. Ltd. constructed a nuclear generating power plant at a cost of $200 million. The plant is expected to last 50 years before being retired from service. The company estimates that at the time the plant is retired from service, $20 million in "decommissioning costs" (costs to dismantle the plant and dispose of the radioactive materials) will be incurred. Straight-line depreciation is computed and charged once per year, at year-end.

During the eleventh year of operation, new regulations governing nuclear waste disposal are enacted. The estimated decommissioning costs increase from $20 million to $24 million.

During the thirty-first year of operation, the estimate of the life of the plant is revised. It will last 60 years in total, not 50 years.

At the end of the thirty-fifth year, the plant is sold to another utility company for $80 million.

a. What is the depreciation charge for the first year?

b. What is the depreciation charge for the eleventh year?

c. What is the depreciation charge for the thirty-first year?

d. Record the journal entry for the sale of the plant at the end of the thirty-fifth year.

PROBLEM 4 FOR SELF-STUDY

Widdicomb Corp. is considering changing from the flow-through method to the deferral method of accounting for the investment tax credit. It expects to acquire assets subject to increasing dollar amounts of investment tax credits each year for the foreseeable future.

Part 1: Indicate the effect on each of the following items in the financial statements two years hence if the deferral, rather than flow-through, method is used, starting now and continuing for the indefinite future.

a. Recorded Cost of Assets Acquired   e. Depreciation Expense
b. Income Taxes Payable   f. Net Income for year
c. Income Tax Expense   g. Retained Earnings
d. Deferred Investment Credits on balance sheet   h. Total Equities

Part 2: Indicate the effect on the financial items (a) to (h) in the financial statements two years hence if the cost-reduction deferral option rather than the deferred-credit deferral option were to be used.

ANSWERS TO SELF-STUDY QUESTIONS AND EXERCISES

True/False

1. F	13. T	25. F	38. T
2. T	14. T	26. T	39. T
3. T	15. T	27. F	40. F
4. F	16. F	28. T	41. F
5. F	17. T	30. F	42. T
6. T	18. T	31. T	43. T
7. F	19. F	32. T	44. T
8. T	20. T	33. T	45. T
9. F	21. F	34. T	
10. T	22. F	35. T	
11. F	23. F	36. F	
12. T	24. T	37. T	

Matching

1. u	6. t	11. c	16. a
2. f	7. m	12. k	17. r
3. g	8. p	13. e	
4. i	9. n	14. o	
5. s	10. w	15. q	

Multiple Choice

1. d	7. a	13. c	19. c
2. b	8. b	14. d	20. c
3. a	9. d	15. d	21. b
4. d	10. d	16. b	22. b
5. b	11. b	17. a	23. a
6. a	12. b	18. a	

Exercises

1. The maximum interest that should be capitalized by Wiley Co. Ltd. is:

$0.14 \times \$4,000,000 = \$560,000$
$0.13 \times \$2,000,000 = \underline{\quad 260,000}$
$\underline{\underline{\$820,000}}$

2. The cost of equipment:

Purchase price	$78,000
Freight	1,500
Major repair	2,300
Rearrangement of machinery	2,000
Rewiring	500
Installation	650
Testing	700
	$85,650

The operating expenses, minor repair, and depreciation would be in the operating expense section of the 19X1 income statement.

3. a. $\qquad$ Depreciation per year $= \dfrac{\$8,000 - \$1,000}{5} = \$1,400$

b.

Year	Book Value at Beginning of Year		Depreciation Rate	Depreciation
1	$8,000	×	0.30	$2,400
2	5,600	×	0.30	1,680
3	3,920	×	0.30	1,176
4	2,744	×	0.30	823
5	1,921	×	0.30	576*
End	1,345			
				$6,655

Because the book value was still $1,345 at the end of Year 5, an additional depreciation of $345 may have been taken to reduce the book value to the $1,000 disposal value.

c.

Year	Hours Produced	Depreciation Rate*	Depreciation
1	240	$5	$1,200
2	280	5	1,400
3	360	5	1,800
4	320	5	1,600
5	200	5	1,000
			$7,000

($8,000 — $1,000) ÷ 1,400 = $5/hour.

4. 19X1: Depreciation $= \dfrac{\$20,000 - \$2,000}{8} = \dfrac{\$18,000}{8} \times 1/2 \text{ year} = \$1,125$

19X2:

Original Cost	$20,000
Less: Depreciation in 19X2	(1,125)
Plus: Improvement	2,500
Book Value X2/1/1	$21,375
Less: Disposal Value	(2,000)
Depreciable Basis	$19,375
Remaining Life	÷ 7.5 years
Depreciation, 19X2	$ 2,583

19X3:

Book Value X3/1/1	$21,375
Less: Depreciation in 19X3	(2,583)
Book Value X3/1/1	$18,792
Less: Revised Disposal Value	(1,000)
Depreciable Basis	$17,792
Remaining Life (revised)	÷ 3
Depreciation, 19X3	$ 5,931

5. a.

	Dr.	Cr.
19X1: Income Tax Expense	$140,000	
Income Tax Payable		$140,000
To record income taxes before		
the investment tax credit.		
Income Tax Payable	$30,000	
Income Tax Expense		$30,000
To record investment tax credit.		

Investment tax credit =
0.10 × $300,000 = $30,000

	Dr.	Cr.
19X2: Income Tax Expense	$140,000	
Income Tax Payable		$140,000
To record income taxes.		

	Dr.	Cr.
b. 19X1: Income Tax Expense	$140,000	
Income Tax Payable		$140,000
To record income taxes before		
investment tax credit.		
Income Tax Payable	$ 30,000	
Income Tax Expense		$ 3,000
Deferred Investment Credit		27,000
To record investment tax credit.		

Investment in Machinery	$300,000
Investment Tax Credit	× 0.10
Total Investment Tax Credit	$ 30,000
Life of Machinery	÷ 10 years
Reduction of Tax Expense per year	$ 3,000
Deferred Investment Credit ($30,000 − $3,000)	$ 27,000

	Dr.	Cr.
19X2: Income Tax Expense	$140,000	
Income Tax Payable		$140,000
To record income taxes before invest-		
ment tax credit.		
Deferred Investment Credit	$ 3,000	
Income Tax Expense		$ 3,000
To record investment tax credit.		

SUGGESTED SOLUTION TO PROBLEM 1
FOR SELF-STUDY

a. First truck recorded at $19,200. Second truck recorded at $15,000, with $4,200 debited to expense or loss.

b. At the time the first truck was acquired, Purdy Inc. knew it would have to make the "repair." The purchase price was presumably reduced because of the known cost to be incurred. At the time of acquisition, the cost was anticipated to be required in order to produce the expected service potential of the asset. The fact that the cost is $4,200, rather than "about $4,000," seems not to violate the Purdy Inc.'s expectations at the time it acquired the truck. If the repair had cost significantly more than $4,000 (say, $7,000), the excess would have been loss or expense.

   The second truck was assumed to be operable when the parties agreed on the purchase price. The cost of the repair is incurred to bring about the level of service potential already thought to have been acquired. There are no more future benefits after the repair than had been anticipated at the time of acquisition. Therefore, the $4,200 is expense or loss.

SUGGESTED SOLUTION TO PROBLEM 2
FOR SELF-STUDY

(Note that three items are included in more than one account.)

(1) a, b, d, j, l, m, o
(2) c, e, f, g, i, k, l, n, o, p
(3) —
(4) h, i, s
(5) i, q, r

Comments and Explanations

f. The reduction in cost of materials and supplies will reduce the cost of the buildings. The actual accounting entries depend on the method used to record the potential discount. These issues are not discussed in this book, but see Problem 26 at the end of Chapter 7.

h. Although one capitalizes explicit interest, one may not capitalize opportunity-cost interest or interest imputed on one's own funds used. The adjusting entry credits Real Estate and debits Interest Revenue or its contra. In any case, the debit reduces income, removing the revenue that had been recognized by the company.

i. Computation of the amounts to be allocated requires an estimate. Once the amounts are estimated, they are debited to Building or to Depreciation Expense and Work-in-Process Inventory, as appropriate for the regular company operations.

j. Credit to Land account, reducing its cost.

l. Allocate to Land and Building on the basis of estimates of how time was spent. Given the description, most of these costs are probably for the building. If all of the salaries had been debited to Real Estate, some must be reclassified as Salary Expense.

m. Part of the cost of the land.

n. Capitalized as part of the Building account for the same reasons that interest during construction is capitalized. Some accountants would treat this item as expense.

p. Most accountants would treat this as an expense or loss for the period. Others would treat it as part of the cost of the building for the same reason that the explicit insurance cost is capitalized. If, however, the company was irrational in acquiring insurance policies with deductible clauses, this item is expense or loss. Accounting usually assumes that most managements make rational decisions most of the time.

q. Debit to Machinery and Equipment account, an asset account separate from Building.

r. Treat the same as preceding item; installation costs are part of the cost of the asset. See Chapter 2.

s. The effect of recognizing revenue is reversed. The Real Estate account is credited and Construction Revenue or its contra is debited.

SUGGESTED SOLUTION TO PROBLEM 3 FOR SELF-STUDY

(Dollar amounts in millions.)

a. $4.4 per year = ($200 + $20)/50 years.

b. $4.5 per year = ($200 + $20 + $4 − $4.4 per year × 10 years)/40 years remaining life
$$= (\$224 − \$44)/40$$
$$= \$180/40$$

c. $3.0 per year = ($180 − $4.5 × 20 years)/30 years remaining life
$$= (\$180 − \$90)/30$$
$$= \$90/30$$

d. Accumulated depreciation at time of sale
$$= (\$4.4 × 10) + (\$4.5 × 20) + (\$3.0 × 5) = \$149.0$$

December 31 of Year 35		
Cash	80.0	
Accumulated Depreciation on Power Plant	149.0	
Power Plant		200.0
Gain on Disposal of Plant		29.0

SUGGESTED SOLUTION TO PROBLEM 4 FOR SELF-STUDY

Part 1: Larger under the deferral method than under the flow-through method: **(c)**, **(d)**. Smaller under the deferral method than under the flow-through method: **(f)**, **(g)**. The same under both methods: **(a)**, **(b)**, **(e)**, **(h)**.

Part 2: Larger under the cost-reduction option than under the deferred-credit option: **(c)**, **(d)**. Smaller under the cost-reduction option than under the deferred-credit option: **(a)**, **(e)**. The same under both methods: **(b)**, **(f)**, **(g)**, **(h)**.

ASSIGNMENT MATERIAL

QUESTIONS

1. Review the meaning of the key terms listed on page 505–506.

2. a. "Accounting for depreciating assets would be greatly simplified if accounting periods were only long enough or the life of the assets short enough." What is the point of the quotation?
   b. "The major purpose of depreciation accounting is to provide funds for the replacement of assets as they wear out." Do you agree? Explain.

3. "Showing both acquisition cost and accumulated depreciation amounts separately provides a rough indication of the relative age of the firm's long-lived assets."
   a. Assume that the Poyfer Co. Ltd. acquired an asset with a depreciable cost of $100,000 several years ago. Accumulated depreciation as of December 31, recorded on a straight-line basis, is $60,000. The depreciation charge for the year is $10,000. What is the asset's depreciable life? How old is the asset?
   b. Assume straight-line depreciation. Devise a formula that, given the depreciation charge for the year and the asset's accumulated depreciation, can be used to determine the age of the asset.

4. a. What is the effect of capitalizing interest on reported net income summed over all the periods of the life of a given self-constructed asset, from building through use, until eventual retirement? Contrast with a policy of expensing interest as incurred.
   b. Consider a company engaging in increasing dollar amounts of self-construction activity each period over periods in which interest rates do not decline. What is the effect on reported income each year of capitalizing interest in contrast to expensing interest as incurred?

EXERCISES

5. *Classification of expenditures as asset or expense.* For each of the following expenditures or acquisitions, indicate the type of account debited. Classify the accounts as asset other than product cost, product cost (Work-in-Process Inventory), or expense. If the account debited is an asset account, specify whether it is current or noncurrent.
   a. $150 for repairs of office machines.
   b. $1,500 for emergency repairs to an office machine.
   c. $250 for maintenance of delivery trucks.
   d. $5,000 for a machine acquired in return for a three-year note.

   e. $4,200 for research staff salaries.
   f. $3,100 for newspaper ads.
   g. $6,400 for wages of factory workers engaged in production.
   h. $3,500 for wages of factory workers engaged in installing equipment.
   i. $2,500 for salaries of office work force.
   j. $1,000 for legal fees in acquiring an ore deposit.
   k. $1,200 for a one-year insurance policy beginning next month.
   l. $1,800 for Treasury Bills, to be sold to pay the next installment due on income taxes.
   m. $4,000 for royalty payment on a patent used in manufacturing.
   n. $10,000 for purchase of a trademark.
   o. $100 filing fee for copyright registration application.

6. *Journal entries for trade-in transactions and depreciation.* On April 30, Year 6, the Tico Wholesale Co. Ltd. acquired a new machine with a fair market value of $14,000. The seller agreed to accept the company's old machine, $7,000 in cash, and a 12 percent, one-year note for $4,000 in payment.

   The old machine was purchased on January 1, Year 1 for $10,000. It was estimated that the old machine would be useful for eight years, after which it would have a disposal value of $400. It is estimated that the new machine will have a service life of ten years and a disposal value of $800.

   Assuming that the Tico Co. Ltd. uses the straight-line method of depreciation and closes its books annually on December 31, give the entries that were made in Year 6.

7. *Computations and journal entries for retirement of plant.* On July 1, Year 2, a building and land were purchased for $96,000 by The Hub, a retail clothing store. Of this amount, $40,000 was allocated to the land and the remainder to the building. The building is depreciated on a straight-line basis.

   On July 1, Year 24 (no additions or retirements having been recorded in the meanwhile), the net book value of the building was $25,200. On March 31, Year 25, the building and site were sold for $60,000. The fair market value of the land was $50,000 on this date.

   The firm closes its books annually on June 30. Give the entries required on March 31, Year 25. (*Hint:* First compute what the annual depreciation charges must be, on the basis of the facts given.)

8. *Journal entries for plant acquisition, depreciation, and retirement.* Journalize the following transactions:
   a. A piece of office equipment is purchased for $850 cash.
   b. Depreciation for one year of $170 is recorded.
   c. The equipment is sold for $400. At the time of the sale, the Accumulated Depreciation shows a balance of $340. Depreciation of $170 for the year of the sale has not yet been recorded.

9. *Journal entries for revising estimate of life.* Give the journal entries for the following selected transactions of the Eagle Manufacturing Co.

Inc. The company uses the straight-line method of calculating depreciation and closes its books annually on December 31.

a. A machine is purchased on November 1, Year 9 for $30,000. It is estimated that it will be used for ten years and that it will have a disposal value of $600 at the end of that time. Give the journal entry for the depreciation at December 31, Year 9.

b. Record the depreciation for the year ending December 31, Year 10.

c. In August Year 15, it is decided that the machine will probably be used for a total of twelve years and that its disposal value will be $400. Record the depreciation for the year ending December 31, Year 19.

d. The machine is sold for $1,000 on March 31, Year 20. Record the entries of that date, assuming that depreciation is recorded as indicated in part (c).

10. *Straight-line depreciation, working backwards.* On March 1, one of the buildings owned by the Metropolitan Storage Co. Ltd. was destroyed by fire. The cost of the building was $100,000. The balance in the Accumulated Depreciation account at January 1 was $38,125. A service life of 40 years with a zero disposal value had been estimated for the building. The company uses the straight-line method. The building was not insured.

a. Give the journal entries made on March 1.

b. If there have been no alterations in the service life estimate, how many years ago was the building acquired?

11. *Journal entries to correct accounting errors.* Give correcting entries for the following situations. In each case, the firm uses the straight-line method of depreciation and closes its books annually on December 31. Recognize all gains and losses currently.

a. A cash register was purchased for $300 on January 1, Year 1. It was depreciated at a rate of 10 percent of original cost per year. On June 30, Year 6, it was sold for $200, and a new cash register was acquired for $500. The bookkeeper made the following entry to record the transaction:

Store Equipment	$300	
Cash in Bank		$300

b. A used truck was acquired for $4,000. Its cost, when new, was $6,000, and the bookkeeper made the following entry to record the purchase:

Truck	$6,000	
Accumulated Depreciation		$2,000
Cash		4,000

c. A testing mechanism was purchased on April 1, Year 4 for $600. It was depreciated at a 10 percent annual rate. On June 30, Year 6, it was stolen. The loss was not insured, and the bookkeeper made the following entry:

Theft Loss	$600	
Testing Mechanism		$600

12. *Journal entries for acquisition of asset with a note and subsequent recognition of depreciation and interest.* The Grogan Manufacturing Company Ltd. started business on January 1, Year 3. At that time, it acquired machine A for $20,000, which it paid by cheque.

Because of an expansion in the volume of business, machine B, costing $25,000, was acquired on September 30, Year 4. A cheque for $15,000 was issued, with the balance to be paid in annual installments of $2,000 plus interest at the rate of 12 percent on the unpaid balance. The first installment is due on September 30, Year 5.

On June 30, Year 5, machine A was sold for $13,000 and a larger model, machine C, was acquired for $30,000.

All installments are paid on time.

All machines have an estimated life of ten years with an estimated disposal value equal to 10 percent of acquisition cost. The company closes its books on December 31. The straight-line method is used.

Prepare dated journal entries to record all transactions through December 31, Year 5, including year-end adjustments but excluding closing entries.

13. *Cost of self-constructed assets.* The Dickhaut Manufacturing Co. Ltd. purchased a plot of land for $90,000 as a plant site. There was a small office building on the plot, conservatively appraised at $20,000, which the company will continue to use with some modification and renovation. The company had plans drawn for a factory and received bids for its construction. It rejected all bids and decided to construct the plant itself. Below are listed additional items that management feels should be included in plant asset accounts:

(1) Materials and Supplies	$200,000
(2) Excavation	12,000
(3) Labour on Construction	140,000
(4) Cost of Remodelling Old Building into Office Building	13,000
(5) Interest on Money Borrowed by Dickhaut[a]	6,000
(6) Interest on Dickhaut's Own Money Used	9,000
(7) Cash Discounts on Materials Purchased	7,000
(8) Supervision by Management	10,000
(9) Workers' Compensation Insurance Premiums	8,000
(10) Payment of Claims for Injuries Not Covered by Insurance	3,000
(11) Clerical and Other Expenses of Construction	8,000
(12) Paving of Streets and Sidewalks	5,000
(13) Architect's Plans and Specifications	4,000

(14) Legal Costs of Conveying Land 2,000
(15) Legal Costs of Injury Claim 1,000
(16) Income Credited to Retained Earnings Account, Being the Difference
Between the Foregoing Cost and the Lowest Contractor's Bid 11,000

ᵃ This interest is the entire amount of interest paid during the construction period.

Show in detail the items to be included in the following accounts: Land, Factory Building, Office Building, and Site Improvements. Explain why you excluded any items that you did not include in the four accounts.

14. Calculations for various depreciation methods. Calculate the depreciation charge for the first and second years of the asset's life in each of the following cases.

Asset	Cost	Estimated Disposal Value	Life (years)	Depreciation Method
a. Blast Furnace	$800,000	$25,000	20	Declining-Balanceᵃ
b. Hotel	500,000	50,000	45	Straight-Line
c. Tractor	18,000	1,500	10	Declining-Balanceᵃ
d. Delivery Truck	22,000	5,200	6	Straight-Line

ᵃ The declining-balance rate is double the straight-line rate.

15. *Calculations for various depreciation methods.* On January 1, Year 5, the Central Production Company Ltd. acquired a new turret lathe for $36,000. It was estimated to have a useful life of four years and no disposal value. The company closes its books annually on December 31. Indicate the amount of the depreciation charge for each of the four years under:
   a. The straight-line method.
   b. The declining-balance method at twice the straight-line rate.

16. *Amount of interest capitalized during construction.* Chan Ltd. builds some of its own chemical processing plants. At the start of the year, the Construction-in-Process account had a balance of $1 million. Construction activity occurred uniformly throughout the year. At the end of the year, the balance was $5 million. The borrowings of the company during the year were as follows:

New Construction Loans at 20 Percent per Year	$ 2,000,000
Old Bond Issues Maturing at Various Times, Averaging 10 Percent Rate	8,000,000
Total Interest-Bearing Debt	$10,000,000

   a. Compute the amount of interest to be capitalized into the Construction-in-Process account for the year.
   b. Present journal entries for interest for the year.

17. *Calculations for various depreciation methods.* A machine is acquired for $8,900. It is expected to last eight years and to be operated for 25,000 hours during that time. It is estimated that its disposal value will be $1,700 at the end of that time. Calculate the depreciation charge for each of the first three years using:
    a. The straight-line (time) method.
    b. The declining-balance method using a 25 percent rate.
    c. The units-of-production method. Operating times are as follows: first year, 3,500 hours; second year, 2,000 hours; third year, 5,000 hours.

18. *Revision of estimated service life changes depreciation schedule.* The Slowpoke Shipping Co. Ltd. buys a new car for $10,000 on January 1, Year 4. It is estimated that it will last six years and have a disposal value of $1,000. Early in Year 6, it is discovered that the car will last only an additional two years, or four years in total. The company closes its books on December 31. Present a table showing the depreciation charges for each year from Year 4 to Year 7 and give the adjusting entry made in Year 6. Follow the instructions for each of the depreciation methods listed below:
    a. The straight-line method.
    b. The decliing-balance method with depreciation at twice the straight-line rate. The remaining undepreciated cost less disposal value is to be written off in the last year.

19. *Retirement of plant assets.* The Lindahl Manufacturing Co. Ltd. acquires a new machine for $7,200 on July 1, Year 1. It is estimated that it will have a disposal value of $900. The company closes its books annually on June 30.
    a. Compute the depreciation charges for each year of the asset's life assuming the straight-line method.
    b. If the machine were sold for $700 on October 30, Year 6, give the journal entries that would be made on that date.

20. *Trade-in transactions.* The Twombly Co. Ltd. purchased a new panel truck in May Year 3. The truck cost $18,600. It was estimated that the truck would be driven for 200,000 kilometres before being traded in and that its disposal value at that time would be $2,600.

    Odometer readings are as follows:

December 31, Year 3	24,000
December 31, Year 4	100,000
December 31, Year 5	164,000
June 16, Year 6	196,000

On June 16, Year 6, the truck was traded in for a new one with a list price of $22,000. The old truck had a fair market value of $2,600, but the dealer allowed $3,000 on it toward the list price of the new one. The balance of the purchase price was paid by cheque.

a. Compute the depreciation charges for each year through Year 5, using a "production" or "use" method.

b. Record the entries for June 16, Year 6, assuming that the list price of the new truck is unreliable whereas the fair market value of the old truck is reliable.

c. Record the entries for June 16, Year 6, assuming that there were no reliable estimates for the fair market value of the old truck.

21. *Exchange of nonmonetary assets.* Assume Etherington Co. trades in a used machine for a new machine that has a cash purchase price of $28,000. The old machine originally cost $22,000 and has $16,000 of accumulated depreciation. The vendor is allowing $7,500 as a trade-in allowance. Etherington pays the balance in cash. Prepare the journal entry for the trade-in under the following assumptions:

a. The assets are similar.

b. The assets are dissimilar.

22. *Amortization of intangibles.* For each of the following unrelated situations, calculate the annual amortization expense and prepare the related journal entry:

a. A two-year-old patent was acquired for $600,000. The patent will probably be commercially exploitable for another eight years. Within months of the acquisition, a major competitor is found to be using the patented process without authorization. The other firm agrees to an out-of-court settlement of $1,000,000.

b. A research discovery within the firm led to the development of a new production process, and a patent was successfully obtained. The company incurred about $40,000 in legal fees associated with the patent application. The company has received a firm offer of $500,000 for the patent. Company policy is to amortize intangibles over ten years.

23. *Journal entries for investment tax credit.* The Libby Co. Inc. has income tax expense, before any investment tax credits, of $50,000 each year. At the start of the first year, it acquires an asset with a depreciable life of four years. Assume that the asset qualifies for an investment credit of $4,000.

a. Record income taxes and the entries related to the investment tax credit for the four years of the asset's life using the flow-through method.

b. Record entries related to income taxes and the investment tax credit for the four years of the asset's life using the deferral method.

24. *Whether a single asset account or separate asset accounts are used affects classification of expenditures as repairs or improvements.* Lafleur Inc. purchased a delivery truck for $20,000 at the start of Year 1. The truck is expected to last for four years, but the engine is expected to be replaced at the end of Year 2 at a cost of $6,000. Lafleur Inc. must choose between depreciating the truck as a single unit or as two separate assets — the engine and the rest of the truck. The company uses straight-line depreciation for financial reporting.

    a. Compute total expense for each of the four years of the truck's life, depreciating the entire cost of $20,000 in a single asset account.

    b. Compute total expense for each year of the truck's life, depreciating the engine and the rest of the truck in separate asset accounts.

25. *Working backwards to derive proceeds of disposition of plant.* Balance sheets of Rasmussen Company at the beginning and end of the year contained the following data:

	End of Year	Beginning of Year
Property, Plant, and Equipment (at cost)	$350,000	$300,000
Accumulated Depreciation	(165,000)	(170,000)
Net Book Value	$185,000	$130,000

During the year, machinery and equipment was sold at a gain of $2,000. New machinery and equipment was purchased at a cost of $80,000. Depreciation charges on machinery and equipment for the year amounted to $20,000.

    Calculate the proceeds received from the sale of the machinery and equipment.

PROBLEMS AND CASES

26. *Allocation of cost in "basket" purchases.* In each of the following situations, compute the amounts of gain or loss to be shown on the income statement for the year, as well as the amount of asset to be shown on the balance sheet as of the end of the year. Show the journal entry or entries required, and provide reasons for your decisions.

    a. A company wishes to acquire a five-acre site for a new warehouse. The land it wants is part of a ten-acre site that the owner insists be purchased as a whole for $18,000. The company purchases the land, spends $2,000 in legal fees for rights to divide the site into five-acre plots, and immediately offers half of the land for resale. The two best offers are:

    (1) $12,000 for the east half, and

    (2) $13,000 for the west half.

    The company sells the east half.

    b. The same data as in part (a), except the two best offers are:

    (1) $5,000 for the east half, and

    (2) $12,000 for the west half.

    The company sells the west half.

27. *Composite depreciation versus individual-item depreciation.* The Alexander Company Inc. acquired three used machine tools for a total price of $49,000. Costs to transport the machine tools from the seller to Alexander Company's factory were $1,000. The machine tools were renovated, installed, and put to use in manufacturing the firm's products. The costs of renovation and installation were as follows:

	Machine Tool A	Machine Tool B	Machine Tool C
Renovation Costs	$1,700	$800	$950
Installation Costs	300	550	250

The machine tools have the following estimated lives: tool A — four years; tool B — ten years; tool C — six years.

   a. Assume that each machine tool is capitalized in a separate asset account and that the remaining life of each machine tool is used as the basis for allocating the joint costs of acquisition. Compute the depreciable cost of each of the three machine tools.

   b. Present journal entries to record depreciation charges for Years 1, 5, and 8, given the assumption in part (a). Use the straight-line method.

   c. Assume that the three machine tools are treated as one composite asset in the accounts. If management decides to depreciate the entire cost of the composite asset on a declining balance basis with a rate of 20 percent, what is the depreciation charge for each year?

28. *Investment tax credits for a firm growing to equilibrium.* Refer to the data in Exercise 23 for the Libby Co. Inc. Assume that, each year, the Babiak Equilibrium Co. Ltd. acquires an asset with a depreciable life of four years. Each year, the asset acquired qualifies for an investment tax credit of $4,000, and income tax expense before any investment tax credits is $50,000.

   a. Record entries related to income taxes and the investment tax credit for each of the first five years using the flow-through method.

   b. Record entries related to income taxes and the investment tax credit for each of the first five years using the deferral method.

   c. Assuming that Babiak Equilibrium Co. Ltd.'s income taxes, asset acquisitions, and investment tax credits continue in the following years as in the first four years, describe the effects on the financial statements of the two methods of accounting for the investment tax credit.

   d. Assume the same data as in part (c), but that the new asset's cost increases by 10 percent each year and that the amount of the investment tax credit earned increases by 10 percent each year. Describe the effects on the financial statements of the two methods of accounting for the investment tax credit.

29. *Choosing between the deferral and flow-through methods for the investment credit.* Three companies have each recently made investments in equipment designed to save fuel. The equipment purchased by each company costs $200,000 and has a ten-year service life. In all three cases, the company was entitled to $10,000 investment tax credit when it purchased the asset during the current year. The income taxes otherwise payable of all three companies were reduced by $10,000 during the current year. In all three companies, management had made careful studies of the costs and benefits of acquiring the new equipment.

Management of Company A decided that the equipment purchased would provide operating cost savings with a present value of $250,000. The company is delighted to acquire the asset.

Management of Company B decided that the equipment it purchased would provide operating cost savings with a present value of $190,000. The equipment was worth acquiring only because of the investment tax credit.

Management of Company C decided that the equipment it purchased provided operating cost savings with a present value of $196,000. The equipment was acquired only because the investment tax credit made the investment worthwhile.

a. Discuss the considerations the management of each of these companies might give to accounting for the investment tax credit.

b. What can you conclude from this problem about the method of accounting for the investment tax credit that reflects managerial decisions?

30. *Capitalizing versus expensing advertising costs: effects on financial statements and rate of return.* The Consumer Products Co. Ltd. has $300,000 of total assets. The Consumer Products Co. Ltd. has been earning $45,000 per year and generating $45,000 per year of cash flow from operations. Each year, the Consumer Products Co. Ltd. distributes its earnings by paying cash of $45,000 to owners. Management of the Consumer Products Co. Ltd. believes that a new advertising campaign now will lead to increased sales over the next four years. The anticipated net cash flows of the project are as follows:

Beginning of Year	Net Cash Inflow (outflow)
1	($24,000)
2, 3, and 4	10,000 each year

Assume that the advertising campaign is undertaken, that cash flows are as planned, and that the Consumer Products Co. Ltd. makes payments to owners of $45,000 at the end of the first year and $47,000 at the end of each of the next three years. Assume that there are no interest expenses in any year. Ignore any income tax effects.

a. Compute net income and the rate of return on assets of the Consumer Products Co. Ltd. for each of the four years, assuming that advertising expenditures are expensed as they occur. Use the year-end balance of total assets in the denominator of the rate-of-return calculation.

b. Compute net income and the rate of return on assets of the Consumer Products Co. Ltd. for each year of the project, assuming that advertising costs are capitalized and then amortized on a straight-line basis over the last three years. Use the year-end balance of total assets in the denominator of the rate of return on assets.

c. How well has the management of the Consumer Products Co. Ltd. carried out its responsibility to its owners? On what basis do you make this judgment? Which method of accounting seems to reflect performance more adequately?

31. *Accounting for intangibles.* In Year 1, Epstein Inc. acquired the assets of Falk Limited. The assets of Falk Limited included various intangibles. Discuss the accounting for the acquisition in Year 1, and in later years, for each of the following items.
    a. Registration of the trademark Thyrom® for thyristors expires in three years. Epstein Inc. thought that the trademark had a fair market value of $100,000. It expects to continue making and selling Thyrom thyristors indefinitely.
    b. The design patent covering the ornamentation of the containers for displaying Thyrom expires in five years. Epstein Inc. thought that the design patent had a fair market value of $30,000 and expects to continue making the containers indefinitely.
    c. An unpatented trade secret on a special material used in manufacturing thryistors was viewed as having a fair market value of $200,000.
    d. Refer to the trade secret in part (c). Suppose that, in Year 2, a competitor discovers the trade secret, but does not disclose the secret to other competitors. How should the accounting policies be changed?
    e. During Year 1, Epstein Inc. produced a sales promotion film, *Using Thyristors for Fun and Profit*, at a cost of $45,000. The film is licensed to purchasers of thyristors for use in training their employees and customers. The film is copyrighted.

32. *Expensing versus capitalizing advertising costs of firm advertising every year.* Equilibrium Ltd. plans to spend $60,000 at the beginning of each of the next several years advertising the company's brand names and trademarks. As a result of the advertising expenditure for a given year, aftertax income (not counting advertising expense) is expected to increase by $24,000 a year for three years, including the year of the expenditure itself. Equilibrium Ltd. has other aftertax income of $20,000 per year. The controller of Equilibrium Ltd. wonders what will be the effect on the financial statements of following one of two accounting policies with respect to advertising expenditures:
    (1) Expensing the advertising costs in the year of expenditures.
    (2) Capitalizing the advertising costs and amortizing them over three years, including the year of the expenditure itself.
    Assume that the Company does spend $60,000 at the beginning of each of four years and that the planned increase in income occurs. Ignore income tax effects.
    a. Prepare a four-year condensed summary of net income, assuming that policy (1) is followed and advertising costs are expensed as incurred.
    b. Prepare a four-year condensed summary of net income, assuming that policy (2) is followed and advertising costs are capitalized and amortized over three years. Compute also the amount of Deferred Advertising Costs (asset) to be shown on the balance sheet at the end of each of the four years.

    c. In what sense is policy **(1)** a conservative policy?

    d. What will be the effect on net income and on the balance sheet if Equilibrium Ltd. continues to spend $60,000 each year and the effects on aftertax income continue as in the first four years?

33. ***Betterments versus repairs or maintenance.*** The balance sheet of Woolf's Department Store Ltd. shows a building with an original cost of $800,000 and accumulatd depreciation of $660,000. The building is being depreciated on a straight-line basis over 40 years. The remaining depreciable life of the building is seven years. On January 2 of the current year, an expenditure of $28,000 was made on the street-level display windows of the store. Indicate the accounting for the current year if the expenditure of $28,000 was made under each of the following circumstances. Each of these cases is to be considered independently of the others, except where noted. Ignore income tax effects.

    a. Management decided that improved display windows would make the store's merchandise seem more attractive. The windows are a worthwhile investment.

    b. A violent hailstorm on New Year's Day destroyed the display windows previously installed. There was no insurance coverage for this sort of destruction. The new windows installed are physically identical to the old windows. The old windows had a book value of $28,000 at the time of the storm.

    c. Vandals destroyed the display windows on New Year's Day. There was no insurance coverage for this sort of destruction. The new windows installed are physically identical to the old windows. The old windows had a book value of $28,000 at the time of destruction.

    d. The old displays contained windows constructed of nonshatterproof glass. Management had previously considered replacing its old nonshatterproof windows with new ones but had decided that there was zero benefit to the firm in doing so. New shatterproof windows were installed because a new law was passed requiring that all stores have shatterproof windows on the street level. The alternative to installing the new windows was to shut down the store. In responding to this part, assume zero benefits result from the new windows. Part **(e)** below considers the more realistic case of some benefits.

    e. Management had previously considered replacing its old, nonshatterproof windows with new ones, but decided that the new windows would produce future benefits of only $7,000 and so were not a worthwhile investment. However, a new law [see part **(d)**] now requires them to do so (or else shut down), and the new windows are installed.

34. ***Capitalizing versus expensing: if capitalized, what amortization period?*** In each of the following situations, compute the amounts of revenue, gain, expense, and loss to be shown on the income statement for the year and the amount of asset to be shown on the balance sheet as of the end of the year. Show the journal entry or entries required, and provide reasons for your decisions. Straight-line amortization is used. The reporting period is the calendar year. The situations are independent of each other, except where noted.

a. Because of a new fire code, a department store must install an additional fire escape on its building. Management had previously considered installing the additional fire escape. It had rejected the idea because it had instead already installed a modern sprinkler system, which was even more cost-effective. The new code gives management no alternative except to close the store. The fire escape is acquired for $28,000 cash on January 1. The building is expected to be demolished seven years from the date the fire escape was installed.

b. Many years ago, a firm acquired shares of stock in Seagram Co. Ltd. for $100,000. On December 31, the firm acquired a building with an appraised value of $1 million. The company paid for the building by giving up its shares in Seagram Co. Ltd. at a time when equivalent shares traded on the Toronto Stock Exchange for $1,050,000.

c. Same data as part **(b)**, except that the shares represent ownership in Small Timers, Inc., whose shares are traded on a regional stock exchange. The last transactions in shares of Small Timers, Inc. occurred on December 27. Using the prices of the most recent trades, the shares of Small Timers, Inc. given in exchange for the building have a market value of $1,050,000.

d. A company decides that it can save $3,500 a year for ten years by switching from small panel trucks to larger delivery vans. To do so requires remodelling costs of $18,000 for various garages. The first fleet of delivery vans will last for five years, and the garages will last for twenty years. The garages are remodelled on January 1.

e. A company drills for oil. It sinks ten holes during the year at a cost of $1 million each. Nine of the holes are dry, but the tenth is a gusher. By the end of the year, the oil known to be recoverable from the gusher has a net realizable value of $40 million, and another oil company has offered to buy the well for $40 million. No oil was extracted during the year.

f. A company manufactures aircraft. During the current year, all sales were to the government under defence contracts. The company spent $400,000 on institutional advertising to keep its name before the business community. It expects to resume sales of small jet planes to corporate buyers in twenty years.

g. A company runs a large laboratory that has, over the years, found marketable ideas and products worth tens of millions of dollars. On average, the successful products have a life of ten years. Expenditures for the laboratory this year were $1,500,000.

h. A textile manufacturer gives $250,000 to the Textile Engineering Department of a local university for basic research in fibres. The results of the research, if any, will belong to the general public.

i. On January 1, an automobile company incurs costs of $6 million for specialized machine tools necessary to produce a new model automobile. Such tools last for six years, on average, but the new model automobile is expected to be produced for only three years.

j. On January 1, an airline purchased a fleet of airbuses for $100 million cash. The airbuses have an expected useful life of ten years and no disposal value. At the same time, the airline purchased spare parts for use with those airbuses for $20 million cash. The spare parts have no use, now or in the future, other than replacing broken or worn-out airbus parts. During the first year of operation, no spare parts were used.

k. Refer to the data in part (j). In the second year of operation, $1 million of spare parts were used.

35. *Effect on net income of changes in estimates for depreciable assets.* A major airline has $3 billion of assets, including airplanes costing $2.5 billion with net book value of $1.6 billion. It earns income before income tax equal to approximately 6 percent of total assets. Airplanes have been depreciated for financial reporting purposes on a straight-line basis over ten-year lives to a disposal value equal to 10 percent of original cost. The airline has announced a change in depreciation policy; it will use fourteen-year lives and disposal values equal to 12 percent of original cost. Assume that the airplanes are all four years old.

What will be the approximate impact on net income of the change in depreciation policy? Compute both dollar and percentage effects.

36. *Capital cost allowance.* Prepare the Year 2 CCA schedule for the Dumpty Co. Ltd. from the following information about events occurring in Year 2, using the CCA rates in the chapter.
    (1) The undepreciated capital cost as of December 31, Year 1 for Class 6 was $6,700; Class 8, $62,750; and Class 10, $43,800.
    (2) Proceeds from the sale of a truck were $6,000. This amount was less than the original capital cost.
    (3) Proceeds from the sale of a specialized machine were $12,000, which was $1,000 more than the capital cost.
    (4) Purchases during the year: Class 8, $16,000; Class 10, $8,000; and special water pollution equipment, $8,400.
    (5) A lease for five years with a five-year renewal option was signed, and $16,000 was paid for improvements to the premises.
    (6) A patent with five years' life remaining was purchased for $7,500.
    (7) The last asset included in Class 6, a galvanized building, was sold for $12,700, which was less than its original capital cost.
    (8) The company claimed the maximum CCA for the year ended December 31, Year 2.

37. *Analysis of financial statement disclosure of effects of depreciation policy.* A recent annual report on Caterpillar Tractor Company contained the following statement of depreciation policy:

Depreciation is computed principally using accelerated methods for both income tax and financial reporting purposes. These methods result in a larger allocation of the cost of buildings, machinery, and equipment to operations in the early years of the lives of assets than does the straight-line method.

Then Caterpillar discloses the amounts for "Buildings, Machinery, and Equipment — Net" as they would appear if the straight-line method had always been used. Exhibit 8.4 shows these amounts and other data from the financial statements for three recent years.

EXHIBIT 8.4
Excerpts from Annual Report of Caterpillar Tractor Company
(dollar amounts in millions)
(Problem 37)

	Year 3	Year 2	Year 1
Buildings, Machinery, and Equipment—Net:			
As Reported	$3,339	$3,300	$2,928
If Straight-Line Depreciation Were Used	4,020	3,894	3,431
Depreciation Expense Reported	505	448	370

a. What amounts would be reported for depreciation expense for Years 2 and 3 if the straight-line method had always been used?

b. Now assume a 40 percent tax rate, that straight-line depreciation had been used always for both income tax and financial reporting purposes, and that Buildings, Machinery, and Equipment — Net on the balance sheet amounted to $4,020 at the end of Year 3. What other items on the balance sheet for the end of Year 3 would probably change and by how much?

38. *Straight-line depreciation is probably too "conservative"; it usually writes off an asset's cost faster than future benefits disappear.* (This problem requires material from Appendix A.) Assets are acquired for their future benefits — the future cash flows they produce, either cash inflows or savings of cash outflows. As the near-term cash flows are received, the future benefits decline, but the future cash flows come closer to being received, *increasing* the value of the future benefits. The present value of future cash flows may, in total, increase or decrease during any one year. This problem explores changes in the present value of future cash flows with the passage of time and illustrates the phenomenon that, for many business projects, the present value of future benefits (that is, future cash flows) declines at a rate much slower than that implied by straight-line depreciation.

Pasteur Limited plans to acquire an asset that will have a ten-year life and promises to generate cash flows of $10,000 per year at the end of each of the ten years of its life. Given the risk of the project that uses the asset, Pasteur Limited judges that a 12 percent rate is appropriate for discounting its future cash flows. Using a 12 percent discount rate, the present value of $1 received at the end of each of the next ten years is $5.65022 (see Table B.4 on page 1069, ten-period row, 12 percent column). Because the project is expected to generate $10,000 per year, the present value of the cash flows is $56,502 (= $10,000 × 5.65022). Assume that Pasteur Limited purchases the asset for exactly $56,502 at the beginning of Year 1. Exhibit 8.5 shows for each year the present value of the cash flows remaining at the beginning of each year of the asset's life. The numbers in column (3) are $10,000 multiplied by the number appearing in Table 4, 12 percent column, for the number of

EXHIBIT 8.5
Pattern of Expiration of Future Benefits Measured as the Net Present Value of Future Cash Flows
(Problem 38)

Assumed Data
Asset cost $56,502 and has ten-year life.
Asset yields $10,000 per year of cash inflow.
Discount rate = 12 percent per year.

Beginning of Year (1)	Years Remaining (2)	Present Value of Remaining Cash Flows (3)	Percentage of Present Value of Cash Flows Remaining (4)	Percentage of Loss in Value During Preceding Year (5)	Straight-Line Depreciation for Preceding Year (6)
1	10	$56,502	100%		
2	9	53,282	94	6%	10%
3	8	49,676	88	6	10
4	7	45,638	81	7	10
5	6	41,114	73	8	10
6	5	36,048	64	9	10
7	4	30,373	54	10	10
8	3	24,018	43	11	10
9	2	16,901	30	13	10
10	1	8,929	16	14	10
11	0	0	0	16	10
Total				100%	100%

Column (3) from Table B.4 (Appendix B), 12 percent column, row corresponding to number in column (2), here multiplied by $10,000.
Column (4) = number in column (3)/$56,502.
Column (5) = column (4) preceding year − column (4) this year.

periods remaining in the asset's life. Column (4) shows the percentage of the asset's present value of the cash flows remaining, and column (5) shows the precentage loss in present value of cash flows during the preceding year. Column (6) shows the percentage writeoff in cost each year using straight-line depreciation — 10 percent per year. Note that the decline in present value of cash flows is less than straight-line in the first five years, but greater in the last four years.

a. Construct an exhibit similar to Exhibit 8.5 for an asset with a five-year life promising $10,000 of cash flows at the end of each year. Use a discount rate of 15 percent per year. The asset cost is $33,522. Compare the resulting decline in present value with straight-line depreciation.

b. Now consider another asset with a five-year life with risk appropriate for a 15 percent discount rate. This asset also has net present value of cash flows of $33,522, but the expected cash flows are $11,733 at the end of the first year, $10,767 at the end of the second year, $9,722 at the end of the third year, $8,716 at the end of the fourth year, and $7,710 at the end of the fifth year. Construct an exhibit similar to Exhibit 8.5 for this asset. You should find that the present value of future cash flows disappears at the rate of 20 percent per year of $33,522, the initial present value.

c. Using the results of your work above, comment on the nature of conservatism of straight-line depreciation.

39. *Income tax advantage of capital cost allowances.* Griffin Co. Limited purchased for $10,000 an asset that has a useful life of ten years, no disposal value, and is included in Classs 8 for income tax purposes. What is the first-year tax advantage (computed to the nearest dollar) of the income tax method over the straight-line method, assuming a constant tax rate of 50 percent? What is the tax advantage over the life of the asset, ignoring present value and assuming the asset is one of several in Class 8?

40. *Effects of recording errors on financial statements.* O'Keefe Company manufactures small machine tools. Its inventory turnover (= cost of goods sold ÷ average inventory during year) is about 3. The company uses a FIFO cost flow assumption. During the current year, inventory increased. The firm depreciates its plant assets over seven years, using the straight-line method. Below are described several transactions and the incorrect way these events were recorded. Indicate the effect of the mistake (overstatement, understatement, no effect) on each of the following items:
(1) Plant Assets (net of depreciation), end of current year.
(2) Selling, General, and Administrative Expenses for the current year.
(3) Cost of Goods Sold for the current year.
(4) Total Assets, end of next year.
(5) Net Income for next year.
(6) Owners' Equity, end of next year.
For example, if the effect of recording is that net income is too low, the right response is "understatement."
   a. During the current year, expenditures for testing a new factory machine were debited to Work-in-Process Inventory.
   b. During the current year, the company completed self-construction of a warehouse for finished goods, but it failed to charge any general supervisory overhead costs of construction to the plant account. All costs were expensed.
   c. The local electric utility installed new time-of-day metering devises to enable peak-load pricing of electricity. The O'Keefe Company paid the utility a $5,000 deposit, which will be returned in three years if the meters have not been negligently damaged by the company. O'Keefe Company debited this payment to Work-in-Process Inventory.
   d. Maintenance cost of office machines was debited to Accumulated Depreciation on Plant Assets.
   e. Maintenance of factory machines was debited to Accumulated Depreciation on Plant Assets.
   f. In the current year, O'Keefe acquired new land to be used for a warehouse. It incorrectly debited the cost of independent appraisals of the property to general expenses rather than to a plant account.

g. O'Keefe Company carried out a significant rearrangement of its factory plant layout during the current year and properly accounted for all costs that were recorded. A bill from Stephens Moving Company will not arrive until the next year. When it is paid, the amount will be debited to a general expense account.

41. *Trade-ins (adapted from a problem by S. Zeff).* Werner Company traded in a machine for an essentially identical machine. The journal entry, which correctly reflects the application of proper accounting practice, was as follows:

Machine	$33,400	
Accumulated Depreciation	12,700	
Loss on Disposition	3,700	
Machine		$29,800
Cash		20,000

a. What is the fair market value of the old machine?
b. Suppose that all of the facts of the trade-in were the same, except that the amount of cash given was $15,000 instead of $20,000, changing the $3,700 loss to a $1,300 gain. Give the journal entry that should be made.

42. *Comparing depreciation methods.* The Hobson Company has been in business since July 19X0, providing a gravel hauling service. Six trucks were purchased on July 1, 19X0 at a cost of $35,000 each. These trucks were expected to have a useful life of eight years and a 10 percent disposal value. They have been depreciated on a straight-line basis.

On April 1, 19X1, one of the drivers experienced a brake failure and overturned his truck. At this time, the truck was written off. The driver sued the company for negligence, charging that the company had not maintained the trucks properly. The suit was successful, and the Hobson Company was ordered on November 16, 19X2 to pay $100,000 in damages.

On January 20, 19X3, when the accountant was preparing the financial statements, she recommended that the production method would provide a better matching of truck depreciation expense to revenue. At the date of purchase, each truck was estimated to have a useful economic life of 80,000 kilometres. Hauling contracts had been somewhat erratic; total kilometres for all trucks in 19X0, 19X1, and 19X2 were 12,000, 55,000, and 40,000 respectively.

Income was reported to be $96,000 and $136,000 in 19X0 and 19X1, respectively. In 19X3, income before depreciation was $154,000.

a. Prepare a journal entry to record the writeoff of the truck on April 1, 19X1.
b. What would be the difference in income for each of the three years if depreciation had been calculated using the production method rather than the straight-line method? Show all supporting calculations.

c. What would be a valid rationale for using the production method in this case? Be specific.

d. What is the required accounting treatment for the $100,000 in damages that Hobson Company was ordered to pay in 19X2?

Adapted with permission from the Society of Management Accountants of Canada.

43. *Limitations of generally accepted accounting principles.* Mr. Goldwin runs an antiques store in Kingston, Ontario. His store has established a reputation that the antiques in stock will always appreciate in value. When Mr. Goldwin applied for a bank loan, the bank manager assessed the store as having $500,000 worth of goodwill and inventory appreciation, although it is not recorded in the books. Mr. Goldwin discussed the bank manager's statements with his accountant and asked to have the goodwill recorded. His accountant replied, "Conventional accounting principles result in many assets being carried at values that do not reflect their true economic value to the firm. In addition, many of the firm's assets are not recorded at all."

a. Explain the accountant's statement and include a discussion of why accounting principles have not been altered to correct this situation. Include in your explanation a recommendation, with reference to generally accepted accounting principles, regarding whether the goodwill should be recorded.

Adapted with permission from the Society of Management Accountants of Canada.

DECISION CASE 8-1

Acme Trucking Ltd. recently expanded its operations into Alberta by purchasing 60 percent of the shares of Alberta Transport Ltd. from the estate of the company's founder. The remaining shares are held by members of the founder's family, who do not wish to sell their shares at this time.

Shortly after gaining control through the share purchase, in order to permit the expansion of the Alberta operations, Alberta Transport, on Acme's direction and financing, sold its existing warehouse and purchased for $400,000 a replacement frame warehouse with greater storage capacity. For the coming year, Alberta expected to use only 60 percent of the warehouse, but over the next ten years, the steady increase in business was expected to result in full capacity use. Because of the ample supply of warehouse space in Alberta, there did not appear to be an alternative use for the excess capacity during this time. The warehouse had been constructed on leased land with 40 years to expire on the lease. At the expiration of the lease, the disposal value of the warehouse was expected to be $20,000 in excess of the costs of demolition.

In the past, Alberta Transport had recorded depreciation on frame buildings equal to the maximum capital cost allowance of 10 percent. Bill Buck, the president of Acme, questions this policy and has asked you to consider either the continuation of the policy or some other alternative (or alternatives) that would present a fair set of financial statements that could be used:

1. To evaluate the performance of Jack Doe, the new manager of Alberta Transport.
2. To report on the results of the company's operations to the minority shareholders.
3. To minimize the payments of corporate income tax.

Before finalizing a policy proposal on depreciation, you collect the following information that may be relevant to the policy:

1. Jack Doe will be evaluated on the return on investment (R.O.I.) achieved on net operating assets (less current liabilities).
2. The minority shareholdings were expected to be purchased by Acme over the next two years. Consequently, it was considered to be in Acme's interest to minimize the reported income, because this policy might encourage the founder's family to sell its shares at a lower price.
3. Sixty percent of Alberta Transport's reported income is to be included in the financial statements of Acme. Because Bill Buck has a ten-year contract with a profit-sharing clause, he was interested in increasing the income of Acme during this period.
4. It was in the interest of all parties to minimize the payments for corporate income tax.

Prepare a statement of depreciation policy that would be suitable for the new warehouse of Alberta Transport, indicating in full the reasons for the policy recommended.

CHAPTER NINE

LIABILITIES: A TEMPORARY SOURCE OF CAPITAL

CHAPTER OUTLINE

- Basic Concepts of Liabilities
- Contingencies — Potential Obligations
- Current Liabilities
- Long-Term Liabilities
- Mortgages and Interest-Bearing Notes
- Bonds
- Unifying Principles of Accounting for Long-Term Liabilities

This chapter and the next two examine the accounting concepts and procedures for the right-hand side of the balance sheet, which shows the sources of a firm's financing. The funds used to acquire assets come from two sources: owners and nonowners. Chapter 11 discusses shareholders' equity. This chapter and Chapter 10 discuss obligations incurred by a business that result from raising funds from nonowners. Banks and creditors providing debt on a long-term basis understand their role as providers of funds. Suppliers and employees, who do not require immediate cash payment of goods provided or services rendered, usually do not think of themselves as contributing to a firm's funds, but they do. Likewise, customers who advance cash to a firm before delivery of a good or service provide funds to the firm. The obligations of a business to these nonowning contributors of funds are **liabilities**.

liabilities
Present obligations resulting from past transactions that require the firm to pay money, provide goods, or perform services in the future.

BASIC CONCEPTS OF LIABILITIES

In accounting, an obligation is generally recognized as a liability of an entity if it has three essential characteristics:[1]

---

[1] *CICA Handbook*, section 1000.29. See also "Elements of Financial Statements of Business Enterprises" in *Statement of Financial Accounting Concepts No. 3* (Stamford, Conn: Financial Accounting Standards Board, 1980), par. 29.

1. The obligation involves a probable future sacrifice of resources — a future transfer of cash, goods, or services or the foregoing of a future cash receipt — at a specified or determinable date. The cash equivalent value of resources to be sacrificed must be measurable with reasonable precision.

2. The entity has little or no discretion to avoid the transfer.

3. The transaction or event giving rise to the entity's obligation has already occurred.

A thorough understanding of liabilities requires knowledge of compound interest and present value computations. In these computations, payments made at different times are made comparable by taking into account the interest that cash can earn over time. Appendix A at the back of the book introduces the computations.

Example 1 Miller Corporation's employees have earned wages and salaries that will not be paid until the next day, two weeks after the end of the current accounting period. Miller Corporation's suppliers are owed substantial amounts for goods sold to Miller Corporation, but these debts are not due for 10 to 30 days after the end of the period. Miller Corporation owes the federal government for taxes, but the payments are not due until the fifteenth of next month. Each of these items meets the three criteria to be a liability. Thus, they are shown as liabilities under titles such as Wages Payable, Salaries Payable, Accounts Payable, and Taxes Payable.

Example 2 When Miller Corporation sells television sets, it gives a warranty to repair or replace any faulty parts within one year after sale. This obligation meets the three criteria of a liability. Because some television sets will surely need repair, the future sacrifice of resources is probable. The obligation to make repairs is Miller Corporation's. The transaction giving rise to the obligation, the sale of the television set, has already occurred.

The amount is not known with certainty, but Miller Corporation has had sufficient experience with its own television sets to be able to estimate with reasonable precision what the expected costs of repairs or replacements will be. The repairs or replacements will occur within a time span, one year, known with reasonable precision. Miller Corporation will thus show Estimated Liability for Warranty Payments on its balance sheet.

Example 3 Miller Corporation signs a binding contract to supply certain goods to a customer within the next six months. In this case, there is an obligation, definite time, and definite amount (of goods, if not cash), but there has been no past or current transaction. Chapter 2 pointed out that accounting does not recognize assets or liabilities for executory contracts — the mere exchange of promises where there is no mutual performance. Without some mutual performance, there is no current or past benefit. Thus, no liability is shown in this case.

Example 4 Facts are the same as in Example 3, except that the customer has made a $10,000 cash deposit on signing the order. Here, there has been more than an exchange of promises. The customer has paid cash and Miller Corporation has accepted it. It will show a liability called Advances from Customers in the amount of $10,000. The remainder of the order is still executory and is not recognized in accounting. Such arrangements are called "partially executory contracts."

Example 5 Miller Corporation has signed a three-year, noncancellable lease with a computer manufacturer to make payments of $3,000 per month for use of a computer system with a three-year life. Definite amounts are due at definite times, and a transaction has occurred — a computer system has been received. Therefore, Miller Corporation will show a liability called Obligation Under Capital Leases on its balance sheet.

Example 6 Miller Corporation is the defendant in a lawsuit alleging damages of $10 million. The lawsuit was filed by customers who claim to have been injured by misleading advertising about Miller Corporation's television sets. Lawyers retained by the corporation think that there is an adequate defence to the charges. Because there is no obligation to make a payment at a reasonably definite time, there is no liability. The notes to the financial statements will disclose the existence of the lawsuit, but no liability will be shown on the balance sheet.

Example 7 Miller Corporation has signed a contract promising to employ its president for the next five years and to pay the president a salary of $250,000 per year. The salary is to be increased in future years at the same rate as that of the Consumer Price Index, published by the government. Miller Corporation has an obligation to make payments (although the president may quit at any time without penalty). The payments are of reasonably certain amounts and are to be made at definite times. At the time the contract is signed, no mutual performance has occurred. The contract is purely executory. Because a transaction is deemed not to have taken place, no liability appears on the balance sheet. A liability will, of course, arise as the president performs services over time.

Example 8 Miller Corporation has signed a contract with Horizon Oil Pipe Line Limited to ship at least 10,000 barrels of crude oil per month for the next three years. Miller Corporation must pay for the shipping services, whether or not it actually ships oil. An arrangement such as this, called a *throughput contract*, is not recorded as a liability because the event giving rise to the obligation is viewed as being the actual shipment, which has not yet occurred. Such an obligation is merely disclosed in notes. Similarly, long-term obligations for so-called take-or-pay contracts, where the "purchaser" is obliged to pay for certain quantities of goods, whether or not the purchaser actually takes delivery of them, is not a formal liability, but must be disclosed. Both throughput and take-or-pay contracts are viewed as executory.

VALUATION

In *historical*-cost accounting, liabilities appear on the balance sheet as the present value of payments to be made in the future. The interest rate used in computing the present-value amount throughout the life of a liability is the interest rate that the specific borrower was required to pay at the time the liability was initially incurred. That is, the *historical* interest rate is used.

As Chapter 2 mentions, most current liabilities appear at the amount payable because the difference between the amount ultimately payable and its present value is immaterial.

CLASSIFICATION

Liabilities are generally classified on the balance sheet as *current* or *noncurrent*. The criterion generally used for dividing current from noncurrent liabilities is the length of time that will elapse before payment must be made. The dividing line between the two is one year, or the length of the operating cycle if more than one year.

CONTINGENCIES — POTENTIAL OBLIGATIONS

One of the criteria used by the accountant to recognize a liability is the probability of a future sacrifice of resources. The world of business and law is full of uncertainties. At any given time, a firm may find itself potentially liable for events that have occurred in the past. Contingencies of this nature are not recognized as accounting liabilities. They are potential future obligations rather than current obligations. The potential obligations arise from events that occurred in the past but the outcome of which is not now known. Whether an item becomes a liability, and how large a liability it will become, depends on a future event, such as the outcome of a lawsuit.

Suppose that a company is sued for damages in a formal court proceeding for an accident involving a customer who was visiting the company. The suit is not scheduled for trial until after the close of the accounting period. If the company's lawyers and auditors agree that the outcome is likely to be favourable for the company or that, if unfavourable, the amount of the damage settlement will not be large, no liability will be recognized on the balance sheet. The notes to the financial statements must disclose, however, significant contingencies.

The *CICA Handbook* recommends that an estimated loss from a contingency should be recognized in the accounts only if both of the following conditions are met:[2]

(a) Information available prior to the issuance of the financial statements indicates that the chance is high that a future event will confirm that an asset had been impaired or that a liability had been incurred.

(b) The amount of the loss can be reasonably estimated.

An example is that of a toy manufacturer who has sold products for which a safety hazard has been discovered. The toy manufacturer thinks it likely that liabilities have been incurred. Test (b) would be met if experience or other information enabled the manufacturer to make a reasonable estimate of the loss. The journal entry would be:

Loss on Damage Claim	$50,000	
Estimated Liability for Damages		$50,000
To recognize estimated liability for expected damage arising from safety hazard of toys sold.		

---

[2] *CICA Handbook*, section 3290.

The debit in the above entry is to a loss account (presented among other expenses on the income statement), and the credit is to an estimated liability, which should be treated as a current liability (similar to the Estimated Warranty Liability account), on the balance sheet. In practice, an account with the title "Estimated Liability for Damages" would seldom, if ever, appear in published financial statements, because it would be perceived as an admission of guilt. Such an admission would likely have an adverse effect on the outcome of the lawsuit. The liability account would be combined with others for financial statement presentation.

contingent liability
A potential obligation, the eventual occurrence of which usually depends on some future event beyond the control of the firm.

The term **contingent liability** is used only when the item is not recognized in the accounts but rather in the footnotes. (A note receivable sold *with* recourse, described in Chapter 6, gives rise to another example of a contingent liability.)

Footnote disclosure is required when the existence of a contingent liability is likely (the chance is high) but the amount cannot be reasonably estimated; when there exists an explosure to loss in excess of the amount accrued; or when the occurrence of the confirming future event is not determinable.

The annual report of ABC Services Ltd. illustrates the disclosure of contingent liabilities as follows:

> Commitments and Contingencies (*in part*)
>
> An action was commenced against the Company by XYZ Corporation Limited claiming damages for alleged breach of contract in the amount of $5,000,000. A court decision, upheld on appeal, that there was an enforceable agreement has been rendered in favour of the plaintiff. The issue of the amount of damages has not been considered. Provision for loss is not currently determinable. Any loss would be treated as a prior period adjustment.

If a contingency arises that may result in a gain to a company and whether or not the above conditions for recognition are met, the *CICA Handbook* recommendations prohibit the accrual of the gain.

CURRENT LIABILITIES

Current liabilities are those due within one year, or the current operating cycle if more than one year. They include accounts payable to creditors, payroll accruals, short-term notes payable, taxes payable, and a few others. Current liabilities are continually discharged and replaced with new ones in the course of business operations.

These obligations may not be paid for several weeks or months after the current balance sheet date. Their present value is therefore less than the amount that will be paid. Nevertheless, these items are shown at the full amount to be paid, because the difference is usually so small that separate accounting for the difference and subsequent interest expense is judged to be not worth the trouble.

ACCOUNTS PAYABLE TO CREDITORS

Companies seldom pay for goods and services when they are received. Payment is usually deferred until a bill is received from the supplier. Even then, the bill might not be paid immediately but, instead, accumulated with other bills until a specified time of the month when all bills are paid. Because explicit interest is not paid on these accounts, management tries to obtain as much capital as possible from its creditors by delaying payment as long as possible. Failure to pay creditors according to schedule can, however, lead to poor credit ratings and restrictions on future credit.

WAGES, SALARIES, AND OTHER PAYROLL ITEMS

When employees earn wages, they owe part of their earnings to governments for income and other taxes. Employees may also owe other amounts for union dues and insurance plans. The amounts, although wage expense of the employer, are not paid directly to employees, but are paid on their behalf to the governments, unions, and insurance companies.

In addition, the employer must pay various payroll taxes and may have agreed to pay for other fringe benefits relating to wages earned. Employers owe Unemployment Insurance and Canada Pension Plan (CPP) contributions, the rates of which vary over time, so the amounts used in this book are only approximately correct.

Employers in most provinces are required to provide paid vacations or vacation pay to employees. The employer must accrue the costs of the earned but unused vacations (including the payroll taxes and fringe benefits on them) at the time the employees earn them, not at the later time when employees take vacations and are paid. In this way, the accountant charges each quarter of the year with a portion of the cost of vacations, rather than allocating all to the summer when most employees take the majority of their vacation days.

Example 9 Assume that employees earn $100,000, that the employees' withholding rates for income taxes average 24 percent, and that employees owe 8 percent of their wages for Unemployment Insurance and CPP. In addition, employees owe a total of $500 for union dues (to be withheld by the employer) and $3,000 for health insurance plans.

The employer must make Unemployment Insurance and CPP payments of $9,400 and $4,500, respectively, to provide life and health insurance coverage. Employees have earned vacation pay estimated to be $4,000; estimated employer payroll taxes and fringe benefits are 18 percent of the gross amount.

The journal entries below record these wages. If some of the wages were earned by production workers, some of the debits would be to Work-in-Process Inventory, rather than to Wage and Salaries Expense. Although three journal entries are used (one for payments to employees, one for employer payroll taxes, and one for the accrual for estimated vacation pay), in practice, these might be prepared as eleven separate entries or even as a single entry.

Wages and Salaries Expense	$100,000	
Withholding Taxes Payable		$24,000
Payroll Taxes Payable		8,000
Withheld Dues Payable to Union		500
Insurance Premiums Payable		3,000
Wages and Salaries Payable		64,500
Record wage expense.		

Wages and Salaries Expense	$ 13,900	
Payroll Taxes Payable		$ 9,400
Insurance Premiums Payable		4,500

Employer's expense for amounts not payable directly to employees.

| Wages and Salaries Expense | $ 4,720 | |
| Estimated Vacation Wages and Fringes Payable | | $ 4,720 |

Estimate of vacation pay and fringes thereon earned
during the current period: 0.18 × $4,000 = $720.

On payday, the employer pays $64,500 to employees, discharging the direct liability to them. The employer writes cheques at various times to the federal government, the union, and the insurance companies. The insurance might be paid in advance with the debit being made to Prepaid Insurance; if so, the credits when wages are recorded will be to the Prepaid Insurance account. The amounts paid to employees taking vacation are debited to the liability account, Estimated Vacation Wages and Fringes Payable, not to an expense account.

SHORT-TERM NOTES AND INTEREST PAYABLE

Businesses obtain interim financing for less than a year from banks or other creditors in return for a short-term note called a *note payable*. Chapter 6 discusses such notes from the point of view of the lender, or note holder. The treatment of these notes by the borrower is the mirror image of the treatment by the lender. Where the lender records an asset, the borrower records a liability. When the lender records interest receivable and revenue, the borrower records interest payable and expense.

INCOME TAXES PAYABLE

Businesses organized as corporations must pay income taxes based on their taxable income from business activities. In contrast, business entities organized as partnerships or sole proprietorships do not pay income taxes. Instead, the income declared by the individual partners or sole proprietor on the personal income tax return is taxed. Each partner or sole proprietor adds his or her share of business income to income from all other (non-business) sources in preparing an individual income tax return.

The details of the income tax on corporations are subject to change. The rates and schedules of payments mentioned below should not be taken as an indication of the exact procedure in force at any particular time, but rather as an indication of the type of accounting procedures that are involved. Throughout the remainder of the book, a corporate income tax rate of 40 percent is used in almost all illustrations for ease of calculation.

Companies must pay income taxes on a monthly basis throughout the year. The monthly installment is based on the lesser of the amount paid in the prior year and the company's estimate of the taxes to be paid during the current year. The final payment for a year is made two or three months after the fiscal year-end. This is frequently described as "pay-as-you-go" taxation.

Example 10 The fiscal year of Bongo Ltd. begins on January 1 and ends on December 31. The Year 6 income tax payable by Bongo Ltd. was $60,000, and the company estimates the Year 7 income tax payable will be $45,000. The company is required to make twelve monthly payments of $3,750 ($= ^1/_{12} \times$ $45,000) commencing in January Year 7 as Year 7 income tax installments. A final payment, equal to the taxes payable according to the income tax return (say, $47,000) less the twelve installments, is due on March 31, Year 8.

The journal entries made for Bongo Ltd. to record Year 6 income tax related transactions follow:

Year 7			
Monthly	Income Tax Payable — Year 7	$ 3,750	
Entry	Cash		$ 3,750
	To record the installment payments on Year 7 income tax ($^1/_{12} \times$ $45,000).		
December	Income Tax Expense	$47,000	
	Income Tax Payable — Year 7		$47,000
	To record Year 7 income tax payable.		
Year 8			
March 31	Income Tax Payable — Year 7	$ 2,000	
	Cash		$ 2,000
	To record the final payment due on Year 7 income tax [$47,000 − 12 × $3,750].		

DEFERRED PERFORMANCE LIABILITIES

Another current liability arises when customers make advance payments for goods or services to be delivered in the future. This liability, unlike the preceding ones, is discharged by delivering goods or services rather than by paying cash. This liability represents "unearned," and therefore unrecognized, revenue; that is, cash is received before the goods or services are furnished to the customer.

An example of this type of liability is the advance sale of theatre tickets for, say, $200. Upon the sale, the following entry is made:

Cash	$200	
Advances from Customers		$200
To record sale of tickets for future performances.		

These deferred performance obligations qualify as liabilities. The account credited is called Advances from Customers or Liability for Advance Sales. After the theatre performance, or after the tickets have expired, revenue is recognized and the liability is removed by recording the following entry:

Advances from Customers	$200	
Performance Revenue		$200
Service has been rendered and revenue is recognized.		

Deferred performance liabilities arise also in connection with the sale of magazine subscriptions, transportation tickets, and service contracts.

PRODUCT WARRANTIES

Most firms today must guarantee the quality of their products in order to sell the product. It would be unthinkable to buy a car or a television without such a guarantee of product performance. This guarantee is called a *product warranty* and can run from 30 days to the lifetime of the consumer.

Accounting for warranties would be trivial if entries were made only as claims were submitted. The matching principle, however, attempts to place the estimated cost of warranty service on sales in the same income statement as that of the associated revenue. A firm must therefore estimate two quantities: the percentage of units sold that will come back for service in the warranty period, and the average cost of honouring each warranty claim.

Assume that Eckel Ltd. sells cellular phones for $2,000 each and offers a one-year warranty against defects. Past experience indicates that 4 percent of the units will prove defective and that the average repair cost for each is $70. This past year, 40,000 phones were sold, and 500 of these have already been returned for service. The accrued liability for product warranties at the end of the year will be calculated as follows:

Number of units sold	40,000
Rate of defective units	×0.04
Total units expected to fail	1,600
Less units already failed	(500)
Number of units sold this year expected to still fail in warranty period	1,100
Average repair cost per unit	×$70
Estimated liability for product warranties at year-end	$77,000

The journal entry at year-end will be:

Product Warranty Expense	$77,000	
Estimated Liability for Product Warranty		$77,000

As each unit is subsequently brought in for repair, the liability will be debited, and the credit will go to Cash, Supplies, Labour, and so on.

PROVINCIAL SALES TAXES (PST) AND THE GOODS AND SERVICES TAX (GST)

A major revenue source for government is the imposition of sales taxes on the sale of most goods and services. The federal government levies a 7 percent goods and services tax (GST), and most provinces levy a provincial sales tax (PST). The PST rate varies between provinces. Although these taxes are levied on consumers and are referred to as consumption taxes, retailers and service providers are forced to act as collection agents for the

DISCUSSION CASE 20

The Bad Guys vs. the Good Guys

At the XIII World Congress of Accountants in Tokyo last October [1987] ... Akio Morita, co-founder and chairman of the giant Sony Corporation, opened his keynote address with an anecdote about his most memorable "tangle" with the accounting profession.

Sony, then in its infancy, was struggling to establish itself in a war-ravaged country, and Morita and his co-founder, Masaru Ibuka, decided the ideal product to make its reputation with was a machine that could record sound on a long piece of magnetic tape.

"We were set on developing and manufacturing Japan's first tape-recorder," Morita explained, "although at the time we didn't even know what material the tape should be made of. We were confident, however, that if we succeeded, our prospects would be promising.

"We took our idea to our chief (in fact, our only) financial officer. He listened carefully to our plan and then proceeded to show us that, based on our financial situation at the time, and the development cost we had projected, it would be disastrous if we were to commit ourselves to such an expensive high-risk venture.

"It looked as though our first step toward the development of Japan's first tape recorder would have to be the development of our chief financial officer. So Mr. Ibuka and I invited this gentleman out one evening for what we called a 'discussion' — to a cozy little restaurant next to our office. At that time, the only way to obtain 'alcoholic instruments of persuasion' was on the black market, but on this occasion, we considered it an R&D cost.

"Well, it was a good discussion, and by the end of the evening we'd managed to convince our CFO that the tape-recorder wasn't really such a dangerous idea after all. That was my first indication that numbers sometimes look different at different times."

That incident may be 40 years old, but it illustrates a characteristic of accountants criticized even today. Morita wasn't really referring to any tendency on the part of accountants to succumb to alcoholic persuasion. I expect we can hold our own in that regard. He was referring to the tendency of many of us to focus on costs and short-term benefits when long-term vision is called for.

"In my experience with accountants," said Morita, "when they are told of an idea for a new product, they immediately do a cost analysis. Their cost estimates, in most cases, are very high, and they are reluctant to give their support." Still, he allowed, accountants have their place.

"The tension between the product developer, who is burning with an idea, and the financial officer whose job is to keep the company from shoving all the chips into the middle of the table

(continued)

(continued)

at one time, is a very common occurrence in business: the engineer versus the accountant; the spenders versus the savers; the good guys versus the bad guys. I am not saying which is which. The truth is, we really need each other. And if an organization is working the way it should, we complement each other."

But good management goes far beyond number crunching, says Morita. It's about taking risks — even when the numbers might speak against it.

"There is no accounting system in the world that could have justified the decision we made to commit ourselves to an extremely expensive digital-recording developmental program, for example. What numbers we did see at the time indicated we were crazy to go on with it, but we didn't seek justification.

"I think sometimes management worries too much about justification through numbers. Instead, I tell my people that good managers develop a sense

of intuition, hunch or sixth sense when it comes to decision making. In order to make a rational decision, you have to know all of the facts and figures and the environment surrounding the facts. But it is impossible for a person to know everything. So in order to run the business, I tell them, 'Take risks based on the numbers, but also have faith in your sixth sense. Don't let the facts and the figures, the elements of justification, turn you away from a new idea.'"

It's a good message for accountants everywhere to ponder as we open the page on a new year.

References

Nelson Luscombe, "The Bad Guys vs. the Good Guys," *CA Magazine*, January 1988. Reprinted with permission of *CA Magazine*, published by the Canadian Institute of Chartered Accountants, Toronto.

Discussion Question

What is Mr. Morita trying to tell accountants?

---

government. The GST alone generates more than $20 billion a year in revenue for the government.

Assume that an item is sold for $1,000 in a province where the PST rate is 8 percent. The sale would be recorded as follows:

Cash (or Accounts Receivable)	$1,150	
Sales		$1,000
GST Payable		70
PST Payable		80

When remittance is made to the government, the liabilities are debited and cash credited. The retailer is allowed to reduce the GST remitted by any GST it had to pay on its own purchases. The governments may also allow the remittances to be reduced by a minor amount to compensate the retailer partially for the expenses incurred in actually collecting the tax.

LONG-TERM LIABILITIES

The principal long-term liabilities are mortgages, notes, bonds, and leases. The significant differences between long-term and short-term, or current, liabilities are that (1) interest on long-term liabilities is ordinarily paid at regular intervals during the life of a long-term obligation, whereas interest on short-term debt is usually paid in a lump sum at maturity; (2) the principal of long-term obligations is often paid back in installments, or (3) special funds are accumulated by the borrower for retiring long-term liabilities.

Accounting for all long-term liabilities generally follows the same procedures. Those procedures are outlined next and illustrated throughout the rest of this chapter and Chapter 10.

PROCEDURES FOR RECORDING LONG-TERM LIABILITIES

Long-term liabilities are initially recorded at the present value of all promised payments to be made using the market interest rate at the time the liability is incurred. This market interest rate is also used to compute the amount of interest expense throughout the life of the liability. A portion (perhaps all) of each cash payment represents interest expense. Any excess of cash payment over interest expense is used to reduce the liability itself (often called the **principal**). If a given payment is not sufficient to discharge the entire interest expense that has accrued since the last payment date, the liability principal increases by the excess of interest expense over cash payment.

Retirement of long-term liabilities can occur in several ways, but the process is the same. The net amount shown on the books for the obligation is debited, the asset given up in return (usually cash) is credited, and any difference is recognized as a gain or loss on retirement of the debt.

MORTGAGES AND INTEREST-BEARING NOTES

In most Canadian provinces, a **mortgage** is considered a lien on property, which may be registered with a government agency as security for a loan made by the "mortgagee" to the borrower. The lien may be removed when the mortgage is paid in full. The mortgaged property is **collateral** for the loan.[3] The customary terminology designates the lender as the "**mortgagee**" and the borrower as the "**mortgagor**."[4]

As long as the mortgagor meets the obligations under the mortgage agreement, the mortgagee does not have the ordinary rights of an owner to possess and use the property. If the mortgagor defaults on either the principal or interest payments, the mortgagee can usually arrange to have the property sold for his or her benefit through a process called **foreclosure**.

---

[3] Accountants are generally careful to use the word *collateral*, rather than *security*, in this context. Whether the loan is "secured" is a matter of legal judgment; moreover, accountants do not wish to imply that the value of the collateral will be sufficient to satisfy the debt, as "secured" might imply.

[4] When you borrow money to finance your home purchase, you give the bank a mortgage, not vice versa.

principal
The face value of a financing transaction. Interest is charged or earned on this amount.

mortgage
A claim given by the borrower (mortgagor) to the lender (mortgagee) against the borrower's property in return for a loan.

collateral
Assets pledged by a borrower that will be given up if the loan is not paid.

mortgagee
The term used to refer to the lender in mortgage situations.

mortgagor
The term used to refer to the borrower in mortgage situations.

foreclosure
The revocation by a lender of a borrower's right to redeem his or her property as a consequence of the borrower's failure to remit required payments (as on a mortgage).

The mortgagee has first rights to the proceeds from the foreclosure sale for satisfying any unpaid claim. If there is an excess, it is paid to the mortgagor. If the proceeds are insufficient to pay the remaining loan, the lender becomes an unsecured creditor of the borrower for the unpaid balance.

A note is similar to a mortgage except that no property is typically pledged as collateral.

ACCOUNTING FOR MORTGAGES AND INTEREST-BEARING NOTES

Some of the more common problems in accounting for mortgages are presented in the following illustration.

On October 1, Year 1, the Western Co. Ltd. borrows $125,000 for five years from the Home Insurance Company to obtain funds for additional working capital. As collateral, Western Co. Ltd. gives Home Insurance Company a mortgage on several parcels of land that it owns and that are on its books at a cost of $50,000. Interest is charged on the unpaid balance of the loan principal at an interest rate of 12 percent per year compounded semiannually. Payments are due on April 1 and October 1 of each year. Western agrees to make ten payments over the five years of the mortgage so that when the last payment is made on October 1, Year 6, the loan and all interest will have been paid. The first nine payments are to be $17,000 each. The tenth payment is to be just large enough to discharge the balance of the loan. The Western Co. Ltd. closes its books annually on December 31. (The derivation of the semiannual payment of $17,000 is shown in Example 11 in Appendix A, page 1045.)

The entries from the time the mortgage is issued through December 31, Year 2, are as follows:

10/1/Year 1	Cash	$125,000	
	Mortgage Payable		$125,000
	Loan obtained from Home Insurance Company for five years at 12 percent compounded semiannually.		

As Example 11 in Appendix A shows, $125,000 is approximately equal to the present value of ten semiannual cash payments of $17,000, each discounted at 12 percent compounded semiannually.

12/31/Year 1	Interest Expense	$3,750	
	Interest Payable		$3,750
	Adjusting entry: Interest expense on mortgage from 10/1/Year 1 to 12/31/Year 1.		

Interest expense on the loan for the first six months is $7,500 (= 0.06 × $125,000). To simplify the calculations, accounting typically assumes that the interest accrues evenly over the six-month period. Thus, interest expense for October, November, and December is half of the $7,500, or $3,750.

4/1/Year 2	Interest Expense	$3,750	
	Interest Payable	3,750	
	Mortgage Payable	9,500	
	Cash		$17,000
	Cash payment made requires an entry. Interest expense on mortgage from 1/1/Year 2 to 4/1/Year 2, payment of six months' interest, and reduction of loan by the difference, $17,000 − $7,500 = $9,500.		

After the cash payment of April 1, Year 2, the unpaid principal of the loan is $115,500 (= $125,000 − $9,500). Interest expense during the second six-month period is based on this unpaid principal amount.

10/1/Year 2	Interest Expense	$ 6,930	
	Mortgage Payable	10,070	
	Cash		$17,000
	Cash payment made requires an entry. Interest expense for the period 4/1/Year 2 to 10/1/Year 2 is $6,930 [= 0.12 × ($125,000 − $9,500) × ½]. The loan is reduced by the difference, $17,000 − $6,930 = $10,070.		
12/31/Year 2	Interest Expense	$3,163	
	Interest Payable		$3,163
	Adjusting entry: Interest expense from 10/1/Year 2 to 12/31/Year 2 = [0.12 × ($125,000 − $9,500 − $10,070) × ³/₁₂].		

AMORTIZATION SCHEDULE

Exhibit 9.1 presents an *amortization schedule* for this mortgage. For each period, it shows the balance at the beginning of the period, the interest for the period, the payment for the period, the reduction in principal for the period, and the balance at the end of the period. (The last payment, $16,782 in this case, often differs slightly from the others because of the cumulative effect of rounding errors.) *All* long-term liabilities have analogous amortization schedules, which aid in understanding the timing of payments to discharge the liability. Amortization schedules for various long-term liabilities appear throughout this chapter and Chapter 10.

BONDS

Whenever funds can be borrowed from one lender, the firm usually issues mortgages or notes. When larger amounts are needed, the firm may have to borrow from the general investing public with a bond issue. Bonds are used primarily by corporations and governmental units. The distinctive features of a bond issue are as follows:

1. A **bond indenture**, or agreement, is drawn up that shows in detail the terms of the loan and the rights and duties of the borrower and other parties to the contract. Bond indentures typically limit the borrower's

bond indenture
The contract between an issuer of bonds and the bondholders.

EXHIBIT 9.1

**Amortization Schedule for $125,000 Mortgage (or Note),
Repaid in Ten Semiannual Installments of $17,000,
Interest Rate of 12 Percent, Compounded Semiannually**

Six-Month Period (1)	Loan Balance Start of Period (2)	Interest Expense for Period (3)	Payment (4)	Portion of Payment Reducing Principal (5)	Loan Balance End of Period (6)
0					$125,000
1	$125,000	$7,500	$17,000	$ 9,500	115,500
2	115,500	6,930	17,000	10,070	105,430
3	105,430	6,326	17,000	10,674	94,756
4	94,756	5,685	17,000	11,315	83,441
5	83,441	5,006	17,000	11,994	71,448
6	71,448	4,287	17,000	12,713	58,734
7	58,734	3,524	17,000	13,476	45,259
8	45,259	2,715	17,000	14,285	30,974
9	30,974	1,858	17,000	15,142	15,832
10	15,832	950	16,782	15,832	0

*Note: In preparing this table, calculations were rounded to the nearest cent. Then, for presentation, results were
rounded to the nearest dollar.*
Column (2) = Column (6) from previous period.
Column (3) = 0.06 × Column (2).
Column (4)   Given, except row 10, where it is the amount such that Column (4) = Column (2) + Column (3).
Column (5) = Column (4) − Column (3).
Column (6) = Column (2) − Column (5).

Bond certificates
Engraved certificates representing the legal obligation.

trustee
An external party, usually a trust company or bank, that performs fiduciary services for an organization.

registrar and disbursing agent
One who receives the borrower's interest and principal payments and distributes the funds to the bondholder.

coupon bonds
Bonds with a coupon attached, which the bondholder detaches and deposits with the bank in order to receive the interest.

right to declare dividends and to make other distributions to owners in order to provide better protection to bondholders.

2. **Bond certificates** are used. Engraved certificates are prepared, each one representing a portion of the total loan. The usual minimum denomination in business practice is $1,000, although smaller denominations are occasionally used. Some government bonds are issued in denominations as small as $50.

3. If property is pledged as collateral for the loan (as in a mortgage bond), a **trustee** is named to represent the bondholders; the trustee is usually a trust company.

4. An agent (usually a trust company) is appointed to act as **registrar and disbursing agent**. The borrower deposits interest and principal payments with the disbursing agent, who distributes the funds to the bondholders.

5. Some bonds are **coupon bonds**. Coupons attached to the bond certificate represent promises to make interest payments throughout the life of the bond. When a coupon comes due, the bondholder cuts it off and deposits it with a bank. The bank sends the coupon through the bank clearing system to the disbursing agent for payment, which is deposited in the bondholder's account at the bank.

6. Bonds are frequently *registered as to principal*, which means that the holder's name appears on the bond certificate and on the records of the registrar. Sometimes, both the principal and interest of bonds are registered, in which case the interest payments are mailed directly to the bondholder and coupons are not used. **Registered bonds** are easily replaced if lost, but the transfer from one holder to another is cumbersome. Unregistered bonds, which are called *bearer bonds*, may be transferred merely by delivery, whereas registered bonds have to be assigned formally from one holder to another.

7. The entire bond issue is usually issued by the borrower to an investment banking firm, or to a group of investment bankers known as an **investment syndicate**, which takes over the responsibility of reselling the bonds to the investing public. Members of the syndicate usually bear the risks and rewards of interest-rate fluctuations while the bonds are being sold to the public.

TYPES OF BONDS

Mortgage bonds carry a mortgage on real estate as collateral for the repayment of the loan. *Collateral trust bonds* are usually secured by shares and bonds of other corporations. The most common type of corporate bond, except in the railroad and public utility industries, is the **debenture bond**. This type carries no special collateral; instead, it is issued on the general credit of the business. To give added protection to the bondholders, provisions are usually included in the bond indenture that limit the dividends that can be declared or the amount of subsequent long-term debt that can be incurred. **Convertible bonds** are debentures that the holder can exchange, possibly after some specific period of time has elapsed, for a specific number of shares. A detailed discussion of accounting for convertible bonds is presented in Chapter 11.

Almost all bonds provide for the payment of interest at regular intervals, usually semiannually. The amount of interest is typically expressed as a percentage of the principal. For example, a 12 percent, ten-year, semiannual coupon bond with face amount of $1,000 promises to pay $60 every six months. Here, we assume, the first payment occurs six months after the issue date. A total of twenty payments are made. At the time of the final $60 coupon payment, the $1,000 principal is also due. The coupon rate is 12 percent in this case. The principal amount of a bond is its face, or par, value. The terms **face value** and **par value** are synonymous in this context. In general, the par value multiplied by the coupon rate equals the amount of cash paid per *year*, whether in quarterly, semiannual, or annual installments. By far, the majority of corporate bonds provide for semiannual coupon payments. A bond can be issued as subsequently traded in the marketplace for amounts below par, at par, or above par.

PROCEEDS OF A BOND ISSUE

The amount received by the borrower will usually differ from the par value of the bonds issued. The difference arises because the coupon rate printed on the bond certificates differs from the interest rate the market requires

---

Registered bonds
Bonds for which the issuing corporation (or trustee) keeps a record of owners to whom they mail interest payments on a regular basis.

investment syndicate
A group that receives bonds issued by a borrower, then resells them to the investing public.

Mortgage bonds
Bonds secured by a mortgage.

debenture bond
A bond that has no specific property pledged as security for its repayment (i.e., a bond secured only by the general reputation of the issuing company).

Convertible bonds
Bonds allowing the holder to convert the bonds to capital stock under prescribed terms.

face value
The principal amount shown on the face of a bond certificate to be repaid at maturity. If interest has been accruing, face value is interest plus principal; if the interest has been paid periodically, face value is simply the principal. Sometimes called the "maturity value" or "par value."

par value
Used interchangeably with the term "face value."

bond discount
From the standpoint of the issuer of a bond at the issue date, the excess of the par value of a bond over its initial sales price; at later dates, the excess of par over the sum of the initial issue price plus the portion of discount already amortized. From the standpoint of a bondholder, the difference between par value and selling price when the bond sells below par.

bond premium
The amount by which the issue price (or current selling price) is higher than face value.

given the risk of the borrower, the general level of interest rates in the economy, and other factors. Whatever the market rate, at time of issue or at any time thereafter, the annual cash payments for a bond remain the product of the face value multiplied by the coupon rate. If the coupon rate is less than the rate the market requires the firm to pay, the bonds will sell for less than par. The difference between par and selling price is called **bond discount**. The issuer will pay the full amount at maturity. The difference between the face amount and the initial issue proceeds is part of the interest the market requires the borrower to pay. Even though the payment occurs at maturity, the accounting procedures are designed to record that interest systematically over the life of the bond. If the coupon rate is larger than the rate the market requires, the bonds will sell above par. The difference between selling price and par is called the **bond premium**.

The presence of a discount or premium in and of itself indicates nothing about the credit standing of the borrower. A firm with a credit standing that would enable it to borrow funds at 11 percent might issue 10 percent bonds that would sell at a discount, whereas another firm with a lower credit standing, requiring it to pay 11.5 percent on loans, might issue bonds at 14 percent that would sell at premium.

Issued at Par

The Macaulay Corporation issues $100,000 face value of 12 percent semiannual coupon bonds. The bonds are dated July 1, Year 1. The principal amount is repayable on July 1, Year 6, or five years later. Interest payments (coupons) are due on July 1 and January 1 of each year. The coupon payments promised at each interest payment date total $6,000. Figure 9.1 presents a time line for the borrower's cash flows associated with this bond. Assuming that the issue was taken by Penman & Co. Inc., investment banker, on July 1, Year 1, at a rate to yield 12 percent compounded semiannually, the calculation of the proceeds to Macaulay would be as follows. (Appendix A at the back of the book explains the present value calculations.)

The issue price would be stated as 100.0 (that is, 100 percent of par), which implies that the market interest rate was 12 percent compounded semiannually, the same as the coupon rate.

(a) Present value of $100,000 to be paid at the end of five years (Appendix B, Table B.2, page 1067, shows the present value of $1 to be received in ten periods at 6 percent per period to be $0.55839; $100,000 × 0.55839 = $55,839.)	$ 55,839
(b) Present value of $6,000 to be paid each six months for five years (Appendix B, Table B.4, page 1069, shows the present value of an ordinary annuity of $1 per period for ten periods discounted at 6 percent to be $7.36009; $6,000 × 7.36009 = $44.161.)	44,161
Total Proceeds	$100,000

FIGURE 9.1

Time Line for Five-Year Semiannual Coupon Bonds, 12 Percent Annual Coupons; $100,000 Par Value Issued at Par

+$100,000										−$100,000
	−$6,000	−$6,000	−$6,000	−$6,000	−$6,000	−$6,000	−$6,000	−$6,000	−$6,000	−$6,000
7/1/	1/1/	7/1/	1/1/	7/1/	1/1/	7/1/	1/1/	7/1/	1/1/	7/1/
Year 1	Year 2	Year 2	Year 3	Year 3	Year 4	Year 4	Year 5	Year 5	Year 6	Year 6

Issued at Less than Par

Assume that these same bonds were issued at a price to yield 14 percent compounded semiannually. The promised cash flows after July 1, Year 1, associated with these bonds (payments of periodic interest plus repayment of principal) are identical to those in the time line shown in Figure 9.1. These future cash flows would be discounted to their present value, however, using a 14 percent discount rate compounded semiannually. The calculation of the issue proceeds (that is, initial market price) would be as follows. (Why it is that "12 percent" bonds can be issued to yield 14 percent is discussed below and on pages 560–62.)

(a) Present value of $100,000 to be paid at the end of five years (Present value of $1 to be received in ten periods at 7 percent per period is $0.50835; $100,000 × 0.50835 = $50,835.)	$50,835
(b) Present value of $6,000 to be paid each six months for five years (Present value of an ordinary annuity of $1 per period for ten periods, discounted at 7 percent per period = $7.02358; $6,000 × 7.02358 = $42,141.)	42,141
Total Proceeds	$92,976

If the issue price were stated on a conventional pricing basis in the market at 92.98 (92.98 percent of par), the issuing price would be $92,980. This amount implies a market yield of approximately 14 percent compounded semiannually.

Issued at More than Par

Assume that the bonds were issued at a price to yield 10 percent compounded semiannually. The cash flows, after July 1, Year 1, would again be identical to those shown in Figure 9.1. They would be discounted at 10 percent compounded semiannually to calculate their present value. The calculation of the proceeds would be as follows:

(a) Present value of $100,000 to be paid at the end of five years (Present value of $1 to be received in ten periods at 5 percent per period is $0.61391; $100,000 × 0.61391 = $61,391.)	$ 61,391
(b) Present value of $6,000 to be paid each six months for five years (Present value of an ordinary annuity of $1 per period for ten periods, discounted at 5 percent per period = $7.72173; $6,000 × 7.72173 = $46,330.)	46,330
Total Proceeds	$107,721

If the issue price were stated on a conventional pricing basis in the market at 107.72 (107.72 percent of par), the issuing price would be $107.720.[5] The price would imply a market yield of approximately 10 percent compounded semiannually.

BOND TABLES

Bond amortization tables
Tables used to look up the periodic amortization amount for bond premium or discount.

These tedious calculations need not be made every time a bond issue is analyzed. **Bond amortization tables** show the results of calculations like those just described. Examples of such tables are included in Tables B.5 and B.6 on pages 1068 and 1069. Table B.5 shows the price for 10 percent, semiannual coupon bonds as a percent of par for various market interest rates (yields) and years to maturity. Table B.6 shows market rates and implied prices for 12 percent, semiannual coupon bonds. (Some modern electronic calculators make the calculations represented by these tables in a few seconds.)

The percentages of par shown in these tables represent the present value of the bond indicated. Because the factors are expressed as a percent of par, they have to be multiplied by ten to find the price of a $1,000 bond. If you have never used bond tables before now, turn to Table B.6 and find in the fifth-year row the three difference prices for the three different market yields used in the preceding examples. Notice further that a bond will sell at par if, and only if, it has a market yield equal to its coupon rate.

These tables are useful whether a bond is being issued by a corporation or resold later by an investor. The approach to computing the market price will be the same in either case, although the years to maturity will be less than the original term of the bond when it is resold. The following generalizations can be made regarding bond prices:

1. When the market interest rate equals the coupon rate, the market price will equal par.
2. When the market interest rate is greater than the coupon rate, the market price will be less than par.
3. When the market interest rate is less than the coupon rate, the market price will be greater than par.

ACCOUNTING FOR BONDS ISSUED AT PAR

The following illustration covers the more common problems associated with bonds issued at par.

We use the data presented in the previous sections for the Macaulay Corporation, where the bonds were issued at par, and we assume that the

---

[5] In many contexts, bond prices are quoted in dollars plus thirty-seconds of a dollar. A bond selling for about 107.721 percent of par would be quoted at 107 $^{23}/_{32}$, which would be written as 107.23. In order to read published bond prices, you must know whether the information after the "decimal" point refers to fractions expressed in one-hundredths or in thirty-seconds. (If you are reading published bond prices and see any number larger than 31 after the decimal point, you can be sure that one-hundredths are being used. If you see many prices, but none of the numbers shown after the point are larger than 31, you can be reasonably sure that thirty-seconds are being used.)

books are closed semiannually on June 30 and December 31. The entry at the time of issue would be:

7/1/Year 1	Cash	$100,000	
	Debenture Bonds Payable		$100,000
	$100,000 of 12-percent, five-year bonds issued at par.		

The entries for interest would be made at the end of the accounting period and on the interest payment dates. Entries through January 1, Year 2 would be:

12/31/Year 1	Interest Expense	$6,000	
	Interest Payable		$6,000
	To accrue six months' interest.		
1/1/Year 2	Interest Payable	$6,000	
	Cash		$6,000
	To record payment of six months' interest.		

Bond Issued Between Interest Payment Dates

The actual date that a bond is issued seldom coincides with one of the payment dates. Assuming that these same bonds were actually brought to market on September 1, rather than July 1, and were issued at par, the purchaser of the bond would be expected to pay Macaulay Corporation for two months' interest in advance. After all, on the first coupon, Macaulay Corporation promises a full $60, for six months' interest, but would have had the use of the borrowed funds for only four months. The purchasers of the bonds would pay $100,000 plus two months' interest of $1,000 (= 0.12 × $100,000 × $^2/_{12}$) and would get $2,000 back when the first coupons were redeemed. The journal entries made by Macaulay Corporation, the issuer, would be:

9/1/Year 1	Cash	$102,000	
	Bonds Payable		$100,000
	Interest Payable		2,000
	To record issue of bonds at par between interest payment		
	dates. The purchasers pay an amount equal to interest		
	for the first two months but will get it back when		
	the first coupons are redeemed.		

ACCOUNTING FOR BONDS ISSUED AT LESS THAN PAR

The following illustrates the more common problems associated with bonds issued for less than par.

Assume the data presented for the Macaulay Corporation, where 12 percent, $100,000 par-value, five-year bonds were issued to yield approximately 14 percent compounded semiannually. The issue price was shown previously to be $92,976. The journal entry at the time of issue would be:

7/1/Year 1	Cash	$92,976	
	Discount on Bonds Payable[6]	7,024	
	Bonds Payable		$100,000
	$100,000 of 12-percent, five-year bonds issued at 92.976.		

The issuance of these bonds for $92,976, instead of the $100,000 par value, indicates that 12 percent is not a sufficiently high rate of interest for the bonds to induce purchasers to pay the full par value in the open market. If purchasers of these bonds paid the full $100,000 par value, they would earn only 12 percent compounded semiannually, the coupon rate. Purchasers desiring a rate of return of 14 percent would postpone their purchases until the market price dropped to $92,976. At this price, purchasers of the bonds would earn the 14 percent return they require. The return would be composed of ten $6,000 coupon payments over the next five years plus $7,024 (= $100,000 − $92,976) as part of the payment at maturity.

For Macaulay Corporation, the total interest expense over the life of the bonds would equal $67,024 (periodic interest payments totalling $60,000 plus $7,024 paid at maturity). Two methods of allocating the total interest expense of $67,024 to the periods of the loan would be the effective-interest method and the straight-line method.

INTEREST EXPENSE UNDER THE EFFECTIVE-INTEREST METHOD

effective-interest method
A systematic method for computing interest expense (or revenue) that makes the interest expense for each period divided by the amount of the net liability (asset) at the beginning of the period equal to the yield rate on the bond at the time of issue (acquisition).

Under the **effective-interest method**, interest *expense* each period is equal to the market interest rate at the time that bonds were initially issued (14 percent compounded semiannually, in this example) multiplied by the *net book value* of the liability[7] at the beginning of the interest period. For example, interest expense for the period from July 1, Year 1 to December 31, Year 1, the first six-month period, is $6,508 [= 0.07 × ($100,000 − $7,024)]. The bond indenture provides that only $6,000 (= 0.06 × $100,000) need be paid on January 2, Year 2. This amount is equal to the coupon rate times the par value of the bonds. The difference between the interest expense of $6,508 and the interest currently payable of $6,000 is deducted

[6] Bond discount may be considered a contra liabiliity account, reducing the liability below its face (redemption) value, or as a deferred charge classified as a noncurrent asset. The advocates of the contra liability view consider that the liability should be shown at the present value of the bond face value discounted at the bond yield rate at the date of issue. This objective is accomplished by deducting the bond discount from the face value on the balance sheet. The advocates of the deferred charge view consider that bond discount represents a prepayment of interest by the company at the issue date in lieu of larger regular interest payments over the life of the bond. Further, they declare that the liability to repay is the face value and may become due at any time if the company fails to meet its interest payments and other commitments. Consequently, the liability is shown at its face value and the discount as a noncurrent asset at amortized value. *CICA Handbook* sections 1520 and 3070 imply that the deferred charge alternative be adopted. To be consistent, unamortized bond premium would be considered as a deferred credit.

[7] The net book value is par value of bonds payable less bond discount, or plus bond premium.

DISCUSSION CASE 21

The Credit Card Mentality

Our nation thrives on credit. Most sales today are on credit. [Chapter 6 deals with sales on account and the need to establish valuation allowances.] Fortunately, this problem is disappearing for most companies that sell at the retail level. Instead of setting up accounts in the store for customers and worrying about collectibility, we just say "will that be cash or charge?" (that is, "will it be cash or Visa, Mastercard, or American Express?"). For a fixed monthly fee these credit card companies take the worry out of sales — collectibility is their problem.

Today, civilization as we know it could not exist without the credit card. The colour of your card is even a symbol of your social status. "Some people need an American Express Gold Card and its $10,000 limit of pure power. Others need that platinum card with its $100,000 spending limit to feel really powerful."

A new credit card is out that puts all others to shame. A plastic card has been issued to members of the United States Congress which members insert into a computer terminal to vote on bills. As Congressman DioGuardi says:

"I've got a card that puts those two to shame. My Congressional voting card. This is the most expensive credit card in the world. The card has no limit ... Last year our national debt reached 2 trillion dollars — the established limit. And what did we do? We decided to raise the limit. You see, we've got a credit card mentality in this country."

References
Reprinted with permission from Joseph J. DioGuardi, "Why Doesn't the Government Understand Accounting?" *Financial Executive*, Sept./Oct. 1988, copyright 1988 by Financial Executives Institute, Morristown, New Jersey.

Discussion Question
What are the negative implications of the credit card mentality in Canada?

from bond discount. The journal entry made on December 31, Year 1 to recognize interest for the last six months of Year 1 is:

12/31/Year 1	Interest Expense	$6,508	
	Interest Payable		$6,000
	Discount on Bonds Payable		508
	To recognize interest expense for six months.		

The Interest Payable account is shown as a current liability on the balance sheet at the end of Year 1. Discount on Bonds Payable of $6,516 (= $7,024 − $508) is reported as a noncurrent asset or as a contra account to Bonds Payable.

On January 2, Year 2, the first periodic cash payment is made.

1/2/Year 2	Interest Payable	$6,000	
	Cash		$6,000
	To record payment of interest for six months.		

Interest expense for the second six months, from January 1, Year 2 through June 30, Year 2, is $6,544 (= 0.07 × $93,484). Interest expense for the second six months of $6,544 is larger than the $6,508 for the first six months because the recorded net book value of the liability at the beginning of the second six months is larger. The journal entry on July 1, Year 2 to record interest expense is shown on page 566.

7/1/Year 2	Interest Expense	$6,544	
	Interest Payable		$6,000
	Discount on Debenture Bonds Payable		544
	To recognize interest expense for six months.		

An amortization schedule for these bonds over their five-year life is shown in Exhibit 9.2.

The effective-interest method of recognizing interest expense on a bond has the following financial statement effects.

1. On the income statement, interest expense will be a constant percentage of the recorded net liability at the beginning of each interest period. This percentage will be equal to the market interest rate for these bonds when they were initially issued. When bonds are issued for less than par value, the *dollar amount* of interest expense will increase each period as the recorded net principal amount increases.

2. On the balance sheet at the end of each period, the net balance of the bonds less the unamortized discount will be the present value of the *remaining* cash outflows discounted at the market rate of interest when the bonds were initially issued. For example, on July 1, Year 2, the present value of the remaining cash payments is as follows:

Present value of July 1, Year 2, interest payment	$ 6,000
Present value of eight remaining semiannual interest payments discounted at 14 percent, compounded semiannually (Table B.4, page 1069, shows the present value of an ordinary annuity of $1 per period for eight periods discounted at 7 percent to be $5.97130; $6,000 × 5.97130 = $35,827)	35,827
Present value of $100,000 to be paid at the end of four years (Table B.2, page 1067, shows the present value of $1 to be paid at the end of eight periods discounted at 7 percent to be $0.58201; $100,000 × 0.58201 = $58,201)	58,201
Total Present Value	$100,028
Less: Amount Shown as Current Liability	($6,000)
Equals Par Value of Bonds Less Bond Discount	$ 94,028

EXHIBIT 9.2

Effective-Interest Amortization Schedule for $100,000 of 12 Percent, Five-Year Bonds Issued for 92.976 Percent of Par to Yield 14 Percent, Interest Payable Semiannually

Semiannual Journal Entry

Dr. Interest Expense	Amount in Column (3)
Cr. Cash	Amount in Column (4)
Cr. Discount on Debenture Bonds Payable	Amount in Column (5)

Period (six-month intervals) (1)	Net Liability at Start of Period (2)	Effective Interest: 7 Percent per Period (3)	Coupon Rate: 6 Percent of Par (4)	Bond Discount Amort-ization (5)	Bond Discount At End of Period (6)	Net Liability at End of Period (7)
0					$7,024	$ 92,976
1	$92,976	$ 6,508	$ 6,000	$ 508	6,516	93,484
2	93,484	6,544	6,000	544	5,972	94,028
3	94,028	6,582	6,000	582	5,390	94,610
4	94,610	6,623	6,000	623	4,767	95,233
5	95,233	6,666	6,000	666	4,101	95,899
6	95,899	6,713	6,000	713	3,388	96,612
7	96,612	6,763	6,000	763	2,625	97,375
8	97,375	6,816	6,000	816	1,809	98,191
9	98,191	6,873	6,000	873	936	99,064
10	99,064	6,936	6,000	936	0	100,000
Total		$67,024	$60,000	$7,024		

Note: In preparing this table, calculations were rounded to the nearest cent. Then, for presentation, results were rounded to the nearest dollar.

Column (2) = Column (7) from previous period.
Column (3) = 0.07 × Column (2).
Column (4) = Given.
Column (5) = Column (3) − Column (4).
Column (6) = Column (6) from previous period − Column (5) of this period.
Column (7) = Column (2) + Column (5).

The amount $94,028 appears in column (7) of Exhibit 9.2 for the net liability at the end of the second six-month period.

INTEREST EXPENSE UNDER THE STRAIGHT-LINE METHOD

The second method for recording interest expense over the life of the bond issue is the **straight-line amortization method**. Under this method, total interest expense (periodic coupon payments plus any amount paid at the time of maturity) is spread evenly over the life of the bonds. In the example of Macaulay Corporation, total interest expense is $67,024 [= ($6,000 × 10) + ($100,000 − $92,976)]. Interest expense each six months will therefore be $6,702.40 (= $67,024/10). The journal entry to record interest expense at the end of each six months is shown on page 566.

straight-line amortization method
The method of recording interest expense whereby the total interest expense is spread evenly over the life of the bond.

Interest Expense	$6,702.40	
Interest Payable		$6,000.00
Discount on Debenture Bonds Payable		702.40
To recognize interest expense for six months.		

The straight-line method of computing interest expense is computationally easier than the effective-interest method. However, it has two theoretical weaknesses:

1. When bonds are issued for less than par value, interest expense will be a decreasing percentage of the net bond liability (par value less unamortized discount) at the beginning of each period. That is, interest expense (numerator) will be constant but the net bond liability (denominator) will increase as the maturity date approaches. In contrast, the effective-interest method provides an amount for interest expense that is a constant percentage of the beginning-of-the-period net liability.

2. The balance sheet values of the bonds less the bond discount that are presented each period will not equal the present value of the remaining cash flows relating to the bond discounted at the historical-interest rate.

PREFERRED METHOD OF AMORTIZING BOND DISCOUNT

Theoretically, the effective-interest method is superior. If the results are not materially different, companies may employ the straight-line method. Notice that, under both methods, if the bonds are held to maturity, the discount or premium is fully amortized so that the carrying value of the bond equals the face value at retirement.

ACCOUNTING FOR BONDS ISSUED FOR MORE THAN PAR

The following discussion illustrates the more common problems associated with bonds issued for more than par.

Assume the data presented for the Macaulay Corporation, in which 12 percent, $100,000 par-value, five-year bonds were issued to yield approximately 10 percent compounded semiannually. The issue price (derived previously) is $107,721. The journal entry at the time of issue is:

7/1/Year 1	Cash	$107,721	
	Debenture Bonds Payable		$100,000
	Premium on Debentures Bonds Payable		7,721
	$100,000 of 12 percent, five-year bonds issued at 107.721.		

The firm borrows $107,721. The issuance of these bonds for $107,721, instead of the $100,000 par value, indicates that 12 percent is a higher rate of interest for the bonds than the purchasers demand. If purchasers of these bonds paid the $100,000 par value, they would earn 12 percent compounded semiannually, the coupon rate. Purchasers requiring a rate of return of only 10 percent will bid up the market price to $107,721. At this price, purchasers of the bonds will earn only the 10 percent demanded return. The return comprises ten $6,000 coupon payments over the next five years reduced by $7,721 (= $107,721 − $100,000) loaned but not repaid at maturity.

For Macaulay Corporation, the total interest expense over the life of the bonds is equal to $52,279 (periodic interest payments totalling $60,000 less $7,721 not repaid at maturity.) Two methods of allocating the total interest expense of $52,279 to the periods of the loan are the effective-interest method and the straight-line method.

INTEREST EXPENSE UNDER THE EFFECTIVE-INTEREST METHOD

Under the effective-interest method, interest *expense* each period is equal to the market interest rate at the time the bonds were initially issued (10 percent compounded semiannually, in this example) multiplied by the net recorded liability at the beginning of the interest period. For example, interest expense for the period from July 1, Year 1 to December 31, Year 1, the first six-month period, is $5,386 [= 0.05 × ($100,000 + $7,721)]. The bond indenture provides that $6,000 (= 0.06 × $100,000) be paid on January 1, Year 2. This amount is equal to the coupon rate times the par value of the bonds. The difference between the payment of $6,000 and the interest expense of $5,386 reduces the amount to be paid at maturity. The journal entry made on December 31, Year 1 to recognize interest for the last six months of Year 1 is:

12/31/Year 1	Interest Expense	$5,386	
	Premium on Bonds Payable	614	
	Interest Payable		$6,000
	To recognize interest expense for six months.		

The Interest Payable account will be shown as a current liability on the balance sheet at the end of Year 1. Bonds Payable of $100,000 and Premium on Bonds Payable of $7,107 (= $7,721 − $614) appear in noncurrent liabilities.

On January 1, Year 2, the first periodic cash payment is made.

1/01/Year 2	Interest Payable	$6,000	
	Cash		$6,000
	To record payment of interest for six months.		

Interest expense for the second six months, from January 1, Year 2 through June 30, Year 2, is $5,355 (= 0.05 × $107,107). Interest expense for the second six months of $5,355 is smaller than the $5,386 for the first six months because the unpaid balance of the net liability at the beginning of the second six months is smaller. The journal entry on June 30, Year 2 to record interest expense is shown on page 568.

7/01/Year 2	Interest Expense	$5,355	
	Premium on Bonds Payable	645	
	Interest Payable		$6,000
	To recognize interest expenses for six months.		

An amortization schedule for these bonds over their five-year life appears in Exhibit 9.3.

The effective-interest method of recognizing interest expense on a bond has the following financial statement effects:

1. On the income statement, interest expense will be a constant percentage of the recorded net liability at the beginning of each interest period. This percentage will be equal to the market interest rate when the bonds were initially issued. When bonds are issued for more than par value, the *dollar amount* of interest expense will decrease each period as the unpaid principal amount decreases to the maturity value.

2. On the balance sheet at the end of each period, the balance of the bonds plus the unamortized premium will be stated at the present value of

EXHIBIT 9.3
Effective-Interest Amortization Schedule for $100,000 of 12 Percent, Five-Year Bonds Issued for 107.721 Percent of Par to Yield 10 Percent, Interest Payable Semiannually

Semiannual Journal Entry
Dr. Interest Expense   Amount in Column (3)
Dr. Premium on Bonds Payable   Amount in Column (5)
   Cr. Cash   Amount in Column (4)

Period (six-month intervals) (1)	Net Liability at Start of Period (2)	Effective Interest: 5 Percent per Period (3)	Coupon Rate: 6 Percent of Par (4)	Bond Premium Amort- ization (5)	Bond Premium At End of Period (6)	Net Liability at End of Period (7)
0					$7,721	$107,721
1	$107,721	$ 5,386	$ 6,000	$ 614	7,107	107,107
2	107,107	5,355	6,000	645	6,462	106,462
3	106,462	5,323	6,000	677	5,785	105,785
4	105,785	5,289	6,000	711	5,074	105,074
5	105,074	5,254	6,000	746	4,328	104,328
6	104,328	5,216	6,000	784	3,544	103,544
7	103,544	5,177	6,000	823	2,721	102,721
8	102,721	5,136	6,000	864	1,857	101,857
9	101,857	5,093	6,000	907	950	100,950
10	100,950	5,050	6,000	950	0	100,000
Total		$52,279	$60,000	$7,721		

Column (2) = Column (7) from previous period.
Column (3) = 0.05 × Column (2).
Column (4)   Given.
Column (5) = Column (4) − Column (3).
Column (6) = Column (6) from previous period − Column (5) of this period.
Column (7) = Column (2) − Column (5).

the *remaining* cash flow discounted at the market rate of interest when the bonds were initially issued. For example, on June 30, Year 2, the present value of the remaining cash payments will be as follows:

Present value of July 1, Year 2, interest payment	$ 6,000
Present value of eight remaining semiannual interest payments discounted at 10 percent, compounded semiannually (Table B.4, page 1069, shows the present value of an ordinary annuity of $1 per period for eight periods discounted at 5 percent to be $6.46321; $6,000 × 6.46321 = $38,779)	38,779
Present value of $100,000 to be paid at the end of four years (Table B.2, page 1067, shows the present value of $1 to be paid at the end of eight periods discounted at 5 percent to be $0.67684; $100,000 × 0.67684 = $67,684	67,684
Total Present Value	$112,463
Less: Amount Shown as Current Liability	(6,000)
Equals Amount Shown for Debenture Bonds Payable Plus Bond Premium	$106,463

The amount $106,462, different because of rounding effects, appears in column (7) of Exhibit 9.3 for the liability at the end of the second six-month period.

PREMIUM ON BONDS PAYABLE ACCOUNT

Accounting has traditionally shown Bonds Payable at par value with a liability adjunct account, Premium on Bonds Payable, carrying the amount to add to par value to show book value. If the Premium on Bonds Payable account were used, the balance sheet on June 30, Year 2, after two semiannual interest periods, would show:

Bonds Payable — Par Value	$100,000
Plus: Premium on Bonds Payable	6,462
Bonds Payable — Net Book Value	$106,462

INTEREST EXPENSE UNDER THE STRAIGHT-LINE METHOD

Under the straight-line method, total interest expense (periodic coupon payments reduced by the excess of initial issue proceeds over amounts paid at maturity) is spread evenly over the life of the bonds. In the example for Macaulay Corporation, total interest expense is $52,279 [= ($6,000 × 10) − ($107,721 − $100,000)]. Interest expense each six months will therefore be $5,227.90 (= $52,279/10). The journal entry to record interest expense at the end of each six months is:

Interest Expense	$5,227.90	
Premium on Bonds Payable	772.10	
Interest Payable		$6,000.00
To recognize interest expense for six months.		

The straight-line method of computing interest expense is computationally easier than the effective-interest method. However, it has two theoretical weaknesses:

1. When bonds are issued for more than par value, interest expense will be an increasing percentage of the net bond liability at the beginning of each period. That is, interest expense (numerator) will be constant but the net bond liability (denominator) will decrease as the maturity date approaches. In contrast, the effective-interest method provides an amount for interest expense that is a constant percentage of the beginning-of-the-period net liability.

2. The net amount at which the bonds are stated on the balance sheet each period will not equal the present value of the remaining cash flows relating to the bond discounted at the historical-interest rate.

BOND RETIREMENT

Many bonds remain outstanding until the stated maturity date. Refer to Exhibit 9.2, the Macaulay example, where the 12 percent coupon bonds were issued to yield 14 percent. The company pays the final coupon, $6,000, and the face amount, $100,000, on the stated maturity date. The entries are:

7/1/Year 6	Interest Expense	$ 6,936	
	Cash		$6,000
	Bonds Payable		936
	See row 10 of Exhibit 9.2		
	Bonds Payable	$100,000	
	Cash		$100,000
	Retirement at maturity of bonds.		

Retirement Before Maturity

A firm sometimes purchases its own bonds on the open market before maturity. Because market interest rates constantly change, the purchase price will seldom equal the recorded book value of the bonds. Assume that Macaulay Corporation originally issued its bonds at par to yield 12 percent compounded semiannually. Assume that three years later, on July 1, Year 4, interest rates in the marketplace have increased so that the market then requires a 15 percent interest rate to be paid by Macaulay Corporation. Refer to Table B.6 on page 1071, two-year row, 15 percent column, which shows that 12 percent bonds with two years until maturity will sell in the marketplace for 94.9760 percent of par if the current interest rate is 15 percent compounded semiannually.

The marketplace is not constrained by the principles of historical-cost accounting. Even though Macaulay Corporation shows the Bonds Payable on the balance sheet at $100,000, the marketplace puts a price of only $94,976 on the entire bond issue. From the point of view of the marketplace, these bonds are the same as two-year bonds issued on July 1, Year 4 at an effective yield of 15 percent, so they carry a discount of $5,024 (= $100,000 − $94,976).

If, on July 1, Year 4, Macaulay Corporation purchased $10,000 of par value of its own bonds, it would have to pay only $9,498 (= 0.94976 × $10,000) for those bonds. It would make these journal entries at the time of purchase:

7/1/Year 4	Interest Payable	$ 6,000	
	Cash		$6,000
	To record payment of coupons, as usual.		
	Bonds Payable	$10,000	
	Cash		$9,498
	Gain on Retirement of Bonds		502
	To record purchase of bonds for less than the current amount shown in the accounting records.		

In the second journal entry, a gain arises because the firm is able to retire a liability recorded at one amount, $10,000, for a smaller cash payment, $9,498. This gain actually occurred as interest rates increased between Year 1 and Year 4. In historical-cost accounting, the gain is reported only when realized — in the period of bond retirement. This phenomenon is analogous to a firm's purchasing temporary investments, holding those investments as prices increase, selling the investments in a subsequent year, and reporting all of the gain in the year of sale. It is caused by the historical-cost accounting convention of recording amounts at historical cost and not recording increases in wealth until those increases are realized in arm's-length transactions with outsiders.

During the 1970s, interest rates increased. Many companies had issued bonds at prices near par with coupon rates of only 3 or 4 percent per year in the 1960s. When interest rates in the 1970s jumped to 12 or 15 percent per year, these bonds sold in the marketplace for substantial discounts from par value. Many companies repurchased their own bonds, recording substantial gains in the process.

Because there is no alternative in historical-cost accounting to showing a gain (or loss) on bond retirement (the debits must equal the credits), and because the gain (or loss) does not meet the criteria of an extraordinary item, generally accepted accounting principles[8] require that all gains or losses on bond retirements be recorded as unusual items in arriving at the net income before extraordinary items. This unusual item must be recorded separately only if it is abnormal in size. This ruling enables companies to manage their reported income before extraordinary items by repurchasing bonds.

SPECIAL PROVISIONS FOR BOND RETIREMENT

Serial Bonds The bond indenture may require the issuing firm to make a special provision for retiring the bond issue. There are two major types of retirement provisions. One provides that certain portions of the principal amount will come due on a succession of maturity dates; the bonds of such

---

[8] *CICA Handbook*, section 3480.

serial bonds
Bonds for which the maturity dates are staggered over a series of years.

sinking funds
Cash and other assets accumulated and segregated for some specific purpose, such as retiring debt.

callable bonds
Bonds for which the issuer reserves the right to pay a specific amount to retire the bond before the maturity date. Usually, the issuer must pay a premium to retire the bonds early. Also called redeemable bonds.

call price
A price set a few percentage points above the par value; declines as the maturity date approaches.

issues are known as **serial bonds**. (The bonds considered so far in this chapter are not serial bonds.)

Sinking-Fund Bonds   The other major type of retirement provision in bond indentures requires the firm to accumulate a fund of cash or other assets that will be used to pay the bonds when the maturity date arrives or to reacquire and retire portions of bond issue. Funds of this type are commonly known as **sinking funds**, although *bond-retirement funds* would be a more descriptive term. The trustee of the bond issue usually holds the sinking fund. It appears on the balance sheet as a noncurrent asset in the "Investments" section.

Refunded Bonds   Some bond indentures make no provision for installment repayment or for accumulating sinking funds for the payment of the bonds when they come due. Such bonds are usually well protected with property held by the trustees as collateral or by the high credit standing of the issuer. Under these circumstances, the entire bond liability may be paid at maturity out of cash in the bank at that time. Quite commonly, however, this procedure is not followed. Instead, the bond issue is *refunded* — a new set of bonds is issued to obtain the funds to retire the old ones when they come due.

Callable Bonds   A common provision gives the issuing company the right to retire portions of the bond issue before maturity if it so desires, but does not require it to do so. To facilitate such reacquisition and retirement of the bonds, the bond indenture can provide that the bonds shall be **callable bonds**. That is, the issuing company has the right to reacquire its bonds at prices specified in the bond indenture. When the bonds are called for redemption, the trustee will notify the holder to present all remaining coupons and the bond principal for payments equal to the call price plus accrued interest.

The **call price** is usually set a few percentage points above the par value and declines as the maturity date approaches. Because the call provision may be exercised by the issuing company at a time when the market rate of interest is less than the coupon rate, callable bonds usually are sold in the marketplace for something less than otherwise similar, but noncallable, bonds.

Assume, for example, that a firm had issued 12 percent, semiannual coupon bonds at par, but the market interest rates and the firm's credit standing at a later date would currently allow it to borrow at 10 percent. If $100,000 par value bonds issued at par were called at 105, the entry, in addition to the one to record the accrued interest expense, would be:

Bonds Payable	$100,000	
Loss on Retirement of Bonds	5,000	
Cash		$105,000
Bonds called and retired.		

A gain or loss recognized on bond retirement is generally classified as an unusual item in the income statement.

When bonds are retired, the entire book value of the bonds at the time of retirement must be removed from the accounting records. Suppose that

$100,000 par-value bonds were issued for more than par value several years ago and that the book value of the bonds is now $103,500. If $10,000 par-value bonds were called at 105, the entry to record the retirement would be:

Bonds Payable	$10,000	
Premium on Bonds Payable	350	
Loss on Retirement of Bonds	150	
Cash		$10,500
Partial retirement of bonds originally issued for more than par value.		

The market rate of interest a firm must pay depends on two factors: the general level of interest rates and its own credit-worthiness. If the market rate of interest has risen since bonds were issued (or the firm's credit rating has declined), the bonds will sell in the market at less than issue price. A firm that wants to retire such bonds does not *call* them, because the call price is typically greater than the face value. Instead, the firm will probably purchase its bonds in the open market and realize a gain on the retirement of bonds.

UNIFYING PRINCIPLES OF ACCOUNTING FOR LONG-TERM LIABILITIES

Long-term liabilities are obligations to pay fixed amounts at definite future times more than one year in the future. The obligations appear on the balance sheet at the present value of the future payments. The present value computations use the historical rate of interest — the market interest rate on the date the obligation was incurred.

The same method of accounting is used for all long-term liabilities and related expenses — the effective-interest method. The liability is initially recorded at the cash equivalent value received, which will equal the present value of the future contractual payments using the interest rate relevant for the borrower on the date the loans begins. At any subsequent interest accrual or interest payment date, Interest Expense is computed by multiplying the book value of the net liability by the historical interest rate. The amount of interest expense increases liabilities. The amount of any cash payment made reduces the liabilities. The difference between interest expense and the cash payment decreases the discount or premium on bonds payable.

Amortization schedules, such as those in Exhibits 9.1, 9.2, 9.3, and 9.4, as well as in Chapter 10, illustrate this unchanging procedure for a variety of long-term liabilities.

SUMMARY

A liability is an obligation by an entity involving a probable future sacrifice of resources. The amount of the obligation and the timing of its payment can be estimated with reasonable certainty. The transaction causing the obligation to arise has already occurred.

Accounting for long-term liabilities is accomplished by recording these obligations at their present value at the date the obligation is incurred (which equals the cash equivalent value received at the time of the borrowing), then showing the change in that present value as the maturity date of the obligation approaches. In historical-cost accounting, the interest rate used throughout the life of the liability is the firm's borrowing rate at the time the liability was originally incurred. Retirement of long-term liabilities can be brought about in a variety of ways but, in each case, the process is the same. The net obligation is offset against what is given in return (usually cash), with gain or loss on retirement recognized as appropriate.

KEY TERMS

Liabilities
Contingent liability
Principal
Mortgage
Collateral
Mortgagee
Mortgagor
Foreclosure
Bond indenture
Bond certificates
Trustee
Registrar and disbursing agent
Coupon bonds
Registered bonds
Investment syndicate

Mortgage bonds
Debenture bond
Convertible bonds
Face value
Par value
Bond discount
Bond premium
Bond amortization tables
Effective-interest method
Straight-line amortization method
Serial bonds
Sinking funds
Callable bonds
Call price

SELF-STUDY MATERIAL

This section contains questions, exercises, and problems to help you assess your understanding of Chapter 9. Careful review of this material will assist you in completing the homework assignments. Solutions are found at the end of the section.

QUESTIONS AND EXERCISES

True/False

For each statement, place a T or and F in the space provided to indicate whether the statement is true or false.

_____ 1. Discount on Bonds Payable should be classified as a contra account to Bonds Payable.

F 2. A manufacturing company guarantees its product against defects for one year. Because neither the amount due nor the due date is known with certainty, the liability for the warranty need not be disclosed.

T 3. Current liabilities are those due within the current operating cycle, which is normally one year.

_____ 4. The process of issuing new bonds to obtain funds to retire old bonds as they come due is known as *calling the old bond issue.*

_____ 5. When a company has the right to retire portions of a bond issue before the bonds' maturity date, the bonds are said to be *callable.*

_____ 6. For a bond issued at a discount, the amount of interest expense reported on the income statement each period will be decreasing under the effective-interest method of rcognizing interest expense.

T 7. Generally accepted accounting principles require the straight-line method of recognizing interest expense.

_____ 8. A bond sold at a discount will have a higher effective rate of interest than that of a bond sold at premium.

_____ 9. Bonds that are due on a succession of maturity dates are known as *serial bonds.*

_____ 10. A fund of cash or other assets that will be used to retire bonds is commonly known as a *sinking fund.*

_____ 11. When bonds are sold at a discount, the difference between the face value and the amount of the proceeds represents additional interest that will be paid as a part of the face value at maturity.

_____ 12. The effect of amortizing the premium on bonds payable is to increase the interest expense over the amount actually paid as interest.

_____ 13. Notes to the financial statements may be used to report contingent liabilities.

_____ 14. One difference between current and noncurrent liabilities is that interest on short-term liabilities is ordinarily paid at regular intervals during the life of the short-term obligation.

_____ 15. On retiring bonds that were originally issued at a discount, the appropriate portion of the unamortized discount also must be retired.

_____ 16. The Gweru Company Ltd. issued bonds at a discount. If the company uses the straight-line method of amortization, the bond interest expense reported in the income statement will be the same amount each year.

_____ 17. For a bond sold a premium, the annual cash payment for interest exceeds the annual interest expense.

_____ 18. If a liability can be retired for an amount that is less than the amount owed, a loss will be reported by the party paying off the liability.

_____ 19. A debenture is a bond contract that is secured by property.

_____ 20. Another difference between current and noncurrent liabilities is that either the principal of long-term obligations is paid back in installments, or special funds are accumulated by the borrower for retiring the liability.

_____ 21. Amortization of bond discount or premium by the straight-line method results in a changing rate of interest each period.

_____ 22. Under the effective-interest method, interest expense each period is equal to the historical interest rate times the net book value of the liability at the beginning of the interest period.

_____ 23. Contingent liabilities are liabilities that are known to exist but that are uncertain in amount.

_____ 24. Under the straight-line method of recognizing interest expense, a bond liability is shown on the balance sheet at the present value of future cash outflows discounted at the historical market rate of return.

_____ 25. The terms *face value* and *par value* are synonymous and refer to the principal amount of a bond.

_____ 26. If the coupon rate of interest is higher than the market interest rate, bonds will sell at discount.

_____ 27. Coupon bonds have coupons for the interest payments attached to the bond certificate.

_____ 28. A bond that is registered as to principal will have the bond owner's name on the bond certificate.

_____ 29. When the market rate of interest exceeds the coupon rate stated on bonds, the bonds will sell at a premium.

_____ 30. The historical interest rate is the market interest rate at the time the debt was initially issued.

_____ 31. Long-term liabilities net of unamortized premium or discount are recorded initially at the present value of all payments.

_____ 32. The discount on bonds payable represents additional interest that will be paid at the bond's maturity.

_____ 33. For a bond sold at a discount, the amount of cash paid for interest will be more than the amount of interest expense recorded.

_____ 34. In mortgage contracts, the lender is known as the mortgagee, and the borrower is known as the mortgagor.

_____ 35. Liabilities are generally classified on the balance sheet as current or by inderterminate term.

_____ 36. Current liabilities are valued on the balance sheet at their present value at the date and not at the amount that will be paid.

Matching

From the list of terms, select one term that is most closely associated with one descriptive phrase or statement that follows and place the letter for that term in the space provided.

a. bond principal
b. contingent liability
c. debenture bond
d. discount on bonds payable

e. effective-interest method
f. historical interest rate
g. liability
h. mortgage

i. premium on bonds payable
j. refunding
k. serial bonds

l. sinking fund
m. straight-line method

g 1. An obligation that involves a probable future sacrifice of resources, that results from a past transaction or event, and for which the entity has little or no discretion to avoid the transfer.

h 2. Contract in which the borrower pledges certain property as collateral security to the lender, with the provision that the title reverts to the lender if the loan or interest is not paid.

a 3. Face value or par value.

e 4. When allocated over the life of the bond, interest expense is increased.

j 5. New bonds are issued to obtain the funds to retire the old bonds when they come due.

b 6. A potential future obligation that arises from an event that has occurred in the past but for which the outcome is not yet known.

m 7. This method of interest expense recognition results in periodic interest expense that is constant over the life of the loan.

e 8. This method of interest expense recognition results in an interest charge each period that results in a constant interest rate.

k 9. Portions of the principal amount come due on a succession of maturity dates.

f 10. The market interest rate at the time the debt was issued.

a 11. This type of bond carries no specific collateral; instead, it is issued on the general credit of the business.

i 12. When allocated over the life of the bond, interest expense is decreased.

l 13. Cash or other assets are accumulated and used to pay the bonds when they mature.

Multiple Choice

Choose the best answer for each question or problem and enter the identifying letter in the space provided.

a 1. If the Hawkins Company Inc. issued bonds due in ten years at a discount, this indicates that:
a) the market rate of interest exceeded the coupon rate at the time the bonds were issued
b) the coupon rate of interest exceeded the market rate at the time the bonds were issued
c) the coupon rate equalled the market rate of interest at the time the bonds were issued
d) none of the above

c 2. The Zerke Corporation issued bonds on January 1, 19X1 that mature in ten years. The par value of the bonds was $100,000, and they were sold at 108 percent of par. If the premium is amortized by the straight-line method, the net long-term liability for the bonds on December 31, 19X1 will be:
a) $100,000
b) $106,400
c) $107,200
d) $108,000

d 3. Both the employer and the employee must make contributions for:
a) Unemployment Insurance premiums
b) Canada Pension Plan
c) employee's income tax
d) both a and b

C 4. The Johnson Corporation sold ten-year, 10 percent coupon bonds (face amount, $100,000) on January 1, 19X1 for 97 percent of their face value. Over the bonds' ten-year life, how much interest expense, in total, will the Johnson Corporation report in its income statement?
   a) $97,000
   b) $100,000
   c) $103,000
   d) $200,000

a 5. The Coral Corporation guarantees its product against defects for one year. In what year should the corporation report the warranty expense?
   a) in the year that the product is sold
   b) in the year that the product becomes defective and is repaired or replaced
   c) the cost of the warranty is included in the product's selling price; therefore, warranty expense is never recorded
   d) none of the above

C 6. The account Premium on Bonds should be shown on the balance sheet as a:
   a) contra account to Bonds Payable
   b) current liability
   c) noncurrent deferred credit
   d) none of the above

a 7. Coty Corporation issued a 7 percent, $100,000 bond issue at a price to yield the market interest rate of 8 percent. The bond pays interest semiannually. How much cash would be paid to Coty at the first interest payment date?
   a) $3,500
   b) $4,000
   c) $7,000
   d) $8,000

b 8. The Benin Corporation issued an 8 percent bond when the market interest rate was also 8 percent. The Benin bonds should have sold:
   a) at a discount
   b) at par
   c) at a premium
   d. cannot be determined with information given

a 9. If bonds are issued at a discount, the net long-term liability reported on the balance sheet:
   a) increases each year during the life of the bond issue
   b) decreases each year during the life of the bond issue.
   c) remains at the maturity value throughout the life of the bond issue
   d) remains at the issue price throughout the life of the bond issue

C 10. On July 1, 19X1, Lynn Limited, which publishes a weekly news magazine, sold 4,000 two-year subscriptions for $10 each. On its income statement for the year ending December 31, 19X1, what amount from the July 1 transaction should be reported as revenue?
   a) $2,500
   b) $5,000
   c) $10,000
   d) $20,000

____ 11. Which of the following is not descriptive of an executory contract?
   a) it involves an exchange of promises
   b) there is no mutual performance
   c) there is no current or past benefit
   d) a liability is recorded

____ 12. Kris Corporation purchased land for $15,000 and signed an 8 percent mortgage note for $10,000. Mortgage payments are $200 per month. Which of these statements is false?
   a) a portion of each payment represents interest expense
   b) the interest expense portion of each payment inceases over the mortgage term
   c) an excess of cash payment over interest expense is used to reduce the principal
   d) the interest expense portion of the first monthly payment will be $66.67

____ 13. These bonds can be exchanged for a specific number of common shares
   a) mortgage bonds
   b) debenture bonds
   c) convertible bonds
   d) collateral trust bonds

____ 14. On March 1, 19X1, Alan-Stein Inc. issued $100,000, 9 percent bonds that mature on January 1, 19X1. The bonds pay interest semiannually on January 1 and July 1. The bonds were sold on March 1, and cash of $101,500 was received. Which of these statements is correct?
   a) the bonds sold at par
   b) the bonds sold at a discount
   c) the bonds sold at a premium
   d) no conclusion about the selling price of the bonds can be determined from the information given

____ 15. On October 1, 19X1, Wyatt Limited issued $1 million, 12 percent bonds at par. The bonds pay interest semiannually on January 1 and July 1. For the year ending December 31, 19X1, Wyatt would report how much interest expense from this bond issue on its income statement?
   a) $120,000
   b) $60,000
   c) $30,000
   d) interest expense on this bond issue for 19X1 cannot be determined from the information given

____ 16. The June Company Ltd., which recognizes interest expense by the straight-line method, issued ten-year, 15 percent bonds (face amount, $100,000) on January 1, 19X1. On its 19X1 income statement, June reports bond interest expense of $14,200. For what amount were the bonds issued on January 1, 19X1?
   a) $92,000
   b) $100,000
   c) $108,000
   d) none of the above

____ 17. The Weaver Corporation issued a 14 percent, $100,000 bond issue at 108. The bond premium is being amortized on a straight-line basis over the bonds' ten-year life. On December 31, 19X1, the bond liability is carried on the balance sheet at $104,800. How many years has the bond issue been outstanding?
   a) four years
   b) five years
   c) six years
   d) none of the above

____ 18. The Chapman Corporation sold a $1 million bond issue at 103 percent of its par value. If the company recognizes interest expense by the effective-interest method:
   a) interest expense on the bond issue will increase each year
   b) interest expense on the bond issue will decrease each year
   c) interest expense on the bond issue will be the same amount each year
   d) none of the above

____ 19. When a bond issue is sold, the proceeds from the sale of the bonds equal:
   a) the present value of the maturity
   b) the present value of all the future interest payments during the life of the bond issue
   c) the sum of a and b

____ 20. Hume Limited had sales of typewriters totalling $50,000 for the year ending December 31, 19X1, its first year of operation. Hume provides free warranty service for eighteen months after the sale and estimates warranty costs to be 6 percent of sales. For the year, expenditures made for warranty repairs totalled $500. What should be the balance in the warranty liability account on December 31, 19X1 balance sheet?
   a) $500
   b) $2,500
   c) $3,000
   d) none of the above

____ 21. The Scotty Company Inc. issued $100,000 of par-value bonds several years ago. On January 1, 19X1, the bond premium account has a balance of $6,000 when $50,000 of the bonds are called at 104. What is the amount of the gain or loss on the retirement of the bonds?
   a) $1,000 gain
   b) $2,000 gain
   c) $4,000 gain
   d) $4,000 loss

____ 22. Refer to question 21. The balance in the bond premium account on January 1, 19X1, after the retirement of the $50,000 of bonds, would be:
   a) 0
   b) $3,000
   c) $6,000
   d) none of the above

____ 23. If bonds are issued at a premium and interest expense is recognized under the effective-interest method:
   a) the amount of premium amortized each year will increase
   b) the amount of the liability reported on the balance sheet will increase each year
   c) the amount of interest expense reported on the income statement will increase each year
   d) all of the above are true statements

____ 24. Which of these accounts would usually be classified as a long-term liability?
   a) Deferred Warranty Liability
   b) Premium on Bonds Payable
   c) Magazine Subscription Fees Received in Advance
   d) Witholding Taxes Payable

___ 25. Which of the following would be an example of an executory contract?
   a) a company sold a one-year subscription to its publication and received the subscription price in cash
   b) a customer places an order for merchandise to be picked up and paid for in one week
   c) a company sold an appliance and gave a warranty to replace defective parts within one year after sale.
   d) a company borrowed money from a bank to purchase a delivery van

___ 26. The Kick Corporation issued 10 percent, ten-year bonds several years ago when the market interest rate was 8 percent. The market interest rate is now 12 percent, and Kick purchases its own bonds in the market and retires them. Kick should report:
   a) a gain on the transaction
   b) a loss on the transaction
   c) neither a gain nor a loss
   d) cannot be determined from the information given

___ 27. The balance in the Estimated Warranty Liability account at the end of the period:
   a. represents the costs incurred for repairs made
   b. represents the estimated cost of repairs to be made under warranties in effect at that time
   c. should be identical to the balance in the Warranty Expense account
   d) should be closed to Retained Earnings, so that warranty costs and revenues will be matched

___ 28. A bond that is issued on the general credit of the business is commonly known as a:
   a) mortgage bond
   b) collateral trust bond
   c) debenture bond
   d) none of the above

___ 29. Which method of interest expense recognition results in a constant interest rate each period?
   a) straight-line method
   b) effective-interest method
   c) periodic-interest method
   d) none of the above

Exercises

1. The Roger Co. Inc. issued $400,000 of 10 percent, ten-year bonds for $354,120 on January 1, 19X1. Interest is paid semiannually on July 1 and January 1.

   Prepare 19X1 entries relative to the bond issue, assuming (a) that the bonds were sold to yield the market interest rate of 12 percent and (b) that interest expense is recognized on an effective-interest basis.

2. The Diamond Company Ltd. issued $500,000 of 12 percent, ten-year bonds at 104 on July 1, 19X1. Interest is paid semiannually on January 1 and July 1.

   Prepare 19X1 entries relative to the bond issue, assuming that interest expense is recognized on a straight-line basis.

3. Hammond Inc. provides a warranty on its product for one year after sale. Warranty costs are estimated to be 5 percent of the selling price. In 19X1, the company had sales of $150,000, which were subject to the warranty. During January 19X2, parts costing $3,600 were used to make repairs covered under warranty.

   Prepare entries for 19X1 and 19X2 for the sale and related warranty transactions.

4. The Marina Company Inc., on December 31, 19X5, has outstanding $200,000 of 4 percent bonds, which mature on December 31, 19X10. The bonds, which were sold to Marina on January 1, 19X1, have an unamortized discount of $6,000 on December 31, 19X5, the last interest payment date. On January 1, 19X6, Marina purchased $100,000 of its bonds in the open market for $82,000 and retired the bonds.

Prepare the January 1, 19X6 entry to record the retirement of the bonds.

PROBLEM 1 FOR SELF-STUDY

On June 30, Year 0, Avner Incorporated issues a three-year, $100,000 note bearing interest at the rate of 15 percent per year. That is, Avner Incorporated promises to pay $15,000 on June 30, Year 1; $15,000 on June 30, Year 2; and $115,000 on June 30, Year 3. The market rate of interest the date the note is issued is 10 percent.

a. compute the proceeds Avner Incorporated receives for its note.

b. Prepare an amortization schedule similar to that in Exhibit 9.1 for the life of the note.

c. Prepare journal entries that would be made on three dates: the date of issue; six months after the date of issue (assuming the books were closed then); and one year after the date of issue, assuming an interest payment is made then.

PROBLEM 2 FOR SELF-STUDY

Generally accepted accounting principals require that long-term monetary net liabilities be stated at the present value of the future cash flows discounted at the market rate of interest appropriate to the monetary items at the time they were initially recorded. Obligations under warranties are excluded from this rule, and warranties are stated at the estimated cost of providing warranty goods and services in the future.

Assume that the estimated future costs of a three-year warranty plan on products sold during Year 1 are as follows:

Year	Expected Cost
2	$ 500,000
3	600,000
4	900,000
Total	$2,000,000

Actual costs coincided with expectations in terms of timing and amount.

a. Prepare the journal entries for each of the Years 1 through 4 for this warranty plan following current generally accepted accounting principles.

b. Now assume that generally accepted accounting principles allow these liabilities to be shown at their present value. Prepare the journal entries for each of Years 1 through 4 for this warranty plan assuming that the warranty liability is stated at the present value of the future costs discounted at 10 percent. To simplify the calculations, assume that all warranty costs are incurred on December 31 of each year.

c. What theoretical agruments can be offered for the valuation basis in (b)?

ANSWERS TO SELF-STUDY QUESTIONS AND EXERCISES

True/False

1. F	10. T	19. F	28. T
2. F	11. T	20. T	29. F
3. T	12. F	21. T	30. T
4. F	13. T	22. T	31. T
5. T	14. F	23. F	32. T
6. F	15. T	24. F	33. F
7. F	16. T	25. T	34. T
8. F	17. T	26. F	35. F
9. T	18. F	27. T	36. F

Matching

1. g	5. j	9. k	13. l
2. h	6. b	10. f	
3. a	7. m	11. c	
4. d	8. e	12. i	

Multiple Choice

1. a	9. a	17. a	25. b
2. c	10. c	18. b	26. a
3. d	11. d	19. c	27. b
4. c	12. b	20. b	28. c
5. a	13. c	21. a	29. b
6. c	14. a	22. b	
7. a	15. c	23. a	
8. b	16. c	24. b	

Exercises

1.

		Dr.	Cr.
1/ 1:	Cash	$354,120	
19X1	Discount on Bonds Payable	45,880	
	Bonds Payable		$400,000
	To record sale of bonds at a discount.		
7/ 1:	Interest Expense	$ 21,247	
19X1	Discount on Bonds Payable		$ 1,247
	Cash		20,000
	To record interest expense and amortization of discount.		

Interest expense: $354,120 ×
0.06 = $21,247

		Dr.	Cr.
12/31:	Interest Expense	$ 21,322	
19X1	Discount on Bonds Payable		$ 1,322
	Interest Payable		20,000
	To record interest expense and amortization of discount.		

Interest expense: ($354,120 + $1,247) ×
0.06 = $21,322

2. 7/1:   Cash $520,000
      19X1   Bonds Payable $500,000
                 Premium on Bonds Payable   20,000
             To record sale of bonds at a premium.

      12/31: Interest Expense $ 29,000
      19X1   Premium on Bonds Payable   1,000
                 Interest Payable $ 30,000
              To record interest expense and amortization of
              premium.

3. 19X1   Cash (or Accounts Receivable) $150,000
              Warranty Expense   7,500
                 Sales $150,000
                 Estimated Warranty Liability   7,500
              To record sale and warranty
              liability.

      19X2:   Estimated Warranty Liability $ 3,600
                 Parts Inventory $ 3,600
              To record parts used in performing warranty work.

4. 1/ 1: Bonds Payable $100,000
      19X1   Gain on Retirement of Bonds $ 15,000
                 Discount on Bonds Payable   3,000
                 Cash   82,000
             To record retirement of bonds.

SUGGESTED SOLUTION TO PROBLEM 1
FOR SELF-STUDY

---

a. Present value of three payments of $15,000, discounted at 10 percent; see
   Table B.4, page 1069, three-period row, 10 percent column: $15,000 × 2.48685 $37,303
   Present value of one payment of $100,000 discounted at 10 percent for
   three periods; see Table B.2, page 1067, three-period row, 10 percent column:
   $100,000 × 0.75131   75,131
   Net Proceeds from Issue of Note $112,434

---

b. See Exhibit 9.4.

---

c. 6/30/Year 0: Cash $112,434
      Note Payable $100,000
      Premium on Note Payable   12,434
   Proceeds of issue of note.

   12/31/Year 0: Interest Expense $ 5,622
      Interest Payable $ 5,622
   See Exhibit 9.4; accrual of six months' interest = $11,243/2.

   6/30/Year 1: Interest Expense $ 5,621
   Interest Payable   5,622
   Premium on Note Payable   3,757
      Cash $ 15,000
   Interest expense for the remainder of the first year and
   cash payment made. Excess of cash payment over
   interest expense reduces note premium.

EXHIBIT 9.4
Amortization Schedule for Note with Face Value of $100,000 Issued for
$112,434, Bearing Interest at the Rate of 15 Percent of Face Value per
Year, Issued to Yield 10 Percent
(Problem 1 for Self-Study)

June 30 Year (1)	Loan Balance Start of Period (2)	Interest Expense for Period (3)	Payment (4)	Note Premium Amort- ization (5)	Note Premium At End of Period (6)	Net Loan Balance End of Period (7)
0					$12,434	$112,434
1	$112,434	$11,243	$ 15,000	$3,757	8,677	108,677
2	108,677	10,868	15,000	4,132	4,545	104,545
3	104,545	10,455	115,000	4,545	0	0

Column (2) = Column (7) from previous period.
Column (3) = 0.10 × Column (2).
Column (4)   Given.
Column (5) = Column (4) − Column (3) except Year 3.
Column (6) = Column (6) from previous period − Column (5) of this period.
Column (7) = Column (2) − Column (5) − $100,000 in Year 3.

SUGGESTED SOLUTION TO PROBLEM 2
FOR SELF-STUDY

a. Year 1	Warranty Expense		$2,000,000	
	Estimated Warranty Liability			$2,000,000
Year 2	Estimated Warranty Liability		$ 500,000	
	Cash and Other Accounts			$ 500,000
Year 3	Estimated Warranty Liability		$ 600,000	
	Cash and Other Accounts			$ 600,000
Year 4	Estimated Warranty Liability		$ 900,000	
	Cash and Other Accounts			$ 900,000

b. The present value of the future costs amounts on December 31, Year 1, discounted at 10 percent, is:

Year 2	$500,000 × 0.90909	$ 454,545
Year 3	$600,000 × 0.82645	495,870
Year 4	$900,000 × 0.75131	676,179
	Total	$1,626,594

Year 1	Warranty Expense	$1,626,594	
	Estimated Warranty Liability		$1,626,594
Year 2	Interest Expense	$ 162,659	
	Estimated Warranty Liability		$ 162,659
	0.10 × $1,626,594 = $162,659.		

Year 2	Estimated Warranty Liability	$ 500,000	
	Cash and Other Accounts		$ 500,000
Year 3	Interest Expense	$ 128,925	
	Estimated Warranty Liability		$ 128,925
	0.10 × ($1,626,594 + $162,659 −		
	$500,000) = $128,925.		
Year 3	Estimated Warranty Liability	$ 600,000	
	Cash and Other Accounts		$ 600,000
Year 4	Interest Expense	$ 81,818	
	Estimated Warranty Liability		$ 81,818
	0.10 × ($1,626,594 + $162,659 −		
	$500,000 + $128,925 − $600,000) =		
	0.10 × $818,178 = $81,818.		
Year 4	Estimated Warranty Liability	$ 899,996	
	Interest Expense	4	
	Cash and Other Accounts		$ 900,000
	There is a rounding error of $4 in the Estimated		
	Warranty Liability account at the end of Year 4.		
	Interest expense for Year 4 is therefore increased		
	by $4.		

c. The goods and services provided under the warranty plan must first be acquired for cash. Thus, even though customers will receive goods and services, the firm must expend cash at some point. To be consistent with monetary liabilities, these amounts should be discounted to their present value.

ASSIGNMENT MATERIAL

QUESTIONS

1. Review the meaning of the key terms listed on page 574.

2. For each of the following items, indicate whether the item meets all of the criteria of a liability. If so, how is it valued?
    a. Interest accrued but not paid on a note.
    b. Advances from customers for goods and services to be delivered later.
    c. Firm orders from customers for goods and services to be delivered later.
    d. Mortgages payable.
    e. Bonds payable.
    f. Product warranties.
    g. Fifteen-year cancellable lease on an office building.
    h. Damages the company must pay if a pending lawsuit is lost.
    i. Cost of restoring strip-mining sites after mining operations are completed.
    j. Contractual promises to purchase natural gas for each of the next ten years.

3. Describe the similarities and differences between the allowance method for uncollectables (see Chapter 6) and the allowance method for estimated warranty costs.

4. Generally accepted accounting principles (GAAP) specifically require the accrual of earned but unpaid wages and fringe benefits thereon. GAAP specifically require the accrual of earned but unused vacation pay under most circumstances. GAAP do not mention fringe benefits attached to vacation pay. Explain why this book might say that accrual of these items is required even though there is no specific pronouncement that mentions such a requirement.

5. A noted accountant once remarked that the optimal number of faulty TV sets for the XYZ Electric Co. Ltd. to sell is "not zero," even if XYZ promises to repair all faulty XYZ sets that break down, for whatever reason, within two years of purchase. Why could the optimal number be "not zero"?

6. A private school has a reporting year ending June 30. It hires teachers for a ten-month period, September of one year through June of the following year. It contracts to pay teachers in twelve monthly installments over the period September of one year through August of the next year. For the current academic year, the total contractual salaries to be paid to teachers is $360,000. How should this amount be accounted for in the financial statements issued June 30, at the end of the academic year?

7. While shopping in a store on July 5, Year 1, a customer slipped on the floor and sustained back injuries. On January 15, Year 2, the customer sued the store for $1 million. The case came to trial on April 30, Year 2. The jury's verdict was rendered on June 15, Year 2, with the store being found guilty of gross negligence. A damage award of $400,000 was granted to the customer. The store, on June 25, Year 2, appealed the decision to a higher court on the grounds that certain evidence had not been admitted by the lower court. The higher court ruled on November 1, Year 2 that the evidence should have been admitted. The lower court reheard the case beginning on March 21, Year 3. Another jury, on April 20, Year 3, again found the store guilty of gross negligence and awarded $500,000. On May 15, Year 3, the store paid the $500,000 judgment. When should a loss from these events be recognized by the supermarket? Explain your reasoning.

8. What factors determine the amount of money a firm actually receives when it offers a bond issue to the market?

9. A call premium is the difference between the call price of a bond and its par value. What is the purpose of such a premium?

10. The Discount on Bonds Payable account has a debit balance and, as such, could be treated as deferred charge or as a liability contra. Present the reasons supporting each alternative.

11. If a company borrows $1,000,000 by issuing, at par, twenty-year, 10 percent bonds with semiannual coupons, the total interest expense over the life of the issue is $2,000,000 (= 20 × 0.10 × $1,000,000). If a company undertakes a twenty-year mortgage or note with an implicit borrowing rate of 10 percent, the annual payments are $1,000,000/8.51356 = $117,460. (See Table B.4, page 1069, twenty-period row, 10 percent column.) The total mortgage payments are $2,349,200 (= 20 × $117,460), and the total interest expense over the life of the note or mortgage is $1,349,200 (= $2,349,200 − $1,000,000).

    Why are the amounts of interest expense different for these two means of borrowing for the same length of time at identical interest rates?

12. The following questions compare the effective-interest method and the straight-line method of accounting for interest expense on bonds.
    a. Which method gives higher interest expense in the first year for a bond issued at less than par value?
    b. Which method gives higher interest expense in the first year for a bond issued at more than par value?
    c. Which method gives higher interest expense in the last year for a bond issued at less than par value?
    d. Which method gives higher interest expense in the last year for a bond issued at more than par value?
    e. Which method involves the larger adjustment to net income in deriving funds provided by operations in the first year for a bond issued at more than par value?
    f. Which method involves the larger adjustment to net income in deriving funds provided by operations in the first year for a bond issued at less than par value?

g. What are the relative advantages and disadvantages of the straight-line method versus the effective-interest method of accounting for interest expense on a bond?

13. Are high-quality, long-term bonds always sound investments? A friend has $20,000 to invest to pay for a child's education expenses. The funds will be needed in four years. The friend believes that the 10 percent, semiannual coupon bonds of the Canadian government maturing in the year 2010 would be as safe and sound an investment as any available. What advice can you give?

14. Critics of historical-cost accounting for long-term debt argue that the procedures give management unreasonable opportunity to "manage" income with the timing of bond retirements. What phenomenon do these critics have in mind?

15. What purposes are served by restrictions placed on borrowing firms by bond indentures?

EXERCISES

16. *Journal entries for payroll.* During the current period, office employees earned wages of $200,000. Of this amount, $38,000 must be withheld from payments for income taxes, and 8 percent must be deducted for Social Insurance taxes. The employer must pay 11 percent of gross wages for Social Insurance taxes. The employer has promised to contribute 4 percent of gross wages to a profit-sharing fund, the proceeds from which are used to pay workers when they retire. Employees earned vacation pay estimated to be $9,000; estimated fringes are 20 percent of that amount.
   a. Prepare journal entries for these wage-related items.
   b. What is total wage and salary expense?

17. *Journal entries for payroll.* Prepare journal entries for the following wages, fringes, and accruals of Bages Limited. Factory employees earned $90,000 and office employees earned $60,000. The company must pay $27,000 to the government for withheld income taxes and 8 percent to the government for withheld Social Insurance taxes. The employer also owes 11 percent for Social Insurance taxes. The employer pays all costs of insurance plans; it owes $5,000 for health and life insurance premiums. The employer awards paid vacations to employees who have been working for a year or more. During the current period, employees earning 90 percent of the gross wages are expected to earn paid vacations, which is estimated to be 4 percent of their gross wages. Payroll taxes and fringe benefits are estimated to be 20 percent of vacation pay.

18. *Journal entries for estimated warranty liabilities and subsequent expenditures.* A new product introduced by Junn Corp. carries a two-year warranty against defects. The estimated warranty costs as a percentage of dollar sales are 3 percent in the year of sale and 5 percent in the next year. Sales (all on account) and actual warranty expenditures

(all paid in cash) for the first two years of the product's life were as follows:

	Sales	Actual Warranty Expenditures
Year 1	$400,000	$10,000
Year 2	500,000	35,000

    a. Prepare journal entries for the events of Year 1 and Year 2. Closing entries are not required.

    b. What is the balance in the Estimated Warranty Liability account at the end of Year 2?

19. **Using bond tables.** The Gonedes Co. Ltd. issues 12 percent, semiannual coupon bonds maturing in ten years. The face amount of the bonds is $1 million. The net cash proceeds to Gonedes Co. Ltd. from the bond issue amounts to $944,907.

    What interest rate will be used in applying the effective interest method over the life of this bond issue?

20. **Using bond tables.** Refer to Table B.6 on page 1071 for 12 percent, semiannual coupon bonds issued to yield 13 percent per year, compounded semiannually. All of the questions below refer to $1 million face value of such bonds.

    a. What are the initial issue proceeds for bonds issued to mature in 30 years?

    b. What is the book value of those bonds after five years?

    c. What is the book value of the bonds when they have twenty years until maturity?

    d. What are the initial issue proceeds of bonds issued to mature in twenty years? [Compare to your answer in part (c).]

    e. Write an equation for interest expense for the last six months before maturity.

    f. If the market rate of interest on the bonds is 14 percent, what is the market value of the bonds when they have twenty years to maturity?

    g. When the bonds have ten years until maturity, they trade in the market for 112.46 percent of par. What will be the effective market rate at that time?

21. **Using bond tables; computing interest expense.** Refer to Table B.5, page 1070, for 10 percent, semiannual coupon bonds. On January 1, Year 1, Souverain Limited issued $1 million of face-value, 10 percent, semiannual coupon bonds maturing in twenty years (on December 31, Year 20) at a price to yield 14 percent per year, compounded semiannually. Use the effective interest method of computing interest expense.

    a. What were the proceeds of the original issue?

    b. What was the interest expense for the first half of Year 1?

    c. What was the interest expense for the second half of Year 1?

    d. What was the book value of the bonds on January 1, Year 6 (when the bonds have fifteen years until maturity)?

    e. What was the interest for the first half of Year 6?

22. **Gain or loss on bond retirement.** Refer to the data in Exercise 21.
    a. By what amount did cash used for debt service differ from interest expense?
    b. On January 1, Year 11 (when bonds have ten years to maturity), $100,000 face value of bonds are purchased in the open market and retired. The market rate of interest at the time of purchase is 12 percent compounded semiannually. What gain or loss will Souverain Limited report?

23. **Journal entry for short-term note payable.** On December 1, the O'Brien Co. Ltd. obtained a 90-day loan for $15,000 from the Twin City Bank at an annual interest rate of 12 percent. On the maturity date, the note was renewed for another 30 days, with a cheque being issued to the bank for the accrued interest. The O'Brien Co. Ltd. closes its books annually at December 31.
    a. Present entries on the books of the O'Brien Co. Ltd. to record the issue of the note, the year-end adjustment, the renewal of the note, and the payment of cash at maturity of the renewed note.
    b. Present entries at maturity date of the original note for the following variations in the settlement of the note of the O'Brien Co. Ltd.
    (1) The original note is paid at maturity.
    (2) The note is renewed for 30 days; the new note bears interest at 15 percent per annum. Interest on the old note was not paid at maturity.

24. **Partial amortization schedule for note.** The Holmes Sales Co. Inc. sells a building lot to N. Wolfe on September 1 for $27,000. The down payment is $3,000, and minimum payments of $265 a month are to be made on the contract. Interest at the rate of 12 percent per annum on the unpaid balance is deducted from each payment, and the balance is applied to reduce the principal. Payments are made as follows: October 1, $265; November 1, $265; December 1, $600; January 2, $265.
    Prepare a partial amortization schedule showing payments, interest and principal, and remaining liability at each of these dates. Round amounts to the nearest dollar.

25. **Partial amortization schedule for mortgage.** Lynne Michals secures a mortgage loan of $112,000 from the Jones Trust Co. Ltd. The terms of the mortgage require monthly payments of $1,660. The interest rate to be applied to the unpaid balance is 9 percent per year.
    Prepare a partial amortization schedule showing payments, interest and principal, and remaining liability for the first four months of the loan. Round amounts to the nearest dollar.

26. **Journal entries for effective interest and straight-line methods of computing bond interest.** On October 1, Year 1, Howell Stores, Inc. issues twenty-year, first mortgage bonds with a face value of $1,000,000. The proceeds of the issue are $1,060,000. The bonds bear interest at the rate of 10 percent per year, payable semiannually at April 1 and October 1. Howell Stores Inc. closes its books annually at December 31. Round amounts to the nearest dollar.
    a. Present dated journal entries related to the bonds from October 1, Year 1 through October 1, Year 2, inclusive. Assume that Howell

Stores, Inc. uses the straight-line method to recognize interest expense.

b. Repeat instructions for part (a), but assume that the company uses the effective-interest method. The effective-interest rate to be used is 9.3 percent, compounded semiannually.

27. *Amortization schedule for bonds.* Hanouille Inc. issues 10 percent, semiannual coupon bonds maturing five years from the date of issue. Interest of 5 percent of the face value of $100,000 is payable January 1 and July 1. The bonds are issued to yield 12 percent, compounded semiannually.

a. What are the initial issue proceeds received by Hanouille Inc.?

b. Construct an amortization schedule for this bond issue, similar to that in Exhibit 9.2.

c. By how much does interest expense for the first year (note *year*, not first six-month period) of the bond's life under the effective interest method differ from that under the straight-line method?

d. Assume that at the end of the third year of the bond's life, $10,000 face value of bonds are called and retired for 103 percent of par. Give the journal entry to record the retirement.

28. *Accounting for bond issue and subsequent interest including journal entries.* The Central Power Company Ltd. issued $2 million bonds in two series, A and B. Each series had face amount of $1 million and was issued at prices to yield 11 percent. Issue A contained 10 percent, semi-annual coupons. Issue B contained 12 percent, semiannual coupons. Issues A and B both mature 30 years from issue date.

Answer the following questions for issue A. Round amounts to the nearest dollar.

a. What is the issuing price of the bonds?

b. Make the journal entry for the date of bond issue.

c. Using the effective-interest method, show the journal entries made on the first semiannual interest payment date.

d. Repeat part (c) for the second and third payment dates.

e. Show the semiannual entry if straight-line method is used.

29. *Accounting for bond issue and subsequent interest including journal entries.* Refer to the data in Exercise 28. Work through the Exercise for issue B.

30. *Liability for sales tax.* The new bookkeeper for Courtis Company forgot to set up a special account for the 5 percent provincial sales tax and included the tax in sales. Eighty percent of the company's sales are subject to sales tax; the remainder are sales to tax-exempt wholesalers. The sales account has a balance of $834,288 at the end of the period. Make the appropriate entry to remit the sales tax and correctly state revenues. What is the correct amount of Sales?

31. *Liability for product warranties.* Kennedy Corp. sells a product with a one-year warranty. At December 31, 19X1 after closing adjustments, the liability account has a balance of $60,000, reflecting 800 units sold this past year still expected to come in for warranty service. The expected failure rate for this product is 3 percent and the average war-

ranty cost per item serviced equals 5 percent of selling price. Of the items sold in 19X1, 1,300 were returned for service before year-end. What was the amount of 19X1 sales?

PROBLEMS AND CASES

32. *Allowance method for warranties; reconstructing transactions.* Colantoni Co. Inc. sells appliances, all for cash. All acquisitions of appliances during a year are debited to the Merchandise Inventory account. The company provides warranties on all of its products, guaranteeing to make repairs within one year of the date of sale as required for any of its appliances that break down. The company has many years of experience with its products and warranties.

The schedule shown in Exhibit 9.5 contains trial balances for the Colantoni Co. Inc. at the end of Year 1 and Year 2. The trial balances for the end of Year 1 are the Adjusted Preclosing Trial Balance (after all adjusting entries have been properly made) and the final Postclosing Trial Balance. The trial balance shown for the end of Year 2 is taken before any adjusting entries of any kind, although entries have been made to the estimated Liability for Warranty Repairs account during Year 2 as repairs have been made. Colantoni Co. Inc. closes its books once each year.

At the end of Year 2, the management of Colantoni Co. Inc. analyzes the appliances sold within the preceding twelve months. All appliances in the hands of customers that are still covered by warranty are clas-

EXHIBIT 9.5
COLANTONI CO. INC.
(Problem 32)

Trial Balance — End of Year 1	Adjusted Preclosing Dr.	Adjusted Preclosing Cr.	Postclosing Dr.	Postclosing Cr.
Estimated Liability for Warranty Repairs		$ 6,000		$ 6,000
Merchandise Inventory	$ 100,000		$100,000	
Sales		800,000		
Warranty Expense	18,000			
All Other Accounts	882,000	194,000	110,000	204,000
Totals	$1,000,000	$1,000,000	$210,000	$210,000

Trial Balance — End of Year 2	Unadjusted Trial Balance Dr.	Unadjusted Trial Balance Cr.
Estimated Liability for Warranty Repairs	$ 15,000	
Merchandise Inventory	820,000	
Sales		$1,000,000
Warranty Expense	—	—
All Other Accounts	265,000	100,000
Totals	$1,100,000	$1,100,000

sified as follows: those sold on or before June 30 (more than six months old); those sold after June 30, but on or before November 30 (more than one month, but less than six months old); and those sold on or after December 1. One-half of 1 percent of the appliances sold more than six months ago are estimated to require repair, 5 percent of the appliances sold one to six months before the end of the year are estimated to require repair, and 8 percent of the appliances sold within the last month are assumed to require repair. From this analysis, management estimated that $5,000 of repairs still would have to be made in Year 3 on the appliances sold in Year 2. Ending inventory on December 31, Year 2 is $120,000

a. What was the total of acquisitions of merchandise inventory during Year 2?
b. What is the cost of goods sold for Year 2?
c. What was the dollar amount of repairs made during Year 2?
d. What is the Warranty Expense for Year 2?
e. Give journal entries for repairs made during Year 2, for the warranty expense for Year 2, and for cost of goods sold for Year 2.

33. *Nonmonetary liabilities; reconstructing transactions.* The Myrtle Lunch sells coupon books that patrons may use later to purchase meals. Each coupon book sells for $17 and has a face value of $20. That is, each book can be used to purchase meals with menu prices of $20. On July 1, redeemable unused coupons with face value of $1,500 were outstanding. During July, 250 coupon books were sold; during August, 100; during September, 100. Cash receipts exclusive of coupons were $1,200 in July, $1,300 in August, and $1,250 in September. Coupons with a face value of $2,700 were redeemed by patrons during the three months.

a. If the Myrtle Lunch had a net income of $500 for the quarter ending September 30, how large were expenses?
b. What effect, if any, do the July, August, and September coupon sales and redemptions have on the right-hand side of the September 30 balance sheet?

34. *Nonmonetary liabilities; journal entries.* The Lambert Co. Ltd. sells service contracts to repair copiers at $300 per year. When the contract is signed, the $300 fee is collected and the Service Contract Fees Received in Advance account is credited. Revenues on contracts are recognized on a quarterly basis during the year in which the coverage is in effect. On January 1, 1,000 service contracts were outstanding. Of these, 500 expired at the end of the first quarter, 300 at the end of the second quarter, 150 at the end of the third quarter, and 50 at the end of the fourth quarter. Sales and service during the year came to these amounts (assume that all sales occurred at the beginning of the quarter):

	Sales of Contracts	Service Expenses
First Quarter	$120,000 (400 contracts)	$50,000
Second Quarter	240,000 (800 contracts)	60,000
Third Quarter	90,000 (300 contracts)	45,000
Fourth Quarter	60,000 (200 contracts)	55,000

a. Prepare journal entries for the first three quarters of the year for the Lambert Co. Ltd. Assume that quarterly reports are prepared on March 31, June 30, and September 30.

b. What is the balance in the Service Contract Fees Received in Advance account on December 31?

35. *Journal entries for purchase with existing mortgage; subsequent interest entries.* On June 1, the Loebbecke Co. Inc. purchases a warehouse from F.S. Brandon for $600,000, of which $100,000 is assigned to the land and $500,000 to the building. There is a mortgage on the property payable to the Hamilton Life Insurance Co. Ltd., which, together with the accrued interest, will be assumed by the purchaser. It bears interest at the rate of 12 percent per year. The balance due on the mortgage is $240,000. The principal of the mortgage will be paid on April 1 and October 1 of each year in installments of $20,000 each. The principal payments of $20,000 are in addition to the interest of 6 percent per six-month period on the outstanding balance. A ten-year second mortgage for $150,000 is issued to F.S. Brandon; it bears interest at the rate of 15 percent per year, payable on June 1 and December 1. A cheque is drawn to complete the purchase.

The Loebbecke Co. Inc. closes its books once a year on December 31. Prepare journal entries for June 1, October 1, and December 1.

36. *Accounting for investment in bonds.* On April 1, Year 1, the Oliver Co. Ltd. acquired $1,000,000 par value of bonds of Bret Corp. for $1,398,000. Costs of acquisition amounted to an additional $2,000. The bonds bear interest at 15 percent per year, payable on March 31 and September 30, and mature on March 31, Year 10. Use the straight-line method to recognize interest revenue.

a. Present journal entries on the books of the Oliver Co. Ltd. from April 1, Year 1 through March 31, Year 2, inclusive. Assume that the books are closed annually on December 31.

b. Present the journal entry (or entries) for the sale of the bonds on August 1, Year 4 at 103.5 plus accrued interest.

37. *Operations of a syndicate and risk of interest rate fluctuations.* During October 1979, MBI arranged with a syndicate of investment bankers to borrow $1 billion. MBI and the syndicate reached agreement on MBI's borrowing rate and the amounts the syndicate would pay to MBI on a Friday. Over the weekend, the Bank of Canada took actions that drastically increased interest rates. The members of the syndicate were responsible for any difference between the amount they had obligated themselves to pay to MBI and the amount for which they could sell the bonds during the following week.

a. Did the syndicate gain or lose by the change in interest rates over the weekend?

b. What sorts of actions might members of the syndicate take to insulate themselves from involuntary speculation in interest rates over the weekend?

38. *Managing income and the debt-equity ratio through bond retirement.* Meyney Limited issued $40 million of 5 percent, semiannual coupon bonds many years ago at par. The bonds now have twenty

years until scheduled maturity. Because market interest rates have risen to 12 percent, the market value of the bonds has dropped to 63 percent of par. Mayney Limited has $5 million of current liabilities and $35 million of owners' equity in addition to the $40 million of long-term debt in its financial structure. The debt-equity ratio is 56 percent [= ($40 + $5)/($5 + $40 + $35)]. (Owners' equity includes an estimate of the current year's income.) The president of Meyney Limited is concerned about boosting reported income for the year, which is about $8 million for the year in the absence of any other actions. Also, the debt-equity ratio appears to be larger than that of other firms in the industry. The president wonders what would be the impact on net income and the debt-equity ratio of issuing at par new 12 percent, semiannual coupon bonds to mature in twenty years and using the proceeds to retire the outstanding bond issue. Assume that such action is taken and that any gain on bond retirement is a nontaxable capital gain.

   a. Prepare the journal entries for the issue of new bonds in amount required to raise funds to retire the old bonds and retirement of the old bonds.
   b. What is the effect on income for the year? Give both dollar and percentage amounts.
   c. What is debt-equity ratio after the transaction?

39. *Financial institutions holding bonds of issuers in financial difficulties may find the book value and the market of the bonds to be quite different; should this change be recognized in accounting; troubled debt restructuring.* On January 1, Year 1, First National Bank (FNB) acquired $10 million of face value bonds issued on that date by the Occidental Oceanic Power Systems (OOPS). The bonds carry 12 percent, semiannual coupons and were to mature twenty years from the issue date. The bonds were issued by OOPS, and purchased by FNB, at par.

   By Year 6, OOPS was in severe financial difficulty and threatened to default on the bonds. After much negotiation with FNB (and other creditors), it agreed to repay the bond issue, but only on less burdensome terms. OOPS agreed to pay 5 percent per year, semiannually, for 25 years and to repay the principal on January 1, Year 31, or 25 years after the negotiation. FNB will receive $250,000 each six months starting with July 1, Year 6 and $10 million on January 1, Year 31. By January 1, Year 6, OOPS was being charged 20 percent per year, compounded semiannually, for its new long-term borrowings.

   a. What is the value of the bonds that FNB holds? That is, what is the present value of the newly promised cash payments when discounted at OOPS' current borrowing rate?
   b. Consider two accounting treatments for this negotiation:
      (1) Write down the bonds to the value computed in part (a) and base future interest revenue computations on that new book value and the new historical interest rate of 20 percent per year, compounded semiannually. (What loss would FNB recognize?)
      (2) Make no entry to record the negotiation and record interest revenue as the amount of cash, $250,000, received semiannually.
         Over the new life of the bond issue, how will total income vary as a function of the method chosen?
   c. Which of these two methods would you recommend and why?

DECISION CASE 9-1

Your Aunt Maud recently received an inheritance and is considering the purchase of $50,000 to $100,000 in shares of Feltham Inc. or Mattesich Ltd. She has given you condensed financial statements of these two companies for the current period, presented in Exhibit 9.6.

EXHIBIT 9.6
FELTHAM INC. AND MATTESICH LTD.
Condensed Financial Statements

Balance Sheet
December 31, Year 11
(thousands of dollars)

	Feltham Inc.	Mattesich Ltd.		Feltham Inc.	Mattesich Ltd.
Current Assets	$ 542	$ 268	Current Liabilities	$ 268	$ 133
Plant and Equipment	2,051	1,027	Bonds Payable	800	400
Bond Discount	77	—	Bond Premium	—	28
			Shareholders' Equity	1,602	734
	$2,670	$1,295		$2,670	$1,295

Income Statement
Year Ended December 31, Year 11
(dollars in thousands, except per share amounts)

	Feltham Inc.	Mattesich Ltd.
Sales	$2,398	$1,204
Less: Cost of Sales	(1,439)	(722)
Gross Profit	$ 959	$ 482
Selling and Administrative Expenses	(501)	(253)
Operating Profit	$ 458	$ 229
Bond Interest	(56)	(30)
Net Income Before Income Tax	$ 402	$ 199
Income Tax	(161)	(80)
Net Income	$ 241	$ 119
Earnings per Share	$ 2.41	$ 1.19

Having been advised in advance of Aunt Maud's interest, you made inquiries about the operations of the two companies and find that the operations of the two companies are similar; the only differences between the two companies appear to relate to size and financing activities. The financial statements appear to reflect the operating similarities. The companies own similar productive assets of the same age.

You determine that one difference between the two companies is their bond financing. On January 1, Year 2, both companies issued bonds with interest payable annually on December 31. Feltham Inc. issued at par $800,000, 7 percent bonds maturing on December 31, Year 11; and Mattesich Ltd. issued at 110.59, $400,000, 8 percent bonds maturing on December 31, Year 21. On December 31, Year 11, Feltham Inc. redeemed the 7 percent issue primarily from the proceeds of an issue at 90.33 of $800,000, 14 percent bonds maturing on December 31, Year 21, yielding a return of 16 percent.

Both companies follow the policy of amortizing the bond premium or discount by the effective-interest method.

The shares of Feltham Inc. are currently trading $15.00 per share, and the shares of Mattesich Ltd. at $7.40 per share.

Which company's shares would you advise Aunt Maud to purchase? Explain how you arrived at your recommendation.

CHAPTER TEN

LIABILITIES: ADVANCED TOPICS

CHAPTER OUTLINE

- Contracts and Long-Term Notes: Interest Imputation
- Leases
- Off-Balance-Sheet Financing
- Pensions
- Summary of Corporate Pension Accounting by Employer
- Income Tax Accounting and Deferred Income Taxes
- An International Perspective

Chapter 9 discussed the concept of an accounting liability and described the accounting for current liabilities, long-term bonds, and long-term notes. This chapter examines more controversial issues in liability recognition, valuation, and accounting. The chapter discusses the accounting for long-term notes payable where the historical interest rate must be imputed, the accounting for leases and pensions, off-balance-sheet financing, and problems in accounting for income taxes and pensions. The accounting issues associated with these topics are complex and are explored more fully in intermediate accounting texts.

carrying charges
The costs of borrowing, including interest and service charges.

implicit interest
Interest not explicitly paid or received. All arms-length transactions involving the deferred payment or receipt of cash involve interest, whether explicitly mentioned or not.

CONTRACTS AND LONG-TERM NOTES:
INTEREST IMPUTATION

Real estate is often purchased on a *land contract*. Equipment is frequently acquired on the installment plan, and the liability is called an *equipment contract*. Such contracts usually require periodic payments. Sometimes the contract provides for an explicit interest rate. Many contracts, however, do not state an explicit interest rate. Instead, so-called **carrying charges** are added to the purchase price and the total is divided over a certain number of months without any specific charge being indicated for interest. The "principal" or "face amount" in this case actually includes **implicit interest**.

Long-term liabilities carrying no explicit interest should be stated at the present value of the future cash payments.[1] The interest rate used in discounting is the rate appropriate to the particular borrower given the amount and terms of the borrowing arrangement at the time the liability is recorded. It is called the **imputed interest rate**. The difference between the present value and the face value of the liability represents interest to be recognized over the period of the loan. The next two sections discuss two acceptable ways to compute the present value of the liability and the amount of imputed interest.

imputed interest rate
The prevailing rate of interest currently used in the economy. This rate is used as the basis for making present value calculations on financial instruments.

BASE INTEREST RATE ON MARKET VALUE OF ASSET

The first approach uses the market value of the asset acquired as a basis for computing the present value of the liability. For example, assume that a piece of equipment can be bought for $10,520 cash. The equipment is purchased in return for a single-payment note with face amount of $16,000 payable in three years. The implied interest rate is about 15 percent per year. (That is, $1.15^3 \times 10,520$ is approximately equal to $16,000.) The journal entry using this approach would be:[2]

Equipment	$10,520	
Note Payable		$10,520

The record purchase of equipment using the known cash price.
The amount for the note is inferred from the known cash
price of the equipment.

At the end of each accounting period that intervenes between the acquisition of the equipment and repayment of the note, journal entries would be made for depreciation of the equipment. These are not shown. Journal entries must also be made to recognize interest expense. Assume that the

---

[1] The CICA has applied the concept of present value in a limited way because of the uncertainties of estimating future cash flows and selecting a discount rate. The concept is applied in the *CICA Handbook* recommendation on capitalizing capital leases and pensions considered later in this chapter. On the other hand, the application of the concept to future income tax assets and liabilities is explicitly rejected. It appears that the *CICA Handbook* would recommend the use of present value as a general practice only where the future cash flows and the discount rate can be reasonably and objectively estimated. At the time of writing, the *CICA Handbook* does not include a recommendation on the use of present value for discounting long-term liabilities, except when determining the fair value of noncurrent assets or obligations in business combinations. In this limited case, discounting may be considered an aid in valuation.

[2] An alternative approach to recording this transaction would be:

Equipment	$10,520	
Discount on Notes Payable	5,480	
Note Payable		$16,000

This would change the amortization entry (1) to:

Interest Expense	$1,578	
Discount on Note Payable		$1,578

Both approaches satisfy the accounting objectives of (a) systematic amortization and (b) making the carrying value of the note equal the face value at maturity.

note was issued at the beginning of a year. The entries for the three years would be:

(1) Interest Expense	$ 1,578	
Notes Payable		$ 1,578
Entry made one year after issuance of note. Interest is 0.15 × $10,520. The amount is not paid in cash but is added to the principal amount of the liability.		
(2) Interest Expense	$ 1,815	
Notes Payable		$ 1,815
Entry made one year after entry above, two years after issuance of note. Interest is 0.15 × ($10,520 + $1,578).		
(3) Interest Expense	$ 2,087	
Note Payable		$2,087
Entry made one year after entry above, three years after issuance of note. Interest is 0.15 × ($10,520 + $1,578 + $1,815). Balance in note payable now $16,000 (= $10,520 + $1,578 + $1,815 + $2,087).		
(4) Note Payable	$16,000	
Cash		$16,000
To repay note at maturity.		

Of the $16,000 paid at maturity, $5,480 represents interest accumulated on the note since its issue.

USE OF MARKET INTEREST RATE TO ESTABLISH MARKET VALUE OF ASSET AND PRESENT VALUE OF NOTE

If the firm purchased used equipment with the same three-year note, it might be unable to establish a reliable estimate of the current market value of the asset acquired. The firm would then use the interest rate it would have to pay for a similar loan in the open market to find the present value of the note. This is the second acceptable method for quantifying the amount of the liability and computing the imputed interest. Suppose that the market rate for notes such as the one above is 12 percent compounded annually, rather than 15 percent. The present value at 12 percent per year of the $16,000 note due in three years is $11,388 (= $16,000 × 0.71178; see Table B.2 on page 1067, three-period row, 12 percent column). The entry to record the purchase of used equipment financed with the note would be:

Equipment	$11,388	
Note Payable		$11,388
To record purchase of equipment. Cost of equipment is inferred from known interest rate.		

Entries would be made at the end of each period to recognize interest expense and to increase the principal amount of the liability. After the third period, the principal amount of the liability would be $16,000.

TOTAL EXPENSE IS INDEPENDENT OF INTEREST RATE

In the first case, the equipment is recorded at $10,520 and there is $5,480 of imputed interest. In the second case, the equipment is recorded at $11,388 and there is $4,612 of imputed interest. The total expense over the combined lives of the note and the equipment — interest plus depreciation — is the same, $16,000, no matter which interest rate is used. Over long enough time periods, total expense equals the total cash expenditure; accrual accounting changes only the timing of the expense recognition.

LONG-TERM NOTES HELD AS RECEIVABLES

A note that is the long-term liability of the borrower is a long-term asset of the lender, who will show the asset in the Long-Term Note Receivable account at its present value. The rate at which the lender discounts the note should, in theory, be the same as that used by the borrower but, in practice, the two rates sometimes differ. The lender's accounting mirrors the borrower's; the lender has interest revenue where the borrower has interest expense.

LEASES

Many firms acquire rights to use assets through long-term noncancellable leases. A company might, for example, agree to lease an office for five years, or an entire building for forty years, promising to pay a fixed periodic fee for the duration of the lease. Promising to make an irrevocable series of lease payments commits the firm just as surely as does a bond indenture or mortgage, and the accounting is similar in many cases.

This section examines two methods of accounting for long-term, noncancellable leases: the operating lease method and the capital lease method. The accounting for leases is based on the concept that the party that carries substantially all of the risks and benefits should reflect the asset in its financial statements.

To illustrate these two methods, suppose that Myers Inc. wants to acquire a computer that has a three-year life and costs $45,000. Assume that Myers Inc., can borrow money for three years at 15 percent per year. The computer manufacturer is willing to sell the equipment for $45,000 or to lease it for three years. Myers Inc. is responsible for maintenance and repair of the computer whether it is leased or purchased.

Assume that the lease is signed on January 1, Year 1 and that payments on the lease are due on December 31, Year 1, Year 2, and Year 3. In practice, lease payments are usually made in advance, but the computations in the example are simpler if we assume payments at the end of the year. Compound interest computations show that each lease payment must be $19,709. (The present value of $1 paid at the end of this year and each of the next two years is $2.28323 when the interest rate is 15 percent per year. See Table B.4, page 1069. Because the lease payments must have a present value of $45,000, each payment must be $45,000/2.28323 = $19,709.)

CHOOSING THE ACCOUNTING METHOD

When a journal entry debits an asset account and credits a liability account, the debt-equity ratio (total liabilities ÷ total equities) increases, making the company appear more risky. Given a choice, most companies prefer not to show an asset and a related liability on the balance sheet, as would be required for either an installment purchase or capital lease, where both the asset and liability appear on the balance sheet. Many managements also prefer to recognize expenses later rather than sooner for financial reporting. These preferences have led companies to structure asset acquisitions so that the financing takes the form of an operating lease.

The *CICA Handbook* has established relatively stringent requirements for accounting for long-term noncancellable leases. A lease must be accounted for as a capital lease if it meets any one of three conditions.[3]

1. There is reasonable assurance that the lease will retain ownership of the leased property by the end of the lease term. This would imply either an agreement for transfer of title or a bargain purchase option.

2. The lease term is of such duration that substantially all of the economic benefits of the property will accrue to the lessee. As a rule of thumb, when the lease term extends more than 75 percent of the economic life of the asset, this is deemed to have occurred.

3. The lessor has substantially recouped its investment in the asset by the return generated by this lease. If the present value of the lease payments at the signing date exceeds 90 percent of the fair market value of the asset, this is considered to have occurred.

Each of these conditions indicates that the risks and rewards of ownership of the asset have passed to the lessee. Thus, in economic substance, the lessee has acquired an asset and agreed to pay for it over an extended period. It is therefore appropriate that the lessee's books show the asset and associated liability.

D I S C U S S I O N   C A S E   2 2

Accounting Across Borders

With the globalization of business and capital markets, there is an ever-increasing need for international comparability of financial statements. Comparable financial statements would bring benefits to U.S. and foreign companies in three main areas of business and finance:

• First, *in conducting competitive surveillance. Because of growing foreign competition, CFOs of U.S. companies are users of*   *(continued)*

---

[3] *CICA Handbook*, section 3065.

(continued)

both their own and other companies' financial statements. It is difficult, if not impossible, to understand the strengths and weaknesses of one's company vis-à-vis its foreign competitors without the solid grasp of relative profitability, liquidity, and financial "staying power" that comparable financial statements can provide.

- *Second, in managing relationships with customers, suppliers, and others.* To cope with today's rapid pace of change in technology and volatility in world markets, companies need to manage for maximum flexibility. More than ever before, this demands a careful assessment of the financial wherewithal of foreign customers. It also means constantly staying on top of alternative sources of overseas supply and potential foreign business partners for international alliances and joint ventures.

- *Third, in raising capital abroad or investing in foreign securities.* Companies have more options today in terms of both investing and financing. This relatively recent development has come about as a result of increased capital mobility and an easing of restrictions on foreign investors by local securities regulators. Examples of the latter include the SEC's Rule 144A, which eases restrictions on private placements by foreign companies, and its multijurisdictional agreement, which eases restrictions on some Canadian companies.

Growing numbers of companies are taking advantage of these new options to gain a higher rate of return or lower cost of capital, to diversify their investment portfolios or shareholder bases, or to raise capital abroad because it gives them valuable local publicity for brand names and markets. Whatever the reason, the result is that growing numbers of corporate treasurers — both U.S. and foreign — need to understand other countries' financial statements to facilitate raising capital or managing investments.

In all three of these areas, the lack of comparable financial statements is a problem — probably an even bigger problem than most companies realize. Financial statements are similar in appearance, a similarity that masks very fundamental — and very important — differences in accounting principles.

For example, Telefonica, Spain's largest industrial company and a veteran filer of 20-Fs ever since they floated the world's first multi-country simultaneous offering in the mid-1980s, reported 1990 net income under U.S. GAAP of 176 billion pesetas, more than double the 76 billion pesetas it reported under Spanish GAAP. The difference was due mainly to an add-back of the incremental depreciation on assets carried at historical cost for U.S. GAAP, but written up to more recent market values under Spanish GAAP. The effect of this difference in basis on shareholders' equity, however, went in the opposite direction, resulting in an equity of about 15 percent less under U.S. GAAP as the book value of the assets was marked back to cost.

(continued)

(continued)

In another example, in 1989, the year in which U.S.-based SmithKline Beckman merged with U.K.-based Beecham, SKB's post-merger earnings, properly prepared in accordance with the U.K.'s Companies Act, were £130 million. This was quite a bit more than the £87 million that appeared in their U.S. annual report as a result of reconciliation procedures accepted by the SEC.

The difference resulted primarily from the income statement effects of different asset bases arising from treating the merger as a pooling for U.K. purposes and as a purchase for U.S. purposes. Even more troubling, the differences resulted in shareholders' equity of £3.5 billion in the U.S., but a negative £300 million in the U.K. After the release of these figures, SmithKline's stock in the U.S. was trading at 17 percent below the shares listed on the London exchange. The disparity was not surprising, given the startling differences in reported results under the two different sets of accounting rules.

Not-So-Easy Answers

What can be done to make the results more comparable? There are several possibilities:

• The standard-setting bodies of the world can take the initiative in reaching agreements as to common accounting treatments. Through a network of bilateral and multilateral cooperation, the FASB and its counterparts around the world could hammer out a series of agreements similar to the reciprocity agreements the SEC is working out with other securities regulators. The SEC is already in the trial stage of its reciprocity agreement with Canada. If the results are positive, it will consider expanding the agreement to the U.K.

• The securities regulators of the world could agree to acknowledge the authority of some transnational organization in international standard setting. The organization most likely to succeed is the International Accounting Standards Committee. Formed in 1973, IASC's early standards were very liberal because they were intended to accommodate the accounting principles of virtually every country. By being so liberal, IASC's standards gained acceptance, but they offered little hope of international comparability.

The emergence of the International Organization of Securities Commissions has forced IASC to take a different stance. IOSCO was formed in 1975 to promote the free flow of capital across borders. To remove the barriers set up by differences in accounting standards, IOSCO told IASC that it would enforce IASC's standards if IASC would reduce the number of acceptable treatments in its existing standards and fill in the gaps for any standards that are missing. To achieve this objective, on January 1, 1989, IASC issued E32, a sweeping set of guidelines designed to eliminate alternatives. It has also set out to beef up its financial resources and

(continued)

(continued)

staffing to address the many issues that remain.

If successful, this effort could mean some unexpected, maybe even unpopular changes for U.S. companies. This fall, IASC plans to issue an exposure draft, to become effective immediately, that would eliminate LIFO as a method of inventory valuation. And, as this issue [March/April 1992] of *Financial Executive* goes to press, IASC is preparing to issue an exposure draft on pooling of interest, with the hope of introducing a new standard in mid-1993.

• Some future alternatives can be developed, evolving from a combination of fine-tuning of one or both of the above possibilities. One suggestion might be for the FASB to work with IASC, as well as other such bodies as Britain's Accounting Standards Committee, the Japanese Business Accounting Deliberation Council, and the European Commission. Such cooperation could include researching, identifying, and developing new standards that address emerging issues common to multinationals. By becoming more involved in setting international standards, the FASB could enhance its role in shaping new standards that protect U.S. companies from potentially unfair accounting and reporting requirements.

Let me suggest some of the criteria a truly viable solution must include:

First, it must provide for broad, rather than narrow, standards. International standards shouldn't try to close every loophole that could possibly jeopardize comparability. The loophole-closing approach leads straight into the temptation to issue standards that are costly to comply with, are difficult to understand, and emphasize form over substance. Broad standards are far preferable.

I say this because I believe preparers will make responsible judgments even in the absence of detailed guidance. And because I know there are areas in which the SEC has already demonstrated that it can be tolerant of differences (e.g., inventory accounting and how it is applied), and history shows the public has suffered no harmful effects as a result.

The switch to broad, rather than detailed, standards would be a fundamental change for U.S. companies, but one that could bring us closer to our goal of useful, comparable financial statements. Specifically, it would help level the playing field when it comes to the cost of preparing financial statements (for U.S. companies, the cost would be less than it is under U.S. GAAP), and users would benefit as well because the resulting financial statements would be likely to have fewer standard-specific disclosures and therefore be less complex to read.

Second, the solution must provide for harmonization without constraining local standard-setters such as the FASB and FEE (a European accounting standard-setter) from dealing with emerg-

(continued)

(continued)

ing conditions or trends in their respective regions or from improving accounting for issues already covered under existing GAAP. The approach being pursued by IASC leaves unanswered some important questions about the role of national standard-setters such as the FASB. Because the FASB is unique as a private-sector standard-setter, its role in IASC's process is difficult to define. Additionally, the IASC process has implications for purely domestic standard-setting. One longer-term possibility is that local standard-setters could confine their efforts to issues where there is a consensus that greater guidance is needed and issues that are not dealt with by IASC. The latter would include country-specific kinds of issues such as accounting for OPEB, since benefits such as retiree health care are provided by the government, rather than employers, in most other countries.

Third, the solution must find a way to prioritize the harmonization of the wide range of country-to-country differences that exist today. At the SEC's request, Price Waterhouse participated in a survey of six major accounting principles in eight countries. We researched the depth of diversity and the extent of differences in cost of compliance in the area of consolidations. Other accounting firms have conducted similar research in the areas of accounting for income taxes, pensions, leasing, business combinations, and foreign currency translation. While the scope of the principles covered by this research is obvi-ously not all-inclusive, our analysis of the findings shows there is currently considerable diversity between the U.S. and other countries around the world in accounting for pensions, leases, and business combinations. The results of the survey should be available within the next several months.

Clearly, there will be many opinions as to priorities. And, just as clearly, the issue of setting priorities is a knotty one. In today's volatile global marketplace, one wonders if comparability of accounting principles alone will be enough to protect investors and managers from the kinds of unpleasant surprises we read about in the business press. Without an early warning system that addresses this concern, I doubt that comparable financial statements alone will ever fully meet user needs.

Your Right to Know

Companies in all industries are faced with risks and uncertainties, the level and complexity of which are greater today than ever before. The advent of more intense foreign competition, with today's rapid pace of technology and volatile economic and political conditions, have all added new complexities to the judgments management must make in order to prepare financial statements in a global business environment. Without an understanding of these underlying judgments, users of financial statements cannot realistically

(continued)

(continued)

assess the extent to which an enterprise is in danger of failing or of suffering severe financial setbacks in the near term.

Suppose, for example, the management of a local savings and loan invests in fixed-rate mortgages because it believes interest rates will stay stable or decline, certainly a high-risk strategy, especially in today's uncertain economy. Yet, the S&L's financial statements would be perfectly acceptable today without any disclosure of the risks and uncertainties associated with its interest-rate assumptions. If you were using the financials as a basis for your personal investing decisions, wouldn't you want to know the facts about the bank's assumptions, so you could make your own informed judgment about the risks involved? Or if a bank decides not to diversify its lending and investing activities, it may face more risk than other banks. If you were using the bank's financials as a basis for your company's investing decisions, wouldn't you want to know the facts about its decision not to diversify?

Let's take a completely different issue. Suppose you are evaluating an aggressive competitor, trying to assess its competitive strengths and weaknesses. And suppose the competitor is highly dependent on a supplier of a critical component not available from other suppliers. Wouldn't you want that information to be readily apparent from the company's financial statements? Wouldn't you want to know even if the current level of purchases

was not "material" in a monetary sense?

Finally, say you are evaluating a potential foreign acquisition that has had to make a particularly tough estimate — the allowance for doubtful accounts, inventory obsolescence, or the resolution of a lawsuit, for example. Your targeted company has made its best estimate, but it could still be wrong, possibly by a material amount. Wouldn't you want to know about this situation? And doesn't the goal of truly comparable financial statements demand the disclosure of such risks and uncertainties?

Obviously, some of these points would be disclosed if the company were a U.S. company, especially one subject to the disclosure requirements of the SEC. But I believe the only effective way to make this kind of information available for multinational companies is to get disclosure requirements out of securities law and into international accounting standards.

I recognize the difficulties inherent in developing an accounting standard on disclosure of management's judgments in these areas. Perhaps the thorniest issue is how to segregate the significant matters that warrant reporting from the host of lesser generic risks and uncertainties that do not. This difficulty notwithstanding, I believe an accounting standard that prescribes uniform disclosure of such matters is fast becoming an absolute necessity — just as important, if not more important, than the

(continued)

(continued)

elimination of alternatives or filling in of gaps in IASC's standards.

The important task of developing this standard is one that could fall to either IASC or the local standard-setters such as the FASB. The AICPA's task force on risks and uncertainties is reviewing a report on these issues, and the AICPA plans to issue an exposure draft late this year [1992] or early next year addressing the task force's report. A final statement that would take effect December 31, 1993, is possible by early 1993.

Very briefly, the AICPA task force report recommends two key disclosures: a discussion of significant, change-sensitive estimates used by management to measure assets and liabilities at the reporting date, and information about current vulnerability to risk due to concentrations, for example, of assets, customers, or suppliers.

These are not terribly onerous reporting requirements, but at the same time the risks inherent in any company's financial statements would be difficult to understand without an appreciation of them.

There is little doubt in my mind that we are about to enter a new era of accounting. The growing need for international comparability and the complexity of today's global business world will force accounting standard-setters to come to grips with some important new issues. Within the next decade, I am hopeful we will have in place both international standards and improved disclosures that will help users better assess financial statements issued anywhere in the world and better prepare them for possible adverse effects in the near-term future.

References

Reprinted with permission from Shaun F. O'Malley, "Accounting Across Borders," *Financial Executive*, March/April 1992, copyright 1992 by Financial Executives Institute, Morristown, New Jersey.

Discussion Question

What is the new era the author is alluding to? Do you believe his prognosis is accurate?

---

sales-type lease
A lease that, from the point of view of the lessor, transfers substantially all of the benefits and risks incident to ownership of the property to the lessee; at the inception of the lease, the fair value of the leased property is greater or less than its carrying amount, thus giving rise to a profit or loss to the lessor (usually a manufacturer or dealer).

direct financing lease
A lease that, from the point of view of the lessor, transfers substantially all of the benefits and risks incident to ownership of the property to the lessee; at the inception of the lease, the fair value of leased property is the same as its carrying amount.

EFFECTS ON LESSOR

The lessor uses the same criteria for classifying a lease as a capital lease or an operating lease as does the lessee. However, the term *capital lease* is replaced by **sales-type lease** or **direct financing lease**. A lessee who is a manufacturer or dealer usually enters into a sales-type lease, whereas a financing intermediary usually enters into a direct financing lease. At the time that a sales-type lease is signed, the lessor recognizes revenue in an amount equal to the present value of all future lease payments and recognizes expense (analogous to cost of goods sold) in an amount equal to the book value of the leased asset. The difference between the revenue and expense is the lessor's gain or loss on the *sale* of the asset. The lease receivable is recorded as any other long-term receivable at the present value of the future cash flows. Interest revenue is then recognized over the collection period of the payments. When a direct financing lease is signed, only interest revenue is recognized. Lessors tend to prefer sales-type lease accounting because it enables the recognition of a gain on the *sale* of the asset on the date the lease is signed. Under the operating lease method, all lease revenue is recognized gradually over time as lease payments are received.

OPERATING LEASE METHOD

In an **operating lease**, the owner, or lessor, transfers the rights to use the property to the lessee for specified periods of time. At the end of the lease period, the property is returned to the lessor. For example, car rental companies lease cars by the day or week on an operating basis. If the Myers Inc. lease is cancellable and Myers Inc. can stop making payments and return the computer at any time, the lease is considered an operating lease. No entry would be made on January 1, Year 1 when the lease is signed, and the following entry would be made on December 31, Year 1, Year 2, and Year 3:

Rent Expense	$19,709	
Cash		$19,709
To recognize annual expense of leasing computer.		

operating lease
A lease whereby the lessor retains the usual risks and rewards of owning the property, and the lessee charges payments to Rent Expense.

CAPITAL-LEASE METHOD

If this lease meets the criteria listed on page 604, it would be accounted for as a **capital lease**.[4] This treatment recognizes the signing of the lease as the simultaneous acquisition of a long-term asset, called a **leasehold**, and the incurring of a long-term liability for lease payments. At the time the lease is signed, both the leasehold and the liability are recorded on the books at the present value of the liability, $45,000 in the example, which is also the fair value of the leased property.

The entry made at the time Myers Inc. signed its three-year, noncancellable lease would be:

Computer Leasehold — (Asset)	$45,000	
Obligation under Capital Lease (Liability)		$45,000
To recognize acquisition of asset and the related liability.		

capital lease
A lease that transfers to the lessee substantially all of the benefits and risks related to ownership of the property. The lessee records the leased property as an asset and establishes a liability for the lease obligation.

leasehold
The rights transferred from the lessor to the lessee by a lease.

At the end of the year, two separate entries must be made. The leasehold is a long-term asset and, like most long-term assets, it must be amortized over its useful life. The first entry made at the end of each year recognizes the amortization of the leasehold asset. Assuming that Myers Inc. uses

---

[4] *CICA Handbook*, section 3065.

straight-line amortization of its leasehold, the entries made at the end of Year 1, Year 2, and Year 3 would be:

Amortization Expense (on Computer Leasehold)	$15,000	
Computer Leasehold (Asset)		$15,000

(An alternative treatment credits a contra-asset account, Accumulated Amortization of Computer Leasehold.)

The second entry made at the end of each year recognizes the lease payment, which is part payment of interest on the liability and part reduction in the liability itself. The entries made at the end of each of the three years would be:

December 31, Year 1

Interest Expense	$ 6,750	
Obligation Under Capital Lease (Liability)	12,959	
Cash		$19,709

To recognize lease payment, interest on liability for year ($0.15 \times \$45,000 = \$6,750$) and reduction in liability. The present value of the liability after this entry is $32,041 = \$45,000 - \$12,959$.

December 31, Year 2

Interest Expense	$ 4,806	
Obligation Under Capital Lease (Liability)	14,903	
Cash		$19,709

To recognize lease payment, interest on liability for year ($0.15 \times \$32,041 - \$4,806$) and the reduction in liability. The present value of the liability after this entry is $17,138 = \$32,041 - \$14,903$.

December 31, Year 3

Interest Expense	$ 2,571	
Obligation Under Capital Lease (Liability)	17,138	
Cash		$19,709

To recognize lease payment, interest on liability for year ($0.15 \times \$17,138 = \$2,571$) and the reduction in liability. The present value of the liability after this entry is zero ($= \$17,138 - \$17,138$).

Exhibit 10.1 shows the amortization schedule for this lease. Note that its form is exactly the same as in the mortgage amortization schedule shown in Exhibit 9.2. The underlying principle uses the effective-interest method of computing interest each period.

ACCOUNTING METHOD DETERMINES TIMING, BUT NOT AMOUNT, OF TOTAL EXPENSE

Notice that, in the capital lease method, the total expense over the three years is $59,127 (= $45,000 (= $15,000 + $15,000 + $15,000) for amortization expense and $14,127 (= $6,750 + $4,806 + $2,571) for interest expense.

EXHIBIT 10.1
Amortization Schedule for $45,000 Lease Liability, Repaid in Three Annual Installments of $19,709 Each, Interest Rate 15 Percent, Compounded Annually

Annual Journal Entry

Dr. Interest Expense   Amount in Column (3)
Dr. Obligation Under Capital Lease (Liability) Amount in Column (5)
    Cr. Cash   Amount in Column (4)

Year (1)	Lease Liability Start of Year (2)	Interest Expense for Year (3)	Payment (4)	Portion of Payment Reducing Lease Liability (5)	Lease Liability End of year (6)
0					$45,000
1	$45,000	$6,750	$19,709	$12,959	32,041
2	32,041	4,806	19,709	14,903	17,138
3	17,138	2,571	19,709	17,138	0

Column (2) = Column (6) previous period.
Column (3) = 0.15 × Column (2).
Column (4)   Given.
Column (5) = Column (4) − Column (3).
Column (6) = Column (2) − Column (5).

This is exactly the same as the total expense recognized under the operating lease method described above ($19,709 × 3 = $59,127). The capital lease method recognizes expense sooner than does the operating lease method, as summarized in Exhibit 10.2. But, over long enough time periods, expense is equal to the cash expenditure. One difference between the operating lease method and the capital method is the *timing* of the expense recognition.

EXHIBIT 10.2
Comparison of Expense Recognized under Operating and Capital Lease Methods

Year	Expense Recognized Each Year Under	
	Operating Lease Method	Capital Lease Method
Year 1	$19,709	$21,750 (= $15,000 + $ 6,750)
Year 2	19,709	19,806 (= 15,000 + 4,806)
Year 3	19,709	17,571 (= 15,000 + 2,571)
Total	$59,127[a]	$59,127 (= $45,000[b] + $14,127[c])

[a] *Rent expense.*
[b] *Amortization expense.*
[c] *Interest expense.*

The other difference is that the capital lease method recognizes both the asset (leasehold) and the liability on the balance sheet, while the operating lease does not.

OFF-BALANCE-SHEET FINANCING[5]

Firms generally obtain debt financing either directly from banks and other financial institutions, or by issuing bonds to investors. These arrangements result in a debit to cash and a credit to a liability account, and increase the debt-equity ratio. Under some other financing arrangements, the resulting obligations do not have to be recorded on the balance sheet as liabilities.

KEEPING DEBT OFF THE BALANCE SHEET

executory contract
An agreement providing for payment by a payor to a payee upon the performance of an act or service by the payee, such as a labour contract. Obligations under such contracts generally are not recognized as liabilities.

To be an accounting liability, an obligation must be incurred for a past or current benefit received — the event or transaction giving rise to the obligation must already have happened. If the obligation arises from an **executory contract**, in which both parties have exchanged promises but there has been no event by which economic risk is transferred, accounting typically does not recognize a liability. This criterion for recognizing a long-term liability focuses on the transfer of risks and rewards of ownership, not just on the undertaking of commitments to make fixed payments.

Example   Miller Corporation wants to acquire land costing $25 million, on which it will build a shopping centre. It could borrow the $25 million from its bank, paying interest at 12 percent, and buy the land outright from the seller. If it did so, both an asset and a liability would appear on the balance sheet. Instead, it borrows $5 million and purchases for $5 million from the seller an option to buy the land from the seller at any time within the next six years for the price of $20 million. The option costs Miller Corporation $5 million immediately and provides for continuing "option" payments of $2.4 million per year, which is equal to Miller Corporation's borrowing rate multiplied by the remaining purchase price of the land: $2.4 million = 0.12 × $20 million. Although Miller Corporation need not continue payments and can let the option lapse at any time, it also has an obligation to begin developing on the site immediately. Because Miller Corporation has invested a substantial sum in the option, will invest more, and will begin immediately developing the land, Miller Corporation is almost certain to exercise its option before it expires. The seller of the land can take the option contract to the bank and borrow $20 million, paying interest at Miller Corporation's borrowing rate, 12 percent per year. The continuing option payments from Miller Corporation will be sufficient to enable the seller to make its payments to the bank. Some accountants would view Miller Corporation as having acquired an option for $5 million, rather than having acquired land costing $25 million in return for $5 million cash and a liability of

---

[5] This section was developed from materials by Richard Dieter, David L. Landsittel, John E. Stewart, and Arthur R. Wyatt, all of Authur Andersen & Co. See Landsittel and Stewart, "Off-Balance-Sheet Financing; Commitments and Contingencies," in *Handbook of Modern Accounting*, 3rd ed., edited by S. Davidson and R.L. Weil (New York: McGraw-Hill, 1983), Chap. 26.

$20 million. As a result, Miller Corporation keeps $20 million of "debt" off the balance sheet until it borrows more funds to exercise the option.

The techniques for **off-balance-sheet financing** generally exploit the requirement that, for there to be a liability in accounting, there must have been mutual performance. That is, benefits must have been received in the past obligating the firm to make payments in the future. When the mutual performance will occur in the future (as in executory contracts), accounting typically does not recognize a liability. In the example above, the buyer is viewed as not yet having performed beyond having purchased an option, even though the terms of the option make its eventual exercise by Miller Corporation a virtual certainty. Similarly, accounting views the seller as having sold only an option, not the land itself. On the other hand, arguing that substance takes precedence over form, many accountants would view the risks and rewards of ownership as having passed to Miller and would insist on recording the full $25 million.

off-balance-sheet financing
Structuring transactions so that the rights to assets are obtained without formal recognition of the full financing impact. An application of the executory contract concept.

WHY REMOVE DEBT FROM THE BALANCE SHEET?

When debt is left off the balance sheet, ratios (such as the debt-equity ratio) that have proved useful to analysts for many years will appear more favourable to the borrower. One motive may be to prevent an adverse debt-equity ratio from developing later. The entity may foresee reaching the danger point in its debt-equity relations on the basis of historical standards. Future credit ratings might be lowered and future borrowing costs might increase.

ACCOUNTING'S RESPONSE

The accounting profession has begun to recognize that certain off-balance-sheet financing arrangements have the economic substance of notes or bonds and should be recognized as accounting liabilities. The Accounting Standards Board has dealt with the transactions on a case-by-case basis, without having promulgated principles to deal with all such transactions. For leases (discussed earlier in this chapter), the accounting profession attempted for more than ten years to develop a set of criteria that specify clearly which lease obligations must be recognized as liabilities. Some accountants think that there will never be a satisfactory solution until accounting requires the recording of a liability whenever there is an obligation to pay a reasonably definite amount at a reasonably definite time, independent of the executory nature of the contract. It appears that the accounting profession is moving in the direction of limiting the circumstances in which off-balance-sheet financing is acceptable practice.

PENSIONS

Under a **pension plan**, an employer promises to make payments to employees after retirement. Private pension plan systems have grown so rapidly in number and size over the last several decades that the major asset of many individuals is the present value of their pension benefits, and a significant obligation of many firms results from their pension promises. The

pension plan
A plan established by a company to pay benefits to its employees after they retire.

basic operations of a pension plan are simple, but the concepts can be lost in a variety of details. In a pension plan, the employer:[6]

1. Sets up a pension plan, specifying the eligibility of employees, the types of promises to employees, the method of funding, and the pension plan administrator.

2. Computes a pension expense each period according to some formula. The employer debits Pension Expense for that amount and credits Pension Liability. This process is called "expensing pension obligations."

3. Transfers cash to the plan administrator each period according to some formula. The employer debits Pension Liability and credits Cash. This process is called "funding pension liabilities." The amounts funded in this step are usually, but *not* necessarily, the same as the amounts expensed in step (2).

The preceding steps constitute the employer's accounting for pensions. The employer is sometimes called the "plan sponsor." The following steps are carried out by the pension plan administrator.

1. The administrator receives cash each period from the plan sponsor. In the accounting records of the administrator, Cash is debited and Liability for Payments to Employees is credited.

2. Funds received are invested to generate income. The income is not part of the employer's (sponsor's) income for the period, but is reported by the administrator in separate financial statements of the pension plan.

3. The administrator makes payments to those entitled to receive them. The administrator debits Liability for Payments to Employees and credits Cash.

INTRODUCTION TO PENSION PLANS

There are almost as many different kinds of pension plans as there are employers who have them. The basic variables of a pension plan are the following:

1. Its requirement for contributions by employers and employees.
2. Vesting provisions.
3. Funding provisions.
4. The kinds of promises made by the employer.
5. Treatment of *accrued actuarial obligation*, if any.

Each of these variables is explained and discussed.

Contributions

noncontributory plan A pension plan whereby only the employer makes payments to a pension fund; contrast with contributory plan.

contributory plan A pension plan whereby employees, as well as employers, make payments to a pension fund. Note that the provisions for vesting are applicable to the employer's payments.

Under a **noncontributory plan**, the employee makes no explicit contribution of funds to the pension plan; only the employer contributes. Under a **contributory plan**, both the employee and the employer contribute, but

---

[6] *CICA Handbook*, sections 3460 and 4100.

they do not necessarily contribute equal amounts. Employees retain a claim to their explicit contributions under virtually all plans. The employee's rights to the employer's contributions are determined by the *vesting* provisions. The rest of this section considers contributions made under noncontributory plans or, where the plan is contributory, only the employer's contributions.

Vesting Provisions

An employee's rights under a pension plan may be fully vested or partially vested. When the rights are *fully vested*, the pension benefits purchased with the employer's contributions cannot be taken away from the employees. If the rights are not vested, the employee will lose rights to the employer's contributions if he or she leaves the company. Under *partially vested* plans, rights vest gradually. For example, an employee in the fifth year of work might have no vested rights, but by the time he or she has been employed for fifteen years, all rights will be vested. The nature of vesting provisions will influence the present value of the expected pension liabilities generated during an accounting period. If employees leave their jobs and their benefits are only partially vested, their rights — and therefore the employer's liabilities — are less than they would be if the benefits were fully vested.

Funding Provisions

A pension plan may be *fully funded* or *partially funded*. Under a fully funded plan, the employer sets aside cash, or pays cash to an outside trustee, such as an insurance company, equal to the present value of all expected pension liabilities. Partially funded plans have cash available in an amount less than the present value of all pension obligations.

EMPLOYER PROMISES

Employers make essentially two different kinds of pension promises to employees:

1. A few employers make promises about the amounts to be contributed to the pension plan without specifying the benefits to be received by retired employees. Such plans are referred to as **defined-contribution plans**.[7] Employer inputs, or contributions to the plan, are defined. The amounts eventually received by employees depend on the investment performance of the pension fund.

2. Most employers make promises about the amount each employee will receive during retirement on the basis of wages earned and number of years of employment. The plan does not specify the amounts the employer will contribute to the plan. Such plans are called **defined-benefit plans**.[8] Payments to employees are defined. The employer must make contributions to the plan so that those amounts plus their earnings are large enough to make the promised payments.

defined-contribution plans
Money purchase (pension) plans or other arrangements, based on formula or discretion, whereby the employer makes cash contributions to eligible individual employee accounts under the terms of a written plan document.

defined-benefit plans
Pension plans whereby the employer promises specific benefits to each eligible employee. The amounts usually depend on a formula that takes into account such things as the employee's earnings, years of employment, and age.

---

[7] Also called *money-purchase* or *cost-based* plans.
[8] Also called *unit-benefit* or *benefit-based* plans.

Defined-Contribution Plans

In a defined-contribution plan, the employer promises to contribute an amount determined by formula to each employee's pension account. An employer, for example, promises to contribute between 6 and 12 percent of income before the contribution (the exact amount depending on some other factors) to the pension plan each year. An employee's share in the company's pension fund depends on his or her annual compensation. Another employer might agree to contribute an amount equal to 5 percent of an employee's salary to a pension fund. Subject to reasonable investment risks, the funds are managed to produce as large a series of payments as is possible during the employee's retirement. No specific promises are made to employees about the amount of the eventual pension. Inputs are defined; total outputs depend on investment performance. In a defined-contribution plan, the investment and actuarial risks are carried by the employees.

The accounting for defined-contribution plans is straightforward. If the employer contributes $75,000 to a trustee to be managed for employees' retirement benefits, the journal entry is:

Pension Expense	$75,000	
Cash		$75,000

Other than the periodical overseeing of the activities of the plan administrator to ensure that investment policies are being carried out prudently, the employer's obligations under the pension plan are largely completed once the cash is paid to the plan administrator. Neither the assets of the pension plan nor the amounts expected to be paid to retired employees appear in the employer's financial statements. The income from pension fund investments each period is not included in the net income of the employer, but in separate financial statements of the plan.

Defined-Benefit Plans

In a defined-benefit plan, the employer promises the employee a series of payments at retirement based on a formula. The typical formula takes into account the employee's length of service and some measure of average earnings. For example, the employer might promise to pay during retirement an annual pension equal to a stated percent of the average annual salary earned during the five highest-paid working years for all employees. The percentage might increase by 2 percent points for each year of service, so that an employee with 35 years of service would get a pension equal to 70 percent of his or her average salary during the five highest-paid working years. The defined-benefit formula in this case is:

$$\begin{matrix} \text{Pension Benefit} & & \text{Average Salary for} \\ \text{per Year During} & = 0.02n \times & \text{the Five Highest-Paid} \\ \text{Retirement} & & \text{Years of Employment} \end{matrix}$$

where n is the number of years of the employee's employment. Payments are defined by formula; the exact amount to be paid later to employees is not known currently and therefore must be estimated. This amount depends on factors such as mortality, inflation, and future wages. In a defined-benefit plan, the investment and actuarial risks are carried by the employer.

The employer must set aside funds to fulfil its pension obligations to employees and report expenses for these amounts. The amount depends on, among other factors, the rate of return to be earned on pension fund investments. Because defined-benefit pension plans are based on numerous estimates, accounting for such plans must cope with faulty estimates as they become apparent.

Comparison of Types of Promises

Most corporate pension plans are defined-benefit plans. Some employees prefer a defined-benefit plan because it reduces the employee's risk in planning for retirement. Employers tend to prefer defined-contribution plans because of the reduced uncertainty of pension expenses and contributions. The plan used in any given firm is likely to be the result of labour-management negotiations.

ACCOUNTING FOR DEFINED-BENEFIT PLANS

The overriding principle that determines the accounting for defined-benefit pension plans is that the pension expense recognized in a period is a function of trying to match the total cost of the pension plan with the years in which employees provide service to the organization. The computation of the expense is *not*, however, tied to actual funding payments made to the pension plan.

An actuary for the pension plan estimates the number of eligible service years accumulated by employees to date. The projected benefits the company will incur as a result of this service are calculated by an algorithm called the defined-benefit formula, such as the one shown above. The present value of benefits payable and attributable to service rendered to date is the principal component of the expense recognized for the current period. We will call this component the *normal cost*.

Adjustments to the Current Expense

In addition to the normal cost, other components that affect the calculation of the current period expense include the amortization of:

1. Adjustments arising from amendments to the plan or to assumptions underlying the plan, such as when past service costs are recognized.

2. Experience gains or losses on the plan.

3. The difference between the value of the pension fund assets and the present value of the accrued pension benefits, calculated at the time when the recommendations of the *CICA Handbook* are first applied.[9]

---

[9] The current rules on accounting for pensions were implemented in December 1986. Previously, most companies recognized an expense equal to the funding requirement for the year.

PAST SERVICE COSTS

The recognition of an obligation for past service costs by an employer is going to increase its costs of providing pension benefits to its employees. How should these additional costs be recognized for accounting purposes? A liability for these costs is not recognized in the accounting records. Instead, the total additional cost of this past service obligation is amortized over the remaining service life of the employees entitled to past service benefits as an increment to the normal pension expense shown each year.

For example, if it was determined that the company had an additional obligation of $900,000 and the remaining service life of employees was fifteen years, the pension expense for each of the next fifteen years would increase by $60,000 ($900,000/15).

Other Pension Plan Adjustments

When estimating the liability for future pensions, a company must make assumptions about such things as investment returns, employee turnover, salary and wage changes, and mortality rates. Periodically, these assumptions are compared with the experience. The difference between an assumption and the experience may be a result of a short-term fluctuation or evidence of a long-run trend. Short-term fluctuations will be considered experience gains or losses and may be automatically corrected in the future. Long-term trends are not self-correcting and will require changes to the original assumptions. Both experience gains or losses and changes in pension liabilities resulting from changes in assumptions will require an adjustment to pension expense. Generally accepted accounting principles (GAAP) require that these adjustments normally be amortized over the expected average remaining service life of the employee group covered by the pension plan.[10]

SUMMARY OF CORPORATE PENSION ACCOUNTING BY EMPLOYER

Total corporate pension expense for a period under a defined-benefit plan is made up of the sum of the charge for current service benefits earned during the period plus the charge for the gradual recognition of past service costs, gains and losses, and amounts arising from changes in assumptions.

GAAP require certain minimum disclosures for pension plans by the employer. The notes to the balance sheet must disclose[11] the present value of accrued pension benefits attributable to services rendered to date and the market value of the pension fund assets.

In addition, it may be desirable to disclose the current period expense and accrual, the basis of valuing pension assets, assumptions used in determining the expense and accrual, the method and period used to amortize adjustments to the plan, a general description of the plan, and the date of the most recent actuarial valuation.

---

[10] *CICA Handbook*, section 3460.
[11] *CICA Handbook*, section 3460.

DISCUSSION CASE 23

Corporate Graphs Open to "Misuse," Expert Says

Bar graphs, pie graphs, column graphs, line graphs.

They sprout like spring flowers in annual company reports, transforming acres of numbers into something almost anyone can grasp.

But experts warn some graphs can be hazardous to your financial health.

The Canadian Institute of Chartered Accountants is launching a project to set guidelines for financial graphics, which they say can sometimes confuse and even mislead.

"They're capable of misuse," said Jerry Trites, a partner at the Halifax office of Peat Marwick Thorne chartered accountants.

"So we felt that the whole area, because of the capabilities for misstating things, needed to be studied."

Trites recently headed an Institute committee that examined the common failings of annual reports — among them that financial graphics can be too much of a free-for-all.

"Companies are using them very liberally," said Paul-Emile Roy, senior manager of research studies at the Institute.

"And there don't seem to be any benchmarks against which they can assess the quality of their . . . graphical presentations."

A 1989 study found that of 319 annual reports of major corporations, eight percent contained at least one graph that presented numbers in a way that covered up bad results.

And a related survey of 120 annual reports found almost 26 percent of the graphs distorted data by more than 10 percent.

"Improperly constructed graphs can significantly influence users' perceptions of corporate performance," Trites's committee concluded.

Toronto accountant Phil Creighton, who for 20 years has helped run contests to select Canada's best annual reports, said that even if a graph faithfully reflects the numbers, it can still distort.

"You can make a nice, slow, steady earnings increase appear to be radical by simply pulling up the vertical axis" of a chart, he said.

New benchmarks for financial graphics will never eliminate shoddy presentations, but chartered accountants "would at least like to make it consistent garbage," Creighton said.

The Institute study, intended to produce guidelines rather than standards, is expected to be complete by the end of this year [1992], Roy said.

At the same time, the Institute is promoting the use of graphics as a way to help ordinary investors understand complex data, Trites said.

With commercial software now available to do sophisticated

(continued)

(continued)

graphic work, companies should consider experimenting, he said.

For example, Trites's committee tried to stir interest in a technique in which human-like faces quickly convey financial information.

The mouth on the face might change from a smile to a frown in tandem with the change in the ratio from one fiscal period to the next. Or the eyes might appear wider and more worried-looking as the company takes on debt.

In the meantime, the Institute is helping to revive an awards program that selects the best of more than 200 annual reports in Canada to encourage improve-

ments. Last year's [1991] awards were cancelled because of costs.

The awards, sponsored by the institute, the National Investor Relations Institute and the *Financial Post* will likely encourage further experimentation with graphical presentations of financial results.

References

Dean Beeby, "Corporate Graphs Open to 'Misuse,' Expert Says." *The Canadian Press,* as appearing in the *Kitchener-Waterloo Record,* May 2, 1992, pp. B5–B6.

Discussion Question

What are the pros and cons of using graphical presentations of financial data?

Income Tax Accounting and Deferred Income Taxes

As discussed throughout this book, a firm often selects different methods of accounting for financial and tax reporting. In most cases, the *total amount* of revenue or expense recognized over the life of an asset or other item will be the same for these two purposes. However, the *timing* of recognition may differ. For example, the total depreciation recognized for both financial and tax reporting over a company's life is its acquisition cost. In the early years, tax depreciation (capital cost allowance) for an asset may exceed depreciation recognized for financial reporting, so that taxable income will be less than financial statement income before taxes. In later years, capital cost allowance (CCA) may be less than depreciation so that taxable income will exceed income before taxes.[12]

The use of different accounting methods for financial and tax reporting creates a problem in measuring income tax *expense* each period:

1. Should income tax expense be equal to the income taxes actually payable each period based on taxable income, or

2. Should income tax expense be equal to the income taxes that would have been payable had the methods of accounting used for financial reporting also been used for tax reporting?

---

[12] The term *financial statement income,* although descriptive, is somewhat cumbersome. Throughout this section, the term *book income* is used to refer to net income before taxes reported in the financial statements, and *taxable income* is used to refer to the amount reported on the income tax return. Similarly, the terms *book purposes* and *tax purposes* differentiate the financial statements from the income tax return.

ILLUSTRATION

Assume that Burns, Inc. pays income taxes at the rate of 40 percent of taxable income. Burns purchased a plant asset for $100,000 that has a five-year estimated life and an estimated disposal value of zero. This asset produces an excess of revenues over operating expenses (other than depreciation and taxes) of $30,000 a year. That is, after paying for the costs of running and maintaining the asset, the firm enjoys a $30,000-per-year excess of revenue over expenses (except depreciation and taxes). Burns uses straight-line depreciation for financial reporting and claims the maximum CCA for tax purposes.

A firm calculates the maximum CCA by applying the appropriate rate (in this case, 50 percent) to the undepreciated capital cost, reduced to one-half in the year of acquisition. Because this asset is the only asset in the class, the undepreciated capital cost remaining in this class can be claimed in the year of disposal (Year 5).

Thus, in the first year the new plant asset is used, depreciation for financial reporting will be $20,000 (= $100,000/5) and the CCA claimed on the tax return will be $25,000 (= 0.5 × $100,000 × 0.5). In addition to the $30,000 from the plant asset, other pretax income for each year is $70,000.

Exhibit 10.3 summarizes the computation of taxes for tax purposes and for financial reporting.

The first column in Exhibit 10.3 shows the tax return for the first, second, and fifth years. Note that nothing changes over time other than the CCA deduction and taxes payable. As CCA increases from Year 1 to Year 2, taxes payable decrease. As CCA decreases from Year 2 to Year 5, taxes payable increase. The middle column shows book income resulting from an income statement (not allowed by GAAP) where income tax expense is equal to income taxes payable. Note that pretax book income is the same, $80,000, in all years, but that aftertax net income increases from $50,000 in Year 1 to $55,000 in Year 2, then declines to $43,750 by Year 5. The pattern results from fluctuations in income taxes over the five years: $30,000; $25,000; $32,500; $36,250; $36,250. [All five of these numbers appear in column (8) in Exhibit 10.4, discussed later.]

Those who set GAAP are uncomfortable with the notion that reported income (as in the middle column) will fluctuate merely because different accounting methods are used for tax and for book purposes. Consequently, in this case, GAAP require that *the income tax expense for financial reporting be based on pretax book income, not on taxes actually payable.* The third column of Exhibit 10.3 shows the required accounting treatment. Note that aftertax net income in each year equals that of the first year, just as pretax income in each year equals that of the first year.

RATIONALE FOR DEFERRED TAX ACCOUNTING

Relative to straight-line depreciation, maximum CCA "borrows" income tax deductions in the early years from later years (as we demonstrate in Exhibit 10.4). The fluctuation in taxable income is predictable during the first year, because it results from a difference in the depreciation methods used in financial statements and the tax return. The tax reduction in the first two years, relative to the last three years, is a difference that will reverse with

EXHIBIT 10.3
Deferred Income Tax Computations for Burns, Inc.

	Tax Return	Book Income Using Taxes Payable (not acceptable)	Financial Reporting (required)
First Year			
Other Pretax Income	$70,000	$70,000	$70,000
Excess of Revenues over Expenses Except			
Depreciation from Plant Asset	30,000	30,000	30,000
CCA or Depreciation	(25,000)	(20,000)	(20,000)
Income Before Taxes	$75,000	$80,000	$80,000
Income Taxes Currently Payable			
(at 40 percent)	$30,000		
Income Tax Expense (at 40 percent):			
On Taxable Income		(30,000)	
On Pretax Book Income			(32,000)
Net Income		$50,000	$48,000
Second Year			
Other Pretax Income	$70,000	$70,000	$70,000
Excess of Revenues over Expenses Except			
Depreciation from Plant Asset	30,000	30,000	30,000
CCA or Depreciation	(37,000)	(20,000)	(20,000)
Income Before Taxes	$62,500	$80,000	$80,000
Income Taxes Currently Payable			
(at 40 percent)	$25,000		
Income Tax Expense (at 40 percent):			
On Taxable Income		(25,000)	
On Pretax Book Income			(32,000)
Net Income		$55,000	$48,000
Fifth Year			
Other Pretax Income	$70,000	$70,000	$70,000
Excess of Revenues over Expenses Except			
Depreciation from Plant Asset	30,000	30,000	30,000
CCA or Depreciation	(9,375)	(20,000)	(20,000)
Income Before Taxes	$90,625	$80,000	$80,000
Income Taxes Currently Payable			
(at 40 percent)	$36,250		
Income Tax Expense (at 40 percent):			
On Taxable Income		(36,250)	
On Pretax Book Income			(32,000)
Net Income		$43,750	$48,000

the mere passage of time. GAAP require that the reported net income be the same in each year, because pretax income on the financial statements is the same each year.[13] The required accounting matches income tax expense and pretax book income rather than income tax expense and taxable

---

[13] Section 3470 of the *CICA Handbook* states that the account credited should be viewed as a "deferred credit" and not as a liability. The issue of whether deferred income tax is a liability is discussed later in this section.

EXHIBIT 10.4
Summary of Deferred Income Tax Credit Account for Burns, Inc.

Annual Journal Entry

Dr. Income Tax Expense		Amount in Column (5)
Dr. Deferred Income Tax Credit		Amount in Column (9)
or { Cr. Deferred Income Tax Credit		Amount in Column (10)
Cr. Income Taxes Payable		Amount in Column (8)

Year (1)	Income Before Depreciation and Tax Expenses (2)	Financial Statements			Tax Returns			Deferred Income Tax Liability Account		
		Depreciation Expense (3)	Pretax Income (4)	Tax Expense (5)	CCA Deduction (6)	Pretax Income (7)	Taxes Payable (8)	Debit (9)	Credit (10)	Credit Balance at Year-End (11)
1	$100,000	$ 20,000	$ 80,000	$ 32,000	$ 25,000	$ 75,000	$ 30,000		$2,000	$2,000
2	100,000	20,000	80,000	32,000	37,500	62,500	25,000		7,000	9,000
3	100,000	20,000	80,000	32,000	18,750	81,250	32,500	500		8,500
4	100,000	20,000	80,000	32,000	9,375	90,625	36,250	4,250		4,250
5	100,000	20,000	80,000	32,000	9,375	90,625	36,250	4,250		0
		$100,000	$400,000	$160,000	$100,000	$400,000	$160,000			

Column (4) = Column (2) − Column (3).
Column (5) = 0.40 × $80,000.
Column (6) = CCA Year 1 (0.5 × 50% × $100,000); Year 2 [50% × ($100,00 − $25,000)]; Year 3, 4 (50% × prior year CCA); Year 5—remainder.
Column (7) = Column (2) − Column (6).
Column (8) = Column (7) × 0.40.
Column (9) and (10) = Column (5) − Column (8); if positive, appears in Column (10); if negative, appears in Column (9).
Column (11) = Sum of entries in Column (10) reduced by Column (9).

income. The rationale is that income taxes will become payable in future years when the difference between book and taxable income reverses. This future cash outflow is an expense of the current period to be matched against pretax book income much the same as future warranty costs are an expense of the period when the warranted product is sold.

TIMING DIFFERENCES AND PERMANENT DIFFERENCES

In general, the problem of accounting for income taxes arises from differences in timing between financial reporting of revenues and expenses and tax reporting of these items. A **timing difference** is any item of revenue or expense that appears on the financial statements in one period but on the tax return in a different period. The total amounts appearing over time on the financial statements and the tax return are identical; only the timing differs. The following list shows some of the ways in which the timing differences can arise:

1. Depreciation for tax purposes is different from that shown in the financial records in a given period because either different depreciation methods or different asset lives, or both, are used for the two purposes. Total depreciation over a company's entire life is the same for book and for tax purposes.

2. Income from installment sales is recognized in the financial records in the year of sale, but recognized for tax purposes in the year when cash is collected from customers. Total income from the installment sales is the same for book and for tax; only their timing of recognition differs.

3. Income from long-term construction projects is recognized in financial records on the percentage-of-completion basis but on tax returns under the completed contract basis. Total income is again the same for book and for tax, but its timing of recognition differs.

Some differences between reported income and taxable income will never reverse because the tax laws single them out for special treatment. These include items of revenue that are never taxed and expenses that are never deductible in computing income taxes payable. An example is income earned on shares owned in another Canadian company held as assets. Income tax-exempt income is part of reported income but is never part of taxable income. Differences between reported income and taxable income that never reverse are called **permanent differences**. Permanent differences do not require special accounting for income taxes.

ACCOUNTING PROCEDURES FOR INCOME TAXES WHERE TIMING DIFFERENCES EXIST

Where there are timing differences for depreciation because the straight-line method is used for financial reporting but the maximum CCA is claimed for taxes, GAAP require **income tax expense** on the financial statements be computed as though straight-line depreciation were used on the tax return. Under such an assumption, income tax expense would be $32,000 each year. Because only $30,000 would be payable in the first year

---

timing difference
A difference between taxable income and pretax income reported in the income statement that will be reversed in a subsequent period. It requires an entry in the Deferred Income Tax account. Examples are the use of accelerated depreciation for tax returns and straight-line depreciation for financial reporting. Contrast with permanent difference.

permanent differences
Differences between reported income and taxable income that will never be reversed and therefore, require no entry in the Deferred Income Tax (liability) account. Contrast with timing difference.

income tax expense
The expense shown for income taxes in the income statement.

and $25,000 would be payable in the second year, the following entries would be made:

Income Tax Expense	$32,000	
Income Tax Payable		$30,000
Deferred Income Tax Credit		2,000
First year income tax entry; expense is larger than cash payment; deferred credit is created.[14]		

Income Tax Expense	$32,000	
Income Tax Payable		$25,000
Deferred Income Tax Credit		7,000
Second year income tax entry; expense exceeds cash payment; deferred credit is increased.		

For this one asset, the $2,000 tax not paid in the first year and the $7,000 not paid in the second year are not forgiven by the government. Instead, these payments are merely delayed. If Burns had only this one asset, the additional taxes would be paid in later years. The bottom portion of Exhibit 10.3 shows the computation of Income Taxes Payable in the fifth year to be $36,250. Because the financial statements will have Income Tax Expense computed under the assumption that straight-line depreciation is used on the tax return, the reported Income Tax Expense will remain $32,000. Because the actual tax payment must be $36,250, however, the journal entry to recognize the income tax expense for the fifth year is:

Income Tax Expense	$32,000	
Deferred Income Tax Credit	4,250	
Income Tax Payable		$36,250
Fifth-year income tax entry; expense is less than cash payment; deferred credit is reduced.		

The amounts of expense not paid in cash in the early years are credited to the Deferred Income Tax Credit account. Later, when cash payments exceed reported expense, the liability account is debited and its balance reduced. Exhibit 10.4 shows a summary of the entries in Burns's Deferred Income Tax Credit account for the five years during which it uses the plant asset. Observe that the total tax expense in column (5) shown on the financial statements over the asset's life is the same as the total taxes payable in column (8), but that claiming maximum CCA on the tax returns defers payment and thus leads to a lower present value of taxes paid.

SUMMARY OF INCOME TAX ACCOUNTING FOR TIMING DIFFERENCES

Income tax *expense* always refers to the financial statements; income taxes *payable* refers to the amount on the tax return.

---

[14] *CICA Handbook*, section 3470.

Income taxes payable
The amount of income taxes currently owing to Revenue Canada.

Deferred Income Taxes
Income taxes that are nominally owing to Revenue Canada, but that, because of timing differences between revenue and expense recognition policies of GAAP and the Income Tax Act, are not a liability in the current period.

Income taxes payable computed on the tax return are based on accounting principles, acceptable under the Income Tax Act, that are selected by the firm to minimize the present value of the cash burden for income taxes. Income tax expense shown in the financial statements results from a measure of taxable income computed using the financial statement's accounting principles for timing differences, rather than the tax return's accounting principles. The excess of income tax expense over income tax payable, if any, is credited to the **Deferred Income Taxes** balance sheet account. The excess of income taxes payable over income tax expense, if any, is debited to the Deferred Income Taxes balance sheet account. If the Deferred Income Taxes account has a credit balance, it appears on the balance sheet among the equities, usually as a liability. If the Deferred Income Taxes account has a debit balance, it appears on the balance sheet among the assets.

DISCLOSURE OF DEFERRED INCOME TAXES IN FINANCIAL STATEMENTS

Notes to financial statements contain a wealth of information about income taxes. Among the items of information included is the amount of deferred tax expense for the year caused by each of the several important timing differences.

Typically, the financial statements do not disclose the amount of deductions claimed on the tax return. The information in the notes about deferred taxes can be used to deduce many of them. For example, the financial statements of Burns, Inc. for the first year in our example show depreciation expense of $20,000. The notes disclose both that the deferred tax expense caused by depreciation timing differences is $2,000 and that the income tax rate is 40 percent of pretax income. From these data, we can deduce that depreciation claimed on the tax return exceeded depreciation expense on the financial statements by $5,000 (= $2,000 ÷ 0.40). Thus, depreciation claimed on the tax return must have been $25,000 (= $20,000 + $5,000).

CRITICISMS OF THE ACCOUNTING FOR DEFERRED INCOME TAXES

The accounting for deferred income taxes has been subject to criticism for many years. The Accounting Standards Committee is currently considering changing the requirements for accounting for timing differences because of the following criticisms.

Benefits Ignored   Deferred tax accounting for timing differences conceals the benefit conveyed by tax rules that delay tax payments. Note that the income statements of Burns, Inc. would look the same as the third column in Exhibit 10.3 if it were to use straight-line depreciation on the tax return. (In fact, Income Tax Expense on Burns's financial statement is computed *assuming* that straight-line depreciation is used on the tax return.) Taxes paid later are less burdensome than taxes paid sooner, but deferred tax accounting conceals this exploitation of the benefits.

Payments Deferred Indefinitely   A going concern claiming maximum CCA on the tax return may be able to defer payment of deferred taxes indefinitely. Taxes are levied on overall operations, not on individual assets. Although timing differences for earlier timing differences do reverse, new acquisitions create new timing differences that offset the reversals if asset acquisitions at least remain level over time in dollar amounts. If increasing amounts are spent each year on new assets, the new timing differences will exceed the reversing timing differences and the credit balance in the deferred tax account will grow. If the firm continues to acquire depreciable assets each year (in dollar amounts no less than those it acquired in the preceding year), then, in every year, Income Taxes Payable will *be less than or equal to* Income Tax Expense computed as GAAP require. In no year will there be a net debit entry to the Deferred Income Tax account on the balance sheet.

Tax payments will exceed tax expense (as in Years 3, 4, and 5 of the Burns example) only when the firm stops acquiring new assets while it continues to earn taxable income. Few firms shrink in size (as is required for the income taxes payable to exceed income tax expense) and at the same time remain profitable. Most shrinking firms owe no taxes because they fail to earn taxable income.

The deferred tax is probably not going to be paid and, if it is, the time when payment is finally made is uncertain.[15]

Not an Obligation   The amount on the balance sheet for deferred income taxes is not an obligation (to the government or to anyone else). The government levies taxes on taxable income as shown on the tax return and only as it is earned. It does not automatically levy a tax because depreciation deductions decline. The government does not suggest to Burns, Inc. in Years 1 and 2 that the firm will also be profitable in Years 3, 4, and 5 and that it has in Years 1 and 2 a liability for taxes due in Years 3, 4, and 5.

Uncertain Amount   Another, but less important, criticism of deferred tax accounting is that if the firm does find at some future date that it has income taxes payable that are greater than income tax expense, it is unlikely that the tax rate on the income will be the same as the rate at the time the

---

[15] Whether timing differences actually reverse remains a controversial question among accounting writers. A majority agree with GAAP on the matter of computing and recognizing deferred income taxes. They argue that the reasons offered against recognizing deferred income tax liabilities also support a conclusion that Accounts Payable are not liabilities either. After all, accounts payable are never paid off in the aggregate for a going concern; in fact, the amount of Accounts Payable usually grows over time.

The critical difference between accounts payable and income taxes, however, is that income taxes are levied on the income of a firm as a whole. Losses or deductions from one project can offset gains or income from another. The government does not tax a firm asset by asset. If a firm shrinks and become bankrupt, having no taxable income, the government will not ask for income tax payments; creditors (those who are due to be paid for the Accounts Payable) will be entitled to payment (or partial payment) from the remaining assets as the firm winds down its business. Accounts Payable do have significance as liabilities even though they may increase year after year. There has been empirical work on this issue of whether there are any, many, or few firms that find taxes payable exceeding tax expense because of reversals of depreciation timing differences. The interested reader can refer to the interchange in the *Journal of Accountancy*, April 1977, pages 53–59. The data show that for 3,100 companies over nineteen years (nearly 60,000 company-years), there are about 700 cases (slightly over 1 percent) of a firm's remaining profitable while its depreciable assets shrink in size for the year.

To avoid facing the question of whether the liability will ever be paid, *CICA Handbook*, section 3470, refers to the item as a "deferred credit" rather than as a liability.

deferred tax expense was originally computed. Tax rates change periodically. Even if aggregate timing differences eventually reverse at a time when the firm has taxable income, the tax rate for that period will not be currently estimable with reasonable precision in most cases.

Undiscounted Amount   Finally, note that obligations for deferred income taxes are shown as undiscounted amounts, not at the present value for those amounts. All other long-term obligations reported on the balance sheet are shown at the present value of the future cash payments. The present value is computed using the historical interest rate appropriate for the firm, as borrower, on the date the obligation is first recorded. The valuation method to be used for deferred income taxes is also under study by the Accounting Standards Committee.

LOSS CARRYBACK AND CARRYFORWARD

taxable loss
A loss recognizable for income tax purposes, but not necessarily on the income statement.

loss carryback
A provision of the Income Tax Act that allows losses to be applied against taxable income of previous years by refiling an amended return if there is insufficient taxable income in the current period to fully absorb the loss.

loss carryforward
A provision of the Income Tax Act that allows unused losses to be applied against taxable income of future years.

A company incurring a **taxable loss** for the year is permitted under the Income Tax Act to use the loss to reduce the taxable income of the preceding three years. If the loss is in excess of the taxable income of the preceding three years, the excess may be applied to reduce taxable income in the succeeding seven years. This section of the Act is called the **loss carryback** or **loss carryforward** provision, and is an attempt to achieve equity by having the government participate in corporate losses as well as corporate income.

A tax loss that reduces the taxable income of a preceding year results in a refund of a portion of the taxes paid for the prior year. This refund will be recorded as a current asset and will reduce the loss for the current year.

When the taxable loss for a year exceeds the taxable income of the preceding three years, a company may apply the unused balance of the tax loss to reduce taxable income for any of the succeeding seven years. To realize the benefit from the loss carryforward, a company must earn taxable income during the succeeding seven years against which it can apply the loss carryforward. In view of the current year's tax loss, the presence of future taxable income is uncertain. Consequently, GAAP[16] ordinarily prohibit a company from anticipating the potential future benefit from a tax loss carryforward in its financial statements. To disclose the potential benefit from the loss carryforward, the company will include the following information in a footnote:

1. The amount of the loss carryforward(s) for tax purposes.
2. The expiration date(s) of the loss carryforward(s).

On the rare occasions in which a company is "virtually certain" of realizing a tax benefit from the loss carryforward, the company should treat the potential tax refund in the same fashion as that resulting from a loss carryback. Virtual certainty requires that several stringent conditions be satisfied.

---

[16] *CICA Handbook*, section 3470.

For a company that did not record the potential tax reduction of a loss carryforward because its realization was not "virtually certain," a further statement presentation problem arises if, in the future year, a tax reduction is realized by the application of the loss carryforward. In this case, GAAP require that the company present the tax recovery resulting from the loss carryforward in the income statement in the year when it is realized.

An illustration of the problem of loss carryback and carryforward based on data of ACO Ltd. for a seven-year period from the date of incorporation follows:

Net income (loss) before income tax of the company for year	
Year 1	$ 4,000
Year 2	6,000
Year 3	3,000
Year 4	5,000
Year 5	(33,000)
Year 6	16,000
Year 7	8,000

During the period, the corporate tax rate was 40 percent and the taxable income or loss equalled accounting income or loss reported above. The company was not virtually certain of receiving a tax benefit from a loss carryforward at the end of Year 5.

The condensed income statements of the company for the seven-year period, in accordance with GAAP, are presented in Exhibit 10.5.

EXHIBIT 10.5
ACO LTD.
Income Statement for the Years Ended December 31, Year 1 to Year 7

	Year 7	Year 6	Year 5	Year 4	Year 3	Year 2	Year 1
Net Income (Loss) Before the Undernoted	$8,000	$16,000	$(33,000)	$5,000	$3,000	$6,000	$4,000
Income Tax (Expense) Recoverable	(3,200)	(6,400)	5,600[a]	(2,000)	(1,200)	(2,400)	(1,600)
Net Income Before Extraordinary Item	4,800	9,600	na[d]	na[d]	na[d]	na[d]	na[d]
Income Tax Reductions Realized Because of Loss in Year Ended December 31, Year 5	1,200[c]	6,400[b]	na[d]	na[d]	na[d]	na[d]	na[d]
Net Income (Loss)	$6,000	$16,000	$(27,400)	$3,000	$1,800	$3,600	$2,400

[a] 40% × ($6,000 + $3,000 + $5,000).
[b] 40% × $16,000.
[c] 40% × [$33,000 − ($6,000 + $3,000 + $5,000 + $16,000)].
[d] Not applicable; heading would not appear in the income statement.

AN INTERNATIONAL PERSPECTIVE

With the exception of those in the United States and Canada, firms in most industrialized countries account for leases as operating leases and do not specify criteria for distinguishing capital leases from operating leases. Firms often lease rather than purchase assets through borrowing because they are unable to take full advantage of income tax deductions from accelerated depreciation and interest. Such lessee firms expect the lessor to claim the tax deductions and pass along some of the benefits realized through lower lease payments. Thus, these firms prefer the operating lease method for tax purposes. Because of book/tax conformity requirements in many of these countries (for example, France, Japan, and Germany), such firms account for the leases as operating leases for financial reporting as well. Lessors likewise prefer the operating lease method, both because it permits them to claim depreciation and because they avoid recognizing a gain on the "sale" of leased property that occurs when they use the capital lease method. Such gains would be immediately subject to income taxes.

Countries that permit firms to select different methods of accounting for financial and tax reporting (for example, the United States, Canada, and Great Britain) require deferred tax accounting. Firms provide deferred taxes for all timing (temporary) differences in the United States and Canada, whereas firms in Great Britain provide deferred taxes only when a firm expects that a liability for deferred taxes will be paid in a short period of time. The book/tax conformity requirement in France, Japan, and Germany largely eliminates the need for deferred tax accounting.

Accounting for income taxes is currently one of the most controversial issues facing the accounting profession. In the 1980s, the International Federation of Accountants issued a standard requiring a move from the *deferral* method to the *liability* method. The details need not concern us; the liability method was simply deemed to be theoretically more sound. The United States promulgated a standard requiring the liability method, and Canada issued an Exposure Draft calling for similar change. Reaction from the accounting profession and industry was swift and hostile — the new standard was a computational nightmare. This has led to a moratorium on the adoption of the liability method. Thus, we see the tradeoff between conceptual elegance and practicality that accountants must face.

KEY TERMS

Carrying charges
Implicit interest
Imputed interest rate
Sales-type lease
Direct financing lease
Operating lease
Capital lease
Leasehold
Executory contract
Off-balance-sheet financing
Pension plan
Noncontributory plan

Contributory plan
Defined-contribution plans
Defined-benefit plans
Timing difference
Permanent differences
Income tax expense
Income taxes payable
Deferred Income Taxes
Taxable loss
Loss carryback
Loss carryforward

SELF-STUDY MATERIAL

This section contains questions, exercises, and problems to help you assess your understanding of Chapter 10. Careful review of this material will assist you in completing the homework assignments. Solutions are found at the end of the section.

QUESTIONS AND EXERCISES

True/False

For each statement, place a T or an F in the space provided to indicate whether the statement is true or false.

_____ 1. Income tax management attempts to maximize the present value of cash payments for income taxes.

_____ 2. In a noncontributory pension plan, only the employee contributes to the pension fund.

_____ 3. The amounts to be contributed to the pension plan by the employer are defined in a defined-benefit plan.

_____ 4. Under a defined benefit plan, total corporate pension expense consists only of current service costs.

_____ 5. In an operating lease, the lessor transfers the rights to use the property to the lessee for a specified period of time.

_____ 6. Many firms prefer the operating lease method because the reported income is higher in the earlier years of the lease than it would be under the capital lease method.

_____ 7. If the present value of the contractual lease payments equals or exceeds 75 percent of the fair market value of the asset at the time the loan is signed, GAAP requires that the lease be accounted for as a capital lease.

_____ 8. Current service cost is the present value of pension liabilities generated by employees' service during the period.

_____ 9. If a lease is considered to be, in substance, an installment purchase of property, the property and the unpaid obligation should be accounted for under the operating lease method.

_____ 10. If the lease term extends for at least 75 percent of the leased asset's life, the lease should be accounted for as an operating lease.

_____ 11. A visitor to Nova Scotia who rents a car for two weeks rents it under an operating lease arrangement.

_____ 12. An interest rate may have to be imputed for a long-term liability that has no interest rate stated for the obligation.

_____ 13. If a pension plan is funded, cash is set aside to pay the future liability.

_____ 14. Under the capital lease method, the lessee merely records annual rent expense when the lease payment is made.

_____ 15. Lessors prefer to account for a lease as an operating lease because it enables the recognition of a gain on the "sale" of the leased asset.

_____ 16. A way to determine the present value of a long-term liability that has no explicitly stated interest rate is to use the market value of the asset acquired when the long-term liability was incurred.

_____ 17. When a pension plan is adopted, current employees may receive credit for services rendered to the company before the pension plan is adopted. On adoption of the pension plan, the employer records a long-term liability for the cost of past service.

_____ 18. Off-balance-sheet financing is preferred by lessees because the leased asset and corresponding obligation are left off the balance sheet.

_____ 19. The capital lease method recognizes expenses later than does the operating lease method.

_____ 20. Past service obligations may result when the terms of a pension plan are changed.

_____ 21. In a defined-contribution plan, the benefits to be received by retired employees are not defined.

_____ 22. The recognition of a lease asset and obligation on the books of the lessee will increase the lessee's debt-equity ratio.

Matching

From the list of terms, select one term that is most closely associated with one descriptive phrase or statement that follows and place the letter for that term in the space provided.

a. capital lease method
b. current service costs
c. defined-benefit plan
d. defined-contribution plan
e. imputed interest rate
f. lessee

g. lessor
h. noninterest-bearing note
i. off-balance-sheet financing
j. operating lease method
k. past service obligation
l. vesting provisions

_____ 1. Landlord.

_____ 2. This treatment recognizes the signing of a lease as the simultaneous acquisition of a long-term asset and the incurring of a long-term liability.

_____ 3. Cost assigned annually for the pension benefits earned during a given year.

_____ 4. The amounts to be paid to an employee on retirement are based on a formula that usually takes into account the employee's length of service and average earnings.

_____ 5. The amounts to be contributed to the pension plan by the employer are defined, but the benefits to be received by retired employees are not defined.

_____ 6. This time is not recognized as a liability in the accounting records, but its amount is disclosed in the notes to the financial statements and is amortized and funded over a given period of time.

_____ 7. Tenant.

_____ 8. A note that carries no explicitly stated interest rate.

_____ 9. Under this method, the owner, or lessor, merely sells the rights to use the property to the lessee for specified periods of time.

_____ 10. Determine the employee's rights to the employer's contribution to a pension plan.

_____ 11. Results in more favourable debt-equity ratios and may favourably affect future credit ratings and future borrowing costs.

_____ 12. Interest rate appropriate to the particular borrower, given the amount and terms of the borrowing arrangement.

Multiple Choice

Choose the best answer for each question or problem and enter the identifying letter in the space provided.

_____ 1. An entry such as this one indicates that the lessee has accounted for the lease in what manner?

Interest Expense	xx	
Liability: Obligation Under Capital Lease	xx	
Cash		xx

a) sales-type lease
b) operating lease
c) capital lease
d) none of the above

_____ 2. A lease must be accounted for as a capital lease if it meets any one of three conditions. Which of the following is *not* one of the conditions?
a) The discounted value of the contractual lease payments are 90 percent of more of the fair value of the asset when the lease is signed.
b) The lease transfers ownership of property to lessee.
c) The lease term is 90 percent or more of the estimated economic life of the leased property.
d) Each of the above is a condition that, if met, would cause the lease to be capitalized.

_____ 3. An employee is likely to prefer this type of pension plan because it reduces the employee's risk in planning for retirement.
a) nonvesting plan
b) defined-contribution plan
c) nonfunded plan
d) defined-benefit plan

_____ 4. The formation or sweetening of a pension plan usually creates employer obligations to pay pensions for past years' work. These obligations are called:
a) current service costs
b) funded costs
c) vested costs
d) none of the above

_____ 5. On January 2, 19X1, Windland Inc. purchased land and gave in exchange a $50,000 noninterest-bearing note, which is due in five years. Using a 10 percent imputed interest rate, the land and the note payable were both recorded at $31,050. Assuming that Windland recognizes interest under the effective-interest method, interest expense for 19X2 would be:
a) $3,790
b) $3,105
c) $3,415.50
d) $5,000

_____ 6. Refer to question 5. At what amount would the note payable be recorded on the December 31, 19X2 balance sheet?
a) $50,000
b) $31,050
c) $34,155
d) none of the above

_____ 7. Which of the following is *not* a perceived advantage of off-balance-sheet financing?
a) the debt-equity ratio will be higher
b) future credit ratings might be higher
c) future borrowing costs might be lower
d) all of the above are perceived advantages of off-balance-sheet financing

_____ 8. Generally, the accounting treatment for leases favoured by lessors and lessees is:
a) both generally prefer operating leases
b) both generally prefer capital leases
c) lessors prefer capital leases, while lessees prefer operating leases
d) lessors prefer operating leases, while lessees prefer capital leases

_____ 9. This method of recording leases recognizes the signing of the lease as the acquisition of a long-term asset and the incurring of a long-term liability for lease payments:
a) operating lease method
b) capital lease method
c) rental lease method
d) none of the above

_____ 10. Under this method of recording leases, the lessee must amortize the leasehold over its useful life and must recognize each lease payment as part payment of interest and part principal:
a) operating lease method
b) capital lease method
c) rental lease method
d) none of the above

_____ 11. On July 1, 19X1, Bill sold to Daryl a hectare of land in exchange for Daryl's $4,000 noninterest-bearing note due in three years. The fair market value of the land is determined to be $3,100. What is the present value of Daryl's obligation to Bill on July 1, 19X1?
a) $3,100
b) $3,250
c) $4,000
d) none of the above

_____ 12. Refer to question 11. Assume that the difference between the present value and the face value of the liability is to be amortized by the straight-line method. What amount would be amortized for the period July 1 to December 31, 19X1?
a) $100
b) $300
c) $900
d) none of the above

_____ 13. On January 1, 19X1, Burnace Limited leased a building and recorded the leasehold asset and the liability at $42,124, which is the present value of five end-of-year payments of $10,000 each discounted at 6 percent. The asset has a useful life of five years and a zero disposal value. On December 31, 19X1, when the first lease payment is made, Burnace should record interest expense of:
a) 0
b) $1,575.20
c) $7,876
d) none of the above

_____ 14. Refer to question 13. Assuming straight-line amortization, on December 31, 19X1, Burnace should report the book value of the leasehold asset on its balance sheet in the amount of:
   a) $50,000
   b) $33,699.20
   c) $42,124
   d) none of the above

Exercises

1. On January 2, 19X1, Kwe-Kwe Company Inc. purchased machinery and gave in exchange a $90,000 noninterest-bearing note due in three years. Assuming that a 14 percent interest rate has been imputed for this transaction, the present value of the note on January 2, 19X1 is $60,750. Kwe-Kwe recognizes interest expense under the effective-interest method.

   Record the appropriate entries for the note from January 2, 19X1 until the note is paid on maturity on January 2, 19X4.

2. On January 2, 19X1, the Mutare Co. Ltd. leased a machine for four years. Annual rentals of $25,000 are to be paid at the end of each calendar year. The present value on January 2, 19X1 of the four lease payments, discounted at 8 percent, is $82,800. The asset's useful life is four years, and its disposal value is zero.

   Prepare all 19X1 entries relative to the lease of the machine if Mutare records the lease by the capital lease method. Also, prepare the 19X2 entry for the lease payment.

PROBLEM 1 FOR SELF-STUDY

The Chang Company purchased a truck from Guttman's Auto Agency. The truck had a list price of $25,000, but discounts of 10 to 15 percent from list price are common in purchases of this sort. Chang Company paid for the truck by giving a noninterest-bearing note due two years from the date of purchase. The note had a face value of $28,730. The rate of interest that Chang Company paid to borrow on secured two-year loans ranged from 10 to 15 percent during the period when the purchase occurred.

a. Record the acquisition of the truck on Chang Company's books, assuming that the fair market value of the truck was computed using 10 percent discount from list price.

b. What imputed interest rate will be used throughout the loan for computing interest expense if the acquisition is recorded as in part (a)?

c. Record the acquisition of the truck on Chang Company's books, assuming that the estimated interest rate Chang Company must pay to borrow is deemed reliable and is 12 percent per year.

d. Record the acquisition of the truck on Chang Company's books, assuming that the interest rate Chang Company must pay to borrow is 1 percent per month.

e. Prepare journal entries to record the loan and to record interest over two years, assuming that the track is recorded at $23,744 and the interest rate implicit in the loan is 10 percent per year.

f. Throughout, this book has stressed that over long enough time periods, total expense is equal to cash outflow. In what sense is the total expense for this transaction the same, independent of the interest rate (and, therefore, the interest expense)?

PROBLEM 2 FOR SELF-STUDY

Landlord Co. Ltd., as lessor, entered into a long-term lease agreement with Tenant Limited, as lessee. The present value of the lease payments and the fair value of the property exceeded the lessor's cost of manufacturing the asset. Both companies accounted for the lease as an operating lease, whereas both companies should have accounted for it as a capital lease. What effect — understated, overstated, or none — will this error have on each of the following items in the financial statements of each of the companies for the first year of the lease?

a. Current assets

b. Liabilities

c. Revenue

d. Expense

e. Net income

f. Retained earnings

PROBLEM 3 FOR SELF-STUDY

Rachel Limited adopted a defined benefit pension plan at the beginning of 19X1. An actuarial valuation at this date showed the following:

Accrued benefits	$8,000,000
Market value of pension fund assets	9,000,000
Expected coverage remaining service life of employees	25 years
Rate of return expected on invested fund assets	7%
Expected salary increase rate	8%
Funding requirement for 19X1	$250,000
Increasing in accrued benefits attributable to 19X1 service rendered	160,000
Estimated benefit payments for 19X1	50,000

a. Calculate 19X1 pension expense.

b. What amount will be shown on Rachel's balance sheet?

c. Give the journal entries made in 19X1. (Assume that all assumptions are realized, so no experience gain or loss occurs.)

PROBLEM 4 FOR SELF-STUDY

The accounting records of Wilson Incorporated disclose the following data on book and taxable income for Year 1 through Year 4:

	Year 4	Year 3	Year 2	Year 1
(1) Pretax Book Income	$90,000	$90,000	$90,000	$90,000
(2) Timing differences (Reducing) or Increasing Book Income to Taxable Income	$ 5,000	$15,000	($10,000)	($20,000)

The income tax rate is 40 percent of taxable income.

a. Compute taxable income on which income taxes are payable.

b. Compute the book amount on which income tax expense is based for each year.

c. Give the journal entries to record income tax expense, income taxes payable, and deferred income taxes for each year.

d. Compute aftertax net income for each year.

e. What is the balance in the Deferred Income Taxes account on the balance sheet at the end of Year 4?

PROBLEM 5 FOR SELF-STUDY

The Dominiak Co. Inc. reports the following information about its financial statements and tax return for a year:

Depreciation Expense from Financial Statements	$270,000
Financial Statement Pretax Income	160,000
Income Tax Expense from Financial Statements	36,000
Income Taxes Payable from Tax Returns	24,000

Taxable income is taxed at a rate of 40 percent. Permanent differences result from dividend income from Canadian companies that is revenue in the financial statements but is exempt from income taxes. Timing differences result from claiming the maximum capital cost allowance for tax returns and straight-line depreciation for financial reporting.

Reconstruct the financial statements and the tax return for the year, identifying the components of timing differences and permanent differences.

ANSWERS TO SELF-STUDY QUESTIONS AND EXERCISES

True/False

1. F	7. F	13. T	19. F
2. F	8. T	14. F	20. T
3. F	9. F	15. F	21. T
4. F	10. F	16. T	22. T
5. T	11. T	17. F	
6. T	12. T	18. T	

Matching

1. g	4. c	7. f	10. l
2. a	5. d	8. h	11. i
3. b	6. k	9. j	12. e

Multiple Choice

1. c	5. c	9. b	13. d
2. c	6. d	10. b	14. b
3. d	7. a	11. a	
4. d	8. c	12. d	

Exercises

1.

		Dr.	Cr.
01/02 19X1	Machinery Note Payable	$60,750	$60,750

To record purchase of machine in exchange for a noninterest-
bearing note.

12/31 19X1	Interest Expense Note Payable	$ 8,505	$ 8,505

To record interest expense for 19X1

Interest $= 0.14 \times \$60,750 = \$8,505$

12/31 19X2	Interest Expense Note payable	$ 9,696	$ 9,696

To record interest expense for 19X2.

Interest $= 0.14 \times (\$60,750 + \$8,505) = \$9,696$

12/31 19X3	Interest Expense Note Payable	$11,049	$11,049

To record interest expense for 19X3.

Interest $= \$90,000 - \$60,750 - \$8,505 - \$9,696 =$
$\$11,049$

01/12 19X4	Note Payable Cash	$90,000	$90,000

To record payment of note at maturity.

2.

		Dr.	Cr.
01/02 19X1	Asset: Machine Leasehold Liability: Obligation Under Capital Lease	$82,800	$82,800

To record leasehold asset and liability.

12/31 19X1	Amortization of Asset: Machine Leasehold Accumulated Amortization: Machine Leasehold	$20,700	$20,700

To record amortization of asset leasehold.

Amortization $= \dfrac{\$82,800}{4} = \$20,700$

12/31 19X1	Interest Expense Liability: Obligation Under Capital Lease Cash	$ 6,624 18,376	$25,000

To record payment of interest and principal.

Interest $= 0.08 \times \$82,800 = \$6,624$

12/31 19X2	Interest Expense Liability: Obligation Under Capital Lease Cash	$ 5,154 19,846	$25,000

To record payment of interest and principal.

Interest $= 0.08 (\$82,800 - \$18,376) = \$5,154$

SUGGESTED SOLUTION TO PROBLEM 1 FOR SELF-STUDY

(See Appendix A, page 1038 for present value computation.)

a. Truck	$22,500	
Note Payable		$22,500
0.90 × $25,000 = $22,500		

b. $28,730/$22,500 = 1.27689. The truck has fair market value of $22,500 (= 0.90 × $25,000);

$(1 + r)^2 = 1.27689$ implies that $r = \sqrt{1.27689} - 1 = 0.13$ or 13 percent per year. That is, $22,500 grows to $28,730 in two years when the interest rate is 13 percent per period.

c. Truck	$22,903	
Note payable		$22,903
$(1.12)^{-2} = 0.79719; 0.79719 × $28,730 = $22,903.$		

d. $(1.01)^{-24} = 0.78757.$ (See Table B.2, page 1067, 24 period row, 1 percent column.) $0.78757 × $28,730 = $22,627.$

Truck	$22,627	
Note Payable		$22,627

e. Truck	$23,744	
Note Payable		$23,744
Year 1		
Interest Expense (= 0.10 × $23,744)	$ 2,374	
Note Payable		$ 2,374
Year 2		
Interest Expense [= 0.10 × ($23,744 + $2,374)]	$ 2,612	
Note Payable		$ 2,612

f. Total expense equals interest expense on note *and* depreciation on truck. Interest expense is $28,730 less the amount at which the truck is recorded. Depreciation expense is equal to the amount at which the truck is recorded less estimated disposal value. Thus, over the life of the truck, or two years, whichever is longer, the total expense equals $28,730 less disposal value of the truck.

SUGGESTED SOLUTION TO PROBLEM 2
FOR SELF-STUDY

	Tenant Limited	Landlord Co. Ltd.
a. Current Assets	None	Understated[a]
b. Liabilities	Understated	None
c. Revenue	None	Understated[b]
d. Expense	Understated	Understated[b]
e. Net Income	Overstated	Understated[b]
f. Retained Earnings	Overstated	Understated[b]

[a] Lease receivables are part current and part noncurrent.
[b] In a capital lease, the lessor treats the signing of the lease as an installment sale. The lessor has sales revenue, cost of goods sold, and a new asset, the long-term receivable.

SUGGESTED SOLUTION TO PROBLEM 3
FOR SELF-STUDY

a. Components for the 19X1 expense

Costs related to current services rendered		$160,000
Amortization of experience gains/losses		nil
Amortization of adjustments arising from plan amendments or changes in assumptions		nil

Amortization of the net pension asset (surplus) arising on implementation of the current pension plan

$$\left(\frac{\$90,000,000 - \$8,000,000}{25 \text{ years}}\right)$$ (40,000)

Interest on the accrued pension benefits

Opening balance	$8,000,000	
Accrual for current year service	160,000	
Benefit payments this year	(25,000)	
	$8,135,000	
@8%		650,800

Interest on the pension fund assets

Opening balance	$9,000,000	
Funding contributions[a]	125,000	
Benefit payments this year[a]	(25,000)	
@7%		(637,000)
Net expense		$133,800

[a] The $50,000 in benefit payments are assumed to occur evenly throughout the year. For interest calculations, the mid-year point is chosen ($50,000 ÷ 2 = $25,000). The same assumption is used for funding contributions.

b. The balance sheet would show a liability of $33,800:

$133,800	expense
(100,000)	funding requirement
$ 33,800[b]	

[b] If the expense is less than the funding requirement, the difference is shown as a deferred charge (CICA Handbook, section 3460.57).

c. The compound journal entry for 19X1 is:

Pension Expense	$133,800	
Cash		$100,000
Liability for pension benefits		33,800

SUGGESTED SOLUTION TO PROBLEM 4 FOR SELF-STUDY

a. Taxable income on the tax return each year is line (1) plus or minus line (2). Year 1 — $70,000; Year 2 — $80,000; Year 3 — $105,000; Year 4 — $95,000.

b. Income tax expense for each year is based on line (1) — $90,000 for each year.

c. See Exhibit 10.6.

d. See Exhibit 10.6

e. $4,000 credit = $8,000 credit + $4,000 credit − $6,000 debit − $2,000 debit.

EXHIBIT 10.6
WILSON INCORPORATED
(Suggested Solution to Problem 4 for Self-Study)

	Year 4		Year 3		Year 2		Year 1
Journal Entries							
Income Tax Expense[a]	$36,000		$36,000		$36,000		$36,000
Deferred Income Taxes	2,000		6,000		—		—
Income Taxes Payable[b]		$38,000		$42,000		$32,000	$28,000
Deferred Income Taxes		—		—		4,000	8,000
Income Statement							
Pretax Book Income	$90,000		$90,000		$90,000		$90,000
Income Tax Expense	(36,000)		(36,000)		(36,000)		(36,000)
Net Income	$54,000		$54,000		$54,000		$54,000

[a] 0.40 of amounts in answer to part (b).
[b] 0.40 of amounts in answer to part (a).

SUGGESTED SOLUTION TO PROBLEM 5 FOR SELF-STUDY

EXHIBIT 10.7
Illustration of Timing Differences and Permanent Differences
Dominiak Co. Inc.
(Suggested Solution to Problem 5 for Self-Study)

	Financial Statements	Type of Difference	Income Tax Return
Operating Income Except Depreciation	$360,000 (6)	—	$360,000 (4)
Depreciation	(270,000) (g)	Timing	(300,000) (3)
Dividend Income	70,000 (5)	Permanent	—
Taxable Income	—		$ 60,000 (2)
Pretax Income	$160,000 (g)		
Income Taxes Payable at 40 Percent			$ 24,000 (g)
Income Tax Expense at 40 Percent of $90,000 = $160,000 − $70,000, which is Book Income Excluding Permanent Differences	(36,000) (g)		
Net Income	$124,000 (1)		

Order and derivation of computations:
(g) Given.
(1) $124,000 = $160,000 − $36,000.
(2) $60,000 = $24,000/0.40.
(3) Timing difference for depreciation is ($36,000 − $24,000)/0.40 = $30,000. Because income taxes payable are less than income tax expense, we know that capital cost allowance deducted on tax return exceeds depreciation expense on financial statements. Thus, the capital cost allowance deduction on the tax return is $300,000 = $270,000 + $30,000.
(4) $360,000 = $300,000 + $60,000.
(5) Taxable income on financial statements is $90,000 = $36,000/0.40. Total financial statement income before taxes, including permanent differences, is $160,000. Hence, permanent differences are $160,000 − $90,000 = $70,000.
(6) $160,000 + $270,000 − $70,000 = $360,000. See also (4), for check.

ASSIGNMENT MATERIAL

QUESTIONS

1. Review the meaning of the key terms listed on page 633.

2. In what sense is the historical-cost accounting for noncurrent liabilities subsequent to the date of issuance based on costs?

3. Brealey Limited negotiated a five-year loan for $1 million with its bank. The terms of the loan require that the interest rate can be changed as the bank chooses, but that the company can repay the loan at any time. Interest is to be paid quarterly. How should Brealey Limited classify this note on its balance sheet?

4. Demonstrate that the amortization schedule in Exhibit 10.1 conforms to the "unifying principles of accounting for long-term liabilities" described on page 573 of Chapter 9.

5. Why is the question, "Who enjoys the potential rewards and bears the risks of an asset?" important for lease accounting?

6. In what ways is the economic substance of a capital lease by a lessee similar to, and different from, that of an installment purchase?

7. Distinguish between the lessee's accounting for a capital lease and for an installment purchase.

8. In what sense is the total expense from a lease independent of the method of accounting for it by the lessee?

9. Why do many managements find off-balance-sheet financing attractive?

10. What are the economic and accounting differences between a defined-benefit pension plan and a defined-contribution plan?

11. Why does the amendment ("sweetening") of a defined-benefit plan ordinarily increase the past service obligation, whereas a change with the same cost in a defined-contribution plan does not?

12. The Hicks Co. Ltd. is adopting a defined-benefit pension plan. Who, the employee or the Hicks Co. Ltd., is more likely to bear the risks and rewards of fluctuating market returns on funds invested to pay the pension?

13. "Deferred income taxes might be viewed as an interest-free loan from the government." Do you agree?

14. Most firms report income tax expense that is a lower percentage of book, pretax income than the statutory tax rate. One cause of this is the investment tax rate. What is another cause?

15. Under what circumstances will the Deferred Income Taxes account reduce to a zero balance? Under what circumstances can deferred taxes represent an asset rather than a liability?

16. You have been called to testify before a parliamentary committee on income taxation. One committee member states, "My staff has added up all of the amounts shown for deferred taxes on the balance sheets of Canada's 500 largest corporations. If we collected these amounts immediately, we could reduce the national deficit by $50 billion. Since I have to pay my taxes immediately each year or be charged arrears interest, why shouldn't corporations be treated the same?" Respond to this statement.

17. Some individuals have called for adoption of a "taxes payable" approach to accounting for income taxes whereby the balance sheet records only the actual liability for current taxes owing. These individuals claim that because empirical research shows that only 15 percent of deferred tax liabilities ever turn into real liabilities, deferred tax accounting is a make-work project for accountants. Comment on this assertion.

EXERCISES

18. *Nature of liabilities.*
    a. For each of the following items, indicate whether the item meets all of the criteria of the accountant's usual definition of a liability.
    b. If the item is recognized as a liability, how is the amount of the liability computed?
    (1) Fifteen-year cancellable lease on an office building.
    (2) Twenty-year noncancellable lease on a factory building.
    (3) Anticipated future cost of restoring strip-mining sites after mining operations are completed.
    (4) Obligation to pay pensions under defined-benefit formula for labour services during current year.
    (5) Obligation to pay pensions under defined-benefit formula with retroactive credit given to employees for labour services provided before the plan was adopted.

19. *Journal entries for equipment contract with imputed interest.* Refer to the example on page 601 of this chapter where equipment is acquired in exchange for a single-payment note for $16,000 due in three years. The issuer of the note pays 12 percent interest for borrowing of this sort. The present value of the note on the date of issue is $11,388. Assume that the note is issued on January 1, Year 1 and that the firm closes its books annually.

    Provide adjusting entries for the end of Years 1, 2 and 3 and an entry for the payment of the note at maturity.

20. *Pension disclosures.* The *CICA Handbook* (section 3460.61) recommends rather than requires several pension-related disclosures, such as the pension expense for the period, the amount of the deferred charge or accrual, the basis of valuing fund assets, the salary and interest rate assumptions, the method and amortization period for all adjustments,

a general description of the plan, the date of the most recent actuarial valuation, and any matters that might affect comparability.

Go to the library and photocopy the pension footnote(s) from the annual report of any Canadian public corporation. Prepare for class discussion a critique of how its disclosure compares with these guidelines.

21. *Amortization schedule for note where explicit interest differs from market rate of interest.*   On January 1, Year 1, the beginning of the fiscal year, Garstka Limited acquires a computer from Berney's Computer Store. The cash price (fair market value) of the computer is $50,568. Garstka Limited gives a three-year, interest-bearing note with maturity value of $60,000. The note requires annual interest payments on December 31 of 9 percent of face value, $5,400 per year. The interest rate implicit in the note is 16 percent per year.
    a. Prepare an amortization schedule for the note.
    b. Prepare journal entries for Garstka Limited over the life of the note.

22. *Operating lease accounting (adapted from CPA Examination).*   The Jackson Co. Ltd. manufactured a piece of equipment at a cost of $7 million, which is held for resale from January 1 to June 30 at a price of $8 million. On July 1, Jackson leased the equipment to the Crystal Co. Ltd. The lease is appropriately recorded as an operating lease for accounting purposes. The lease is for a three-year period. Equal monthly payments under the lease are $115,000 and are due on the first of the month. The first payment was made on July 1. The equipment is being depreciated on a straight-line basis over an eight-year period with no disposal value expected.
    a. What expense should Crystal record as a result of the above facts for the current year ending December 31? Show supporting computations in good form.
    b. What income or loss before income taxes should Jackson record as a result of the above facts for the year ending December 31? Show supporting computations in good form.

23. *Understanding pension disclosures in financial statements.*   From the notes to financial statements of Imperial Oil Ltd., determine the following:
    a. The type of plan.
    b. The expense for pension costs shown in the 1986 income statement.
    c. How much the company actually pays into the pension plan each year.
    d. The adequacy of the pension fund in relation to Imperial Oil's obligations to its employees for its *regular* pension plans.
    e. Are the pension numbers reported by Imperial Oil for 1986 and 1985 comparable? Are any caveats to readers in order?

IMPERIAL OIL LTD.
In Summary of Accounting Policies

Retirement plans
The company's pension plans cover almost all employees. Pension-benefit obligations are determined annually by independent actuaries using the

projected-unit-credit method. Valuation of assets is based on market values at December 31 of each year. The amounts contributed by the company to the plans are established according to accepted actuarial procedures. Prior to 1986, the amount funded was also the pension expense for the year. In 1986, the Canadian Institute of Chartered Accountants published new standards for accounting for pension plans. As a result, starting in 1986 the amount expensed is determined on the accrual basis, which reflects the service of employees for the year rather than the amount contributed by the company to the plans.

Note to Financial Statements

16. *Employee retirement plans*

The pension plan cover almost all company employees and generally are based on length of service and on average earnings during the final three years of employment. The plans are funded by the company based on actuarial valuation, the most recent being December 31, 1985. As well, the amounts include the company's share of the pension plans for the Syncrude joint venture.

Funded status at December 31	1984	1985	1986
	(millions of dollars)		
Market value of assets	1057	1296	1319
Accumulated benefit obligation (1)	842	898	1067
Assets excess	215	298	252
Unearned benefit obligation (1)	308	328	222
(Unfunded liability) Surplus	(93)	70	30

The benefit obligation for 1986 is affected by the 1986 early-retirement program and an updating of the actuarial assumptions.

The surplus/unfunded liability is credited/charged to expense over the average remaining service life of employees, which is currently seventeen years.

In addition, actuarially determined obligations to surviving spouses (which are paid directly by the company) amount to $150 million at December 31, 1986.

Annual pension expense

In accordance with new accounting standards, the pension expense for 1986 is calculated on the accrual basis rather than the funding basis used in prior years. (See summary of significant accounting policies.)

	1984	1985	1986
	(millions of dollars)		
Current service cost	—	—	33
Interest cost	—	—	5
Plan amendment amortization	—	—	1
Expense for 1984 and 1985 based on funding method	32	34	—
Pension expense before 1986 early-retirement program	32	34	39
Expense of 1986 early-retirement program (2)	—	—	109
Total pension expense	32	34	148

Assumptions

The measurement of the retirement obligation and expense involves making assumptions about economic and other factors over an extended future period. In order to aid in understanding the information provided above, the following provides the most significant assumptions and their impact:

	1984	1985	1986
Rate of return on the plan's assets (percent)	7.0	7.0	8.5
Salary escalation rate (percent)	5.0	5.0	6.0
			(millions of dollars)
Impact of a 1 percent increase in rate of return on			
total benefit obligation (1)			(160)
annual expense			(9)
Impact of a 1 percent increase in salary escalation on			
total benefit obligation (1)			22
annual expense			1

(1) The total benefit obligation is the amount the pension fund needs to have invested at the assumed rate of return (currently 8.5 percent) in order to be able to pay pensions for service rendered to date. This obligation has two parts. The accumulated benefit obligation is based on current salaries and the unearned benefit obligation is the estimated additional amount due to salary escalation by the time of retirement.

(2) This amount is part of the work-force reduction program included in unusual items.

Source: 1986 Annual Report of Imperial Oil Ltd.

24. *Computation of pension expense.* The actuaries of Campbell Corporation have provided the following information on its pension plan as of 12/31/19X0:

	12/31/19X0[a]
Average service life remaining of employees covered by the plan	20 years
Expected salary rate increase	6%
Rate of return expected on fund assets	7%
Funding requirement for 19X1	$800,000
Increase in accrued benefits attributable to 19X1 service rendered	$200,000
Estimate of benefits to be paid out in 19X1	$100,000
Market value of fund assets at 12/31/19X0	$6,000,000
Accrued benefits at 12/31/19X0	$7,000,000

[a] *Campbell adopted a defined benefit plan at this date.*

Compute the 19X1 pension expense and the amount to be shown on the balance sheet at 12/31/19X1.

25. *Computations and journal entries for income taxes with both timing and permanent differences.* Joyce Inc. reported the following amounts for book and tax purposes for its first three years of operations:

	Year 3	Year 2	Year 1
Pretax Book Income	$440,000	$280,000	$300,000
Taxable Income	340,000	320,000	240,000

The differences between book and taxable income are attributable to the use of different depreciation methods. The income tax rate was 40 percent during all years.
   a. Give the journal entry to record income tax expense for each year.
   b. Assume, for this part, that $10,000 of dividend income from Canadian companies was included in the pretax book income amounts shown above for each year but properly excluded from taxable income. Give the journal entry to record income tax expense for each year.

26. *Income tax timing difference from differing methods of revenue recognition.* Refer to the data in Exhibit 4.3 on page 235 showing income over a five-year period under various methods of revenue and income recognition. Use the methods of accounting indicated below for financial statements and for tax returns. Assume an income tax rate of 40 percent. Compute income tax expense, income taxes payable, and deferred income taxes for each period. Put this information into journal entry form.
   a. Use the percentage-of-completion method on the financial statements and the completed contract method on the tax return.
   b. Use the cost-recovery-first method on the financial statement and the installment method on the tax return.

27. *Deriving permanent and timing differences from financial statement disclosures.* Gigondas Corp. reports the following information for a year:

Financial Statement Pretax Income	$106,000
Income Tax Expense	52,000
Income Taxes Payable for This Year	16,000
Income Tax Rate on Taxable Income	40 Percent

The company has both permanent and timing differences between book and taxable income.
   a. What is the amount of timing differences for the year? Give the amount and whether the effect is to make reported income larger or smaller than taxable income.
   b. What is the amount of permanent differences for the year? Give the amount and whether the effect is to make reported income larger or smaller than taxable income.

PROBLEMS AND CASES

28. *Comparing expense for operating lease with capital lease.* Maher Co. Ltd. has calculated that the annual payment in arrears to amortize a $1 million loan over twenty-five years at 15 percent interest is $154,700.
    a. What is rent expense for the first year of an operating lease when the rent payment is $154,700?
    b. What is lease expense for the first year of a twenty-five-year capital lease for use of an asset costing $1 million requiring annual payments in arrears of $154,700? Use straight-line amortization of leasehold.
    c. How much larger in percentage terms is the lessee's expense in the first year under the capital lease than under the operating lease?

29. *Criteria for classifying leases as operating or capital.* Assume that Rich's Department Stores Inc. is about to sign for separate leases for stores in four separate shopping centres. Each of the stores would cost $20 million if purchased outright and has an economic life of twenty years. Assume that the company currently must pay interest at the rate of 15 percent per year on long-term borrowing when sound collateral backs the loan. The lease payments are to be made at the end of each year in all four cases.

    On the basis of the information given here, decide whether each of the four leases requires accounting as operating leases or as capital leases. Give your reasoning.

	Lease Term	Annual Lease Payment
a. Cumberland Mall	16 Years	$2,500,000
b. Normandale Centre	16 Years	2,600,000
c. Eastbrook Haven	12 Years	3,300,000
d. Peachtree Parkview	12 Years	3,400,000

30. *Comparison of borrow/buy with operating and capital leases.* The Carom Co. Ltd. plans to acquire, as of January 1, Year 1, a computerized cash register system that costs $100,000 and has a five-year life and no disposal value. The company is considering two plans for acquiring the system.
    (1) Outright purchase. To finance the purchase, $100,000 of par value, 10 percent, semiannual coupon bonds will be issued January 1, Year 1 at par.
    (2) Lease. The lease requires five annual payments to be made on December 31, Year 1, Year 2, Year 3, Year 4, and Year 5. The lease payments are such that they have a present value of $100,000 on January 1, Year 1 when discounted at 10 percent per year.

    Straight-line amortization methods will be used for all depreciation and amortization computations for assets.
    a. Certify that the amount of the required lease payment is $26,380 by constructing an amortization schedule for the five payments.

Note that there will be a $2 rounding error in the fifth year. Nevertheless, you may treat each payment as being $26,380 in the rest of the problem.

b. What balance sheet amounts will be affected if plan (1) is selected? If plan (2) is selected, the lease is cancellable, and the operating lease treatment is used? If plan (2) is selected, the lease is noncancellable, and the capital lease treatment is used?

c. What will be the total depreciation and interest expenses for the five years under plan (1)?

d. What will be the total expenses for the five years under plan (2) if the lease is accounted for as an operating lease? As a capital lease?

e. Why are the answers in part (d) the same? Why are the answers in part (c) different from those in part (d)?

f. What will be the total expenses for Year 1 under plan (1)? Under plan (2) accounted for as an operating lease? Under plan (2) accounted for as a capital lease?

g. Repeat part (f) for the fifth year, Year 5.

31. *Analysis of risks and rewards of lease contracts.* Pacific Eastern Air Lines (PEA) leased three aircraft in Year 1 from Sally Leasing Limited (Sally). The aircraft had a purchase price of $6.64 million each. The leases covered thirteen-year terms, were noncancellable, contained no purchase options, and required monthly payments of $71,115. The rental cost per month of $71,115 was several hundred dollars less than PEA would have had to pay for conventional financing at the then-prevalent interest rate.

a. What, if anything, did PEA give up in return for its saving of several hundred dollars per month for thirteen years? What, if anything, did Sally get for giving up several hundred dollars per month for thirteen years?

b. Who bore the risks and rewards of ownership in these leases?

c. Verify that the interest rate implicit in the lease contract is about three-fourths of 1 percent per month.

d. Assume that section 3065 of the *CICA Handbook* had been in effect when these leases were signed. To ascertain how the leases would be accounted for, what further information would you need?

32. *Possible accounting treatments for past service obligations.* When a company adopts a defined-benefit pension plan giving credit to current employees for past service, an obligation, perhaps in large amounts, arises. This amount is currently disclosed in notes and is only gradually recognized in the balance sheet.

Assume that the amount is immediately credited to a liability when it comes into existence. What accounts might be debited? Give justifications for debiting an asset account or an expense account, or directly debiting Retained Earnings.

33. *Analysis of attempts to achieve off-balance-sheet financing [adapted from "Off-Balance-Sheet Financing," Case 3.1 in* Accounting and Auditing Case Studies *(The Trueblood Professors' Seminar), The Touche Ross Foundation and The American Accounting Association,*

1983, pp. 21–22]. Container Limited has developed a process for manufacturing plastic bottles at a cost lower than any competitor's. Gigantic Drugs, Inc. has offered to purchase enough of the bottles so that Container will have to build a new plant just to fill Gigantic's orders. The new plant will be built next to Gigantic's plant, with a conveyor belt to carry the bottles into Gigantic's plant. Container will operate the plant. The problem is that Container does not have, and is unable to raise, sufficient funds to finance construction of the new plant. Gigantic is willing to provide its financial backing to raise the necessary funds, but has insufficient cash to finance the project. Moreover, it is unwilling to borrow the funds if doing so will increase the recorded debt on its balance sheet because of potential default on some of its own debt covenants and some other new plans it has to raise funds by borrowing. The financial executives of Container and Gigantic have devised two plans to finance the plant while attempting to satisfy Gigantic's requirements. Under both plans, Container will create a subsidiary, Borrower Inc., to borrow all of the funds required from a bank to build the plant.

Plan 1 Borrower will lease the plant to Gigantic for forty years with lease payments matched in size and timing to Borrower's debt service payments to the bank. Gigantic is sufficiently solvent and profitable that its promised lease payments and the plant itself will induce a bank to provide 100 percent financing at Gigantic's borrowing rate. Borrower will contract with Container to manage the new plant.

Plan 2 Gigantic will sign a contract to purchase bottles from the new plant. It will buy all of the bottles produced by the plant when it operates at normal capacity. Contractual payments will cover all variable manufacturing costs, debt service on the bank loan, and the payments to Container to manage the new plant. If Gigantic does not wish to purchase the entire output of the plant, and if Borrower is unable to sell the bottles to other bottle users, Gigantic will agree to make a cash payment to Borrower for the difference so that Borrower can meet all of its cash obligations. Any cash that Borrower can generate from selling bottles to other bottle users for amounts larger than variable manufacturing costs will reduce the payments Gigantic makes to Borrower.

Discuss these two plans from two perspectives:
a. Consider the auditor who must decide whether each arrangement requires recognition on the balance sheet, or footnote disclosure is sufficient.
b. Consider an investment banker who is planning to bid on the new bond issue Gigantic will use to raise funds for a different purpose. The banker must take into account, among other things, Gigantic's entire financial structure.

34. *Analysis of take-or-pay contract including capitalization of future payments and possible losses.* Natural gas pipelines sign take-or-pay contracts with producers of natural gas. Under these contracts the pipelines agree to purchase the natural gas in fixed (or computable) quantities at fixed (or computable) prices or to pay for the gas even if they do not take delivery. By the mid-1980s, there was a large quantity of

natural gas contracted for relative to the amounts that could be sold by the pipelines. A *Business Week* article on the subject said:

> Most of the unfavorable contracts were hastily signed after the cold winters of 1977 and 1978, when the gas shortage assumed crisis proportions. The pipeline industry faced the prospect of . . . lawsuits over its inability to supply contracted-for fuel. . . . Aggressively bidding for new supplies, the pipelines bought their way out of the problem — and into an even greater mess. They now find themselves stuck with massive numbers of "take-or-pay" agreements. . . . The fear of another icy, gasless winter, some say, drove pipeline executives to close one bad deal after another. Tenneco . . . had 4 billion cu. ft. per day of gas available for delivery and sales of just over 2 billion cu. ft. per day. . . . [The] costs [of natural gas had] soared to $3.48 per thousand cu. ft. . . . and price escalators in many contracts threaten to keep costs rising, especially after [price] controls expire . . . .

The financial statements of Tenneco showed total assets of $17.4 billion, current liabilities of $6.9 billion, long-term debt of $5.0 billion, and owners' equity of $5.5 billion. Notes to the statements indicate that some of Tenneco's take-or-pay contracts extend twenty-five years into the future.

a. Compute the long-term debt ratio [= long-term debt/(long-term debt + owners' equity)] from the financial statement data.

b. Compute the present value of the obligation to take 4 billion cubic feet of gas per day for ten years. Assume a price of $3.50 per thousand cubic feet, a year of 300 business days, and a discount rate of 15 percent per year. Payments occur at year-end.

c. Assume that these contractual payments are capitalized on the balance sheet and that an asset is recorded in the same amount. Compute the long-term debt ratio.

d. Now assume that Tenneco will be able to sell only 60 percent of the contracted for gas. The other 40 percent will be paid for, but because it is not taken, there is no offsetting asset for this amount, only a loss. Assume that the loss is tax-deductible and assume an income tax rate of 46 percent. Recompute owners' equity and the long-term debt ratio for the financial data given above.

35. *Attempts to achieve off-balance-sheet financing* (adapted from materials by Richard Dieter, David L. Landsittel, John E. Stewart, and Arthur R. Wyatt). Brion Limited wishes to raise $50 million cash but, for various reasons, does not wish to do so in a way that results in a newly recorded liability. It is sufficiently solvent and profitable that its bank is willing to lend up to $50 million at the prime interest rate. Brion Limited's financial executives have devised six different plans, described below.

Transfer of Receivables with Recourse Brion Limited will transfer to Credit Corp. its long-term accounts receivable, which call for payments over the next two years. Credit Corp. will pay an amount equal to the present value of the receivables less an allowance for uncollectables and a discount because it is paying now, but will collect cash later. Brion Limited must repurchase from Credit Corp. at face value any receivables that become uncollectable in excess of the allowance. In addition, Brion Limited may repurchase any of the receivables not yet due at face value less a discount specified by formula and based on the prime rate at the time of transfer. (This option permits Brion Limited to benefit if an unexpected drop in interest rates occurs after the transfer.) The accounting issue is whether the transfer is a sale (whereby Brion Limited debits Cash, credits Accounts Receivable, and debits expense or loss on transfer) or merely a loan collateralized by the receivables (whereby Brion Limited debits Cash and credits Notes Payable at the time of transfer).

Product Financing Arrangement   Brion Limited will transfer inventory to Credit Corp., which will store inventory in a public warehouse. Credit Corp. may use the inventory as collateral for its own borrowing, the proceeds of which will be used to pay Brion Limited. Brion Limited will pay storage costs and will repurchase all of the inventory within the next four years at contractually fixed prices plus interest accrued for the time elapsed between the transfer and later repurchase. The accounting issue is whether the inventory is sold to Credit Corp., with later repurchases treated as new acquisitions for Brion's inventory, or whether the transaction is merely a loan, with the inventory remaining on Brion's balance sheet.

Throughput Contract   Brion Limited requires a branch line of a railroad to be built from the main rail line to carry raw material directly to its own plant. It could, of course, borrow the funds and build the branch line itself. Instead, it signs an agreement with the railroad to ship specified amounts of material each month for ten years. Even if it does not ship the specified amounts of material, it will pay the agreed shipping costs. The railroad will take the contract to its bank and, using it as collateral, borrow the funds to build the branch line. The accounting issue is whether Brion Limited should debit an asset for future rail services and credit a liability for payments to the railroad. The alternative is to make no accounting entry except when Brion makes payments to the railroad.

Construction Partnership   Brion Limited and Mission Inc. will jointly undertake to build a plant to manufacture chemicals both need in their own production process. Each will contribute $5 million to the project, called Chemical. Chemical will borrow another $40 million from a bank, with only Brion guaranteeing the debt. Brion and Mission are each to contribute equally to future operating expenses and debt service payments of Chemical but, in return for its guaranteeing the debt, Brion will have an option to purchase Mission's interest for $20 million four years hence. The accounting issue is whether Brion Limited should recognize a liability for the funds borrowed by Chemical; because of the debt guarantee, debt service payments will ultimately be the responsibility of Brion Limited. Alternatively, the debt guarantee is a commitment merely to be disclosed in notes to Brion Limited's financial statements.

Research and Development Partnership   Brion Limited will contribute a laboratory and preliminary finding about a potentially profitable gene-splicing discovery to a partnership called Venture. Venture will raise funds by selling the remaining interest in the partnership to outside investors for $2 million and borrowing $48 million from a bank, with Brion Limited guaranteeing the debt. Although Venture will operate under the management of Brion Limited, it will be free to sell the results of its further discoveries and development efforts to anyone, including Brion Limited. Brion Limited is not obligated to purchase any of Venture's output. The accounting issue is whether the liability should be recognized by Brion Limited. (Would it make any difference if Brion Limited had either the *option* to purchase or an *obligation* to purchase the results of Venture's work?)

Hotel Financing   Brion Limited owns and operates a profitable hotel. Brion could use the hotel as collateral for a conventional mortgage loan. Instead, it considers selling the hotel to a partnership for $50 million cash. The partnership will sell ownership interests to outside investors for $5 million and borrow $45 million from a bank on a conventional mortgage loan, using the hotel as collateral. Brion Limited guarantees the debt. The accounting issue is whether Brion Limited should record the liability for the guaranteed debt of the partnership.

Consider each of these proposed arrangements from the viewpoint of the auditor (who must decide whether the transaction will result in a liability to be recorded or whether footnote disclosure will suffice) and from the viewpoint of an investment banker (who must assess the financing structure of Brion Limited in order to make a competitive bid on a proposed new underwriting of Brion Limited common shares).

36. *Behaviour of deferred income tax account when new assets are acquired every year.*   Equilibrium Co. Ltd. adopted a program of purchasing a new machine each year. It claims the maximum capital cost allowance using a rate of 40 percent on its income tax return and straight-line depreciation on its financial statements. Each machine costs $15,000 installed and has an economic life of five years for financial reporting.
    a. Calculate the capital cost allowance claimed on the tax return for each of the first seven years.
    b. Calculate depreciation for each year using the straight-line method of depreciation.
    c. Calculate the annual difference between capital cost allowance claimed and depreciation charges using the results form parts **(a)** and **(b)**.
    d. Calculate the annual increase in the Deferred Income Taxes account for the balance sheet by multiplying the tax rate, 40 percent, by the amount found in part **(c)**.
    e. Calculate year-end balances for the Deferred Income Taxes account on the balance sheet.
    f. If Equilibrium Co. Ltd. continues to follow its policy of buying a new machine every year for $15,000, what will happen to the balance in the Deferred Income Taxes account on the balance sheet?

37. *Accounting for deferred income taxes using net present values of payments expected to be made.*   The Accounting Standards Board is considering changing the requirements and procedures for accounting for deferred income taxes. Assume that it will require that firms record income tax expense and liability for the *present value* of payments to be

made when timing differences reverse. In all respects, the methods will conform to the principles of historical-cost accounting for liabilities.

Describe the estimates firms will have to make, the journal entries that will be required on first recording the deferred tax liability, and the subsequent entries in subsequent periods as the reversal approaches and occurs.

38. *Tax loss carryback and carryforward.* Taxco Ltd. is subject to a corporate income tax rate of 40 percent. Assume that it pays all income taxes and receives all rebates in the year that the income tax return is filed. The taxable income (loss) for each of the Years 1 through 7, before considering the loss carryback and carryforward provisions of the Income Tax Act, are:

Year	Taxable Income (Loss)
1	$20,000
2	(7,000)
3	18,000
4	6,000
5	(29,000)
6	4,000
7	7,000

Prepare a schedule of income payments made, or rebates received, for each of the Years 2 to 7, inclusive.

39. *Tax loss carryback and carryforward.* Goren Limited reports taxable income, before application of loss carryback and carryforward, for the first seven years of operations as follows:

Year	Profit (Loss)
1	$ 3,000
2	6,000
3	(11,000)
4	(6,000)
5	4,000
6	11,000
7	(6,000)

What is the taxable income (loss) for each year, as originally submitted and as revised, after applying the loss carryback, carryforward provisions of the Income Tax Act?

DECISION CASE 10-1

Shifty Moving Ltd. is considering the acquisition of a warehouse to provide storage for its moving customers. R.U. Shifty, the president and sole shareholder, has designed a suitable frame building, which he can have constructed for $100,000 on land leased for forty years. He is considering alternative methods of financing the construction.

Shifty Moving Ltd. is subject to a 40 percent marginal rate of income tax.

R.U. Shifty has approached an insurance company that is prepared to lend Shifty Moving $100,000 in exchange for a first mortgage for the same amount bearing interest at 12 percent, with payments of principal and interest of $12,130 per year in arrears. The mortgage would be paid in full in forty years.

As an alternative, Shifty is considering financing the warehouse from a trust fund established for his children by his father. He and his two unmarried sisters are the trustees of the fund. His sisters follow his advice, because Shifty pays them an annual gift of $1,600 a month as a balm to his conscience for paying them only 20 percent of the real value of the shares in Shifty Moving Ltd.; these shares were willed to the three of them by their father.

Shifty has considered that the trust fund can purchase the building and lease it to the company for $12,130 per year in arrears on a forty-year lease. Shifty Moving Ltd. would pay all taxes and maintenance costs, and the building would have no value in forty years' time.

Shifty has heard that, if he considers the lease a "capital lease," he will be required to record the asset and liability on his books and present them in his financial statements in a similar fashion to that necessary if he were to choose the mortgage issue alternative. Ont the other hand, if he considers the lease to be an "operating lease," he need not show the asset and liability in his financial statements.

Because of his indirect control of the trust fund, Shifty determines that the lease could be written so that it might be considered either as a capital lease or as an operating lease. In either case, the annual payment, in arrears, would be $12,130 over a period of forty years.

Evaluate the alternative methods of financing the construction (mortgage purchase, capital lease, operating lease).

CHAPTER ELEVEN

SHAREHOLDERS' EQUITY: A PERMANENT SOURCE OF CAPITAL

CHAPTER OUTLINE

- Incorporating Acts
- Capital Contributions
- Issuances of Shares for Cash
- Costs of Issuing Shares
- Share Subscriptions
- Issuances of Shares for Assets Other than Cash
- Treasury Shares
- Reacquisition of Shares by Redemption
- Retained Earnings
- Dividend Policy
- Other Changes in Shareholders' Equity Accounts
- Reporting Income and Retained Earnings Adjustments
- Disclosure of Changes in Shareholders' Equity
- An International Perspective

The economic resources of a firm come from two major sources. Non-owners provide funds to a firm; the sources of these funds are shown on the balance sheet as *liabilities*, discussed in Chapters 9 and 10. Owners provide funds; the sources of these funds are shown on the balance sheet as **owners' equity**.

owners' equity
The interest or claim of an entity's owners in the entity's assets; equal to assets less liabilities.

Assets = Claims to Assets
or
Assets = Liabilities + Owners' Equity

There are three different legal forms that a business can practice under in Canada: sole proprietorship, partnership, and corporation. *Owners' equity* is a general term that encompasses all three types of business organization. Because we will be discussing only the corporation in this chapter, we will use the more specific term **shareholders' equity**.

shareholders' equity
Proprietorship or owners' equity of a limited company. Assets less liabilities.

Corporations dominate the economic activity of Canada. Although fewer than 20 percent of Canadian businesses are incorporated, those companies generate more than 75 percent of the gross sales. There are three major advantages to incorporation:

1. The corporate form provides the owner (shareholder) with limited liability. That is, should the corporation become insolvent, creditors' claims are limited to the assets of the corporate entity. The corporation's creditors cannot claim the assets of the individual owners. On the other hand, creditors of partnerships and sole proprietorships have a claim on both the owners' personal and the business assets to settle such firms' debts.[1]

2. The corporate form allows the raising of funds by the issuing of shares. The general public can acquire the shares in varying amounts. Individual investments can range from a few dollars to hundreds of millions of dollars.

3. The corporate form makes transfer of ownership interests relatively easy, because individual shares can be sold by current owners to others without interfering with the ongoing operations of the business. Changes in ownership do not affect the continuity of the management and of operations.

There are also disadvantages to incorporation. The major disadvantage is double taxation — corporations must pay income tax on earnings whether or not earnings are distributed to shareholders. Remaining earnings, distributed as dividends, are taxed again in the shareholders' hands.[2] Another disadvantage is that corporations are generally subject to more government regulation and supervision than unincorporated businesses face.

This chapter discusses the accounting for capital contributed by owners; the accounting for income earned by the firm, which may be retained or distributed to owners; and other changes in shareholders' equity accounts.

INCORPORATING ACTS

A corporation is an artificial legal "person" created with the approval of government. As such, it can sue, be sued, enter into contracts, and pay income taxes as would an individual. A firm may choose to be incorporated federally under the jurisdiction of the **Canada Business Corporations Act (CBCA)** or provincially under one of the provincial corporations acts. Variations exist in the rules among these acts, especially with respect to the accounting and disclosure of capital transactions. The most significant of these involve whether par-value shares and treasury shares are allowed. Throughout this chapter, we will differentiate between CBCA and non-CBCA requirements.

Canada Business Corporations Act (CBCA) An act of the federal Parliament that establishes rules for incorporating businesses and for conduct of affairs by incorporated companies.

---

[1] Note that, with small firms, the directors/owners are often required to guarantee the firm's liabilities.

[2] Dividends received from Canadian corporations are eligible for a dividend tax credit. Depending on the individual's personal tax rate, this can largely eliminate the double taxation.

PUBLIC VERSUS PRIVATE CORPORATIONS

public corporations
Companies whose shares are traded on a public stock exchange.

Two fundamentally different types of corporations exist in Canada: **public corporations** and **private corporations**. Although the terms were created under the predecessor Canada Corporations Act and have been discontinued in the CBCA, they are still widely used.

A public company offers its shares to the general public and is usually listed on one of the five Canadian stock exchanges. Most of the large companies in Canada are public, although there are some exceptions, such as the T. Eaton Company. A private company is a *closely held company*. This means that its shares are owned by a small number of people and that they are not marketed to the general public or sold on public stock exchanges.

private corporations
Limited, closely held companies whose shares are not listed on a recognized stock exchange or otherwise available to the public investor.

From an accounting perspective, the key distinction between these two types of companies is that private companies are not legally required to have an annual audit, unless a shareholder requests one, and are not required to file annual financial statements with the Director of Companies or with the provincial securities commission. In order to qualify for this exemption, the corporation must meet a size test imposed by the CBCA. The corporation must have gross revenues of less than $10 million and total assets under $5 million.

Two implications arise from these exemptions. First, small, closely held companies can escape much of the costly bureaucratic red tape that large corporations face. Second, because most Canadian companies are small, closely held companies, the public has no access to their financial statements.

CAPITAL CONTRIBUTIONS

A corporation is a legal entity separate from its owners. Individuals or other entities make capital contributions under a contract between themselves and the corporation. Because those who contribute funds receive and hold share certificates, they are known as **shareholders**.[3] The rights and obligations of a shareholder are governed by:

shareholders
Those who hold the shares of a corporation (i.e., the owners).

1. The corporation laws of the jurisdiction in which incorporation takes place.

2. The **articles of incorporation** or *charter*. This is a contract between the firm and a provincial or the federal government under whose laws the business is incorporated. The enterprise is granted the privileges of operating as a corporation for certain stated purposes and of obtaining its capital through the issue of shares.

articles of incorporation
A document prepared on incorporation that sets forth the structure and purposes of the corporation and specifics regarding shares to be issued.

3. The bylaws of the corporation. The board of directors adopts bylaws, which are the rules and regulations governing the internal affairs of the corporation.

4. The share contact. Each type of share capital has its own provisions regarding such matters as voting, sharing in earnings, distribution of earnings, and sharing in assets in case of dissolution.

---

[3] The terminology in the United States is *stockholder* (and *stock* instead of *shares*). Many Canadian companies now use the term *capital stock* instead of *share capital*.

Some closely held corporations have a small number of shareholders and operate much like a partnership. The few people involved agree to the amount of capital to be contributed, elect each other to be members of the board of directors and officials to the firm, and agree on policies regarding dividends and salaries. They may restrict the transfer of shares to outsiders, and may even become liable for debts of the corporation by endorsing its notes and bonds.

In the case of large, widely held corporations, the effect of the corporation's beginning a separate legal entity is more pronounced. Officials and directors may own few or no shares in the corporation. Actual control is likely to be in the hands of a few individuals or a group who own or control enough shares to elect a majority of the board of directors. Most "minority" shareholders think of their shareholdings merely as passive investments, and they participate little, if at all, in the conduct of the affairs of the corporation. The shareholders assume no obligation for the debts of the business. Shares change hands at the will of the shareholders, and the record of who owns shares is usually kept by a trust company.

CLASSES OF SHARES

Corporations are often authorized to issue more than one class of shares, each representing ownership in the business. Most shares issued are either *common* or *preferred*. Occasionally, there may be several classes of common or preferred shares, each with different rights and privileges. All corporations must have at least one class of shares. They are usually called "common shares," but they may be designated by another name, such as Class A shares. Preferred shares may, but need not be, issued by a corporation.

Common shares have the claim to earnings of the corporation after commitments to preferred shareholders have been satisfied. Frequently, common shares are the only voting shares of the company. In the event of corporate dissolution, all of the proceeds of asset disposition, after the setting of claims of creditors and required distributions to preferred shareholders, are distributable to the common shareholders.

Preferred shares have special privileges. Although these privileges vary considerably from issue to issue, a preferred share usually entitles its holder to receive dividends at a certain rate, which must be paid before dividends can be paid to common shareholders. Sometimes, though, these dividends may be postponed or omitted.

DIVIDEND PREFERENCE

The amount of dividends to be paid may be specified in dollars per share or as a percentage of the stated share value. However, the dividend becomes a legal obligation to the shareholders only if declared.

Preferred dividends are usually **cumulative** — that is, regular dividends to preferred shareholders omitted in past years must be paid in addition to the current year's dividend before any distribution is made to common shareholders. For example, a company might decide not to declare a dividend in an unprofitable year. If a $6 preferred stock dividend was one year in arrears and a dividend was declared in the current year, preferred share-

Common shares
Basic ownership class of corporate capital stock, carrying the right to vote, to share in earnings, to participate in future issuances of shares, and to share in any liquidation proceeds after prior claims have been settled.

Preferred shares
A class of corporate capital stock that typically receives priority over common shares in dividend payments and distribution of assets if the corporation is liquidated.

cumulative (dividends)
A feature associated with some classes of shares such that they are entitled to receive any dividends in arrears before any distributions can be made to the common shareholders.

holders would receive $12 per share before common shareholders received anything. If a preferred share is noncumulative, omitted dividends do not carry forward. Because investors normally consider the cumulative feature attractive, noncumulative preferred shares are rarely issued.

Dividends in arrears (that is, omitted in past years) on cumulative preferred shares are not an accounting liability and do not appear in the liability section of the balance sheet. They do not become an obligation of the corporation until the board of directors formally declares such dividends. Any arrearages are typically disclosed to investors in a footnote to the balance sheet.

Ordinarily, preferred shareholders receive a fixed amount and do not participate further in distributions made by the corporation. In rare circumstances, however, the corporation may decide to make the preferred share a **participating share**. This feature is illustrated in the footnote taken from an annual report of a Canadian company, shown here as Exhibit 11.1.

To show the impact of different share classes and **share dividend preferences**, assume that the company in Exhibit 11.1 makes the following dividend distributions:

1. $1,000,000
2. $2,500,000
3. $10,000,000

Exhibit 11.2 calculates the dividends payable to Class A and to Class B shareholders. Although the participation feature in Exhibit 11.2 involves two classes of common shares, the accounting would be similar if participating preferred shares were involved.

Many preferred shares issued by corporations in recent years have been **redeemable shares**. Redeemable preferred shares can be reacquired by the corporation at a specified price, which may vary according to a present time schedule. Redeemability is commonly thought to be for the benefit of the corporation. If financing becomes available at a lower cost than the rate fixed for the preferred shares, a corporation may wish to reduce the relatively fixed commitment of preferred dividends (as compared to common). It can do so by exercising its option to redeem the preferred shares. This option is valuable to the corporation but makes the shares less attractive to potential owners. Other things being equal, nonredeemable shares will be issued for a higher price than will redeemable shares. Thus, the degree to which the corporation benefits by making shares redeemable is not clear-cut.

Preferred shares with a conversion feature also have become increasingly popular. **Convertible preferred shares** may be converted by their owner into a specified amount of common shares at specified times. The conversion privilege may appear advantageous to both the individual shareholder and the corporation. The preferred shareholder enjoys the security of a relatively assured dividend as long as the preferred shares are held. The shareholder also has the opportunity to realize capital appreciation by converting the shares into common shares if the market price of the common shares rises sufficiently. Because of this feature, the change in the market price of convertible preferred shares will often parallel changes in the market price of the common shares.

Dividends in arrears
Dividends on cumulative preferred shares that have not been declared in accordance with the preferred share contract. Such arrearages must usually be cleared before dividends on common shares can be declared.

participating share
A preferred share on which dividends may be paid in addition to the minimum preferred dividends, usually after dividends on common shares have reached a certain level.

share dividend preferences
The privileges associated with a given class of shares regarding its rights to receive dividends in relation to the residual common class of shares.

redeemable shares
Shares that are redeemable at the discretion of the issuing company.

Convertible preferred shares
Shares of one class that can be exchanged at the option of the holder for shares of another class.

EXHIBIT 11.1
Example of Note Disclosure for Capital Stock

Capital stock (note 10)	19X2	19X1
	63,168	61,135

Note to financial statements

10. Capital Stock

Authorized

The Corporation is authorized to issue:

(a) an unlimited number of Class "A" nonvoting shares without nominal or par value (the "Class 'A' shares");

(b) an unlimited number of Class "B" common shares without nominal or par value (the "Class 'B' shares"); and

(c) an unlimited number of preference shares without nominal or par value, which shall rank in priority to the Class "A" and Class "B" shares and may be issued from time to time in series with the designation, right, privileges, restrictions, and conditions attaching to each series as and in the manner set out in its Articles.

The holders of the Class "A" shares are entitled, voting separately as a class on the basis of one vote per share, to elect annually three members of the Board of Directors of the Corporation. Subject to applicable law, the holders of the Class "A" shares do not otherwise have a right to vote at meetings of shareholders but are entitled to notice of and to attend all shareholders' meetings except class meetings of the holders of another class of shares. The holders of the Class "B" shares are entitled to one vote per share at all meetings of shareholders.

In each fiscal year, the holders of the Class "A" shares are entitled to receive noncumulative dividends aggregating $0.10 per share before any dividends may be paid on the Class "B" shares. No further dividends can be paid to the holders of the Class "A" shares until dividends aggregating $0.10 per share have been declared or paid on the Class "B" shares, and thereafter the Class "A" shares and the Class "B" shares participate equally as to all dividends declared. The former rate of $0.20 per share was adjusted to reflect the 2:1 stock split on July 18, 19X1.

In the event of the liquidation, dissolution or winding-up of the Corporation, the holders of the Class "A" shares and the holders of the Class "B" shares would be entitled to share equally, share for share, in all distributions of the assets of the Corporation.

Issued and outstanding

At March 31, the following shares were issued and outstanding:

	19X2		19X1	
	Shares	Amount	Shares	Amount
Class "A"	18,384,157	$ 53,952	18,265,054	$ 51,919
Class "B"	10,182,538	9,216	10,182,538	9,216
	28,566,695	$ 63,168	28,447,592	$ 61,135

The firm may also benefit from the conversion option. By including it in the issue, the company is usually able to specify a lower dividend rate on the preferred than otherwise would have been required to issue the shares for a given price; alternatively, the corporation can hold the dividend rate constant and realize a higher issue price.

In recent years, a number of firms have issued *term preferred shares*. The holder of these shares is allowed to trade them with the firm for cash or

EXHIBIT 11.2
Illustration of Impact of Dividend Preference Features

(1)	Class A	Class B
Outstanding shares	18,384,157	10,182,538
Dividend declared: $1,000,000		
Payable to Class A	$1,000,000	
(5.43¢ per share)		
Payable to Class B		—
(2)		
Outstanding shares	18,384,157	10,182,538
Dividend declared: $2,500,000		
Payable to Class A (10¢/share)	$1,838,416	
Payable to Class B (6.5¢/share)		$661,584
(3)	**Class A**	**Class B**
Outstanding shares	18,384,157	10,182,538
Dividend declared: $10,000,000		
Payable to Class A (10¢/share)	$1,838,416	
Payable to Class B (10¢/share)		$1,018,254
Remainder allocated equally		
(25¢/share [rounded])*	4,597,105	2,546,225

$7,143,330/(18,384,157 + 10,182,538) = 25.01 cents

bonds at specified dates and prices or conversion ratios. Although term preferred shares have many of the attributes of bonds, a *CICA Guideline* recommends that companies classify them in shareholders' equity. However, the guideline requires that the unique characteristics of term preferred shares be clearly disclosed in the financial statements.

On the balance sheet, the full disclosure concept [4] requires each class of share to be shown separately, disclosing the authorized and issued shares. Full details of each class of shares authorized must be presented. The issued share capital will disclose the number of shares outstanding, the amount attributable to capital from the shares issued, and, where the shares are not fully paid for, the details of the amounts outstanding. The company will also disclose, if relevant, details of shares issued or redeemed during the year, commitments to issue or resell shares, and the amount of preferred dividends in arrears. Customarily, preferred shares are listed before common shares in the balance sheet.

PAR- AND NO-PAR-VALUE SHARES

Par value and no par value are legal terms. **Par value** is a dollar value given to each share as specified by the articles of incorporation of a company. It does not necessarily mean that the share will sell at that price. The Canada Business Corporations Act requires the use of shares of **no par value**, wherein the entire proceeds from the sale of the shares is the amount shown in the Common Share account. Companies incorporated in some

Par value
The dollar value given to each share as specified by the articles of incorporation of a company.

no par value
A type of share where the entire proceeds from the sale of shares is credited to the common share account.

---
[4] *CICA Handbook*, section 3240.

provinces may issue par-value shares, and the term is still used in the United States. This section briefly describes its use.

For companies in jurisdictions where the incorporating act permits it, the corporate charter may stipulate a par value for each share of any class. This value can be set at any amount; it rarely has any relationship to the market value of the share.

A **share premium** is the amount in excess of par value received when a corporation issues shares. The excess of par value over the amount received may be called a **share discount**. In some jurisdictions, people purchasing shares for less than par value may have a liability for the discount should creditor claims remain unsatisfied after the company's liquidation. Shares are rarely sold at a discount — in certain areas, this practice is even forbidden.

To record differences between amounts received for shares and par value, the accountant uses appropriately descriptive accounts. When an amount greater than par value is received, one may use the account Premium on Stock. The account Discount on Stock can be used when a discount is involved.

To illustrate, let us assume that, in its first year of operations, a corporation had the following transactions:

1. Sold 1,000 shares of $100 par value, preferred stock at $107 per share.

2. Sold 1,000 shares of $100 par value, preferred stock at $98 per share.

The two journal entries would be:

Cash	$107,000	
Preferred Shares		$100,000
Premium on Preferred Shares[5]		7,000
Cash	$ 98,000	
Discount on Preferred Shares	2,000	
Preferred Shares		$100,000

Thus, no matter what the selling price of a share, under a par-value system, only the par value is recorded in the share account itself.

ISSUANCES OF SHARES FOR CASH

In issuing its shares, a corporation may use the services of an investment broker, often called an underwriter, who is a specialist in marketing securities to investors. The broker may underwrite an issue of shares — that is, the broker buys the shares from the corporation and resells them to investors. The corporation does not risk being unable to sell its shares. The underwriter bears this risk in return for the profits generated by selling the shares to investors at a price higher than that paid to the corporation. An investment broker who is unwilling to underwrite an issue of shares may

share premium
The amount in excess of par value received when a corporation issues shares.

share discount
The amount by which the par value of a share exceeds its selling price. In most jurisdictions, issuing shares at a discount is prohibited.

---

[5] Part of contributed surplus.

best efforts basis
An arrangement whereby an investment dealer undertakes to sell as many shares as possible on a commission basis, rather than underwriting the shares.

organization costs
Expenditures incurred in launching a business (usually a corporation) or in issuing shares; may include lawyers' fees, various registration fees paid to government, and other start-up costs.

subscription contracts
Agreements made between companies and prospective purchasers of its shares that arrange an installment payment plan.

handle them on a **best efforts basis**. In such a case, the broker agrees to sell as many shares as possible at a set price, but the corporation bears the risk of unsold shares.

COSTS OF ISSUING SHARES

In order to issue and market its shares, a company may incur legal fees; accounting fees; underwriting commissions; and mailing, registration, and advertising costs. It is common practice to treat these costs as a reduction of the net proceeds received for the share issuance. Theoretically, a company will benefit for many years from these expenditures and should set them up as an intangible asset called **organization costs**. This asset is amortized systematically over 40 years or less.

SHARE SUBSCRIPTIONS

Sometimes, a corporation sells shares directly to investors rather than through an investment broker. The corporation may obtain signatures of prospective purchasers on **subscription contracts** before issuing shares. Frequently, such contracts provide for installment payments. When subscriptions are obtained, the corporation debits an asset account, Share Subscriptions Receivable. Instead of crediting the regular Common Shares account, the firm credits a temporary paid-in capital account called Common Shares Subscribed. The use of a temporary account signifies that the shares have not yet been paid for or issued. The CBCA does not allow the issue of shares until they are fully paid for. Until the shares are paid for, the account is shown separately in the shareholders' equity section of the balance sheet. Share Subscriptions Receivable appears with the current assets. After all payments have been received and the shares are issued, the corporation debits the temporary account, Common Shares Subscribed, and credits the regular account, Common Shares.

To illustrate the journal entries for share subscription transactions, let us assume that 500 shares were sold on subscription for $120 a share, paid in installments of $40 and $80. The entries would be:

To record receipt of subscriptions
Share Subscriptions Receivable — Common	$60,000	
Common Shares Subscribed		$60,000
Received subscriptions for 500 shares at $120 per share.		

To record collection of first installment
Cash	$20,000	
Share Subscriptions Receivable — Common		$20,000
Collected first installment of $40 per share.		

To record collection of final installment and issuance of shares
Cash	$40,000	
Share Subscriptions Receivable — Common		$40,000
Collected first installment of $80 per share.		

Common Shares Subscribed	$60,000	
Common Shares		$60,000
To record issuance of 500 shares.		

ISSUANCES OF SHARES FOR ASSETS OTHER THAN CASH

When shares are issued for property other than cash or for services, the accountant must carefully determine the amount recorded. This type of transaction involving the exchange of two non-monetary assets was introduced in Chapter 8 under the heading "Trade-In Transactions." The general valuation principle applied is that property or services acquired should be recorded at their current fair value or at the fair value of the shares issued, whichever is more clearly determinable. If the shares are actively traded on a securities exchange, the market price of the shares issued may indicate an appropriate value. For example, if the current market price is $140 per share and 500 shares are issued for a parcel of land, this land may be valued, in the absence of other price indicators, at $70,000. An effort should be made, however, to determine a fair value for the property. Certainly, all aspects of the transaction should be carefully scrutinized to ascertain that the number of shares issued was objectively determined. Obviously, if no market value for the shares is available, one would seek an independently determined value for the property or services received.

Assuming that the property's market value is the best indicator of its fair value, the entry to record the transaction will be:

Land	$70,000	
Common Shares		$70,000
To record issuance of 500 shares for land valued at $70,000.		

TREASURY SHARES

The term **treasury shares** refers to shares that a corporation, of itself, purchased on the open market. A company might do this to attempt to influence the market price of the shares, to buy out a particular shareholder, or to have shares on hand to satisfy employee stock options.

The CBCA allows a corporation to acquire its own share options as long as the solvency of the corporation is not impaired. However, the act requires immediate cancellation of these shares, which means that a CBCA company would not have treasury shares on its balance sheet.

treasury shares
Capital stock of a company acquired on the open market by the company. Such reacquisitions result in a reduction of shareholders' equity, and are usually shown on the balance sheet as contra to shareholders' equity.

PROVINCIAL CORPORATIONS ACTS

Some of the provincial corporations acts do allow the use of treasury shares. For companies incorporated under these acts, the *CICA Handbook* requires the following accounting treatment for treasury shares.

The acquired shares are set up at cost, debiting Treasury Shares and crediting Cash. Treasury Shares is deducted from total Shareholders' Equity in the balance sheet. Suppose a corporation had outstanding 2,000 shares of no-par-value common stock originally issued at $100 per share, then repurchased 100 shares at $120 per share. The entry for the repurchase is shown on page 670.

Treasury Shares	$12,000	
Cash		$12,000
To resale purchase of 100 shares of treasury stock at $120 per share.		

The corporation may accept any price for the reissue of treasury shares. Treasury share transactions are not part of a firm's normal operating activities, and any additional capital obtained from reissuing such shares at more than cost is not regarded as earnings and is not added to retained earnings. The corporation should regard any additional amounts paid by subsequent purchasers as excess capital. Therefore, increases in capital from the reissue of purchased treasury shares should be credited to an account called Contributed Surplus: Treasury Shares. Decreases on reissue of treasury shares at less than cost offset previously recorded credits to Contributed Surplus: Treasury Shares, or, if that is not possible, Retained Earnings.

Let us assume that 50 shares of the treasury shares reacquired were resold by the corporation at $130 per share. The entry to record the reissue would be:

Cash	$6,500	
Treasury Shares		$6,000
Contributed Surplus: Treasury Shares		500
To record resale of 50 shares of treasury stock at $130 per share.		

Observe that Treasury Shares is credited at the cost price of $120 per share, a basis consistent with the original debit to the account. The excess over cost is credited to Contributed Surplus: Treasury Shares. If a balance sheet were prepared after this transaction, the shareholders' equity section would appear as shown below (assuming retained earnings of $40,000):

Shareholders' Equity

Common Shares, No Par Value, authorized and issued 2,000 shares;	
50 shares in treasury, 1,950 shares outstanding	$200,000
Contributed Surplus: Treasury Shares	500
Retained Earnings	40,000
	$240,500
Less: Treasury Shares (50 shares) at Cost	(6,000)
Total Shareholders' Equity	$234,500

Note that the $200,000 stated value of all issued stock is shown, although 50 shares are no longer outstanding. The total cost of the 50 shares, however, is later deducted from total shareholders' equity.

In the above shareholders' equity situation, the corporation apparently has $40,000 retained earnings unfettered by any legal restrictions; the entire amount can be distributed as dividends if the corporation's cash position permits. In some jurisdictions, however, the corporation must restrict (reduce) the retained earnings available for declaration of dividends by the cost of any treasury shares held. Then, in our illustration, only $34,000 in retained earnings would be available for dividends, and the reason would be disclosed in the shareholders' equity section.

CONTRIBUTED SURPLUS

The previous section introduced an account called Contributed Surplus: Treasury Shares. Under the CBCA, any capital contributed other than through the issue of shares should be shown as **Contributed Surplus**. Shareholders' Equity may, therefore, show three subheadings: Capital Stock, Contributed Surplus, and Retained Earnings. Other examples of transactions creating contributed surplus include redemption of shares and certain dividend transactions.

Contributed Surplus
Capital contributions from sources other than the issuance of shares; includes donated capital.

DONATED CAPITAL

Sometimes, corporations receive donations of assets from shareholders or from governmental units. How should these donations be reflected in the accounts?

A donation from a shareholder is really an additional investment by the shareholder and, as a result, represents **Donated Capital** (sometimes referred to as Contributed Surplus), a shareholders' equity account.

Under GAAP, donations from outsiders are not part of capital but are, in fact, an income item. The donation or government assistance either relates to one period or is treated as deferred revenue (or deferred government assistance), which is amortized to income.

Donated Capital
Donations of actual assets from shareholders or from governmental entities.

REACQUISITION OF SHARES BY REDEMPTION

The CBCA treats redemption of callable preferred shares and acquisition of common shares in the open market in the same way: solvency must be maintained by the corporation and the reacquired shares must be cancelled.

Assume that the Arctic Corporation had the following equity accounts:

Preferred Shares	
2,000,000 no-par-value shares redeemable at $1.50	$1,000,000
Common Shares	
500,000 no-par-value shares	$4,000,000
Retained Earnings	$5,000,000

The CBCA states that when a corporation redeems its own shares, the stated capital account maintained *for the class or series of shares acquired* is to be reduced on a *proportionate* basis.

The amount to be deducted from the stated capital would be calculated as:

$$\left(\frac{\text{stated capital before acquisition}}{\text{number of shares before acquisition}} \right) \times \text{number of shares acquired}$$

Assume that 100,000 preferred shares were redeemed at the call price of $1.50. Using this formula, we calculate the amount by which the capital stock account would be reduced as follows:

$$\left(\frac{\$1,000,000}{2,000,000}\right) \times 100,000 = \$50,000$$

The remainder of the $150,000 call price would be charged against Retained Earnings. If a Contributed Surplus account existed, it would be drawn down first. The entry on this redemption would be:

Preferred Shares	$ 50,000	
Retained Earnings	100,000	
Cash		$150,000

It is important to remember that any type of capital transaction, such as the redemption or issue of shares, affects only capital accounts and is never a determinant of current net income.

SHOULD A FIRM RAISE NEW FUNDS BY ISSUING SHARES OF BONDS?

A major consideration in the issue of common or preferred shares is that dividends are not deductible in calculating taxable income. Bond interest is, however, deductible. Thus, the aftertax accounting cost of borrowing may be less than the aftertax accounting cost of issuing shares, even though the interest rate of the bonds is higher than the dividend rate. Exhibit 11.3 illustrates this phenomenon. The accounting figures, however, do not reflect the economic costs of risk. When bonds are issued, both preferred and common shares become more risky, because bondholders have a claim on future cash flows senior to the claim of shareholders. When preferred shares are issued, common shares become more risky. When shares become more risky, all else being equal, the rate of return on those shares required by the market increases. (For a given dollar amount of return from an investment in a share, this means that the price of the share must fall.) Even though a project financed with a bond issue may result in a larger earnings-per-share increase than one financed by a common stock issue, one cannot conclude that raising new funds by borrowing is better than raising new funds with share issues. Leverage (the raising of funds by borrowing) is a two-edged sword.

If the new project undertaken by the firm illustrated in Exhibit 11.3 has the same risk characteristics as the other, older projects of the firm, it is likely that the market value after either form of financing will remain at about $20 per share. If so, the return required by the market of the bond-financed firm increases from 12.0 percent to 14.5 percent. Although projected earnings per share increase, so does risk.

EXHIBIT 11.3
Accounting Benefit of Raising New Funds by Borrowing Rather than by Issuing Common Shares (financial leverage)

Current operations—expected to continue
Income Tax Rate: 40 Percent
Net Income: $216,000
Shares Outstanding: 90,000
Market Price per Share: $20.00
Earnings per Share: $2.40 (= $216,000/90,000 shares)

Assumptions About New Project
Requires New Funds of $1,000,000
Generates Income Before Financing Charges and Taxes of $200,000 per Year

Assumptions About New Financing Options
Issue $1,000,000 of Bonds at Par with Annual Coupon Rate of 12.5 Percent
or Issue 50,000 New Common Shares at $20 Each

Pro Forma Income Statements After New Financing

	Issue Bonds	Issue Shares
Income from New Project Before Interest and Taxes	$200,000	$200,000
Less: Interest Expense (= 0.125 × $1,000,000)	(125,000)	—
Less: Additional Income Taxes at 40 Percent	(30,000)	(80,000)
Additional Income	$ 45,000	$120,000
Current Income	216,000	216,000
Revised Income	$261,000	$336,000
Shares Outstanding	90,000	140,000
Earnings per Share	$2.90	$2.40
Rate of Return on Market Value of Share of $20	14.5%	12.0%

DISCUSSION CASE 24

When Two Plus Two Equals Three

As anyone who's ever had reason to regret falling for a sales pitch knows only too well, form may promise substance but doesn't always deliver. What you see isn't always what you get.

As I write this, this morning's *Toronto Star* headline blares: "RCMP probing alleged fraud of $22 million at failed banks" and underneath it, reporter Diane Francis unravels a tale of loans by the now-defunct Canadian Commercial and Northland banks to Insurance Premium Finance, an Alberta corporation. Those loans were made on the basis of insurance policies that — according to an affidavit filed by CCB's receiver, Coopers & Lybrand — never existed or, perhaps more correctly, existed but in counterfeit or forged form only.

(continued)

(continued)

The story reminded me of something Mike Mackenzie had said when I interviewed him a week earlier, just after the government announced his appointment as Canada's new Inspector General of Banks and soon-to-be first Superintendent of Financial Institutions ... It was related to the form over substance idea, but had an added dimension.

Called the "real world versus the symbolic world" concept, Mike first heard of it from an old professor of his at the Harvard Business School. In essence, it is that the real world is made up of a series of activities like, say, catching fish, which are then processed, sold, cooked and put on the table. Real economic wealth, as the argument goes, can come only from activities that provide jobs to create products. Those products, in turn, require manufacturing facilities and the funds to build them, thus stimulating investment and contributing to a vibrant economy.

The symbolic world, by contrast, is the world overlying this economic structure: an elaborate superstructure comprising activities engaged in by bankers, brokers, investment dealers, insurance companies, lawyers and, yes — dare we say it? — even chartered accountants. This is the world that produces not fish on the table but symbols such as "earnings per share" and "return on investment."

"Both worlds are necessary," Mike's professor told him. "But if the symbolic world departs too much from the real world, there could be trouble ahead."

The student, now occupying a super-regulatory role over the financial institutions of this country, echoes his mentor's concerns: "I'm not saying that banks and insurance companies don't offer real products to real people, because they do," Mike admits. "But I have this uneasy feeling that so much of our brainpower and so much of our investment has gone into this 'overhead' world rather than into the true, economic world. I suspect if you could measure the amount of credit, money movement velocity and financial products, and assign a number to the amount of those available, and another to the real economic world, you'd find that the former world is getting bigger in relation to the underlying real world."

Bank of Montreal Chairman Bill Mulholland said as much recently in connection with the rash of corporate takeovers in this country. In his "Chairman's Letter to Shareholders," in the bank's latest annual report, he writes: "Corporate takeovers are not bad *per se* or even necessarily unconstructive. Sometimes two plus two does equal five, but equally it can sometimes equal only three. . . .

"Corporate takeover activity should not only serve a basic economic purpose — that is, provide net value added — but it must be seen to do so.

Those engaged in this activity argue, sometimes correctly, he says, that they serve a legitimate economic and social purpose by identifying areas of opportunity and, by their actions, force a more

(continued)

(continued)

efficient use of capital. "Even when true, this is a tough argument to sell," he says. "Try selling it to the employees of a business that is dismembered or a business that is dismembered or a plant that is shut down to help finance the acquisitor's purchase or to turn a quick profit."

Mulholland is even more graphic in a *Maclean's* interview with Peter Newman. "Who has put up a new factory, brought in a new mine, put up a new pulp mill in the past five or 10 years?" he asks. "I can count them on my fingers. It's sick. The world's monetary system is flooded with liquidity, but it ain't being productively employed the way it used to be. People are finding it's cheaper making money with money than to make better goods or new products, or bring in new

resources. . . . This wave of take-overs without productive investment is wrong, just *wrong*."

As a citizen, taxpayer and bank depositor in this country, I'm heartened to hear such concerns expressed by individuals of the stature and influence of Mike Mackenzie and Bill Mulholland. And as a CA, I'm particularly pleased I can call one of them a professional colleague.

References
Nelson Luscombe, "When Two Plus Two Equals Three," *CA Magazine*. Reprinted with permission of *CA Magazine*. Published by the Canadian Institute of Chartered Accountants, Toronto.

Discussion Question
What is meant by "the real world versus the symbolic world"? What is the fundamental problem alluded to by the author?

RETAINED EARNINGS

After a new business has established itself and is profitable, it usually generates additional shareholders' equity from undistributed earnings. These undistributed earnings represent the accumulated periodic net income that remains after dividends have been declared and are called **retained earnings**.

A common misconception about retained earnings is that it represents a fund of cash available for distribution or expansion. Earnings from operations usually involve cash at some stage: goods are sold to customers, the cash is collected, more goods are acquired, bills are paid, more sales are made, and so on. Assets generated by earnings do not, however, remain in the form of cash.[6] Only under most unrealistic conditions, with net plant and equipment, inventories, receivables, and liabilities remaining at con-

retained earnings
Net income over the life of a company less all dividends (including capitalization though stock dividends); shareholders' equity less contributed capital.

---

[6] For many businesses, increased net income is frequently associated with decreased cash, whereas contraction of net income may be accompanied by an increase in cash. In the first stages of a business decline, cash may start to build up from the liquidation of inventories and receivables that have not been replaced, as well as from postponing replacement or expansion of plant. When conditions improve, inventories and receivables are expended, a new plant may be acquired, and a cash shortage may develop.

stant amounts, would earnings correspond to the increase in cash. The statement of changes in financial position shows how the funds provided by operations and other sources are used during a period.

A well-managed firm keeps its cash at a reasonable minimum. If cash starts to accumulate, the firm may pay some obligations, increase its inventory, buy more equipment, or declare dividends. Thus, there is no way of knowing how retaining earnings affects the individual asset and liability accounts. The only certain statement is that an increase in retained earnings results in increased *net assets* (that is, an increase in the excess of all assets over all liabilities).

CASH DIVIDENDS

Cash Dividends
Dividends paid in cash rather than in stocks or nonmonetary assets.

The shareholders of a corporation do not directly control distributions of corporate assets generated by net income. Corporate bylaws almost always delegate the authority to declare dividends to the board of directors. When a dividend is declared, the entry is:

Retained Earnings[7]	$150,000	
Dividends Payable		$150,000
To record declaration of dividends.		

Sometimes an account called Dividends or Dividends Declared is debited. The Dividends account is a temporary account and is closed to Retained Earnings at the end of the period.

Once the board of directors declares a dividend, the dividend becomes a legal liability of the corporation. Dividends Payable is shown as a current liability on the balance sheet if the dividends have not been paid at the end of the accounting period. When the dividends are paid, the entry is:

Dividends Payable	$150,000	
Cash		$150,000
To record payment of dividends.		

property dividend
A distribution of a corporation's assets other than cash to its shareholders.

A distribution of a corporation's assets other than cash to its shareholders is called a *dividend in kind* or a **property dividend**. Such dividends are accounted for just like cash dividends, except that when the dividend is paid, the asset given up, unlike cash, is credited. The amount debited to Retained Earnings is the fair market value of the assets distributed, and the asset is credited for its book value. Any gain or loss resulting is part of income for the period.

---

[7] We follow the practice of debiting Retained Earnings directly when dividends of any type are declared. Some firms debit a temporary account called Dividends Declared and close this to Retained Earnings at the end of the period.

STOCK DIVIDENDS

The retention of earnings may lead to a substantial increase in shareholders' equity, which represents a relatively permanent commitment by shareholders to the business. The commitment is relatively permanent because the net assets generated have been invested in operating assets such as inventories and plant. To indicate such a permanent commitment of reinvested earnings, the board of directors may declare a **stock dividend**. The accounting involves a debit to Retained Earnings and a credit to the capital accounts. When a stock dividend is issued, shareholders receive additional shares in proportion to their existing holdings. If a 5 percent stock dividend is issued, each shareholder receives one additional share for every twenty shares held before the dividend.

stock dividend
Additional shares issued by a corporation to its current shareholders in proportion to their ownership interests.

The usual accounting practice is to base the valuation of the newly issued shares on the market value of the shares issued. For example, the directors of a corporation may decide to issue a stock dividend of 10,000 additional shares with a par value of $10 per share at a time when the market price of a share is $38. The entries would be:

Retained Earnings	$380,000	
Stock Dividend Distributable		$380,000
Declaration of a stock dividend using market price of shares to quantify the amounts ($38 × 10,000 shares = $380,000)		
Stock Dividend Distributable[8]	$380,000	
Common Stock		$100,000
Contributed Surplus		280,000
Issue of the stock dividend.		

The stock dividend relabels a portion of the retained earnings that had been legally available for dividend declarations as a more permanent form of shareholders' equity. A stock dividend formalizes the fact that some of the funds represented by past earnings have been used for plant expansion, to replace assets at increased prices, or to retire bonds. Such funds are therefore unavailable for cash dividends.

Stock dividends have little economic substance for shareholders; the same ownership is spread over more pieces of paper. If the distributed shares are of the same type as those held before, each shareholder's proportionate interest in the capital of the corporation and proportionate voting power has not changed. Although the book value per common share (total common shareholders' equity divided by number of common shares outstanding) decreases, a proportionally larger number of shares will be held, so the total book value of each shareholder's interest will remain unchanged. The market value per share should decline but, all else being equal, the total market value of an individual's shares will not change. To describe such a distribution of shares as a "dividend" — meaning a distribution of earnings — is potentially misleading. It is, nevertheless, generally accepted terminology.

---

[8] If the declared dividend has not been issued at the balance sheet date, this account appears as an addition to the capital stock section.

DIVIDEND POLICY

The directors, in considering whether or not to declare cash dividends, must conclude both (1) that the declaration of a dividend is legal and (2) that it is financially expedient.

STATUTORY LIMITS ON DIVIDENDS

Corporation law limits directors' freedom to declare dividends. These limitations are designed to protect creditors, whose interests might be jeopardized because neither shareholders nor directors are liable for debts of the corporation.

Generally, the laws provide that dividends may not be declared if a company is currently or potentially insolvent, or if the dividend is paid out of capital. The Canada Business Corporations Act prohibits a company from declaring a dividend if there are reasonable grounds for believing that the company is, or would after the payment be, unable to pay its liabilities as they become due (the test of solvency), or if the realizable value of the company's assets would thereby be less than the aggregate of its liabilities and capital of all classes (the test of capital).

For most companies, these statutory limits have little influence on the accounting for shareholders' equity and dividends. A balance sheet does not spell out all of the legal details of amounts available for dividends, but it should disclose information necessary for the user to apply the legal rules of the jurisdiction in which the business is incorporated. For example, statutes can provide that "treasury shares may be acquired only with retained earnings." That is, dividends cannot exceed the amount of Retained Earnings reduced by the cost of treasury shares. If treasury shares are acquired under these circumstances, the amount of this limit on dividends should appear as a footnote to the balance sheet.

The statutory requirements for declaring dividends can be met by building up a balance in retained earnings. Such a balance does not mean that a fund of cash is available for the dividends. Managing cash is a specialized problem of corporate finance; cash for dividends must be anticipated just as well as cash for the purchase of equipment, the retirement of debts, and so on. Borrowing from the bank to pay the regular dividend is not unsound if the corporation's financial condition justifies the resulting increase in liabilities.

CONTRACTUAL LIMITS ON DIVIDENDS

Contracts with bondholders, other lenders, and preferred shareholders often limit dividend payments and thereby compel the retention of earnings. A bond contract might provide that the retirement of the debt be made "out of earnings." Such a provision involves curtailing dividends so that the necessary debt service payments, plus any dividends, will not exceed the amount of net income for the period. Such a provision forces the shareholders to increase their investment in the business by limiting the amount of dividends that might otherwise be made available to them. Financial statement notes must disclose significant limitations on dividend declarations. For example, a recent balance sheet of the Great Lakes Forest Products Ltd. contains the following footnote:

4. Dividend Restriction
Certain of the indentures relating to the company's long-term debt contain covenants limiting dividends. The most restrictive of these requires that, after any dividend is declared, working capital (which for these purposes is before the deduction of the current portion of long-term debt) must be over $10 million and shareholders' equity must be over $50 million.

DIVIDENDS AND CORPORATE FINANCIAL POLICY

Dividends are seldom declared up to the maximum legal limit. The directors may allow the retained earnings to increase as a matter of corporate financial policy for several reasons:

1. Earnings are not reflected in a corresponding increase of available cash.
2. Restricting dividends in prosperous years may permit continued dividend payments in poor years.
3. Funds may be needed for expansion of working capital or plant and equipment.
4. Reducing the amount of borrowings, rather than paying dividends, may seem prudent.

The statement of changes in financial position helps the reader understand how funds provided by earnings and other sources have been used.

Stabilization of Dividends

Many corporate shareholders want to receive a predictable cash return. To accommodate such shareholders and to create a general impression of stability, directors commonly attempt to declare a regular dividend. They try to maintain the regular dividend through good years and bad. When earnings and financial policy permit, they may declare "extra" dividends.

Financial Policy

Some shareholders prefer a policy that restricts dividends in order to finance expansion. When dividends are declared, such shareholders will use the funds received to acquire an equivalent amount of the new shares issued to finance the expansion. These shareholders will be saved transaction costs if earnings are retained. If the corporation pays dividends, the shareholders may pay income taxes on the receipts before they can be reinvested. If the funds are reinvested directly by the corporation, there may be a deferral of, and possibly a permanent avoidance of, personal income taxes.

Other shareholders may want a steady flow of cash but may not wish to sell a portion of their shares to raise cash. Such shareholders will resent being forced to reinvest in the corporation when expansion is financed through the curtailing of dividends. They may change their investment to corporations that declare regular dividends.

How to finance expansion is a problem of managerial finance, not accounting. Research in finance suggests that, within wide limits, what a firm does makes little difference so long as it tends to follow the same policy over time. Shareholders who want earnings reinvested can invest in shares of firms that finance expansion with earnings, whereas others who want a steady flow of cash can invest in shares of firms that regularly pay dividends.

OTHER CHANGES IN SHAREHOLDERS' EQUITY ACCOUNTS

STOCK SPLITS

Stock splits
Additional shares issued by a corporation to its current shareholders in proportion to their ownership interests.

Stock splits (or, more technically, *split-ups*) are like stock dividends. Additional shares are issued to shareholders in proportion to existing holdings. No additional assets are brought into the firm. In a stock split, the par value of all the shares in the issued class is reduced. A corporation may, for example, have 1,000 shares of $10 par value outstanding and, by a stock split, exchange those shares for 2,000 shares of $5 par value (a two-for-one split), or 4,000 shares of $2.50 par value (a four-for-one split), or any number of shares of no par value. If the shares outstanding have no par value, the shareholders keep the existing certificates and receive additional ones.

A stock split generally does not require a journal entry. The amount of retained earnings is not reduced. The amount shown in the share capital account represents a larger number of shares. Of course, the additional number of shares held by each shareholder must be recorded in the subsidiary share capital records. Sometimes, stock splits are accounted for as stock dividends — with a transfer from Retained Earnings to the Contributed Capital account. If so, the amounts are based on the market value of the shares on the date of the split. There is no easy way to distinguish stock splits from stock dividends. Usually, small percentage distributions are treated as stock dividends and larger ones as stock splits.

A stock split (or a stock dividend) usually reduces the market value per share, all other factors remaining constant, in inverse proportion to the split (or dividend). Thus, a two-for-one-split could be expected to result in a 50 percent reduction in the market price per share. Stock splits have therefore usually been used to keep the market prices per share from rising to a price level unacceptable to management. For example, the board of directors might think that a market price of $30 to $40 is an effective trading range for its shares. (This is a purely subjective estimate, and it is almost never supported by convincing evidence.) If the share prices have risen to $60 in the market, the board of directors may declare a two-for-one split. The only certain result of stock splits and dividends is increased record-keeping costs.

STOCK OPTIONS

Stock options
Rights granted by companies to purchase a specified number of shares of their stock for a specified price at specified times; usually granted to employees. Contrast with share warrants.

Stock options are often a part of employee compensation plans. Under such plans, employees are granted an option to purchase shares in their company. Stock options present two kinds of accounting problems: (1) recording the granting of the option and (2) recording its exercise or lapse.

Granting the Option The generally accepted accounting treatment for options usually results in no entry being made at the time the options are granted. The **exercise price** of an option is the price the option holder will have to pay to acquire a share. If the exercise price is equal to the market price of the share on the date the option is granted, the granting of the option is not viewed as resulting in compensation to the employee or expense to the employer, and no entry is made. If the exercise price is less than the market price of the share on the date of the grant, compensation expense may have to be recognized under some circumstances.

Exercise or Lapse When the option is exercised, the conventional entry treats the transaction simply as an issue of shares at the option price.

Cash	$35,000	
Common Shares		$35,000
To record issue of 1,000 no-par-value shares upon exercise of options and receipt of $35,000 cash.		

If the option lapses or expires without being exercised, no entry is required.

Disclosure of Options GAAP require that the terms of options granted, outstanding, and exercised during a period be disclosed in text or notes accompanying the financial statements.[9]

SHARE RIGHTS AND WARRANTS

Opportunities to buy shares may be granted through share rights and share warrants.

Share Rights **Share rights** are similar to stock options, but there are some differences. Stock options are granted to employees, are nontransferable, and are a form of compensation. In contrast, share rights are typically granted to current shareholders and can usually be traded in public markets. They are generally exercisable for only a limited period, but occasionally are good indefinitely. Share rights are ordinarily associated with attempts to raise new capital for a firm from current shareholders. The legal evidence of the right is a certificate called a **share warrant**.

Share rights entitle the owner to purchase shares at a specified price. Journal entries are not necessary when share rights are granted to current shareholders. When the rights are exercised, the entry is like the one to record the issue of new shares at the price paid.

Assume that a corporation issued warrants for $15,000 cash. The entry would be:

Cash	$15,000	
Common Share Rights		$15,000
To record issue of rights to the public.		

exercise price
The price the option holder will have to pay to acquire a share.

Share rights
Rights granted to shareholders on the occasion of a new issue of capital stock, entitling them to purchase their pro rata share of the issue at the stated price and within a stated period of time.

Share warrant
The actual certificate that represents the share rights discussed above.

---

[9] *CICA Handbook*, section 3240.

The Common Share Rights account would normally be included with Contributed Surplus for balance sheet presentation.

If the options to purchase contained in these warrants were exercised and 10,000 common shares of no par value were issued in exchange for the warrants plus $200,000, the entry would be:

Cash	$200,000	
Common Share Rights	15,000	
Common Stock		$215,000
To record the issue of 10,000 shares for $200,000 cash and the redemption of rights.		

If the warrants expired without having been exercised, the entry would be:

Common Share Rights	$15,000	
Contributed Surplus[10]		$15,000
To record expiration of common share rights and the transfer to permanent contributed capital.		

CONVERTIBLE BONDS

Convertible bonds
Bonds incorporating the holder's right to convert the bonds to capital stock under prescribed terms.

Convertible bonds are, typically, semiannual coupon bonds like the ones discussed in Chapter 9 — with one added feature: the holder of the bond can *convert* the bond into shares. The bond indenture specifies the number of shares to be received when the bond is converted, the dates when conversion can occur, and other details. Convertible bonds are usually callable.

Investors often find convertible bonds attractive. The owner is promised a regular interest payment. In addition, should the company business be so successful that its share prices rise on the stock market, the holder of the bond can convert the investment from debt into equity. The creditor has become an owner and can share in good fortune of the company. Of course, an investor does not get something for nothing. Because of the potential participation in the earnings of the company once the bonds are converted into common shares, an investor in the bonds must accept a lower interest rate than would be received if the bonds were not convertible into shares. From the company's point of view, convertible bonds allow borrowing at lower rates of interest than are required on ordinary debt, but the company must promise to give up an equity interest if the bonds are converted. The purchaser of the convertible bond is paying something for the option to acquire common shares later. Thus, a portion of the proceeds from the issue of convertible bonds actually represents a form of capital contribution, even though it is not so recorded.

---

[10] We have been following the practice of debiting and crediting Contributed Surplus in this chapter. It is possible to treat this as being analogous to a control account and keep track of transactions by type. In this instance, the credit would be to Contributed Surplus: Share Rights.

Issue of Convertible Bonds

Suppose, for example, that the Johnson Co. Ltd.'s credit rating allows it to issue $100,000 of ordinary ten-year, 14 percent, semiannual coupon bonds at par. The firm prefers to issue convertible bonds with a lower coupon rate. Assume that Johnson Co. Ltd. issues at par $100,000 of ten-year, 10 percent, semiannual coupon bonds, but each $1,000 bond is convertible into 50 Johnson Co. Ltd. $5 par value common shares. (The entire issue is convertible into 5,000 shares.) The following entry is required:

Cash	$100,000	
Convertible Bonds Payable		$100,000
Issue of convertible bonds at par.		

This entry effectively treats convertible bonds just like ordinary, nonconvertible bonds and records the value of the conversion feature at zero.[11]

Conversion of Bonds

Assume that the common shares of the Johnson Co. Ltd. increase in the market to $30 a share so that one $1,000 bond, which is convertible into 50 shares, can be converted into shares with a market value of $1,500. If the entire convertible issue were converted into common shares at this time, 5,000 shares of $5 par value would be issued on conversion.

The usual entry to record the conversion of bonds into shares ignores current market prices in the interest of simplicity and merely shows the swap of shares for bonds at their book value.

---

[11] Recognizing the value of the conversion feature is not permitted. Table B.5, page 1070 (for 10 percent coupon bonds), indicates that 10 percent, ten-year, semiannual (nonconvertible) coupon bonds sell for about 79 percent of par when the market rate of interest is 14 percent. Thus, if the 10 percent convertible bonds can be issued at par, the conversion feature must be worth about 21 ($=100 - 79$) percent of par. Then, 21 percent of the proceeds from the bond issue is actually a capital contribution by the bond buyers for the right to acquire common shares later. The logical entry to record the issue of these 10 percent convertible bonds at par would be:

Cash	$100,000	
Discount on Bonds Payable	21,000	
Convertible Bonds Payable		$100,000
Contributed Surplus		21,000
Issue of 10 percent semiannual coupon convertible bonds at a time when ordinary 10 percent bonds could be issued for 79 percent of par.		

Notice that the calculation of the amounts for this entry requires that we know what the proceeds would be of an issue of nonconvertible bonds that are otherwise similar to the convertible bonds. Because auditors are often unable to ascertain this information in a reasonably objective manner, this alternative is seldom followed in Canada and is prohibited under GAAP in the United States. The entry is simply a debit to Cash and a credit to Convertible Bonds Payable for $100,000.

If the recommendations of the CICA Exposure Draft on Financial Instruments are adopted, the value-of-conversion option will be separately recognized.

Convertible Bonds Payable	$100,000	
Common Stock		$25,000
Contributed Surplus		75,000
To record conversion of 100 convertible bonds with a book value of $100,000 into 5,000 shares of $5 par value.		

An alternative treatment recognizes that market prices provide information useful in quantifying the market value of the shares issued. Under the alternative treatment, if the market price of a share were $30 and the fair market value of the 5,000 shares issued on conversion were $150,000, the journal entry would be:

Convertible Bonds Payable	$100,000	
Loss on Conversion of Bonds	50,000	
Common Stock		$ 25,000
Contributed Surplus		125,000
To record conversion of 100 convertible bonds into 5,000 shares of $5 par value at a time when the market price of a share is $30.		

The alternative entry results in the same total shareholders' equity: smaller retained earnings (because the Loss on Conversion of Bonds will reduce current net income and thus Retained Earnings), but larger contributed capital. It is the equivalent of the following two entries:

Cash	$150,000	
Common Stock — $5 Par Value		$25,000
Contributed Surplus		125,000
To record issue of 5,000 shares of $5 par value at $30 per share.		

Convertible Bonds Payable	$100,000	
Loss on Retirement of Bonds	50,000	
Cash		$150,000
Retirement by purchase for $150,000 of 100 convertible bonds carried on the books at $100,000.		

POTENTIAL DILUTION OF EARNINGS PER SHARE

Chapter 4, page 240 explained that earnings per common share is conventionally calculated by dividing net income attributable to the common shareholders by the weighted-average number of common shares outstanding during the period. When a firm has outstanding securities that, if exchanged for common shares, would decrease earnings per share as conventionally calculated, the earnings per share calculations become somewhat more complicated. Stock options, share rights, and convertible bonds all have the potential to reduce earnings per share and must be taken into account in calculating earnings per share. These complications are discussed in intermediate accounting books, but are introduced in Problem 37 at the end of this chapter.

DISCUSSION CASE 25

A Telephone Number Says It All

Andrew Agnew, a certified financial analyst addressing a Society of Management Accountants symposium, has pledged for professional accountants to take a lead in promoting fuller disclosure in corporate financial reports.

"Individually, there are numerous companies which have excellent disclosure.... The immediate problem ... is to bring the laggards up to a desirable minimum of disclosure."

Canadian companies are weak in disclosing revenues and profits by product line, their corporate goals and strategies, and their sensitivity to external forces.

He noted that some companies can also be criticized for the way they valued their assets, covered up the details of their involvement in joint ventures, and provided a lack of information about the different segments of their businesses.

Agnew noted that some companies even fail to list their telephone number in the annual report. "To me, this reflects management's state of mind towards shareholders — let's keep them in the dark."

References

"A Telephone Number Says It All," *The Bottom Line*, July 1986, p. 3.

Discussion Question

Why would management want to keep shareholders in the dark?

REPORTING INCOME AND RETAINED EARNINGS ADJUSTMENTS

THE INCOME STATEMENT RECONSIDERED

What is the purpose of the income statement? It is *not* just to show net income for the period. The reader of the financial statements can generally ascertain net income by subtracting the beginning balance of Retained Earnings from its ending balance and adding dividends. The purpose of the income statement is to show the *causes* of income.[12] Then, a company's performance can be compared with other companies or with itself over time, and more informed projections can be made about the future.

To help the reader understand the causes of income, GAAP principles require the separate reporting of certain items in the income statement. Extraordinary items and the results of operations attributable to Discontinued Segments should be separately identified. In addition, the company should separately disclose gains and losses resulting from normal business

[12] Parallel statements can be made about the funds statement. The purpose of the statement of changes in financial position is *not* to report the change in cash for the period. That can be deduced by subtracting the balance in the Cash account at the start of the period from that at the end of the period. The purpose is to report the *causes* of the change in the Cash account.

activities that are both abnormal in size and caused by rare or unusual circumstances.

With this information, the reader is able to select or calculate the measure of income that is relevant to the decision.

DIRECT ADJUSTMENTS TO RETAINED EARNINGS

Nearly all items that cause the total of retained earnings to change during a period result from transactions reported in the income statement for that period. The major exception to this general rule is the declaration of dividends. Dividend declarations are distributions that reduce the balance in the Retained Earnings account but do not affect reported income. There are four other exceptions to the general rule that changes in retained earnings arise from transactions reported in the income statement. These are:

1. Losses from treasury share transactions.
2. Corrections of prior-period errors.
3. Retroactive changes in accounting policy.
4. Other prior-period adjustments that meet restrictive criteria.

Corrections of prior period errors are rare and include mistakes in computation or errors made in a prior year because of lack of information normally available to management. Examples or retained earnings adjustments resulting from changes in accounting policies are changes in lease capitalization, foreign currency translation, basis of consolidation, depreciation method, accounting for exploration and development expenses, and interest capitalization. **Changes in accounting policies** are the most common adjustments to retained earnings.

Except for corrections of prior-period errors and changes in accounting policies, **prior-period adjustments** (which should be rare) should have four characteristics. They should be specifically identified with and directly related to the business activities of particular prior periods; they should depend primarily on decisions or determinations by persons other than management or owners; they should not be attributable to economic events occurring subsequent to the date of the financial statements for such prior periods; and they could not be reasonably estimated before such decisions or determinations. Examples of prior-period adjustments that may meet these criteria would be settlements of claims resulting from litigation and settlements of prior-period income taxes. Prior-period adjustments *should not* include normal adjustments arising from modification of estimates commonly used in accounting, such as adjustments arising from changes in the estimated useful life of fixed assets. They also do not include, regardless of size, bed debt losses, inventory losses, deferred development costs written off, or income tax reductions realized from the carryforward of a loss.

Exhibit 11.4 shows the presentation of prior-period adjustments in the financial statements when a company has been required to pay additional income taxes for prior years.

When presenting the Year 5 comparative financial statements, the company would amend the Year 4 income statement, presented last year, by

Changes in accounting policies
Changes to other accounting methods allowable within the framework of GAAP. The financial statements are retroactively adjusted to reflect such changes.

prior-period adjustments
Adjustments made under rare conditions, primarily to correct errors made in financial statements of prior periods. Each adjustment is made to the opening balance of Retained Earnings.

EXHIBIT 11.4
Prior-Period Adjustment Ltd.
Statement of Retained Earnings for the Year Ended
December 31, Year 5 (amounts in thousands)

	Year 5	Year 4
Retained earnings, beginning of year		
As previously reported	$60,100	$54,100
Adjustments of prior years' income taxes (Note x)	(7,500)	(5,100)
As restated	$52,600	$49,000
Net income for the year	5,300	5,600
	$57,900	$54,600
Dividends	(2,000)	(2,000)
Retained earnings, end of year	$55,900	$52,600

Note x: As a result of income tax reassessments applicable to the Years 1 to 4, the balance of retained earnings at December 31, Year 4 previously reported as $60,100,000 has been restated to show a retroactive charge of $7,500,000 representing the cumulative amount by which income taxes as of December 31, Year 4 had been increased. Of the $7,500,000, $2,400,000 is applicable to Year 4 and has been charged to income for that year. The remaining $5,100,000 is applicable to years prior to January 1, Year 4 and has been charged to retained earnings at that date, previously reported as $54,100,000.

increasing income tax expense by $2,400,000 and decreasing net income by the same amount from the $8 million balance originally reported.

DISCLOSURE OF CHANGES IN SHAREHOLDERS' EQUITY

The changes in all shareholders' equity accounts must be explained in the annual reports to shareholders.[13] As previous chapters have pointed out, the reconciliation of retained earnings may appear in the balance sheet, in a statement of income and retained earnings, or in a separate statement.

AN INTERNATIONAL PERSPECTIVE

The accounting for shareholders' equity in most developed countries closely parallels that in Canada. That is:

1. Contributed capital accounts increase when firms issue shares of common or preferred stock.

2. Revenues, gains, expenses, and losses affect the measurement of periodic income and then transfer to the retained earnings account as part of the closing process.

---

[13] *CICA Handbook*, section 3240.

3. Dividends reduce retained earnings and either reduce corporate assets (cash dividends or dividends in kind) or increase other shareholders' equity accounts (stock dividends).

One major difference between accounting in Canada and abroad is the use of "reserve" accounts in many other countries. Reserve accounts generally have credit balances and appear in the shareholders' equity section of the balance sheet. In Canada, the use of this term is not allowed; "appropriation" is used instead.

Example 1   Japanese accounting standards require that firms declaring dividends transfer from retained earnings to a legal capital reserve account a specified percentage of the dividend each period. Japanese firms make this entry additional to the usual entry for dividends. To illustrate Oji Paper Company declared and paid a ¥10 million dividend during a recent year and made the following entry (amounts in millions):

Retained Earnings	¥10	
Cash		¥10
To record declaration and payment of cash dividend.		

The firm also made the following entry:

Retained Earnings	¥3	
Legal Capital Reserve		¥3
To reclassify 30 percent of dividends out of retained earnings and into a permanent capital account.		

The second entry effectively capitalizes a portion of retained earnings. Including the ¥3 million in a capital account indicates to the reader of the financial statements that the firm may not declare dividends up to the full amount of retained earnings.

Example 2   French accounting standards permit firms to reclassify a portion of retained earnings to a reserve account to indicate that the full amount of retained earnings is temporarily unavailable for dividends. A recent annual report of Société Nationale Elf Acquitaine revealed the following:

Reserves:	
Legal	Fr 100
Long-Term Capital Gains	3,885
Operating Costs	7,300
Unappropriated	5,227

This disclosure indicates that Fr5,227 is available for dividends. The firm has assets totalling Fr11,285 (= Fr100 + Fr3,885 + Fr7,300) that are permanently or temporarily not available for dividends. For example, suppose that the firm is being sued by a customer for Fr2,000. Although the firm feels that it has an adequate defence, the possibility of a loss exists. The firm might make the following entry when the customer files the suit:

Retained Earnings (unappropriated)	Fr2,000	
Operating Risk Reserve		Fr2,000
To reclassify a portion of retained earnings into an operating risk reserve.		

Assume now that the firm loses the suit and incurs an uninsured liability of Fr1,200. The entry, assuming immediate cash payment, is:

Loss from Damage Suit (income statement account)	Fr1,200	
Cash		Fr1,200

Because the suit is now settled, the firm reclassifies the operating risk reserve back to retained earnings.

Operating Risk Reserve	Fr2,000	
Retained Earnings		Fr2,000

A second use of reserve accounts relates to revaluations of assets. Accounting regulations in Great Britain and France permit firms to revalue their plant and other assets periodically.

Example 3   Refer to Exhibit 2.9 on page 118, which shows the balance sheet of Ranks Hovis McDougall PLC, a British company. During the current year, this firm revalued its fixed assets and recognized its brand names as an asset. The offsetting credit is to a revaluation reserve account. The firm will charge (debit) future depreciation and amortization of these revalued amounts to the revaluation reserve account. Neither the initial revaluation, the subsequent depreciation, nor amortization enter the income statement.

Example 4   In Canada, portfolio investments in Long-Term Investments are carried at cost unless a permanent impairment in value is deemed to have occurred, at which point they are written down to market. This contrasts with the U.S. treatment, whereby lower of cost or market is used, but with no income statement impact.

In the U.S.A., when market prices are less than cost, the firm debits the account, Unrealized Loss on Investments in Marketable Equity Securities (and credits a contra account to Investments in Securities). This account appears in the shareholders' equity section of the balance sheet and serves a similar function to that of the revaluation reserve account discussed above. However, accounting practices in the United States discourage the use of the term "reserve" in the title of this account.

Thus, the reader of financial statements issued by firms outside Canada will frequently encounter various "reserve" accounts appearing in the shareholders' equity section of the balance sheet. The reader must be wary of these accounts for the following reasons:

1. Firms rarely set aside assets in the amount of the reserve for the purpose indicated by the title of the reserve (for example, reserve for plant replacement, reserve for business risks). Because of the balance sheet equality of assets and equities, one can only conclude that there are assets in some form (for example, equipment, goodwill) equal to the amount of the reserve.

2. Firms increase and decease reserves for a variety of purposes (reclassifying retained earnings, revaluing assets). The reader should understand the nature of each reserve and the events that cause its amount to change.

A second major difference between Canada and the United States is the use of and accounting for treasury shares. Treasury shares are a normal part of Stockholders' Equity in the financial statements of American companies, because of the popularity of stock options as a part of executive compensation plans.

Only a few of the provincial incorporating acts in Canada allow treasury shares. In a sense, treasury shares became redundant when the Canada Business Corporations Act and other provincial acts moved to no-par-value shares because, at the same time, the upper limits on authorized shares were lifted. If an unlimited supply of new shares can be issued, this removes any need to reacquire shares previously issued.

This chapter has illustrated the use of the cost method for accounting for treasury shares. Another method that is popular in the United States is the par-value method. In this approach, no matter what price is paid to reacquire the share, only the par value is put into the treasury. On subsequent reissue, the share is treated like a brand new issue, with the premium or discount on issue if the proceeds are different from par value.

Overall, there are probably more differences in accounting for Shareholders' Equity among countries than for any other component of the financial statements, because the accounting in this area is dictated more by legal requirements than by accounting concepts.

KEY TERMS

Owners' equity
Shareholders' equity
Canada Business Corporations
   Act (CBCA)
Public corporations
Private corporations
Shareholders
Articles of incorporation
Common shares
Preferred shares
Cumulative (dividends)
Dividends in arrears
Participating share
Share dividend preferences
Redeemable shares
Convertible preferred shares
Par value
No par value
Share premium

Share discount
Best efforts basis
Organization costs
Subscription contracts
Treasury shares
Contributed Surplus
Donated Capital
Retained earnings
Cash dividends
Property dividend
Stock dividend
Stock splits
Stock options
Exercise price
Share rights
Share warrant
Convertible bonds
Changes in accounting policies
Prior-period adjustments

SELF-STUDY MATERIAL

This section contains questions, exercises, and problems to help you assess your understanding of Chapter 11. Careful review of this material will assist you in completing the homework assignments. Solutions are found at the end of the section.

QUESTIONS AND EXERCISES

True/False

For each statement, place a T or an F in the space provided to indicate whether the statement is true or false.

_____ 1. The corporate form provides the owner, or shareholder, with unlimited liability.

_____ 2. Stock options, often a part of compensation plans, offer employees the opportunity to purchase, at some time within a specified number of years in the future, shares in their company at a specified price.

_____ 3. Corrections of errors and prior-period adjustments both result in either a debit or a credit to Retained Earnings.

_____ 4. It is difficult to raise large amounts of funds for corporations because so many shares of relatively small value must be sold.

_____ 5. Common shareholders have the claim to earnings of the corporation after commitments to creditors and preferred shareholders have been satisfied.

_____ 6. Preferred shares are frequently the only voting shares of the company.

_____ 7. Corporation statutes generally provide that dividends must be "paid out of earnings."

_____ 8. Cumulative preferred shares entitle the holder to receive all current and previously postponed dividends before common share dividends can be distributed.

_____ 9. Convertibility is generally a feature of common shares allowing the holder to convert shares into preferred shares at some specified time in the future.

_____ 10. Par-value shares and no-par-value shares have basically the same effect on the recording in the accounts of the issue of share capital.

_____ 11. Treasury shares refer to shares reacquired by the issuing corporation.

_____ 12. Bondholder agreements often place restrictions on dividend payments.

_____ 13. At the end of an accounting period, a well-managed company will always have an increase in cash at least equal to the net income for the period.

_____ 14. Net assets refer to the excess of all assets over all liabilities.

_____ 15. For most companies, the amount and timing of dividend declarations are determined by the shareholders at their annual meeting.

_____ 16. In most cases, corporations pay out dividends equal to net income unless specific restrictions, either legal or financial, are stated in the annual report.

_____ 17. A stock dividend is often referred to as a dividend in kind.

_____ 18. In a stock split, the par value of all shares in the issued class is reduced in proportion to the additional shares issued.

_____ 19. When a company needs additional capital, a major consideration in the decision to issue shares or bonds is that dividends and interest be deductible in calculating taxable income.

_____ 20. Share rights cannot be traded in the open market, because such trading is an exclusive right for employees.

_____ 21. Stock splits and stock dividends are accounted for in the same manner.

_____ 22. Earnings per common share is only a statistic; therefore, share options, share rights, warrants, and convertible bonds are disregarded in the calculation of that ratio.

Matching

From the list of terms, select one term that is most closely associated with one descriptive phrase or statement that follows and place the letter for that term in the space provided.

a. redeemable preferred shares
b. common shares
c. contractual restriction on dividends
d. contributed surplus
e. convertible bonds
f. articles of incorporation
g. cumulative preferred shares
h. net assets

i. par value
j. preferred shares
k. prior-period adjustment
l. share option
m. stock dividends
n. stock split
o. treasury shares

_____ 1. An issue of an additional number of shares to shareholders in proportion to their existing holdings without any additional contribution and without a change in the par value per share.

_____ 2. The voting class of share that also has a residual claim to earnings.

_____ 3. A nominal value per share specified in the articles of incorporation and printed on the face of the share certificates.

_____ 4. Class of share usually entitling the holder to dividends at a certain rate, which must be paid before dividends can be declared and paid to common shareholders.

_____ 5. Shares reacquired by the issuing corporation.

_____ 6. The agreement between the firm and the jurisdiction in which the business is incorporated.

_____ 7. Type of shares that must receive all current and previously postponed dividends before dividends may be issued to other classes of share.

_____ 8. Account title used to designate contributed capital by owners paid in excess of par value.

_____ 9. An issue of additional shares to shareholders in proportion to existing holdings without any additional contributions but with a proportional reduction of the par value of all the shares in the issued class.

_____ 10. An example would be a restriction of dividends imposed by an agreement between bondholders and the corporation.

_____ 11. Type of preferred shares that may be reacquired by the corporation at a specified price, which may vary according to a predetermined time schedule.

_____ 12. Rarely occurring items relating to correction of prior-period errors are treated as a direct adjustment of Retained Earnings at the beginning of the period.

_____ 13. Part of employee compensation plan, which, under GAAP, usually does not require a journal entry at the date of grant.

_____ 14. Type of bonds that may be exchanged for common shares at specified times at the option of the owner.

_____ 15. Excess of all assets over all liabilities of a firm.

Multiple Choice

Choose the best answer for each question or problem and enter the identifying letter in the space provided.

_____ 1. The shareholders' equity account with a normal debit balance is:
   a) Contributed Surplus
   b) Common Shares
   c) Retained Earnings
   d) Treasury Shares

_____ 2. The articles of incorporation are:
   a) the contract between the firm and the jurisdiction in which the business is incorporated
   b) the corporation laws of the jurisdiction in which incorporation takes place
   c) the bylaws of the corporation
   d) the share contract

_____ 3. One feature that is generally not associated with preferred shares is the:
   a) cumulative feature
   b) callable feature
   c) voting right
   d) conversion right

_____ 4. When a corporation reissues treasury shares for a price above their acquisition price, the amount above the acquisition price is credited to:
   a) Contributed Surplus
   b) Treasury Shares
   c) Gain on Sale of Treasury Shares
   d) Retained Earnings

_____ 5. The account Treasury Shares should be disclosed on the balance sheet as a:
   a) short-term investment
   b) contra to total shareholders' equity
   c) deferred share
   d) share-investment account

_____ 6. Which of these distributions usually does not require a debit to Retained Earnings?
   a) cash dividend
   b) dividend in kind
   c) stock dividend
   d) stock split

_____ 7. Which of the following is usually associated with employee compensation plans?
   a) stock options
   b) share rights
   c) share warrants
   d) none of the above

_____ 8. Which of these entries are correct when a company issues convertible bonds?
   a) debit Cash, credit Convertible Bonds Payable
   b) debit Cash, credit Convertible Bonds Payable and Contributed Surplus
   c) neither entry is correct
   d) both entries are correct

9. Which of the following require direct adjustments to Retained Earnings?
   a) extraordinary items
   b) gain or loss from unusual items
   c) prior-period adjustments
   d) none of the above

Exercises

1. From the following accounts, indicate in the space provided the correct debit and credit entries corresponding to the transactions described. Credit entries should be shown in parentheses. The first transaction is answered as an example.

   a. Cash
   b. Common Shares
   c. Common Share Warrants
   d. Contributed Surplus
   e. Dividends Payable
   f. Inventory
   g. Plant Expansion Fund

   h. Preferred Shares
   i. Retained Earnings
   j. Retained Earnings Appropriated
      for Plant Expansion
   k. Treasury Shares
   l. An Account Not Listed
   m. No Formal Journal Entry Required

   __(b)__ 1. Issued common shares at par value for cash.
   _____ 2. A stock dividend is declared and distributed at a time when the market value is above the par value.
   _____ 3. The board of directors authorizes the distribution of a two-for-one stock split.
   _____ 4. Warrants to acquire common shares are issued for cash to the public.
   _____ 5. Half of the warrants in transaction 4 are submitted for redemption with the appropriate cash (the amount exceeds the par value of the shares).
   _____ 6. The remaining warrants from transaction 4 expire without having been exercised.
   _____ 7. Closed Income Summary (credit Balance) to Retained Earnings.
   _____ 8. The board of directors declares a cash dividend to be distributed in three weeks.
   _____ 9. Cash dividend from transaction 8 is paid.
   _____ 10. Preferred shares are issued for cash in excess of the par value of the shares issued.
   _____ 11. Common shares previously issued are reacquired by the corporation, resulting in cash in excess of the price for which the shares were initially sold.
   _____ 12. Half of the shares in transaction 11 are reissued at an amount that exceeds half the purchase price.
   _____ 13. The remaining half of the treasury shares are reissued at an amount that is less than one-half of the purchase price.
   _____ 14. An error was discovered: the inventory at the end of the previous period was understated by $15,000.

2. Record the following entries in the books of Prince-William Corporation.

   a. Issued 1,000 common shares for $15 cash per share. The common shares had a $10 par value per share.

   b. A 10 percent stock dividend on common shares was issued. At the time of issuance, there were 100,000 shares outstanding; each share was currently trading on the open market for $16 per share.

   c. Reacquired 500 common shares, paying $7,000.

   d. Reissued 250 shares obtained in entry c, receiving $13 per share.

   e. Reissued the remaining 250 shares obtained in entry c, receiving $15 per share.

   f. Declared a cash dividend to shareholders totalling $200,000.

g. Granted a stock option to employees to acquire 3,000 shares at $15 a share, the current market price.

h. Employees exercise stock options in entry g to acquire 2,000 shares.

i. The remaining stock options in entry g lapse.

j. The firm issues at par $50,000 of twenty-year bonds, 12 percent, semiannual coupon bonds, each $1,000 bond being convertible into 40 of the company's $10 par-value common shares. The bonds without the convertible feature would have sold for $47,000.

k. Paid cash dividend declared in entry f.

l. Issued share warrants to the public containing rights to purchase 2,000 common shares for $15 each, and received $2,500 cash for the warrants.

m. The rights for 1,000 common shares in entry l were exercised.

n. The remaining rights in entry l expire without being exercised.

o. Net income of $300,000 (balance in Income Summary) is closed to Retained Earnings.

PROBLEM 1 FOR SELF-STUDY

Exhibit 11.5 shows the shareholders' equity account for Lorla Corporation at the end of Year 1 and Year 2. During Year 2, Lorla Corporation issued new shares for $40 a share and reacquired 60 shares for the treasury at $42 per share. Still later in the year, it sold some of the treasury shares. Revenues for Year 2 were $90,100 and net income was $10,100.

EXHIBIT 11.5
Lorla Corporation Shareholders' Equity Accounts

	December 31	
	Year 2	Year 1
Common Shares ($5 par value)	$ 5,500	$ 5,000
Contributed Surplus	33,620	30,000
Retained Earnings	66,500	59,100
	$105,620	$94,100
Less: Cost of Treasury Shares	(840)	—
Total Shareholders' Equity	$104,780	$94,100

Reconstruct all of the transactions involving shareholders' equity accounts for Year 2 and show the journal entries for those transactions.

PROBLEM 2 FOR SELF-STUDY

Patell Limited owns 100,000 shares of Canco Aluminium Limited, which it has held as an investment. The shares had cost $2 million, $20 each, and now have a fair market value of $50 each. Patell Limited declares a dividend in kind, distributing the shares of Canco Aluminium Limited to its shareholders.

a. Prepare the journal entry to record the declaration. Under GAAP, dividends in kind are recorded at the market value, not the cost, of the assets distributed.

b. Prepare a journal entry that would record the dividend using the cost of the shares. This treatment is not generally acceptable.

c. Compare the effects on net income, retained earnings, and total shareholders' equity of the two treatments.

ANSWERS TO SELF-STUDY QUESTIONS AND EXERCISES

True/False

1. F	7. T	13. F	19. F
2. T	8. T	14. T	20. F
3. T	9. F	15. F	21. F
4. F	10. T	16. F	22. F
5. T	11. T	17. F	
6. F	12. T	18. T	

Matching

1. m	5. o	9. n	13. l
2. b	6. f	10. c	14. e
3. i	7. g	11. a	15. h
4. j	8. d	12. k	

Multiple Choice

1. d	4. a	7. a	9. c
2. a	5. b	8. a	
3. c	6. d		

Exercises

1.

1. a, (b)	8. i, (e)
2. i, (b), (d)	9. e, (a)
3. m	10. a, (h), (d)
4. a, (c)	11. k, (a)
5. a, c, (b), (d)	12. a, (k) , (d)
6. c, (d)	13. a, i, (k) *or* a, d, (k)
7. l, (i)	14. f, (i)

2.

	Dr.	Cr.
a. Cash	$15,000	
Common Share Capital		$10,000
Contributed Surplus (Premium on Shares)		5,000
To issue 1,000 common shares for $15 per share.		

b. Retained Earnings $160,000
    Common Share Capital $100,000
    Contributed Surplus (Premium on Shares)   60,000
    To issue a 10 percent stock dividend.

c. Treasury Shares — Common $7,000
    Cash $7,000
    To reacquire 500 common shares.

d. Cash $3,250
    Contributed Surplus (Premium on Shares)   250*
      Treasury Shares — Common $3,500
    To reissue 250 treasury shares.

    *Debit to Retained Earnings would be appropriate if
    balance were insufficient in Contributed Surplus
    (Premium on Shares).

e. Cash $3,750
    Treasury — Shares Common $3,500
    Contributed Surplus   250
    To reissue 250 treasury shares.

f. Retained Earnings $200,000
    Dividends Payable $200,000
    To declare $200,000 cash dividend.

g. No formal journal entry required.

h. Cash $30,000
    Common Share Capital $20,000
    Contributed Surplus (Premium on Shares)   10,000
    To issue 2,000 shares under stock option plan.

i. No formal journal entry required.

j. Cash $50,000
    Convertible Bonds Payable $50,000
    To issue $50,000 par-value, twenty-year, 12 percent,
    semiannual coupon bonds convertible into 40 common
    shares for each $1,000 bond.

k. Dividend Payable $200,000
    Cash $200,000
    To pay cash dividend.

l. Cash $2,500
    Common Share Warrants $2,500
    To issue share warrants.

m. Cash $15,000
    Common Share Warrants   1,250
      Common Shares $10,000
      Contributed Surplus (Premium on Shares)   6,250
    Warrants for 1,000 shares exercised.

n. Common Share Warrants $1,250
    Contributed Surplus $1,250
    To record warrants expiration.

o. Income Summary $300,000
    Retained Earnings $300,000
    To close net income to Retained Earnings.

SUGGESTED SOLUTION TO PROBLEM 1
FOR SELF-STUDY

Cash	$4,000	
Common Shares ($5 par value)		$ 500
Contributed Surplus		3,500

Because the Common Shares account went up by $500 and the par value is $5 per share, 100 shares (= $500/$5 per share) must have been issued. The issue price was $40 per share; hence, the cash raised was $4,000 (= $40 × 100 shares).

Treasury Shares	$2,520	
Cash		$2,520

Acquisition of 60 shares for the treasury at $42 per share; 60 × $42 = $2,520.

Cash	$1,800	
Treasury Shares		$1,680
Contributed Surplus		120

Because the year-end balance in the treasury shares account is $840, 20 shares (= $840/$42 per share) must remain in the treasury. Thus, 40 (= 60 − 20) shares were resold. Because the year-end Contributed Surplus account is $120 [= $33,620 − ($30,000 + $3,500)] larger than is explained by the issue of new shares, a "gain" of $120 must have been realized on the resale of the shares from the treasury. Because 40 shares were resold, the total "gain" was the $120, and the "gain" per share must have been $3 (= $120/40 shares). Thus, the total resale price per share must have been $45 (= $42 + $3). Cash raised must have been $1,800 = $45 per share x 40 shares.

Revenue Accounts	$90,100	
Expense Accounts		$80,000
Retained Earnings		10,100

Closing entries for revenue and expense accounts, given that revenues were $90,100 and net income was $10,000 for the year.

Retained Earnings	$2,700	
Dividends Payable		$2,700

The Retained Earnings account increased by only $7,400 for the year. Dividends must have been $10,000 − $7,400 = $2,700.

SUGGESTED SOLUTION TO PROBLEM 2
FOR SELF-STUDY

a. Retained Earnings	$5,000,000	
Investments		$2,000,000
Gain on Disposition of Investments		3,000,000

    To record the declaration of a dividend in kind recorded at market value. The excess of the market value over cost is recognized.

b. Retained Earnings	$2,000,000	
Investments		$2,000,000

    To record the declaration of a dividend in kind measured at cost.

c. Net income is larger when the dividend is recorded at fair market value. In both cases, Retained Earnings and total shareholders' equity decline by $2 million. The difference is that in the former treatment, income is increased by $3 million, the holding gain on the shares, which offsets the larger debit to Retained Earnings for the larger amount of dividend recognized.

ASSIGNMENT MATERIAL

QUESTIONS

1. Review the meaning of the key terms listed on page 691.

2. Under what circumstances would you expect par-value shares to be issued at a price in excess of par? What is the entry to record such an issue?

3. A construction corporation is attempting to borrow money on a note secured by some of its property. A bank agrees to accept the note, provided that the president of the corporation will personally endorse it. What is the point of this requirement?

4. "Par value of preferred shares is frequently a significant figure, but par value of common shares has little significance." Why may par value of preferred shares be significant?

5. Why is the amount in the Retained Earnings account for a profitable, growing company that has been in business for several decades unlikely to be of much value for predicting future dividend declarations?

6. What are treasury shares? How are they reported on the balance sheet?

7. A certain corporation retained almost all of its earnings, only rarely paying a cash dividend. When some of the shareholders objected, the reply of the president was, "Why do you want cash dividends? You would just have to go to the trouble of reinvesting them. Where can you possibly find a better investment than our own company?" Comment.

8. Compare the position of a shareholder who receives a cash dividend with that of one who receives a stock dividend.

9. At the annual shareholders' meeting, the president of the Santa Cris Corporation make the following statement: "The net income for the year, after taxes, was $1,096,000. The directors have decided that the corporation can afford to distribute only $500,000 as a cash dividend." Are the two sentences of this statement compatible?

10. The text says, "Convertible bonds are usually callable." "The call feature is included so that the issuer can force conversion of the bonds. Explain.

11. Are accumulated, but unpaid, dividends to preferred shareholders (which must be paid before dividends can be declared on common shares) liabilities? Explain.

12. What are prior-period adjustments? Why do some accountants think that GAAP should only rarely allow them?

13. Interest on bonds is deductible for tax purposes; dividends on preferred share issues are not. Assume that a company can raise $100 million either by assuming bonds promising 12 percent annual interest or by issuing preferred shares, convertible into common shares promising 12 percent annual dividends. The firm expects to continue to have income (in excess of all interest payments) taxable at the rate of 40 percent per year.
    a. Which of the two financing methods will show a larger income available for common shares?
    b. Why does this book suggest that, despite the answer above, one financing method is not necessarily preferred to the other?

EXERCISES

14. *Effects of transactions involving shareholders' equity.* Indicate whether each of the following statements is true or false and justify your response. Ignore the effects of income taxes.
    a. Cash dividends reduce the book value per share.
    b. A stock dividend does not affect the Retained Earnings account.
    c. Stock dividends reduce the book value per share.
    d. The declaration of a cash dividend does not reduce the amount of the shareholders' equity.
    e. The distribution of a stock dividend tends to reduce the market value per share.
    f. A stock split generally does not affect the Retained Earnings account.
    g. A stock dividend declaration is usually accompanied by a reduction in par value per share.

15. *Effects of transactions on Retained Earnings and shareholders' equity.* Indicate the effect of each of the following transactions on (1) the balance in the Retained Earnings and (2) the total shareholders' equity.
    a. Bonds are issued at a discount.
    b. A cheque is written to the Receiver General of Canada for additional income taxes levied on past years' income (no previous entry).
    c. A stock split is voted by the directors. The par value per share is reduced from $20 to $5, and each shareholder is given four new shares in exchange for each old share.
    d. The manager is voted a bonus of $35,000 by the directors.
    e. Notes payable in the face amount of $50,000 are paid by cheque.
    f. A dividend in preferred shares is issued to common shareholders (no previous entry).
    g. Securities held as a long-term investment are sold at book value.
    h. A building site is received as a donation by the company from the local chamber of commerce.
    i. A building is sold for less than its book value.

16. *Journal entries for transactions involving shareholders' equity.* Present the journal entries for each of the following transactions. These transactions do not relate to the same set of records.

   a. The no-par-value shares of a corporation are selling on the market at $100 a share. In order to bring the market value down to a "more popular" figure, the board of directors votes to issue four shares to shareholders in exchange for each share already held by them. The shares are issued.

   b. The treasurer of the corporation reports that cash on hand exceeds normal requirements by $300,000. Pending a decision by the board of directors on the final disposition of the funds, temporary investments in marketable securities in the amount of $299,600 are purchased.

   c. The net income for the year is $150,000. The directors vote to issue 1,000 shares of 10 percent, $100 par-value preferred shares as a stock dividend on the 2,500 no-par-value common shares outstanding. The preferred's market price is $102 a share. The common's market price is $50 a share.

   d. After the books are closed and the financial statements are issued, it is discovered that an arithmetic error was made in calculating depreciation on office equipment for the preceding period. The depreciation expense was $8,000 too large.

17. *Analyzing changes in shareholders' equity accounts.* The comparative balance sheet of the Forty-Misty Co. Inc. shows the following data:

	Dec. 31, Year 2	Dec. 31, Year 1
Common Shares	$1,320,000	$1,200,000
Retained Earnings	400,000	460,000
Total Shareholders' Equity	$1,720,000	$1,660,000

During Year 2, common shareholders received $60,000 in cash dividends and $120,000 in stock dividends. A refund on Year 0 taxes of $30,000 was received on March 1, Year 2 and was credited directly to Retained Earnings. A loss on retirement of plant assets of $5,600 occurred during the year and was debited directly to Retained Earnings.

   a. What net income is reported for Year 2, after the accounting was done as described?

   b. What net income should actually be reported for Year 2? Show your calculations.

18. *Analyzing changes in shareholders' equity accounts.* The comparative balance sheet of the Royal Corporation shows the following information:

	Dec. 31, Year 2	Dec. 31, Year 1
Preferred Shares (6 percent)	$ 600,000	$ 750,000
Common Stock	1,550,000	1,400,000
Retained Earnings	372,000	324,000
Total Shareholders' Equity	$2,522,000	$2,474,000

During Year 2, stock dividends of $150,000 were issued to common shareholders. In addition, common shareholders received $70,000 in cash dividends; the preferred shareholders received $36,000 in cash dividends. On July 1, Year 2, preferred shares with a par value of $150,000 were redeemed at 104; that is, $156,000 was paid to retire the shares. The call premium was debited to the Retained Earnings account.

What net income is reported to shareholders for Year 2?

19. *Journal entries for transactions involving shareholders' equity.* Give journal entries for the following transactions.
   a. Outstanding shares are acquired by the issuing corporation for its treasury at a cost of $100,000.
   b. Dividends are declared on preferred shares, $220,000.
   c. A dividend is paid to common shareholders consisting of preferred shares in the same corporation with a par value of $200,000.
   d. A dividend is paid to common shareholders consisting of no-par-value common shares in the same corporation. The amount assigned to these shares is $600,000.
   e. The building is mortgaged for $100,000, and this amount is distributed to the common shareholders as a cash dividend.

20. *Journal entries for transactions involving shareholders' equity and other accounts.* Give journal entries, if required, for the following transactions, which are unrelated unless otherwise specified.
   a. The regular quarterly dividend is declared on the 10 percent, $100 par-value preferred shares. There are 10,000 shares authorized and 8,000 shares issued, of which 1,600 shares have been reacquired and are held in the treasury.
   b. The dividend on the preferred shares [see part (a)] is paid.
   c. A stock dividend of $250,000 of no-par-value common shares is issued to common shareholders.
   d. A building replacement fund of $125,000 is created. The fund is to be used to purchase a new building when the present one becomes inadequate.
   e. Bonds with $500,000 par value are retired at par out of the sinking fund created for that purpose.
   f. The no-par-value common shares of the corporation are selling on the market at $300 a share. In order to bring the market value down to a more popular price and thereby broaden the distribution of its shareholdings, the board of directors votes to issue four extra shares to shareholders for each share already held by them. The shares are issued.

21. *Journal entries for transactions involving shareholders' equity.* Journalize the following transactions.

    a. A cash dividend of $2 a share is declared on the outstanding preferred shares. There are 5,000 shares authorized, 3,000 shares issued, and 100 shares reacquired and held in the treasury.

    b. A cash dividend of $1 a share is declared on the no-par common shares, of which there are 10,000 shares authorized, 7,000 shares issued, and 1,000 shares reacquired and held in the treasury.

    c. The dividend on the preferred shares is paid.

    d. The dividend on the common shares is paid.

22. *Restrictions on dividend declarations.* Daley Limited has total retained earnings of $100 million and has acquired treasury shares at a cost of $25 million. Its loan agreements limit dividend declarations that would reduce retained earnings below $60 million. The corporation laws of the province of Daley Limited's incorporation do not allow dividend declarations if the amount of retained earnings is less than the cost of treasury shares held.

    What is the maximum amount of dividends that Daley Limited can declare?

23. *Stock splits and stock splits accounted for as stock dividends.* The Horngren Co. Ltd. has 5 million common shares outstanding with a par value of $5 per share and retained earnings of $600 million. The common shares have a market price of $80 each. The board of directors wishes to increase the number of shares in circulation to 10 million either by declaring a two-for-one-stock split or by declaring a 100 percent stock dividend to be accounted for as a stock split.

    a. Give journal entries for each of these treatments.

    b. Explain the relative advantages and disadvantages of each.

24. *Transactions to incorporate and run a business.* The following events relate to shareholders' equity transactions of the Richardson Copper Co. Ltd. during the first year of its existence. Present journal entries for each of the transactions.

    a. January 2. Articles of incorporation are filed with the provincial registrar of companies. The authorized share capital consists of 5,000, $100 par-value preferred shares, which offers an 8 percent annual dividend, and 50,000 no-par-value common shares. The original incorporators are issued 100 common shares at $20 per share; cash is collected for the shares.

    b. January 6. A total of 1,600 common shares are issued for cash at $20 per share.

    c. January 8. A total of 3,000 preferred shares are issued at par.

    d. January 9. Certificates for the preferred shares are issued.

    e. January 12. The tangible assets and goodwill of Richardson Copper Works, a partnership, are acquired in exchange for 600 preferred shares and 10,000 common shares. The tangible assets acquired are valued as follows: inventories, $40,000; land, $45,000; buildings, $80,000; and equipment, $95,000.

    f. July 3. The semiannual dividend on the preferred shares outstanding is declared, payable July 25, to shareholders of record on July 12.

g. July 5. Operations for the first six months have been profitable, and the decision is made to expand. The company issues 20,000 common shares for cash at $33 per share.

h. July 25. The preferred shares dividend declared July 3 is paid.

i. October 2. The directors declare a dividend of $1 per share on the common shares, payable October 25, to shareholders of record on October 12.

j. October 25. The dividend on common shares declared on October 2 is paid.

25. *Transactions to incorporate and run a business.* The following data are selected from the records of capital stock and retained earnings of the Wheellock Inc. Present journal entries for these transactions.

a. July 5, Year 1. Articles of incorporation are filed with the director of the Canada Business Corporations Act. The authorized share capital consists of 1,000 Class B preferred shares with a preferred dividend of $6 per share and 10,000 Class A common shares.

b. July 8, Year 1. The company issues 3,000 common shares for cash at $60 per share.

c. July 9, Year 1. The company issues 6,000 common shares for the assets of the partnership of Able and Baker. Their assets are valued as follows: accounts receivable, $30,000; inventories, $60,000; land, $80,000; buildings $90,000; and equipment, $100,000.

d. July 13, Year 1. A total of 750 preferred shares are issued for $75,000.

e. December 31, Year 1. The balance in the Income Summary account, after closing all expense and revenue accounts, is $300,000. That account is to be closed to the Retained Earnings account.

f. January 4, Year 2. The regular semiannual dividend on the preferred shares and a dividend of $2 per share on the common shares are declared. The dividends are payable on February 1.

g. February 1, Year 2. The dividends declared on January 4 are paid.

h. July 2, Year 2. The regular semiannual dividend on the preferred shares is declared. The dividend is payable on August 1.

i. August 1, Year 2. The dividend declared on July 2 is paid.

26. *Accounting for convertible bonds.* On January 2, Year 1, the Ogopogo Corporation issues $1 million of twenty-year, $1,000 par value, 10 percent, semiannual coupon bonds at par. Each $1,000 bond is convertible into 40 no-par-value common shares. The Ogopogo Corporation's credit rating is such that it would have to issue 15 percent, semiannual coupon bonds if the bonds were not convertible and if they were to be issued at par. On January 2, Year 5, the bond issue is converted into common shares. A common share has a market price of $45 a share on January 2, Year 5.

Present the journal entries made on January 2, Year 1 and Year 5, under GAAP, to record the issue and conversion of the issue.

27. *Granting stock options to executives involves an element of compensation.* Suppose that accounting were to require recognition of compensation expense on the date that stock options were granted to an employee. A precise measure of the amount of the compensation expense would not be possible, but various approximations could be made. How might the accountant put a dollar amount on the compen-

sation expense granted through stock options? You may assume that the exercise price is the market price on the date the option is granted.

PROBLEMS AND CASES

28. *Reconstructing transactions involving shareholders' equity.* The Chelex Co. Ltd. began business on January 1. Its balance sheet on December 31 contains the shareholders' equity section shown in Exhibit 11.6.

EXHIBIT 11.6
CHELEX CO. LTD.
Shareholders' Equity as of December 31

Commons Shares ($10 par value)	$ 50,000
Contributed Surplus	78,000
Retained Earnings	10,000
Less: 300 Shares Held in Treasury	(6,000)
Total Shareholders' Equity	$132,000

During the year, Chelex Co. Ltd. engaged in the following share capital transactions:
(1) Issued shares for $25 each.
(2) Acquired a block of 500 shares for the treasury in a single transaction.
(3) Reissued some of the treasury shares.

Assuming that these were all of the share capital transactions during the year, answer the following questions:
a. How many shares were issued for $25?
b. What was the price at which the treasury shares were acquired?
c. How many shares were reissued from the block of treasury shares?
d. What was the price at which the treasury shares were reissued?
e. What journal entries must have been made during the year?

29. *Reconstructing transactions involving shareholders' equity.* The Worman Co. Inc. began business on January 1. Its balance sheet on December 31 contains the shareholders' equity section shown in Exhibit 11.7.

EXHIBIT 11.7
WORMAN CO. INC.
Shareholders' Equity as of December 31

Commons Shares ($5 par value)	$ 50,000
Contributed Surplus	254,800
Retained Earnings	25,000
Less: 600 Shares Held in Treasury	(16,800)
Total Shareholders' Equity	$313,000

During the year, Worman Co. Inc. engaged in the following share capital transactions:

(1) Issued shares for $30 each.

(2) Acquired a block of 1,000 shares for the treasury in a single transaction.

(3) Reissued some of the treasury shares.

Assuming that these were the only share capital transactions during the year, answer the following questions:

a. How many shares were issued for $30 each?

b. What was the price at which the treasury shares were acquired?

c. How many shares were reissued from the block of treasury shares?

d. What was the price at which the treasury shares were reissued?

e. What journal entries must have been made during the year?

30. *Dividends in kind.* In the mid-1970s, American Express Company held shares of Donaldson, Lufkin & Jenrette, Inc. (DLJ) as an investment. These shares had cost about $27 million but had a market value of about $6 million. The shares were carried on the books as a long-term investment at cost. (These events occurred before the FASB issued *SFAS No. 12*, requiring such items to be carried at lower of cost or market.) During a year when its income was about $200 million, American Express distributed the shares of DLJ as a dividend in kind to its own shareholders. The annual report of American Express said that, in management's opinion, the difference between the cost and the market value of the DLJ investment "did not represent a permanent impairment in value. . . . Accordingly, the entire carrying value of the DLJ investment . . . was charged to retianed earnings." Ignore income tax effects.

a. What journal entry did American Express apparently make?

b. What journal entries would have been made had the dividend in kind been recorded at market value of the assets distributed?

c. What are the differences in these two treatments on net income and retained earnings?

31. *Dilutive effects of stock options.* Refer to the schedule reproduced in Exhibit 11.8, which shows employee stock option data for the International Products Co. Ltd. (IP). At December 31, Year 3, there were 2.7 million options outstanding to purchase shares at an average of $54 per share. Total shareholders' equity at December 31, Year 3 was about $2.5 billion.

a. If IP were to issue 2.7 million shares in a public offering at the market price per share on December 31, Year 3, what would be the proceeds of the issue?

b. If IP were to issue 2.7 million shares to employees who exercised all outstanding stock options, what would be the proceeds of the issue?

c. Are IP's shareholders better off under **(a)** or under **(b)**?

d. The text accompanying the stock option data in the IP annual report reads, in part, as appears on page 708.

EXHIBIT 11.8
INTERNATIONAL PRODUCTS CO. LTD.
Disclosure of Employee Stock Options

Stock Options	Shares Subject to Option	Average per Share	
		Option Price	Market Price
Balance at December 31, Year 1	2,388,931	$45	$72
Options Granted	475,286	77	77
Options Exercised	(297,244)	42	76
Options Terminated	(90,062)	45	—
Balance at December 31, Year 2	2,476,911	50	83
Options Granted	554,965	75	75
Options Exercised	(273,569)	42	74
Options Terminated	(58,307)	52	—
Balance at December 31, Year 3	2,700,000	54	77

Option price under these plans is the full market value of International Products common shares on date of grant. Therefore, participants in the plans do not benefit unless the share's market price rises, thus benefiting all share owners.

IP seems to be saying that shareholders are not harmed by these options, whereas your answers to parts **(a)** and **(b)** show shareholders are worse off when options are exercised than when shares are issued to the public. Attempt to reconcile IP's statement with your own analysis in parts **(a)** and **(b)**.

32. *Reporting nonrecurring gains in the income statement.* Dominion Textile Inc. undertook a comprehensive review of the corporation's business units. As a result of this review, the directors decided to discontinue a number of lines of business and to redeploy the corporation's resources to a narrower range of products.

   Accordingly, the corporation deducted $11,500,000 from income as follows:

Writedown of fixed assets		$ 9,600,000
Provision for anticipated cash costs		10,300,000
		19,900,000
Less: Reduction in income taxes		
Deferred	$4,100,000	
Current	4,300,000	(8,400,000)
		$11,500,000

Before considering the above, the corporation reported a loss of $2,900,000.
   a. Give the journal entry made by Dominion Textiles Inc. to record the above event.

b. How do you think the above event should be reported in the financial statements?

33. *Dilution of earnings per share.* In May of Year 1, the A-Tat Co. Ltd. issued 100,000 no-par-value convertible preferred shares for $50 a share. The shares promised a dividend of $6. All shares were issued for cash. These shares were convertible into common shares at a rate of five common shares for each preferred share. The preferred shares are *not* regarded as equivalent to common shares in the calculation of earnings per share.

The company's earnings increased sharply during the next four years, and during January of Year 5, all preferred shares were converted into common shares. One million common shares were outstanding before conversion of the shares. If the conversion had not taken place, the net income to common for Year 5 would have been $3,000,000. Other data are as follows:

	Jan. Year 5	May Year 1
Market Prices:		
A-Tat Common Shares	$ 20	$10
A-Tat $6 Preferred Shares	100	50
Book Value per A-Tat Common Share		
(before conversion of preferred)	18	14

a. Prepare journal entries to record the issuance and conversion of the preferred shares.
b. Compute earnings per common share before conversion of the shares. What was the effect of the conversion on book values and on earnings per common share?
c. Did the conversion of the preferred shares into common shares lead to a dilution of the common shareholders' equity? Explain your reasoning.

34. *Accounting for detachable warrants.* After several years of rapid expansion, the Alcher Co. Ltd. approached the Bank of Nova Montreal for a $1 million, five-year loan. The bank was willing to lend the money at an interest rate of 12 percent per year. Alcher Co. Ltd. then approached an individual investor, who was willing to provide the same funds for only 8 percent per year, provided that the Alcher Co. Ltd. gave the investor an option to purchase 20,000 no-par-value common shares of Alcher Co. Ltd. for $20 per share at any time within five years of the initial date of the loan.

Alcher weighed both opportunities and decided to borrow from the investor. At the time of the loan, the common shares had a market price of $15 per share. Five years after the initial date of the loan, the investor exercised the option and purchased 20,000 shares for $20 each. At that time, the market price of the common shares was $45 each.
a. Did the use of the "detachable warrants" (the technical name for the option granted to the investor) reduce the Alcher Co. Ltd.'s cost of borrowing?

    b. How should the loan and annual interest payments of $80,000 be recorded in the books of the Alcher Co. Ltd. to reflect the economic reality of the transaction?

    c. How might the exercise of the warrants (and the purchase of the 20,000 shares) be recorded?

    d. Did exercise of the option dilute the shareholders' equity of the other shareholders on the date the option was exercised?

    e. What disclosures during the life of the loan do you think are appropriate? Why?

35. Comprehensive review of accounting for shareholders' equity. The shareholders' equity section of the balance sheet of the Reis Corporation at December 31 shown below.

Shareholders' Equity	
Common Shares — $10 Par Value, 500,000 Shares Authorized	
and 100,000 Shares Outstanding	$1,000,000
Contributed Surplus	500,000
Retained Earnings	3,000,000
Total Shareholders' Equity	$4,500,000

    a. Calculate the total book value and the book value per common share as of December 31.

    b. For each of the following transactions or events, give the appropriate journal entry and determine the total book value and the book value per common share of the Reis Corporation after the transaction. The transaction and events are independent of each other, except where noted.

      (1) A 10 percent stock dividend is declared when the market price of Reis Corporation's common shares is $60 per share.

      (2) A two-for-one stock split is declared, and the par value of a common share is reduced from $10 to $5. The new shares are issued immediately.

      (3) Ten thousand common shares of Reis Corporation are purchased on the open market for $50 per share and held as treasury shares.

      (4) Ten thousand common shares of Reis Corporation are purchased on the open market for $30 per share and held as treasury shares.

      (5) The shares acquired in **(3)** are sold for $70 per share.

      (6) The shares acquired in **(3)** are sold for $40 per share.

      (7) The shares acquired in **(3)** are sold for $30 per share.

      (8) Options to acquire 10,000 shares of Reis Corporation are exercised by officers for $15 per share.

      (9) Same as **(8)**, except that the exercise price is $50 per share.

     (10) Convertible bonds with a book value of $300,000 and a market value of $340,000 are exchanged for 10,000 common shares having a market value of $34 per share. No gain or loss is recognized on the conversion of bonds.

     (11) Same as **(10)**, except that gain or loss is recognized on the conversion of bonds into shares. Ignore income tax effects.

c. Using the results from part **(b)**, summarize the transactions and events that result in a reduction in:
   (1) Total book value.
   (2) Book value per share.

36. *Reconstructing events affecting shareholders' equity.* Exhibit 11.9 reproduces the statement of changes in shareholders' equity accounts for Granof Inc. for Year 2.
    a. Identify the most likely events or transaction for each of the events numbered **(1)** to **(6)** in the exhibit.
    b. Prepare journal entries for each of these events or transactions.

EXHIBIT 11.9

GRANOF INC.

Statement of Changes in Shareholders' Equity Accounts for Year 2

	Common Shares					
	Market Value per Share[a]	Number of Shares	Par Value	Contributed Surplus	Retained Earnings	Total Shareholders' Equity
Balances, Dec. 31, Year 1	$100	2,000,000	$12,000,000	$48,000,000	$40,000,000	$100,000,000
Events Causing Changes						
Event (1)	$105	4,000,000	—	—	—	—
Event (2)	$ 40	600,000	1,200,000	22,800,000	(24,000,000)	—
Event (3)	$ 45	100,000	200,000	4,300,000	—	4,500,000
Event (4)	$ 48	50,000	100,000	1,400,000	—	1,500,000
Event (5)	$ 50	—	—	—	45,000,000	45,000,000
Event (6)	$ 53	—	—	—	(6,750,000)	(6,750,000)
Balances, Dec. 31, Year 2		6,750,000	$13,500,000	$76,500,000	$54,250,000	$144,250,000

[a]*Before event.*

37. *Case introducing earnings per share calculations for a complex capital structure.* The Layton Ball Corporation has a relatively complicated capital structure. In addition to common shares, it has issued stock options, warrants, and convertible bonds. Exhibit 11.10 summarizes some pertinent information about these items. Net income for the year is $9,500, and the income tax rate used in computing income tax expense is 40 percent of pretax income.
    a. First, ignore all items of capital except for the common shares. Calculate earnings per common share.
    b. In past years, employees have been issued options to purchase shares. Exhibit 11.10 indicates that the price of the common shares throughout the year was $25, but that the stock options could be exercised at any time for $15 each. The holder of an option is allowed to surrender it along with $15 cash and receive one share in return. Thus, the number of shares would be increased, which would decrease the earnings per share figure. The company would, however, have more cash. Suppose that the holders of options ten-

EXHIBIT 11.10
Layton Ball Corporation
Information on Capital Structure for Earnings per Share Calculation (Problem 37)

Assume the following data about the capital structure and earnings for the Layton Ball Corporation for the year:

Number of Common Shares Outstanding Throughout the Year	2,500 shares
Market Price per Common Share Through the Year	$25
Options Outstanding During the Year:	
Number of Shares Issuable on Exercise of Options	1,000 shares
Exercise Price per Share	$15
Warrants Outstanding During the Year:	
Number of Shares Issuable on Exercise of Warrants	2,000 shares
Exercise Price per Share	$30
Convertible Bonds Outstanding:	
Number (issued fifteen years ago)	100 bonds
Proceeds per Bond at Time of Issue (= par value)	$1,000
Shares of Common Issuable on Conversion (per bond)	10 shares
Coupon Rate (per year)	$4^{1/6}$ percent

dered their options, along with $15 each, to purchase shares, and that the company used the cash to purchase shares for the treasury at a price of $25 each. Compute a new earnings per share figure. (Treasury shares are *not* counted in the denominator of the earnings per share calculation.)

c. Exhibit 11.10 indicates that there are also warrants outstanding in the hands of the public. Anyone who owns such a warrant is allowed to turn in that warrant along with $30 cash and to purchase one share. If the warrants were exercised, there would be more shares outstanding, which would reduce earnings per share. The company would, however, have more cash, which it could use to purchase shares for the treasury, reducing the number of shares outstanding. Suppose that all holders of warrants exercised them. Suppose that the company used the cash to purchase outstanding shares for the treasury. Compute a new earnings per share figure. (Ignore the information about options and the calculation in part **(b)** at this point.) Note that a rational warrant holder would *not* exercise his or her warrants for $30 when a share can be purchased for $25.

d. There are convertible bonds outstanding. A holder of a convertible bond is entitled to trade in that bond for ten shares. If a bond were converted, the number of shares would increase, which would tend to reduce earnings per share. On the other hand, the company would not have to pay interest and thus would have no interest expense on the bond, because it would no longer be outstanding. This would tend to increase income and earnings per share. Suppose that all holders of convertible bonds converted their bonds into shares. Compute a new net income figure (do not forget income tax effects on income of the interest saved) and a new earnings per share figure. (Ignore the information about options and warrants and the calculations in parts **(b)** and **(c)** at this point.)

e. Now consider all of the above calculations. Which sets of assumptions from parts **(b)**, **(c)**, and **(d)** would lead to the lowest possible earnings per share when they are all made simultaneously? Compute a new earnings per share under the most restrictive set of assumptions about reductions in earnings per share.

f. Accountants publish several earnings per share figures for companies with complicated capital structures and complicated events during the year. The *Financial Post*, however, publishes only one figure in its weekly columns (where it reports the price-earnings ratio — the price of a share divided by its earnings per share). Which of the figures computed above for earnings per share do you think should be reported by the *Financial Post* as *the* earnings per share figure? Why?

38. *Stated value.* Brenda's Edit Shoppes, Inc. has the following equity account balances:

Preferred Shares, 40,000 no-par shares issued and outstanding	$ 60,000
Common Shares, 50,000 no-par shares issued and outstanding	100,000
Retained Earnings	40,000

The company reacquires 10,000 of its common shares on the open market at $2.50 per share and retires them. What is the *stated capital* of common shares after this transaction?

39. *Shareholders' equity — transactions, balance sheet presentation, and book value per share.* The shareholders' equity section of the Western Economic Fund Corporation, a crown corporation, at January 1 of the current year appears below:

Preferred Shares, $1.50 Dividend Per Share, No Par Value,	
10,000 shares authorized; 5,200 shares issued and outstanding	$208,000
Common Shares, No Par Value, 200,000 shares authorized;	
60,000 shares issued and outstanding	600,000
Retained Earnings	325,000

During the current year, the following transactions have occurred:

Jan. 10 Issued 11,000 common shares for $13 cash per share.

　　　23 Issued 6,000 common shares at $14 per share.

Mar. 2 The federal government, the majority shareholder, donated $44,200 to Western.

July 15 Issued 1,200 preferred shares to acquire special equipment with a fair market value of $54,000.

Sept. 15 Received subscriptions to 10,000 common shares at $21 per share. One-third of the subscriptions price was received in cash.

Nov. 15   Received the balance due on the September 15 share subscriptions in cash, and issued the share certificates.

Dec. 31   Closed the net income of $95,800 from the Income Summary account to Retained Earnings.

a. Set up T-accounts for the shareholders' equity accounts at the beginning of the year and enter January 1 balances.

b. Prepare general journal entries to record the foregoing transactions, and post to T-accounts (set up any additional T-accounts needed). Determine the ending balances for the shareholders' equity accounts.

c. Prepare the December 31 shareholders' equity section of the balance sheet.

40. *Shareholders' equity — transaction descriptions from account data.* The T-accounts below contain keyed entries representing six transactions involving the shareholders' equity of Lawson, Inc.

		Cash				Deferred Government Assistance	
(1)	29,600	(6)	2,150			(4)	25,000
(2)	40,000						

		Preferred Shares				Land	
(6)	2,250	(1)	29,600	(3)	60,000		
				(4)	25,000		

	Common Shares				Contributed Surplus — Redemption of Shares	
		(2)	40,000		(6)	100
		(3)	60,000			
		(5)	2,160			

	Organization Costs	
(5)	2,160	

a. Using this information, give detailed descriptions for each of the six transactions.

41. *Dividends, share redemptions, and earnings per share.* The Cracker Corporation had the following shareholders' equity at January 1, 19X2.

Common shares, no par value, 100,000 shares outstanding	$1,200,000
$12 Preferred, no par value, 20,000 shares outstanding, cumulative and redeemable at 104	2,000,000
Retained Earnings	1,875,000
	$5,075,000

Although earnings were satisfactory in the past, no cash dividends had been declared in the last two years (that is, in 19X0 and 19X1). In 19X2, however, Cracker Corporation was confident that it would be able to afford to distribute $1,000,000 in cash dividends. After distribution of the dividends, it planned to redeem 5,000 of the preferred shares. This could be accomplished either through a purchase in the market or by "calling" these shares for redemption.

a. Calculate the amount of the dividend that would be paid to the preferred shareholders and to the common shareholders if dividends of $1,000,000 were declared in 19X2.

b. Calculate the effect on assets of calling the preferred stock for redemption.

c. Preferred shares are more like debt security than an equity security. Explain what is meant by this statement.

d. Dividends are said to be a distribution of earnings. Cracker Corporation has a large Retained Earnings balance. How could they not have been able to afford to pay dividends in 19X0 and 19X1?

e. Ignoring the redemption of preferred shares, if earnings for 19X2 were $635,000, calculate the earnings per share for 19X2.

Adapted with permission from the Society of Management Accountants of Canada.

DECISION CASE 11-1

In early January Year 3, B.R. Baine (B.R.), the president of Fanco Ltd., a diversified public company, faced the problem of determining the means of financing a major project recently approved by the board of directors. This project requires an investment of $1,000,000 and is expected to produce an operating income before financing costs and income taxes of $200,000 a year, with the principal returned at the end of the fifth year. Fanco Ltd. is subject to an income tax rate of 40 percent.

The corporate treasurer has advised B.R. that following alternative sources of financing are available:

1. Issue rights to common shareholders to purchase common shares at $20 per share.

2. Arrange a five-year bank loan with 14 percent interest payable annually in arrears.

3. Issue five-year convertible bonds with 10 percent interest payable annually. Each $100 bond would be convertible into 4.5 common shares.

4. Issue cumulative, redeemable, convertible $1.75 preferred shares. The preferred shares are redeemable in five years at their issue price and convertible into common shares on the basis of one common share for each preferred share. The preferred shares would be issued at $25 per share.

B.R. Baine owns no Fanco Ltd. common shares, but is paid an annual bonus of 10,000 times the reported earnings per common share before bonus. The earnings per share for this purpose is calculated by dividing net income less preferred dividends by the common shares outstanding at the fiscal year-end. In Year 2, Fanco Ltd. reported income of $420,000 and earnings per share of $2.10.

After careful consideration, B.R. estimated that it was likely that 20 percent of the bonds or preferred shares would be converted at the end of the first year and a further 40 percent would be converted at the end of each of the third and fifth years.

Determine the form of financing that B.R. should select to maximize his bonus in the first, third, and fifth years of the project.

Decision Case 11-2

Part I

Smith, Jones, and Able had been equal partners in a chain of photographic shops in Hamilton for a number of years. Able was approaching 65 and wished to retire from the business and spend his golden years in Florida. He proposed that he retire from the partnership by changing from a partner to a creditor of the partnership, with his capital to be repaid at the rate of $40,000 per year, plus 10 percent interest on the outstanding balance. At the same time, Jones and Smith thought they should convert the form of business to that of a limited company to provide more permanence and the flexibility to admit new employees as owners through the purchase of shares.

Jones and Smith considered that the book value of the assets and liabilities of the partnership were an inadequate measure of the value of the business, but did provide a list of the assets. To overcome the "historical cost" handicap of the book values, they had each asset and liability individually appraised at current market value and agreed upon by all partners. The following balance sheet presents the book values and agreed appraised values.

Because the business will remain essentially unchanged when Able retires, the partners decided to maintain the present accounting system. The new company, Smith, Jones and Able Ltd., is to issue 5,000 shares of no par value (for a consideration of $30 each) to each of Smith and Jones as partial consideration for their interest in the partnership.

Prepare the journal entries necessary to record the revaluation of assets, the retirement of Able, and the conversion to a limited company.

Part II

Five years later, when the retained earnings of the company amounted to $240,300 and the share capital, $500,000, Smith decided to retire. Rather than have the current shareholders — now increased by the addition of the six store managers — purchase the shares, it was decided to have the company purchase them for $46 a share. The shares would be held for subsequent reissue or cancellation.

1. Prepare the journal entry to record the purchase by the company of the shares of Smith.

2. Prepare the shareholders' equity segment of the balance sheet prepared immediately following the share purchase.

Smith Jones & Able
Balance Sheet
October 31, Year 5

ASSETS		Book Value	Appraised Value
Current Assets:			
Cash on Hand and in Bank		$ 12,500	$ 12,500
Temporary Investments		8,000	12,600
Accounts Receivable		17,600	17,200
Inventory		96,900	99,200
Prepaid Expenses		700	700
Total Current Assets		$135,700	$142,200
Land, Buildings, and Equipment:			
Land		$ 72,000	$169,500
Buildings	$ 68,200		272,000
Furniture and Fixtures	57,500		42,600
Automobiles	14,900		6,700
	$140,000		
Less: Accumulated Depreciation	(61,700)	78,900	
Total Plant and Equipment		$150,900	$490,800
Goodwill		2,500	46,300
Total Assets		$289,100	$679,300
LIABILITIES AND PARTNERS' EQUITY			
Current Liabilities:			
Accounts Payable		$ 6,400	$ 6,400
Accruals		700	700
		$ 7,100	$ 7,100
Mortgage Payable		106,000	98,200
Total Liabilities	$113,500	$105,300	
Partners' Equity:			
Smith		30,100	
Jones		41,300	
Able		104,200	
		$175,600	574,000
		$289,100	$679,300

CHAPTER TWELVE

LONG-TERM INVESTMENTS IN CORPORATE SECURITIES

CHAPTER OUTLINE

- Types of Long-Term Investments
- Portfolio Investments
- Minority Investments
- Majority Investments
- Preparing Consolidated Financial Statements
- Appendix 12.1: Accounting for Corporate Acquisitions

Investments
Expenditures to acquire property or other assets in order to produce revenue; assets so acquired — hence, current expenditures made in anticipation of future income. Most commonly used in the context of securities of other companies held for the long term.

significant influence
The ability to exert influence over the affairs and management policies of a company with less than majority ownership of its voting stock.

For a variety of reasons, corporations often acquire the shares or bonds of other corporations. For example, a corporation may temporarily have excess cash that is not needed for operations. Rather than permit the cash to remain idle in its bank account, the corporation may invest in the common shares of another corporation. Relatively short-term investments of excess cash in corporate securities are usually classified as Temporary Investments and are shown in the Current Assets section of the balance sheet. Chapter 6 discusses the accounting for short-term investments.

A corporation may acquire another corporation's shares for some long-term purpose.[1] For example, a firm may acquire shares of a major raw materials supplier to help assure continued availability of raw materials. Or, a firm may wish to diversify its operations by acquiring a controlling interest in an established firm in some new area of business. Long-term investments in corporate securities are typically classified on the asset side of the balance sheet in a separate section called **Investments**.

TYPES OF LONG-TERM INVESTMENTS

The accounting for long-term investments depends on the extent to which one company is able to exercise **significant influence** over the other. Sig-

---

[1] Industrial firms seldom acquire bonds of other corporations as long-term investments. Consequently, this chapter focuses on long-term investments in capital stock.

nificant influence over the operating and financial decisions of another company is indicated by such things as representation on the board of directors, participation in policy-making processes, material intercompany transactions, interchange of technical personnel, or provision of technical information. The extent of share ownership is one of the determinants of significant influence. Refer to Figure 12.1. Three types of long-term investments can be identified:

1. **Portfolio Investments** — Shares of another corporation are viewed as a good long-term investment and are acquired for the dividends and capital gains (increases in the market price of the shares) anticipated from owning the shares. The percentage owned of the other corporation's shares is not so large that the acquiring company can control or exert significant influence over the other company. Generally accepted accounting principles (GAAP) view investments of less than 20 percent of the voting shares of another company as portfolio investments, unless significant influence is clearly demonstrated.[2]

2. **Minority Investments** — Shares of another corporation are acquired so that the acquiring corporation can exert significant influence over the other company's activities. Because the shares of most publicly held corporations are widely dispersed among numerous individuals, many of whom do not vote their shares, it is possible to exert significant influence over another corporation with ownership of less than a majority of the voting shares. GAAP view investments of between 20 percent and 50 percent of the voting shares of another company as minority investments. However, ownership of 20 percent or more of the voting shares is insufficient by itself to confirm the ability to exercise significant influence.

3. **Majority Investments** — Shares of another corporation are acquired so that the acquiring corporation can control the other company. This control is typically at both the broad policy-making level and at the day-to-day operational level. Ownership of more than 50 percent of the voting shares of another company implies an ability to control, unless there is evidence to the contrary.

Portfolio Investments
All long-term investments in companies that are not subsidiaries, effectively controlled companies, or corporate joint ventures.

Minority Investments
A holding of less than 50 percent of the voting shares in another company. Accounted for with the cost method when it is not effectively controlled, and with the equity method otherwise.

Majority Investments
Shares of another corporation acquired so that the acquiring corporation can control the other company.

FIGURE 12.1
Types of Intercorporate Investments in Securities

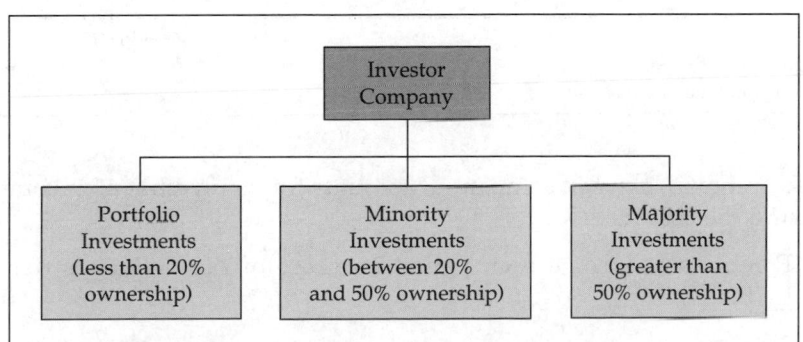

---

[2] *CICA Handbook*, section 3050.

The section that follows discusses the accounting for these three types of investments. **Throughout the chapter, the acquiring corporation is designated P, for *purchaser* or for *parent*, depending on the context; and the acquired corporation is designated S, for *seller* or for *subsidiary*. Unless stated otherwise, company S issues only common shares.**

PORTFOLIO INVESTMENTS

cost method
A method of accounting for portfolio investments where the investment is maintained at cost, not recognizing periodically any share of investee income or loss.

If a firm does not own a sufficient percentage (20 percent or more) of the voting shares of another corporation to control or significantly influence it, the management of the investment involves two activities: (1) awaiting the receipt of dividends and (2) deciding when the investment should be sold for a capital gain or loss. Portfolio investments must be accounted for by using the **cost method** in accordance with GAAP.[3]

The following illustration presents typical transactions in portfolio investments.

Suppose that P acquired 1,000 shares of S (10 percent of the issued shares) for $40,000. The entry to record the acquisition would be:

Investment in S	$40,000	
Cash		$40,000

If, while P held these shares, S paid a dividend of $2 per share, P would make the following entry:

Cash	$2,000	
Dividend Revenue		$2,000

If P sold all of its shares of S, P would debit Cash for the proceeds, credit the Investment in S account to reduce the balance in that account to zero, and credit Gain on Sale of Shares (or debit Loss on Sale of Shares) to complete the entry. If P sold its 1,000 shares of S for $40,500, and they were still recorded at a cost of $40,000, the entry would be:

Cash	$40,500	
Investment in S		$40,000
Gain on Sale of Investment		500

To summarize, when company P accounts for its investment in company S using the cost method:

1. P reports as income each period its share of the dividends declared by S.

---

[3] *CICA Handbook,* section 3050.

2. P reports on the balance sheet the cost of the shares in S.

3. P recognizes gains or losses on the income statement from holding the shares of S at the time the shares are sold.

Under the cost method, the carrying value of the investment usually is *not* affected by changes in the market value of the investment.[4] Because the investment is expected to be held for a long time, there is no point in recognizing market fluctuations that are likely to reverse themselves eventually. However, if a decline in market value below the carrying value were deemed to be a permanent decline, the investment should be written down. If there were subsequent rise in the market value, the carrying value would not be readjusted.

These investments are shown between current assets and capital assets on the balance sheet.

MINORITY INVESTMENTS

Judgment is required in ascertaining when significant influence can be exercised over another company when less than a majority of the voting shares is owned. As a rule of thumb, GAAP presume that one company can significantly influence another company when 20 percent or more of the voting shares of the other company are owned. Significant influence may be present when less than 20 percent are owned but, in these cases, management must demonstrate clearly to the independent accountants that significant influence exists.

Minority investments — those where ownership is between 20 percent and 50 percent — must be accounted for using the **equity method**. Under the equity method, the firm owning shares in another firm recognizes as revenue (expense) in each period its share of the net income (loss) of the other firm. Dividends received from S are recognized not as income, but as a return of capital.

equity method
A method of accounting by parent companies for investments in subsidiaries in which the parent's share of subsidiary income or loss is periodically recorded in the parent company's accounts.

EQUITY METHOD — RATIONALE

The rationale for the equity method when significant influence is present can be best understood by considering the financial statement effects of using the cost method in these circumstances. Under the cost method, P recognizes income or loss on the income statement only when it receives a dividend, when there is a permanent decline in value, or when it sells all or part of the investment. Suppose, as often happens, that S follows a policy of financing its own growing operations through retention of earnings and consistently declares dividends significantly less than its net income. The market price of S's shares will probably increase to reflect the retention of assets generated by earnings. Under the cost method, P will continue to show the investment at acquisition cost, and P's only reported income from

---

[4] Recall from Chapter 6 that investments classified as temporary should be carried at the lower of cost and market.

the investment will be the modest dividends received. P, because of its ownership percentage, can influence the dividend policy of S and thereby the amount of income recognized under the cost method. Under these conditions, the cost method may not reasonably reflect the earnings of S generated under P's influence. The equity method is designed to provide a better measure of a firm's earnings and of its investment when, because of its ownership interest, significant influence can be exerted over the operations of another firm.

EQUITY METHOD — PROCEDURES

Under the equity method, the initial purchase of an investment is recorded at acquisition cost, the same as under the cost method. P treats as revenue, each period, its proportionate share of the periodic earnings, not the dividends, of S. Dividends declared by S are then treated by P as a reduction in its Investment in S.

Suppose that P acquired 30 percent of the outstanding shares of S for $600,000. The entry to record the acquisition would be:

(1) Investment in S	$600,000	
Cash		$600,000
Investment made in 30 percent of S.		

Between the time of the acquisition and the end of P's next accounting period, S would report income of $180,000. P, using the equity method, would record:

(2) Investment in S	$54,000	
Revenue from Investments[5]		$54,000
To record 30 percent of income earned by S, accounted for using the equity method.		

If S paid a dividend of $70,000, P would be entitled to receive $21,000 and would record:

(3) Cash	$21,000	
Investment in S		$21,000
To record dividends received from S, accounted for using the equity method, and the resulting reduction in the investment account.		

Notice that the credit would be to the Investment in S account. P would record income earned by S as an *increase* in investment. The dividend would

---

[5] In practice, this account is frequently called "Equity in Earnings of Unconsolidated Affiliates."

become a return of capital or a *decrease* in investment.[6] P's Investment in S account would now have a balance of $633,000 as follows:

Investment in S			
(1)	600,000	21,000	(3)
(2)	54,000		
Bal.	633,000		

If P now sold one-quarter of its shares for $165,000, P's entry to record the sale would be:

Cash	$165,000	
Investment in S		$158,250
Gain on Sale of Investment		6,750
($^1/_4$ × $633,000 = $158,250.)		

The equity method, as described above, is simple enough to use. To make financial reports that use the equity method more realistic, GAAP require some modification of the entries under certain circumstances, described below.

When the equity method is used, the amount of income recorded by P should be equal to the amount that would have been recognized if S's operations had been consolidated with P's. These modifications will be discussed and illustrated later in the chapter; for our immediate purposes, we note two of them here.

Where either P or S sells goods to the other during the year and the goods have not been resold to other customers by the end of the year, the income from the sales is considered unrealized. The cost of the products recorded by the purchaser will usually exceed the cost to the seller by the amount of the income from the transaction recorded by the seller. In these circumstances, the unrealized income associated with the transaction will be excluded from P's income from Investment in S, and the value of the unsold goods reduced. This concept will be discussed in detail and illustrated later in this chapter.

An additional complication in using the equity method arises when the acquisition cost of P's shares exceeds P's proportionate share of the carrying value of the net assets (= assets minus liabilities) or shareholders' equity

---

[6] Students often have difficulty understanding journal entry (3), particularly the credit by the investor when a dividend is declared by the investee company. The transaction and entries are analogous to an individual's ordinary savings account at a local bank. Assume that you put $600 in a savings account, that interest of 9 percent (or $54) is later added by the bank to the account, and that, still later, you withdraw $21 from the savings account. Journal entries (1) to (3) in the text could be recorded for these three events, with slight changes in the account titles: Investment in S changes to Savings Account, and Revenue from Investments changes to Interest Revenue. The cash withdrawal reduces the amount invested in the savings account. Similarly, the declaration of a cash dividend by an investee company accounted for with the equity method reduces the investor's investment in the company.

goodwill
The value that derives from a firm's ability to earn more than a normal rate of return on its physical assets. Goodwill is recognized in the accounts only when it is acquired through a purchase transaction.

of S at the date of acquisition. For example, assume that P acquires 25 percent of the shares of S for $400,000 when the total shareholders' equity of S is $1 million and the carrying value of the net assets of S equals their fair value. The excess of P's cost over carrying value acquired is $150,000 (= $400,000 − 0.25 × $1,000,000) and is called **goodwill**. Goodwill must be amortized over a period not greater than 40 years. Accounting for goodwill, including its amortization, is discussed later in this chapter.

On the balance sheet, an investment accounted for using the equity method is shown separately in the Investments section. The amount shown will generally be equal to the acquisition cost of the shares plus P's share of S's undistributed earnings since the date the shares were acquired, less any cash dividends received and any amortization of goodwill recorded. On the income statement, P shows its share of S's income as revenue each period. (The financial statements of the investee, S, are not affected by the accounting method used by the investor, P.)

MAJORITY INVESTMENTS

parent
The term referring to the majority investor.

subsidiary
A company which has more than 50 percent of its voting shares owned by another company.

consolidation
Production of financial statements showing the parent and its subsidiaries as a single economic entity.

When one firm, P, owns more than 50 percent of the voting shares of another company, S, P can normally control the activities of S. The majority investor in this case is called the **parent**, and the majority-owned company is called the **subsidiary**. GAAP require majority-owned investments to be combined with those of the parent, except under certain conditions. Such combining is known as **consolidation**. Where these conditions are present, consolidated financial statements are not prepared. Instead, the investment is reported using the equity method.

REASONS FOR LEGALLY SEPARATE CORPORATIONS

There are many reasons why a business firm may prefer to operate as a group of legally separate corporations rather than as a single legal entity. From the standpoint of the parent company, the more important reasons for maintaining legally separate subsidiary companies include the following:

1. To reduce the financial risk. Separate corporations may be used for mining raw materials, transporting them to a manufacturing plant, producing the product, and selling the finished product to the public. If any one part of the total process proves to be unprofitable or inefficient, losses from insolvency will fall only on the owners and creditors of the one subsidiary corporation.

2. To meet more effectively the requirements of corporation laws and tax legislation. If an organization does business in a number of countries or provinces, it is often faced with overlapping and inconsistent taxation, regulations, and requirements. Organizing separate corporations to conduct the operations in the various local areas may be more economical.

3. To expand or diversify with a minimum of capital investment. A firm may absorb another company by acquiring a controlling interest in its

voting shares. The result may be accomplished with a substantially smaller capital investment (as well as with less difficulty, inconvenience, and risk) than if a new plant had been constructed or the firm had geared up for a new line of business.

PURPOSE OF CONSOLIDATED STATEMENTS

For a variety of reasons, then, a single *economic entity* may exist in the form of a parent and several legally separate subsidiaries. (MacMillan Bloedel Limited, for example, consists of about 75 legally separate companies.) A consolidation of the financial statements of the parent and each of its subsidiaries presents the results of operations, financial position, and changes in financial position of an affiliated group of companies under the control of a parent, essentially as if the group of companies were a single entity. The parent and each subsidiary are legally separate entities, but they operate as one centrally controlled economic entity. Consolidated financial statements generally provide more useful information to the shareholders of the parent corporation than would separate financial statements of the parent as investor and each subsidiary as an operating company.

Consolidated financial statements also generally provide more useful information than does use of the equity method. The parent, because of its voting interest, can effectively control the use of all of the subsidiary's assets. Consolidation of the individual assets and equities of both the parent and the subsidiary provides a more realistic picture of the operations and financial position of the single economic entity.

The Canada Business Corporations Act and the corporation statutes of most of the provinces permit companies to replace the separate statements of the parent corporation by consolidated financial statements.

DISCUSSION CASE 26

Cash Management in Canada: How the System Works

The basic principles and objectives of cash management within the United States and Canada are very similar. But despite the similarities, differences in the payment and banking systems in each country have resulted in very different methods being used to meet these objectives. American cash managers who are unfamiliar with these differences often request their Canadian subsidiaries to use specific cash management techniques and services which may be effective in the U.S. but are inappropriate or unnecessary in Canada. Opportunities are often missed because American cash managers are unaware that Canada's nationwide banking and payment systems pro-

(continued)

(continued)

vide cash management benefits that are unavailable in most other countries, including the U.S.

The U.S. [in 1987] has nearly 15,000 banks (of which the top six hold 20 percent of American bank assets), and more than 10,000 thrift institutions.

In the U.S., banks have been restricted geographically and operationally by federal law from setting up an interstate branch network. While there has been a recent emergence of limited interstate branching, it is governed by various restrictive regulations that will hinder the move toward nationwide branching.

In Canada, the chartered banks include nine Schedule A banks and 55 Schedule B banks. All operate within the mandate set out in the federal Bank Act, which allows a nationwide system of branch banking.

The six largest Schedule A banks have a long history of growth and stability. Their extensive on-line systems and advanced automated services have linked their national branch networks coast to coast and have permitted centralization of the financial operations of major corporations. Collectively, these six banks own 97 percent of Canada's 7,000 bank branches, which are located almost everywhere in the country and in many parts of the world.

Most of the Schedule B banks are foreign-bank subsidiaries, which concentrate on specialized lending to specific target markets. Only a few offer a full range of services or comprehensive service delivery networks. Even fewer provide cash management capabilities in Canada.

The remaining members of the Canadian banking system include approximately 70 trust companies and 3,000 credit unions ("near banks").

Although the Canadian payment system has looser geographic restrictions than does the American system, Canadian banks do have legislative restrictions on their activities. Traditionally, the Canadian financial system has been based on the concept of four separate "pillars" — banking, insurance, trusts, and securities — with rigidly defined functions. For example, the Bank Act restrains banks from offering data processing services for non-bank activities, engaging in fiduciary activities, underwriting or handling private placement of corporate securities, and providing investment advice.

This traditional separation of core functions is being revised and does not apply to Canadian bank development outside Canada, where Canadian banks operate trust, securities, and investment or merchant banking subsidiaries in conjunction with their primary functions of commercial and consumer lending.

Check-Clearing System

Check clearing in the U.S. is not centralized. Most checks are cleared through the Federal Reserve and, in addition, there are local clearing houses, automated clearing houses (some under the control of the Federal Reserve and some under private

(continued)

(continued)

control), and "direct-send" arrangements between numerous combinations of correspondent banks. Consequently, when a check is deposited, the funds are held and availability may not be given to the depositor until the check has been withdrawn from the payor's account.

When multiple local banks or out-of-town checks are involved, availability may not be given for two or three days. Because so many banks and near banks operate in the U.S., the "bank float" problem will not soon disappear.

In contrast, the Canadian check and electronic clearing system is controlled by the Canadian Payments Association, whose membership comprises the chartered banks and several other financial institutions. The current 119 members clear their own items and act as clearing agents for other banks or near banks. Although funds transfers may originate with any of the financial institutions, most corporate transactions move through Canada's "Big Six" Schedule A banks and their branches.

The strong nationwide branch system and a long history of financial stability and interaction among the relatively few Canadian banks have fostered a high level of trust among them. This allows same-day settlement and availability for all Canadian dollar items deposited, regardless of the banks involved or where in Canada the bank accounts are located.

The efficiency of the Canadian payment system, which settles checks overnight through the Bank of Canada, has precluded the need for payment techniques such as remote or controlled disbursement.

Multibank Balance Reporting

In the U.S., the larger number of banks and the state branching restrictions have imposed a need for multiple banking relationships, delayed credit for deposits, and caused a need for precise float measurement.

A large corporation may deal with several hundred unaffiliated banks every day. Even a small retail chain with five outlets in one city might have to deal with five or six banks. When it became economically unsound for large corporations to leave surplus funds in non-interest-bearing accounts at all their banks to make payments and to compensate the banks, the need became more critical to monitor these balances daily.

Multibank balance reporting services meet this need to assist American cash managers to determine the consolidated cash positions of their organizations. Once these are confirmed, the funds are mobilized in order to meet corporate financial objectives.

There is less need for multibank balance reporting in Canada because of the national branch networks — even the smallest communities are served by a major bank, and often by more than one. Since the 1970s, Canadian banks have provided their customers with numerous report-

(continued)

(continued)

ing options through on-line multibranch balance reporting. Consequently, the banking needs of a very large Canadian corporation can be fulfilled by dealing with one or two banks.

Intrabank Funds Concentration

In the U.S., deferred availability makes it difficult to accurately determine total funds for use. Complex interbank routines are required even for intracompany movement of collected funds. Typically, an organization's concentration bank must issue and send depository transfer checks (DTCs) to each remote bank to draw down funds. Even electronic DTCs do not provide same-day availability.

Electronic items are cleared separately from checks by means of a network of automated clearing houses. To expedite the settlement of high-value payments, wire transfer systems have been developed. These include Fed-Wire, BankWire, CHIPS, and systems operated by local clearing house associations.

In Canada, electronic items are exchanged at the check clearing points. Intra-bank funds concentration (and disbursement) is simple, quick, and inexpensive because of nationwide branch and on-line computer networks.

The Canadian system allows bank clients to consolidate or disburse their funds electronically. Regardless of geographic distance, deposits made at a local branch can receive same day value through automatic transfers to a concentration branch (or

funds can be disbursed from the concentration account to the field account). This reduces the number of banks (or branches) with which the cash manager must do business and allows easy centralization or disbursement of funds to meet the company's needs.

Although specific features and options differ from bank to bank, Canada's centralized banking system can provide a daily snapshot of the net position of an entire organization and gives full value for the total cash pool. This can reduce a company's overall borrowing requirements because cash-generating subsidiaries can fund those that need cash. The corporation has all the benefits of a central operation, tighter control over bank accounts and funds at the local level, and the maximum use of its funds, without taking away local autonomy in the management of payables and receivables.

Some banks offer enhancements to this service. For example, an automated interest allocation reporting system exists that identifies the suppliers and users of funds within a firm. This information allows company treasurers to act, in effect, as internal bankers for their organizations. It also helps in charging back the interest expense to the subsidiaries that are users of cash and in crediting interest income to those that are contributors of cash. Sophisticated services of this sort can usually be delivered through the head office's bank branch or through an in-office microcomputer.

(continued)

(continued)

Computerized Delivery Systems

The major Canadian banks can provide in-office delivery of bank products through interactive terminal facilities. The systems are similar in their general features, but differ greatly in their specific capabilities. In general, they provide information on balances, transactions, and rates; reports or raw data for various banking services; the ability to input and receive information for payroll preparation or security transactions; and the ability to initiate various types of funds transfers.

On most Canadian in-office delivery systems, the "start-of-day consolidated balance" is a statement of the organization's net position. Generally, it reflects all activity and all check clearings of the previous business day.

Multibank reporting on a Canadian in-office delivery system, as with American systems, is subject to the reliability of the banks reporting into the system. Multibank information may, therefore, be less accurate or timely than multibranch information.

Intrabank services delivered through interactive terminal facilities are accurate and easy to use. This is because many activities — such as offsetting, netting, zero balancing, and money movement — are automatic. Moreover, in the Canadian payment system, features such as availability reports and target balancing are not needed.

Most Canadian in-office delivery systems can be accessed worldwide. This means a multi-national corporation can monitor its Canadian banking network from anywhere in the world.

Disbursement Services

Canadian banks offer a direct deposit service — similar to an ACH credit — that electronically credits payee accounts on specified value dates. This service is particularly useful when combined with the payroll systems available through the major Canadian banks. The Canadian subsidiary of a multinational corporation can provide the payroll service supplier with payment information on magnetic tape or transmit the information directly to the data centers. The payments are prepared and can be distributed throughout the banking system to any branch of any financial institution in Canada. In addition to payrolls, this service is also valuable for pensions, stock dividends, annuities, insurance payments, and almost all recurring payments.

In Canada, there is currently no formal method for corporate-to-corporate electronic payments that is similar to the Corporate Trade Payment program offered by the National Automated Clearing House Association. However, a number of different programs for inter-institutional payments are evolving and standards are being developed. The smaller number of financial institutions in Canada makes domestic interbank funds concentration comparatively easier.

The efficiency of the Canadian payment system in the area of

(continued)

(continued)

disbursement services has afforded less room for creativity; Canadian banks emphasize precise regulation, information, and automation, as opposed to float maximization .

In both countries, the type of collection services required by a company is determined by its customer base and the payment system in which it operates.

In the U.S., the ban on interstate branching has made the lock box service a necessity for corporations that collect payments in more than one state. Corporations with nationwide lock boxes must use a lock box network or cope with the problem of transferring funds through wire transfers or DTCs (both paper and electronic varieties) to their major concentration bank. Availability of funds and mail times are the key to lock box decisions.

In Canada, less emphasis is placed on lock box services. The branch banking system allows the major banks to offer concentration services to enable a company's local offices to collect payments and deposit them at the nearest branch of the company's bank from which the funds are transferred automatically. That allows them same-day value at the concentration branch.

Results from a number of Canadian studies show that mail times are generally longer and more variable than those in the U.S. The use of lock boxes in Canada is justified on the basis of mail time savings and reduced internal processing. Canadian banks can do computerized lock box location analyses to deter-

mine if the savings are worthwhile.

Lengthy mail delays place a premium on intercepting large value northbound and southbound payments in both countries before they cross the border. An American company with Canadian revenues but no sales office in Canada may find it useful to have at least one lock box location in Canada for collecting its Canadian dollar receipts. Depending on the location of the American collection bank, a five- to ten-day cash flow saving could result from the use of a lock box in Canada.

Canadian banks can be paid for financial services with fees or compensating balances. An account analysis in Canada is usually conducted annually and is based on an actual sample from an agreed-upon typical operating period. The amount and type of compensation is agreed upon for the year.

Bank compensation in Canada takes service fees, balances, and Bank of Canada reserve requirements into account. Most banks provide "unbundled" pricing for each of their operating services. This pricing takes the form of a monthly fee and/or a per item charge, as is the case for transaction-based services.

The majority of the differences between Canada and U.S. cash management products are based on the distinctive banking systems that exist in the two countries. The primary Canadian cash management goal is not float management but rather a combination of up-to-date information,

(continued)

(continued)

improved efficiency, and considerable flexibility in reporting formats and bank/business arrangements.

The major Canadian banks offer many sophisticated cash management services that take advantage of the country's national banking structure. American cash managers who seek to structure the cash management procedures of their Canadian subsidiaries should be knowledgeable about the Canadian banking and payment systems and should seek professional advice on available products and services to capitalize on these systems.

References

Reprinted with permission from John Bumister, "Cash Management in Canada: How the System Works," *Financial Executive*, Sept./Oct. 1987, copyright 1987 by Financial Executives Institute, Morristown, New Jersey.

Discussion Question

What is "float" and how do wise financial managers take advantage of it?

CONSOLIDATION POLICY

Consolidated financial statements are generally prepared when the following criteria are met:

1. There are no important restrictions on the ability of the parent to exercise effective control of the subsidiary.
2. There are no legal restrictions prohibiting the consolidation of the subsidiaries.

Ownership of more than 50 percent of the subsidiary's voting shares normally implies an ability to exert control over the activities of the subsidiary.[7] For example, the parent can control the subsidiary's corporate policies and dividend declarations. There may be situations, however, in which control of the subsidiary's activities cannot be carried out effectively, despite the ownership of a majority of the voting shares. For example, the subsidiary may be located in a foreign country that has severely restricted the withdrawal of funds from that country. Or, the subsidiary may be in bankruptcy and under the control of a court-appointed group of trustees. In these cases, the financial statements of the subsidiary probably will not be consolidated with those of the parent. When the parent owns more than 50 percent of the shares and can exercise effective control, but consolidated statements are not prepared, the equity method is normally used.

---

[7] Technically, the key criterion determining the appropriateness of consolidation is control, which is defined as the continuing power to determine the strategic operating, investing, and financing policies without the co-operation of others (*CICA Handbook*, section 1590.03). The circumstances under which 51 percent ownership does not result in effective control are rare, so the majority ownership test is sufficient for our level of discussion.

Historically, if the asset and equity structure of the subsidiary was significantly different from that of the parent, the subsidiary's financial statements were not consolidated with those of the parent. For example, a consolidated statement might not have been prepared if the parent was a manufacturing concern and the subsidiary was a finance or insurance company. Current thinking is that appropriate footnote disclosures can adequately inform readers of the nature and impact of consolidating widely disparate types of entities. The CICA now requires consolidation of all subsidiaries.

Where the consolidated group of companies spans several industries, markets, or geographical areas, segmented reporting should be implemented to ensure no loss of useful information.

UNDERSTANDING CONSOLIDATED STATEMENTS

The remainder of this section discusses the five concepts essential for understanding published consolidated statements:

1. Substitution
2. External relationship
3. Consolidated entity cost
4. Indivisibility
5. Acquisition cost (Goodwill)

Each concept will be defined, explained, and illustrated through to its application to the consolidated balance sheet. The impact of these concepts will be explained briefly as they apply to the consolidated income statement.

Concept of Substitution

The concept of substitution is applied so that the subsidiary's detailed financial data are substituted for the aggregated totals appearing in the parent's single-company financial statements. This substitution is accomplished in the balance sheet by eliminating (1) the balance in the "Investment in S" account appearing on P's balance sheet and (2) the balance in the shareholders' equity section appearing on S's balance sheet, then combining the remaining balances reported on S's balance sheet with the corresponding balances in P's single-company balance sheet. This substitution is accomplished in the income statement by eliminating the "Income from S" from P's income statement and combining the revenues and expenses of S with the corresponding revenues and expenses of P.[8] Where the parent uses the equity basis of accounting for the investment in S, a complete substitution occurs, but where the investment in S is recorded on a cost basis, the balance must be converted to the equity basis to achieve a complete substitution.

---

[8] In some cases (discussed on the following page), additional balances are created or revised valuations occur.

The concept of substitution is applied whenever consolidated financial statements are prepared.

For example, the parent company's balance sheet shows an asset, Investment in S. The balance sheet of S shows its individual assets and liabilities balanced by the shareholders' equity. In the simple case where S has no liabilities, the assets of S are substituted for the Investment in S and combined with the corresponding assets of P.

If the only asset of S was Cash, the Investment in S (a noncurrent asset) would be replaced by Cash (a current asset), increasing the liquidity of P. If, in another case, the only asset of S was land, there would be no change in the liquidity of P. The additional detail provided through the application of the concept of substitution is of significant value to the reader of the financial statements.

If S's balance sheet included liabilities, the amount of the assets would be increased over the previous case by the amount of the liabilities. For example, where S acquired additional land in return for issuing a demand note, the application of this concept would result in a reduction in the liquidity of P, because the total current liability would be increased but not the total current assets.

To understand the eliminations from the right-hand side of the balance sheet, recall that the right-hand side shows the sources of the firm's financing. The subsidiary is financed by creditors (liabilities) and by owners (shareholders' equity). Assume that the parent owns 100 percent of the subsidiary's voting shares. In such a case, the assets on the consolidated balance sheet of the single economic entity are financed by the creditors of both companies and by the parent's shareholders. That is, the liabilities of the consolidated entity are the liabilities of both companies and the shareholders' equity is that of the parent alone. If the shareholders' equity accounts of the subsidiary were added to those of the parent, the financing from the parent's shareholders would be counted twice (once on the parent's books and once on the subsidiary's books). Hence, when the parent's investment account is eliminated from the sum of the two companies' assets, the accounting equation is maintained by eliminating the shareholders' equity accounts of the subsidiary.

The substitution and combination process explained above and the consolidation eliminations referred to below are made on a consolidation work sheet and are not recorded on the books of any of the legal entities being consolidated. The consolidated financial statements are then prepared directly from the work sheet. There are no separate books for the consolidated entity. Exhibit 12.1 summarizes the substitution concept.

Concept of External Relationship

This concept means that the consolidated financial statements show only the results of transactions between the consolidated group of companies and external parties. Account balances resulting from transactions between companies in the consolidated group are eliminated when consolidated statements are prepared. This elimination to balance sheet accounts is accomplished by eliminating all asset balances appearing on one entity's

EXHIBIT 12.1
The Concept of Substitution[a]

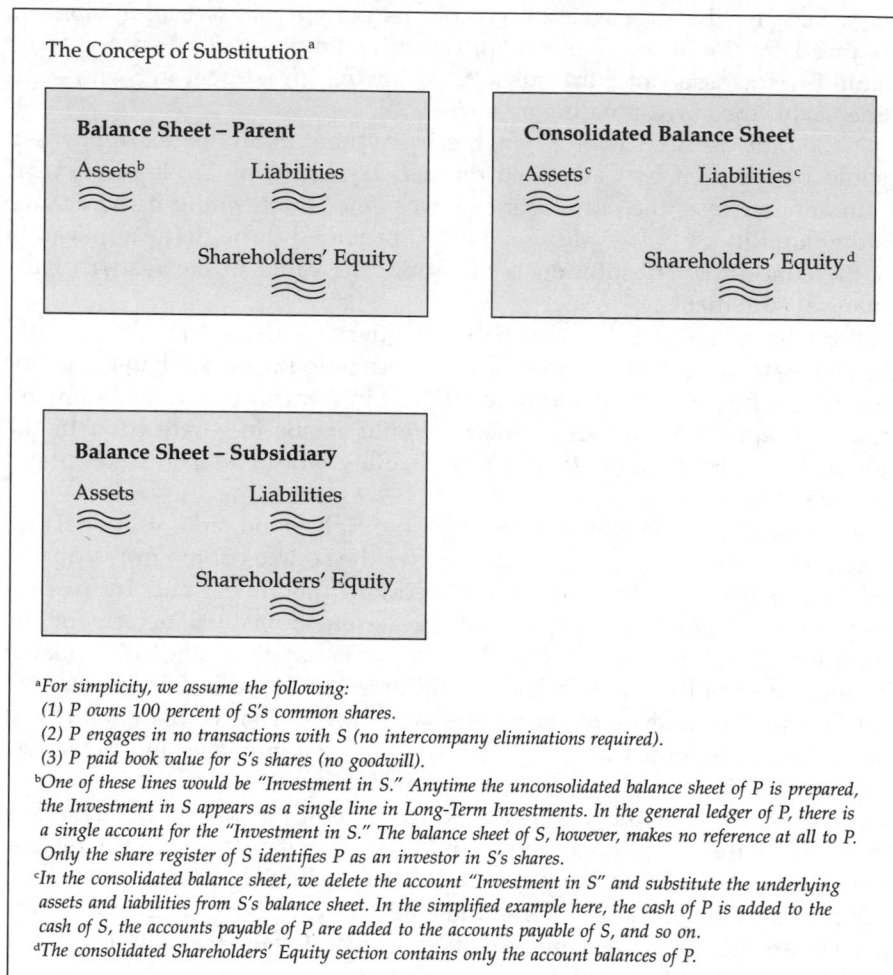

The Concept of Substitution[a]

Balance Sheet – Parent

Assets[b]   Liabilities

                   Shareholders' Equity

Consolidated Balance Sheet

Assets[c]   Liabilities[c]

                   Shareholders' Equity[d]

Balance Sheet – Subsidiary

Assets   Liabilities

                   Shareholders' Equity

[a]*For simplicity, we assume the following:*
  (1) P owns 100 percent of S's common shares.
  (2) P engages in no transactions with S (no intercompany eliminations required).
  (3) P paid book value for S's shares (no goodwill).
[b]*One of these lines would be "Investment in S." Anytime the unconsolidated balance sheet of P is prepared,
  the Investment in S appears as a single line in Long-Term Investments. In the general ledger of P, there is
  a single account for the "Investment in S." The balance sheet of S, however, makes no reference at all to P.
  Only the share register of S identifies P as an investor in S's shares.*
[c]*In the consolidated balance sheet, we delete the account "Investment in S" and substitute the underlying
  assets and liabilities from S's balance sheet. In the simplified example here, the cash of P is added to the
  cash of S, the accounts payable of P are added to the accounts payable of S, and so on.*
[d]*The consolidated Shareholders' Equity section contains only the account balances of P.*

balance sheet that represent claims due from another entity, and eliminating
the corresponding payables from the other entity's balance sheet. The elimination in the income statement is accomplished by eliminating the billed
price of intercompany sales of goods and services from revenue reported
by the entity providing the goods and services, and from the corresponding
cost or expense reported by the receiving entity. This process prevents double counting of receivables and payables and of revenues and expenses that
would otherwise occur.

For example, a parent may lend funds to its subsidiary. If the separate
balance sheets were merely added together, those funds would be counted
twice: once as a note receivable on the parent's books and again as cash or
other asset on the subsidiary's books. Consolidated balance sheets eliminate

intercompany transactions that would not be reported for a single, integrated enterprise. Thus, the note receivable of the parent and the note payable of the subsidiary are eliminated in preparing the consolidated balance sheet. These adjustments are referred to as **intercompany eliminations**.

Concept of Consolidated Entity Cost

The accounting realization principle generally requires a company to defer the recognition of increases in value and recognition of gains until the assets are sold to an independent person in an arm's-length transaction. Legally, each affiliated company is an independent person; assets transferred between them will generally be sold at market price, usually in excess of cost. As a result, realized gains will be reported by the seller, and the purchaser will record the asset at the market value on the date of purchase. Often, however, the asset purchased from an affiliate at market price remains on hand at the balance sheet date. At that time, it may be valued at more than the cost to the affiliated company that first purchased the asset. The historical-cost concept applied to the economic entity requires that the assets owned by members of the consolidated group must be valued at the cost at which they were first acquired by the group. Any unrealized gain must be eliminated.

The elimination of the unrealized gain from the balance sheet is accomplished by eliminating the unrealized gain from the asset to which it is attached and from the retained earnings of the entity that made the sale and recorded the gain. The reduction in the retained earnings of the entity that made the sale results from the elimination from the income statement of this entity of the sales and cost of sales of the merchandise remaining unsold.

For example, suppose that P imported a quantity of cameras from Japan for a laid-down cost of $100 each for sale to retailers for $120 each. A subsidiary, S, which operates a retail camera store, purchased five cameras for $600 (= 5 × $120). These cameras were unsold at the fiscal year-end. S would properly record these cameras in its inventory at $600, because this represents the cost to S. From a consolidated viewpoint, however, the $600 cost includes $100 of gain recognized by P. The cost of the cameras to the consolidated group remains $500. The application of the concept of consolidated entity cost results in a reduction in the consolidated value of the cameras to $500 and the elimination of the $100 unrealized gain from P's consolidated retained earnings and income. As a result, the cost of the assets included in the consolidated balance sheet is defined as cost when first purchased by a member of the affiliate group plus any costs incurred to modify the product subsequent to purchase.

An Illustration We illustrate the concepts of substitution, external relationship, and consolidated entity cost with the data in Exhibit 12.2 for P and S. Columns 1 and 2 show the financial statement amounts for the two separate companies. Column 3 sums columns 1 and 2 for comparison with column 4 — the correct consolidated financial statements.

Eliminating Double Counting of Intercompany Payables For example, suppose that separate company records indicate that $12,000 of S's accounts receivable represent amounts payable by P. Column (3) counts the current

intercompany eliminations
Journal entries to remove the effects of transactions between a parent and its subsidiary prior to preparing consolidated financial statements.

EXHIBIT 12.2
Illustrative Data for Preparation of Consolidated Financial Statements (in thousands)

	Single-Company Statements			Consolidated (See
	Company P (1)	Company S (2)	Combined (3) = (1) + (2)	Exhibit 12.19) (4)
CONDENSED BALANCE SHEETS ON DECEMBER 31				
Assets				
Accounts Receivable	$ 200	$ 25	$ 225	$ 213
Investment in S (at equity)	705	—	705	—
Other Assets	2,150	975	3,125	3,125
Total Assets	$3,055	$1,000	$4,055	$3,338
Equities				
Accounts Payable	$ 75	$ 15	$ 90	$ 78
Other Liabilities	70	280	350	350
Common Shares	2,500	500	3,000	2,500
Retained Earnings	410	205	615	410
Total Equities	$3,055	$1,000	$4,055	$3,338
CONDENSED INCOME STATEMENTS FOR CURRENT YEAR				
Revenues				
Sales	$ 900	$ 250	$1,150	$1,110
Equity in Earnings of				
Company S*	48	—	48	—
Total Revenues	948	250	$1,198	$1,110
Expenses				
Cost of Goods Sold				
(excluding depreciation)	$ 440	$ 80	$ 520	$ 480
Depreciation Expense	230	50	170	170
Administrative Expenses	80	40	120	120
Income Tax Expense	104	32	136	136
Total Expenses	$ 744	$ 202	$ 946	$ 906
Net Income	$ 204	$ 48	$ 252	$ 204
Dividends Declared	(50)	(13)	(63)	(50)
Increase in Retained				
Earnings for the Year	$ 154	$ 35	$ 189	$ 154

An alternative caption would be Revenue from Investments.

assets underlying this transaction twice: once as part of Accounts Receivable on S's books and a second time as Cash (Other Assets) on P's books. Also, the liability shown on P's books appears in the combined amount for Accounts Payable in column (3). The consolidated group does not owe this $12,000 to an outsider. To eliminate double counting on the asset side and to report Accounts Payable at the amount payable to outsiders, the consolidation process must eliminate $12,000 from the amounts for Accounts Receivable and Accounts Payable in column (3). See column (4).

If either company held bonds or long-term notes of the other, the consolidation process would eliminate the investment and related liability in the consolidated balance sheet. It would also eliminate the "borrower's" interest expense and the "lender's" interest revenue from the consolidated income statement.

Eliminating Double Counting of Investment   To consider a more complex example, suppose that P's balance sheet shows an asset, Investment in S. The subsidiary's balance sheet shows its individual assets. When column (3) adds the two balance sheets, the sum shows both P's investment in S's assets and the assets themselves. The consolidation process must eliminate P's account, Investment in S, $705,000, from the sum of the balance sheets. Because the consolidated balance sheet must maintain the accounting equation, the process must make corresponding eliminations of $705,000 from the equities.

The rationale is as follows. S's financing comes from creditors (liabilities of $295,000) and from owners (shareholders' equity of $705,000). In this case, P owns 100 percent of S's voting shares. Thus, the financing for the assets of the consolidated entity comes from the creditors of both companies and from P's shareholders. In other words, the equities of the consolidated entity are the liabilities of both companies but the shareholders' equity of P alone. Column (3) adds the shareholders' equity accounts of S to those of P. It counts the financing from P's shareholders twice (once on the parent's books and once on the subsidiary's books). Hence, when the consolidation process eliminates P's investment account ($705,000) from the sum of the two companies' assets, it eliminates the shareholdres' equity accounts of S ($500,000 of common stock and $205,000 of retained earnings). See column (4).

Eliminating Double Counting of Income   Similarly, the consolidation process must eliminate certain intercompany items from the sum of the income statements so that the consolidated income statement will present the consolidated entity in transactions with outsiders. P's accounts show Equity in Earnings of Company S of $48,000. S's records show individual revenues and expenses that net to $48,000. When column (3) sums the revenues and expenses of the two companies, it counts that income twice. The consolidation process must eliminate the account Equity in Earnings of S. See column (4) for Equity in Earnings.

Eliminating Intercompany Sales   Another example of an intercompany item involves intercompany sales. Separate company records indicate that S sold merchandise to P for $40,000 during the year. None of this inventory remains in P's inventory of December 31. Therefore, the merchandise inventory items sold appear in Sales Revenue of both S's books (sale to P) and on P's books (sale to outsiders). Thus, column (3) overstates sales of the consolidated entity to outsiders. Likewise, Cost of Goods Sold of both companies in column (3) counts twice the $40,000 Cost of Goods Sold by S to P and then by P to outsiders. The consolidation process eliminates the inter-company sale from S to P. See column (4) for Cost of Goods Sold.

Concept of Indivisibility

In many cases, the parent will not own 100 percent of the voting shares of a consolidated subsidiary. The owners of the remaining voting shares are

minority interest
That portion of capital stock in a subsidiary corporation not owned by the controlling (parent) company.

called *external minority shareholders*, or the **minority interest**.[9] These shareholders continue to have a proportionate interest in the net assets (or total assets minus total liabilities) of the subsidiary as shown in the subsidiary's separate corporate records. They also have a proportionate interest in the earnings of the subsidiary.

An issue in the GAAP for consolidated statements is whether the statements should show only the parent's share of the assets and liabilities of the subsidiary (proportionate consolidation), or whether they should show all of the subsidiary's assets and liabilities along with the minority interests in them (full consolidation).

The law clearly establishes that the ownership of shares in the company does not entitle a shareholder to a proportional claim to individual company assets. Further, the parent, with its controlling voting interest, can effectively direct the use of all the assets and liabilities, not merely an amount equal to the parent's percentage of ownership.

The concept of indivisibility rejects the proportionate consolidation alternative and requires that the individual asets and liabilities of a company may not be prorated between the majority and minority shareholders, and that the consolidated financial statements include all of the assets and liabilities of the subsidiary. The consolidated balance sheet and income statement in these instances, however, must disclose the interest of the minority shareholders in the subsidiary that has been consolidated.

The amount of the minority interest shown on the balance sheet is generally the result of multiplying the common shareholders' equity of the subsidiary — reduced by unrealized gains on goods sold by the subsidiary — by the minority's percentage of ownership. For example, if the common shareholders' equity (or assets minus liabilities) of a consolidated subsidiary totals $500,000 and the minority owns 20 percent of the common shares, the minority interest shown on the consolidated balance sheet is $100,000 (= 0.20 × $500,000).

The minority interest is typically presented among the equities on the consolidated balance sheet between the liabilities and shareholders' equity. Usally, the right-hand side of the balance sheet contains only liabilities and owners' equity items, so that the minority interest should appear as one or the other. Because the minority interest has no maturity date, it does not meet the criteria to be a liability, as discussed in Chapter 9. It might be classified as an indeterminate-term liability, much the same as deferred income taxes.

The amount of the minority interest in the subsidiary's income shown on the consolidated income statement is generally the result of multiplying the *subsidiary's* net income by the minority's percentage of ownership. The consolidated income is allocated to show the portions applicable to the parent company and the portion of the subsidiary's income applicable to the minority interest. Typically, the minority interest in the subsidiary's income is shown as a deduction in calculating consolidated net income.

---

[9] Do not confuse this minority interest in a consolidated subsidiary with a firm's own minority investments, discussed earlier. The minority *interest* belongs to others outside the parent and its economic entity. The parent's minority *investments* are those for which the parent owns less than 50 percent of the shares.

Concept of Acquisition Cost (Goodwill)

When a company gains a majority interest in another established company through the purchase of shares, the cost of the shares purchased by the parent will ordinarily differ from their book value calculated from the balance sheet of the subsidiary.

Two issues in the GAAP for consolidated statements arise under these circumstances: the presentation of the difference between the cost and book value of the shares purchased, and the valuation of the assets and liabilities when presented on the consolidated financial statements.

The purchase of majority share interest in a going concern is analogous to purchasing a share of the assets less liabilities of the firm, because, in both cases, the purchaser acquires control over the resources. When the assets of a going concern are purchased and the liabilities assumed, the value of the individual assets and liabilities (usually their fair market value) are ordinarily specified in the sales contract. The sum of the contract values of the individual assets, less the liabilities assumed, ordinarily differ from the total contracted price, the difference being attributed to goodwill. In this case, providing that the contract values for the individual assets and liabilities do not materially differ from the current market prices, the contract values will be considered as cost for accounting purposes, and the goodwill reported as an asset and amortized by a charge to income over a period not exceeding forty years.

The above accounting treatment for the purchase of assets of a going concern is used as a precedent for resolving the accounting issues that arise when majority control of a going concern is acquired through the purchase of shares. The concept of acquisition cost requires that, where a majority interest in a subsidiary is acquired through share purchase, the parent's interest in identifiable assets acquired and liabilities assumed will be based on their fair value at the date of acquisition. An exception is made when the fair value of the acquired interest in the net assets exceeds the total cost of acquiring the shares. In this case, the fair value should be adjusted to equal the total cost of acquisition.

The excess of the acquisition cost over the fair value of the acquired interest in the net assets is recorded as goodwill in the consolidated balance sheet. This goodwill is amortized over its estimated life (not exceeding forty years). For example, suppose that a parent company purchases for $400,000 all of the shares of a company that owns an apartment complex, has assets consisting of the apartment land and buildings with a book value of $100,000, and has no liabilities. Two factors could be identified for causing the difference of $300,000 (= $400,000 − $100,000) between the cost and book value of the shares. The book value of the land and buildings is based on historical cost and fails to consider changes in construction costs and increases in land values. An estimate of $350,000 for the depreciated replacement cost of the land and buildings could be considered the fair value of the assets. The remainder of the purchase price ($50,000) is attributed to the goodwill of the business. On the consolidated balance sheet at the date the shares are purchased, the land and buildings of the subsidiary will be valued at acquisition cost to the parent of $350,000 and goodwill on consolidation recorded at $50,000. The depreciation on the building in the consolidated income statement will subsequently be based on the portion of the acquisition cost allocated to the building.

Where P uses the equity method for recording the investment in S, the goodwill will be amortized by an entry on P's books reducing the balances in the accounts, Investment in S and Income from S, by the amounts of the annual amortization.

DISCUSSION CASE 27

Setting GAAP

Most of the GAAP you encounter in this book are presented to you without discussion of the alternatives they supplant. In some cases, accounting principles have been chosen because they are perceived as generally accepted. In other cases, they are established by fiat — a handbook pronouncement by the CICA.

Mergers and acquisitions are a good example of an economic event in which several plausible accounting alternatives are possible. One of the choices the Accounting Standards Board has had to make involves the problem of what values to use for the assets of the subsidiary when bringing them forward to the consolidated balance sheet.

When less than 100 percent of the shares of S are purchased and consolidated statements are prepared by P, a problem arises in recording the value of the assets of S on the consolidated balance sheet. At least three alternative solutions could be considered. The assets of S could be included in the consolidated balance sheet at their value on S's books; at their fair value at the date P purchased S's shares (the date of acquisition); or at S's book value plus P's proportion of the difference between fair market value

and book value at the date of acquisition.

If S's assets were included in the consolidated balance sheet at S's book value, the concept of acquisition cost would be disregarded on the consolidated balance sheet. Consequently, this alternative has been rejected.

If S's assets (including goodwill) were included in the consolidated balance sheet at the fair market value at the date of acquisition, a portion of the excess would be allocated to the minority interest. Because the minority interest represents the minority shareholders' equity in S *as recorded on S's books* and S does not record the unrealized gain in conformity with the cost principle, the alternative has also been rejected.

If S's assets were included in the consolidated balance sheet at S's book value plus P's share of the difference between book value and fair market value at date of acquisition, the resulting consolidated balance sheet would conform to the concept of acquisition cost and the amount of the minority interest would be based on the book value of S's books. This method is required to be adopted under Canadian GAAP

(continued)

(continued)

(CICA Handbook, section 1600).

To illustrate these alternatives, assume that, in the previous example, the parent company purchased only 80 percent of the shares of S for $230,000.

Under the first alternative, the consolidated balance sheet would include S's land and buildings at the book value of $100,000, minority interest of $20,000 (= 0.20 × $100,000), and goodwill of $240,000 [= $320,000 − (0.80 × $100,000)]. This alternative ignores the fact that the fair market value of S's land and buildings at the date of acquisition was $350,000 and consequently overstates goodwill.

Under the second alternative, the consolidated balance sheet would include S's land and buildings at their fair market value at date of acquisition of $350,000, goodwill of $50,000 (= $400,000 − $350,000), and minority interest of $80,000 (= 0.20 × $400,000). This alternative recognizes the unrealized increase in value of S's land and buildings and the goodwill implied in the purchase price of S's shares. However, these amounts are not recorded on S's balance sheet and do not represent the minority's share in the shareholders' equity

of S of $20,000 (= 0.20 × $100,000).

Under the third alternative, the land and buildings would be valued on the consolidated balance sheet at historical cost plus P's share in the unrealized gain at the date of acquisition of $300,000 [= $100,000 + 0.80 × ($350,000 − $100,000)], the goodwill of $40,000 [= 0.80 × ($400,000 − $350,000)], and minority interest of $20,000 (= 0.20 × $100,000). Another way to calculate the consolidated balance sheet value of the land and buildings is to combine P's share in the market value at the date of acquisition and the minority interest's share of S's book value (0.80 × $350,000 + 0.20 × $100,000 = $300,000).

The amounts appearing on the consolidated balance sheet for land and buildings, goodwill, and minority interest under each of the alternatives are shown below. Note that the net balance under each alternative equals the cost of P's investment in S's shares of $320,000.

It should be noted that the subsidiary would record no change in the valuation of the land and buildings but would continue to report them in its financial statements as depreciated historical cost of $100,000.

	Alternative 1	Alternative 2	Alternative 3
Land and Buildings	$100,000	$350,000	$300,000
Goodwill	240,000	50,000	40,000
Total	$340,000	$400,000	$340,000
Less: Monthly Interest	(20,000)	(80,000)	(20,000)
Cost of S's Shares	$320,000	$320,000	$320,000

Discussion Question

Is Alternative 1, 2, or 3 GAAP in Canada? What are the conceptual arguments favouring these methods?

Consolidated Income and Retained Earnings

The amount of consolidated net income for a period is the same as the amount that would be reported if the parent company used the equity method of accounting for the intercorporate investment. That is, consolidated net income is equal to:

$$\text{Parent Company's Net Income} + \text{Parent's Share of Subsidiary's Net Income} - \text{Unrealized Profit (or Plus Loss) on Intercompany Transactions}$$

Where the subsidiary is accounted for under the equity method, the principal difference between the consolidated income statement relates to the components of income presented. When a consolidated income statement is prepared, the individual revenues and expenses of the subsidiary (less intercompany adjustments) are combined with those of the parent. When the equity method is used for an unconsolidated subsidiary, the parent's share of the subsidiary's net income minus gain (or plus loss) on intercompany transactions is shown on a single line of the income statement with a title such as "Equity in Earnings (Loss) of Unconsolidated Subsidiary."

Similarly, the amount shown on the consolidated balance sheet for retained earnings is the amount that would be reported if the parent company used the equity method of accounting for the intercorporate investment. That is, consolidated retained earnings is equal to:

$$\text{Parent's Retained Earnings} + \text{Parent's Share of the Change in Subsidiary's Retained Earnings Since Acquisition} - \text{Unrealized Profit (or Plus Loss) on Intercompany Transactions}$$

CONSOLIDATION AND EQUITY METHOD COMPARED

The only difference between the consolidation and the equity method is financial statement presentation. Under the equity method, there is one-line disclosure of the investment on the balance sheet and one-line disclosure of the investee earnings[10] on the income statement. Under the consolidation method, the underlying balance sheet accounts are substituted for the one line, "Investment in S," and the underlying revenue and expense accounts are substituted for the one line on the income statement, "Equity in earnings of S." In fact, for 364 days of the year, the parent accounts for subsidiaries using the equity method. Only when year-end consolidated financial statements are to be prepared is it necessary to deviate from the one-line presentation used for investments under the equity method. Because we have said that income reported from the investment must be identical under both equity and consolidation methods, it follows that all of the intercompany eliminations are identical. Exhibit 12.3 summarizes use of the equity method.

LIMITATIONS OF CONSOLIDATED STATEMENTS

The consolidated statements do not replace those of individual corporations; rather, they supplement those statements and aid in their interpre-

---

[10] Assuming that the investee has no extraordinary items in its income statement.

EXHIBIT 12.3
Components of the Investment Account During the Year for Long-Term Intercorporate Investments Using the Equity Method

Investment in S	
(a) Acquisition cost of investment	(c) Cash dividends received
(b) Proportionate share of investee earnings recognized for the period	(d) Amortization of goodwill (excess of purchase price over proportionate share of fair value of net assets acquired)
	(e) Additional depreciation on the fair value increment attributed to undervalued plant assets
	(f) Elimination of unrealized profit on intercompany sales still held in inventory

Underlying Entries	Circumstances
(a) Investment in S Cash	Each time additional shares in S acquired.
(b) Investment in S Revenue from Investments	Made annually on receipt on financial statements from S. If S has a loss, P will record a loss, not revenue.
(c) Cash Investment in S	As dividends received.
(d) Goodwill amortization expense Investment in S	Each financial statement date.
(e) Depreciation expense Investment in S	Each financial statement date.

(f) Sales Revenue (P)
    Inventory (S)
  Sales Revenue (S)
    Inventory (P)
	Each financial statement date.

tation. Creditors must rely on the resources of one corporation and may be misled if forced to rely entirely on a consolidated statement that combines the data of a company in good financial condition with those of one verging on insolvency. A corporation can declare dividends only against its own retained earnings. Shareholders of the subsidiary can judge the ability of S to pay dividends only by looking at the balance sheet of S. Looking at the consolidated balance sheet gives no information on the retained earnings balance for S.

PREPARING CONSOLIDATED FINANCIAL STATEMENTS

This section illustrates the preparation of consolidated financial statements for P and S. Knowing how to construct consolidated financial statements is not essential for learning how to interpret and analyze them. Nevertheless, it helps.

DATA FOR THE ILLUSTRATION

The illustration covers a five-year period during which transactions occur that demonstrate the application of each of the five concepts presented above. For the sake of simplicity, the illustration is limited to the preparation of the consolidated balance sheet.

Work sheets are used to prepare consolidated financial statements. The data include the postclosing trial balances of each company included in the consolidation, as well as supplementary information. The work sheet illustrated in Exhibit 12.6 differs from that adopted in Chapter 3 in the following ways:

1. There is a separate self-balancing work sheet for each financial statement.
2. There is a separate column for each company included in the consolidation. The postclosing trial balances of each single company will be inserted in these columns.
3. The assets are separated from the equities.
4. The two Adjustment columns are replaced by one Elimination column.
5. Only one column is required for the consolidated statement.

Keep in mind that the Elimination entries are recorded only on the work sheet used to prepare the consolidated statements — not in the accounting records of the company. There is no "consolidated" set of books.

YEAR 1 — THE CONCEPT OF SUBSTITUTION

To illustrate the process of substitution and to demonstrate the use of consolidated working papers, the following facts are assumed:

1. P starts a subsidiary company, S, on December 15, Year 1 and pays $60,000 for the shares of the subsidiary. The subsidiary purchases land to construct a building for $20,000 cash, and purchases inventory for $28,000, paying $18,000 on account.
2. The balance sheet of S at December 31, Year 1, the fiscal year-end of both the parent and subsidiary, after the above transactions have been recorded, is shown in Exhibit 12.4:

EXHIBIT 12.4
S's Balance Sheet
December 31, Year 1

ASSETS		EQUITIES	
Cash	$22,000	Accounts Payable	$10,000
Inventory	28,000	**Shareholders' Equity:**	
Land	20,000	Common Shares	60,000
Total Assets	$70,000	Total Equities	$70,000

3. The balance sheet of the parent company at December 31, Year 1 is shown in Exhibit 12.5.

EXHIBIT 12.5
P's Balance Sheet
December 31, Year 1

ASSETS		EQUITIES		
Cash	$ 26,000	Accounts Payable		$ 29,000
Accounts Receivable	37,000	**Shareholders' Equity:**		
Inventory	64,000	Common Shares	$100,000	
Investment in S	60,000	Retained Earnings	58,000	158,000
Total Assets	$187,000	Total Equities		$187,000

The parent company wishes to prepare a consolidated balance sheet that presents the state of affairs as though the two companies were one economic entity.

The parent's investment account equals the parent's ownership of the subsidiary's share capital. Before adding together the single-company balance sheet items to determine consolidated totals, the parent's Investment in S must be eliminated so that the subsidiary's assets and the parent's investment in those assets are not both shown on the consolidated balance sheet.

The shareholders' equity of the consolidated entity is provided by the shareholders of the parent. If the shareholders' equity of the parent and the subsidiary were merely added together, equities would be counted twice.

EXHIBIT 12.6
P's Consolidated Balance Sheet Work Sheet
December 31, Year 1

	Balance Sheets P	Balance Sheets S	Intercompany Eliminations	Consolidated Balance Sheet
ASSETS				
Cash	$ 26,000	$22,000		$ 48,000
Accounts Receivable	37,000	—		37,000
Inventory	64,000	28,000		92,000
Investment in S	60,000	—	A $(60,000)	—
Land	—	20,000		20,000
Total Assets	$187,000	$70,000	$(60,000)	$197,000
EQUITIES				
Accounts Payable	$ 29,000	$10,000		$ 39,000
Common Shares:				
P	100,000	—		100,000
S	—	60,000	A $(60,000)	—
Retained Earnings:				
P	58,000	—		58,000
Total Equities	$187,000	$70,000	$(60,000)	$197,000

Intercompany Eliminations:
A — Parent's Investment in S and the subsidiary's Common Shares.

When the investment account is eliminated to avoid double counting of assets, the subsidiary's shareholders' equity accounts corresponding to the parent's investment are eliminated to avoid double counting of these equities.

To eliminate the parent's investment account and the subsidiary's shareholders' equity accounts, offset the subsidiary's Share Capital against the Investment in S account. The entry in Exhibit 12.6 to eliminate P's investment in S is:

(A) Common Stock	$60,000	
Investment in S		$60,000
To eliminate the investment in S account and the		
Share Capital account of S.		

This entry is entered in the consolidated balance sheet work sheet, Exhibit 12.6. Remember that this entry is not made in the books of either company. The consolidated balance sheet follows in Exhibit 12.7.

EXHIBIT 12.7
P's Consolidated Balance Sheet
December 31, Year 1

ASSETS		EQUITIES		
Cash	$ 48,000	Accounts Payable		$ 39,000
Accounts Receivable	37,000	**Shareholders' Equity:**		
Inventory	92,000	Common Shares	$100,000	
Land	20,000	Retained Earnings	58,000	158,000
Total Assets	$197,000	Total Equities		$197,000

A comparison of the parent company's balance sheet unconsolidated with the consolidated balance sheet shows that the only difference between the two is that the "Investment in S ... $60,000" has been eliminated and the balances of the underlying assets and liabilities have been substituted and aggregated with similar items on the parent company's balance sheet.

Year 2 — The Concept of External Relationship

To illustrate the concept of external relationship, the following facts are assumed during Year 2 for P and S:

1. S carried on an active business, reported an income of $18,000 for the year, and paid a dividend to P, its sole shareholder, of $12,000. P was not so successful and earned only $10,000 from its operations (before recognition of Income from Investment in S). Because funds were required for expansion, P paid no dividends.

2. At December 31, Year 2, P advanced $50,000 to S in return for a note.

3. At December 31, Year 2, P owed S $6,000 on current account.

A parent may sell goods on account or buy goods on account from a subsidiary and treat the resulting obligation as an account receivable or an account payable. The subsidiary will treat the obligation as an account payable or an account receivable. A parent often makes loans to subsidiaries that appear as Note Receivable, Investment in Bonds, or Advances to Subsidiary on the parent's books. The subsidiary would show Note Payable, Bonds Payable, or Advances from Parent on its books. A single company would not show Accounts Receivable and Accounts Payable for departments within the company. The balances resulting from these transactions must be eliminated from the consolidated balance sheet so that the resulting statement will appear as that of a single company.

EXHIBIT 12.8
P's Consolidated Balance Sheet Work Sheet
December 31, Year 2

	Balance Sheets P	Balance Sheets S	Intercompany Eliminations	Consolidated Balance Sheet
ASSETS				
Cash	$ 2,000	$ 3,000		$ 5,000
Accounts Receivable	52,000	27,000		79,000
Accounts Receivable from P		6,000	B $ (6,000)	—
Inventory	76,000	51,000		127,000
Land	—	20,000		20,000
Building[a]	—	72,000		72,000
Investment in S	66,000[b]		C (66,000)	—
Note Receivable from S	50,000		A (50,000)	—
Total Assets	$246,000	$179,000	$(122,000)	$303,000
EQUITIES				
Bank Loan	$ 30,000	$ 40,000		$ 70,000
Accounts Payable	24,000	23,000		47,000
Accounts Payable to S	6,000		B $ (6,000)	—
Note Payable to P		50,000	A (50,000)	—
Common Shares				
P	100,000	—		100,000
S	—	60,000	C (60,000)	—
Retained Earnings:				
P	86,000[c]	—		86,000
S	—	6,000[d]	C (6,000)	—
Total Equities	$246,000	$179,000	$(122,000)	$303,000

Intercompany Eliminations:
A — Intercompany notes.
B — Intercompany current accounts.
C — Parent's Investment in S and the subsidiary's Share Capital and Retained Earnings.

[a]Net of accumulated depreciation.
[b]$60,000 + $18,000 − $12,000 = $66,000.
[c]$58,000 + $10,000 + $18,000 = $86,000.
[d]$18,000 − $12,000 = $6,000.

In Exhibit 12.8, P's Note Receivable consists of $50,000 due from S, and S's Accounts Receivable include $6,000 due from P. The entries to record the elimination of the intercompany receivable and payables in Exhibit 12.8 are:

(A) Note Payable to P	$50,000	
Note Receivable from S		$50,000
(B) Accounts Payable to S	$ 6,000	
Accounts Receivable from P		$ 6,000
To eliminate intercompany payables and receivables.		

Entry (C) is similar to entry (A) in Year 1 and is described at the bottom of the work sheet. The balance sheet data for P and S extracted from their individual postclosing trial balances are shown in the consolidated balance sheet work sheet presented in Exhibit 12.8. The consolidated balance sheet follows in Exhibit 12.9.

EXHIBIT 12.9
P's Consolidated Balance Sheet
December 31, Year 2

ASSETS		EQUITIES		
Cash	$ 5,000	Bank Loan		$ 70,000
Accounts Receivable	79,000	Accounts Payable		47,000
Inventory	127,000	Current Liabilities		$117,000
Current Assets	$211,000	**Shareholders' Equity:**		
Land	20,000	Common Shares	$100,000	
Building (net)	72,000	Retained Earnings	86,000	186,000
Total Assets	$303,000	Total Equities		$303,000

Note that all intercompany balances are excluded from the consolidated balance sheet and that the parent's Shareholders' Equity remains unchanged, because the parent used the equity basis of accounting for investment in the subsidiary.

YEAR 3 — THE CONCEPT OF CONSOLIDATED ENTITY COST

To illustrate the process of implementing the concept of consolidated entity cost, the following events are assumed to occur to P and S in Year 3:

1. During the Year, P incurred a loss of $2,000 from its own operations. S reported earnings of $7,000 from its normal operations plus a $17,000 gain on the sale of land to P, as detailed below. Because the $17,000 gain on the sale of the land has not been realized through sale outside the affiliated group, it was excluded from S's income recorded by P. Neither company paid dividends during the year.

2. To facilitate the financing of the consolidated group, it was decided that S would sell to P the land it purchased in Year 1. The sale was recorded at the current market price of $37,000, and the land was leased by the

parent to the subsidiary for an annual rental of $3,600 per year. The proceeds from the sale of land helped the subsidiary repay the $50,000 Note Payable to the parent.

3. At December 31, Year 3, the subsidiary owed the parent $25,000 on current account.

A common feature of affiliated company activities is the sale of assets from one company to another. As single companies, the sale is usually transacted at the normal market price, which frequently exceeds cost. If the subsidiary had been organized as a department of the parent rather than as a separate legal entity, it is likely that the assets would have been transferred at cost, because the realization convention requires the deferral of revenue and profit until the sale is completed to a person outside the company. As single companies, however, the profit from the sale will be recognized by the vendor, and cost to the purchaser will be the contracted price.

Because one purpose of consolidated statements is to report the results of the economic entity as if it were one legal entity, the cost of the assets transferred, if held by the purchaser at the balance sheet date, must be adjusted to the cost when acquired by the consolidated group. In this way, the asset value appearing on the consolidated balance sheet will appear as if the group were a single company.

In Exhibit 12.10, land is recorded on the single-company postclosing trial balance of P at the $37,000 cost to P. However, because the sale is made between the subsidiary and the parent, the increase in market value cannot be recognized, and the land must be reduced to the cost of $20,000 when purchased by S. The entry to record the elimination of the unrealized profit in Exhibit 12.10 is:

(B) Retained Earnings (S)	$17,000	
Land		$17,000
To eliminate the unrealized profit from the sale of land (= $37,000 − $20,000).		

Entry A is similar to Entry B in Year 2, and Entry C is similar to Entry C in Year 2.

The consolidated balance sheet work sheet of P and S at December 31, Year 3 is presented in Exhibit 12.10, and the consolidated balance sheet in Exhibit 12.11.

YEAR 4 — THE CONCEPT OF INDIVISIBILITY

To illustrate the concept of indivisibility, the following events are assumed to occur to P and S in Year 4:

1. On January 1, P sold for $40,000 the land it had purchased from S in Year 3.

2. On January 1, P sold 20 percent of the shares of S to the senior executives of S for $18,000.

EXHIBIT 12.10
P's Consolidated Balance Sheet Work Sheet
December 31, Year 3

	Balance Sheets P	Balance Sheets S	Intercompany Eliminations		Consolidated Balance Sheet
ASSETS					
Cash	$ 4,000	$ 3,000			$ 7,000
Accounts Receivable	51,000	32,000			83,000
Accounts Receivable from S	25,000		A	$ (25,000)	—
Inventory	84,000	44,000			128,000
Land	37,000	—	B	(17,000)	20,000
Buildingᵃ	—	69,000			69,000
Investment in S	73,000ᵇ		C	(73,000)	—
Total Assets	$274,000	$148,000		$(115,000)	$307,000
EQUITIES					
Bank Loan	$ 30,000	—			$ 30,000
Accounts Payable	53,000	$ 33,000			86,000
Accounts Payable to P		25,000	A	$ (25,000)	—
Common Shares					
P	100,000	—			100,000
S	—	60,000	C	(60,000)	—
Retained Earnings:					
P	91,000ᶜ	—			91,000
S	—	30,000ᵈ	B	(17,000)	—
			C	(13,000)	—
Total Equities	$274,000	$148,000		$(115,000)	$307,000

Intercompany Eliminations:
A — Intercompany current accounts.
B — Reduction in value of land to subsidiary's cost.
C — Parent's Investment in S and the subsidiary's Share Capital and Retained Earnings.

ᵃ*Net of accumulated depreciation.*
ᵇ*$66,000 + $7,000 = $73,000.*
ᶜ*$86,000 − $2,000 + $7,000 = $91,000.*
ᵈ*$6,000 + $7,000 + $17,000 = $30,000.*

EXHIBIT 12.11
P's Consolidated Balance Sheet
December 31, Year 3

ASSETS		**EQUITIES**		
Cash	$ 7,000	Bank Loan		$ 30,000
Accounts Receivable	83,000	Accounts Payable		86,000
Inventory	128,000	Current Liabilities		$116,000
Current Assets	$218,000	**Shareholders' Equity:**		
Land	20,000	Common Shares	$100,000	
Building (net)	69,000	Retained Earnings	91,000	191,000
Total Assets	$307,000	Total Equities		$307,000

3. During the year, P earned income from its normal operations of $5,000 plus $3,000 (= $40,000 − $37,000) from the sale of land. S reported income of $15,000.

4. During the year, P paid a dividend of $14,000 and S paid a dividend of $10,000.

Because P sold 20 percent of the shares of S at January 1, Year 4, minority shareholders of S have been created. These minority shareholders have a 20 percent interest in the net assets and income of S.

The concept of indivisibility requires that the entire assets, liabilities, revenues, and expenses of the consolidated group be combined, because they represent the items under the control of the parent company's shareholders.

EXHIBIT 12.12
P's Consolidated Balance Sheet Work Sheet
December 31, Year 4

	Balance Sheets		Intercompany Eliminations	Minority Interest	Consolidated Balance Sheet
	P	S			
ASSETS					
Cash	$ 47,000	$ 4,000			$ 51,000
Accounts Receivable	43,000	37,000			80,000
Accounts Receivable from S	28,000		A $ (28,000)		—
Inventory	77,000	57,000			134,000
Building[a]	—	66,000			66,000
Investment in S					—
	76,000[b]		B (76,000)		
Total Assets	$271,000	$164,000	$(104,000)		$331,000
EQUITIES					
Accounts Payable	$ 57,000	$ 41,000			$ 98,000
Accounts Payable to P		28,000	A $ (28,000)		—
Common Shares:					
P	100,000	—			100,000
S	—	60,000	B (48,000)	$12,000	—
Retained Earnings:					
P	114,000[c]				114,000
S		35,000[d]	B (28,000)	7,000	—
Minority Interest				$19,000	19,000
Total Equities	$271,000	$164,000	$(104,000)		$331,000

Intercompany Eliminations:
A — Intercompany current accounts.
B — Parent's Investment in S and the parent's share of the subsidiary Share Capital and Retained Earnings.

[a]Net of accumulated depreciation.
[b]$73,000 + $17,000 − $18,000 + (0.80 × $15,000) − (0.80 × $10,000) = $76,000.
[c]$91,000 + $5,000 + $3,000 + $17,000 + (0.80 × $15,000) − $14,000 = $114,000.
[d]$30,000 + $15,000 − $10,000 = $35,000.

The amount of the minority shareholders' interest in the net assets and net income will be their proportional interest in the company in which they hold shares. In Exhibit 12.12, the minority interest in the net assets of S at December 31, Year 4 is $19,000 [= 0.20 × ($60,000 + $35,000)], and their interest in the net income is $3,000 (= 0.20 × $15,000). The minority interest in the net assets is presented in the balance sheet between Liabilities and Shareholders' Equity, and the minority interest in the net income is presented as a deduction in determining consolidated income. In place of an entry to record the minority share of the net assets, it is customary to create an additional column in the consolidated work sheet where the minority share is recorded and totalled.

Entry (A) is similar to entry (A) in Year 3, and entry (B) is similar to entry (C) in Year 3.

The consolidated work sheet at December 31, Year 4 is presented in Exhibit 12.12, and the consolidated balance sheet in Exhibit 12.13.

EXHIBIT 12.13
P's Consolidated Balance Sheet
December 31, Year 4

ASSETS		EQUITIES		
Cash	$ 51,000	Accounts Payable		$ 98,000
Accounts Receivable	80,000	Minority Interest		19,000
Inventory	134,000	**Shareholders' Equity:**		
Current Assets	$265,000	Common Shares	$100,000	
Building (net)	66,000	Retained Earnings	114,000	214,000
Total Assets	$331,000	Total Equities		$331,000

YEAR 5 — THE CONCEPT OF ACQUISITION COST (GOODWILL)

To illustrate the concept of acquisition cost (goodwill), the following events are assumed to occur to P, S, and SS in Year 5:

1. Effective January 1, P sold its remaining shares in S for $90,000. During the year, the parent recorded operating income of $15,000 and paid dividends to its shareholders of $6,000.

2. Using in part the proceeds from the sale of the shares in S, P purchased 60 percent of the shares in SS, one of its major suppliers, for $135,000 on December 31. The balance sheet of SS at the date of acquisition, showing both the book value and the fair value of the identifiable assets, is presented in Exhibit 12.14.

The book value of the 60 percent of the shares of SS purchased by P was $97,800 [= 0.60 × ($100,000 + $63,000)], whereas the cost of the shares purchased was $135,000. The difference (purchase discrepancy) of $37,200 can be attributed to two factors. The balance sheet values of the net assets may differ from their fair value, and other attributes of the company may not be recorded on the balance sheet.

To determine the amount attributed to each of the above two factors, P undertook a detailed examination of the net assets and found that the fair value was $38,000 greater than the book value. P's share of this difference

EXHIBIT 12.14
SS's Balance Sheet
December 31, Year 5

	Book Value	Fair Value	Increase (Decrease)
ASSETS			
Cash	$ 17,000	$ 17,000	—
Accounts Receivable	77,000	76,000	$(1,000)
Inventory	69,000	79,000	10,000
Land	7,000	21,000	14,000
Buildings and Machinery (net)	52,000	67,000	15,000
Total Assets	$222,000	$260,000	$38,000
EQUITIES			
Accounts Payable	$ 59,000	$ 59,000	
Shareholders' Equity			
Common Shares	100,000		
Retained Earnings	63,000		
Total Equities	$222,000		

was $22,800 (= 0.60 × $38,000). The remainder of the difference between the cost of the shares to P and 60 percent of the book value of the net asset, $14,400 (= $37,200 − $22,800), is assumed to be attributed to Goodwill.

To record the parent's share of the net assets at fair value at the date of the share purchase, the following entry is recorded in the consolidated balance sheet work sheet:

(A) Inventory	$6,000	
Land	8,400	
Buildings and Machinery	9,000	
Accounts Receivable		$ 600
Investment in SS		22,800

The purchase discrepancy attributed to Goodwill appears when the following substitution entry is recorded:

(B) Common Shares (SS)	$60,000[a]	
Retained Earnings (SS)	37,800[b]	
Goodwill	14,400[c]	
Investment in SS		$112,200

[a] 60 percent × $100,000 = $60,000.
[b] 60 percent × $63,000 = $37,800.
[c] $135,000 − $22,800 − $60,000 − $37,800 = $14,400.

The consolidated balance sheet work sheet at December 31, Year 5, following the acquisition of SS, is presented in Exhibit 12.15 and the consolidated balance sheet in Exhibit 12.16.

EXHIBIT 12.15
P's Consolidated Balance Sheet Work Sheet
December 31, Year 5

	Balance Sheets P	SS	Intercompany Eliminations and Adjustments	Minority Interest	Consolidated Balance Sheet
ASSETS					
Cash	$ 25,000	$ 17,000			$ 42,000
Accounts Receivable	52,000	77,000	A $ (600)		128,400
Inventory	85,000	69,000	A 6,000		160,000
Land	—	7,000	A 8,400		15,400
Building & Machinery[a]	—	52,000	A 9,000		61,000
Investments in SS	135,000[b]		B (112,200)		—
			A (22,800)		—
Goodwill			B 14,400		14,400
Total Assets	$297,000	$222,000	$ (97,800)		$421,200
EQUITIES					
Accounts Payable	$ 60,000	$ 59,000			$119,000
Common Shares:					
P	100,000				100,000
SS		100,000	B (60,000)	$40,000	
Retained Earnings:					
P	137,000[c]				137,000
SS		63,000	B (37,800)	25,200	
Minority Interest				$65,200	$ 65,200
Total Equities	$297,000	$222,000	$ (97,800)		$421,200

Intercompany Eliminations:

A — To include the parent's interest in the difference between the book value and fair value of identifiable assets at the date of acquisition.

B — Parent's Investment in SS, the parent's share of the subsidiary's Share Capital and Retained Earnings, and a difference attributable to Goodwill.

[a]Net of accumulated depreciation.
[b]Cost of shares at balance sheet date.
[c] $114,000 + $15,000 + ($90,000 − $76,000) − $6,000 = $137,000.

EXHIBIT 12.16
P's Consolidated Balance Sheet
December 31, Year 5

ASSETS		EQUITIES		
Cash	$ 42,000	Accounts Payable		$119,000
Accounts Receivable	128,400	Minority Interest		65,200
Inventory	160,000			
Current Assets	$330,400			
Land	15,400	**Shareholders' Equity:**		
Building and Machinery (net)	61,000	Common Shares	$100,000	
Goodwill	14,400	Retained Earnings	137,000	237,000
Total Assets	$421,200	Total Equities		$421,200

The 40 percent minority interest of SS is presented under the equities between the Accounts Payable and the Shareholders' Equity. It consists of 40 percent of the $163,000 book value of the subsidiary's shareholders' equity.

The consolidated assets are valued at book value to the company plus the parent's share in the difference between book value and fair value of subsidiary's assets.

The following schedule of the Inventory value in the consolidated balance sheet illustrates this calculation.

Book Value of Inventory:		
P		$ 85,000
SS		69,000
Total		$154,000
Excess of Fair Value of Inventory of SS over Book Value:		
Fair Value	$79,000	
Book Value	(69,000)	
Excess	$10,000	
Parent's Interest (60% of $10,000)		$ 6,000
Inventory on Consolidated Balance Sheet		$160,000

The Goodwill presented in the consolidated balance sheet represents the cost of purchasing 60 percent of the shares of SS for $135,000 less 60 percent of the fair value of the net assets at the date of purchase [= $135,000 − 0.60 × ($260,000 − $59,000)]. In the formal consolidated balance sheet, the Goodwill may be described as "Goodwill on purchase of shares of subsidiary SS."

SUMMARY

Businesses acquire shares in other businesses for a variety of reasons and in a variety of ways. The acquisition of shares of another company as long-term investment is generally recorded as follows:

Investment in S	$X	
Cash or Other Consideration Given		$X

The investment account is recorded at the amount of cash given or the market value of other consideration exchanged.

The accounting for the investment subsequent to acquisition depends on the ability of one company, the investor, to exercise significant influence over another. The investor's ownership of 20 percent or more of the voting shares of another company is a major indicator of significant influence. The increase of the investor's ownership of the voting shares to 50 percent usually indicates that the investor (now called the *parent*) controls the other company, which is now called the *subsidiary*. The cost method is used where the investor does not exercise significant influence (generally less than

20 percent ownership). The equity method is used when the investor exercises significant influence but does not control the other company (generally less than 50 percent ownership). Consolidated statements are generally prepared when the parent owns more than 50 percent of the voting shares of the subsidiary. Exhibit 12.17 summarizes the accounting for investments subsequent to the acquisition.

EXHIBIT 12.17
Effects of Various Methods of Accounting for Long-Term Investments in Corporate Securities

Method of Accounting	Balance Sheet	Income Statement
Cost method. Parent unable to exercise significant influence (generally when ownership is less than 20 percent).	Investment account shown at acquisition cost as a noncurrent asset. Unrealized losses that are other than a temporary decline reduce the value of the investment and are charged against income.	Dividends declared by investee shown as revenue of investor. Unrealized losses are reported in the income statement when they are other than a temporary decline in value. Gains and losses (from original cost reduced as noted above) are reported in the income statement as realized in arm's-length transactions with outsiders.
Equity method (generally when parent is able to exercise significant influence but owns not more than 50 percent of the shares).	Investment account shown at cost plus share of investee's net income less share of investee's dividends since acquisition.	Equity in investee's net income shown as revenue in period that investee earns income.
Consolidation (generally when ownership percentage is greater than 50 percent).	Investment account is eliminated and replaced with individual assets and liabilities of subsidiary. Minority interest in subsidiary's net assets shown among equities.	Individual revenues and expenses of subsidiary are combined with those of parent. Minority interest in subsidiary's net income shown as a subtraction.

Under the cost method, income is recognized only when dividends become receivable by the investor or when the securities are sold.

Consolidated statements and the equity method both have the same effect on net income. The parent shows as income its proportional share of the acquired firm's periodic income after acquisition. Income statement amounts of revenues and expenses will be larger under the consolidation method, however, because the revenues and expenses of the acquired company are combined with those of the parent. Balance sheet components will be larger under the consolidation method than under the equity method, because the individual assets and liabilities of the acquired company will be substituted for the investment balance on the parent company's books.

APPENDIX 12.1

ACCOUNTING FOR CORPORATE ACQUISITIONS

In a **corporate acquisition**, one corporation acquires all, or substantially all, of another corporation's common stock in a single transaction. GAAP require one of two methods of accounting for corporate acquisitions: the purchase method or the pooling-of-interests method. Which method is used depends on the structure of the acquisition. The method of accounting for the acquisition affects the *amounts* in the entries on the consolidation work sheet but not the accounting *procedures*.

corporate acquisition
The acquisition of one company by another, creating a parent-subsidiary relationship.

PURCHASE METHOD

The **purchase method** uses acquisition cost accounting. The parent initially records the Investment in Subsidiary account at the amount of cash or the market value of other net assets given in the exchange. The consolidation process allocates any difference between the amount in the investment account on the date of acquisition and the book value of the net assets acquired to individual assets less liabilities. The purpose is to write them up or down to their market values. Any excess of the purchase price over the market values of the individual assets less liabilities becomes goodwill. Thus, the purchase method reports the assets less liabilities of the acquired company at their market values in the consolidated balance sheet at the date of acquisition. The consolidated income statement in subsequent periods will show expenses (depreciation and amortization) based on these market values.

purchase method
A procedure that treats a business combination, from the viewpoint of the acquiring company, as a purchase transaction.

POOLING-OF-INTERESTS METHOD

The **pooling-of-interests method** accounts for a corporate acquisition as the uniting of ownership interests of two companies by exchange of equity (common stock) securities. Accounting views the exchange of equity interests as a change in *form*, not in *substance*; that is, the shareholders of the predecessor companies become shareholders in the new combined enterprise. Each of the predecessor companies continues carrying out its operations as before. Because the substance of neither the ownership interest nor the nature of the activities of the enterprises changes, no new basis of accountability arises. In other words, the book values of the assets and liabilities of the predecessor companies carry over to the new combined, or consolidated, entreprise. Unlike the purchase method, assets and liabilities do not reflect market values at the date of acquisition on the consolidated balance sheet.

pooling-of-interests method
A consolidation method used when an acquirer cannot be identified that adds the asset book values and the equities of the respective firms to create the consolidated financial statements.

ILLUSTRATION OF PURCHASE AND POOLING-OF-INTERESTS METHODS

To illustrate the purchase and pooling-of-interests methods, assume that P and S decide to combine operations. Management estimates that the combination will save $50,000 a year in expenses of running the combined businesses. Columns (1) and (2) in Exhibit 12.18 show abbreviated single-company financial statements for P and S before combination. S has 20,000 shares of stock outstanding that sell for $84 per share in the market. The market value of S as a going concern is $1,680,000 (= $84 × 20,000). As shown in column (3), S's shareholders have $1,230,000 of equity not recorded on the books. Of this $1,230,000 amount, $400,000 results from undervalued noncurrent assets, and $830,000 results from goodwill. P has 100,000 shares outstanding, which have a $5 par value and sell for $42 each in the market. The illustration ignores income taxes.

Purchase Method

To carry out the acquisition, P issues (sells) 40,000 additional shares on the market for $42 each, or $1,680,000 in total, and uses the proceeds to purchase all shares of S for $84 each. P has acquired 100 percent of the shares of S and now owns S.

P will use the purchase method to account for the acquisition of S. P will amortize the revalued asset costs over five years and the goodwill over forty years. Consolidated financial reports under the purchase method appear in Exhibit 12.18 in column (4). The consolidated balance sheet sums columns (1) and (3), except for the shareholders' equity section. Because P issued 40,000 new shares for $42 each, the Common Stock account shows 140,000 shares of $5 par value. The Contributed Surplus account shows former contributed surplus plus the addition arising from the new stock issue: $200,000 + [40,000 × ($42 − $5)] = $1,680,000. The retained earnings of the consolidated enterprise equals P's retained earnings.

The consolidated income statement starts with the combined incomes before consolidation. The cost saving of $50,000 resulting from the more efficient operations of the combination increases net income. Both the additional depreciation expense arising from the asset revaluations and the goodwill amortization expense reduce net income. The projected consolidated net income is $409,250.

Pooling of Interests

Now, examine the accounting for the acquisition as shown in column (5), assuming that it qualifies for the pooling-of-interests method. Assume that P issued the 40,000 shares of stock directly to the owners of S in return for their shares. The owner of a share of S gets two shares of P. The balance sheet items, except for the individual shareholders' equity accounts, sum the single-company amounts from columns (1) and (2). The shareholders' equity after pooling must then equal total shareholders' equity before pooling.

The common stock of the pooled enterprise must equal the par value of the shares outstanding after pooling. After pooling, there are 140,000 shares outstanding with a par value of $700,000. The general rule is that the pooled retained earnings balance is the sum of the retained earnings before pooling. The example illustrates the general rule. The total contributed capital (par value plus contributed surplus) after pooling will generally equal the sum of the capital accounts of the firms before pooling. Thus, the contrib-

EXHIBIT 12.18
Consolidated Statements Comparing Purchase and Pooling-of-Interests Methods

	Historical Cost		S Shown at Current Values	Companies P and S Consolidated at Date of Acquisition	
	P (1)	S (2)	(3)	Purchase (4)	Pooling of Interests (5)
BALANCE SHEETS					
Assets					
Current Assets	$1,500,000	$450,000	$ 450,000	$1,950,000	$1,950,000
Long-Term Assets less					
Accumulated Depreciation	1,700,000	450,000	850,000	2,550,000	2,150,000
Goodwill	—	—	830,000	830,000	—
Total Assets	$3,200,000	$900,000	$2,130,000	$5,330,000	$4,100,000
Equities					
Liabilities	$1,300,000	$450,000	$ 450,000	$1,750,000	$1,750,000
Common Shares ($5 par)	500,000	100,000	100,000	700,000[a]	700,000[a]
Contributed Surplus	200,000	150,000	150,000	1,680,000[b]	250,000[e]
Retained Earnings	1,200,000	200,000	200,000	1,200,000[c]	1,400,000[d]
Unrecorded Equity at Current					
Valuation	—	—	1,230,000	—	—
Total Liabilities and					
Shareholders' Equity	$3,200,000	$900,000	$2,130,000	$5,330,000	$4,100,000
INCOME STATEMENTS (IGNORING INCOME TAXES)[h]					
Precombination Income	$ 300,000	$160,000		$ 460,000	$ 460,000
From Combination:					
Cost Savings (projected)	—			50,000	50,000
Extra Depreciation Expense	—	—		(80,000)[f]	—
Amortization of Goodwill	—	—		(20,750)[g]	—
Net Income	$ 300,000	$160,000		$ 409,250[h]	$ 510,000[h]
Number of Common Shares					
Outstanding	100,000	20,000		140,000	140,000
Earnings per Share	$3.00	$8.00		$2.92	$3.64
RATE OF RETURN RATIOS					
Return on Assets					
(Net Income/Total Assets)	9.4%	17.8%		7.7%	12.4%
Return on Common Shareholders'					
Equity					
(Net Income/Shareholders'					
Equity)	15.8	35.6		11.4	21.7

Assumptions: (1) S has 20,000 shares outstanding that sell for $84 each in the market.
              (2) P's shares sell for $42 each in the market. P issues 40,000 shares for the purpose of acquiring S.

[a]*P's 100,000 original shares plus 40,000 new shares at $5 par.*
[b]*P's $200,000 original additional paid-in capital plus 40,000 × ($42 − $5).*
[c]*P's retained earnings.*
[d]*Sum of P's and S's retained earnings.*
[e]*Plug to equate pooled shareholders' equity to the sum of all the shareholders' equity accounts of the combining companies before combination.*
[f]*1/5 × ($850,000 − $450,000).*
[g]*1/40 × $830,000.*
[h]*As projected.*

uted surplus of the pooled firm is, ordinarily, the plug to equate the pooled capital with the sum of the capital accounts before pooling.

The income statement resulting from a pooling of interests shows the same revenues and cost savings as those following a purchase. There are, however, no extra depreciation and amortization expenses resulting from increased asset valuations and the recognition of goodwill. Consequently, the pooled enterprise projects net income of $510,000 and shareholders' equity of $2,350,000, whereas the identical acquisition accounted for using the purchase method projects smaller income of $409,250 and larger shareholders' equity of $3,580,000. Notice that the earnings-per-share figure — one often scrutinized by financial analysts — under the pooling-of-interests method is 25 percent larger than under the purchase method. The rate of return on shareholders' equity, which Chapter 15 discusses, is 21.7 percent under pooling accounting but only 11.4 percent under purchase accounting.

This example, if anything, understates the difference between the purchase and pooling methods. Notice that S's market value before the merger is less than four times ($1,680,000/$450,000 = 3.7) its book value. In practice, poolings of interests have occurred when the ratio of market value to book value was 10 to 1. Thus, the amortization charges of the purchased subsidiary's assets can be many times larger than the amortization of the pooled subsidiary's assets.

MANAGING EARNINGS

Pooling of interests not only keeps reported expenses from increasing after the merger, but may also allow the management of the pooled companies to manage the reported earnings in an arbitrary way. Suppose that P merges with an old, established firm, F, which produces commercial movie films. F amortized its films made in the 1940s and 1950s so that, by the 1990s, the book value of these films is close to zero. But the market value of the films is much larger than zero because television stations and cable networks find that old movies please their audiences. If P purchases F, the old films will appear on the consolidated balance sheet at the films' current market value. If P merges with F using the pooling-of-interests method, the films will appear on the consolidated balance sheet at their near-zero book values. Then, when P wants to boost reported earnings for the year, it can sell some old movies to a television network and report a large gain. Actually, of course, the owners of F enjoyed this gain when they "sold" their stock to P at their current values, not at the obsolete book values.

Those who defend pooling-of-interests accounting argue that the management of the pooled enterprise has no more opportunity to manage earnings than did the management of F before the pooling. Management of F can sell old movies any time it chooses and report handsome gains. The historical-cost basis of accounting causes the problem because it recognizes gains only when a market transaction has occurred. Defenders of pooling argue that there is no reason to penalize the management of a merged company relative to the management of an established company with many assets undervalued on its books. Opponents of pooling reply that management of F earned the holding gains, whereas pooling allows management of P to realize and report the gains.

In summary, purchase accounting typically reduces the reported income of the combined enterprise because of additional depreciation and amortization expenses. The extra depreciation and amortization expenses result from recognizing increased asset valuations and, perhaps, goodwill. Pooling-of-interests accounting typically reports income for the consolidated enterprise that is greater than it would be for the same consolidated enterprise if it were accounted for as a purchase.

To use pooling, the combining firms must be able to show that no acquirer can be identified. This stringent condition makes pooling very rare in Canada.

KEY TERMS

Investments
Significant influence
Portfolio investments
Minority investments
Majority investments
Cost method
Equity method
Goodwill

Parent
Subsidiary
Consolidation
Intercompany eliminations
Minority interest
Corporate acquisition
Purchase method
Pooling-of-interests method

SELF-STUDY MATERIAL

This section contains questions, exercises, and problems to help you assess your understanding of Chapter 12. Careful review of this material will assist you in completing the homework assignments. Solutions are found at the end of the section.

QUESTIONS AND EXERCISES

True/False

For each statement, place a T or an F in the space provided to indicate whether the statement is true or false.

_____ 1. A company is required to use the cost method to account for its investments in securities of another company regardless of its percentage of ownership.

_____ 2. The consolidation method of reporting investments in shares may be used under the same percentage of ownership as the equity method.

_____ 3. A minority investor owns less than 50 percent of the voting shares of another corporation.

_____ 4. GAAP require that the equity method be used when a company owns 20 to 50 percent of the voting shares of another company.

_____ 5. Under the equity method, the investor company treats as income (or revenue), in each period, its proportionate share of the periodic earnings of the investee company.

_____ 6. Dividends paid to the owner of common shares in an investment accounted for by the equity method are treated as a reduction of the investment account.

_____ 7. When a shareholder owns more than 50 percent of the voting shares of another company, the shareholder is called the "majority investor" or the "parent."

_____ 8. Dividends can legally be declared only from retained earnings of one corporation.

_____ 9. If a company is appropriately using the cost method of accounting for long-term investments in corporate securities, a temporary decline in market value below cost results in a loss to be recognized on the current period income statement.

_____ 10. Consolidated financial statements reflect only transactions between the group of consolidated companies and other entities.

_____ 11. Goodwill is the excess of the cost of an acquisition over the current market value of the net identifiable assets required.

_____ 12. Goodwill may be presented on the balance sheet (not expensed) indefinitely or until the board of directors determines there is no value associated with it.

_____ 13. The entries to eliminate intercompany transactions are made on the books of only the parent company.

_____ 14. There is no difference between a consolidated income statement and the income statement where the subsidiary is accounted for using the equity method.

_____ 15. When the equity method is used for an unconsolidated subsidiary, the parent's share of the subsidiary's net income minus gain (or plus loss) on intercompany transactions is shown on a single line, Equity in Earnings of Unconsolidated Subsidiary.

_____ 16. The account Equity in Earnings of Unconsolidated Subsidiary is not eliminated in the consolidation process.

_____ 17. The amount of the minority interest shown on the balance sheet is generally the result of multiplying the common shareholders' equity of the subsidiary by the minority's percentage of ownership.

_____ 18. Subsidiary companies are those that have equal ownership in the common shares of a third corporation.

_____ 19. Most published financial statements report minority interest as a reduction in the cost of the asset Investment in Shares.

Matching

From the list of terms, select one term that is most closely associated with one descriptive phrase or statement that follows and place the letter for that term in the space provided.

a. consolidated financial statements
b. cost method
c. equity method
d. goodwill
e. intercompany transactions
f. majority investment

g. minority investment
h. minority interest
i. parent
j. portfolio investment
k. subsidiary

_____ 1. Companies normally use this method to account for long-term investments where their ownership is less than 20 percent of the outstanding voting common shares.

_____ 2. The corporation that is subject to control by a parent corporation.

_____ 3. An investment where the percentage of the other corporation's shares owned is not so large that the acquiring company can exert significant influence over the other company.

_____ 4. Statements combining the results of operations, financial position, and changes in financial position of a parent company and its subsidiaries, as if the companies were one economic entity.

_____ 5. An investment through which the shareholder owns greater than 50 percent of the voting shares of another company.

_____ 6. These would be eliminated in preparing consolidated statements.

_____ 7. An investment through which the percentage of the ownership of voting shares is between 20 percent and 50 percent.

_____ 8. The equity of minority shareholders shown in a consolidated balance sheet.

_____ 9. The excess of the cost of the acquisition over the current market value of the net assets acquired.

_____ 10. A corporation exercising control over another through share ownership.

_____ 11. Under this method, the book value of the investment is reduced when dividends are received by the investor company.

Multiple Choice

Choose the best answer for each question or problem and enter the identifying letter in the space provided.

_____ 1. This method is required by GAAP for accounting for investment in common shares of 20 percent to 50 percent.
  a) cost method
  b) equity method
  c) consolidation method
  d) all of the above are acceptable

_____ 2. Which of these account titles is not associated with the use of the cost method?
   a) Portfolio Investment
   b) Loss from Permanent Decline in Portfolio Investment
   c) Equity in Earnings of Portfolio Investment
   d) Dividends from Portfolio Investment

_____ 3. Under the equity method, as the investee company declares dividends, the investor company will:
   a) increase the investment account
   b) increase the investment account
   c) increase the revenue account
   d) decrease the revenue account

_____ 4. Majority investments are generally reported by:
   a) preparation of consolidated statements
   b) application of the equity method
   c) one-line presentations on the balance sheet (as an investment)
   d) application of the cost method

_____ 5. One important reason for continued legal existence of subsidiary companies is:
   a) to reduce the financial risk of one segment becoming insolvent
   b) to meet effectively the requirements of corporation and tax legislation
   c) to expand with a minimum of capital investment
   d) all of the above

_____ 6. The entry to record a decline at year-end in a company portfolio of securities held as long-term investments is:
   a) debit Allowance for Excess of Cost of Investments over Market Value; credit Unrealized Loss on Valuation of Portfolio Investments
   b) debit Unrealized Loss on Valuation of Portfolio Investments; credit Allowance for Excess of Cost of Investments over Market Value
   c) debit Unrealized Loss on Valuation of Portfolio Investments; credit Long-Term Investments
   d) debit Realized Loss on Valuation of Portfolio Investments; credit Long-Term Investments

_____ 7. The cost method is used to account for:
   a) portfolio investments
   b) minority investments
   c) majority investments
   d) none of the above

_____ 8. The ownership percentage of voting shares of minority investments is usually:
   a) zero to 20 percent
   b) 20 to 50 percent
   c) more than 50 percent
   d) 100 percent

_____ 9. Generally, financial statements are consolidated for parent and subsidiary companies for:
   a) portfolio investments
   b) minority investments
   c) majority investments
   d) none of the above

_____ 10. Consolidated financial statements are generally prepared when:
   a) the parent owns more than 50 percent of the voting shares of the subsidiary
   b) there are no important restrictions on the ability of the parent to exercise control over the subsidiary
   c) the asset and equity structure of the subsidiary is not significantly different from that of the parent
   d) all of the above

_____ 11. When the cost of purchasing a majority interest exceeds the book value of the shares acquired:
   a) the excess is presented as goodwill in the consolidated balance sheet
   b) the unamortized excess is allocated to the subsidiary's assets and liabilities included in the consolidated balance sheet
   c) the unamortized excess is presented as goodwill in the consolidated balance sheet
   d) the unamortized excess is allocated to the consolidated subsidiary's assets and liabilities and any unallocated balance is presented as goodwill in the consolidated balance sheet

_____ 12. All of the following accounts would be eliminated in the preparation of consolidated financial statements, except:
   a) Common Share Capital (company P)
   b) Common Share Capital (company S)
   c) Investment in Shares of S (P)
   d) all of the above

_____ 13. All of the following accounts would be eliminated in the preparation of consolidated financial statements, except:
   a) Equity in Earnings of S (P)
   b) Accounts Receivable (Intercompany)
   c) Sales (Intercompany)
   d) Dividends Declared (P)

_____ 14. Which of the following statements is not true?
   a) consolidated net income is the same amount as that which results when the parent uses the equity method for an unconsolidated subsidiary
   b) consolidated retained earnings is the same amount as that which results when the parent uses the equity method for an unconsolidated subsidiary
   c) when a subsidiary's financial statements are not consolidated with those of the parent, the parent's balance sheet will show the investment in the subsidiary's net assets in a single investment account
   d) all of the above are true

_____ 15. The eliminations to remove intercompany transactions are typically made on:
   a) separate books for the consolidated entity
   b) P's books
   c) a consolidated work sheet
   d) S's books

Exercises

1. Prepare general journal entries for each of the transactions on the books of the Clio Corporation:

19X1
Jan. 18:   Purchased 10 percent of the outstanding shraes of Franklin Enterprises Inc. for $40,000. (Use the cost method.)

Feb. 12:   Purchased 30 percent of the outstanding shares of Merritt Limited for $75,000. (Use the equity method.)

Dec. 31: Franklin Enterprises Inc. reported $10,000 of net income and Merritt Limited reported $5,000 of net income. Franklin Enterprises Inc. shares are currently valued at $42,000 (Apply cost method for Franklin Enterprises Inc. and the equity method for Merritt Limited.)

19X2

Jan. 15: Franklin Enterprises Inc. declared and distributed cash dividends totalling $5,000.

Jan. 18: Merritt Limited declared and distributed $3,000 in cash dividends.

Jan. 19: Clio Corporation sold half of its interest in Franklin Enterprises Inc. for $18,000.

Jan. 20: Clio Corporation sold 10 percent of its interest in Merritt Limited for $8,000.

Dec. 31: The remaining Franklin Enterprises Inc. shares are currently valued at $19,000. Because the company reported a loss, this market value decline appeared permanent. (Apply cost method.)

2. On January 2, 19X1, the Prince Company Inc. purchased 80 percent of the common shares of Winston Enterprises Ltd. at book value of $1,200,000. The total common shares of Winston Enterprises Ltd. at that date was $1,125,000, and the Retained Earnings balance was $375,000. During the year, net income of Winston Enterprises Ltd. was $225,000; dividends declared were $90,000. The Prince Company Inc. uses the equity method to account for the investment.

   a. Record the entries Prince Company Inc. would make in 19X1 related to its investment in Winston Enterprises Ltd.
   b. Give the elimination entry for the investment account and for recognition of external minority interest assuming that the consolidation worksheet is based on preclosing financial data.

PROBLEM 1 FOR SELF-STUDY

Reynolds Corporation acquired common shares of companies R, S, and T on January 2 as long-term investments. These are the only long-term investments in securities of Reynolds Corporation. Data relating to the acquisitions are shown below.

Company	Percentage Acquired	Book Value and Market Value of Total Net Assets on January 2	Acquisition Cost	Net Income for Year	Dividends Declared for Year
R	10%	$5,000,000	$ 540,000	$1,000,000	$400,000
S	30	5,000,000	1,700,000	1,000,000	400,000
T	100	5,000,000	5,000,000	1,000,000	400,000

Any goodwill arising from the acquisitions is amortized over ten years.

a. Give the journal entries made to acquire the shares of R and to account for the investment during the year, using the cost method.

b. Give the journal entries made to acquire the shares of S and to account for the investment during the year, using the equity method.

c. Give the journal entries made to acquire the shares of T and to account for the investment during the year, using the equity method.

d. Give the consolidation balance sheet work sheet entry to eliminate the Investment in Shares of T account at the end of the year, assuming that the equity method is used and that the work sheet is based on postclosing trial balance amounts. T had $2,000,000 in its Common Share Capital account throughout the year and a zero balance in Contributed Surplus.

e. Assume that the shares of T had been acquired for $5,500,000, instead of $5,000,000. Give the journal entries made during the year to acquire the shares of T and to account for the investment, using the equity method. Any excess of cost over book value is considered goodwill and is amortized over ten years.

f. Refer to **(e)** above. Give the consolidation work sheet entry to eliminate the Investment in Shares of T account, assuming that the work sheet is based on postclosing trial balance data.

g. Assume that Reynolds Corporation had paid $4,000,000 for 80 percent of the shares of T on January 2. Give the journal entries made during the year to acquire the shares of T and to account for the investment, using the equity method.

h. Refer to **(g)** above. Give the consolidation balance sheet work sheet entries to eliminate the Investment in Shares of T account, assuming that the work sheet is based on postclosing trial balance data. A separate column is used on the work sheet to accumulate the minority interest.

PROBLEM 2 FOR SELF-STUDY

The single-company financial statements of P and S appear in Exhibit 12.2 on page 736. The following additional information affects the preparation of the consolidated financial statements.

1. P acquired 100 percent of the outstanding shares of S for $650,000 cash on January 1, Year 1. At the time of acquisition, the book value of the shareholders' equity of S was $650,000, comprising the following account balances:

S, January 1, Year 1	
Common Shares	$500,000
Retained Earnings	150,000
Total Shareholders' Equity	$650,000

P made the following journal entry on its books at the time of acquisition:

Investment in S	$650,000	
Cash		$650,000

2. P records its investment in the shares of S using the equity method. The Retained Earnings of S have increased since January 1, Year 1, the date of acquisition, by $55,000 (= $205,000 − $150,000). This increase appears in the Investment in S account on P's books: $705,000 = $650,000 + $55,000.

3. At December 31, Year 4, $12,000 of S's accounts receivable represents amounts payable by P.

4. During Year 4, S sold merchandise to P for $40,000. None of that merchandise remains in P's inventory as of December 31, Year 4.

Prepare a consolidated work sheet and the accompanying elimination entries.

PROBLEM 3 FOR SELF-STUDY

Refer to the data for P and S in Exhibit 12.2. Suppose that P had paid $700,000, rather than $650,000 for its 100 percent investment in S. The $50,000 difference in purchase price represents the amount paid for S's assets in excess of their book value, for goodwill, or for both. Assume that on the date of acquisition, January 1, Year 1, the book value of S's recorded assets and liabilities equalled their market values. The fact that P was willing to pay $700,000 for recorded assets having book values and market values equal to $650,000 means that S must have had *unrecorded* assets of $50,000 on January 1, Year 1. The $50,000 of unrecorded assets represents goodwill. GAAP require the owner of goodwill to amortize it over a period not exceeding 40 years. Assume that P chose a forty-year amortization period.

Prepare the journal entries to record amortization of goodwill in Years 1 through 4 and the entry to set up goodwill on the consolidated work sheet in Year 4.

Answers to Questions and Exercises

True/False

1. F	6. T	11. T	16. F
2. F	7. T	12. F	17. T
3. T	8. T	13. F	18. F
4. T	9. F	14. F	19. F
5. T	10. T	15. T	

Matching

1. b	4. a	7. g	10. i
2. k	5. f	8. h	11. c
3. j	6. e	9. d	

Multiple Choice

1. b	5. d	9. c	13. d
2. c	6. c	10. d	14. d
3. b	7. a	11. d	15. c
4. a	8. b	12. a	

Exercises

1.

		Dr.	Cr.
01/18: 19X1	Investment in Frankling Enterprises Inc.	$40,000	
	Cash		$40,000
	Purchased 10 percent of outstanding shares (cost method).		
02/12: 19X1	Investment in Merritt Limited	$75,000	
	Cash		$75,000
	Purchased 30 percent of outstanding shares (equity method).		
12/31: 19X1	Investment in Merritt Limited	$1,500	
	Revenue from Investments		$1,500
	Recognized 30 percent of Merritt Limited income.		
01/15: 19X2	Cash	$500	
	Dividend Revenue		$500
	Received Franklin Enterprises Inc. dividends.		
01/18: 19X2	Cash	$900	
	Investment in Merritt Limited		$900
	Received Merritt Limited dividends.		
01/19: 19X2	Cash	$18,000	
	Loss on Sale of Shares	2,000	
	Investment in Franklin Enterprises Inc.		$20,000
	Sold half of interest in Franklin Enterprises Inc.		
01/20: 19X2	Cash	$8,000	
	Investment in Merritt Limited		$7,560*
	Gain on Sale of Shares	440	
	Sold 10 percent interest of Merritt Limited.		

*($75,000 + $1,500 − $900) × 10%.

12/31:	Holding Loss on Valuation of Portfolio Investments	$1,000	
19X2	Portfolio Investments		$1,000
	Adjusted remaining shares of Franklin Enterprises Inc. to reflect a permanent reduction in market price.		

		Dr.	**Cr.**
2. a.	Investment in Winston Enterprises Ltd.	$1,200,000	
	Cash		$1,200,000
	To record acquisition of common shares.		
	Investment in Winston Enterprises Ltd.	$180,000	
	Equity in Earnings of Winston Enterprises Ltd.		$180,000
	To record 80 percent of Winston Enterprises Ltd.'s earnings.		
	Cash (or Dividend Receivable)	$72,000	
	Investment in Winston Enterprises Ltd.		$72,000
	To record dividends declared by Winston Enterprises Ltd.		
b.	Common Share Capital (Winston)	$900,000	
	Retained Earnings (Winston)	300,000	
	Equity in Earnings of Winston Enterprises Ltd.	180,000	
	Dividends Declared		$ 72,000
	Investment in Winston Enterprises Ltd.		1,308,000
	To eliminate investment account.		
	$1,200,000 + 180,000 − 72,000 = $1,308,000.		
	Common Share Capital	$225,000	
	Retained Earnings	75,000	
	Minority Interest in Earnings	45,000	
	Dividends Declared		$ 18,000
	Minority Interest in Net Assets		327,000
	To recognize external minority interest.		

SUGGESTED SOLUTION TO PROBLEM 1
FOR SELF-STUDY

a. Investment in R	$540,000	
Cash		$540,000
To record acquisition of shares of R.		
Cash and Dividends Receivable	$ 40,000	
Dividends Revenue		$ 40,000
To record dividends received or receivable.		

b. Investment in S	$1,700,000	
Cash		$1,700,000
To record acquisition of shares of S.		
Investment in S	$ 300,000	
Equity in Earnings of S		$ 300,000
To accrue share of S's earnings; $300,000 = 0.30 × $1,000,000.		
Cash or Dividends Receivable	$ 120,000	
Investment in S		$ 120,000
To record dividends received or receivable; $120,000 = 0.30 × $400,000.		

Equity in Earnings of S	$ 20,000	
Investment in S		$ 20,000

To record amortization of goodwill implicit in purchase
price; $20,000 = ($1,700,000 − $1,500,000) ÷ 10.

c. Investment in T	$5,000,000	
Cash		$5,000,000

To record acquisition of Shares of T.

Investment in T	$1,000,000	
Equity in Earnings of T		$1,000,000

To accrue earnings of T;
$1,000,000 = 100% × $1,000,000.

Cash or Dividends Receivable	$ 400,000	
Investment in T		$ 400,000

To record dividends received or receivable.

d. Common Shares (T)	$2,000,000	
Retained Earnings (T) (December 31)	3,600,000	
Investment in T		$5,600,000

To eliminate investment account on consolidation work sheet.

e. Investment in T	$5,500,000	
Cash		$5,500,000

To record acquisition of shares of T.

Investment in T	$1,000,000	
Equity in Earnings of T		$1,000,000

To accrue earnings of T.

Cash or Dividends Receivable	$ 400,000	
Investment in T		$ 400,000

To record dividends received or receivable.

Equity in earnings of T	$ 50,000	
Investment in T		$ 50,000

To record amortization of goodwill implicit in purchase
price; $50,000 = ($5,500,000 − $5,000,000) ÷ 10.

f. Common Shares (T)	$2,000,000	
Retained Earnings (T)	3,600,000	
Goodwill	450,000	
Investment in T		$6,050,000

To eliminate investment account on consolidation
work sheet; $6,050,000 = $5,500,000 + $1,000,000
− $400,000 − $50,000.

g. Investment in T	$4,000,000	
Cash		$4,000,000

To record acquisition of shares of T.

Investment in T	$ 800,000	
Equity in Earnings of T		$ 800,000

To accrue share of T's earnings;
$800,000 = 0.80 × $1,000,000.

Cash or Dividends Receivable	$ 320,000	
Investment in T		$ 320,000

To record dividends received or receivable;
$320,000 = 0.80 × $400,000.

h. Common shares (T)	$1,600,000	
Retained Earnings (T)	2,880,000	
Investment in T		$4,480,000

To eliminate investment account on consolidation
work sheet; $4,480,000 = $4,000,000 +
$800,000 − $320,000.

SUGGESTED SOLUTION TO PROBLEM 2 FOR SELF-STUDY

The journal entries for the eliminations are:

A. Elimination of Parent Company's Investment Account

(1) Common Shares (S)	$500,000	
Retained Earnings, January 1, Year 4 (S)	170,000	
Equity in Earnings of S (P)	48,000	
Dividends Declared (S)		$ 13,000
Investments in S (P)		705,000

B. Elimination of Intercompany Receivables and Payables

(2) Accounts Payable	$12,000	
Accounts Receivable		$12,000

To eliminate intercompany payables and receivables.

C. Elimination of Intercompany Sales and Purchases

(3) Sales	$40,000	
Cost of Goods Sold		$40,000

To eliminate intercompany sales and purchases.

SUGGESTED SOLUTION TO PROBLEM 3 FOR SELF-STUDY

On its separate company books, P would have made the following entry during each of the Years 1 through 4:

Amortization Expense	$1,250	
Investment in S		$1,250

To recognize amortization of goodwill; $1,250 = ($700,000 − $650,000)/40.

In preparing the consolidation work sheet at the end of Year 4, entry (1) would be the same as that shown in Exhibit 12.19. After entry (1), the Investment in Stock of S would still have a debit

EXHIBIT 12.19
P AND S
Work Sheet to Derive Consolidated Financial Statements Based on Data from Preclosing Trial Balances for Year 4

TRIAL BALANCE ACCOUNTS	P Debit	P Credit	S Debit	S Credit	Adjustments and Eliminations Debit	Adjustments and Eliminations Credit	P and S Consolidated Debit	P and S Consolidated Credit
Accounts Receivable	$ 200,000		$ 25,000			(2) $ 12,000	$ 213,000	
Investment in Shares of S	705,000		—			(1) 705,000	—	
Other Assets	2,150,000		975,000				3,125,000	
Accounts Payable		$ 75,000		$ 15,000	(2) $ 12,000			$ 78,000
Other Liabilities		70,000		280,000				350,000
Common Shares		2,500,000		500,000	(1) 500,000			2,500,000
Retained Earnings, January 1, Year 4:								
P		256,000						256,000
S				170,000	(1) 170,000			
Sales		900,000		250,000	(3) 40,000			1,110,000
Equity in Earnings of S		48,000		—	(1) 48,000			
Cost of Goods Sold	440,000		80,000			(3) 40,000	480,000	
Depreciation Expense	120,000		50,000				170,000	
Administrative Expenses	80,000		40,000				120,000	
Income Tax Expense	104,000		32,000				136,000	
Dividends Declared	50,000		13,000			(1) 13,000	50,000	
Totals	$3,849,000	$3,849,000	$1,215,000	$1,215,000	$770,000	$770,000	$4,294,000	$4,294,000

balance of $45,000 [= $50,000 − (4 × $1,250)]. This amount represents the *unamortized good-will* arising from the acquisition. The consolidation process will make a work sheet entry to reclassify this amount from the investment account to goodwill. The entry is as follows:

Goodwill	$45,000	
Investment in S		$45,000
To reclassify goodwill.		

The consolidated balance sheet on December 31, Year 4 will show goodwill of $45,000 [= $50,000 − (4 × $1,250)]. Consolidated net income for Year 4 will now be $202,750 (= $204,000 − $1,250) to reflect amortization expense for Year 4. Consolidated retained earnings will be $405,000 [= $410,000 − (4 × $1,250)].

Assignment Material

Questions

1. Review the meaning of the key terms listed on page 761.

2. Unrealized holding losses from price declines of temporary investments classified as current assets are recognized as they arise in calculating net income. Similar unrealized holding losses from portfolio investments accounted for using the cost method are not recognized as they arise in calculating net income unless the decline is considered to be permanent. What is the rationale for this difference in accounting treatment?

3. Compare and contrast each of the following pairs of accounts:
   a. Dividend Revenue, and Equity in Earnings of Unconsolidated Affiliates.
   b. Equity in Earnings of Unconsolidated Affiliate, and Minority Interest in Earnings of Consolidated Subsidiary.
   c. Minority Interest in Earnings of Consolidated Subsidiary, and Minority Interest in Net Assets of Consolidated Subsidiary.

4. "Dividends received or receivable from another company may be either an item of revenue in calculating net income or a return of capital, depending on the method of accounting used." Explain.

5. Why is the equity method sometimes called a "one-line consolidation"? Consider both the balance sheet and the income statement in your response.

6. Distinguish between minority investments in other companies and the minority interest in a consolidated subsidiary.

7. "Net income will be the same regardless whether an investment in a subsidiary is accounted for using the equity method and not consolidated or whether the subsidiary is consolidated. Total assets will be different, however, depending on whether or not the subsidiary is consolidated." Explain.

Exercises

8. *Amount of income recognized under various methods of accounting for investments.* On January 1, Buyer Limited acquired common shares of X Inc. At the time of acquisition, the book value and fair market value of X Inc.'s net assets were $200,000. During the year, X Inc. earned $50,000 and declared dividends of $40,000. How much income would Buyer Limited report for the year from its investment under the assumption that Buyer Limited:

a. Paid $30,000 for 15 percent of the common shares and uses the cost method for its investment in X Inc.?

b. Paid $40,000 for 15 percent of the common shares and uses the cost method for its investment in X Inc.?

c. Paid $60,000 for 30 percent of the common shares and uses the equity method to account for its investment in X Inc.?

d. Paid $80,000 for 30 percent of the common shares and uses the equity method to account for its investment in X Inc.? Give the maximum income that Buyer Limited can report from the investment.

9. *Consolidation work sheet: intercompany balances.* Listed below are balances of the preclosing trial balances for Billy Ltd. and Tommy Ltd. at December 31, Year 1. On January 1, Year 1, Billy Ltd. purchased all of the outstanding shares of Tommy Ltd. for $125,000. Included in Tommy Ltd.'s December 31 payables is $100,000 due Billy Ltd.

	Billy Ltd.	Tommy Ltd.
Assets		
Cash	$ 15,000	$ 10,000
Accounts Receivable	355,000	130,000
Inventories	100,000	60,000
Net Capital Assets	140,000	80,000
Investment in Tommy Ltd.	145,000	
Equities		
Accounts Payable	150,000	135,000
Common Shares	125,000	100,000
Retained Earnings	440,000	25,000
Dividends	15,000	5,000
Revenues		
Sales	220,000	100,000
Equity in T's Income	25,000	
Expenses		
Cost of Goods Sold	150,000	50,000
Other Expenses	20,000	10,000
Income Tax	20,000	15,000

Required: Prepare consolidated financial statements.

10. *Journal entries to account for investments on an equity basis.* Johnson Corporation made three long-term intercorporate investments on January 2. Data relating to these investments for the year are as follows:

Company	Percentage Acquired	Book Value and Market Value of Net Assets on January 2	Acquisition Cost	Net Income for the Year	Dividends Declared During the Year
X	20%	$2,000,000	$ 400,000	$200,000	$ 80,000
Y	25	3,000,000	800,000	300,000	120,000
Z	30	4,000,000	1,300,000	400,000	160,000

Give the journal entries to record the acquisition of these investments and to apply the equity method during the year. Goodwill is amortized over twenty years.

11. *Journal entries under various methods of accounting for investments.* Maddox Corporation made three long-term intercorporate investments on January 2. Data relating to these investments are as follows:

Company	Percentage Acquired	Book Value and Market Value of Net Assets on January 2	Acquisition Cost	Net Income for the Year	Dividends Declared During the Year
A Ltd.	10%	$1,800,000	$ 200,000	$100,000	$40,000
B Ltd.	25	1,800,000	500,000	100,000	40,000
C Inc.	60	1,800,000	1,400,000	100,000	40,000

Assume that these were the only three intercorporate investments of Maddox Corporation. Goodwill is amortized over forty years.

a. Give the journal entries on Maddox Corporation's books to record these acquisitions of common shares and to account for the intercorporate investments under GAAP. The investment in C Inc. is not consolidated. Be sure to include any required year-end adjusting entries.

b. Assume that the financial statements of C Inc. are consolidated with those of Maddox Corporation, that the investment in C Inc. is accounted for using the equity method, and that the consolidation work sheet is based on postclosing trial balance data. Give the work sheet entry to eliminate the Investment in Shares of C Inc. account on December 31. The Common Stock account of C Inc. has a balance of $1,000,000, and Contributed Surplus has a zero balance.

12. *Consolidated policy and principal consolidation concepts.* The CAR Corporation manufactures computers in Canada. It owns 75 percent of the voting shares of Charles of U.S.A., 80 percent of the voting shares of Alexandre de France (in France), and 90 percent of the voting shares of R Credit Corporation (a finance company). The CAR Corporation prepares consolidated financial statements consolidating Charles of U.S.A., using the equity method for R Credit Corporation, and using the cost method for its investment in Alexandre de France. Data from the annual reports of these companies are given below:

	Percentage Owned	Net Income	Dividends	Accounting Method
CAR Corporation Consolidated	—	$1,000,000	$ 70,000	—
Charles of U.S.A.	75%	100,000	40,000	Consolidated
Alexandre de France	80	80,000	50,000	Cost
R Credit Corporation	90	120,000	100,000	Equity

a. Which, if any, of the companies is incorrectly accounted for by CAR according to GAAP?

Assuming that the accounting for the three subsidiaries shown above is correct, answer the following questions:

b. How much of the net income reported by CAR Corporation Consolidated is attributable to the operations of the three subsidiaries?

c. What is the amount of the minority interest now shown on the income statement, and how does it affect net income of CAR Corporation Consolidated?

d. If all three subsidiaries had been consolidated, what would have been the net income of CAR Corporation Consolidated?

e. If all three subsidiaries had been consolidated, what would be the minority interest shown on the income statement?

13. *Equity method and consolidation elimination entries.* The Hart Co. Ltd. acquired control of Keller Inc. on January 2 by purchasing 80 percent of its outstanding shares for $700,000. The entire excess of cost over book value acquired is attributable to goodwill, which is amortized over forty years. The shareholders' equity account of Keller Inc. appeared as follows on January 2 and December 31 of the current year.

	Dec. 31	Jan. 2
Common Shares	$600,000	$600,000
Retained Earnings	420,000	200,000

Keller Inc. had earnings of $250,000 and declared dividends of $30,000 during the year. The accounts receivable of the Hart Co. Ltd. at December 31 include $4,500, which is due it from Keller Inc. Hart Co. Ltd. accounts for its investment in Keller Inc. on its single-company books using the equity method.

a. Give the journal entries to record the acquisition of the shares of Keller Inc. and to apply the equity method during the year on the books of Hart Co. Ltd.

b. Give the required elimination entries for a consolidation work sheet at the end of the year assuming that the work sheet is based on postclosing trial balance data.

14. *Equity method and consolidation elimination entries.* The Roe Co. Ltd. purchased 80 percent of the common shares of Danver Limited on January 2 at book value, $480,000. The total common stock of Danver Limited at this date was $450,000, and the retained earnings balance was $150,000. During the year, net income of the Danver Limited was $90,000; dividends declared were $36,000. The Roe Co. Ltd. uses the equity method to account for the investment.

a. Give the journal entries made by Roe Co. Ltd. during the year to account for its investment in Danver Limited.

b. Give the elimination entry for the investment account, assuming that the consolidation work sheet is based on postclosing trial balance data.

15. *Equity method and consolidation work sheet entries.* The Little Corp. is a subsidiary of the Butler Co. Inc. and is accounted for using the equity method on the single-company books of the Butler Co. Inc.
  a. Present journal entries for the following selected transactions. Record the set of entries on the books of the Little Corp. separately from the set of entries on the books of the Butler Co. Inc.
    (1) On January 2, the Butler Co. Inc. acquired on the market, for cash, 80 percent of all of the common shares of the Little Corp. The outlay was $325,000. The total share capital outstanding was $300,000; the retained earnings balance was $80,000. The excess of cost over book value acquired is all attributed to goodwill and is amortized over ten years.
    (2) The Little Corp. purchased materials from the Butler Co. Inc. on account at the latter's cost, $23,000.
    (3) The Little Corp. obtained an advance of $9,000 from the Butler Co. Inc. The funds were deposited in the bank.
    (4) The Little Corp. paid $19,000 on the purchases in (2).
    (5) The Little Corp. repaid $7,500 of the loan received from the Butler Co. Inc. in (3).
    (6) The Little Corp. declared and paid a dividend of $24,000 during the year.
    (7) The net income of the Little Corp. for the year was $40,000.
  b. Prepare the adjustment and elimination entries that would be necessary in the preparation of the December 31 consolidated balance sheet, recognizing the effects of only the above transactions. Assume that the work sheet is based on preclosing financial statement data.

16. *Intercompany inventory transactions between consolidated entities.* P Ltd. owns 70 percent of a consolidated subsidiary, S Ltd. During the year, P Ltd.'s sales to S Ltd. amounted to $50,000. The cost of those sales was $35,000. The following data are taken from the two companies' income statements:

	P Ltd.	S Ltd.
Sales	$120,000	$250,000
Cost of Goods Sold	70,000	150,000

  a. Compute consolidated sales and consolidated cost of goods sold for the year, assuming that S Ltd. sold all the goods purchased from P Ltd.
  b. Compare the consolidated sales, cost of goods sold, and gross profit on sales to the sum of the sales, cost of goods sold, and gross profit of the separate companies.

17. *Working backwards to consolidation relationships.* A parent company owns shares in one other company. It has owned them since the other company was formed. The parent company has retained earnings from its own operations independent of intecorporate investments of $100,000. The consolidated balance sheet shows no goodwill and

retained earnings of $160,000. Consider each of the following questions independently of the others.

 a. If the parent owns 80 percent of its consolidated subsidiary, what are the retained earnings of the subsidiary?

 b. If the subsidiary has retained earnings of $96,000, what fraction of the subsidiary does the parent own?

 c. If the subsidiary had not been consolidated but, instead, had been accounted for by the equity method, how much revenue in excess of dividends received would the parent have recognized over the life of the investment?

18. *Working backwards from consolidated income statements.* Sealco Enterprises Inc. published the consolidated income statement for the year that is shown in Exhibit 12.20. The unconsolidated affiliate retained 20 percent of its earnings of $100,000 during the year, having paid out the rest as dividends. The consolidated subsidiary earned $200,000 during the year and declared no dividends.

EXHIBIT 12.20
SEALCO ENTERPRISES INC.
Consolidated Income Statement

Sales		$1,000,000
Less: Cost of Goods Sold		765,000
Gross Profit		$ 235,000
Less: Administrative Expenses	$100,000	
Amortization of Goodwill	5,000	105,000
Operating Income		$ 130,000
Equity in Earnings of Unconsolidated Affiliate		40,000
Net Income Before the Undernoted		$ 170,000
Less: Income Tax Expense Currently Payable	$ 42,000	
Deferred	10,000	52,000
		$ 118,000
Less: Minority Interest in Earnings of Consolidated Subsidiary		30,000
Net Income		88,000

 a. What percentage of the unconsolidated affiliate does Sealco Enterprises Inc. own?

 b. What dividends did Sealco Enterprises Inc. receive from the unconsolidated affiliate during the year?

 c. What percentage of the consolidated subsidiary does Sealco Enterprises Inc. own?

19. *Balance sheet and income effects of alternative methods of accounting for investments.* On January 1, Flexaco acquired common stock of Sun Company. At the time of acquisition, the book value and market value of Sun's net assets were $300 million. During the current year, Sun earned $40 million and declared dividends of $10 million. Indicate the amount shown for Investment in Sun on the balance sheet on December 31 and the amount of income Flexaco would report for the year from its investment under the assumption that Flexaco did the following:

 a. Paid $30 million for a 10 percent interest in Sun and uses the lower of cost or market method. The market value of Sun on December 31 was $300 million.

b. Same as **(a)**, except that the market value of Sun on December 31 was $290 million.

c. Paid $35 million for a 10 percent interest in Sun and uses the lower of cost or market method. The market value of Sun on December 31 was $350 million.

d. Paid $120 million for a 40 percent interest in Sun and uses the equity method.

e. Paid $140 million for a 40 percent interest in Sun and uses the equity method. Flexaco amortizes goodwill over forty years.

20. *Effect of errors on financial statements.* Using the notation O/S (overstated), U/S (understated), or No (no effect), indicate the effects on assets, liabilities, and shareholders' equity of each of the independent errors below. Ignore income tax effects.

a. In applying the cost method to portfolio investments, dividends received were incorrectly credited to the Investment account.

b. In applying the equity method, P correctly accrued its share of S's net income for the year. However, when a dividend was received, Dividend Revenue was credited.

c. P acquired 30 percent of S on January 1 of the current year for an amount in excess of the market value of S's net assets. P correctly accounted for its share of S's net income and dividends for the year, but neglected to amortize any of the excess purchase price.

d. During the current year, P sold inventory items to S, its wholly owned subsidiary, at a profit. These inventory items were sold by S, and P has paid for them before the end of the year. No elimination entry was made for this intercompany sale on the consolidation work sheet. Indicate the effect of this error on consolidated assets, liabilities, and net income.

e. Refer to **(d)**. Assume that one-fourth of these goods were not sold by S during the year and therefore remain in ending inventory.

f. Refer to **(d)**. Assume that S owes P $10,000 for intercompany purchases at year-end. No elimination entry is made for this intercompany debt. Indicate the effect on consolidated assets, liabilities, and net income.

g. P owns 90 percent of S. The minority interest in consolidated subsidiaries is treated as part of shareholders' equity. In preparing a consolidated work sheet, no entry was made to accrue the minority interest's share of S's net income or of S's net assets.

PROBLEMS AND CASES

21. *Consolidation work sheet for wholly owned subsidiary purchased at book value.* The trial balances of High Ltd. and Low Inc. on December 31, Year 6 are shown in Exhibit 12.21.

High Ltd. acquired all of the common shares of Low Inc. on January 1, Year 6 for $80,000. The receivables of High Ltd. and the liabilities of Low Inc. contain $5,000 of advances from High Ltd. to Low Inc.

EXHIBIT 12.21
HIGH LTD. AND LOW INC.
Preclosing Trial Balances

	High Ltd.	Low Inc.
Debits		
Cash	$ 50,000	$ 5,000
Accounts Receivable	80,000	15,000
Investment in Low Inc. (at equity)	90,000	—
Other Assets	360,000	100,000
Cost of Goods Sold	160,000	60,000
Selling and Administrative Expenses	50,000	20,000
Income Tax Expense	40,000	10,000
Totals	$830,000	$210,000
Credits		
Accounts Payable	$ 70,000	$ 30,000
Bonds Payable	100,000	—
Common Shares	150,000	50,000
Retained Earnings	200,000	30,000
Sales Revenue	300,000	100,000
Equity in Earnings of Low Inc.	10,000	—
Totals	$830,000	$210,000

Prepare a consolidation balance sheet work sheet for High Ltd. and Low Inc. as of December 31, Year 6. The elimination column should contain entries to:

(1) Eliminate the investment account.

(2) Eliminate intercompany receivables and payables.

22. *Consolidation work sheet entries for less than wholly owned subsidiary purchased for more than book value.* Refer to the data for High Ltd. and Low Inc. in Problem 21. Give the consolidation balance sheet work sheet elimination entries under each of the following independent situations:

a. High Ltd. paid $100,000, instead of $80,000, for all of the common shares of Low Inc. on January 1, Year 6. The market values of Low Inc.'s recorded assets and liabilities equalled their book values. Goodwill is amortized over ten years.

b. High Ltd. paid $64,000 for 80 percent of the common shares of Low Inc. on January 1, Year 6. The Investment in Shares of Low Inc. account showed a balance of $72,000 on December 31, Year 6.

23. *Consolidation work sheet for less than wholly owned subsidiary purchased for book value.* The preclosing trial balances of L Corp. and M Inc. on December 31, Year 2 are shown in Exhibit 12.22. L Corp. acquired 90 percent of the common shares of M Inc. on January 2, Year 1 for $270,000. On this date, the shareholders' equity accounts of M Inc. were as shown at the top of page 782.

Common Stock	$100,000
Retained Earnings	200,000
Total	$300,000

During Year 2, L Corp. sold merchandise costing $30,000, on account, to M Inc. for $40,000. Of the amount, $10,000 remains unpaid at year-end. M Inc. sold all of the merchandise during Year 2.

 a. Prepare a consolidated balance sheet work sheet for L Corp. and M Inc. for Year 2. The elimination column should contain entries to:

 (1) Eliminate the investment account.

 (2) Eliminate intercompany receivables and payables.

 b. Prepare a consolidated balance sheet as of December 31, Year 2.

EXHIBIT 12.22
L CORP. AND M INC.
Preclosing Trial Balances

	L Corp.	M Inc.
Debits		
Receivables	$ 60,000	$130,000
Investment in M Inc.	319,500	—
Other Assets	761,500	285,000
Cost of Goods Sold	550,000	150,000
Other Expenses	120,000	10,000
Dividends Declared	30,000	15,000
Totals	$1,841,000	$590,000
Credits		
Accounts Payable	$ 80,000	$ 20,000
Other Liabilities	90,000	40,000
Common Shares	400,000	100,000
Retained Earnings	435,000	230,000
Sales Revenue	800,000	200,000
Equity in Earnings of M Inc.	36,000	—
Totals	$1,841,000	$590,000

24. **Consolidation work sheet for less than wholly owned subsidiary purchased for more than book value.** The condensed balance sheets of Ely Corp. and Sims Ltd. at December 31 are shown in Exhibit 12.23.

The receivables of the Ely Corp. and the liabilities of Sims Ltd. contain an advance from the Ely Corp. to Sims Ltd. of $5,500. The Ely Corp. acquired 85 percent of the share capital of Sims Ltd. on the market at January 2 of this year for $80,000. At that date, the balance in the Retained Earnings account of Sims Ltd. was $30,000. Amortize goodwill, if any, over forty years.

Prepare a consolidated balance sheet work sheet for Ely Corp. and Sims Ltd. The elimination column should contain entries to:

(1) Eliminate the Investment in the Sims Ltd. account.

(2) Eliminate intercompany obligations.

EXHIBIT 12.23
Ely Corp. and Sims Ltd.
Balance Sheet Data

	Ely Corp.	Sims Ltd.
Assets		
Cash	$ 60,000	$ 5,000
Receivables	120,000	15,000
Investment in Sims Ltd. (at equity)	88,200	—
Other Assets	540,000	100,000
	$808,200	$120,000
Liabilities and Shareholders' Equity		
Current Liabilities	$250,000	$ 30,000
Common Shares	400,000	50,000
Retained Earnings	158,200	40,000
	$808,200	$120,000

25. *Consolidation work sheet subsequent to year of acquisition.* The condensed balance sheets of R Ltd. and S Ltd. on December 31, Year 2 are shown in Exhibit 12.24. Additional information:

R Ltd. owns 90 percent of the share capital of S Ltd. The shares of S Ltd. were acquired on January 1, Year 1 when S Ltd.'s retained earnings amounted to $20,000.

R Ltd. holds a note issued by S Ltd. in the amount of $8,200.

Excess of cost over book value acquired is all attributable to goodwill, to be amortized over forty years. The company has recorded Year 2 goodwill amortization.

Prepare a work sheet for a consolidated balance sheet.

EXHIBIT 12.24
R Ltd. and S Ltd.
Balance Sheet Data

	R Ltd.	S Ltd.
Assets		
Cash	$ 18,000	$ 13,000
Accounts and Notes Receivable	90,000	25,000
Inventories	220,000	125,000
Investment in S Ltd. (at equity)	312,450	—
Capital Assets	300,000	212,000
Total Assets	$940,450	$375,000
Liabilities and Shareholders' Equity		
Accounts and Notes Payable	$ 55,000	$ 17,000
Dividends Payable	—	12,500
Other Liabilities	143,000	11,000
Common Shares	600,000	250,000
Contributed Surplus	—	50,000
Retained Earnings	$142,450	$ 34,500
Total Liabilities and Shareholders' Equity	$940,450	$375,000

26. *Total consolidated assets, unrealized inventory profit.* The assets included in the balance sheets of Parent Co. Ltd. and Subsidiary Co. Ltd. at December 31, Year 1 are shown in Exhibit 12.25.

EXHIBIT 12.25
PARENT CO. LTD. AND SUBSIDIARY CO. LTD.
Balance Sheet Assets

	Parent Co. Ltd.	Subsidiary Co. Ltd.
ASSETS		
Current Assets		
Cash	$ 40,000	$ 30,000
Accounts Receivable — Customers	88,200	59,000
Advances to Subsidiary Co. Ltd.	8,000	
Inventory	150,000	100,000
Prepaid Expenses	1,800	1,000
Total Current Assets	$288,000	$190,000
Capital Assets		
Land	$100,000	$ 50,000
Buildings	300,000	200,000
Accumulated Depreciation	(140,000)	(60,000)
Equipment	150,000	120,000
Accumulated Depreciation	(68,000)	(40,000)
Total	$342,000	$270,000
Investment in Subsidiary Co. Ltd. (at equity)	300,000	
Total Assets	$930,000	$460,000

Parent Co. Ltd. owns 80 percent of the common shares of Subsidiary Co. Ltd., which it purchased when Subsidiary Co. Ltd. was formed.

All of the inventory of Subsidiary Co. Ltd. was purchased from Parent Co. Ltd. The inventory cost Parent Co. Ltd. $85,000.

The chief accountant of Parent Co. Ltd. must prepare a consolidated balance sheet. Determine the total that will be shown for the asset side of the consolidated balance sheet.

27. *Consolidated balance sheet, unrealized inventory profit.* The condensed balance sheets of Saginaw Co. Limited and Valley Co. Ltd. at December 31, Year 2 are shown in Exhibit 12.26.
Saginaw Co. Limited organized Valley Co. Ltd. one year ago and holds all of the outstanding share capital of the subsidiary.
   a. Prepare the December 31, Year 2 consolidated balance sheet. A consolidation work sheet is not required.
   b. Assume that the following data relate to the next year, which ends December 31, Year 3.

	Saginaw Co. Limited	Valley Co. Ltd.
Net Income (single-company operations)*	$25,000	$10,000
Dividends paid	10,000	5,000

Excluding any income from Valley Co. Ltd.

EXHIBIT 12.26
SAGINAW CO. LIMITED AND VALLEY CO. LTD.
Balance Sheets

	Saginaw Co. Limited	Valley Co. Ltd.
ASSETS		
Current Assets	$ 90,000	$ 50,000
Investment in Valley Co. Ltd.	110,000	
Capital Assets — net	200,000	110,000
Total Assets	$400,000	$160,000
EQUITIES		
Current Liabilities	$ 60,000	$ 30,000
Long-Term Liabilities	40,000	20,000
Shareholders' Equity		
Common Shares	200,000	100,000
Retained Earnings	100,000	10,000
Total Equities	$400,000	$160,000

Compute the consolidated retained earnings as of December 31, Year 3.

   c. In addition to the information provided in **(b)**, assume that Saginaw Co. Limited made intercompany sales to Valley Co. Ltd. of $5,000, on which there was $500 of intercompany profit, and that the goods are included in the December 31, Year 3 inventory of Valley Co. Ltd. Compute the consolidated retained earnings as of December 31, Year 3.

28. *Minority interest.* The condensed balance sheets of Alpha Co. Limited and Gamma Limited at December 31, Year 9 are shown in Exhibit 12.27.

   On December 31, Year 1, Alpha Co. Limited acquired 90 percent of the share capital of Gamma Limited at a cost of $117,000. On this date, the balances of the retained earnings accounts of the two companies were as shown at the top of page 786.

EXHIBIT 12.27
ALPHA CO. LIMITED AND GAMMA LTD.
Condensed Balance Sheets

	Alpha Co. Limited	Gamma Limited
Assets		
Current Assets	$ 34,730	$ 10,100
Investment in Gamma Limited	102,870	
Capital Assets — net	134,500	122,400
Total Assets	$272,100	$132,500
Equities		
Current Liabilities	$ 46,800	$ 18,200
Common Shares	150,000	100,000
Retained Earnings	75,300	14,300
Total Equities	$272,100	$132,500

Alpha Co. Limited	$48,000
Gamma Limited	30,000

    a. Compute the amount of minority interest that would be included in the December 31, Year 9 consolidated balance sheet.

    b. Prepare the Shareholders' Equity section of the December 31, Year 9 consolidated balance sheet.

29. *Consolidation work sheet and balance sheet, minority interest, purchase discrepancy, unrealized inventory profit.* The June 30, Year 8 balance sheets of Vapour Co. Ltd. and Trail Co. Limited are shown in Exhibit 12.28. Vapour Co. Ltd. accounts for its investment in Trail Co. Limited on the equity basis. Vapour Co. Ltd. acquired its 80 percent interest in Trail Co. Limited for $37,000 on July 1, Year 1, on which date the balance of retained earnings of Trail Co. Limited was $1,500. On this date, there was evidence that the land owned by Trail Co. Limited was worth $5,000 more than its book value. Vapour Co. Ltd. had amortized $1,100 of goodwill on acquisition to June 30, Year 8.

EXHIBIT 12.28
Vapour Co. Ltd. and Trail Co. Limited
Balance Sheets

	Vapour Co. Ltd.	Trail Co. Limited
Assets		
Cash	$ 18,400	$ 6,800
Accounts Receivable	46,100	10,200
Advance to Trail Co. Limited	25,000	
Inventory	83,500	18,500
Prepaid Expenses	6,400	2,600
Investment in Trail Co. Limited	40,000	
Land	15,000	6,400
Buildings — net	108,600	20,100
Furniture and Equipment — net	138,900	12,300
Total Assets	$481,900	$76,900
Equities		
Accounts Payable	$ 18,900	$14,200
Income Tax Payable	62,400	4,200
Advance from Vapour Co. Ltd.		25,000
Common Shares	300,000	25,000
Retained Earnings	100,600	8,500
	$481,900	$76,900

    On June 30, Year 8, the inventory of Trail Co. Limited included merchandise purchased from Vapour Co. Ltd. for $6,400, which was $1,500 above cost to Vapour Co. Ltd.

    a. Prepare the consolidated balance sheet work sheet as of June 30, Year 8.

    b. Prepare the consolidated balance sheet as of June 30, Year 8.

30. *Consolidated balance sheets, investment on a cost basis, purchase discrepancy, unrealized inventory profit.* The condensed balance sheets of Par Ltd. and Sub Ltd. at December 31, Year 7 are shown in Exhibit 12.29. Par Ltd. records the Investment in Sub Ltd. on a cost basis and follows the practice of amortizing any goodwill arising from consolidation on a straight-line basis over a twenty-year period.

Prepare a condensed consolidated balance sheet for each of the following separate cases.

   a. The parent purchased all of the shares of the subsidiary for $120,000 when the retained earnings of the subsidiary amounted to $20,000.

   b. The parent purchased 80 percent of the subsidiary's shares for $120,000 when the retained earnings of the subsidiary amounted to $50,000.

   c. On December 31, Year 2, the parent purchased 70 percent of the subsidiary's shares for $120,000 when the retained earnings of the subsidiary amounted to $50,000. At the date of acquisition, the fair value of the land was $10,000 above the book value. Intercompany profit in the inventory of the subsidiary was as follows:

December 31, Year 6	$2,000
December 31, Year 7	3,000

EXHIBIT 12.29
PAR LTD. AND SUB LTD.
Condensed Balance Sheets

	Par Ltd.	Sub Ltd.
Assets		
Current Assets	$ 40,000	$ 30,000
Investment in Sub Ltd.	120,000	—
Capital Assets	220,000	150,000
Total Assets	$380,000	$180,000
Equities		
Current Liabilities	$ 30,000	$ 20,000
Common Shares	240,000	100,000
Retained Earnings	110,000	60,000
Total Equities	$380,000	$180,000

31. *Determine specific consolidated financial statement numbers, purchase discrepancy, minority interest, unrealized inventory profit.* The condensed balance sheets of P Ltd. and S. Ltd. at December 31, Year 7 are shown in Exhibit 12.30. In addition, the following information is provided:

   (1) P Ltd. acquired 80 percent of the shares of S Ltd. on December 31, Year 6 for $160,000. At that date, the balance of shareholders' equity of S Ltd. was $142,500. Neither company issued shares during the year.

EXHIBIT 12.30
P LTD. AND S LTD.
Condensed Balance Sheets
(amounts in thousands)

	P Ltd.	S Ltd.
Assets		
Current Assets	$212	$140
Investment in S Ltd.	158	—
Other Assets	420	180
Total	$790	$320
Equities		
Current Liabilities	$100	$170
Long-Term Debt	200	—
Common Shares	200	100
Retained Earnings	290	50
Total	$790	$320

(2) On May 15, Year 7, P Ltd. sold merchandise to S Ltd. for a price of $60,000. The merchandise had cost P Ltd. $50,000 when purchased on December 20, Year 6. S Ltd. had resold half of the merchandise by December 31, Year 7.

(3) On November 30, Year 7, P Ltd. had advanced S Ltd. $40,000 on a 90-day note. The note was still outstanding at December 31, Year 7.

(4) At December 31, Year 6, the fair value of the land owned by S Ltd. exceeded the book value by $20,000. This was the sole difference between fair value and book value of S Ltd.'s assets at that date. No land was sold during Year 7.

(5) P. Ltd. followed the policy of amortizing goodwill over ten years on a straight-line basis by reducing the book value of the investment in S Ltd.

(6) S Ltd. declared and paid no dividends during Year 7.

a. Calculate the following balances appearing on the consolidated balance sheet at December 31, Year 7. (Show details of your calculation.)
   (i)   Current liabilities
   (ii) Other assets (excluding goodwill on consolidation)
   (iii) Consolidated retained earnings
   (iv) Minority interest
   (v)   Goodwill on consolidation
   (vi) Current assets

b. Determine the income of S Ltd. for the year ended December 31, Year 7.

c. Determine the amount and describe the location of references to minority interest in the Statements of Consolidated Income, Consolidated Balance Sheet, and Consolidated Retained Earnings for the year ended December 31, Year 7.

32. *Effect of accounting methods for investments on financial statements.* Sturdy Manufacturing (S.M.) Limited manufactures heavy-duty industrial equipment and consumer-durable goods. To enable its customers to make convenient credit arrangements, S.M. Limited organized Sturdy Manufacturing Credit Corporation several years ago. S.M. Credit Corporation is 100-percent owned by S.M. Limited. S.M. Limited accounts for its investment in S.M. Credit Corporation using the equity method. S.M. owns shares of many other companies and consolidates several of them in its financial statements. Refer to the comparative balance sheets and income statements for the two companies in Exhibits 12.31 and 12.32.

EXHIBIT 12.31
STURDY MANUFACTURING LIMITED AND CONSOLIDATED AFFILIATES

	(In millions of $) December 31		
Balance Sheet	**Year 3**	**Year 2**	**Year 1**
Investment in S.M. Credit Corporation	$ 260.0	$ 231.9	$ 190.0
Other Assets	7,141.8	6,655.9	6,008.5
Total Assets	$ 7,401.8	$6,887.8	$6,198.5
Total Liabilities	$ 4,317.2	$4,086.0	$3,644.9
Shareholders Equity	3,084.6	2,801.8	2,553.6
Total Equities	$ 7,401.8	$6,887.8	$6,198.5
Income Statement	**Year 3**	**Year 2**	**Year 1**
Sales	$10,387.6	$9,546.4	$8,813.6
Equity in Net Earnings of Credit Corporation	41.1	30.9	19.9
Total Revenues	$10,428.7	$9,577.3	$8,833.5
Expenses	(9,898.7)	(9,105.5)	(8,505.0)
Net Income	$ 530.0	$ 471.8	$ 328.5

a. Given that S.M. Limited accounted for its investment in S.M. Credit Corporation by the equity method, identify, for Year 3, the components of S.M. Limited's income that are attributable to the Credit Corporation's dividends and earnings.

b. Suppose that S.M. Limited had accounted for its investment in the Credit Corporation using the cost method, and that market value has exceeded acquisition cost at all times since acquisition.
   (i) Show the components of S.M. Limited's income from the Credit Corporation, and compute how much larger or smaller S.M. Limited's income would have been for Year 3 than the income that was reported.
   (ii) Identify any S.M. Limited's balance sheet accounts that would have different balances, and calculate the differences from what is shown in the actual statements and what would be shown had the alternative treatment been used.

c. Assume that S.M. Limited had accounted for its investment in the Credit Corporation by consolidating it. Perform the same compu-

EXHIBIT 12.32
STURDY MANUFACTURING CREDIT CORPORATION

| | (In millions of $) December 31 | | |
Balance Sheet	Year 3	Year 2	Year 1
Total Assets	$2,789.5	$2,358.7	$2,157.0
Total Liabilities	$2,529.5	$2,126.8	$1,967.0
Common Shares	$ 110.0	$ 90.0	$ 55.0
Retained Earnings	150.0	141.9	135.0
Shareholders' Equity	$ 260.0	$ 231.9	$ 190.0
Total Equities	$2,789.5	$2,358.7	$2,157.0

Statement of Income and Retained Earnings	Year 3	Year 2	Year 1
Revenues	$ 319.8	$ 280.0	$ 247.5
Less: Expenses	278.7	249.1	227.6
Net Income	$ 41.1	$ 30.9	$ 19.9
Less: Dividends	33.0	24.0	15.0
Earnings Retained for Year	$ 8.1	$ 6.9	$ 4.9
Retained Earnings at January 1	141.9	135.0	130.1
Retained Earnings	$ 150.0	$ 141.9	$ 135.0

tations as required in **(i)** and **(ii)** of **(b)** above for Year 3. Notice that when a 100-percent-owned subsidiary — accounted for with the equity method — is consolidated, the effect on balance sheet totals and subtotals can be summarized as follows:

(1) Total owners' equity on the parent's books remain unchanged.

(2) Total liabilities on the parent's books increases by the amount of the subsidiary's total liabilities (assuming there are no intercompany receivables and payables).

(3) Total assets on the parent's books increases net by an amount equal to the subsidiary's liabilities. (All of the subsidiary's assets are put onto the parent's books, but the parent's investment in the subsidiary, an amount equal to the subsidiary's owners' equity, is removed. The net effect is to increase assets by the amount of the subsidiary's total assets − subsidiary's owners' equity = subsidiary's liabilities.)

d. Compute the following ratios for S.M. from the annual report as published for Year 3.

(1) Rate of return on assets, defined for this purpose as net income divided by total assets at the end of the year. (Insufficient information is given to allow an addback to the numerator for interest payments net of tax effects; ignore that adjustment to net income, which is ordinarily required. Use the year-end balance of total assets for the year's average.)

(2) Debt-equity ratio, defined as total liabilities divided by total equities.

e. For Year 3, compute the two ratios required in part **(d)**, assuming that S.M. had consolidated the Credit Corporation, rather than accounting for it with the equity method. Use the information derived in part (c).

f. Compare the results in parts (d) and (e). What conclusions can you draw from this exercise about comparing financial ratios for companies that consolidated their subsidiaries with those of companies do not?

33. Repeat Problem (32) for Year 2.

34. Repeat Problem (32) for Year 1.

35. *Impact of consolidation policy on debt ratios.* This problem illustrates the impact that consolidation policy can have on financial statements and financial statement analysis. Suppose that Pears, Starbuck & Co. and C.J. Nichols Company are large retailers who have similar operations. Both companies have organized financing subsidiaries. Each subsidiary borrows funds in credit markets and lends the funds to customers who purchase goods or services from the retailers. Each subsidiary is 100 percent owned by its parent company. Pears consolidates its financing subsidiary (Pears, Starbuck Acceptance Corp.) in published financial statements. Nichols uses the equity method for its financing subsidiary (C.J. Nichols Financial Corporation) and shows the separate financial statements of the financing subsidiary in notes to the published financial statements.

In this problem, we focus on the debt ratio, because the effects are easy to illustrate. Other ratios could be used as well. Throughout this book, the debt-equity ratio has been defined as:

$$\text{Debt-Equity Ratio} = \frac{\text{Total Liabilities}}{\text{Total Equities}}$$

Many financial analysts prefer to use a form of the debt ratio such as:

$$\text{Debt Ratio} = \frac{\text{Total } Long\text{-}Term \text{ Debt}}{\text{Total Shareholders' Equity}}$$

Such analysts feel that this version of the debt ratio focuses more attention on the risk of companies being analyzed. (The notion is that the percentage of current liabilities to total equities is, to a large degree, determined by the nature of the business and that, so long as current assets are as large as current liabilities, the percentage of current liabilities in total equities is not important.)

The accompanying Exhibit 12.33 shows pertinent data from recent financial statements for both Pears and Nichols. Both versions of the debt ratio mentioned above are presented. The data for Pears are taken directly from the financial statements. For Nichols, the exhibit shows data from the published balance sheet in column (1), shows data from the statements of the financing subsidiary in column (2), and presents a column for Nichols hypothetical financial statements, assuming consolidation of the financing subsidiary. Column (3) represents the accounting for Nichols that is analogous to Pears' accounting.

a. Complete column (3) for Nichols. (The ratios shown are correct; you can check your work from them.) You may find the summary in part (c) of Problem (32) to be useful.

EXHIBIT 12.33
Effect of Consolidation Policy
(all dollar amounts in millions)

	C.J. Nichols Company			Pears, Starbuck & Co.
	Financial Statements as Issued (1)	Financing Subsidiary Statements as Shown in Notes (2)	Hypothetical Financial Statements if Subsidiary Were Consolidated (3)	Financial Statements as Issued (4)
Total Assets	$3,483.8	$1,458.1	?	$12,711.5
Total Liabilities	1,567.2	1,078.9	?	6,774.6
Long-Term Debt	355.5	517.0	?	1,563.5
Shareholders' Equity	1,916.6	379.2	?	5,936.9
Debt-Equity Ratio (Total Liabilities/Total Equities)	45.0%	72.3%	58.0%	53.3%
Long-Term Debt/Shareholders' Equity	18.5%	136.3%	45.5%	26.3%

b. As measured by the debt ratios (and ignoring other factors — see Problem 19 in Chapter 14), which company appears to be more risky? Which company do you think is more risky and why?

c. Assume that the managements of Nichols and Pears are both considering additional long-term financing to raise funds. Managements of both companies are concerned about how the marketplace will react to new debt financing on the one hand or new common share issues on the other. How are financial analysts who are concerned with risk (as measured in part by debt ratios) likely to react to these two companies? How are managements of the two companies likely to react in making their financing decisions if they anticipate the reaction of financial analysts?

36. *Purchase versus pooling.* (Requires coverage of Appendix 12.1.) P Ltd. and S Inc. decide to combine operations. Management estimates that the combination will save $50,000 a year in expenses of running the combined businesses. Columns (1) and (2) in Exhibit 12.34 show abbreviated single-company financial statements for P Ltd. and S Inc. before combination. S Inc. has 20,000 shares outstanding that sell for $84 per share in the market. The market value of S Inc. as a going concern is, therefore, $1,680,000. As shown in Column (3), S's shareholders have $1,230,000 of equity not recorded on the books. Of this $1,230,000, $400,000 is attributable to undervalued noncurrent assets, and $830,000 is attributable to goodwill. P Ltd. has 100,000 shares outstanding, which have a $5 par value and sell for $42 each in the market. Ignore income taxes throughout this problem.

a. Assume that P Ltd. purchases S Inc. to combine their operations. P Ltd. issues (sells) 40,000 additional shares on the market for $42 each, or $1,680,000 in total, and uses the proceeds to purchase all shares of S Inc. for $84 each. (Each share of S Inc. is, in effect, "sold" for two shares of P Ltd.) P Ltd. has acquired 100 percent of the

EXHIBIT 12.34
Consolidated Statements
Comparing Purchase and Pooling-of-Interest Methods

	Historical Cost		S Inc. Shown at Current Values	P Ltd. & S Inc. Consolidated at Date of Acquisition	
	P Ltd. (1)	S Inc. (2)	Values (3)	Purchase (4)	Pooling of Interests (5)
BALANCE SHEETS					
Assets:					
Current Assets	$1,500,000	$450,000	$ 450,000	$1,950,000	$1,950,000
Long-Term Assets Less					
Accumulated Depreciation	1,700,000	450,000	850,000	?	?
Goodwill	—	—	830,000	?	?
Total Assets	$3,200,000	$900,000	$2,130,000	$5,330,000	$4,100,000
Equities:					
Liabilities	$1,300,000	$450,000	$ 450,000	$1,750,000	$1,750,000
Common Shares	500,000	100,000	100,000	?	?
Contributed Surplus	200,000	150,000	150,000	?	?
Retained Earnings	1,200,000	200,000	200,000	?	?
Unrecorded Equity at Current					
Valuation	—	—	1,230,000	—	—
Total Liabilities and					
Shareholders' Equity	$3,200,000	$900,000	$2,130,000	$5,330,000	$4,100,000

	Actual			Projected	
INCOME STATEMENTS (Ignoring Income Taxes)					
Precombination Income from					
Combination	$ 300,000	$160,000		$ 460,000	$ 460,000
Cost Savings (Projected)	—	—		50,000	50,000
Extra Depreciation Expense	—	—		?	—
Amortization of Goodwill	—	—		?	—
Net Income	$ 300,000	$160,000		$ 409,250	$ 510,000
Number of Common Shares					
Outstanding	100,000	20,000		?	?
Earnings per Share	$3.00	$8.00		?	?
Rate of Return on Assets (Using					
Balances at Merger Date)				?	?
Rate of Return on Owners'					
Equity (Using Balances at					
Merger Date)				?	?

Assumptions: (1) S Inc. has 20,000 shares outstanding that sell for $84 each in the market.
           (2) P Ltd.'s shares sell for $42 each in the market. P Ltd issues 40,000 shares for the purpose of acquiring S Inc.

shares of S Inc. and now owns S Inc. P Ltd.'s acquisition of S Inc. would be accounted for as a purchase. P Ltd. decides to amortize the revalued asset costs over five years and to amortize the goodwill over forty years. Complete column (4) to show the effects of purchase accounting.

b. Assume that P Ltd. issued the 40,000 shares directly to the owners of S Inc. in return for their shares. The merger is treated as a pooling of interests. Complete column (5) to show the effects of pooling accounting.

c. Suggest reasons why managers of business firms involved in corporate acquisition might prefer the pooling-of-interests method.

37. *Determine specific balances on statements for six conditions.*   The condensed, single-company Balance Sheets and Statements of Retained Earnings of P Ltd. and S Ltd. at December 31, Year 1 and Year 2 follow:

P LTD. & S LTD.
Condensed Comparative Balance Sheets
at December 31

	P Ltd.		S Ltd.	
	Year 2	Year 1	Year 2	Year 1
Current Assets	$200,000	$160,000	$ 60,000	$ 40,000
Capital Assets	210,000	240,000	60,000	70,000
Investments (Note A)	220,000	200,000	—	—
Total Assets	$630,000	$600,000	$120,000	$110,000
Current Liabilities	$ 80,000	$ 70,000	$ 15,000	$ 10,000
Common Shares	200,000	200,000	60,000	60,000
Retained Earnings	350,000	330,000	45,000	40,000
Total Equities	$630,000	$600,000	$120,000	$110,000

(Note A) including investment in S Ltd. at amounts indicated below.

P LTD. & S LTD.
Statement of Retained Earnings
Years Ended December 31

	P Ltd.		S Ltd.	
	Year 2	Year 1	Year 2	Year 1
Opening Balance	$330,000	$300,000	$ 40,000	$ 30,000
Plus: Net Income	80,000	90,000	25,000	30,000
Less: Dividends	(60,000)	(60,000)	(20,000)	(20,000)
Closing Balance	$350,000	$330,000	$ 45,000	$ 40,000

When preparing P Ltd.'s financial statements, presented above, the bookkeeper incorrectly recorded the investment in S Ltd. on a cost basis — hence, dividends received from S Ltd. are recorded as income P Ltd.

It is the company's policy to amortize goodwill, if any, on the purchase of S Ltd. shares on a straight-line basis over ten years.

Alternatives A to F below represent unrelated events that occurred during Year 2.

Alternative A
P Ltd. purchased 100 percent of the shares of S Ltd. on January 1, Year 2 for $100,000.

Alternative B

P Ltd. purchased 10 percent of the shares of S Ltd. on January 1, Year 2 for $13,000. At December 31, Year 2, P Ltd. owed S Ltd. $12,000 on current account for merchandise purchased from S Ltd. that remained unsold at December 31. These goods cost S Ltd. $9,000.

Alternative C

P Ltd. purchased 80 percent of the shares of S Ltd. on January 1, Year 2 for $80,000. At December 31, Year 2, P Ltd. owed S Ltd. $13,000.

Alternative D

P Ltd. purchased 60 percent of the shares of S Ltd. on January 1, Year 2 for $63,000.

Alternative E

P Ltd. purchased 30 percent of the shares of S Ltd. on January 1, Year 2 for $36,000. At December 31, Year 2, S Ltd. owed P Ltd. $30,000 on current accounts for merchandise purchased from P Ltd. that remained unsold at December 31. These goods cost P Ltd. $16,000.

Alternative F

P Ltd. purchased 70 percent of the shares of S Ltd. on January 1, Year 2 for $84,000. At that date, it was determined that the land owned by S Ltd. had a fair value of $25,000 in comparison with a book value of $10,000. At December 20, Year 2, P Ltd. sold S Ltd. on account a machine, with a book value of $40,000, for $60,000. The account had not been paid as of December 31, Year 2.

For each of these events, A to F, calculate the amounts that would be reported in the Year 2 financial statements of P Ltd. (prepared in accordance with GAAP) for each of the following captions:

1. Investment in S Ltd.
2. Net Income
3. Minority Interest
4. Goodwill on Consolidation
5. Income from S. Ltd. Investment
6. Total Assets

If the caption does not appear in the financial statements of P Ltd., insert "na" beside the caption.

38. *Determining specific balances on investor's statements.* On January 1, Year 1, P Ltd. purchased shares of X Ltd., Y Ltd., and Z Ltd. These were the only purchases made by P Ltd. in shares of other companies. None of these shares were sold in the next three years. The following information has been extracted from the consolidated balance sheet of P Ltd.:

	December 31	
	Year 3	Year 2
Investment in X Ltd.	$120,000	$120,000
Investment in Z Ltd.	18,000	16,000
Land (owned by Y Ltd.)	89,000	89,000
Minority interest in Y Ltd.	15,000	13,000
Goodwill on consolidation of Y Ltd.	14,000	16,000

In addition, the following information was made available from the footnotes to the financial statements, or direct inquiry:

(1) P Ltd. follows the policy of amortizing goodwill on consolidation on a straight-line basis over ten years.

(2) P Ltd. purchased 90 percent of the shares of Y Ltd. on January 1, Year 1.

(3) During Year 3, the following dividends were paid:

By X Ltd.	$200,000
By Y Ltd.	12,000
By Z Ltd.	7,500

(4) The land presented above was owned by Y Ltd. on January 1, Year 1. At that date, the fair value was $10,000 more than the book value.

(5) During Year 3, the following incomes were reported by the companies:

P Ltd.	$107,000
X Ltd.	240,000
Y Ltd.	not available
Z Ltd.	not available

(6) Income from long-term share investments reported in P Ltd.'s financial statements (prepared in conformity with GAAP) follow:

X Ltd.	$18,000
Y Ltd.	not available
Z Ltd.	5,000

(7) The shares of Z Ltd. were purchased at their book value.

Required: Calculate the following (show details of your calculations):

1. The balance of shareholders' equity of Y Ltd. at December 31, Year 3.
2. The percentage of shares of X Ltd. purchased by P Ltd.
3. The income reported in the financial statements of Y Ltd. for the year ended December 31, Year 3.
4. The cost of the land owned by Y Ltd. referred to above.
5. The percentage of shares of Z Ltd. purchased by P Ltd.
6. The total excess of the cost of shares in Y Ltd. over the book value of these shares on January 1, Year 1.

39. *Purchases versus pooling: balance sheet.* (Requires coverage of Appendix 12.1.) Marmee Company and Small Enterprises agree to

merge at a time when the balance sheets of the two companies appear as follows:

	Marmee Company	Small Enterprises
Assets	$700,000	$312,000
Liabilities	$150,000	$100,000
Common Shares ($1 par)	160,000	64,000
Contributed Surplus	120,000	34,000
Retained Earnings	270,000	114,000
Total Equities	$700,000	$312,000

Marmee issues 50,000 shares with market value of $80,000 to the owners of Small in return for their 64,000 shares, which represent equity of $212,000 (= $312,000 of assets − $100,000 of liabilities). The excess of Marmee's cost ($800,000) over the book value of Small's assets acquired ($212,000) results from Small's book value of assets being $448,000 less than their current value and from $140,000 of goodwill ($800,000 − $212,000 = $448,000 + $140,000).

Prepare consolidated balance sheets as of the merger date, assuming that the merger is treated as:

a. A purchase.

b. A pooling of interests.

40. *Purchasing versus pooling: income statement.* (Requires coverage of Appendix 12.1.) Refer to the data in Problem 39. Partial single-company income statements for Marmee Company and Small Enterprises for the first year after the merger appear as follows:

	Marmee Company	Small Enterprises
Sales	$2,000,000	$1,500,000
Other Revenues	50,000	10,000
Total Revenues	$2,050,000	$1,510,000
Expenses Except Income Taxes	(1,700,000)	(1,300,000)
Pretax Income	$ 350,000	$ 210,000

Make the following assumptions:

(1) The income tax rate for the consolidated firm is 40 percent.

(2) Where necessary, Marmee Comapny amortizes the extra asset costs over five years and the goodwill over forty years in the consolidated statements.

(3) Marmee Company cannot deduct amortization of asset costs and goodwill arising from the purchase from taxable income in calculations for tax returns.

(4) Small Enterprises declared no dividends.

Prepare consolidated income statements and consolidated earnings per share for the first year following the merger. Assume that the merger is treated as:

a. A purchase.
b. A pooling of interests.

DECISION CASE 12-1

"You mean that the company can *increase* its working capital by purchasing shares in Equity Corp.? That's creative accounting!!"

The above remark was made by C. Bartello, the president of Conglo Inc., who was concerned that the working capital of the company would fall below the amount specified in the company's bank loan agreements.

The controller of Conglo Inc. had suggested that, rather than sell the common shares in Equity Corp. for less than their book value, the company purchase an additional 6 percent of the shares for $400,000. This purchase would increase Conglo's common share investment in Equity Corp. from 45 percent to 51 percent. The Investment in Equity Corp. account has a current balance of $3,600,000.

The condensed balance sheet of Equity Corp. at a current date is presented in Exhibit 12.35.

The controller further recommended that, in order to increase the income of Conglo Inc., a portion of the increased working capital be used to purchase an additional 4 percent of the shares of Cost Ltd. for about $800,000. This purchase would increase the investment in the common shares of Cost Ltd. from 17 percent to 21 percent and would enable Conglo Inc. to exercise significant influence over Cost Ltd. The income of Cost Ltd. for the current year was $4,000,000 and was expected to increase by 10 percent each year as a consequence of the company policy of reinvesting about half of each year's income for expansion.

EXHIBIT 12.35
EQUITY CORP.
Condensed Balance Sheet at a Current Date
(thousands of dollars)

Current Assets	$ 5,000	Current Liabilities	$ 2,000
Plant and Equipment (net)	12,000	Noncurrent Liabilities	7,000
		Shareholders' Equity	8,000
Total	$17,000	Total	$17,000

Was the result of the controller's suggestion valid? Did it conform to GAAP?

PART FOUR

SYNTHESIS: ANALYZING FINANCIAL POSITION, CHANGES IN FINANCIAL POSITION, AND THE IMPACT OF ACCOUNTING POLICY CHOICE

THE STATEMENT OF CHANGES IN FINANCIAL POSITION

CHAPTER OUTLINE

- Rationale for the Statement of Changes in Financial Position
- Analysis of the Effects of Transactions on Cash
- Preparation of the Statement of Changes in Financial Position
- Appendix 13.1: Comprehensive Illustration of Statement of Changes in Financial Position

statement of changes in financial position (SCFP)
A financial statement showing the nature of a firm's cash inflows and cash outflows for the period, classified into operating, investing, and financing categories.

funds
Generally, cash or cash and temporary investments. In archaic usage, referred to working capital (current assets less current liabilities).

This chapter discusses the **statement of changes in financial position**, which reports the flows of cash into and out of a business during a period of time. This statement is also sometimes referred to as the "funds statement." This comes from the historical name of the statement, "The Statement of Sources and Applications of Funds." The term "**funds**" was used because firms could define funds as cash or working capital (working capital = current assets − current liabilities).

In 1985, the CICA decided that the definition of funds should be cash only. This change was attributable largely to the fact that, in an increasing number of business failures, analysis of the firm's working capital position failed to point out its solvency problems.

The accounting profession has concluded that the primary objective of financial statements is to assist users in predicting future cash flows. A cash-basis statement of changes in financial position reflects the financial community's growing preoccupation with cash flow analysis and cash management.

RATIONALE FOR THE STATEMENT OF CHANGES IN FINANCIAL POSITION

Recall from Chapter 1 the relation between the principal activities of a business and the two financial statements already discussed, the balance sheet and the income statement. These relations are shown in Figure 13.1.

FIGURE 13.1

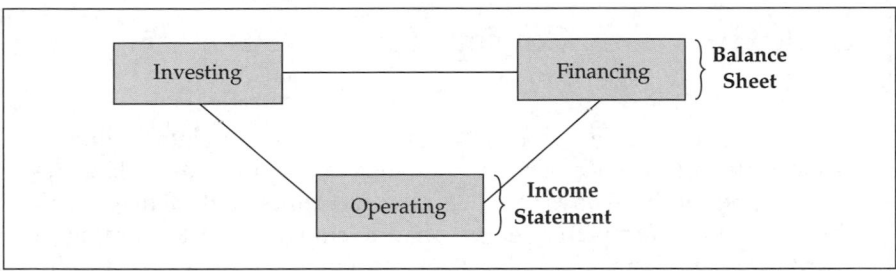

Investing activities, **financing activities**, and **operating activities** might be thought of as three interconnected cog-wheels, each turning on its own, yet connected in important ways with the other activities (Figure 13.2).

Cash ties these three activities together and keeps them running smoothly. If cash cannot be generated in sufficient amounts and at the right times, a firm faces financial difficulty and perhaps even bankruptcy.

Example Banks Corporation was formed during January, Year 1 to operate a computer supply business. Banks obtained financing from creditors and owners and invested the funds in buildings and equipment. The firm has operated profitably since opening, with net income increasing from $3,000 in Year 1 to $20,000 in Year 4. The firm has had increasing difficulty, however, paying its monthly bills as they become due. Management is puzzled about how net income could be increasing while, at the same time, the firm continually finds itself strapped for cash.

Investing activities
Section of the SCFP showing investment requiring cash flow and divestment generating cash flow.

financing activities
Section of the SCFP showing cash flow generated from or spent on capital-raising activities.

operating activities
Section of the SCFP showing the results of operations on cash flow.

FIGURE 13.2

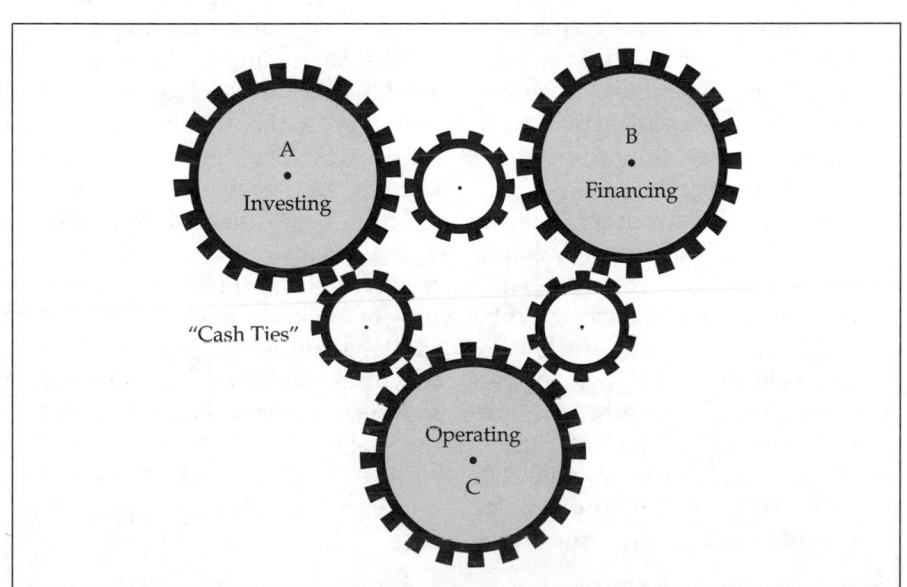

DISCUSSION CASE 28

Cash Flow — A Concept for the '90s

If there is such a thing as being fashionable or trendy in accounting, it is trendy these days to talk about cash flow. Terms frequently heard among business analysts today include "cash flow statements," "cash flow per share," and "cash flow projections." In 1986, the CICA's definition of funds used in the statement of changes in financial position was changed from working capital to cash. Why is cash flow so important and what led to the sudden interest in this concept?

Historically, cash was the bad guy of the balance sheet. Near the beginning of this century, the accounting profession embraced matching and accrual-based accounting as central pillars in accounting. Matching is the attempt to get revenues and all costs associated with generating those revenues into the same income statement. Accrual-based accounting is recognizing expenses as soon as they are incurred and revenues as soon as they are earned, rather than waiting for the cash flow to trigger a recording entry.

Both of these concepts are the antithesis of cash-basis accounting, in which all recording activity in the accounts is triggered by a cash flow in or out of the firm. Your chequebook is a perfect illustration of cash-basis accounting. Accounting pundits, however, saw cash-basis statements as a distortion of the true income measurement. More important,

cash-basis statements allowed management to manipulate reported profits. All management had to do was alter the timing of a disbursement or a cash receipt to radically alter the bottom line on the income statement. We call deliberate efforts by management to change net income by employing accounting tactics "income smoothing" (which has also had a bad name in accounting lore).

Consequently, cash took a back seat to another concept — working capital — which is current assets minus current liabilities. Working capital was supposed to be a better indicator of a firm's solvency because it represented the amount of current assets left over after the day-to-day bills were paid. Thus, in the past, the statement of changes measured changes in working capital, and business schools offered courses not in cash management but in working capital management.

The beginning of the end for working capital came in the mid-1970s, with the collapse of two major U.S. corporations — Penn Central (a railway) and W.T. Grant (a department store chain). These collapses sent shock waves throughout the financial community because traditional working capital analysis had failed to foretell their collapse. Subsequent business failures have brought the financial community to the realization that working capital tells very little about a company's

(continued)

(continued)
solvency. Two of the principal components of working capital, receivables and inventories, do not always convert as readily into cash as we would like to believe. History is full of examples of bankrupt firms with warehouses filled with inventory. Cash pays bills, working capital does not. It's as simple as that.

The accounting profession recognized the pre-eminence of cash in the blue-ribbon American Institute of Certified Public Accountants' study, *The Objectives of Financial Statements*, which concluded that the primary objective of financial statements is to assist users in predicting future cash flows. The culmination of cash's ascendancy came in 1986 when the profession changed the statement of changes from a working-capital basis to a cash basis. With the growing preoccupation with measuring corporate solvency, cash management will continue to play a larger role in financial statement presentation.

Discussion Question

Why is cash flow such a popular concept?

RELATIONSHIP BETWEEN INCOME FLOWS AND CASH FLOWS

Revenues and expenses reported in the income statement for a period differ in amount from cash receipts and disbursements for the period. The differences arise for two principal reasons:

1. The accrual basis of accounting is used in measuring net income. Thus, the recognition of revenues does not necessarily coincide with receipts of cash from customers. Likewise, the recognition of expenses does not necessarily coincide with disbursements of cash to suppliers, employees, and other creditors. As Chapter 3 pointed out, the accrual basis of accounting focuses on the use of assets in generating earnings and not on their associated cash receipts and disbursements.

2. The firm receives cash from sources that are not related directly to operations, such as issuing shares of bonds. Similarly, the firm makes cash disbursements for such things as dividends and the acquisition of equipment that are not related directly to operations during the current period.

To illustrate the differences between income flows and cash flows, refer to the data for Banks Corporation for Year 4 in Exhibit 13.1. Sales revenue reported in the income statement totalled $125,000. However, only $90,000 was collected in cash from customers. The remaining amount of sales was not collected by the end of the year and is reflected in the increase in the Accounts Receivable account on the balance sheet.[1] Likewise, the cost of

---

[1] This example has been simplified for purpose of illustration. In a realistic situation, some of the receipts would have been from collection of receivables existing at the start of the year. Similarly, some of the payments would have been for liabilities existing at the start of the year. To further simplify the example, we have included income tax with "other expenses."

goods sold shown on the income statement totalled $60,000. Only $50,000 cash was disbursed to suppliers during the year. Similar differences between income flows and cash flows can be seen for salaries and for other expenses. Note that there is no specific cash flow associated with depreciation expense during Year 4. Cash was used in some earlier periods for the acquisition of buildings and equipment, but the amount of cash spent earlier was not reported then as an expense in accrual accounting. Rather, it was reflected in the balance sheet as an increase in the asset account for buildings and equipment and shown in the statement of changes in financial position as a use of funds. Now, as the buildings and equipment are being used, the cost of the assets' services used is reported as expense of the period even though there is now no outflow of cash. Although the operating activities generated $20,000 in net income, these activities led to an increase in cash of only $8,000 during Year 4.

The Banks Corporation engaged in other activities affecting cash during Year 4, as is reported in the lower portion of Exhibit 13.1. Cash in the amount of $100,000 was received from the issue of bonds, $10,000 was disbursed for dividends, and $125,000 was disbursed for the acquisition of new equipment. The result of all of the firm's activities is a decrease in cash of $27,000.

EXHIBIT 13.1
BANKS CORPORATION
Income Statement and Statement of
Cash Receipts and Disbursements for Year 4

	Income Statement[a]	Statement of Cash Receipts and Disbursements	
Sales Revenue	$125,000	$ 90,000	Collections from Customers
Less: Expenses			Less: Disbursements
Cost of Goods Sold	$ 60,000	$ 50,000	To Merchandise Suppliers
Salaries	20,000	19,000	To Employees
Depreciation	10,000	0	—
Other	15,000	13,000	To Other Suppliers
Total Expenses	$105,000	$ 82,000	Total Disbursements to Suppliers and Employees
Net Income	$ 20,000	$ 8,000	Net Cash Inflow from Operations
		100,000	Receipts from Issuing Long-Term Bonds
		$108,000	Total Receipts from Operations and Bond Issue
		$ 10,000	Disbursements for Dividends
		125,000	Disbursements for Equipment
		$135,000	Total Disbursements for Dividends and Equipment
		$ 27,000	Net Decrease in Cash

[a]*To facilitate comparison, a single-step income statement is used in this illustration.*

The experience of Banks Corporation is not unusual. Many firms, particularly those growing rapidly, discover that their cash position is deteriorating despite an excellent earnings record. The statement of changes in financial position explains how the financing, investing, and operating activities of a firm affect cash for a period.

OBJECTIVE OF THE STATEMENT OF CHANGES IN FINANCIAL POSITION

The statement of changes in financial position reports the major sources and uses of cash flowing through a firm during a period of time. Figure 13.3 shows the major sources and uses, which are described below.

1. *Sources — Operations.* The net amount of cash generated from selling goods and providing services is one of the most important sources of funds for a financially healthy company. When assessed over several years, cash provided by operations indicates the extent to which the operating or earnings activities have generated more than is used up. The excess from operations can then be used for dividends, acquisition of buildings and equipment, or repayment of long-term debt as necessary.

FIGURE 13.3
Sources and Uses of Cash

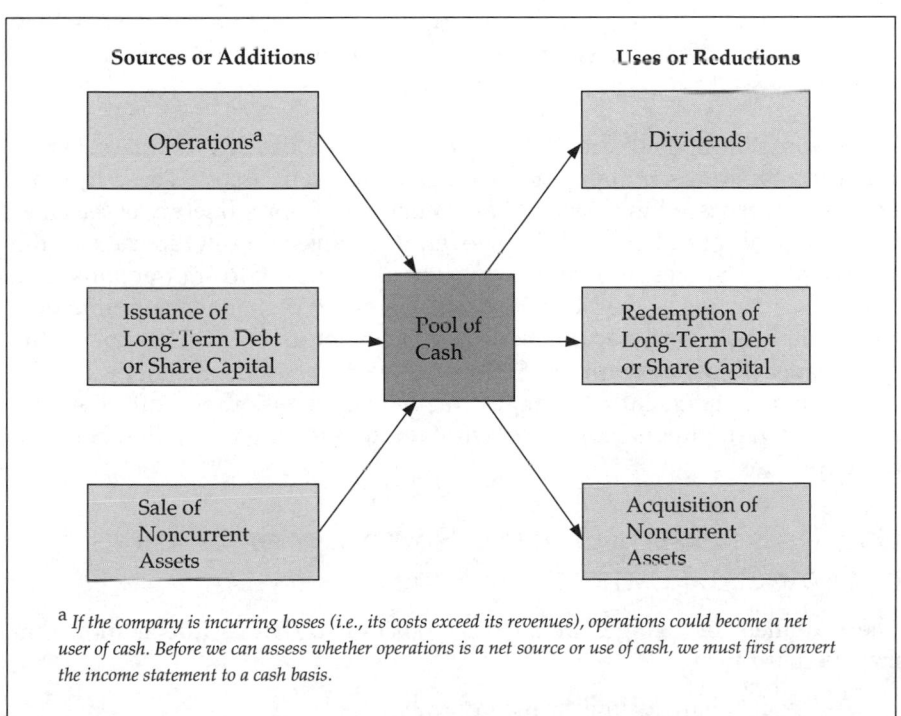

ᵃ *If the company is incurring losses (i.e., its costs exceed its revenues), operations could become a net user of cash. Before we can assess whether operations is a net source or use of cash, we must first convert the income statement to a cash basis.*

2. *Sources — Issuance of Long-Term Debt or Share Capital.* In the long run, a firm must generate most of its cash from operating activities. Potential shareholders are not willing to invest in unprofitable firms. Neither are banks willing to lend large amounts of cash to firms that do not generate profits. A potentially profitable firm finds that it can raise cash by issuing shares to owners or by borrowing. The amount of cash that can be generated by issuing shares or by borrowing is limited, however, by the marketplace's assessment of the firm's prospects.

3. *Sources — Sales of Noncurrent Assets.* The sale of buildings, equipment, and other noncurrent assets increases cash. These sales generally are not a major source of financing for an ongoing firm. The amounts received from the sales are not likely to be sufficient to replace the assets sold.

4. *Uses — Dividends.* Dividends are generally a recurring use of cash. Most publicly held firms are reluctant to omit the payment of dividends, even during a year of poor earnings performance. Because dividends use cash that might otherwise be retained and used elsewhere, they generally increase the need for other forms of financing.

5. *Uses — Redemption of Long-Term Debt or Share Capital.* In most instances, publicly held firms redeem or pay long-term debt at maturity with the proceeds of another debt issue. Thus, these redemptions often have little effect on the *net* change in cash. Some firms also occasionally reacquire, or redeem, their own share capital for various reasons (discussed in Chapter 11).

6. *Uses — Acquisition of Noncurrent Assets.* The acquisition of noncurrent assets, such as buildings and equipment, usually represents the most important continuing use of cash. Such assets must be replaced as they wear out, and additional noncurrent assets must be acquired if a firm is to grow.

Firms sometimes issue long-term debt or shares directly to the seller in acquiring buildings, equipment, or other noncurrent assets. These transactions were discussed in Chapter 8 as exchanges of nonmonetary assets, and technically do not affect cash. However, the transaction is reported in the statement of changes in financial position as though two transactions took place: the issuance of long-term debt or shares for cash, and the immediate use of that cash in the acquisition of noncurrent assets. This is called the **dual transactions assumption**. Such a transaction would normally be disclosed in the statement of changes in financial position as both a source and use of cash of equal amounts, with a note referring to the link between the two items.

USES OF INFORMATION IN THE STATEMENT OF CHANGES IN FINANCIAL POSITION

The statement of changes in financial position provides information that may be used in:

1. Assessing changes in a firm's liquidity.
2. Assessing changes in the structure of a firm's assets and equities.

dual transactions assumption
In presenting the statement of changes in financial position, some transactions not actually involving cash are reported as though cash changed hands, for example, the issue of capital stock in return for land.

Liquidity

Perhaps the most important factor not reported on either the balance sheet or income statement is how the operations of a period affected the liquidity of a firm. It is easy to conclude that increased earnings mean increased cash or other liquid assets. Such a conclusion may not be valid. The successful firm may acquire a new plant and therefore have less cash after a good year than before. On the other hand, increased liquidity can accompany reduced earnings. Consider, for example, a firm that is gradually reducing the scope of its operations. Such a firm is likely to report reduced net income or even losses over time. But because it is not replacing plant and equipment, it is likely to be accumulating cash or other liquid assets.

Structure of Assets and Equities

In addition to providing information about changes in a firm's liquidity during a period, the statement of changes in financial position indicates the major transactions causing changes in the structure of a firm's assets (investments) and its liabilities and shareholders' equity (financing). For example, acquisitions and sales of specific types of assets (buildings, equipment, patents) are reported. Likewise, issues and redemptions of long-term debt and share capital are disclosed. These transactions are difficult to observe by looking at the income statement or the balance sheet or both. For example, the change in the account Buildings and Equipment — Net of Accumulated Depreciation could be attributable to depreciation charges, to acquisition of new buildings and equipment, to disposition of old buildings and equipment, or to a combination of these. The income statement and comparative balance sheets do not provide sufficient information about these three items individually for the reader to disaggregate the net change in the account during the period. A statement of changes in financial position is required to report this information.

"CASH" DEFINED

The *CICA Handbook* defines cash as "cash plus **cash equivalents** net of short-term bank borrowings [emphasis added]."[2] This broader measure gives a more accurate representation of short-term liquidity. To avoid confusion, the phrase **cash position** will be used in this book whenever the CICA definition is employed.

Although the choice of the phrase *cash position* is arbitrary, there is a degree of logical support for its use. The accounting profession has embraced the phrase *statement of financial position*, which is gradually supplanting the traditional phrase *balance sheet*. One of the major functions of this statement is to allow readers to assess the liquidity of the firm. *Cash position* is liquidity under distress conditions. A number of leading Canadian corporations now use the phrase *cash position*.

cash equivalents
Short-term, highly liquid investments that firms acquire with cash in excess of their immediate needs.

cash position
Term used in the statement of changes in financial position to refer to cash plus cash equivalents minus short-term borrowings.

---

[2] *CICA Handbook*, section 1540. Judgment is necessary in deciding what items to include in this algorithm. For instance, if a certificate of deposit was a one-year GIC, noncashable before maturity, it would not be a cash equivalent. Similarly, if a bank note payable was a twelve-month note and not a demand note, it would not be a factor in assessing short-term liquidity.

DISCUSSION CASE 29

Corporate Cash: Why Its Meaning Differs Between Treasurers and Controllers

Everyone knows what cash is. You reach in your pocket, pull out some bills, and that's cash — it's simple. As for money, that's another matter; the monetary aggregates used by economists (M-1, M-2, etc.) are confusing at best. The meaning of cash, as well, is not simple in the corporate world of cash managers (treasurers) and accountants (controllers).

Determining how much cash a corporation has is another task that's not easy. Dictionary definitions of cash are not particularly helpful because they do not take into account the dynamics of either modern cash management or current accounting practices. Also, all corporations do not use the same accounting treatment for cash. The problem of measuring corporate cash is further compounded by the fact that corporate treasurers and controllers use different definitions of cash. These different definitions and different accounting treatments can cause misunderstandings and problems within the corporation, as well as for users of published financial statements.

Different Definitions

Two key objectives of modern corporate cash management are maximization of the return on liquid assets and minimization of the cost of financing the assets used by corporations. The minimization of idle cash balances is basic to the achievement of these objectives. Corporations should either invest all available cash to produce investment income or use cash to reduce debt and the cost of borrowing. One way that corporate cash management groups minimize idle cash is to wait until outstanding checks issued by the corporation are presented for payment at the corporation's banks before depositing money into the bank accounts to cover them.

From a cash management point of view, the objective is to have a bank balance of zero at the end of each day. Banks provide "controlled disbursing" programs to assist corporations in achieving their zero-balance objectives. Many treasurers are so successful at eliminating bank account balances that they are able to consistently maintain a negative account balance (for cash) on the corporation's accounting books.

The negative accounting balance for corporate cash results from the fact that the accepted accounting procedure is to reduce the cash account when checks are issued. When the value of outstanding but uncleared checks exceeds the amount of cash in the corporate bank accounts, the corporation's accounting records show a deficit cash balance. This result is especially likely when a corporation uses a controlled disbursing program to keep bank account balances at zero.

(continued)

(continued)

Public corporations almost always maintain accounting records and financial statements on an accrual basis, in accordance with "generally accepted accounting principles." One of the basis objectives of accrual accounting is to record and report revenues and expenses in the same period in which they are incurred. Standard accounting practice calls for the reduction of the cash account balance and a debit to accounts payable — or some other liability or expense account — when a check is prepared and mailed to the payee. On the other hand, treasury cash management practices recognize a reduction in cash balances only when a bank debits a corporate bank account. The bank's daily reports of cash balances are based upon cash disbursements and do not reflect any outstanding checks that have not been presented for payment. The difference between the treasurer's cash records and the balance in the controller's cash account is simply the timing difference — the number of days it takes for the check to be delivered, deposited, and cleared through the banking system to the company's bank account. In cash management parlance, the dollar amount of outstanding checks is known as "disbursement float."

Deposit float, the mirror image of disbursement float, refers to the receipt of checks rather than the issuance of checks. Generally accepted accounting principles dictate that the accounting cash balance be increased as checks are deposited in the bank. However, the treasurer's cash management staff does not record an increase in cash until the banks have credited the corporate bank accounts with cleared funds.

The preceding sounds basic to anyone familiar with modern corporate cash management practices and accrual accounting. The point is that "cash" takes on different meanings as one moves from the realm of cash management into the world of accounting. If nothing else were involved, these two corporate departments could use different definitions of cash without being concerned about what is being done elsewhere. Unfortunately, neither group can take a myopic view of what cash is. The following section describes a few of the problems that arise from the use of different definitions of cash by treasurers and controllers.

The Problem with Definitions

One of the most important problems associated with the difference in definitions of cash is the economic cost incurred by corporations that are reluctant to publish financial statements showing "bank overdrafts" (outstanding checks in excess of bank balances) on their balance sheet. It is very common for senior corporate executives to establish, as a cash target, the amount of cash they want to show on published financial statements. Unfortunately for these executives, the cash figure cannot be buried in financial statements; U.S. accounting rules require that "cash" be shown on corporate balance sheets as a separate line item.

Under certain conditions, cash can be combined with short-term
(continued)

(continued)

investments, but it may not be combined with other current asset items in published financial statements. Also, the accounting profession insists that the dollar figure reported as cash should be the amount available for the payment of debts — and should not include bank account balances against which checks are outstanding.

It is not entirely clear why most corporate executives believe that a positive cash figure is so desirable. A few large corporations report bank overdrafts without any apparent ill effects. In fact, those familiar with modern cash management practices know that a large positive cash figure on a corporate balance sheet may be a symptom of either poor cash management or window dressing. One reason that has been advanced to justify cash window dressing is that both investors and lending institutions view with disfavor those companies that show either a zero cash balance or bank overdrafts in published financials. However, informal discussions with both investment professionals and bankers suggest that they do not downgrade corporations that report a zero cash figure or book overdrafts. Investment professionals do look at financial ratios, such as the current ratio and quick ratio that include cash, but they do not focus on cash as an important item. If a company's financial ratios are of an investment grade, then investment professionals are not concerned about bank overdrafts on the balance sheet.

Similarly, commercial banks take many objective and subjective factors into account as a part of their loan approval process. In their eyes, the presence of bank overdrafts in financial statements is not sufficient to affect the lending decision. However, a zero cash or overdraft position may be the symptom of fundamental liquidity or profit problems that would cause a bank to reject a loan request.

There is a very real economic cost associated with cash window dressing in published financial statements. In corporations that wish to show a particular balance in the cash amount at the end of financial reporting periods, the treasurer's staff must do two things: First, they must estimate how large a cash deposit will be required to offset the disbursement float on the last day of the reporting period. Second, they must obtain the cash and put it in the bank for at least one day (longer if weekends or holidays follow the end of the accounting period). This idle cash has an economic cost. That is, investments must be foregone or interest must be paid on borrowed funds.

In some cases, the cost can be significant. For example, the cost of $100 million for two days four times per year at 10 percent per year is approximately $219,000. This figure does not include the cost of information systems and staff time.

Some Solutions

Corporations deal with the problem of the economic cost of cash

(continued)

(continued)

window dressing in different ways. A few companies generate improved reported cash balances by changing their accounting treatment rather than by actually increasing the bank balances. These companies have been successful in persuading their accountants and auditors to add disbursement float back to the cash account at the end of the financial reporting period. This adjustment on the asset side of the balance sheet must be accompanied by an offsetting adjustment to liabilities. In some cases, the liability item is descriptive (e.g., "Outstanding Checks in Excess of Bank Balances"), but other companies include the addition to liabilities in a nondescriptive account such as "Accounts Payable."

Making payments with drafts is another way to deal with the problem of the difference between cash and accrual accounting. A draft is a written order (by the company as drawer) instructing a bank (the drawee) to pay a third party (the payee). Legally, a draft is not the same as a check; however, in appearance, a draft is almost indistinguishable from a check. The difference is that a draft is drawn against a bank rather than against a company's bank account. The company need not pay a draft until it is approved by the corporation, honored by the bank, and charged against the corporation's bank account. Consequently, accrual accounting practices do not require a reduction in the cash account balance until the company is charged by the bank.

The disadvantage of drafts (vs. checks) is that the companies issuing them are responsible for verifying signatures and approving the bank's payments to the payees. The verification of signatures on tens of thousands or millions of drafts can be a labor-intensive and expensive activity. However, companies can separately authorize their banks to verify the signatures on drafts. Because signature verification is a normal bank service, this contractual shifting of responsibility for signature verification results in a per-item cost equal to the cost of checks.

How then can the differing objectives and accounting treatments for cash be accommodated with a minimum of effort and cost?

- Continue the current cash management and accounting practices.
- Discontinue window dressing for published financial statements.
- Use drafts rather than checks to pay obligations.
- Adjust the accounting practice to add back issued but uncleared checks to the accounting book balance at the end of financial reporting periods.

References

Reprinted with permission from Richard P. Kramer, "Corporate Cash: Why Its Meaning Differs Between Treasurers and Controllers," *Financial Executive*, Jan./Feb. 1988, copyright 1988 by Financial Executives Institute, Morristown, New Jersey.

Discussion Question

What is "cash window dressing" and why do corporate financial managers engage in it?

STATEMENT FORMAT

Since the CICA introduced the new recommendations for the statement of changes in financial position in 1986, there has been a proliferation of formats for the statement. In our opinion, many of these variations are punitive to readers because sources and applications of cash are mixed together and the statements employ extensive use of bracketed figures.

We believe the format shown in Figure 13.4 displays the clearest presentation, and we will use it consistently throughout this book.

FIGURE 13.4
The Every Firm Statement of Changes in Financial Position
For the year ended 19XX

Cash Provided by		
Operations[a]	$	
Financing Activities	$	
Investing Activities	$	
		$
Cash Applied to		
Financing Activities	$	
Investing Activities	$	
Dividends	$	
		$
Increase (Decrease) in Cash Position[b]		$
Cash Position Beginning of Year		$
Cash Position End of Year		$

[a]Schedule of reconciliation of net income to cash flow provided here.
[b]Cash position is defined as cash plus cash equivalents net of short-term bank borrowings.

ANALYSIS OF THE EFFECTS OF TRANSACTIONS ON CASH

ALGEBRAIC FORMULATION

The effects of various transactions on cash might be seen by re-examining the accounting equation. In doing so, the following notation is used:

$\quad$ C— cash
NCA— noncash assets
$\quad$ L— liabilities
$\quad$ SE— shareholders' equity
$\quad$ Δ— the change in an item, whether positive (an increase) or negative (a decrease) from the beginning of a period to the end of the period.

The accounting equation states that:

$$\text{Assets} = \text{Liabilities} + \text{Shareholders' Equity}$$
$$C + NCA = L + SE$$

Furthermore, this equation must be true for balance sheets constructed at both the start of the period and the end of the period. If the start-of-the-period and end-of-the-period balance sheets maintain the accounting equation, the following equation must also be valid:

$$\Delta C + \Delta NCA = \Delta L + \Delta SE$$

By rearranging terms in this equation, we obtain the equation for changes in cash:

$$\Delta C = \Delta L + \Delta SE - \Delta NCA$$

The left-hand side of the above equation represents the change in cash. The right-hand side of the equation, reflecting changes in all noncash accounts, must also be equal in amount to the net change in cash. The equation states that increases (decreases) in cash (left-hand side) are equal to, or caused by, the increases in liabilities plus the increases (decreases) in shareholders' equity less the increases (decreases) in noncash assets (right-hand side). Next, we illustrate how the changes in the accounts on the right-hand side bring about the change in cash on the left-hand side.

ILLUSTRATION OF TRANSACTIONS ANALYSIS

We can analyze some typical transactions to demonstrate how the equation is maintained and how cash is affected.

Assume that the following events occur during Year 4 for the Banks Corporation, considered earlier in Exhibit 13.1.

1. Merchandise costing $70,000 is acquired on account.
2. Merchandise costing $60,000 is sold to customers on account for $125,000.
3. Salaries of $19,000 are paid in cash.
4. Other expenses of $13,000 are paid in cash.
5. Cash collections of customers' accounts total $90,000.
6. Cash payments to suppliers of merchandise total $50,000.
7. Salaries earned but not paid as of December 31, Year 4 are accrued, $1,000.
8. Other expenses not paid as of December 31, Year 4 are accrued, $2,000.
9. Depreciation for Year 4 is recorded, $10,000.
10. Long-term debt is issued for cash, $100,000.
11. Dividends of $10,000 are declared and paid.
12. Equipment costing $125,000 is acquired for cash.

The effects of these transactions on cash are analyzed in Exhibit 13.2. Cash decreased by $27,000 during Year 4. Both sides of the equation show this net change. The net change in cash during a period (left-hand side of the equation at the top of Exhibit 13.2) can therefore be explained, or analyzed, by focusing on the changes in noncash accounts (right-hand side of the equation). For Banks Corporation, the net decrease in cash position of $27,000 is explained as follows.

Increases in Cash Position:	
From Operations	$ 8,000
From Issuing Long-Term Debt	100,000
Total Increases	$108,000
Decreases in Cash Position:	
For Dividends	$ 10,000
For Acquisition of Equipment	125,000
Total Decreases	$135,000
Net Decrease in Cash Position	$ 27,000

Note that the recording of depreciation for the period does not affect cash. A noncash asset is decreased and shareholders' equity is decreased. Cash is not affected. (Cash was reduced in the period in which the noncurrent asset was purchased.)

The information necessary to prepare the statement of changes in financial position could be developed using the transactions analysis approach illustrated in Exhibit 13.2. This approach quickly becomes cumbersome, however, as the number of transactions increases. The next section describes an alternative procedure for preparing the statement of changes in financial position that uses the T-account discussed in previous chapters.

PREPARATION OF THE STATEMENT OF CHANGES IN FINANCIAL POSITION

As with the balance sheet and income statement, knowing how to prepare a statement of changes in financial position is not essential in order to use it effectively. Nevertheless, learning how to construct this statement facilitates understanding of its rationale and content. This section presents a step-by-step procedure for preparing the statement of changes in financial position. This procedure is then illustrated using the transactions of Banks Corporation for Year 4.

Unlike the balance sheet and income statement, the statement of changes in financial position is not generated as a regular output of a firm's record-keeping system. The statement of changes in financial position is usually prepared with a work sheet or other analysis after the balance sheet and income statement have been prepared.

THE PROCEDURE AND AN ILLUSTRATION

Step 1   Obtain balance sheets for the beginning and end of the period covered by the statement of changes in financial position. Exhibit 13.3 presents the comparative balance sheets of Banks Corporation for December 31, Year 3 and Year 4.

Step 2   Prepare a T-account work sheet. An example of such a T-account work sheet is shown in Exhibit 13.4. At the top of the work sheet is a master T-account titled Cash Position.[3] Note that this T-account has sections

---

[3] The account title reflects the expanded definition of "cash" that is used by the CICA (see footnote 2).

EXHIBIT 13.2
Analysis of the Effects of Banks Corporation's Transactions
During Year 4 on Cash and Noncash Accounts (amounts in thousands)

Transactions	Changes in Cash ΔC	=	ΔL	+	ΔSE	−	ΔNCA
					Effect on Cash		
					Changes in Noncash Accounts		
(1) Merchandise costing $70,000 is acquired on account, increasing a noncash asset and a noncash liability	$ 0	=	$ 70	+	0	−	(+$ 70)
(2) Merchandise costing $60,000 is sold to customers on account for $125,000, increasing a noncash asset, accounts receivable, by $125,000, decreasing the noncash asset, inventory, by $60,000, and increasing shareholders' equity by $65,000 (= $125,000 − $60,000)	0	=	0	+	$65	−	(+$125) (−$ 60)
(3) Salaries of $19,000 are paid in cash, decreasing cash and shareholders' equity	(−$ 19)	=	0	+	(−$19)	−	0
(4) Other expenses of $13,000 are paid in cash, decreasing cash and shareholders' equity	(−$ 13)	=	0	+	(−$13)	−	0
(5) Cash collections of customers' accounts total $90,000, increasing cash and decreasing the noncash asset, accounts receivable	$ 90	=	0	+	0	−	(−$ 90)
(6) Payments to suppliers of merchandise total $50,000, decreasing cash and a liability	(−$ 50)	=	(−$ 50)	+	0	−	0
(7) Salaries of $1,000 earned but not paid as of December 31, Year 4 are accrued, increasing a liability and decreasing shareholders' equity	0	=	$ 1	+	(−$ 1)	−	0
(8) Other expenses of $2,000 not paid as of December 31, Year 4 are accrued, increasing a liability and decreasing shareholders' equity	0	=	$ 2	+	(−$ 2)	−	0
(9) Depreciation for Year 4 of $10,000 is recorded, decreasing shareholders' equity and noncash assets	0	=	0	+	(−$10)	−	(−$ 10)
Total from operations	$ 8	=	$ 23	+	$20	−	$ 35
(10) Long-term debt is issued for $100,000, increasing cash and a liability	$100	=	$100	+	0	−	0
(11) Dividends of $10,000 are declared and paid, decreasing cash and shareholders' equity	(−$ 10)	=	0	+	(−$10)	−	0
(12) Equipment costing $125,000 is acquired for cash, decreasing cash and increasing noncash assets	(−$125)	=	0	+	0	−	(+$125)
Net change in cash and noncash accounts	−$ 27	=	$123	+	$10	−	$160

labelled Operations, Financing, Investing, and Dividends. Transactions affecting cash during the period are classified under one of these headings to aid in the preparation of the statement of changes in financial position. This procedure is explained later in this section. The beginning and ending

EXHIBIT 13.3
BANKS CORPORATION
Comparative Balance Sheets for December 31,
Year 3 and Year 4 (amounts in thousands)

	December 31, Year 4	December 31, Year 3
ASSETS		
Current Assets:		
Cash	$ 3	$ 30
Accounts Receivable	55	20
Merchandise Inventory	50	40
Total Current Assets	$108	$ 90
Noncurrent Assets:		
Buildings and Equipment (Cost)	$225	$100
Accumulated Depreciation	(40)	(30)
Total Noncurrent Assets	$185	$ 70
Total Assets	$293	$160
EQUITIES		
Current Liabilities:		
Accounts Payable — Merchandise Suppliers	$ 50	$ 30
Accounts Payable — Other Suppliers	12	10
Salaries Payable	6	5
Total Current Liabilities	$ 68	$ 45
Noncurrent Liabilities:		
Bonds Payable	$100	$ 0
Shareholders' Equity:		
Common Shares	$100	$100
Retained Earnings	25	15
Total Owners' Equity	$125	$115
Total Equities	$293	$160

amounts of cash are then entered in the master T-account. The beginning and ending amounts of cash for Banks Corporation are $30,000 and $3,000, respectively. The check marks indicate that the figures are balances. The number at the top of the T-account is the opening balance; the one at the bottom is the closing balance. Note that the T-account Cash Position is another means of expressing the left-hand side of the equation for changes in cash in Exhibit 13.2.

After the T-account for Cash Position has been prepared (as at the top of Exhibit 13.4), the work sheet is completed by preparing T-accounts for *each* noncash asset and liability and shareholders' equity account. Enter the beginning and ending balances in each account for the period as given in Exhibit 13.3. The lower portion of Exhibit 13.4 shows the T-accounts for each noncash account. Note that the sum of the changes in these individual T-accounts is another means of expressing the right-hand side of the equation for changes in cash in Exhibit 13.2.

Step 3 Explain the change in the master cash account between the beginning and end of the period by explaining, or accounting for, the change in

EXHIBIT 13.4
Preliminary T-Account Work Sheet for Banks Corporation

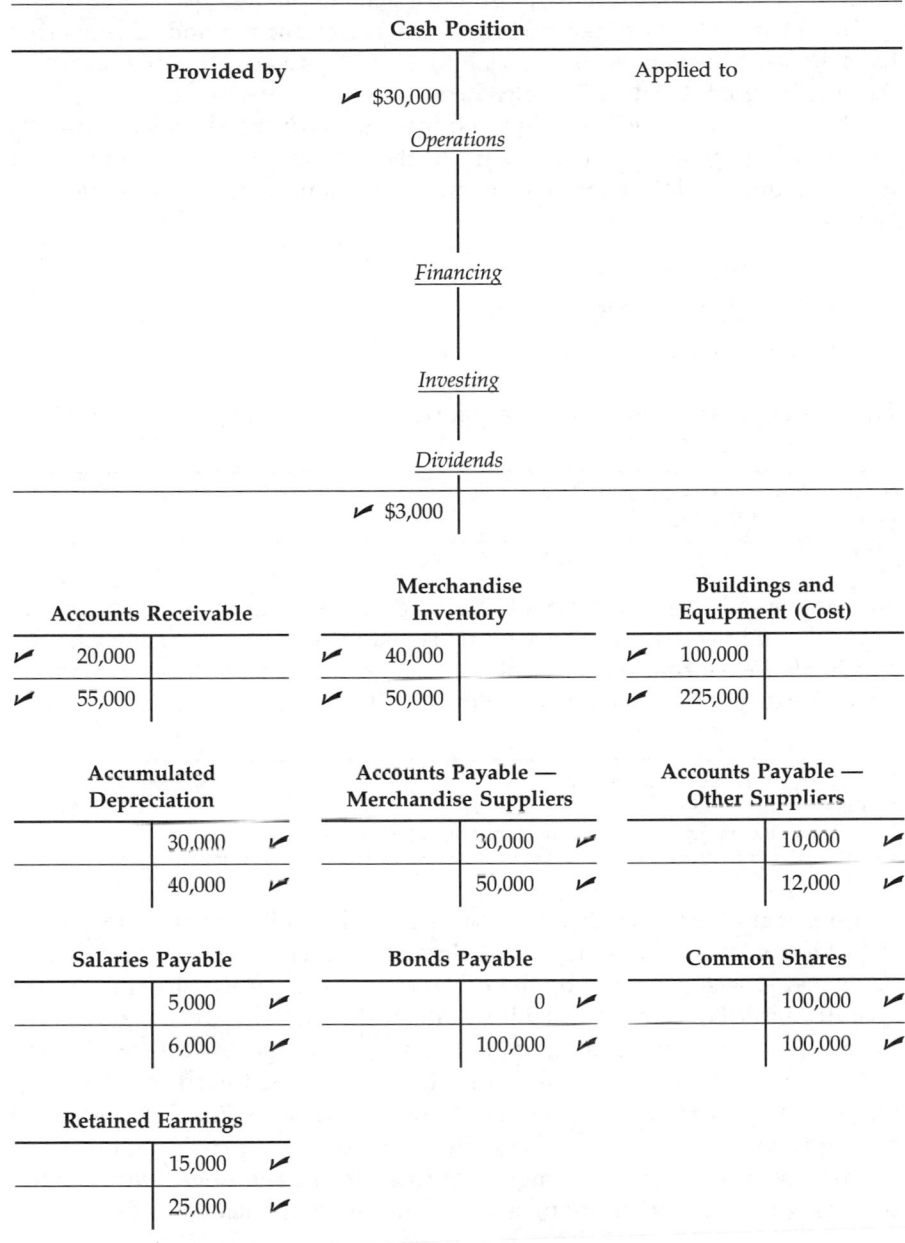

Cash Position

Provided by		Applied to
	✓ $30,000	
	Operations	
	Financing	
	Investing	
	Dividends	
	✓ $3,000	

Accounts Receivable		Merchandise Inventory		Buildings and Equipment (Cost)	
✓ 20,000		✓ 40,000		✓ 100,000	
✓ 55,000		✓ 50,000		✓ 225,000	

Accumulated Depreciation		Accounts Payable — Merchandise Suppliers		Accounts Payable — Other Suppliers	
	30,000 ✓		30,000 ✓		10,000 ✓
	40,000 ✓		50,000 ✓		12,000 ✓

Salaries Payable		Bonds Payable		Common Shares	
	5,000 ✓		0 ✓		100,000 ✓
	6,000 ✓		100,000 ✓		100,000 ✓

Retained Earnings	
	15,000 ✓
	25,000 ✓

analytical entries Entries made on a work sheet rather than in the formal accounting records for the purpose of explaining (and reconciling) the transactions supporting the statement of changes in financial position.

the balance of each noncash account during the period. This step is accomplished by *reconstructing the entries originally recorded in the accounts during the period*. The reconstructed entries are written in the appropriate T-accounts on the work sheet. These reconstructed entries are called **analytical entries**. Once the net change in each of the noncash accounts has been accounted for, sufficient information will have been generated to account

T-account method
A popular method of preparing the statement of changes in financial position that involves constructing T-accounts as surrogates for the underlying general ledger accounts and then analyzing the changes to these T-accounts.

for the net change in cash. That is, if the changes in the right-hand side of the cash equation have been explained, the causes of the changes in cash itself on the left-hand side will also have been explained.

These three steps are referred to as the **T-account method** of preparing the statement of changes in financial position. There are other methods, but these will be left to more advanced courses.

The process of reconstructing the transactions during the year is usually easiest if information supplementary to the balance sheet is accounted for first. Assume the following information concerning Banks Corporation for Year 4:

1. Net income is $20,000.

2. Depreciation expense is $10,000.

3. Dividends declared and paid total $10,000.

The analytical entry to record the information concerning net income is:

(1) Cash Position (Operations — Net Income)	$20,000	
Retained Earnings		$20,000

To understand this entry, review the process of recording revenues and expenses and the closing entries for those temporary accounts from Chapter 3. All of the journal entries that together record the process of earning $20,000 net income are equivalent to the following single journal entry:

Net Assets (= Assets − Liabilities)	$20,000	
Retained Earnings		$20,000
Summary entry equivalent to recording earnings of $20,000.		

The summary journal entry debits Net Assets. The initial assumption at this stage of preparing the statement of changes in financial position is that all of the net assets generated by the earnings process were cash. Thus, in the analytic entry (1) above, the debit results in showing a provisional increase in cash from operations in an amount equal to net income for the period.

Not all of the items recognized as expenses and deducted in calculating net income, however, decrease cash (refer to Exhibit 13.1). The portion of the expenses that does not affect cash is added to the provisional increase in cash to calculate the net amount of cash from operations. One expense not using cash is depreciation, as illustrated in analytical entry (2).

(2) Cash Position (Sources: Operations — Depreciation Expense Addback)	$10,000	
Accumulated Depreciation		$10,000

Because depreciation expense was deducted in calculating net income but did not reduce cash, the amount of depreciation expense must be added back to net income in calculating the amount of cash provided by operations. A more complete explanation is provided on pages 821 to 824.

The supplementary information concerning dividends of $10,000 declared and paid is recorded in analytical entry (3).

---

(3) Retained Earnings $10,000
        Cash Position (Uses: Dividends) $10,000
      Dividends reduce retained earnings and cash.

Dividends create a classification problem within the operating/investing/financing format. Some firms treat dividends as a financing activity, some as an operating activity, and some as a separate category altogether. Because the logic supporting their inclusion as operating or financing activities is weak, we support the classification of dividends as a separate item on the statement of changes in financial position.

Once the supplementary information has been reflected in the T-accounts, it is necessary to make inferences about the reasons for the remaining changes in the noncash accounts on the balance sheet. (If the statement of changes in financial position were being prepared for an actual firm, such inferences might not be necessary, because sufficient information regarding the change in each account would likely be available from the firm's accounting records.) The changes in noncash accounts are explained in the order of their appearance.

The Accounts Receivable account shows an increase of $35,000. The analytical entry to record this assumed information in the work sheet is:

---

(4) Accounts Receivable $35,000
        Cash Position (Uses: Operations — Subtractions) $35,000

The operations of the period generated sales. Not all of these sales resulted in an increase in cash. Some of the sales resulted in an increase in Accounts Receivable. Because we start the statement of changes in financial position with net income, in deriving the amount of cash from operations, we must *subtract that portion of revenues not producing cash* (that is, the excess of sales on account over cash collections from customers).

The next noncash account showing a change is that for Merchandise Inventory. That account shows an increase during the year of $10,000. As the operations of the firm have expanded, so has the amount carried in inventory. The analytical entry of the work sheet to explain the change in Merchandise Inventory is:

---

(5) Merchandise Inventory $10,000
        Cash Position (Uses: Operations — Subtractions) $10,000

Banks Corporation found it necessary to increase the amount of inventory carried to make possible increased future sales. An increase in inventory is ordinarily an operating use of cash. Because we start the statement of changes in financial position with net income, in deriving cash from operations, we must subtract from net income the incremental investment in inventories during the year (that is, the excess of purchases over the cost of goods sold).

The next noncash account showing a change is that for Buildings and Equipment (Cost). The Buildings and Equipment (Cost) account shows a net increase of \$125,000 (= \$225,000 − \$100,000). Because we have no other information, we must assume or deduce that buildings and equipment costing \$125,000 were acquired during the year. The analytical entry is:

(6) Buildings and Equipment (Cost)	\$125,000	
Cash Position (Uses: Investing — Acquisitions of Buildings and Equipment)		\$125,000

Acquisition of buildings and equipment is a nonoperating use of cash.

The next noncash account showing a change is that for Accounts Payable — Merchandise Suppliers. As the amounts carried in inventory have increased, so have the amounts owned to suppliers of inventory. The analytical entry to explain the increase in the amount of Accounts Payable — Merchandise Suppliers is:

(7) Cash Position (Sources: Operations — Additions)	\$20,000	
Accounts Payable — Merchandise Suppliers		\$20,000

Ordinarily, acquiring inventory requires cash. Suppliers who allow a firm to pay later for goods (and services) received now are effectively supplying the firm with cash. Thus, an increase in the amount of accounts payable for inventory results from a transaction in which inventory increased but cash did not decrease, which is equivalent to saying that an increase in payables provides cash, even if only temporarily. The increase in cash resulting from increased payables for inventory is an operating source of funds.

The next noncash account showing a change is Accounts Payable — Other Suppliers. As the scope of operations has increased, so has the amount owed to others. The analytical entry to explain the increase in the amount of Accounts Payable — Other Suppliers is:

(8) Cash Position (Sources: Operations — Additions)	\$2,000	
Accounts Payable — Other Suppliers		\$2,000

The reasoning behind this entry is the same as that for entry (7). Creditors who permit a firm to owe them effectively provide cash. The same reasoning applies to an increased amount of Salaries Payable, the next noncash account showing a change. The analytical entry to record the increase in Salaries Payable is:

(9) Cash Position (Sources: Operations — Additions)	\$1,000	
Salaries Payable		\$1,000

Employees who do not demand immediate payment for salaries earned have provided their employer with cash, at least temporarily.

The final noncash account showing a change not yet explained is Bonds Payable. It shows a net increase of $100,000 for the year. Because no other information is given, it must be assumed that bonds were issued during the year. The analytical entry is:

(10) Cash Position (Sources: Financing — Bond Issue)	$100,000	
Bonds Payable		$100,000

Exhibit 13.5 presents the completed T-account work sheet for Banks Corporation for Year 4. All changes in the noncash T-accounts have been explained with the ten entries. If the work is correct, the causes of the change in the Cash Position account will have been presented in the entries in the master Cash Position account.

Step 4 The final step is the preparation of a formal statement of changes in financial position. Exhibit 13.6 presents the statement for Banks Corporation. The statement is prepared directly from the information provided in the master T-account for Cash Position in the completed work sheet.

The first item disclosed in the statement is the amount of cash generated by operations. In deriving cash from operations, published annual reports typically start with net income. Expenses not using cash are then added to net income, and revenues not providing cash are subtracted to obtain cash from operations. If the reconciliation of net income to cash provided by operations is placed in a separate schedule below the main statement, a much "cleaner" looking statement results. Exhibit 13.6 illustrates this format. Because depreciation expense is added to net income to calculate cash provided by operations, some readers of financial statements incorrectly conclude that depreciation expense is a source of cash. As Exhibit 13.2 illustrated, the recording of depreciation expense does not affect cash. A noncash asset is decreased and a shareholders' equity account is decreased. Cash is not affected. Cash from operations results from selling goods and services to customers. If no sales are made, there will be no cash provided by operations regardless how large the depreciation charge may be.

A definition of the components of Cash Position should always be provided somewhere on the face of the statement.

Depreciation Is Not a Source of Funds

To demonstrate that depreciation is not a source of funds, refer to the income statement of Banks Corporation (Exhibit 13.1) and the cash flow from the operations section of the statement of changes in financial position (Exhibit 13.6). Exhibit 13.7 reproduces them in condensed form. Suppose that depreciation for Year 4 had been $25,000 rather than $10,000. Then, the condensed income statement and cash flow from operations would appear as in Exhibit 13.8. Note that the total cash flow from operations remains $8,000, which is the difference between receipts from revenues and all expenses that did use cash. The only effects on cash of transactions involv-

EXHIBIT 13.5
Completed T-Account Work Sheet for Banks Corporation

		Cash Position		
Provided by				**Applied to**
		✓ $30,000		

Operations

Net Income	(1)	20,000	35,000 (4)	Increased Accounts Receivable
Depreciation Expense	(2)	10,000	10,000 (5)	Increased Merchandise
Increased Accounts Payable				Inventory
to Merchandise Suppliers	(7)	20,000		
Increased Accounts Payable				
to Other Suppliers	(8)	2,000		
Increased Salaries Payable	(9)	1,000		

Financing

Bonds Issued	(10)	100,000	

Investing

	125,000 (6)	Acquisition of Buildings
		and Equipment

Dividends

10,000 (3)	

✓ $3,000	

Accounts Receivable			Merchandise Inventory			Buildings and Equipment (Cost)	
✓ 20,000		✓ 40,000		✓ 100,000	
(4) 35,000		(5) 10,000		(6) 125,000	
✓ 55,000		✓ 50,000		✓ 225,000	

Accumulated Depreciation			Accounts Payable — Merchandise Suppliers			Accounts Payable — Other Suppliers	
	30,000 ✓		30,000 ✓		10,000 ✓
	10,000 (2)		20,000 (7)		2,000 (8)
	40,000 ✓		50,000 ✓		12,000 ✓

Salaries Payable			Bonds Payable			Retained Earnings			
	5,000 ✓		0 ✓			15,000 ✓
	1,000 (9)		100,000 (10)	(3)	10,000	20,000 (1)
	6,000 ✓		100,000 ✓			25,000 ✓

ing long-term assets are that (1) cash is typically used when a long-term asset is acquired, and (2) cash is provided when the asset is sold.

An alternative procedure for deriving cash flow from operations is to list all revenue items that provide cash and then subtract all expense items that use cash. The right-hand column of Exhibit 13.1 illustrates this

EXHIBIT 13.6
BANKS CORPORATION
Statement of Changes in Financial Position
For the Year Ended December 31, 19X4

Cash Provided by	
Operations[a]	$ 8,000
Investing Activities	—
Financial Activities	
Sale of bonds	100,000
	$108,000
Cash Applied to	
Investing Activities	
Acquisition of plant assets	$125,000
Financing Activities	—
Dividends	10,000
	$135,000
Net Decrease in Cash Position[b]	$(27,000)
Cash Position Beginning of Year	30,000
Cash Position End of Year	$ 3,000

[a]Cash provided by operations:

Net Income	$ 20,000
Add (deduct) noncash items	
Depreciation expense	10,000
Working Capital Accounts	
Cash provided by net increases in accounts payable and salaries payable	23,000
Cash applied to net increases in accounts receivable and inventory	(45,000)
Cash Provided by Operations	$ 8,000

[b]Cash Position is defined as cash plus cash equivalents net of short-term bank borrowings.

EXHIBIT 13.7
BANKS CORPORATION
Year 4
Depreciation $10,000

Income Statement		**Cash Flow from Operations**	
Revenues	$125,000	Net Income	$20,000
Expenses Except Depreciation	(95,000)	Additions:	
	$ 30,000	Depreciation	10,000
Depreciation Expense	(10,000)	Other	23,000
		Subtractions	(45,000)
		Cash Flow Provided by	
Net Income	$ 20,000	Operations	$ 8,000

approach. This alternative presentation is appealing because depreciation expense does not appear as an element in the calculation of cash flow provided by operations. The latter presentation, although acceptable, is rarely used in published financial statements. If this approach were followed for Banks, cash flow from operations would be computed as follows.

Collections from Customers		
Opening balance Accounts Receivable	$ 20,000	
+ Sales	125,000	
− Receivables at end of period	(55,000)	
		$90,000
Payments to Suppliers and Creditors		
(from data on p. 813, $19,000 + $13,000 + $50,000)		($82,000)
Cash Flow from Operations		$ 8,000

EXHIBIT 13.8
BANKS CORPORATION
Year 4
Depreciation $25,000

Income Statement		Cash Flow from Operations	
Revenues	$125,000	Net Income	$ 5,000
Expenses Except Depreciation	(95,000)	Additions:	
	$ 30,000	Depreciation	25,000
Depreciation Expense	(25,000)	Other	23,000
		Subtractions	(45,000)
		Cash Flow Provided by	
Net Income	$ 5,000	Operations	$ 8,000

EXTENSION OF THE ILLUSTRATION

The illustration for Banks Corporation considered so far in this chapter is simpler than the typical published statement of changes in financial position in at least four respects:

1. There were only a few balance sheet accounts whose changes are to be explained.

2. Several types of more complex transactions that affect the source of cash from operations were not involved.

3. Each transaction involved only one debit and one credit.

4. Each explanation of a noncash account change involved only one analytical entry on the work sheet, except for the Retained Earnings account.

Suppose that the firm sold some of its buildings and equipment during the year. Assume that the firm disposes of existing buildings and equipment at their book value; the cash proceeds from disposition are equal to acquisition cost less accumulated depreciation of the assets. With this assumption, there will be no gain or loss on disposition.

Reconsider the Banks Corporation example with the following new information. Banks Corporation sold some equipment during Year 4. This equipment cost $10,000 and was sold for $3,000 at a time when accumulated depreciation on the equipment sold was $7,000. The actual entry made during the year to record the sale of the equipment was as follows:

Cash	$3,000	
Accumulated Depreciation	7,000	
Buildings and Equipment (Cost)		$10,000
Journal entry for sale of equipment.		

Assume that the comparative balance sheets as shown in Exhibit 13.3 are correct and thus that the net decrease in cash for Year 4 is still $27,000. The entries in the T-accounts must be altered to reflect this new information. The following entry in the T-account work sheets would be required to recognize the effect of the sale of equipment:

(1a) Cash Position (Sources — Sale of Equipment)	$3,000	
Accumulated Depreciation	7,000	
Buildings and Equipment (Cost)		$10,000

The debit to Cash Position (Sources: Sale of Equipment) shows the proceeds of the sale.

As a result of entry (1a), the T-accounts for Buildings and Equipment (Cost) and Accumulated Depreciation would appear as follows:

Buildings and Equipment (Cost)				**Accumulated Depreciation**	
✔ 100,000				30,000	✔
	10,000	(1a)	(1a)	7,000	
✔ 225,000				40,000	✔

When the time comes to explain the change in the account Buildings and Equipment (Cost), the T-account indicates that there is an increase of $125,000 and a credit entry (1a) of $10,000 to recognize the sale of equipment. The net increase in the Buildings and Equipment (Cost) account can be accounted for, given the decrease already entered, only by assuming that new buildings and equipment have been acquired during the period for $135,000.

The reconstructed entry to complete the explanation of the change in this account would be as follows:

(6a) Buildings and Equipment (Cost)	$135,000	
Cash Position (Uses: Acquisition of		
Buildings and Equipment)		$135,000

Likewise, when the change in the T-account for Accumulated Depreciation is explained, there is a net credit change of $10,000 and a debit entry (1a) of $7,000 to recognize the sale. Thus, the depreciation charge for Year 4 must have been $17,000. The reconstructed entry to complete the explanation of the change in the Accumulated Depreciation account would be as follows on page 826.

| (2a) Cash Position (Source — Depreciation Expense Addback) | $17,000 | |
| Accumulated Depreciation | | $17,000 |

Exhibit 13.9 presents a revised T-account work sheet for Banks Corporation incorporating the new information on the sale of equipment.

EXHIBIT 13.9
Revised T-Account Work Sheet for Banks Corporation

Cash Position					
Provided by			**Applied to**		
		✔ $30,000			
		Operations			
Net Income	(1)	20,000	35,000	(4)	Increased Accounts Receivable
Depreciation Expense	(2a)	17,000	10,000	(5)	Increased Merchandise Inventory
Increased Accounts Payable to Merchandise Suppliers	(7)	20,000			
Increased Accounts Payable to Other Suppliers	(8)	2,000			
Increased Salaries Payable	(9)	1,000			
		Financing			
Bonds Issued	(10)	100,000			
		Investing			
Sale of Equipment	(1a)	3,000	135,000	(6a)	Acquisition of Buildings and Equipment
		Dividends			
			10,000	(3)	Dividends Declared and Paid
		✔ $3,000			

Accounts Receivable				Merchandise Inventory				Buildings and Equipment (Cost)			
✔	20,000			✔	40,000			✔	100,000		
(4)	35,000			(5)	10,000			(6a)	135,000	10,000	(1a)
✔	55,000			✔	50,000			✔	225,000		

Accumulated Depreciation				Accounts Payable — Merchandise Suppliers				Accounts Payable — Other Suppliers			
		30,000	✔			30,000	✔			10,000	✔
(1a)	7,000	17,000	(2a)			20,000	(7)			2,000	(8)
		40,000	✔			50,000	✔			12,000	✔

Salaries Payable				Bonds Payable				Retained Earnings			
		5,000	✔			0	✔			15,000	✔
		1,000	(9)			100,000	(10)	(3)	10,000	20,000	(1)
		6,000	✔			100,000	✔			25,000	✔

ANALYSIS OF STATEMENT OF CHANGES IN FINANCIAL POSITION

The principal questions that the statement of changes in financial position is designed to answer include the following:

1. What is the relation between the various sources of cash (operations, new financing, sale of noncurrent assets)?

2. What is the relation between the various uses of cash (dividends, reduction in financing, acquisition of noncurrent assets)?

3. What is the relation between the total sources and the total uses of cash?

In analyzing the statement of changes in financial position, it is often useful to express each source as a percentage of total sources and each use as a percentage of total uses. Such an analysis appears in Exhibit 13.10 for General Products Limited. Because the percentages for any particular year can be significantly affected by a large debt or common stock issue in that year, it is often useful to combine the data for several years, as is done in the far-right column of Exhibit 13.10.

EXHIBIT 13.10
GENERAL PRODUCTS LIMITED
Statement of Changes in Financial Position
(amounts in millions)

	19X2		19X1		19X0		Combined	
Cash Provided by								
Operations	$1,963	83.0%	$2,322	88.6%	$1,742	79.0%	$6,027	83.8%
Financing Activities	258	10.9	198	7.5	289	13.1	745	10.4
Investing Activities	143	6.0	102	3.9	173	7.8	418	5.8
Total Sources	$2,364	100.0%	$2,622	100.0%	$2,204	100.0%	$7,190	100.0%
Cash Applied to								
Dividends	$ 670	22.6%	$ 624	24.9%	$ 570	25.8%	$1,864	24.6%
Reduction in Financing	214	7.2	253	13.6	582	26.4	1,049	13.8
Investing Activities	2,077	70.1	1,543	61.5	1,055	47.8	4,675	61.6
Total Uses	$2,961	100.0%	$2,420	100.0%	$2,207	100.0%	$7,588	100.0%

Note the following regarding General Products Limited:

1. Approximately 84 percent of the funds needed over the three-year period were generated from operations. Such a percentage is characteristic of a financially healthy firm.

2. Approximately 60 percent of the funds used were for the acquisition of plant, equipment, and other noncurrent assets. Such percentages are likewise typical of a manufacturing firm experiencing significant growth.

3. More funds were obtained from operations than were paid out as dividends. Thus, the firm is not liquidating itself, or shrinking. Instead, the excess cash generated from operations is being used for replacement and growth of assets.

General Products Limited is a sound, financially healthy company. For a contrast, refer to Problem 27 at the end of the chapter, which involves analysis of the statement of changes in financial position for a financially troubled company.

SUMMARY

The statement of changes in financial position is as important to the information needs of financial statement users as the income statement and balance sheet.[4] The statement of changes in financial position reports the flows of cash into and out of a business during a period, and shows how management actually deployed the resources entrusted to it. The procedures for preparation are as follows:

Step 1   Obtain a balance sheet for the beginning and end of the period for which the statement of changes in financial position is to be prepared.

Step 2   Prepare a T-account work sheet. At the top of the work sheet is a master T-account for cash position. The T-account has sections labelled Operations, Investing, Financing, and Dividends. The beginning and ending balances of cash position are entered in the master T-account. The T-account work sheet is completed by preparing a T-account for each balance sheet account other than cash position and entering the beginning and ending balances.

Step 3   Explain the change in the cash position account between the beginning and end of the period by explaining, or accounting for, the changes in the other balance sheet accounts. This step is accomplished by reconstructing the entries originally made in the accounts during the period and entering them in appropriate T-accounts on the work sheet. Once the changes in these other balance sheet accounts have been explained, the change in cash position will have been explained.

Step 4   Prepare a statement of changes in financial position using information in the T-account work sheet.

The statement of changes in financial position helps explain the major reasons for a change in a firm's liquidity. In particular, it shows the relation between net income and cash generated by operations. The statement also reports the reasons for significant shifts in the structure of a firm's assets (changes in receivables, inventories, plant and equipment) and in the structure of a firm's liabilities and shareholders' equity (changes in accounts payable, bonds payable, common stock, retained earnings). These types of information are difficult to observe from a balance sheet or income statement alone.

The statement of changes in financial position is basically derived from an analysis of changes in balance sheet accounts during the accounting

---

[4] Technically, the *CICA Handbook* strongly recommends but does not require a statement of changes in financial position. Some incorporating acts, such as the Canada Business Corporations Act, do require such a statement. *Financial Reporting in Canada* shows that virtually 100 percent of public companies present this statement.

period. If the double-entry recording process has been applied properly, the net change in cash (or other definition of funds) should equal the net change in all noncash accounts. By reconstructing the entries made in noncash accounts and explaining their net change during the period, the net change in cash is also explained.

The statement of changes in financial position usually begins with net income for the period. Adjustments are then made for revenues not providing cash and expenses not using cash. The result is cash generated by operations. Other sources (new financing, sale of noncurrent assets) are then shown. From the total soures are subtracted the uses of cash (dividends, reductions in financing, acquisition of noncurrent assets) to derive the net change in cash for the period.

When analyzing a statement of changes in financial position, the focus is on the relations between the various sources, among the various uses, and between the total sources and total uses. A financially healthy firm typically obtains a majority of its funds from operations and invests a large percentage in plant and equipment.

Chapter 13 constitutes an introduction to the statement of changes in financial position. Appendix 13.1 introduces some complexities and works through a comprehensive illustration.

APPENDIX 13.1

COMPREHENSIVE ILLUSTRATION OF STATEMENT OF CHANGES IN FINANCIAL POSITION

Data for Church Corporation for Year 2 is used in this comprehensive illustration of the statement of changes in financial position. Exhibit 13.11 presents a comparative balance sheet as of December 31, Year 1 and Year 2; Exhibit 13.12 presents an income statement for Year 2; Exhibit 13.13 presents the T-accounts; and Exhibit 13.14 presents the completed statement of changes in financial position. In the sections that follow, each of the line items in Exhibit 13.14 is discussed.

CASH POSITION

From Exhibit 13.11, cash position can be computed:

	Cash Position Beginning of Year 2	Cash Position End of Year 2
Cash	$ 1,150	$1,050
Certificates of Deposit	1,800	980
Temporary Investments	—	—
Short-term bank indebtedness	(2,000)	(2,750)
	$ 950	($ 720)

EXHIBIT 13.11
CHURCH CORPORATION
Consolidated Balance Sheet

	December 31	
	Year 1	Year 2
ASSETS		
Current Assets:		
Cash	$ 1,150	$ 1,050
Certificate of Deposit	1,800	980
Accounts Receivable (net)	3,400	4,300
Inventory	1,500	2,350
Prepayments	800	600
Total Current Assets	$ 8,650	$ 9,280
Investments:		
Investment in Company A (15%)	$ 1,200	$ 1,200
Investment in Company B (40%)	2,100	2,420
Total Investments	$ 3,300	$ 3,620
Capital Assets:		
Land	$ 1,000	$ 1,000
Buildings	8,600	8,900
Equipment	10,840	11,540
Less: Accumulated Depreciation	(6,240)	(6,490)
Total Capital Assets	$14,200	$14,950
Patent	$ 2,550	$ 2,550
Less: Accumulated Amortization	(600)	(750)
Total Intangible Assets	$ 1,950	$ 1,800
Total Assets	$28,100	$29,650
LIABILITIES AND SHAREHOLDERS' EQUITY		
Current Liabilities:		
Bank Notes Payable	$ 2,000	$ 2,750
Accounts Payable	2,250	3,000
Warranties Payable	1,200	1,000
Advances from Customers	600	900
Total Current Liabilities	$ 6,050	$ 7,650
Noncurrent Liabilities:		
Bonds Payable	$ 2,820	$ 1,370
Capitalized Lease Obligation	1,800	2,100
Deferred Taxes	550	650
Total Noncurrent Liabilities	$ 5,170	$ 4,120
Minority Interest in Consolidated Subsidiary	$ 200	$ 230
Shareholders' Equity:		
Preferred Shares	$ 1,000	$ 1,200
Common Shares	2,000	2,100
Contributed Surplus	4,000	4,200
Retained Earnings	9,930	10,530
Total	$16,930	$18,030
Less: Cost of Treasury Shares	(250)	(380)
Total Shareholders' Equity	$16,680	$17,650
Total Liabilities and Shareholders' Equity	$28,100	$29,650

EXHIBIT 13.12
CHURCH CORPORATION
Consolidated Income Statement for Year 2

Revenues:	
Sales	$10,500
Interest and Dividends	320
Equity in Earnings of Affiliate	480
Gain on Sale of Equipment	50
Total Revenues	$11,350
Expenses:	
Cost of Goods Sold	$ 6,000
Selling and Administration	3,550
Interest	450
Income Taxes	300
Total Expenses	$10,300
Net Income Before Minority Interest	$ 1,050
Less: Minority Interest in Earnings	(50)
Net Income	$ 1,000

These numbers become the starting and ending balances in the master T-account for cash position and on the statement of changes in financial position. Exhibit 13.13 presents a T-account work sheet for Church Corporation for Year 2.

Item 1: Gain on Sale of Equipment   The accounting records indicate that a machine originally costing $60 and on which accumulated depreciation of $450 had been taken was sold for $180 during Year 2. The journal entry made to record this sale was as follows:

(1) Cash	$180	
Accumulated Depreciation	450	
Equipment		$600
Gain on Sale of Equipment		30

The cash proceeds of $180 are shown as an increase in cash from an investing activity. The $30 gain on the sale is included in net income. To avoid overstating the amount of cash derived from this sale, the $30 gain must be subtracted from net income in computing cash from operations.

(1) Cash (Investing — Sale of Equipment)	$180	
Accumulated Depreciation	450	
Equipment		$600
Cash (Operations — Gain on Sale of Equipment Subtraction)		30

Note that all cash proceeds are classified as investing activities and none are classified as operating activities. Most firms acquire and sell plant assets with the objective of providing a capacity to carry out operations rather than as means of generating operating income.

EXHIBIT 13.13
CHURCH CORPORATION
T-Account Work Sheet

Cash Position

✔ $950

Operations

Net Income	(10)	1,000	50	(15)	Bond Premium Amortization
Depreciation Expense Addback	(11)	700	30	(1)	Gain on Sale of Equipment
Amortization Expense Addback	(12)	150	320	(16)	Equity in Undistributed Earnings
Minority Interest in Consolidated Subsidiary	(13)	50	900	(20)	Increase in Accounts Receivable
Deferred Taxes	(14)	100	850	(21)	Increase in Inventories
Decrease in Prepayment	(19)	200	200	(22)	Decrease in Warranties Payable
Increase in Accounts Payable	(17)	750			
Increase in Advances from Customers	(18)	300			

Investing

Sale of Equipment	(1)	180	1,300	(6)	Acquisition of Equipment
			300	(3)	Acquisition of Building Through Capital Lease

Financing

Capital Lease Obligation Incurred in Acquisition of Building	(3)	300	300	(5)	Conversion of Long-Term Bonds into Common Shares
Long-Term Bonds Issued	(2)	400	1,500	(7)	Retirement of Long-Term Debt
Preferred Shares Issued	(4)	200	130	(8)	Acquisition of Common Shares
Common Shares Issued on Conversion of Bonds	(5)	300			

Dividends 420 (9)

✔ 720

Accounts Receivable			
✔	3,400		
(20)	900		
✔	4,300		

Inventories			
✔	1,500		
(21)	850		
✔	2,350		

Prepayments			
✔	800		
		200	(19)
✔	600		

Investment in Company A			
✔	1,200		
✔	1,200		

Investment in Company B			
✔	2,100		
(16)	320		
✔	2,420		

Land			
✔	1,000		
✔	1,000		

Buildings			
✔	8,600		
(3)	300		
✔	8,900		

Equipment			
✔	10,840		
(6)	1,300	600	(1)
✔	11,540		

Accumulated Depreciation			
		6,240	✔
(1)	450	700	(11)
		6,490	✔

EXHIBIT 13.13 (continued)

Patent		Accumulated Amortization	
✔ 2,550			600 ✔
			150 (12)
✔ 2,550			750 ✔

Accounts Payable		Warranties Payable		Advances from Customers	
	2,250 ✔		1,200 ✔		600 ✔
	750 (17)	(22) 200			300 (18)
	3,000 ✔		1,000 ✔		900 ✔

Bonds Payable		Capitalized Lease Obligation		Deferred Taxes	
	2,820 ✔		1,800 ✔		550 ✔
(15) 50	400 (2)		300 (3)		100 (14)
(5) 300					
(7) 1,500					
	1,370 ✔		2,100 ✔		650 ✔

Minority Interest in Consolidated Subsidiary		Preferred Shares		Common Shares	
	200 ✔		1,000 ✔		2,000 ✔
(9) 20	50 (13)		200 (4)		100 (5)
	230 ✔		1,200 ✔		2,100 ✔

Contributed Surplus		Retained Earnings		Treasury Stock	
	4,000 ✔		9,930 ✔	✔ 250	
	200 (5)	(9) 400	1,000 (10)	(8) 130	
	4,200 ✔		10,530 ✔	✔ 380	

If plant assets are sold at a loss instead of a gain, the loss must be added back to net income in deriving cash flow from operations. The typical worksheet entry would be as follows:

Cash (Investing — Sale of Equpiment)	$X	
Accumulated Depreciation	X	
Cash (Operations — Loss on Sale of Equipment Addback)	X	
Equipment		$X

Item 2: Long-Term Bonds Issued Long-term bonds totalling $400 were issued during Year 2.

(2) Cash (Financing — Long-Term Bonds Issued)	$400	
Bonds Payable		$400

EXHIBIT 13.14
CHURCH CORPORATION
Consolidated Statement of Changes in Financial Position for Year 2

Cash Provided by			
Operations[a]			$ 900
Investing Activities			
(1) Sale of equipment			180
Financing Activities			
(2) Long-term bonds issued		$ 400	
(3) Capital lease obligation incurred		300	
(4) Preferred shares issued		200	
(5) Common shares issued		300	
			1,200
			$ 2,280
Cash Applied to			
Investing Activities			
(6) Acquisition of equipment		$(1,300)	
(3) Acquisition of building through capital lease		(300)	
			(1,600)
Financing Activities			
(7) Retirement of long-term debt		$(1,500)	
(5) Conversion of long-term bonds and common shares		(300)	
(8) Treasury shares acquired		(130)	
			(1,930)
(9) Dividends			(420)
			$(3,950)
Increase (Decrease) in Cash Position			$(1,670)
Cash Position at Beginning of Year			950
Cash Position at End of Year			$ (720)

[a]*Cash provided by operations:*

(10) Net Income	*$ 1,000*
Add (deduct) items not affecting cash flow	
(11) Depreciation	*700*
(12) Amortization of patent	*150*
(13) Minority interest in consolidated earnings	*50*
(14) Deferred taxes	*100*
(15) Amortization of bond premium	*(50)*
(1) Gain on sale of equipment	*(30)*
(16) Equity in undistributed earnings of affiliate	*(320)*
	1,600
Working Capital Accounts	
Cash provided by net increases in Accounts Payable (17) and Advances on Contracts (18)	*1,050*
Cash provided by net decrease in Prepayments (19)	*200*
Cash applied to net increase in Receivables (20) and Inventory (21)	*(1,750)*
Cash applied to net decrease in Warranties Payable (22)	*(200)*
Cash Provided by Operations	*$ 900*

Item 3: Acquisition of Building Through Capital Lease   A long-term lease was signed during Year 2 for a building. This lease was classified as a capital lease and recorded in the accounts as follows:

(3) Building	$300	
Capitalized Lease Obligations		$300

Note that this entry does not affect cash. It does affect the investing and financing activities of Church Corporation and can be shown either in the statement of changes in financial position or in a supplementary schedule. Church Corporation indicates the transaction in its statement of changes in financial position with the following work sheet entry:

(3) Cash (Investing — Acquisition of Building Through Capital Lease)	$300	
Cash (Financing — Capital Lease Obligation Incurred in Acquisition of Building)		$300

Item 4: Preferred Shares Issued   Preferred shares totalling $200 were issued during the year.

(4) Cash (Financing — Preferred Share Issued)	$200	
Preferred Shares		$200

Item 5: Conversion of Debt to Common Shares   The conversion of debt to common shares is a transaction that does not directly affect cash but represents a financing transaction. It is disclosed as a source and as an application in offsetting amounts. An analysis of the balance sheet for Church Corporation shows that Contributed Surplus increased by $200. It can be inferred that the conversion of bonds into common shares resulted in the following entry:

Bonds Payable	$300	
Common Shares		$100
Contributed Surplus		200

(5) Cash (Financing — Conversion of Long-Term Bonds into Common Shares)	$300	
Cash (Financing — Issue of Common Shares in Bond Conversion)		$300

Item 6: Acquisition of Equipment   Equipment costing $1,300 was acquired during Year 2. The analytical entry for this investing activity is as follows:

(6) Equipment	$1,300	
Cash (Investing — Acquisition of Equipment)		$1,300

Item 7: Retirement of Long-Term Debt   Church Corporation retired $1,500 of long-term debt at maturity, and the work sheet entry is as follows:

(7) Bonds Payable	$1,500	
Cash (Financing — Retirement of Long-Term Debt)		$1,500

DISCUSSION CASE 30

Should Companies Be Made To Air Their Forecasts?

Stop talking about yesterday. How do you see tomorrow?

Investors, stock market analysts and securities regulators constantly urge this upon the often reluctant bosses of companies with shares available for trading.

One such advocate is Stanley Beck, chairman of the Ontario Securities Commission. He says the commission is thinking of introducing a sweeping requirement that companies tell investors, in some detail, of trends and events that may affect how they'll do in the future.

He and many others say that the now-extensive discussion of the past and the present doesn't really represent good corporate disclosure.

The key to investor decisions — to buy, ignore, sell or continue to own a stock — hinges less on history than on the future and what the company plans for it. That will determine whether or not the company will prosper and whether or not the investors make money on their investments.

So, it's natural that there's a pressure for such information, especially because it's sure to exist. Any company will have its own formal or informal analysis of the trends and a program for coping with them.

The normal corporate impulse, though, is to be secretive. Forecasts are dicey. It's easy to be wrong and no one likes to risk the embarrassment of being wrong in public.

Another thing: corporate judgments of the future are subject to constant alteration, especially in times as uncertain as these. That would put a heavy burden on the company to keep updating its disclosures. And, when an earlier analysis is wrong, and a company changes its view, some investors are bound to be angry, even suspicious of motives. They made decisions on the basis of one forecast and now they're left out on a limb! The results differ from the forecasts and the company has changed its tune.

Shareholders may ask antagonistic questions at the next annual meeting. Analysts may make pointed comments.

Obviously, this is not an easy matter for companies, no matter how eager they are to build a good reputation for good disclosure. Still, they have little choice but to do more future thinking for the public. The pressure is too great to resist.

That's clear from the comments of the judges in the latest *Financial Post* contest for the best corporate annual reports, held last November [1985]. One judge had cited as a "common omission" any "clear statement or discussion of corporate goals and strategies" — a future-oriented topic. Another wanted "more specific information about objectives and plans." Said another, "all too often companies still say

(continued)

(continued)

little of substance about the future or they bury comments about the outlook."

In a general sense, it's true that much of business is in a constant state of being dragged kicking and screaming into the information age. With honourable exceptions, companies with shares in the public's hands are slow to venture on to new frontiers in providing clear, comprehensive details on themselves.

It has always taken pressure from regulators to achieve much progress. Disclosure does, after all, take money and time. It sometimes edges into the area of telling competitors more than is comfortable.

While voluntary efforts to play fair with investors are reasonably widespread among larger corporations — many small resource companies are simply disgusting — it has long been clear that most executives have to be pushed.

Indeed, voluntarism can be a problem. It's better that all should be forced to meet certain standards, otherwise the secretive, bad guy may win an advantage. But it's wrong to hang shareholders or prospective shareholders out to dry. They deserve a generous flow of material useful for making good choices.

If that bothers a company — and it can be hurtful or embarrassing at times — it should leave the arena. It shouldn't expect to enjoy the benefits of having public shareholders and escape any drawbacks.

As to the future, let's consider a certain irony concerning Canada Trustco. The big trust company was the winner of the grand prize for best-in show of *The Financial Post*'s contest.

Canada Trustco, despite its own objections, was recently [1985] taken over by Genstar. That makes the trust firm's marvelous disclosure policies less meaningful for investors. Now that Genstar has snapped up almost all of Canada Trustco's shares, it has only about 1,200 shareholders compared with the earlier 6,700.

The latest (as of this writing) monthly report to Canada Trustco Shareholders, signed by chairman Arthur Mingay and president Mervyn Lahn, says of the future:

"The emerging Canada Trust" (assuming its merger with the large Canada Permanent, also controlled by Genstar) "will be both bigger and better — a unique and significant competitor . . . ideally positioned . . ."

Well, maybe. But these same executives would have had a different attitude a few months earlier. Then they were bitterly resisting any thought that Canada Trustco should be taken over, merged with some other company or controlled by a single owner. They thought that was bad for Canada and the company.

You can see that opinions about the future do indeed change radically in a short time.

References

Jack McArthur, "Should Companies Be Made To Air Their Forecasts?" *The Bottom Line*, January 1986.

Discussion Question

Given that investors value forecasts so highly, why are they not a required component of annual reports?

If the debt had been retired before maturity, it is likely that a gain or loss would have been recognized. The gain or loss would have been eliminated from net income in computing cash flow from operations, and the full amount of cash used to retire the debt would have been classified as a financing activity.

Item 8: Acquisition of Common Shares   Common shares costing $130 were acquired during Year 2.

(8) Treasury Shares	$130	
Cash (Financing — Acquisition of Common Shares)		$130

Item 9: Dividends   Church Corporation declared and paid $400 of dividends to its shareholders during Year 2. In addition, a consolidated subsidiary paid $20 of dividends to minority shareholders (see discussion of Item 13). The analytical entry is as follows:

(9) Retained Earnings	$400	
Minority Interest in Consolidated Subsidiary	20	
Cash (Dividends)		$420

Item 10: Net Income   The income statement indicates that net income for the period was $1,000. The work sheet entry presumes that cash is provisionally increased by the amount of net income.

(10) Cash (Operations — Net Income)	$1,000	
Retained Earnings		$1,000

Item 11: Depreciation Expense Addback   Internal records indicate that depreciation of $500 was included in cost of goods sold and depreciation of $200 was included in selling and administrative expenses. None of this $700 of depreciation required an operating cash outflow during Year 2. Thus, it must be added back to net income in deriving cash flow from operations.

(11) Cash (Operations — Depreciation Expense Addback)	$700	
Accumulated Depreciation		$700

Item 12: Amortization of Patent   The treatment of patent amortization is identical to that of depreciation. Company records indicate that patent amortization of $150 was recorded during Year 2 and was included in cost of goods sold. The work sheet entry is as follows:

(12) Cash (Operations — Amortization Expense Addback)	$150	
Accumulated Amortization		$150

Item 13: Minority Interest in Consolidated Earnings   The financial statement in Exhibits 13.11, 13.12, and 13.14 are consolidated statements for Church Corporation and its majority-owned subsidiaries. Church does not own all of the shares of some of its consolidated subsidiaries. The minority shareholders in these subsidiaries have a claim on the earnings of their respective subsidiaries. The income statement in Exhibit 13.13 indicates that the minority interest in earnings of $50 has been subtracted in computing consolidated net income. This amount does not use cash and must be added back to net income to compute cash flow from operations. The analytical entry on the work sheet is as follows:

(13) Cash (Operations — Minority Interest)	$50	
Minority Interest in Consolidated Subsidiary		$50

The balance sheet in Exhibit 13.12 indicates that the account titled Minority Interest in Consolidated Subsidiary increased during Year 2 by $30 (= $230 − $200). Because the account increased by $50 for the minority interest in earnings, dividends of $20 must have been paid to these shareholders during the year. The work sheet entry for these dividends is discussed in conjunction with the consideration of dividends (Item 9).

Item 14: Deferred Income Taxes   Notes to the financial statements of Church Corporation indicate that income tax expense of $300 comprises $200 of currently payable taxes and $100 of deferred income taxes. The $100 of deferred income taxes reduced net income but did not require a cash outflow during Year 2. This amount must therefore be added back to net income.

(14) Cash (Operations — Future Tax Addback)	$100	
Deferred Income Taxes		$100

Item 15: Amortization of Bond Premium   Included in Bonds Payable on the balance sheet is one series of bonds that were initially issued at a premium (that is, the coupon rate exceeded the required market rate of interest). The bond premium must be amortized over the life of the bonds as a reduction in interest expense. The entry made in the accounting records for this bond during the period was as follows:

(15) Interest Expense	$300	
Bonds Payable	50	
Cash		$350

Cash of $350 was expended even though only $300 of interest expense had been subtracted in computing net income. An additional $50 must be subtacted from net income to derive cash flow from operations.

(15) Bonds Payable	$50	
Cash (Operations — Bond Premium Amortization Subtraction)		$50

Note that cash used for interest expense is classified as an operating, not a financing, activity because it is viewed as a cost of carrying out operations.

Item 16: Equity in Undistributed Earnings of Affiliate   The balance sheet indicates that Church Corporation owns 40 percent of the common stock of Company B. During Year 2, Company B earned $1,200 and paid $400 of dividends. Church Corporation made the following entries on its books during the year:

(16) Investment in Company B	$480	
Equity in Earnings of Affiliate		$480
Cash	$160	
Investment in Company B		$160
(0.40 × $400 = $160; 0.40 × $1,200 = $480)		

Net income of Church Corporation in Exhibit 13.14 includes $480 of equity income. Only $160 of cash was received. Thus, a subtraction of $320 (= $480 − $160) must be made from net income in deriving cash from operations.

(16) Investment in Company B	$320	
Cash (Operations — Equity in Undistributed		
Earnings Subtraction)		$320

The investment in Company A shown in the balance sheet in Exhibit 13.12 is accounted for using the cost method. During Year 2, dividends of $100 were received and included in Interest and Dividends on the income statement. Because these dividends provided cash, no adjustment is made to net income in computing cash flow from operations.

Item 17: Increase in Accounts Payable   An increase in accounts payable indicates that more costs were incurred on account and cash payments delayed than the amount paid during Year 2 for previous purchases on account. This increase in accounts payable, a credit change in an operating current liability account, implicitly increases cash from operations.

(17) Cash (Operations — Increase in Accounts Payable)	$750	
Accounts Payable		$750

Item 18: Increase in Advances from Customers   The $300 increase in customer advances means that $300 more cash was received during Year 2 than was recognized as revenue. The excess must be added to net income in deriving cash flow from operations.

(18) Cash (Operations — Increase in Advances on Contracts)	$300	
Advances from Customers		$300

Item 19: Decrease in Prepayments Because prepayments decreased by $200 during Year 2, less cash was expended during Year 2 for new prepayments than was amortized from prepayments of earlier years. Thus, $200 must be added to net income for this credit change in an operating current asset account.

(19) Cash (Operations — Decrease in Prepayments)	$200	
Prepayments		$200

Item 20: Increase in Accounts Receivable The increase in accounts receivable indicates that less cash was collected from customers than the amount shown for sales on account. Thus, the increase in accounts receivable, a debit change in an operating current asset account, must be subtracted from net income.

(20) Accounts Receivable	$900	
Cash (Operations — Increase in Accounts Receivable)		$900

Note that this entry automatically incorporates the effect of any change in the Allowance for Uncollectable Accounts. Separate work sheet entries could be made for the change in gross accounts receivable and allowance for uncollectable accounts.

Item 21: Increase in Inventories The increase in inventories indicates that more merchandise was purchased than was sold during Year 2. Thus, more cash was used than was shown for cost of goods sold.[5] A subtraction from net income is required for this debit change in an operating current asset account.

(21) Inventories	$850	
Cash (Operations — Increase in Inventories)		$850

Item 22: Decrease in Warranties Payable Recall that Warranties Payable is increased for the estimated cost of future warranty services on products sold during the period and is decreased by the actual cost of warranty services performed. During Year 2, $200 more in costs was incurred and paid in cash than was included in expenses on the income statement. This decrease in Warranties Payable, a debit change in an operating current liability account, must be subtracted from net income.

(22) Warranties Payable	$200	
Cash (Operations — Decrease in Warranties Payable)		$200

Cash flow from operations is $900 for Year 2.

---

[5] To correctly compute the cash flow effect, the change in accounts payable must also be considered. See Item 17.

KEY TERMS

Statement of changes in financial
  position
Funds
Investing activities
Financing activities
Operating activities

Dual transactions assumption
Cash equivalents
Cash position
Analytical entries
T-account method

SELF-STUDY MATERIAL

This section contains questions, exercises, and problems to help you assess your understanding of Chapter 13. Careful review of this material will assist you in completing the homework assignments. Solutions are found at the end of this section.

QUESTIONS AND EXERCISES

True/False

For each statement, place a T or an F in the space provided to indicate whether the statement is true or false.

_____ 1. The statement of changes in financial position is sometimes referred to as the "funds statement."

_____ 2. Since 1986, the most commonly used definition of "funds" is working capital.

_____ 3. Whenever there are sales on account, the amount of sales revenue will always exceed the amount of cash receipts.

_____ 4. The statement of changes in financial position, although it provides useful information to readers, is not considered a major financial statement.

_____ 5. One of the most important factors not reported on the balance sheet and income statement is how the operations of the period affected the liquidity of the firm.

_____ 6. Dividends are an example of a cash disbursement that does not affect operations.

_____ 7. Because the exchange of a piece of land for a new machine does not involve cash, it should not be included in a statement of changes in financial position.

_____ 8. The fact that the balance in cash increased over time does not necessarily mean that the cash generated from operations was positive.

_____ 9. Depreciation is added back to net income in a statement of changes in financial position because it is a source of cash.

_____ 10. One difference between the income statement and the statement of changes in financial position is that the former is based upon the accrual basis of accounting and the latter is usually prepared on a cash basis.

_____ 11. Cash provided from operations is considered a source of cash but could also be considered a use of cash when a company experiences a net loss.

_____ 12. Working capital is defined as current assets minus current liabilities.

_____ 13. If the balance in Accounts Receivable increases over the year, it indicates that the sales revenue exceeds the cash receipts.

_____ 14. Cash receipts from operations are the only source of funds for a company.

_____ 15. The declaration of dividends has no effect on cash.

_____ 16. The accounting equation expresses the change in a company's cash in the following manner:

$$\Delta C = \Delta L + \Delta SE + \Delta NCA$$

_____ 17. When all other things remain the same, an increase in noncash assets causes cash to decline.

_____ 18. In determining cash provided from operations, depreciation expense is added to the net income, because it represents a fund of cash set aside during the year for the replacement of long-lived assets.

_____ 19. A transaction involving an exchange of one piece of land for another piece of land most likely would not be disclosed in the firm's income statement or balance sheet, especially if there were no gain or loss.

_____ 20. Retirement of long-term debt is an example of a use of cash.

_____ 21. It is correct to asume that, if a firm has a loss for a period of time, the firm has also decreased its liquidity.

_____ 22. If the beginning and ending balances in a Building T-account are the same, no transactions affecting this account could have taken place during the year.

_____ 23. If the only noncurrent item to change was a decrease in shareholders' equity, cash must have increased.

_____ 24. The most important source of cash for successful firms is the return on funds invested in profitable securities.

_____ 25. Like the balance sheet and income statement, the statement of changes in financial position is generated as a regular output of the firm's recordkeeping system.

_____ 26. An increase in accounts payable is added to net income in determining the cash provided from operations.

_____ 27. A decrease in inventory is added to net income in calculating the cash provided from operations.

_____ 28. A reason that revenues and expenses differ from cash receipts and disbursements is that the accrual basis of accounting is used in determining net income.

_____ 29. The statement of changes in financial position is related to both the balance sheet and the income statement, but also discloses information that is unavailable or only partially available by analysis of the balance sheet and income statement alone.

_____ 30. Accumulated depreciation increased by $10,000 during the year. As long as no depreciable assets have been retired during the year, this $10,000 increase can be completely attributed to depreciation expense.

_____ 31. A possible explanation for the following analytical entry taken from a T-account work sheet is that bonds were issued for cash:
Cash $XX
   Bonds Payable $XX

_____ 32. If a creditor allows a firm to owe money on account, this is in effect a use of cash to the firm.

Matching

For each transaction, indicate whether it would be a source of cash, a use of cash, or have no direct effect on cash; place the letter for that answer in the space provided. (Hint: Use the CICA definition of "cash.")

a = source of cash; b = use of cash; c = no direct effect

_____ 1. Issuance of share capital

_____ 2. Sale of temporary investments, with no gain or loss

_____ 3. Borrowing on a 60-day note payable

_____ 4. Issuance of 10-year bonds

_____ 5. Return of inventory to suppliers for credit

_____ 6. Recording of depreciation expense

_____ 7. Receipt of cash for delivery of merchandise next month

_____ 8. Acceptance of a 30-day note for an overdue account receivable

_____ 9. Early retirement of bonds due in 4 years

_____ 10. Prepayment for a 1-year insurance policy

_____ 11. Recognition of accrued interest expense, payable in 30 days, on long-term notes

_____ 12. Sale of used equipment

_____ 13. Sale of inventory on account

_____ 14. Payment of dividends previously declared

_____ 15. Purchase of equipment for cash

_____ 16. Accrual of income taxes to be paid in following year

_____ 17. Declaration of dividends to be paid in 30 days

_____ 18. Expiration of insurance policy 1 year after purchase

_____ 19. Collection of 1-year note receivable

_____ 20. Purchase of a plot of land in exchange for a mortgage payable

_____ 21. Signing a short-term demand note to cover a bank overdraft

Multiple Choice

Choose the best answer for each question or problem and enter the identifying letter in the space provided.

_____ 1. Which transaction is shown on a statement of changes in financial position but does not affect cash directly?
a) sale of bonds for cash
b) exchange of land for shares
c) collection of customer accounts
d) dividends paid to owners

_____ 2. Which transaction involves a use of cash?
a) declaration of dividends
b) acceptance of a note for an overdue account
c) issuance of shares
d) retirement of long-term debt

_____ 3. Bonds Payable had the following balances at the beginning and end of 19X1: January 1: $100,000; January 31: $140,000. In addition, $60,000 of bonds were retired in 19X1. How much was issued during the year?
a) $100,000
b) $20,000
c) $160,000
d) $180,000

_____ 4. The Faryl Co. Inc. had a net loss of $160,000 in 19X1. The following facts are also given:

Dividends Paid	$ 40,000
Depreciation Expense	30,000
Increase in Accounts Payable	15,000
Issuance of Shares	100,000
Retirement of Debt	150,000

What was the amount of cash provided (or used) from operations?

    a) ($115,000)
    b) ($205,000)
    c) ($75,000)
    d) $65,000

_____ 5. Referring to question 4, what was the net increase (decrease) in cash for 19X1?
    a) $215,000
    b) $10,000
    c) ($105,000)
    d) ($165,000)

_____ 6. During 19X1, the Darling Linda Doll Co. Ltd. had a net income of $100,000. Depreciation expense was $3,000. In addition, selected balance sheet accounts showed the following changes:

Accounts Receivable	$ 6,000 increase
Accounts Payable	2,000 increase
Building	8,000 decrease
Bonds Payable	16,000 increase

What was the amount of cash flow provided by operations?
    a) $100,000
    b) $119,000
    c) $99,000
    d) $103,000

_____ 7. Kurt Limited had these selected amounts taken from its balance sheet:

	Building	Accumulated Depreciation
1/1 19X1	$800,000	$200,000
12/31 19X1	785,000	225,000

During 19X1, a building having a cost of $100,000 was purchased. Was any building sold during the year and, if so, what was its original cost?
    a) no building was sold in 19X1
    b) yes, but its cost cannot be determined
    c) yes, and its original cost was $85,000
    d) yes, and its original cost was $115,000

_____ 8. Which statement expresses the purpose of the statement of changes in financial position?
    a) to summarize all of the major transactions causing changes in the structure of a firm's assets and liabilities
    b) to report on the flow of all resources into and out of the business during a period of time
    c) to provide information concerning the financing and investing activities of a business
    d) all of the above

_____ 9. The balance in the Accumulated Depreciation account was $30,000 on January 1, 19X1 and $20,000 on December 31, 19X1. During 19X1, an asset costing $100,000 (accumulated depreciation of $80,000) was sold for $20,000. What was the depreciation expense for 19X1?
    a) $10,000
    b) $90,000
    c) $110,000
    d) $70,000

_____ 10. Which statement is true concerning depreciation expense?
   a) depreciation expense increases the expenses for a period but does not use cash
   b) depreciation expense is added back to net income in determining funds provided from operations because it had originally been subtracted in computing net income but was not a use of cash
   c) depreciation expense is not a source of funds
   d) all of the above are true

_____ 11. During 19X1, the following changes took place:

Current Liabilities	$75,000 increase
Noncurrent Liabilities	45,000 decrease
Owners' Equity	51,000 decrease
Noncurrent Assets	42,000 increase
Current Assets (other than cash)	18,000 increase

What has been the increase (decrease) in cash for 19X1?
   a) ($57,000)
   b) $30,000
   c) $39,000
   d) ($81,000)

_____ 12. The following items were found on an income statement: Sales of $600,000, Depreciation Expense of $320,000, Income Taxes of $160,000, and Other Expenses of $100,000. In addition, common shares were issued for $80,000 cash during the year. What was the amount of cash provided from operations, assuming that all noncash working capital balances did not change during the year?
   a) $20,000
   b) $100,000
   c) $420,000
   d) $340,000

Exercises

1. Several key transactions, along with other relevant information, are supplied for Latka Limited in 19X1. Prepare the statement of changes in financial position for 19X1.
   a. Net income for 19X1 was $100,000.
   b. Depreciation expense for the year was $25,000, and patent amortization was $500.
   c. Dividends of $18,000 were paid in December.
   d. A total of 10,000 preferred shares were issued for a total cash consideration of $350,000.
   e. Bonds payable in the amount of $80,000, previously classified as long-term, were reclassified as current because they were due in 19X2.
   f. A piece of land was acquired for $20,000.
   g. A $2,500 loan was made to one of the company's officers to be repaid in 19X3.
   h. A long-term investment that originally cost $1,100 was sold for $1,100.
   i. A used piece of equipment was sold for $8,500. It had an original cost of $20,000 and accumulated depreciation of $11,500.
   j. The following changes occurred in other noncash working capital accounts:

Accounts Receivable	$27,000 increase
Inventory	16,000 decrease
Accounts Payable	11,000 decrease

2. Financial statement data for Zebco Inc. are presented for the years ended December 31, 19X1 and December 31, 19X2.

ZEBCO INC.
Comparative Balance Sheets

| | Year-end December 31 | | | |
	19X2		19X1	
Assets				
Current Assets:				
Cash	$ 40,000	$	42,000	
Accounts Receivable	60,000		34,000	
Inventories	100,000	$200,000	66,000	$142,000
Fixed Assets:				
Land	$20,000		0	
Equipment (cost)	120,000		$154,000	
Less Accumulated Depreciation	(60,000)	80,000	(64,000)	90,000
Intangibles:				
Goodwill		20,000		22,000
Total Assets		$300,000		$254,000
Liabilities				
Current Liabilities:				
Accounts Payable	$ 58,000		$ 48,000	
Notes Payable	70,000		0	
Interest Payable	2,000	$130,000	2,000	$50,000
Long-Term Liabilities:				
Notes Payable, due in 19X3		0	70,000	
Total Liabilities		$130,000	$120,000	
Shareholders' Equity				
Share Capital	$ 80,000		$ 50,000	
Retained Earnings	90,000	$170,000	84,000	$134,000
Total Liabilities and Shareholders' Equity		$300,000		$254,000

ZEBCO INC.
Income Statement
For the Year Ended December 31, 19X2

Sales		$100,000
Deduct Expenses:		
Depreciation	$ 14,000	
Amortization of Goodwill	2,000	
Bad Debts Expense	1,400	
Interest Expense	2,600	
Other Expenses	20,000	40,000
Net Income Before Income Tax		$ 60,000
Income Tax		24,000
Net Income		$ 36,000

ZEBCO INC.
Retained Earnings Statement
For the Year Ended December 31, 19X2

Retained Earnings 1/1 19X2	$ 84,000
Plus: Net Income	36,000
	120,000
Less: Dividends	30,000
Retained Earnings 12/31 19X2	$ 90,000

Additional Information: There were no purchases of equipment during 19X2. Equipment was sold in 19X2 for its book value.

Prepare a T-account work sheet and a statement of changes in financial position of 19X2.

ANSWERS TO QUESTIONS AND EXERCISES

True/False

1. T	9. F	17. T	25. F
2. F	10. T	18. F	26. T
3. F	11. T	19. T	27. T
4. F	12. T	20. T	28. T
5. T	13. T	21. F	29. T
6. T	14. F	22. F	30. T
7. F	15. T	23. F	31. T
8. T	16. F	24. F	32. F

Matching

1. a	7. a	13. c	19. a
2. a	8. c	14. b	20. c
3. c	9. b	15. b	21. c
4. a	10. b	16. c	
5. c	11. c	17. c	
6. c	12. a	18. c	

Multiple Choice

1. b	4. a	7. d	10. d
2. d	5. c	8. d	11. d
3. a	6. c	9. d	12. d

Exercises

1. **LATKA LIMITED**
Statement of Changes in Financial Position
For the Year Ended December 31, 19X1

Cash Provided By			
Operations:			
Net Income			$100,000
Additions:			
Decrease in Inventory		$16,000	
Depreciation Expense		25,000	
Patent Amortization		500	41,500
			$141,500
Subtractions:			
Increase in Accounts Receivable		$27,000	
Decrease in Accounts Payable		11,000	(38,000)
			$103,500

Financing Activities:	
Issue of Shares	350,000
Investing Activities:	
Sale of Investment	1,100
Sale of Equipment	8,500
Total Sources	$463,100
Cash Applied To	
Dividends	$ 18,000
Investing Activities:	
Purchase of Land	20,000
Financing Activities:	
Loan to Officers	2,500
Total Uses	40,500
Increase in Cash Position	$422,600

2. ZEBCO INC.
T-Account Work Sheet

Cash Position

Sources			Uses	
	42,000			
		Operations		
(1) Net Income	36,000	26,000	Accounts Rec. Incr.	(4)
(2) Depreciation	14,000	34,000	Inventories	(5)
(3) Amortization	2,000			
(6) Accounts Payable Incr.	10,000			
		Financing		
(10) Sale of Shares	30,000			
		Investing		
(9) Sale of Equipment	16,000	20,000	Purchase of Land	(8)
		Dividends		
		30,000		(7)
	40,000			

Accounts Receivable				**Inventories**				**Land**		
	34,000				66,000				0	
(4)	26,000		(5)		34,000		(8)		20,000	
	60,000				100,000				20,000	

Equipment				**Interest Payable**			**Accounts Payable**		
154,000	34,000	(9)			2,000			48,000	
								10,000	(6)
120,000					2,000			58,000	

Goodwill				**Acc. Depreciation**				**Notes Payable**	
22,000	2,000	(3)	(9)	18,000	64,000				70,000
					14,000	(2)			
20,000					60,000				70,000

Share Capital				Retained Earnings		
	50,000				84,000	
	30,000	(10)	(7)	30,000	36,000	(1)
	80,000				90,000	

ZEBCO INC.
Statement of Changes in Financial Position
For the Year Ended December 31, 1986

Cash Provided By		
Operations:		
Net Income	$36,000	
Additions:		
Depreciation Expense	14,000	
Amortization of Goodwill	2,000	
Increase in Accounts Payable	10,000	
Subtractions:		
Increase in Accounts Receivable	(26,000)	
Increase in Inventories	(34,000)	
Total Sources from Operations		$ 2,000
Financing Activities:		
Sale of Share Capital		30,000
Investing Activities:		
Sale of Equipment		16,000
Total Sources of Cash		$48,000
Cash Applied To		
Dividends		$30,000
Investing Activities:		
Purchase of Land		20,000
Uses of Cash		$50,000
Net Decrease in Cash Position		($ 2,000)

PROBLEM 1 FOR SELF-STUDY

Exhibit 13.15 presents a comparative balance sheet for Fisher Corporation as of December 31, Year 1 and Year 2. During Year 2, no plant and equipment was sold and no dividends were declared or paid.

Prepare a T-account work sheet for the preparation of a statement of changes in financial position.

PROBLEM 2 FOR SELF-STUDY[6]

Exhibit 13.16 presents comparative balance sheets for Smith Corporation as of December 31, Year 1 and Year 2. The following information pertains to Smith Corporation for Year 2:

1. Net Income was $200,000.

2. Dividends declared and paid were $120,000.

---

[6] Although working capital is no longer used as a definition of "funds" in Canada, this exercise is useful in helping students understand the relationship between cash and working capital.

EXHIBIT 13.15
FISHER CORPORATION
Comparative Balance Sheet
December 31, Year 1 and Year 2
(amounts in thousands)
(Problem 1 for Self-Study)

	December 31			December 31	
	Year 2	Year 1		Year 2	Year 1
ASSETS			**LIABILITIES AND SHAREHOLDERS' EQUITY**		
Current Assets:			**Current Liabilities:**		
Cash	$ 25	$10	Accounts Payable	$ 40	$30
Accounts Receivable	20	15	Total Current Liabilities	$ 40	$30
Merchandise Inventories	25	20			
Total Current Assets	$ 70	$45	**Long-Term Debt:**		
			Bonds Payable	$ 15	$10
Capital Assets	$ 60	$50	Total Liabilities	$ 55	$40
Less: Accumulated			**Shareholders' Equity:**		
Depreciation	(30)	(25)	Common Shares	$ 20	$10
Total Capital Assets	$ 30	$25	Retained Earnings	25	20
Total Assets	$100	$70	Total Shareholders'		
			Equity	$ 45	$30
			Total Liabilities and		
			Shareholders' Equity	$100	$70

3. Depreciation expense totalled $80,000.

4. Buildings and equipment originally costing $50,000 and with accumulated deprecation of $40,000 were sold for $10,000.

   a. Prepare a T-account work sheet for the preparation of a statement of changes in financial position, defining "funds" as cash.

   b. Prepare a T-account work sheet for the preparation of a statement of changes in financial position, defining "funds" as working capital.

   c. Convert working capital provided by operations to cash flow provided by operations.

SUGGESTED SOLUTION TO PROBLEM 1 FOR SELF-STUDY

Exhibit 13.17 presents a completed T-account work sheet for Fisher Corporation.

SUGGESTED SOLUTION TO PROBLEM 2 FOR SELF-STUDY

Exhibit 13.18 shows the analytical entries posted to Exhibits 13.19 and 13.20. Note that the changes to current assets and current liabilities posted to Exhibit 13.19 as analytical entries 5, 6, 7, 10, 11,

EXHIBIT 13.16
SMITH CORPORATION
Comparative Balance Sheets
December 31, Year 1 and Year 2
(amounts in thousands)

	December 31	
	Year 2	Year 1
ASSETS		
Current Assets:		
Cash	$ 40	$ 70
Accounts Receivable	420	320
Merchandise Inventories	470	360
Prepayments	70	50
[hm1p]To tal Current Assets	$1,000	$ 800
Capital Assets:		
Land	$ 250	$ 200
Building and Equipment (net of accumulated depreciation of $800 and $840)	1,150	1,000
Total Capital Assets	$1,400	$1,200
Total Assets	$2,400	$2,000
LIABILITIES AND SHAREHOLDERS' EQUITY		
Current Liabilities:		
Accounts Payable	$ 440	$ 320
Income Taxes Payable	80	60
Other Current Liabilities	360	170
Total Current Liabilities	$ 800	$ 550
Noncurrent Liabilities:		
Bonds Payable	200	250
To tal Liabilities	$1,080	$ 800
Shareholders' Equity		
Common Shares	$ 540	$ 500
Retained Earnings	780	700
Total Shareholders' Equity	$1,320	$1,200
Total Liabilities and Shareholders' Equity	$2,400	$2,000

and 12 are not posted to Exhibit 13.20, in which "funds" are defined as working capital.[7] Exhibit 13.19 presents a completed T-account work sheet for Smith Corporation with funds defined as cash. Exhibit 13.20 presents a completed T-account work sheet with "funds" defined as working capital. Exhibit 13.21 shows the conversion of working capital provided by operations to cash flow provided by operations.

[7] Before 1986, this was the prevalent definition of "funds" in Canada.

EXHIBIT 13.17
T-Account Work Sheet for Fisher Corporation
Funds Defined as Cash
(amounts in thousands)

	Cash Position	
Provided by	✔ 10	**Applied to**

Operations

Depreciation Expense	(4) 5	5 (1) Increased Accounts Receivable
Increase Accounts Payable to		
Merchandise Suppliers	(5) 10	5 (2) Increased Merchandise Inventories
Net Income	(8) 5	

Financing

Long-Term Bonds Issued	(6) 5	
Shares Issued	(7) 10	

Investing

		10 (3) Capital Assets Purchased
	✔ 25	

Accounts Receivable				**Merchandise Inventories**				**Capital Assets**	
✔	15			✔	20			✔	50
(1)	5			(2)	5			(3)	10
✔	20			✔	25			✔	60

Accumulated Depreciation				**Accounts Payable**				**Bonds Payable**	
	25	✔			30	✔			10	✔
	5	(4)			10	(5)			5	(6)
	30	✔			40	✔			15	✔

Common Shares				**Retained Earnings**		
	10	✔			20	✔
	10	(7)			5	(8)
	20	✔			25	✔

QUESTIONS AND EXERCISES FOR APPENDIX 13.1

True/False

For each statement, place a T or an F in the space provided to indicate whether the statement is true or false.

_____ 1. For the statement of changes in financial position, "cash" is defined as cash and cash equivalents less short-term borrowings.

EXHIBIT 13.18
Analytical Entries for Smith Corporation
for Exhibits 13.19 and 13.20
(amounts in thousands)

Entry 13.19	Exhibit 13.20	T-Account	Amount Dr.	Cr.	Comment
(1)	(1)	Cash (Operations)	$200		Net income.
		Retained Earnings		$200	
(2)	(2)	Retained Earnings	120		Dividends.
		Cash (Other)		120	
(3)	(3)	Cash (Operations)	80		Depreciation expense.
		Bldgs. and Equip. — Net		80	
(4)	(4)	Bldgs. and Equip. — Net	40		Sale of buildings and
		Cash (Other)	10		equipment.
		Bldgs. and Equip. — Net		50	
(5)	—	Accounts Receivable	100		Accounts receivable increase.
		Cash (Operations)		100	
(6)	—	Merchandise Inventories	110		Merchandise inventories
		Cash (Operations)		110	increase.
(7)	—	Prepayments	20		Prepayments increase.
		Cash (Operations)		20	
(8)	(5)	Land	50		Purchase of land.
		Cash (Other)		50	
(9)	(6)	Bldgs. and Equip. — Net	240		Purchase of buildings and
		Cash (Other)		240	equipment.
(10)	—	Cash (Operations)	120		Accounts payable increase.
		Accounts Payable		120	
(11)	—	Cash (Operations)	20		Income tax payable increase.
		Income Tax Payable		20	
(12)	—	Cash (Operations)	190		Other current liabilities
		Other Current Liabilities		190	increase.
(13)	(7)	Bonds Payable	50		Noncurrent bonds payable
		Cash (Other)		50	decrease.
(14)	(8)	Cash (Other)	40		Share issue.
		Common Stock		40	

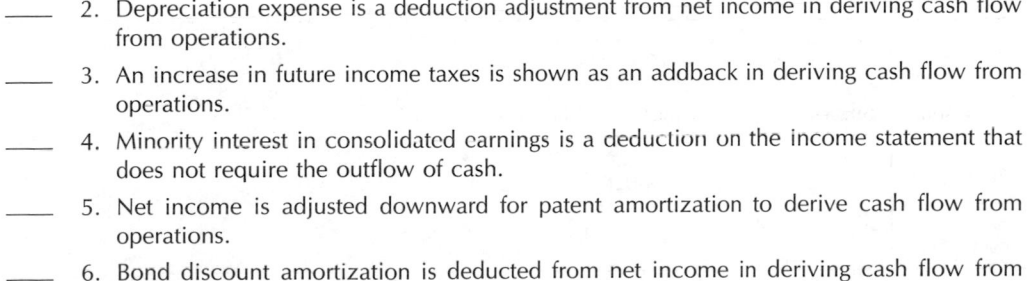

_____ 2. Depreciation expense is a deduction adjustment from net income in deriving cash flow from operations.

_____ 3. An increase in future income taxes is shown as an addback in deriving cash flow from operations.

_____ 4. Minority interest in consolidated earnings is a deduction on the income statement that does not require the outflow of cash.

_____ 5. Net income is adjusted downward for patent amortization to derive cash flow from operations.

_____ 6. Bond discount amortization is deducted from net income in deriving cash flow from operations.

EXHIBIT 13.19
Revised T-Account Work Sheet for Smith Corporation
Funds Defined as Cash
(amounts in thousands)

Cash Position

Provided by				Applied to
	✔ 70			
	Operations			
Net Income	(1) 200		100 (5)	Accounts Receivable Increase
Depreciation Expense	(3) 80		110 (6)	Inventories Increase
Accounts Payable Increase	(10) 120		20 (7)	Prepayments Increase
Income Tax Payable Increase	(11) 20			
Other Current Liabilities Increase	(12) 190			
	Financing			
Share Issue	(14) 40			
			50 (13)	Bonds Payable Decrease
	Investing			
Bldgs. and Equip. Sale	(4) 10		50 (8)	Land Purchase
			240 (9)	Bldgs. and Equip. Purchase
	Dividends			
			120 (2)	
	✔ 40			

Accounts Receivable			Merchandise Inventories			Prepayments	
✔ 320			✔ 360			✔ 50	
(5) 100			(6) 110			(7) 20	
✔ 420			✔ 470			✔ 70	

Land			Buildings and Equipment — Net			Accounts Payable	
✔ 200			✔ 1,000				320 ✔
(8) 50			(4) 40	80 (3)			120 (10)
			(9) 240	50 (4)			
✔ 250			✔ 1,150				440 ✔

Income Taxes Payable			Other Current Liabilities			Bonds Payable	
	60 ✔			170 ✔		250 ✔	
	20 (11)			190 (12)	(13) 50		
	80 ✔			360 ✔		200 ✔	

Common Shares			Retained Earnings	
	500 ✔			700 ✔
	40 (14)	(2) 120		200 (1)
	540 ✔			780 ✔

EXHIBIT 13.20
T-Account Work Sheet for Smith Corporation
Funds Defined as Working Capital
(amounts in thousands)

Working Capital		
Sources		**Uses**
	✔ 250	

Operations

Net Income	(1) 200	
Depreciation Expense	(3) 80	

Financing

Share Issue	(8) 40	50 (5) Bonds Payable Decrease

Investing

Bldgs. and Equip. Sale	(4) 10	240 (6) Bldgs. and Equip. Purchase
		50 (7) Land Purchase

Dividends

		120 (2)
	✔ 120	

Land			Buildings and Equipment — Net				Bonds Payable	
✔ 200			✔ 1,000					250 ✔
(5) 50			(4) 40	80 (3)	(7) 50			
			(6) 240	50 (4)				
✔ 250			✔ 1,150					200 ✔

Common Shares			Retained Earnings		
	500 ✔			700 ✔	
	40 (8)	(2) 120		200 (1)	
	540 ✔			780 ✔	

_____ 7. Loss on sale of machinery is added to net income in deriving cash flow from operations.

_____ 8. Sale of equipment without a gain or loss is not shown on the statement of cash flows.

_____ 9. A decrease in prepaid insurance would be shown as an addback to net income on the statement of changes in financial position.

_____ 10. An example of a deduction adjustment in net income in deriving cash flow from operations would be a decrease in accounts receivable.

_____ 11. An increase in inventory would be presented in the investing section of the statement of changes in financial position.

_____ 12. Decreases in accounts payable would be shown as an addback adjustment to net income in deriving cash flow from operations.

_____ 13. Equity in undistributed earnings of an affiliate would be deducted from net income in deriving cash flow from operations.

_____ 14. An acquisition of a building by incurring a capital lease obligation would be shown as both an investing and financing activity on the statement of changes in financial position.

EXHIBIT 13.21
Smith Corporation Conversion
of Working Capital Provided by
Operations to Cash Flow Provided by Operations
(amounts in thousands)

Working Capital Provided by Operations	$280
Plus:	
Increase in Accounts Payable	120
Increase in Income Taxes Payable	20
Increase in Other Current Liabilities	190
Less:	
Increase in Accounts Receivable	(100)
Increase in Merchandise Inventories	(110)
Increase in Prepayments	(20)
Cash Provided by Operations	$380

_____ 15. Acquisition of treasury stock should be presented in the investing section of the statement of changes in financial position.

_____ 16. The conversion of long-term bonds into common stock would not be presented on the statement of changes in financial position.

_____ 17. Short-term bank borrowing and long-term bonds issued would both be presented in the financing activities section of the statement of changes in financial position.

_____ 18. Dividends paid would not be presented in the statement of changes in financial position.

_____ 19. Cash proceeds from the sale of a building would be presented in the investing section of the statement of changes in financial position.

_____ 20. A purchase of a long-term investment in stock of another company would be presented in the financing section of the statement of changes in financial position.

Matching

For each transaction below, indicate the line(s) of the statement of changes in financial position where the effect would be presented and place the letter(s) for your answer in the space provided. Place an X if the effect would not be shown on the statement. Ignore income tax effects. (Hint: remember the CICA definition of "cash.")

A = Operating Section
B = Investing Activity (Source)
C = Investing Activity (Application)
D = Financing Activity (Source)
E = Financing Activity (Application)
F = Dividends (Application)

_____ 1. Depreciation recorded on equipment.

_____ 2. Marketable securities purchased for cash.

_____ 3. Discount on bonds payable is amortized.

_____ 4. Increase in the balance of accounts payable.

_____ 5. Land is acquired by giving cash.

_____ 6. Equity is undistributed earnings of affiliate is recognized.

_____ 7. The future income tax (credit) is increased for the year.

_____ 8. Acquisition of a building and land by entering into a lease meeting the capital lease criteria.

_____ 9. Paid dividends for the year.

_____ 10. Warranties payable increased during the year.

_____ 11. Preferred stock is converted into common stock.

_____ 12. Borrowed cash from the bank by issuing short-term note payable.

_____ 13. Amortization of patent recorded.

_____ 14. Sale of equipment for cash with a loss recognized.

_____ 15. Minority interest in net income for the period is deducted on the income statement.

_____ 16. Treasury stock is purchased for cash.

_____ 17. Long-term investments are sold for cash with a gain recognized.

_____ 18. Treasury stock is sold for an amount greater than its repurchase price.

_____ 19. Salaries are paid during the year.

_____ 20. New equipment is purchased by issuing a long-term note payable.

_____ 21. Accounts receivable increased during the year.

_____ 22. Land was acquired by issuing preferred stock.

_____ 23. Unearned revenue was reduced during the year.

_____ 24. Prepaid rent was increased during the year.

_____ 25. Retirement of long-term debt at maturity by using bond sinking fund.

Multiple Choice

Choose the best answer for each of the following questions and enter the identifying letter in the space provided.

_____ 1. The statement of changes in financial position is typically prepared:
a) before the balance sheet is prepared
b) after the balance sheet but before the income statement
c) after the income statement is prepared but before the balance sheet
d) after both the balance sheet and income statement are prepared

_____ 2. Each of the following is an addback to net income in deriving cash flow from operations except:
a) depreciation expense
b) amortization of patent
c) minority interest in consolidated earnings
d) all of the above

_____ 3. Each of the following is an addback to net income in deriving cash flow from operations except:
a) decrease in future income taxes
b) decrease in prepaid insurance
c) decrease in accounts receivable
d) increase in accounts payable

_____ 4. Each of the following is a deduction from net income in deriving cash flow from operations except:
a) increase in accounts receivable
b) loss on sale of equipment
c) amortization of bond premium
d) decrease in accounts payable

_____ 5. Each of the following is a deduction from net income in deriving cash flow from operations except:
a) decrease in warranties payable
b) increase in inventories
c) increase in accounts payable
d) all of the above

_____ 6. Each of the following is an addback to net income in deriving cash flow from operations except:
a) gain on sale of building
b) loss on sale of building
c) total proceeds from sale of building
d) all of the above

_____ 7. Each of the following is an addback to net income in deriving cash flow from operations except:
a) loss of sale equipment
b) equity in affiliate's losses
c) amortization of bond premium
d) all of the above

_____ 8. Each of the following is a deduction from net income in deriving cash flow from operations except:
a) gain on sale of building
b) gain of sale of equipment
c) gain on sale of temporary investments
d) all of the above

_____ 9. Each of the following would be presented in the investing section of the statement of changes in financial position except:
a) acquisition of equipment
b) acquisition of building
c) proceeds from sale of equipment
d) all of the above

_____ 10. Each of the following would be presented in the investing section of the statement of changes in financial position except:
a) proceeds from sale of land
b) proceeds from sale of equipment
c) proceeds from sale of marketable securities
d) all of the above

_____ 11. Which of the following would be presented in the investing section of the statement of changes in financial position?
a) acquisition of equipment through a capital lease
b) acquisition of treasury stock
c) retirement of long-term debt
d) none of the above

_____ 12. Which of the following would be presented in the financing section of the statement of changes in financial position?
a) long-term bonds payable issued
b) long-term notes payable issued
c) short-term notes payable issued (six-month note)
d) all of the above

_____ 13. Which of the following would be presented in the investing section of the statement of changes in financial position?
   a) retirement of long-term debt
   b) retirement of preferred stock
   c) acquisition of treasury stock
   d) none of the above

_____ 14. Which of the following transactions could be shown as an investing and financing activity?
   a) acquisition of building for cash
   b) common stock issued upon conversion of bonds
   c) acquisition of equipment by issuing a long-term note payable
   d) both b and c

_____ 15. Which of the following transactions would be presented in the financing section of the statement of changes in financial position?
   a) dividends paid
   b) dividends received
   c) interest paid
   d) none of the above

_____ 16. Which of the following would not be shown on the statement of changes in financial position?
   a) stock dividends paid
   b) early retirement of debt
   c) reissue of treasury stock
   d) none of the above

Exercises

1. Below is a list of several key transactions that may or may not affect the presentation of the statement of changes in financial position. You are to prepare the reconstruction work sheet entries (in journal form) to explain the change in cash and the other balance sheet accounts. Label the cash entries in a way that identifies the section of the statement of changes in financial position in which the item would appear. Explanations for the entries are not necessary. The first is answered as an example.
   a. Internal records indicate that $1,200 of depreciation is included in income determination for the period.

   Example answer:
   Cash (Operations — Addback) $1,200
      Accumulated Depreciation $1,200
   b. The income statement indicates that net income of the period was $5,000.
   c. Goodwill amortization amounted to $700 for the year.
   d. Equipment was acquired for $5,000, giving a long-term capital lease.
   e. Preferred stock totalling $3,000 was issued during the year.
   f. The company declared and paid $2,000 of dividends to its shareholders during the year. A consolidated subsidiary paid $100 dividends to its minority shareholders.
   g. The company sold for $250 a piece of equipment originally costing $1,000 on which accumulated depreciation of $700 had been taken.
   h. The company purchased treasury stock, $2,500.
   i. Accounts payable decreased by $200 during the year.
   j. The company borrowed $5,000 from the bank by giving a long-term note payable.
   k. Accounts receivable decrease by $150 during the year.
   l. Minority interest in earnings for the period was $200.
   m. Amortization of bond discount for the year was $75.

2. Your client, LOL, Inc., provides you with the income statement and comparative balance sheet data below. The client indicates that long-term investments were sold during the year at book value and new property and plant were acquired costing $210,000. You are to prepare a T-account work sheet and reconstruct entries originally made and enter them in appropriate T-accounts. You do not have to prepare the formal statement of changes in financial position.

LOL, INC.
Income Statement
For the Year Ended December 31, 19X2

Sales	$880,000	
Other Revenues	40,000	$920,000
Less:		
Cost of Goods Sold	$260,000	
Selling Expenses	26,000	
Depreciation Expenses	84,000	
Income Taxes	10,000	
Loss on Sale of Property and Plan	24,000	404,000
Net Income		516,000
Dividends		40,000
Income Retained in Business		$476,000

LOL, INC.
Comparative Balance Sheet Data
As of December 31, 19X2 and 19X1

	19X1	19X2
Cash	$ 321,600	$ 76,800
Accounts Receivable	246,400	98,000
Inventories	225,000	123,000
Long-Term Investments	180,000	194,000
Property and Plant	480,000	425,000
	$1,453,000	$917,600
Accounts Payable	$ 200,000	$134,600
Bonds Payable	100,000	149,800
Accumulated Depreciation	60,000	104,000
Capital Stock	350,000	262,200
Retained Earnings	743,000	267,000
	$1,453,000	$917,600

3. Comparative balance sheets as of December 31, 19X1 and 19X2 and the income statement for the year ended December 31, 19X2 for Lindsay, Inc. are presented below:

LINDSAY, INC.
Comparative Balance Sheets
December 31, 19X1 and 19X2

	19X1	19X2
Cash	$ 50,100	$ 174,000
Temporary Investments	33,500	15,400
Accounts Receivable, net	48,000	90,000
Inventory	62,820	105,820
Total Current Assets	$194,420	$ 385,220
Investment in Carter Co.	122,440	133,960
Plant Assets	610,200	730,600
Accumulated Depreciation	(30,000)	(32,500)
Total Assets	$897,060	$1,217,280

	19X1	19X2
Accounts Payable	$ 32,440	$ 110,892
Warranties Payable	10,000	9,000
Total Current Liabilities	$ 42,440	$ 119,892
Bonds Payable	100,000	230,000
Discount on Bonds Payable	(4,600)	(4,300)
Future Income Taxes	1,020	1,692
Preferred Stock	60,000	—
Common Stock	160,000	220,000
Retained Earnings	538,200	649,996
Total Liabilities and Shareholders' Equity	$897,060	$1,217,280

LINDSAY, INC.
Income Statement
For Year Ended December 31, 19X2

Sales	$485,614
Gain on Sale of Temporary Investments	4,800
Gain on Sale of Land	21,400
Equity in Carter Co. Earnings	11,760
	$523,574
Cost of Goods Sold	$296,814
Depreciation	2,500
Other Expenses	96,464
	$395,778
Net Income	$127,796

Additional information:

1. Lindsay, Inc. declared and paid $16,000 dividends during the year.

2. Land with a book value of $42,600 was sold during the year.

3. Equipment costing $163,000 was purchased during the year.

4. Bonds payable were issued at par.

5. Goodwill of $240 was amortized. The goodwill was attributed to the investment in Carter Co., a 30-percent owned company.

6. During the year, the preferred shareholders elected to exercise their conversion privilege. The conversion ratio was one preferred stock ($10 par) to two common shares ($5 par).
   a. Prepare a T-account work sheet for the preparation of a statement of changes in financial position.
   b. Prepare a formal statement of changes in financial position for the year ended December 31, 19X2.

ANSWERS TO QUESTIONS AND EXERCISES FOR APPENDIX 13.1

True/False

1. T	6. F	11. F	16. F
2. F	7. T	12. F	17. F
3. T	8. F	13. T	18. F
4. T	9. T	14. T	19. T
5. F	10. F	15. F	20. F

Matching

1. A	8. C, D	15. A	22. C, D
2. X	9. F	16. E	23. A
3. A	10. A	17. B, A	24. A
4. A	11. D, E	18. D	25. B, E
5. C	12. X	19. A	
6. A	13. A	20. C, D	
7. A	14. A, B	21. A	

Multiple Choice

1. d	5. c	9. d	13. d
2. d	6. a	10. c	14. c
3. a	7. c	11. a	15. d
4. b	8. c	12. d	16. a

Exercises

1.

	Dr.	Cr.
a. Cash (Operations — Addback)	$1,200	
Accumulated Depreciation		$1,200
b. Cash (Operations — Net Income)	$5,000	
Retained Earnings		$5,000
c. Cash (Operations — Addback)	$700	
Accumulated Amortization		$700
(or Goodwill)		
d. Cash (Financing — Capital lease		
obligation to acquire equipment)	$5,000	
Cash (Investing — Acquisition of		
equipment by issuing capital lease)		$5,000
e. Cash (Financing — Issue preferred stock)	$3,000	
Preferred Stock		$3,000
f. Retained Earnings	$2,000	
Minority Interest in Consolidated Subsidiary	100	
Cash (Dividends)		$2,100
g. Cash (Investing — Sale of Equipment)	$250	
Accumulated Depreciation	700	
Cash (Operations — Addback)	50	
Equipment		$1,000
h. Treasury Stock	$2,500	
Cash (Financing — Reacquisition of stock)		$2,500
i. Accounts Payable	$200	
Cash (Operations — Deduction)		$200

j.	Cash (Financing — Issue note payable)	$5,000	
	Long-term Note Payable		$5,000
k.	Cash (Operations — Addback)	$150	
	Accounts Receivable		$150
l.	Cash (Operations — Addback)	$200	
	Minority Interest in		
	Consolidated Subsidiary		$200
m.	Cash (Operations — Addback)	$75	
	Discount on Bonds Payable		$75

2. LOL, INC.
T-Account Work Sheet

Cash Position

		76,800	
		Operations	
Net Income	(a) 516,000	148,400 (g)	Increase in Accounts Receivable
Depreciation Expense	(b) 84,000	101,200 (h)	Increase in Inventories
Loss of Sale of Property and Plant	(e) 24,000		
Increase in Accounts Payable	(i) 65,400		
		Investing	
Sale of Long-Term Investments	(c) 14,000	210,000 (d)	Acquisition of Property
Sale of Property and Plant	(e) 3,000		
		Financing	
Issue Capital Stock	(k) 87,800	49,800 (j)	Retire Bonds Payable
		Dividends	
		40,000 (f)	
	321,600		

Accounts Receivable

	98,000		
(g)	148,400		
	246,400		

Inventories

	123,800		
(h)	101,200		
	225,000		

Long-Term Investments

194,000	14,000	(c)
180,000		

Property and Plant

	425,000	155,000	(e)
(d)	210,000		
	480,000		

Accounts Payable

		134,600	
		65,400	(i)
		200,000	

Bonds Payable

(j)	49,800	149,800	
		100,000	

Accumulated Depreciation

(e)	128,000	104,000	
		84,000	(b)
		60,000	

Capital Stock

		262,200	
		87,800	(k)
		350,000	

Retained Earnings

(f)	40,000	267,000	
		516,000	(a)
		743,000	

3. a.

LINDSAY, INC.
T-Account Work Sheet

			Cash Position			

			83,600			

Operations

Net Income	(1)	127,796	21,400	(3)	Gain on Sale of Land
Goodwill Amort.	(6)	240	11,760	(8)	Equity in Carter Co. Earnings
Depreciation	(9)	2,500	42,000	(10)	Incr. in Accts. Rec.
Increase in Accts. Pay.	(12)	78,452	43,000	(11)	Incr. in Inventory
Bond Disc. Amort.	(14)	300	1,000	(13)	Decr. in Warranties Payable
Deferred Income Taxes	(15)	672			

Investing

| Sale of Land | (3) | 64,000 | 163,000 | (4) | Acquisition of Equipment |

Financing

Issue Bonds Payable (5) 130,000			60,000	(7)	Conversion of Preferred
Issue Common Stock upon					Stock to Common Stock
Conversion of Preferred Stock	(7)	60,000			

Dividends

| | | | 16,000 | (2) | |

| | | | 189,400 | | | |

Accounts Receivable		**Inventory**		**Investment in Carter Co.**	
	48,000			62,820				122,440	240	(6)
(10)	42,000		(11)	43,000		(8)	11,760		
	90,000			105,820			133,960		

Plant Assets		**Accumulated Depreciation**		**Accounts Payable**	
	610,200	42,600			30,000				32,440
(4)	163,000				2,500	(9)			78,452
	730,600				32,500				110,892

Warranties Payable		**Bonds Payable**		**Discount on Bonds Payable**	
(13)	1,000	10,000			100,000		4,600		
					130,000	(5)		300	(14)
		9,000			230,000		4,300		

Deferred Income Taxes		**Preferred Stock**		**Common Stock**	
		1,020	(7a)	60,000	60,000			160,000	
		672 (15)						60,000	(7a)
		1,692						220,000	

Retained Earnings	
(2)	16,000	538,200	
		127,796	(1)
		649,996	

b. **LINDSAY, INC.**
Statement of Changes in Financial Position
For the Year Ended December 31, 19X2

Cash Provided by		
Operations:		
Net Income	$127,796	
Noncash Revenues, Expenses, Gains, and		
Loans Included in Income:		
Gain on Sale of Land	(21,400)	
Goodwill Amortization	240	
Depreciation	2,500	
Equity in Carter Co. Earnings	(11,760)	
Increase in Account Receivable	(42,000)	
Increase in Accounts Payable	78,452	
Increase in Inventory	(43,000)	
Decrease in Warranties Payable	(1,000)	
Bond Discount Amortization	300	
Future Income Taxes	672	
Cash Flow from Operations		$ 90,800
Investing Activities:		
Sale of Land		64,000
Financing Activities:		
Issue Bonds Payable	$130,000	
Issue Common Stock Upon Conversion		
of Preferred Stock	60,000	190,000
Total Sources of Cash	$344,800	
Cash Applied to Dividends		$ 16,000
Investing Activities:		
Acquisition of Equipment		163,000
Financing Activities:		
Conversion of Preferred Stock to Common Stock		60,000
Total Applications of Cash		$239,000
Net Increase in Cash Position		$105,800
Cash Position, Beginning of Year		$ 83,600
Cash Position, End of Year		$189,400

ASSIGNMENT MATERIAL

QUESTIONS

1. Review the meaning of the key terms listed on page 842.

2. "The reporting objective of the income statement under the accrual basis of accounting and the reporting objective of the statement of changes in financial position could be more easily accomplished by issuing a single income statement using the cash basis of accounting." Evaluate this proposal.

3. The text indicates that the statement of changes in financial position provides information about changes in the structure of a firm's assets and equities. Of what value is information about the structure of a firm's assets and equities?

4. The text states that the statement of changes in financial position can be used for assessing changes in both (1) liquidity and (2) the structure of assets, liabilities, and shareholders' equity. The acquisition of equipment by assuming a noncurrent liability is a transaction that must be disclosed (using the dual transactions assumption) even though it does not involve cash. This disclosure is made primarily for the second rather than the first use of the statement of changes in financial position listed above. Explain.

5. One writer stated, "Depreciation expense is the chief source of cash for growth in industries." A reader criticized this statement by replying: "The fact remains that if the companies listed had elected, in any year, to charge off $10 million more depreciation than they did charge off, they would not thereby have added one dime to the total of their cash available for plant expansion or for increasing inventories or receivables. Therefore, to speak of depreciation expense as a source of cash has no significance in a discussion of fundamentals." Comment on these statements, ignoring income tax effects.

6. A firm generated net income for the current year, but cash flow relating to operations was negative. How can this happen?

7. A firm operated at a net loss for the current year, but cash flow relating to operations was positive. How can this happen?

8. The acquisition of equipment by assuming a mortgage is a transaction that must be disclosed either in the statement of changes in financial position or in a supplemental schedule. Of what value is information about the disclosure of this type of transaction?

Exercises

9. *Effect of various transactions on cash.* Prepare a work sheet with the following headings.

Effect of Transaction or Event on:

Transaction or Event	Cash	Other Current Assets	Noncurrent Assets	Current Liabilities	Noncurrent Liabilities	Shareholders' Equity

a. For each of the transactions or events listed below, indicate the effect on the balance sheet categories shown in the work sheet.
   (1) Purchase of merchandise on account, $5,000.
   (2) Payment of $4,000 of amount due for purchases in **(1)**.
   (3) Sale of merchandise to customers on credit. Selling price is $7,000; cost of goods sold is $3,500.
   (4) Collection of $5,500 of amount due from customers from sales in **(3)**.
   (5) Depreciation expense for the period is $600.
   (6) Employees earn salaries of $1,200 [also see transaction **(7)**].
   (7) Employees are paid $1,100 of amount due in **(6)**.
   (8) Insurance premium of $200 is paid for coverage to begin next period.
   (9) Income taxes for the period are accrued, $900 [also see transaction **10)**].
   (10) Income taxes of $600 are paid.
   (11) Bonds payable are issued, $200.
   (12) Equipment costing $1,500, and on which $1,000 of depreciation had been taken, is sold for $500.
   (13) Equipment costing $300 is acquired for cash.
   (14) Equipment costing $200 is acquired and a noncurrent liability of $200 is assumed for the purchase price.
   (15) Dividends of $700 are declared and paid.
b. Indicate whether each of the transactions or events affecting cash relates to an operating, financing, or investing activity.

10. *Calculating cash provided by operations.* The following items were found in the financial statements of Maher Company Ltd. for Year 2:

Sales	$90,000
Depreciation Expense	45,000
Income Taxes	10,000
Other Expenses	20,000
Common Shares Issued During Year	17,500

The changes in current asset and current liability accounts were as follows on page 870.

Accounts Receivable	$45,000 Increase
Merchandise Inventories	30,000 Increase
Prepayments	5,000 Decrease
Accounts Payable	15,000 Increase
Income Taxes Payable	7,500 Decrease

Compute the amount of cash provided by operations.

11. *Calculating cash provided by operations.* Compute the amount of cash provided by operations in each of the independent cases below.

	a	b	c	d
Net Income (Loss)	$100	$50	$70	$(40)
Depreciation Expense	15	10	12	18
Increase (Decrease) in:				
Accounts Receivable	20	15	(10)	12
Merchandise Inventories	25	(10)	15	15
Prepayments	10	(3)	4	(6)
Accounts Payable	15	10	(20)	14
Income Taxes Payable	18	(8)	14	(16)
Other Current Liabilities	12	(9)	(7)	11

12. *Working backwards from changes in buildings and equipment account.* The comparative balance sheet of the Kanodia Co. Ltd. showed a balance in the Buildings and Equipment account at December 31, Year 5 of $24,600,000; at December 31, Year 4, the balance was $24,000,000. The Accumulated Depreciation account showed a balance of $8,600,000 at December 31, Year 5 and $7,600,000 at December 31, Year 4. The statement of changes in financial position reports that expenditures for buildings and equipment for the year totalled $1,300,000. The income statement indicates a depreciation charge of $1,200,000 for the year. Buildings and equipment were sold during the year at their book value.

Calculate the acquisition cost and accumulated depreciation of the buildings and equipment retired during the year and the proceeds from their disposition.

13. *Preparing statement of changes in financial position; working backwards from changes in plant asset accounts.* The balance in the Capital Assets account was $200 on January 1 and $260 on December 31. The balance in the Accumulated Depreciation account was $120 on January 1 and $140 on December 31. During the year, equipment costing $25 and with accumulated depreciation of $15 was sold for $10. No dividends were paid during the year, nor were there any changes in the Bonds Payable or the Common Stock accounts. Cash provided by operations totalled $80, and the net change in cash for the year was an increase of $5.

Prepare a statement of changes in financial position for the year.

14. *Preparing statement of changes in financial position using changes in balance sheet accounts.* The accounting records of Kropp Corporation reveal the following for the current year.

Account	Amount	Change
Cash	$120	Increase
Accounts Receivable	15	Increase
Merchandise Inventories	20	Decrease
Capital Assets	50[a]	Increase
Accumulated Depreciation	10	Increase
Accounts Payable	25	Increase
Bonds Payable	20	Increase
Common Shares	30	Increase
Retained Earnings	80[b]	Increase

[a]*There were no dispositions of Capital Assets during the year.*
[b]*Net income was $130; dividends were $50.*

Prepare a statement of changes in financial position, explaining the change in cash for the year.

15. *Preparing statement of changes in financial position using changes in balance sheet accounts.* The accounting records of Baker Corporation reveal the following for the current year.

Account	Amount	Change
Cash	$75	Decrease
Accounts Receivable	40	Increase
Merchandise Inventories	30	Increase
Capital Assets	60[a]	Increase
Accumulated Depreciation	20[a]	Increase
Accounts Payable	25	Decrease
Bonds Payable	35[b]	Decrease
Common Shares	45	Increase
Retained Earnings	50[c]	Increase

[a]*Equipment costing $15 and with accumulated depreciation of $12 was sold for $3 during the year.*
[b]*Bonds with a face value and book value of $50 were retired during the year at no gain or loss.*
[c]*Dividends declared and paid totalled $20 during the year.*

Prepare a statement of changes in financial position, explaining the change in cash for the year.

16. *Reformulating statement of changes in financial position.* Guerrero Corporation has prepared the statement of changes in financial position appearing in Exhibit 13.22. Recast this statement into a properly formulated statement of changes in financial position as shown in Figure 13.4.

EXHIBIT 13.22
GUERRERO CORPORATION
Statement of Changes in Financial Position
for the Current Year

Cash Provided by	
Proceeds from Issue of Bonds	$ 20,000
Proceeds from Issue of Common Stock	30,000
Proceeds from Sale of Equipment	4,000
Net Income	40,000
Depreciation Expense	10,000
Increase in Accounts Payable	15,000
Total Sources	$119,000
Cash Applied to	
Acquisition of Equipment[a]	$ 60,000
Payment of Dividends	12,000
Repayment of Bonds Payable	8,000
Increase in Accounts Receivable	16,000
Increase in Merchandise Inventory	11,000
Total Uses	$107,000
Net Change in Cash	$ 12,000

[a]*In addition, equipment costing $25,000 was acquired and a noncurrent liability assumed for the purchase price.*

17. *Effect of various transactions on statement of changes in financial position.* Exhibit 13.23 shows a *simplified* statement of changes in financial position for a period. Eleven of the lines in the statement are numbered. Other lines are various subtotals and grand totals; these are to be ignored in the remainder of the problem. Assume that the accounting cycle is complete for the period and that all of the financial statements have been prepared. Then it is discovered that a transaction has been overlooked. That transaction is recorded in the accounts, and all of the financial statements are corrected. For each of the following transactions, indicate which of the numbered lines of the statement of changes in financial position are affected. Define "funds" as cash. If net income, line (1) is affected, be sure to indicate whether it decreases or increases. Ignore income tax effects.
   a. Depreciation expense on office computer.
   b. Purchase of machinery for cash.
   c. Declaration of a cash dividend on common shares; the dividend was paid by the end of the fiscal year.
   d. Issue of common shares for cash.
   e. Proceeds of sale of common share investment, a noncurrent asset, for cash. The investment was sold for book value.
   f. Amortization of patent, treated as an expense.
   g. Amortization of patent, charged to production activities. The items being produced have not yet been completed.
   h. Acquisition of a factory site by issue of share capital.
   i. Purchase of inventory on account.
   j. Uninsured fire loss of merchandise inventory.
   k. Collection of an account receivable.

EXHIBIT 13.23
Simplified Statement of
Changes in Financial Position

Cash Provided by

Operations

Net Income	(1)
Addback for Expenses and Losses Not Using Working Capital	(2)
Additions for Decreases in Current Asset Accounts Other than Cash and for Increase in Current Liability Accounts	(3)
Subtractions for Revenues and Gains Not Producing Working Capital from Operations	(4)
Subtractions for Increases in Current Asset Accounts Other than Cash and for Decreases in Current Liability Accounts	(5)
Total Cash Provided by Operations [= (1) + (2) + (3) − (4) − (5)]	$

Financing Activities

Increases in Debt or Capital Stock	(6)

Investing Activities

Proceeds from Dispositions of Noncurrent Assets	(7)
Total "Other" Sources of Cash [= (6) + (7)]	$
Total Sources of Cash	$

Cash Applied to

Dividends	(8)
Financing Activities	
Reduction in Debt or Capital Stock	(9)
Investing Activities	
Acquisition of Noncurrent Assets	(10)
Total Uses of Cash [= (8) + (0) + (10)]	$
Change in Cash for the Period	(11)

l. Issue of bonds for cash.

m. Proceeds from sale of equipment. The equipment was sold for its book value.

PROBLEMS AND CASES

18. *Preparing statement of changes in financial position.* Exhibit 13.24 presents a comparative balance sheet for Bragg Corporation as of the beginning and end of the current year. During the year, there were no dispositions of property, plant, and equipment, and no dividends were declared or paid.

    Prepare a statement of changes in financial position for Bragg Corporation for the current year, supporting the statement with a T-account work sheet.

19. *Preparing statement of changes in financial position.* Condensed financial statement data for the Harris Company for the current year appear in Exhibits 13.25 and 13.26. During the current year, equipment costing $10,000 and with $8,000 of accumulated depreciation was sold for $2,000.

EXHIBIT 13.24
BRAGG CORPORATION
Comparative Balance Sheet

	December 31	January 1
ASSETS		
Current Assets:		
Cash	$ 10,000	$ 6,000
Accounts Receivable	82,000	72,000
Merchandise Inventories	110,000	95,000
Total Current Assets	$202,000	$173,000
Capital Assets	$425,000	$350,000
Less: Accumulated Depreciation	(135,000)	(123,000)
Total Capital Assets	$290,000	$227,000
Total Assets	$492,000	$400,000
LIABILITIES AND SHAREHOLDERS' EQUITY		
Current Liabilities:		
Accounts Payable	$121,000	$ 95,000
Income Taxes Payable	15,000	10,000
Total Current Liabilities	$136,000	$105,000
Long-Term Debt:		
Bonds Payable	75,000	50,000
Total Liabilities	$211,000	$155,000
Shareholders' Equity:		
Common Shares	$106,000	$105,000
Retained Earnings	175,000	140,000
Total Shareholders' Equity	$281,000	$245,000
Total Liabilities and Shareholders' Equity	$492,000	$400,000

EXHIBIT 13.25
HARRIS CO. LTD.
Comparative Balance Sheets

	December 31	January 1
Assets		
Cash	$ 24,000	$ 20,000
Accounts Receivable	58,000	52,000
Inventory	81,000	79,000
Land	15,000	15,000
Buildings and Equipment (Cost)	415,000	400,000
Less: Accumulated Depreciation	(252,000)	(240,000)
Total Assets	$341,000	$326,000
Liabilities and Shareholders' Equity		
Accounts Payable for Inventory	$ 65,000	$ 62,000
Interest Payable	4,000	6,000
Mortgage Payable	55,000	60,000
Common Shares	130,000	120,000
Retained Earnings	87,000	78,000
Total Liabilities and Shareholders' Equity	$341,000	$326,000

EXHIBIT 13.26
HARRIS CO. LTD.
Statement of Income and Retained Earnings
For the Current Year

Sales		$200,000
Less: Cost of Goods Sold		100,000
Gross Profit		$100,000
Less: Operating Expenses		
Wages and Salaries	$30,000	
Depreciation	20,000	50,000
Net Income Before Income Tax		$ 50,000
Income Tax Expense		11,000
Net Income		$ 39,000
Dividends on Common Shares		30,000
Addition to Retained Earnings for Year		$ 9,000
Retained Earnings, January 1		78,000
Retained Earnings, December 31		$ 87,000

EXHIBIT 13.27
PERKERSON SUPPLY CO. INC.
Comparative Balance Sheets

	December 31	January 1
ASSETS		
Current Assets:		
Cash	$ 162,000	$ 179,000
Accounts Receivable	526,000	473,000
Inventory	604,000	502,000
Total Current Assets	$1,292,000	$1,154,000
Capital Assets:		
Land	$ 315,000	$ 297,000
Buildings and Machinery	4,773,000	4,339,000
Less: Accumulated Depreciation	(2,182,000)	(1,987,000)
Total Capital Assets	$2,906,000	$2,649,000
Total Assets	$4,198,000	$3,803,000
LIABILITIES AND SHAREHOLDERS' EQUITY		
Current Liabilities:		
Accounts Payable	$ 279,000	$ 206,000
Income Taxes Payable	145,000	137,000
Other Short-Term Payables	363,000	294,000
Total Current Liabilities	$ 787,000	$ 637,000
Noncurrent Liabilities:		
Bonds Payable	967,000	992,000
Total Liabilities	$1,754,000	$1,629,000
Shareholders' Equity		
Common Shares	$ 852,000	$ 836,000
Retained Earnings	1,592,000	1,338,000
Total Shareholders' Equity	$2,444,000	$2,174,000
Total Liabilities and Shareholders' Equity	$4,198,000	$3,803,000

Prepare a statement of changes in financial position for the year, supporting the statement with a T-account work sheet. Define "funds" as cash.

20. *Preparing statement of changes in financial position.* Financial statement data for the Perkerson Supply Co. Inc. for the current year appear in Exhibit 13.27.

Additional information:

(1) Net income for the year was $324,000; dividends declared and paid were $70,000.
(2) Depreciation expense for the year was $305,000 on buildings and machinery.
(3) Machinery originally costing $125,000 and with accumulated depreciation of $110,000 was sold for $15,000.

Prepare a statement of changes in financial position for the Perkerson Supply Co. Inc. for the year with "funds" defined as cash. Support the statement with a T-account work sheet.

21. (This problem should not be attempted until Problem **(20)** has been completed.) Refer to Problem **(20)** concerning the Perkerson Supply Co. Inc. Convert cash provided by operations to working capital provided by operations.

EXHIBIT 13.28
VICTORIA LTD.
Postclosing Trial Balance
Comparative Data

	December 31	January 1
Debits:		
Cash	$ 55,000	$ 62,000
Accounts Receivable	163,000	135,000
Inventory	262,000	247,000
Plant and Equipment (cost)	1,389,000	1,362,000
Total Debits	$1,869,000	$1,806,000
Credits:		
Accounts Payable	$ 75,000	$ 72,000
Accumulated Depreciation	573,000	508,000
Long-Term Debt	215,000	200,000
Capital Stock	509,000	509,000
Retained Earnings	497,000	517,000
Total Credits	$1,869,000	$1,806,000
Income Statement Data		
Sales	$1,338,000	
Cost of Goods Sold (excluding depreciation)	932,000	
Selling and Administrative Expenses	313,000	
Depreciation Expense (manufacturing)	93,000	
Interest Expense	20,000	

22. Refer to Problem (20) concerning the Perkerson Supply Co. Inc. Work through the problem using a definition of "funds" as working capital.

23. *Preparing income statement and statement of changes in financial position.* Condensed financial statement data for Victoria Ltd. for the year appear in Exhibit 13.28.

Expenditures on new plant and equipment for the year amounted to $121,000. Old plant and equipment that had cost $94,000 were sold during the year. It was sold for cash at book value.
  a. Prepare an income statement (including a reconciliation of retained earnings) for the year.
  b. Prepare a statement of changes in financial position for Victoria Ltd. for the year, defining "funds" as cash. Support the statement of changes in financial position with a T-account work sheet.

24. *Preparing statement of changes in financial position.* Exhibit 13.29 presents a comparative balance sheet for Psilos Corporation as of the beginning and end of the current year. Additional information related to the year is shown at the top of the next page.

EXHIBIT 13.29
PSILOS CORPORATION
Comparative Balance Sheet

	December 31	January 1
ASSETS		
Current Assets:		
Cash	$ 16,000	$ 28,000
Accounts Receivable	109,000	125,000
Merchandise Inventories	163,000	147,000
To tal Current Assets	$288,000	$300,000
Capital Assets:	$240,000	$210,000
Less: Accumulated Depreciation	(85,000)	(87,000)
Total Capital Assets	$155,000	$123,000
Total Assets	$443,000	$423,000
LIABILITIES AND SHAREHOLDERS' EQUITY		
Current Liabilities:		
Accounts Payable	$175,000	$177,000
Income Taxes Payable	30,000	23,000
Total Current Liabilities	$205,000	$200,000
Long-Term Debt:		
Bonds Payable	75,000	50,000
Total Liabilities	$280,000	$250,000
Shareholders' Equity		
Common Shares	$ 10,000	$ 10,000
Retained Earnings	153,000	163,000
Total Shareholders' Equity	$163,000	$173,000
Total Liabilities and Shareholders' Equity	$443,000	$423,000

Net Income	$40,000
Dividends Declared and Paid	50,000
Capital Assets Acquired:	
For Cash	40,000
By Assuming Long-Term Debt	15,000
Proceeds from Sale of Capital Assets Sold at Book Value	5,000

Prepare a statement of changes in financial position for Psilos Corporation for the current year, supporting the statement with a T-account work sheet.

25. *Preparing statement of changes in financial position over two-year period.* Condensed financial statement data of the Alberta Co. Ltd. for the years ending December 31, Year 1, Year 2, and Year 3 are presented in Exhibits 13.30 and 13.31.

EXHIBIT 13.30
ALBERTA CO. LTD.
Postclosing Trial Balance
Comparative Data

	12/31/Year 3	12/31/Year 2	12/31/Year 1
Debits:			
Cash	$ 97,000	$ 87,000	$ 55,000
Accounts Receivable	105,000	120,000	110,000
Merchandise Inventories	140,000	115,000	125,000
Total Current Assets	$ 342,000	$ 322,000	$ 290,000
Capital Assets	1,875,000	1,679,000	1,616,000
Total Debits	$2,217,000	$2,001,000	$1,906,000
Credits:			
Accounts Payable	$ 83,000	$ 80,000	$ 81,000
Accumulated Depreciation	745,000	720,000	697,000
Bonds Payable	135,000	90,000	106,000
Common Shares	514,000	423,000	377,000
Retained Earnings	740,000	688,000	645,000
Total Credits	$2,217,000	$2,001,000	$1,906,000

EXHIBIT 13.31
ALBERTA CO. LTD.
Income and Retained Earnings
Statement Data

	Year 3	Year 2
Sales	$970,000	$910,000
Interest and Other Revenue	7,000	5,000
Cost of Goods Sold (excluding depreciation)	413,000	370,000
Selling and Administrative Expenses	301,000	320,000
Depreciation	98,000	87,000
Income Taxes	66,000	55,000
Dividends Declared	47,000	40,000

a. Prepare a statement of changes in financial position for Year 2. Support the statement with a T-account work sheet. The original cost of the capital assets sold during Year 2 was $108,000. These assets were sold for cash at their net book value.

b. Prepare a T-account work sheet and a statement of changes in financial position for Year 3. Capital assets were sold during the year at book value. Expenditures on new capital assets amounted to $318,000 during Year 3.

26. **Working backwards through statement of changes in financial position.** The Quinta Co. Ltd. presents the postclosing trial balance shown in Exhibit 13.32 and statement of changes in financial position shown in Exhibit 13.33 for Year 5.

EXHIBIT 13.32
QUINTA CO. LTD.
Postclosing Trial Balance
December 31, Year 5

Debit Balances:

Cash	$ 25,000
Accounts Receivable	220,000
Merchandise Inventories	320,000
Land	40,000
Buildings and Equipment	500,000
Investments (noncurrent)	100,000
Total Debits	$1,205,000

Credit Balances:

Accumulated Depreciation	$ 200,000
Accounts Payable	280,000
Other Current Liabilities	85,000
Bonds Payable	100,000
Common Shares	200,000
Retained Earnings	340,000
Total Credits	$1,205,000

Investment, equipment, and land were sold for cash at their net book value. The accumulated depreciation of the equipment sold was $20,000.

Prepare a balance sheet for the beginning of the year, January 1, Year 5.

27. **Interpretative case using statement of changes in financial position** *(adapted from a problem by Leonard Morrissey).* RV Suppliers, Incorporated, founded in January Year 1, manufactures "Kaps." A "Kap" is a relatively low-cost camping unit attached to a pickup truck. Most units consist of an extruded aluminum frame and a fibreglass skin.

After a loss in its initial year, the company was barely profitable in Year 2 and Year 3. More substantial profits were realized in Years 4 and 5, as indicated in the financial statements shown in Exhibits 13.34 and 13.35.

EXHIBIT 13.33
QUINTA CO. LTD.
Statement of Changes in Financial Position
For Year Ended December 31, 19X5

Cash Provided by		
Operations		
Net Income		$200,000
Additions:		
Depreciation Expense		60,000
Increase in Accounts Payable		25,000
Subtractions:		
Increase in Accounts Receivable		(30,000)
Increase in Merchandise Inventories		(40,000)
Decrease in Other Current Liabilities		(45,000)
Total Sources from Operations		$170,000
Financing Activities		
Common Share Issue	$60,000	
Bond Issue	40,000	
Investing Activities		
Sale of Investments	$40,000	
Sale of Buildings and Equipment	15,000	
Sale of Land	10,000	
Total Sources of Cash		$335,000
Cash Applied to		
Dividends		$200,000
Investing Activities		
Acquisition of Buildings and Equipment		130,000
Total Uses of Cash		$330,000
Increase in Cash During the Year		$ 5,000

EXHIBIT 13.34
RV SUPPLIERS, INCORPORATED
Income Statements
(amounts in thousands)

	Year 6	Year 5	Year 4
Net Sales	$247.4	$424.0	$266.4
Cost of Goods Sold	210.6	314.6	191.4
Gross Profit	$ 36.8	$109.4	$ 75.0
Operating Expenses[a]	55.2	58.4	35.5
Income (loss) Before Income Taxes	$(18.4)	$ 51.0	$ 39.5
Income Taxes	(5.0)	16.4	12.3
Net Income (loss)	$(13.4)	$ 34.6	$ 27.2

[a]Includes depreciation expense of $1.7 in Year 4, $4.8 in Year 5, and $7.6 in Year 6.

EXHIBIT 13.35
RV SUPPLIERS, INCORPORATED
Balance Sheet
(amounts in thousands)

	Dec. 31 Year 6	Dec. 31 Year 5	Dec. 31 Year 4
ASSETS			
Current Assets:			
Cash	$ 5.2	$ 12.0	$ 14.0
Accounts Receivable	24.2	55.6	28.8
Inventories	81.0	85.6	54.0
Income Tax Recoverable	5.0	0	0
Prepayments	5.6	7.4	4.8
Total Current Assets	$121.0	$160.6	$101.6
Capital Assets — Net (Note 1)	72.2	73.4	30.2
Total Assets	$193.2	$234.0	$131.8
LIABILITIES AND SHAREHOLDERS' EQUITY			
Current Liabilities:			
Bank Notes Payable	$ 70.0	$ 52.0	$ 10.0
Accounts Payable	17.4	53.4	31.6
Income Taxes Payable	0	7.0	5.8
Other Current Liabilities	4.4	6.8	4.2
Total Current Liabilities	$ 91.8	$119.2	$ 51.6
Shareholders' Equity:			
Capital Shares	$ 44.6	$ 44.6	$ 44.6
Retained Earnings	56.8	70.2	35.6
Total Shareholders' Equity	$101.4	$114.8	$ 80.2
Total Liabilities and Shareholders' Equity	$193.2	$234.0	$131.8

Note 1	Year 6	Year 5	Year 4
Acquisitions	$ 11.8	$ 48.4	$ 13.4
Depreciation Expense	(7.6)	(4.8)	(1.7)
Book Value and Sales Proceeds from Retirements	(5.4)	(0.4)	(0.4)
Net Change in Capital Assets	$ (1.2)	$ 43.2	$ 11.3

However, in Year 6, ended just last month, the company suffered a loss of $13,400. Sales dropped from $424,000 in Year 5 to $247,400 in Year 6. The outlook for Year 7 is not encouraging. Potential buyers continue to shun pickup trucks in preference to more energy-efficient small foreign and domestic automobiles.

How did the company finance its rapid growth during the year ended December 31, Year 5? What were the sources and uses of cash during the year? Similarly, how did the company manage its financial affairs during the abrupt contraction in business during the year just ended last month?

Problems and Cases Requiring Study of Appendix 13.1

28. *Effect on statement of changes in financial position.* Refer to Exhibit 13.23, where a simplified statement of changes in financial position is presented. For each of the transactions that follow, indicate the number(s) of the line(s) in Exhibit 13.23 that would be affected. If net income is affected, be sure to indicate if it increases or decreases. Ignore income tax effects. (See page 873.)

 a. Long-term bonds are retired, using funds in a bond sinking fund.

 b. A cash dividend is received from an unconsolidated subsidiary accounted for using the equity method.

 c. Accounts are written off as uncollectable when the allowance method is used.

 d. Marketable securities are purchased for cash.

 e. Land is sold for an amount greater than its acquisition cost.

 f. A firm's annual cash contribution to a bond sinking fund is made.

 g. A fully amortized patent is written off.

 h. Land is given in settlement of annual legal fees of the corporate lawyer.

 i. Preferred stock is converted into common stock.

 j. Inventory items are written down to reflect a lower of cost for market valuation.

 k. The Deferred Income Tax (Credit) account is increased for the year.

 l. The Premium on Bonds Payable account is amortized for the year.

 m. A majority interest in the common stock of a supplier is acquired by issuing long-term convertible bonds.

 n. The liability account Rental Fees Received in Advance is reduced when the rental services are provided.

 o. A 10 percent stock dividend is declared and issued.

 p. Long-term debt maturing within the next year is reclassified as a current liability.

 q. Provision is made for estimated uncollectable accounts when the allowance method is used.

 r. Income is recognized using the percentage-of-completion method for long-term contracts.

 s. Land is donated to a firm by a local government as an inducement to locate manufacturing facilities in the area.

 t. Long-term investments in securities are written down to reflect a permanent decline in value.

 u. Research and development costs are paid during the period.

 v. Depreciation is recorded on selling and administrative facilities.

 w. Depreciation is recorded on manufacturing facilities.

 x. Treasury stock is sold for an amount less than its repurchase price.

 y. A three-month loan is obtained from a local bank.

EXHIBIT 13.36
TAYLOR CORPORATION
Changes in Account Balances Between December 31, Year 4 and December 31, Year 5

	December 31	
	Year 5	Year 4
DEBIT BALANCES		
Cash	$ 145,000	$ 186,000
Accounts Receivable	255,000	273,000
Inventories	483,000	538,000
Securities Held for Plant Expansion Purposes	150,000	—
Machinery and Equipment	927,000	647,000
Leasehold Improvements	87,000	87,000
Patents	27,800	30,000
Totals	$2,074,800	$1,761,000
CREDIT BALANCES		
Allowance for Uncollectable Accounts	$ 16,000	$ 17,000
Accumulated Depreciation of Machinery and Equipment	416,000	372,000
Allowance for Amortization of Leasehold Improvements	58,000	49,000
Accounts Payable	232,800	105,000
Cash Dividends Payable	40,000	—
Current Portion of 6-Percent Serial Bonds Payable	50,000	50,000
6-Percent Serial Bonds Payable	250,000	300,000
Preferred Shares	90,000	100,000
Common Shares	500,000	500,000
Retained Earnings	422,000	268,000
Totals	$2,074,800	$1,761,000

29. *Preparation of statement of changes in financial position (adapted from CPA examination).* The management of Taylor Corporation, concerned over a decrease in cash, has provided you with the comparative analysis of changes in account balances between December 31, Year 4 and December 31, Year 5, shown in Exhibit 13.36.

During Year 5, the following transactions occurred:
(1) New machinery was purchased for $386,000. In addition, certain obsolete machinery, having a book value of $61,000, was sold for $48,000. No other entries were recorded in Machinery and Equipment or related accounts other than provision for depreciation.
(2) Taylor paid $2,000 of legal costs in a successful defense of a new patent, which was correctly debited to the Patents account. Amortization of patents amounting to $4,200 was recorded.
(3) Preferred shares, par value $100, were purchased at 110 and subsequently cancelled. The premium paid was charged to retained earnings.
(4) On December 10, Year 5, the board of directors declared a cash dividend of $0.20 per share payable to holders of common shares on January 10, Year 6.
(5) A comparative analysis of retained earnings as of December 31, Year 5 and Year 4 is presented as follows on the next page.

| | December 31 | |
	Year 5	Year 4
Balance, January 1	$268,000	$131,000
Net Income	195,000	172,000
	$463,000	$303,000
Dividends Declared	(40,000)	(35,000)
Premium on Preferred Stock Repurchased	(1,000)	—
Balance, December 31	$422,000	$268,000

(6) Accounts totalling $3,000 were written off as uncollectable during Year 5.

a. Prepare a T-account work sheet for preparation of a statement of changes in financial position.

b. Prepare a formal statement of changes in financial position for Taylor Corporation for the year ending December 31, Year 5.

30. *Preparation of statement of changes in financial position* (adapted from CPA examination). Feltham Company has prepared its financial statements for the year ended December 31, Year 6 and for the three months ended March 31, Year 7. You have been asked to prepare a statement of changes in financial position for the three months ended March 31, Year 7. The company's balance sheet data at December 31, Year 6 and March 31, Year 7 are shown in Exhibit 13.37, and its income statement data for the three months ended March 31, Year 7 are shown in Exhibit 13.38. You have previously satisfied yourself about the correctness of the amounts presented.

Your discussion with the company's controller and a review of the financial records have revealed the following information:

(1) On January 8, Year 7, the company sold marketable securities for cash. These securities had been held for more than six months. No marketable securities were purchased during Year 7.

(2) The company's preferred shares are covertible into common shares at a rate of one share of preferred to two shares of common. The preferred shares and common shares have par values of $2 and $1, respectively.

(3) On January 17, Year 7, three acres of land were condemned. An award of $32,000 in cash was received on March 22, Year 7. Purchase of additional land as a replacement is not contemplated by the company.

(4) On March 25, Year 7, the company purchased equipment for cash.

(5) On March 29, Year 7, bonds payable were issued by the company at par for cash.

(6) The investment in the 30-percent-owned company included an amount attributable to goodwill of $3,220 at December 31, Year 6. Goodwill is being amortized at an annual rate of $480.

a. Prepare a T-account work sheet for the preparation of statement of changes in financial position, defining "funds" as cash and cash equivalents.

b. Prepare a formal statement of changes in financial position for Feltham Company for the three months ending March 31, Year 7.

EXHIBIT 13.37
FELTHAM COMPANY
Balance Sheet

	Dec. 31, Year 6	Mar. 31, Year 7
Cash	$ 25,300	$ 87,400
Marketable Securities	16,500	7,300
Accounts Receivable (net)	24,320	49,320
Inventory	31,090	48,590
Total Current Assets	$ 97,210	$192,610
Land	40,000	18,700
Building	250,000	250,000
Equipment	—	81,500
Accumulated Depreciation	(15,000)	(16,250)
Investment in 30-Percent-Owned Company	61,220	66,980
Other Assets	15,100	15,100
Total Assets	$448,530	$608,640
Accounts Payable	$ 21,220	$ 17,330
Dividend Payable	—	8,000
Income Taxes Payable	—	34,616
Total Current Liabilities	$ 21,220	$ 59,946
Other Liabilities	186,000	186,000
Bonds Payable	50,000	115,000
Discount on Bonds Payable	(2,300)	(2,150)
Deferred Income Taxes	510	846
Preferred Shares	30,000	—
Common Shares	80,000	110,000
Dividends Declared	—	(8,000)
Retained Earnings	83,100	146,998
Total Equities	$448,530	$608,640

EXHIBIT 13.38
FELTHAM COMPANY
Income Statement Data for the Three Months Ended March 31, Year 7

Sales	$242,807
Gain on Sale of Marketable Securities	2,400
Equity in Earnings of 30-Percent-Owned Company	5,880
Gain on Condemnation of Land	10,700
Total Revenues	$261,787
Cost of Sales	$138,407
General and Administration Expenses	22,130
Depreciation	1,250
Interest Expense	1,150
Income Taxes	34,952
Total Expenses	$197,889
Net Income	$ 63,898

31. *Preparation of statement of changes in financial position* (adapted from CPA examination). Exhibit 13.39 presents a comparative statement of financial position for McGuffin Corporation as of December 31, Year 1 and Year 2. Exhibit 13.40 presents an income statement for Year 2. The following additional information has been obtained.

(1) On February 2, Year 2, McGuffin issued a 10 percent stock dividend to shareholders of record on January 15, Year 2. The market price per share of the common stock on February 2, Year 2 was $15.

(2) On March 1, Year 2, McGuffin issued 3,800 common shares for land. The common shares and land had current market values of approximately $40,000 on March 1, Year 2.

EXHIBIT 13.39
McGuffin Corporation
Statement of Financial Position

	December 31	
	Year 2	Year 1
ASSETS		
Current Assets:		
Cash	$ 100,000	$ 90,000
Accounts Receivable (net of allowance for doubtful accounts of $10,000 and $8,000, respectively)	210,000	140,000
Inventories	260,000	220,000
Total Current Assets	$ 570,000	$ 450,000
Land	325,000	200,000
Plant and Equipment	580,000	633,000
Less: Accumulated Depreciation	(90,000)	(100,000)
Patents	30,000	33,000
Total Assets	$1,415,000	$1,216,000
LIABILITIES AND SHAREHOLDERS' EQUITY		
Liabilities:		
Current Liabilities:		
Accounts Payable	$ 260,000	$ 200,000
Accrued Liabilities	200,000	210,000
Total Current Liabilities	$ 460,000	$ 410,000
Deferred Income Taxes	140,000	100,000
Long-Term Bonds (due December 15, Year 13)	130,000	180,000
Total Liabilities	$ 730,000	$ 690,000
Shareholders' Equity:		
Common Shares, Par Value $5, Authorized 100,000 Shares, Issued and Outstanding 50,000 and 42,000 Shares, Respectively	$ 250,000	$ 210,000
Contributed Surplus	233,000	170,000
Retained Earnings	202,000	146,000
Total Shareholders' Equity	$ 685,000	$ 526,000
Total Liabilities and Shareholders' Equity	$1,415,000	$1,216,000

EXHIBIT 13.40
McGUFFIN CORPORATION
Income Statement for the Year Ended December 31, Year 2

Sales	$1,000,000
Expenses:	
Cost of Goods Sold	$ 560,000
Salary and Wages	190,000
Depreciation	20,000
Amortization	3,000
Loss on Sale of Equipment	4,000
Interest	16,000
Miscellaneous	8,000
Total Expenses	$ 801,000
Income Before Income Taxes and Extraordinary Item	$ 199,000
Income Taxes	
Current	$ 50,000
Deferred	40,000
Provision for Income Taxes	$ 90,000
Income Before Extraordinary Item	$ 109,000
Extraordinary Item — Gain on Repurchase of Long-Term Bonds	
(net of $10,000 income tax)	12,000
Net Income	$ 121,000
Earnings per Share:	
Income Before Extraordinary Item	$2.21
Extraordinary Item	0.24
Net Income	$2.45

(3) On April 15, Year 2, McGuffin repurchased long-term bonds with a face and book value of $50,000. The gain of $22,000 was reported as an extraordinary item on the income statement.

(4) On June 30, Year 2, McGuffin sold equipment costing $53,000, with a book value of $23,000, for $19,000 cash.

(5) On September 30, Year 2, McGuffin declared and paid a $0.04 per share cash dividend to shareholders of record on August 1, Year 2.

(6) On October 10, Year 2, McGuffin purchased land for $85,000 cash.

(7) Future income taxes represent timing differences relating to the use of different depreciation methods for income tax and financial statement reporting.

a. Prepare a T-account work sheet for the preparation of statement of changes in financial position.

b. Prepare a formal statement of changes in financial position for McGuffin Corporation for the year ended December 31, Year 2.

32. *Preparation of statement of changes in financial position* (*adapted from CPA examination*). The comparative balance sheets for the Crandall Corporation are shown in Exhibit 13.41.

The following additional information relates to Year 5 activities.

(1) The Retained Earnings account was analyzed as follows:

Retained Earnings, December 31, Year 4		$758,200
Add Net Income After Extraordinary Items (loss of $3,000)		236,580
Subtotal		$994,780
Deduct:		
Cash Dividends	$130,000	
Loss on Reissue of Treasury Shares	3,000	
Stock Dividend	100,200	(233,200)
Retained Earnings, December 31, Year 5		$761,580

(2) On January 2, Year 5, marketable securities costing $110,000 were sold for $127,000. The proceeds from this sale, the funds in the bond sinking fund, and the amount received from the issuance of the 8 percent debentures were used to retire the 6 percent mortgage bonds. Any gain or loss on the retirement is taxed currently at 40 percent.

EXHIBIT 13.41
CRANDALL CORPORATION
Comparative Balance Sheets
December 31, Year 5 and Year 4

	Year 5	Year 4
ASSETS		
Cash	$ 141,900	$ 165,300
Marketable Securities (at cost)	122,800	129,200
Accounts Receivable (net)	312,200	371,200
Inventories	255,200	124,100
Prepayments	23,400	22,000
Bond Sinking Fund	—	63,000
Investment in Subsidiary (at equity)	134,080	152,000
Plant and Equipment (net)	1,443,700	1,534,600
Total Assets	$2,433,280	$2,561,400
EQUITIES		
Accounts Payable	$ 238,100	$ 213,300
Notes Payable — Current	—	145,000
Accrued Payables	16,500	18,000
Income Taxes Payable	97,500	31,000
Deferred Income Taxes (noncurrent)	127,900	128,400
6-Percent Mortgage Bonds Payable (due Year 17)	—	300,000
Premium on Mortgage Bonds	—	10,000
8-Percent Debentures Payable (due Year 25)	125,000	—
Common Shares, $10 Par Value	1,033,500	950,000
Contributed Surplus	67,700	51,000
Retained Earnings	761,580	758,200
Treasury Shares — at Cost of $3 per Share	(34,500)	(43,500)
Total Equities	$2,433,280	$2,561,400

(3) The treasury shares were reissued on February 28, Year 5. All "losses" on the reissue of treasury shares are charged to retained earnings.

(4) The stock dividend was declared on October 31, Year 5, when the market price of Crandall Corporation's shares was $12 per share.

(5) On April 30, Year 5, a fire destroyed a warehouse that cost $100,000, on which depreciation of $65,000 had accumulated. The loss was not insured.

(6) Plant and equipment transactions consisted of the sale of a building at its book value of $4,000 and the purchase of machinery for $28,000.

(7) Accounts receivable written off as uncollectable were $16,300 in Year 4 and $18,500 in Year 5. Expired insurance was $4,100 recorded in Year 4 and $3,900 in Year 5.

(8) The subsidiary, which is 80 percent owned, reported a loss of $22,400 for Year 5.

a. Prepare a T-account work sheet for Crandall Corporation for Year 5, defining "funds" as cash and cash equivalents.

b. Prepare a formal statement of changes in financial position for the year ending December 31, Year 5.

33. **Effects on funds statement.** Indicate the effect on Cash Provided by Operations of the following independent transactions. Include the effects of income taxes, assuming a rate of 40 percent of pretax income, that the accounting methods used on the tax return are the same as on the financial statements, and that taxes have been paid in cash.

a. A firm using the lower of cost and market basis for inventories writes ending inventory down by $100,000.

b. A firm has been using FIFO. It switches to weighted-average cost at the end of the current year and finds that the cost of goods sold is $200,000 larger than it would have been under FIFO.

34. **Funds statement effects.** Refer to the Simplified Statement of Changes in Financial Position Statement for a Period in Exhibit 13.23, on page 873. Eleven of the lines in the statement are numbered. Ignore the unnumbered lines in responding to the questions below.

Assume that the accounting cycle is complete for the period and that all of the financial statements have been prepared. Then it is discovered that a transaction has been overlooked. That transaction is recorded in the accounts, and all of the financial statements are corrected. Define "funds" as cash.

For each of the following transactions or events, indicate which of the numbered lines of the funds statement would be affected and by how much. Ignore income tax effects.

a. Estimated uncollectables equal to 1 percent of the year's sales of $1 million are recognized. An entry is made increasing the Allowance for Doubtful Accounts.

b. The specific account receivable of Eli Worman in the amount of $2,000 is written off by a firm using the allowance method.

c. The specific account receivable of Eli Worman in the amount of $3,000 is written off by a firm using the direct writeoff method.

d. A firm owns temporary investments. Dividends of $30,000 are declared on the shares owned. The payment will be received next period.

e. The portfolio of temporary investments acquired this period has a market value of $60,000 less than their net amount shown on the balance sheet at the end of the current accounting period. An entry is made changing the allowance account contra to the current asset, temporary investments.

f. The market value of the same portfolio of temporary investments referred to in part (e) has increased $40,000 by the end of the next period.

35. *Analysis of statement of changes in financial position; change definition of funds to exclude inventories.* For many years, Standard Motors Corporation (SM) defined "funds" as working capital (= current assets − current liabilities) in its statement of changes in financial position. Exhibit 13.42 presents condensed excerpts of SM's funds statements for several recent years with "funds" defined as working capital. During this five-year period, SM changed the definition of "funds" to cash and temporary investments. Today, companies present the funds statement with "funds" defined as cash or cash plus temporary investments net of short-term borrowings. One implication of the difference is that changes in inventories become sources of uses of funds, rather than mere alterations of the components of funds.

EXHIBIT 13.42
STANDARD MOTORS CORPORATION
Excerpts from Statement of Changes in Financial Position
with Working Capital Definition of Funds
(dollars amounts in millions)

	Year 5	Year 4	Year 3	Year 2	Year 1
Total Working Capital Provided by Current Operations	$5,589.0	$4,807.6	$3,726.7	$5,758.8	$6,479.7
Increase (Decrease) in Working Capital Items by Element:					
Cash and Temporary Investments	$1,805.5	($2,394.5)	$ 728.8	($1,068.4)	$ 814.8
Accounts and Notes Receivable	(778.8)	(125.1)	(1,262.0)	(608.3)	957.6
Inventories	(1,038.5)	(72.3)	(844.1)	499.6	401.0
Prepaid Expenses and Deferred Income Taxes	341.1	820.6	243.1	(259.9)	(131.1)
Accounts Payable	99.0	268.0	(586.4)	307.0	893.3
Loans Payable	543.3	51.3	(752.4)	466.2	57.3
Accrued Liabilities	(474.3)	498.7	(1,065.9)	(590.0)	(773.1)
Increase (decrease) in Working Capital Items	$ 497.3	($ 953.3)	($3,538.9)	($1,253.8)	$2,219.8

Derive funds provided by operations for SM, defining "funds" as cash plus temporary investments. Treat changes in working capital accounts other than cash and temporary investments as *operating* sources and uses of funds. Analyze the apparent differences in changes in liquidity by comparing your statements to those in Exhibit 13.42. Try to form an opinion about which funds statement you as an analyst would prefer to use.

DECISION CASE 13-1

Bill Wanda had been a successful public accountant before his death four years ago. On his death, his wife, Kit, was left with a portfolio of securities along with the proceeds of a life insurance policy and a mortgage-free house to look after herself and her three children. In the past, the investment portfolio had paid sufficient interest and dividends to provide Kit's major source of income. During the last year, Kit's cash needs had increased as a result of growing children and rising price levels. At the same time, the dividends from one of her major shareholdings, Price Sisters Ltd, had declined. She had read in the president's report of the company that the dividends had been reduced in order to fund the company's expansion program, because the profit potential was large — as evidenced by the increased profits reported in Year 4. Kit interpreted this statement to mean that the company's net income was increasing but, she said, "The income is meaningless to me since I can't buy food with it."

The comparative balance sheets and income statements of Price Sisters Ltd. for Year 4, included in the company's Annual Report, is presented in Exhibits 13.43 and 13.44.

During Year 4, 10 autos and trucks (one-third of the fleet) with an original cost of $33,000 were replaced for a cost of $52,000, after deducting the trade-in allowance (equal to their net book value) of $13,000. In addition, the fleet was expanded to 36 vehicles with the purchase of 6 additional vehicles for $39,000.

Explain to Kit Wanda why the dividends have been cut in half at the same time that the net income has increased by three-quarters over that reported in the previous year. Is Price Sisters Ltd. in a better financial position at December 31, Year 4 than it was in at December 31, Year 3? If not, why not?

DECISION CASE 13-2

H.R. Franck was admitted to the Law Society of Nova Scotia on November 15, Year 4 and immediately set up her own practice in Halifax. Because she was uncertain about the amount of business she would have, she arranged with a recently qualifed chartered accountant, C.M. Lindsay, to share office space and secretarial and reception facilities. Franck and Lindsay agreed that they would pay for the secretarial services used by both at the rate of $10 per hour and that the remainder of the office costs would be shared equally. Each of them deposited $40,000 in a joint account to pay for the

EXHIBIT 13.43
PRICE SISTERS LTD.
Comparative Balance Sheets
As of December 31
(amounts in thousands)

	Year 4		Year 3	
ASSETS				
Current Assets:				
Cash		$ 21		$ 22
Accounts Receivable		533		410
Inventory		540		427
		$1,094		$ 859
Plant and Equipment	$2,624		$1,980	
Less: Accumulated Depreciation	(1,397)	1,227	(1,217)	763
Autos and Trucks	$ 203		$ 132	
Less: Accumulated Depreciation	(69)	134	(48)	84
		$2,455		$1,706
LIABILITIES AND SHAREHOLDERS' EQUITY				
Current Liabilities:				
Bank Loan		$ 391		$ 100
Accounts Payable		332		251
		$ 723		$ 351
Bonds Payable		740		540
Shareholders' Equity:				
Share Capital	$ 500		$ 500	
Retained Earnings	492	992	315	815
		$2,455		$1,706

EXHIBIT 13.44
PRICE SISTERS LTD.
Condensed Comparative Income Statement
Years Ended December 31
(amounts in thousands)

	Year 4	Year 3
Sales	$3,604	$2,772
Less: Cost of Sales[a]	2,172	1,675
Gross Profit	$1,432	$1,097
Expenses[a]	1,015	841
Net Income Before Income Tax	$ 417	$ 256
Income Tax	200	133
Net Income	$ 217	$ 123
Deduct Dividends	40	80
Addition to Retained Earnings	$ 177	$ 43

[a]Including depreciation of $221,000 (plant and equipment, $180,000; autos and trucks, $41,000) for each year.

costs of furniture and equipment, joint supplies used by the secretary, and monthly expenses. At the end of each month, Lindsay prepared a statement of joint operating expenses, and each of them reimbursed the joint account for her portion.

Franck and Lindsay were responsible for furnishing their own offices and purchasing their own letterhead stationery.

An analysis of Franck's bank statements from the opening of her practice on December 1, Year 4 to November 30, Year 5 follows:

Deposits:

Collection of Fees Billed	$ 22,600
Receipt of Trust Funds from Clients	30,100
Loan from Parents	40,000
Demand Loan from Bank	20,000
Deposit of Personal Funds	6,000
Total Deposits	$118,700

Withdrawals:

Share of Office Expenses to October 31, Year 5	$ 19,800
Purchase of Letterhead	900
Transfer to Joint Account	40,000
Purchase of Office Equipment	6,500
Personal Withdrawals	10,800
Law Society Fees, Year 5	360
Payment of Trust Funds on Behalf of Clients	26,400
Bank Interest	1,600
Bank Charges	200
Payments on Demand Loan	4,000
Total Withdrawals	$110,560

The bank statement for December Year 5 includes the following items that may relate to the year ended November 30, Year 5.

Payment of trust funds held for clients	$ 600
Payment of joint expenses for November, Year 5	3,100
Payment of letterhead purchased on October 15, Year 5 (cheque dated November 25)	300

Approximately one-third of the letterhead stationery purchased during the year was on hand on November 30. The fees billed but not collected at November 30 were $8,200 and included one for $700 that had been billed in December Year 4 — which Franck does not expect to collect because her client was found guilty and is currently serving a five-year sentence.

Franck's parents loaned her $40,000 interest free, but Franck felt a moral obligation to repay the loan in a couple of years with interest at 10 percent compounded annually.

Franck estimates that the billings accumulated for the cases she had worked on but has neither completed not billed by November 30 amount to $1,400.

Franck has been living comfortably for the past year and, with a bank balance of about $8,000, considers she has begun a successful practice.

To eliminate the need for two sets of records, Franck has decided to claim the maximum capital cost allowance for 20 percent of her furniture when calculating taxable income, and to record depreciation in an equal amount.

Prepare a report for Franck, with supporting schedules, analyzing the degree of financial success she has achieved as a lawyer to November 30, Year 5.

CHAPTER FOURTEEN

SIGNIFICANCE AND IMPLICATIONS OF ALTERNATIVE ACCOUNTING POLICIES

CHAPTER OUTLINE

- Summary of Generally Accepted Accounting Policies
- The Firm's Selection of Alternative Accounting Policies
- An Illustration of the Effects of Alternative Accounting Policies on a Set of Financial Statements
- Assessing the Effects of Alternative Accounting Policies on Investment Decisions
- An International Perspective
- Development of Accounting Principles

Accounting policies
The policies, principles, and accounting methods employed by an organization that collectively determine the content and format of the financial statements.

Accounting policies are the specific principles and the methods used in their application that are selected by a company as being most appropriate in the circumstances.[1] Previous chapters have described and illustrated most of the important accounting policies currently employed in preparing financial statements. This chapter focuses on the following questions:

1. What criteria should a firm employ in selecting its accounting policies from among those that are considered "generally acceptable"?

2. What are the effects of using alternative accounting policies on the principal financial statements?

3. What are the effects of using alternative accounting policies on investors' decisions to invest their capital resources?

One who understands the significance and implications of alternative generally accepted accounting policies is a more effective reader and interpreter of published financial statements. Throughout this chapter, we use the terms *accounting policies*, *methods*, and *procedures* interchangeably.

---

[1] *CICA Handbook*, section 1505.

SUMMARY OF GENERALLY ACCEPTED ACCOUNTING POLICIES

This section lists the major currently acceptable accounting policies, most of which have been discussed in previous chapters. These accounting policies might be classified into two broad groups on the basis of the flexibility permitted to firms in selecting alternative methods of accounting for a specific item. In some instances, the firm has wide flexibility in choosing among alternative methods, such as in the selection of depreciation methods. In other instances, the specific conditions associated with a transaction or event dictate the method of accounting that must be used. For example, the method of accounting for investments in the common shares of other firms depends on the presence of significant influence of which the percentage of share ownership is partial evidence. Although a list of major currently acceptable accounting policies is given below, remember that a particular firm does not have wide flexibility in selecting its accounting methods in all instances.

Revenue Recognition A firm may recognize revenue at the time goods are sold or services are rendered, as is typically done under the accrual basis of accounting, at the time cash is collected (installment method or cost-recovery-first method), or as production progresses (percentage-of-completion method for long-term contracts).

Doubtful Accounts The amount that a firm recognizes as bad debts expense under the allowance method depends partly on the method used to make the estimate. A firm may estimate the expense as a percent of sales or by estimating the amount of the allowance for doubtful accounts. Several alternative methods are available when applying the second alternative.

Inventories A firm may cost inventories on one of several bases: acquisition cost, lower of acquisition cost and market, standard cost, and, in the case of some byproducts and precious minerals, net realizable value. When the cost of the specific goods sold cannot be ascertained, the firm must make a cost flow assumption. The cost flow assumption may be FIFO, LIFO, or weighted average, although LIFO may not be used when determining taxable income.

Investments in Securities A firm accounts for investments in the common shares of other firms using either the cost method or the equity method, or else prepares consolidated statements. The method used depends primarily on the degree of influence exercised by one firm over another. The percentage ownership of the voting shares is *prima facie* evidence of influence.

Machinery, Equipment, and Other Depreciable Assets These plant assets may be depreciated using the straight-line, declining-balance, compound interest, or units-of-production method. Estimates of service lives and disposal values of similar assets may differ among firms. The depreciation recorded in the financial statements is disregarded when determining taxable income, but is replaced by a company's capital cost allowance claimed, ordinarily the maximum allowed in the Income Tax Act.

Intangible Resources Development Cost The costs incurred in creating intangible resources, such as preproduction costs or store opening costs, can be treated as an expense in the year the costs are incurred, or capitalized and amortized over some period of years. Thus, advertising and some development costs may be either capitalized when incurred and subsequently amortized, or expensed when incurred. Research costs, however, must be recognized as an expense in the year in which the costs are incurred.

Leases   A firm may set up as an asset and subsequently amortize as a capital lease the rights to the use of property acquired under lease or give no recognition to the lease except at the time that lease payments are due each period (operating lease method). Likewise, the lessor can set up the rights to receive future lease payments as a receivable at the inception of the lease (capital lease method), or give no recognition to the lease except to the extent that lease payments become due each period (operating lease method). Whether the capital or operating lease method is used depends on such factors as the life of the lease relative to the life of the leased asset and the present value of the lease payments relative to the market value of the leased property. The facts of each lease agreement determine the method to be used. Both the lessor and the lessee will generally use the same method for any lease.

Interest Revenue and Expense on Long-Term Investments and Debt   Most firms recognize interest revenue and expense on long-term investments and debt using the effective-interest method, although the straight-line method can be used.

The preceding list of alternative acceptable accounting policies is not exhaustive. Also, remember that a firm does not always have a choice of methods. The factors that a firm might consider in selecting its accounting policies are discussed below.

THE FIRM'S SELECTION OF ALTERNATIVE ACCOUNTING POLICIES

The methods of accounting used for *income tax* and *financial reporting* purposes generally do not have to be the same. Because the firm might pursue different objectives for financial and tax reporting, the selection of accounting policies for each type of reports is discussed separately.

FINANCIAL REPORTING PURPOSES

Accurate Presentation

accuracy in presentation
A desirable attribute of financial statements.

One of the criteria for assessing the usefulness of accounting information is **accuracy in presentation** of the underlying events and tansactions. This criterion might be used by the firm as a basis for selecting its methods of accounting. For example, "assets" have been defined as resources having future service potential, and "expenses" as a measurement of the services consumed during the period. In applying the accuracy criterion, the firm would select the inventory cost flow assumption and depreciation method that most accurately measures the pattern of services consumed during the period and the amount of services still available at the end of the period.

As a basis for selecting accounting methods, this approach has at least one serious limitation. The accountant can seldom directly observe the services consumed and the service potential remaining. Without this information, the accountant cannot ascertain which accounting policies lead to the most accurate presentation of the underlying events. This criterion can serve only as a normative criterion toward which the development and selection of accounting policies should be directed.

Conservatism

In choosing among alternative, generally acceptable methods, the firm might select the set that provides the most conservative measure of net income. Considering the uncertainties involved in measuring benefits received as revenues and services consumed as expenses, some have suggested that a conservative measure of earnings should be provided, thereby reducing the possibility of unwarranted optimism by users of financial statements. As a criterion for selecting accounting policies, **conservatism** implies that methods should be chosen that minimize cumulative reported earnings. That is, expenses should be recognized as quickly as possible, and the recognition of revenue should be postponed as long as possible. This reporting objective would lead to selecting the declining-balance depreciation method, selecting the LIFO cost flow assumption if periods of rising prices are anticipated, and expensing of intangible development costs in the year incurred.

conservatism
An accounting principle dictating that judgmental determinations in accounting should tend toward understatement rather than overstatement of assets and income.

The rationale for conservatism as a reporting objective has been challenged. Over the whole life of the firm, income is equal to cash receipts minus cash expenditures. Thus, to the extent that net income of earlier periods is smaller, earnings of later periods must be larger. The "later" periods when income must be larger may, however, be many periods later, sometimes even the last period of the firm's existence. Also, some statement users may be misled by earnings reports based on conservative reporting policies. Consider, for example, investors who sell shares because they consider that the firm is not operating in a sufficiently profitable manner with the resources available, when earnings reported in a less conservative manner would not have induced the sale. Or, consider the potential investors who do not purchase securities because they are misled by the published "conservative" statement of earnings.

Profit Maximization

A reporting objective having an effect opposite to conservatism might be employed in selecting among alternative generally accepted accounting policies. Somewhat loosely termed **profit maximization,**[2] this criterion suggests the selection of accounting methods that maximize cumulative reported earnings. That is, revenue should be recognized as quickly as possible, and the recognition of expense should be postponed as long as possible. For example, the straight-line method of depreciation would be used and, when periods of rising prices were anticipated, the FIFO cost flow assumption would be selected. The use of profit maximization as a reporting objective

profit maximization
The doctrine that a given set of operations should be accounted for in order to make reported net income as large as possible; contrast with conservatism.

---

[2] The concept of profit maximization as a reporting objective is not the same as the profit-maximization dictum of microeconomics.

is an extension of the notion that the firm is in business to generate profits and that the firm should present as favourable a report on performance as possible within currently acceptable accounting methods. Profit maximization is subject to a similar, but mirror-image, criticism as is levelled at the use of conservatism as a reporting objective. Reporting income earlier under the profit maximization criterion must mean that smaller income will be reported in some later period.

Income Smoothing

income smoothing
A method of timing business transactions or choosing accounting principles so that variations in reported income from year to year are reduced from what they would otherwise be. Although income smoothing is an objective of some managements, it is not an official accounting principle or reporting objective.

A final reporting objective that might be used in selecting accounting policies is referred to as **income smoothing**. This criterion suggests the selection of accounting methods that result in the smoothest earnings trend over time. As is discussed later in this chapter, empirical research has shown that changes in stock prices are related to changes in earnings. Advocates of income smoothing suggest that if a company can minimize fluctuations in earnings, the perceived risk of investing in its shares will be reduced and, all else being equal, its share price will be higher. Note that this reporting criterion suggests that net income, not revenues and expenses individually, is to be smoothed. As a result, the firm must consider the total pattern of its operations before selecting the appropriate accounting methods. For example, the straight-line method of depreciation may provide the smoothest amount of depreciation expense on a machine over its life. If, however, the productivity of the machine declines with age so that revenues decrease in later years, net income using the straight-line method may not provide the smoothest net income stream. In this case, perhaps the declining-balance method should be used.

Summary

The principal message of this section is that accurate presentation, although perhaps a desirable reporting objective, is not the sole consideration in selecting accounting policies. As a result, firms may select from among the methods included in the set of generally acceptable accounting policies using whatever reporting criteria they choose.

Where does this flexibility permitted in selecting accounting policies leave the user of financial statements? The *CICA Handbook*[3] requires firms to disclose the accounting policies used in preparing financial statements. The general custom in Canada is that the first footnote to the financial statements is entitled "Summary of Significant Accounting Policies." The effect of alternative accounting policies on investment decisions is discussed later in this chapter.

INCOME TAX REPORTING PURPOSES

least and latest rule
Pay the lowest amount of taxes as late as possible within the law to minimize the present value of tax payments for a given set of operations.

In selecting accounting procedures for income tax purposes, the corporation's objective should be to select those methods that minimize the present value of the stream of income tax payments. The operational rule, sometimes called the **least and latest rule**, is to pay the lowest amount of taxes as late as possible within the law. The least and latest rule generally trans-

---

[3] *CICA Handbook*, section 1505.

lates into a policy of recognizing expenses as quickly as possible and postponing the recognition of revenue as long as possible. This policy might be atlered somewhat if income tax rates are expected to change, if the firm had losses in earlier years, or if the firm is a sole proprietorship or partnership where earnings of the firm are subject to graduated income tax rates of the owners.

The desire to recognize expenses as quickly as possible suggests claiming the maximum capital cost allowance and immediate expensing of research and development, advertising, and similar costs. Using the installment basis of recognizing revenue, where permitted by the Income Tax Act and Regulations, is generally desirable for income tax purposes because it results in postponing the recognition of revenue and the resulting income tax payments until cash is collected.

DISCUSSION CASE 31

What Investors Want in an Annual Report

What influences investor decisions, and how do annual reports fit into that decision-making process? Such questions prompted the Financial Executives Research Foundation to commission a study on the subject in 1986. The initial results were reported at the FEI conference on Current Financial Reporting Issues by Errol Alexander, director, corporate financial services, of SRI International, which conducted the study.

The findings revealed the decision-making process to be a complex one, and corporate executives were found to have some misperceptions. For example, that individual investors want less information. "There is a grain of truth in that there is a lot of information that investors do not know what to make of," said Alexander. However, when you talk to them, he added, they show that they do want "more information, but they want it to be more usable, more palatable,

more in tune with the way they think." He also said they did not want "to be denied information they think is available to others." Survey respondents particularly did not want "different versions of the annual report for different audiences."

When asked to indicate additional information they would like to see in annual reports, investors cited company reputation, company outlook, potential risk, and industry outlook. Business segment information was not rated important by individual investors, Alexander said. In talking to CEOs and CFOs of 26 companies, he also reported, "these people were all very comfortable with the credibility level of their annual report. [However,] both professional and individual investors say very much otherwise."

But why, then, do these same investors say that annual reports "are the most frequently used
(continued)

(continued)

source of information"? The answer, Alexander said, is because they are so available. But while they are used, he reported, they are not influential in the decision-making process. "No one relies heavily on information in the annual report unless he can confirm it through other means," he explained. For example, in talking to professional investors, he said, "rarely did one say 'annual report' without saying '10 K' in the same or next sentence."

Asked to characterize the readers of annual reports, Alexander described individual investors as "scanners" and professionals as "selective." Both types of investors, he said, ranked financial statements the highest in importance, in contrast to corporate executives, who believe the letter to shareholders is the most important part of the annual report and the most read. Investors did not agree. "They want to know what's really going on," Alexander said, and they see innate biases "that push the chairman's letter way down on the list of what's important."

It is important to investors, Alexander said, to know the company's plans for the future. In addition, professional investors want to know the company's view of its competitive standing, even though they will confirm this information from other sources as well. They would also like to see projections and forecasts in annual reports, even though they will generate their own from other sources. On the other hand, individual investors, the study reports, would like to

see more key financial ratios, along with a short explanation.

Alexander cited a seeming conflict: individual investors said that annual reports could be improved by being shorter and less redundant, but they also said they desired more information in clearer detail. The answer, he said, was that these investors want more information of the right kind, which can be in keeping with shorter, less redundant information. However, he said that the most frequently cited area for improvement "was frank reporting of poor company performance."

Further details can be found in the FERF study, now available, Alexander said. He concluded by saying that management needed to set a primary objective for its annual report — that it be a stewardship document or a document to influence investors, for example. Then a primary target audience should be selected, and the report written to accommodate the characteristics and information needs of that primary audience. Finally, put one person in charge of the entire report — the letter, the narrative, and the financials. That person, he said, should have a working understanding of public relations and marketing as well as the financial side of the business.

References

Reprinted with permission from "What Kind of Annual Do Investors Need?" *Business Talk*, Sept./Oct., 1987, copyright 1987 by Financial Executives Institute, Morristown, New Jersey.

Discussion Question

What do investors want in an annual report? Should their desires be accommodated?

AN ILLUSTRATION OF THE EFFECTS OF ALTERNATIVE ACCOUNTING POLICIES ON A SET OF FINANCIAL STATEMENTS

This section illustrates the effects of using different accounting policies on a set of financial statements. The illustration has been constructed so that the accounting policies used create significant differences in the financial statements. Therefore, inferences should not be drawn from this example about the usual magnitude of the effects of alternative methods.

THE SCENARIO

On January 1, two corporations are formed to purchase two similar merchandising businesses. The two firms are alike in all respects, except for their methods of accounting. Conservative Limited chooses the accounting policies that will minimize its reported net income. High Flyer Inc. chooses the accounting policies that will maximize its reported net income. The following events occur during the year.

1. Both corporations issue 2 million no-par-value shares on January 1 for $23 million cash.

2. On January 1, both firms acquire the equipment of their predecessors for $18 million cash. The equipment has a fair value of $14 million and an estimated life of ten years with no disposal value, creating goodwill valued at $4 million.

3. Both firms make the following purchases of merchandise inventory:

Date	Units Purchased	Unit Price	Cost of Purchases
January 1	170,000	$60	$10,200,000
May 1	190,000	$63	11,970,000
September 1	200,000	$66	13,200,000
Total	560,000		$35,370,000

4. During the year, both firms sell 420,000 units at an average price of $100 each. All sales are made for cash.

5. During the year, both firms have selling, general, and administrative expenses, excluding depreciation and amortization of goodwill, of $7.1 million.

6. The income tax rate is assumed to be 46 percent.

ACCOUNTING POLICIES USED

The methods of accounting used by each firm in preparing its financial statements are described below.

Inventory Cost Flow Assumption Conservative Limited makes a LIFO cost flow assumption, whereas High Flyer Inc. makes a FIFO assumption. Both firms use the FIFO method when deriving taxable income, because

LIFO is not permitted for income tax purposes. Because the beginning inventory is zero, the cost of goods available for sale by each firm is equal to the purchases during the year of $35,370,000. Both firms have 140,000 units in ending inventory. Conservative Limited therefore reports a cost of goods sold of $26,970,000 [= $35,370,000 − (140,000 × $60)], whereas High Flyer Inc. reports a cost of goods sold of $26,130,000 [= $35,370,000 − (140,000 × $66)].

Depreciation   Conservative Limited decides to claim the maximum capital cost allowance, using a rate of 20 percent, for income tax purposes and to record depreciation on its books in an equal amount. High Flyer Inc. decides to use the straight-line method in reporting income to shareholders but to claim the maximum capital cost allowance in its tax return. Conservative Limited therefore reports depreciation expense of $2.8 million (= 0.2 × $14,000,000), whereas High Flyer Inc. reports depreciation expense of $1.4 million (= $1/10$ × $14,000,000) to shareholders and $2.8 million on its tax return.

Amortization of Goodwill   Conservative Limited decides to amortize goodwill on a straight-line basis over five years. High Flyer Inc. decides to amortize goodwill over the maximum period allowed of forty years on a straight-line basis. A taxpayer may claim 50 percent of goodwill purchased as an expense for tax purposes at a straight-line rate of 10 percent. Each company claims the maximum deduction. Conservative Limited therefore reports goodwill amortization of $800,000 (= $4,000,000/5), High Flyer Inc. reports goodwill amortization of $100,000 (= $4,000,000/40), and both companies claim the maximum income tax deduction of $200,000 (= 10% × 0.5 × $4,000,000).

COMPARATIVE INCOME STATEMENTS

Exhibit 14.1 presents comparative income statements for Conservative Limited and High Flyer Inc. for the year ending December 31. Conservative Limited reports a larger deduction for cost of sales and amortization of goodwill in its financial statements than it is allowed to deduct from its income tax return. The difference in cost of sales and one-half the diffrence in amortization of goodwill are viewed as timing differences. The taxes currently payable exceed the deduction from income and a deferred income tax debit is recorded. High Flyer Inc. reports larger deductions from revenues on the income tax return than it reports to shareholders. The difference for depreciation on equipment is viewed as a timing difference. A portion of the income tax expense shown on the income statement of High Flyer Inc. is not payable currently, and therefore a deferred tax liability will appear on the balance sheet. In this illustration, net income and earnings per share of High Flyer Inc. are almost double the amounts shown for Conservative Limited.

COMPARATIVE BALANCE SHEETS

Exhibit 14.2 presents comparative balance sheets for Conservative Limited and High Flyer Inc. as of December 31. Merchandise inventory, goodwill, and equipment (net), as well as total assets of Conservative Limited, are

EXHIBIT 14.1
Comparative Income Statements Based on Different Accounting
Policies for the Year Ending December 31
(amounts in thousands, except for per-share amounts)

	Conservative Limited		High Flyer Inc.	
	Financial Statement	Tax Return	Financial Statement	Tax Return
Sales Revenue	$42,000.0	$42,000.0	$42,000.0	$42,000.0
Less: Cost of Goods Sold	26,970.0[b]	26,130.0[b]	26,130.0	26,130.0
Gross Profit	$15,030.0	$15,870.0	$15,870.0	$15,870.0
Less: Expenses				
Depreciation on Equipment	$ 2,800.0	$ 2,800.0	$ 1,400.0[c]	$ 2,800.0[c]
Goodwill Amortized	800.0[d]	200.0[d]	100.0[d]	200.0[d]
Other Selling and Administrative	7,100.0	7,100.0	7,100.0	7,100.0
Total Expenses	$10,700.0	$10,100.0	$ 8,600.0	$10,100.0
Net Income Before Income Tax	$ 4,330.0	$ 5,770.0	$ 7,270.0	$ 5,770.0
Income Tax Expense:				
Currently Payable	$ 2,654.2		$ 2,654.2	
Deferred[e]	(478.4)		713.0	
Total[a]	$ 2,175.8		$ 3,367.2	
Net Income	$ 2,154.2		$ 3,902.8	
Earnings per Share (2,000,000 shares outstanding)	$ 1.08		$ 1.95	
[a]Computation of Income Tax Expense: Net Income Before Income Tax	$ 4,330.0	$ 5,770.0	$ 7,270.0	$ 5,770.0
Plus: Permanent Timing Difference, Goodwill Amortization:				
(0.5 × $800)	400.0			
(0.5 × $100)			50.0	
Total	$ 4,730.0	$ 5,770.0	$ 7,320.0	$ 5,770.0
Income Tax on Current Income (at 46%)	$ 2,175.8		$ 3,367.2	
Income Tax Currently Payable (at 46%)		$ 2,654.2		$ 2,654.2
Income Taxes Deferred by Timing Differences:				
[b]For Cost of Goods Sold				
[0.46 × ($26,130 − $26,970)]	($ 386.4)			
[c]For Depreciation [0.46 × ($2,800 − $1,400)]			$ 644.0	
[d]For Goodwill Amortization				
{0.46 × [$250 − (0.5 × $800)]}	(92.0)			
{0.46 × [$200 − (0.5 × $100)]}			69.0	
[e]Total Income Taxes	($ 478.4)		$ 713.0	

stated at lower amounts than those of High Flyer Inc. There is no real difference between the economic positions of the two companies. They each hold identical assets and owe identical amounts. One apparent difference is shown in the balances of deferred income taxes. This difference arises not as a result of different current or deferred income tax payments, but because of differences in reported income.

The differences in the amounts at which merchandise inventory, equipment (net), and goodwill are stated result from the different accounting methods used by the two companies. The amounts shown for Conservative Limited are smaller than the corresponding amounts for High Flyer Inc.

EXHIBIT 14.2
Comparative Balance Sheets Based on Alternative Accounting
Policies, December 31
(amounts in thousands)

	Conservative Limited	High Flyer Inc.
Assets		
Cash	$ 1,875.8	$ 1,875.8
Merchandise Inventory	8,400.0	9,240.0
Deferred Income Taxes (current)	386.4	—
Equipment	14,000.0	14,000.0
Less: Accumulated Depreciation	(2,800.0)	(1,400.0)
Goodwill	3,200.0	3,900.0
Deferred Income Taxes (noncurrent)	92.0	—
Total Assets	$25,154.2	$27,615.8
Equities		
Deferred Income Taxes	$ —	$ 713.0
Common Shares	23,000.0	23,000.0
Retained Earnings	2,154.2	3,902.8
Total Equities	$25,154.2	$27,615.8

because a larger portion of the costs incurred during the period by Conservative Limited has been recognized as an expense.

In the assets section of the balance sheet, Conservative Limited also shows debit balances of Deferred Income Taxes of $386.4 and $92 arising from differences in cost of sales and goodwill amortization, respectively, for financial and tax reporting. High Flyer Inc. also reports deferred income taxes on the balance sheet resulting from differences in the timing of depreciation on equipment in the financial statements and income tax return.

Note the effect of using alternative accounting policies on the ratio rate of return on total assets (= net income/total assets). Conservative Limited reports a smaller amount of net income but also a smaller amount of total assets. One might expect, then, that the rates of return on total assets of the two firms would approximate each other more closely than either net income or total assets individually. Significant differences in the ratio for the two firms are still observable, however, in this illustration. The rate of return on total assets of Conservative Limited is 8.9 percent (= $2,154,200/ [($23,000,000 + $25,154,200)/2]); for High Flyer Inc., it is 15.4 percent (= $3,902,800/[($23,000,000 + $27,615,800)/2]).

COMPARATIVE STATEMENTS OF CHANGES IN FINANCIAL POSITION

Exhibit 14.3 presents comparative statements of changes in financial position for Conservative Limited and High Flyer Inc. Despite the differences in income between the two companies, they report the same amount of cash used in operations. Because the firms are alike in all respects except

EXHIBIT 14.3
**Comparative Statements of Changes in Financial Position for the Year
Ending December 31
(amounts in thousands)**

	Conservative Limited	High Flyer Inc.
Cash Provided by		
Financing Activities:		
Issue of common shares	$ 23,000.0	$ 23,000.0
Cash Applied to		
Operations:		
Net Income	$ 2,154.2	$ 3,902.8
Add (deduct):		
Depreciation expense	2,800.0	1,400.0
Goodwill amortization	800.0	100.0
Deferred Income Taxes	(478.4)	713.0
Increase in merchandise inventory	(8,400.0)	(9,240.0)
	($ 3,124.2)	($ 3,124.2)
Investment Activities:		
Acquisition of Subsidiary	(18,000.0)	(18,000.0)
	(21,124.2)	(21,124.2)
Net Increase in Cash[a] Position	$ 1,875.8	$ 1,875.8

[a]*In this illustration, there are no cash equivalents or bank indebtedness, so cash position is equivalent to cash alone.*

for their method of accounting, the amount of the cash flow from operations is a more valued report for comparing the two companies than is the amount of net income.

Note that the differences in depreciation methods, inventory cost flow assumptions, and goodwill amortization methods do not affect the cash used in operations. As long as these firms use the same methods for the above on their income tax returns, cash flows will be the same. Thus, the statement of changes in financial position tends to be affected much less by alternative generally accepted accounting policies than are the balance sheet and the income statement.

MORAL OF THE ILLUSTRATION

In order to interpret published financial statements, you must be aware of which accounting policies from the set of alternative generally accepted accounting policies are used. When reports of several companies are compared, the amounts shown should be adjusted where possible for the different accounting methods used. The techniques for making some of these adjustments were illustrated in previous chapters (for example, LIFO to FIFO cost flow assumption, equity method to consolidated statements). The notes to the financial statements will disclose the accounting policies used, but not necessarily the data required to make appropriate adjustments.

DISCUSSION CASE 32

How Readable Are Our Annual Reports?

The annual report is the main formal medium for the messages corporations wish to convey to their shareholders and other interested parties each year. Although newspapers often pre-empt the report as a timely source of information, it contains a comprehensive, credible database prepared and issued by the company involved.

Recipients review the report for guidance on many aspects related to the company's past, present and future behaviour. But communications of this guidance will be effective only if the readers understand the messages the preparers of the report intended to convey.

Studies have shown that, although the rest of the report receives some attention, shareholders spend most of the review time reading the chairman's address because of its general overview and less technical orientation. To ensure effective communication, therefore, companies should pay particular attention to the content, organization and readability of this address.

One way for report preparers to gauge communication effectiveness is to use readability formulas. These are quantitative methods for predicting whether certain text material is likely to be understood by a target audience.

Although there are more than five dozen variations of read-

ability formulas, a simple two-variable (a word variable and a sentence variable), general-purpose formula is usually sufficient. It is believed that the length of a word is related to a reader's speed of recognition and that sentence length is related to memory span. While neither variable necessarily causes reading difficulty, each has been found to be a good index of such difficulty.

One popular formula used in accounting studies is the Flesch reading ease measurement. This formula is equal to the constant number 206.835 less 0.846 times the word length (the number of syllables per 100 words of sampled prose) and then less 1.015 times sentence length (the average sentence length in the sampled passage).

The result of the equation is a reading ease score ranging from zero to 100 — the closer the score to zero, the more incomprehensible the writing.

Validated comprehension tests have shown that prose scoring between 0–30 is very difficult to read — equivalent to scientific writing — and the reader needs to have a postgraduate degree to understand it. A score of 30–50 means the passage is still difficult — equivalent to academic literature — and requires at least an undergraduate education on the part of the reader. A score above 50 makes the message compre-

(continued)

(continued)

hensible to the majority of the readers.

To determine whether the annual report can be easily read and understood, several sample passages of 100 words should be selected at random. Count the number of sentences and words in each passage and calculate the average sentence length across all passages. Next, count the number of syllables in each passage and average it across the sample passages. Finally, insert the two results into the formula to yield the measure of reading ease.

I have conducted a series of studies on readability levels for Canadian annual reports for the years 1982, 1983 and 1984. I randomly selected 100-word prose passages from the chairman's address of 46 different year-end 1982 reports, 96 1983 reports and 65 1984 reports.

What I found was surprising. Contrary to expectations, the chairman's address was not easy to read. For all three years, the over-all average reading ease score for this section bordered on difficult to very difficult, with a score of 31.17. Only seven of 207 reports scored more than 50— 96% of the sampled chairman's addresses were written on a level akin to scientific and academic writing! Fully 42% of the addresses seem to require readers to have postgraduate degrees to understand them.

But do most annual report recipients have the educational background to easily understand the chairman's address? If we look at the education of the adult Canadian population, based on

1981 census statistics, the chairman's address appears to be beyond the comprehension of 92% of the population.

It doesn't look quite so bad if we use the education levels of the Canadian investor population (as reported by the Toronto Stock Exchange's 1984 Shareholder Profile Study): 44% of shareholders have at least part of a university education. They should, therefore, be able to understand most of the intended messages.

Although readability formulas are based on two fundamental variables, they don't examine important matters, such as reader interest, and design format, such as length of type line, hyphenated words, long paragraphs, confusing punctuation, full pages of type, style and size of typeface, illustration and colour. Nor do they measure word frequency, concept density and level of abstraction, or whether there is logical organization, coherence and flow of ideas.

But the formulas are a quick way for those responsible for annual report preparation to get some indication of how easy it is to read their reports. If the reports fail the test, chances are that many readers will fail to get the message.

References

John Courtis, "How Readable Are Our Annual Reports?" *The Bottom Line*, June 1986.

Discussion Question

What level of technical training in accounting should be expected of financial statement users?

ASSESSING THE EFFECTS OF ALTERNATIVE ACCOUNTING POLICIES ON INVESTMENT DECISIONS

Previous sections of this chapter emphasized the flexibility that firms have in selecting accounting procedures and the possible effects of using different accounting procedures on the financial statements. We now focus briefly on a related and important question: do investors accept financial statement information as presented, or do they somehow filter out all or most of the differences in the financial statements of various firms resulting from differences in the methods of accounting employed? If investors accept financial statement information as presented, without adjustments for the methods of accounting used, then two firms, otherwise identical except for the accounting procedures employed, might receive a disproportionate amount of capital funds. Thus, the use of alternative accounting policies could lead to a misallocation of resources in the economy. On the other hand, if investors make adjustments for the different accounting procedures in analyzing the financial statements of various firms, perhaps the policy maker need not be concerned over the variety of acceptable accounting policies. If investors do make such adjustments, increased disclosure of the procedures followed may be more important than greater uniformity in accounting policies.

The question regarding the effect of alternative accounting policies on investment decisions has been the subject of extensive debate among public accountants, academicians, personnel in government agencies, and financial statement users.

Those who believe that investors can be misled point to examples in which the market price of particular firms' shares have decreased dramatically after the effects of using specific accounting procedures have been carefully analyzed and reported in the financial press.[4] In these examples, it is often difficult, however, to judge if the price change is attributable to the disclosure of the effects of using particular accounting procedures or to other, more temporary factors affecting the specific firm, its industry, or all firms in the economy. Also, it is difficult to generalize on the effects of using alternative accounting policies on investment decisions from isolated and anecdotal examples.

An expanding number of empirical research studies, on the other hand, have provided support for the view that investors at the aggregate market level are rarely misled by the accounting methods employed. This research has developed from the theory and empirical evidence that the stock market is efficient, in the sense that market prices adjust quickly and in an unbiased manner to new information.[5] Unlike the examples supporting the view that investors are misled, these empirical studies have been based on data for a large number of firms over long time periods. Also, an effort is made in

---

[4] For several examples, see Abraham J. Briloff, *More Debits Than Credits* (New York: Harper & Row, 1976). For an analysis of these examples, see George Foster, "Briloff and the Capital Market," *Journal of Accounting Research* (Spring 1979), pp. 262–74.

[5] See Eugene F. Fama, "Efficient Capital Markets: A Review of Theory and Empirical Work," *Journal of Finance* (May 1970), pp. 383–417.

these studies to control for the effects of economy-wide and industry effects on market price changes.

Several studies have shown that changes in earnings and changes in market prices are associated and, therefore, indicate that information contained in the financial statements is used by investors in making their resource allocation decisions.[6] Several studies have examined the effects of *changes* in the methods of accounting on market prices,[7] and a third group of studies looked at *differences* in the methods of accounting across firms.[8] The results of these last two groups of studies have been mixed, with several studies supporting the position that investors are misled and several studies supporting the position that they are not misled. The methodology employed in many of these studies has been extensively criticized, so the full implications are not clear.[9]

Research into the question regarding the effects of alternative accounting policies on investment decisions has not progressed sufficiently for any consensus to have been reached. The research that has been conducted has been described here briefly to emphasize an important point. It is not obvious, as it might first appear, that the current flexibility permitted firms in selecting accounting policies necessarily misleads investors and results in a misallocation of resources.[10]

---

[6] See, for example, Ray Ball and Philip Brown, "An Empirical Evaluation of Accounting Income Numbers," *Journal of Accounting Research* (Autumn 1968), pp. 159–78; William H. Beaver, "The Information Content of Annual Earnings Announcements," *Empirical Research in Accounting: Selected Studies, 1968*, Supplement to Vol. 6, *Journal of Accounting Research* (Autumn 1968), pp. 67–92; Robert G. May, "The Influence of Quarterly Earnings Announcements on Investor Decisions as Reflected in Common Stock Price Changes," *Empirical Research in Accounting: Selected Studies, 1977*, Supplement to Vol. 9, *Journal of Accounting Research*, pp. 119–63.

[7] See, for example, Ray Ball, "Changes in Accounting Techniques and Stock Prices," *Empirical Research in Accounting: Selected Studies, 1972*, Supplement to Vol. 10, *Journal of Accounting Research* (Autumn 1968), pp. 1–38; Robert S. Kaplan and Richard Roll, "Investor Evaluation of Accounting Information: Some Empirical Evidence," *Journal of Business* (April 1972), pp. 225–57; Shyam Sunder, "Relationships Between Accounting Changes and Stock Prices: Problems of Measurement and Some Empirical Evidence," *Empirical Research in Accounting: Selected Studies, 1973*, Supplement to Vol. 11, *Journal of Accounting Research*, pp. 1–45.

[8] See, for example, Robert E. Jensen, "An Experimental Design for Study of Effects of Accounting Variations in Decision Making," *Journal of Accounting Research* (Autumn 1966), pp. 224–38; Thomas R. Dyckman, "On the Investment Decision," *The Accounting Review* (April 1964), pp. 285–95; John L. O'Donnell, "Relationships Between Reported Earnings and Stock Prices in the Electric Utility Industry," *The Accounting Review* (January 1965), pp. 135–43.

[9] For a review of these studies, see Ray Ball and George Foster, "Corporate Financial Reporting: A Methodological Review of Empirical Research," *Studies in Current Methodologies in Accounting: A Critical Evaluation*, Supplement to Vol. 20 (1982), *Journal of Accounting Research*, pp. 117–48; Baruch Lev and James A. Ohlson, "Market-Based Empirical Research: A Review, Interpretation, and Extension," Ibid., pp. 249–322.

[10] For a description of the theoretical framework and a summary of the empirical work behind this position, see Nicholas J. Gonedes and Nicholas Dopuch, "Capital Market Equilibrium, Information-Production, and Selecting Accounting Techniques: Theoretical Framework and Review of Empirical Work," *Studies on Financial Accounting Objectives: 1974*, Supplement to Vol. 12, *Journal of Accounting Research* (Autumn 1968), pp. 48–129; and Robert S. Kaplan, "Information Content of Financial Accounting Numbers: A Survey of Empirical Evidence," in *Symposium of Impact of Accounting Research in Financial Accounting and Disclosure on Accounting Practice*, ed. by T. Keller and R. Abdel-khalik (Durham: Duke University Press, 1978).

AN INTERNATIONAL PERSPECTIVE

The increasing internationalization of business increases the need for comparable financial statement information about firms operating in different countries. The International Accounting Standards Committee (IASC), a voluntary association of professional accounting bodies from countries around the world, attempts to harmonize international accounting principles. Its pronouncements, although not binding on IASC countries, have helped to reduce the diversity of accounting principles among countries. The close relation between financial and tax reporting in certain countries (for example, France and Germany) impedes the effectiveness of the IASC. Changes in financial accounting principles sometimes reduce taxable income and therefore tax revenues. Changing accounting principles in these cases is more complex.

Previous chapters discussed GAAP for various accounts for six major industrialized countries. Exhibit 14.4 summarizes these accounting principles. Acceptable accounting principles change periodically, so some inaccuracies may exist in the information in Exhibit 14.4. The following summarizes the differences in accounting principles that remain.

Inventories Only the United States and Japan permit a LIFO cost flow assumption for inventories. Most other countries do not allow LIFO. Even in Japan, firms seldom use LIFO.

Leases Canada and the United States require the capitalization of some leases, while other countries account for all leases as operating leases. With leasing increasing in importance, several countries are now examining the operating/capital lease issue.

Deferred Taxes Canada and the United States require deferred tax accounting for timing differences between book and taxable income. Great Britain requires deferred tax accounting only for those timing differences that will likely reverse in the near future. France, Japan, and Germany have a few timing differences between book and taxable income, so deferred tax issues do not arise often.

Investments in Securities Most countries use the lower of cost and market valuation method for investments in securities representing less than 20 percent ownership. In some countries, however, the write-down to market occurs only when the firm considers the market value decline to be permanent. Most countries require the equity method for investments that represent a 20 percent to 50 percent ownership interest. Japan and Germany, however, account for such investments using the cost method. Common practice prepares consolidated financial statements for majority-owned subsidiaries, except in Japan.

Corporate Acquisitions Canada, the United States, and Great Britain permit the pooling-of-interest method under certain circumstances, whereas other countries permit only the purchase method. Practice varies widely on the amortization of goodwill arising in a corporate acquisition.

EXHIBIT 14.4
Summary of GAAP for Major Industrialized Countries

	Canada	United States	France	Japan	Great Britain	Germany
Marketable Securities (current asset)	Lower of cost and market	Lower of cost and market	Lower of cost and market	Cost (unless price declines considered permanent)	Lower of cost and market	Lower of cost and market
Bad Debts	Allowance method	Allowance method	Allowance method for identifiable uncollectable accounts	Allowance method	Allowance method	Allowance method for identifiable uncollectable accounts
Inventories—Valuation	Lower of cost and market	Lower of cost and market	Lower of cost and market	Lower of cost and market	Lower of cost and market	Lower of cost and market
—Cost Flow Assumption	FIFO, average	FIFO, LIFO, average	FIFO, average	FIFO, LIFO, average	FIFO, average	Average (unless physical flow is FIFO or LIFO)
Fixed Assets—Valuation	Acquisition cost less depreciation	Acquisition cost less depreciation	Acquisition cost less depreciation[a]	Acquisition cost less depreciation	Acquisition cost less depreciation[b]	Acquisition cost less depreciation
—Depreciation	Straight-line, accelerated	Straight-line, declining-balance, sum-of-the-years'-digits	Straight-line, accelerated	Straight-line, declining-balance, sum-of-the-years'-digits	Straight-line, declining-balance, sum-of-the-years'-digits	Straight-line, accelerated
Research and Development	Expensed when incurred	Expensed when incurred	Generally expensed when incurred, but may be capitalized and amortized	Expensed when incurred or capitalized and amortized	Expensed when incurred	Expensed when incurred
Leases	Operating and capital lease methods	Operating and capital lease methods	Operating lease method	Operating lease method	Operating lease method	Operating lease method
Deferred Taxes	Deferred tax accounting required	Deferred tax accounting required	Book/tax conformity generally required so deferred tax accounting not an issue	Book/tax conformity generally required so deferred tax accounting not an issue	Deferred tax accounting required based on probability that liability or asset will crystalize in near future	Book/tax conformity generally required so deferred tax accounting not an issue

EXHIBIT 14.4 (continued)

	Canada	United States	France	Japan	Great Britain	Germany
Investments in Securities: 0%–20%	Cost (unless price declines considered permanent)	Lower of cost and market	Lower of cost and market[a]	Cost (unless price declines considered permanent)	Lower of cost and market	Cost (unless price declines considered permanent)
20%–50%	Equity method	Equity method	Equity method	Cost (unless price declines considered permanent)	Equity method	Cost (unless price declines considered permanent)
Greater than 50%	Consolidation generally required	Consolidation required	Consolidation required	Consolidation not required (except in certain filings with the Ministry of Finance)	Both parent company and group (consolidated) financial statements presented	Consolidation required
Corporate Acquisitions: Accounting Method	Purchase method (pooling permitted only when acquirer cannot be identified)	Purchase and pooling-of-interests methods	Purchase method	Purchase method	Purchase and pooling-of-interests methods	Purchase method
Amortization of Goodwill	Amortized over maximum of 40 years	Amortized over maximum of 40 years	Amortization required	Amortized over maximum of 5 years	Goodwill either written off immediately against a retained earnings reserve or capitalized and amortized over its expected useful life.	Amortized over period of 4 to 15 years

[a]GAAP in France permit periodic revaluations of tangible fixed assets and investments to current market values. However, the book/tax conformity requirement in France results in immediate taxation of unrealized gains. As a consequence, revaluations are unusual.

[b]GAAP in Great Britain permit periodic revaluations of land, buildings, and certain intangibles to current market values. The firm credits a revaluation reserve account, a component of shareholders' equity.

DEVELOPMENT OF ACCOUNTING PRINCIPLES

Chapter 5 indicated that the development of "generally accepted accounting principles" (GAAP) is essentially a political process. Various persons or groups have power or authority in the decision process, including the federal and provincial legislatures and the provincial securities commissions, the courts, professional accounting organizations and their members, business firms, and financial statement users. Although Parliament has the ultimate authority to specify acceptable accounting methods for federally incorporated companies, it has delegated that authority to the Accounting Standards Board (ASB) of the CICA. The majority of the provincial securities commissions have similarly delegated their authority to the ASB. In the United States and the United Kingdom, the legislatures have occasionally determined accounting principles. In those countries, the role of the private sector versus the public sector in setting accounting policies and regulating professional accounting practice continues to be the subject of extensive public debate.

In Canada, on the other hand, governments have not publicly influenced accounting principles and, consequently, the controversy has not arisen. However, the Northland-Commercial Bank failure in the 1980s raised public questions about the degree to which current GAAP protected the public interest. The provincial securities commissions have undoubtedly felt pressure to take a more active role in standard-setting. The Ontario Securities Commission has begun issuing technical bulletins on accounting issues that will have an increasing impact on GAAP.

SUMMARY

The structure of accounting policies might be depicted as shown in Figure 14.1. The "universe" of possible accounting policies is encircled by a broken line because of the difficulty in defining the relative size, or boundaries, of circle A. The process of specifying the policies designated as *generally acceptable* (the subset of policies from circle A represented by circle B) is political in nature. The federal and provincial legislatures have the legal authority to make the selection, but most of the responsibility for doing so has, in effect, been delegated to the Accounting Standards Board. The individual firm's selection of accounting policies (the subset of policies from circle B represented by Circle C) might be based on a criterion of accurate presentation. However, because benefits received and services consumed are seldom observable events and are therefore difficult to measure, reaching consensus on which generally accepted accounting policies provide an accurate or fair presentation is difficult. This chapter suggests that a firm might pursue a specific reporting objective, such as conservatism, profit maximization, or income smoothing, in selecting its accounting policies.

Before we can know whether circle B should be widened or narrowed, we must learn whether investors accept financial statement information as presented or whether investors make adjustments to recognize the effects of using alternative accounting policies. This question has been, and continues to be, the subject of extensive research.

FIGURE 14.1
Structure of Accounting Policies

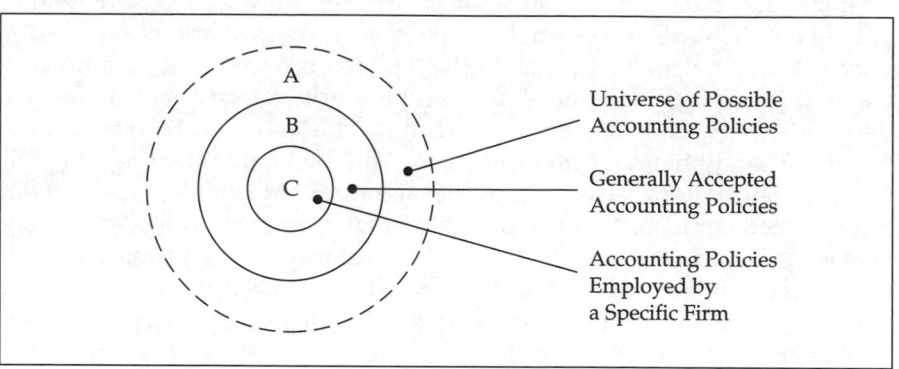

Key Terms

Accounting policies
Accuracy in presentation
Conservatism
Profit maximization
Income smoothing
Least and latest rule

SELF-STUDY MATERIAL

This section contains questions, exercises, and problems to help you assess your understanding of Chapter 14. Careful review of this material will assist you in completing the homework assignments. Solutions are found at the end of the section.

QUESTIONS AND EXERCISES

True/False

For each statement, place a T or an F in the space provided to indicate whether the statement is true or false.

_____ 1. Research has proved conclusively that investors adjust for the use of different accounting procedures in analyzing the financial statements of various firms; therefore, the concern over the variety of policies available to firms is unwarranted.

_____ 2. The development of accounting policies has been shown to be essentially a political process.

_____ 3. In accounting, policies are judged on their general acceptability by the preparers and users of accounting reports.

_____ 4. There is a great deal of flexibility in choosing among depreciation methods for financial reporting purposes.

_____ 5. A deferred tax liability will most likely result from the handling of depreciation for financial reporting and taxes.

_____ 6. It is unlikely that any single generally accepted accounting policy could accomplish both the financial reporting objectives of conservatism and profit maximization.

_____ 7. Assuming no change in income tax rates, claiming maximum capital cost allowance for tax purposes instead of using the straight-line method will significantly improve the present value of tax savings from depreciation over the life of an asset.

_____ 8. The investment tax credit is a deductible expense in the compution of income tax.

_____ 9. Research costs must be expensed in the year in which the costs are incurred for financial reporting purposes, even though the costs may provide benefits to future periods.

_____ 10. If the FIFO inventory method is employed for tax purposes, it must also be used for financial reporting purposes.

_____ 11. When the amount of doubtful accounts can be reasonably estimated, the direct writeoff method is not allowed for financial reporting.

_____ 12. If a firm wants a conservative yet acceptable set of financial statements, it should record depreciation equal to the maximum capital cost allowance.

_____ 13. The methods of accounting for income tax purposes and financial accounting purposes can never be different.

_____ 14. It has been proved conclusively that firms using conservative accounting policies will be undervalued by investors in the stock market.

_____ 15. For financial reporting purposes, the investment tax credit is accounted for by either the flow-through method or the deferral method.

_____ 16. A firm always has wide flexibility in its selection of accounting methods.

_____ 17. For lessees, all leases are treated as operating leases, but for lessors, they are treated as capital leases.

_____ 18. The accountant should always try to use the accounting policies that lead to the most accurate set of financial statements.

_____ 19. All methods allowed for tax reporting purposes are also allowed for financial reporting purposes.

_____ 20. When accounting for interest expense, it is acceptable to use either the straight-line method or the effective-interest method.

_____ 21. The production method is used more frequently than any other depreciation method because of its smoothing effect on net income over time.

_____ 22. Generally accepted accounting policies require revenue to be usually recognized at time of sale.

_____ 23. Over the entire life of a firm, the LIFO inventory method will show the same cumulative profits as the FIFO method.

_____ 24. The general rule in selecting accounting methods for tax purposes is to postpone revenue recognition and to recognize expenses as soon as possible. If tax rates are expected to rise significantly, the reverse of this rule may be appropriate.

_____ 25. When the income reporting for tax purposes is greater than the net income reported for financial statement purposes, Future Income Tax Debits will generally appear on the balance sheet.

Matching

From the list of objectives for financial accounting and tax reporting, select the objectives that can be most closely associated with each of the accounting and valuation methods that follows and place the letter for that objective in the space provided. (An objective may be used more than once, and more than one objective may be applicable to each method. You may assume that inflation has occurred in the past and is expected to continue in the future.)

a. conservatism

b. accurate presentation

c. income smoothing

d. profit maximization

e. tax minimization

f. none of the above

_____ 1. cost reduction (investment tax credit)

_____ 2. capitalization of prepaid advertising costs

_____ 3. claiming maximum capital cost allowance

_____ 4. straight-line method

_____ 5. LIFO method

_____ 6. flow-through method

_____ 7. operating method (accounting for leases)

_____ 8. FIFO method

_____ 9. double-declining-balance method

_____ 10. installment sales method

_____ 11. percentage-of-sales method for uncollectable accounts

_____ 12. expensing of research costs

_____ 13. percentage-of-completion method

_____ 14. weighted-average inventory method

Multiple Choice

Choose the best answer for each question or problem and enter the identifying letter in the space provided.

_____ 1. Which financial accounting objective would seem to be the closest to the objectives of tax reporting?
   a) conservatism
   b) fair presentation
   c) accuracy
   d) profit maximization

_____ 2. For which account would the use of lower of cost and market not be acceptable?
   a) Inventory
   b) Land
   c) Temporary Investments
   d) it would be acceptable for all accounts above

_____ 3. The use of a straight-line method of amortization would be acceptable for:
   a) Building
   b) Patent
   c) Goodwill
   d) all of the above

_____ 4. Liberal Limited and Low Gear Company Inc. are identical in all respects, except that Liberal Limited uses FIFO and Low Gear Company Inc. uses weighted average in costing its inventories. Prices have been rising steadily over the last several years. Which statement would be incorrect in comparing the financial statements of these two companies?
   a) the inventory for Liberal Limited would be higher than the inventory for Low Gear Company Inc.
   b) the Retained Earnings for Liberal Limited would be higher than the Retained Earnings for Low Gear Company Inc.
   c) the net income in the current year for Liberal Limited would be higher than the net income for Low Gear Company Inc.
   d) the tax liability for Liberal Limited would be less than the tax liability for Low Gear Company Inc.

_____ 5. Which generally accepted accounting policy would be appropriate if the firm's objective was to present accounting information in a conservative manner?
   a) lower of cost and market
   b) expensing of exploration costs when incurred
   c) amortization of organization costs over minimum time period
   d) all of the above would be appropriate

_____ 6. Which account may appear on a company's balance sheet when the income for financial and tax reporting are different?
   a) Future Income Tax Debits
   b) Deferred Investment Credit
   c) Income Taxes Due Currently
   d) all of the above

_____ 7. In order to minimize the present value of income tax payments, which course of action should a firm take?
   a) use the weighted-average inventory method instead of FIFO in periods of rising prices

b) depreciate plant assets on the straight-line method rather than the maximum capital cost allowance

c) capitalize exploration costs instead of expensing them

d) all of the above

_____ 8. The Not Too Hot Radiator Company Inc. has decided to use straight-line depreciation in its financial statements and to claim maximum capital cost allowance on its tax return. Which statement concerning Not Too Hot's financial statements would be correct?

a) the net cash flow from operations will be less than it would have been if straight-line had been used for tax purposes as well as financial statement purposes

b) the income tax expense presented on the income statement in the early years of the assets' useful lives will be less than the tax payment

c) future income taxes (account with a credit balance) will be shown as a deferred credit on the balance sheet

d) all of the above statements are correct

_____ 9. If a firm wanted to smooth its income as a means of minimizing large fluctuations in the price of its shares, which method would be employed to help accomplish this objective?

a) weighted average for inventory

b) percentage-of-completion method for long-term construction contracts

c) straight-line amortization of patents

d) all of the above might smooth income in appropriate circumstances

_____ 10. The method of accounting for exploration costs of a mineral resource that would best attain the objective of income tax accounting would be to:

a) expense in total when incurred

b) capitalize only those costs related to mineral deposits

c) capitalize all costs associated with productive as well as nonproductive mineral deposits

d) none of the above

_____ 11. Which of these instances is not an example of a firm having flexibility in the choice of methods for financial reporting?

a) accounting for depreciation

b) accounting for investment tax credit

c) accounting for inventories

d) accounting for the investment in common shares

_____ 12. For financial reporting, when is revenue normally recognized?

a) at point in sale

b) while cash is being collected

c) after all cash has been collected

d) at the end of each year

Exercises

1. Indicate the accounting policy that would more likely lead to profit maximization.

   a. FIFO, LIFO, or weighted-average method, when prices are falling

   b. straight-line or double-declining-balance method in the first year of an asset's life

   c. deferral or flow-through method in year of purchase

   d. effective-interest or straight-line method, in the last year of an outstanding bond that was issued at face value

e. double-declining-balance or straight-line method in the last year of an asset's life

f. expensing versus capitalization of prepaid advertising, in the year prepaid

g. point-of-sale or installment sale method in the year of sale

2. Answer exercise 1 so that the methods are being considered for tax reporting and the purpose is to minimize taxes.

3. Name the generally accepted accounting policy or method described below:

a. a way of valuing inventory that recognizes the reduction of value below original cost

b. the preferable method for amortizing bond discounts

c. the method that accounts for a lease as for a purchase

d. the usual accounting for investments in common shares when the percentage of ownership is less than 20 percent

e. the method of recognizing income from long-term construction contracts that results in the most fluctuations in earnings over several periods

f. the required accounting treatment for most research costs

4. On January 1, 19X1, the Wilkie Company Ltd. is organized and 100,000 shares of $100 par value are issued at par. Following is the company's balance sheet for January 1, 19X1:

Assets		Equities	
Cash	$2,500,000	Common Shares	$10,000,000
Land	3,500,000		
Equipment	4,000,000		
Total Assets	$10,000,000	Total Equities	$10,000,000

Merchandise inventory is purchased and sold during 19X1 as follows:

Date of Purchase	Units Purchased	Unit Price	Units Sold
Jan. 3	10,000	$100	9,500
Jun. 6	18,000	110	16,000
Nov. 10	20,000	120	17,000
	48,000		42,500

Merchandise sales totalled $11 million during 19X1. In addition, long-term contracts were signed to produce machinery for the Capitalized Corporation. None of the machinery was completed during 19X1, but on the basis of the percentage of work completed, $1 million of profits have been earned.

The land was acquired for $2 million for speculation. Wilkie Company Ltd. believes that there is oil on the property and has spent $1 million on exploration costs.

The equipment was bought on January 1 and is being used in a building that has been leased by the Wilkie Company Ltd. for 30 years. The estimated life of the equipment is 20 years, and its expected disposal value is $500,000. The equipment qualifies for the 10 percent investment tax credit.

To promote the company in its first year of operations, Wilkie spent $2 million on an extensive advertising campaign. Three-quarters of the advertising expenditure is expected to benefit the company in future years. Other operating expenses for 19X1 were $1.2 million. Assume a tax rate of 40 percent. Also, assume that any method used for financial accounting purposes will also be used for tax purposes (with the exception of the investment tax credit and depreciation).

The president of Wilkie believes that maximizing reported profits results in maximizing the earnings per share. The controller is concerned about misleading potential investors by reporting possibly overstated profits. He would rather take a conservative approach, at least until the firm has proven itself. You are to prepare comparative income statements for the first year of operation, selecting those methods that would be most appropriate to (a) maximize profits for the president and (b) show conservative profits for the controller. Also, (c), specify what you would do with each item in order to minimize income taxes.

5. Presented here are the financial statements and notes for Grinnel Co. Inc. for 19X2:

GRINNEL CO. INC.
Balance Sheets
December 31, 19X1 and 19X2

	12/31 19X1	12/31 19X2
Assets		
Current Assets:		
Cash	$ 80,000	$ 52,000
Accounts Receivable (net)[a]	120,000	150,000
Inventory	80,000	60,000
	$ 280,000	$ 262,000
Capital Assets:		
Land	$ 300,000	$ 340,000
Building[b]	750,000	700,000
Accumulated Depreciation	(100,000)	(120,000)
	$ 950,000	$ 920,000
Total Assets	$1,230,000	$1,182,000
Liabilities and Shareholders' Equity		
Current Liabilities:		
Accounts Payable	$ 50,000	$ 70,000
Notes Payable[c]	100,000	0
Dividends Payable	20,000	0
Deferred Investment Tax Credit	10,000	0
	$ 180,000	$ 70,000
Shareholders' Equity:		
Common Shares, Par Value	$ 200,000	$ 200,000
Retained Earnings	850,000	912,000
	$1,050,000	$1,112,000
Total Liabilities and Shareholders' Equity	$1,230,000	$1,182,000

[a]All sales are on account and no accounts were written off as definitely uncollectable during the year.
[b]On January 1, 19X2, part of the building was destroyed by a fire. No other additions or retirements took place during 19X2 in the Building account.
[c]The notes were paid off on July 1, 19X2.

GRINNELL CO. INC.
Income Statement
For the Year Ended December 31, 19X2

Sales		$950,000
Cost of Goods Sold		400,000
Gross Profit		$550,000
Operating Expenses:		
Depreciation	$ 50,000	
Selling & Administrative	210,000	
Bad Debts Expense	50,000	310,000
Operating Income		$240,000
Nonoperating Items:		
Loss from Fire	$ 15,000	
Interest Expense	5,000	20,000
Income Before Tax		$220,000
Income Tax	$ 88,000	
Less: Investment Tax Credit	10,000	78,000
Net Income		$142,000
Earnings per Share		$14.20

GRINNELL CO. INC.
Retained Earnings Statement
For the Year Ended December 31, 19X2

Retained Earnings 1/1 19X2	$850,000
Net Income	142,000
	$992,000
Dividends Declared	80,000
Retained Earnings 12/31 19X2	$912,000

a. How much cash was collected on account during 19X2?

b. Which method of accounting for bad debts was being used by Grinnell Co. Inc.?

c. If the balance in the Allowance for Doubtful Accounts was $15,000 on January 1, 19X2, what would be its balance on December 31, 19X2?

d. Was there any land purchased or sold during 19X2? If so, how much?

e. What was the book value of the building destroyed by the fire?

f. If the company was able to salvage some of the building after the fire, what were the proceeds from salvage for the company?

g. Grinnell is using brand new equipment and furniture. Was it purchased or leased? Why?

h. How much inventory was purchased during 19X2?

i. How much was paid on account for inventory purchases? Assume all purchases are made on account.

j. What interest rate was being paid on the notes outstanding on January 1, 19X2?

k. How many dollars in dividends were paid to shareholders during 19X2?

l. How many shares were outstanding in December 31, 19X2, and what was the par value of the shares?

m. Was the deferral or the flow-through method used for the investment tax credit in 19X2? Explain.

n. What was the tax rate in 19X2?

o. How much cash was provided from operations?

MASTER REVIEW PROBLEM FOR SELF-STUDY

Presented below is a set of financial statements for Batch Corporation, including a consolidated income statement (Exhibit 14.5) and a consolidated statement of changes in financial position (Exhibit 14.7) for Year 2, and a comparative consolidated balance sheet (Exhibit 14.6) on December 31, Year 1 and Year 2. Following the financial statements is a series of notes providing additional information on certain items in the financial statements. Respond to each of the questions listed, using information from the financial statements and notes. It is suggested that you study the statements and notes carefully before attempting to respond to the questions.

a. Temporary investments costing $180,000 were sold during Year 2. Ascertain the price at which these securities were sold.

EXHIBIT 14.5
BATCH CORPORATION
Consolidated Income Statement for Year 2
(amounts in thousands)

Sales		$12,000
Less: Cost of Goods Sold		7,200
Gross Profit		$ 4,800
Less: Operating Expenses		
Selling and Administrative	$2,689	
Loss on Sale of Equipment	80	2,769
Operating Profit		$ 2,031
Less: Financial Expenses		
Interest Expense (Notes 7 and 8)	561	
Unrealized Loss from Price Decline of:		
Temporary Investments	20	
Portfolio Investments	15	
	$ 596	
Financial Income:		
Equity in Income of Unconsolidated Affiliates:		
Klatt Credit Corporation	$ 160	
Johnson Corporation	140	
Total	$ 300	
Dividend Revenue	20	
Gain on Sale of Temporary Investments	30	
	$ 350	246
Net Income Before Income Taxes and Minority Interest		$ 1,785
Income Tax Expense		720
Net Income Before Minority Interest		$ 1,065
Minority Interest in Earnings of McCutcheon Corporation		40
Net Income		$ 1,025

EXHIBIT 14.6
BATCH CORPORATION
Consolidated Balance Sheets
December 31, Year 1 and Year 2
(amounts in thousands)

	December 31, Year 2	December 31, Year 1
ASSETS		
Current Assets:		
Cash	$ 2,739	$ 1,470
Temporary Investments (Note 2)	550	450
Accounts Receivable (net; Note 3)	2,850	2,300
Inventories (Note 4)	3,110	2,590
Prepayments	970	800
Total Current Assets	$10,219	$ 7,610
Investments (Note 5):		
Investment in Maher Corporation (10 percent)	$ 185	$ 200
Investment in Johnson Corporation (30 percent)	410	310
Investment in Klatt Credit Corporation (100 percent)	930	800
Total investments	$ 1,525	$ 1,310
Capital Assets:		
Land	$ 500	$ 400
Buildings	940	800
Equipment	3,800	3,300
Total Cost	$ 5,240	$ 4,500
Less: Accumulated Depreciation	(930)	(1,200)
Net Capital Assets	$ 4,310	$ 3,300
Goodwill (Note 6)	80	90
Total Assets	$16,134	$12,310
LIABILITIES AND SHAREHOLDERS' EQUITY		
Current Liabilities:		
Note Payable (Note 7)	$ 1,000	$ —
Accounts Payable	2,425	1,070
Salaries Payable	600	800
Interest Payable	400	300
Income Taxes Payable	375	250
Total Current Liabilities	4,800	2,420
Long-Term Liabilities:		
Bonds Payable (Note 8)	$ 6,000	$ 6,000
Premium less Discount on Bonds Payable	209	209
Total Long-Term Liabilities	6,209	6,209
Deferred Income Taxes	940	820
Minority Interest	214	180
Shareholders' Equity:		
Common Shares (no par value)	$ 1,800	$ 1,300
Contributed Surplus	5	—
Retained Earnings	2,186	1,411
Total	$ 3,991	$ 2,711
Less: Treasury Shares (at cost)	(20)	(30)
Total Shareholders' Equity	$ 3,971	$ 2,681
Total Liabilities and Shareholders' Equity	$16,134	$12,310

EXHIBIT 14.7
BATCH CORPORATION
**Consolidated Statement of Changes in Financial Position for Year 2
(amounts in thousands)**

Cash[a] Provided by		
Operations		
Net Income		$1,025
Additions:		
Depreciation	560	
Deferred Income Taxes	120	
Loss on Sale of Equipment	80	
Minority Interest in Undistributed Earnings of Consolidated Subsidiaries	34	
Unrealized Loss from Price Decline of Portfolio Investments	15	
Amortization of Discount on Bonds	28	
Amortization of Goodwill	10	
Increase in Notes Payable	1,000	
Increase in Accounts Payable	1,355	
Increase in Interest Payable	100	
Increase in Income Taxes Payable	125	
Subtractions:		
Equity in Earnings of Affiliates and Subsidiaries in Excess of Dividends Received	(180)	
Amortization of Premium on Bonds	(28)	
Increase in Accounts Receivable	(550)	
Increase in Inventories	(520)	
Increase in Prepayments	(170)	
Decrease in Salaries Payable	(200)	
Cash Provided by Operations		$2,804
Financing Activities		
Common Shares Issued	$ 500	
Treasury Shares Sold	15	
Investing Activities		515
Sale of Equipment		150
Total Sources of Cash		$3,469
Cash Applied to		
Dividends		$ 250
Investing Activities:		
Acquisition of Assets:		
Investment in Johnson Corporation	$ 50	
Land	100	
Building	300	
Equipment	1,400	
		1,850
Total Applications of Cash		$2,100
Net Increase in Cash Position		$1,369
Cash Position Beginning of Year		$1,920
Cash Position End of Year		$3,289

[a]*"Cash" is defined for purposes of this statement as cash plus cash equivalents net of short-term bank indebtedness.*

b. Refer to **(a)**. Compute the cost of temporary investments purchased during Year 2.

c. What was the amount of specific customers' accounts written off as uncollectable during Year 2?

d. Assume that all sales are made on account. Compute the amount of cash collected from customers during the year.

e. Compute the cost of units completed and transferred to the financial goods storeroom during Year 2.

f. Direct labour and overhead costs incurred in manufacturing during the year totalled $4,500,000. Determine the cost of raw materials purchased during Year 2.

g. What would cost of goods sold have been if current cost rather than weighted-average cost had been used?

h. Prepare an analysis that explains the causes of the changes in each of the three intercorporate investment accounts.

i. Assume that Klatt Credit Corporation has been consolidated with Batch Corporation instead of being treated as an unconsolidated subsidiary. Prepare a condensed consolidated balance sheet on December 31, Year 2 and a condensed consolidated income statement for Year 2 for Batch Corporation and Klatt Credit Corporation.

j. Prepare an analysis that explains the change in each of the following four accounts during Year 2: Land, Building, Equipment, and Accumulated Depreciation.

k. Give the journal entry made on Batch Corporation's books on January 2, Year 1, when it acquired McCutcheon Corporation.

l. Compute the book value of the net assets of McCutcheon Corporation on January 2, Year 1.

m. Compute the total amount of dividends declared by McCutcheon Corporation during Year 2.

n. The 4 percent bonds payable were initially priced to yield 6 percent compounded semiannually. The 10 percent bonds were initially priced to yield 8 percent compounded semiannually. The 8 percent bonds were issued at par. Using the appropriate present value tables in Appendix B at the back of the book, demonstrate that $208,640 was the correct balance for the bond premium less discount at December 31, Year 1.

o. Calculate the amount of interest expense and any change in the bond discount or premium for Year 2 on each of the three long-term bond issues.

p. Compute the amount of income taxes actually paid during Year 2.

q. Prepare an analysis explaining the change during Year 2 in each of the following accounts: Contributed Surplus, Retained Earnings, Treasury Shares.

Note 1: Summary of Significant Accounting Policies

Basis of Consolidation The financial statements of Batch Corporation are consolidated with McCutcheon Corporation, an 80-percent-owned subsidiary acquired on January 2, Year 1. Klatt Credit Corporation, a wholly owned finance subsidiary, is excluded from the consolidation because the inclusion would not provide more informative presentation to the shareholders. The investment is accounted for on an equity basis, and condensed financial statements are presented in Note 5.

Temporary Investments Temporary investments are stated at the lower of acquisition cost and market.

Accounts Receivable Doubtful accounts of customers are accounted for using the allowance method.

Inventories Inventories are valued at the lower of weighted-average cost and replacement cost.

Investments Investments of less than 20 percent of the outstanding common shares of other companies are accounted for using the cost method. Investments of greater than or equal to 20 percent of the outstanding common shares of unconsolidated affiliates and subsidiaries are accounted for using the equity method.

Buildings and Equipment   Depreciation for financial reporting purposes is calculated using the straight-line method. For income tax purposes, the maximum capital cost allowance is claimed.

Goodwill   Goodwill is amortized over a period of ten years.

Interest on Long-Term Debt   Interest expense on bonds payable is recognized using the effective-interest method.

Deferred Income Taxes   Future income taxes are provided for timing differences between book income and taxable income.

Note 2: Temporary investments are shown net of an allowance for market price declines below acquisition cost of $50,000 on December 31, Year 1 and $70,000 on December 31, Year 2.

Note 3: Accounts receivable are shown net of an allowance for doubtful accounts of $200,000 on December 31, Year 1, and $250,000 on December 31, Year 2. Bad debts expense of $120,000 is included in Selling and Administrative expenses.

Note 4: Inventories consist of the following:

	December 31, Year 2	December 31, Year 1
Raw Materials	$ 380,000	$ 330,000
Work in Process	530,000	460,000
Finished Goods	2,200,000	1,800,000
Total	$3,110,000	$2,590,000

The current cost of inventories exceeded the amounts determined on a weighted-average basis by $420,000 on December 31, Year 1 and $730,000 on December 31, Year 2.

Note 5: Condensed financial statements for Klatt Credit Corporation, a wholly owned, unconsolidated subsidiary, are shown below.

Note 6: On January 2, Year 1, Batch Corporation acquired 80 percent of the outstanding common shares of McCutcheon Corporation by issuing 20,000 shares of Batch Corporation. The Batch Corporation shares were selling on January 2, Year 1, for $40 a share. Any difference between the acquisition price and the book value of the net assets acquired was considered goodwill and is being amortized over a period of ten years from the date of acquisition.

Note 7: The note payable included under current liabilities is a one-year note due on January 2, Year 3. The note requires annual interest payments on December 31 of each year. The interest expense on this note for Year 2 was $101,000.

Note 8: Bonds payable are the following:

	December 31, Year 2	December 31, Year 1
4 percent bonds due December 31, Year 7, with interest payable semiannually	$2,000,000	$2,000,000
10 percent bonds due December 31, Year 11, with interest payable semiannually	3,000,000	3,000,000
8 percent bonds due on December 31, Year 17, with interest payable semiannually	1,000,000	1,000,000
Total	$6,000,000	$6,000,000

The interest expense of the bonds payable for Year 2 was $460,000.

KLATT CREDIT CORPORATION
(Note 5) (amounts in thousands)

	December 31, Year 2	December 31, Year 1
Balance Sheet		
Cash and Temporary Investments	$ 840	$ 760
Accounts Receivable (net)	7,400	6,590
Other Assets	1,260	1,050
Total Assets	$9,500	$8,400
Notes Payable Due Within One Year	$4,300	$3,900
Long-Term Note Payable	3,100	2,620
Other Liabilities	1,170	1,080
Common Shares	100	100
Contributed Surplus	300	300
Retained Earnings	530	400
Total Equities	$9,500	$8,400

Statement of Income and Retained Earnings	Year 2
Revenues	$680
Expenses	520
Net Income	$160
Less Dividends	(30)
Retained Earnings, December 31, Year 1	400
Retained Earnings, December 31, Year 2	$530

Note 9: The change in issued share capital during the year was as follows:

	Number of Shares	Amount
December 31, Year 1	50,000	$1,300,000
Issued for Cash	10,000	500,000
December 31, Year 2	60,000	$1,800,000

ANSWERS TO QUESTIONS AND EXERCISES

True/False

1. F	8. F	15. F	22. T
2. F	9. T	16. F	23. T
3. T	10. F	17. F	24. T
4. T	11. T	18. F	25. T
5. T	12. T	19. F	
6. T	13. F	20. T	
7. T	14. F	21. F	

Matching

1. a, c	5. a, c	9. a	13. c, d
2. d	6. d	10. a, e	14. c
3. e	7. f	11. a, c	
4. c, d	8. d	12. a, e	

Multiple Choice

1. a	4. d	7. a	10. a
2. b	5. d	8. c	11. b
3. d	6. a	9. d	12. a

Exercises

1. a. LIFO
    b. straight-line
    c. flow-through
    d. neither; because the bond was issued at face value, there is no discount or premium to amortize
    e. double-declining-balance
    f. capitalization
    g. point-of-sale

2. a. FIFO
    b. double-declining-balance
    c. flow-through
    d. neither, because there is no discount or premium to amortize
    e. straight-line
    f. expensing
    g. installment sales

3. a. lower of cost and market
    b. effective-interest
    c. capital lease
    d. lower of cost and market
    e. completed contract
    f. expense when incurred

4. **WILKIE COMPANY LTD.**
    Comparative Income Statements
    Based on Different Accounting Principles
    For the Year Ending December 31, 19X1

	(a) Profit Maximization (for President)	(b) Conservative (for Controller)
Revenue:		
Sale of Merchandise	$11,000,000	$11,000,000
Profit on Long-Term Contract	1,000,000	—
Total Revenue	$12,000,000	$11,000,000
Cost of Goods Sold	4,720,000[a]	4,830,000[a]
Gross Profit	$ 7,280,000	$ 6,170,000
Expenses:		
Depreciation on Equipment	$ 175,000[b]	$ 400,000[b]
Advertising	500,000[c]	2,000,000[c]
Exploration Costs	—[d]	1,000,000[d]
Other Operating Expenses	1,200,000	1,200,000
Total Expenses Before Income Taxes	$1,875,000	$4,600,000
Net Income Before Income Taxes	$5,405,000	$1,570,000

Income Tax Expense:

Tax on Current Income (at 40%)	$2,162,000	$ 628,000
Tax Credit for Investment in Equipment	400,000[e]	20,000[e]
Total Income Tax	$1,762,000	$ 608,000
Net Income	$3,643,000	$ 962,000
Earnings per share		
(100,000 shares outstanding)	$36.43	$9.62

Supporting Schedules

[a]Profit-Maximization Approach: FIFO

$$10,000\ u \times \$100 = \$1,000,000$$
$$18,000\ u \times\ \ 110 =\ \ 1,980,000$$
$$14,500\ u \times\ \ 120 =\ \ 1,740,000$$
$$\underline{\$4,720,000}$$

Conservative Approach: LIFO

$$20,000\ u \times \$120 = \$2,400,000$$
$$18,000\ u \times\ \ 110 =\ \ 1,980,000$$
$$4,500\ u \times\ \ 100 =\ \ \ \ 450,000$$
$$\underline{\$4,830,000}$$

[b]Profit-Maximization Approach: Straight-Line Method

$$(\$4,000,000 - \$500,000) \div 20 = \$175,000$$

Conservative Approach: Double-Declining-Balance Method

$$(\$4,000,000 \times \tfrac{1}{20} \times 2) = \$4,000,000 \times 0.10 = \$400,000$$

[c]Profit-Maximization Approach: Partial Capitalization

$$\tfrac{1}{4} \times \$2,000,000 = \$500,000$$

The remaining $1.5 million is capitalized and will be allocated to those periods that are expected to benefit from the expenditure.

Conservative Approach: Expense all of the $2 million expenditure in the year incurred.

[d]Profit Maximization Approach: Capitalization of $1 million.

All exploration costs are capitalized as part of the cost of the expected mineral deposit. Whenever oil is discovered, the cost will be amortized on the basis of the estimated productive output of the wells.

Conservative approach: Expense all of the $1 million expenditure.

[e]Profit Maximization Approach: Flow-Through Approach

$$0.10 \times \$4,000,000 = \$400,000$$

Conservative Approach: Cost-Reduction Approach

$$0.10 \times \$4,000,000 = \$400,000 \div 20\ \text{years} = \$20,000$$

---

c. For tax purposes, in order to minimize income taxes:

1. Because LIFO may *not* be used when computing taxable income, the company would use the annual weighted-average method of inventory valuation.
2. The company would claim maximum capital cost allowance.
3. The entire amount of advertising and exploration costs would be deducted immediately.
4. The flow-through method would be used for the investment credit.

5. a.

Accounts Receivable 1/1 19X2	$ 120,000
Sales on Account	950,000
	$1,070,000

Less:
Bad Debts	(50,000)
Cash Collections	(?)
Accounts Receivable 12/31 19X2	$150,000

The cash collections are $870,000.
($1,070,000 − $50,000 − $150,000)

b. The allowance method, because there was a bad debts expense for 1986 ($50,000) and no accounts were written off; the direct writeoff method was not being used.

c.
Balance 1/1 19X2	$15,000
Plus: Bad Debts for 19X2	50,000
	$65,000
Less: Writeoffs during 19X2	0
Balance 12/31 19X2	$65,000

d. The land account increased by $40,000 during 19X2. This increase most likely represented a purchase.

e.
Building 1/1 19X2		$750,000
Building 12/31 19X2		(700,000)
Cost of Building Destroyed		$ 50,000
Accumulated Depreciation 1/1 19X2	$100,000	
Accumulated Depreciation 12/31 19X2	120,000	
Increase for 19X2	$ 20,000	
Depreciation for 19X2	50,000	
Accum. Dep. for Building Destroyed		(30,000)
Book Value of Building Destroyed		$ 20,000

f.
Book Value	$ 20,000
Disposal	(?)
Loss from Fire	$ 15,000

The proceeds from disposal were $5,000.

g. Leased, because there are no accounts for machinery and furniture in the Capital Assets section of the balance sheet.

h.
Inventory Balance 1/1 19X2	$ 80,000
Plus: Purchases	?
Total Available	$
Less: Inventory Balance 12/31 19X2	(60,000)
Cost of Goods Sold	$400,000

Purchases were $380,000. ($400,000 + $60,000 − $80,000)

i.
Accounts Payable 1/1 19X2	$ 50,000
Plus: Purchases on Account	380,000
Total to be paid	$430,000
Less: Accounts Payable 12/31 19X2	(70,000)
Amount paid on account	$360,000

j.
Interest Expense: 1/1 19X2 to 7/1 19X2 (6 months)	$ 5,000
	× 2
Annual Interest	$ 10,000
Notes Payable	÷ $100,000
Interest Rate	10%

k.

Dividends Declared in 19X2	$ 80,000
Dividends Payable 1/1 19X2 (and paid in 19X2)	20,000
Dividends Paid in 19X2	$100,000

l.

Net Income	$142,000
Shares Outstanding	÷ ?
Earnings per Share	= 14.20

The number of shares outstanding was 10,000. ($142,000 ÷ $14.20)
The par value of a share was $20. ($200,000 par value ÷ 10,000 shares)

m. The deferral method, because there was a credit against taxes in 19X2, yet there were no plant assets purchased in that year. The credit must have related to purchases of a previous year. In addition, there was a deferred investment tax credit account on the books on January 1, 19X2 for the same amount.

n. The tax rate was 40 percent ($88,000 ÷ $220,000).

o.

Net Income		$142,000
Additions:		
Depreciation	$ 50,000	
Loss from Fire	15,000	
Reduction in Inventory	20,000	
Increase in Accounts Payable	20,000	105,000
Deductions:		
Increase in Accounts Receivable	$ 30,000	
Decrease in Notes Payable	100,000	
Decrease in Deferred Investment Tax Credit	10,000	(140,000)
Cash Provided by Operations		$107,000

SUGGESTED SOLUTION TO MASTER REVIEW PROBLEM FOR SELF-STUDY

The source of the data is shown in parentheses as follows: Balance Sheet — BS; Income Statement — IS; Statement of Changes — SC; Question — Q; Answer — A; Note — N.

a.

Cost of Temporary Investments Sold (Q, A)	$180,000
Gain on Sale (IS)	30,000
Selling Price	$210,000

b.

Temporary Investments at Cost on December 31, Year 1 ($450,000 + $50,000) (BS)	$500,000
Plus: Purchases	?
Less? Cost of Temporary Investments Sold (Q, A)	(180,000)
Temporary Investments at Cost on December 31, Year 2 ($550,000 + $70,000) (BS)	$620,000

The cost of temporary investments purchased during Year 2 was $300,000.

c.

Allowance for Doubtful Accounts, December 31, Year 1 (N, 2)	$200,000
Plus: Bad Debts Expense During Year 2 (N, 2)	120,000
Less: Specific Customers' Accounts Written Off as Uncollectable During Year 1	(?)
Allowance for Doubtful Accounts, December 31, Year 2 (N, 2)	$250,000

Specific customers' accounts written off as uncollectable during Year 2 totalled $70,000.

d.

Gross Accounts Receivable December 31, Year 1[a]	$ 2,500
Plus: Sales During the Year (IS)	12,000
Less: Gross Accounts Receivable December 31, Year 2[b]	(3,100)
Accounts Collected or Written Off	$11,400
Less: Writeoffs (A, c)	(70)
Cash Collected During Year	$11,330

[a]$2,300 + $200.(BS + N, 2)
[b]$2,850 + $250.(BS + N, 2)

e.

Finished Goods Inventory, December 31, Year 1 (N, 4)	$1,800,000
Plus: Cost of Units Completed During the Year	?
Less: Cost of Units Sold During the Year (IS)	(7,200,000)
Finished Goods Inventory, December 31, Year 2 (N, 4)	$2,200,000

The cost of units completed was $7,600,000.

f.

Work-in-Process Inventory, December 31, Year 1 (N, 4)	$ 460,000
Plus: Cost of Raw Materials Used	?
Plus: Direct Labour and Manufacturing Overhead Costs Incurred (Q, f)	4,500,000
Less: Cost of Units Completed (A, e)	(7,600,000)
Work-in-Process Inventory, December 31, Year 2 (N, 4)	$ 530,000

The cost of raw materials used during Year 2 was $3,170,000.

Raw Materials Inventory, December 31, Year 1 (N, 4)	$ 330,000
Plus: Cost of Raw Material Purchased	?
Less: Cost of Raw Materials Used (A, f)	(3,170,000)
Raw Materials Inventory, December 31, year 2 (N, 4)	$ 380,000

The cost of raw materials purchased was $3,220,000.

g.

	Weighted-Average	Difference	Current Cost
Inventory, December 31, Year 1	$ 2,590,000[a]	$420,000[c]	$ 3,010,000
Purchases Plus Costs Incurred	7,720,000[b]	—	7,720,000
Goods Available	$10,310,000	$420,000	$10,730,000
Less: Inventory, December 31, Year 2	(3,110,000)[a]	(730,000)[c]	(3,840,000)
Cost of Goods Sold	$ 7,200,000	($310,000)	$ 6,890,000

[a](BS).
[b]{$3,220,000 [(A, f) + $4,500,000 (Q, f)]}
[c]N, 4.

Cost of goods sold under Current Cost would have been $6,890,000.

h. **Investment in Maher Corporation (cost method)**

Balance, December 31, Year 1 (BS)	$200,000
Plus: Additional Investments (SC)	—
Less: Sales of Investments (SC)	—
Less: Increase in Unrealized Loss on Valuation of Investments (SC)	(15,000)
Balance, December 31, Year 2 (BS)	$185,000

Investment in Johnson Corporation (equity method)

Balance, December 31, Year 1 (BS)	$310,000
Plus: Additional Investments (SC)	50,000
Plus: Equity in Earnings (IS)	140,000
Less: Sale of Investments (SC)	—
Less: Dividend Received (plug)	(90,000)
Balance, December 31, Year 2 (BS)	$410,000

Investment in Klatt Credit Corporation (equity method)

Balance, December 31, Year 1 (BS)	$800,000
Plus: Additional Investments (SC)	—
Plus: Equity in Earnings (IS)	160,000
Less: Sale of Investments (SC)	—
Less: Dividends Received (plug)	(30,000)
Balance, December 31, Year 2 (BS)	$930,000

i.

Balance Sheet	Batch Corp.	Klatt Credit Corp.	Eliminations	Consolidated
Cash and Temporary Investments	$ 3,289	$ 840		$ 4,129
Accounts Receivable	2,850	7,400		10,250
Investment in Klatt Credit Corporation	930	—	$(930)	—
Other Assets	9,065	1,260		10,325
Total Assets	$16,134	$9,500	$(930)	$24,704
Notes Payable:				
Due Within 1 Year	$ 1,000	$4,300		$ 5,300
Long-Term	6,209	3,100		9,309
Other Liabilities	3,800	1,170		4,970
Deferred Income Taxes	940	—		940
Minority Interest	214			214
Common Shares	1,800	100	$(100)	1,800
Contributed Surplus	5	300	(300)	5
Retained Earnings	2,186	530	(530)	2,186
Treasury Shares	(20)	—		(20)
Total Equities	$16,134	$9,500	$(930)	$24,704
Income Statement				
Revenues	$12,000	$ 680		$12,680
Equity in Earnings of Unconsolidated				
Affiliates	300	—	$(160)[a]	140
Expenses	(11,275)	(520)		(11,795)
Net Income	$ 1,025	$ 160	$(160)	$ 1,025

[a] The credit entry for $160 would be made to the Investment account in Klatt Credit Corporation. Because the entry above — to eliminate the investment account — was made to postclosing trial balance data, this $160 debit is implicitly included in the debit of $530 made to the Retained Earnings account.

j. **Land**

Balance, December 31, Year 1 (BS)	$ 400,000
Plus: Acquisitions (SC)	100,000
Less: Disposals (SC)	—
Balance, December 31, Year 2 (BS)	$ 500,000

Building

Balance, December 31, Year 1 (BS)	$ 800,000
Plus: Acquisition (SC)	300,000
Less: Disposals (SC)	(160,000)
Balance, December 31, Year 2 (BS)	$ 940,000

Equipment

Balance, December 31, Year 1 (BS)	$3,300,000
Plus: Acquisitions (SC)	1,400,000
Less: Disposals (plug)	(900,000)
Balance, December 31, Year 2 (BS)	$3,800,000

Accumulated Depreciation

Balance, December 31, Year 1 (BS)	$1,200,000
Plus: Depreciation for Year 2 (SC)	560,000
Less: Accumulated Depreciation on Building (plug)	(160,000)
Less: Accumulated Depreciation on Equipment Sold (see below)	(670,000)
Balance, December 31, Year 2 (BS)	$ 930,000
Selling Price of Equipment Sold (SC)	$ 150,000
Loss on Sale of Equipment (SC)	80,000
Book Value of Equipment Sold	$ 230,000
Cost of Equipment Sold (above)	$ 900,000
Less: Accumulated Depreciation on Equipment Sold (plug)	(670,000)
Book Value of Equipment Sold (above)	$ 230,000

k.	Investment in McCutcheon Corporation (N, 6)	$800,000
	Common Shares (20,000 × $40) (N, 6)	$800,000

l.	Cost of Investment in McCutcheon Corporation (A, k)	$800,000
	Goodwill $80,000 + (2 × $10,000) (BS + SC)	(100,000)
	Book Value of Net Assets Acquired	$700,000

80 percent acquired (N, 6); therefore, book value of McCutcheon on date of acquisition is $700,000/0.80 = $875,000.

m.	Minority Interest in McCutcheon Corporation, January 2, Year 2 (BS)	$180,000
	Plus: Minority Interest in Earnings of McCutcheon Corporation (IS)	40,000
	Less: Minority Interest in Dividends of McCutcheon Corporation (plug)	(6,000)
	Minority Interest in McCutcheon Corporation, December 31, Year 2 (BS)	$214,000

Total dividends declared were $30,000 (= $6,000/0.20).

n.	**10 Percent Bond Issue**	
	Discounted Present Value[a] at December 31, Year 1:	
	Interest payments for 10 years (= $150,000 × 13.59033) (N, 8)	$2,038,550
	Par value at end of 10 years (= $3,000,000 × 0.45639) (N, 8)	1,369,170
	Total	$3,407,720
	Less: Par Value (N, 8)	(3,000,000)
	Premium	$ 407,720

4 Percent Bond Issue

Discounted Present Value[b] at December 31, Year 1:

Interest payments for 6 years (= $40,000 × 9.9540) (N, 8)	$ 398,160
Par value at end of 6 years (= $2,000,000 × 0.70138) (N, 8)	1,402,760
Total	$1,800,920
Less: Par Value (N, 8)	(2,000,000)
Discount	(199,080)
Net Bond Premium at December 31, Year 1	$ 208,640

[a]*At 8 percent compounded semiannually.*
[b]*At 6 percent compounded semiannually.*

	Net Liability Beginning of the Period	Market Interest Rate	Interest Expense	Interest Payable	Bond Premium or Discount	
					Reduction During Period	Balance End of Period
o.						
4 Percent						
Bond Issue						
January 1, Year 2	$1,800,920[b]	0.03[a]	$ 54,028	$ 40,000	$14,028	$185,052
July 1, Year 2	1,814,948	0.03[a]	54,448	40,000	14,448	170,604
Total			$108,476	$ 80,000	$28,476	
10 Percent						
Bond Issue						
January 1, Year 2	3,407,720[b]	0.04[a]	$136,309	$150,000	$13,691	$394,029
July 1, Year 2	3,394,029	0.04[a]	135,761	150,000	14,239	379,790
Total			$272,070	$300,000	$27,930	
8 Percent						
Bond Issue						
January 1, Year 2	1,000,000[a]	0.04[a]	$ 40,000	$ 40,000	$ 0	$ 0
July 1, Year 2	1,000,000	0.04[a]	40,000	40,000	$ 0	$ 0
Total			$ 80,000	$ 80,000	$ 0	

[a]*(Q, 4).*
[b]*(A, n).*

p.	Income Taxes Payable, December 31, Year 1 (BS)	$250,000
	Plus: Current Income Tax Expenses for Year 2 (see below)	600,000
	Less: Cash Payment during Year 2	?
	Income Taxes Payable, December 31, Year 2 (BS)	$375,000
	Total Income Tax Expense (IS)	$720,000
	Less: Increase in Deferred Income Taxes ($940 − $820) (BS)	(120,000)
	Current Income Tax Expense	$600,000

Cash payments for income taxes totalled $475,000 during Year 2.

		Contributed Surplus	Retained Earnings	Treasury Shares
q.	Balance, December 31, Year 1 (BS)	—	$1,411,000	$30,000
	Treasury Shares Sold	$5,000[b]	—	(10,000)[a]
	Net Income (IS)	—	$1,025,000	—
	Dividends (SC)	—	(250,000)	—
	Balance, December 31, Year 2 (BS)	$5,000	$2,186,000	$20,000

[a]*(plug).*
[b]*[$15,000 (SC) − $10,000].*

ASSIGNMENT MATERIAL

QUESTIONS

1. Review the meaning of the key terms listed on page 916.

2. A critic of accounting stated: "The financial statements are virtually useless because firms have too much latitude in selecting from among generally accepted accounting methods." Another critic of accounting reacted: "I agree that the financial statements are useless, but it is because there is too little latitude in the way certain transactions are accounted for under generally accepted accounting principles." Respond to these statements.

3. "The controversy over alternative generally accepted accounting policies could be solved by requiring all firms to use the same methods of accounting in their financial statements that they use in their tax return." Respond to this proposal.

4. If net income over long enough time periods is equal to cash-in minus cash-out, why not allow the timing of cash flows to dictate revenue and expense recognition and eliminate alternative generally accepted accounting policies?

5. "The total reported net income over long enough time periods will be the same regardless whether a firm follows a conservative strategy or a profit-maximizing strategy in selectings its accounting methods." Explain.

6. "The statement of changes in financial position is affected less by the use of alternative accounting policies than the balance sheet and income statement." Explain.

7. If capital markets react quickly and in an unbiased manner to the release of information, including information contained in the financial statements, what is the benefit of analyzing a set of financial statements?

EXERCISES

8. *Identifying generally accepted accounting policies.* Indicate the generally accepted accounting policy, or method, described in each of the following statements. Explain your reasoning.
   a. This inventory cost flow assumption results in reporting the largest net income during periods of rising prices.
   b. This method of accounting for doubtful accounts recognizes the implied income reduction in the period of sale.

c. This method of accounting for long-term investments in the securities of unconsolidated subsidiaries or other corporations usually requires an adjustment to net income to calculate cash provided by operations in the statement of changes in financial position.

d. This method of accounting for long-term leases by the lessee gives rise to a noncurrent liability.

e. This inventory cost flow assumption results in approximately the same balance sheet amount as the FIFO flow assumption.

f. This method of recognizing interest expense on bonds provides a uniform annual rate of interest expense over the life of the bond.

g. During periods of rising prices, this inventory valuation basis produces approximately the same results as the acquisition cost valuation basis.

h. When specific customers' accounts are deemed uncollectable and written off, this method of accounting results in a decrease in the current ratio.

i. This method of depreciation generally provides the largest amounts of depreciation expense during the first several years of an asset's life.

j. This method of recognizing income from long-term contracts generally results in the least fluctuation in earnings over several periods.

k. When specific customers' accounts are deemed uncollectable and are written off, this method of accounting has no effect on working capital.

l. Under this method of accounting for long-term leases of equipment by the lessor, an amount for depreciation expense on the leased equipment will appear on the income statement.

m. This method of recognizing interest expense on bonds provides a uniform annual amount of interest expense over the life of the bonds.

9. *Identifying generally accepted accounting policies.* Indicate the accounting policy, or procedure, apparently being used to record each of the following independent transactions. Indicate your reasoning.

a. Bad Debt Expense		X	
Accounts Receivable			X
b. Cash		X	
Dividend Income			X
c. Income Taxes Payable — Current		X	
Deferred Investment Tax Credits			X
d. Unrealized Loss from Price Declines in Temporary			
Investments		X	
Allowance to Reduce Temporary Investments to Market			X
e. Cash		X	
Investment in Unconsolidated Subsidiary			X
Dividend declared and received from unconsolidated			
subsidiary.			
f. Bad Debt Expense		X	
Allowance for Doubtful Accounts			X

10. *Identifying generally accepted accounting policies.* Indicate the accounting policy, or procedure, apparently being used to record each of the following independent transactions. Give your reasoning.

a. Rent Expense (for lease contract)	X	
Cash		X
b. Advertising Expense	X	
Deferred Advertising Costs		X
c. Investment in Unconsolidated Subsidiary	X	
Equity in Earnings of Unconsolidated Subsidiary		X
d. Allowance for Doubtful Accounts	X	
Accounts Receivable		X
e. Loss from Price Decline for Inventories	X	
Merchandise Inventories		X
f. Liability Under Long-Term Lease	X	
Interest Expense	X	
Cash		X

11. *Identifying effects of generally accepted accounting policies on reported income.* Indicate the accounting policy that provides the smallest amount of earnings in each of the following cases.
    a. FIFO, LIFO, or weighted-average cost flow assumption for inventories during periods of rising prices.
    b. FIFO, LIFO, or weighted-average cost flow assumption for inventories during periods of declining prices.
    c. Cost or equity method of accounting for minority investments in the securities of unconsolidated subsidiaries where dividends declared by the subsidiary are less than its earnings.
    d. Declining-balance or straight-line depreciation method during the first one-third of an asset's life.
    e. Declining-balance or straight-line depreciation method during the last one-third of an asset's life.
    f. Percentage-of-completion or installment method of revenue recognition.
    g. The valuation of inventories at acquisition cost or lower of cost and market.
    h. Cost or equity method of accounting for long-term investments in the securities of unconsolidated subsidiaries where the investee realizes net losses and does not pay dividends.
    i. Effective interest or straight-line method of recognizing interest expense on bonds in the first year that bonds originally issued at a discount are outstanding.
    j. Effective interest or straight-line method of recognizing interest expense on bonds in the last year that bonds originally issued at a discount are outstanding.

Problems and Cases

12. *Impact of capitalizing and amortizing versus expensing when incurred.* South Co. Ltd. and North Corp. incur $50,000 of advertising costs each

year. South Co. Ltd. expenses these costs immediately, whereas North Corp. capitalizes the costs and amortizes them over five years.

   a. Compute the amount of advertising expense and deferred advertising costs each firm would report beginning in the first year that advertising costs are incurred and continuing for six years.

   b. For this part, assume that the amount of advertising costs incurred by each firm increases by $10,000 each year. Repeat part **(a)**.

   c. Comment on the differences noted in parts **(a)** and **(b)**.

13. *Impact of alternative accounting policies on two firms.* On January 1, Year 1, two corporations are formed to operate merchandising business. The firms are alike in all respects except for their methods of accounting. Ruzicka Limited chooses the accounting policies that will minimize its reported net income. Murphy Inc. chooses the accounting policies that will maximize its reported net income but, where different procedures are permitted, will use acounting methods that minimize its taxable income. The following events occur during Year 1.

   (1) Both companies issue 500,000 no-par-value common shares for $6 per share on January 2, Year 1.

   (2) Both firms acquire equipment on January 2, Year 1 for $1,650,000 cash. The equipment is estimated to have a ten-year life and zero disposal value.

   (3) Both firms engage in extensive sales promotion activities during 1982, incurring costs of $400,000.

   (4) The two firms make the following purchases of merchandise inventory.

Date	Units Purchased	Unit Price	Cost of Purchase
January 2	50,000	$6.00	$ 300,000
April 2	60,000	6.20	372,000
August 15	40,000	6.25	250,000
November 30	50,000	6.50	325,000
Total	200,000		$1,247,000

   (5) During the year, both firms sell 140,000 units at an average price of $15 each.

   (6) Selling, general, and administrative expenses, other than advertising, total $100,000 during the year.

Ruzicka Limited uses the following accounting methods (for both book and tax purposes): weighted-average inventory cost flow assumption, declining-balance depreciation method, with a rate of 20 percent, immediate expensing of the costs of sales promotion.

Murphy Inc. uses the following accounting methods: FIFO inventory cost flow assumption for both book and tax purposes, the straight-line depreciation method for book and the declining-balance method for tax purposes, with a rate of 20 percent, capitalization and amortization of the costs of the sales promotion campaign over four years for book and immediate expensing for tax purposes.

a. Prepare comparative income statements for the two firms for Year 1. Include separate computations of income tax expense. The income tax rate is 40 percent.

b. Prepare comparative balance sheets for the two firms as of December 31, Year 1. Both firms have $1 million of outstanding accounts receivable on this date and a single current liability for income taxes payable for the year.

c. Prepare comparative statements of changes in financial position for the two firms for Year 1, defining "funds" as cash.

14. *Impact of two sets of alternative accounting principles on net income and cash flows.* The Langston Corporation is formed on January 2, Year 1 with the issuance at par of 100,000 $10-par-value common shares for cash. During Year 1, the following transactions occur.

(1) The assets of the Dee's Department Store are acquired on January 2, Year 1 for $800,000 cash. The market values of the identifiable assets received are as follows: accounts receivable, $200,000; merchandise inventory, $400,000 (200,000 units); store equipment, $150,000; goodwill, $50,000.

(2) Merchandise inventory is purchased during Year 1 as follows:

Date	Units Purchased	Unit Price	Cost of Purchase
April 1	30,000	$2.10	$ 63,000
August 1	20,000	2.20	44,000
October 1	50,000	2.40	120,000
Total	100,000		$227,000

(3) During the year, 210,000 units are sold at an average price of $3.20.

(4) Extensive training programs are held during the year to acquaint previous employees of Dee's Department Store with the merchandising policies and procedures of Langston Corporation. The costs incurred in the training programs total $50,000.

(5) Selling, general, and administrative costs incurred and recognized as an expense during Year 1 are $80,000.

(6) The store equipment is estimated to have a five-year useful life and zero disposal value.

(7) The income tax rate is 40 percent. Ten percent of half of the goodwill arising from a corporate acquisition is deductible in computing taxable income, and the remaining 50 percent is a permanent difference, not a timing difference. Ignore investment tax credit provisions in this problem.

The management of Langston Corporation is uncertain about the accounting methods that should be used in preparing its financial statements. The choice has been narrowed to two sets of accounting methods, and you have been asked to determine net income for Year 1 using each set.

Set A consists of the following accounting methods (for book and tax purposes): weighted-average inventory cost flow assumption, declining-balance depreciation method at double the straight-line rate, immediate expensing of the costs of the training program, and amortization of goodwill over ten years.

Set B consists of the following accounting methods: FIFO inventory-costing assumption, straight-line depreciation for book and declining-balance for tax purposes, capitalization and amortization of the costs of the training program over five years for book and immediate expensing for tax purposes, and amortization of goodwill over forty years.

a. Calculate net income for Year 1 under each set of accounting methods.

b. Calculate cash flow from operations under each set of accounting methods. Assume that accounts receivable at year-end total $160,000.

15. *Impact of alternative accounting principles on net income, Year 2.* Net income of Miller Corporation for the year ending December 31, Year 2 is $600,000, based on the accounting methods actually used by the firm. You have been asked to determine the amount of net income that would have been reported under several alternative accounting methods. The income tax rate is 40 percent, and the same accounting methods are used for financial reporting and income tax purposes unless otherwise indicated. Each of the following questions should be considered independently.

a. Miller Corporation acquired a machine costing $300,000 on January 2, Year 2. The machine was depreciated during Year 2 using the straight-line method on the basis of a five-year useful life and zero disposal value. What would net income have been if the declining-balance depreciation method, with a rate of 40 percent, had been used? Ignore the investment tax credit.

b. Miller Corporation used the cost method of accounting for its 18 percent investment in the common shares of General Tools Corporation. During Year 2, General Tools Corporation earned $200,000 and paid dividends of $50,000. The market value of General Tools Corporation was the same at the end of Year 2 as it was at the beginning of Year 2. What would net income have been during Year 2 if Miller Corporation used the equity method for financial reporting purposes? Ignore income tax.

c. Miller Corporation used the FIFO inventory cost flow assumption. Under FIFO, the January 1, Year 2 inventory was $300,000, and the December 31, Year 2 inventory was $320,000. Under LIFO, the January 1, Year 2 inventory would have been $240,000 and the December 31, Year 2 inventory would have been $230,000. What would net income have been if the LIFO inventory costing assumption had been used?

16. *Computation of cash provided by operations.* The income statement of Garrett Corporation for Year 2 appears in Exhibit 14.8.

Current income tax expense has been reduced by $40,000 for amortization of deferred investment tax credits. The investment credit realized during Year 2 and added to the Deferred Investment Tax Credit account on the balance sheet is $60,000.

EXHIBIT 14.8
GARRETT CORPORATION
Income Statement for the Year Ended December 31, Year 2

Sales Revenue		$5,000,000
Less: Cost of Goods Sold (Note 1)		3,000,000
Gross Profit		$2,000,000
Operating Expenses (Note 1)		800,000
Net Operating Income		$1,200,000
Equity in Earnings of Unconsolidated Affiliate (Note 2)		300,000
		$1,500,000
Financial Expense:		
Interest Expense	$200,000	
Less: Interest Income	130,000	
	$ 70,000	
Dividend Income (Note 3)	60,000	10,000
Income Before Income Tax and Minority Interest		$1,490,000
Income Tax Expense (Note 4)		700,000
Income Before Minority Interest		$ 790,000
Minority Interest in Income of Consolidated Subsidiary		160,000
Net Income		$ 630,000

Analysis of Changes
in Working Capital Accounts

Increase (decrease) in Current Assets:	
Cash	$ 70,000
Temporary Investments	30,000
Accounts Receivable	430,000
Merchandise Inventories	370,000
Decrease (increase) in Current Liabilities	
Accounts Payable	(320,000)
Income Taxes Payable	(120,000)
Increase in Working Capital	$460,000

Determine the amount of cash provided by operations for Garret Corporation during Year 2. Your analysis should begin with net income of $630,000.

Note 1: Depreciation charges of $200,000 and $100,000 are included in Cost of Goods Sold and Operating Expenses, respectively.

Note 2: Garrett Corporation owns 30 percent of the outstanding common shares of Knowles Corporation. During Year 2, Knowles Corporation earned $1,000,000 and declared dividends of $400,000.

Note 3: Garrett Corporation owns 10 percent of the outstanding common shares of Williams Corporation. During Year 2, Williams Corporation earned $2,000,000 and declared dividends of $600,000.

Note 4: Income Tax Expense is composed of the following:

Current	$500,000
Deferred	200,000
Total	$700,000

17. *Preparation of financial statements from comprehensive data.* The data in Exhibit 14.9 are taken from the adjusted trial balances of the Hickory Merchandising Co. Ltd. as of December 31, Year 1 and Year 2. The square brackets indicate amounts to be found in the solution of the problem.

EXHIBIT 14.9
HICKORY MERCHANDISING CO. LTD.
Adjusted Trial Balance

	December 31, Year 2		December 31, Year 1	
Accounts Payable	—	$ 98,715	—	$ 97,320
Accounts Receivable—Net	$ 617,530	—	$ 580,335	—
Accruals and Withholdings Payable	—	99,700	—	99,800
Administrative Expenses	447,260	—	449,160	—
Bonds Payable (6%)	—	277,000	—	275,000
Cash	149,485	—	114,080	—
Common Shares	—	[ ]	—	100,000
Contributed Surplus	—	[ ]	—	700,000
Cost of Goods Sold	3,220,390	—	3,207,840	—
Depreciation Expense	48,825	—	45,710	—
Dividends on Common Shares—Cash and Stock	[ ]	—	50,000	—
Dividends on Preferred Shares—Cash	6,000	—	6,000	—
Dividends Payable	—	[ ]	—	—
Gain on Sale of Plant	—	[ ]	—	—
Income Tax Expense	122,675	—	104,975	—
Income Tax Payable	—	111,675	—	104,975
Interest Expense on Bonds	[ ]	—	20,000	—
Interest Expense on Notes	3,100	—	2,900	—
Interest and Dividend Revenue	—	18,070	—	16,010
Inventories	633,690	—	616,120	—
Investments in Subsidiaries	162,000	—	162,000	—
Notes Payable	—	53,400	—	51,500
Notes Receivable	68,400	—	65,600	—
Plant and Equipment—Net	[ ]	—	391,880	—
Preferred Shares	—	100,000	—	100,000
Prepaid Insurance	7,640	—	8,240	—
Retained Earnings	—	[ ]	—	[ ]
Royalties Revenue	—	44,285	—	37,020
Sales	—	4,605,275	—	4,552,320
Selling Expenses	656,230	—	642,530	—
	$6,739,860	$6,739,860	$6,467,370	$6,467,370

Additional data:

(1) Preferred shares: 6 percent, cumulative, $100 par value; 2,000 shares authorized.

(2) Common shares: $1 par value; 150,000 shares authorized.

(3) On January 10, Year 2, a 10 percent stock dividend was declared on common shares, issuable in common shares. The market price per share was $10 and the dividend was capitalized at $10 per share.

(4) On March 31 and September 30, Year 2, dividends of 25 cents per share were declared. The dividends were payable on April 20 and October 20, Year 2, respectively. On December 31, Year 2, an extra dividend of 12$^1/_2$ cents per share was declared payable on January 20, Year 3. Note that all dividends, in cash and in shares, have been debited to Dividends accounts, not to Retained Earnings.

(5) Plant and equipment items having a cost of $39,240 and accumulated depreciation of $32,570 were retired and sold for $15,000. Acquisitions during Year 2 amounted to $71,500.

(6) The bonds are thirty-year bonds and mature on June 30, Year 14. All bonds issued remain outstanding; straight-line amortization is used.

a. Prepare a well-organized comparative statement of income and retained earnings.

b. Prepare a well-organized comparative balance sheet.

c. Prepare a well-organized statement of changes in financial position defining "funds" as cash.

18. *Preparation of three principal financial statements from comprehensive data.* The data in Exhibit 14.10 are taken from the records of the Barr Sales Inc.

Additional information:

(1) During the year, the company retired fully depreciated fixtures that had cost $2,000. These were the only dispositions of furniture and fixtures.

(2) Furniture and fixtures acquired on May 10, Year 2 were financed one-third down, one-third due May 10, Year 3, and one-third due May 10, Year 4.

(3) On December 9, Year 2, the company sold a parcel of land it had purchased on January 14, Year 2 at a cost of $8,000.

(4) On June 15, Year 2, the company purchased additional investments at a cost of $3,200. This was the only acquisition during the year. All investments are shown at cost, because market value exceeds cost.

(5) Merchandise was delivered during the year on customers' deposits in the amount of $1,200. All other deliveries were on account.

(6) On January 2, Year 2, the board of directors declared a 5 percent stock dividend, capitalized at $11 per share. On January 2, Year 2, there were 5,000 shares outstanding, and 15,000 shares authorized.

(7) On June 20, Year 2 and December 20, Year 2, the board of directors declared the regular semiannual cash dividend of $0.50 per share.

(8) On June 30, Year 2, the company issued 250 shares for cash.

(9) Note that all dividends, both in cash and in shares, were debited to Dividends on Common Shares, not to Retained Earnings.

EXHIBIT 14.10
BARR SALES INC.
Trial Balance Data

	December 31	
	Year 2 Adjusted Trial Balance	Year 1 Postclosing Trial Balance
Accounts Payable — Merchandise	$ 8,400	$ 9,160
Accounts Receivable	25,100	25,900
Accumulated Depreciation	4,600	5,600
Allowance for Doubtful Accounts	400	430
Cash	27,802	21,810
Common Shares (no par value)	59,500	54,000
Cost of Goods Sold	155,000	
Deposits by Customers	420	
Depreciation	1,000	
Dividends on Common Shares (both in cash and in shares)	8,125	
Dividends Payable	2,750	2,500
Furniture and Fixtures	21,000	20,000
Gain on Sale of Land	1,500	
Income Tax Expense	3,600	
Income Tax Payable	3,600	2,400
Installment Contracts Payable	2,000	
Interest Expense on Mortgage	482	
Interest Revenue on Investments	500	
Interest Payable on Mortgage	50	
Interest Receivable	50	30
Investments	14,000	15,000
Loss on Sales of Investments	300	
Merchandise Inventory	33,450	31,150
Mortgage Payable (5%)	10,122	10,140
Other Expenses	27,093	
Prepaid Rent	300	
Rent Expense	3,600	
Retained Earnings	28,860	28,860
Sales	210,000	
Sales Commissions	12,400	
Sales Commissions Payable	600	800

a. Prepare a well-organized statement of income and retained earnings for Year 2.

b. Prepare a well-organized comparative balance sheet.

c. Prepare a well-organized statement of changes in financial position for Year 2, defining "funds" as cash.

19. *Impact of alternative accounting principles on debt ratio.* In this problem, we focus on the following definition:

$$\text{Debt Ratio} = \frac{\text{Total Long-Term External Financing}}{\text{Shareholders' Equity}}$$

Many analysts use this ratio to assess the risk in the financial structure of a corporation. The higher the debt ratio, other things being equal, the greater the risk. Many analysts construct ratios from the conventional, historical-cost financial statements without adjustment. This problem illustrates how the assessment of the relative risk of companies can change as more sophisticated analysis of the financial statements is undertaken. In this problem, various adjustments to the conventional financial statements are made and new versions of the debt ratio are compared.

Data for four companies are presented in Exhibit 14.11. The methods are illustrated with the data for General Products Limited. The reader is to prepare answers for the three other companies. All data are taken from the financial statements of the various companies for the same year. All dollar amounts are in millions. Income tax effects are ignored, except where noted.

EXHIBIT 14.11
(amounts in millions)

	General Products Limited	Dell Enterprises Inc.	Consolidated-Spadina Inc.	John Kramer Limited
1. Long-Term Debt	$1,000	$4,418	$546	$289
2. Deferred Tax Credits (balance sheet)	1,242	1,819	223	88
3. Shareholders' Equity	8,200	5,731	626	449
4. Excess of Current Value over Book Value of:				
Inventory	2,358	(1)	4	2
Plant & Equipment	3,017	4,604	363	325
5. Pension Costs Not Recorded	2,046	—	—	10

a. Compute the debt ratio for each of the companies. Include future income taxes with long-term financing in the numerator. For General Products Limited, the debt ratio is:

$$\frac{\$1,000 + \$1,242}{\$8,200} = 27.3\%$$

Which companies appear to be significantly different from the others in terms of financial structure and risk? Discuss.

b. Chapter 10 suggests that certain items shown as liabilities should not be, whereas certain other items not shown as liabilities should be. These two "errors" do not necessarily cancel each other out.
  (i) First, note that, in most cases, Deferred Income Taxes are not likely even to be paid and ought, in our opinion, to be reclassified as shareholders' equity. We can reflect this reclassification in the financial statements by making the following entry:

Deferred Income Taxes	$1,242	
Shareholders' Equity		$1,242

Amount is that shown in line 2 of Exhibit 14.11.

After adjusting for deferred income taxes only, General Products Limited's debt ratio is:

$$\frac{\$1,000}{\$8,200 + \$1,242} = \frac{\$1,000}{\$9,442} = 10.6\%$$

Case-by-case analysis might be required in practice to find out if some of the companies' timing differences are likely to reverse in the foreseeable future. Our analysis of these companies' items does not reveal any such significant potential reversals.

(ii) The unrecognized prior service cost for pension plans meets all of the criteria to be a (long-term) liability, but is not shown as such. The amount is merely disclosed in the notes. To bring this number onto the balance sheet, the financial statements are adjusted with the following entry, which ignores income tax effects:

Shareholders' Equity	$2,046	
Pension Liability		$2,046

This figure, $2,046 million, is the amount shown in General Products Limited's notes to the financial statements for unamortized prior-service costs.

After adjusting for the pension liability only, General Products Limited's debt ratio is:

$$\frac{\$1,000 + \$1,242 + \$2,046}{\$8,200 - \$2,046} = \frac{\$4,288}{\$6,154} = 69.7\%$$

Make the adjustments suggested above and recompute the debt ratio for each of the other three companies. Compute the ratios on a cumulative and noncumulative basis; that is, compute the debt ratio after making each individual adjustment to the ratios computed in (a), and then, after taking all the adjustments together, compute the percentage change in the ratio for each company. On which of the companies did each of these adjustments have the most impact?

c. What can you infer from this exercise about the debt ratio computed from published financial statements?

20. *Comprehensive review problem.* The principal objective of this book has been to help you develop a sufficient understanding of the accounting process that generates financial statements for external users so that the resulting statements can then be interpreted, analyzed, and evaluated. This problem has been designed partly as a review of the material covered in the book and partly as a means of assessing your progress toward this objective. A partial set of financial statements of Calmes Corporation for Year 2, including consolidate comparative balance sheets at December 31, Year 1 and Year 2, and a consolidated statement of income and retained earnings for Year 2, is presented in Exhibits 14.12 and 14.13. A series of discussion questions and short problems relating to the financial statements of Calmes Corporation is presented on pages 952 to 955. We suggest that you study the financial statements before responding to these questions and problems.

Part I — Financial Statement Interpretation

For each of the accounts or items listed below and appearing on the consolidated balance sheets and income statement of the Calmes Cor-

EXHIBIT 14.12
CALMES CORPORATION
Consolidated Statement of Income and Retained Earnings for the Year Ended December 31, Year 2

Sales Revenue		$6,000,000
Less: Cost of Goods Sold		2,500,000
Gross Profit		$3,500,000
Income from Completed Contracts		960,000
		$4,460,000
Less: Operating Expenses	$1,500,000	
Depreciation on Plant and Equipment and Amortization of Leased Property Rights	500,000	
Amortization of Intangibles	100,000	
Bad Debts	60,000	
General Corporate Expenses	100,000	2,260,000
Operating Income		$2,200,000
Other Income:		
Equity in Earnings of Unconsolidated Subsidiaries and Affiliates:		
Calmes Finance Corporation	900,000	
Richardson Ltd.	50,000	
Anthony Inc.	$1,000,000	
Gain on Sale of Machinery and Equipment	100,000	1,100,000
		$3,300,000
Less: Interest Expense		300,000
Income Before Income Tax		$3,000,000
Income Tax:		
Current	$ 700,000	
Deferred	100,000	800,000
Income Before Minority Interest		$2,200,000
Minority Interest in Earnings		200,000
Net Income		$2,000,000
Less: Dividends on Preferred Shares		60,000
Dividends on Common Shares		840,000
Increase in Retained Earnings		$1,100,000
Retained Earnings, January 1, Year 2		1,400,000
Retained Earnings, December 31, Year 2		$2,500,000
Basic Earnings per Common Share (based on 1,000,000 average shares outstanding)		$1.94
Fully Diluted Earnings per Share (assuming conversion of preferred shares)		$1.25

EXHIBIT 14.13
CALMES CORPORATION
Consolidated Balance Sheets
December 31

	Year 2	Year 1
ASSETS		
Current Assets:		
Cash	$ 50,000	$ 100,000
Temporary Investments at Lower of Cost and Market (market value, $160,000)	150,000	—

EXHIBIT 14.13 (continued)

	Year 2	Year 1
Accounts Receivable	300,000	250,000
Merchandise Inventory	700,000	600,000
Accumulated Costs Under Contracts in Process in Excess of Progress Billings	200,000	150,000
Prepayments	100,000	100,000
Total Current Assets	$ 1,500,000	$1,200,000
Investments (at equity):		
Calmes Finance Corporation (100% owned)	$ 2,000,000	$1,100,000
Richardson Ltd. (50% owned)	500,000	450,000
Anthony Inc. (25% owned)	100,000	50,000
Total Investments	$ 2,600,000	$1,600,000
Capital Assets:		
Property, Plant and Equipment:		
Land	$ 250,000	$ 200,000
Building	2,000,000	2,000,000
Machinery and Equipment	4,000,000	3,650,000
Property Rights Acquired Under Lease	750,000	750,000
Total	$ 7,000,000	$6,600,000
Less: Accumulated Depreciation and Amortization	(2,000,000)	(1,900,000)
Total Property, Plant and Equipment	$ 5,000,000	$4,700,000
Intangible Assets:		
Discount on Bonds Payable	$ 176,000	$ 200,000
Patent	200,000	250,000
Goodwill	700,000	750,000
Total Intangible Assets	$ 1,076,000	$1,200,000
Total Capital Assets	$10,176,000	$8,700,000
LIABILITIES AND SHAREHOLDERS' EQUITY		
Current Liabilities:		
Notes Payable	$ 250,000	$ 200,000
Accounts Payable	350,000	330,000
Salaries Payable	150,00	120,000
Income Taxes Payable	200,000	150,000
Rent Received in Advance	50,000	—
Other Current Liabilities	200,000	100,000
Total Current Liabilities	$ 1,200,000	$ 900,000
Long-Term Debt:		
Bonds Payable	$ 2,000,000	$2,000,000
Equipment Mortgage Indebtedness	176,000	650,000
Obligation Under Capital Lease	500,000	550,000
Deferred Income Taxes	$ 800,000	$ 700,000
Total Long-Term Debt	$ 3,476,000	$3,900,000
Minority Interest in Subsidiary	$ 500,000	$ 300,000
Shareholders' Equity:		
Convertible Preferred Shares	$ 1,000,000	$1,000,000
Common Shares	1,000,000	1,000,000
Contributed Surplus	1,000,000	900,000
Retained Earnings	2,500,000	1,400,000
Total	$ 5,500,000	$4,300,000
Less: Cost of Treasury Shares	(500,000)	(700,000)
Total Shareholders' Equity	$ 5,000,000	$3,600,000
Total Liabilities and Shareholders' Equity	$10,176,000	$8,700,000

poration, describe **(1)** the nature of the account or item (that is, the transaction or conditions that resulted in its recognition), and **(2)** the valuation method used in determining its amount. Respond in descriptive terms rather than by using specific numbers from the financial statements of the Calmes Corporation. The first one is provided as an example.

a. Accumulated Costs under Contracts in Progress in Excess of Progress Billings — *The Calmes Corporation is providing services of some type to specific customers under contract. All costs incurred under the contracts are accumulated in this current asset account. When customers are billed periodically for a portion of the contract price, this account is credited. The account, therefore, reflects the excess of costs incurred to date on uncompleted contracts over the amounts billed to customers. Because the account does not include any income or profit from the contracts (that is, "accumulated costs"), the firm is apparently using the completed contract method rather than the percentage-of-completion method of recognizing revenues.*

b. Investment in Calmes Finance Corporation
c. Property Rights Acquired Under Lease
d. Goodwill
e. Rent Received in Advance
f. Deferred Income Taxes (balance sheet)
g. Minority Interest in Subsidiary (balance sheet)
h. Treasury Shares
i. Bad Debts Expense (income statement)

Additional information:
The balance of the allowance for doubtful accounts was $80,000 at December 31, Year 1 and $50,000 at December 31, Year 0.

Part II — Financial Statement Analysis

a. The Calmes Corporation used the LIFO cost flow assumption in determining its cost of goods sold and beginning and ending merchandise inventory amounts. If the FIFO cost flow assumption had been used, the beginning inventory would have been $900,000 and the ending inventory would have been $850,000. Compute the actual gross profit of the Calmes Corporation for Year 2 if FIFO had been used (ignore income tax effects). Calmes Corporation used the periodic inventory method.

b. Refer to **(a)**. What can be said about the quantity of merchandise inventory at the beginning and end of Year 2 and the direction of price changes during Year 2? Explain.

c. The Calmes Corporation accounts for its three intercorporate investments in unconsolidated subsidiaries under the equity method. The shares in each of these companies were acquired at book value at the time of acquisition. What were the total dividends declared by these three companies during Year 2? How can you tell?

d. The Calmes Corporation accounts for its three intercorporate investments in unconsolidated subsidiaries under the equity method. The shares in each of these companies were acquired at book value at the time of acquisition. Give the journal entry (entries) that was (were) made during Year 2 in applying the equity method.

e. The building was acquired on January 1, Year 1. It was estimated to have a 40-year useful life and zero disposal value at that time. Determine the amount of depreciation expense on this building for Year 2, assuming that the declining-balance method is used.

f. Machinery and equipment costing $500,000, and with a book value of $100,000, were sold for cash during Year 2. Give the journal entry to record the disposition.

g. The bonds payable carry 6 percent annual coupons. Interest is paid on December 31 of each year. Give the journal entry made on December 31, Year 2 to recognize interest expense for Year 2, assuming that Calmes Corporation uses the effective-interest method.

h. Refer to (g). What was the effective or market interest rate on these bonds on the date they were issued? Explain.

i. The only timing difference between net income and taxable income during Year 2 was in the amount of depreciation expense. If the income tax rate was 40 percent, determine the difference between the depreciation deduction reported on the tax return and the depreciation expense reported on the income statement.

j. Give the journal entry that explains the change in the treasury shares account assuming that there were no other transactions affecting common or preferred shares during Year 2.

k. If the original amount of the patent acquired was $500,000, and the patent is being amortized on a straight-line basis, when was the patent acquired?

l. The shares of Anthony Inc. were acquired on December 31, Year 1. If the same amount of shares in Anthony Inc. were held during the year, but the amount represented only *15 percent* ownership of Anthony Inc., how would the financial statements have differed? Disregard income tax effects.

m. During Year 2, Calmes paid $85,000 to the lessor of property represented on the balance sheet by "Property Rights Acquired Under Lease." Property rights acquired under lease have a ten-year life and are being amortized on a straight-line basis. What was the total expense reported by Calmes Corporation during Year 2 from using the leased property?

n. How would the financial statements have differed if the Calmes Corporation accounted for temporary investments on the lower of cost and market basis and the market value of these securities had been $130,000 instead of $160,000 at the end of Year 2? Disregard income tax effects.

o. If the Minority Interest in Subsidiary represents a 20 percent interest in Calmes Corporation's only consolidated subsidiary, what was the *total* amount of dividends declared by this subsidiary during Year 2? How can you tell?

p. Refer to the earnings-per-share amounts in the income statement of Calmes Corporation. How many common shares would be issued if all of the outstanding preferred shares were converted into common shares?

EXHIBIT 14.14

CALMES CORPORATION

Consolidated Statement of Changes in Financial Position for the Year Ended December 31, Year 2

Cash Provided by

Operations:

(3) _____	......	$ _____
Add Expenses and Deductions Not Using Cash:		
(4) _____	......	_____
(5) _____	......	_____
(6) _____	......	_____
(7) _____	......	_____
(8) _____	......	_____
Add Credit Changes in Operating Current Asset and Current Liability Accounts:		
(9) _____	......	_____
(10) _____	......	_____
(11) _____	......	_____
(12) _____	......	_____
(13) _____	......	_____
(14) _____	......	_____
Subtract Revenues and Additions Not Providing Cash:		
(15) _____	......	_____
(16) _____	......	_____
Subtract Debit Changes in Operating Current Asset and Current Liability Accounts:		
(17) _____	......	_____
(18) _____	......	_____
(19) _____	......	_____
(20) _____	......	_____
Cash Provided by Operations		$1,774,000
New Financing:		
(21) _____	......	_____
(22) _____	......	_____
Total Sources of Cash		$2,274,000

Cash Applied to

Reduction in Financing:

(23) _____	......	_____
(24) _____	......	_____
(25) _____	......	_____
Acquisition of Assets:		
(26) _____	......	_____
(27) _____	......	_____
Total Uses of Cash		$2,324,000
Decrease in Cash		$ 50,000

q. Insert the missing items of information numbered (3) to (27) in the statement of changes in financial position of the Calmes Corporation in Exhibit 14.14. Be sure to include both descriptions of the missing items and their amounts. Provide supporting calculations for each of the missing items in the statement.

r. On January 2, Year 3, the Calmes Corporation requested its bank to grant a six-month loan for $300,000. If approved, the loan would be granted on January 10, Year 3. As the bank's senior credit analyst, you have been asked to assess the liquidity of the Calmes Corporation and present a memorandum summarizing your conclusions. Include any ratios and any other information from the financial statements that you consider relevant. Also include a summary of information not disclosed in the financial statements that you think the loan officer should consider before making a final decision.

Part III — Financial Statement Evaluation

a. The treasurer of the Calmes Corporation recently remarked, "The value or worth of our company on December 31, Year 2 is $5,000,000, as measured by total shareholders' equity." Describe briefly at least three reasons why the difference between recorded total assets and recorded total liabilities on the balance sheet does not represent the firm's value or worth.

b. The accounting profession has been criticized for permitting several "generally accepted accounting policies" for the same or similar transactions. What are the major arguments for **(1)** narrowing the range of acceptable policies and **(2)** continuing the present system of permitting business firms some degree of flexibility in selecting their accounting methods?

21. *Comprehensive review problem.* Partial financial statements of Tuck Corporation for Year 2 are presented in Exhibit 14.15 (consolidated statement of income and retained earnings) and Exhibit 14.16 (consolidated balance sheet). Also shown are a statement of accounting policies and a set of notes to the financial statements. After studying these financial statements and notes, respond to each of the following questions.

a. Prepare an analysis that explains the change in Temporary Investments account during Year 2.

b. Calculate the proceeds from sales of temporary investments during Year 2.

c. Calculate the amount of the provision for doubtful accounts made during Year 2.

d. Give the journal entry(s) to account for the change in the Investments in Thayer Corporation — Net account during Year 2.

e. Calculate the amount of income or loss from the investment in Thayer Corporation during Year 2.

f. Give the journal entry(s) to account for the change in the Investment in Tuck Credit Corporation account during Year 2.

g. Assume that Tuck Credit Corporation had been consolidated with Tuck Corporation on December 31, Year 2. Calculate the amount of (1) total assets, (2) total liabilities, and (3) net income.

h. Prepare an analysis that identifies the factors and the amounts that explain the change in the Minority Interest in Subsidiary account on the balance sheet.

i. Calculate the balance in the Investment in Harvard Corporation account on Tuck Corporation's books on December 31, Year 2, assuming that the equity method had been used.

j. Calculate the amount of cash received during Year 2 for rental fees.

k. Calculate the actual cost of goods and services required to service customers' warranties during Year 2.

EXHIBIT 14.15

TUCK CORPORATION

Consolidated Statement of Income and Retained Earnings for the Year Ended December 31, Year 2

Sales		$4,000,000
Less: Cost of Goods Sold (Note 1)		2,530,000
Gross Profit		$1,470,000
Less: Operating Expenses		
Selling and Administrative (Note 1)	$1,092,205	
Warranty Expense	46,800	
	$1,139,005	
Less: Gain on Sale of Equipment	3,000	1,136,005
Operating Profit		$ 333,995
Plus: Financial Income (net)		
Rental Revenue	$ 240,000	
Dividend Revenue	8,000	
Equity in Income of Unconsolidated Subsidiary and Affiliate	102,000	
	$ 350,000	
Less: Financial Expenses		
Interest	$ 165,995	
Loss on Sale of Temporary Investments	8,000	
Unrealized Loss on Portfolio Investment	5,000	
	$ 178,995	171,005
Income Before the Undernoted		$ 505,000
Income Tax Expense		200,000
Income Before Minority Interest		$ 305,000
Minority Interest in Income of Consolidated Subsidiary		10,000
Consolidated Net Income		$ 295,000
Less: Dividends Declared		(120,000)
Increase in Retained Earnings for Year 2		$ 175,000
Retained Earnings, December 31, Year 1		204,000
Retained Earnings, December 31, Year 2		$ 379,000

EXHIBIT 14.16

TUCK CORPORATION

Consolidated Comparative Balance Sheets

	December 31	
	Year 2	**Year 1**
ASSETS		
Current Assets:		
Cash	$ 280,000	$ 240,000
Temporary Investments (Note 2)	141,000	125,000
Accounts Receivable—Net (Note 3)	1,509,600	1,431,200
Inventories	1,525,315	1,257,261
Prepayments	32,000	28,000
Total Current Assets	$3,487,915	$3,081,461
Investments: (Note 4)		
Investment in Thayer Corporation—Net (15% owned)	$ 87,000	$ 92,000
Investment in Hitchcock Corporation (30% owned)	135,000	120,000
Investment in Tuck Credit Corporation (100% owned)	298,000	215,000
Total Investments	$ 520,000	$ 427,000

EXHIBIT 14.16 (continued)

	Year 2	Year 1
Capital Assets:		
Property, Plant, and Equipment: (Note 5)		
Land	$ 82,000	$ 82,000
Building	843,000	843,000
Equipment	1,848,418	497,818
Leasehold	98,182	98,182
Total Plant Assets at Cost	$2,871,600	$1,521,000
Less: Accumulated Depreciation and Amortization	(413,000)	(376,000)
Total Property, Plant, and Equipment	$2,458,600	$1,145,000
Intangible Assets:		
Discount on 8 Percent Bonds Payable	$ 168,680	—
Goodwill—Net	$ 34,000	$ 36,000
Total Capital Assets	$6,669,195	$4,689,461
LIABILITIES AND SHAREHOLDERS' EQUITY		
Current Liabilities:		
Note Payable (Note 6)	$ 200,000	$ 100,000
Accounts Payable	723,700	666,100
Rental Fees Received in Advance	58,000	46,000
Estimated Warranty Liability	78,600	75,200
Interest Payable on Notes	2,000	1,500
Dividends Payable	30,000	25,000
Income Taxes Payable—Current	160,000	140,000
Total Current Liabilities	$1,252,300	$1,053,800
Noncurrent Liabilities:		
Bonds Payable (Note 7)	$2,000,000	$1,000,000
Mortgage Payable (Note 8)	280,943	299,947
Obligation Under Capital Lease (Note 9)	56,229	62,064
Premium on 6 Percent Bonds Payable	99,823	104,650
Deferred Income Taxes	145,000	130,000
Total Noncurrent Liabilities	$2,581,995	$1,596,661
Total Liabilities	$3,834,295	$2,650,461
Minority Interest in Subsidiary	$ 36,500	$ 32,000
Shareholders' Equity:		
Convertible Preferred Shares, $100 Par Value (Note 10)	$ 200,000	$ 700,000
Common Shares, $10 Par Value (Note 11)	1,650,000	1,000,000
Contributed Surplus	583,600	130,000
Retained Earnings	379,000	204,000
Total	$2,812,600	$2,034,000
Less: Cost of Treasury Shares (Note 12)	(14,200)	(27,000)
Total Shareholders' Equity	$2,798,400	$2,007,000
Total Liabilities and Shareholders' Equity	$6,669,195	$4,689,461

l. Refer to Note 8. Calculate the amount of interest expense on the $1 million, 6 percent bonds for Year 2.

m. Give the journal entry(s) that accounts for the change in the Mortgage Payable account during Year 2.

n. The income tax rate is 40 percent. Calculate the capital cost allowance claimed for income tax purposes for Year 2.

o. Give the journal entry made on July 1, Year 2 upon conversion of the preferred shares.

p. Give the journal entry(s) to account for the change in the Treasury Shares account during Year 2.

q. Prepare a T-account work sheet for the preparation of a statement of changes in financial position, defining "funds" as cash.

Notes to the Financial Statements

Note 1: Summary of Significant Accounting Policies

Basis of Consolidation   The financial statements of Tuck Corporation are consolidated with Harvard Corporation, a 90-percent-owned subsidiary acquired on January 2, Year 0.

Temporary Investments   Temporary Investments are stated at lower of acquisition cost and market.

Accounts Receivable   Doubtful accounts of customers are accounted for using the allowance method.

Inventories   Inventories are measured using a LIFO cost flow assumption.

Investments   Investments of less than 20 percent of the outstanding common shares of other companies are accounted for using the cost method. Investments of greater than or equal to 20 percent of the outstanding common shares of unconsolidated affiliates and subsidiaries are accounted for using the equity method.

Building, Equipment, and Leaseholds   Depreciation for financial reporting purposes is calculated using the straight-line method. For income tax purposes, the company claims the maximum capital cost allowance.

Goodwill   Goodwill arising from investments in Harvard Corporation is amortized over a period of twenty years.

Interest Expense on Long-Term Debt   Interest expense on long-term debt is recognized using the effective-interest method.

Deferred Income Taxes   Future income taxes are provided for timing differences between book and taxable income. All timing differences relate to depreciation.

Note 2: Cost of goods sold and selling and administrative expenses include depreciation and amortization of $56,000.

Note 3: Temporary Investments costing $35,000 were sold during Year 2. No dividends were received from temporary investments during Year 2.

Note 4: Accounts receivable are shown net of an allowance for doubtful accounts of $128,800 on December 31, Year 1 and $210,400 on December 31, Year 2. A total of $63,000 of accounts were written off as uncollectable during Year 2.

Note 5: Condensed balance sheet data for Tuck Credit Corporation, a wholly owned, unconsolidated credit subsidiary, are shown below:

	December 31, Year 2	December 31 Year 1
Total Assets	$478,000	$375,000
Total Liabilities	$180,000	$160,000
Shareholders' Equity	$298,000	$215,000

Net income of Tuck Credit Corporation for Year 2 was $87,000. Dividends declared and paid during Year 2 totalled $24,000.

Note 6: Equipment with a cost of $23,000 and a book value of $4,000 was sold during Year 2. This was the only disposition of capital assets during the year.

Note 7: A 90-day, 9 percent note with a face amount of $100,000 was paid with interest at maturity on January 30, Year 2. On December 1, Year 2, Tuck Corporation borrowed $200,000 from its local bank, promising to repay the principal plus interest at 12 percent in six months.

Note 8: Bonds Payable on the balance sheet is composed of the following:

	December 31, Year 2	December 31, Year 1
$1,000,000, 6 percent, semiannual coupon bonds, due December 31, Year 16, priced at $1,125,510 to yield 5 percent, compounded semiannually, at the time of issue	$1,000,000	$1,000,000
$1,000,000, 8 percent, semiannual coupon bonds, due December 31, Year 21, priced at $828,409 to yield 10 percent, compounded semiannually, at the time of issue	$1,000,000	—
Total	$2,000,000	$1,000,000

Note 9: Mortgage Payable represents a mortgage on buildings requiring equal installment payments of $40,000 on December 31 of each year. The loan underlying the mortgage bears interest of 7 percent, compounded annually. The final installment payment is due on December 31, Year 12.

Note 10: The Obligation Under Capital Lease represents a twenty-year, noncancellable lease on certain equipment. The lease requires annual payments in advance of $10,000 on January 2 of each year. The last lease payment will be made on January 2, Year 8. The lease is capitalized at the lessee's borrowing rate (at the inception of the lease) of 8 percent.

Note 11: Each preferred share is convertible into five common shares. On July 1, Year 2, holders of 5,000 preferred shares exercised their options. The conversion was recorded using book values.

Note 12: On October 1, Year 2, 40,000 common shares were issued on the open market for $15 per share.

Note 13: Treasury Shares are composed of the following:

December 31, Year 1: 2,250 shares at $12 per share	$27,000
December 31, Year 2: 450 shares at $12 per share	$ 5,400
550 shares at $16 per share	8,800
	$14,200

DECISION CASE 14-1

Champion Clothiers, Inc. owns and operates eighty retailing establishments throughout Quebec and the Maritimes, specializing in quality men's and women's clothing. The company was established many years ago by Jean-Pierre Champion and has been run by a member of the Champion family ever since. Currently, Roger Champion, grandson of the founder, is president and chief executive officer. The company's shares are held by members of the Champion family.

The setting for this case is March 1993. The following conversation takes place between Roger Champion and the company's accountant, Tom Morrissey.

Champion (president): "Tom, you said on the telephone that the financial statements for 1992 were now complete. How much did we earn last year?"

Morrissey (accountant): "Net income was $800,000, with earnings per share at $1.60. With the $1.20 per share earned in 1990 and $1.38 earned in 1991, we have maintained our 15 percent growth rate in profits."

Champion: "That sounds great! Tom, at our board meeting next week, I am going to announce that the Champion family has decided to take the company public. We will be issuing shares equal to a 40 percent stake in the company early in 1994. It is important that our earnings for 1993 continue to reflect the growth rate we have been experiencing. By my calculations, we need an earnings per share for 1993 in the neighbourhood of $1.84. Does this seem likely?"

Morrissey: "I'm afraid not. Our current projections indicate an earnings per share around $1.65 for this year. Major unexpected style changes earlier this year have left us with obsolete inventory that will have to be written off. In addition, increased competition in several of our major markets is putting a squeeze on margins. Even the acquisition of Green Trucking Limited in June of this year will not help earnings that much."

Champion: "I know you accountants have all kinds of games you can play to doctor up the numbers. There must be something we can do to increase earnings to the desired level. What about our use of LIFO for inventories?"

Morrissey: "We have been using LIFO in the past because it reduces income during a period of rising prices. The more recent, higher acquisition costs of inventory items are used in computing cost of goods sold in the income statement. The older, lower acquisition prices are used in the valuation of inventory on the balance sheet. We could switch to FIFO for 1993. That would add about $0.21 to earnings per share. Because LIFO is not allowed for tax purposes, there would be no additional taxes to pay. However, income tax expense would be increased by about $50,000, and an offsetting increase in deferred income tax would be recorded."

Champion: "FIFO certainly more closely approximates the physical flow of our goods. If we decide to stay on LIFO, is there anything we can do in applying the LIFO method that would prop up earnings?"

Morrissey: "We now classify our inventory very broadly into two LIFO groups, or pools: one for men's clothing and one for women's clothing. We do this to minimize the possibility of dipping into an old LIFO layer. As you will recall, if we sell more than we purchase during a given period, we dip into an old LIFO layer. These LIFO layers are valued using acquisition costs of the year the layer was added. Some of these layers reflect costs of the mid-'50s. When we dip into one of these layers, we have to use these old, lower costs in figuring cost of goods sold and net income. By defining our LIFO pools broadly to include our dollar investment in men's clothing and our dollar investment in women's clothing, we minimize the profitability of liquidating an old LIFO layer. We could define our LIFO pools more narrowly to increase the possibility of dipping. We could then let the inventory of particular items run down at the end of the year, dip into the LIFO layer to increase earnings, and then rebuild the inventory early in the next year. I suspect we could add about $0.02 a share to 1993 earnings if we went with narrower pools."

Champion: "We own all of our store buildings and display counters. Is there anything we can do with depreciation expense?"

Morrissey: "We now depreciate these items using the fastest writeoff permitted by tax law. However, we do not have to calculate depreciation for financial reporting the same as we do for tax reporting. We could depreciate these items over the expected economic life of each asset. That should add about $0.04 to earnings per share for 1990. We could also use the straight-line depreciation method for financial reporting. While our depreciable assets probably decrease in value faster than the straight-line method would indicate, we would be using the depreciation method that most of our competitors use for financial reporting. The use of straight-line depreciation would add another $0.08."

Champion: "Now you're talking. What else can we do?"

Morrissey: "In previous years, we have charged all interest accrued to expense. We could capitalize a portion of this interest as a cost of the plant under construction. For 1993, this would add another $0.10 per share. There is also one thing we can do very easily with our pension plan to improve earnings. When we adopted the pension plan two years ago, we gave all employees credit for their service before adoption. This created an immediate obligation for past service. We are amortizing this obligation as a charge against earnings over a five-year period. Generally accepted accounting practice permits us to use fifteen years, the average remaining work life of our employees, instead of five years as the amortization period; that switch would increase earnings per share by $0.05 for 1993."

Champion: "All of the things you have suggested deal with the selection or application of accounting methods. Can we do anything with the timing of expenditures to help 1993 earnings?"

Morrissey: "Well, painting and other maintenance of our stores scheduled for the last quarter of this year could be postponed until the first quarter of next year. That would add $0.02 to earnings per share. In addition, we anticipate running a major advertising campaign just after Christmas. While the advertising expenditure will be made in 1993 and will reduce earnings per share by $0.07, all of the benefits of the campaign will be realized in greater sales early in 1994."

Champion: "I hadn't realized how much flexibility we had for managing our earnings. Before we decide which choices to make, can you think of any other avenues open to us?"

Morrissey: "We could always sell off assets on which we have potential gain. For example, we hold some temporary investments that we purchased last year. Selling those securities would net us an additional $0.02 in earnings per share. In addition, we own two parcels of land that we hope to use some day for new stores. These parcels could be sold at a gain of $0.04 per share."

Champion: "It strikes me that these alternatives could increase earnings per share for 1993 to the $2.00-plus range. This level is a lot more appealing than the $1.65 per share anticipated for the year. Will we have to do anything to earnings per share for prior years if we adopt any of these alternatives?"

Morrissey: "I have set out in Exhibit 14.17 the impact of each of the choices on earnings per share for 1993, as well as any retroactive adjustment required for prior years. This summary should be helpful as we decide our strategy."

How much do you think Champion Clothiers should report as earnings per share for 1993?

EXHIBIT 14.17
CHAMPION CLOTHIERS, INC.
Alternative Strategies for Managing Earnings per Share

	Impact on Earnings per Share			
	1993	**1992**	**1991**	**1990**
Actual or Anticipated	$1.65	$1.60	$1.38	$1.20
Adoption of FIFO	+0.21	+0.20	+0.17	+0.15
Use of Narrower LIFO Pools	+0.02	+0.02	+0.03	+0.02
Use of Longer Depreciable Lives	+0.04	—	—	—
Adoption of Straight-Line Depreciation	+0.08	+0.07	+0.06	+0.05
Capitalizing Interest on Construction in Progress	+0.10	+0.06	+0.04	+0.02
Amortization of Pension Obligation over 15 Years	+0.05	—	—	—
Deferral of Maintenance	+0.02	—	—	—
Deferral of Advertising	+0.07	—	—	—
Sale of Temporary Investments	+0.02	—	—	—
Sale of Land	+0.04	—	—	—

DECISION CASE 14-2

The Coffee Mill is a retail business specializing in gourmet teas and coffees, which are imported through a broker. The owner began the business on January 1, Year 1, when she contributed $50,000 of personal savings to the business. The Coffee Mill is a private corporation. The owner and sole shareholder holds 100 shares with no par value.

Sales receipts for the past year totalled $65,000, including $2,400 received for gift certificates yet to be redeemed at the Coffee Mill. Purchases in the past year were made in three lots as follows:

		Coffee		Tea	
Lot #	Date	Quantity (kg)	Cost ($/kg)	Quantity (kg)	Cost ($/kg)
1	January 1	1,000	$1.65	500	$1.24
2	April 15	2,500	1.85	700	1.45
3	November 15	3,400	2.05	900	1.62

The prices on these products are subject to many different variables in the international market. Ending inventory consists of 1,500 kilograms of coffee and 230 kilograms of tea.

The Coffee Mill is located in 800 square feet of retail space in a small shopping centre. It signed a five-year lease at $20 per square foot. As an incentive, the landlord offered the business the first year's rent free. Coffee Mill is responsible for its share of the operating costs incurred by the Mall Merchants' Association, which total $6.50 per square foot. Both the rent and the operating costs are expressed in annual terms. One-twelfth of this total is payable monthly to the landlord.

During Year 1, the owner of the Coffee Mill received a monthly salary of $2,000. The owner's husband and daughter each spent about twenty hours per week assisting in the store and running errands. Because the owner had been very concerned with conserving cash, no payment had been made for this help. Extra personnel had been hired over the Christmas season at a cost of $1,600, based on a rate of $5 per hour. Promotion and advertising costs amounted to $6,400. Supplies costing $1,500 had been purchased on account.

The Coffee Mill has been in operation for exactly one year. The owner is considering opening a second shop, for which she would require a bank loan.

a. The bank manager has requested that you prepare a balance sheet and an income statement for the Coffee Mill's first year of operations. He also wishes to have your comments regarding any accounting problems encountered and the assumptions you have made in preparing the above statements.

Adapted with the permission of the Society of Management Accountants of Canada.

CHAPTER FIFTEEN

INTRODUCTION TO FINANCIAL STATEMENT ANALYSIS

preparer's perspective
The viewpoint of the accountant preparing the financial statements.

user's perspective
The perspective of the user of the financial statements. According to the decision usefulness paradigm, the preparer should try to reflect this perspective as much as possible.

financial statement analysis
The use of various methods of comparing financial statements between periods and between companies to assess financial performance and financial position.

general-purpose statements
Statements prepared for general release to the public, which implies they must attempt to service the information needs of diverse groups — a classical dilemma of accounting.

CHAPTER OUTLINE

- General-Purpose Financial Statements
- Other Sources of Financial Information
- Objectives of Financial Statement Analysis
- Usefulness of Ratios
- Analysis of Profitability
- Analysis of Risk
- Measures of Long-Term Liquidity Risk
- Limitations of Ratio Analysis

Most of this book has examined accounting from a **preparer's perspective**. We have examined the four basic financial statements in depth and have considered both the rules governing their preparation and the concepts underlying these rules. In this chapter, we turn to the **user's perspective** — we shift our orientation to that of the user of financial statement information by looking at a technique called **financial statement analysis**.

GENERAL-PURPOSE FINANCIAL STATEMENTS

Many individuals and groups are interested in the data appearing in a firm's financial statements, including managers, owners, prospective investors, creditors, labour unions, environmentalists, government regulatory bodies, and the general public. We refer to the financial statements as **general-purpose statements** because they must try to serve the information needs of all parties in society. As preparers of financial statements, we generally recognize that the needs of investors and creditors are foremost, and attempt to make servicing their information requirements our first priority. In this chapter, we will refer primarily to investor/creditor needs, although there are other legitimate users.

Even with this focus, some tradeoffs necessarily occur. For instance, current market values are more relevant to the decision models of investors and creditors than are historical costs. However, the need for objectivity takes precedence over the need for decision relevance and we publish historical-cost-based financial statements. Another important need of these user groups is to receive information about the firm on a timely basis, but published financial statements are anything but timely. It is not uncommon for there to be a six-month lag between the year-end date and the publication date. Because of this lack of timely preparation, the financial statements are sometimes referred to as *historical records*. Interim financial statements, press releases, stock market analyst's reports, and personal interviews serve as more timely (although not more objective) sources of information. One of the most famous research studies in accounting[1] estimated that only 15 percent of the information contained in published financial statements is new information. Such findings support the concept of financial statements as primarily stewardship reports.

Before we relegate published financial statements to the scrap heap, however, we must consider the value added to society by audited financial information. Other sources of information may be more timely, but these sources are useful only because we know they will eventually be validated by the year-end financial statements containing the independent auditor's report. These audited statements provide credibility and, therefore, many investors and creditors use financial statements as their primary information source.

OTHER SOURCES OF FINANCIAL INFORMATION

The published annual report containing the financial statements is only one of numerous information sources available to investors and creditors. Widely held companies must also issue quarterly financial statements if they are listed on a public stock exchange. A special type of financial report called a *prospectus* is issued by a firm attempting to sell new issues of securities to the public. These sales brochures contain financial statements for the previous five years, *pro forma* financial statements showing the intended use of the capital raised, and substantial descriptive information about the company. The prospectus must be approved by the provincial securities commission before being released to the public.

Personal interviews with company management, contacts with research organizations, trade association data, and subscriptions to financial newsletter services that publish analyses of firms also represent information sources for individuals. Useful information can also be obtained from financial newspapers such as *The Financial Post*, *Business Week*, and *The Bottom Line*. Industry data for comparison purposes is available from agencies such as the Financial Post, Dun & Bradstreet, Barron's, and Moody's. Even Statistics Canada compiles a wealth of data on Canadian business firms.

---

[1] Ray Ball and Phillip Brown, "An Empirical Evaluation of Accounting Income Numbers," *Journal of Accounting Research* (Autumn 1968), pp. 159–78.

OBJECTIVES OF FINANCIAL STATEMENT ANALYSIS

The first question likely to be raised in analyzing a set of financial statements is, "What do I look for?" The response to this question requires an understanding of investment decisions.

To illustrate, assume that you recently inherited $25,000 and must decide what to do with the bequest. You have narrowed the investment decision to purchasing either a certificate of deposit at a local bank or common shares of Heywood Corporation, currently selling for $40 per share. Your decision will be based on the **return** anticipated from each investment and the **risk** associated with that return.

return
The profit or payback generated by a given level of investment. Other uses of the term in accounting include a schedule of information required by governmental bodies, or the physical return of merchandise.

risk
A measure of the variability of the return on investment.

The bank is currently paying interest at the rate of 10 percent annually on certificates of deposit. Because it is unlikely that the bank will go out of business, you are virtually certain of earning 10 percent each year.

The return from investing in the common shares of Heywood Corporation has two components. First, the firm paid a cash dividend in their most recent year of $0.625 per share, and it is anticipated that this dividend will continue in the future. Second, the market price of the shares is likely to change between the date the shares are purchased and the date in the future when they are sold. The difference between the eventual selling price per share and the $40 purchase price, often called a *capital gain*, is a second component of the return from buying the shares.

The return from the common share investment is more risky than the interest on the certificate of deposit. Future dividends and market price changes are likely to be associated, at lease partially, with the profitability of the firm. Future income might be less than is currently anticipated if competitors introduce new products that erode Heywood Corporation's share of its sales market. Future income might be greater than currently anticipated if Heywood Corporation makes important discoveries or introduces successful new products.

The market price of Heywood Corporation's shares will probably be affected also by economy-wide factors such as inflation and changes in international tensions. Also, specific industry factors, such as raw materials shortages or government antitrust actions, may influence the market price of the shares. Because most individuals prefer less risk to more risk, you will probably demand a higher expected return from the purchase of Heywood Corporation's shares than if you invest the inheritance in a certificate deposit.

Theoretical and empirical research has shown that the expected return from investing in a firm is, in part, related to its expected profitability.[2] A firm's past operating, or earnings, performance is analyzed as a basis for forecasting its future profitability.

Investment decisions also require that the risk associated with the expected return be assessed.[3] A firm may find itself with a shortage of cash and be unable to repay a short-term loan coming due. Or the amount of long-term debt in the capital structure may be so large that a firm has

---

[2] Ray Ball and Phillip Brown, "An Empirical Evaluation of Accounting Income Numbers," *Journal of Accounting Research*, (Autumn 1968), pp. 159–78.

[3] Modern finance makes a distinction between systematic (market) risk and nonsystematic (firm-specific) risk. The discussion in this chapter does not differentiate between these two dimensions of risk.

difficulty meeting the required interest and principal payments. The financial statements provide information for assessing how these and other elements of risk affect expected return.

Most financial statement analysis, therefore, is directed at some aspect of a firm's *profitability* or its *risk*.

USEFULNESS OF RATIOS

The various items in financial statements may be difficulat to interpret in the form in which they are presented. For example, the profitability of a firm may be difficult to assess by looking at the amount of net income alone. It is helpful to compare earnings with the assets or capital required to generate those earnings. This relation, and other important ones between various items in the financial statements, can be expressed in the form of **ratios**. Some ratios compare items within the income statement; some use only balance sheet data; others relate items from more than one of the three principal financial statements. Ratios are useful tools of financial statement analysis because they conveniently summarize data in a form that is more easily understood, interpreted, and compared.

Ratios are, by themselves, difficult to interpret. For example, does a rate of return on common shares of 8.6 percent reflect a good performance? Once calculated, the ratios must be compared with some standard. Several possible standards might be used:

1. The planned ratio for the period being analyzed.
2. The corresponding ratio during the preceeding period for the same firm.
3. The corresponding ratio for a similar firm in the same industry.
4. The average ratio for other firms in the same industry.

Difficulties encountered in using each of these bases for comparison are discussed later in this chapter.

The sections that follow describe several ratios useful for assessing profitability and various dimensions of risk. To demonstrate the calculation of various ratios, we use data for Heywood Corporation for Years 2 through 4 as shown in Exhibit 15.1 (comparative balance sheets), Exhibit 15.2 (comparative income statements), and Exhibit 15.3 (comparative statements of changes in financial position). Our analysis for Heywood Corporation is based on a study of the changes in its various ratios over the three-year period. Such an analysis is referred to as *time-series analysis*. Comparison of a given firm's ratios with those of other firms for the same period is referred to as *cross-sectional analysis*, which involves comparing a given firm's ratios with those of other firms for a particular period.

ANALYSIS OF PROFITABILITY

The operating activities of a firm are carried out in order to generate net income. Three measures of **profitability** discussed in this section are:

ratios
A ratio is the number resulting when one number is divided by another. Ratios are generally used to assess aspects of profitability, solvency, and liquidity.

profitability
Three measures of profitability are (1) Rate of return on assets, (2) Rate of return on common shareholders' equity, and (3) Earnings per share.

EXHIBIT 15.1
HEYWOOD CORPORATION
Comparative Balance Sheets
(amounts in millions)

	December 31			
	Year 4	Year 3	Year 2	Year 1
ASSETS				
Cash	$ 12	$ 8	$ 14	$ 10
Accounts Receivable (net)	76	46	36	26
Inventories	83	46	30	14
Total Current Assets	$171	$100	$ 80	$ 50
Land	$ 60	$ 60	$ 30	$ 20
Building	190	150	150	150
Equipment	313	276	192	70
Less: Accumulated Depreciation	(84)	(66)	(52)	(40)
Total Noncurrent Assets	$479	$420	$320	$200
Total Assets	$650	$520	$400	$250
LIABILITIES AND SHAREHOLDERS' EQUITY				
Accounts Payable	$ 50	$ 35	$ 30	$ 25
Salaries Payable	20	15	13	10
Income Taxes Payable	20	10	7	5
Total Current Liabilities	$ 90	$ 60	$ 50	$ 40
Bonds Payable	150	100	50	50
Total Liabilities	$240	$160	$100	$ 90
Common Stock ($10 par value)	$160	$160	$150	$100
Contributed Surplus	120	120	100	20
Retained Earnings	130	80	50	40
Total Shareholders' Equity	$410	$360	$300	$160
Total Liabilities and Shareholders Equity	$650	$520	$400	$250

1. Rate of return on assets.

2. Rate of return on common shareholders' equity.

3. Earnings per common share.

RATE OF RETURN ON ASSETS

rate of return on assets
Net income plus after-tax interest charges plus minority interest in income divided by average total assets. Perhaps the single most useful ratio for assessing management's overall operating performance.

The **rate of return on assets** is a measure of a firm's performance in using assets to generate earnings independent of the financing of those assets. In terms of the three principal business activities (investing, financing, and operating) discussed in previous chapters, the rate of return on assets relates the results of *operating* performance to the *investments* that a firm has made without regard to how the acquisition of those investments was *financed*.

The rate of return on assets is calculated as follows:

$$\frac{\text{Net Income} + \text{Interest Expense (\textit{Net of Income Tax Savings})}}{\text{Average Total Assets}}$$

Because the rate of return on assets measures a firm's performance in using assets independent of the financing of those assets, the earnings figure used

EXHIBIT 15.2
HEYWOOD CORPORATION
Comparative Income Statements
(amounts in millions)

	Years Ended December 31		
	Year 4	Year 3	Year 2
Sales Revenue	$475	$310	$210
Less: Cost of Goods Sold	280	179	119
Gross Profit	$195	$131	$ 91
Less: Operating Expenses			
Selling	$ 46	$ 38	$ 36
Administrative	15	13	12
Depreciation	18	14	12
Total Operating Expenses	$ 79	$ 65	$ 60
Operating Profit	$116	$ 66	$ 31
Less: Interest	16	10	5
Net Income Before Income Tax	$100	$ 56	$ 26
Income Tax Expense	40	22	10
Net Income	$ 60	$ 34	$ 16

payments or distributions to the providers of capital. Because interest is a payment to a provider of capital, interest expense should not be deducted in measuring the return on total assets. To derive income before interest charges, it is usually easier to start with net income and add to that figure. The amount added to net income is not, however, the interest expense shown on the income statement. Because interest expense is deductible in calculating taxable income, interest expense does not reduce *aftertax* net income by the full amount of interest expense. The amount added back to net income is interest expense reduced by income tax savings.

For example, interest expense for Heywood Corporation for Year 4, as shown in Exhibit 15.2, is $16 million. The income tax rate is assumed to be 40 percent of pretax income. The income taxes saved, because interest is deductible in computing taxable income, is $6.4 million (= 0.40 × $16 million). The amount of interest expense net of income tax savings that is added back to net income is therefore $9.6 million (= $16 million − $6.4 million). There is no need to add back dividends paid to shareholders, because they are not deducted as an expense in calculating net income.

Because the earnings rate *during the year* is being computed, the measure of investment should reflect the average amount of assets in use during the year. A crude, but usually satisfactory, figure for average total assets is one-half the sum of total assets at the beginning and at the end of the year.

The calculation of rate of return on assets for Heywood Corporation for Year 4 is shown on the next page.[4]

---

[4] Throughout the remainder of this chapter, we omit reference to the fact that the amounts for Heywood Corporation are in millions of dollars.

EXHIBIT 15.3
HEYWOOD CORPORATION
Comparative Statements of Changes in Financial Position
(amounts in millions)

	For the Year Ended December 31		
	Year 4	Year 3	Year 2
Cash Provided by			
Operations			
Net Income	$ 60	$ 34	$ 16
Additions:			
Depreciation Expense	18	14	12
Increase in Accounts Payable	15	5	5
Increase in Salaries Payable	5	2	3
Increase in Income Taxes Payable	10	3	2
Subtractions:			
Increase in Accounts Receivable	(30)	(10)	(10)
Increase in Inventories	(37)	(16)	(16)
Cash Provided by Operations	$ 41	$ 32	$ 12
Financing Activities			
Issuance of Bonds	50	50	—
Issuance of Common Shares	—	30	130
Total Sources	$ 91	$112	$142
Cash Applied to			
Dividends	$ 10	$ 4	$ 6
Investing Activities			
Purchase of Land	—	30	10
Purchase of Building	40	—	—
Purchase of Equipment	37	84	122
Total Uses	$ 87	$118	$138
Increase (Decrease) in Cash Position	$ 4	$ (6)	$ 4

$$\frac{\text{Net Income} + \text{Interest Expense } (Net\ of\ Income\ Tax\ Savings)}{\text{Average Total Assets}}$$

$$= \frac{\$60 + (\$16 - \$6.4)}{^1/_2\,(\$520 + \$650)} = 11.9\%$$

Thus, for each dollar of assets used, the management of Heywood Corporation was able to earn $0.119 during Year 4 before payments to the suppliers of capital. The rate of return on assets was 5.8 percent in Year 2 and 8.7 percent in Year 3. Thus, the rate of return has increased steadily during this three-year period.

One might question the rationale for a measure of return that is independent of the means of financing. After all, the assets must be financed and the cost of that financing must be covered if the firm is to be profitable.

The rate of return on assets is of particular concern to lenders, or creditors, of a firm. These creditors have a senior claim on earnings and assets relative to common shareholders. Creditors receive their return in the form of interest. This return typically comes from earnings generated from assets

DISCUSSION CASE 33

Good-Looking Balance Sheets Can Be Assets for Companies

Lenders judge businesses by their financial statements. So common sense dictates that they look as good as possible. Year-end is "the one time of the year they take a picture of your company," says Steven N. Delit, of the New York CPA firm of Delit Friedman & Co., "and you want it to look its best."

There are a number of perfectly legitimate things a business can do to put the best face on its balance sheet. Some can be done near the end of the year, but it is better to operate a company with financial results in mind all the time.

Business owners need "an element of perspicacity" about producing a good balance sheet each year, says James McNeil Stancil, a professor of finance at the University of Southern California. As an example, he cites a company that borrows regularly against its receivables from a finance company, as many companies do.

The business normally takes cash it collects on its receivables and promptly pays off the finance company. One day its bank balance is impressive, the next it is anemic. If it has a skimpy bank balance the last day of the year, Mr. Stancil says, its balance sheet will look bad. It wouldn't matter that the company "has $5 million of assets," he says. "Someone will look at the cash account and say, 'My God! You are broke!'"

That can be avoided by having the finance company agree to slower repayment for a week or more near year-end, so the business can accumulate late cash for its balance sheet.

Ratio analysis is a common way lenders analyze balance sheets. Most familiar is the current ratio, computed by dividing current assets — cash accounts receivable, inventory — by current liabilities, or debt due within a year.

A company can strengthen this ratio by paying off current debt. If a business has, say, $40,000 cash (its only current asset) and $20,000 of current liabilities, its current ratio is 2:1. If $10,000 of the cash is used to reduce debt, however, the ratio improves significantly to 3:1.

A financial statement can be enhanced by borrowing long term to pay off short-term debt. "If you can get debt out of short term into long term, it cleans up the balance sheet," says Edward H. Pendergast, chairman of Kennedy & Lehan CPAs Inc., North Quincy, Mass. But this isn't mere window dressing, he says. "The company is much stronger because it is more liquid. Current demands on the business have been reduced considerably."

Bankers look carefully at the equity a small business has in relationship to debt. "There's nothing like equity," says the executive vice president of a $7 billion bank. "It's your cushion in the event something comes up that could damage the company." In the past, nothing less than a

(continued)

(continued)

one-to-one debt equity ratio would satisfy most banks. Nowadays, debt one and a half times greater than equity is usually acceptable. And some banks won't balk if it exceeds this, says David F. Nasman, president of Bellingham National Bank, Tacoma, Wash.

High debt-equity ratios could be acceptable. Mr. Nasman says, for a young company "that is strong and operating and growing well." But, he says, a bank would view with alarm "a company in business for 25 years whose debt-equity ratio starts to slide." The difference, he says, is that the young profitable company probably can "increase the equity along the way."

Profits left in the business become retained earnings and increase equity. However, small business owners usually try to minimize profits for income tax purposes, and often do this by paying themselves year-end bonuses. One way to satisfy tax considerations and bolster the financial statement is for the owner to take the bonus, providing the company a tax deduction, and then loan the money back to the company.

"If you indicate that the company doesn't have to pay the owner back for a year," says Herbert C. Speiser, a partner at Touche Ross & Co., CPAs, "a banker will consider it equity."

Such a solution isn't always possible, however. "Sometimes tax planning goes against the financial statement," says Irwin Math, a partner in the CPA firm of Laventhol & Horwath. "Sometimes I tell a client to pay taxes and strengthen your statement." In some small companies this means valuing year-end inventory as high as possible to maximize profits, and thus incur higher taxes.

Manufacturers should try to reduce raw materials inventory by turning it into finished goods, Mr. Math says. Large year-end raw-materials inventory suggests "you have a problem of not being able to sell your product," he says. A bulge in finished-goods inventory looks better because "finished goods are what you can convert to cash quickly."

However, when the business is having a terrible year, says John J. O'Leary, partner in the accounting firm of Alexander Grant & Co., "you can't pull a rabbit out of a hat in the last quarter." Don't wait for year-end to tell the bank the business is in trouble, he says. "It rubs bankers the wrong way."

Henry R. Pearson, a Dallas CPA, says he doesn't window dress statements for clients. "We dress down; we are very conservative." The way to impress lenders is to repay them on time, he says. "If you're not paying your debts," he says, "no matter what you say to your banker he isn't going to be happy."

References

Sanford L. Jacobs, "Good-Looking Balance Sheets Can Be Assets for Companies," *Wall Street Journal*, Sept. 23, 1985, p. 31. Reprinted by permission of *Wall Street Journal*, © 1985 Dow Jones & Company, Inc. All rights reserved worldwide.

Discussion Question

Are the window-dressing practices described in this article ethical? Are they effective?

before any other suppliers of capital receive a return (for example, dividends). When extending credit or providing debt capital to a firm, creditors want to be sure that the return generated by the firm on that capital (assets) exceed its cost.

The rate of return on assets is also useful to common shareholders in assessing financial leverage, a topic discussed later in this chapter.

DISAGGREGATING THE RATE OF RETURN ON ASSETS

One means of studying changes in the rate of return on assets is to disaggregate the ratio into two other ratios as follows:

$$\begin{array}{c} \text{Rate of} \\ \text{Return} \\ \text{on Assets} \end{array} = \begin{array}{c} \text{Profit Margin Ratio} \\ \text{(before interest expense} \\ \text{and related income tax effects)} \end{array} \times \begin{array}{c} \text{Total Assets} \\ \text{Turnover} \\ \text{Ratio} \end{array}$$

or

$$\frac{\begin{array}{c}\text{Net Income +}\\ \text{Interest Expense}\\ \text{(\textit{Net of Income Tax}}\\ \text{\textit{Savings})}\end{array}}{\begin{array}{c}\text{Average Total}\\ \text{Assets}\end{array}} = \frac{\begin{array}{c}\text{Net Income + Interest Expense}\\ \text{(\textit{Net of Income Tax Savings})}\end{array}}{\text{Revenues}} \times \frac{\text{Revenues}}{\begin{array}{c}\text{Average Total}\\ \text{Assets}\end{array}}$$

The **profit margin ratio** is a measure of a firm's ability to control the level of costs, or expenses, relative to revenues generated. By holding down costs, a firm will be able to increase the profits from a given amount of revenue and thereby improve its profit margin ratio. The **total assets turnover ratio** is a measure of a firm's ability to generate revenues from a particular level of investment in assets or, to put it another way, the total assets turnover measures a firm's ability to control the level of investment in assets for a particular level of resources.

Exhibit 15.4 shows the disaggregation of the rate of return on assets for Heywood Corporation for Year 2, Year 3, and Year 4 into profit margin and total assets turnover ratios. Much of the improvement in the rate of return on assets between Year 2 and Year 3 results from an increase in the proft margin ratio from 9.1 percent to 12.9 percent. The total assets trunover ratio remained relatively stable between these two years. On the other hand, most of the improvement in the rate of return on assets between Year 3 and Year 4 can be attributed to the increased total assets turnover. The firm was able to generate $0.81 of sales from each dollar invested in assets during Year 4 as compared to $0.67 of sales per dollar of assets in Year 3. The increased total assets turnover, coupled with an improvement in the profit margin ratio, permitted Heywood Corporation to increase its rate of return on assets during Year 4. We must analyze the changes in profit margin ratio and total assets turnover ratio in greater depth to pinpoint the causes of the changes in Heywood Corporation's profitability over this three-year period. We return to this analysis shortly.

Improving the rate of return on assets can be accomplished by increasing the profit margin ratio, the rate of asset turnover, or both. Some firms, however, may have little flexibility in altering one of these components. For example, a firm committed under a three-year labour union contract may

profit margin ratio
A measure of a firm's ability to control the level of costs, or expenses, relative to revenues generated.

total assets turnover ratio
A measure of a firm's ability to generate revenues from a particular level of investment in assets, or to put it another way, the total assets turnover measures a firm's ability to control the level of investment in assets for a particular level of resources.

EXHIBIT 15.4
Disaggregation of Rate of Return on Assets for
Heywood Corporation for Year 2, Year 3, and Year 4

	Net Income + Interest Expense Net of Income Tax Savings ÷ Average Total Assets	=	Net Income + Interest Expense Net of Income Tax Savings ÷ Revenues	×	Revenues ÷ Average Total Assets

$$\text{Year 2:} \quad \frac{\$16 + (\$5 - \$2)}{^1/_2(\$250 + \$400)} = \frac{\$16 + (\$5 - \$2)}{\$210} \times \frac{\$210}{^1/_2(\$250 + \$400)}$$

$$5.8\% = 9.1\% \times 65\%$$

$$\text{Year 3:} \quad \frac{\$34 + (\$10 - \$4)}{^1/_2(\$400 + \$520)} = \frac{\$34 + (\$10 - \$4)}{\$310} \times \frac{\$310}{^1/_2(\$400 + \$520)}$$

$$8.7\% = 12.9\% \times 67\%$$

$$\text{Year 4:} \quad \frac{\$60 + (\$16 - \$6.4)}{^1/_2(\$520 + \$650)} = \frac{\$60 + (\$16 - \$6.4)}{\$475} \times \frac{\$475}{^1/_2(\$520 + \$650)}$$

$$11.9\% = 14.7\% \times 81\%$$

have little control over wage rates paid. Or a firm operating under market- or government-imposed price controls may not be able to increase the prices of its products. In these cases, the opportunities for improving the profit margin ratio may be limited. In order to increase the rate of return on assets, the level of investment in assets such as inventory, plant, and equipment must be reduced or, to put it another way, revenues per dollar of assets must be increased.

ANALYZING CHANGES IN THE PROFIT MARGIN RATIO

Profit, or net income, is measured by subtracting various expenses from revenues. To identify the reasons for a change in the profit margin ratio, changes in a firm's expenses relative to revenues must be examined. One approach is to express individual expenses and net income as a percentage of revenues producing a common-size statement. Such an analysis is presented in Exhibit 15.5 for Heywood Corporation. Note that we have altered somewhat the conventional income statement format in this analysis by subtracting interest expense (net of its related income tax effects) as the last expense item. The percentages on the line, Income Before Interest and Related Income Tax Effect, correspond (except for rounding) to the profit margin ratios (before interest and related tax effects) shown in Exhibit 15.4.

The analysis in Exhibit 15.5 indicates that the improvement in the profit margin ratio over the three years for Heywood Corporation can be attributed primarily to decreases in selling, administrative, and depreciation expenses as a percentage of sales. The reasons for these decreasing percentages should be explored further with management. Does the decrease in selling expenses as a percentage of sales reflect a reduction in the rate

EXHIBIT 15.5
Net Income and Expenses as a Percentage of Sales for
Heywood Corporation for Year 2, Year 3, and Year 4

	Years Ended December 31		
	Year 4	Year 3	Year 2
Sales	100.0%	100.0%	100.0%
Less: Cost of Goods Sold	58.9	57.7	56.7
Gross Profit	41.1%	42.3%	43.3%
Less: Operating Expenses			
Selling	9.7%	12.3%	17.1%
Administrative	3.2	4.2	5.7
Depreciation	3.8	4.5	5.7
Total Operating Expenses	16.7%	21.0%	28.5%
Operating Profit	24.4%	21.3%	14.8%
Income Taxes at 40 Percent	9.7	8.4	5.7
Income Before Interest and Related Income Tax Effect	14.7%	12.9%	9.1%
Interest Expense Net of Income Tax Effect	2.1	1.9	1.5
Net Income	12.6%	11.0%	7.6%

of advertising expenditures that could hurt future sales? Does the decrease in depreciation expense as a percentage of sales reflect a failure to expand plant and equipment as sales have increased? On the other hand, do these decreasing percentages merely reflect the realization of economies of scale as fixed selling, administrative, and depreciation expenses are being spread over a larger number of units?[5] The amount or trend in a particular ratio cannot, by itself, be the basis for investing or not investing in a firm. Ratios merely indicate areas where additional analysis is required. For example, the increasing percentage of cost of goods sold to sales should be explored further. It may reflect a successful, planned pricing policy of reducing gross profit (selling price less cost of goods sold) in order to increase the volume of sales. On the other hand, the replacement cost of inventory items may be increasing without corresponding increases being made in selling prices. Or, the firm may be accumulating excess inventories that are physically deteriorating or becoming obsolete.

ANALYZING CHANGES IN THE TOTAL ASSETS TURNOVER RATIO

The total assets turnover ratio depends on the turn over ratios for its individual asset components. Three turnover ratios are commonly calculated: accounts receivable turnover, inventory turnover, and fixed asset turnover.

Accounts Receivable Turnover

The rate at which accounts receivable turnover gives an indication of their nearness to being converted into cash. The **accounts receivable turnover** is

accounts receivable turnover
The rate at which accounts receivable turn over gives an indication of their nearness to being converted into cash. Calculated by dividing net sales on account by average accounts receivable.

---

[5] This phenomenon is called *operating leverage* and is discussed more fully in managerial accounting textbooks.

calculated by dividing net sales on account by average accounts receivable. For Heywood Corporation, the accounts receivable turnover for Year 4, assuming all sales are on account (that is, none are for immediate cash), is calculated as follows:

$$\frac{\text{Net Sales on Account}}{\text{Average Accounts Receivable}} = \frac{\$475}{\frac{1}{2}(\$46 + \$76)} = 7.8 \text{ times per year}$$

The concept of accounts receivable turnover is often expressed in terms of the average number of days receivables are outstanding before cash is collected. The calculation divides the accounts receivable turnover ratio into 365 days. The average number of days that account receivable are outstanding for Heywood Corporation for Year 4 is 46 days (= 365 days/7.8 times per year). Thus, on average, accounts receivable are collected approximately one and one-half months after the date of sale. The interpretation of this average collection period depends on the terms of sale. If the terms of sale are "net 30 days," the accounts receivable turnover indicates that collections are not being made in accordance with the stated terms. Such a ratio would warrant a review of the credit and collection activity for an explanation and for possible corrective action. If the firm offers terms of "net 45 days," the results indicate that accounts receivable are being handled better.

Inventory Turnover

inventory turnover ratio
A financial ratio indicating how many times a firm sells its inventory stock in a year, measured as Cost of Goods Sold/Average Inventory.

The **inventory turnover ratio** is considered to be a significant indicator of the efficiency of operations for many businesses. It is calculated by dividing cost of goods sold by the average inventory during the period. The inventory turnover of Heywood Corporation for Year 4 is calculated as follows:

$$\frac{\text{Cost of Goods Sold}}{\text{Average Inventory}} = \frac{\$280}{\frac{1}{2}(\$46 + \$83)} = 4.3 \text{ times per year}$$

Thus, inventory is typically on hand an average of 84 days (= 365 days/ 4.3 times per year) before it is sold.

The interpretation of the inventory turnover figure involves two opposing considerations. Management would like to sell as many goods as possible with a minimum of capital tied up in inventories. An increase in the rate of inventory turnover between periods would seem to indicate more profitable use of the investment in inventory. On the other hand, management does not want to have so little inventory on hand that shortages result and customers are turned away. An increase in the rate of inventory turnover in this case may mean a loss of customers and thereby offset any advantage gained by decreased investment in inventory. Some tradeoffs are therefore required in deciding the optimum level of inventory for each firm, and thus the desirable rate of inventory turnover.

The inventory turnover ratio is sometimes calculated by dividing sales, rather than cost of goods sold, by the average inventory. As long as there is a relatively constant relationship between selling price and cost of goods sold, changes in the *trend* of the inventory turnover can usually be identified with either measure. It is inappropriate to use sales in the numerator if the inventory turnover ratio is to be used to calculate the average number of days inventory is on hand until sale.

Plant Asset Turnover

The **plant asset turnover ratio** is a measure of the relationship between sales and the investment in plant assets such as property, plant, and equipment. It is calculated by dividing revenues by average plant assets during the year. The plant assets turnover ratio for Heywood Corporation for Year 4 is:

$$\frac{\text{Sales}}{\text{Average Plant Assets}} = \frac{\$475}{\frac{1}{2}(\$420 + \$479)} = 1.1 \text{ times per year}$$

plant asset turnover ratio Number of dollars of sales generated per dollar of plant assets. Equal to sales divided by average plant assets.

Thus, for each dollar invested in plant assets during Year 4, $1.10 was generated in revenues.

Changes in the plant asset turnover ratio must be interpreted carefully. Investments in plant assets (for example, production facilities) are often made several periods before the time when sales are generated from products manufactured in the plant. Thus, a low or decreasing rate of plant asset turnover may be indicative of an expanding firm preparing for future growth. On the other hand, a firm may cut back its capital expenditures if the near-term outlook for its products is poor. Such action could lead to an increase in the plant asset turnover ratio.

We noted earlier that the total assets turnover for Heywood Corporation was relatively steady between Year 2 and Year 3 but increased dramatically in Year 4. Exhibit 15.6 presents the four turnover ratios we have discussed for Heywood Corporation over this three-year period. The accounts receivable turnover ratio increased steadily over the three years, indicating either more careful screening of credit applications or more effective collection efforts. The inventory turnover ratio decreased during the three years. Coupling this result with the increasing percentage of cost of goods sold to sales shown in Exhibit 15.5 indicates that there may be excessive investments in inventories that are physically deteriorating or becoming obsolete.

EXHIBIT 15.6
Asset Turnover Ratios for Heywood Corporation for Year 2, Year 3, and Year 4

	Year 4	Year 3	Year 2
Total Assets Turnover	0.81	0.67	0.65
Accounts Receivable Turnover	7.6	7.8	0.68
Inventory Turnover	4.3	4.7	5.4
Plant Asset Turnover	1.1	0.8	0.8

Most of the increase in total assets turnover between Year 3 and Year 4 can be attributed to an increase in the plant assets turnover. We note in the statement of changes in financial position for Heywood Corporation in Exhibit 15.3 that total capital expenditures on land, building, and equipment have decreased over the three-year period, possibly accounting for the increase in the plant assets turnover. The reasons for this decrease should be investigated.

Summary of the Analysis of the Rate of Return on Assets

This section began by stating that the rate of return on assets is a useful measure for assessing a firm's performance in using assets to generate earnings. The rate of return on assets was then disaggregated into profit margin and total assets turnover components. The profit margin ratio was, in turn, disaggregated by relating various expenses and net income to sales. The total assets turnover was further analyzed by calculating turnover ratios for accounts receivable, inventory, and plant assets.

The analysis revealed the following:

1. The rate of return on assets increased steadily over the three-year period from Year 2 to Year 4.

2. The improved rate of return on assets can be attributed to an increasing profit margin over all three years and an improved total asset turnover during Year 4.

3. The improved profit margin is in large measure attributable to a decrease in the percentage of selling expenses to sales. The reason for this decrease should be explored further to ascertain whether advertising and selling efforts are being curtailed currently in a way that might adversely affect future sales.

4. The changes in the total assets turnover reflect the effects of increasing accounts receivable and plant asset turnover and a decreasing inventory turnover. The increasing plant asset turnover might be attributable to a reduction in the level of investment in new property, plant, and equipment that could hurt future productive capacity and should be explored further. The decreasing rate of inventory turnover coupled with the increasing percentage of cost of goods sold to sales may be indicative of inventory control problems (buildup of obsolete inventory) and should likewise be explored further.

RATE OF RETURN ON COMMON SHARE EQUITY

rate of return on common shareholders' equity (Net Income − Preferred Dividends) divided by Average Common Shareholders' Equity.

A second measure of profitability is the **rate of return on common shareholders' equity**. The rate of return on common shareholders' equity measures a firm's performance in using assets to generate earnings but, unlike the rate of return on assets, explicitly considers the financing of those assets. Thus, this measure of profitability incorporates the results of operating, investing, and financing decisions. This measure of profitability is of primary interest to investors in a firm's common shares. The rate of return on common shareholders' equity is calculated as follows:

$$\frac{\text{Net Income} - \text{Dividends on Preferred Shares}}{\text{Average Common Shareholders' Equity}}$$

To calculate the amount of earnings assignable to common shareholders' equity, the earnings allocable to any preferred share equity — usually the dividends on preferred shares declared during the period — must be deducted from net income. The capital invested during the period by common shareholders can be calculated by averaging the aggregate par value of common shares, contributed surplus on common shares, and retained earnings (or by deducting the equity of preferred shareholders from total shareholders' equity) at the beginning and end of the period.

The rate of return on common share equity of Heywood Corporation for Year 4 is calculated as:

$$\frac{\text{Net Income} - \text{Dividends on Preferred Shares}}{\text{Average Common Shareholders' Equity}} = \frac{\$60 - \$0}{\frac{1}{2}(\$360 + \$410)} = 15.6\%$$

The rate of return on common shareholders' equity was 7.0 percent in Year 2 and 10.3 percent in Year 3. Thus, like the rate of return on assets, the rate of return on common shareholders' equity increased dramatically over the three years.

RELATIONSHIP BETWEEN RETURN ON ASSETS AND RETURN ON COMMON SHAREHOLDERS' EQUITY

Figure 15.1 graphs the two measures of rate of return discussed thus far for Heywood Corporation for Year 2, Year 3, and Year 4. In each year, the rate of return on common shareholders' equity exceeded the rate of return on assets. What accounts for this relation?

Recall that the rate of return on assets measures the profitability of a firm *before* any payments to the suppliers of capital. This return on assets must then be allocated among the various providers of capital. Creditors are allocated an amount equal to any contractual interest to which they have a claim. Preferred shareholders, if any, are allocated an amount equal to the stated dividend rate on the preferred shares. *Any remaining return* belongs to the common shareholders. That is, common shareholders have a residual claim on all earnings after creditors and preferred shareholders have received amounts contractually owed them. Thus,

$$\begin{array}{c} \text{Rate of Return} \\ \text{on Assets} \end{array} \rightarrow \begin{array}{c} \text{Return to} \\ \text{Creditors} \\ \text{(interest)} \end{array} + \begin{array}{c} \text{Return to} \\ \text{Preferred} \\ \text{Shareholders} \\ \text{(dividends)} \end{array} + \begin{array}{c} \text{Return to} \\ \text{Common} \\ \text{Shareholders} \\ \text{(residual)} \end{array}$$

We can now see how the rate of return on common shareholders' equity can be larger than the rate of return on assets. The rate of return on assets must exceed the aftertax cost of debt capital (Heywood Corporation has no preferred stock outstanding). For Year 4, the rate of return on assets was 11.9 percent and the aftertax cost of debt was 4.8 percent [= (1 − 0.4)($16)/ 0.5($160 + $240); see Exhibits 15.1 and 15.2]. This excess return belongs to the common shareholders.

The common shareholders earned a higher return only because the shareholders undertook more risk in their investment. They were placed in a riskier position because the firm incurred debt obligations with fixed payment dates. The phenomenon of common shareholders trading extra risk for a potentially higher return is called *financial leverage* and is described below.

FIGURE 15.1
Rates of Return for Heywood Corporation

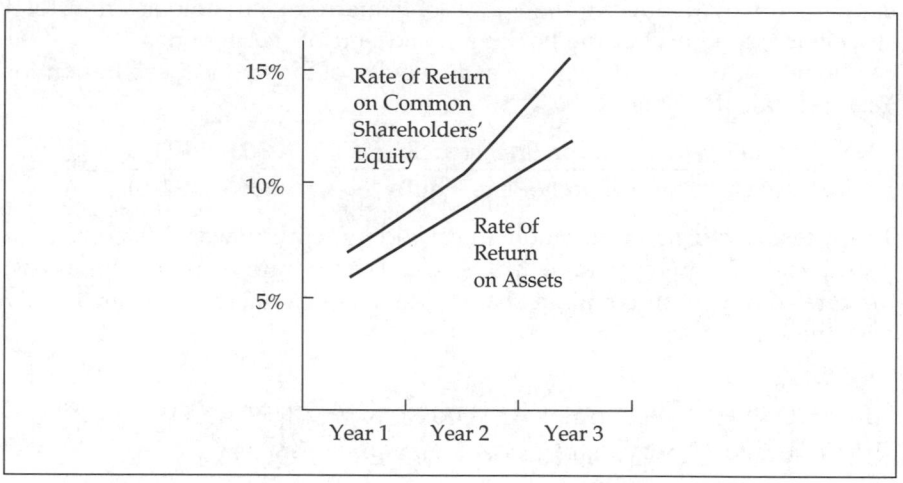

FINANCIAL LEVERAGE — TRADING ON THE EQUITY

financial leverage
Financing with debt
and preferred shares to
increase the potential
return to the residual
common shareholders'
equity.

Financing with debt and preferred shares to increase the potential return to the residual common shareholders' equity is referred to as **financial leverage** or *trading on the equity*. So long as a higher rate of return can be earned on assets than is paid for the capital used to acquire those assets, the rate of return to common shareholders can be increased. Exhibit 15.7 explores this phenomenon. Leveraged Limited and No-Debt Limited both have $100,000 of assets. Leveraged Limited borrows $40,000 at a 10 percent annual rate. No-Debt Limited raises all its capital from common shareholders. Both companies pay income taxes at the rate of 40 percent.

Consider first a "good" earnings year. Both companies earn $10,000 before interest charges (but after taxes except for tax effects of interest charges).[6] This represents a rate of return on assets for both companies of 10 percent:

$$\frac{\$10,000}{\$100,000} = 10\%$$

Leveraged Limited's net income is $7,600:

$10,000 - (1 - 0.40 \text{ tax rate}) \times (0.10 \text{ interest rate} \times \$40,000 \text{ borrowed}) = \$7,600$

The net income represents a rate of return on common shareholders' equity of 12.7 percent:

$$\frac{\$7,600}{\$60,000} = 12.7\%$$

Net income of No-Debt Limited is $10,000, representing a rate of return on shareholders' equity of 10 percent. Leverage increased the rate of return to shareholders of Leveraged Limited, because the capital contributed by the long-term debtors earned 10 percent but required an aftertax interest pay-

---

[6] That is, income before taxes and before interest charges is $16,667; $10,000 = (1 − 0.40) × $16,667.

EXHIBIT 15.7
Effects of Leverage on Rate of Return of Shareholders' Equity
(income tax rate is 40 percent of pretax income)

| | Long-Term Equities | | Income After Taxes but Before Interest Charges[a] | Aftertax Interest Charges[b] | Net Income | Rate of Return on Total Assets[c] (Percent) | Rate of Return on Common Share-holders' Equity |
	Long-Term Borrowing at 10 Percent per Year	Share-holders' Equity					
Good Earnings Year							
Leveraged Limited	$40,000	$ 60,000	$10,000	$2,400	$ 7,600	10.0%	12.7%
No-Debt Limited	—	100,000	10,000	—	10,000	10.0	10.0
Neutral Earnings Year							
Leveraged Limited	40,000	60,000	6,000	2,400	3,600	6.0	6.0
No-Debt Limited	—	100,000	6,000	—	6,000	6.0	6.0
Bad Earnings Year							
Leveraged Limited	40,000	60,000	4,000	2,400	1,600	4.0	2.7
No-Debt Limited	—	100,000	4,000	—	4,000	4.0	4.0

[a]But not including any income tax savings caused by interest charges. Income before taxes and interest for good year is $16,667; for neutral year, $10,000; for bad year, $6,667.
[b]$40,000 (borrowed) × 0.10 (interest rate) × [1 − 0.40 (income tax rate)]. The numbers shown in the preceding column for aftertax income do not include the effects of interest charges on taxes.
[c]In each year, the rate of return on assets is the same for both companies as the rate of return on common shareholders' equity for No-Debt Limited: 10%, 6%, and 4%, respectively.

ment of only 6 percent [= (1 − 0.40 tax rate) × (0.10 interest rate)] This additional 4 percent return on each dollar of assets increases the return to the common shareholders.

Although leverage increased the return to the common share equity during the "good" earnings year, the increase would be larger if a larger proportion of the assets were financed with long-term borrowing and the firm were made more risky. For example, assume that the assets of $100,000 were financed with $50,000 of long-term borrowing and $50,000 of shareholders' equity. Net income of Leveraged Limited in this case would be:

$10,000 − (1 − 0.40 tax rate) × (0.10 × $50,000 borrowed) = $7,000

The rate of return on common share equity would be:

$$\frac{\$7,000}{\$50,000} = 14\%$$

This rate compares with a rate of return on common share equity of 12.7 percent when long-term debt was only 40 percent of the total capital provided.

Financial leverage increases the rate of return on common share equity when the rate of return on assets is higher than the aftertax cost of debt. The greater the proportion of debt in the capital structure, however, the greater the risk borne by the common shareholders. Debt cannot, of course, be increased without limit. As more debt is added to the capital structure, the risk of default or insolvency becomes greater. Lenders, including investors in a firm's bonds, will require a higher and higher return (interest rate) to compensate for this additional risk. A point will be reached when the aftertax cost of debt will exceed the rate of return that can be earned on assets. At this point, leverage can no longer increase the potential rate of return to common share equity. For most large manufacturing firms, liabilities represent between 30 percent and 60 percent of total capital.

The leverage ratio is a measure of the financial leverage practised by the firm on behalf of common shareholders during a year. The leverage ratio is calculated by dividing the total assets by the common shareholders' equity averaged over the year. The leverage ratio for No-Debt Limited is 1(= $100,000/$100,000); for Leveraged Limited, it is 1.7 (= $100,000/ $60,000).

Exhibit 15.7 also demonstrates the effect of leverage in a "neutral" earnings year and in a "bad" earnings year. In the "neutral" earnings year, the rate of return to common shareholders is neither increased nor decreased by leverage, because the return on assets is 6 percent and the aftertax cost of long-term debt is 6 percent. In the "bad" earnings year, the return on assets of 4 percent is less than the aftertax cost of debt of 6 percent. The return on common share equity therefore drops — to only 2.7 percent — below the rate of return on assets. Clearly, financial leverage can work in two ways. It can enhance owners' rate of return in good years, but owners run the risk that bad earnings years will be even worse than they would have been without the borrowing.

DISAGGREGATING THE RATE OF RETURN ON COMMON SHAREHOLDERS' EQUITY

The rate of return on common shareholders' equity can be disaggregated into several components in a manner similar to the disaggregation of the rate of return on assets. The rate of return on common shareholders' equity might be disaggregated as follows:

$$\begin{matrix} \text{Rate of Return} \\ \text{on Common} \\ \text{Shareholders'} \\ \text{Equity} \end{matrix} = \begin{matrix} \text{Profit Margin Ratio} \\ \text{(after interest} \\ \text{expense and} \\ \text{preferred dividends)} \end{matrix} \times \begin{matrix} \text{Total} \\ \text{Assets} \\ \text{Turnover} \\ \text{Ratio} \end{matrix} \times \begin{matrix} \text{Leverage} \\ \text{Ratio} \end{matrix}$$

The profit margin percentage indicates the portion of the revenue dollar left over for the common shareholders after all operating costs have been covered and all claims of creditors and preferred shareholders have been subtracted. The total assets turnover, as discussed earlier, indicates the revenues generated from each dollar of assets. The **leverage ratio** indicates the extent to which capital (= total assets) has been provided by common shareholders. The larger the leverage ratio, the smaller the portion of capital provided by common shareholders and the larger the proportion provided by creditors and preferred shareholders. Thus, the larger the leverage ratio, the greater the extent of financial leverage.

The disaggregation of the rate of return on common shareholders' equity ratio for Heywood Corporation for Year 4 is as follows:

leverage ratio
The proportion of the company's assets provided by creditors vs. shareholders. More commonly known as the debt to equity ratio. A firm having a high ratio is said to be highly leveraged.

$$\frac{\$60}{\frac{1}{2}(\$360 + \$410)} = \frac{\$60}{\$475} \times \frac{\$475}{\frac{1}{2}(\$520 + \$650)} \times \frac{\frac{1}{2}(\$520 + \$650)}{\frac{1}{2}(\$360 + \$410)}$$

$$15.6\% \quad = 12.6\% \times \quad 0.81 \quad \times \quad 1.5$$

Exhibit 15.8 shows the disaggregation of the rate of return on common shareholders' equity for Heywood Corporation for Year 2, Year 3, and Year 4. Most of the increase in the rate of return on common shareholders' equity can be attributed to an increasing profit margin over the three-year period plus an increase in total assets turnover in Year 4. The leverage ratio remained reasonably stable over this period.

EXHIBIT 15.8
Disaggregation of Rate of Return
on Common Shareholders' Equity for Heywood Corporation

Year	Rate of Return on Common Shareholders' Equity	=	Profit Margin	×	Total Assets Turnover	×	Leverage Ratio
Year 2	7.0%	=	7.6%	×	0.65	×	1.4
Year 3	10.3%	=	11.0%	×	0.67	×	1.4
Year 4	15.6%	=	12.6%	×	0.81	×	1.5

EARNINGS PER COMMON SHARE

Basic earnings per share for Heywood Corporation for Year 4 is calculated as follows:

$$\frac{\text{Net Income} - \text{Preferred Share Dividend}}{\text{Weighted Average Number of Common Shares Outstanding During the Period}} = \frac{\$60 - \$0}{16\ \text{shares}^7} = \$3.75\ \text{per share}$$

Basic earnings per share were $1.28 (= $16/12.5) for Year 2 and $2.19 (= $34/15.5) for Year 3.

If a firm has securities outstanding that can be converted into or exchanged for common shares, it may be required to present two earnings per share amounts: **basic earnings per share** and **fully diluted earnings per share**. For example, some firms issue convertible bonds or convertible preferred shares that can be exchanged directly for common shares. Also, many firms have employee stock option plans under which the company's common shares may be acquired by employees under special arrangements. If these convertible securities were converted or stock options were exercised and additional common shares were issued, the amount conventionally shown as basic earnings per share would probably decrease, or become *diluted*. When a firm has outstanding securities that, if exchanged for common shares, would decrease earnings per share by a material amount, a dual presentation of basic and fully diluted earnings per share is required.[8]

basic earnings per share
The amount of current earnings attributable to each common share outstanding during the period. This calculation does not take into account the potential effects of dilutive securities.

fully diluted earnings per share
The earnings per share of a corporation with a complex capital structure calculated on the assumption that all shareholders with dilutive securities converted them into common shares.

---

[7] Exhibit 15.1 indicates that the par value of a common share is $10 and that the common stock account has a balance of $160 million throughout 1982. The shares outstanding were therefore 16 million.

[8] *CICA Handbook*, section 3500.

Interpreting Basic Earnings per Share

Basic earnings per share has been criticized as a measure of profitability because it does not consider the amount of assets or capital required to generate that level of earnings. Two firms with the same earnings and same basic earnings per share will not be equally profitable if one of the firms requires twice the amount of assets or capital to generate the earnings than does the other firm.

Basic earnings per share amounts are also difficult to interpret when comparing firms. For example, assume that two firms have identical earnings, common shareholders' equity, and rates of return on common shareholders' equity. One firm may have a lower basic earnings per share simply because it has a larger number of shares outstanding (owing perhaps to the use of a lower par value for its shares or from different earnings retention policies; see Problem 21 at the end of this chapter).

PRICE-EARNINGS RATIO

price-earnings ratio
The market price per common share divided by the related earnings per share.

Basic earnings per share amounts are often compared with the market price of the shares. This is usually expressed as a **price-earnings ratio** (= market price per share/basic earnings per share). For example, the common shares of Heywood Corporation are selling for $40 per share at the end of Year 4. The price-earnings ratio, also called the P/E ratio, is 10.67 to 1 (= $40/$3.75). This ratio is often presented in tables of stock market prices and in financial periodicals. The relationship is sometimes expressed by saying that "the shares are selling at 10.7 times earnings."

The relation between earnings and market price per share might be expressed as a rate (= earnings per share/market price per share). This calculation, 9.4 percent (= $3.75/$40) for Heywood Corporation, is less common than the price-earnings ratio.

SUMMARY OF PROFITABILITY ANALYSIS

Three broad measures for assessing a firm's profitability have been discussed in this chapter. Because the rate of return on assets and rate of return on common shareholders' equity relate earnings to some measure of the capital required to generate those earnings, most of our attention has been focused on the two profitability measures.

Figure 15.2 summarizes the analysis discussed. On the most general level, the concern is with overall measures of profitability and the effectiveness of financial leverage. On the next level, the overall measures of profitability are disaggregated into profit margin, asset turnover, and leverage components. On the third level, the profit margin and asset turnover ratios are further disaggregated to gain additional insights into reasons for changes in profitability. The depth of analysis required in any particular case depends on the differences or changes in profitability observed.

ANALYSIS OF RISK

The second parameter in investment decisions after profitability is risk. There are various factors that affect the risk of business firms:

FIGURE 15.2
Profitability Ratios

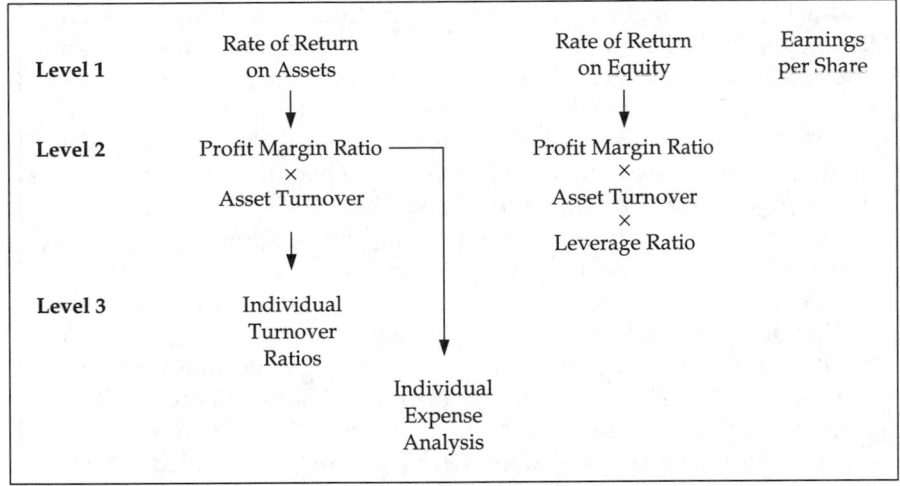

1. Economy-wide factors, such as increased inflation or interest rates, unemployment, or recession.

2. Industry-wide factors, such as increased competition, lack of availability of raw materials, changes in technology, or increased government antimonopoly actions.

3. Firm-specific factors, such as labour strikes, loss of facilities because of fire or other casualty, or poor health of key managerial personnel.

The ultimate risk is that a firm will be forced into bankruptcy and creditors and investors will lose the capital they provided to the firm.

DISCUSSION CASE 34

Securities Analysis — Art or Science?

The prediction of corporate economic performance by financial statement analysis is one of the most heavily researched of all human endeavours. A whole industry of financial analysts has been spawned by investors' unquenchable thirst for predictive information. Most investment brokers and securities analysts use the techniques illustrated in this chapter. There are, however, some additional methods in use — some uncontroversial and some controversial. These include the statisticians, the bullionists, the hemliners, and the tippers.

Interviewing of corporate financial executives is a standard tool in the financial analyst's

(continued)

(continued)

kit. Theoretically, an individual investor could call on a company and ask for information. In reality, this task is left to financial analysts. An American department store chain, J.C. Penney, reported that in one year it granted 1,500 one-hour interviews to analysts. Consequently, some large firms hire someone full-time just to talk to these analysts.

One of the oldest forms of corporate predictive tools, charting, is based on the premise that if you chart economic activity long enough, cycles will be discernible. These sawtooth diagrams, often seen in movies and cartoons, are examples of charting. Chartists eventually go looney because they discover cycles within cycles within cycles, all depending on how long a time horizon has been taken.

Statisticians have refined charting using a rigorous method called time series analysis, which is, simply stated, regression over time. Despite a period of academic popularity, the latest view is that the behaviour of most securities can be depicted as a random walk (i.e., its future behaviour is unpredictable.)

Bullionists believe that stock market performance and the price of gold bullion are inversely related. When the economy is deteriorating (along with the companies responsible for the economy), people flee paper investments and put their funds into gold and diamonds.

Hemlining has reappeared several times in the twentieth century. A hemliner believes that stock market prices move in the same direction as women's hemlines. It is unknown how many people use this technique.

The tipper is the most popular of all techniques. Most investments today are based on "hot tips." Few investors have not suffered the pangs of remorse after failing to act on one of these tips and then seeing the company's stock price take off like a rocket. Strangely enough, those tips we do act on usually blow up on the launching pad. Where do tips come from? Some come from the people who do financial statement analysis. But most come from something called *insider information.* Somebody knows somebody who knows somebody inside the company who has access to important information not yet known to the public. For instance, when a gold mining company strikes a motherlode, there is an interval of time before this information is made public, and if the company's shares are purchased before this release, a killing can be made because the share prices will surely jump later on. One problem with acting on insider information is that it is illegal.

In summary, there are numerous techniques available for predicting stock performance. However, if someone attempts to sell you advice based on any of these approaches, ask yourself one question first: If the methods work, why does this person have to peddle advice for a living?

Discussion Question

If you had saved $10,000 to invest in shares, how would you pick a stock?

When assessing risk, the focus is generally on the relative *liquidity* of a firm. Cash and near-cash assets provide a firm with the resources needed to adapt to these various dimensions of risk as potential losses arise. That is, liquid resources provide a firm with *financial flexibility*. Cash is also the connecting link that permits the operating, investing, and financing activities of a firm to continue operating smoothly and effectively.

When assessing liquidity, time is of critical importance. Consider the following three questions:

1. Does a firm have sufficient cash to repay a loan due tomorrow?

2. Will the firm have sufficient cash to repay a note due in six months?

3. Will the firm have sufficient cash to repay bonds due in five years?

In answering the first question, the analysis would probably focus on the amount of cash on hand and in the bank relative to obligations coming due tomorrow. In answering the second question, consideration would be given to the amount of cash expected to be generated from operations during the next six months, as well as to any new borrowing, relative to obligations coming due during that period. In answering the third question, the focus would shift to the longer-run cash-generating ability of the firm relative to the amount of long-term debt that would become due.

MEASURES OF SHORT-TERM LIQUIDITY RISK

This section discusses four measures for assessing *short-term liquidity risk*: (1) current ratio, (2) quick ratio, (3) operating cash flow to current liabilities ratio, and (4) working capital turnover ratio.

CURRENT RATIO

The **current ratio** is calculated by dividing current assets by current liabilities. It is commonly expressed as a ratio such as "2 to 1" or "2:1," meaning that current assets are twice as large as current liabilities. The current ratio of Heywood Corporation on December 31, Year 1, Year 2, Year 3, and Year 4 is:

current ratio
Current assets divided by current liabilities.

$$\frac{\text{Current Assets}}{\text{Current Liabilities}} = \frac{\text{Current}}{\text{Ratio}}$$

$$\text{December 31, Year 1:} \quad \frac{\$\ 50}{\$\ 40} = 1.25 \text{ to } 1.0$$

$$\text{December 31, Year 2:} \quad \frac{\$\ 80}{\$\ 50} = 1.60 \text{ to } 1.0$$

$$\text{December 31, Year 3:} \quad \frac{\$100}{\$\ 60} = 1.67 \text{ to } 1.0$$

$$\text{December 31, Year 4:} \quad \frac{\$171}{\$\ 90} = 1.90 \text{ to } 1.0$$

This ratio is presumed to indicate the ability of the firm to meet its current obligations, and is therefore of particular significance to short-term creditors. Although an excess of current assets over current liabilities is generally considered desirable from the creditor's viewpoint, changes in the trend of the ratio may be difficult to interpret. For example, when the current ratio is larger than 1 to 1, an increase of equal amount in both current assets and current liabilities results in a decline in the ratio, whereas equal decreases result in an increased current ratio.

In a recession period, business is contracting, current liabilities are paid, and even though the current assets may be at a low point, the ratio may go to high levels. In a boom period, just the reverse effect might occur. In other words, a very high current ratio may accompany unsatisfactory business conditions, whereas a falling ratio may accompany profitable operations.

Furthermore, the current ratio and the quick ratio below are susceptible to "window dressing"; that is, management can take deliberate steps to produce a financial statement that presents a better current ratio at the balance sheet date than the average or normal current ratio. For example, toward the close of a fiscal year, normal purchases on account may be delayed. Or, loans to officers, classified as noncurrent assets, may be collected and the proceeds used to reduce current liabilities. These actions may be taken so that the current ratio will appear as favourable as possible in the annual financial statements at the balance sheet date.

Although the current ratio is probably the most common liquidity ratio presented in statement analysis, there are limitations in its use, as discussed above. Its trends are difficult to interpret and, if overemphasized, it can easily lead to undersirable business practices as well as misinterpretation of financial condition.

QUICK RATIO

quick ratio
The total of cash, marketable securities, and receivables divided by current liabilities.

A variation of the current ratio, usually known as the **quick ratio** or *acid-test ratio*, is computed by including in the numerator of the fraction only those current assets that could be converted quickly into cash. The numerator customarily includes cash, temporary investments, and receivables, but it is advisable to make a study of the facts in each case before deciding whether or not to include receivables and to exclude inventories. In some businesses, the inventory of merchandise might be converted into cash more quickly than the receivables of other businesses.

Assuming that the accounts receivable of Heywood Corporation are included but that inventory is excluded, the quick ratio on December 31, Year 1, Year 2, Year 3, and Year 4 is:

$$\frac{\text{Cash, Accounts Receivable}}{\text{Current Liabilities}} = \frac{\text{Quick}}{\text{Ratio}}$$

$$\text{December 31, Year 1: } \frac{\$36}{\$40} = 0.90 \text{ to } 1.0$$

$$\text{December 31, Year 2: } \frac{\$50}{\$50} = 1.0 \text{ to } 1.0$$

$$\text{December 31, Year 3: } \frac{\$54}{\$60} = 0.90 \text{ to } 1.0$$

$$\text{December 31, Year 4: } \frac{\$88}{\$90} = 0.98 \text{ to } 1.0$$

Whereas the current ratio increased steadily over the period, the quick ratio remained relatively constant. The increase in the current ratio results primarily from a buildup of inventories.

OPERATING CASH FLOW TO CURRENT LIABILITIES

Both the current ratio and quick ratio can be criticized in that they are calculated using amounts at a specific point in time. If financial statement amounts at that particular time are unusually large or small, the resulting ratios will not reflect more normal conditions.

To overcome these deficiencies, the **operating cash flow to current liabilities ratio** can be calculated. The numerator of this ratio is cash provided by operations for the year. The denominator is average current liabilities for the year. The operating cash flow to current liabilities ratios for Heywood Corporation for Year 2, Year 3, and Year 4 are as follows:

operating cash flow to current liabilities ratio The numerator of this ratio is cash provided by operations for the year. The denominator is average current liabilities for the year.

	$$\frac{\text{Cash Provided by Operations}}{\text{Average Current Liabilities}} =$$	Operating Cash Flow to Current Liabilities
Year 2	$$\frac{\$12}{\frac{1}{2}(\$40 + \$50)} =$$	26.7%
Year 3	$$\frac{\$32}{\frac{1}{2}(\$50 + \$60)} =$$	58.2%
Year 4	$$\frac{\$41}{\frac{1}{2}(\$60 + \$90)} =$$	54.7%

A ratio of 40 percent or more[9] is common for a healthy firm. Thus, the liquidity of Heywood Corporation improved dramatically between Year 2 and Year 3. The decrease between Year 3 and Year 4 is due primarily to a buildup in current liabilities (which, in turn, is probably related to the buildup in inventories, noted above).

WORKING CAPITAL TURNOVER RATIO

The **operating cycle** of a firm is a sequence of activities in which:

1. Inventory is purchased on account from suppliers.
2. Inventory is sold on account to customers.
3. Customers pay amounts due.
4. Suppliers are paid amounts due.

operating cycle The time period between the acquisition of raw materials or merchandise and the recovery of cash from the related sale.

This cycle occurs continually for most business firms. The longer the cycle, the longer the time that funds are tied up in receivables and inventories. The interest cost on funds required to carry receivables and inventory reduces net income and hurts profitability. Funds tied up in receivables and inventory also have negative effects on the short-run liquidity of a firm. The more quickly inventory and receivables are turned into cash, the more liquid is a firm.

[9] Cornelius Casey and Norman Bartczak, "Operating Cash Flow Data and Financial Distress: Some Empirical Evidence," *Journal of Accounting Research* (Spring 1985), pp. 384–401.

**working capital
turnover ratio**
The ratio of sales to
working capital.

The **working capital turnover ratio** is a measure of the length of the operating cycle. It is calculated by dividing sales by the average working capital for the year. Working capital is equal to current assets minus current liabilities. The working capital turnover ratio for Heywood Corporation is as follows:

	$\dfrac{\text{Sales}}{\text{Working Capital}}$	=	Working Capital Turnover Ratio
Year 2	$\dfrac{\$210}{\frac{1}{2}(\$10 + \$30)}$	=	10.5 times
Year 3	$\dfrac{\$310}{\frac{1}{2}(\$30 + \$40)}$	=	8.9 times
Year 4	$\dfrac{\$475}{\frac{1}{2}(\$40 + \$81)}$	=	7.9 times

The turnover rate has decreased over the three-year period, primarily because inventories net of currrent liabilities increased faster than sales.

The working capital turnover ratio is often converted to the number of days required for one revolution of the operating cycle by dividing the turnover ratio into 365 days. Thus, working capital turned over on average every 34.8 days (= 365/10.5) during Year 2. The corresponding amounts for Year 3 and Year 4 were 41.0 days and 46.2 days, respectively.

The working capital turnover ratio varies significantly across firms depending on the nature of their businesses. The working capital turnover for grocery stores is approximately 12 times per year, whereas for a construction company the turnover is sometimes less than 1. When using the working capital turnover ratio to evaluate short-term liquidity, the analyst must be aware of the type of business in which the firm is involved.

SUMMARY OF SHORT-TERM LIQUIDITY ANALYSIS

The current and quick ratios give snapshot measures of liquidity at particular points in time. These ratios for Heywood Corporation are at reasonably adequate levels at the end of each year, although they indicate a buildup of inventories in Year 4.

The cash flow from operations to current liabilities and the working capital turnover ratios provide measures of short-term liquidity for a period of time. Both ratios indicate a significant improvement in liquidity between Year 2 and Year 3, owing primarily to increased cash flow from operations. Both ratios decreased during Year 4, owing to the buildup of inventory. However, the levels of the ratios during Year 4 do not yet indicate serious short-term liquidity problems for Heywood Corporation. Given the growth rate in sales during the past two years (approximately 50 percent per year), a buildup of inventories may be justified.

MEASURES OF LONG-TERM LIQUIDITY RISK

Measures of *long-term liquidity risk* are used in evaluating the firm's ability to meet interest and principal payments on long-term debt and similar obligations as they become due. If the payments cannot be made on time, the firm becomes *insolvent* and may have to be reorganized or liquidated.

Perhaps the best indicator for assessing long-term liquidity risk is a firm's ability to generate profits over a period of years. If a firm is profitable, it will either generate sufficient capital from operations or be able to obtain needed capital from creditors and shareholders. The measures of profitability discussed previously are therefore applicable for this purpose as well. Three other commonly used measures of long-term liquidity are debt ratios, the cash flow from operations to total liabilities ratio, and the number of times that interest charges are earned.

DEBT RATIOS

There are several variations of the debt ratio, but the one most commonly encountered in financial analysis is the **long-term debt ratio**. It reports the portion of the firm's long-term capital that is furnished by debt holders. To calculate this ratio, divide total long-term debt by the sum of total long-term debt and total shareholders' equity.

Another form of the debt ratio is the **debt-equity ratio**. To calculate the debt-equity ratio, divide total liabilities (current and noncurrent) by total equities (liabilities plus shareholders' equity = total assets).

Exhibit 15.9 shows the two forms of the debt ratio for Heywood Corporation on December 31, Year 1, Year 2, Year 3, and Year 4. In general, the higher these ratios, the higher the likelihood that the firm may be unable to meet fixed interest and principal payments in the future. The decision for most firms relates to how much financial leverage, with its attendant risk, they can afford to assume. Funds obtained from issuing bonds or borrowing from a bank have a relatively low interest cost but require fixed, periodic payments that increase the likelihood of bankruptcy.

In assessing the debt ratios, analysts customarily vary the standard in direct relation to the stability of the firm's earnings and cash flow from operations. The more stable the earnings, and cash flow, the higher the debt ratio that is considered acceptable or safe. The debt ratios of public utilities

long-term debt ratio
Reports the portion of the firm's long-term capital that is furnished by debt holders. To calculate this ratio, divide total long-term debt by the sum of total long-term debt and total shareholders' equity.

debt-equity ratio
The total liabilities divided by total equities. Sometimes the denominator is merely total shareholders' equity. Sometimes the numerator is restricted to noncurrent debt.

EXHIBIT 15.9
HEYWOOD CORPORATION
Debt Ratios

$\dfrac{\text{Total Long-Term Debt}}{\begin{array}{c}\text{Total Long-Term Debt}\\\text{Plus Shareholders'}\\\text{Equity}\end{array}}$	=	Long-Term Debt Ratio	$\dfrac{\text{Total Liabilities}}{\begin{array}{c}\text{Total Liabilities Plus}\\\text{Shareholders'}\\\text{Equity}\end{array}}$	=	Debt-Equity Ratio
Dec. 31, Year 1: $\dfrac{\$\,50}{\$210}$	=	24%	Dec. 31, Year 1: $\dfrac{\$\,90}{\$250}$	=	36%
Dec. 31, Year 2: $\dfrac{\$\,50}{\$350}$	=	14%	Dec. 31, Year 2: $\dfrac{\$100}{\$400}$	=	25%
Dec. 31, Year 3: $\dfrac{\$100}{\$460}$	=	22%	Dec. 31, Year 3: $\dfrac{\$160}{\$520}$	=	31%
Dec. 31, Year 4: $\dfrac{\$150}{\$560}$	=	27%	Dec. 31, Year 4: $\dfrac{\$240}{\$650}$	=	37%

are customarily high, frequently on the order of 60 to 70 percent. The stability of public utility earnings and cash flow makes these ratios acceptable to many investors who would be dissatisfied with such high leverage for firms with less stable earnings and cash flows. The debt ratios of Heywood Corporation are about average for an industrial firm.

Because several variations of the debt ratio appear in corporate annual reports, care in comparing debt ratios among firms is necessary.

CASH FLOW FROM OPERATIONS TO TOTAL LIABILITIES RATIO

The debt ratios give no recognition to the varying liquidity of assets for covering various levels of debt. The cash flow from operations to total liabilities ratio overcomes this deficiency. This cash flow ratio is similar to the one used in assessing short-term liquidity risk, but here all liabilities (both current and noncurrent) are included in the denominator. The **cash flow from operations to debt ratio** for Heywood Corporation is:

cash flow from operations to debt ratio
Similar to cash flow ratio used in assessing short-term liquidity risk, but here all liabilities (both current and noncurrent) are included in the denominator.

	$\dfrac{\text{Cash Flow from Operations}}{\text{Average Total Liabilities}}$	=	Cash Flow from Operations to Debt Ratio
Year 2	$\dfrac{\$12}{{}^{1}/_{2}(\$90 + \$100)}$	=	12.6%
Year 3	$\dfrac{\$32}{{}^{1}/_{2}(\$100 + \$160)}$	=	24.6%
Year 4	$\dfrac{\$41}{{}^{1}/_{2}(\$160 + \$240)}$	=	20.5%

A ratio of 20 percent or more is normal for a financially healthy company. Thus, the long-term liquidity risk decreased significantly between Year 2 and Year 3 but increased again in Year 4. The level of the ratio in Year 4, though, is still adequate.

INTEREST COVERAGE — TIMES INTEREST CHARGES EARNED

Another measure of long-term solvency is the *number of times that interest charges are earned*, or *covered*. This ratio is calculated by dividing net income before interest and income tax expenses by interest expense. For Heywood Corporation, the **times interest earned ratios** for Year 2, Year 3, and Year 4 are:

times interest earned ratios
Ratios of pretax income plus interest charges to interest charges.

$$\frac{\text{Net Income Before Interest and Income Taxes}}{\text{Interest Expense}} = \frac{\text{Times Interest}}{\text{Charges Earned}}$$

$$\text{Year 2: } \frac{\$16 + \$5 + \$10}{\$5} = 6.2 \text{ times}$$

$$\text{Year 3: } \frac{\$34 + \$10 + \$22}{\$10} = 6.6 \text{ times}$$

$$\text{Year 4: } \frac{\$60 + \$16 + \$40}{\$16} = 7.3 \text{ times}$$

Thus, whereas the bonds payable increased sharply during the three-year period, the growth in net income before interest and income taxes was sufficient to provide increasing coverage of the fixed interest charges.

The purpose of this ratio is to indicate the relative protection of bondholders and to assess the probability that the firm will be forced into bankruptcy by a failure to meet required interest payments. If periodic repayments of principal on long-term liabilities are also required, the repayments might also be included in the denominator of the ratio. The ratio would then be described as the *number of times that fixed charges were earned*, or *covered*.

The times interest or fixed charges earned ratios can be criticized as measures for assessing long-term liquidity risk, because the ratios use earnings rather than cash flows in the numerator. Interest and other fixed payment obligations are paid with cash, not with earnings. When the value of the ratio is relatively low (for example, 2 to 3 times), some measure of cash flows, such as cash flows from operations, may be preferable in the numerator.

SUMMARY OF LONG-TERM LIQUIDITY ANALYSIS

The focus of long-term liquidity analysis is on the amount of debt, particularly long-term debt, in the capital structure and the adequacy of earnings and cash flows for debt service — making interest and principal payments as they become due. Although both short- and long-term debt of Heywood Corporation have increased over the three-year period, increases in sales, earnings, and cash flows from operations all appear to be increasing sufficiently to cover the current levels of debt.

LIMITATIONS OF RATIO ANALYSIS

For convenient reference, Exhibit 15.10 summarizes the calculation of the ratios discussed in this chapter. The analytical computations discussed in this chapter have a number of limitations that should be kept in mind by anyone preparing or using them. Several of the more important limitations are the following:

1. The ratios are based on financial statement data and are therefore subject to the same criticisms as the financial statements (for example, use

EXHIBIT 15.10
Summary of Financial Statement Ratios

Ratio	Numerator	Denominator
Profitability Ratios		
Rate of Return on Assets	Net Income + Interest Expense (net of tax effects)[a]	Average Total Assets During the Period
Profit Margin Ratio (before interest effects)	Net Income + Interest Expense (net of tax effects)[a]	Revenues

[a]*If a consolidated subsidiary is not owned entirely by the parent corporation, the minority interest share of earnings must also be added back to net income. See the description in Chapter 12.*

EXHIBIT 15.10 (continued)

Ratio	Numerator	Denominator
Various Expense Ratios	Various Expenses	Revenues
Total Assets Turnover Ratio	Revenues	Average Total Assets During the Period
Accounts Receivable Turnover Ratio	Net Sales on Accounts	Average Accounts Receivable During the Period
Inventory Turnover Ratio	Cost of Goods Sold	Average Inventory During the Period
Plant Asset Turnover Ratio	Revenues	Average Plant Assets During the Period
Rate of Return on Common Shareholders' Equity	Net Income — Preferred Stock Dividends	Average Common Shareholders' Equity During the Period
Profit Margin Ratio (after interest expense and preferred dividends)	Net Income — Preferred Stock Dividends	Average Common Shareholders' Equity During the Period
Leverage Ratio	Average Total Assets During the Period	Average Common Shareholders' Equity During the Period
Earnings per Share of Stock[b]	Net Income — Preferred Stock Dividends	Weighted-Average Number of Common Shares Outstanding During the Period
Short-Term Liquidity Ratios		
Current Ratio	Current Assets	Current Liabilities
Quick or Acid-Test Ratio	Highly Liquid Assets (ordinarily, cash, temporary investments, and receivables)[c]	Current Liabilities
Cash Flow from Operations to Current Liabilities Ratio	Cash Provided by Operations	Average Current Liabilities During the Period
Working Capital Turnover Ratio	Revenues	Average Working Capital During the Period
Long-Term Liquidity Ratios		
Long-Term Debt Ratio	Total Long-Term Debt	Total Long-Term Debt Plus Shareholders' Equity
Debt-Equity Ratio	Total Liabilities	Total Equities (liabilities plus shareholders' equity)
Cash Flow from Operations to Total Liabilities Ratio	Cash Provided by Operations	Average Total Liabilities During the Period
Times Interest Charges Earned	Net Income Before Interest and Income Taxes	Interest Expense

[b]*This calculation can be more complicated when there are convertible securities, options, or warrants outstanding.*
[c]*Receivables could conceivably be excluded for some firms and inventories included for others. Such refinements are seldom employed in practice.*

of acquisition cost rather than current replacement cost or net realizable value; the latitude permitted firms in selecting from among various generally accepted accounting policies).

2. Changes in many ratios are highly associated with each other. For example, the changes in the current ratio and quick ratio between two different times are often in the same direction and approximately proportional. It is therefore not necessary to compute all of the ratios to assess a particular factor.

3. When comparing the size of a ratio between periods for the same firm, one must recognize conditions that have changed between the periods being compared (for example, different product lines or geographical markets served, changes in economic conditions, changes in prices).

4. When comparing ratios of a particular firm with those of similar firms, one must recognize differences between the firms (for example, use of different methods of accounting, differences in the method of operations, type of financing, and so on).

Results of financial statement analyses cannot be used by themselves as direct indications of good or poor management. Such analyses merely indicate areas that might be investigated further. For example, a decrease in the turnover of raw materials inventory, ordinarily considered to be an undesirable trend, may reflect the accumulation of scarce materials that will keep the plant operating at full capacity during shortages when competitors have been forced to restrict operations or to close down. Ratios derived from financial statements must be combined with an investigation of other facts before valid conclusions can be drawn.

SUMMARY

This chapter began by raising the question, "Should you invest your inheritance in a certificate of deposit or in the common shares of Heywood Corporation?" Analysis of Heywood Corporation's financial statements indicates that it has been a growing, profitable company with few indications of either short-term liquidity or long-term liquidity problems. At least three additional inputs are necessary before making the investment decision. First, consideration must be given to other sources of information besides the financial statements to determine if information relevant for projecting rates of return or for assessing risk needs to be considered. Second, you must decide your attitude toward, or willingness to assume, risk. Third, you must decide if you think the stock market price of the shares makes them an attractive purchase.[10] It is at this stage in the investment decision that the analysis becomes particularly subjective.

---

[10] Other important factors cannot be discussed here, but are in finance texts. Perhaps the most important question of all is how a particular investment fits in with the investor's entire portfolio. Modern research suggests that the suitability of a potential investment depends more on the attributes of the other components of an investment portfolio and the risk attitude of the investor than on the attributes of the potential investment itself.

KEY TERMS

Preparer's perspective
User's perspective
Financial statement analysis
General-purpose statements
Return
Risk
Ratios
Profitability
Rate of return on assets
Profit margin ratio
Total assets turnover ratio
Accounts receivable turnover
Inventory turnover ratio
Plant asset turnover ratio
Rate of return on common
   shareholders' equity

Financial leverage
Leverage ratio
Basic earnings per share
Fully diluted earnings per share
Price-earnings ratio
Current ratio
Quick ratio
Operating cash flow to current
   liabilities ratio
Operating cycle
Working capital turnover ratio
Long-term debt ratio
Debt-equity ratio
Cash flow from operations to
   debt ratio
Times interest earned ratios

SELF-STUDY MATERIAL

This section contains questions, exercises, and problems to help you assess your understanding of Chapter 15. Careful review of this material will assist you in completing the homework assignments. Solutions are found at the end of this section.

QUESTIONS AND EXERCISES

True/False

For each statement, place a T or an F in the space provided to indicate whether the statement is true or false.

_____ 1. If the inventory of a company turns over 5 times each year, the average number of days that merchandise is held during the year is seventy-three days.

_____ 2. The long-term debt ratio is calculated by dividing total liabilities by total equities.

_____ 3. A point will be reached where financial leverage can no longer increase the potential rate of return to common shareholders' equity.

_____ 4. The quick ratio is a measure of the relationship between sales and the investment in plant assets.

_____ 5. If the average number of days that an accounts receivable is outstanding is about forty-six days, the accounts receivable turnover for the year is about 6 times.

_____ 6. A dual presentation of basic and fully diluted earnings per share is required when a firm has outstanding securities that, if exchanged for more common shares, would decrease earnings per share by a material amount.

_____ 7. In some situations, it may be preferable to compute times interest charges earned by using cash flows rather than earnings in the numerator.

_____ 8. In computing the quick ratio, inventories are usually omitted from the listing of assets that can be converted into cash quickly.

_____ 9. The current ratio is susceptible to window dressing through completion of certain transactions just before the end of the period.

_____ 10. A person concerned with the long-term liquidity risk of a firm is primarily interested in whether the firm will have sufficient cash available to pay current debt.

_____ 11. In computing the rate of return on assets, the denominator should reflect average total assets during the year.

_____ 12. Basic earnings per share is the amount of earnings per share reflecting the maximum dilution that would occur if all options, warrants, and convertible securities outstanding at the end of the accounting period were exchanged for common shares.

_____ 13. The operating cash flow to average current liabilities is a measure of profitability.

_____ 14. Financial leverage increases the rate of return on common shareholders' equity when the rate of return on assets is less than the aftertax cost of debt.

_____ 15. Rate of return on assets is computed using income before deducting any payment or distributions to the providers of capital.

_____ 16. The cash flow from operations to total liabilities ratio is one measure of long-term liquidity risk.

_____ 17. To determine the amount of earnings assignable to common shareholders, any dividends on preferred shares declared during the period must be deducted from net income.

_____ 18. If the common shares of the Garrett Co. Ltd. are selling for $50 per share and the earnings per share for the current year is $2, the price-earnings ratio is 100 to 1.

_____ 19. The rate of return can be disaggregated into two other ratios as follows:

$$\text{Rate of Return} = \text{Profit Margin Ratio} \times \text{Current Ratio}$$

_____ 20. The shorter the time that funds are tied up in receivables and inventories, the shorter the operating cycle.

_____ 21. The leverage ratio indicates the extent to which total assets have been provided by common shareholders.

_____ 22. The rate of return on assets measures the profitability of a firm before any payments to the suppliers of capital.

_____ 23. Ratios are more meaningful if they are compared to a budgeted standard or an industry standard, rather than used on their own.

_____ 24. Improving the rate of return on assets can be accomplished by increasing the profit margin ratio, the rate of asset turnover, or both.

_____ 25. To compute the rate of return on common shareholders' equity, dividends on preferred shares must be added to net income.

Matching

From the list of terms, select one term that is most closely associated with each of the descriptive phrases or statements and place the letter for that term in the space provided.

a. accounts receivable turnover
b. current ratio
c. debt-equity ratio
d. basic earnings per share
e. financial leverage
f. inventory turnover
g. liquidity
h. long-term debt ratio
i. operating cash flow to current liabilities

j. operating cycle
k. plant asset turnover
l. profit margin ratio
m. quick ratio
n. rate of return on assets
o. rate of return on common shareholders' equity
p. times interest charges earned
q. total assets turnover
r. working capital turnover ratio

_____ 1. Measures how many times in each period that accounts receivable are turned over (or converted to cash).

_____ 2. Indicates the proportion of a firm's long-term capital that is provided by creditors.

_____ 3. A measure of how long funds are tied up in receivables and inventory.

_____ 4. Refers to the "nearness of cash" of a firm's assets.

_____ 5. Indicates the number of times that an average inventory has been sold during the period.

_____ 6. Measures management's performance in generating earnings that are assignable to the common shareholders' equity.

_____ 7. Refers to a firm's financing with debt and preferred shares to increase the return to the common shareholders' equity.

_____ 8. This ratio generally includes cash, temporary investments, and accounts receivable in its numerator.

_____ 9. This ratio has been found to be useful in predicting bankruptcy.

_____ 10. Provides a measure of the revenue generated for each dollar invested in plant assets.

_____ 11. This ratio assess management's operating performance independently of financing decisions.

_____ 12. Is computed by dividing net income attributable to common shares by the average number of common shares outstanding during the period.

_____ 13. This ratio is supposed to indicate the ability of the firm to meet its current obligations.

_____ 14. This ratio is a measure of a firm's ability to control the level of costs, or expenses, relative to revenues generated.

_____ 15. Provides a measure of the revenue generated for each dollar invested in assets.

_____ 16. This ratio is a measure of the length of the operating cycle.

_____ 17. This ratio indicates the proportion of total capital supplied by creditors.

_____ 18. This ratio is used to indicate the relative protection of bondholders and to assess the probability that the firm will be forced into receivership by a failure to meet required interest payments.

Multiple Choice

Choose the best answer for each question or problem and enter the identifying letter in the space provided.

_____ 1. Assume that the current ratio of the Sanyati Corp. is 2.5 to 1. What effect would an equal dollar increase in current assets and current liabilities have on the current ratio?
   a) increase the current ratio
   b) decrease the current ratio
   c) no effect on the current ratio
   d) answer cannot be determined from information given

_____ 2. Which of these transactions would result in an increase in a company's current ratio?
   a) declaring cash dividend payable next period
   b) paying long-term debt
   c) paying accounts payable
   d) borrowing money on a six-month note

_____ 3. Which of the following is a measure of the length of the operating cycle?
   a) quick ratio
   b) working capital turnover ratio
   c) current ratio
   d) debt-equity ratio

_____ 4. The rate of return on assets can be disaggregated into two other ratios. Which of the following is one of the two ratios?
   a) plant asset turnover ratio
   b) debt-equity ratio
   c) profit margin ratio
   d) inventory turnover ratio

_____ 5. Which of the following is not used to assess short-term liquidity risk?
   a) accounts receivable
   b) working capital turnover ratio
   c) current ratio
   d) quick ratio

_____ 6. The Taylor Company Inc. sells on credit with terms of "net 30 days." If the company's credit policy and collection activity is working efficiently, how many times should the company's accounts receivable turn over in a year?
   a) approximately 6 times
   b) approximately 8 times
   c) approximately 10 times
   d) approximately 12 times

_____ 7. Comparisons of a given firm's ratios with those of other firms for a particular period is refered to as:
   a) time-series analysis
   b) defensive-interval analysis
   c) cross-section analysis
   d) none of the above

_____ 8. This ratio is a useful measure for assessing a firm's performance in using assets to generate earnings:
   a) profit margin ratio
   b) financial leverage
   c) rate of return on assets
   d) working capital

_____ 9. If a company's rate of return on assets is 20 percent and the profit margin percentage is 5 percent, the company's total assets turnover must be:
   a) 1
   b) 4
   c) 5
   d) 20

_____ 10. In computing the rate of return on assets, interest expense net of income tax savings is added to net income. Assume that Mickey Limited has interest expense of $10 million and net income of $25 million. Assume that the income tax rate is 45 percent. In computing the rate of return on assets, the numerator would be:
   a) $29.5 million
   b) $30.5 million
   c) $35 million
   d) none of the above

_____ 11. Which of the following is not a component of the rate of return on common shareholders' equity?
   a) leverage ratio
   b) profit margin ratio
   c) total assets turnover ratio
   d) all three of the above ratios are components of the rate of return on common shareholders' equity

_____ 12. In computing the quick ratio, which of the following items is customarily excluded from the numerator?
   a) Cash
   b) Inventory
   c) Temporary Investments
   d) Accounts Receivable

_____ 13. Which of these ratios would not be used in assessing a firm's long-term liquidity risk?
   a) debt-equity ratio
   b) long-term debt ratio
   c) times interest charges earned
   d) current ratio

____ 14. Which of these ratios would probably not be used to analyze the total assets turnover ratio?
   a) plant asset turnover
   b) accounts receivable turnover
   c) inventory turnover
   d) long-term debt ratio

____ 15. A company wants to increase its rate of return on assets from 8 percent to 14 percent. It is believed that the firm's total assets turnover of 0.667 cannot be easily increased at the present time. What must the profit margin percentage be to achieve the desired 14 percent rate of return on assets?
   a) 7 percent
   b) 14 percent
   c) 21 percent
   d) 28 percent

____ 16. Which of the following is not a measure of profitability?
   a) rate of return on assets
   b) working capital turnover ratio
   c) rate of return on common shareholders' equity
   d) earnings per common share

____ 17. The phenomenon whereby common shareholders trade extra risk for a potentially higher return is called:
   a) financial leverage
   b) operating leverage
   c) trading on the equity
   d) both a and c are correct

____ 18. Financial leverage can increase the return to common shareholders as long as:
   a) the rate of return earned on assets equals the rate paid for the capital used to acquire those assets
   b) the rate of return earned on assets is less than the rate paid for the capital used to acquire those assets
   c) the rate of return earned on assets exceeds the rate paid for the capital used to acquire those assets
   d) the firm has a good earnings year

Exercises

1. The comparative balance sheets for 19X1 and 19X2 along with the 19X2 income statement for Larry's Garden Shop Inc. are as follows:

LARRY'S GARDEN SHOP INC.
Comparative Balance Sheets

	Year Ended December 31	
	19X2	**19X1**
Assets		
Cash	$ 50,000	$ 15,000
Accounts Receivable	100,000	150,000
Inventory	300,000	200,000
Capital Assets	700,000	735,000
Total Assets	$1,150,000	$1,100,000

Liabilities and Shareholders' Equity

Current Liabilities	$ 225,000	$ 250,000
5% Mortgage Payable	400,000	415,000
Common Shares (150,000 shares outstanding)	300,000	300,000
Retained Earnings	225,000	135,000
Total Liabilities and Equities	$1,150,000	$1,100,000

LARRY'S GARDEN SHOP INC.
Income Statement
For Year Ended December 31, 19X2

Sales on Account		$900,000
Less: Cost of Sales		500,000
Gross Profit		$400,000
Less: Expenses		
Salary Expense	$165,000	
Depreciation Expense	35,000	
Interest Expense	20,000	
Total Expenses		220,000
Income Before Taxes		$180,000
Income Tax Expense (50% rate)		90,000
Net Income		$ 90,000

Compute the following ratios for Larry's Garden Shop Inc. for 19X2.
  a. current ratio
  b. quick ratio (Inventory cannot be quickly converted to cash.)
  c. debt-equity ratio
  d. rate of return on assets
  e. rate of return on common shareholders' equity
  f. earnings per common share
  g. profit margin ratio
  h. total assets turnover
  i. times interest charges earned
  j. inventory turnover
  k. average number of days inventory on hand
  l. accounts receivable turnover
  m. average collection period for accounts receivable
  n. long-term debt ratio
  o. plant asset turnover ratio
  p. leverage ratio
  q. working capital turnover ratio
  r. gross profit ratio

2. Bailey Limited's balance sheet indicates that the company has $2 million of 7 percent debt and total shareholders' equity of $1 million.

   Griffin Incorporated's balance sheet indicates that the company has no debt and total shareholders' equity of $3 million.

   Assume that both companies are identical in all respects except for this difference. If both companies report income before interest and taxes of $400,000 and the tax rate is 40 percent, compute:

   a. the rate of return on assets for both companies
   b. the rate of return on common shareholders' equity

   Explain any difference in the computed ratios for the two companies.

PROBLEM 1 FOR SELF-STUDY

Exhibit 15.11 presents a comparative balance sheet for McCall Ltd. as of December 31, Year 1 and Year 2, and Exhibit 15.12 presents an income statement for Year 2. Using information from these financial statements, compute the following ratios. (The income tax rate is 40 percent. Cash provided by operations totals $3,300.)

a. Rate of return on assets
b. Profit margin ratio (before interest and related tax effects)
c. Cost of goods sold to sales percentage
d. Selling expense to sales percentage
e. Total assets turnover
f. Accounts receivable turnover

EXHIBIT 15.11
McCALL LTD.
December 31, Year 1 and Year 2

	December 31	
	Year 2	Year 1
ASSETS		
Current Assets:		
Cash	$ 750	$ 600
Accounts Receivable	4,300	3,600
Merchandise Inventories	7,900	5,600
Prepayments	380	300
Total Current Assets	$13,330	$10,100
Capital Assets:		
Land	$ 600	$ 500
Buildings and Equipment	10,070	9,400
Total Capital Assets	$10,670	$ 9,900
Total Assets	$24,000	$20,000
LIABILITIES AND SHAREHOLDERS' EQUITY		
Current Liabilities:		
Notes Payable	$ 4,000	$ 2,000
Accounts Payable	3,300	3,500
Other Current Liabilities	1,900	1,500
Total Current Liabilities	9,200	7,000
Noncurrent Liabilities:		
Bonds Payable	2,800	4,000
Total Liabilities	$12,000	$11,000
Shareholders' Equity:		
Preferred Shares	$ 1,000	$ 1,000
Common Shares	4,300	3,500
Retained Earnings	6,700	4,500
Total Shareholders' Equity	$12,000	$ 9,000
Total Liabilities and Shareholders' Equity	$24,000	$20,000

EXHIBIT 15.12
McCALL LTD.
Income and Retained Earnings Statement
For Year 2

Sales		$30,000
Less: Cost of Sales		18,000
Gross Profit		$12,000
Less: Operating Expenses		
Selling	$4,500	
Administrative	1,800	6,300
Operating Profit		$ 5,700
Less: Interest Expense		700
Net Income before Income Tax		$ 5,000
Income Tax		2,000
Net Income		$ 3,000
Less: Dividends		
Preferred	$ 100	
Common	700	800
Increase in Retained Earnings for Year 2		$ 2,200
Retained Earnings, December 31, Year 1		4,500
Retained Earnings, December 31, Year 2		$ 6,700

  g. Inventory turnover

  h. Plant asset turnover

  i. Rate of return on common shareholders' equity

  j. Profit margin (after interest)

  k. Leverage ratio

  l. Current ratio (both dates)

 m. Quick ratio (both dates)

  n. Cash flow from operations to current liabilities

  o. Working capital turnover

  p. Long-term debt ratio (both dates)

  q. Debt-equity ratio (both dates)

  r. Cash flow from operations to total liabilities.

  s. Time interest charges earned

PROBLEM 2 FOR SELF-STUDY

Exhibit 15.13 presents a ratio analysis for Abbott Corporation for Year 1 to Year 3.

  a. What is the likely explanation for the decreasing rate of return on assets?

  b. What is the likely explanation for the increasing rate of return on common shareholders' equity?

  c. What is the likely explanation for the behaviour of the current and quick ratios?

  d. What is the likely explanation for the decreases in the two cash flow from operations to liabilities ratios?

EXHIBIT 15.13
Ratio Analysis for Abbott Corporation

	Year 3	Year 2	Year 1
Rate of Return on Assets	9.2%	9.6%	10.0%
Profit Margin (before interest and related tax effects)	6.1%	6.1%	6.0%
Total Assets Turnover	1.5	1.6	1.7
Cost of Goods Sold/Revenues	62.6%	62.3%	62.5%
Selling Expenses/Revenues	10.4%	10.2%	10.3%
Interest Expense/Revenues	2.5%	2.0%	1.5%
Accounts Receivable Turnover	4.2	4.3	4.3
Inventory Turnover	3.6	3.4	3.2
Plant Asset Turnover	0.6	0.7	0.8
Rate of Return on Common Shareholders' Equity	14.5%	14.2%	14.0%
Profit Margin (after interest)	4.6%	4.9%	5.1%
Leverage Ratio	2.1	1.8	1.6
Current Ratio	1.2	1.3	1.4
Quick Ratio	1.0	0.9	1.0
Cash Flow from Operations to Current Liabilities	36.4%	37.3%	38.2%
Working Capital Turnover	5.2	5.0	4.8
Long-Term Debt Ratio	43.3%	33.8%	37.5%
Debt-Equity Ratio	52.4%	44.4%	37.5%
Cash Flow from Operations to Total Liabilities	11.1%	13.4%	16.3%
Times Interest Charges Earned	4.1	5.1	6.7

ANSWERS TO QUESTIONS AND EXERCISES

True/False

1. T	8. T	15. T	22. T
2. F	9. T	16. T	23. T
3. T	10. F	17. T	24. T
4. F	11. T	18. F	25. F
5. F	12. F	19. F	
6. T	13. F	20. T	
7. T	14. F	21. T	

Matching

1. a	6. o	11. n	16. r
2. h	7. e	12. d	17. c
3. j	8. m	13. b	18. p
4. g	9. i	14. l	
5. f	10. k	15. q	

Multiple Choice

1. b	6. d	11. d	16. b
2. c	7. c	12. b	17. d
3. b	8. c	13. d	18. c
4. c	9. b	14. d	
5. a	10. b	15. c	

Exercises

1. a. Current Ratio $= \dfrac{\text{Current Assets}}{\text{Current Liabilities}}$

$$= \dfrac{\$450,000}{\$225,000} = 2{:}1$$

b. Quick Ratio $= \dfrac{\text{Cash} + \text{Receivables} + \text{Temporary Investments}}{\text{Current Liabilities}}$

$$= \dfrac{\$50,000 + \$100,000}{\$225,000} = 0.667{:}1$$

c. Debt-Equity Ratio $= \dfrac{\text{Total Liabilities}}{\text{Total Liabilities} + \text{Shareholders' Equity}}$

$$= \dfrac{\$625,000}{\$1,150,000} = 0.543$$

d. Rate of Return on Assets $= \dfrac{\text{Net Income} + \text{Interest Expense (net of income tax savings)}}{\text{Average Total Assets}}$

$$= \dfrac{\$90,000 + \$10,000}{{}^{1}/_{2}(\$1,150,000 + \$1,100,000)} = 0.089$$

e. Rate of Return on Common Shareholders' Equity

$$= \dfrac{\text{Net Income} - \text{Dividends on Preferred Shares}}{\text{Average Common Shareholders' Equity During Period}}$$

$$= \dfrac{\$90,000}{{}^{1}/_{2}(\$525,000 + \$435,000)} = 0.1875$$

f. Earnings per Common Share

$$= \dfrac{\text{Net Income} - \text{Preferred Share Dividends}}{\text{Weighted-Average Number of Common Shares Outstanding During Period}}$$

$$= \dfrac{\$90,000}{150,000} = \$0.60$$

g. Profit Margin Ratio $= \dfrac{\text{Net Income} + \text{Interest Expense (net of tax effects)}}{\text{Revenues}}$

$$= \dfrac{\$90,000 + \$10,000}{\$900,000} = 0.11$$

h. Total Assets Turnover $= \dfrac{\text{Revenues}}{\text{Average Total Assets During Period}}$

$$= \dfrac{\$900,000}{{}^{1}/_{2}(\$1,150,000 + \$1,100,000)} = 0.8$$

i. Times Interest Charges Earned $= \dfrac{\text{Net Income Before Interest and Income Taxes}}{\text{Interest Expense}}$

$$= \dfrac{\$200,000}{\$20,000} = 10 \text{ times}$$

j. Inventory Turnover $= \dfrac{\text{Cost of Goods Sold}}{\text{Average Inventory During Period}}$

$$= \dfrac{\$500,000}{{}^{1}/_{2}(\$300,000 + \$200,000)} = 2$$

k. Average Number of Days Inventory on Hand $= \dfrac{365}{\text{Inventory Turnover}}$

$$= \dfrac{365}{2} = 182.5$$

l. Accounts Receivable Turnover $= \dfrac{\text{Net Sales on Account}}{\text{Average Accounts Receivable During Period}}$

$$= \dfrac{\$900,000}{\frac{1}{2}(\$100,000 + \$150,000)} = 7.2$$

m. Average Collection Period for Accounts Receivable $= \dfrac{365}{\text{Accounts Receivable Turnover}}$

$$= \dfrac{365}{7.2} = 50.7 \text{ days}$$

n. Long-Term Debt Ratio $= \dfrac{\text{Total Long-Term Debt}}{\text{Total Long-Term Debt} + \text{Shareholders' Equity}}$

$$= \dfrac{\$400,000}{\$400,000 + \$525,000} = 0.43$$

o. Plant Asset Turnover Ratio $= \dfrac{\text{Revenues}}{\text{Average Plant Assets During Period}}$

$$= \dfrac{\$900,000}{\frac{1}{2}(\$700,000 + \$735,000)} = 1.25$$

p. Leverage Ratio $= \dfrac{\text{Average Total Assets During Period}}{\text{Average Common Shareholders' Equity During Period}}$

$$= \dfrac{\frac{1}{2}(\$1,150,000 + \$1,100,000)}{\frac{1}{2}(\$525,000 + \$435,000)} = 2.34$$

q. Working Capital Turnover Ratio $= \dfrac{\text{Revenues}}{\text{Average Working Capital During Period}}$

$$= \dfrac{\$900,000}{\frac{1}{2}(\$225,000 + \$115,000)} = 5.29$$

r. Gross Profit Ratio $= \dfrac{\text{Gross Profit}}{\text{Sales}} = \dfrac{\$400,000}{\$900,000} = 0.44$

2. a. Computation of Net Income for:

	Bailey	Griffin
Income Before Interest and Taxes	$400,000	$400,000
Interest Expense	(140,000)	0
Income Before Taxes	$260,000	$400,000
Tax Expense	(104,000)	(160,000)
Net Income	$156,000	$240,000

Rate of Return on Assets $= \dfrac{\text{Net Income} + \text{Interest Expense (net of income tax savings)}}{\text{Average Total Assets}}$

Bailey: $\dfrac{\$156,000 + \$84,000}{\$3,000,000} = 0.08$

Griffin: $\dfrac{\$240,000}{\$3,000,000} = 0.08$

b. Rate of Return on Common Shareholders' Equity

$$= \frac{\text{Net Income} - \text{Preferred Share Dividends}}{\text{Average Shareholders' Equity}}$$

Bailey: $\dfrac{\$156,000}{\$1,000,000} = 0.156$

Griffin: $\dfrac{\$240,000}{\$3,000,000} = 0.08$

The rate of return on assets is 8 percent for both companies. Bailey is using financial leverage to increase the return to its common shareholders. Griffin has financed its assets through common shareholders' equity and is not using any financial leverage. Bailey's return on common shareholders' equity is 15.6 percent, which is greater than the company's rate of return on assets of 8 percent.

SUGGESTED SOLUTION TO PROBLEM 1 FOR SELF-STUDY

a. Rate of return on assets $= \dfrac{\$3,000 + (1 - 0.40)(\$700)}{0.5(\$20,000 + \$24,000)} = 15.5\%$

b. Profit margin ratio $= \dfrac{\$3,000 + (1 - 0.40)(\$700)}{\$30,000} = 11.4\%$

c. Cost of goods sold to sales percentage $= \dfrac{\$18,000}{\$30,000} = 60.0\%$

d. Selling expense to sales percentage $= \dfrac{\$4,500}{\$30,000} = 15.0\%$

e. Total assets turnover $= \dfrac{\$30,000}{0.5(\$20,000 + \$24,000)} = 1.4$ times per year

f. Accounts receivable turnover $= \dfrac{\$30,000}{0.5(\$3,600 + \$4,300)} = 7.6$ times per year

g. Inventory turnover $= \dfrac{\$18,000}{0.5(\$5,600 + \$7,900)} = 2.7$ times per year

h. Plant asset turnover $= \dfrac{\$30,000}{0.5(\$9,900 + \$10,670)} = 2.9$ times per year

i. Rate of return on common shareholders' equity $= \dfrac{\$3,000 - \$100}{0.5(\$8,000 + \$11,000)} = 30.5\%$

j. Profit margin (after interest) $= \dfrac{\$3,000 - \$100}{\$30,000} = 9.7\%$

k. Leverage ratio $= \dfrac{0.5(\$20,000 + \$24,000)}{0.5(\$8,000 + \$11,000)} = 2.3$

l. Current ratio

December 31, Year 1: $\dfrac{\$10,100}{\$7,000} = 1.4{:}1$

December 31, Year 2: $\dfrac{\$13,330}{\$9,200} = 1.4{:}1$

m. Quick ratio

December 31, Year 1: $\dfrac{\$4,200}{\$7,000} = 0.6:1$

December 31, Year 2: $\dfrac{\$5,050}{\$9,200} = 0.5:1$

n. Cash flow from operations to current liabilities $= \dfrac{\$3,300}{0.5(\$7,000 + \$9,200)} = 40.7\%$

o. Working capital turnover $= \dfrac{\$30,000}{0.5(\$3,100 + \$4,130)} = 8.3$ times per year

p. Long-term debt ratio

December 31, Year 1: $\dfrac{\$4,000}{\$13,000} = 30.8\%$

December 31, Year 2: $\dfrac{\$2,800}{\$14,800} = 18.9\%$

q. Debt-equity ratio

December 31, Year 1: $\dfrac{\$11,000}{\$20,000} = 55.0\%$

December 31, Year 2: $\dfrac{\$12,000}{\$24,000} = 50.0\%$

r. Cash flow from operations to total liabilities $= \dfrac{\$3,300}{0.5(\$11,000 + \$12,000)} = 28.7\%$

s. Times interest charges earned $= \dfrac{\$3,000 + \$2,000 + \$700}{\$700} = 8.1$ times

SUGGESTED SOLUTION TO PROBLEM 2 FOR SELF-STUDY

a. Given that the profit margin (before interest expense and related tax effects) is stable over the three years, the decreasing rate of return on assets is attributable to a decreasing total assets turnover. The decreasing total assets turnover is caused primarily by a decreasing plant asset turnover (the accounts receivable turnover is stable while the inventory turnover increased). Explanations for a decreasing plant asset turnover include (1) acceleration of capital expenditures in anticipation of higher sales in the future, and (2) decreasing use of plant capacity so that depreciation expense must be covered by fewer units sold.

b. Given that the rate of return on assets is decreasing, the increasing rate of return on common shareholders' equity must be owing to increased financial leverage. The increased financial leverage is evident from the leverage ratio, as well as the percentage of interest expense to sales and the difference between the profit margin measures before and after interest expense.

c. Because the primary difference between the current and quick ratios relates to inventories, the decreasing current ratio coupled with a stable quick ratio must be caused by more efficient inventory management. This explanation is supported by the increasing inventory turnover.

d. Given the stability of the profit margin (before interest expense and related tax effects) and the accounts receivable turnover, and given the increased inventory turnover, we must look to the impact of interest expense on operating cash flows for the explanation. The increasing debt load has decreased the profit margin (after interest) and drained greater and greater amounts of cash for interest payments. These drains on operating cash flows coupled with increasing amounts of debt, particularly long-term debt, have driven the cash flow ratios down.

ASSIGNMENT MATERIAL

QUESTIONS

1. Review the meaning of the key terms listed on page 996.

2. Describe several factors that might limit the comparability of a firm's financial statement ratios over several periods.

3. Describe several factors that might limit the comparability of one firm's financial statement ratios with those of another firm in the same industry.

4. "I can understand why interest expense is added back to net income in the numerator of the rate of return on assets, but I don't see why an adjustment is made for income taxes." Provide an explanation.

5. One company president stated: "The operations of our company are such that we must turn inventory over once every four weeks." Another company president in a similar industry stated: "The operations of our company are such that we can live comfortably with a turnover of four times each year." Explain what these two company presidents probably had in mind.

6. It has been suggested that, for any given firm at a particular time, there is an optimal inventory turnover ratio. Explain.

7. Under what circumstances will the rate of return on common shareholders' equity be greater than the rate of return on assets? Under what circumstances will it be less?

8. A company president recently stated: "The operations of our company are such that we can effectively use only a small amount of financial leverage." Explain.

9. Define "financial leverage." As long as a firm's rate of return on assets exceeds its aftertax cost of borrowing, why doesn't the firm increase borrowing to as close to 100 percent of financing as possible?

10. Illustrate with amounts how a decrease in working capital can accompany an increase in the current ratio.

EXERCISES

11. *Calculation and disaggregation of rate of return on assets.* The following data are taken from the most recent annual reports of Manitoba Ltd. and Ontario Inc.

a. Calculate the rate of return on assets for each company.
b. Disaggregate the rate of return in part (a) into profit margin and total assets turnover components.
c. Comment on the relative profitability of the two companies.

	Manitoba Ltd.	Ontario Inc.
Revenues	$2,000,000	$2,400,000
Expenses Other than Interest and Income Taxes	1,700,000	2,150,000
Interest Expense	100,000	50,000
Income Tax Expense at 40 Percent	80,000	80,000
Net Income	120,000	120,000
Average Total Assets During the Year	1,500,000	1,000,000

12. **Profitability analysis for two types of retailers.** The following information is taken from the annual reports of two companies; one is a retailer of quality men's clothes and the other is a discount household goods store. Neither company had any interest-bearing debt during the year. Identify which of these companies is likely to be the clothing retailer and which is likely to be the discount store. Explain.

	Company A	Company B
Sales	$3,000,000	$3,000,000
Net Income	60,000	300,000
Average Total Assets	600,000	3,000,000

13. **Analysis of accounts receivable for two companies.** The following information relates to the activities of Quebec Corporation and N.B. Corporation for the current year.

	Quebec Corp.	N.B. Corp.
Sales on Account	$4,050,000	$2,560,000
Accounts Receivable, January 1	960,000	500,000
Accounts Receivable, December 31	840,000	780,000

a. Compute the accounts receivable turnover of each company.
b. Compute the average number of days that accounts receivable are outstanding for each company.
c. Which company is managing its accounts receivable more efficiently?

14. **Analysis of inventories over four years.** The following information relates to the activities of Carlson Corporation.

	Year 4	Year 3	Year 2	Year 1
Sales	$8,000	$5,000	$2,500	$1,000
Cost of Goods Sold	5,120	3,150	1,550	600
Average Inventory	2,050	1,170	550	200

    a. Compute the inventory turnover for each year.

    b. Compute the average number of days that inventories are held for each year.

    c. How well has Carlson Corporation been managing its inventories?

15. *Analysis of plant assets over four years.* The following information relates to Steele Limited.

	Year 4	Year 3	Year 2	Year 1
Sales	$3,000	$1,500	$800	$500
Average Plant Assets	2,630	1,290	670	400
Expenditures on Plant Assets	2,700	1,200	500	250

    a. Compute the plant asset turnover for each year.

    b. How well has Steele Limited been managing its investment in plant assets?

16. *Calculation and disaggregation of rate of return on common shareholders' equity.* The following data are taken from the financial statements of N.S. Corporation.

	Year 4	Year 3	Year 2	Year 1
Revenues	$2,750	$2,500	$2,250	$2,000
Net Income	220	200	180	160
Average Total Assets	809	694	592	500
Average Common Shareholders' Equity	1,517	1,333	1,160	1,000

    a. Calculate the rate of return on common shareholders' equity.

    b. Disaggregate the rate of return on common shareholders' equity into profit margin, total assets turnover, and leverage components.

    c. How has the profitability of N.S. Corporation changed over the four years?

17. *Profitability analysis for three companies.* The data below show five items from the financial statements for three companies for a recent year in millions of dollars.

	Company A	Company B	Company C
For Year			
Revenues	$3,438	$ 632	$3,137
Income Before Interest and Related Taxes[a]	96	303	107
Net Income to Common Shareholders[b]	77	215	27
Average During Year			
Total Assets	1,041	3,058	1,774
Common Shareholders' Equity	615	946	509

[a]*Net Income + Interest Charges × (1 − Tax Rate).*
[b]*Net Income − Preferred Stock Dividends.*

a. Compute the profit margin (after interest) ratio for each company. Which company seems to be the most successful according to this ratio?

b. How many dollars of sales on average does each of the companies make for each dollar's worth of average assets held during the year?

c. Compute the rate of return on assets for each company. Which company seems to be the most successful according to this ratio?

d. Compute the rate of return on common shareholders' equity for each company. Which company seems to be the most successful according to this ratio?

e. The three companies are a provincial utilities company, a medium-sized grocery store chain, and a huge retail chain. (Dollar amounts shown are actually in thousands.) Which of the companies corresponds to A, B, and C? What clues did you use in reaching your conclusion?

18. *Relation of profitability to financial leverage.*
    a. Compute the ratio of return on common shareholders' equity in each of the following independent cases.

Case	Total Assets	Interest-Bearing Debt	Common Shareholders' Equity	Rate of Return on Assets	Aftertax Cost of Interest-Bearing Debt
A	$200	$100	$100	6%	6%
B	$200	$100	$100	8%	6%
C	$200	$120	$ 80	8%	6%
D	$200	$100	$100	4%	6%
E	$200	$ 50	$100	6%	6%
F	$200	$ 50	$100	5%	6%

b. In which cases is leverage working to the advantage of the common shareholders?

19. *Analysis of financial leverage.* The Borrowing Co. Ltd. has total assets of $100,000 during the year. It has borrowed $20,000 at a 10 percent annual rate and pays income taxes at a rate of 40 percent of pretax income. Shareholders' equity is $80,000.

a. What must net income be for the rate of return on shareholders' equity to equal the rate of return on assets?

b. What is the rate of return on common shareholders' equity for the net income determined in part (a)?

c. What must income before interest and income taxes be to achieve this net income?

d. Repeat parts **(a)**, **(b)**, and **(c)**, assuming borrowing of $80,000 and common shareholders' equity of $20,000.

e. Compare the results from the two different debt-equity relations. What generalizations can be made?

20. *Ratio analysis of profitability and risk.* Refer to the data below for the Adelsman Co. Inc.

	Year 3	Year 2	Year 1
Rate of Return on Common Shareholders' Equity	11%	10%	8%
Earnings per Share	$4.40	$4.00	$3.00
Net Income/Total Interest Expense[a]	4	5	10
Debt-Equity Ratio (liabilities/all equities)	60%	50%	20%

[a]*Note that this computation does not represent "times interest earned," as defined in the chapter.*

The income tax rate was 40 percent in each year and 100,000 common shares were outstanding throughout the period.

a. Did the company's profitability increase over the three-year period? How can you tell? (*Hint*: Compute the rate of return on assets.)

b. Did risk increase? How can you tell?

c. Are shareholders better off in Year 3 than in Year 1?

21. *Interpreting changes in earnings per share.* A Inc. and B Ltd. both start Year 1 with $1 million of shareholders' equity and 100,000 common shares outstanding. During Year 1, both companies earn net income of $100,000, a rate of return of 10 percent on common shareholders' equity. A Inc. declares and pays $100,000 of dividends to common shareholders at the end of Year 1, whereas B Ltd. retains all of its earnings, declaring no dividends. During Year 2, both companies earn net income equal to 10 percent of shareholders' equity at the beginning of Year 2.

a. Compute earnings per share for A Inc. and for B Ltd. for Year 1 and for Year 2.

b. Compute the rate of growth in earnings per share for A Inc. and B Ltd., comparing earnings per share in Year 2 with earnings per share in Year 1.

c. Using the rate of growth in earnings per share as the criterion, determine which company's management is doing a better job for its shareholders. Comment on this result.

22. *Working backwards from profitability ratios to financial statement data.* The revenues of Lev Limited were $1,000 for the year. A financial analyst computed the following ratios for Lev Limited, using the year-end balances for balance sheet amounts. The Lev Limited has no preferred shares outstanding.

Debt-Equity Ratio (all liabilities/all equities)	73¹/₃%
Income Tax Expense as a Percentage of Pretax Income	40%
Net Income as a Percentage of Revenue	12%
Rate of Return on Common Shareholders' Equity	10%
Rate of Return on Assets	6%

From this information, compute each of the following items.
a. Interest expense
b. Income tax expense
c. Total expenses
d. Net income
e. Total assets
f. Total liabilities

23. *Effect of financing strategy on earnings per share (CMA adapted).* The Virgil Co. Ltd. is planning to invest $10 million in an expansion program that is expected to increase income before interest and taxes by $2.5 million. Currently, Virgil Co. Ltd. has total equities of $40 million, 25 percent of which is debt and 75 percent of which is shareholders' equity, represented by one million shares. The expansion can be financed with the issuance of 200,000 new shares at $50 each or by issuing long-term debt at an annual interest rate of 10 percent. The following is an excerpt from the most recent income statement.

Earnings Before Interest and Taxes	$10,500,000
Less: Interest Charges	500,000
Earnings Before Income Taxes	$10,000,000
Income Taxes (at 40 percent)	4,000,000
Net Income	$ 6,000,000

Assume that Virgil Co. Ltd. maintains its current earnings on its present assets, achieves the planned earnings from the new program, and that the tax rate remains at 40 percent.
a. What will be earnings per share if the expansion is financed with debt?
b. What will be earnings per share if the expansion is financed by issuing new shares?
c. At what level of earnings before interest and taxes will earnings per share be the same, regardless of which of the two financing programs is used?
d. At what level of earnings before interest and taxes will the rate of return on shareholders' equity be the same, regardless of which of the two financing plans is used?

24. *Relation between book and market rates of return.* Net income attributable to common shareholders' equity of Quebec Corporation during the current year was $250,000. Earnings per share were $0.50 during

the period. The average common shareholders' equity during the year was $2,500,000. The market price at year-end was $6.00.

    a. Calculate the rate of return on common shareholders' equity for the year.

    b. Calculate the rate of return currently being earned on the market price of the shares (the ratio of earnings per common share to market price per common share).

    c. Why is there a difference between the rates of return calculated in parts **(a)** and **(b)**?

25. *Calculation and interpretation of short-term liquidity ratios.* The following data are taken from the financial statements of Maloney Corporation.

For the Year	Year 4	Year 3	Year 2	
Revenues	$281	$270	$245	
Cash Flow from Operations	137	105	79	

On December 31	Year 4	Year 3	Year 2	Year 1
Quick Assets	$350	$330	$225	$200
Current Assets	455	420	375	320
Current Liabilities	350	300	250	200

    a. Compute the current and quick ratios as of December 31 of each of the Years 1 through 4.

    b. Compute the cash flow from operations to current liabilities ratio and the working capital turnover ratio for each of the Years 2 through 4.

    c. How has the short-term liquidity risk of Maloney Corporation changed over the three-year period?

26. *Calculating changes incurrent ratio and working capital.* Merchandise inventory costing $30,000 is purchased on account. Indicate the effect (increase, decrease, no effect) of this transaction on (1) working capital and (2) the current ratio, assuming that current assets and current liabilities immediately before the transaction were as follows:

    a. Current assets, $120,000; current liabilities, $120,000.

    b. Current assets, $120,000; current liabilities, $150,000.

    c. Current assets, $120,000; current liabilities, $80,000.

27. *Relation of profitability to short-term liquidity.* Following is a schedule of the current assets and current liabilities of the Lewis Company Ltd.

	December 31	
	Year 2	Year 1
Current Assets:		
Cash	$ 355,890	$ 212,790
Accounts Receivable	389,210	646,010

	Year 2	Year 1
Inventories	799,100	1,118,200
Prepayments	21,600	30,000
Total Current Assets	$1,565,800	$2,007,000
Current Liabilities:		
Accounts Payable	$ 152,760	$ 217,240
Accrued Payroll, Taxes, etc.	126,340	318,760
Notes payable	69,500	330,000
Total Current Liabilities	$ 348,600	$ 866,000

During Year 2, the Lewis Company Ltd. operated at a loss of $100,000. Depreciation expense during Year 2 was $30,000.
  a. Calculate the current ratio for each date.
  b. Calculate the amount of cash provided by operations for Year 2.
  c. Explain how the improved current ratio is possible under the Year 2 operating conditions.

28. *Calculation and interpretation of long-term liquidity ratios.* The following data are taken from the financial statements of Saskatchewan Corporation.

For the Year	Year 4	Year 3	Year 2
Net Income Before Interest and Income Taxes	$360	$325	$200
Cash Flow from Operations	184	155	115
Interest Expense	60	50	40

On December 31	Year 4	Year 3	Year 2	Year 1
Current Liabilities	$ 362	$ 304	$ 250	$ 200
Total Liabilities	1,018	822	650	500
Total Assets	1,818	1,522	1,250	1,000

  a. Compute the long-term debt ratio and the debt-equity ratio at the end of each of the Years 1 through 4.
  b. Compute the cash flow from operations to total liabilities ratio and the times interest charges earned ratio for each of the Years 2 through 4.
  c. How has the long-term liquidity risk of Saskatchewan Corporation changed over this three-year period?

29. *Effect of various transactions on financial statement ratios.* Indicate the immediate effects (increase, decrease, no effect) of each of the independent transactions below on (1) rate of return on common shareholders' equity, (2) current ratio, and (3) debt-equity ratio. State any necessary assumptions.
  a. Merchandise inventory costing $205,000 is purchased on account.
  b. Merchandise inventory costing $120,000 is sold on account for $150,000.
  c. Collections from customers on accounts receivable total $100,000.

    d. Payments to suppliers on accounts payable total $160,000.

    e. A machine costing $40,000, on which $30,000 of depreciation had been taken, is sold for $10,000.

    f. Dividends of $80,000 are declared. The dividends will be paid during the next accounting period.

    g. Common shares are issued for $75,000.

    h. A machine costing $60,000 is acquired. Cash of $10,000 is given, and a note for $50,000 payable for five years from now is signed for the balance of the purchase price.

30. *Effect of various transactions on financial statement ratios.* Indicate the effects (increase, decrease, no effect) of the independent transactions below on (1) earnings per share, (2) working capital, and (3) quick ratio, where accounts receivable are *included* but merchandise inventory is *excluded* from "quick assets." State any necessary assumptions.

    a. Merchandise inventory costing $240,000 is sold on account for $300,000.

    b. Dividends of $160,000 are declared. The dividends will be paid during the next accounting period.

    c. Merchandise inventory costing $410,000 is purchased on account.

    d. A machine costing $80,000, on which $60,000 depreciation had been taken, is sold for $20,000.

    e. Merchandise inventory purchased for cash in the amount of $7,000 is returned to the supplier because it is defective. A cash reimbursement is received.

    f. A total of 10,000 no-par-value common shares were issued on the last day of the accounting period for $15 per share. The proceeds were used to acquire the assets of another firm composed of the following: accounts receivable, $30,000; merchandise inventory, $60,000; plant and equipment, $100,000. The acquiring firm also agreed to assume current liabilities of $40,000 of the acquired company.

31. *Profitability analysis for three companies.* The following data show five items from the financial statements of three companies for a recent year.

	Company A	Company B	Company C
For Year			
Revenues	$28,947,200	$13,639,900	$9,716,900
Income Before Interest and Related Taxes[a]	4,295,800	824,600	156,400
Net Income to Common Shareholders[b]	2,915,800	522,600	148,600
Average During Year			
Total Assets	77,107,200	10,885,000	1,532,400
Common Shareholders' Equity	29,769,200	5,118,800	743,830

[a]*Net Income + Interest Expense × (1 − Tax Rate).*
[b]*Net Income − Preferred Stock Dividends.*

a. Compute the profit margin ratio (after interest) for each company. Which company seems to be the most successful according to this ratio?

b. On average, how many dollars of sales does each of the companies earn for each dollar's worth of assets held during the year?

c. Compute the rate of return on assets for each company. Which company seems to be the most successful according to this ratio?

d. Compute the rate of return on common shareholders' equity for each company. Which company seems to be the most successful according to this ratio?

e. One of the companies is a utility and the other two are in retailing. Identify the utility firm and provide rationale.

PROBLEMS AND CASES

32. *Calculations of profitability and risk ratios.* The following data are taken from the financial statements of the Press Co. Inc.:

	December	January
Current Assets	$210,000	$180,000
Noncurrent Assets	275,000	255,000
Current Liabilities	78,000	85,000
Long-Term Liabilities	75,000	30,000
Common Shares (10,000 shares)	300,000	300,000
Retained Earnings	32,000	20,000

	Operations
Net Income	$72,000
Interest Expense	3,000
Income Taxes (40 percent rate)	48,000
Cash Provided by Operations	30,970
Dividends Declared	60,000

Calculate the following ratios:
a. Rate of return on assets
b. Rate of return on common shareholders' equity
c. Earnings per common share
d. Current ratio (both months)
e. Cash flow from operations to current liabilities
f. Debt-equity ratio (both months)
g. Cash flow from operations to total liabilities
h. Times interest charges earned

33. *Calculation of profitability and risk ratios.* The comparative balance sheets, income statement, and statement of changes in financial position of the Solo Corporation for the current year are shown in Exhibits 15.14, 15.15, and 15.16.

EXHIBIT 15.14
SOLO CORPORATION
Comparative Balance Sheets

	December 31	January 1
ASSETS		
Current Assets:		
Cash	$ 3,000	$ 30,000
Accounts Receivable	55,000	20,000
Merchandise Inventory	50,000	40,000
Total Current Assets	$108,000	$ 90,000
Noncurrent Assets:		
Buildings and Equipment (cost)	$225,000	$100,000
Accumulated Depreciation	(40,000)	(30,000)
Total Noncurrent Assets	$185,000	$ 70,000
Total Assets	$293,000	$160,000
LIABILITIES AND SHAREHOLDERS' EQUITY		
Current Liabilities:		
Accounts Payable — Merchandise Suppliers	$ 50,000	$ 30,000
Accounts Payable — Other Suppliers	12,000	10,000
Salaries Payable	6,000	5,000
Total Current Liabilities	$ 68,000	$ 45,000
Noncurrent Liabilities:		
Bonds Payable	100,000	0
Total Liabilities	$168,000	$ 45,000
Shareholders' Equity:		
Common Shares ($10 par value)	$100,000	$100,000
Retained Earnings	25,000	15,000
Total Shareholders' Equity	$125,000	$115,000
Total Liabilities plus Shareholders' Equity	$293,000	$160,000

EXHIBIT 15.15
SOLO CORPORATION
Income Statement for the Current Year

Sales		$125,000
Less: Cost of Goods Sold		60,000
Gross Profit		$ 65,000
Less: Operating Expenses		
Salaries	$19,667	
Depreciation	10,000	29,667
Operating Profit		$ 35,333
Less: Interest Expense		2,000
Net Income before Income Tax		$ 33,333
Income Tax Expense		13,333
Net Income		$ 20,000

EXHIBIT 15.16
SOLO CORPORATION
Statement of Changes in Financial Position
for the Current Year

Cash Provided by	
Operations	
Net Income	$ 20,000
Additions:	
Depreciation Expense	10,000
Increase in Accounts Payable:	
Merchandise Suppliers	20,000
Other Suppliers	2,000
Increase in Salaries Payable	1,000
Subtractions:	
Increase in Accounts Receivable	(35,000)
Increase in Merchandise Inventory	(10,000)
Cash Provided by Operations	$ 8,000
Financing Activities	
Proceeds from Long-Term Bonds Issued	100,000
Total Sources of Cash	$108,000
Cash Applied to	
Dividends	$ 10,000
Investing Activities	
Acquisition of Buildings and Equipment	125,000
Total Uses of Cash	$135,000
Net Decrease in Cash During the Year	$ 27,000

    a. Calculate the ratios listed in Exhibit 15.10 in the chapter for Solo Corporation for the current year. You may omit expense ratios. Balance sheet ratios are to be computed at the end of the year.

    b. Was Solo Corporation successfully leveraged during the current year?

    c. Assume that the bonds were issued on November 1. At what annual interest rate were the bonds apparently issued?

    d. If Solo Corporation earns the same rate of return on assets next year as it realized this year, and issues no more debt, will the firm be successfully leveraged next year?

34. *Calculation of profitability and risk ratios.* Comparative balance sheets, income statement, and statement of changes in financial position of Nykerk Electronics Corporation for the current year are presented in Exhibits 15.17, 15.18, and 15.19, respectively.

    a. Calculate the ratios listed in Exhibit 15.10 for Nykerk Electronics Corporation for the current year. You may omit expense ratios. Balance sheet ratios are to be computed at the end of the year.

    b. Was Nykerk Electronics Corporation successfully leveraged during the year?

EXHIBIT 15.17
NYKERK ELECTRONICS CORPORATION
Comparative Balance Sheets

	(thousands of dollars)	
	December 31	January 1
ASSETS		
Current Assets:		
Cash	$ 1,600	$ 1,400
Accounts Receivable (net)	2,600	2,500
Inventories	7,300	6,900
Total Current Assets	$11,500	$10,800
Noncurrent Assets:		
Plant and Equipment	$ 5,200	$ 4,500
Less: Accumulated Depreciation	(1,300)	(1,000)
Net Plant and Equipment	$ 3,900	$ 3,500
Land	1,200	1,200
Total Noncurrent Assets	5,100	4,700
Total Assets	$16,600	$15,500
LIABILITIES AND SHAREHOLDERS' EQUITY		
Current Liabilities:		
Accounts Payable	$ 1,600	$ 1,700
Accrued Payables	800	900
Income Taxes Payable	300	200
Notes Payable	1,900	1,200
Total Current Liabilities	$ 4,600	$ 4,000
Long-Term Liabilities:		
Bonds Payable (8 percent)	$ 2,000	$ 2,100
Mortgage Payable	200	200
Total Long-Term Liabilities	$ 2,200	$ 2,300
Total Liabilities	$ 6,800	$ 6,300
Shareholders' Equity:		
Preferred Shares (6 percent, $100 par)	$ 2,000	$ 2,000
Common Shares ($1 par)	3,000	3,000
Total Contributed Capital	$ 5,000	$ 5,000
Retained Earnings	4,800	4,200
Total Shareholders' Equity	$ 9,800	$ 9,200
Total Liabilities and Shareholders' Equity	$16,600	$15,500

EXHIBIT 15.18
NYKERK ELECTRONICS CORPORATION
**Statement of Income and Retained Earnings
for the Current Year**

	(thousands of dollars)
Sales	$26,500
Less: Sales Allowance, Returns, and Discounts	600
Net Sales	$25,900
Less: Cost of Goods Sold	20,500
Gross Profit	$ 5,400

EXHIBIT 15.18 (continued)

	(thousands of dollars)	
Less: Operating Expenses		
Selling Expenses	$2,120	
Administrative Expenses	1,000	
Depreciation	300	3,420
Operating Profit		$ 1,980
Financial Income:		
Interest Income	$ 200	
Less: Interest Expense	180	20
Net Income Before Income Tax		$ 2,000
Income Tax Expense		800
Net Income		$ 1,200
Retained Earnings, January 1		4,200
		$ 5,400
Less: Dividends Paid		
On Preferred Shares	$ 120	
On Common Shares	480	600
Retained Earnings, December 31		$ 4,800

EXHIBIT 15.19
NYKERK ELECTRONICS CORPORATION
Statement of Changes in Financial Position
for the Current Year

	(thousands of dollars)
Cash Provided by	
Operations	
Net Income	$1,200
Additions:	
Depreciation Expense	300
Increase in Income Taxes Payable	100
Subtractions:	
Increase in Accounts Receivable	(100)
Increase in Inventories	(400)
Decrease in Accounts Payable	(100)
Decrease in Accrued Payables	(100)
Cash Provided by Operations	$ 900
Financing Activities	
New Financing by Bank Note	700
Total Sources of Cash	$1,600
Cash Applied to	
Dividend on Preferred Shares	$ 120
Dividend on Common Shares	480
Investing Activities	
Purchase of Plant and Equipment	700
Financing Activities	
Redemption of Bonds Payable	100
Total Uses of Cash	$1,400
Increase in Cash for the Year	$ 200

35. *Analysis of profitability and risk for two companies.* Exhibits 15.20 and 15.21 present the income statements and balance sheets of Toronto Corporation and Regina Corporation.

Cash flow provided by operations was $600,000 for Toronto Corporation and $550,000 for Regina Corporation.

Assume that the balances in asset and equity accounts at year-end approximate the average balances during the period. The income tax rate is 40 percent. On the basis of this information, which company is:

a. More profitable?

b. Less risky in terms of short-term liquidity?

c. Less risky in terms of long-term liquidity?

Use financial ratios, as appropriate, in your analysis.

EXHIBIT 15.20
Income Statements for the Current Year

	Toronto Corp.	Regina Corp.
Sales	$4,300,000	$3,000,000
Less: Cost of Goods Sold	2,800,000	1,400,000
Gross Profit	$1,500,000	$1,600,000
Less: Selling and Administrative Expenses	330,000	580,000
Operating Profit	$1,170,000	$1,020,000
Interest Expense	100,000	200,000
Net Income Before Income Tax	$1,070,000	$ 820,000
Income Tax Expense	428,000	328,000
Net Income	$ 642,000	$ 492,000

EXHIBIT 15.21
Balance Sheets December 31

	Toronto Corp.	Regina Corp.
ASSETS		
Cash	$ 100,000	$ 50,000
Accounts Receivable (net)	700,000	400,000
Merchandise Inventory	1,200,000	750,000
Plant and Equipment (net)	4,000,000	4,800,000
Total Assets	$6,000,000	$6,000,000
LIABILITIES AND SHAREHOLDERS' EQUITY		
Accounts Payable	$ 572,000	$ 172,000
Income Taxes Payable	428,000	328,000
Long-Term Bonds Payable (10 percent)	1,000,000	2,000,000
Common Shares	2,000,000	2,000,000
Retained Earnings	2,000,000	1,500,000
Total Liabilities and Shareholders' Equity	$6,000,000	$6,000,000

36. *Detective analysis: identify company.* In this problem, you become a financial analyst/detective. The condensed financial statements in Exhibit 15.22 are constructed on a percentage basis. In all cases, total sales revenues are shown as 100.00%. All other numbers were divided by sales revenue for the year. The thirteen companies (all corporations except for the accounting firm) shown here represent the industries listed on page 1026.

EXHIBIT 15.22
Data for Ratio Detective Exercise

| | Company Numbers | | | | | | |
	(1)	(2)	(3)	(4)	(5)	(6)	(7)
Balance Sheet at End of Year							
Current Receivables	0.31%	29.11%	6.81%	25.25%	3.45%	38.78%	17.64%
Inventories	7.80	0.00	3.14	0.00	6.45	14.94	20.57
Net Plant and Equipment	8.50	9.63	11.13	19.88	49.87	15.59	37.60
All Other Assets	2.16	7.02	25.59	32.93	24.05	15.54	30.07
Total Assets	18.77%	45.76%	46.67%	78.06%	83.82%	84.85%	105.88%
Cost of Plant and Equipment (gross)	14.64%	14.80%	19.57%	29.03%	79.03%	24.80%	59.73%
Current Liabilities	6.08%	9.82%	6.41%	17.49%	14.83%	35.28%	27.68%
Long-Term Liabilities	2.12	7.96	0.00	0.00	0.00	8.33	1.33
Shareholders' Equity	10.58	27.98	40.25	60.57	69.00	41.24	76.86
Total Equities	18.78%	45.76%	46.66%	78.06%	83.83%	84.85%	105.87%
Income Statement for Year							
Revenues	100.00%	100.00%	100.00%	100.00%	100.00%	100.00%	100.00%
Cost of Goods Sold (excluding depreciation) or Operating Expenses[a]	78.97	53.77	48.21	59.07	68.62	60.88	33.29
Depreciation	1.04	1.39	1.72	2.07	4.07	1.09	3.02
Interest Expense	0.16	0.52	0.00	0.08	0.02	1.35	0.73
Advertising Expense	3.72	0.00	11.43	0.06	4.39	2.93	2.28
Research and Development Expense	0.00	1.00	0.00	0.00	0.15	0.00	9.06
Income Taxes	1.28	0.53	9.59	6.52	7.87	3.78	8.55
All Other Items (net)	13.34	18.88	18.58	24.52	6.40	24.39	27.66
Total Expenses	98.51%	76.09%	89.53%	92.32%	91.52%	94.42%	84.59%
Net Income	1.50%	23.92%	10.47%	7.68%	8.49%	5.59%	15.41%

| | Company Numbers | | | | | |
	(8)	(9)	(10)	(11)	(12)	(13)
Balance Sheet at End of Year						
Current Receivables	12.94%	9.16%	25.18%	27.07%	13.10%	653.94%
Inventories	15.47	56.89	79.53	0.00	1.62	0.00
Net Plant and Equipment	70.29	28.36	19.22	2.64	251.62	2.88
All Other Assets	18.37	26.42	24.72	223.91	23.68	200.37
Total Assets	117.07%	120.83%	148.65%	253.62%	290.02%	857.19%
Cost of Plant and Equipment (gross)	167.16%	42.40%	35.08%	4.45%	320.90%	3.81%
Current Liabilities	19.37%	33.01%	20.42%	161.37%	28.01%	377.56%
Long-Term Liabilities	20.62	34.07	36.09	10.62	115.50	280.79
Shareholders' Equity	77.09	53.74	92.13	81.63	146.51	198.83
Total Equities	117.08%	120.82%	148.64%	253.62%	290.02%	857.18%

EXHIBIT 15.22 (continued)

	Company Numbers					
	(8)	(9)	(10)	(11)	(12)	(13)
Income Statement for Year						
Revenues	100.00%	100.00%	100.00%	100.00%	100.00%	100.00%
Cost of Goods Sold (excluding depreciation) or Operating Expenses[a]	81.92	57.35	42.92	82.61	45.23	47.69
Depreciation	5.81	1.90	1.97	0.05	14.55	0.00
Interest Expense	1.23	2.69	3.11	1.07	7.15	24.33
Advertising Expense	0.00	6.93	13.04	0.00	0.00	0.00
Research and Development Expense	0.76	0.00	0.00	0.00	0.71	0.00
Income Taxes	2.15	7.47	10.63	3.92	8.73	12.89
All Other Items (net)	3.81	14.82	17.99	2.97	11.51	−5.57
Total Expenses	95.68%	91.16%	89.66%	90.62%	87.88%	79.34%
Net Income	4.32%	8.84%	10.34%	9.38%	12.11%	20.65%

[a]Represents operating expenses for the following companies: Advertising/public opinion survey firm, insurance company, finance company, and the public accounting partnership.

a. Advertising and public opinion survey firm
b. Beer brewery
c. Department store chain (which carries its own receivables)
d. Distiller of hard liquor
e. Drug manufacturer
f. Finance company (lends money to consumers)
g. Grocery store chain
h. Insurance company
i. Manufacturer of tobacco products, mainly cigarettes
j. Public accounting (CA) partnership
k. Soft drink bottler
l. Steel manufacturer
m. Utility company

Use whatever clues you can to match the companies in Exhibit 15.22 with the industries listed above. You may find it useful to refer to average industry ratios compiled by Dun & Bradstreet. Copies of this document can be found in most libraries.

37. *Interpretation of ratio analysis.* Exhibit 15.23 presents a ratio analysis for Sarwark Limited.
   a. What is the likely explanation for the stable rate of return on assets coupled with the decreasing rate of return on common shareholders' equity?
   b. What is the likely reason for the increasing plant asset turnover?

38. *Interpretation of ratio analysis.* Exhibit 15.24 presents a ratio analysis for Widdicombe Corporation for Year 1 through Year 3.
   a. What is the likely explanation for the increasing rate of return on assets coupled with the decreasing rate of return on shareholders' equity?
   b. How effectively has the firm been managing its inventories?
   c. What is the likely explanation for the increasing total assets turnover?

EXHIBIT 15.23
Ratio Analysis for Sarwark Limited

	Year 3	Year 2	Year 1
Rate of Return on Assets	9.9%	10.2%	10.1%
Profit Margin (before interest and related tax effects)	9.6%	10.0%	11.9%
Total Assets Turnover	1.03	1.02	0.85
Cost of Goods Sold/Revenues	73.8%	73.9%	72.4%
Selling and Administrative/Revenues	10.5%	10.4%	10.5%
Interest Expense/Revenues	4.0%	3.5%	2.1%
Income Tax Expense/Revenues	3.8%	4.1%	4.2%
Accounts Receivable Turnover	4.6	4.7	4.6
Inventory Turnover	3.7	3.6	3.7
Plant Asset Turnover	1.7	1.5	1.2
Rate of Return on Common Shareholders' Equity	14.7%	15.2%	15.5%

	Year 3	Year 2	Year 1
Current Ratio	1.2:1	1.4:1	1.6:1
Quick Ratio	0.5:1	0.7:1	0.9:1
Total Liabilities/Total Liabilities and Shareholders' Equity	60.0%	48.0%	42.0%
Long-Term Liabilities/Total Liabilities and Shareholders' Equity	25.0%	26.0%	25.0%
Revenues as Percentage of Year 1 Revenues	130%	115%	100%
Assets as Percentage of Year 1 Assets	125%	113%	100%
Capital Expenditures as Percentage of Year 1 Capital Expenditures	120%	112%	100%

EXHIBIT 15.24
Ratio Analysis for Widdicombe Corporation

	Year 3	Year 2	Year 1
Rate of Return on Assets	12%	11%	10%
Profit Margin (before interest and related taxes)	14%	16%	18%
Total Asset Turnover	0.86	0.69	0.56
Cost of Goods Sold/Revenues	65%	63%	62%
Selling and Administrative/Revenues	10%	10%	8%
Interest Expense/Revenues	8%	12%	16%
Income Tax Expense/Revenues	7%	5%	4%
Accounts Receivable Turnover	2.4	2.5	2.6
Inventory Turnover	2.5	2.8	3.2
Fixed Asset Turnover	0.7	0.5	0.3
Rate of Return on Common Shareholders' Equity	14%	16%	18%
Profit Margin (after interest)	10%	10%	10%
Asset Turnover	0.86	0.69	0.56
Leverage Ratio	1.6	2.3	3.2
Revenues as Percentage of Year 1 Revenues	99%	102%	100%
Assets as Percentage of Year 1 Assets	105%	104%	100%
Net Income as Percentage of Year 1 Net Income	99%	102%	100%
Capital Expenditures as Percentage of Year 1 Capital Expenditures	85%	90%	100%

39. *Case analysis of bankruptcy.*   On October 2, 1975, W.T. Grant Company filed for bankruptcy. At that time, it reported assets of $1.02 billion and liabilities of $1.03 billion. The company had operated at a profit for most years before 1974, but it reported an operating loss of $177 million for its fiscal year January 31, 1974, to January 31, 1975.

   The accompanying Exhibits 15.25 through 15.28 contain:

1. Balance sheets, income statements, and statements of cash flows for W.T. Grant Company for the 1971 through 1975 fiscal periods.

2. Additional financial information about W.T. Grant Company, the retail industry, and the economy for the same period.

Prepare an analysis that explains the major causes of Grant's collapse. Assume an income tax rate of 48 percent.

EXHIBIT 15.25
W.T. GRANT COMPANY
Comparative Balance Sheet

	January 31				
	1971	1972	1973	1974	1975
Assets					
Cash and Marketable Securities	$ 34,009	$ 49,851	$ 30,943	$ 45,951	$ 79,642
Accounts Receivable	419,731	477,324	542,751	598,799	431,201
Inventories	260,492	298,676	399,533	450,637	407,357
Other Current Assets	5,246	5,378	6,649	7,299	6,581
Total Current Assets	$719,478	$831,299	$ 979,876	$1,102,686	$ 942,781
Investments	23,936	32,367	35,581	45,451	49,764
Capital Assets (net)	61,832	77,173	91,420	100,984	101,932
Other Assets	2,382	3,901	3,821	3,862	5,790
Total Assets	$807,628	$944,670	$1,110,698	$1,252,983	$1,082,267
Equities					
Short-Term Debt	$246,420	$237,741	$ 390,034	$ 453,097	$ 600,695
Accounts Payable	118,091	124,990	112,896	103,910	147,211
Current Deferred Taxes	94,489	112,846	130,137	133,057	2,000
Total Current Liabilities	$459,000	$475,577	$ 633,067	$ 690,064	$ 749,906
Long-Term Debt	32,301	128,432	126,672	220,336	216,341
Noncurrent Deferred Taxes	8,518	9,664	11,926	14,649	—
Other Long-Term Liabilities	5,773	5,252	4,694	4,195	2,183
Total Liabilities	$505,592	$618,925	$ 776,359	$ 929,244	$ 968,430
Preferred Stock	$ 9,600	$ 9,053	$ 8,600	$ 7,465	$ 7,465
Common Stock	18,180	18,529	18,588	18,599	18,599
Contributed Surplus	78,116	85,195	86,146	85,910	83,914
Retained Earnings	230,435	244,508	261,154	248,461	37,674
Total	$336,331	$357,285	$ 374,488	$ 360,435	$ 147,652
Less: Cost of Treasury Stock	(34,295)	(31,540)	(40,149)	(36,696)	(33,815)
Total Shareholders' Equity	$302,036	$325,745	$ 334,339	$ 323,739	$ 113,837
Total Equities	$807,628	$944,670	$1,110,698	$1,252,983	$1,082,267

EXHIBIT 15.26
W.T. GRANT COMPANY
Statement of Income and Retained Earnings

	Years Ended January 31				
	1971	**1972**	**1973**	**1974**	**1975**
Sales	$1,254,131	$1,374,811	$1,644,747	$1,849,802	$1,761,952
Concessions	4,986	3,439	3,753	3,971	4,238
Equity in Earnings	2,777	2,383	5,116	4,651	3,086
Other Income	2,874	3,102	1,188	3,063	3,376
Total Revenues	$1,264,768	$1,383,735	$1,654,804	$1,861,487	$1,772,652
Cost of Goods Sold	$ 843,192	$ 931,237	$1,125,261	$1,282,945	$1,303,267
Selling, General, and Administration	329,768	373,816	444,377	518,280	540,953
Interest	18,874	16,452	21,127	51,047	199,238
Taxes: Current	21,140	13,487	9,588	(6,021)	(19,439)
Deferred	11,660	13,013	16,162	6,807	(98,027)
Other Expenses	557	518	502	—	24,000
Total Expenses	$1,225,191	$1,348,523	$1,617,017	$1,853,058	$1,949,992
Net Income	$ 39,577	$ 35,212	$ 37,787	$ 8,429	$ (177,340)
Dividends	(20,821)	(21,139)	(21,141)	(21,122)	(4,457)
Other	—	—	—	—	(28,990)
Change in Retained Earnings	$ 18,756	$ 14,073	$ 16,646	$ (12,693)	(210,787)
Retained Earnings — Beginning of Period	211,679	230,435	244,508	261,154	248,461
Retained Earnings — End of Period	$ 230,435	$ 244,508	$ 261,154	$ 248,461	$ 37,674

EXHIBIT 15.27
W.T. GRANT COMPANY
Statement of Changes in Financial Position

	Years Ended January 31				
	1971	**1972**	**1973**	**1974**	**1975**
Cash Provided by Financing Activities					
New Financing:					
Short-Term Bank Borrowing	$ 64,288	—	$ 152,293	$ 63,063	$ 147,898
Issue of Long-Term Debt	—	$ 100,000	—	100,000	—
Sale of Common Stock:					
To Employees	5,218	7,715	3,492	2,584	886
On Open Market	—	2,229	174	260	—
Other Sources (net)	—	—	2,307	—	—
Total Sources of Cash	$ 69,506	$ 109,944	$ 158,266	$ 165,907	$ 148,784
Cash Applied to Operations:					
Net Income	$ 39,577	$ 35,212	$ 37,787	$ 8,429	$(177,340)
Additions:					
Depreciation and Other	9,619	10,577	12,004	13,579	14,587
Decrease in Accounts Receivable	—	—	—	—	121,351
Decrease in Inventories	—	—	—	—	43,280
Increase in Accounts Payable	13,947	6,900	—	—	42,028
Increase in Deferred Taxes	14,046	18,357	17,291	2,920	—
Subtractions:					
Equity in Earnings and Other	(2,470)	(1,758)	(1,699)	(1,344)	(16,993)
Increase in Accounts Receivable	(51,464)	(57,593)	(65,427)	(56,047)	—
Increase in Inventories	(38,365)	(38,184)	(100,857)	(51,104)	—
Increase in Prepayments	(209)	(428)	(1,271)	(651)	(11,032)
Decrease in Accounts Payable	—	—	(12,093)	(8,987)	—
Decrease in Deferred Taxes	—	—	—	—	(101,078)
Cash Used by Operations	$ 15,319	$ 26,917	$ 114,265	$ 93,205	$ 85,197

EXHIBIT 15.27 (continued)

			Years Ended January 31		
	1971	1972	1973	1974	1975
Financing Activities					
Reduction in Financing:					
Repayment of Short-Term Borrowing (net)	—	$ 8,680	—	—	—
Retirement of Long-Term Debt	$ 1,538	5,143	$ 1,760	$ 6,336	$ 3,995
Reacquisition of Preferred Stock	948	308	252	618	—
Reacquisition of Common Stock	13,224	—	11,466	133	—
Dividends	20,821	21,138	21,141	21,122	4,457
Total for Reductions in Financing	$ 36,531	$ 35,269	$ 34,619	$ 28,209	$ 8,452
Investing Activities					
Investments in Noncurrent Assets:					
Capital Assets	$ 16,141	$ 25,918	$ 26,250	$ 23,143	$ 15,535
Investments in Securities	436	5,951	2,040	5,700	5,182
Total for Investments	$ 16,577	$ 31,869	$ 28,290	$ 28,843	$ 20,717
Other Uses (net)	$ 47	$ 47	—	642	$ 727
Total Uses of Cash	$ 68,474	$ 94,102	$ 177,174	$ 150,899	$ 115,093
Increase (decrease) in Cash	$ 1,032	$ 15,842	$ (18,908)	$ 15,008	$ 33,691

EXHIBIT 15.28
Additional Information

			Fiscal Years Ending January 31		
	1971	1972	1973	1974	1975
W.T. GRANT COMPANY					
Range of Stock Price, Dollar per Share[a]	41⅞–70⅝	34¾–48¾	9⅞–44⅜	9⅝–41	1½–12
Earnings per Share in Dollars	$2.64	$2.25	$2.49	$0.76	$(12.74)
Dividends per Share in Dollars	$1.50	$1.50	$1.50	$1.50	$0.30
Number of Stores	1,116	1,168	1,208	1,189	1,152
Total Store Area, Thousands of Square Feet	38,157	44,718	50,619	53,719	54,770

	1970	1971	1972	1973	1974
RETAIL INDUSTRY[b]					
Total Chain Store Industry Sales in Millions of Dollars	$6,969	$6,972	$7,498	$8,212	$8,714

	1970	1971	1972	1973	1974
AGGREGATE ECONOMY[c]					
Gross National Product in Billions of Dollars	$1,075.3	$1,107.5	$1,171.1	$1,233.4	$1,210
Bank Short-Term Lending Rate	8.48%	6.32%	5.82%	8.30%	11.28%

[a]*Source:* Standard and Poor's Stock Reports.
[b]*Source:* Standard Industry Surveys.
[c]*Source:* Survey of Current Business.

DECISION CASE 15-1

In February Year 6, the president of Alba Ltd. is preparing for a meeting of the finance committee of the board of directors to discuss the financial plans of the company for the coming year. He wants to continue to expand the company's activities, but will need more funds provided for the purpose from outside the company. He has asked you to play the role of representative of the financial community to evaluate the attached financial statements of the company for the four preceding years. He would like you, in turn, to represent the views of a bank credit officer considering an expansion of the loan to the company, an investment manager of an insurance company considering a purchase of the company's bonds, and a stock broker advising his clients who are present or potential shareholders of the company.

ALBA LTD.
Comparative Balance Sheets
December 31, Year 2 to Year 5

	(thousands of dollars)			
	Year 5	Year 4	Year 3	Year 2
ASSETS				
Current Assets:				
Cash	$ 48	$ 29	$ 21	$ 212
Accounts Receivable	882	709	601	541
Inventories	2,903	1,183	789	578
Total Current Assets	$3,833	$1,921	$1,411	$1,331
Capital Assets:	$4,917	$3,884	$2,853	$2,491
Less: Accumulated Depreciation	(1,915)	(1,643)	(1,472)	(1,499)
Net Capital Assets	$3,002	$2,241	$1,381	$ 992
Total	$6,835	$4,162	$2,792	$2,323
LIABILITIES AND SHAREHOLDERS' EQUITY				
Current Liabilities:				
Bank Loan	$1,609	$ 518	$ 386	$ 238
Trade Accounts Payable	974	471	272	184
Other Liabilities	146	79	39	17
Total Current Liabilities	$2,729	$1,068	$ 697	$ 439
Long-Term Debt	2,542	1,558	702	526
Total Liabilities	$5,271	$2,626	$1,399	$ 965
Shareholders' Equity:				
Common Share Capital	$1,000	$1,000	$1,000	$1,000
Retained Earnings	564	536	393	358
Total Shareholders' Equity	$1,564	$1,536	$1,393	$1,358
Total	$6,835	$4,162	$2,792	$2,323

ALBA LTD.
Comparative Income Statements
For the Years Ended December 31, Year 2 to Year 5

	(thousands of dollars)			
	Year 5	Year 4	Year 3	Year 2
Sales	$9,658	$7,853	$6,647	$5,942
Less: Cost of Sales	5,796	4,709	3,991	3,560
Gross Profit	$3,862	$3,144	$2,656	$2,382
Expenses	3,329	2,621	2,158	1,918
	$ 533	$ 523	$ 498	$ 464
Interest	479	248	104	83
Net Income Before Income Tax	$ 54	$ 275	$ 394	$ 381
Income Tax (48 percent)	26	132	189	183
Net Income	$ 28	$ 143	$ 205	$ 198
Deduct Dividends Paid	—	—	170	160
Increase in Retained Earnings	$ 28	$ 143	$ 35	$ 38

Prepare calculations and notes that you would take to the meeting with the president.

Do you think that any of the above members of the financial community would be willing to provide funds to the company? If not, what do you recommend the company should do during the next few years?

DECISION CASE 15-2

Western Printers had operated a commercial printing business in Vancouver since it was founded by P.R. Robson several years ago. Robson suffered a heart attack in July Year 3 and retired from active interest in the business, delegating complete responsibility to Phil Grange, who had joined the company in Year 1. A month ago, Robson died, and willed the majority interest in the company to his son, Barry, who is currently completing his final year studying philosophy at university. Barry Robson has approached you to advise him whether Grange has been performing in a competent fashion and should be retained or replaced.

Barry Robson has with him condensed financial statements of the company for the past few years and, for the same period, comparative data for the printing industry. A review of these statements leads you to the conclusion that the financial statements for Year 5 and Year 6 attached are representative of the financial statements of both the company and the industry for the past few years.

Condensed Income Statement
For Year Ended December 31, Year 6

	Western Printers Ltd. (thousands)	Total Industry (millions)
Sales	$212.2	$237.5
Cost of Sales	141.1	160.6
Gross Profit	$ 71.1	$ 76.9
Selling and Administrative Expenses	53.3	61.1
Operating Income	$ 17.8	$ 15.8
Interest Paid	$ 3.1	$ 1.5
Less: Interest and Dividends Received	0.3	0.6
Net Interest Expense	$ 2.8	$ 0.9
Net Income Before Income Tax	$ 15.0	$ 14.9
Income Tax	4.4	4.4
Net Income	$ 10.6	$ 10.5
Dividends	2.7	4.4
Addition to Retained Earnings	$ 7.9	$ 6.1

1. From the information available, advise Barry Robson whether he should retain Phil Grange as manager of the company, look for a replacement, or make some modification of these alternatives.

2. List the four most important additional pieces of financial information that you would consider necessary to confirm these impressions.

Condensed Balance Sheet
For Years Ended December 31, Year 5 and Year 6

	Western Printers Ltd. (thousands)		Total Industry (millions)	
	Year 6	Year 5	Year 6	Year 5
ASSETS				
Current Assets:				
Cash	$ 30	$ 24	$ 7	$ 11
Temporary Investments (at market value)	11	9	9	9
Accounts Receivable	34	30	36	40
Inventory	26	20	29	24
	$101	$ 83	$ 81	$ 84
Land	$ 3	$ 3	$ 4	$ 5
Buildings	$111	$109	$136	$122
Less: Accumulated Depreciation	(64)	(56)	(74)	(66)
	$ 47	$ 53	$ 62	$ 56
Total	$151	$139	$147	$145
LIABILITIES AND SHAREHOLDERS' EQUITY				
Current Liabilities:				
Bank Loan	$ 18	$ 18	$ 9	$ 11
Accounts Payable	7	7	18	16
Due to Finance Companies	18	14	1	3
Taxes Payable	4	4	5	5
	$ 47	$ 43	$ 33	$ 35
Mortgages	—	—	12	14
	$ 47	$ 43	$ 45	$ 49
Shareholders' Equity:				
Share Capital	$ 30	$ 30	$ 32	$ 32
Retained Earnings	74	66	70	64
Total Shareholders' Equity	$104	$ 96	$102	$ 96
Total	$151	$139	$147	$145

COMPOUND INTEREST CONCEPTS AND APPLICATIONS

Money is a scarce resource that its owner can use to command other resources. Like owners of other scarce resources, owners of money can permit borrowers to rent the use of their money for a period of time. Payment for the use of money differs little from other rental payments, such as those made to a landlord for the use of property or to a car rental agency for the use of a car. Payment for the use of money is called *interest*. Accounting is concerned with interest because it must record transactions in which the use of money is bought and sold.

Accountants and managers are concerned with interest calculations for another, equally important, reason. Expenditures for an asset most often do not occur at the same time as the receipts for services produced by that asset. Money received sooner is more valuable than money received later. The difference in timing can affect whether or not acquiring an asset is profitable. Amounts of money received at different times are different commodities. Managers use interest calculations to make amounts of money to be paid or received at different times comparable. For example, an analyst might compare two amounts to be received at two different times by using interest calculations to find the equivalent value of one amount at the time the other is due.

Contracts involving a series of money payments over time, such as bonds, mortgages, notes, and leases, are evaluated by finding the *present value* of the stream of payments. The present value of a stream of payments is a single amount of money at the present time that is the economic equivalent of the entire stream.

COMPOUND INTEREST CONCEPTS

The quotation of interest "cost" is typically specified as a percentage of the amount borrowed per unit of time. Examples are 12 percent per year and 1 percent per month, which are not the same. Another example occurs in the context of discounts on purchases. The terms of sale "2/10, net/30" is equivalent to 2 percent for twenty days because, if the discount is not taken, payment can be delayed and the money can be used for up to an extra 20 (= 30 − 10) days.

The amount borrowed or loaned is called the **principal**. To "compound" interest means that the amount of interest earned during a period is added to the principal and the principal for the next interest period is larger.

For example, if you deposit $1,000 in a savings account that pays **compound interest** at the rate of 6 percent per year, you will earn $60 by the end of one year. If you do not withdraw the $60, then $1,060 will be earning interest during the second year. During the second year, your principal of $1,060 will earn $63.60 interest: $60 on the initial deposit of $1,000 and $3.60 on the $60 earned the first year. By the end of the second year, you will have $1,123.60.

When only the original principal earns interest during the entire life of the loan, the interest due at the time the loan is repaid is called **simple interest**. In simple interest calculations, interest on previously earned interest is ignored.[1] The use of simple interest calculations in accounting arises in the following way. If you borrow $10,000 at a rate of 12 percent per year, but compute interest for any month as $100 ($= \$10,000 \times 0.12 \times \frac{1}{12}$), you are using a simple interest calculation. Nearly all economic calculations involve compound interest.

The "force," or effect, of compound interest is more substantial than many people realize. For example, compounded annually at 8 percent, money "doubles itself" in less than nine years. Put another way, if you invest $100 at 8 percent compounded annually, you will have $200 in nine years.

Problems involving compound interest generally fall into two groups with respect to time: first, there are the problems for which we want to know the future value of money invested or loaned today; second, there are the problems for which we want to know the present value, or today's value, of money to be received or paid at later dates. In addition, the accountant must sometimes compute the interest rate implicit in certain payment streams, and determine identical combined payments of principal and interest to repay a debt over a specified period.

principal
An amount on which interest is charged or earned.

compound interest
Interest calculated on principal plus previously undistributed interest.

simple interest
Interest calculated on principal where interest earned during periods before maturity of the loan is neither added to the principal nor paid to the lender. Interest = Principal $\times$ Interest rate $\times$ Time.

FUTURE VALUE

If $1.00 is invested today at 12 percent compounded annually, it will grow to $1.12000 at the end of one year, $1.25440 at the end of two years, $1.40493 at the end of three years, and so on according to the formula

$$F_n = P(1 + r)^n$$

where
F_n represents the accumulation of future value,
P represents the one-time investment today,
r is the interest rate per period, and
n is the number of periods from today.

The amount F_n is the future value of the present payment, P, compounded at r percent per period for n periods. Table B.1, page 1066, shows the future

---

[1] If interest earned may be withdrawn, then compounded interest techniques are relevant. The withdrawn interest can be invested elsewhere to earn additional interest

values of $P = \$1$ for various numbers of periods and for various interest rates. Extracts from that table are shown here in Table A.1.

TABLE A.1 (Excerpt from Table B.1)
Future value of \$1 at 6 percent and 12 percent per period
$F_n = P(1 + r)^n$

Number of Periods = n	Rate = r	
	6%	12%
1	1.06000	1.12000
2	1.12360	1.25440
3	1.19102	1.40493
10	1.79085	3.10585
20	3.20714	9.64629

SAMPLE PROBLEMS IN COMPUTING FUTURE VALUE

Example 1 How much will $1,000 deposited today at 6 percent compounded annually be worth ten years from now?

One dollar deposited today at 6 percent will grow to $1.79085; therefore, $1,000 will grow to $1,000(1.06)^{10} = \$1,000 \times 1.79085 = \$1,790.85$

Example 2 Macaulay Corporation deposits $10,000 in an expansion fund today. The fund will earn 12 percent per year. How much will the $10,000 grow to in twenty years if the entire fund and all interest earned on it are left on deposit in the fund?

One dollar deposited today at 12 percent will grow to $9.64629 in twenty years. Therefore, $10,000 will grow to $96,463 (= \$10,000 \times 9.64629$) in twenty years.

PRESENT VALUE

The preceding section developed the tools for computing the future value, F_n, of a sum of money, P, deposited or invested today. P is known; F_n is calculated. This section deals with the problems of calculating how much principal, P, has to be invested today in order to have a specified amount, F_n, at the end of n periods. The future amount, F_n, the interest rate, r, and the number of periods, n, are known; P is to be found. In order to have $1 one year from today when interest is earned at 6 percent, P of $0.94340 must be invested today. That is, $F^1 = P(1.06)^1$ or $\$1 = \$0.94340 \times 1.06$. Because $F_n = P(1 + 4)^n$, dividing both sides of the equation by $(1 + r)^n$ yields:

$$\frac{F_n}{(1 + r)^n} = P$$

or

$$P = \frac{F_n}{(1 + r)^n} = F_n(1 + r)^{-n}$$

PRESENT VALUE TERMINOLOGY

The number $(1 + r)^{-n}$ is the present value of \$1 to be received after n periods when interest is earned at r percent per period. The term **discount** is used in this context as follows: The **discounted present value** of \$1 to be received n periods in the future is $(1 + r)^{-n}$ when the **discount rate** is r percent per period for n periods. The number r is the discount *rate* and the number
$(1 + r)^{-n}$ is the discount *factor* for n periods. A discount factor $(1 + r)^{-n}$ is merely the reciprocal, or inverse, of a number, $(1 + r)^n$, in Table A.1. Therefore, tables of discount factors are not necessary for present value calculations if tables of future values are at hand, and vice versa. But present value calculations are so frequently needed that tables of discount factors are as widely available as tables of future values. Portions of Table B.2 (page 1067), which shows discount factors or, equivalently, present values of \$1 for various numbers of periods, appear in Table A.2.

TABLE A.2 (Excerpt from Table B.2)
Present value of \$1 at 6 percent and 12 percent per period
$P_n = F(1 + r)^{-n}$

Number of Periods = n	Rate = r	
	6%	12%
1	.94340	.89286
2	.89000	.79719
3	.83962	.71178
10	.55839	.32197
20	.31180	.10367

SAMPLE PROBLEMS IN DETERMINING PRESENT VALUES

Example 3 What is the present value of \$1 due ten years from now if the interest (equivalently, the discount) rate r is 6 percent per year?

From Table A.2, 6 percent column, ten-period row, the present value of \$1 to be received ten periods hence at 6 percent is \$0.55839.

Example 4 (This example is used in Chapter 10.) You issue a noninterest-bearing note that promises to pay \$16,000 three years from today in exchange for used equipment. How much is that promise worth today if the discount rate appropriate for such notes is 12 percent per period?

One dollar received three years hence discounted at 12 percent has a present value of \$0.71178. Thus, the promise is worth $\$16,000 \times 0.71178 = \$11,388$.

CHANGING THE COMPOUNDING PERIOD — NOMINAL AND EFFECTIVE RATES

"Twelve percent, compounded annually" is the price for a loan; this means that interest is added to or *converted* into principal once a year at the rate

---

discount
In the context of compound interest, bonds, and notes, the difference between face or future value and present value of a payment. In the context of sales and purchases, a reduction in price granted for prompt payment.

discounted present value
Using present value techniques to adjust future cash flows to their monetary equivalent today by recognizing the time value of money.

discount rate
Interest rate used to convert future payments to present value.

of 12 percent. Often, however, the price for a loan states that compounding is to take place more than once a year. A bank may advertise that it pays 6 percent, compounded quarterly. This means that, at the end of each quarter, the bank credits savings accounts with interest calculated at the rate 1.5 percent (= 6 percent/4). The interest payment can be withdrawn or left on deposit to earn more interest.

If $10,000 is invested today at 12 percent compounded annually, its future value one year later is $11,200. If the rate of interest is stated as 12 percent compounded semiannually, 6 percent interest is added to the principal every six months. At the end of the first six months, $10,000 will have grown to $10,600, so that the accumulation will be $10,600 × 1.06 = $11,236 by the end of the year. Notice that 12 percent compounded *semiannually* is equivalent to 12.36 percent compounded *annually*.

Suppose that the price is quoted as 12 percent, compounded quarterly. Then, an additional 3 percent of the principal will be added to, or converted into, principal every three months. By the end of the year, $10,000 will grow to $10,000 × $(1.03)^4$ = $10,000 × 1.12551 = $11,255. Twelve percent compounded quarterly is equivalent to 12.55 percent compounded annually. If 12 percent is compounded monthly, $1 will grow to $1 × $(1.01)^{12}$ = $1.12683, and $10,000 will grow to $11,268. Thus, 12 percent compounded monthly is equivalent to 12.68 percent compounded annually.

For a given **nominal rate**, such as the 12 percent in the examples above, the more often interest is compounded or converted into principal, the higher the **effective rate** of interest is paid. If a nominal rate, r, is compounded m times per year, the effective rate is $1 + r/m)^m - 1$.

In practice, to solve problems that require computation of interest quoted at a nominal rate of r percent per period compounded m times per period for n periods, merely use the tables for the rate r/m and $m × n$ periods. For example, 12 percent compounded quarterly for five years is equivalent to the rate found in the interest tables for r = 12/4 = 3 percent for $m ×$ n = 4 × 5 = 20 periods.

Some banks advertise that they compound interest daily or even continuously. The mathematics of calculus provides a mechanism for finding the effective rate when interest is compounded continuously. If interest is compounded continuously at nominal rate r per year, the effective annual interest rate is $e^r - 1$, where e is the base of the natural logarithms. Tables of values of e^r are widely available.[2] Six percent per year compounded continuously is equivalent to 6.1837 percent compounded annually; 12 percent per year compounded continuously is equivalent to 12.75 percent compounded annually. Do not confuse the **compounding period** with the payment period. Some banks, for example, compound interest daily but pay interest quarterly.

SAMPLE PROBLEMS IN CHANGING THE COMPOUNDING PERIOD

Example 5   What is the future value five years hence of $600 invested at 12 percent compounded semiannually?

---

[2] See, for example, Sidney Davidson and Roman L. Weil, eds., *Handbook of Modern Accounting*, 3rd ed. (New York: McGraw-Hill Book Company, 1983), chap. 9, Exhibit 1.

---

nominal rate
The annual rate of interest payable on a bond. This rate is stated on the bond agreement.

effective rate
The current rate of interest in the market for a bond or note receivable. When issued, the bond or note is priced to yield the market rate of interest at date of issuance.

compounding period
The time period for which interest is calculated. At the end of the period, the interest may be paid to the lender or added (that is, converted) to principal for the next interest-earning period, which is usually a year or some portion of a year.

Twelve percent compounded two times per year for five years is equivalent to 6 percent per period compounded for ten periods. Table A.1 shows the value of $F_{10} = (1.06)^{10}$ to be 1.79085. Six hundred dollars, then, would grow to $600 \times 1.79085 = \$1,074.51$.

Example 6   How much money must be invested today at 12 percent compounded semiannually in order to have \$10,000 ten years from today?

Twelve percent compounded two times a year for ten years is equivalent to 6 percent per period compounded for twenty periods. The *present* value (Table A.2) of \$1 received twenty periods hence at 6 percent per period is \$0.31180. That is, \$0.31180 invested today for twenty periods at an interest rate of 6 percent per period will grow to \$1. To have \$10,000 in twenty periods (ten years), \$3,118 (= \$10,000 $\times$ \$0.31180) must be invested today.

Example 7   A local department store offers its customers credit and advertises its interest rate at 18 percent per year, compounded monthly at the rate of $1\frac{1}{2}$ percent per month. What is the effective annual interest rate?

One-and-one-half percent per month for 12 months is equivalent to $(1.015)^{12} - 1 = 19.562$ percent per year. See Table B.1 (page 1066), twelve-period row, $1\frac{1}{2}$ percent column, where the factor is 1.19562.

Example 8   If prices increased at the rate of 6 percent during each of two consecutive six-month periods, how much did prices increase during the entire year?

If a price index is 100.00 at the start of the year, it will be 100.00 $\times$ $(1.06)^2$ = 112.36 at the end of the year. The price change for the entire year is $(112.36/100.00) - 1 = 12.36$ percent.

ANNUITIES

An *annuity* is a series of equal payments made at the beginning or end of equal periods of time. Examples of annuities include monthly rental payments, semiannual corporate bond coupon (or interest) payments, and annual payments to a lessor under a lease contract. Armed with an understanding of the tables for future and present values, you can solve any annuity problem. Annuities arise so often, however, and their solution is so tedious without special tables that annuity problems warrant special study and the use of special tables.

TERMINOLOGY FOR ANNUITIES

The terminology used for annuities can be confusing because not all writers use the same terms. Definitions of the terms used in this text follow.

An annuity whose payments occur at the *end* of each period is called an **ordinary annuity** or an *annuity in arrears*. Semiannual corporate bond coupon payments are usually paid in arrears; that is, the first payment does not occur until after the bond has been outstanding for six months.

An annuity whose payments occur at the *beginning* of each period is called an **annuity due** or an *annuity in advance*. Rent is usually paid in advance, so that a series of rental payments is an annuity due.

ordinary annuity
An annuity whose payments occur at the end of each period.

annuity due
An annuity whose first payment is made at the start of period 1 (or at the end of period 0). Contrast with ordinary annuity.

deferred annuity
An annuity whose first payment is made sometime after the end of the first period.

perpetuities
An annuity whose payments continue forever. The present value of a perpetuity in arrears is p/r, where p is the periodic payment and r is the interest rate per period.

time line
A horizontal line labelled with dates and cash flows constructed for the purpose of clarifying the relationship between the two for an annuity.

A **deferred annuity** is one whose first payment is at some time later than the end of the first period.

Annuities can be paid forever. Such annuities are called **perpetuities**. A perpetuity can be in arrears or in advance. The only difference between the two is the timing of the first payment.

Annuities can be confusing. Their study is made easier with a **time line**, such as the one shown below.

	$30	$30	$30	$30	$30	$30
End of Period	0	1	2	3	4	5	6 ↑

A time line marks the end of each period, numbers the periods, shows the payments to be received or paid, and shows the time at which the annuity is valued. The time line above represents an ordinary annuity (in arrears) for six periods of $30 to be valued at the end of period 6. The end of period 0 is "now." The first payment is to be received or paid one period from now.

ORDINARY ANNUITIES (ANNUITIES IN ARREARS)

The future values of ordinary annuities are shown in Table B.3 (page 1068), portions of which Table A.3 reproduces.

TABLE A.3 (Excerpt from Table B.3)
Future value of an ordinary annuity of $1 at 6 percent and 12 percent

$$F_A = \frac{[(1 + r)^n - 1]}{r}$$

Number of	Rate = r	
Periods = n	6%	12%
1	1.00000	1.00000
2	2.06000	2.12000
3	3.18360	3.37440
5	5.63709	6.35285
10	13.18079	17.54874
20	36.78559	72.05244

Consider an ordinary annuity for three periods at 6 percent. The time line for the future value of such an annuity is:

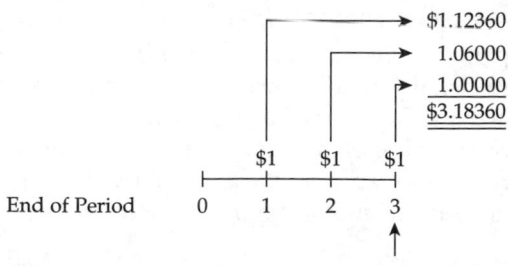

	$1	$1	$1
End of Period	0	1	2	3 ↑

The $1 received at the end of the first period earns interest for two periods, so it is worth $1.2360 at the end of period 3. (See Table A.1.) The $1 received at the end of the second period grows to $1.06 by the end of period 3, and the $1 received at the end of period 3 is, of course, worth $1 at the end of period 3. The entire annuity is worth $3.18360 at the end of period 3. This is the amount shown in Table A.3 for the future value of an ordinary annuity for three periods at 6 percent. The future value of an ordinary annuity is calculated as follows:

$$\begin{array}{c}\text{Future Value of}\\\text{Ordinary}\\\text{Annuity}\end{array} = \begin{array}{c}\text{Periodic}\\\text{Payment}\end{array} \times \begin{array}{c}\text{Factor for the Future}\\\text{Value of an Ordinary}\\\text{Annuity of \$1}\end{array}$$

Thus,

$$\$3.18360 = \$1 \times 3.18360$$

Table B.4 (page 1069) shows the present value of ordinary annuities. Table A.4 reproduces excerpts from Table B.4.

TABLE A.4 (Excerpt from Table B.4)
Present value of an ordinary annuity of $1 per period at 6 percent and 12 percent

$$P_A = \frac{[1 - (1 + r)^{-n}]}{r}$$

Number of Periods = n	Rate = r	
	6%	12%
1	.94340	.89286
2	1.83339	1.69005
3	2.67301	2.40183
5	4.21236	3.60478
10	7.36009	5.65022
20	11.46992	7.46944

The time line for the present value of an ordinary annuity of $1 per period for three periods, discounted at 6 percent, is:

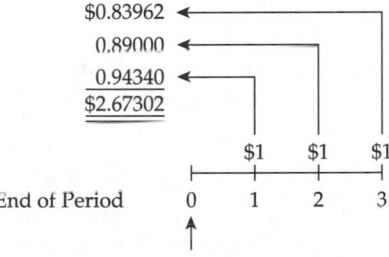

The $1 to be received at the end of period 1 has a present value of $0.94340, the $1 to be received at the end of period 2 has a present value of $0.89000, and the dollar to be received at the end of the third period has a present value of $0.83962. Each of these numbers comes from Table A.2. The present value of the annuity is the sum of these individual present values, $2.67302, shown in Table A.4 as 2.67301 (our calculation differs beause of rounding).

The present value of an ordinary annuity for n periods is the sum of the present value of $1 received one period from now plus the present value of $1 received two periods from now, and so on until we add on the present value of $1 received n periods from now. The present value of an ordinary annuity is calculated as follows:

$$
\begin{array}{c}
\text{Present Value} \\
\text{of an} \\
\text{Ordinary Annuity}
\end{array}
=
\begin{array}{c}
\text{Periodic} \\
\text{Payment}
\end{array}
\times
\begin{array}{c}
\text{Factor for the} \\
\text{Present Value of} \\
\text{an Ordinary Annuity} \\
\text{of \$1}
\end{array}
$$

Thus,

$$\$2.67302 \quad = \quad \$1 \quad \times \quad 2.67302$$

SAMPLE PROBLEMS INVOLVING ORDINARY ANNUITIES

Example 9 An individual plans to invest $1,000 at the end of each of the next ten years in a savings account. The savings account accumulates interest of 12 percent compounded annually. What will be the balance in the savings account at the end of ten years?

The time line for this problem is:

The symbol x denotes the amount to be calculated. Table A.3 indicates that the factor for the future value of an annuity at 12 percent for ten periods is 17.54874. Thus,

$$
\begin{array}{c}
\text{Future Value} \\
\text{of an} \\
\text{Ordinary Annuity}
\end{array}
=
\begin{array}{c}
\text{Periodic} \\
\text{Payment}
\end{array}
\times
\begin{array}{c}
\text{Factor for the Future} \\
\text{Value of an Ordinary} \\
\text{Annuity of \$1}
\end{array}
$$

$$x \quad = \quad \$1,000 \quad \times \quad 17.54874$$

$$x \quad = \quad \$17,549$$

Example 10 An individual wishes to receive $60 every six months, starting six months hence, for the next five years. How much must be invested today in a savings account if the interest rate on the savings account is 12 percent compounded semiannually?

The time line is:

The factor from Table A.4 for the present value of an annuity at 6 percent (= 12 percent per year/2 semiannual periods per year) for 10 (= 2 periods per year × 5 years) periods is 7.36009. Thus,

$$
\begin{matrix}
\text{Present Value} \\
\text{of an} \\
\text{Ordinary Annuity}
\end{matrix}
=
\begin{matrix}
\text{Periodic} \\
\text{Payment}
\end{matrix}
\times
\begin{matrix}
\text{Factor for the} \\
\text{Present Value of an} \\
\text{Ordinary Annuity of \$1}
\end{matrix}
$$

$$x = \$60 \times 7.36009$$
$$x = \$441.61$$

If \$441.61 is invested today, the principal plus interest compounded on the principal will provide sufficient funds so that \$60 can be withdrawn every six months for the next five years.

Example 11   (Western Co. Ltd. mortgage example, from Chapter 9.) A company borrows \$125,000 from a bank. The interest rate on the loan is 12 percent compounded semiannually. The company agrees to repay the loan in equal semiannual installments over the next five years. The first payment is to be made six months from now. What is the amount of the required semiannual payment?

The time line is:

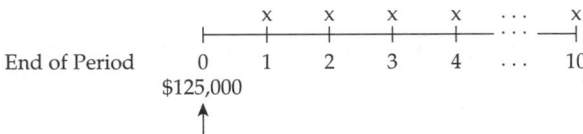

This problem is similar to Example 10 because both involve periodic payments in the future that are discounted to today. In Example 10, the periodic payments were given and the present value was computed. In Example 11, the present value is given and the periodic payment is computed. Table A.4 indicates that the present value of annuity at 6 percent (= 12 percent per year/2 semiannual periods per year) for 10 (= 2 periods per year × 5 years) periods is 7.36009. Thus,

$$
\begin{matrix}
\text{Present Value} \\
\text{of an} \\
\text{Ordinary Annuity}
\end{matrix}
=
\begin{matrix}
\text{Periodic} \\
\text{Payment}
\end{matrix}
\times
\begin{matrix}
\text{Factor for the} \\
\text{Present Value of an} \\
\text{Ordinary Annuity of \$1}
\end{matrix}
$$

$$\$125,000 = x \times 7.36009$$
$$x = \frac{\$125,000}{7.36009}$$
$$x = \$16,983$$

Because the periodic payment is being calculated, the present value amount of \$125,000 must be divided by the present value factor. (You may wish to turn to Exhibit 9.1, page 556, to study the amortization table for this loan. The amount of each semiannual payment shown here is \$17,000 rather than \$16,983, but the last payment is less than \$17,000.)

Example 12   (Myers Inc. lease example, from Chapter 10.) A company signs a lease acquiring the right to use property for three years. Lease payments of $19,709 are to be made annually at the end of this and the next two years. The discount, or interest, rate is 15 percent per year. What is the present value of the lease payments?

The time line is:

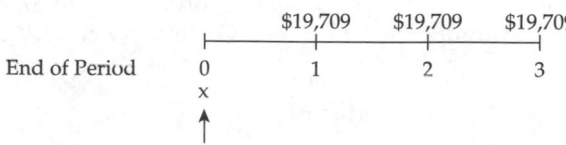

The factor from Table B.4 for the present value of an annuity at 15 percent for three periods is 2.28323. Thus,

$$
\begin{array}{ccc}
\text{Present Value} & & \text{Factor for the} \\
\text{of an} & = \text{Periodic} \times & \text{Present Value} \\
\text{Ordinary Annuity} & \text{Payment} & \text{of an Ordinary} \\
& & \text{Annuity of \$1}
\end{array}
$$

$$x = \$19{,}709 \times 2.28323$$

$$x = \$45{,}000$$

In the Myers Inc. example in Chapter 10, the cost of the equipment is given at $45,000 and the periodic rental payment is computed with an annuity factor. Thus,

$$
\begin{array}{ccc}
\text{Present Value} & & \text{Factor for the} \\
\text{of an} & = \text{Periodic} \times & \text{Present Value of} \\
\text{Ordinary Annuity} & \text{Payment} & \text{an Annuity of} \\
& & \$1
\end{array}
$$

$$\$45{,}000 = x \times 2.28323$$

$$x = \frac{\$45{,}000}{2.28323}$$

$$x = \$19{,}709$$

Example 13 (Pension funding example.) A company is obligated to make annual payments to a pension fund at the end of the next 30 years. The present value of those payments is to be $100,000. What must the annual payment be if the fund is projected to earn interest at the rate of 8 percent per year?

This time line is:

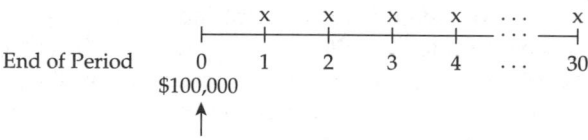

Table B.4 indicates that the factor for the present value of $1 paid at the end of the next 30 periods at 8 percent per period is 11.25778. Thus,

$$\begin{array}{ccc} \text{Present Value} \\ \text{of an} \\ \text{Ordinary Annuity} \end{array} = \begin{array}{c} \text{Periodic} \\ \text{Payment} \end{array} \times \begin{array}{c} \text{Factor for the} \\ \text{Present Value of an} \\ \text{Ordinary Annuity of \$1} \end{array}$$

$$\$100,000 = x \times 11.25778$$

$$x = \frac{\$100,000}{11.25778}$$

$$x = \$8,883$$

Example 14 Mr. Mason is 62 years old. He wishes to invest equal amounts on his sixty-third, sixty-fourth, and sixty-fifth birthdays so that, starting on his sixty-sixth birthday, he can withdraw $5,000 on each birthday for ten years. His investments will earn 8 percent per year. How much should be invested on the sixty-third through sixty-fifth birthdays?

The time line for this problem is:

		x	x	x	–$5,000	–$5,000	⋯	–$5,000
End of Year	62	63	64	65	66	67	⋯	75

On his sixty-fifth birthday, Mr. Mason needs to have accumulated a fund equal to the present value of an annuity of $5,000 per period for ten periods, discounted at 8 percent per period. The factor from Table B.4 for 8 percent and ten periods is 6.71008. Thus,

$$\begin{array}{ccc} \text{Present Value} \\ \text{of an} \\ \text{Ordinary Annuity} \end{array} = \begin{array}{c} \text{Periodic} \\ \text{Payment} \end{array} \times \begin{array}{c} \text{Factor for the} \\ \text{Present Value of an} \\ \text{Ordinary Annuity of \$1} \end{array}$$

$$x = \$5,000 \times 6.71008$$

$$x = \$33,550$$

The time line now appears as follows:

				$33,550				
		x	x	x	–$5,000	–$5,000	⋯	–$5,000
End of Year	62	63	64	65	66	67	⋯	75

The question now becomes: How much must be invested on Mr. Mason's sixty-third, sixty-fourth, and sixty-fifth birthdays to accumulate to a fund of $33,550 on his sixty-fifth birthday? The factor for the future value of an annuity for three periods at 8 percent is 3.24640. Thus,

$$\begin{array}{ccc} \text{Future Value} \\ \text{of an} \\ \text{Ordinary Annuity} \end{array} = \begin{array}{c} \text{Periodic} \\ \text{Payment} \end{array} \times \begin{array}{c} \text{Factor for the} \\ \text{Future Value of an} \\ \text{Ordinary Annuity of \$1} \end{array}$$

$$\$33,550 = x \times 3.24640$$

$$x = \frac{\$33,550}{3.24640}$$

$$x = \$10,335$$

In the solution above, all calculations are expressed in terms of equivalent amounts on Mr. Mason's sixty-fifth birthday. That is, the present value of an annuity of $5,000 per period for ten periods at 8 percent is equal to the future value of an annuity of $10,335 per period for three periods at 8 percent and both of these amounts are equal to $33,550. The problem could have been worked through by selecting any specific date between Mr. Mason's sixty-second and seventy-fifth birthdays.

One possibility is to express all calculations in terms of equivalent amounts on Mr. Mason's sixty-second birthday. To solve the problem in this way, first find the present value on Mr. Mason's *sixty-fifth* birthday of an annuity of $5,000 per period for ten periods ($33,550 = $5,000 × 6.71008). Discount $33,550 back three periods using Table B.2 for the present value of $1 ($26,633 = $33,550 × 0.79383). The result is the present value of the payments to be made to Mr. Mason *measured as of his sixty-second birthday*. Then find the amounts that must be invested by Mr. Mason on his sixty-third, sixty-fourth, and sixty-fifth birthdays that have a *present value* on his sixty-second birthday equal to $26,633. The calculation is as follows:

$$\begin{array}{ccc} \text{Present Value} & & \text{Factor for the} \\ \text{of an} & = \dfrac{\text{Periodic}}{\text{Payment}} \times & \text{Present Value of an} \\ \text{Ordinary Annuity} & & \text{Ordinary Annuity of \$1} \end{array}$$

$$\$26{,}633 = x \times 2.57710$$

$$x = \$10{,}335$$

The amount $10,335 is the same as that found above.

PERPETUITIES

A periodic payment to be received forever is called a *perpetuity*. Future values of perpetuities are undefined. If $1 is to be received at the end of every period and the discount rate is r percent, the present value of the perpetuity is $\$1/r$. This expression can be derived with algebra or by observing what happens in the expression for the present value of an ordinary annuity of $\$A$ per payment as n, the number of payments, approaches infinity:

$$P_A = \frac{A[1 - (1 + r)^{-n}]}{r}$$

As n approaches infinity, $(1 + r)^{-n}$ approaches zero, so that P_A approaches $A(1/r)$. If the first payment of the perpetuity occurs now, the present value is $A[1 + 1/r]$.

EXAMPLES OF PERPETUITIES

Example 15 The Canadian government offers to pay $30 every six months forever in the form of a perpetual bond. What is that bond worth if the discount rate is 15 percent compounded semiannually?

Fifteen percent compounded semiannually is equivalent to 7.5 percent per six-month period. If the first payment occurs six months from now, the present value is $30/0.075 = 400. If the first payment occurs today, the present value is $30 + $400 = 430.

Example 16 Every two years, Ms. Young gives $10,000 to a university to provide a scholarship for an entering student in a two-year business administration course. If the university credits 6 percent per year to its investment accounts, how much must Ms. Young give to the university to provide such a scholarship every two years forever, starting two years hence?

A perpetuity in arrears assumes one payment at the end of each period. Here, the period is two years; 6 percent compounded once a year over two years is equivalent to a rate of $(1.06)^2 - 1 = 0.12360$, or 12.36 percent compounded once per two-year period. Consequently, the present value of the perpetuity paid in arrears every two years is $80,906 (= $10,000/ 0.12360). A gift of $80,906 will be sufficient to provide a $10,000 scholarship forever. If the first scholarship is to be awarded now, the gift must be $90,906 (= $80,906 + $10,000).

IMPLICIT INTEREST RATES — FINDING INTERNAL RATES OF RETURN

In the preceding examples, given the interest rate and stated cash payments, a future value or a present value was computed. Or, the required payments were computed given their known future value or their known present value. In some calculations, the present or future value and the periodic payments are known; the implicit interest rate is to be found. For example, Chapter 10 illustrates a case in which the cash price of some equipment is known to be $10,520 and the asset was acquired using a note. The note is noninterest-bearing, has a face value of $16,000, and matures in three years. In order to compute interest expense over the three-year period, the implicit interest rate must be found. The time line for this problem is:

$$
\begin{array}{ccccc}
+\$10,520 & 0 & 0 & -\$16,000 \\
\vdash & + & + & \dashv \\
\text{End of Year} \quad 0 & 1 & 2 & 3
\end{array}
$$

The implicit interest rate is r, such that:

(I)
$$\$10,520 = \frac{\$16,000}{(1 + r)^3}$$

(II)
$$0 = \$10,520 - \frac{\$16,000}{(1 + r)^3}$$

That is, the present value of $16,000 discounted three periods at r percent per period is $10,520. The present value of all current and future cash flows nets to zero when future flows are discounted at r per period. In general, the only way to find such an r is a trial-and-error procedure. In a case where r appears only in one term, as here, r can be found analytically. Here, $r = (\$16,000/\$10,520)^{1/3} - 1 = 0.1507 = 15.1$ percent.

The general procedure is called "finding the internal rate of return" or "finding the implicit interest rate" of a series of cash flows. The **internal rate of return** of a series of cash flows is the discount rate that equates the net present value of that series of cash flows to zero. The steps in finding the internal rate of return are as follows:

1. Make an educated guess, called the "trial rate," at the internal rate of return. If you have no idea what to guess, try zero.

2. Calculate the present value of all the cash flows (including the one at the end of the Year 0).

3. If the present value of the cash flows is zero, stop. The current trial rate is the internal rate of return.

4. If the amount found in step 2 is less than zero, try a larger interest rate as the trial rate and go back to step 2.

5. If the amount found in step 2 is greater than zero, try a smaller interest rate as the new trial rate and go back to step 2.

The iterations below illustrate the process for the example in equation (II).

Iteration Number	Trial Rate $= r$	Net Present Value: Right-Hand Side of (II)
1	0.0%	($5,500)
2	10.0	(1,521)
3	15.0	(20)
4	15.5	116
5	15.2	34
6	15.1	7

With a trial rate of 15.1 percent, the right-hand side is close enough to zero so that 15.1 percent can be used as the implicit interest rate. Continued iterations would find trial rates even closer to the true rate, which is about 15.0739 percent.

Finding the internal rate of return for a series of cash flows can be tedious and should not be attempted unless one has at least a calculator. An exponential feature, the feature that allows the computation of $(1 + r)$ raised to various powers, helps.[3]

SAMPLE PROBLEM INVOLVING IMPLICIT INTEREST RATES

Example 17   The Alexis Co. Inc. acquires a machine with a cash price of $10,500. It pays for the machine by giving a note promising to make payments equal to 7 percent of the face value, $840, at the end of each of the next three years and a single payment of $12,000 in three years. What is the implicit interest rate in the loan?

---

[3] There are ways to guess the trial rate that will approximate the true rate in fewer iterations than the method described here. If you want to find internal rates of return efficiently with successive trial rates, refer to a mathematical reference book to learn about the "Newton search" method, sometimes called the "method of false position."

The time line for this problem is:

	$10,500	–$840	–$840	–$12,840
End of Period	0	1	2	3

The implicit interest rate is r, such that:[4]

(III) $$\$10,500 = \frac{\$840}{(1 + r)} + \frac{\$840}{(1 + r)^2} + \frac{\$12,840}{(1 + r)^3}$$

The internal rate of return, to the nearest tenth of 1 percent, is found to be 12.2 percent:

Iteration Number	Trial Rate	Right-Hand Side of (III)
1	7.0%	$12,000
2	15.0	9,808
3	11.0	10,827
4	13.0	10,300
5	12.0	10,559
6	12.5	10,428
7	12.3	10,480
8	12.2	10,506
9	12.1	10,532

SUMMARY

Accountants typically deal with four kinds of compound interest problems: those involving the present or future value of a single payment or of a series of payments. In working through annuity problems, you will find drawing a line helpful in deciding which particular kind of annuity is involved.

KEY TERMS

Principal
Compound interest
Simple interest
Discount
Discounted present value
Discount rate
Nominal rate
Effective rate

Compounding period
Ordinary annuity
Annuity due
Deferred annuity
Perpetuities
Time line
Internal rate of return

[4] Compare this formulation to that in equation (I), above. Note that the left-hand side is zero in one case but not in the other. The left-hand side can be either a nonzero number or zero, depending on what seems convenient for the particular context.

SELF-STUDY MATERIAL

This section contains questions, exercises, and problems to help you assess your understanding of Appendix A. Careful review of this material will assist you in completing the homework assignments. Solutions are found at the end of the section.

QUESTIONS AND EXERCISES

True/False

For each statement, place a T or an F in the space provided to indicate whether the statement is true or false.

_____ 1. The future amount of an annuity increases if the compounding period is changed from a semiannual to a quarterly basis.

_____ 2. For a given instrument, the higher the interest rate, the lower the future amount.

_____ 3. If a company invests $20,000 for five years with interest at 8 percent compounded annually, the amount of interest earned each year will increase.

_____ 4. The lower the interest rate, the lower the future amount of a present value.

_____ 5. The future value of a single payment increases if the period of compounding is changed from a semiannual to a quarterly basis.

_____ 6. The amount of simple interest earned each period on an amount invested at interest rate, r, increases over time.

_____ 7. With the same rate of annual interest, a semiannual compounding procedure will result in a larger future amount than will a quarterly compounding procedure.

_____ 8. The present value of a single amount decreases as the rate of discount decreases.

_____ 9. The higher the interest rate, the lower the present value of a future amount

_____ 10. Grady Inc. invested funds in a savings account that earns interest at a rate of 8 percent, compounded quarterly. The interest rate, therefore, is 12 percent per quarter.

_____ 11. For a given future amount and a given interest rate, r, the shorter the period of discounting, the higher the present value.

_____ 12. An annuity with payments at the beginning of each period is called an "annuity due."

Matching

From the list of terms, select one term that is most closely associated with one descriptive phrase or statement that follows and place the letter for that term in the space provided.

a. annuity due
b. compound interest
c. deferred annuity
d. future value of a single sum
e. interest
f. internal rate of return

g. ordinary annuity
h. perpetuity
i. present value of a single sum
j. principal
k. simple interest

_____ 1. A periodic payment to be received forever.

_____ 2. Interest is computed on the principal and on any interest computed previously that has not been paid.

_____ 3. An annuity with a first payment at some time later than the end of the first period.

_____ 4. An annuity with payments occurring at the beginning of each period.

_____ 5. The discount rate that equates the net present value of a series of cash flows to zero.

_____ 6. Interest is computed on the amount of the principal only.

_____ 7. $P = F_n(1 + r)^{-n}$

_____ 8. Payment for the use of money.

_____ 9. Amount borrowed or loaned.

_____ 10. $F_n = P(1 + r)^{-n}$

_____ 11. An annuity with payments occurring at the end of each period.

Multiple Choice

Choose the best answer for each question or problem and enter the identifying letter in the space provided.

_____ 1. Cliff Howadel inherited $5,000 from his uncle. He plans to invest the money in a note that earns 20 percent annually. When the note matures in ten years, how much money (rounded to the nearest dollar) will Howadel receive?
  a) $129,793
  b) $20,962
  c) $30,950
  d) none of the above

_____ 2. Ron Ward is planning an extended vacation when he graduates from school. If he can invest his money and it earns 8 percent compounded quarterly, what amount (rounded to the nearest dollar) should be invested now in order for the investment to grow to $6,000 in four years?
  a) $4,410
  b) $8,237
  c) $4,371
  d) none of the above

_____ 3. On January 1, 19X1, Welde Limited purchased a machine and gave in exchange a three-year, noninterest-bearing note for $20,000. Assuming that the appropriate rate of interest for such a note is 12 percent, the present value of the note (rounded to the nearest dollar) on January 1, 19X1 is:
  a) $12,800
  b) $14,236
  c) $15,200
  d) none of the above

_____ 4. Robbins Company Inc. purchased an annuity that will pay the company $1,000 every quarter forever. If the discount rate is 9 percent compounded quarterly, what did Robbins pay (rounded to the nearest dollar) for this annuity?
  a) $44,444
  b) $11,111
  c) $61,111
  d) none of the above

_____ 5. Claire Peoples invested $60,000 in a savings account on January 1, 19X1. The investment will earn 10 percent. Peoples wants to treat the investment as an annuity and withdraw funds at the end of each year for eight years. The amount she can withdraw each year (rounded to the nearest dollar) is:
a) $8,942
b) $5,247
c) $11,247
d) $16,077

_____ 6. Rudolphe Company Ltd. enters into a lease contract and agrees to pay $5,000 at the beginning of each year for five years. This is an example of:
a) a deferred annuity
b) an ordinary annuity
c) an annuity in arrears
d) an annuity due

_____ 7. On January 1, 19X1, Mitzie Co. Ltd. purchased some farm land and agreed to make annual payments of $2,000 each December 31 for the next fifteen years. If the appropriate interest rate is 5 percent, at what amount (rounded to the nearest dollar) should the land be recorded on the books of Mitzie?
a) $37,198
b) $20,759
c) $30,000
d) none of the above

_____ 8. On January 1, 19X1, Maggard Inc. borrowed $567 and signed a five-year note for $1,000. The appropriate interest rate is 12 percent. How much interest expense (rounded to the nearest dollar) on this note should Maggard report for 19X1?
a) $120
b) $68
c) $87
d) none of the above

_____ 9. The Glorions Company Ltd. has a $10,000 debt, which will come due in five years. The company wants to make a series of five payments at the end of each of the next five years in an amount such that $10,000 will have accumulated to pay the debt when it matures. Assuming an interest rate of 10 percent, determine the amount (rounded to the nearest dollar) of each of the five payments.
a) $2,638
b) $1,638
c) $1,295
d) none of the above

_____ 10. The Anderson Company Inc. has $50,000 to invest. One investment will yield returns of $3,000 each year for four years. The $50,000 investment will be returned at the end of the fourth year. An alternative investment will yield returns as follows: Year 1: $7,000; Years 2 and 3: $2,000; and Year 4: $1,000. The alternative investment will also return the $50,000 investment at the end of the fourth year. Which investment would be more profitable?
a) the first investment
b) the alternative investment
c) the two are equally profitable because each promises a return of $12,000
d) none of the above

___ 11. Gill Corp. issued on January 1 a $100,000 bond issue that pays 10 percent interest, compounded semiannually. The interest on the bond is an example of:
   a) an annuity due
   b) a perpetuity
   c) a deferred annuity
   d) an ordinary annuity

___ 12. Refer to question 11. Assume that the bond will mature in ten years. If the market interest rate is 12 percent and the bond is paying 10 percent interest, determine the present value (rounded to the nearest dollar) of the future interest payments discounted at the market interest rate.
   a) $56,502
   b) $57,350
   c) $61,446
   d) $62,311

___ 13. Refer to questions 11 and 12. Determine the present value (rounded to the nearest dollar) of the bond's $100,000 maturity value.
   a) $37,689
   b) $61,391
   c) $55,839
   d) $31,180

___ 14. Larrays Ltd. invested $5,000 in a savings account on January 1, 19X1. The investment will earn 12 percent compounded quarterly. The balance (rounded to the nearest dollar) in the savings account on December 31, 19X5 will be
   a) $8,812
   b) $8,768
   c) $9,031
   d) none of the above

___ 15. Sara Miller deposits $250 in her savings account every six months. If she makes deposits every July 1 and December 31, and the account earns 6 percent interest compounded semiannually, what amount (rounded to the nearest dollar) will she have in her account on December 31 of the fifth year?
   a) $2,133
   b) $2,819
   c) $2,866
   d) none of the above

___ 16. Refer to question 15. Instead of depositing $250 every six months, Miller deposits $125 every quarter, beginning on March 31. If she makes that same deposit every quarter and the account earns 6 percent interest compounded quarterly, what amount (rounded to the nearest dollar) will she have in her account on December 31 of the fifth year?
   a) $2,890
   b) $2,146
   c) $2,725
   d) none of the above

Exercises

1. Compute the future amount at the end of Year 5 for each of the following:
   a. $10,000 invested today that will earn 20 percent interest annually
   b. $10,000 invested today that will earn 20 percent, compounded semiannually
   c. $10,000 invested today that will earn 20 percent, compounded quarterly

2. Compute the present value today of $100,000 to be received in ten years if:
   a. the interest rate is 12 percent, compounded annually
   b. the interest rate is 12 percent, compounded semiannually
   c. the interest rate is 12 percent, compounded quarterly.

3. Compute the future amount at the end of Year 6 for each of the following annuities:
   a. $5,000 is invested at the end of each year for six years: the interest rate is 10 percent, compounded annually
   b. $2,500 is invested at the end of every six months for six years: the interest rate is 10 percent, compounded semiannually

4. Compute the present value today for each of the following annuities:
   a. $10,000 to be received at the end of each year for ten years: the interest rate is 8 percent, compounded annually
   b. $2,500 to be received at the end of each quarter for ten years: the interest rate is 8 percent, compounded quarterly

5. How much should be invested at the end of each year to accumulate $250,000 at the end of Year 20? The interest rate is 15 percent, compounded annually.

6. A purchase of stereo equipment costing $1,750 was financed for three years, with payments to be made at the end of each month. The finance charge was quoted as an annual rate of 18 percent. Compute the amount for each of the monthly payments.

ANSWERS TO QUESTIONS AND EXERCISES

True/False

1. T	4. T	7. F	10. T
2. F	5. T	8. F	11. T
3. T	6. F	9. T	12. T

Matching

1. h	4. a	7. i	10. d
2. b	5. f	8. e	11. g
3. c	6. k	9. j	

Multiple Choice

1. c	5. c	9. b	13. d
2. c	6. d	10. b	14. c
3. b	7. b	11. d	15. c
4. a	8. b	12. b	16. a

? on page 1066).

future
state.

,32,197

.. × 0.31180 = $31,180

..le B.2

c. $n = 40$ $100,000 × 0.30656 = $30,656
   $r = 3$
   Table B.2

3. a. $n = 6$ $5,000 × 7.71561 = $38,578.05
   $r = 10$
   Table B.3

   b. $n = 12$ $2,500 × 15.91713 = $39,792.83
   $r = 5$
   Table B.3

4. a. $n = 10$ $10,000 × 6.71008 = $67,100.80
   $r = 8$
   Table B.4

   b. $n = 40$ $2,500 × 27.35548 = $68,388.70
   $r = 2$
   Table B.4

5. $n = 20$ Periodic Payment × 102.44358 = $250,000
   $r = 15$ Periodic Payment = $\dfrac{\$250,000}{102.44358}$
   Table B.3
             = $2,440.37

6. $n = 36$ Periodic Payment × 27.66068 = $1,750
   $r = 1.5$ Periodic Payment = $\dfrac{\$1,750}{27.66068}$
   Table B.4
             = $63.27

ASSIGNMENT MATERI

QUESTIONS

1. Review the key terms listed on page 1051.

2. What is interest?

3. Distinguish between simple and compound interest.

4. Distinguish between the discounted present value of a stream of
   payments and their net present value. If there is no distinction, so

5. Distinguish between an annuity due and an ordinary annuity.

6. Describe the "implicit interest rate" for a series of cash flows and
   procedure for finding it.

7. Does the present value of a given amount to be paid in ten years
   increase or decrease if the interest rate increases? What if the amount
   were due in five years? Twenty years? Does the present value of an
   annuity to be paid for ten years increase or decrease if the discount
   rate decreases? What if the annuity were for five years? Twenty years?

8. Rather than pay you $100 a month for the next twenty years, the person
   who injured you in an automobile accident is willing to pay a single
   amount now to settle your claim for injuries. Would you rather an
   interest rate of 6 percent or 12 percent be used in computing the present
   value of the lump-sum settlement? Comment or explain.

EXERCISES

9. **Effective interest rates.** State the rate per period and the number of
   periods, in each of the following:
   a. 12 percent per annum, for five years, compounded annually.
   b. 12 percent per annum, for five years, compounded semiannually.
   c. 12 percent per annum, for five years, compounded quarterly.
   d. 12 percent per annum, for five years, compounded monthly.

10. Compute the future value of:
    a. $100 invested for five years at 4 percent compounded annually.
    b. $550 invested for fifteen periods at 2 percent compounded once per
       period.
    c. $200 invested for eight years at 3 percent compounded semi-
       annually.
    d. $2,500 invested for fourteen years at 8 percent compounded
       quarterly.
    e. $600 invested for three years at 12 percent compounded monthly.

11. Compute the present value of:
  a. $100 due in 30 years at 4 percent compounded annually.
  b. $250 due in 8 years at 8 percent compounded quarterly.
  c. $1,000 due in 2 years at 12 percent compounded monthly.

12. Compute the amount (future value) of an ordinary annuity (an annuity in arrears) of:
  a. 13 rents of $100 at 1½ percent per period.
  b. 8 rents of $850 at 6 percent per period.
  c. 28 rents of $400 at 4 percent per period.

13. Mr. Adams has $500 to invest. He wants to know how much it will amount to if he invests it at:
  a. 6 percent per year for 21 years.
  b. 8 percent per year for 33 years.

14. Ms. Black wishes to have $15,000 at the end of eight years. How much must she invest today to accomplish this purpose if the interest rate is:
  a. 6 percent per year?
  b. 8 percent per year?

15. Mr. Case plans to set aside $4,000 each year, the first payment to be made on January 1, 1993, and the last on January 1, 1998. How much will he have accumulated by January 1, 1998 if the interest rate is:
  a. 6 percent per year?
  b. 8 percent per year?

16. Ms. David wants to have $450,000 on her sixty-fifth birthday. How much must she deposit on each birthday from her fifty-eighth to sixty-fifth, inclusive, in order to receive this amount? Assume an interest rate of:
  a. 8 percent per year.
  b. 12 percent per year.

17. If Mr. Edwards invests $900 on June 1 of each year from 1993 to 2003, inclusive, how much will he have accumulated on June 1, 2004 (note that one year elapses after last payment) if the interest rate is:
  a. 5 percent per year?
  b. 10 percent per year?

18. Mr. Frank has $145,000, with which he purchased an annuity on February 1, 1993. The annuity consists of six annual payments, the first to be made on February 1, 1994. How much will he receive in each payment? Assume an interest rate of:
  a. 8 percent per year.
  b. 12 percent per year.

19. In the preceding Exercises 10 to 18, you have been asked to compute a number. First, you must decide what factor from the tables is appropriate; then, you use that factor in the appropriate calculation. Notice that the last step could be omitted. You could write an arithmetic expression showing the factor you want to use without actually copying down the number and doing the arithmetic. For example, define the following notation: $T(i, p, r)$ means Table i (B.1, 2, 3, or 4), row p

sufficient income that any loss from disposing of or depreciating the "old" machine can be used to offset other taxable income. Ignore the investment tax credit.

How much, at a minumum, must the "old" machine fetch on resale at this time to make purchasing the new machine worthwhile?

38. *Computation of present value of cash flows; untaxed acquisition, no change in tax basis of assets.* The balance sheet of Lynch Limited shows assets of $1,000,000, net, and shareholders' equity of $1,000,000. The assets are all depreciable assets with remaining lives of twenty years. The income statement for the year shows revenues of $700,000, depreciation of $50,000 (= $1,000,000/twenty years), no other expenses, income taxes of $260,000 (40 percent of pretax income of $650,000), and net income of $390,000.

Zeff Incorporated is considering purchasing all of the stock of Lynch Limited. It is willing to pay an amount equal to the present value of the cash flows from operations for the next twenty years discounted at a rate of 10 percent per year.

The transaction will not be taxable; that is, after the purchase, the tax basis of the assets of Lynch Limited will remain unchanged, so that depreciation charges will remain at $50,000 per year and income taxes will remain at $260,000 per year. Revenues will be $700,000 per year for the next twenty years.

a. Compute the annual cash flows produced by Lynch Incorporated.
b. Compute the maximum amount Zeff Incorporated should be willing to pay.

39. *Computation of present value of cash flows; taxable acquisition, changing tax basis of assets.* Refer to the data in Problem 38. Assume now that the acquisition is taxable, so that the tax basis of the assets acquired changes after the purchase. If the purchase price is $V, depreciation charges will be $V/20 per year for twenty years. Income taxes will be 40 percent of pretax income.

What is the maximum Zeff Incorporated should be willing to pay for Lynch Limited?

COMPOUND INTEREST, ANNUITY, AND BOND TABLES

TABLE B.3
Future Value of Annuity of $1 in Arrears

$$F = \frac{(1 + r)^n - 1}{r}$$

r = interest rate; n = number of payments

No. of Payments = n	1%	2%	3%	4%	5%	6%	7%	8%	10%	12%	14%	15%	16%	18%	20%	25%
1	1.00000	1.00000	1.00000	1.00000	1.00000	1.00000	1.00000	1.00000	1.00000	1.00000	1.00000	1.00000	1.00000	1.00000	1.00000	1.00000
2	2.01000	2.02000	2.03000	2.04000	2.05000	2.06000	2.07000	2.08000	2.10000	2.12000	2.14000	2.15000	2.16000	2.18000	2.20000	2.25000
3	3.03010	3.06040	3.09090	3.12160	3.15250	3.18360	3.21490	3.24640	3.31000	3.37440	3.43960	3.47250	3.50560	3.57240	3.64000	3.81250
4	4.06040	4.12161	4.18363	4.24646	4.31013	4.37462	4.43994	4.50611	4.64100	4.77933	4.92114	4.99338	5.06650	5.21543	5.36800	5.76563
5	5.10101	5.20404	5.30914	5.41632	5.52563	5.63709	5.75074	5.86660	6.10510	6.35285	6.61010	6.74238	6.87714	7.15421	7.44160	8.20703
6	6.15202	6.30812	6.46841	6.63298	6.80191	6.97532	7.15329	7.33593	7.71561	8.11519	8.53552	8.75374	8.97748	9.44197	9.92992	11.25879
7	7.21354	7.43428	7.66246	7.89829	8.14201	8.39384	8.65402	8.92280	9.48717	10.08901	10.73049	11.06680	11.41387	12.14152	12.91590	15.07349
8	8.28567	8.58297	8.89234	9.21423	9.54911	9.89747	10.25980	10.63663	11.43589	12.29969	13.23276	13.72682	14.24009	15.32700	16.49908	19.84186
9	9.36853	9.75463	10.15911	10.58280	11.02656	11.49132	11.97799	12.48756	13.57948	14.77566	16.08535	16.78584	17.51851	19.08585	20.79890	25.80232
10	10.46221	10.94972	11.46388	12.00611	12.57789	13.18079	13.81645	14.48656	15.93742	17.54874	19.33730	20.30372	21.32147	23.52131	25.95868	33.25290
11	11.56683	12.16872	12.80780	13.48635	14.20679	14.97164	15.78360	16.64549	18.53117	20.65458	23.04452	24.34928	25.73290	28.75514	32.15042	42.56613
12	12.68250	13.41209	14.19203	15.02581	15.91713	16.86994	17.88845	18.97713	21.38428	24.13313	27.27075	29.00167	30.85017	34.93107	39.58050	54.20766
13	13.80933	14.68033	15.61779	16.62684	17.71298	18.88214	20.14064	21.49530	24.55271	28.02911	32.08865	34.35192	36.78620	42.21866	48.49660	68.75958
14	14.94742	15.97394	17.08632	18.29191	19.59863	21.01507	22.55049	24.21492	27.97498	32.39260	37.58107	40.50471	43.67199	50.81802	59.19592	86.94947
15	16.09690	17.29342	18.59891	20.02359	21.57856	23.27597	25.12902	27.15211	31.77248	37.27971	43.84241	47.58041	51.65951	60.96527	72.03511	109.6868
16	17.25786	18.63929	20.15688	21.82453	23.65749	25.67253	27.88805	30.32428	35.94973	42.75328	50.98035	55.71747	60.92503	72.93901	87.44213	138.1086
17	18.43044	20.01207	21.76159	23.69751	25.84037	28.21288	30.84022	33.75023	40.54470	48.88367	59.11760	65.07509	71.67303	87.06804	105.9306	173.6537
18	19.61475	21.41231	23.41444	25.64541	28.13238	30.90565	33.99903	37.45024	45.59917	55.74971	68.39407	75.83636	84.14072	103.7403	128.1167	218.0446
19	20.81090	22.84056	25.11687	27.67123	30.53900	33.75999	37.37896	41.44626	51.15909	63.43968	78.96923	88.21181	98.60323	123.4135	154.7400	273.5558
20	22.01900	24.29737	26.87037	29.77808	33.06595	36.78559	40.99549	45.76196	57.27500	72.05244	91.02493	102.44358	115.3798	146.6280	186.6880	342.9447
22	24.47159	27.29898	30.53678	34.24797	38.50521	43.39229	49.00574	55.45676	71.40275	92.50258	120.4360	137.63164	157.4150	206.3448	271.0307	538.1011
24	26.97346	30.42186	34.42647	39.08260	44.50200	50.81558	58.17667	66.76476	88.49733	118.1552	158.6586	184.16784	213.9776	289.4945	392.4842	843.0330
26	29.52563	33.67091	38.55304	44.31174	51.11345	59.15638	68.67647	79.95442	109.1818	150.3339	208.3327	245.71197	290.0883	405.2721	567.3773	1319.489
28	32.12910	37.05212	42.93092	49.96758	58.40258	68.52811	80.69769	95.33883	134.2099	190.6989	272.8892	327.10408	392.5028	566.4809	819.2233	2063.952
30	34.78489	40.56808	47.57542	56.08494	66.43885	79.05819	94.46079	113.2832	164.4940	241.3327	356.7869	434.74515	530.3117	790.9480	1181.881	3227.174
32	37.49407	44.22703	52.50276	62.70147	75.29883	90.88978	110.2181	134.2135	201.1378	304.8477	465.8202	577.10046	715.7475	1103.496	1704.109	5044.710
34	40.25770	48.03380	57.73018	69.85791	85.06696	104.1838	128.2588	158.6267	245.4767	384.5210	607.5199	765.36535	965.2698	1538.688	2456.118	7884.609
36	43.07688	51.99437	63.27594	77.59831	95.83632	119.1209	148.9135	187.1022	299.1268	484.4631	791.6729	1014.34568	1301.027	2144.649	3539.009	12321.95
38	45.95272	56.11494	69.15945	85.97034	107.7095	135.9042	172.5610	220.3159	364.0434	609.8305	1030.998	1343.62216	1752.822	2988.389	5098.373	19255.30
40	48.88637	60.40198	75.40126	95.02552	120.7998	154.7620	199.6351	259.0565	442.5926	767.0914	1342.025	1779.09031	2360.757	4163.213	7343.858	30088.66
45	56.48107	71.89271	92.71986	121.0294	159.7002	212.7435	285.7493	386.5056	718.9048	1358.230	2590.565	3585.12846	4965.274	9531.577	18281.31	91831.50
50	64.46318	84.57940	112.7969	152.6671	209.3480	290.3359	406.5289	573.7702	1163.909	2400.018	4994.521	7217.71628	10435.65	21813.09	45497.19	280255.7
100	170.4814	312.2323	607.2877	1237.624	2610.025	5638.368	12381.66	27484.52	137796.1	696010.5	3502323.	783 × 10⁴	174 × 10⁵	857 × 10⁵	414 × 10⁶	196 × 10⁸

Note: To convert from this table to values of an annuity in advance, determine the annuity in arrears above for one more period and subtract 1.00000.

TABLE B.4
Present Value of Annuity of $1 in Arrears

$$P_A = \frac{1 - (1+r)^{-n}}{r}$$

r = discount rate; n = number of payments

No. of Payments = n	½%	1%	1½%	2%	3%	4%	5%	6%	7%	8%	10%	12%	15%	20%	25%
1	.99502	.99010	.98522	.98039	.97087	.96154	.95238	.94340	.93458	.92593	.90909	.89286	.86957	.83333	.80000
2	1.98510	1.97040	1.95588	1.94156	1.91347	1.88609	1.85941	1.83339	1.80802	1.78326	1.73554	1.69005	1.62571	1.52778	1.44000
3	2.97025	2.94099	2.91220	2.88388	2.82861	2.77509	2.72325	2.67301	2.62432	2.57710	2.48685	2.40183	2.28323	2.10648	1.95200
4	3.95050	3.90197	3.85438	3.80773	3.71710	3.62990	3.54595	3.46511	3.38721	3.31213	3.16987	3.03735	2.85498	2.58873	2.36160
5	4.92587	4.85343	4.78264	4.71346	4.57971	4.45182	4.32948	4.21236	4.10020	3.99271	3.79079	3.60478	3.35216	2.99061	2.68928
6	5.89638	5.79548	5.69719	5.60143	5.41719	5.24212	5.07569	4.91732	4.76654	4.62288	4.35526	4.11141	3.78448	3.32551	2.95142
7	6.86207	6.72819	6.59821	6.47199	6.23028	6.00205	5.78637	5.58238	5.38929	5.20637	4.86842	4.56376	4.16042	3.60459	3.16114
8	7.82296	7.65168	7.48593	7.32548	7.01969	6.73274	6.46321	6.20979	5.97130	5.74664	5.33493	4.96764	4.48732	3.83716	3.32891
9	8.77906	8.56602	8.36052	8.16224	7.78611	7.43533	7.10782	6.80169	6.51523	6.24689	5.75902	5.32825	4.77158	4.03097	3.46313
10	9.73041	9.47130	9.22218	8.98259	8.53020	8.11090	7.72173	7.36009	7.02358	6.71008	6.14457	5.65022	5.01877	4.19247	3.57050
11	10.67703	10.36763	10.07112	9.78685	9.25262	8.76048	8.30641	7.88687	7.49867	7.13896	6.49506	5.93770	5.23371	4.32706	3.65640
12	11.61893	11.25508	10.90751	10.57534	9.95400	9.38507	8.86325	8.38384	7.94269	7.53608	6.81369	6.19437	5.42062	4.43922	3.72512
13	12.55615	12.13374	11.73153	11.34837	10.63496	9.98565	9.39357	8.85268	8.35765	7.90378	7.10336	6.42355	5.58315	4.53268	3.78010
14	13.48871	13.00370	12.54338	12.10625	11.29607	10.56312	9.89864	9.29498	8.74547	8.24424	7.36669	6.62817	5.72448	4.61057	3.82408
15	14.41662	13.86505	13.34323	12.84926	11.93794	11.11839	10.37966	9.71225	9.10791	8.55948	7.60608	6.81086	5.84737	4.67547	3.85926
16	15.33993	14.71787	14.13126	13.57771	12.56110	11.65230	10.83777	10.10590	9.44665	8.85137	7.82371	6.97399	5.95423	4.72956	3.88741
17	16.25863	15.56225	14.90765	14.29187	13.16612	12.16567	11.27407	10.47726	9.76322	9.12164	8.02155	7.11963	6.04716	4.77463	3.90993
18	17.17277	16.39827	15.67256	14.99203	13.75351	12.65930	11.68959	10.82760	10.05909	9.37189	8.20141	7.24967	6.12797	4.81219	3.92794
19	18.08236	17.22601	16.42617	15.67846	14.32380	13.13394	12.08532	11.15812	10.33560	9.60360	8.36492	7.36578	6.19823	4.84350	3.94235
20	18.98742	18.04555	17.16864	16.35143	14.87747	13.59033	12.46221	11.46992	10.59401	9.81815	8.51356	7.46944	6.25933	4.86958	3.95388
22	20.78406	19.66038	18.62082	17.65805	15.93692	14.45112	13.16300	12.04158	11.06124	10.20074	8.77154	7.64465	6.35866	4.90943	3.97049
24	22.56287	21.24339	20.03041	18.91393	16.93554	15.24696	13.79864	12.55036	11.46933	10.52876	8.98474	7.78432	6.43377	4.93710	3.98111
26	24.32402	22.79520	21.39863	20.12104	17.87684	15.98277	14.37519	13.00317	11.82578	10.80998	9.16095	7.89566	6.49056	4.95632	3.98791
28	26.06769	24.31644	22.72672	21.28127	18.76411	16.66306	14.89813	13.40616	12.13711	11.05108	9.30657	7.98442	6.53351	4.96967	3.99226
30	27.79405	25.80771	24.01584	22.39646	19.60044	17.29203	15.37245	13.76483	12.40904	11.25778	9.42691	8.05518	6.56598	4.97894	3.99505
32	29.50328	27.26959	25.26714	23.46833	20.38877	17.87355	15.80263	14.08404	12.64656	11.43500	9.52638	8.11159	6.59053	4.98537	3.99683
34	31.19555	28.70267	26.48173	24.49859	21.13184	18.41120	16.19290	14.36814	12.85401	11.58693	9.60857	8.15656	6.60910	4.98984	3.99797
36	32.87102	30.10751	27.66068	25.48884	21.83225	18.90828	16.54685	14.62099	13.03521	11.71719	9.67651	8.19241	6.62314	4.99295	3.99870
38	34.52985	31.48466	28.80505	26.44064	22.49246	19.36736	16.86789	14.84602	13.19347	11.82887	9.73265	8.22099	6.63375	4.99510	3.99917
40	36.17223	32.83469	29.91585	27.35548	23.11477	19.79277	17.15909	15.04630	13.33171	11.92461	9.77905	8.24378	6.64178	4.99660	3.99947
45	40.20720	36.09451	32.55234	29.49016	24.51871	20.72004	17.77407	15.45583	13.60552	12.10840	9.86281	8.28252	6.65429	4.99863	3.99983
50	44.14279	39.19612	34.99969	31.42361	25.72976	21.48218	18.25593	15.76186	13.80075	12.23348	9.91481	8.30450	6.66051	4.99945	3.99994
100	78.54264	63.02888	51.62470	43.09835	31.59891	24.50500	19.84791	16.61755	14.26925	12.49432	9.99927	8.33323	6.66666	5.00000	4.00000

Note: To convert from this table to values of an annuity in advance, determine the annuity in arrears above for one less period and add 1.00000.

TABLE B.5
Bond Values in Percent of Par:
10 Percent Semiannual Coupons

$$\textit{Bond value} = 10/r + (100 - 10/r)(1 + r/2)^{-2n}$$
$$r = \text{yield to maturity}; \quad n = \text{years to maturity}$$

Market Yield Percent per Year Compounded Semiannually

Years to Maturity	8.0	9.0	9.5	10.0	10.5	11.0	12.0	13.0	14.0	15.0	20.0
0.5	100.9615	100.4785	100.2387	100.0	99.7625	99.5261	99.0566	98.5915	98.1308	97.6744	95.4545
1.0	101.8861	100.9363	100.4665	100.0	99.5368	99.0768	98.1666	97.2691	96.3840	95.5111	91.3223
1.5	102.7751	101.3745	100.6840	100.0	99.3224	98.6510	97.3270	96.0273	94.7514	93.4987	87.5657
2.0	103.6299	101.7938	100.8917	100.0	99.1186	98.2474	96.5349	94.8613	93.2256	91.6267	84.1507
2.5	104.4518	102.1950	101.0899	100.0	98.9251	97.8649	95.7876	93.7665	91.7996	89.8853	81.0461
5.0	108.1109	103.9564	101.9541	100.0	98.0928	96.2312	92.6399	89.2168	85.9528	82.8398	69.2772
9.0	112.6593	106.0800	102.9803	100.0	97.1339	94.3770	89.1724	84.3513	79.8818	75.7350	58.9929
9.5	113.1339	106.2966	103.0838	100.0	97.0393	94.1962	88.8419	83.8979	79.3288	75.1023	58.1754
10.0	113.5903	106.5040	103.1827	100.0	96.9494	94.0248	88.5301	83.4722	78.8120	74.5138	57.4322
15.0	117.2920	108.1444	103.9551	100.0	96.2640	92.7331	86.2352	80.4120	75.1819	70.4740	52.8654
19.0	119.3679	109.0250	104.3608	100.0	95.9194	92.0976	85.1540	79.0312	73.6131	68.8015	51.3367
19.5	119.5845	109.1148	104.4017	100.0	95.8854	92.0357	85.0509	78.9025	73.4701	68.6525	51.2152
20.0	119.7928	109.2008	104.4408	100.0	95.8531	91.9769	84.9537	78.7817	73.3366	68.5140	51.1047
25.0	121.4822	109.8810	104.7461	100.0	95.6068	91.5342	84.2381	77.9132	72.3985	67.5630	50.4259
30.0	122.6235	110.3190	104.9381	100.0	95.4591	91.2751	83.8386	77.4506	71.9216	67.1015	50.1642
40.0	123.9154	110.7827	105.1347	100.0	95.3175	91.0345	83.4909	77.0728	71.5560	66.7690	50.0244
50.0	124.5050	110.9749	105.2124	100.0	95.2666	90.9521	83.3825	76.9656	71.4615	66.6908	50.0036

TABLE B.6
Bond Values in Percent of Par:
12 Percent Semiannual Coupons

$$\text{Bond value} = 12/r + (100 - 12/r)(1 + r/2)^{-2n}$$
$$r = \text{yield to maturity; } n = \text{years to maturity}$$

Market Yield Percent per Year Compounded Semiannually

Years to Maturity	8.0	9.0	10.0	11.0	11.5	12.0	12.5	13.0	14.0	15.0	20.0
0.5	101.9231	101.4354	100.9524	100.4739	100.2364	100.0	99.7647	99.5305	99.0654	98.6047	96.3636
1.0	103.7722	102.8090	101.8594	100.9232	100.4600	100.0	99.5433	99.0897	98.1920	97.3067	93.0579
1.5	105.5502	104.1234	102.7232	101.3490	100.6714	100.0	99.3348	98.6758	97.3757	96.0992	90.0526
2.0	107.2598	105.3813	103.5459	101.7525	100.8713	100.0	99.1387	98.2871	96.6128	94.9760	87.3205
2.5	108.9036	106.5850	104.3295	102.1351	101.0603	100.0	98.9540	97.9222	95.8998	93.9312	84.8369
5.0	116.2218	111.8691	107.7217	103.7683	101.8620	100.0	98.1816	96.4056	92.9764	89.7039	75.4217
9.0	125.3186	118.2400	111.6896	105.6230	102.7585	100.0	97.3432	94.7838	89.9409	85.4410	67.1944
9.5	126.2679	118.8899	112.0853	105.8033	102.8449	100.0	97.2642	94.6326	89.6644	85.0614	66.5403
10.0	127.1807	119.5119	112.4622	105.9752	102.9266	100.0	97.1898	94.4907	89.4060	84.7083	65.9457
15.0	134.5841	124.4333	115.3724	107.2669	103.5353	100.0	96.6489	93.4707	87.5910	82.2844	62.2923
19.0	138.7357	127.0750	116.8679	107.9024	103.8283	100.0	96.3995	93.0104	86.8065	81.2809	61.0694
19.5	139.1690	127.3445	117.0170	107.9643	103.8565	100.0	96.3760	92.9675	86.7351	81.1915	60.9722
20.0	139.5855	127.6024	117.1591	108.0231	103.8832	100.0	96.3539	92.9272	86.6683	81.1084	60.8838
25.0	142.9644	129.6430	118.2559	108.4658	104.0822	100.0	96.1930	92.6377	86.1993	80.5378	60.3407
30.0	145.2470	130.9570	118.9293	108.7249	104.1960	100.0	96.1053	92.4835	85.9608	80.2609	60.1314
40.0	147.8308	132.3480	119.5965	108.9655	104.2982	100.0	96.0313	92.3576	85.7780	80.0614	60.0195
50.0	149.0100	132.9248	119.8479	109.0479	104.3316	100.0	96.0093	92.3219	85.7307	80.0145	60.0029

Index

To the Owner of this Book

We are interested in your reaction to *Financial Accounting*, Fifth Canadian Edition, by Brian Gaber, Sidney Davidson, Clyde P. Stickney, and Roman L. Weil. With your comments, we can improve this book in future editions. Please help us by completing this questionnaire.

1. What was your reason for using this book?
   _____ university course   _____ personal interest
   _____ college course   _____ other (specify)
   _____ continuing education course

2. If you used this text for a program, what was the name of the program?

3. Which school do you attend?

4. Approximately how much of the book did you use?

   _____ $^1/_4$ _____ $^1/_2$ _____ $^3/_4$ _____ all

5. Which chapters or sections were omitted from your course?

6. What are the best aspects of this book?

7. Is there anything that should be added?

8. Did you find the self-study material in each chapter a valuable addition to this book?

9. Did the running glossary and use of colour make the book easier to use?

10. Please add any comments or suggestions.

(fold here)

0116870399-M8Z4X6-BR01

Scott Duncan
Editorial Director
College Division
DRYDEN CANADA
55 HORNER AVENUE
TORONTO, ONTARIO
M8Z 9Z9

(tape shut)